Spain

KT-510-480

THE ROUGH GUIDE

written and researched by
Mark Ellingham and John Fisher

with
Graham Kenyon and Jules Brown

revised and updated by
Philip Cooper, Adam Coulter, Marc Dubin,
Wendy Ferguson, Ricardo Figueiras, Geoff Garvey,
Joanna Howard, Phil Lee and James Wilson

additional accounts by
Guy Barefoot, Manuel Domínguez,
Teresa Farino and Gordon McLachlan

THE ROUGH GUIDES

Our continued thanks to everyone who has contributed **letters, comments, accounts and suggestions** over the years, and especially to this 1994 edition. In particular: Marie-Laure Amalric, Pat and Sylvia Bacon, WS Bagshaw, John P Berger, Tim Bradley, TW Buck, Fiona Bullock, Rev. Peter Burtwell, Sara Butler, Christine and Ian Campbell, Steve Carr, Patrick Carter, Suzannah Carver, Hugh Clarke, Sue Clarke, AJ Cragg, Jenny Doe, Andrew Downing, Marja Dullaart, Jan Duvekot, Tom and Thelma Eley, Julie Escott, Rebecca Ferguson, Rona Fergusson, Teresa Flower, Neil Froom, Amanda Goldin, A Gough-Yates, Nancy Gordon, Barbara and Mike Harding, DA Hardy, Angus Haywood, John Hemingway, Lucy Henry, Colin Hogarth, Christine Holloway, Alison Hudson, Claire Hunt, Charlotte Hunter, Caroline Jepson, Chris and Angela Kenny (as ever), Colin Kerr, Andrew Knowlman, P Larder, Esther Leslie, Uwe Lorentzen, Sally-Ann Lynch, Gordon Macdonald, Engelen Maersk, Norman Martin, Duncan Maxwell, Peter Minshull, Stephen Minton, John Moore, Gillian C More, Katharine Murphy, Phebe Paine, Fiona Pardey, Derek Pearce, RH Pell, Pim Piers, Emma Pitkethly, Jonathan Pocock, Allen Potter, Wendy Pullem, Adam Pyke, Andrew Pyke, Liz Raymont, James Rimmer, Susan Ross, David Rumsey, Pau Sandham, Gavin Schmidt, Kamrah Sepehri, Frank Sierowski, Marguerite and Martyn Skinner, GJ and KL Slay, Ciarán Slevin, Sebastian Smedley-Aston, TJ Snow, Pernille Holm Sorenson, Barry C Smith, Iain S Smith, Conxa Sondellas, Miles Thompson, Richard Thompson, GK Thomson, Sharon Unitt, Gabriella Vergés, Magda Walker, NC Walker, E Wallace, John L Watt, Martin Webber, Richard B White, Juli Wileman, Richard Williams, Sarah Williams, Stella Wisbling, Helen Windrath, Richard Winscoo, CD Wood, Christopher Wood, Mike Wood, and Nicola Young.

Spain

THE ROUGH GUIDE

Rough Guide Spain Credits

Text editors:	Jo Mead and Jules Brown
Series editor:	Mark Ellingham
Editorial:	Martin Dunford, John Fisher, Jonathan Buckley, Greg Ward, Graham Parker, Samantha Cook
Production:	Susanne Hillen, Andy Hilliard, Gail Jammy, Vivien Antwi, Alan Spicer
Cartography:	Melissa Flack
Publicity:	Richard Trillo
Finance:	Celia Crowley, Simon Carloss

On this sixth (¡oyé!) edition, special **thanks** to Jo Mead for editing brilliantly at the deep end, and to Jules Brown for helping to pull it all together; to Melissa for sorting out the maps – and Anaya for rights; to James Wilson, Joanna Howard, Wendy Ferguson and Ricardo Figuerias, Phil Lee (of course!), Adam Coulter, Philip Cooper, Geoff Garvey, Marc Dubin and Chris Stewart for sterling updates; to Amanda Tomlin and Andrew Tibber for proofreading; Colette Doyle and Lizzie Holden for their expert assistance; to Pol Ferguson, Damien Rea, Greg Ward and Steve Trott for their original contributions; and, above all, to Pilar Vazquez and Esteban Pujals, without whom nothing would have been the same.

This sixth edition published 1994 by Rough Guides Ltd, 1 Mercer Street, London WC2H 9QJ. Distributed by The Penguin Group:

Penguin Books Ltd, 27 Wrights Lane, London W8 5TZ
Penguin Books USA Inc., 375 Hudson Street, New York 10014, USA
Penguin Books Australia Ltd, 487 Maroondah Highway, PO Box 257, Ringwood, Victoria 3134, Australia
Penguin Books Canada Ltd, 10 Alcorn Avenue, Toronto, Ontario, Canada M4V 1E4
Penguin Books (NZ) Ltd, 182–190 Wairau Road, Auckland 10, New Zealand

Previous editions published in the UK by Harrap Columbus and Routledge & Kegan Paul.
Previous edition published in the United States and Canada as *The Real Guide Spain*.

Illustrations in Part One and Part Three by Ed Briant
Basics illustration by Simon Fell. Contexts illustration by David Loftus
Maps © Anaya (Madrid), adapted and reprinted by permission.
Typeset in Linotron Univers and Century Old Style to an original design by Andrew Oliver.
Printed in the United Kingdom by Cox & Wyman Ltd (Reading).

A catalogue record for this book is available from the British Library.

ISBN 1-85828-081-8

CONTENTS

Introduction viii

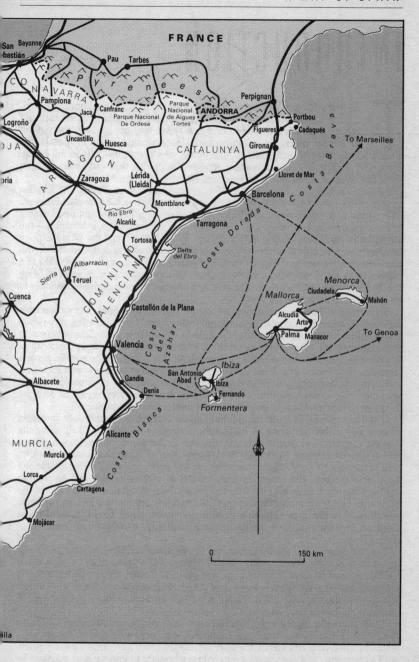

FRANCE

San
Bayonne
bastián
Pau
Tarbes
CO
NAVARRA
Pamplona
Pyrenees
Perpignan
Logroño
Jaca
Canfranc
Parque
Nacional
de Aigües
Tortes
ANDORRA
Portbou
Cadaqués
OJA
Uncastillo
Huesca
CATALUNYA
Figueres
Girona
AR
AGÓN
Lérida
(Lleida)
Montblanc
Barcelona
ria
Zaragoza
Rio Ebro
Alcañiz
Tarragona
oria
Sierra de Albarracin
Teruel
COMUNIDAD
VALENCIANA
Delta
del Ebro
Lloret de Mar
Cuenca
Castellón de la Plana
Costa Brava
Costa Dorada
Menorca
Ciudadela
Mahón
Mallorca
Alcudia
Arta
Palma
Manacor
To Marseilles
Valencia
Costa del Azahar
Albacete
Gandía
Denia
San Antonio
Abad
Ibiza
Ibiza
Fernando
Formentera
To Genoa
MURCIA
Alicante
Costa Blanca
Murcia
Lorca
Cartagena
Mojácar
illa

0   150 km

INTRODUCTION

T he first edition of this guide was published in 1983: only a decade ago but, looking back, almost another world. Spain, then, was emerging spectacularly and traumatically from the Franco era. Tejero had just fired his shots at the parliament ceiling, in an unsuccessful coup attempt, while in Madrid and Barcelona, the *movida* – the belated "happening" and liberation – was in full swing. Rural and provincial Spain, meanwhile, appeared stuck in a timewarp, little changed since the 1950s or, occasionally, so it seemed, from the last century.

All that has changed. Spain in the 1990s is firmly in western Europe. Its socialist government – considered daring and radical on its election – is the new establishment. There have been boom years, which reverberated down to building and development in even the smallest villages. In 1992, there was the famous triple whammy – the Olympics in Barcelona, Madrid as "European City of Culture", and the World Expo in Sevilla – alongside official celebration (and some critical analysis) of the five-hundredth anniversary of Columbus's expedition to the Americas. There is now something of a hangover, as world recession catches up. The Spanish economy, after years of being the fastest-growing in Europe, is stagnant, and unemployment has risen drastically to an estimated 20 percent of the workforce.

Such realities, however, are almost a measure of how much Spain has moved from its isolation under Franco into the European mainstream. They also tell a very partial truth. Spaniards tend not to speak of *La España* – Spain – but *Las Españas*; come to that, they even talk of the capital in the plural – *Las Madriles*, the Madrids. Regionalism is almost an obsession and perhaps the most significant change in the post-Franco era has been the creation of a dozen *autonomías* – autonomous regions – with their own governments, budgets and cultural ministries. The old days of a unified nation, governed with a firm hand from Madrid, seem to have gone forever, as the separate kingdoms which made up the original Spanish state reassert themselves.

If you are coming to Spain for the first time, this regional diversity – of language, culture and artistic traditions, of landscapes, as well as politics – is likely to be the biggest surprise. The monuments, too, span an extraordinary range, from a history which takes in Romans, Moors and the "Golden Age" of Renaissance imperialism, as well as the regions' very different twentieth-century developments. Touring Castile and León, you confront the classic Spanish images of vast cathedrals and *reconquista* castles – literally hundreds of the latter; in the northern mountains of Asturias and the Pyrenees, tiny, almost organic Romanesque churches dot the hillsides and villages; Andalucía has the great Moorish palaces and mosques of Granada, Sevilla and Córdoba; in Barcelona there are the amazing *modernista* (Art Nouveau) creations of Antoni Gaudí.

Not that Spain is just about monuments. For most visitors, the landscape holds just as much fascination – and variety. The evergreen *rías* or estuaries of Galicia could hardly be more different from the high, arid plains of Castile, or the gulch-like desert landscapes of Almería. Spain is also one of the most mountainous countries in Europe, and there is superb walking and wildlife in a dozen or more *sierras* – and above all in the Picos de Europa and Pyrenees.

Then, of course, there are the Spaniards and their infectious enthusiasm for life. In the cities there is always something happening – in bars and clubs, on the streets – while the music and arts scenes are more vibrant than they have been for many years, with a resurgent "new flamenco", a film industry brought to international attention by the anarchic Pedro Almodóvar, and a superb array of modern galleries, including a trio devoted to the century's greatest Spanish artists, Picasso, Miró and Dalí. Even in out of the way places there's a surprising range of nightlife and entertainment, not to mention the daily pleasures of a round of *tapas*, moving from bar to bar, having a beer, a glass of wine or a *fino* (dry sherry) and a bite of the house speciality.

Another, almost limitless, source of diversion are the traditional fiestas. They include established events like the great April *feria* in Sevilla, the pyrotechnic extravaganzas of *Las Fallas* in Valencia, and the running of the bulls in Pamplona, as well as thousands of local events, celebrating a town or village saint's day. As often as not, you'll happen on these quite unawares, to be carried away on a tide of exuberant street partying, concerts, and any number of bizarre activities, from parades of devils to full-blown tomato-throwing battles.

Where to go: some highlights

The identity and appeal of each of the regions is explored in the chapter introductions, and, if you're travelling around, there's a lot to be said for concentrating on one or two provinces, getting a feel for their individuality and character. If you want a broader sweep, though, definite **highlights** of Spanish travel include:

Barcelona. The Catalan capital is a must for the fantasy architecture of Antoni Gaudí; the great promenading street of the Ramblas; the Picasso museum; designer clubs and nightlife, par excellence; and, not least, FC Barcelona – the football team.

Madrid is not as pretty as Barcelona, by a long way, but has an irrepressible style and fantastic bars, both traditional and modern, plus Spain's top three art galleries – the Prado, the new Museo Thyssen-Bornemisza, and the Centro Reina Sofía (now housing Picasso's *Guernica*).

Sevilla. Home of flamenco and all the clichés of the Spanish south; beautiful city quarters and major Christian and Moorish monuments; extraordinary festivals in Easter week, and, afterwards, at the April *feria*.

Toledo. Capital of medieval Spain and stunningly preserved, with synagogues, former mosques and an amazing cathedral; also houses a number of works by El Greco.

Salamanca. Spain's oldest university city remains a small, largely academic place, untouched by suburbs, and packed with Gothic and Renaissance buildings.

Moorish monuments. The best are in the Andalucían cities: the Alhambra palace in Granada, perhaps the most sensual building in Europe; the Mezquita, a former mosque, in Córdoba; and the Alcázar and Giralda tower in Sevilla.

Cathedrals, churches and monasteries. A tour of the top five cathedrals will take you through the Castilian cities of Toledo, León, Burgos, Salamanca and Segovia. Gorgeous Romanesque churches are to be seen along the pilgrim route to Santiago, in the Pyrenees, and at Oviedo. Aragón has superb Mudéjar (Moorish-crafted) churches and towers. Santiago de Compostela is the highpoint of Spanish Baroque. The palace-monastery of El Escorial is the greatest expression of the late Renaissance in Spain.

Beaches. There is a lot more to Spanish beaches than the over-developed *costas*. Excellent and much less frequented strands are to be found around Cádiz and Almería in the south, and along the Asturian and Galician coasts in the north. If you want action and nightlife, it's hard to beat the island of Ibiza, home of the Balearic Beat.

Medieval towns. Small-scale towns, once grand, now hardly significant, are often Spain at its best. Rewarding itineraries could include: Ciudad Rodrigo (Old Castile), Baeza and Úbeda (Andalucía), Trujillo and Cáceres (Extremadura), Albarracín (Aragón).

Roman sites. Mérida has the most significant sites and a superb museum; Segovia's aqueduct is stunning; other rewarding Roman ruins and sites include Italica (near Sevilla), Carmona, Tarragona and Empúries.

Trekking. Key areas are the Pyrenees – which spread across the regions of the Basque country, Aragón (perhaps the best areas) and Catalunya – and the Picos de Europa in Cantabria and Asturias.

Wildlife and national parks. Favourite parks include Monfragüe (in Extremadura) and Ordesa (in the Aragonese Pyrenees). For more details, see the Contexts section of this book.

When to go

Overall, spring and autumn are ideal times for a trip – though the weather varies enormously from region to region. The high plains of the centre suffer from fierce extremes, stiflingly hot in summer, bitterly cold and swept by freezing winds in winter. The Atlantic coast, in contrast, has a temperate pattern with depressions rolling in off the ocean, a permanent tendency to damp and mist, and a relatively brief, humid summer. The Mediterranean south is warm virtually all year round, and in parts of Andalucía positively subtropical, attracting off-season visitors even in December.

In high summer the other factor worth considering is **tourism** itself. Spain plays host to some thirty million tourists a year – one for every resident – and all the better known resorts are packed from June to September, as are the major sights. August, Spain's own holiday month, sees the coast at its most crowded and the cities, by contrast, half empty – and half-closed. Whatever time of year, though, smaller, inland towns see few visitors, and, as noted above, there are beaches beyond the major holiday *costas*. There's no need to feel trapped.

AVERAGE MAXIMUM TEMPERATURES °C (°F)

	Jan	March	May	July	Sept	Nov
Madrid	9	15	21	31	25	13
Castile	(49)	(59)	(70)	(88)	(77)	(56)
Málaga	17	19	23	29	29	20
Costa del Sol	(63)	(67)	(74)	(84)	(84)	(68)
Sevilla	15	21	26	35	32	20
Inland Andalucía	(59)	(69)	(79)	(95)	(90)	(68)
Pontevedra	14	16	20	25	24	16
Galicia	(58)	(61)	(68)	(77)	(75)	(61)
Santander	12	15	17	22	21	15
Cantabrian coast	(54)	(59)	(63)	(72)	(70)	(59)
Barcelona	13	16	21	28	25	16
Catalunya	(56)	(61)	(70)	(83)	(77)	(61)
Cap Bagur	14	16	20	27	25	16
Costa Brava	(57)	(61)	(68)	(80)	(77)	(62)
Alicante	16	20	26	32	30	21
Costa Blanca	(61)	(68)	(78)	(90)	(86)	(70)
Mallorca	14	17	22	29	27	18
Balearic Islands	(58)	(63)	(72)	(84)	(81)	(65)

Note that these are all *maximum temperatures* – and whilst Sevilla, the hottest city in Spain, can soar into the nineties at midday in summer, it is a fairly comfortable 23–27°C (75–80°F) through much of the morning and late afternoon. Equally, bear in mind that temperatures in the north, in Galicia for example, can approach freezing point at night in winter, whilst mountainous regions can get extremely cold at any time of year.

PART ONE

THE
BASICS

GETTING THERE FROM NORTH AMERICA

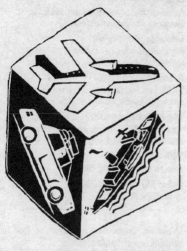

There is a fair variety of scheduled and charter flights from most parts of North America to Madrid, often with connections on to Barcelona. Occasionally, however – and especially if you're coming from Canada – you'll still find it cheaper to route via London, picking up an inexpensive onward flight from there (see "Getting there from Britain", following, for all the details). If Spain is part of a longer European trip, you'll also want to check out details of the *Eurail* pass, which must be purchased in advance of your arrival and can get you by train from anywhere in Europe to Spain.

FROM THE US

Leaving aside discounted tickets, the cheapest way to go is with an **Apex** (Advance Purchase Excursion) ticket, although these carry certain restrictions: you have to book – and pay – at least 21 days before departure, spend at least seven days abroad (maximum stay three months), and you tend to get penalized if you change your schedule. There are also winter **Super Apex** tickets, sometimes known as "Eurosavers" – slightly cheaper than an ordinary Apex, but limiting your stay to between 7 and 21 days. Some airlines also issue **Special Apex** tickets to those under 24, often extending the maximum stay to a year.

However, discount outlets can usually do better than any Apex fare. They come in several forms. **Consolidators** buy up large blocks of tickets that airlines don't think they'll be able to sell at their published fares, and sell them at a discount. Besides being cheap, consolidators normally don't impose advance purchase requirements (although in busy times you'll want to book ahead just to be sure of getting a ticket), but they do often charge very stiff fees for date changes. Also, these companies' margins are pretty tiny, so they make their money by dealing in volume – don't expect them to entertain lots of questions.

Discount agents – such as *STA*, *Council Travel*, *Nouvelles Frontières*, or others listed on p.6 – also wheel and deal in blocks of tickets offloaded by the airlines, but they typically offer a range of other travel-related services such as travel insurance, rail passes, youth and student ID cards, car rentals, tours and the like. These agencies tend to be most worthwhile to students and under-26s, who can often benefit from special fares and deals. **Travel clubs** are another option for those who travel a lot – most charge an annual membership fee, which may be worth it for discounts on air tickets, car rental and the like. You should also check the travel section in the Sunday *New York Times*, or your own major local newspaper, for current bargains, and consult a good travel agent.

Regardless of where you buy your ticket, the **fare** will depend on season. Fares to Spain (like the rest of Europe) are highest from around early June to the end of August, when everyone wants to travel; they drop during the "shoulder" seasons, September–October and April–May, and you'll get the best deals during the low season, November through March (excluding Christmas). Note that flying on weekends ordinarily adds $50 to the round-trip fare; price ranges quoted in the sections below assume midweek travel.

DIRECT FLIGHTS

Iberia flies direct to Madrid from New York, Chicago, Miami and Los Angeles, and to Barcelona from New York. The best deals on high season prices range from around $1000 for the JFK–Madrid flight to almost $1250 for a midweek APEX fare from Los Angeles to Madrid; low

AIRLINES IN NORTH AMERICA

Air France ☎800/237-2747.
Flies from many cities to Paris and then on to Madrid, Barcelona, Málaga and Sevilla.

American Airlines ☎800/433-7300.
Dallas and Miami to Madrid.

British Airways ☎800/247-9297 (in Canada, ☎800/668-1059).
Flies from many cities to London, with connections to Madrid, Barcelona, Bilbão and Málaga.

Continental Airlines ☎800/231-0856.
Newark to Madrid.

Delta Airlines ☎800/241-4141.
Atlanta to Barcelona.

Iberia ☎800/772-4642.
Flies direct from New York, Miami, LA, Toronto and Montréal to Madrid, Barcelona, Málaga and Sevilla; many other internal connections possible.

KLM ☎800/374-7747.
Numerous flights, via Amsterdam, to Madrid, Barcelona, Málaga and Alicante.

Lufthansa ☎800/645-3880.
Flights from many cities to Madrid, Barcelona, Valencia, Málaga and Bilbão, all via Frankfurt.

Sabena ☎800/955-2000.
Flights from East Coast cities to Brussels and on to Madrid, Barcelona, Málaga and Bilbão.

TAP Air Portugal ☎800/221-7370.
New York, Boston, Toronto and Montréal to Madrid and Barcelona, via Lisbon.

TWA ☎800/892-4141.
New York to Madrid and Barcelona.

United Airlines ☎800/538-2929.
Washington DC to Madrid.

---

season prices are around $450 less. One advantage of *Iberia* is that it offers connecting flights to almost anywhere in Spain, often very good value if booked with your transatlantic flight.

As for other carriers, *Continental* and *TWA* also offer direct flights from **New York/Newark** to Madrid and Barcelona at much the same price; *United* has flights to Madrid out of **Washington, DC** (also around $550 in low season, $1000 peak); *American* flies regularly out of **Miami** ($650/$1050), Chicago ($650/$1100) and **Dallas-Ft. Worth** ($700/$1300); and *Delta* flies to Barcelona out of its **Atlanta** hub (about $550/$1000). Coming from anywhere else in the US, a connecting flight on the same airline should add only $50–200 from Midwest cities, $150–200 from the West Coast (a connecting flight with a different carrier may run to $300–500).

FLIGHTS VIA OTHER EUROPEAN CITIES

You may also find very good deals on **routings via other major European cities** with the airlines of those countries: *KLM* via Amsterdam, *Lufthansa* via Frankfurt, *TAP* via Lisbon, *British Airways* via London, or *Sabena* via Brussels, for example. These vary constantly according to the special deals on offer: remember, though, that you may be better off continuing with a locally bought flight, or overland (especially if you plan to buy a rail pass). The widest range of deals is on the New York–London route, served by dozens

of airlines. Competition is intense, so look for bargains especially out of season.

FROM CANADA

From Canada, you've got considerably less choice in **direct flights** to Spain – in fact at the time of writing there's only one choice, *Iberia*, which operates a daily service originating in **Toronto** and stopping in **Montréal**. The APEX fare, at around CDN$750 in low season, CDN$1000 in peak season, isn't bad, and this fare is valid for travel to Barcelona, Madrid and most other Spanish cities. Connecting flights to Toronto or Montréal will add about CDN$200–500 to the above fares. West of the Rockies you're probably better off flying **Vancouver–London** (from CDN$750–1050 return) and then continuing on to Madrid, or alternatively getting a flight from Seattle.

Discount travel agents deal mainly in flights **via London** (usually using a combination of airlines) or **via Lisbon** (on *TAP Air Portugal*). There are several other possibilities using other European national airlines via their respective capitals (see airlines box). Fares are generally in line with those of *Iberia's*.

Travel CUTS is the most reliable student/youth agency, with some deals for non-students, too; or check the travel ads in your local newspaper and consult a good travel agent.

CITY BREAKS AND PACKAGE TOURS

Package tours may not sound like your kind of travel, but don't dismiss the idea out of hand. It's true that tours arranged in North America tend to be of the everybody-on-the-bus group variety, but many agents can put together very flexible deals, sometimes amounting to no more than a flight plus car or rail pass and accommodation; if you're planning to travel in moderate or luxury style, and especially if your trip is geared around special interests, such packages can work out cheaper than the same arrangements made on arrival. A package can also be great for your peace of mind, if only just to ensure a worry-free first week while you're finding your feet on a longer tour (of course, you can jump off the itinerary any time

you like). Most companies will expect you to book through a local travel agent, and since it costs the same you might as well.

Plenty of tour companies offer whirlwind itineraries around Spain. Most of these also offer independent **city breaks**, although the accommodation tends to be in pretty pricey hotels, costing upwards of $150 per person for a typical three-night stay. A more structured **escorted tour** will run in the neighbourhood of $100 a night per person – even more if you're staying in the historic *paradores*.

A few American companies run **trekking** (backpacking) and biking trips to the Pyrenees and the sierras of Andalucía, which cost at least as much as escorted tours due to all the logistics

TOUR OPERATORS IN NORTH AMERICA

Abercrombie & Kent 1520 Kensington Rd, Oak Brook, IL (☎800/323-7308). *Treks in the Pyrenees and bike tours in Andalucía.*

Central Tours 73 Ferry St, Newark, NJ 07105 (☎800/783-9882). *Fly-drives, city packages.*

Contiki Holidays 300 Plaza Alicante, Suite 900, Garden Grove, CA (☎800/466-0610). *Bus tours for under-35s.*

Cosmos/Global Gateway 92–25 Queens Blvd, Rego Park, NY11374 (☎800/221-0090). *Budget tour operator; book through travel agent only.*

Discover Spain 2200 Fletcher Ave, Fort Lee, NJ 07024 (☎800/227-5858). *City breaks, parador tours and Costa del Sol packages.*

EC Tours 10153 1/2 Riverside, Toluca Lake, CA 91602 (☎800/388-0877). *City packages, parador tours, pilgrimages.*

Europe Through the Back Door Tours 109 Fourth Ave. N, Box C-20009, Edmonds, WA 98020 (☎206/771-8303). *Travel club that runs budget bus tours, sells Eurail passes and publishes its own excellent newsletter.*

Europe Train Tours 198 Boston Post Rd, Mamoroneck, NY 10543 (☎800/551-2085). *Rail specialist.*

Friendly Holidays 575 Anton Blvd, #790, Costa Mesa, CA 92626 (☎800/221-9748). *City packages, parador tours.*

Himalayan Travel 112 Prospect St, Stamford CT 06901(☎800/225-2380). *Trekking in the Sierra Nevada and Alpujarras.*

Ibero Travel 109–19 72nd St, Forest Hills, NY 11375 (☎800/654-2376). *Fly-drives, apartments, paradores.*

Jet Vacations 1775 Broadway, New York, NY 10019 (☎800/538-2999). *European package specialist.*

Kesher Tours 370 Lexington Ave, New York, NY (☎800/582-8330). *Jewish heritage tours.*

MI Travel 450 Seventh Ave, Suite 1805, New York, NY (☎800/848-2314). *City and Costa packages, tours, paradores.*

Mountain Travel-Sobek 6420 Fairmount Ave, El Cerrito, CA 94530 (☎800/227-2384). *Treks in the Pyrenees and the Sierra Nevada.*

Munditour International 3935 NW 26th St, Miami, FL33142(☎800/327-7011). *Major packager of Spanish tours.*

Petrabax 6464 Sunset Blvd, #570, Hollywood, CA 90028 (☎800/634-1188). *Historic city tours, parador tours.*

Sun Holidays, 26 Sixth St, Stamford, CT 0690 (☎800/243-2057). *City packages, parador tours, Costa del Sol packages.*

Travel Bound 599 Broadway, New York, NY 10012 (☎800/456-8656). *Extensive range of Spanish tour itineraries.*

Welcome Tours 99 Tulip Ave, Suite 208, Floral Park, NY 11001 (☎800/274-4400). *City and regional tours, paradores and Costa del Sol packages.*

Wilderness Travel 801 Allston Way, Berkeley, CA 94710 (☎800/368-2794). *Treks in the Pyrenees and the Basque country.*

involved, and at least one can put you on skis in the Pyrenees. Packages to the **beaches** of the Costa del Sol are offered by several operators.

RAIL PASSES

The **Eurail Pass** is not likely to pay for itself if you travel only in Spain, though if you're planning a longer European trip it may prove useful. The pass, which must be purchased before arrival in Europe, allows unlimited free train travel in Spain and sixteen other countries. The **Eurail Youthpass** (for under-26s) costs US$578 for one month or $768 for two; if you're 26 or over you'll have to buy a first-class pass, available in 15-day ($498), 21-day ($648), one-month ($798), two-month ($1098) and three-month ($1398) increments.

You stand a better chance of getting your money's worth out of a Eurail **Flexipass**, which is good for a certain number of travel days in a two-month period. This, too, comes in under-26 and first-class versions: 5 days cost $255/$348; 10 days, $398/$560; and 15 days, $540/$740.

A further alternative is to attempt to buy an *InterRail Pass* in Europe (see "Getting there from Britain") – most agents don't check residential qualifications, but once you're in Europe it'll be too late to buy a *Eurail Pass* if you have problems. North Americans are also eligible to purchase the more specific **Spain Flexipass** (see "Getting around", p.22); all these passes can be reserved through *Rail Europe*, 226 Westchester Ave, White Plains, NY 10604 (☎800/438-7245) or youth-oriented travel agents (see below).

DISCOUNT AGENTS, CONSOLIDATORS AND TRAVEL CLUBS IN NORTH AMERICA

Council Travel Head Office, 205 E 42nd St, New York, NY 10017 (☎800/743-1823). *Nationwide US student travel organization with branches (among others) in San Francisco, Washington DC, Boston, Austin, Seattle, Chicago, Minneapolis.*

Discount Travel International, Ives Bldg, 114 Forrest Ave, Suite 205, Narberth, PA 19072 (☎800/334-9294). *Discount travel club.*

Encore Travel Club 4501 Forbes Blvd, Lanham, MD 20706 (☎301/459-8020). *East Coast travel club.*

Interworld 800 Douglass Rd, Miami, FL 33134 (☎305/443-4929). *Southeastern US consolidator.*

Moment's Notice 425 Madison Ave, New York, NY 10017 (☎212/486-0503). *Discount travel club.*

New Frontiers/Nouvelles Frontières 12 E 33rd St, New York, NY 10016 (☎800/366-6387); 1001 Sherbrook East, Suite 720, Montréal, H2L 1L3 (☎514/526-8444). *French discount travel firm. Other branches in LA, San Francisco and Québec City.*

STA Travel ☎800/777-0112 (nationwide). *Worldwide specialist in independent travel with offices in Los Angeles, San Francisco, Boston.*

Stand Buys 311 W Superior St, Chicago, IL 60610 (☎800/255-0200). *Midwestern travel club.*

Travel Cuts Head Office: 187 College St, Toronto, ON M5T 1P7 (☎416/979-2406). Others include: MacEwan Hall Student Centre, University of Calgary, Calgary, AL T2N 1N4 (☎403/282-7687);

12304 Jasper Ave, Edmonton, AL T5N 3K5 (☎403/488 8487); 6139 South St, Halifax, NS B3H 4J2 (☎902/494-7027); 1613 rue St Denis, Montréal, PQ H2X 3K3 (☎514/843-8511); 1 Stewart St, Ottawa, ON K1N 6H7 (☎613/238-8222); 100–2383 CH St Foy, St Foy, G1V 1T1 (☎418/654-0224); Place Riel Campus Centre, University of Saskatchewan, Saskatoon S7N 0W0 (☎306/975-3722); 501–602 W Hastings, Vancouver V6B 1P2 (☎604/681-9136); University Centre, University of Manitoba, Winnipeg R3T 2N2 (☎204/269-9530). *Canadian student travel organization.*

Travelers Advantage 49 Music Sq, W Nashville, TN 37204 (☎800/344-2334). *Reliable travel club.*

Travac 989 Sixth Ave, New York, NY 10018 (☎800/872-8800). *US consolidator.*

Unitravel 1177 N Warson Rd, St Louis, MO 63132 (☎800/325-2222). *US consolidator.*

Worldwide Discount Travel Club 1674 Meridian Ave, Miami Beach, FL 33139 (☎305/534-2082). *Florida-based travel club.*

GETTING THERE FROM BRITAIN

The most convenient way of getting to Spain is to **fly** – flights take around two hours to Madrid and an hour and a half to Barcelona compared with a minimum of 24 hours by train to Barcelona. **Trains** – and **driving** to Spain – are set to become easier, though, with the opening of *Le Shuttle* cross-channel services, and there are also **direct ferry services** from Plymouth to Santander and from Portsmouth to Bilbão.

BY AIR

There's a vast number of flights from Britain to Spain throughout the year. Out of season, or if you're prepared to book at the last minute, they can be very good value indeed – often as little as £80–100 return to Málaga, Alicante or Mallorca (generally the three cheapest destinations), though more likely £150 in the height of summer.

CHARTER FLIGHTS
Charters are usually block-booked by package holiday firms, but even in the middle of August they're rarely completely full and spare seats are often sold off at discounts. For an idea of current prices and availability, contact any high street travel agent, or a specialist agency or operator. The widest selection of ads for London departures is invariably found in the classified pages of the London listings magazine *Time Out*. For departures **from other British airports** check the local evening papers and *The Sunday Times* and *Observer*. The agents and operators listed in the box on p.8 make a good start.

The independent travel specialists, *STA Travel*, offer a range of special discount flights, most frequently to Madrid and Barcelona, while **students** – and anyone **under 26** – can also try *Campus Travel*; they offer return flights to Barcelona for £145, Málaga for £132 and Madrid £83 (this flight is open to all travellers). Student union travel bureaux can usually fix you up with flights through one of these operators, and they're both worth calling for charters, too – whether you're a student or not.

The major disadvantage of charter flights is the fixed return date – a maximum of four weeks from the outward journey. Some return charters are good value even if you only use half, but for more flexibility you'll probably want to buy a ticket for a scheduled flight.

SCHEDULED FLIGHTS
Iberia, Spain's national airline, and **British Airways** have the widest range of **scheduled flights**, including regular services to Santiago, Bilbão and Sevilla, as well as the more common Spanish destinations. Both airlines also fly direct from Manchester into Madrid and Barcelona. **GB Airways** (part of *British Airways*) also flies direct to Gibraltar.

Scheduled flights are rarely the cheapest option but some of their special offers can be highly competitive, especially if you need the greater **flexibility** of a scheduled airline. They offer, for example, open-jaw flights (fly in to one

SAMPLE SCHEDULED FLIGHT PRICES TO SPAIN		
	Low	High
From **London** to:		
Madrid	£157	£230
Barcelona	£175	£216
Málaga	£191	£254
Bilbão	£142	£195
Gibraltar	£189	£219
From **Manchester** to:		
Madrid	£175	£232
Barcelona	£165	£226
Málaga	£235	£264
Bilbão	£254	£307
Gibraltar	£209	£239

AIRLINES, AGENTS AND OPERATORS

AIRLINES

Iberia 29 Glasshouse St, London W1R 5RG (☎071/ 830 0011); Birmingham ☎021/643 1953; Manchester ☎061/436 6444; Glasgow ☎041/248 6581.

British Airways 156 Regent St, London W1R 5TA (☎081/897 4000).

AGENTS AND OPERATORS

APA Travel 138 Eversholt St, London NW1 (☎071/387 5337). *Spanish flight specialists.*

Aventura 42 Greenlands Rd, Staines, Middlesex TW18 4LR (☎0784/459 018). *Horse-riding and mule-trekking in the Sierra Nevada.*

B&B Abroad 5 World's End Lane, Green Street Green, Orpington, Kent BR6 6AA (☎0689/857 838). *Specialist operator with a wide range of bed and breakfast accommodation from rustic farmhouses to luxurious country manors. Also has hotel accommodation.*

Campus Travel 52 Grosvenor Gardens, London SW1(☎071/730 3402); 541 Bristol Rd, Selly Oak, Birmingham (☎021/414 1848); 39 Queen's Rd, Clifton, Bristol (☎0272/292 494); 5 Emmanuel St, Cambridge (☎0223/324 283); 53 Forest Rd, Edinburgh (☎031/668 3303); 166 Deansgate, Manchester (☎061/273 1721); 13 High St, Oxford (☎0865/242 06)7. Also in YHA shops and on university campuses throughout Britain. *Youth/student specialist.*

Exodus Expeditions 9 Weir Road, London SW12 0LT (☎081/675 5550). *Walking and riding in Andalucía, Majorca and the Pyrenees.*

Explore Worldwide Ltd, 1 Frederick St, Aldershot, Hants GU11 1O (☎0252/344 161). *Walking in Andalucía, Sierra Nevada and Picos de Europa.*

Individual Travellers Bignor, Pulborough, W Sussex RH20 1QD (☎07987/416). *Farmhouses, cottages and village houses all over Spain.*

Keytel International 402 Edgware Rd, London W2 1ED (☎071/402 8182).*Main agents for the paradores.*

Magic of Spain 227 Shepherd's Bush Road, London W6 7AS (☎081/748 7575). *High quality, out-of-the-way hotels and paradores.*

Mundi Color 276 Vauxhall Bridge Rd, London SW1 (☎071/828 6021). *Spanish specialists for flights, packages and city breaks.*

Owners Abroad Astral Towers, Bettsway, London Road, Crawley, West Sussex (☎0293/554 444). *Charter flights.*

Portland Holidays 218 Great Portland St, London W1 (☎071/388 5111). *Costa Brava packages.*

Sherpa Expeditions 131a Heston Rd, Hounslow, Middlesex TW5 0RD (☎081/577 2717). *Trekking in the Sierra Nevada, the Alpujarras and Pyrenees.*

Springways Travel 258 Vauxhall Bridge Rd, London SW1(☎071/253 5577). *Good prices on charters.*

STA Travel 86 Old Brompton Road, London SW7 (☎071/937 9921); 117 Euston Road, London NW1; 25 Queen's Road, Bristol BS8 1QE (☎0272/294 399); 38 Sidney Street, Cambridge CB2 3HX (☎0223/66966); 36 George Street, Oxford OX1 2OJ (☎0865/792 8000); 75 Deansgate, Manchester M3 2BW (☎061/834 0668). *Independent travel specialists; discounted flights.*

Time Off 2a Chester Close, Chester Street, London SW1 (☎071/235 8070). *City breaks.*

Travellers Way Hewell Lane, Tardebigge, Bromsgrove, Worcs B60 1LP (☎0527/836 791). *Tailor-made holidays and city breaks all over Spain, especially Andalucía.*

Waymark Holidays 44 Windsor Road, Slough SL1 2EJ (☎0753/516 477). *Walking holidays in Andalucía and along the Camino de Santiago.*

---

airport, back from another); Fly-Drive deals; and inexpensive connections from most regional UK airports. The cheapest tickets with *Iberia* or *BA* go by various names at different times of the year, but they are usually only valid for one month, require you to stay at least one Saturday night, and don't allow for change or cancellation. Consequently there's no great difference between these and a charter ticket but prices are

competitive: fares start from around £157 return from London to Madrid in low season to £230 in July and August.

For a more flexible ticket, such as BA's *Excursion* fare, which is valid for six months, can be upgraded and is fully refundable, you're looking at around £344 from London to Madrid (£374 from Manchester) and £314 from London to Barcelona (£344 from Manchester).

PACKAGES AND CITY BREAKS

Package holiday deals can be worth looking at, especially if you book early, late or out of season. While the cheaper, mass market packages may seem to restrict you to some of the worst parts of the coast, remember that there's no compulsion to stick around your hotel. Get a good enough deal and it can be worth it simply for the flight – with transfer to a reasonably comfortable hotel laid on for a night or two at each end. Bargains can be found at virtually any high street travel agent.

City breaks are often available at excellent package rates and destinations on offer include Barcelona, Madrid, Sevilla and Granada, flying from London or Manchester. Prices start at around £200 for three days (two nights); adding extra nights or upgrading your hotel is possible, too, usually at a fairly reasonable cost. The prices always include return flights and bed and breakfast in a centrally located one-, two- or three-star hotel. Again, ask your travel agent for the best deal, and check the addresses in the box opposite.

Fly-Drive deals are well worth considering, too, as a combined air ticket and car rental arrangement can be excellent value. There are also some very good (and very attractive) deals available in **villas and apartments**, especially from companies who specialize in off-the-beaten-track farmhouses and the like. Several companies have started offering a range of *casas rurales*, on a similar basis to French *gîtes*. Other specialist companies offer an enticing range of **trekking holidays**, or, moving upmarket, tours based around the country's historic *paradores*.

BY TRAIN

From London to **San Sebastián** (for Madrid, Old Castile and the northwest) or **Barcelona** takes just under 24 hours by train, though once through trains from London to Paris are in operation using the Channel Tunnel (see p.10) you can expect the time to drop a little. Currently, departures are from Victoria station around 9am, changing trains (and stations, from Nord to Austerlitz) in Paris around 6–8pm and again at the Spanish border (at Hendaye/Irún or Cerbere/Port Bou) around dawn. It's an efficient approach, and can be an interesting one if you stop over en route.

OTHER ROUTES

Two exciting (but more expensive) alternatives are the minor routes which cross the central Pyrenees to enter Aragón at Canfranc or Catalunya at Puigcerdà On the first of these *British Rail* will issue a ticket only as far as Oloron in France, from where you have to cross the border by bus. Similarly on the Catalan route, *British Rail* fares are sold only as far as the French station at Bourg-Madame, just over the frontier from Puigcerdà, where you must change trains. On both routes you may have to spend the night at either of the border towns if you want to see the mountains in daylight.

TICKETS AND PASSES

A **standard rail ticket** from London to Madrid will currently cost you £198 return, to Barcelona £167 return, to San Sebastián £170 return. Tickets are bookable through some travel agents or at London's Victoria station.

The alternative for **under-26s** is a discounted **BIJ** ticket from *Eurotrain* (through *Campus Travel*) or *Wasteels*. These can be booked for journeys from any British station to any major station in Europe; like full-price tickets, they remain valid for two months and allow as many stopovers as you want along a pre-specified route (which can be different going out and coming home). The current return fare from London to Barcelona is £165, to Madrid £195 (via Hendaye), to San Sebastián £168 (via Hendaye), and to Málaga and Sevilla £217. You might consider instead *Eurotrain's* **Spanish Explorer Ticket** (£202), valid for two months on the London – Paris – Toulouse – Biarritz – San Sebastián – Madrid – Barcelona – Lyon – Paris – London route; again, you can stop off anywhere along the way.

If you plan to travel extensively in Europe by train, there are better value options than simply buying a return ticket. Under-26s can invest in an **InterRail pass** from *British Rail* or a travel agent; the only restriction is that you must have been resident in Europe for at least six months.

TRAIN INFORMATION

British Rail European information line ☎071/ 834 2345

Eurotrain 52 Grosvenor Gds, London SW1 ☎071/730 3402

Wasteels, Victoria Station, London SW1 ☎071/ 834 7066

BUS INFORMATION

Eurolines *National Express*, 164 Buckingham Palace Rd, London SW1 ☎071/730 0202

This comes in two forms; either an *InterRail Global* pass, valid for one month's unlimited travel in 26 European countries including Spain (£249), or an *InterRail Zonal* pass, whereby the 26 countries are split into seven zones and you choose which countries you want the pass to be valid for – Spain is grouped with Portugal and Morocco. A fifteen-day pass for any one zone costs £179; any two zones, valid for one month, costs £209, any three, also for one month, £229. In addition all *InterRail* passes offer discounts on rail travel in the UK, on Channel ferries, and on ferries from Spain to the Balearics and Morocco. Since Spain has an extensive rail network this is basically a bargain though be prepared (see p.22) to pay various and unpredictable supplements on some of the Spanish services; there are also one or two private lines on which passes are not valid.

BY BUS

The main **bus route** from Britain to Spain is from London to Barcelona (daily in season, 3 times a week out; 26hr) and Alicante (3 times a week; 35hr) via the Costa Brava. There are also two buses a week to Algeciras (43hr), via Paris, San Sebastián (24hr), Madrid (32hr; more buses run this far in season), Málaga (38hr) and the Costa del Sol; at least two a week to Zaragoza (27hr) via Pamplona (25hr); and two to Santiago (36hr) along the north coast. Fares start at around £68 single, £121 return (to Barcelona or San Sebastián), rising to £85 single, £149 return for the Costa del Sol destinations in peak season, with a ten percent reduction if you're under 26.

All these routes are operated by *Eurolines* in Britain and by *Iberbus/Linebus* and *Julia* in Spain. In both Britain and Spain tickets are bookable through most major travel agents; *Eurolines* sells tickets and through-transport to London at all British *National Express* bus terminals.

To San Sebastián or Barcelona the journey is long but quite bearable – just make sure you take along enough to eat, drink and read, and a small amount of French and Spanish currency for coffee and the like. There are stops for around twenty minutes every four to five hours and the routine is also broken by the Dover–Calais/Boulogne ferry (which is included in the cost of the ticket). Any further and you may well find that air tickets in fact compare very favourably price and comfort-wise.

BY CAR, FERRY AND LE SHUTTLE

The coach routes follow the most direct roads from London to Spain: if you plan to **drive** them yourself, unless you're into non-stop rally motoring, you'll need to roughly double their times. There are now two **direct ferry sailings** to **Bilbāo** and **Santander** from Britain. See the box opposite for ferry company addresses, or contact your local travel agent for the latest ticket and sailing details.

LE SHUTTLE AND CROSS-CHANNEL SERVICES

The opening of **Le Shuttle** service through the Channel Tunnel won't significantly affect travel times for drivers to Spain, though it will of course speed up the cross-Channel section of the journey. Le Shuttle is due to operate trains 24 hours a day carrying cars, motorcycles, coaches and their passengers, taking 35 minutes between Folkestone and Calais. At peak times, services will operate every fifteen minutes, making advance bookings unnecessary; during the night, services are hourly. Through trains will eventually connect London with Paris in just over three hours. Return fares from May to August cost £280–310 per vehicle (passengers included), with discounts in the low season on either side.

Traditional cross-Channel options are the **ferry** or **hovercraft** links between **Dover** and Calais or Boulogne, or, if you're headed for the northwest of Spain, ferries to Le Havre (from Portsmouth), Cherbourg (from Portsmouth and Weymouth), St Malo (from Portsmouth) or even Roscoff (from Plymouth). Any of these cuts out the trek round or through Paris, and opens up some interesting detours around Brittany and the French Atlantic coast. Ferry **prices** vary according to the time of year and, for motorists, the size of your car. The Dover–Calais/Boulogne runs, for example, start at about £70 one-way for a car, two adults and two kids, but this figure doubles in high season. Foot passengers should be able to cross for about £20–30.

TO SANTANDER AND BILBÃO

The direct car and passenger ferry services from England to Spain are convenient but expensive.

The ferry from **Plymouth to Santander** is operated by *Brittany Ferries*, takes 24 hours and runs twice weekly for most of the year (less often from December to mid-March). Ticket prices vary

FERRY COMPANIES AND LE SHUTTLE

Brittany Ferries Millbay Docks, Plymouth (☎0752/221 321); Wharf Rd, Portsmouth (☎0705/827 701); New Harbour Rd, Poole (☎0202/671 100).
To Santander, St Malo, Roscoff, Cherbourg and Caen.

Hoverspeed International Hoverport, Dover, Kent (☎0304/240 101); also in London (☎081/554 7061).
To Boulogne and Calais.

P&O European Ferries Channel House, Channel View Rd, Dover (☎0304/203 388); Continental Ferry Port, Mile End, Portsmouth (☎0705/772 244)

also in London (☎081/575 8555).
To Calais, Cherbourg, Le Havre and Bilbão.

Sally Line Argyle Centre, York St, Ramsgate, Kent (☎0843/595 522); 81 Piccadilly, London W1 (☎081/858 1127).
To Dunkerque.

Stena Sealink Line Charter House, Park St, Ashford, Kent (☎0233/647 047).
To Calais, Cherbourg and Dieppe.

Le Shuttle Customer Services Centre (Information and ticket sales ☎0303/271 100).

---

enormously according to the season and the number of passengers carried; one-way fares start at around £111 for a car plus £48 per person mid-season. Foot passengers will pay around £50 one way, and everyone has to book some form of accommodation; cheapest is a pullman seat (from £3.50 off season), and two- and four-berth cabins are available for around £50–70 each. Tickets are best booked in advance, through any major travel agent.

P&O has recently started a twice-weekly ferry service from **Portsmouth to Bilbão**. The journey takes approximately 30 hours and leaves Portsmouth on Saturdays and Tuesdays. A mid-season return for a car and up to five passengers costs £638; foot passengers £129 (children £54). All prices include a cabin.

HITCHING

Hitching on major French routes – and Spanish ones too – can be dire, and stopping people and asking directly for lifts in cafés is about the only technique that works. At all events don't try to hitch from the Channel ports to Paris (organize a lift while you're still on the ferry) nor (still worse) out of Paris itself. If you can afford it, perhaps the best approach is to buy a train ticket to somewhere south of Paris and set out from there. Lille or Orléans are reasonably well poised for Barcelona; Tours or Chartres for San Sebastián.

Freewheelers (☎091/222 0090) is a Newcastle-based **lift-sharing service**, which can arrange lifts from all over the UK to Spain. It is free to drivers and costs passengers a few pounds in fees plus any arrangements with the driver.

GETTING THERE FROM IRELAND

Summer charter flights to the Costa del Sol and Costa Brava are easy to pick up from either Dublin or Belfast, while year-round scheduled services operate to Madrid and Barcelona. However, other package holidays or city breaks are often routed via London, with an add-on fare from Ireland for the connection. Students, and anyone under the age of 31, should contact *USIT*, which generally has the best discount deals on flights and train tickets. For *InterRail* details, see pp.9–10).

Iberia has direct **scheduled flights** from Dublin to Madrid costing from £IR225 return in the low season (Jan–Feb) to £IR271 in July and

August, and to Barcelona costing from £IR197–237. These cheapest fares have several restrictions – you must stay at least one Saturday night, and can only stay for a maximmum of one month – and if you want to change your departure date you can do so only once by paying an upgrade fee of £IR30.

There are direct once-a-week summer **charter flights** to the Costa del Sol (Málaga) and the Costa Brava from Belfast (around £269 return) and Dublin (IR£239–269), with prices at their highest during August and dropping a little in the months either side. If you're prepared to book at the last minute, you'll often get much better flight-only deals than this, though obviously you can't guarantee the departure date you want.

For a two-week **package** to the Costa del Sol or Costa Brava (based on four people in a self-catering apartment), you can expect to pay from £315 (low season) to £409 (high) from Belfast; from IR£285 (low) to IR£395 (high) from Dublin. **City breaks** out of Belfast run from £209–285 for three days (two nights) in Barcelona and from £189 –289 in Madrid; you can book a city break from Dublin, but it basically means sorting out a city break deal from London with your travel agent, which will then be able to sell you a connecting, add-on Dublin–London flight from IR£59–89, depending on which London airport you fly into.

If you're really trying to get to Spain in the cheapest possible way, you might find that budget flights from Dublin (with *Ryanair, Aer*

USEFUL ADDRESSES IN IRELAND

AIRLINES

British Airways 60 Dawson St, Dublin (☎800/626 747); 9 Fountain Centre, College St, Belfast (☎0232/245 151).

Iberia 54 Dawson St, Dublin 2 (☎01/677 9846)

Aer Lingus, 42 Grafton St, Dublin (☎01/637 0011); 46 Castle St, Belfast (☎0232/245 151).

AGENTS AND OPERATORS

Joe Walsh Tours 8–11 Baggot St, Dublin (☎01/678 9555). General budget fares agent.

Thomas Cook, 118 Grafton St, Dublin (☎01/677 1721); 11 Donegall Place, Belfast (☎0232/240 833). Package holiday and flight agent, with occasional discount offers.

USIT O'Connell Bridge, 19–21 Aston Quay, Dublin 2 (☎01/778 117); 10–11 Market Parade, Cork (☎021/270 900); 31a Queen St, Belfast (☎0232/242 562) Student and youth specialist for flights and trains.

Lingus and *British Midland*) or Belfast (*British Airways* and *British Midland*) to London, plus a last-minute London charter flight, will save you a few pounds, but don't count on it. Buying a

Eurotrain ticket (from *USIT*) from Dublin to London will slightly undercut the plane's price, but by this time you're starting to talk about a journey of days and not hours.

GETTING THERE FROM AUSTRALIA & NEW ZEALAND

There are no direct flights to Spain from Australia or New Zealand, but by combining services some airlines now offer travel to

Madrid (and sometimes Barcelona) in conjunction witrh a stopover in Europe. While this means a journey of around 24 hours' flying time – not counting time spent waiting for connections – this is a good way to see places on the way if you're not rushed for time. *British Airways, Aeroflot* and *Japanese Airlines* provide the most direct services.

As destinations in Europe are "common rated" – you pay the same fare whatever your destination – some airlines offer free flight coupons, car rental or accommodation if you book these extras with your ticket. Choose carefully, though, as these perks are impossible to alter later. Alternatively, you could buy the cheapest possible flight to anywhere in Europe and make your way to Spain by standby flight, train or bus, but this rarely works out as cheaply as buying a discounted flight airfare all the way. For extended

---

AIRLINES

Aeroflot 388 George St, Sydney (☎02/233 7911). *Low fares from Sydney via Moscow to Madrid twice a week; for a little more you can fly to Singapore on Singapore Airlines and connect with Aeroflot there..*

Air France 12 Castlereagh St, Sydney (☎02/233 3277); 57 Fort St, Auckland (☎09/303 1229). *One weekly from Sydney and Auckland to Madrid or Barcelona via Pacific islands..*

British Airways 64 Castelreagh St, Sydney (☎02/258 3300). *Use the free European flight included in the London ticket price to reach Madrid or Barcelona . Daily to London from Sydney.*

Garuda 120 Albert St, Auckland (☎09/366 1855). *Combined services with KLM; flights to Madrid via Jakarta and Amsterdam.*

Japanese Airlines 17 Bligh St, Sydney (☎02/233 4500). *Flies from Sydney via Tokyo to Madrid three times a week, and includes one night's accommodation in Tokyo.*

KLM 5 Elizabeth St, Sydney (☎02/231 6333). *Combines services with Singapore Airlines or Lufthansa/Air Lauda for Madrid via Amsterdam.*

Lufthansa 143 Macquarie St, Sydney (☎02/367 3800). *Combines with KLM and Air Lauda to Europe; use the free flight coupons (booked with main ticket and not alterable) from hub European cities to reach Spain.*

Malaysian Airlines 388 George St, Sydney (☎02/231 5066). *Once weekly to Madrid via Kuala Lumpur and London.*

Qantas Qantas House, 154 Queen St, Auckland (☎09/303 2506). *Three times a week from Auckland via Rome to Madrid..*

Singapore Airlines 17 Bridge St, Sydney (☎02/236 0111). *Combined services with KLM (see above).*

Thai International, Kensington Swan Building, 22 Fanshawe St, Auckland (☎09/377 0268). *Spanish connections from Bangkok via London.*

AUSTRALIAN DISCOUNT AGENTS

Anywhere Travel 345 Anzac Parade, Kingsford, Sydney (☎02/663 0411).

Brisbane Discount Travel 360 Queen St, Brisbane (☎07/229 9211).

Discount Travel Specialists Shop 53, Forrest Chase, Perth (☎09/221 1400).

Flight Centres Circular Quay, Sydney (☎02/241 2422); Bourke St, Melbourne ☎03/650 2899; plus other branches nationwide except the Northern Territory.

Passport Travel 320b Glenfarrie Rd, Malvern, Melbourne (☎03/824 7183).

STA Travel 732 Harris St, Sydney (☎02/212 1255); 256 Flinders St, Melbourne (☎03/347 4711); other offices in Townsville and state capitals.

Topdeck Travel 45 Grenfell St, Adelaide (☎08/410 1110).

Tymtro Travel Suite G12, Wallaceway Shopping Centre, Chatswood, Sydney (☎02/411 1222).

NEW ZEALAND DISCOUNT AGENTS

Budget Travel PO Box 505, Auckland (☎09/309 4313).

Flight Centres National Bank Towers, 205–225 Queen St, Auckland (☎09/309 6171); Shop 1M, National Mutual Arcade, 152 Hereford St, Christchurch (☎09/379 7145); 50–52 Willis St, Wellington (☎04/472 8101); other branches countrywide.

STA Travel Traveller's Centre, 10 High St, Auckland (☎09/309 9995); 233 Cuba St, Wellington (☎04/385 0561); 223 High St, Christchurch (☎03/379 9098); other offices in Dunedin, Palmerston North and Hamilton.

---

trips, Round the World (RTW) tickets, valid for up to a year, are a good option – especially from New Zealand, where airlines offer fewer bonuses to fly with them.

FARES

Fares change according to the time of year you travel. December and January is high season; February, and October through to mid-November the low season; and the rest of the year the shoulder season. The current lowest standard return fares to Madrid (low/high season) are around A$2000/2200 from eastern Australia; A$1990/2200 from Perth; NZ$2200/2600 from Auckland.

While charging heavily for cancellations or alterations, **discount agents** can usually provide far better prices than these – from A$1700/NZ$2155 for a low-season fare. Full-time students, and those under 26 or over 60, can also make big savings through specialist agents. Some are listed above, and you'll find others in the travel sections of the major Saturday papers.

RED TAPE AND VISAS

Citizens of most EC countries (and of Norway, Sweden, Finland and Iceland) need only a valid national identity card to enter Spain for up to ninety days. Since Britain has no identity card system, however, British citizens do have to take a passport. US citizens require a passport but no visa and can stay for up to six months; other European, Canadian and New Zealand citizens also require a passport and can stay for up to ninety days. Australians need a visa, but can get one on arrival which is valid for thirty days.

To stay longer, EC nationals (and citizens of Norway, Sweden, Finland and Iceland) can apply for a *permiso de residencia* (residence permit) once in Spain. You'll have to either produce proof that you have sufficient funds (officially 5000ptas a day) to be able to support yourself without working – easiest done by keeping bank exchange forms every time you change money – or you'll have to have a contract of employment (*contrato de trabajo*) or become self-employed (for example as a teacher), which involves registering at the tax office. Other nationalities will either need to get a special visa from a Spanish consulate before departure (see below for addresses), or can apply for one ninety-day extension, showing proof of funds.

CUSTOMS

Customs and duty-free restrictions vary throughout Europe, with subtle variations even within the European Community.

Since the inauguration of the EC Single Market, travellers entering Britain from another EC country do not have to make a declaration to Customs at their place of entry. You can effectively bring in as much duty-paid wine or beer as you can carry (the legal limits being 90 litres of wine or 110 of beer), though there are still restrictions on the volume of tax- or duty-free goods you can bring into the country. The current duty-free allowance for EC citizens is 200 cigarettes, one litre of spirits and five litres of wine; for non-EC residents the allowances are usually 200 cigarettes, one litre of spirits and two litres of wine.

Residents of the USA and Canada can take up to 200 cigarettes and one litre of alcohol home, as can **Australian** citizens, while **New Zealanders** must confine themselves to 200 cigarettes, 4.5 litres of beer or wine, and just over one litre of spirits.

INSURANCE

As an EC country, Spain has free reciprocal health agreements with other member states (to take advantage, you should carry form E111, available over the counter from main post offices). Even so, some form of travel insurance is still all but essential. With insurance you'll be able to claim back the cost of any drugs prescribed by pharmacies, and European policies generally cover your baggage/tickets in case of theft, so long as you get a report from the local police. North American policies – see below – are more complex and restrictive.

EUROPEAN INSURANCE COVER

In Britain and Ireland, travel insurance schemes (from around £20 a month) are sold by almost every travel agent and bank, or consider a specialist insurance firm. Policies issued by *Campus Travel* (see p.8 for address), *Endsleigh Insurance* (97–107 Southampton Row, London WC1; ☎071/436 4451), or *Columbus Travel Insurance* (17 Devonshire Square, London EC2; ☎071/375 0011) are all good value. If you're going skiing in the Pyrenees, or engaging in any other high risk outdoor activity, you'll probably have to pay an extra premium; ask your insurers for advice.

NORTH AMERICAN INSURANCE

In the **US and Canada**, insurance tends to be much more expensive, and may be medical cover

only. Before buying a policy, check that you're not already covered by existing insurance plans. **Canadians** are usually covered by their provincial health plans; holders of **ISIC cards** and some other student/teacher/youth cards are entitled to $3000 worth of accident coverage and sixty days ($100 per day) of hospital in-patient benefits for the period during which the card is valid.

Students will often find that their student health coverage extends during the vacations and for one term beyond the date of last enrolment. Bank and credit cards (particularly *American Express*) often have certain levels of medical or other insurance included, and travel insurance may also be included if you use a major credit or charge card to pay for your trip. **Homeowners' or renters'** insurance often covers theft or loss of documents, money and valuables while overseas, though conditions and maximum amounts vary from company to company.

Only after exhausting the possibilities above might you want to contact a specialist travel insurance company; your travel agent can usually recommend one. Travel insurance offerings are quite comprehensive, anticipating everything from charter companies going bankrupt to delayed or lost baggage, by way of sundry illnesses and accidents. **Premiums** vary widely, from the very reasonable ones offered primarily through student/youth agencies (*STA*'s policies range from about $50–70 for fifteen days to $500–700 for a year, depending on the amount of financial cover), to those so expensive that the cost for anything more than two months of coverage will probably equal the cost of the worst possible combination of disasters. Note also that very few insurers will arrange on-the-spot payments in the event of a major expense or loss; you will usually be reimbursed only after going home. If you're planning on doing any **trekking, mountaineering or skiing** while abroad, you'll need to take out an additional rider to cover these activities – this will add an extra thirty to fifty percent to the premium.

None of these policies insure against **theft** of anything while overseas. North American travel policies apply only to items **lost** from, or **damaged** in, the custody of an identifiable, responsible third party – hotel porter, airline, luggage consignment, etc. Even in these cases you will have to contact the local police to have a complete report made out so that your insurer can process the claim. If you are travelling via London it might be better to take out a British policy, available instantly and easily (though making the claim may prove more complicated).

TRAVELLERS WITH DISABILITIES

Spain is not exactly at the forefront of providing facilities for travellers with disabilities. That said, there are accessible hotels in the major cities and resorts and, by law, all new public buildings are required to be fully accessible. The staging of the 1992 Paralympic Games in Barcelona has done much to help attitudes and facilities there; and there are also a number of active and forceful groups of disabled people: *ONCE*, the Spanish organization for the blind, is particularly active, its huge lottery bringing with it considerable power.

Transport is still the main problem, since buses are virtually impossible for wheelchairs and trains only slightly better (though there are wheelchairs at major stations and wheelchair spaces in some carriages). *Hertz* has cars with hand controls available in Madrid and Barcelona (with advance notice), and taxi drivers are usually helpful. The *Brittany Ferries* crossing from Plymouth to Santander offers good facilities if you're **driving to Spain** (as do most cross-Channel ferries).

Once out of the cities and away from the coast, the difficulties increase. Road surfaces in the mountain regions can be rough and toilet facilities for disabled motorists are a rare sight. If you've got the money, *paradores* are one answer to the problem of unsuitable **accommodation**. Many are converted from castles and monasteries and although not built with the disabled guest in mind, their grand scale – with plenty of room to manoeuvre a wheelchair inside – tends to compensate.

CONTACTS FOR TRAVELLERS WITH DISABILITIES

General

Spanish National Tourist Office (See p.18 for addresses). *Publishes a fact sheet, listing a avriety of useful addresses and some accessible accommodation.*

Organización Nacional de Ciegos de España (*ONCE***)**, c/de Prado 24, Madrid (☎91/589 46 00); c/Calabria 66–76, Barcelona 08015 (☎93/325 92 00). *Sells braille maps and can arrange trips for blind people; write for details.*

Institut Municipal de Disminuits c/Comte d'Urgell 240, 3°/A, Barcelona (☎93/439 66 00)

Britain

Holiday Care Service 2 Old Bank Chambers, Station Rd, Horley, Surrey RH6 9HW (☎0293/774535). *Information on all aspects of travel.*

Mobility International, 228 Borough High St, London SE1 1JX (☎071/403 5688). *Information, access guides, tours and exchange programmes.*

RADAR 25 Mortimer St, London W1N 8AB (☎071/637 5400). *A good source of advice on holidays and travel abroad.*

North America

Information Center for People with Disabilities Fort Point Place, 27–43 Wormwood St, Boston, MA 02210 (☎617/727-5540). *Clearing house for information, including travel.*

Jewish Rehabilitation Hospital 3205 Place Alton Goldbloom, Montréal, Québec H7V 1R2 (☎514/688-9550). *Guidebooks and travel information.*

Kéroul 4545 Ave Pierre de Coubertin, CP 1000, Montréal H1V 3R2 (☎512/252-3104). *Travel for mobility-impaired people.*

Mobility International USA Box 10767, Eugene, OR 97440 (☎503/343-1284). *Information, access guides, tours and exchange programmes.*

Travel Information Center Moss Rehabilitation Hospital, 1200 West Tabor Rd, Philadelphia, PA 19141 (☎215/456-9900). *Access information.*

INFORMATION AND MAPS

The Spanish National Tourist Office (SNTO) produces and gives away an impressive variety of maps, pamphlets and special interest leaflets. Visit one of their offices before you leave and stock up, especially on city plans, as well as province-by-province lists of hotels, *hostales* and campsites.

INFORMATION OFFICES

In Spain itself you'll find SNTO offices in virtually every major town (addresses are detailed in the *Guide*) and from these you can usually get more specific local information. SNTO offices are often supplemented by separately administered provincial or municipal **Turismo** bureaux. These vary enormously in quality, but while they are generally extremely useful for regional information, and local maps, they cannot be relied on to know anything about what goes on outside their patch.

Spanish Turismo **hours** are usually Mon–Fri 9am–1pm and 3.30–6pm, Sat 9am–1pm – but you can't always rely on the official hours, especially in the more out-of-the-way places.

In the main cities, branches of the department store, *El Corte Ingles*, also provide information services and useful free maps.

MAPS

In addition to the various free leaflets, the one extra you'll want is a reasonable **road map**. This is best bought in Spain, where you'll find a good selection in most bookshops (*librerías*) and at street kiosks or petrol stations. Among the best are those published by *Editorial Almax*, which also produces reliable indexed **street plans** of the main cities.

Good alternatives, especially if you're shopping before arrival, are the 1:800,000 map put out by *RV* (*Reise und Verkehrsverlag*, Stuttgart) and packaged in Spain by *Plaza & Janes*, or less detailed offerings from *Michelin*, *Firestone* or *Rand McNally*. The most comprehensive **city**

SNTO OFFICES ABROAD

Britain 57–58 St James's St, London SW1A 1LD (☎071/499 0901 or 499 1169). *The number is invariably engaged; write or visit.*

Australia 203 Castlereagh St, Suite 21a, PO Box A685, Sydney, NSW (☎02/ 264 79 66).

Belgium 18 Rue de la Montagne, 1000 Bruxelles (☎02/512 57 35).

Canada 102 Bloor St W, 14th Floor, Toronto, Ontario (☎416/961 31 31).

Denmark Store Kongensgade 1–3, Kobenhavn (☎33/15 11 65).

France Ave Pierre 1er de Serbie 43, 75381 Paris (☎61 47 23 37).

Netherlands Laan Van Meerdevoort 8, 2517 Den Haag (☎070/46 59 00).

Norway Ruselökkveien 26, 0251 Oslo 2 (☎22 83 40 92).

Portugal Rua Camilo Costelo Branco 34, 1000 Lisbon (☎01/54 19 92).

Sweden Grev Turegatan 7, 1TR, 114-46 Stockholm (☎08/611 41 36).

USA 665 Fifth Ave, New York, NY 10022 (☎212/759 88 22); 8383 Wilshire Boulevard, Suite 960, Beverly Hills, CA 90211 (☎213/658 7188); Water Tower Place, Suite 915 East, 845 North Michigan Ave, Chicago, IL 60611 (☎312/642 1992); 1211 Brickell Ave #1850, Miami, FL 33131 (☎305/358 1992).

MAP OUTLETS

IN THE UK

London *National Map Centre*, 22–24 Caxton St, SW1 (☎071/222 4945); *Stanfords*, 12–14 Long Acre, WC2 (☎071/836 1321); *The Travellers Bookshop*, 25 Cecil Court, WC2 (☎071/836 9132).

Edinburgh *Thomas Nelson and Sons Ltd*, 51 York Place, EH1 3JD (☎031/557 3011).

Glasgow *John Smith and Sons*, 57–61 St Vincent St (☎041/221 7472).

Note: maps by **mail or phone order** are available from *Stanfords* (☎071/836 1321).

IN NORTH AMERICA

Chicago *Rand McNally*, 444 N Michigan Ave, IL 60611(☎312/321-1751).

Montréal *Ulysses Travel Bookshop*, 4176 St-Denis (☎514/289-0993).

New York *British Travel Bookshop*, 551 Fifth Ave, NY 10176 (☎1-800/448-3039 or 212/490-6688); *The Complete Traveler Bookstore*, 199 Madison Ave, NY 10016 (☎212/685-9007); *Rand McNally*, 150 E 52nd St, NY 10022 (☎212/758-7488); *Traveler's Bookstore*, 22 W 52nd St, NY 10019 (☎212/664-0995).

San Francisco *The Complete Traveler Bookstore*, 3207 Fillmore St, CA 92123 (☎415/923-1511); *Rand McNally*, 595 Market St, CA 94105 (☎415/777-3131).

Santa Barbara *Map Link, Inc*, 25 E Mason St, CA 93101 (☎805/965-4402).

Seattle *Elliot Bay Book Company*, 101 S Main St, WA 98104 (☎206/624-6600).

Toronto *Open Air Books and Maps*, 25 Toronto St, M5R 2C1 (☎416/363-0719).

Vancouver *World Wide Books and Maps*, 1247 Granville St (☎604/687-3320).

Washington DC *Rand McNally*, 1201 Connecticut Ave NW, Washington DC 20036 (☎202/223-6751).

Note: *Rand McNally* now has 24 stores across the US; call ☎1-800/333-0136 (ext 2111) for the address of your nearest store, or for **direct mail** maps.

IN AUSTRALIA AND NEW ZEALAND

Adelaide *The Map Shop*, 16a Peel St, Adelaide, SA 5000 (☎08/231 2033).

Brisbane *Hema*, 239 George St, Brisbane, QLD 4000 (☎07/221 4330).

Melbourne *Bowyangs*, 372 Little Bourke St, Melbourne, VIC 3000 (☎03/670 4383).

Perth *Perth Map Centre*, 891 Hay St, Perth, WA 6000 (☎09/322 5733).

Sydney *Travel Bookshop*, 20 Bridge St, Sydney, NSW 2000 (☎02/241 3554).

---

street plans are the fold-out *Falkplans*, covering all the suburbs and with full street indexes; they are available for Madrid, Barcelona and Sevilla.

Serious **trekkers** can get more detailed maps from *La Tienda Verde* at c/Maudes 38, Madrid, and *Libreria Quera* at c/Petritxol 2, Barcelona. Both of these stores – and many other bookshops in Spain, and a few specialists overseas – stock the full range of **topographical maps** issued by two government agencies: the *IGN* (*Instituto Geográfico Nacional*), and the *SGE* (*Servicio Geográfico del Ejército*). They are available at scales of 1:200,000, 1:100,000, 1:50,000 and even occasionally 1:25,000. The various *SGE* series are considered to be more up to date, although neither are hugely reliable.

A Catalunya-based company, *Editorial Alpina*, produces useful 1:40,000 or 1:25,000 map-**booklets** for most of the Spanish mountain and foothill areas of interest, and these are also on sale in many bookshops; the relevant editions are noted in the text where appropriate.

COSTS, MONEY AND BANKS

Although people still think of Spain as a budget destination, hotel prices have increased considerably over the last three or four years, and if you're spending a lot of your time in the cities, you can expect to spend easily as much as you would at home, if not more. However, there are still few places in Europe where you'll get a better deal on the cost of simple meals and drink.

On average, if you're prepared to buy your own picnic lunch, stay in inexpensive *pensiones* and hotels, and stick to local restaurants and bars, you could get by on £15–20/US$23–30 a day. If you intend to upgrade your accommodation, experience the city nightlife and eat fancier meals then you'll need more like £40/$60 a day. On £50–60/$75–90 a day and upwards you'll only be limited by your energy reserves – though of course if you're planning to stay in four- and five-star hotels or Spain's magnificent *paradores*, this figure won't even cover your room.

Room prices vary considerably according to season. In the summer you'll find little below 1500ptas (£7/$11) single, 2000ptas (£9/$14) double, and 1800ptas single, 2500ptas double (£11.50/$18) might be a more realistic average. Campsites start at around 400ptas (£2/$3.30) a night per person (more like 600ptas in some of the major resorts), plus a similar charge for a tent.

The cost of **eating** can vary wildly, but in most towns there'll be restaurants offering a basic three-course meal for somewhere between 750 and 1500ptas (£3.50–7/$5.50–11). As often as not, though, you'll end up wandering from one bar to the next sampling *tapas* without getting round to a real sit-down meal – this is certainly tastier though rarely any cheaper (see "Eating and Drinking"). Drink, and wine in particular, costs ridiculously little: £3/$5 will see you through a night's very substantial intake of the local vintage.

Long-distance **transport**, if used extensively, may prove a major expense. Although prices compare well with the rest of Europe, Spain is a very large country. Madrid to Sevilla, for example – a journey of over 500km – costs around 3500ptas (£17/$25) by bus or train. Urban transport almost always operates on a flat fare of 150–250ptas (70p–£1.20/$1–1.80).

All of the above, inevitably, are affected by where you are and when. The big cities and tourist resorts are invariably more expensive than remoter areas, and certain regions tend also to have higher prices – notably the industrialized north, Euskadi, Catalunya and Aragón, and the Balearic Islands. Prices are hiked up, too, to take advantage of special events. Despite official controls, you'd be lucky to find a room in Sevilla during its April *feria*, or in Pamplona for the running of the bulls, at less than double the usual rate. As always, if you're travelling alone you'll end up spending much more than you would in a group of two or more – sharing rooms saves greatly. An *ISIC* student card is worth having – it'll get you free or reduced entry to many museums and sites as well as occasional other discounts – and a *FIYTO* youth card (available to anyone under 26) is almost as good.

One thing to look out for on prices generally is the addition of sales tax – **IVA** – which may come as an unexpected extra when you pay the bill for food or accommodation, especially in more expensive establishments.

MONEY AND THE EXCHANGE RATE

The Spanish currency is the peseta, indicated in this book as "ptas". **Coins** come in denominations of 1, 5, 10, 25, 50, 100, 200 and 500 pesetas; **notes** as 1000, 2000, 5000 and 10,000 pesetas. The only oddity is that in a shop when paying for something, you'll often be asked for a *duro* (5ptas) or *cinco duros* (25ptas).

The **exchange rate** for the Spanish peseta is currently around 215 to the pound sterling, 140 to the US dollar. You can take in as much money as you want (in any form), although amounts over a million pesetas must be declared, and you can only take up to 500,000 pesetas out unless you can prove that you brought more with you in the first place. Not, perhaps, a major holiday worry.

TRAVELLERS' CHEQUES AND CREDIT CARDS

Probably the safest and easiest way to carry your funds is in **travellers' cheques** – though watch out for occasionally outrageous commissions; 500–600ptas per transaction isn't unusual. If you have an ordinary British bank account (or virtually any European one) you can use **Eurocheques** with a Eurocheque card in many banks and can also write out cheques in pesetas in shops and hotels.

Most Eurocheque cards, many Visa, Mastercard (Access) or British automatic bank cards, and US cards in the Cirrus or Plus systems, can also be used for **withdrawing cash** from ATMs in Spain: check with your bank to find out about these reciprocal arrangements – the system is highly sophisticated and can usually give instructions in a variety of languages.

Leading **credit cards** are recognized too, and are useful for such extra expenses as car rental, as well as for cash advances at banks. American Express, and Visa, which has an arrangement with the Banco de Bilbão, are the most useful; Mastercard is less widely accepted.

CHANGING MONEY

Spanish **bancos** (banks) and **cajas de ahorro** (savings banks) have branches in all but the smallest towns, and most of them should be prepared to change travellers' cheques (albeit occasionally with reluctance for certain brands, and almost always with hefty commissions). The *Banco Central Hispano* and *Banco Bilbão Vizcaya* are two of the most efficient and widespread; all handle Eurocheques, change most brands of travellers' cheques, and give cash advances on credit cards; commissions at the *Banco Central Hispano* are generally the lowest. Elsewhere you may have to queue up at two or three windows, a twenty-to-thirty-minute process.

Banking hours are Mon–Fri 9am–2pm, Sat 9am–1pm (except from June to September when banks close on Saturday). Outside these times, it's usually possible to change cash at larger hotels (generally bad rates, low commission) or with travel agents, who may initially grumble but will eventually give a rate with the commission built in – useful for small amounts in a hurry.

In tourist areas you'll also find specialist *casas de cambio*, with more convenient hours (though rates vary), and most branches of *El Corte Inglés*, a major department store found throughout Spain, have efficient exchange facilities open throughout store hours and offering competitive rates and generally a much lower commission than the banks (though they're worse for cash).

American Express offices can also be useful; their addresses are given in the *Guide* for cities where they have representation.

GETTING AROUND

Most of Spain is well covered by both bus and rail networks and for journeys between major towns there's often little to choose between them in cost or speed. On shorter or less obvious routes buses tend to be quicker and will also normally take you closer to your destination; some train stations are several kilometres from the town or village they serve and you've no guarantee of a connecting bus. Approximate journey times and frequencies can be found in the "Travel details" at the end of each chapter, and local peculiarities are also pointed out in the text of the *Guide*. Car rental may also be worth considering, with costs among the lowest in Europe.

BUSES

Unless you're travelling on a rail pass, **buses** will probably meet most of your transport needs; many smaller villages are accessible only by bus, almost always leaving from the capital of their province. Service varies in quality, but on the whole the buses are reliable and comfortable enough, with prices pretty standard at around 600ptas per 100km. The only real problem involved is that many towns still have no main bus station, and buses may leave from a variety of places (even if they're heading in the same direction, since some destinations are served by more than one company). Where a new terminal has been built, it's often on the outer fringes of town. As far as possible, departure points are detailed in the text or the "Travel Details".

One important point to remember is that all public transport, and the bus service especially, is drastically reduced on **Sundays and holidays** – it's best not even to consider travelling to out-of-

the-way places on these days. The words to look out for on timetables are *diario* (daily), *laborables* (workdays, including Saturday), and *domingos y festivos* (Sundays and holidays).

TRAINS

RENFE, the Spanish rail company, operates a horrendously complicated variety of train services. An ordinary train, much the same speed and cost as the bus, will normally be described as an *expreso* or *rapido*. *Semi-directos* and *tranvías* (mostly short-haul trains) are somewhat slower. Intercity expresses, in ascending order of speed and luxury, are known as *Electrotren*, *Talgo* or *Pendular*. The latter two categories, complete with muzak and air-conditioning, cost as much as sixty to seventy percent more than you'd pay for a standard second-class ticket; *Electrotren* tickets cost forty to fifty percent more. The new high speed train from Madrid to Córdoba and Sevilla, the *AVE*, costs around double the basic fare.

In recent years many bona fide train services have been phased out in favour of buses operated jointly by *RENFE* and a private bus company. This is particularly the case when the connection is either indirect or the daily train or trains leave(s) at inconvenient times. On some routes the rail buses outnumber the conventional departures by a ratio of four to one. Prices are the same as on the trains, and these services usually leave and arrive from the bus stations/stops of the towns concerned.

RAIL PASSES

InterRail (see pp.9–10) and **Eurail** (p.6) **passes,** and **BIJ** tickets, are valid on all *RENFE* trains, but there's a supplement payable for travelling on any of the intercity expresses, and sometimes on *expresos* and *rapidos* too. The apparently random nature of these **surcharges** – which seem to depend on the individual train guard – can be a source of considerable irritation. It's better to know what you're letting yourself in for by reserving a seat in advance, something you'll be obliged to do in any case on some trains. For 400ptas (including a 200ptas *suplemento fijo*), you'll get a large, computer-printed ticket which will satisfy even the most unreasonable of guards.

If you're using the trains extensively in Spain, but not outside the country, you might consider a **RENFE Tarjeta Turística**, accepted on all trains – and currently the only pass available within Spain. Three days' second-class travel in any 30-day period costs 15,400ptas (£72/$110); 5 days' costs 24,200ptas (£112/$173); and 10 days' costs 37,400ptas (£173/$267). First-class passes are also available, costing around another 30 percent more. British and Irish residents can buy a **Eurodomino** pass before arrival allowing 3, 5 or 10 days travel in one month within Spain. Youth prices are 3 days (£78), 5 days (£127), 10 days (£204); adult prices are 3 days (£97), 5 days (£151) and 10 days (£240). North Americans can buy a similar Spain **Flexipass** before arrival, allowing 3 days ($145) or 5 days ($225) unlimited travel in a month, or 10 days in two months ($345). See p.6 for details of where to buy the pass

TICKETS AND FARES

RENFE also offers a whole range of **discount fares** on its *días azules* ("blue days" – which cover most of the year, with the exception of peak holiday weekends). If you're over 65, travelling with children under 12, in a group of eleven or more, or planning a return to be done on the same or separate 'Blue Day,' you can get between twelve and fifty percent off.

Tickets can be bought at the stations between sixty days and fifteen minutes before departure from the *venta anticipada* window, or in the final two hours from the *venta inmediata* window. Don't leave it to the last minute, though, as there are usually long lines. There may also be separate windows for *largo recorrido* (long-distance) trains and *regionales* or *cercanías* (locals). If you board the train without a ticket the conductor may charge you up to double the normal fare; if you don't have the cash, they'll call the police.

Most larger towns have a much more convenient *RENFE* office in the centre as well, which sell **tickets in advance** and dish out schedule pamphlets; you can also buy the *Guía RENFE* timetable here (and at major stations) – useful if you plan to travel extensively by train. You can also buy tickets at travel agents which display the *RENFE* sign – they have a sophisticated computer system which can also make seat reservations; the cost is the same as at the station. For long journeys, a reserved seat is a worthwhile precaution, as many trains are very crowded.

You can change the departure date of an electronically issued, reserved-seat, long-distance (*largo recorrido*) ticket without penalty up to fifteen minutes before your originally scheduled departure. An actual cancellation and a refund of the same sort of ticket entails losing fifteen percent of the purchase price if it's done more than 24 hours in advance.

DRIVING AND VEHICLE RENTAL

Whilst getting around on public transport is easy enough, you'll obviously have a great deal more freedom if you have your **own car**. Major roads are generally good, especially in the north, and traffic, while a little hectic in the cities, is generally well behaved – though Spain does have one of the highest incidences of traffic accidents in Europe. But you'll be spending more (even with a full car); petrol prices are only marginally lower than in Britain (almost double US prices), and in the big cities at least you'll probably want to pay extra for a hotel with parking, or be forced to stay on the outskirts. Also, vehicle crime is rampant – never leave anything visible in the car.

Most foreign **driver's licences** are honoured in Spain – including all EC, US and Canadian ones – but an International Driver's Licence (available in Britain from the AA or RAC) is an easy way to set your mind at rest. If you're bringing your own car, you must have a green card from your insurers, and a bail bond or extra coverage for legal costs is also worth having, since if you do have an accident it'll be your fault, as a foreigner, regardless of the circumstances. Without a bail bond both you and the car could be locked up pending investigation.

Away from main roads you yield to vehicles approaching from the right, but rules are not too strictly observed anywhere. Speed limits are posted – maximum on urban roads is 60kph, other roads 90kph, motorways 120kph – and (on the main highways at least) speed traps are common. If you're stopped for any violation, the Spanish police can and usually will levy a stiff on-the-spot fine before letting you go on your way, especially since as a foreigner you're unlikely to want, or be able, to appear in court.

VEHICLE RENTAL

Hiring a car lets you out of many of the hassles, and it's not too expensive. You'll find a choice of companies in any major town, with the biggest ones – *Hertz, Avis* and *Europcar* – represented at

SPAIN: TRAINS

CAR RENTAL AGENCIES

Britain

Avis ☎081/848 8733.

Budget ☎0800/181 181.

Europcar/InterRent ☎0345/222 525.

Hertz ☎081/679 1799.

Holiday Autos ☎071/491 1111.

North America

Avis ☎800/331-1212.

Budget ☎800/527-0700.

Europe by Car ☎800/223-1516.

Hertz ☎800/654-3131.

Holiday Autos ☎800/442-7737.

National Car Rental ☎800/CAR-RENT.

the airports as well as in town centres. You'll need to be 21 or over (and have been driving for at least a year), and you're looking at from 5000ptas per day for a small car (less by the week, special rates at the weekend). **Fly-Drive deals** with *Iberia* and other operators can be good value if you know in advance that you'll want to rent a car. The big companies all offer schemes, but you'll often get a better deal through someone who deals with local agents. *Holiday Autos* (see box for number) are one of the best, substantially undercutting the large companies. If you're going in high season try and book well in advance.

Renting **motorcycles** (from 3000–4000ptas a day, cheaper by the week) is also possible. You have to be 14 or over to ride a machine under 75cc, 18 for one over 75cc and crash helmets are compulsory. Note that mopeds and motorcycles are often rented out with insurance that doesn't include theft – always check with the company first. You will generally be asked to produce a driving licence as a deposit.

Taxis in city areas are incredibly good value and are certainly the safest way to travel late at night. Make full use of them, particularly in Madrid and Barcelona.

HITCHING

As in most other countries today, we do not recommend hitching in Spain as a safe method of getting around.

If you are determined to hitch, be warned that the road down the east coast (Barcelona–Valencia–Murcia) is notoriously difficult, and trying to get out of either Madrid or Barcelona

can prove to be a nightmare (you're best off taking a bus out to a smaller place on the relevant road). On the other hand, thumbing on back roads is often surprisingly productive; the fewer cars there are, the more likely they are to stop.

Regionally there's considerable variation as well: the Basque country, and the north in general, often prove quite easy, whereas Andalucía tends to involve long (and very hot) waits. In summer, always carry some water with you and some kind of hat or cap – lifts too often dry up at some shadeless junction in the middle of nowhere.

CYCLING

Taking your own bike can be an inexpensive and flexible way of getting around, and of seeing a great deal of the country that would otherwise pass you by. Do remember, though, that Spain is one of the most moutainous countries in Europe. The Spanish are keen cycle fans – though their interest is mainly in racing, and active cycling is largely restricted to racing club members – which means that you'll be well received and find reasonable facilities. There are bike shops in the larger towns and parts can often be found at auto repair shops or garages – look for Michelin signs. Cars tend to hoot before they pass, which can be alarming at first but is useful once you're used to it. Cycle-touring guides to the better areas (especially in the north) can be found in good bookshops – in Spanish, of course.

Getting your bike there should present few problems. Most airlines are happy to take them as ordinary baggage provided they come within your allowance (though it's sensible to check first; crowded charters may be less obliging). Deflate the tyres to avoid explosions in the unpressurised hold. Spanish trains are also reasonably accessible, though bikes can only go on a train with a guard's van (*furgón*) and must be registered – go to the *Equipajes* or *Paquexpres* desk at the station. If you are not travelling with the bike you can either send it as a package or buy an undated ticket and use the method above. Most *hostales* seem able to find somewhere safe for overnight storage.

FLYING

Both *Iberia* and the smaller, slightly cheaper *Aviaco* operate an extensive network of internal flights. While these are quite reasonable by international standards, they still work out very pricey, and are only really worth considering if you're in an extraordinary hurry and need to cross the entire peninsula. The main exception is getting to, and between, the Balearic Islands, where flights are only marginally more expensive than the ferries. In peak season you may well have to reserve long in advance for these (see *The Balearic Islands* for more details).

HEALTH MATTERS

No inoculations are required for Spain, though if you plan on continuing to North Africa, typhoid and polio boosters are highly recommended. The worst that's likely to happen to you is that you might fall victim to an upset stomach. To be safe, wash fruit and avoid *tapas* dishes that look like they were cooked last week.

PHARMACIES, DOCTORS AND HOSPITALS

If you should become ill, it's easiest for minor complaints to go to a ***farmacia*** – they're listed in the phone book in major towns and you'll also find one in virtually every village. Pharmacists are highly trained, willing to give advice (often in English), and able to dispense many drugs which would be available only on prescription in most other countries. They keep usual shop hours (ie 9am–1pm & 4–8pm), but some open late and at weekends while a rota system keeps at least one open 24 hours. The rota is displayed in the window of every pharmacy, or you can check in one of the local newspapers under *Farmacias de guardia*.

EMERGENCY TELEPHONE NUMBER

Dial ☎091 in an emergency.

In more serious cases you can get the address of an English-speaking doctor from the nearest relevant consulate, or with luck from a *farmacia*, the local police or *Turismo*. In **emergencies** dial ☎091 for the *Servicios de Urgencia*, or look up the *Cruz Roja Española* (Red Cross) which runs a national ambulance service. Treatment at hospitals for EC citizens in possession of form E111 (see "Insurance", p.16) is free; otherwise you'll be charged at private hospital rates, which can be as much as 14,000ptas per visit. Accordingly, it's essential to have comprehensive travel insurance.

CONTRACEPTIVES

Condoms no longer need to be smuggled into Spain – as during the Franco years. Along with the pill, they're available from most *farmacias* and increasingly from vending machines in bars. AIDS (*SIDA*) has definitely reached Spain.

COMMUNICATIONS: POST, PHONES AND MEDIA

Post offices (*Correos*) are generally found near the centre of towns and are open from 8am–noon and again from 5–7.30pm, though big branches in large cities may have considerably longer hours and usually do not close at midday. Except in the cities there's only one post office in each town, and queues can be long: stamps are also sold at tobacconists (look for the brown and yellow *Tabac* sign).

You can have letters sent **poste restante** (*Lista de Correos*) to any Spanish post office: they should be addressed (preferably with ·the surname underlined and in capitals) to *Lista de Correos* followed by the name of the town and province. To collect, take along your passport and, if you're expecting mail, ask the clerk to check under all of your names – letters are often to be found filed under first or middle names.

American Express in Madrid and Barcelona will hold mail for a month for customers, and have special windows for mail pickup.

Outbound mail is reasonably reliable, with letters or cards taking around five days to a week to the UK, a week to ten days to North America.

PHONES

Spanish public **phones** work well and have instructions in English. If you can't find one, many bars also have pay phones you can use. Cabins take 5-, 25-, or 100-ptas pieces or phone cards of 1000ptas or 2000ptas, which you can buy in tobacconists: in old-style phones, rest the coins in the groove at the top and they'll drop when someone answers; in the newer cabins follow the automatic instructions displayed. Spanish provincial (and some overseas) dialling codes are displayed in the cabins. The **ringing tone** is long, **engaged** is shorter and rapid; the standard Spanish response is *digáme* (speak to me).

For **international calls**, you can use almost any cabin (marked *teléfono internacional*) or go to a **Telefónica** office where you pay afterwards. International and domestic rates are slightly cheaper after 10pm, and after 2pm on Saturday and all day Sunday. If you're using a cabin to call abroad, you're best off putting at least 200ptas in to ensure a connection, and make sure you have a good stock of 100-ptas pieces.

If you want to make a **reverse charge call** (*cobro revertido*), you'll have to go to a *Telefónica*, where you can expect queues at cheap rate times. Some hotels will arrange reverse charge calls for you, but as with all phone calls from hotels you'll often be stung for an outrageous surcharge.

MEDIA

British newspapers and the *International Herald Tribune* are on sale in most large cities and resorts. There are also various English-language magazines produced by and for the expatriate communities on the *costas*; all are of limited interest though occasionally they carry details of local events and entertainment. The monthly *Lookout* on the Costa del Sol is one of the best, with travel articles and interesting background on Spanish affairs.

Of the **Spanish newspapers** the best are *El País* and *El Mundo*, both of which are liberal in outlook and have good arts and foreign news coverage, including comprehensive regional "what's on" listings and supplements each Friday. *El País* is rather too closely supportive of the government for many tastes but has exceptional (and independent) columnists such as Manuel Vázquez Montalban. Other national papers include *ABC*, solidly elitist with a hard moral line against divorce and abortion; the Catholic *Ya*; *Diario 16* and Barcelona's *La Vanguardia*, both of which are centrist. The regional press is generally run by local magnates and is predominantly right-

---

PHONING ABROAD FROM SPAIN

To Britain: dial ☎07, wait for the International tone, then 44 + area code minus first 0 + number.

To US: dial ☎07, wait for the International tone, then 1 + area code + number.

PHONING ABROAD TO SPAIN

From Britain: dial ☎010 + 34 + area code + number.

From US: dial ☎011 + 34 + area code + number.

USEFUL TELEPHONE NUMBERS

Directory Enquiries ☎003	Alarm call ☎096
International Operator (Europe) ☎008	Weather ☎094
International Operator (rest of the world) ☎005	

AREA CODES WITHIN SPAIN

Balearic Islands ☎971	Gibraltar ☎350	Málaga ☎952	Sevilla ☎954
Barcelona ☎93	Girona ☎972	Oviedo ☎98	Valencia ☎96
Bilbão ☎94	Granada ☎958	Salamanca ☎923	Zaragoza ☎976
Burgos ☎947	León ☎987	San Sebastián ☎943	
Cádiz ☎956	Madrid ☎91	Santiago ☎981	

wing, though often supporting local autonomy movements. Nationalist press includes *Avui* in Catalunya, printed largely in Catalan, and the Basque papers *El Diario Vasco*, *Deia* and *Egin*, the latter a supporter of ETA, and mostly in *Euskera*.

Spain's most interesting **magazine** is *Ajo Blanco*, a monthly from Barcelona, providing a generally stimulating mix of politics, culture and style. The more arty and indulgent *El Europeo*, a massive quarterly publication from Madrid, can also be worth a browse. And of course, Spain is the home of *Holá* – the original of *Hello*.

TV AND RADIO

You'll inadvertently catch more **TV** than you expect sitting in bars and restaurants, and on the whole it's a fairly entertaining mix. Soaps are a particular speciality, either South American *tele-novas*, which take up most of the daytime programming, or well-travelled British or Australian exports. Sports fans are well catered for, with regular live coverage of **football** and basketball matches. In the football season, you can watch live matches from the Spanish, Italian and British leagues, mainly on Canal 5; they are shown in many bars.

If you have a **radio** which picks up short wave you can tune in to the *BBC World Service*, broadcasting in English for most of the day on frequencies between 12MHz (24m) and 4MHz (75m). You may also be able to receive *Voice of America* and American Forces' stations.

ACCOMMODATION

Simple, reasonably priced rooms are still very widely available in Spain, and in almost any town you'll be able to get a double for around 2000–3000ptas (£9–14/ $14–21), a single for 1500–2500ptas (£7– 11.50/$11–18). Only in major resorts and a handful of "tourist cities" (like Toledo or Sevilla) need you pay more.

We've detailed where to find places to stay in most of the destinations listed in the *Guide*, and given a price range for each (see p.30), from the most basic rooms to luxury hotels. As a general rule, all you have to do is head for the cathedral or main square of any town, invariably surrounded by an old quarter full of accommodation possibilities. In Spain, unlike most countries, you don't seem to pay any more for a central location (this goes for bars and cafés, too), though you do tend to get a comparatively bad deal if you're travelling on your own as there are relatively few single rooms. Much of the time you'll have to negotiate a reduction on the price of a double.

It's often worth **bargaining** over room prices, since the regulated prices don't necessarily mean much. In high season you're unlikely to have much luck (although many hotels do have rooms at different prices, and tend to offer the more expensive ones first) but at quiet times you may get quite a discount, even at fancier places. If there are more than two of you, most places have rooms with three or four beds at not a great deal more than the double-room price – a bargain, especially if you have children.

FONDAS, PENSIONES, HOSTALES AND *HOTELES*

The one thing all travellers need to master is the elaborate variety of types and places to stay. Least expensive of all are *fondas* (identifiable by a square blue sign with a white **F** on it, and often positioned above a bar), closely followed by *casas de huéspedes* (**CH** on a similar sign), *pensiones* (**P**) and, less commonly, *hospedajes*. Distinctions between all of these are rather blurred, but in general you'll find food served at both *fondas* and *pensiones* (some of which may offer rooms only on a meals-inclusive

ACCOMMODATION PRICE SYMBOLS

All the establishments listed in this book have been price-graded according to the following scale. The prices quoted are for the **cheapest available double room in high season**; effectively this means that anything in the ① and most places in the ② range will be without private bath, though there's usually a washbasin in the room. In the ③ category and above you will probably be getting private facilities. Remember, though, that many of the budget places will also have more expensive rooms including en suite facilities. Youth hostels are graded under ① as the price per person is less than half of the category's upper limit.

Note that in the more upmarket *hostales* and *pensiones*, and in anything calling itself a hotel, you'll pay a **tax** (*IVA*) of six percent on top of the room price.

① Under 2000ptas	③ 3000–4500ptas	⑤ 7500–12,500ptas
② 2000–3000ptas	④ 4500–7500ptas	⑥ Over 12,500ptas

basis). *Casas de huéspedes* – literally "guest houses" – were traditionally for longer stays; and to some extent, particularly in the older family seaside resorts, they still are.

Slightly more expensive but far more common are **hostales** (marked **Hs**) and **hostal-residencias** (**HsR**). These are categorized from one star to three stars, but even so prices vary enormously according to location – in general the more remote, the less expensive. Most *hostales* offer good functional rooms, usually with private shower, and, for doubles at least, they can be excellent value. The *residencia* designation means that no meals other than perhaps breakfast are served.

Moving up the scale you finally reach fully-fledged **hoteles** (**H**), again star-graded by the authorities (from one to five). One-star hotels cost no more than three-star *hostales* – sometimes they're actually less expensive – but at three stars you pay a lot more, at four or five you're in the luxury class with prices to match. Near the top end of this scale there are also state-run **paradores**: beautiful places, often converted from castles, monasteries and other minor Spanish monuments. If you can afford them these are almost all wonderful. Even if you can't afford to stay, the buildings are often worth a look in their own right, and usually have pleasantly classy bars.

Outside all of these categories you will sometimes see **camas** (beds) and **habitaciones** (rooms) advertized in private houses or above bars, often with the phrase "*camas y comidas*" (beds and meals). If you're travelling on a very tight budget these can be worth looking out for – particularly if you're offered one at a bus station and the owner is prepared to bargain with you.

There are also **casas rurales** (rural houses), a new scheme established along the lines of French *gîtes*. Accommodation at these can vary from B & B at a farmhouse to a rental cottage. Local Turismos have details.

YOUTH HOSTELS, MOUNTAIN REFUGES AND MONASTERIES

Albergues Juveniles (youth hostels) are rarely very practical, except in northern Spain (especially the Pyrenees) where it can be difficult for solo, short-term travellers to find any other bed in summer. Only about twenty Spanish hostels stay open all year – the rest operating just for the summer (or spring and summer) in temporary premises – and in cities they tend to be inconveniently located. The most useful are detailed in the *Guide*, or you can get a complete list (with opening times and phone numbers) from the *YHA*. Be warned that they tend to have curfews, are often block-reserved by school groups and demand production of a *YHA* card (though this is generally available on the spot if you haven't already bought one from your national organization). At 800–1000ptas a person, too, you can quite easily pay more than for sharing a cheap double room in a *fonda* or *casa de huespedes*.

In isolated **mountain areas** the *Federacion Español de Montañismo*, c/Alberto Aguilar 3, Madrid 15 (☎91/445 13 82) or Apodaca 16, Madrid 4, and three Catalunya-based clubs (the *FEEC*, the *CEC* and the *UEC*) run a number of **refugios**: simple, cheap dormitory-huts for climbers and trekkers, generally equipped only with bunks and a very basic kitchen. Again off the beaten track, it is sometimes possible to stay at Spanish **monasterios** or **conventos**. Often severely underpopulated, these may let empty cells for a

YOUTH HOSTEL ASSOCIATIONS

Australia *Australian Youth Hostels Association*, Level 3, 10 Mallett St, Camperdown, NSW ☎02/565-1325.

Canada *Canadian Hostelling Association*, Room 400, 205 Catherine St, Ottawa, ON K2P 1C3 ☎613/748-5638.

England and Wales *Youth Hostel Association* (*YHA*), Trevelyan House, 8 St Stephen's Hill, St Alban's, Herts AL1 ☎07278/45047. London shop and information office: 14 Southampton St, London WC2 ☎071/836 1036.

Ireland *An Oige*, 39 Mountjoy Square, Dublin 1 ☎01/363111.

New Zealand *Youth Hostels Association of New Zealand*, PO Box 436, Christchurch 1 ☎03/799-970.

Northern Ireland *Youth Hostel Association of Northern Ireland*, 56 Bradbury Place, Belfast, BT7 ☎0232/324733.

Scotland *Scottish Youth Hostel Association*, 7 Glebe Crescent, Stirling, FK8 2JA ☎0786/51181.

USA *American Youth Hostels* (*AYH*), 733 15th St NW 840, PO Box 37613, Washington, DC 20005 ☎202/783-6161.

small charge. You can just turn up and ask – many will take visitors regardless of sex – but if you want to be sure of a reception it's best to approach the local Turismo first, and phone ahead. There are some particularly wonderful monastic locations in Galicia, Catalunya and Mallorca.

Those following the **Camino de Santiago** can also take advantage of monastic accommodation specifically reserved for pilgrims along the route and some of the best places are detailed in the text.

Monasteries and youth hostels aside, if you have any **problems** with Spanish rooms – overcharging, most obviously – you can usually produce an immediate resolution by asking for the *libra de reclamaciones* (complaints book). By law all establishments must keep this and bring it out for regular inspection by the police. Nothing is ever written in them .

CAMPING

There are some 350 authorized **campsites** in Spain, predominantly on the coast. They usually work out at about 400ptas (£2/$3.30) plus the same again for a tent (once again, discriminating against solo travellers) and a similar amount for each car or caravan, perhaps twice as much for a van. Only a few of the best sited or most popular sites are significantly more expensive. Again

we've detailed the most useful in the text, but if you plan to camp extensively then pick up the free *Mapa de Campings* from the National Tourist Board, which marks and names virtually all of them. A complete *Guía de Campings*, listing full prices, facilities and exact locations, is available at most Spanish bookshops.

Camping outside campsites is legal – but with certain restrictions. You're not allowed to camp "in urban areas, areas prohibited for military or touristic reasons, or within 1km of an official campsite". What this means in practice is that you can't camp on tourist beaches (though you can, discreetly, nearby) but with a little sensitivity you can set up a tent for a short period almost anywhere in the countryside. Whenever possible ask locally first.

If you're planning to do a lot of camping, an **international camping carnet** is a good investment, available from home motoring organizations, or from one of the following: in Britain, the *Camping and Caravan Club*, 32 High St, London, E15 2PF ☎081/503 0426; in the US, the *Family Campers and RVers*, 4804 Transit Rd, Building 2, Depew, NY 14043 ☎800/245-9755; and in Canada, *Family Campers and RVers*, 51 W 22nd St, Hamilton, Ontario LC9 4N5 ☎800/245-9755. The carnet serves as useful identification and covers you for third party insurance when camping.

EATING AND DRINKING

There are two ways to eat in Spain: you can go to a *restaurante* or *comedor* (dining room) and have a full meal, or you can have a succession of *tapas* (small snacks) or *raciones* (larger ones) at one or more bars.

At the bottom line a *comedor* – where you'll get a basic, filling, three-course meal with a drink, the **menú del día** – is the cheapest option, but they're often tricky to find, and drab places when you do. Bars tend to work out pricier but a lot more interesting, allowing you to do the rounds and sample local or house specialities.

BREAKFAST, SNACKS AND SANDWICHES

For **breakfast** you're best off in a bar or café, though some *hostales* and *fondas* will serve the "Continental" basics. The traditional Spanish breakfast is *churros con chocolate* – long tubular doughnuts (not for the weak of stomach) with thick drinking chocolate. But most places also serve *tostadas* (toasted rolls) with oil (*con aceite*) or butter (*con mantequilla*) – *y mermelada* (and jam), or more substantial egg dishes (*huevos fritos* are fried eggs). *Tortilla* (potato omelette) also makes an excellent breakfast.

Coffee and pastries (*pastas*) or doughnuts (*donuts*) are available at most cafés, too, though for a wider selection of cakes you should head for one of the many excellent *pastelerías* or *confiterías*. In larger towns, especially in Catalunya, there will often be a *panadería* or *croissantería* serving quite an array of appetizing (and healthier) baked goods besides the obvious

bread, croissants and pizza. For ordering coffee see p.37.

Some bars specialize in **sandwiches** (*bocadillos*), and as they're usually outsize affairs in French bread, they'll do for breakfast or lunch. In a bar with *tapas* (see below), you can have most of what's on offer put in a sandwich, and you can often get them prepared (or buy the materials to do so) at grocery shops. Incidentally a *sandwich* is a toasted cheese and ham sandwich, usually on sad processed bread.

TAPAS

One of the advantages of eating in **bars** is that you are able to experiment. Many places have food laid out on the counter, so you can see what's available and order by pointing without necessarily knowing the names; others have blackboards (see box opposite). *Tapas* are small portions, three or four small chunks of fish or meat, or a dollop of salad, which traditionally used to be served up free with a drink. These days you have to pay for anything more than a few olives (where you do get free food now, it will often be called a *pincho*), but a single helping rarely costs more than 200–400ptas unless you're somewhere very flashy. *Raciones* are simply bigger plates of the same, and can be enough in themselves for a light meal; *pinchos morunos* (small kebabs) are often also available. (Make sure you make it clear whether you want a *racion* or just a *tapa*.) The more people you're with, of course, the better; half a dozen *tapas* or *pinchos* and three *raciones* can make a varied and quite filling meal for three or four people.

Tascas, *bodegas*, *cervecerías* and **tabernas** are all types of bar where you'll find *tapas* and *raciones*. Most of them have different sets of prices depending on whether you stand at the bar to eat (the basic charge) or sit at tables (up to fifty percent more expensive – and even more if you sit out on a terrace).

Wherever you have *tapas*, it is important to find out what is the local **"special"** and to order it. Spaniards will commonly move from bar to bar, having just the one dish that they consider each bar does well. A bar's "non-standard" dishes, these days, can all too often be microwaved – which is not a good way to cook fried squid.

TAPAS AND OTHER SNACKS

The most usual **fillings for sandwiches** are *lomo* (loin of pork), *tortilla* and *calamares* (all of which may be served hot), *jamón* (*York* or, much better, *serrano*), *chorizo*, *salchicha* (and various other regional sausages – like the small, spicy Catalan *butifarras*), *queso* (cheese) and *atún* (tuna – probably canned).

Standard *tapas* and *raciones* might include:

Aceitunas	Olives	Gambas	Shrimp
Albóndigas	Meatballs	Habas	Beans
Anchoas	Anchovies	Habas con jamón	Beans with ham
Berberechos	Cockles	Hígado	Liver
Boquerones	Fresh anchovies	Huevo cocido	Hard-boiled egg
Calamares	Squid	Jamón serrano	Dried ham
Callos	Tripe	Jamón York	Regular ham
Caracoles	Snails	Mejillones	Mussels
Carne en salsa	Meat in tomato sauce	Navajas	Razor clams
Champiñones	Mushrooms, usually fried in garlic	Patatas alioli	Potatoes in mayonnaise
		Patatas Bravas	Spicy fried potatoes
Chorizo	Spicy sausage	Pimientos	Peppers
Cocido	Stew	Pincho moruno	Kebab
Empanadilla	Fish/meat pastie	Pulpo	Octopus
Ensaladilla	Russian salad (diced vegetables in mayonnaise)	Riñones al Jerez	Kidneys in sherry
		Salchicha	Sausage
		Sepia	Cuttlefish
Escalibada	Aubergine (eggplant) and pepper salad	Tortilla Española	Potato omelette
		Tortilla Francesa	Plain omelette

MEALS AND RESTAURANTS

Once again, there's a multitude of distinctions. You can sit down and have a full meal in a *comedor*, a *cafetería*, a *restaurante* or a *marisquería* – all in addition to the more food-oriented bars.

Comedores are the places to seek out if your main criteria are price and quantity. Sometimes you will see them attached to a bar (often in a room behind), or as the dining room of a *pensión* or *fonda*, but as often as not they're virtually unmarked and discovered only if you pass an open door. Since they're essentially workers' cafés they tend to serve more substantial meals at lunchtime than in the evenings (when they may be closed altogether). When you can find them – the tradition, with its family-run business and marginal wages, is on the way out – you'll probably pay around 600–1300ptas for a ***menú del día*** or ***cubierto***, a complete meal of three courses, usually with wine.

Replacing *comedores* to some extent are ***cafeterías***, which the local authorities now grade from one to three cups (the ratings, as with restaurants, seem to be based on facilities offered rather than the quality of the food). These can be good value, too, especially the self-service places, but their emphasis is more northern European and the light snack-meals served tend to be dull. Food here often comes in the form of a ***plato combinado*** – literally a combined plate – which will be something like egg and chips or *calamares* and salad (or occasionally a weird combination like steak and a piece of fish), often with bread and a drink included. This will generally cost in the region of 500–900ptas. *Cafeterías* often serve some kind of *menú del día* as well. You may prefer to get your *plato combinado* at a bar, which in small towns with no *comedores* may be the only way to eat inexpensively.

Moving up the scale there are ***restaurantes*** (designated by one to five forks) and ***marisquerías***, the latter serving exclusively fish and seafood. *Restaurantes* at the bottom of the scale are often not much different in price to *comedores*, and will also generally have *platos combinados* available. A fixed-price *cubierto*, *menú del día* or *menú de la casa* (all of which mean the same) is often better value, though: two or three courses plus wine and bread for 600–1500ptas. Move above two forks, however, or find yourself

UNDERSTANDING SPANISH MENUS

As with *tapas* and *raciones*, **restaurant dishes** vary enormously from region to region. The list below is no more than a selection, with the main Spanish dishes and a handful of local specialities. Wherever possible you'll do best by going for the latter; some are mentioned in the regional chapters that follow, others you'll simply see people eating. *Quisiera uno asi* (I'd like one like that) can be an amazingly useful phrase.

BASICS

Aceite	Oil	*Huevos*	Eggs	*Pimienta*	Pepper
Ajo	Garlic	*Mantequilla*	Butter	*Sal*	Salt
Arroz	Rice	*Miel*	Honey	*Vinagre*	Vinegar
Azúcar	Sugar	*Pan*	Bread		

MEALS

Almuerzo	Lunch	*Cuchara*	Spoon	*Mesa*	Table
Botella	Bottle	*Cuchillo*	Knife	*Platos*	Mixed plate
Carta	Menu	*La Cuenta*	The bill	combinados	
Cena	Dinner	*Desayuno*	Breakfast	*Tenedor*	Fork
Comedor	Dining room	*Menú del día/*	Fixed-price	*Vaso*	Glass
		cubierto	set meal		

SOUPS (*SOPAS*) AND STARTERS

Caldillo	Clear fish soup	*Sopa d'ajo*	Garlic soup
Caldo	Broth	*Sopa de cocido*	Meat soup
Caldo verde or gallego	Thick cabbage-based broth	*Sopa de gallina*	Chicken soup
Ensalada (mixta/verde)	(Mixed/green) salad	*Sopa de mariscos*	Seafood soup
Gazpacho	Cold tomato and cucumber	*Sopa de pescado*	Fish soup
	soup	*Sopa de pasta (fideos)*	Noodle soup
Pimientos rellenos	Stuffed peppers	*Verduras con patatas*	Boiled potatoes with
			greens

FISH (*PESCADOS*)

Anchoas	Anchovies (fresh)	*Mero*	Perch
Anguila/Angulas	Eel/Elvers	*Pez espada*	Swordfish
Atún	Tuna	*Rape*	Monkfish
Bacalao	Cod (often salt)	*Raya*	Ray, skate
Bonito	Tuna	*Rodaballo*	Turbot
Boquerones	Small, sardine-like fish	*Salmonete*	Mullet
Chanquetes	Whitebait	*Sardinas*	Sardines
Lenguado	Sole	*Trucha*	Trout
Merluza	Hake		

SEAFOOD (*MARISCOS*)

Almejas	Clams	*Nécora*	Sea-crab
Arroz con Mariscos	Rice with seafood	*Ostras*	Oysters
Calamares (en sutinta)	Squid (in ink)	*Paella*	Classic Valencian dish
Centollo	Spider-crab		with saffron rice,
Cigalas	King prawns		chicken, seafood, etc
Conchas finas	Large scallops	*Percebes*	Goose-barnacles
Gambas	Prawns/shrimps	*Pulpo*	Octopus
Langosta	Lobster	*Sepia*	Cuttlefish
Langostinos	King prawns	*Vieiras*	Scallops
Mejillones	Mussels	*Zarzuela de*	Seafood casserole
		mariscos	

SOME COMMON TERMS

al ajillo	in garlic	*alioli*	with mayonnaise
asado	roast	*cazuela, cocido*	stew
a la Navarra	stuffed with ham	*en salsa*	in (usually tomato) sauce
a la parilla/plancha	grilled	*frito*	fried
a la Romana	fried in batter	*guisado*	casserole
al horno	baked	*rehogado*	baked

MEAT (*CARNE*) AND POULTRY (*AVES*)

Callos	Tripe	*Hamburguesa*	Hamburger
Carne de buey	Beef	*Hígado*	Liver
Cerdo	Pork	*Lacón con grelos*	Trotter with turnips
Chuletas	Chops	*Lengua*	Tongue
Cochinillo	Suckling pig	*Lomo*	Loin (of pork)
Codorniz	Quail	*Pato*	Duck
Conejo	Rabbit	*Pavo*	Turkey
Cordero	Lamb	*Perdiz*	Partridge
Escalopa	Escalope	*Pollo*	Chicken
Fabada Asturiana/	Hot pot with butter	*Riñones*	Kidneys
Fabes a la Catalana	beans, black pudding, etc	*Ternera*	Veal

VEGETABLES (*LEGUMBRES*)

Acelga	Chard	*Judías verdes, rojas, negras*	Green, red, black beans
Alcachofas	Artichokes		
Arroz a la Cubana	Rice with fried egg and tomato sauce	*Lechuga*	Lettuce
		Lentejas	Lentils
Berenjenas	Aubergine/eggplant	*Menestra/Panache de verduras*	Mixed vegetables
Cebollas	Onions		
Champiñones/Setas	Mushrooms	*Nabos/Grelos*	Turnips
Coliflor	Cauliflower	*Patatas (fritas)*	Potatoes (fries)
Esparragos	Asparagus	*Pepino*	Cucumber
Espinacas	Spinach	*Pimientos*	Peppers/capsicums
Garbanzos	Chickpeas	*Pisto manchego*	Ratatouille
Habas	Broad/fava beans	*Puerros*	Leeks
Judías blancas	Haricot beans	*Repollo*	Cabbage
		Tomate	Tomato
		Zanahoria	Carrot

FRUIT (*FRUTAS*)

Albaricoques	Apricots	*Melocotónes*	Peaches
Cerezas	Cherries	*Melón*	Melon
Chirimoyas	Custard apples	*Naranjas*	Oranges
Ciruelas	Plums, prunes	*Nectarinas*	Nectarines
Dátiles	Dates	*Peras*	Pears
Fresas	Strawberries	*Piña*	Pineapple
Granada	Pomegranate	*Plátanos*	Bananas
Higos	Figs	*Sandía*	Watermelon
Limón	Lemon	*Toronja/Pomelo*	Grapefruit
Manzanas	Apples	*Uvas*	Grapes

UNDERSTANDING SPANISH MENUS (cont.)

DESSERTS (*POSTRES*)

Arroz con leche	Rice pudding	*Helados*	Ice cream
Crema catalana	Catalan crème caramel	*Melocotón en almíbar*	Peaches in syrup
		Membrillo	Quince paste
Cuajada	Cream-based dessert served with honey	*Nata*	Whipped cream
		Natillas	Custard
Flan	Crème caramel	*Yogur*	Yogurt

CHEESE

Cheeses (*quesos*) are on the whole local, though you'll get the hard, salty *Queso manchego* everywhere. Mild sheep's cheese (*queso de oveja*) from the León province is widely distributed and worth asking for.

---

in one of the more fancy *marisquerías* (as opposed to a basic seafront fish-fry place), and prices can escalate rapidly. In addition, in all but the most rock-bottom establishments it is customary to leave a small tip: the amount is up to you, though ten percent of the bill is quite sufficient. Service is normally included in a *menú del día*. The other thing to take account of in medium and top-price restaurants is the addition of **IVA**, a six percent tax on your bill. It should say on the menu if you have to pay this.

You'll find numerous recommendations, in all price ranges, in the main body of the *Guide*. Spaniards generally eat very late, so most of these places serve food from around 1 until 4pm and from 8pm to midnight. Many restaurants **close on Sunday evening**.

WHAT TO EAT

Our food glossary should give you an idea of what's on offer and help you cope when faced with a restaurant menu. Local specialities are highlighted in the *Guide*, too. It's possible to make a few generalizations about Spanish food. If you like **fish and seafood** you'll be in heaven in Spain as this forms the basis of a vast array of *tapas* and is fresh and excellent even hundreds of miles from the sea. It's not cheap, unfortunately, so rarely forms part of the lowest priced menus (though you may get the most common fish – cod, often salted, and hake – or squid) but you really should make the most of what's on offer. Fish stews (*zarzuelas*) and rice-based *paellas* (which also contain meat, usually rabbit or chicken) are often memorable in seafood restaurants. *Paella* comes originally from Valencia and is still best there, but you'll find versions of it all over Spain.

Meat is most often grilled and served with a few fried potatoes and a couple of salad leaves, or cured or dried and served as a starter or in sandwiches. *Jamón Serrano*, the Spanish version of Parma ham, is superb, though the best varieties, from Extremadura and the southwest, are extremely expensive. In country areas game is very much on the menu, too – you may find the baby animal specialities of central Spain like *cochinillo* (suckling pig) less appetizing.

Vegetables rarely amount to more than a few fries or boiled potatoes with the main dish (though you can often order a side dish à la carte). It's more usual to start your meal with a **salad**, or, in the north especially, you may get hearty vegetable soups or a plate of boiled potatoes and greens as a starter. **Dessert** in the cheaper places is nearly always fresh fruit or *flan*, the Spanish *crème caramel*. There are also various varieties of *pudin* – rice pudding or assorted blancmange mixtures. Even in fancy restaurants you'll find little better – stick to fruit and cheese.

VEGETARIANS

Vegetarians have a fairly hard time of it in Spain: there's always something to eat, but you may get weary of eggs and omelettes (*tortilla francesa* is a plain omelette, *con champiñones* with mushrooms). In the big cities you'll find vegetarian restaurants and ethnic places which serve vegetable dishes. Otherwise, superb fresh produce is always available in the markets and shops, and cheese, fruit and eggs are available everywhere. In restaurants you're faced with the extra problem that pieces of meat – especially ham, which the Spanish don't seem to regard as real meat – are often added to vegetable dishes to "spice them up".

The phrase to get to know is *Soy vegetariano. Hay algo sin carne?* (I'm a vegetarian. Is there anything without meat?); you may have to add *y sin Mariscos* (and without seafood) *y sin jamón* (and without ham) to be really safe.

If you're a vegan, you're either going have to be not too fussy or accept weight loss if you're away for any length of time. Some salads and vegetable dishes are strictly vegan, but they're few and far between. Fruit and nuts are widely available, though, nuts being sold by street vendors everywhere.

ALCOHOLIC DRINKS

Vino (wine), either *tinto* (red), *blanco* (white) or *rosado/clarete* (rosé), is the invariable accompaniment to every meal and is, as a rule, extremely inexpensive. The most common bottled variety is *Valdepeñas*, a good standard wine from the central plains of New Castile; *Rioja*, from the area round Logroño, is better but a lot more expensive. Both are found all over the country. There are also scores of local wines – some of the best in Catalunya (*Bach, Sangre de Toro* and the champagne-like *Cava*) and Galicia (*Ribeiro, Fefiñanes* and *Albariño*) – but you'll rarely be given any choice unless you're at a good restaurant.

Otherwise it's whatever comes out of the barrel, or the house-bottled special (ask for *caserío* or *de la casa*). This can be great, it can be lousy, but at least it will be distinctively local. In a bar, a small glass of wine will generally cost around 50–100ptas; in a restaurant, if wine is not included in the menu, prices start at around 300–350ptas a bottle. If it is included you'll usually get a whole bottle for two people, a *media botella* (a third to a half of a litre) for one.

The classic Andalucian wine is **sherry** – *Vino de Jerez*. This is served chilled or at *bodega* temperature – a perfect drink to wash down *tapas* – and, like everything Spanish, comes in a perplexing variety of forms. The main distinctions are between *fino* or *Jerez seco* (dry sherry), *amontillado* (medium), and *oloroso* or *Jerez dulce* (sweet), and these are the terms you should use to order. Similar – though not identical – are *montilla* and *manzanilla*, dry sherry-like wines from the provinces of Córdoba and Huelva. These too are excellent and widely available.

Cerveza, lager-type beer, is generally pretty good, though more expensive than wine. It comes in 300-ml bottles (*botellines*) or, for about the same price, on tap – a *caña* of draught beer is a small glass, a *caña doble* larger. Many bartenders will assume you want a *doble*, so if you don't, say so. Local brands, such as *Cruz Campo* around Sevilla or *Alhambra* in Granada, are often better than the national ones.

Equally refreshing, though often deceptively strong, is *sangría*, a wine-and-fruit punch which you'll come across at fiestas and in tourist bars; *tinto de verano* is basically the same red wine and soda or lemonade combination.

In mid-afternoon – or even at breakfast – many Spaniards take a *copa* of **liqueur** with their coffee. The best are *anís* (like Pernod) or *coñac*, excellent local brandy with a distinct vanilla flavour (try *Magno, Soberano*, or *103* to get an idea of the variety).

Most **spirits** are ordered by brand name, since there are generally less expensive Spanish equivalents for standard imports. *Larios Gin* from Málaga, for instance, is about half the price of *Gordon's Gin* . Specify *nacional* to avoid getting an expensive foreign brand. Spirits can be very expensive at the trendier bars; however, wherever they are served, they tend to be staggeringly generous – the bar staff pouring from the bottle until you suggest they stop.

Mixed drinks are universally known as *Cuba Libre* or *Cubata*, though strictly speaking this is rum and Coke. Juice is *zumo*; orange, *naranja*; lemon, *limón*; tonic is *tónica*.

SOFT DRINKS AND HOT DRINKS

Soft drinks are much the same as anywhere in the world, but try in particular *granizado* (slush) or *horchata* (a milky drink made from tiger nuts or almonds) from one of the street stalls that spring up everywhere in summer. You can also get these drinks from *horchaterías* and from *heladerías* (ice cream – *helados* – parlours), or in Catalunya from the wonderful milk bars known as *granjas*. Although you can drink the **water** almost everywhere it usually tastes better out of the bottle – inexpensive *agua mineral* comes either sparkling (*con gas*) or still (*sin gas*).

Café (coffee) – served in cafés, *heladerías* and bars – is invariably espresso, slightly bitter and, unless you specify otherwise, served black (*café solo*). If you want it white ask for *café* cortado (small cup with a drop of milk) or café con leche (made with lots of hot milk). For a large cup ask for a doble or grande. Coffee is also frequently mixed with brandy, cognac or whisky, all such concoctions being called carajillo. Té

(tea) is also available at most bars, although bear in mind that Spaniards usually drink it black. If you want milk it's safest to ask for it afterwards, since ordering té con leche might well get you a glass of milk with a teabag floating on top.

DRINKS AND BEVERAGES					
Hot drinks		**Soft drinks**		**Alcohol**	
Coffee	Café	Water	Agua	Beer	Cerveza
Espresso coffee	Café solo	Mineral water	Agua mineral	Champagne	Champan
White coffee	Café con leche	. . . (sparkling)	. . .(con gas)	Wine	Vino
Decaff	Descafeinado	. . (still)	. . .(sin gas)		
Tea	Té	Milk	Leche		
Drinking	Chocolate	Juice	Zumo		
chocolate		Tiger nut drink	Horchata		

OPENING HOURS AND PUBLIC HOLIDAYS

Almost everything in Spain – shops, museums, churches, tourist offices – closes for a siesta of at least two hours in the hottest part of the day. There's a lot of variation (and the siesta tends to be longer in the south) but basic summer working hours are 9.30am–1.30pm and 4.30–7.30pm. Certain shops do now stay open all day, and there is a move towards "normal" working hours. Nevertheless, you'll get far less aggravated if you accept that the early afternoon is best spent asleep, or in a bar, or both.

Museums, with very few exceptions, follow the rule above, with a break between 1 and 4 in the afternoon. Their summer schedules are listed in the Guide; watch out for Sundays (most open mornings only) and Mondays (most close all day). Admission charges vary, but there's usually a big reduction or free entrance if you show an ISIC or FIYTO card. Anywhere run by the Patrimonio Nacional, the national organization which preserves monuments, is free to EC citizens on Wednesday – you'll need your passport to prove your nationality. This includes some of the most important buildings in Spain, such as El Escorial and the Royal Palace in Madrid.

Getting into **churches** can present more of a problem. The really important ones, including most cathedrals, operate in much the same way as museums and almost always have some entry

charge to see their most valued treasures and paintings, or their cloisters. Other churches, though, are usually kept locked, opening only for worship in the early morning and/or the evening (between around 6–9pm). So you'll either have to try at these times, or find someone with a key. This is time-consuming but rarely difficult, since a sacristan or custodian almost always lives nearby and most people will know where to direct you. You're expected to give a small tip, or donation. For all churches "decorous" dress is required, ie no shorts, bare shoulders, etc.

PUBLIC HOLIDAYS

Public holidays can (and will) disrupt your plans at some stage. There are fourteen national holidays, listed in the box, and scores of local festivals (different in every town and village, usually marking the local saint's day); any of them will mean that everything except bars (and hostales, etc.) locks its doors.

In addition, **August** is Spain's own holiday month, when the big cities – especially Madrid – are semi-deserted, and many of the shops and restaurants, even museums, close. In contrast, it can prove nearly impossible to find a room in the more popular coastal and mountain resorts at these times; similarly, seats on planes, trains and buses at this time should if possible be booked in advance.

SPANISH NATIONAL HOLIDAYS

January 1, New Year's Day

January 6, Epiphany

Good Friday

Easter Sunday

Easter Monday

May 1, May Day/Labour Day

Corpus Christi (early or mid-June)

June 24, Día de San Juan, the king's name-saint

July 25, Día de Santiago

August 15, Assumption of the Virgin

October 12, National Day

November 1, All Saints

December 6, Día de la Constitución

December 8, Immaculate Conception

Christmas Day

FIESTAS, THE BULLFIGHT, FOOTBALL AND MUSIC

It's hard to beat the experience of arriving in some small Spanish village, expecting no more than a bed for the night, to discover the streets decked out with flags and streamers, a band playing in the plaza and the entire population out celebrating the local fiesta. Everywhere in the country, from the tiniest hamlet to the great cities, will take at least one day off a year to devote to partying. Usually it's the local saint's day, but there are celebrations, too, of harvests, of deliverance from the Moors, of safe return from the sea – any excuse will do.

Each festival is different. In the Basque country there will often be bulls running through the streets, and the ancient Basque sports which resemble nothing so much as Scottish Highland games; in Andalucía horses, *flamenco* and the guitar are an essential part of any cele-

bration; in Valencia you'll see stylized battles between Christians and Moors, huge bonfires and stunning fireworks. But there is always music, dancing, traditional costume and an immense spirit of enjoyment. The main event of most fiestas is a parade, either behind a revered holy image, or a more celebratory affair with fancy costumes and *gigantones*, grotesque giant carnival figures which run down the streets terrorizing children.

Although these take place throughout the year – and it is often the obscure and unexpected event which proves to be most fun – there are certain occasions which stand out. *Semana Santa* (Easter week) and **Corpus Christi** (in early June) are celebrated all over the country with magnificent religious processions. Easter, particularly, is worth trying to coincide with – head for Sevilla, Málaga, Granada or Córdoba, where huge pasos, floats of wildly theatrical religious scenes, are carried down the streets, accompanied by weirdly hooded penitents atoning the year's misdeeds.

Among the biggest and best known of the other **popular festivals** are: the Cádiz *carnavales* (first to third week of February); the *Fallas de San José* in Valencia (March 12–19); Sevilla's enormous *April Feria* (a week at the end of the month); Jerez's Horse Fair (early May); the *Romería del Rocío*, an extraordinary pilgrimage to El Rocío near Huelva (arriving there on Whitsunday); Pamplona's riotous *Fiesta de San Fermín*, most famous of the bull-runnings (July 6–14); the Feast of St James at Santiago de Compostela (July 25); and the mock battles

> **Note** that saints' day festivals – indeed all Spanish celebrations – can **vary in date**, often being observed over the weekend closest to the dates given in our "Fiestas" listings at the beginning of each chapter.

between Christians and Moors in Elche (August 10–15), ending with a centuries-old mystery play.

The list is potentially endless, and although you'll find the major events detailed at the beginning of each chapter we can't pretend that this is an exhaustive list. Local tourist offices should have more information about what's going on in their area at any given time. Outsiders are always welcome at Spanish festivals, the one problem being that during any of the most popular you'll find it difficult and expensive to find a bed. If you're planning to coincide with a festival, try and book your accommodation well in advance.

BULLFIGHTS

Bullfights are an integral part of many Spanish festivals. In the south, especially, any village that can afford it will put on a *corrida* for an afternoon, while in big cities like Madrid or Sevilla, the main festival times are accompanied by a week-long (or more) season of prestige fights.

Los Toros, as Spaniards refer to bullfighting, is big business. Each year an estimated 24,000 bulls are killed before a live audience of over thirty million, and many more on televison. It is said that 150,000 people are involved, in some way, in the industry, and the top performers, the **matadores**, are major earners, on a par with the country's biggest pop stars. There is some opposition to the activity from animal welfare groups but it is not widespread: if Spaniards tell you that bullfighting is controversial, they are likely to be referring to practices in the trade. In recent years, bullfighting critics (who you will find on the *arts* pages of the newspapers) have been expressing their perennial outrage at the widespread but illegal shaving of bulls' horns prior to the *corrida*. Bulls' horns are as sensitive as fingernails, a few millimetres in, and deter the animal from charging; they affect the creature's balance, too, reducing the danger for the *matador* still further.

Notwithstanding such abuse (and there is plenty more), *Los Toros* maintain their **aficionados** throughout the country. Indeed, they are on the rise, with the elaborate language of the *corrida* quite a cult among the young, as the days of Franco's patronage of bullfighting are forgotten, and TV stations paying big money for major events. To *aficionados* (a word that implies more knowledge and appreciation than "fan"), the bulls are a culture and a ritual – one in which the emphasis is on the way man and bull "perform" together – in which the art is at issue rather than the cruelty. If pressed on the issue of the slaughter of an animal, they generally fail to understand. Fighting bulls are, they will tell you, bred for the industry; they live a reasonable life before they are killed; and, if the bullfight went, so too would the bulls.

Whether you attend a *corrida*, obviously, is down to your own feelings and ethics. If you spend any time at all in Spain during the season (which runs from March through October), you will encounter *Los Toros*, at least on a bar TV, and that will as likely as not make up your mind. If you decide to go, try to see the biggest and most prestigious that is on, in a major city, where star performers are likely to despatch the bulls with "art" and a successful, "clean" kill. There are few sights worse than a matador making a prolonged and messy kill, while the audience whistles. Established and popular **matadores** include Enrique Ponce, Cesar Rincon, Victor Mendes, Joselito, Litri, Paco Ojeda, Ortega Cano, José María Manzanares and Finito de Cordoba. Two new stars in the headlines are El Cordobes – a young pretender of spectacular technique who claims to be his legendary namesake's illegitimate son – and Cristina Sanchez, the first woman to make it into the top flight for many decades. If you have the chance to see one, the most exciting and skilfull performances of all are by **mounted matadores**, or *rejoneadores*; this is the oldest form of *corrida*, developed in Andalucía in the seventeenth century.

THE *CORRIDA*

The *corrida* begins with a **procession**, to the accompaniment of a *paso doble* by the band. Leading the procession are two *algauziles* or "constables", on horseback and in traditional costume, followed by the three *matadores*, who will each fight two bulls, and their *cuadrillas*, their personal "team" each comprising two mounted *picadores* and three *banderilleros*. At the back are the mule teams who will drag off the dead bulls.

Once the ring is empty, the *algauzil* opens the *toril* (the bulls' enclosure) and the first bull appears – a moment of great physical beauty – to be "tested" by the *matador* or his *banderilleros* using pink and gold capes. These preliminaries conducted (and they can be short, if the bull is ferocious), the **suerte de picar** ensues, in which the *picadores* ride out and take up position at opposite sides of the ring, while the bull is distracted by other *toreros*. Once they are in place, the bull is made to charge one of the horses; the *picador* drives his short-pointed lance into the bull's neck, while it tries to toss his padded, blindfolded horse, thus tiring the bull's powerful neck and back muscles. This is repeated up to three times, until the horn sounds for the *picadores* to leave. For most neutral spectators, it is the least acceptable and most squalid stage of the corrida, and it is clearly not a pleasant experience for the horses, who have their vocal cords cut out.

The next stage, the **suerte de banderillas**, involves the placing of three sets of *banderillas* (coloured sticks with barbed ends) into the bull's shoulders. Each of the three *banderilleros* delivers these in turn, attracting the bull's attention with the movement of his own body rather than a cape, and placing the *banderillas* whilst both he and the bull are running towards each other. He then runs to safety out of the bull's vision, sometimes with the assistance of his colleagues.

Once the banderillas have been placed, the **suerte de matar**, begins, and the *matador* enters the ring alone, having exhanged his pink and gold cape for the red one. He (or she) salutes the president and then dedicates the bull either to an individual, to whom he gives his hat, or to the audience by placing his hat in the centre of the ring. It is in this part of the *corrida* that judgments are made and the performance is focused, as the *matador* displays his skills on the (by now exhausted) bull. He uses the movements of the cape to attract the bull, while his body remains still. If he does well, the band will start to play, while the crowd *olé* each pass. This stage lasts around ten minutes and ends with the kill. The *matador* attempts to get the bull into a position where he can drive a sword between its shoulders and through to the heart for a *coup de grâce*. In practice, they rarely succeed in this, instead taking a second sword, crossed at the end, to cut the bull's spinal cord; this causes instant death.

If the audience are impressed by the *matador's* performance, they will wave their handkerchiefs and shout for an award to be made by the president. He can award one or both ears, and a tail – the better the display, the more pieces he gets – while if the matador has excelled himself, he will be carried out of the ring by the crowd, through the *puerta grande*, the main door, which is normally kept locked. The bull, too, may be applauded for its performance, as it is dragged out by the mule team.

Tickets for *corridas* are 2000ptas and up – much more for the prime seats and prestigious fights. The cheapest seats are *gradas*, the highest rows at the back, from where you can see everything that happens without too much of the detail; the front rows are known as the *barreras*. Seats are also divided into *sol* (sun), *sombra* (shade), and *sol y sombra* (shaded after a while), though these distinctions have become less relevant as more and more bullfights start later in the day, at 6pm or 7pm, rather than the traditional 5pm. The *sombra* seats are more expensive not so much for the spectators' personal comfort as the fact that most of the action takes place in the shade.

On the way in, you can rent **cushions** – two hours sitting on concrete is not much fun. Beer and soft drinks are sold inside.

ANTI-BULLFIGHT GROUPS

If you want to know more about the international **opposition to bullfighting**, contact the *World Society for the Protection of Animals*, 2 Langley Lane, London SW8 1TJ ☎071/793 0540; PO Box 190, Boston, MA 02130 ☎617/522-7000; PO Box 15, Toronto, Ontario, M5J 2HT ☎416/369-0044. Spain's Anti-Bullfight Committee (*Comité Antitaurino*) can be contacted by mail via: Apartado 3098, 50080 Zaragoza.

FOOTBALL

To foreigners, the bullfight is easily the most celebrated of Spain's spectacles. In terms of popular support in modern Spain, however, it ranks far below **futbol** (soccer). If you want the excitement of a genuinely Spanish afternoon out, a football stadium will usually have more passion than anything you'll find in the Plaza de Toros.

For many years, the country's two dominant teams have been **Real Madrid** and **F.C. Barcelona**, and these have shared the League and Cup honours more often than is healthy. At the time of writing, Barcelona are in the ascendant, having won the league in 1992 and 1993 – each time after Real, in the lead, lost their last game of the season against their bogey-team, Tenerife. Recently, however, both teams have faced a bit more oppositon than usual from clubs like **Atletico Bilbão**, **Sporting Gijón**, **Atletico Madrid**, **Real Sociedad** (the Basque team from San Sebastián, managed by a Welshman, John Toshack), **Real Zaragoza**, and, a new force at present, **Deportivo La Coruña** (from Galicia). **Sevilla**, where Maradona finished his European career, are the main team in Andalucía, though currently in the doldrums.

With the exception of a few big games – the Madrid derbies between Real and Atletico, and games between these teams and Barcelona – **tickets** are pretty easy to get; they start at around 1200ptas for First Division games. Trouble is very rare: English fans, in particular, will be amazed at the easygoing family atmosphere and mixed sex crowds.

If you don't go to a game, the atmosphere can be pretty good **watching on TV** in a local bar, especially in a city whose team is playing away. Many bars advertise the matches they screen, which can include Sunday afternoon **English league and cup games**, if they have Canal 5.

MUSIC

An account of Spain's diverse music appears in the *Contexts* section of this guide. Enough to say, here, that you should catch all that is going on. You will see and hear plenty of regional specialities at any of the country's fiestas.

Traditional *flamenco* – the country's most famous sound – is best witnessed in its native Andalucía, and particularly at one of the major fiestas. There are also some specifically *flamenco* festivals in the summer, most notably at Cartagena and around Granada. Clubs and bars which feature *flamenco* performers tend on the whole to be expensive and tourist-oriented, while the *peñas* (clubs) are often members-only affairs. However, it is possible to find accessible places which cater for aficionados, and in Andalucía itself almost any *flamenco* guitarist you come

across is likely to be extremely good. Just watch the cost of the drinks. In recent years, there has been an exciting development in the shape of new *flamenco* bands, some of whom have attempted introducing jazz, rock and African elements into their music. Some of the best artists in this field are to be seen in Madrid.

If you're anywhere in Spain between about December 18 and January 3, watch for performances in local churches of *villancicos*. These are Christmas carols in local style – they can be *flamenco*, waltz or polyphonic – and are sung by fairly large *coral/rondalla* groups of instrumentalists and vocalists of both sexes. When they're good they're extremely beautiful, and it's obviously a non-boozy, family-oriented spectacle.

Rock music in Spain may tend to follow British and American trends, but the scene is livelier – and less slavishly derivative – than in almost any other west European country, at its best drawing from a broad range of influences in which traditional Spanish and Latin American rhythms play a major part. There are some excellent home-grown bands and regular gigs in most of the big cities, especially in the north.

In Madrid, you'll find the more promising **clubs** and **venues** listed in the following chapter. Both Madrid and Barcelona attract major **international concerts** from time to time, usually staged in their giant football stadiums. Wherever you are, keep an eye out for posters or check the entertainments sections in the local press – you'll find local bands airing their talents at just about any fiesta.

Because of relatively large expatriate populations, Madrid and Barcelona are also good places to hear **Latin American and African** music – again, keep your eye out for posters and check the club and dance-hall listings in the local papers.

There are several excellent **jazz festivals** in the summer: notably in San Sebastián in the middle of July, and in Barcelona, Santander and Sitges.

Worth checking out, too, is the International Festival of Guitar in Córdoba (early July), where most of the great **classical guitarists** put in an appearance along with exponents of Latin American and *flamenco* styles.

TROUBLE, THE POLICE AND SEXUAL HARASSMENT

While you're unlikely to encounter any trouble during the course of a normal visit, it's worth remembering that the Spanish police, polite enough in the usual course of events, can be extremely unpleasant if you get on the wrong side of them. There are three basic types: the Guardia Civil, the Policía Municipal, and the Policía Nacional, all of them armed.

AVOIDING TROUBLE

Almost all the problems tourists encounter are to do with **petty crime** – pickpocketing and bagsnatching – rather than more serious physical confrontations, so it's as well to be on your guard and know where your possessions are at all times. Sensible **precautions** include: carrying bags slung across your neck, not over your shoulder; not carrying anything in zipped pockets facing the street; having photocopies of your passport, and leaving passport and tickets in the hotel safe; and noting down travellers' cheque and credit card numbers. There are also several ploys to be aware of and situations to avoid as you do the rounds of the city.

• Thieves often work in pairs, so watch out for people standing unusually close if you're studying postcards or papers at stalls; keep an eye on your wallet if it appears you're being distracted. **Ploys** (by some very sophisticated operators) include: the "helpful" person pointing out birdshit (shaving cream or something similar) on your jacket while someone relieves you of your money; the card or paper you're invited to read on the street to distract your attention; the move by someone in a café for your drink with one hand (the other hand's in your bag as you react to save your drink).

• If you have a **car** don't leave anything in view when you park it; take the radio with you. Vehicles are rarely stolen, but luggage and valuables left in cars do make a tempting target and rental cars are easy to spot.

• **Looking for hotel rooms**, don't leave any bags unattended anywhere. This applies especially to blocks where the hotel or *hostal* is on the higher floors and you're tempted to leave baggage in the hallway or ground floor lobby.

WHAT TO DO IF YOU'RE ROBBED

If you're robbed, you need to **go to the police** to report it, not least because your insurance company will require a police report. Don't expect a great deal of concern if your loss is relatively small – and expect the process of completing forms and formalities to take ages. In the unlikely event that you're **mugged**, or otherwise threatened, *never* resist; hand over what's wanted and go straight to the police, who on these occasions will be more sympathetic .

THE POLICE

There are three basic types of **police**: the *Guardia Civil*, the *Policía Municipal* and the *Policía Nacional*, all of them armed.

The *Guardia Civil*, in green uniforms, are the most officious and the ones to avoid. Though their role has been cut back since they operated as Franco's right hand, they remain a reactionary force (it was a *Guardia Civil* colonel, Tejero, who held the Cortes hostage in the February 1981 failed coup).

If you do need the police – and above all if you're reporting a serious crime such as rape – you should always go to the more sympathetic *Policía Municipal*, who wear blue-and-white uniforms with red trim. In the countryside there may be only the *Guardia Civil*, though they're usually helpful, they are inclined to resent the suggestion that any crime exists on their turf and you may end up feeling as if you are the one who stands accused.

The brown-uniformed **Policía Nacional** are mainly seen in cities, armed with submachine guns and guarding key installations such as embassies, stations, post offices and their own barracks. They are also the force used to control crowds and demonstrations.

OFFENCES

There are a few **offences** you might commit unwittingly that it's as well to be aware of.

• In theory you're supposed to carry some kind of **identification** at all times, and the police can stop you in the streets and demand it. In practice they're rarely bothered if you're clearly a foreigner.

• **Nude bathing** or **unauthorized camping** are activities more likely to bring you into contact with officialdom, though a warning to cover up or move on is more likely than any real confrontation. **Topless** tanning is commonplace at all the trendier resorts, but in country areas, where attitudes are still very traditional, you should take care not to upset local sensibilities.

• Spanish **drug laws** are in a somewhat bizarre state at present. After the socialists came to power in 1983, cannabis use (possession of up to 8gm of what the Spanish call *chocolate*) was decriminalized. Subsequent pressures, and an influx of harder drugs, have changed that policy and – in theory at least – any drug use is now forbidden. You'll see signs in some bars saying "*no porros*" (no joints), which you should heed. However, the police are in practice little worried about personal use. Larger quantities (and any other drugs) are a very different matter.

Should you be **arrested** on any charge you have the right to contact your **consulate** (see "Listings" in the *Guide* for individual cities), and although they're notoriously reluctant to get involved they are required to assist you to some degree if you have your passport stolen or lose all your money. If you've been detained for a drugs offence, don't expect any sympathy or help from your consulate.

SEXUAL HARASSMENT

Spain's macho image has faded dramatically in the post-Franco years and these days there are relatively few parts of the country where foreign women, travelling alone, are likely to feel threatened, intimidated, or attract unwanted attention.

Inevitably, the **big cities** – like any others in Europe – have their no-go areas, where street crime and especially drug-related hassles are on the rise, but there is little of the pestering and propositions that you have to contend with in, say, the larger French or Italian cities. The outdoor culture of *terrazas* (terrace bars) and the tendency of Spaniards to move around in large, mixed crowds, filling central bars, clubs and streets late into the night, help to make you feel less exposed. If you are in any doubt, there are always taxis – plentiful and reasonably priced.

The major **resorts** of the *costas* have their own artificial holiday culture. The Spaniards who hang around in discos here or at fiesta fairgrounds pose no greater or lesser threat than similar operators at home. The language barrier simply makes it harder to know who to trust. "*Dejame en paz*" (leave me in peace) is a fairly standard rebuff.

Predictably, it is in **more isolated regions**, separated by less than a generation from desperate povery (or still starkly poor), that most serious problems can occur. Since the last edition of this book, we have had two reports of women being followed and attacked in remote parts of Andalucía. You do need to know a bit about the land you're travelling around.

In some areas you can walk for hours without coming across an inhabited farm or house, and you still come upon shepherds working for nothing but the wine they take to their pastures. It's rare that this poses a threat – help and hospitality are much the norm – but you are certainly more vulnerable. That said, **trekking** is becoming more popular in Spain as a whole and many women happily tramp the footpaths, from Galicia to the Sierra Nevada. In the south, especially, though, it is worth finding rooms in the larger villlages, or, if you camp out, asking permission to do so on private land, rather than striking out alone.

WORK

Tape and Visas" (p.15). A word of warning: police are cracking down on people without visas and may ask for passport/residence papers on the spot, especially out of tourist season.

Other options are to try advertising **private lessons** (better paid at 1500–2500ptas an hour, but harder to make a living at) on the *Philologia* noticeboards of university faculties.

Another possibility, so long as you speak good Spanish, is **translation work**, most of which will be business correspondence – look in the Yellow Pages under *Traductores*. If you intend doing agency work, you'll usually need access to a fax and a PC.

TEMPORARY WORK

If you're looking for **temporary work** the best chances are in the **bars and restaurants** of the big Mediterranean resorts. This may help you have a good time but it's unlikely to bring in very much money; pay (often from British bar owners) will reflect your lack of official status or work permit. If you turn up in spring and are willing to stay through the season you might get a better deal – also true if you're offering some special skill like windsurfing (there are schools sprouting up all along the coast). Quite often there are jobs at **yacht marinas**, too, scrubbing down and repainting the boats of the rich; just turn up and ask around, especially from March until June

As a foreigner you've no hope at all of work on harvests – France is much more viable. Students, however, can get various types of community work through the *Viajesu* agency in Madrid (c/ Fernandes de los Ríos; near Moncloa metro). Much of this is very low paid, often food and bed only, but it can be an interesting way to spend the summer and learn Spanish.

Unless you've some particular skill and have applied for a job advertized in your home country such as au pair work, the only real chance of long-term work in Spain is in language schools. However, there is much less work about than in the boom years of the early 1980s – schools are beginning to close down rather than open – and you'll need to persevere if you're to come up with a rewarding position. You'll need a TEFL (Teaching English as a Foreign Language) or ESL (English as a Second Language) certificate to give yourself any kind of chance.

TEACHING AND OFFICE WORK

Finding a teaching job is mainly a question of pacing the streets, stopping in at every language school around and asking about vacancies. For the addresses of schools look in the Yellow Pages under *Idiomas* or *Escuelas Idiomas*.

If you intend to stay in Spain longer than three months, you'll also need a visa – see "Red

DIRECTORY

ADDRESSES are written as: c/Picasso 2, 4° izda. – which means Picasso street (*calle*) no. 2, fourth floor, left- (*izquierda*) hand flat or office; dcha. (*derecha*) is right; cto. (*centro*) centre. Other confusions in Spanish addresses result from the different spellings, and sometimes words, used in Catalan, Basque and Gallego – all of which are to some extent replacing their Castilian counterparts – and from the gradual removal of Franco and other fascist heroes from the main avenidas and plazas. On this latter front, Avenidas del Generalísimo are on the way out all over the country (often changing to "Libertad" or "España"); so too are José Antonios, General Molas, Falanges, and Caudillos. Note that a lot of maps – including the official ones – haven't yet caught up; nor have a handful of right-wing-controlled towns. In some towns dual numbering systems are also in effect, and looking at the plates it's difficult to tell which is the old and which the new scheme.

AIRPORT TAX You can happily spend your last pesetas – there's no departure tax.

BAGGAGE If you are camping, or travelling long-term, you may need a backpack, but for shorter visits you're better off with something smaller and lighter. A nylon duffel bag is big enough to hold a sleeping bag and adequate clothes, and much easier to load on buses, trains and planes.

CONSULATES Practically every nation has an embassy in Madrid: there are also British consulates in Barcelona, Alicante, Bilbão, Ibiza, Malaga, Palma de Mallorca, Sevilla, Tarragona and of course Gibraltar; US representation outside the capital is confined to Barcelona, Sevilla and Valencia.

ELECTRICITY Current in most of Spain is 220 volts AC (just occasionally it's still 110V): most European appliances should work as long as you have an adaptor for European-style two-pin plugs. North Americans will need this plus a transformer.

FEMINISM The Spanish women's movement, despite having to deal with incredibly basic issues (like trying to get contraception available on social security), is radical, vibrant and growing fast. Few groups, however, have permanent offices, and if you want to make contact it's best to do so through the network of feminist bookshops in the major cities. Some of the more established are: Madrid – Librería de Mujeres, c/San Cristóbal 17 (near Plaza Mayor); Barcelona – Librería de les Dones, c/Llado 10; Valencia – Librería Dona, c/Gravador Esteve 34; Sevilla Librería Feminista, c/Zaragoza 36; Granada – Librería Mujer, c/Carnicería 1.

FILM Movie-going remains a remarkably cheap and popular entertainment, with crowded cinemas in every town. The majority of what's screened is the usual Hollywood fare poorly dubbed into Spanish, but in the cities you will find more exciting options and some films in their original language with subtitles. Look for *voz* or *versión original* (*subtitulada*), abbreviated "v.o.", in the listings; "v.e." means *versión español*. An account of Spanish cinema is to be found in the *Contexts* section of this book.

FISHING Fortnightly permits are easily and cheaply obtained from any *ICONA* office – there's one in every big town (addresses from the local Turismo).

GAY LIFE Ibiza is now Europe's major gay resort, surpassing even Greek Mykonos, and attitudes there, and in the major cities and resorts, are fairly relaxed. Madrid, Barcelona, Sitges and Cádiz in particular have large gay communities and a thriving scene. The age of consent is 18.

KIDS/BABIES don't pose great travel problems. *Hostales*, *pensiones* and *restaurantes* generally welcome them and offer rooms with three or four beds; *RENFE* allows children under three to travel free on trains, with half price for those under seven; and some cities and resorts – Barcelona is particularly good – have long lists or special pamphlets on kids' attractions. As far as babies go, food seems to work out quite well (*hostales* often prepare food specially – or will let you use the kitchen to do so) though you might want to bring powdered milk – babies, like most Spaniards, are pretty contemptuous of the UHT (ultra heat-treated) stuff generally available. If you're travelling in the north, or out of season, however, bear in mind that most *hostales* (as opposed to more expensive hotels) don't have any heating systems – and it can get cold. Disposable nappies and other standard needs are very widely available. Many *hostales* will be prepared to baby-sit, or at least to listen out for trouble. This is obviously more likely if you're staying in an old-fashioned family-run place than in the fancier hotels.

LANGUAGE COURSES are offered at most Spanish universities, and in a growing number of special language schools for foreigners. For details overseas and a complete list write to a branch of the Spanish Institute: the London one is at 102 Eaton Square, London SW1 (☎01/235 1484) – other addresses from the nearest tourist office. Many American universities have their own courses based in Spain – or try the Education Office of Spain, 150 Fifth Avenue #600, New York, NY 10011 (☎212/741-5144).

LAUNDRIES You'll find a few self-service launderettes (*lavanderías automáticas*) in the major cities, but they're rare – you normally have to leave your clothes for the full (and somewhat expensive) works. Note that you're not allowed by law to leave laundry hanging out of windows over a street. A dry cleaner is a *tintorería*.

LUGGAGE After a long period of absence following terrorist actions in the late 1970s, self-service *consignas* are back at most important Spanish train stations. You'll find lockers large enough to hold most backpacks, plus a smaller bag, which cost about 200ptas a day. (Put the coin in to free the key.) These are not a viable alternative for long-term storage, however, as they're periodically emptied out by station staff. Bus terminals have manned *consignas* where you present a claim stub to get your gear back; cost is about the same.

SKIING There are resorts in the Pyrenees, Sierra Nevada, and outside Madrid and Santander, all detailed in the relevant chapters. The SNTO's *Skiing in Spain* pamphlet is also useful. If you want to arrange a weekend or more while you're in Spain, *Viajes Ecuador* (the biggest travel firm in the country, with branches in most cities) is good for arranging cheap all-inclusive trips.

SWIMMING POOLS Even quite small Spanish towns have a public swimming pool, or *piscina municipal* – a lifesaver in the summer and yet another reason not to keep exclusively to the coast.

TIME Spain is one hour ahead of the UK, six hours ahead of Eastern Standard Time, nine hours ahead of Pacific Standard Tme, except for brief periods during the changeovers to and from daylight saving. In Spain the clocks go back in the last week in March and forward again in the last week in September.

TOILETS Public ones are averagely clean but very rarely have any paper (best to carry your own). They're often squat-style. They are most commonly referred to and labelled *Los Servicios*, though signs may point you to *baños*, *aseos*, *retretes* or *sanitarios*. *Damas* (Ladies) and *Caballeros* (Gentlemen) are the usual distinguishing signs for sex, though you may also see the confusing *Señoras* (Women) and *Señores* (Men).

FRANCE

7. CANTABRIA AND ASTURIAS

8. GALICIA

6. EUSKADI: THE BASQUE PROVINCES AND NAVARRA

ANDORRA

5. OLD CASTILE AND LEóN

11. CATALUNYA

9. ARAGÓN

10. BARCELONA

1. MADRID

2. AROUND MADRID

PORTUGAL

3. NEW CASTILE AND EXTREMADURA

12. VALENCIA AND MURCIA

4. ANDALUCíA

13. BALEARIC ISLANDS

0   250 km

CHAPTER ONE

MADRID

Madrid became Spain's capital simply through its geographical position at the centre of Iberia. When Felipe II moved the seat of government here in 1561 his aim was to create a symbol of the unification and centralization of the country, and a capital from which he could receive the fastest post and communications from each corner of the nation. The site itself had few natural advantages – it is 300km from the sea on a 650-metre-high plateau, freezing in winter, burning in summer – and it was only the determination of successive rulers to promote a strong central capital that ensured Madrid's survival and development.

Nonetheless, it was a success, and today, Madrid is a vast, predominantly modern city, with a population of some five million and growing. Pretty it isn't, especially on the journey in, through an ugly stream of concrete-block suburbs. However the streets at the heart of the city are a pleasant surprise, with odd pockets of medieval buildings and narrow atmospheric alleys, dotted with the oddest of shops and bars, and interspersed with eighteenth-century Bourbon squares. By comparison with the historic cities of Spain – Toledo, Salamanca, Sevilla, Granada – there may be few sights of great architectural interest, but the monarchs did acquire outstanding picture collections, which formed the basis of the **Prado** museum. This has long ensured Madrid a place on the European art-tour, and the more so since the 1990s' arrival – literally down the street – of the **Reina Sofía** and **Thyssen-Bornemisza** galleries, state-of-the-art homes to fabulous arrays of modern Spanish painting (including Picasso's *Guernica*) and European and American masters.

As you get to grips with the place you soon realize that it's the inhabitants – the **Madrileños** – that are the capital's key attraction: hanging out in the traditional cafés or the summer *terrazas*, packing the lanes of the Sunday Rastro flea market, or playing hard and very, very late in a thousand **bars**, clubs, discos and *tascas*. Whatever Barcelona or San Sebastian might claim, the Madrid scene, immortalised in the movies of Pedro Almodovar, remains the most vibrant and fun in the country. It is also in better shape than for many years past, after a £500m ($800m) refurbishment for its role as 1992 European Capital of Culture; two years on, most of the projects have been completed.

The city's development

Arriving in modern Madrid can be a depressing experience for it is enclosed by some of the world's dreariest suburbs: acres of high-rise concrete seemingly dumped without thought on to the dustiest parts of the plain. The great spread to suburbia was encouraged under Franco, who also extended the city northwards along the spinal route of the Paseo de la Castellana, to accommodate his ministers and minions during development extravaganzas of the 1950s and 1960s. Large, impressive, and unbelievably sterile, these constructions leave little to the imagination; but then, you're unlikely to spend much time in these parts of town.

In the centre, things are very different. The oldest streets at the very heart of Madrid are crowded with ancient buildings, spreading out in concentric circles which reveal the development of the city over the centuries. Only the cramped street plan gives much clue as to what was here before Madrid became the **Habsburg** capital (in 1561), but the narrow alleys around the Plaza Mayor are still among the city's liveliest and

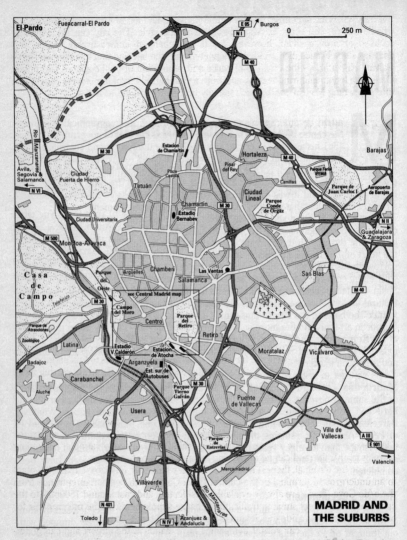

**MADRID AND
THE SUBURBS**

most atmospheric. Later growth owed much to the French tastes of the **Bourbon**
dynasty in the eighteenth century, when for the first time Madrid began to develop a
style and flavour of its own.

The early **nineteenth century** brought invasion and turmoil to Spain as Napoleon
established his brother Joseph on the throne. Madrid, however, continued to flourish,
gaining some very attractive buildings and squares. With the onset of the twentieth
century, the capital became the hotbed of the political and intellectual discussions
which divided the country; *tertulias* (political/philosophical discussion circles) sprang
up in cafés across the city (some of them are still going) as the country entered the
turbulent years of the end of the monarchy and the foundation of the Second Republic.

The **Civil War**, of course, caused untold damage, and led to forty years of isolation, which you can still sense in Madrid's idiosyncratic style. The city can no longer be accused of provincialism, however, for it has changed immeasurably in the two decades since Franco died, guided by a poet-mayor, the late and much lamented Tierro Galván. His efforts – the creation of parks and renovation of public spaces and public life – have left an enduring legacy, and were a vital ingredient of the *movida Madrileño*, the "happening Madrid", with which the city broke through in the 1980s.

Orientation, arrival and information

The city's layout is pretty straightforward. At the heart of Madrid – indeed at the very heart of Spain since all distances in the country are measured from here – is the **Puerta del Sol**. Around it lie the oldest parts of Madrid, neatly bordered to the west by the **Río Manzanares**, to the east by the park of **El Retiro**, and to the north by the city's great thoroughfare, the Gran Vía.

Within this very compact area, you're likely to spend most of your time. The city's three big museums – the **Prado**, **Thyssen-Bornemisza** and **Reina Sofía** – lie in a "magic triangle" just west of El Retiro, while over towards the river are the oldest, Habsburg parts of town – centred around the beautiful arcaded **Plaza Mayor**. After Gran Vía, the most important streets (*calles* – abbreviated as c/) are **c/de Alcala** and its continuation, **c/Mayor**, which cut right through the centre from the main post office at **Plaza de Cibeles** to the Bourbon **Palacio Royal**.

Arrival

If Madrid is your first stop in Spain, by **air, train or bus**, you are likely to arrive some way from the centre. Transport into the centre, however, is relatively easy and efficient.

If you are **driving**, be prepared for a long trawl around the streets to find parking, or – a lot safer – put your car in one of the many signposted *parkings*. If you are staying more than a couple of weeks, you can get long-term parking rates at neighbourhood garages.

By air

The **Aeropuerto de Barajas** is 16km east of the city, at the end of Avenida de Americas; it has two terminals, one for *vuelos internacionales*, the other for *nacionales* (domestic services). The journey to/from central Madrid is highly variable, depending on rush hour traffic and can take anything from 20 minutes to an hour.

Outside the terminal, there is a shuttle bus every half-hour (4.45am–1.15am; 300ptas) to an underground terminal in the central Plaza Colón, with pedestrian entrance from the c/de Goya. **Taxis** are always available outside, too, and cost around 1500ptas to the centre, unless you get stuck in traffic; they charge supplements on the metered fair for baggage, for going outside the city limits and for night (11pm–6am) trips.

Half a dozen or so **car rental** companies have stands at the airport and can generally supply clients with maps and directions. Other airport facilities include 24hr currency exchange, a tourist office and hotel reservations desk. See "Listings" for addresses and phone numbers of car rental offices in the city.

By train

Trains **from France** and **north/northeast Spain** arrive at the **Estación de Chamartín**, a modern terminal isolated in the north of the city; it has usual big station facilities, including currency exchange. A metro line connects Chamartín with the centre, plus there are regular connections by *tranvía* with the much more central Estación de Atocha; just take any *tranvía* headed in that direction.

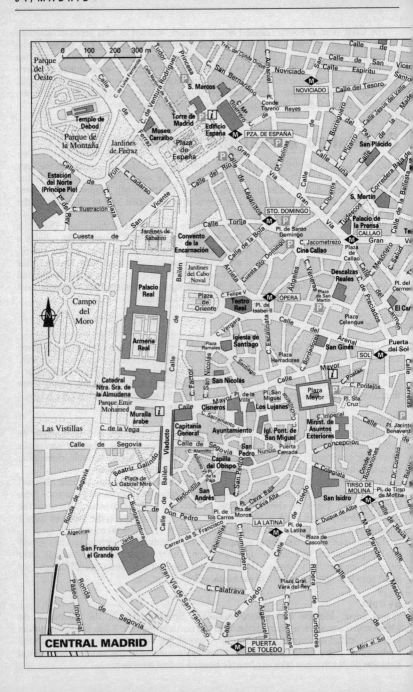

CENTRAL MADRID

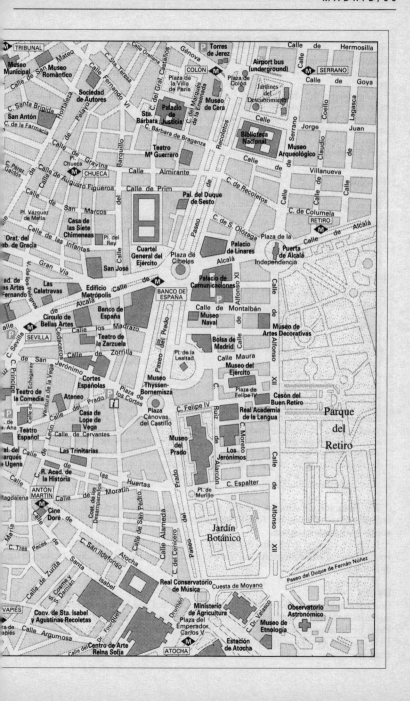

MADRID'S FIESTAS

Look out for **fiestas** whenever you're in Madrid: there are dozens, some of which involve the whole city, others just an individual *barrio*. The more important dates are listed below.

Also well worth checking out are cultural festivals organized by the city-council, and in particular the **Veranos de la Villa** (July–September), a programme of exhibitions, concerts (classical, rock, flamenco), theatre and cinema. Many events are free and they are often open-air, taking place in the parks and squares. One of the nicest venues is the courtyard of the Antiguo Cuartel del Conde Duque (Mº Ventura Rodriguez), where weekly flamenco recitals are held. Full programmes are published in the monthly *En Madrid* tourist hand-out.

February

Carnaval – the week before Lent – is the excuse for a lot of partying.

March/April

Easter Week *Semana Santa* is celebrated in Madrid but with more spirit and processional activity in Toledo.

May

2 *Fiesta de los Dos de Mayo* in Malasaña. Bands and partying around the Plaza Dos de Mayo – a bit low-key in recent years, having been the funkiest festival in the city in the 1980s.

15 The *Fiestas de San Isidro* – Madrid's patron saint – spread for a week either side of this date, and are among the country's biggest festivals. A non-stop round of carnival events: bands, parades and loads of free entertainment. There is a band each night in the Jardines Vistillas (south of the Palacio Real), and the evenings there start out with *chotis* (waltz) music and dancing. The fiestas also herald the start of the bullfighting season.

June

13 *Fiesta de la Ermita de San Antonio de la Florida*; events around the church.

17–24 *Fiestas de San Juan*. Bonfires and fireworks in El Retiro

July

9–16 Local fiesta in Chamberí.

August

15 *Fiesta de la Virgen de la Paloma* in La Latina *barrio*. Main activity takes place around the Plaza de la Paja and Las Vistillas.

October

Festivales de Otoño (autumn festival) around the city.

December

31 New Year's Eve (*nochevieja*) is celebrated at bars, restaurants and parties all over the city, and there are bands in some of the squares. Puerta del Sol is the traditional place to gather, waiting for the strokes of the clock (and swallowing a grape on each strike).

The **Estación de Atocha**, recently expanded and imaginatively remodelled, has two separate terminals: one for **Toledo** and other local services, the other for all points in **south and eastern Spain**.

If you're coming **from the northwest** – Galicia, Salamanca and points en route – you'll arrive at the **Estación del Norte** (aka Principe Pio), fairly close to the centre near the Royal Palace.

By bus

Bus terminals are scattered throughout the city, but the largest – used by all of the international bus services – is the **Estación Sur de Autobuses** at c/Canarias 17 (Mº Palos de Frontera), five blocks south of Atocha train station, down the Paseo de las Delicias. For details of others, see the "Travel Details" section at the end of this chapter.

Information and maps

There are year-round **Turismo** offices at the following locations: **Barajas International Airport** (Mon–Sat 9am–8pm); **Estación de Chamartín** (Mon–Sat 9am–8pm); **Plaza Mayor 3** (Mon–Sat 10am–2pm & 4–8pm); **Torre de Madrid**, c/ Princesa 1/Plaza de España (Mon–Fri 9am–7pm, Sat 9.30am–1.30pm); **c/Duque de Medinaceli 2** (Mon–Fri 9am–7pm, Sat 9.30am–1.30pm).

In the **summer**, Turismo posts operate at popular tourist spots such as the Puerta del Sol and the Prado, and there are **guides** (in blue and yellow uniforms) on call outside the Palacio Real, *Ayuntamiento* and Prado, and in the Plaza Mayor and Puerta del Sol. You can **phone for information** on 901 300 600 (English spoken).

Free **maps** of Madrid are available from any of the Turismos detailed above. However, if you intend to do more than a day's sightseeing, you would be well advised to invest in the *Almax Madrid Centro* map (200ptas), available from just about any kiosk in the city; this is very clear, 1:10,000 in scale, fully street-indexed, and has a colour plan of the metro on the reverse. The area covered on this represents just about everything of interest; if you want more, *Almax* does a rather less clear, 1:12,000 scale *Madrid Ciudad* that goes right out into the suburbs. Again, it's widely available.

Safety and crime

As far as safety goes, there's little cause for concern. Central Madrid is so populated – and so busy at just about every hour of the day and night – that it never seems to carry any "big city" threat. Which is not to say that **crime** is not a problem, nor that there aren't sleazy pockets to be avoided. Madrid has a big drug problem, all too evident around the Plaza de España and some of the streets just north of Gran Vía. Drugs, it is reckoned, account for ninety percent of crimes in Madrid, and if you are unlucky enough to be threatened for money, it's unwise to resist.

Tourists in Madrid, as everywhere, are prime targets for pickpockets and petty thieves. The main shopping areas, and anywhere with crowds, are their favourite haunts; burger bars and the Rastro market seem especially popular. Unless you have rented expensive garage space, drivers may well find that they get their cars broken into and the radio stolen. The **police** are sympathetic and will give you a report form for insurance claims. In emergency, dial ☎091 or ☎092; English is spoken on these numbers.

Getting around

Madrid is a pretty easy city to get around. The central areas are walkable; the metro is modern and efficient, buses serve out of the way districts, and taxis are always available.

If you're using public transport extensively and staying long-term, monthly **passes** are worthwhile; they must be ordered before the month in question and put into service before the tenth of the month. It's also worth checking what deals are available in the form of three-day or weekly *metro-tour* passes: these can be good value, but the system seems to change every few months. If you have an *InterRail* or *Eurail* pass, you can use the *RENFE* urban and suburban trains (*cercanias*) free of charge – they're an alternative to the metro for some longer city journeys.

The metro

The **metro** is by far the quickest way of getting around Madrid and the system serves most places you're likely to want to get to. It runs from 6am until 1.30am; the flat fare is 125ptas for any journey, or 550ptas for a ten-trip (*bono diez viajes*) ticket. You can get a free colour map of the system (*plano del metro*) at any station.

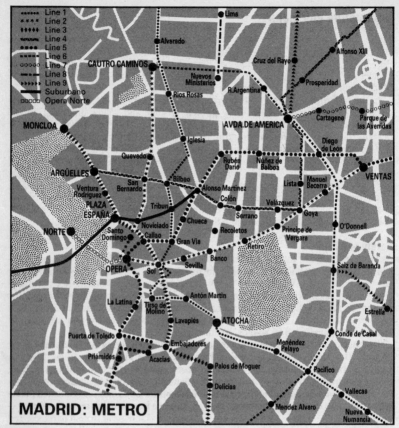

MADRID: METRO

Map legend:
- ••••• Line 1
- ×××× Line 2
- ✦✦✦✦ Line 3
- ⌇⌇⌇ Line 4
- ●●●● Line 5
- ⌇⌇⌇ Line 6
- ○○○○○ Line 7
- —•— Line 8
- ►►►► Line 9
- ——— Suburbano
- □□□□ Opera Norte

Buses

The urban **bus network** is comprehensive but complicated: in the text, where there's no metro stop, we've indicated which bus to take. There are information booths in the Plaza de Cibeles and Puerta del Sol, which dispense a huge routemap (*plano de los transportes de Madrid*), and – along with other outlets – sell bus passes. Fares are the same as for buses, at 125ptas a journey, or 550ptas for a ten-trip (*bono diez viajes*) ticket. When you get on a bus, you punch your ticket in a machine by the driver.

Buses run from 6am to midnight. In addition, there are several **all-night** lines around the central area: departures are half-hourly midnight–2am, hourly 2–6am, from Plaza de Cibeles and Puerta del Sol.

Taxis

One of the best things about Madrid is that there are thousands of taxis – and they're reasonably cheap; 400ptas will get you most places within the centre and, although it's common to round up the fare, you're not expected to tip. In any area in the centre, day and night, you should be able to wave down a taxi (available ones have a green light on top of the cab) in a couple of minutes. To phone for a taxi, call ☎547 82 00, ☎405 13 13 or ☎445 90 08.

Accommodation

Madrid has a lot of **accommodation**, and – business hotels apart – most of it is pretty central. It is, on the whole, pretty functional, too. Few places, at any price range, have much character, and you're basically paying for location and facilities. At the lower end of the range, there are **bargains** to be had, with double rooms as low as 2000ptas a night – and less if you are looking for an extended stay. Move up a few notches and you can find plenty of places at around 4000–5000ptas a night, offering a comfortable room with a private bath or (more often) shower. Few places, however, justify paying prices much higher than that and, assuming money is limited and Madrid is not your only destination in Spain, you'd be better off splashing out for luxury elsewhere.

If you prefer to have others find you a room, there is an **accommodation service**, *Brujula*, with offices at the airport, the Estación Sur de Autobuses, Atocha and Chamartín train stations, and in the centre, above the main Turismo office, on the sixth floor of the Torre de Madrid (☎248 97 05). The service covers the whole of Spain and is free apart from long-distance phone-calls.

ACCOMMODATION PRICE SYMBOLS

The symbols used in our hotel listings denote the following price ranges:

① Under 2000ptas	③ 3000–4500ptas	⑤ 7500–12,500ptas
② 2000–3000ptas	④ 4500–7500ptas	⑥ Over 12,500ptas

See p.30 for more details.

Pensiones, hostales and hotels

The main factor to consider in choosing a hotel is location. If you want to be at the heart of the old town, you'll probably choose the areas around Plaza de Santa Ana or Plaza Mayor; if you're into nightlife, Malasaña or Chueca may appeal; if you want a bit of class, then there are the Paseo del Prado or Serrano areas. From a cursory glance at the listings below, you'll note that buildings in the more popular hotel/*hostal* areas often house two or three separate establishments, each on separate **floors**; these are generally independent of each other. Floors (*pisos*) are written as 1º (1st floor in British parlance, 2nd in American), 2 º, etc. A problem with some of the *hostales* in larger buildings – on Gran Vía, for example – is that they are often inaccessible at night, unless you've been given a front door key, as there's not always an entryphone or doorbell at street level. If you book a room and intend to arrive after, say, 9pm, check that you will be able to get in.

AROUND ATOCHA STATION

Much of the cheapest accommodation in Madrid is to be found in the area immediately around the Estación de Atocha. However, the *pensiones* closest to the station are often grim, catering for migrants from the south looking for work, and the area can be a little threatening after dark. The two below, however, are good safe choices.

Hostal Buelta, c/Drumen, first to the left as you walk up Atocha (☎539 98 07). A decent place, handy for the station. ③.

Pensión Mollo, c/Atocha 104 (☎528 71 76). This is the closest reasonable *hostal* to the station on the way up c/Atocha; convenient if you're heavily laden. ②.

AROUND PLAZA DE SANTA ANA

Plaza de Santa Ana is at the heart of Madrid nightlife, with cafés open until very late at night. The recommendations following are all within a block or two of the square. The metro stations Antón Martín, Sevilla and Sol are all close by.

Hostal Alonso, c/Espoz y Mina 17 (☎531 56 79). Basic but good value and well positioned. ②.

Hostal Los Ángeles, c/Cruz 14 (☎532 90 90). A comfortable, modest place. ③.

Hostal Escadas (☎429 63 81), **Hostal Lido** (☎429 62 07) and **Hostal Internacional** (☎429 62 09), all at c/Echegaray 5. A trio of decent *hostales* in a street that has some of Madrid's most memorable bars and restaurants. ③.

Hostal Filo, Plaza de Santa Ana 15 (☎522 40 56). Pleasant rooms overlooking the square. ④.

Gran Hotel Reina Victoria, Plaza del Ángel 7 (☎531 60 00). A lovely old hotel in a historic building, where the bullfighters stay when they're in town. Rooms are a hefty 24,000ptas a night, but this is the pick of Madrid's class hotels in this price range. ⑥.

Hotel Inglés, c/Echegaray 8 (☎429 65 51). A three-star hotel that has seen better days, but remains comfortable and very reasonably priced for what you get. ⑤.

Hostal Regional, c/del Príncipe 18 (☎522 33 73). Comfortable place in elegant old building off Plaza de Santa Ana. *Hostal Carreras* (☎522 00 36), a couple of floors below, has similar standards and prices but more noise; *Hostal Villar* (☎531 66 00) in the same building, has similar prices and more rooms (so more chance of a vacancy), but seems less friendly. All ③.

Pensión Romero, c/León 13 (☎429 51 39). Comfortable and good value. ③.

Pensión La Torre, c/Espoz y Mina 8 (☎531 00 79). Cuban-run, friendly and quiet. ③.

SOL, OPERA AND PLAZA MAYOR

This really is the heart of Madrid and prices, not surprisingly, are a bit higher, though you can still find bargains in the slightly battered streets towards the Plaza Mayor.

Hostal Americano, Puerta del Sol 11 (☎522 28 22). Nothing wrong with this *hostal*, but you're paying extra for the location. ④.

Hostal Caritel, c/Arenal 26 (☎247 31 29). One of several reasonable *hostales* at the Opera end of Arenal; has a range of rooms with and without bath. ③–④.

Hotel Carlos V, c/Maestro Vitoria 5 (☎531 41 00). Three-star, turn-of-the-century hotel, just off c/ Preciados behind the Descalzas Reales monastery. Not always the quietest location but probably the best central hotel at this price (12500ptas a double). ⑤.

Hostal Cruz Sol, Plaza Santa Cruz 6 (☎532 71 97). Slightly run-down, but in a quiet position just east of Plaza Mayor. ③.

Pensión Jeyma, c/Arenal 24 (no phone). Best budget option in this area – a friendly place with big if basic rooms. ①.

Hostal La Macarena, Cava de San Miguel 8 (☎265 92 21). A fine, family-run *hostal*, in a characterful alley just off the Plaza Mayor. ④.

Hostal Montalvo, c/Zaragoza 6 (☎265 59 10). Between Plaza Santa Cruz and Plaza Mayor; clean and friendly, with good views. ③.

Hotel Paris, c/Alcalá 2 (☎521 64 96). Old-fashioned two-star hotel right on the Puerta del Sol. Very good value for so central a position. ⑤.

Hostal Riesgo, c/Correo (☎522 26 92). Old style place in a street just off Sol. All rooms with private bathrooms. ③.

Hostal Rifer (☎5323197) and **Hostal Riosol** (☎532 31 42), both c/Mayor 5. These two are good value, with a few less expensive bath-less rooms; located just off Puerta del Sol. ③.

AROUND PASEO DEL PRADO

This is a quieter area, though still very central, which hosts some of the city's most expensive hotels – as well as the following more modest options.

Hostal Aguadulce, Plaza de las Cortes 3 (☎429 83 65). This is in a wonderful position – the square is the beginning of Carrera de San Jerónimo – but it is very small. If you turn up to find it full, there are several other *hostales* in the same building. ④.

Hostal Coruña (☎429 25 43) and **Hostal Sud-Americana** (☎429 25 64), Paseo del Prado 12. This pair of *hostales* are very reasonable places, considering they're almost opposite the Prado. The *Sud-Americana* has the better rooms. ③.

Pensión Guerra, Carrera de San Jerónimo 3 (☎522 55 77). Located at the noisier, Puerta del Sol end of the street; it has a wide range of room prices. ②.

Hostal María de Molina, Carrera San Jerónimo 11 (☎429 66 38). A good choice in a building with several *hostales*. ④.

Hostal Mondragón (☎429 68 16), Carrera San Jerónimo 32. Again, the best value *hostal* in a building that includes several others. Has a range of rooms at various prices. ②–③.

ALONG GRAN VÍA

The huge old buildings along the Gran Vía – which stretches all the way from Plaza de España to c/de Alcalá – hide a vast array of hotels and *hostales* at every price, often with a delightfully decayed elegance, though also noisy from outside traffic.

Hostal Alcázar Regis (☎247 93 17; ③), **Hostal Buenos Aires** (☎542 22 50), Gran Vía 61 – at the Plaza de España end of the street. The *Alcázar Regis* is excellent value (③); the *Buenos Aires* more comfortable (④).

Hostal Andorra, Gran Vía 33, 7º (☎532 31 16). Smart, clean and quiet, with bathrooms in all the rooms. ④.

Hostal Atlántico (☎522 64 80) and **Hostal California** (☎522 47 03), Gran Vía 38. Well placed but somewhat pricey three-star *hostales*. ④–⑤.

Hostal Continental (☎521 46 40), **Hostal Hispania**, (☎221 60 72), **Hostal Josefina** (☎521 81 31), **Hostal Miami** (☎521 14 64), **Hostal Tánger** (☎521 75 85), **Hostal Valencia** (☎522 11 15), Gran Vía 44. Take your pick from these: all are reasonable, the *Continental* and *Tánger* are ③, the others ④.

NORTH OF GRAN VÍA

North of Gran Vía, there are further wedges of *hostales* on and around **c/ Fuencarral** and **c/Hortaleza**, near Mº Gran Vía, and **c/Luna**, behind Mº Callao. Fuencarral itself can be almost as noisy as Gran Vía, however, so ask for a room facing away from the street; the higher the street numbers, the further these streets are from Gran Vía – and the nearer to Malasaña (see below).

Hostal Breogán (☎522 81 53), **Hostal Krise** (☎231 15 12) and **Hostal Ribadavia** (☎531 10 58), c/Fuencarral 25. A trio of clean, friendly places run by the same management. ③.

Hostal Ducal, c/Hortaleza 3, 2º (☎521 10 43). A pleasant *hostal* with flower-laden verandas overlooking the city; all rooms with showers. ③.

Hostal Julia (☎522 41 76) and **Hostal Nueva Montaña** (☎521 60 85), c/de la Luna 30. A couple of respectable cheapies. ②.

Hostal del Mar (☎531 72 55), **Hostal Luna** (☎532 45 85) and **Hostal Santo Domingo** (☎531 52 90), c/de la Luna 6. These are all decent value *hostales*. ③.

Hostal Medieval, c/Fuencarral 46 (☎522 25 49). Well-run, friendly place with a range of rooms. ④.

Hostal Pizarro, c/Pizarro 14 (☎532 71 97). A comfortable, fairly upmarket hostal on a street just off c/de la Luna. ④.

Hostal Serrano (☎448 89 87) and **Hostal Sil** (☎448 89 72), c/Fuencarral 95. The building is in a slightly quieter area near Mº Tribunal – very handy for Malasaña. ③–④.

Hostal Zamoran (☎532 20 60) and **Hostal Nuestra Señora de Sonsoles** (☎532 75 23), c/Fuencarral 18. These are not far from Gran Vía and have comfortable and fairly pleasant rooms. Respectively, ③ and ④.

MALASAÑA

Malasaña, centred around Plaza Dos de Mayo, is an old working class district, and one of the main nightlife areas of Madrid. The *hostales* here tend towards the basic, but if you stay here you'll get a feel for what the city is really like – and you'll still be in walking distance of the sights.

Hostal Centro, c/Palma 11, 1º (☎447 00 47). A reasonable budget choice. ②.

Hostal Gallardo, c/Espíritu Santo 18 (☎531 02 64). Good value *hostal*, recently refurbished, with bathrooms and TVs in all the rooms. ③.

Hostal Los Gallegos, c/Palma 43 (☎522 09 25). A friendly, family-run place. ②.

Hostal Maravillas, c/Manuel Malasaña 23, 1º (☎448 40 00). A lively location with low-priced rooms. ②.

Hostal Palma, c/Palma 17 (☎447 54 88). Basic but clean rooms, behind Mº Tribunal. ③.
Hostal El Paraiso, c/San Andres 38, 3º (☎447 95 60). Not quite all its name suggests. ②.
Hostal Los Perales, c/Palma 61 (☎222 71 91). Best budget option in a building with several *hostales*. ②.

CHUECA AND SANTA BARBARA

Chueca, east of Fuencarral, has another cluster of *hostales*. The neighbourhood is another nightlife centre: more so, these days, than Malasaña, with lots of music bars and a *zona gay*. Plaza Chueca, however, is also a hangout for junkies and dealers. The northern reaches of Chueca, around Plaza Santa Barbara (Mº Alonso Martínez), are unintimidating and still full of nightlife.

Hostal Asunción, Plaza Santa Barbara 8 (☎410 25 28). Large, pleasant rooms. ③.
Hostal Barajas, c/Augusto Figueroa 17 (☎532 40 78). An unusually fancy *hostal* for this area, with bathrooms and TVs in all the rooms. ④.
Hostal Domínguez, c/Santa Brígida 1 (☎232 15 47). Just off c/Fuencarral; rooms are a bit dark, but the location is handy. ②.
Hostal El Pinar, c/San Bartolomé 2, 4º (☎531 01 34). A good *hostal* that charges some of the lowest per person rates in the city. ②.
Hostal La Víanesa, c/San Marcos 26 (☎532 70 71). This is a clean and friendly place with some excellent value rooms. ③.
Hostal Santa Bárbara, Plaza Santa Barbara 4 (☎445 73 34). Nice, old-fashioned *hostal* in a good location. Worth the money. ④.

RECOLETOS AND SALAMANCA

This is Madrid at its most chi-chi: the Bond Street/Rue de Rivoli region of smart shops and equally well-heeled apartment blocks. It's a safe, pleasant area but the pavements are notorious for dog shit – poodles being almost as ubiquitous here as fur coats.

Residencia Don Diego, c/Velazquez 65. This is a comfortable little hotel – and quite reasonably priced for the area, with doubles around 10,000ptas. ⑤.
Hotel Serrano, c/Marques de Villamejor 8 (☎435 52 00; Mº Ruben Dario). A small modern hotel, handily sited between c/Velazquez and Paseo de la Castellana. Rooms look out onto a back court-yard so are fairly quiet. Doubles from 15,000ptas. ⑥.

Youth hostels

Madrid has two **youth hostels** – one reasonably central, the other some way out. To get into the former, try to book ahead if at all possible.

Hostel Santa Cruz de Marcenado, c/Santa Cruz de Marcenado 28 (☎547 45 32; Mº Argüelles). This is twenty minutes' walk (or an easy metro ride) north of the centre, just off our map, east of c/ de la Princesa (top left). It is a modern, reasonably pleasant building, with good local bars, and maintains a 1.30am curfew.
Hostel Richard Schirmann, in the Casa de Campo (☎463 56 99; Mº Lago or bus #33). Not very convenient (about 45min from *Sol*) but friendly, comfortable and clean with plenty of fresh air and an enjoyably noisy bar. You can call and they'll pick you up at the Lago metro station, roughly 1km away; you certainly shouldn't walk there alone after dark.

Campsites

There are half a dozen campsites within 30km of Madrid, but (following the closure of *Camping Madrid* – which is still listed in some camping guides) just one that is "local".

Camping Osuna, Avenida de Logroño, out near the airport (☎741 05 10; Mº Canillejas, then bus #105). Friendly, with good facilities, reasonable prices and plenty of shade, but the ground is rock-hard and, with planes landing and taking off overhead, it's extremely noisy.

> The phone code for Madrid and its municipal area is ☎91

The City

Madrid's main sights occupy a compact area between the **Palacio Real** (Royal Palace) and the gardens of **El Retiro**. The great trio of museums – the **Prado**, **Thyssen** and **Reina Sofía** – are ranged along the Paseo del Prado, over towards the Retiro. The oldest part of the city, an area known as **Madrid de los Austrias**, after the Habsburg monarchs who built it, is centred on the gorgeous, arcaded **Plaza Mayor**, just to the east of the Palacio Real.

If you have very limited time, you might well do no more sightseeing than this. However, monuments are not really what Madrid is about, and to get a feel for the city you need to branch out a little, and experience the contrasting character and life of the various *barrios*. The most central and rewarding of these are the areas **around Plaza de Santa Ana and c/de las Huertas**, east of Puerta del Sol; **La Latina and Lavapiés**, south of Plaza Mayor, where the sunday market, **El Rastro**, takes place; and **Malasaña and Chueca**, north of Gran Vía. By happy circumstance, these *barrios* have some of Madrid's finest concetrations of *tapas* bars and restaurants (see p.83).

Sol, Plaza Mayor and Opera: Madrid of the Austrias

Madrid de los Austrias – Habsburg Madrid – was a mix of formal planning, at its most impressive in the expansive and theatrical Plaza Mayor, and areas of shanty-town development, knocked up as the new capital gained an urban population. The central area of old Madrid still relects both characteristics, with its twisting grid of streets, alleyways and steps, and its Flemish-inspired architecture of red brick and grey stone, slate-tiled towers, and Renaissance doorways.

Puerta del Sol

The obvious starting point for exploring Habsburg Madrid (and most other areas of the centre) is the **Puerta del Sol** (Mº Sol). This square marks the epicentre of the city – and, indeed of Spain. It is from here that all distances are measured, and here that six of Spain's *Rutas Nacionales* (the roads known as N1, to Burgos, N2, to Zaragoza, etc) officially begin. On the pavement outside the clocktower building on the south side of the square, a stone slab shows **Kilometre Zero**.

The square is a popular meeting place, especially by the fountain, or at the corner of c/del Carmen, with its statue of a bear pawing a bush – the city's emblem. These apart, there's little of note, though the square fulfils something of a public role when there's a demonstration or celebration. At the New Year, for example, it is packed with people waiting for the clock to chime midnight. The square's main business, however, is shopping, with giant branches of the **department stores** *El Corte Inglés* and *Galerías Preciados* to be found in c/de Preciados, at the top end of the square.

Plaza Mayor

Follow c/Mayor (the "Main Street" of the medieval city) west from the Puerta del Sol and you could easily walk right past Madrid's most important landmark: **Plaza Mayor**. This is set back from the street and, entered by stepped passageways, appears all the more grand in its continuous sweep of arcaded buildings. It was planned by Felipe II, the monarch who made Madrid the capital, as the public meeting place of the city, and was finished thirty years later in 1619, during the reign of Felipe III, who sits astride the stallion in the central statue. The architect was Juan Gómez de Mora, who was responsible for many of the civic and royal buildings in this quarter.

The square, with its hundreds of balconies, was designed as a theatre for public events, and it has served this function throughout its history. It was the scene of the Inquisition's *autos-da-fé* (trials of faith) and the executions which followed; kings were crowned here; festivals and demonstrations passed through; plays by Lopé de Vega and others received their first performances; bulls were fought; and gossip was spread. The more important of the events would be watched by royalty from their apartments in the central **Casa Panadería**, a palace (now municipal offices) named after the bakery which it replaced. It was rebuilt after a fire in 1692 and decorated with a delightful – and to modern eyes, highly kitsch – array of allegorical figures, recently restored to their full glory.

Nowadays, Plaza Mayor is primarily a tourist haunt, full of outdoor cafés and restaurants (best stick to a drink). However, an air of grandeur clings to the place and the plaza still performs public functions. In the summer months it becomes an outdoor theatre and music stage; in the autumn there's a book fair; and in the winter, just before Christmas, it becomes a bazaar for festive decorations and religious regalia. Every Sunday, too, stamp sellers and collectors convene to talk philately together while their numismatic counterparts rummage through boxes of rare coins in an open-air market.

In the alleys just below the square, such as calle Cuchilleros, are some of the city's oldest *mesones*, or taverns. Have a drink in these in the early evening and you are likely to be serenaded by passing *tunas* – musicians and singers dressed in traditional costume of knickerbockers and waistcoats who wander around town playing and passing the hat. These men-only troupes are attached to various faculties of the university and are used by students to supplement their grants.

Plaza de la Villa, San Miguel and San Ginés

Further west along Calle Mayor, towards the Royal Palace, is **Plaza de la Villa**, a perfect example of three centuries of Spanish architectural development. Its oldest surviving building is the fifteenth-century **Torre de los Lujanes**, a fine Mudéjar (Moors working under Christian rule) tower, where Francis I of France is said to have been imprisoned in 1525 after his capture at the battle of Pavia (in Italy). Opposite is the **Casa de Cisneros**, built by a nephew of Cardinal Cisneros in the sixteenth-century Plateresque ("silversmith") style. Finally, fronting the square is the old townhall, the **Ayuntamiento**, begun in the seventeenth century, but remodelled in a Baroque mode.

Baroque is taken even further around the corner in c/San Justo, where the parish church of **San Miguel** shows the unbridled imagination of the eighteenth-century Italian architects who designed it.

Another fine – but much more ancient – church is **San Ginés**, north of Plaza Mayor on c/del Alcalá. This is of Mozarabic origin (built by Christians under Moorish rule) and has an El Greco canvas of the money changers being chased from the temple. It is open only during services. Alongside the church, in somewhat uneasy juxtaposition, stands a cult temple of the twentieth century, the *Joy Eslava* disco, and, behind it, the

Chocolatería San Ginés, a Madrid institution, which at one time catered for the early rising worker but now churns out *churros* and hot chocolate for the late night club crowd (see p.93).

Descalzas Reales and Encarnación convents

A couple of blocks north of San Ginés is one of the hidden treasures of Madrid, the **Convento de las Descalzas Reales**. This was founded by Juana de Austria, daughter of the emperor Carlos (Charles) V, sister of Felipe II, and, at age nineteen, already the widow of Prince Don Juan of Portugal. In her wake came a succession of titled ladies (*Descalzas Reales* means Barefoot Royals), who brought fame and, above all, fortune. The place is unbelievably rich, though beautiful and tranquil, too, and still in use as a monastery, with shoeless nuns tending patches of vegetable garden.

Whistle-stop guided **tours** (Tues–Thurs & Sat 10.30am–12.30pm & 4–5.15pm, Fri & Sun 10.30am–12.30pm; 350ptas) conduct visitors through the cloisters and up an incredibly fancy stairway to a series of chambers packed with art and treasures of every kind. The dormitories are perhaps the most outstanding feature, decorated with a series of Flemish tapestries based on designs by Rubens and a striking portrait of Saint Francis by Zurbarán. These were the sleeping quarters for all the nuns – who included, for a time, Saint Teresa of Ávila – except for the Empress María of Germany, who endowed the convent with her own luxurious private chambers. The other highlight of the tour is the *Joyería* (Treasury), piled high with jewels and relics of uncertain provenance. The nuns kept no records of their gifts, so no one is quite sure what many of the things are – there is a bizarre cross-sectional model of Christ – nor which bones came from which saint. Whatever, it's an exceptional hoard.

Tickets to the Descalzas Reales admit you to the **Convento de la Encarnación** (same hours), over towards the Palacio Real. This was founded a few years after Juana's convent, by Margarita, wife of Felipe III, though substantially rebuilt towards the end of the eighteenth century. It houses an extensive but disappointing collection of seventeenth-century Spanish art.

Opera: Plaza de Oriente and the cathedral

West of Sol, c/del Arenal leads to the **Teatro Real** or **Opera**, which gives this area its name (M° Opera). It was built in the mid-nineteenth century and almost sunk a few decades later as a result of subsidence caused by underground canals. At present, it's again shrouded in plastic and scaffolding, amid a major restoration programme.

Around the back, the opera house is separated from the Palacio Real by the **Plaza de Oriente**, a surprisingly under-used square, perhaps due to a hangover from the bad old days when Franco used to address crowds here; neo-Fascists still gather here on the anniversary of his death in November. The square's main distinction – and the focus of its life – is the elegant *Café del Oriente*, whose summer *terraza* is one of the stations of Madrid nightlife. The café (which is also a prestigious restaurant) looks as traditional as any in the city but was in fact opened in the 1980s, by a priest, Padre Lezama, who ploughs his profits into various charitable schemes.

The café apart, the dominant feature of Plaza de Oriente are statues: forty-four of them, depicting Spanish kings and queens, which were designed originally to go on the palace facade but found to be too heavy (some say too ugly) for the roof to support. The **statue of Felipe IV** on horseback, in the centre of the square, clearly belongs on a different plane; it was based on designs by Velázquez, and Galileo is said to have helped with the calculations to make it balance.

Facing the Palacio Real to the south, across the shadeless Plaza Armería, is Madrid's newly-inauguarated cathedral, **Nuestra Señora de la Almudena** (closed 1.30–5pm). This was planned centuries ago, bombed out in the civil war, worked upon at intervals since, and eventually opened for business in 1993 by Pope John Paul II. Its neoclassical bulk is as indistinguished inside as out, though the boutique-like Capilla Opus Dei has, at least, novelty value amid an array of largely unfilled chapel alcoves.

South again from here, c/Bailén crosses c/Segovia on a high **viaduct** which was constructed as a royal route from the palace to the church of San Francisco el Grande, avoiding the rabble and river which both flowed below. Close by is a patch of **Moorish wall** from the medieval fortress here, which the original royal palace replaced. Across the aqueduct, the gardens of *Las Vistillas* ("the views") beckon, with their summer *terrazas* (terrace cafés) looking out across the river.

El Palacio Real

The **Palacio Real** or Royal Palace scores high on statistics. It claims more rooms than any other European palace; a library with one of the biggest collections of books, manuscripts, maps and musical scores in the world; and an armoury with an unrivalled collection of weapons dating back to the fifteenth century.

Times for **guided tours** in various languages (Mon–Sat 9am–6.15pm; winter 9am–5.15pm, Sun 9am–2.15pm; closed occasionally for state occasions), which are compulsory for the main apartments, are posted by the entrance on the Plaza de las Armas, facing the cathedral. The tours have been abbreviated in recent years, now taking in just thirty (rather than ninety) rooms and apartments, but they are still a pretty hard slog, rarely allowing much time to contemplate the extraordinary opulence: acres of Flemish and Spanish tapestries, endless Rococo decoration, bejewelled clocks and pompous portraits of the monarchs.

The palace and outhouses

The Habsburg's original palace burned down on Christmas Day 1734. Its replacement, the current building, was based on drawings made by Bernini for the Louvre. It was constructed in the mid-eighteenth–century and was the principal royal residence from then until Alfonso XIII went into exile in 1931; both Joseph Bonaparte and the Duke of Wellington also lived here briefly. The present royal family inhabits a considerably more modest residence in the western outskirts of the city, using the Palacio Real only on state occasions.

On the tour, you will find yourself, sooner or later, in the **Sala del Trono** (Throne Room). This is the highlight for most visitors, the guide's explanations allowing time to admire the new thrones installed for Juan Carlos and Sofía, the current monarchs, as well as the splendid ceiling by Tiepolo, a giant fresco representing the glory of Spain – an extraordinary achievement for an artist by then in his seventies.

The palace outbuildings and annexes include the **Armería Real**, a huge room full of guns, swords and armour, with such curiosities as El Cid's sword and the suit of armour worn by Carlos V in his equestrian portrait by Titian in the Prado. Especially fascinating are the complete sets of armour, with all the original spare parts and gadgets for making adjustments. The **Biblioteca Real** (Royal Library) is equally staggering, including a first edition of *Don Quixote* among its countless volumes. There is also an eighteenth-century **Farmácia**, a curious mixture of alchemist's den and laboratory, whose walls are lined with jars labelled for various remedies.

Gardens and the coach museum

Immediately north of the palace the **Jardines Sabatini**, the royal gardens, are also open to the public, while to the rear is the larger park of the **Campo del Moro** (access only from the far west side off the Paseo de la Virgen del Puerto).

In the latter is the **Museo de Carruajes** (Tues–Sat 10am–1.30pm, Sun 9am–3.30pm; separate ticket), a collection of state coaches and the like from the sixteenth century to the present.

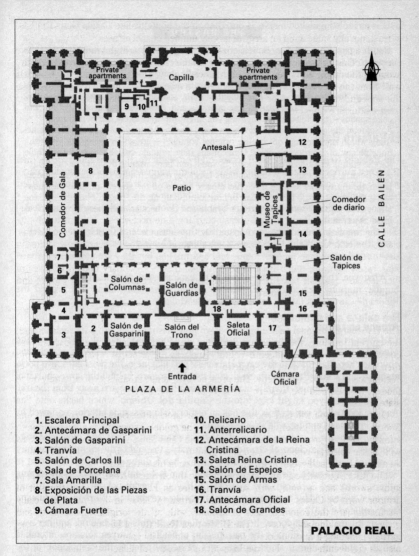

1. Escalera Principal
2. Antecámara de Gasparini
3. Salón de Gasparini
4. Tranvía
5. Salón de Carlos III
6. Sala de Porcelana
7. Sala Amarilla
8. Exposición de las Piezas de Plata
9. Cámara Fuerte
10. Relicario
11. Anterrelicario
12. Antecámara de la Reina Cristina
13. Saleta Reina Cristina
14. Salón de Espejos
15. Salón de Armas
16. Tranvía
17. Antecámara Oficial
18. Salón de Grandes

PALACIO REAL

South of Plaza Mayor: La Latina, Lavapiés and El Rastro

The areas south of Plaza Mayor have traditionally been tough, working-class districts, with tenement buildings thrown up to accommodate the huge expansion of the population in the eighteenth and nineteenth centuries. In many places these old houses survive, huddled together in narrow streets, but the character of **Latina** and **Lavapiés** is beginning to change as their inhabitants, and the districts themselves, become younger and more fashionable. The streets of Cava Baja and Cava Alta, for example, in La Latina, include some of the city's most fashionable bars and restaurants.

THE RASTRO

Madrid's flea maket, **El Rastro**, is as much part of the city's weekend ritual as a mass or a *paseo*. This gargantuan, thriving, thieving shambles of a street market sprawls south from Mº Latina to the Ronda de Toledo, especially along Ribera de Curtidores. Through it, crowds flood between 10am and 3pm every Sunday and increasingly on Fridays and Saturdays too. On offer are secondhand clothes, military surplus items, budgies and canaries, sunshades, razor blades, fine antiques and Taiwanese transistors, cutlery and coke spoons – in fact just about anything you might (or more likely, might not) need.

Some of the goods – broken telephone dials, plastic shampoo bottles half-full of something which may or may not be the original contents – are so far gone that you can't imagine any of them ever selling. Other items may be quite valuable, but on the whole it's the stuff of markets around the world you'll find here: pseudo-designer clothes, bags and T-shirts. Don't expect to find fabulous bargains, or the hidden Old Masters of popular myth; the serious antique trade has mostly moved off the streets and into the shops along the street, while the real junk is now found only on the fringes. Nonetheless, the atmosphere of the Rastro is always enjoyable and the bars around these streets are as good as any in the city.

One warning: keep a tight grip on your bags, pockets, cameras (best left at the hotel), and jewellery. The Rastro rings up a fair percentage of Madrid's tourist thefts.

Whatever, these are attractive *barrios* to explore, and particularly so during the Sunday morning flea market, **El Rastro**, which takes place along and around the Ribera de Curtidores (Mº La Latina or Tirso de Molina).

Around La Latina

La Latina is a short walk from Plaza de la Villa (see above) and, if you're exploring Madrid de los Austrias, it's a natural continuation. Some of the squares, streets and churches here date back to the early Habsburg period. One of the most attractive pockets is around **Plaza Paja**, an acacia-shaded fountain square, behind the large church of San Andrés. In summer, there is usually a *terraza* here, tucked well away from the traffic. If it is open, you might look into the **Capilla del Obispo**, which backs onto San Andrés; long under restoration, this has an elaborate Renaissance interior, endowed by one of Ferdinand and Isabella's counsellors.

Over to the west of here is one of Madrid's grandest, richest and most elaborate churches, **San Francisco el Grande**. Built towards the end of the eighteenth century as part of Carlos III's renovations of the city, it has a dome even larger than that of Saint Paul's in London. Inside (Tues–Sat 11am–1pm & 4–7pm) are paintings by, among others, Goya and Zurbarán, and frescoes by Bayeu. They're not all that easy to see, however, as scaffolding is in place for a painfully slow restoration. Work is scheduled to be completed in 2012.

The Ribera de Curtidores, heart of the Rastro, begins just behind another vast church, **San Isidro**. Isidro is the patron saint of Madrid – his remains are entombed within – and his church acted as the city's cathedral prior to the completion of the Almudena by the Palacio Real. Relics apart, its chief attribute is size – it's as bleak as it is big. Next door is the **Instituto Real**, a school which has been in existence considerably longer than the church and counts among its former pupils such literary notables as Calderón de la Barca, Lope de Vega, Quevedo and Jacinto Benavente.

If you continue to the end of **Ribera de Curtidores**, whose antique shops (some, these days, extremely upmarket) stay open all week, you'll see a large arch, the **Puerta de Toledo**, at one end of the Ronda de Toledo. The only surviving relation to the Puerta de Alcalá in the Plaza Independencia, this was built originally as a triumphal arch to honour the conquering Napoleon. After his defeat in the Peninsular Wars, it became a symbol of the city's freedom. Just in front of the arch, the **Mercado Puerta Toledo**, once the city's fish market, is now a classy and expensive emporium of designer clothing, gifts, furniture and antiques. It's an attractive development, worth looking into for the architecture and occasional entertainment.

Lavapiés and the Cine Doré

A good point to start exploring **Lavapiés** is the Plaza Tirso de Molina (Mº Tirso de Molina). From here, you can follow c/Mesón de Paredes, stopping for a drink at *Taverna António Sanchéz*, at no. 13, down to **La Corrala**, on the corner of c/ Sombrerete. This is one of many traditional *corrales* – tenement blocks – in the quarter, built with balconied apartments opening onto a central patio. Plays – especially farces and *zarzuelas* (a kind of operetta) – used to be performed regularly in Spanish *corrales*, and the open space here usually hosts a few performances in the summer. It has been well renovated and declared a national monument.

From Lavapiés, you are not far from the Centro de Arte Reina Sofía (see p.76), while to the north of the quarter, near Mº Antón Martin, is the **Cine Doré**, the oldest cinema in Madrid, dating from 1922, with a late modernista/art nouveau facade. It has been converted to house the *Filmoteca Nacional*, an art-film centre, and has a pleasant and inexpensive café.

West of Sol: Plaza de Santa Ana and Huertas

The **Plaza de Santa Ana/Huertas** area forms a triangle, bordered to the east by the Paseo del Prado, to the north by c/Alcalá, and along the south by c/Atocha, with the Puerta del Sol at the western tip. The city reached this district after extending beyond the Royal Palace and the Plaza Mayor, so the buildings date predominantly from the nineteenth century. Many of them have literary associations: there are streets named after Cervantes and Lope de Vega (where one lived and the other died), and the *barrio* is host to the Atheneum club (literary guild), Círculo de las Bellas Artes (Fine Arts Institute), Teatro Nacional, and the Cortes (parliament). Just to the north, there is also an important museum, the **Academía de Bellas Artes de San Fernando**.

For most visitors, though, the major attraction is that in this district are some of the best and most beautiful bars and *tascas* in the city. They are concentrated particularly around Plaza de Santa Ana, which – following a rather seedy period – has been smart- ened up by the council and is now one of the finest squares of the city.

Santa Ana and around

The bars around **Plaza de Santa Ana** (Mº Sol) really are sights. In the square itself, the dark panelled **Cerveceria Alemana** has hardly changed since the turn of the century, and was a firm favourite of Hemingway. It's a place to drink beer and go easy on *tapas* (the *empanadillas* are good), if you don't want to run up a significant bill. **Viva Madrid**, on the corner at c/Manuel Fernández y Gonzalez 7, should be another port of call, if only to admire the fabulous tilework, original zinc bar and a ceiling supported by wooden caryatids. Another notable place is the *Bar Torero* of the **Gran Hotel Reina Cristina**, the smart hotel flanking Plaza de Santa Ana; this is where bullfighters stay, when in town, and the bar is packed with taurine memorabilia.

One block east from here is **c/Echegaray** – of which more in the restaurant and bar sections on p.85 and p.93 – where the highlight is **Los Gabrieles** at no. 17. This is a bar with museum-piece *azulejos*, endowed by sherry companies in the late nineteenth century and fabulously inventive: there are skeletons climbing over barrels, Goya- esque idylls with sherry and bulls, and a superb co-opting of Vélazquez's *Los Borrachos*.

Huertas, the Cortes and the Círculo de Bellas Artes

Huertas is a slightly more classy area, though **c/de las Huertas** itself is workaday enough – and again packed with bars. North of the street, and parallel, are two streets named after the greatest figures of Spain's seventeenth-century literary golden age, **Cervantes** and **Lope de Vega**. Bitter rivals in life, both are probably spinning in their graves now, since Cervantes is interred in the **Convento de las Trinitarias** on the street named after Lope de Vega, while the latter's house, the **Casa de Lope de Vega** (Tues–Sun 11am–2pm, closed mid-July to mid-Aug), finds itself on c/de Cervantes. The latter is well worth visiting for its reconstruction of life in seventeenth-century Madrid.

A block to the north is **Las Cortes Españolas**, an unpreposessing nineteenth–century building where the congress (the lower house) meets. Sessions can be visited by appointment only, though anyone can turn up (with a passport) for a tour on Saturday mornings. You are shown the bullet holes left by mad Colónel Tejero and his Guardia Civil associates in the abortive coup attempt of 1981.

Cut across to c/de Alcalá from the Plaza de las Cortes and you will emerge close to the **Círculo de Bellas Artes**, a strange-looking 1920s building crowned by a statue of Pallas Athene. This is Madrid's best arts centre, and includes a theatre, music hall, exhibition galleries, cinema and a very pleasant bar – all marble and leather decor, with a nude statue reclining in the middle of the floor. It attracts Madrid's arts-media crowd but is not in the least exclusive, nor expensive, and there's an adjoining *terraza*, too. The *Círculo* is theoretically a members-only club, but it issues 100ptas day membership on the door, for which you get access to all areas.

Calle Alcalá to Cibeles

At the Circulo, you are on the corner of Gran Vía (see p.79), and only a hundred metres to the east, c/del Alcalá meets the Paseo del Prado at the **Plaza de la Cibeles**. The wedding-cake building on the far side of this square is Madrid's main post office, the aptly entitled **Palacio de Comunicaciones**. Constructed from 1904 to 1917, it is vastly more imposing than the parliament and runs the Palacio Real pretty close: a fabulous place, flanked by polished brass postboxes for each provinces and preserving a totally Byzantine system within, where scores of counters each offer just one particular service, from telegrams to string, and, until quite recently, scribes.

Awash in a sea of traffic in the centre of the square is a **fountain** and statue of the goddess Cibeles, which survived the bombardments of the Civil War by being swaddled from helmet to hoof in sandbags. It was designed, as were the two other fountains gushing magnificently along the Paseo del Prado, by Ventura Rodríguez, who is honoured in modern Madrid by having a metro station and a street named after him.

Madrid's three principal art museums, the **Prado**, **Thyssen-Bornemisza** (see p.74) and **Centro de Arte Reina Sofía** (see p.76), all lie to the south of here, along the Paseo del Prado. To the north, on Paseo de Recoletos, are a couple of the city's most lavish **traditional cafés**, the *Café Gijón* at no. 21 and *Café El Espejo* at no. 31 (see p.88).

Real Academia de Bellas Artes de San Fernando

Art buffs who have some appetite left after the Prado, Thyssen and Reina Sofía, will find the Real Academia de Bellas Artes de San Fernando, at c/Alacalá 13 (Tues–Sat 11am–1pm & 5–8pm, Sun 11am–1pm), next on their list. Admittedly, you have to plough through a fair number of dull academic canvases, but there are hidden gems, particularly in the second and third rooms. They include a group of small panels by **Goya**, especially *The Burial of the Sardine*; portraits of the monks of the Merced order by Zurbarán and others; and a curious *Family of El Greco*, which may be by the great man or his son. Two other rooms are devoted to foreign artists, especially Rubens. Upstairs, there is a series of engravings by Picasso, and, scattered throughout the museum, is a dismembered *Massacre of the Innocents* by sculptor José Ginés.

Museo del Prado

The **Museo del Prado** (M° Banco de España/Atocha; Tues–Sat 9am–7pm, Sun 9am–
2pm; 400ptas, students/EC citizens under 21 free) is Madrid's premier tourist attraction, and one of the oldest and greatest collections of art in the world. Originally
opened to the public in 1819, it houses all the finest works collected by Spanish royalty
– for the most part avid, discerning, and wealthy buyers – as well as Spanish paintings
gathered from other sources over the past two centuries: 7000 paintings in all, of which
around 1500 (still a pretty daunting tally) are on permanent display.

The museum's highlights are its Flemish collection – including almost all of **Bosch**'s
best work – and of course its incomparable display of Spanish art, especially **Velázquez**
(including *Las Meninas*), **Goya** (including the *Mayas*), and **El Greco**. There's also a
huge section of **Italian painters (Titian**, notably) collected by Carlos V and Felipe II,
both great patrons of the Renaissance, and a strong showing of later Flemish pictures
collected by Felipe IV. Even in a full day you couldn't hope to do justice to everything
here, and it's perhaps best to make a couple of more focused visits. If you are tempted
to get your money's worth out of the long opening hours, however, there's a decent
cafetería in the basement.

ORGANIZATION, CATALOGUES AND ENTRANCES
Major reorganization for the installation of air-conditioning and much-needed lighting
improvement has been going on for years now, so you may find displays moved or
temporarily closed. What follows is, by neccessity, only a brief guide to the museum
contents. Illustrated **guides and catalogues** describing and explaining the paintings
are on sale in the museum shop, and there are useful **notes** (100ptas) on Velázquez,
Goya and El Greco available in their respective galleries.

There are two main **entrances** to the museum: the **Puerta de Goya**, opposite the
Hotel Ritz on c/Felipe IV, and the **Puerta de Murillo**, on Plaza de Murillo, opposite
the botanical gardens. The former takes you up to the first floor (US second floor),
with the Italian Renaissance, giving way to the main Spanish collections; the latter is a
ground floor entrance which steers you past Goya's *Black Paintings* towards Bosch and
the other Flemish galleries.

Spanish painting
The Prado's collections of Spanish painting begins on the ground floor, where rooms
51a and 51b house cycles of twelfth-century **Romanesque frescoes**, reconstructed
from a pair of churches from the Mozarabic (Muslim rule) era in Soria and Segovia.
Early panel paintings – exclusively religious fourteenth- and fifteenth-century works
– include a huge *retablo* by Nicolás Francés; the anonymous *Virgin of the Catholic
Monarchs*; Bermejo's *Santo Domingo de Silos*; and Pedro Berruguete's *Auto da Fé*.

At present, the ground floor also shows the Prado's holdings of **José Ribera** (1591–
1625), who worked mainly in Naples, and was influenced .there by Caravaggio. His
masterpieces are considered *The Martyrdom of St Bartholomew* and the dark, realist
portrait of *Archimedes*. Housed, too, on the ground floor (in rooms 66 and 67) are
Goya's *Black Paintings*, though these are probably best seen after you've visited the
rest of his work on the floor above.

THE GOLDEN AGE: VELAZQUEZ AND EL GRECO
Upstairs, to the left of the Puerta de Goya entrance, and beyond the Italian galleries (see
below), are the Prado's collections from Spain's Golden Age: the late sixteenth and
seventeenth centuries under Habsburg rule. They are prefigured, in the early rooms, by
a collection of paintings by **El Greco** (1540–1614), the Cretan born artist who worked in
Toledo from the 1570s. You really have to go to Toledo to appreciate fully his extraordi-

nary genius, but the portraits and religious works here, ranging from the Italianate *Trinity* to the visionary late *Adoration of the Shepherds* are a good introduction.

With rooms 12, 14 and 15, you confront the greatest painter of Habsburg Spain, **Diego Velázquez** (1599–1660). Born in Portugal, Velazquez became court painter to Felipe IV, whose family is represented in many of the works: "I have found my Titian", Felipe is said to have remarked of his appointment. Velazquez's masterpiece, *Las Meninas*, has room 12 to itself, displayed alongisde studies for the painting: Manet remarked of it, "After this I don't know why the rest of us paint", and the French poet Théophile Gautier asked "But where is the picture?", because it seemed to him a continuation of the room. *Las Hilanderas*, showing the royal tapestry factory at work, *Christ Crucified*, *Los Borrachos* (The Drunkards) and *The Surrender of Breda* (note the compositional device of the lances) are further magnificent works. In fact almost all of the fifty works on display (around half of the artist's surviving output) warrant close attention. Don't overlook the two small panels of the *Villa Medici*, painted in Rome in 1650, in virtually impressionist style.

In the adjacent rooms are examples of just about every significant Spanish painter of the seventeenth century, including many of the finest works of **Francisco Zurbarán** (1598–1664), **Bartlomé Esteban Murillo** (1618–82), **Alonso Cano** (1601–67), **Juan de Valdes Leal** (1622–1660), and **Juan Carreño (1641–85)**. Note, in particular, Carreño's portrait of the last Habsburg monarch, the drastically inbred and mentally retarded *Carlos II*, rendered with terrible realism.

GOYA

The final suite of Spanish rooms (19–23 and 32–39) provides an awesome and fabulously complete overview of the works of **Francisco de Goya** (1746–1828), the greatest painter of Bourbon Spain, and an artist whom many see as the inspiration and forerunner of impressionism and modern art. He was an enormously versatile artist: contrast the voluptuous *Maja Vestida* and *Maja Desnuda* (The Clothed and Naked Belles) with the horrors depicted in *Dos de Mayo* and *Tres de Mayo* (on-the-spot portrayals of the rebellion against Napoleon in the streets of Madrid and the subsequent reprisals). Then again, there are the series of pastoral cartoons – designs for tapestries – and, downstairs, the extraordinary *Black Paintings*, a series of murals painted on the walls of his home by the deaf and embittered painter in his old age. His many portraits of his patron, Carlos IV, are remarkable for their lack of any attempt at flattery while those of Queen María Luisa, whom he despised, are downright ugly.

Italian painting

The Prado's early Italian galleries (rooms 2–11 & 40–44) are distinguished principally by **Fra Angelico**'s *Annunciation* (c1445) and by a trio of panels by **Botticelli** (1445–1510). The latter illustrate a deeply unpleasant story from the *Decameron* about a woman hunted by hounds; the fourth panel (in London) is a happier conclusion.

With the sixteenth–century Renaissance, and especially its Venetian exponents, the collection really comes into its own. There are major works by **Raphael** (1483–1520), including a fabulous *Portrait of a Cardinal*, and masterpieces from the Venetians, **Tintoretto** (1518–94), **Veronese** (1528–88) and **Caravaggio** (1573–1610). The most important group of works, however, are by Titian (Tiziano; 1487–1576). These include portraits of the Spanish emperors, *Carlos V* and *Felipe II* (Charles's suit of armour is preserved in the Palacio Real), and a famous, much-reproduced piece of erotica, *Venus, Cupid and the Organist*, a painting originally owned by a bishop.

Flemish and German painting (ground floor)

The biggest name in the Flemish collections is **Hieronymus Bosch** (1450–1516), known in Spain as El Bosco. The Prado has several of his greatest triptychs: the early-

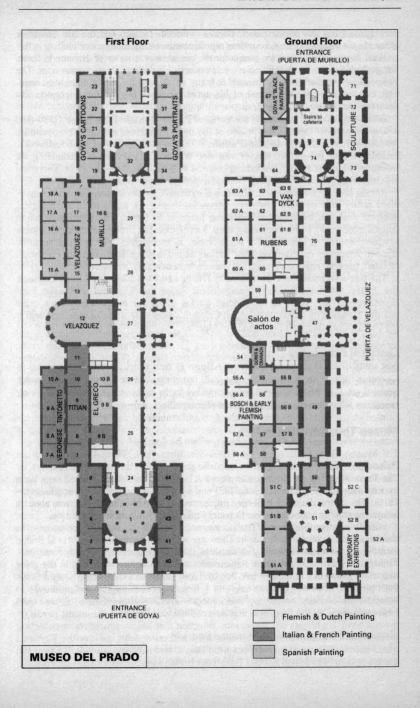

First Floor

GOYA'S CARTOONS

23 39 38
22 37 GOYA'S PORTRAITS
21 36
20 35
19 34
32

18 A 18
17 A 17 VELAZQUEZ
16 A 16
15 A 15
13
12 VELAZQUEZ
11
10 A 10 10 B
9 A 9 TITIAN
8 A 8
7 A 7
VERONESE TINTORETTO

16 B MURILLO
29
28
27
26
EL GRECO
9 B
25
8 B
7 B

6 44
5 43
4 1 42
3 41
2 40
24

ENTRANCE
(PUERTA DE GOYA)

Ground Floor
ENTRANCE
(PUERTA DE MURILLO)

67 GOYA'S BLACK PAINTINGS
66
65
64
Stairs to cafeteria
71 SCULPTURE
72
74
73

63 A 63 63 B VAN DYCK
62 A 62 62 B
61 A 61 61 B RUBENS
60 A 60
75

59
Salón de actos
47
54 DÜRER & CRANACH
55 A 55 55 B
56 A 56
BOSCH & EARLY FLEMISH PAINTING
57 A 57 57 B
58 A 58
56 B
49
PUERTA DE VELAZQUEZ

50
51 C 52 C
51 B 51 52 B
52 A
51 A
TEMPORARY EXHIBITIONS

Flemish & Dutch Painting

Italian & French Painting

Spanish Painting

MUSEO DEL PRADO

period *Hay Wain*, the middle-period *Garden of Earthly Delights* and the late *Adoration of the Magi* – all familiar from countless reproductions but infinitely more chilling in the original. Bosch's hallucinatory genius for the macabre is at its most extreme in these but reflected here in many more of his works, including three versions of *The Temptations of Saint Anthony* (though only the smallest of these is definitely an original). Don't miss, either, the amazing table-top of *The Seven Deadly Sins*, displayed without a label in the centre of the room.

Bosch's visions find an echo in the works of **Pieter Breughel the Elder** (1520–69), whose Triumph of Death must be one of the most frightening canvases ever painted. Another elusive painter, **Joachim Patinir**, is represented by four of his finest works. From an earlier generation, **Rogier van der Weyden's** *Deposition* is outstanding; its monumental forms make a fascinating contrast with his miniature-like *Pietà*. There are also important works by Memling, Bouts, Gerard David and Massys.

Among later Flemish painters, **Rubens** is extensively represented, though he supervised rather than executed the most interesting works – a series of 18 mythological subjects designed for Felipe IV's hunting lodge in El Pardo. There are, too, a fine collection of works by his contemporaries, Van Dycks, Jan Bruegel and David Teniers – whose scenes of lowlife get a whole room to themselves. For political reasons, Spanish monarchs collected very few works painted in seventeenth-century Protestant Holland; the only important exception is an early Rembrandt, *Artemesia*.

The **German rooms** are dominated by **Dürer (1471–1528)** and **Lucas Cranach the Elder** (1472–1553). Durer's magnificent *Adam* and *Eve* was only saved from destruction at the hands of the prudish Carlos III by the intervention of his court painter, Mengs. The most interesting of Cranach's works are a pair of paintings depicting Carlos V hunting with Ferdinand I of Austria.

Casón del Beun Retiro

Just south of the Prado is the **Casón del Buen Retiro**, which used to house Picasso's *Guernica* (now in the Reina Sofía – see p.76) but is now devoted to nineteenth-century Spanish art. It is included in the entrance ticket to the main museum but, considering the riches which have gone before, is not of compelling interest.

Museo Thyssen-Bornemisza

The **Museo Thyssen-Bornemisza** (Tues–Sun 10am–7pm; 600ptas) occupies the old Palacio de Villahermosa, diagonally opposite the Prado, at the end of the Carrera de San Jerónimo. This prestigious site played a large part in Spain's acquisition – for a knock-down $350m (£230m) in June 1993 – of what many argue was the world's greatest private art trove after that of the British royals: 700-odd paintings accumulated by father-and-son ⌐erman-Hungarian industrial magnates. Another trumpcard was Baron Thyssen's current (5th) wife, "Tita" Cervera, a former Miss Spain, once married to Tarzan actor Lex Barker, who steered the works to Spain against the efforts of Prince Charles, the Swiss and German governments, the Getty foundation, and other suitors.

Tita's portrait – a kitsch (and dangerously anorexic) stunner – hangs in the great hall of the museum, alongside her husband and King Juan Carlos and Queen Sofía. Pass beyond, however, and you are into seriously premier league art: **medieval to seventeenth-century** on the top floor, **rococo and neoclassicism to fauves and expressionists** on the first floor, and **surrealists, pop art and the avant garde** on ground level. Highlights are legion in a collection that has an almost stamp-collecting mentality in its examples of every major artist and movement, but how the Thyssens got hold of classic works by everyone from Duccio and Holbein, through El Greco and Caravaggio, to Schiele and Rothko, takes your breath away.

The museum

The **museum**, which has had no expense spared on its design, with stucco walls (Tita wanted pink) and marble floors, has a handy **bar and cafeteria** in the basement and allows re-entry, so long as you get your hand stamped at the exit desk. There is also a **shop**, where you can buy the first instalments of the 15-volume catalogue of the Baron's collection. Around half of the collection is now on show here, or at the Monastir de Pedralbes in Barcelona, which houses around 80 works of Sacred Art (see p.550).

EUROPEAN OLD MASTERS: THE SECOND FLOOR

Take a lift to the second floor and you will find yourself at the chronological beginning of the museum's collections: European painting (and some sculpture) from the fourteenth to eighteenth centuries. The core of these collections was accumulated in the 1920s and 1930s by the present baron's father, Heinrich, who was a friend of the art critics Bernard Berenson and Max Friedländer.

He was clearly well advised. The early paintings include incredibly good (and rare) devotional panels by the Sienese painter **Duccio di Buoninsegna**, and the Flemish artists, **Jan van Eyck** and **Rogier van der Weyden**. You then move into a fabulous array of Renaissance portraits, which include three of the very greatest of the period: **Ghirlandaio**'s *Portrait of Giovanna Tornabuoni*, Hans Holbein's *Portrait of Henry VIII* (the only one of many variants in existence which is definitely genuine), **Raphael**'s *Portrait of a Young Man*. A *Spanish Infanta* by **Juan de Flandes** may represent the first of Henry VIII's wives, Catherine of Aragón, while the *Young Knight* by **Carpaccio** is one of the earliest known full-length portraits. Beyond these is a collection of **Dürers** and **Cranachs** to rival that in the Prado, and as you progress through this extraordinary panoply, display cases along the corridor contain scarcely less spectacular works of sculpture, ceramics and gold- and silverwork.

Next in line are **Titian** and **Tintoretto**, and a couple of paintings by **El Greco**, one early, one late, which make an interesting comparison with each other and with those in the Prado. **Caravaggio**'s monumental *St Catherine of Alexandria* is the centrepiece of an important display of works by followers of this innovator of chiaroscuro. And finally, as you reach the eighteenth century, there is a room of flawless **Canaletto** views of Venice.

AMERICANS, IMPRESSIONISTS AND EXPRESSIONISTS: THE FIRST FLOOR

The present baron, Heine Thyssen, began collecting, according to his own account, to fill the gaps in his late father's collection, after it was split among his siblings. He too started with old masters – his father thought nineteenth and twentieth-century art was worthless – but in the 1960s started on German expressionists, closely followed by Cubists, Futurists, Vorticists and De Stijl, and also American art of the nineteenth century. The first floor, then, is largely down to him.

After a comprehensive round of seventeenth–century Dutch painting of various genres, rococo and neoclassicism, you reach the **American painting** in rooms 29 and 30. The collection, one of the best outside the US, concentrates on landscapes and includes James Goodwyn Clonney's wonderful *Fishing Party on Long Island Sound*, and works by James Whistler, Winslow Homer and John Singer Sargent. It is followed by a group of European **Romantics and Realists**, including Constable's *The Lock* – the only English painting in the museum, bought not so long ago for £10.8m ($14m).

Impressionism and **post-Impressionism** is another strong point of the collection, especially in the choice of paintings by Vincent van Gogh, which include one of his last and most gorgeous works, *Les Vessenots*. **Expressionist** representatives, meanwhile, include an unusually pastoral Edvard Munch, *Evening*, Egon Schiele's Mondrian-like *Houses on the River*, and some stunning work by Ernst Ludwig Kirchner, Wassily Kandinsky and Max Beckmann.

AVANT GARDES: THE GROUND FLOOR

Works on the ground floor run from the beginning of the twentieth century through to around 1970. The good baron doesn't, apparently, like contemporary art: "If they can throw colours, I can be free to duck", he explained, following the gallery's opening.

The most interesting work in his "experimental avant garde" sections is from the **Cubists**. There is an inspired, side-by-side hanging of parallel studies by Picasso (Man with a Clarinet), Braque and Mondrian. **Later choices** – a scattering of Joan Miró, Jackson Pollock, Magritte and Dalí, Rauschenberg and Liechtenstein, do less justice to their artists and movements, though there is a great work by Edward Hopper, and a fascinating **Lucien Freud** *Portrait of Baron Thyssen*, posed in front of the Watteau Pierrot hanging upstairs.

Centro de Arte Reina Sofía

It is fortunate that the **Centro de Arte Reina Sofía** (Mon & Wed–Sat 10am–9pm, Sun 10am–2.30pm, closed Tues; 400ptas), facing Atocha station at the end of Paseo del Prado, keeps different opening hours and days to its neighbours. For this leading exhibition space and permanent gallery of modern Spanish art – its centrepiece is Picasso's greatest picture, *Guernica* – is another essential stop on the Madrid art circuit, and one that really mustn't be seen after a Prado–Thyssen overdose.

The museum, a vast former hospital, is a kind of Madrid response to the Pompidou centre in Paris. Transparent lifts shuttle visitors up the outside of the building, whose levels feature a cinema, excellent art book and design shops, a print, music and photographic library, restaurant, bar and café, as well as the exhibition halls (top floor) and the collection of twentieth century art (second floor).

The Permanent Collection

It is for **Picasso's Guernica** that most visitors come to the Reina Sofía, and rightly so. Superbly displayed, this icon of twentieth century Spanish art and politics carries a shock that defies all familiarity. Picasso painted it in response to the bombing of the Basque town of Guernica, by the German Luftwaffe, acting in concert with Franco, in the Spanish Civil War. In the preliminary studies, displayed around the room, you can see how he developed its symbols – the dying horse, the woman mourning her dead, the bull, the sun, the flower, the light bulb – and then return to the painting to marvel at how it all is made to work.

The work was first exhibited in Paris in 1937, as a part of a Spanish Republican Pavilion in the Expo there, and was then loaned to the Museum of Modern Art in New York, until, as Picasso put it, Spain had rid itself of fascist rule. The artist never lived to see that time but in 1981, following the restoration of democracy, the painting was. amid much controversy, moved to Madrid to hang (as Picasso had stipulated) in the Prado. Its recent transfer to the Reina Sofía, in 1992, again prompted much soul-searching and protest, though for anyone who saw it in the old prado annexe, it looks truely liberated in its present setting.

Guernica hangs in Room 7, midway around the permanent collection, although Picasso himself is actually a starting point: symbolically, no painter represented here was born before Picasso (in 1881). It is preceded by strong sections on **Cubism** and the **Paris School**, in the first of which Picasso is again well represented, alongside an intriguing straight Cubist work by Salvador Dalí. There are good collections of other Avant garde Spaniards of the 1920s and 30s, too, including Juan Gris.

In the post-*Guernica* halls, **Dalí**'s more familiar surrealism seems trite and **Miró** less engaging than usual. However, the museum is still in a formative state, and may yet respond to critics who have pointed out the absence of the Spanish realists like Antonio López – the recent subject of a hugely popular retropsective in the temporary gallery.

There are, already, interesting works by **Tapiès** and **Chillida**, and the final rooms are stimulating: entitled **"Proposals"**, they comprise an evolving display of contemporary art, both Spanish and foreign.

Parque del Retiro and around

When you get tired of sightseeing, Madrid's many parks provide a great place to escape for a few hours. The most central and most popular of them is **El Retiro**, a delightful mix of formal gardens and wider open spaces. Around it, in addition to the Prado, Thyssen and Reina Sofia galleries, are a number of the city's **smaller museums**, plus a startlingly peaceful **Jardines Botánicos**.

Parque del Retiro

Originally the grounds of a royal retreat (*retiro*), the **Parque del Retiro** has been public property for more than a hundred years; the palace itself burned down in the eighteenth century. In its 330 acres you can jog (there is a council-sponsored track), row in the lake of **El Estanque** (you can rent boats by the Monumento a Alfonso XII), picnic (though not on the grass), have your fortune told, and – above all – promenade. The busiest day is Sunday, when half of Madrid, spouses, in-laws and kids turn out for the *paseo*. Dressed for show, the families stroll around among the various activities, nodding at neighbours and building up an appetite for a long Sunday lunch.

Strolling aside, there's almost always something going on in the park, including a good programme of **concerts** and **ferias** organized by the city council. Concerts tend to be held in the Jardines de Cecilio Rodríguez, in the southeast of the park. The most popular of the fairs is the *Feria del Libro* (Book Fair), held in early June, when every publisher and half the country's bookshops set up stalls and offer a 25 percent discount on their wares. In the summer months free **films** are shown in the evenings in the area known as La Chopera, in the southwest corner of the park, while on Saturdays and Sundays there are **puppet shows** by the Puerta de Alcalá entrance (1pm, 7pm & 8pm). On Sundays, you can often watch groups of Catalans performing their counting-dance, the **Sardana**.

Travelling art exhibitions are frequently housed in the beautiful **Palacio de Velázquez** (no relation to Diego) and the nearby **Palacio de Cristal** and **Casa de Vacas** (normal hours for these are Tues–Sat 10am–2pm and 5–7pm, Sun 10am–2pm). Look out, too, for **El Angel Caido** (Fallen Angel), the world's only public statue to Lucifer, in the south of the park. A number of **stalls and cafés** along the Salón del Estanque sell drinks, *bocadillos* and *pipas* (sunflower seeds), and there are *terrazas*, too, for *horchata* and *granizados*. The park has a very safe reputation, at least by day. In the late evening – in summer, the park stays open all night (access is through the c/ Alfonso XII entrance) – it's best not to wander alone. Note also that the area east of La Chopera is known as a cruising ground for gay prostitutes.

Puerta de Alcalá to San Jerónimo: some minor museums

Leaving the park at the northwest corner takes you to the Plaza de la Independencia, in the centre of which is one of the two remaining gates from the old city walls. Built in the late eighteenth century, the **Puerta de Alcalá** was the biggest in Europe at that time and, like the bear and bush, has become one of the city's monumental emblems.

South from here, you pass the **Museo de Artes Decorativas** (M° Banco de España/Retiro; Tues–Fri 9.30am–3pm, Sat & Sun 10am–2pm; 200ptas), which has its entrance on c/Montalbán. The furniture and decorations here are not very thrilling but there are some superb azulejos and other decorative ceramics.

A couple of blocks west, in a corner of the Naval Ministry, at c/Montalbán 2, is a **Museo Naval** (Tues–Sun 10.30am–1.30pm; free), strong, as you might expect, on

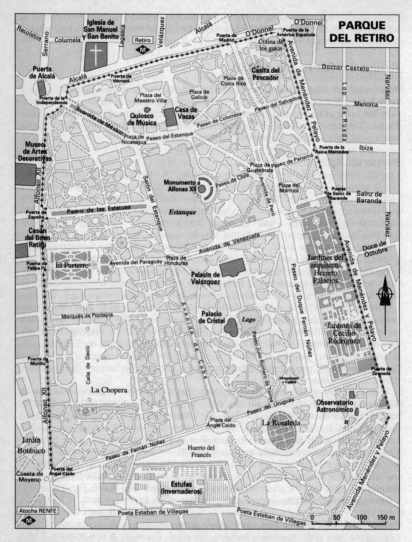

PARQUE DEL RETIRO

models, charts and navigational aids from or relating to the Spanish voyages of discovery. The army has its museum, the **Museo del Ejército**, just to the south of here at c/ Méndez Núñez 1 (Tues–Sun 10am–2pm; 100ptas). It is a traditional display, packed with arms and armour (including a sword of El Cid and *conquistador* breastplates), and models and memorabilia of various battles, from earliest times to the Civil War – in which Franco, here, remains the good guy.

South again, past the Prado's Casón del Buen Retiro annexe (part of the original Retiro palace), is **San Jerónimo el Real**, Madrid's society church, where in 1975 Juan Carlos (like his predecessors) was crowned. Opposite is the **Real Academia**

Española de la Lengua (Royal Language Academy), whose job is to make sure that the Spanish language is not corrupted by foreign or otherwise unsuitable words; the results are entrusted to their official dictionary – a work that bears virtually no relation to the Spanish you'll hear spoken on the streets.

The Botanical Gardens and Atocha

Immediately south of the Prado are the delightful, shaded **Jardines Botanicos** (daily 10am–8pm; 100ptas). Opened in 1781 by Carlos III (known as *El Alcalde* – "the mayor" – for his urban improvement programmes), they once contained over 30,000 plants. The numbers are down these days, though they were well renovated in the 1980s, after years of neglect, and the worldwide collection of flora is fascinating for any amateur botanist. Under an edict issued when the gardens were opened, *Madrileños* are still theoretically entitled to help themselves to cuttings of any plant or medicinal herb.

On the other side of the botanical gardens is the sloping **Cuesta de Moyano**, lined with bookstalls. You can buy anything here, new or old, from secondhand copies of Captain Marvel to Cervantes or Jackie Collins. There's always something of interest, often quite a selection of dog-eared paperbacks in English, and usually one or two surprises. You'd be lucky to find anything valuable, but prices are low and it's a pleasant stroll. Though at its busiest on Sundays, some of the stalls are open every day.

Across the way – and worth a look even if you're not travelling out of Madrid – is the **Estación de Atocha**. It is actually two stations, old and new: the former, a glorious 1880s glasshouse, recently revamped as a kind of tropical garden. It is a wonderful sight from the walkways above, and train buffs will want to take a look at the high-speed AVE trains (Sevilla in two and a half hours) on the stations beyond.

Lastly in this area, the **Real Fábrica de Tapices** at c/Fuenterrabia 2 (Mº Menéndez Pelayo; Mon–Fri 9.30am–12.30pm; closed Aug) still turns out handmade tapestries, many of them based on the Goya cartoons in the Prado. They are fabulously expensive but there's no charge for a tour of the manufacturing process.

The Gran Vía, Chueca and Malasaña

The **Gran Vía**, Madrid's great thoroughfare, runs from Plaza de Cibeles to Plaza de España, effectively dividing the old city to the south from the newer parts northwards. Permanently jammed with traffic and crowded with shoppers and sightseers, it's the commercial heart of the city, and – if you spare the time to look up – quite a monument in its own right, with its turn of the century palace-like banks and offices, and the huge hand-painted posters of the cinemas. Look out, too, for the Moorish-style **Telefónica** building, which was the chief observation post for the Republican artillery during the Civil War, when the Nationalist front line stretched across the Casa de Campo. And don't miss a cocktail at the art deco **Museo Chicote** at Gran Vía 12.

North of the Telefónica, c/de Fuencarral heads north to the Glorieta de Bilbao. To either side of this street are two of Madrid's most characterful *barrios*: **Chueca**, to the east, and **Malasaña**, to the west. Their chief appeal lies in an amazing concentration of bars, restaurants and, especially, nightlife. However, there are a few reasons – bars included – to look around here by day.

Chueca

Plaza de Chueca (Mº Chueca) teeters on the verge of infamy, due to its popularity with drug dealers and prostitutes. But if this sounds like a place to avoid at all costs, then you're not in key with Madrid: it is one of those squares that has its addicts but also a strong neighbourhood feel, with kids and grannies giving a semblance of innocence by day. It is also fronted by one of the best old-style *vermut* bars in the city, *Bodega Ángel Sierra*, on c/Gravina at the northwest corner.

From Plaza de Chueca **east to Paseo Recoletos** (the beginning of the long Paseo de la Castellana) are some of the city's most enticing streets. Offbeat restaurants, small private art galleries, and odd corner shops are to be found here in abundance and the **c/Almirante** has some of the city's most fashionable clothes shops too. On the parallel c/de Prim, **ONCE**, the national association for the blind, has its headquarters. *ONCE* is financed by a lottery, for which the blind are employed as ticket-sellers, and many come here to collect their allocation of tickets. The lottery has become such a major money-spinner that the organisation is now one of the wealthiest businesses in Spain; oddly, perhaps, it is the sponsor of one of the world's top cycling teams.

To the south, the Ministry of Culture fronts the **Plaza del Rey**, which is also worth a look for the other odd buildings surrounding it, especially the **Casa de las Siete Chimenas** (House of seven chimneys), which is supposedly haunted by a mistress of Felipe II who disappeared in mysterious circumstances.

To the north, on the edge of the Santa Barbara *barrio*, is the **Sociedad de Autores** (Society of Authors), housed in the only significant *modernista* building in Madrid, designed by José Grasés Riera, part of the Gaudí school. Nearby, the **Museo Romántico**, at c/San Mateo 13, (Mº Tribunal; Tues–Sat 9am–3pm, Sun 10am–2pm; 200ptas), has its admirers, for its late Romantic era furnishings, though casual visitors are unlikely to be impressed. The **Museo Municipal** at c/Fuencarral 78 (Mº Tribunal; Tues–Fri 9am–8pm, Sat & Sun 10am–2pm; 200ptas) is more interesting for its models and maps of old Madrid, showing the incredible expansion of the city in this century. The building itself has a superb Churrigueresque facade.

Malasaña

The heart, in all senses, of **Malasaña** is the **Plaza Dos de Mayo**, named after the insurrection against Napoleonic forces on May 2, 1808; the rebellion and its aftermath are depicted in a series of Goyas at the Prado. The surrounding district bears the name of one of the martyrs of the uprising, fifteen-year-old Manuela Malasaña, who is also commemorated in a street (as are several other heroes of the time). On the night of May 1 all of Madrid shuts down to honour its heroes, and the plaza is the scene of festivities lasting well into the night.

More recently, the quarter was the focus of the *Movida Madrileña*, the "happening scene" of the late 1970s and early 1980s. As the country relaxed after the death of Franco and the city developed into a thoroughly modern capital under the leadership of the late lamented mayor, Tierno Galván, Malasaña became the mecca of the young. Bars appeared behind every doorway, drugs were sold openly in the streets, and there was an extraordinary atmosphere of new-found freedom. Times have changed – and *chocolate* (dope) sellers are less tolerated by residents and police alike – but the *barrio* retains a somewhat alternative feel, with its bar custom spilling onto the streets, and an ever-lively scene in the Plaza Dos de Mayor *terrazas*.

There are no regular sights in this quarter but the streets have an interest of their own, some fine traditional bars – *Casa Camacho* at c/San Andrés 2 is another great place for *vermut*, and there are some wonderful old shop signs and architectural details. The best of all is the **old pharmacy** on the corner of c/San Andres and c/San Vicente Ferrer, with its irresisitible 1920s azulejo scenes depicting cures for diarrhoea, headaches and suchlike.

Plaza de España, Parque del Oeste and Casa de Campo

The **Plaza de España** (Mº Plaza de España), at the west end of Gran Vía, was home, until the recent flurry of corporate building in the north of Madrid, to the city's two tallest buildings – the **Torre de Madrid**, which houses the main tourist office and has a top storey bar, and **Edificio de España**. These rather stylish 1950s buildings look over an elaborate monument to Cervantes in the middle of the square, which in turn overlooks the bewildered bronze figures of Don Quixote and Sancho Panza.

The plaza itself is a rather seedy place, and something of a junky hangout. However, to its north, **c/Martín de los Héros** is a lively place, day and night, with three of the city's best cinemas, and behind them is the **Centro Princesa**, with shops, clubs, bars and a twenty-four hour branch of the ubiquitous *VIPS* – just the place to have your film developed at 4am, or a bite to eat before heading onto a small hours club.

A block to the west is the **Museo Cerralbo**, c/Ventura Rodríguez 17 (Mº Ventura Rodríguez; Tues–Sun 10am–2pm; closed Aug; 200ptas), an elegant mansion, endowed with its collections by the Marqués de Cerralbo. The rooms, stuffed with paintings, furniture, armour and artefacts, provide insights into the lifestyle of the nineteenth-century aristocracy, though there is little of individual note.

Parque del Oeste – and Goya's Ermita frescoes

The **Parque del Oeste** stretches northwest from the Plaza de España, following the railway tracks of the Estación del Norte up to the suburbs of Moncloa and Ciudad Universitaria. On its south side, ten minutes' walk from the square, is the **Templo de Debod**, a fourth-century BC Egyptian temple given to Spain in recognition of the work done by Spanish engineers on the Aswan High Dam (which inundated its original site). Reconstructed here stone by stone, it seems comically incongruous but provides a good concert venue nonetheless. In summer, there are numerous *terrazas* in the park, while, year-round, a **teleférico** (mornings: daily 11.30am–2.30pm; afternoons: Mon–Thur 4.30–9.30pm, Fri & Sat 4.30pm–1.30am, Sun 3.30–10pm; 425ptas return) shuttles its passengers high over the river to the middle of the Casa de Campo (see below). It was built to rival Barcelona's *teleférico* but doesn't quite have the topography to match.

Rail lines to Galicia and other parts of the north terminate at the **Estación del Norte**, a quietly spectacular construction of white enamel, steel and glass which enjoyed a starring role in Warren Beatty's film *Reds*. About 300m from the station along the Paseo de la Florida – or a shorter walk from the Estación Teleférico – is the *Casa Mingo* restaurant (see "Restaurants"), an institution for chicken and cider take-outs for the Casa de Campo, and, almost alongside it, the **Ermita de San Antonio de la Florida** (Mº Norte; often closed for restoration work but nominally open Mon, Tues, Thurs–Sat 11am–1pm & 3–7pm, Sun 11am–1pm).

This little church on a Greek cross plan was built by an Italian, Felipe Fontana, between 1792 and 1798, and decorated by **Goya**, whose frescoes are the main reason to visit. In the dome is a depiction of a miracle performed by Saint Anthony of Padua. Around it (in a reversal of convention), heavenly bodies of angels and cherubs hold back curtains to reveal the main scene: the saint resurrecting a dead man to give evidence in favour of a prisoner falsely accused of murder (the saint's father). Beyond this central group, Goya created a gallery of highly realist characters – their models were court and society figures – while for a lesser fresco of the angels adoring the Trinity in the apse, he took prostitutes as his models. The *ermita* also houses the artist's mausoleum.

Casa de Campo

If you want to jog, play tennis, swim, picnic, go to the fairground, or see pandas, then the **Casa de Campo** is the place to head. This enormous (4300-acre) expanse of heath and scrub is in parts surprisingly wild for a place so easily accessible from the city; other sections have been tamed for more conventional pastimes. Far larger and more natural than the city parks, the Casa de Campo can be reached by Metro (Mº Batán or Mº El Lago), various buses, or the aforementioned cable car. The walk from the Estación del Norte station via the Puente del Rey isn't too strenuous either.

Throughout the park there are picnic tables and café/bars; a **jogging track** with exercise posts; a municipal, open-air **swimming pool** (summer only; 8am–8pm;

300ptas – close to Mº El Lago); tennis courts; and rowing boats to hire on the **lake** (again near Mº Lago). In summer, **concerts** are held at the lakeside *Rockodromo*.

Sightseeing attractions include a **Zoo** (10am–8pm daily), which is perenially popular and pretty good, and, adjoining it, a large if not tremendously inspired amusement park, the **Parque de Atracciones**. Both are easiest reached by bus (#33 from Plaza de Oriente), which will take you right to the gates; the Batán metro station is a fifteen-minute walk through scrubland.

Salamanca and the Paseo de la Castellana

Salamanca, the area north of the Parque del Retiro, is a smart address for apartments and, even more so, for shops. The *barrio* is the haunt of *pijos* – universally-denigrated rich kids, from families who made it good under Franco – and the grid of streets between c/Goya and c/José Ortega y Gassett contain most of the city's designer emporiums. The buildings are largely modern and undistinguished, though there are a scattering of musuems and galleries that might tempt you up here, in particular the **Lazaro Galdiano**, the pick of Madrid's smaller museums.

Taking the area from south to north, the first point of interest is **Plaza de Colón** (Mº Colón), endowed at street level with a statue of Columbus (Cristóbal Colón) and some huge stone blocks arranged as a megalithic monument to the discovery of the Americas. Below it is the 1970s **Centro Cultural Villa de Madrid**, which is still a good place for film and theatre and occasional exhibitions. Across the square, if your taste runs to tableaux of matadors being gored, or vain attempts to recognise Juan Carlos, there is diversion at the **Museo de Cera** (daily 10.30am– 1.30pm & 4–8.30pm), a pretty lamentable wax museum.

Off the square, too, with its entrance at c/Serrano 13, is the **Museo Arqueológico Nacional** (Mº Serrano; Tues–Sat 9.30am–8.30pm, Sun 9.30am–2.30pm; 200ptas). As the national collection, this has some impressive pieces, among them the celebrated Celto-Iberian busts known as *La Dama de Elche* and *La Dama de Baza*, and a wonderfully rich hoard of Visigothic treasures found at Toledo. The exhibition, however, is very old fashioned and rooms are often closed for somnolent rearrangement. In the gardens, downstairs to the left of the main entrance, is a reconstruction of the Altamira Caves, with their prehistoric wall paintings.

The **Museo Lázaro Galdiano** (Mº Rubén Dario; Tues–Sun 10am–2pm; closed Aug), is some way north at c/Serrano 122. This former private collection was given to the state by José Galdiano in 1948 and spreads over the four floors of his former home. It is a vast jumble of artwork, with some very dodgy attributions, but includes some really exquisite and valuable pieces. Among painters represented are Bosch (two works: one, *Saint John the Evangelist on Patmos*, is important, the other may not be genuine), Gerard David, Dürer (perhaps) and Rembrandt, as well as a host of Spanish artists, including Berruguete, Murillo, Zurbarán and Velázquez. El Greco – whose *Adoration of the Magi* was painted long before he arrived in Spain – and Goya are also particularly well represented. *The Saviour*, hidden away in a room of Renaissance sculpture on the ground floor, is a beautiful little picture which the museum claims as a Leonardo da Vinci, though, sadly, no one else seems to agree. Other exhibits include a collection of clocks and watches, many of them once owned by Carlos V.

Not far to the west of here, across the Paseo de la Castellana, is another enjoyable gallery, the **Museo Sorolla**, c/General Martínez Campos 37 (Mº Rubén Dario; Tues–Sun 10am–2.30pm; closed Aug). It is a large collection of work by the painter Joaquín Sorolla (1863–1923), displayed in his old home and studio. The best works are striking, impressionistic plays on light and texture, others just obsessively preoccupied with beaches, naked bodies, and their reflections and refractions in the water.

Further north along Castellana, you reach the **Zona Azca**, Madrid's newest business quarter, with its tallest skyscraper – the 43-storey Torre Picasso (1989) – and corporate headquarters. Just beyond it, and easily the most famous sight up here, is the **Santiago Bernabeu** football stadium, home of Real Madrid and the Spanish national side.

El Pardo

Franco had his principal residence at **EL PARDO**, a former royal hunting ground, 9km northwest of central Madrid. A garrison still remains at the town – where most of the Generalísimo's staff were based – but the stigma has lessened over the years, and this is now a popular excursion for *Madrileños*, who come here for long lunches in the *terraza* restaurants, or to play tennis or swim at one of the nearby sports centres.

The tourist focus is the **Palacio del Pardo** (guided tours Mon–Sat 10am–12.15pm & 3–5.30pm, Sun 10am–1pm; closed Tues), rebuilt by the Bourbons on the site of a hunting lodge of Carlos V. The interior is pleasant enough, with its chapel and theatre, a portrait of Isabella la Católica by her court painter Juan de Flandes, and an excellent collection of tapestries, many after the Goya cartoons at the Prado. Guides detail the uses Franco made of them, though passing over some of his stranger habits. He kept by his bed, for instance, the hand of Saint Teresa of Ávila. Tickets to the palace are valid also for the **Casita del Príncipe**, though this cannot be entered from the gardens and you must return to the main road. Like the *casitas* (pavilions) at El Escorial, this was built by Juan de Villanueva, and is highly ornate.

You can reach El Pardo by local **bus** (every 10mins during the day, from c/Hilarión Escalava; Mº Moncloa), or by any city **taxi**.

Restaurants and tapas bars

The sections below review Madrid's best places for **eating and drinking**, essentially in conjunction with each other. They don't include out-and-out bars, where *Madrileños* go later in the evening to drink, dance, listen to music, and, of course, to be seen; those follow in the next section, on nightlife.

Entries here include *bares*, *cafés*, *cervecerías* (beerhalls), *marisquerías* (seafood bars) and *restaurantes* but have been divided simply between **"tapas bars"** and **"restaurants"**, depending on whether they concentrate more on sit-down meals or bar food. Sometimes this division is arbitrary, as many places have a bar area, where you can get *tapas*, together with a more formal *comedor* (canteen) or *restaurante* out the back or upstairs. At almost any of our recommendations you could happily eat your fill – money permitting – though at bars *Madrileños* usually eat just a *tapa* or share a *ración* of the house speciality, then move on to repeat the procedure down the road.

Hours

The hours for having **cañas y copas**, drinks and *tapas* are from around noon to 2pm and 7pm to 10pm, though most bars will do you a snack at most hours of the day, and they generally stay open till midnight or beyond. Summer hours are generally later than winter, and Sundays are early to bed.

Restaurant meals (*comidas*) are taken very late: few *Madrileños* will start lunch before 2pm or dinner much before 10pm, and if you turn up much earlier you may find yourself alone, or the restaurant (in the evening) not yet open. On the other hand, most people do arrive for dinner by 10.30pm and you may not be admitted much later; Madrid being Madrid, though, there are quite a number of late-night options and the listings magazines all have sections for restaurants open past midnight (*despues medianoche/de madrugada*). Many restaurants close on Sundays and/or Mondays.

Cuisines

Madrid's restaurants and bars offer every regional style of **Spanish cooking**: Castilian for roasts (*horno de asar* is a woodburning oven) and stews (such as the meat and chickpea *cocido*), Gallego for seafood, Andaluz for fried fish, Levantine (Valencia/Alicante) for *paella* and other rice (*arroz*) based dishes, Asturian for winter stews like *fabada*, Basque for the ultimate gastronomy (and correspondingly high prices).

Over the last few years, dozens of **foreign cuisines** have appeared. There are some good Peruvian, Argentinian and Italian places and a scattering of enjoyable Indonesian and Japanese restaurants. With a few honourable exceptions, though, Indian and Chinese restaurants are dire, as too, alas, are most of the Mexican and Brazilian ones.

Sol, Plaza Mayor and Opera

The central area is the most varied in Madrid in terms of price and choice of food. Indeed there can be few places in the world which rival the streets around Puerta del Sol for sheer number of places to eat and drink. Around the smarter **Opera** district, you need to be more selective, while on **Plaza Mayor** itself, stick to drinks.

TAPAS BARS

Ángel Suárez, c/Vergara – just south of the Teatro Real (Mº Opera). Old-fashioned *taberna* with reasonably priced *tapas*.

Las Bravas, c/Espoz y Mina 13 (Mº Sol). As the name suggests, *patatas bravas* (spicy potatoes) are the *tapa* to try at this bar, just south of Puerta del Sol; the *tortilla* is tasty, too. On the outside of the bar are novelty mirrors, a hangover from when this was a barbers and the subject of a story by Valle Inclan.

Casa del Abuelo, c/de la Victoria (Mº Sol). A tiny, highly atmospheric bar serving just their sweet rich red house wine and prawns cooked four ways (try them *al ajilo* – in garlic).

Casa del Labra, c/de Tetuan – opposite El Corte Ingles (Mº Sol). Order a drink at the bar and a *ración* of cod at the counter to the right of the door. (See also restaurants, below).

Casa Vasca, c/Victoria 2 (Mº Sol). Basque stuffed peppers and grilled sardines await.

La Gaditana, c/Cadiz 10 (Mº Sol). A sign outside claims this is the world's largest bar, as you "enter in Cadiz and leave in Barcelona": true enough, as it's at the corner of the two streets. Speciality is fried fish, Andaluz style.

Lhardy, Carrera de San Jerónimo 8 (open to 8pm; closed Sun & hols; Mº Sol). *Lhardy* is one of Madrid's most famous and expensive restaurants – a beautiful place but with greatly overpriced food. Downstairs, however, there's a wonderful bar, where you can snack on a fabulous array of canapes, *fino* and *consommé*, without breaking the bank.

Mejillonera El Pasaje, Pasaje Matheu (Mº Sol). Mussels (*mejillones*) served in every way conceivable at one of many bars on this pedestrian-only alleyway between c/Espoz y Mina and c/Victoria, south of Puerta del Sol.

La Menorquina, c/Mayor – on Puerta del Sol (Mº Sol). Good for breakfast or snacks – try one of their *napolitanas* (filled croissants).

Meson del Champiõnes and **Meson de la Tortilla**, c/Cuchilleros (Mº Sol). These are two of the oldest tavernas in Madrid, just down the steps at the southwest corner of Plaza Mayor. They specialize, as you'd imagine, in mushrooms and tortilla, respectively.

Museo del Jamón, Carrera de San Jerónimo 6 (Mº Sol). The largest branch of this Madrid chain, from whose ceilings are suspended hundreds of *jamónes* (hams). The best – and they are not cheap – are the *jabugos* from the Sierra Morena.

RESTAURANTS

El Abuelo, c/Nuñez de Arce 3 (Mº Sol). There's a *comedor* at the back of this spit-and-sawdust bar, where you can order a selection of delicious and inexpensive *raciones* and a jug of house wine. Inexpensive.

Arco Mayor, Plaza de la Provincia 3 – off the southeast corner of Plaza Mayor (☎364 01 49; open daily until 4am; Mº Sol). It's good to know that if you want a *paella* towards dawn, nobody here will turn a hair. Expensive.

El Botín, c/Cuchilleros 17 (☎266 42 17; Mº Tirso de Molina). This is one of the city's oldest restaurants, established in 1725, highly picturesque, and favoured by Hemingway. Inevitably, it's a tourist haunt but not such a bad one, with creditable if not tremendously inspired roasts – especially suckling pigs (*cochinillo*) and lamb (*lechal*). The *menú* is 3500ptas but you could eat for less. Moderate to expensive.

Café de Chinitas, c/Torija 7 (☎547 15 02; closed Sun; Mº Santo Domingo). An old established *tablao flamenco*, where you can eat well and listen to some authentic flamenco singers and guitarists. The sessions start at 9.30pm and run to 2.30am – sometimes later if things are swinging. Food is typically *Madrileña*. Moderate to expensive, depending on who's playing and whether there's an admission fee.

Casa Ciriaco, c/Mayor 84 (☎248 50 66; closed Thurs & Aug; Mº Opera). An attractive old-style *taberna*, long reputed for traditional Castilian dishes – trout, chicken and so on, served up in old-style portions. The *menú* is 1800ptas; main *carta* dishes a bit less. Moderate.

Casa Gallega, c/Bordadores 11 (☎541 90 55; Mº Opera/Sol). An airy and welcoming *marisquería* that has been importing seafood on overnight trains from Galicia since it opened in 1915. Costs vary greatly according to the rarity of the fish or shellfish that you order. Gallego staples like *pulpo* (octopus) and *pimientos de Padron* (tiny, randomly piquant peppers) are brilliantly done and inexpensive but the more exotic seasonal delights will raise a bill for two well into five figures. Expensive.

Casa del Labra, c/Tetuan 12 (☎531 00 81; closed Sun & hols; Mº Sol). A great, traditional place, where the Spanish socialist party was founded. The restaurant is through the bar on the right: an old panelled room, with classic *Madrileña* food. Moderate to expensive.

Prego, Costanilla de los Angeles (☎559 20 57; open daily; Mº Opera). One of Madrid's best Italian restaurants, and good for veggies, too, with its range of fresh pasta. Moderate.

Taberna del Alabardero, c/Felipe V 6 (☎547 25 77; open daily; Mº Opera). A fine *taberna* in one of the nicest streets in this area, just behind the Plaza de Oriente. The cooking is Basque and, considering this, prices are relatively low. Moderate.

Around Santa Ana and Huertas

You must spend at least an evening eating and drinking at the historic, tiled bars in this central area. Restaurants are good, too, and frequented as much by locals as tourists.

TAPAS BARS

Casa de las Gambas, c/Álvarez Gato – just north of Plaza de Santa Ana (Mº Sol). As you'd expect, the speciality is prawns (*gambas*), grilled with garlic.

Cerveceria Alemana, Plaza de Santa Ana (Mº Sol). Stylish old beerhouse frequented by Hemingway and, these days, seemingly every other American tourist. Order a *caña* and go easy on the *tapas*, as the bill can mount up fast.

Cerveceria Santa Ana, Plaza de Santa Ana (Mº Sol). This is cheaper than the *Alemana*, has tables outside, friendly service, and a good selection of *tapas*.

La Fidula, c/Huertas 57 (M° Antón Martín). A fine bar where you can sip *fino* to the accompaniment of classical tunes, performed from the tiny stage.

Los Gabrieles, c/Echegaray (M° Sol). This tiled bar is a Madrid monument and it's worth going earlier than is cool to appreciate the fabulous tableaux, created by sherry companies in the 1880s. Drinks are not too pricey, considering the venue; *tapas* don't go much beyond olives and crisps. Very crowded after 10pm, especially at weekends.

La Trucha, c/Manuel Fernández y González 3 (M° Antón Martín). If you're not going to end up at the restaurant here (see below), at least call in for a *tapa* at the bar. Smoked fish and *pimientos de Padron* are specialities. Usually very crowded.

La Venencia, c/Echegaray (M° Sol). For a real taste of old Madrid, this is a must: a long, narrow bar, serving just *fino* (dry sherry), cheese, and delicious cured tuna and pork. Decoration is unchanged for decades, with ancient barrels and posters.

Viva Madrid, c/Manuel Fernández y González 7 (M° Antón Martín). Another fabulous tiled bar – both outside and in – with wines and sherry, plus basic *tapas*. Open to 2.30am and always crowded.

RESTAURANTS

Casa Alberto, c/Huertas 18 (☎429 93 56; closed Mon; M° Antón Martín). Traditional *taberna* with a zinc bar and a small dining room at the back. Vast portions. Inexpensive.

Domine Cabra, c/Huertas 54 (☎429 43 65; closed Sun night; M° Antón Martín). An interesting mix of traditional and modern, with *Madrileña* standards given the *nueva cocina* treatment. Moderate.

Donzoko, c/Echegaray 3 (☎429 57 20; closed Sun; M° Sevilla). A very reasonable value Japanese restaurant with decent *sushi* and delicious *tempura*. Moderate.

La Trucha, c/Manuel Fernández y González 3 – off c/Echegaray (☎429 58 33; M° Antón Martín). This is a treat: call in to reserve a table while you have drinks at nearby *Los Gabrieles* and *La Venencia*, then fight your way through the bar to a half dozen tables at the back (or in the basement). Highlights include the *plato de verbena* (salmon and caviar canapes) and *fritura variada* (a huge platter of fried fish); decline the house wine and order a bottle instead. Moderate.

La Zamoranita, c/Santa María 15 – parallel to c/Huertas (M° Antón Martín). A good, basic *comedor* with simple home cooking. (Exceptionally) inexpensive.

Gran Vía and Plaza de España

On the **Gran Vía** burger bars fill most of the gaps between shops and cinemas. However, head a few blocks in and there's plenty on offer, including a good cluster of ethnic restaurants on c/San Bernardino (north of the Plaza de España). Nearby, on c/Princesa, there is also one of Madrid's very best restaurants, *Juan de Alzate*.

TAPAS BARS

Cervecería La Mina, c/Martín de los Heros 27 (M° Plaza de España). Pleasant bar with a range of *tapas* and *bocadillos*.

Stop Madrid, c/Hortaleza 11 (M° Gran Vía). An old-time spit-and-sawdust bar, revitalised, with Belgian beers as well as *vermut* on tap; *tapas* are largely *jamón* and *chorizo*.

RESTAURANTS

Adrish, c/San Bernardino 1 (☎559 58 14; closed Sun; M° Gran Vía). One of the city's better Indian restaurants, nicely decorated and with a vast selection of dishes. The cooking is mild, so if you like your curries hot, let the waiter know. Moderate.

Bali, c/San Bernardino 6 (☎541 91 22; closed Sun night & Mon; M° Gran Vía). Indonesian food; speciality is the all-encompassing *rijsttafel*. Moderate.

Hanil, c/San Bernardino 1 (☎559 58 14; closed Sun; M° Gran Vía). Korean cuisine: very light dishes, expertly prepared and presented. Smart and friendly. Moderate.

Jaun de Alzate, c/Princesa 18 (☎547 00 10; closed Sat lunch, Sun & Aug; M° Ventura Rodriguez). Celebrated and highly individual *nueva cocina* from a Basque chef, Iñaki Izaguirre. Sauces are refined, ingredients sublime and portions sensibly generous. If you want to try the range, there is a *menú gastronomico* at 5000ptas. Expensive.

MADRID'S VEGETARIAN RESTAURANTS

Madrid can be an intimidating city for veggies, given the mass of pigs, fish and seafood on display in bar and restaurant windows and counters. However, you can order vegetables separately at just about any restaurant in the city – Argentine steakhouses, perhaps, excepted – and there is good pizza and pasta to be had at a number of Italian places.

More crucially, the capital now has half a dozen decent and inexpensive **vegetarian restaurants**, scattered about the centre. These include:

Artemisa, c/Ventura de la Vega 4 (☎429 50 92; closed Sun night; Mº Sol). A popular place (you may have to wait for a table), best for its veggie pizzas and an imaginative range of salads. No smoking – even more of a novelty than veggie food in Madrid. Inexpensive.

Biotika, c/Amor de Diós 3 – just off c/ Huertas (☎429 07 80; closed Sun night; Mº Antón Martín). Stylish veggie cooking, based on tofu, rice and cereals. Inexpensive.

La Cosecha, c/Santa Barbara 11 (☎532 05 01; open daily; Mº Tribunal). Run by the chief of the Spanish Yoga Foundation, this is a bit of a centre for green/new age type activities. The food is tasty and wholesome, both at the modest set lunch

(1000ptas) and more elaborate dinners (1800ptas). Specials include a vegetarian *paella*. Inexpensive.

El Granero de Lavapiés, c/Argumosa 10 (open Mon–Fri 1–4pm only; Mº Lavapiés). Excellent macrobiotic and vegetarian fare in a very pleasant Latina street. Inexpensive.

La Granja, c/de Velarde (Mº Tribunal). A cosy, inexpensive café-restaurant that is again completely non-smoking. Meals work out around 1000ptas a head, and there's a cocktail night each Thursday. Inexpensive.

Vegetariano, c/Marqués de Santa Ana (☎532 09 27; closed Sun night & Mon; Mº Tribunal). Another place that's best for salads. Inexpensive.

Machupichu, c/de los Infantes 10 (☎521 80 81; closed Mon; Mº Gran Vía). A Peruvian–Salvadorian restaurant, with well-prepared spicy dishes (try the *cebiche*) and a *terraza* for eating outside in summer. Moderate.

Plata, c/Jardines 11 (closed Sun; Mº Gran Vía). One of the cheapest restaurants in the city, always packed out for lunch and dinner. Go for the *menú*, like almost everyone else, and don't let the surly service put you off. Inexpensive.

La Latina and Lavapiés: the Rastro area

South from Sol and Huertas are the quarters of **La Latina** and **Lavapiés** – where the Rastro takes place on a Sunday. The tiny streets here retain tall nineteenth–century (and older) houses, an appealing neighbourhood feel, and a great selection of bars and restaurants. There's a fair bit of nightlife action here, too, and *terrazas* in summer on the edge of the quarter in the Jardines las Vistillas (see box on p.91) and in the pretty Plaza de la Paja – just north of the church of San Andres.

TAPAS BARS

Almacen de Vinos, c/Calatrava 21 (Mº La Latina). A neighbourhood *tapas* bar in the best tradition. Well worth a call.

Barranco, San Isidro Labrador 14 (Mº La Latina). Come here for *gambas* after a trek around the Rastro. Very popular.

Los Caracoles, Plaza Cascorro 18 (Mº La Latina). Good for a range of *tapas* as well as its namesake *caracoles* (snails).

Cervecería el Doblete, Costanilla de San Andres 10 (Mº Latina). A trendy new bar, open late night, with nice canapés.

CAFÉ LIFE

Madrid has a number of cafés that are institutions. They serve food but are much more places to drink coffee, or have a *copa* or *caña*, read the papers, or meet up; the latter can sometimes be a semi-formal *tertulia* – a kind of discussion/drinking group, popular among Madrid intellectuals of the past and revived in the 1980s. Many cafés also have summer – or all-year – *terrazas* (outside terraces), though be aware that sitting outside puts up the prices. Good choices include:

Café Barbieri, Plaza Lavapiés (Mº Lavapiés). Well-known café with a vaguely intellectual reputation. It's a relaxed place with unobtrusive music, lots of wooden tables, old-style decor, newspapers to read, and a wide selection of coffees.

Café El Botánico, c/Espalter/Plaza Murillo (Mº Atocha). A quiet place to sit with a drink, opposite the south entrance of the Prado.

Café Central, Plaza del Angel 10 (Mº Sol). A jazz club by night but a regular café by day, again with newspapers supplied.

Círculo de Bellas Artes, c/de Alcalá 42 (Mº Banco de España). You pay 100ptas for day membership to the Círculo, which gives access to exhibitions, and to a most luxurious bar, where you can loll on sofas and have drinks at normal prices. Outside, covered by an awning, there is also a year-round *terraza*.

Café Comercial, Glorieta de Bilbao (Mº Bilbao). One of the city's most popular meeting points – a lovely traditional café, well poised for the Chueca/Santa Barbara area.

Café del Espejo, Paseo de Recoletos 31 (Mº Colón). Opened in 1978 but you wouldn't guess it – mirrors, gilt, and a wonderful glass pavilion.

Café Gijón, Paseo de Recoletos 21 (Mº Banco de España). A famous literary café – and a centre of the intellectual/arty *movida* in the 1980s – decked out in Cuban mahogany and mirrors. Has a summer *terraza*.

Café León, c/Alcalá near the Puerta de Alcalá (Mº Retiro). This is the pick of the bunch in the Recoletos/Retiro area – a great café, preserving much of its nine-teenth-century atmosphere of gossip and intrigue.

Cafe Manuela Malasaña, c/San Vicente Ferrer 29 (Mº Tribunal). Wonderful mirrors and fittings and a very civilized atmosphere, with *tertulias*, in different languages, most nights.

Café de Oriente, Plaza de Oriente (Mº Retiro). An elegant, traditional style café founded a decade or so ago by a priest, as part of a charity rehab programme. Has a popular *terraza*.

Taberna Antonio Sánchez, c/Meson de Paredes 13 (Mº Tirso de Molina). Stuffed bulls head – one of which killed Antonio Sanchéz, the son of the founder – and a wooden interior decorate this seventeenth–century bar. Lots of finos on offer, plus *jamón* and *queso tapas*.

RESTAURANTS

La Cacharrería, c/Morería 9 (☎365 39 30; closed Sun & Aug; Mº Latina). An Argentine restaurant – which means vast steaks and huge plates of chops – all expertly grilled. Order a salad to start as veggies aren't exactly abundant. Moderate.

Casa Lucio, c/Cava Baja 35 (☎265 32 52; closed Sat lunch & Aug; Mº Latina). *Madrileños* come here for the expected: classic Castilian dishes like *cocido*, *callos* (tripe) and roasts, cooked to perfection. Prices have gone up a bit since the king visited but you can still eat well for under 5000ptas, if you're careful. Booking is essential. Expensive.

El Economico, c/Argumosa (Mº Lavapiés) Traditional, workmen's *comedor* with an unbeatable 600ptas lunchtime *menú*. Inexpensive.

El Frontón, c/Tirso de Molina 7–1º – entrance is just off the square (Mº Tirso de Molina). An old and charming neighbourhood restaurant, where publishers and the like settle down for a long after-noon's lunch. Wide range of classic Castilian dishes – all delicious. Moderate.

Logroñes, c/ Duque de Alba (Mº Tirso de Molina). A down to earth place serving excellent, hearty fair from La Rioja region. Inexpensive.

Posada de la Villa, c/Cava Baja 9 (☎266 18 60; closed Sun night; Mº Latina). The most attractive-looking restaurant in Latina, spread over three floors of a seventeenth-century mansion. Cooking is typically *Madrileña*, including superb roast lamb. Reckon on a good 5000ptas per person for the works – though you could get away with less. Expensive.

El Schotis, c/Cava Baja 11 (☎265 32 30; closed Mon & Aug; Mº Latina). A long-established, *tasca* with an old-style bar up front. Like other places on this street, cooking is typically Castilian, with lots of red meat and roasts, but there's also fish and seafood. Moderate.

Viuda de Vacas, c/Cava Alta 23. Highly traditional restaurant with quality Castilian fare. Inexpensive to moderate.

Chueca and Santa Barbara

Chueca – and Santa Barbara to its north – have some superb traditional old bars and bright new restaurants, and a vast amount of nightlife. The southern part of Chueca, however, around the metro station, and south to Gran Vía, is also quite a big drug area, which can leave you feeling a little uneasy after dark.

TAPAS BARS
Bodega Ángel Sierra, c/Gravina 2, on Plaza Chueca (Mº Chueca). One of the great bars of Madrid, with a traditional zinc counter, constantly washed down. Everyone drinks *vermut*, which is on tap and delicious, and free *tapas* of the most exquisite *boquerones al vinaigre* are despatched (*raciones*, too, for the greedy – though they are expensive).

Cervecería Santa Barbara, Plaza Santa Barbara 8 (Mº Alonso Martinez). A popular meeting place in this part of town, with *cañas* and prawns to keep you going.

RESTAURANTS
Al Hoceima, c/Farmacia 8 (☎531 94 11; closed Mon; Mº Chueca). An elegant little Moroccan restaurant, with decent *couscous* and *tajines* (casseroles). Moderate.

Anapurna, c/Zurbano 5 (☎308 32 49; closed Sun & hols; Mº Alonso Martinez). To say this is the best Indian restaurant in Madrid is faint praise – however, *Anapurna* could hold its own in London, especially if you go for the *tandoori* dishes or *thali*. Moderate.

Carmencita, c/Libertad 16 (☎531 66 12; closed Sun & hols; Mº Chueca). A beautiful old restaurant, dating to 1830, with panelling, brass, marble tables – and a new Basque-influenced chef. Lunch *menú* is a bargain 1200ptas. Inexpensive to moderate.

La Carreta, c/Barbieri 10 (☎532 70 42; open everyday to 5am; Mº Chueca). An Argentinian restaurant, heavy on steaks and red meat. From Wed–Sun there's a trio playing tango; on Tues you can learn to dance. Moderate.

Casa Gades, c/Conde de Xiquena 4 (☎532 30 51; Mº Chueca). A very attractive restaurant in a fashionable area on the edge of Chueca, owned by the flamenco dancer Antonio Gades. Food is a mix of Spanish and Italian. Moderate.

El Comunista (Tienda de Vinos), c/Augusto Figueroa – between Libertad and Barbieri. A long-established *comedor*, which has got a bit fancier in recent years. Its unofficial (but always used) name dates back to its time as a student haunt under Franco. Inexpensive.

Nabucco, c/Hortaleza 108 (☎410 06 11; Mº Alonso Martínez). A pleasant little Italian restaurant that serves up pukka pizzas and a few pasta dishes. Open till 1am at weekends. Inexpensive.

La Tasca Suprema, c/Argensola 7 (☎308 03 47; closed Sun & Aug; Mº Alonso Martínez). A very popular neighbourhood local, worth booking ahead. Castilian home-cooking to a T, including *cocido* on Mon & Thurs. Inexpensive.

Malasaña and north to Bilbão

Malasaña is another characterful area, with a big nightlife scene and dozens of bars. Further north, the area around Plaza de Olavide – a real neighbourhood square – offers some good value places, well off any tourist trails.

TAPAS BARS

Casa Camacho, c/San Andrés 2 – just off Plaza Dos de Mayo (Mº Tribunal). An irresistible old bodega, with a traditional bar counter, *vermut* on tap, and basic *tapas*. An ideal place to start the evening. Packed out at weekends.

Croissantería, c/Corredera Alta de San Pablo – just off Plaza San Ildefonso (Mº Tribunal). Some of the best stuffed croissants in the city, plus ice cream and coffee.

Taberna La Nueva, c/Arapiles 7 (Mº Quevedo). An attractive, century-old *taberna* with an extensive range of *tapas*.

RESTAURANTS

Balear, c/Sagunto 18 (☎447 91 15; Mº Iglesia). This Levantine restaurant serves only rice-based dishes. They're superb; there's an inexpensive house *cava*; and you can turn up any time before midnight. What more could you want? Moderate.

Creperie Petite Bretagne, c/San Vicente Ferrer 9 (☎581 77 74; Mº Tribunal). Tiny place with good *crêpes*, open until after midnight. Inexpensive.

Fernández, c/Palma 6 (Mº Tribunal). As simple as they come – and always packed with locals and low-budget travellers. Inexpensive.

La Gata Flora, Plaza Dos de Mayo 1 (☎521 20 20; Mº Tribunal). Argentine-Italian cooking of a pretty high quality, considering the low prices. Serves until midnight on weekdays, 1am on Fridays and Saturdays. Inexpensive.

La Giralda, c/Hartzenbusch 12 (☎445 77 79; closed Sun & hols; Mº Bilbao). An Andaluz fish and seafood restaurant of very high quality: perfectly cooked *chipirones*, *calamares*, and all the standards, plus wonderful *mero*. A second branch, across the road at no.15, does a similarly accomplished job on *pescados fritos*. Moderate to expensive, depending on your order.

La Glorieta, c/Manuel Malasaña 37 (☎448 40 16; closed Sun night & Mon; Mº Bilbao). Modern Spanish cooking – imaginative and tasty. Moderate.

El Rincón de Mondoñedo, c/Cardenal Cisneros 6 (closed Sun; Mº Bilbao). A Gallego café-restaurant with formica tables – as unpretentious as they come – but serving superb *pulpo*, *pimientos de Padron*, and other staples of the region. Moderate.

Taberna Griega, c/Tesoro 6 (☎532 18 92; Mº Tribunal). Enjoyable Greek restaurant, with live bouzouki music most nights. Open until well after midnight. Inexpensive.

La Zamorana, c/Galielo 21 (☎447 11 69; closed Sat lunch & Sun; Mº San Bernardo). An attractive, titled restaurant, with good value Basque cooking – including lots of dishes based on *bacalao* (dried cod). Moderate (just about).

Paseo del Prado, Recoletos and Retiro

This is a fancier area with few bars of note but some extremely good restaurants, well worth considering, even if you're not staying in the hotels *Ritz* and *Palace*, facing each other across the Neptune fountain in the Plaza Canovas del Castillo.

RESTAURANTS

Al Mounia, c/Recoletos 5 (☎435 08 28; closed Sun, Mon & Aug; Mº Banco de España). Moroccan cooking at its best – indeed, it is equalled only by a couple of restaurants in Paris and Marrakesh. Be sure to try the bastilla (pigeon pie). Expensive.

La Ancha, c/de Zorrilla 7 (☎429 81 86; closed Sun & hols; Mº Sevilla). Highly regarded restaurant in a rather gloomy street behind the Cortes – and hence popular with politicians. Traditional, mahogany-panelled decor, and imaginative variations on traditional castilian dishes. Good value lunchtime menú. Moderate to expensive.

Paradis Madrid, c/Marqués de Cubas 14 (☎429 73 03; closed Sat lunch, Sun & Aug; Mº Banco de España). There are paradises in Barcelona and New York – the chain is run by a Catalan duo – and the American influence is apparent in designerish details like a *carta* for olive oils. Nonetheless, the cooking is light, Mediterranean and tasty; try the wonderful *arroz negro* with seafood. Stays open till 1.30am, if it's busy. Moderate.

Viridiana, c/Juan de Mena 14 (☎523 44 78; closed Sun & Aug; Mº Retiro). A bizarre temple of Madrid *nueva cocina*, offering mouthwatering creations like *solomillo* (sirloin) with black truffles

TERRAZAS AND CHIRINGUITOS

Madrid is a different city during summer, as temperatures soar into the hundreds, and life moves outside – and becomes even more late night. In July and August, those Madrileños who haven't headed for the coast meet up with each other, from 10pm onwards, at one or other of the city's immensely popular **terrazas**. These can range from a few tables set up outside a café, or alongside a **chiringuito** – a makeshift bar – in one of the squares, to extremely trendy (and extremely expensive) designer bars, which form the summer annexe of one or other of the major clubs or *discotecas*. Most places offer cocktails, in addition to regular drinks, and the better or more traditional ones also serve *horchata* (an almond-ish milk shake) and *granizado* (crushed-ice lemon). A few of the *terrazas* operate year-round.

Terrazas run by the **clubs** – such as *Stella*, *Hanoi* and *Zanizibar* – vary their sites year by year, often locating way out from the centre, and necessitating long and expensive taxi rides. Still, if you *do* want to run into Pedro Almodóvar, Alaska and their chums, you'll have to track down *Stella* – wherever it currently is.

Paseo de Recoletos and Paseo la Castellana

The biggest concentration of *terrazas* are to be found up and down the grass strip in the middle of the Paseo de Recoletos and its continuation, Paseo de la Castellana. On the nearer reaches of Paseo de Recoletos are *terrazas* of the **old-style cafés** *Gran* (no. 8), *Gijón* (no. 21) and *Espejo* (no. 31), which are popular meeting points for Madrileños of all kinds.

Past Plaza de Colón, the **trendier terrazas** begin, most pumping out music, and some offering entertainment – especially midweek, when they need to attract custom. They are extremely posey places, with clubbers dressing up for a night's cruise along the length – an expensive operation, with cocktails at 1000ptas a shot, and even a caña costing 600ptas. If you want to take in a good selection, walk up from Plaza de Colón for around 500m. Alternatively, take a taxi or the metro up to Plaza de Lima, where you'll find *Castellana 99* – a fashionable *terraza* and bar that's open year-round. For some reason, most of the Castellana *terrazas* are known only by their (approximate) street number.

Elsewhere in Madrid

Antiguo Cuartel del Conde Duque (Mº Ventura Rodriguez). This is a beautiful patio, inside an old military barracks. The council puts on weekly flamenco recitals in July–Aug, with a small admission charge, but most nights there's free entry.

Jardines de Conde Duque, at the corner of c/de Conde Duque and c/Santa Cruz del Marcenado (Mº Ventura Rodriguez). The summer base of *Zanzibar* in recent years.

Jardines Las Vistillas, c/Bailén – on the south side of the viaduct (Mº Latina – though it's not very close). This area, due south of the royal palace, has a number of *terrazas* and *chiringuitos*. It's named for the "little vistas" to be enjoyed in the direction of the Guadarrama mountains to the northwest.

Paseo del Pintor Rosales (Mº Arguelles). There is a clutch of late-night *terrazas* around the base of the teleférico,

with views across the river to the Casa de Campo.

Plaza de Comendadoras (Mº Ventura Rodriguez). One of the city's nicest squares, this has a couple of *terrazas* – attached to the *Café Moderno* and to a not very good Mexican restaurant.

Plaza Dos de Mayo (Mº Tribunal). The *chiringuito* on Malasaña's main square is always diverting.

Plaza de Olavide (Mº Quevedo). This is an attractive neighbourhood square, with more or less year-round terrazas belonging to four or five cafés and *tapas* bars.

Plaza de Oriente (Mº Opera). The *Café de Oriente terraza* is a station of Madrid nightlife.

Plaza de Santa Ana (Mº Sol). Several of the *cervecerías* here have seats outside and there's a *chiringuito* in the middle of the square from June to September.

and *mero* with *cêpes*, while also conducting pyrotechnic experiments (dishes often arrive decorated with small incendiary devices). You'll need to go to the bank first, as main courses are around 2500ptas and no cards are accepted. Expensive.

Salamanca

Salamanca is Madrid's equivalent of Bond Street or Fifth Avenue, full of designer shops and expensive looking natives. Recommendations below are correspondingly pricey but high quality.

TAPAS BARS

José Luís, c/Serrano 89 (Mº Serrano). A very chi-chi bar with dainty and delicious sandwiches laid out along the bar. You take what you fancy, in the safe knowledge that the barman will have notched up another few hundred pesetas on your account.

RESTAURANTS

El Amparo, Callejón Puigcerdá 8 (☎431 64 56; closed Sat lunch & Sun; Mº Serrano). Most critics rate this among the top five Madrid restaurants – and you'll need to book a couple of weeks ahead to get a table. If you strike lucky, the rewards are faultless Basque cooking from a woman chef, Carmen Guasp – Guaspi to the Spanish media. Main dishes are around the 3000ptas mark so expect a bill of at least 6000ptas a head. Expensive.

Casa Portal, c/Dr. Castelo 26 (☎574 20 26; closed Mon night & hols & Aug; Mº Goya). Superlative Asturian cooking – go for the *fabada* (beans and sausage stew) or *besugo* (bream). Moderate.

El Pescador, c/José Ortega y Gasset 75 (☎402 12 90; closed Sun & Aug; Mº Lista). This is one of the city's top seafood restaurants, run by Gallegos and with specials flown in from the Atlantic each morning. The clientele can be a bit initimidating – it is reputedly one of Felipe Gonzalez's favourites – but you'll rarely experience better seafood cooking. Expensive.

Suntory, Paseo de la Castellana 36 (☎577 37 33; closed Sun & hols; Mº Rúben Dario). An authentic and upmarket Japanese restaurant, where a mixed *sushi* will set you back around 3000ptas. Expensive.

Teatriz, c/Hermosilla 15 (☎577 53 79; closed Sat lunch, Sun & Aug; Mº Serrano). As the name suggests, this was once a theatre, and the lay-out has been maintained by designers Philipe Stark and Mariscal – as trendy a European combination as could be conceived. Although primarily a nightspot (see p.95), there's a fine restaurant in the old "circle", with light, nouvelle cuisine influenced dishes. (Surprisingly) moderate.

The west

Picnicking in the Casa de Campo aside, the west doesn't hold much in the way of culinary interest. However one excellent restaurant deserves a mention.

RESTAURANTS

Casa Mingo, Paseo de la Florida 2 – next to the chapel of San Antonio de la Florida (☎547 79 18; Mº Norte). A famous Asturian café-restaurant where you eat roast chicken – which is basically all they serve – washed down with sidra (cider), and followed up by *yemas* (candied egg yolk) or aged Roquefort-like cheese (*cabrales*). Good value and great fun. You can also buy a take-out (chicken and cider) for a picnic in the Casa de Campo, if you prefer. Moderate.

Nightlife

Madrid **nightlife** is a pretty serious phenomenon. This is the only city in Europe where you can get caught in traffic jams at 4am, when the clubbers are either going home or moving on to the dance-past-dawn discos. In the summer months, there's even nighttime horseracing (see box on p.96).

CHOCOLATE BEFORE BED

If you stay up through a Madrid night, then you must try one of the city's great institutions – the **Chocolatería San Ginés** on Pasadizo de San Ginés, off c/de Arenal between the Puerta del Sol and Teatro Real. Established in 1894, this serves *chocoláte con churros* to perfection – just the thing after a night's excess. There's an almost mythical Madrileño custom of winding up at San Ginés after the clubs close (not that they do any longer), before heading home for a shower and then off to work. And why not?

San Ginés is open Tues–Sun 1am–7.30am & Fri–Sun 7–10pm – the latter for weekend shoppers. The *chocoláte* is half the price in the 7–10pm session.

As with everything *Madrileño*, there is a bewildering variety of types of nightlife venue – all of which are covered, to some degree, in the area-reviews following. Most common are the **discobares** – bars of all musical and sexual persuasion, whose unifying feature is background (occasionally live) rock, dance or salsa music. These get going from around 11pm and will stay open routinely to 2 or 3am, as will the few quieter **cocktail bars** and **pubs**.

Discotecas – which we've separated in the listings – are rarely worth investigating until around 1am (the *madrugada* – early morning). Most of them pick their clientele through a dress code exclusivity and you may at times need to ingratiate yourself with the doorman. Being foreign, oddly enough, seems to make it easier to get in. Entry charges are quite common and quite hefty (500–1000ptas) at *discotecas* (and some of the more disco-like *discobares*) but tend to cover you for a first drink.

Places with regular **live music** – rock, jazz, flamenco, salsa and classical – are covered in the "Performance" section, following on p.97.

Bars

Madrid's bar scene has, if anything, got more frenetic over the past couple of years, largely due to the appearance of *bakalao*, a Spanish (originally Ibizan) version of house music. In both *discobares* or *discotecas*, it's horribly popular, and *Madrileños* have taken to the idea of all night raving with unmitigated enthusiasm.

Perhaps in reaction to *bakalao*, the more traditional bar scene has revived and expanded, too. In the listings below, you'll find a fair number of *bares de copas* (drinking bars) where the music is restrained – and even a couple with chamber orchestras.

SOL, OPERA AND PLAZA DE SANTA ANA

Carbones, c/Manuel González – off c/Echegaray (Mº Sol). A cafe by day and *discobar* at night. The music selection is one of the best you can find in Madrid, and beers are modestly priced. Small, so very packed at weekends.

No se lo digas a nadie, c/Ventura de la Vega 7 (Mº Sol). This was founded (and is still run) by a women's co-op, though it has mellowed a bit in recent years (the toilets no longer proclaim *nosotros* and *ellos* – "us" and "them"). Nonetheless, it retains a political edge, hosting benefit events from time to time, and has a different atmosphere from other bars in this area. There is no door policy or dress code and reasonably priced drinks. Upstairs there's a pool table and plenty of places to sit, downstairs is a disco playing mainly dance music.

Palacio de Gaviria, c/Arenal 9 (Mº Opera; Mon–Sat 8pm–3am, Sun 7pm–midnight; ☎526 60 69). An aristocratic nineteenth–century palace where you can wander through a sequence of extravagant salons and listen to a chamber concert most nights in the ballroom. It's pricey: entrance is 3000ptas if there's a concert – and drinks 1500ptas a shot.

Salon del Prado, c/Prado 4 (Mº Sol). A very elegant café-bar which again hosts classical concerts – on Thursday nights at 11pm. Turn up early if you want a table.

GAY AND LESBIAN MADRID

Much of Madrid's nightlife has a big gay imput and gays will feel at home in most of the listings in our clubs/discotecas section. However, around Plaza Chueca, graffiti-plastered walls proclaim the existence of a *Zona Gay*, and the surrounding streets, especially c/de Pelayo, harbour at least a dozen exclusively gay bars and clubs, and a café that's traditionally gay – the *Café Figueroa* at c/Augusto Figueroa 17. Wandering about, be aware that Chueca is also something of a drug centre, so taxis are best late at night. The lesbian scene, such as it is, has a current focus in Lavapiés.

Chueca bars and *discotecas*

Bachelor, c/de la Reina. One of Madrid's best known gay discobars: very plush and catering for an older, smarter crowd with a bit of money. 1000ptas entrance.

Bar LL, c/de Pelayo (Mº Chueca). There's a bar at the front and a more intimate room at the back, where people sit around and talk or watch hard-core gay porn on the video screen. Slightly older crowd, mainly singles. The bar offers free entry to an all-night **sauna**, *Cristal*, at c/ Augusto Figueroa 17.

Cruising, c/Perez Galdos 5 (Mº Chueca). This *discobar* is strictly for leather boys, with a dark room and bar upstairs and a small, intimate disco below. It has a slightly tense atmosphere and you have to order your drinks at the door before you come in.

Leather and **Cuero**, both c/de Pelayo (Mº Chueca). The names imply a leather scene but both these bars have a mixed gay crowd.

Lesbian bars and *discotecas*

Fragil, c/Lavapiés 11 (Mº Lavapiés). A lively lesbian *discobar*.

Medea, c/de la Cabeza 33 (Mº Lavapiés/ Antón Martín). The city's premier lesbian

disco – though accompanied men are admitted. Entrance charge (900pts) includes a cabaret on Thurs and Sun. Smart decor, great music, pool table.

Sherazade, c/Santa Maria 18 – parallel with Huertas (Mº Antón Martín). For neo-hippies: rugs to sit on, Moroccan tea, and (tobacco) hubble-bubble pipes.

Taberna del Leon de Oro, c/del Leon 10 (Mº Antón Martín). Popular Irish bar, serving Guinness and Newcastle Brown Ale to homesick foreign residents.

GRAN VÍA

Museo Chicote, Gran Vía 12 (Mon–Sat 1.30pm–3am; Mº Gran Vía). *Chicote* is a piece of design history, virtually unaltered since it opened in 1931, full of art deco lines and booths. They will mix you any cocktail, alcoholic or not. Busiest after midnight.

El Cock, c/de la Reina 16 – just behind Museo Chicote (Mº Gran Vía). Former gay disco, now a smart and very *moda* bar, styled like a gentlemen's club. The music is good, there's no dancing, and you have to knock to get in. *Cañas* or wine cost around 600ptas.

El Morocco, c/Marqués de Leganes 7 (Mº Santo Domingo). The latest venture by rock singer Alaska, long-time mover of the *movida*, and mate of Pedro Almodovar. The crowds here could well be from an Almodovar movie (it's likely that some, at least, have acted in one), and they get a club in their own image, including a cabaret show at 2am, the odd (and odd is the word) band, and a dancefloor open till 9am. There's an occasional entrance charge and you'll need to look the part to get past the doorman.

LA LATINA/LAVAPIÉS

Avapies, c/Lavapiés 5 (Mº Lavapiés). Excellent music and nightly cabaret around 10pm. Closes at 2am.

Maravillita, c/Zurita 39 (Mº Lavapiés). Loud music, even louder clientele. Open till late.

CHUECA/SANTA BARBARA

Cliche, c/del Barquillo (M⁰ Chueca). Best of many bars along this street – a relaxed yet funky place, with clientele as eclectic as the decor, and all ages from 15 to 50. Open till 3am.

La Fabrica de Pan, c/Regueros (M⁰ Chueca). Deep in the heart of Chueca, this has a relaxed atmosphere and good music. On any day of the week you'll find people drinking till 4am, or playing board games in the room at the back. Perhaps best enjoyed during the week, as it's a small place and gets packed at weekends. *Cañas* are a modest 350ptas.

Impacto, c/Campoamor 3 (M⁰ Alonso Martínez). Inside this is a mini-labyrinth of little rooms and bars around every corner. A fairly trendy, slightly older crowd. Reasonably priced drinks and a good variety of music, despite the lack of dancefloor. Door policy of sorts.

Ricks, c/de las Infantas 26 (M⁰ Banco de España). This mixed straight/gay *discobar* gets wild at weekends when every available space is used for dancing – and at weekends it keeps going as late as 7am (4am during the week). Open and light, with a friendly atmosphere and fine music from house classics to disco to hi-NRG – plus table football at the back.

MALASAÑA AND A BIT NORTH

Al Lab Oratorio, c/de Colón 14 (M⁰ Tribunal). A famous 80s bar with very loud rock music on the sound system, and often live on a little stage downstairs. No entry charge but the drinks are expensive.

Café del Foro, c/San Andres 38 (M⁰ Tribunal). An expensive but enjoyable bar with live music or some form of entertainment most nights. Attracts a slightly older, fairly smart crowd. Open from 6.30pm till 3 or 4am.

The Harp, c/Jesus del Valle (M⁰ Tribunal). Irish bar with Guinness on tap; riotous and packed at weekends. Occasional live music.

Hotel California, c/San Vicente Ferrer 28 (M⁰ Tribunal). Film set interior with lots of intimate booths. Rock music, but not deafening, and a varied crowd. Fairly expensive drinks.

Kiks Mode, c/Manuela Malasaña 20 (M⁰ Tribunal). Shrine to Bob Marley with reggae on the sound system and live downstairs some nights; mixed crowd, smoky atmosphere.

Pepe Botella, c/San Andres 12 – on Plaza Dos de Mayo (M⁰ Tribunal). Formerly a restaurant, now a relaxed wine-bar, with friendly staff, decent music and no fruit machine.

Bar Plaza Dos de Mayo, Plaza Dos de Mayo (M⁰ Tribunal). An old-style wood and tiles bar, which gets packed at weekends. Good music, regular prices, and opens up in the summer so you can watch the goings-on in the square.

Vía Lactea, c/Velarde 18 (M⁰ Tribunal). Call in here to see where the *movida* began. *Vía Lactea* was a key meeting place for Spain's designers, directors, pop stars and painters in the 80s, and it retains its original decor from the time, billiard tables included.

TRAFALGAR/QUEVEDO

Casa Quemeda, c/Cardenal Cisneros 56 (M⁰ Quevedo). Unusual for this bar-packed area in that it's old – all-wood decor – and very peaceful. There's a car stuck in the window — one of the first assembly line models produced in the country. *Sangria* at a modest 900ptas a jug.

Warhol's Club, c/Luchana 20 (M⁰ Quevedo). Very popular *discobar* open until 10am – and until noon on Sundays. It is spread over two floors, with lots of chrome, glass, video screens, and ultra-violet lighting. Attracts an early-20s crowd. No door policy.

SALAMANCA

Avion Club, c/Hermosilla 99 (7pm–3am; M⁰ Goya). This was one of the most popular clubs in the gloomy post-Civil War years, when it was adopted by the remains of the left. It hasn't changed an iota in the last sixty years and even the pianist, at 90-odd, is virtually original.

Teatriz, c/Hermosilla 15 (café noon–3pm, bars 9pm–3am; closed Sat lunch, Sun & Aug; M⁰ Serrano). This former theatre, redesigned by the Catalan, Mariscal, together with Philipe Stark, is as elegant a club as any in Europe. There are bars on the main theatre levels, watched over by a restaurant in the circle. Down in the basement there's a library-like area and small disco. Drinks are fairly pricey (1500ptas for spirits) but there's no entrance charge.

A MIDSUMMER'S NIGHT AT THE RACES

Since 1992, Thursday nights in August and September have presented a curious spectacle as up to 15,000 Madrileños head out for a night at the **Hipódromo** racecourse, 7km out from the centre on Carretera de La Coruña. The first race starts at midnight and for the next three hours punters can watch the horses trot around the paddock and gamble on the results.

The more serious posers, with their English dress and binoculars, keep up a semblance of horseracing etiquette but most people are here for the novelty of an alternative location to amuse themselves in the early morning. There are twenty or so *terraza* bars (drink prices are steep with a *caña* at 600ptas), lots of snack stalls, and even a proper restaurant.

Free buses (marked *Hipódromo*) leave from Plaza Moncloa (Mº Moncloa) from 10.30pm until 1am. Getting back, you're on your own, so save that last 2000ptas for the taxi.

Discotecas

Discotecas – or clubs – aren't always that different from *discobares*, though they tend to be bigger and flashier, with a lot of attention to the lights, sound system and decor, and stay open very late – most until 4am, some till 6am, and one till noon. In summer, many of the trendier clubs suspend operations and set up outdoor *terrazas* (see p.91).

SOL, OPERA AND PLAZA DE SANTA ANA

Banos, c/Independencia (Mº Opera). Large disco with an unpretentious atmosphere and a good selection of music. No door policy or dress code and reasonably priced drinks.

Changoo, Plaza de Santa Ana (Mº Sol). Modern, spacious, chrome-decor disco on two floors. Upstairs is a small bar and dancefloor, usually playing house; downstairs is the main bar and seating; toilets are bizarre. Smart crowd and door policy.

Joy Eslava, c/Arenal 11 (Mº Sol). This big-name disco is frequented by musicians, models and media folk, for whom the 2000ptas entry and rigorous door policy hold no fears. If you can't get in – and 3–5am is the hippest time here – console yourself with the *Chocolatería San Gines* (see box), on the street behind.

Stella, c/Arlaban 7 (Mº Sevilla). This has been one of Madrid's trendiest discos right from its launch by Alaska (see *El Morocco* – under "Bars"). It attracts a gay/straight mix and gets going from about 4am; music is (or was) an inspired blend of House and tacky 70s disco, and if it all palls, there's a bowling alley downstairs. You'll need to dress up.

GRAN VÍA

El Calentito, c/Jacometrezo 15 (Mº Callao). This is a fine place for an experience of wild, abandoned Madrid. It is tiny and cramped with strictly South American sounds: be prepared to dance with anyone! Drinks are modest. Open from midnight but doesn't really get going till 4am. The entrance is easily missed – look out for the painted window.

Xenon, Plaza Callao (Mº Callao). One of the biggest discos in town: all black and chrome design, dance sounds, plus a huge video screen. Door policy requires cool costumes and you need a lot of cash to service the bar.

CHUECA/SANTA BARBARA

Boccacio, c/Marques Enseneda 16 (Mº Colón). This is an all-nighter: it kicks off about midnight with a business-type crowd, then around 5am a younger, trendier crew take over and go on till noon – the latest it gets here in Madrid. Plush interior with a bar upstairs and a disco down, playing mainly *bakalao*. Entrance is 1000ptas for men, free for women.

Pacha, c/de Barcelo 11 (Mº Tribunal). An eternal survivor on the Madrid disco scene. Once a theatre and still very theatrical, it is exceptionally cool during the week, less so at the weekend when the out-of-towners take over.

MALASAÑA AND A BIT NORTH

La Habana, c/San Vicente Ferrer 23 (Mº Tribunal). A spacious, un-posey disco that plays exclusively Latin American sounds. If you can't *salsa*, just sit back and watch uninhibited displays from those who really are the business.

Provisional, c/Fernandez de los Rios 59 (Mº Quevedo). A club for serious and sweaty *bakalao* revels. Open from 11pm till 5am.

Rajaja, c/Trafalgar 10 (Mº Bilbao). A little maze inside, with lots of dark corners around a small dancefloor. Strict door policy but reasonably priced drinks and a *terraza* in summer.

MONCLOA

Cats, c/Julia Romeo 4 (Mº Guzman El Bueno). Moncloa is a popular student area, towards the end of c/de la Princesa, and it has a good range of bars and discos. This is one of the best: a large bar surrounded by various dance floors, podiums and chill-out areas. Young crowd and emphasis firmly on dancing, to house and *bakalao*. Open till 5.30am.

OUT WEST

Aqualung Universal, Paseo de la Ermita del Santo 40 (midnight–5am). This is a disco and aquapark for all-night raving, if you suddenly thought you'd rather be in Ibiza than Madrid. It's located across the river, over the Puente de Sevoia: a 20-minute taxi ride from the centre.

Performance: music, theatre and film

Most nights in Madrid, you could take in performances of **flamenco**, **salsa**, **rock** (local and imported), **jazz**, **classical music** and **opera** at one or other of the city's venues. Often, it's the smaller, offbeat clubs that are the more enjoyable, though there are plenty of big auditoria – including the football stadiums and bullring – for big name concerts. In summer, events are supplemented by the council's **Veranos de la Villa** cultural programme. This also encompasses **theatre** and **film**, both of which have fairly healthy year-round scenes.

Flamenco

Flamenco has undergone something of a revival in Madrid in the 90s, in large part due to the "new flamenco" artists, unafraid to mix it with a bit of blues, jazz, even rock. The club listings below span the range between purist flamenco and crossover experiments and most artists – even major stars – appear in them. Paco de Lucía is a rare exception – when he plays with his band in Madrid, it's usually in the bullring, Las Ventas.

Clubs and cafés include:

Café de Chinitas, c/Torija 7 (☎248 51 35; Mº Opera). One of the oldest flamenco clubs in Madrid, with a dinner-dance spectacular. It is very touristy and expensive but the music is authentic. Reservations are essential, though you may get in late when people start to leave (at this time you don't have to eat and the entrance fee includes your first drink).

Candela, c/del Olmo 2 (Mº Antón Martín). A legendary bar frequented by musicians; the late, great Camarón de la Isla is reputed to have sung here until 11am on one occasion.

Caracol, c/Bernardino Obregón 18 (☎530 80 55; Mº Embajadores). The top names tend to appear here, so it's worth making a reservation as early as possible. Almost any night here you are guaranteed an *¡¡actuación especial!!*, as they disarmingly put it.

Casa Patas, c/Canizares 10 (Mº Lavapiés). A small club that gets its share of big names.

The Revolver Club, c/Galileo 26 (Mº Arguelles). This (mainly rock) venue hosts brilliant flamenco nights on Mondays, from 10.30pm. It is associated with the new flamenco sound.

La Solea, Cava Baja 27 (Tues–Sun 10pm–3am; Mº La Latina). This brilliant, long-established flamenco bar is the genuine article. People sit around in the salon, pick up a guitar or start to sing and gradually the atmosphere builds up until everyone else is clapping or dancing. Has to be seen to be believed.

MADRID LISTINGS – AND THE *MADRUGADA*

Listings information is in plentiful supply in Madrid. The newspapers *El Pais* and *El Mundo* have excellent daily listings, and on Fridays both publish supplements devoted to events, bars and restaurants in the capital. Of the two, the **Guía El Pais** is the better – a compact little handbook, full of previews and details of the week's exhibitions, films, theatre, and concerts, and with extensive listings of clubs, bars and restaurants (including opening hours and average prices – usually on the high side of what you'll spend).

If your time in Madrid doesn't coincide with the Friday *El País* supplement, or you want maximum info, pick up the weekly listings magazine **Guía del Ocio** (100ptas) at any kiosk. It's not quite as clear or discriminating as *El País*, but functional enough. The *Ayuntamiento* also publishes a monthly "What's On" pamphlet, **En Madrid**, which is free from any of the tourist offices. Lastly, if you're into **shopping**, the **Guía de Compras** (twice yearly; 490ptas) has exhaustive reviews for just about everything you might want to buy in Madrid.

One word that might perplex first-timers in Madrid – and which crops up in all the listings magazines – is **madrugada**. This refers to the hours between midnight and dawn and, in this supremely late-night/early-morning city, is a necessary adjunct to announcements of important events. *Tres de la madrugada* means an event is due to start at 3am.

Rock and blues

Madrid is very much on the international rock tour circuit and you can catch big (and small) American and British acts in front of enthusiastic audiences. One of the more endearing Spanish habits is to translate all foreign names – including rock bands: thus, just as Prince Charles is always known as Principe Carlos, U2 are, of course, U–Dos. **Tickets** for most big rock concerts are sold by *Madrid Rock*, Gran Vía 25 (Mº Callao; daily 10am–10pm; all cards).

In the smaller clubs, you have a chance of seeing a very wide range of local bands. Madrid has long been the heart of the Spanish rock scene (see "Music" in *Contexts*).

CLUBS

La Croqueta, c/ de la Hileras (Mº Opera). Small, smokey blues bar, where people sit around in the near dark watching the band perform on a tiny stage. Live music most nights.

Maravillas, c/San Vicente Ferrer 33 (Mº Tribunal). Small but usually uncrowded venue where bands play anything from jazz to funk to reggae, often till around 4am.

The Revolver Club, c/Galileo 26 (Mº Arguelles). The city's best small-scale venue, with an ever diverse mix of people and music. There's a band on almost every night, from the latest British indie sensation, to the hippest of local talent, to old funksters from the US, to "new flamenco" (on Mondays). Post-gig music varies, though it's generally rock based. Entry fee most nights. Open till 6am. Jewellery and clothes market on a Sunday afternoon.

Siroco, c/San Dimas 3 (Mº Noviciado). Live bands most nights at this popular little club, not far north of Gran Vía.

Ya'sta, c/Valverde 10 (Mº Gran Vía). A weird and wonderful place for terminal insomniacs. Most nights there's a a jam session from local rock musicians, then a disco plays rock and funk until about 7am. The door policy gets strict from 4am, so best turn up early.

MAJOR CONCERT VENUES

Aqualung Universal, Paseo de la Ermita del Santo 48. Rock and salsa concerts are often held at this disco and aquapark, located across the river, over the Puente de Sevoia. It's a 20-minute taxi ride from the centre.

Auditorio Parque de Attracciones, Casa de Campo (Mº Lago). Open air summer venue.

Plaza de Toros de las Ventas, Las Ventas (Mº Ventas). The bull ring is a pretty good concert venue, put to good use in the summer festival. Tickets are usually one price, though you can pay more for a (good) reserved seat (*asiento reservado*).

Teatro Monumental, c/de Atocha 65 (Mº Atocha). A large theatre, where rock and flamenco events are often held. Tickets are sold for stalls (*butaca de patio*) or a series of dizzying circles (*entresuelo*).

See "Listings" (under "Football") for transport details for the **football stadiums**, Estadio Bernabeu and Estadio Vicente Calderón.

Latin music

Madrid attracts big-name Latin artists and if you happen to coincide with the summer festival you'll stand a good chance of catching someone of the stature of salsa legend Joe Arroyo, or – a huge star in Spain – Jean Luís Guerra from the Dominican Republic. Gigs by the likes of these tend to take place at the venues listed above. The local scene is a good deal more low-key but there's enjoyable salsa, nonetheless, in a handful of clubs.

Massai, c/Victoria 6 (Mº Sol). Nightly salsa.

Café del Mercado in the Centro Artesano Puerta de Toledo (Mº Puerta de Toledo). Live music every day and a *Gran Baile de Salsa* every Friday and Saturday at 2am.

Oba-Oba, c/Jacometrezo 4 (Mº Callao). Samba and lambada.

Salsipuedes, c/Puebla 6 (Mº Callao). Serious *salsa* dancing to a live orchestra most weekdays. Strict door policy. Open from 11pm to 6am.

Jazz

Madrid doesn't rank with London, Paris or New York on the jazz front but the clubs are friendly, unpretentious places .

Café Central, Plaza del Angel 10 (Mº Sol). This got voted no. 6 in a recent "Best Jazz Clubs of the World" poll in *Wire* magazine. It's certainly an attractive venue – small and relaxed – and it gets the odd big name, plus strong local talent.

Bar Clamores, c/Albuquerque (Mº Bilbao). A large, low-key and enjoyable jazz bar with accomplished (if not very famous) artists, not too exorbitant drinks and a nice range of snacks. Last set finishes around 1.30am, though the bar stays open to 4am.

Café Jazz Populart, c/de las Huertas 22 (Mº Antón Martín). Nightly sets from jazz and blues bands. It's open from 6pm, gets cooking around 11pm and stays open till 2am or so.

Jazz Madrid, c/San Vicente Ferrer (Mº Tribunal). A trendy and fairly expensive venue, spread over two floors in Malasaña.

Ragtime, c/Ruiz (Mº Bilbao). Small, intimate venue which puts on mainly trad jazz. Good atmosphere and reasonably priced.

Classical music and opera

The **Teatro Royal** – Madrid's opera house – has been under scaffolding for most of the 1990s but is scheduled to reopen some time in 1995. When it does, it will be the city's prestige venue, along with the **Auditoria Nacional de Musica**, home of the Orquesta Nacional de España. Equally enjoyable are the salons and small auditoriums for chamber orchestras and groups.

Venues include:

Auditorio Nacional de Musica, c/Principe de Vergara 146 (Mº Cruz del Rayo). This is the home of the Spanish orchestra and host to most international visiting orchestras.

Centro de Arte Reina Sofía, c/Santa Isabel (Mº Atocha). The new arts centre often has programmes of contemporary music.

Fundación Juan March, c/Castelló 99 (M⁰ Núñez de Balboa). A small auditorium used for recitals two or three times a week.

Palacio de Gaviria, c/Arenal 9 (M⁰ Opera; Mon–Sat 8pm–3am, Sun 7pm–midnight; ☎526 60 69). A nineteenth–century palace which has chamber concerts most nights. See p.93.

Salon del Prado, c/Prado 4 (M⁰ Sol). Another café venue which hosts classical musicians on Thursday nights at 11pm.

Teatro Real, Plaza Isabel II (M⁰ Opera). Madrid's opera house.

Film

Cines – cinemas or movie houses – can be found all over the central area. Major releases (which make it here well before London) are dubbed into Spanish, though a number of cinemas have regular **original language** screenings, with subtitles; these are listed in a separate *versión original/subtitulada* (*v.o.*) section in the newspapers. **Tickets** for films cost around 600ptas but most cinemas have a *dia de espectador* (usually Mon or Wed) with 400ptas admission. Be warned that on Sunday night half of Madrid goes to a movie and queues can be long.

Interesting cinemas/screens include:

Alphaville, **Renoir** and **Lumière**, c/Martín de los Heros – just north of the Plaza de España (M⁰ Plaza de España). This trio of multi-screen cinemas, within 200m of each other, show regular *v.o.* films.

La Chopera in the Parque del Retiro. Free open-air screenings on summer nights.

Filmoteca/Cine Doré, c/Santa Isabel 3 (M⁰ Antón Martín). A beautiful old cinema, now home to an art film centre, with imaginative programmes of classic and contemporary films, all shown in *v.o.* In summer, there are open-air screenings on a little *terraza* – they're very popular, so buy tickets in advance.

Cinés Ideal, c/Doctor Cortezo 6 (M⁰ Sol/Tirso de Molina). Six-screen complex which shows most films in *v.o.*

Sala Olimpia, Plaza de Lavapiés. Another cinema with open-air screenings in summer and a fairly alternative programme.

Theatre and cabaret

The theatre scene is more exciting in Barcelona (where there are some very wacky companies) than in Madrid. Nonetheless, you can catch anything from Lope de Vega to contemporary and experimental productions, and there's also a new wave of cabaret and comedy acts. Interesting venues include:

Teatro Alfil, c/Pez 10 (M⁰ Noviciado). Alternative theatre and comedy.

Círculo de Bellas Artes, c/ de Alcalá (M⁰ Sevilla). The Círculo includes a beautiful old theatre which puts on adventurous productions.

Centro Cultural de la Villa, Plaza de Colón (M⁰ Colón). Arts centre where you're likely to see some of the more experimental companies on tour.

Teatro Español, Plaza de Santa Ana (M⁰ Sol or Antón Martín). Classic Spanish theatre.

Shopping

Shopping districts in Madrid are pretty defined. The biggest range of stores are along Gran Vía and around Puerta del Sol, which is where the **department stores** – *El Corte Inglés* and *Galerias Preciados* – have their main branches. For **fashion** (*moda*), the smartest addresses are c/de Serrano, c/de Goya and c/de Velázquez, north of the Retiro, while more alternative designers are to be found in Malasaña and Chueca (c/ Almirante, especially). The **antiques** trade is centred down towards the Rastro, on and

LATE NIGHT SHOPPING

Madrid has three chains of late-night shops – the oddly-named **Bob's**, **Vip's** and **7 Eleven** – that stay open into the small (and not so small) hours. Each of them sells papers, cigarettes, groceries, books, CDs: the kind of things you need to pop in for at 2am. Larger branches of *Bob's* and *Vip's* also have café-restaurants, one-hour photo developing, and suchlike.

Central branches include:

Bob's (Sun–Thur 9am–1.30am, Fri, Sat & festivals 9am–3am): Serrano 41 (Mº Serrano); Glorieta de Quevedo (Mº Quevedo); Miguel Angel 11 (Mº Rúben Darío).

Vip's (daily 9am–3am): Gran Vía 43 (Mº Gran Vía); Velázquez 84 & 136 (Mº Velázquez); Miguel Angel 11 (Mº Rúben Darío).

7 Eleven (daily 24hrs): c/Atocha 44 (Mº Atocha).

around c/Ribera de Curtidores, while for **general weirdness**, it's hard to beat the shops just off Plaza Mayor, where luminous saints rub shoulders with surgical supports and fascist memorabilia.

Most areas of the city have their own *mercados del barrio* – indoor **markets**, devoted mainly to food. Among the best and most central are those in Plaza San Miguel (just west of Plaza Mayor); behind the Gran Vía in Plaza de Mostenses; on c/Gravina in Chueca; and on c/Barcelo in Malasaña. The city's biggest market is, of course, the **Rastro** – the flea market – which takes place on Sundays in Latina, south of Plaza Mayor. For details of this great Madrid institution, see p.68. Other specialized markets include a secondhand **book market** on the Cuesta de Moyano, at the southwest corner of El Retiro.

Artesania: crafts, fans, guitars, hats, perfumes and toys

El Arco de los Cuchilleros, Plaza Mayor 9 – by the steps (Mº Sol; Mon–Sat 11am–8pm, Sun 11am–2.30pm). The location of this shop may be at the heart of tourist Madrid but the goods are a far cry from the swords, lace and castanets that fill most shops in the region. *El Arco* handles thirty or so workshops and artesans, who reflect Spanish artesania at its most innovative and contemporary. They encompass ceramics (six of Madrid's top potters), leather (from Oviedo), wood (including some fine games), jewellery and textiles.

Alvarez Goméz, c/Serrano 14 (Mº Serrano; Mon–Sat 9.30am–2pm & 4.45–8.15pm; all cards). *Goméz* have been making the same perfumes in the same bottles for the past century. The scents – carnations, rose, violets – are as simple and straight as they come.

Conde Hermanos, c/Felipe II 2 (Mº Opera; Mon–Fri 9.30am–1.30pm & 4.30–8pm; *Visa/Amex*); **José Ramírez**, c/Concepción Jerónima (Mº Tirso de Molina; Mon–Fri 10am–2pm & 5–8pm, Sat 10am–2pm). Two of the most renowned guitar workshops in Spain. Prices start at around 14,000ptas and head skywards for the quality models and fancy woods.

Fundación de Gremios, Plaza de la Independencia 4 (Mº Retiro; Mon–Fri 9.30am–2pm & 4.30–7.30pm, Sat 10am–2pm; *Amex/Visa*). A shop for a group of artesans working in various mediums – textiles, stone, metals. It is mostly traditional material but there are a few modern designs, including rugs by Mariscal.

Casa Jiménez, c/Preciados 42 (Mº Callao; Mon–Sat 10am–1.30pm & 5–8pm; *Amex/Visa*). If you want a fan (*abanico*) that's a work of art, this is the place.

Puck, c/Duque de Sesto 30 (Mº Goya; Mon–Sat 10am–1.30pm & 4.30–8pm; *Visa*). This is the best – indeed, about the only decent – toyshop in central Madrid.

Casa Yustas, Plaza Mayor 30 (Mº Callao; Mon–Fri 9.45am–1.30pm & 4.30–8pm, Sat 9.45am–1.30pm; no cards). Madrid's oldest hatshop, established in 1894. Pick from traditional designs for men's and women's hats (*sombreros*), caps (*gorras*) and berets (*boinas*).

Books, comics and maps

Casa de Libro, Gran Vía (Mº Gran Vía; ; Mon–Sat 10am–8.30pm; all cards). The city's biggest bookstore: three floors covering just about everything, including a wide range of fiction in English.

Librería Antonio Machado, c/Fernando VI 17 (Mº Alonso Martínez; Mon–Sat 10am–2pm & 5–8pm; all cards). The city's best literary bookshop.

Madrid Cómics, c/Silva 17 (Mº Callao; Mon–Sat 9am–10pm, Sun 11am–8pm; *Visa*). Good for a browse through one of Spain's most popular artforms. There is a happy hour, with 10 percent discount, from 9–10pm.

La Tienda Verde, c/Maudes 23 & 38 (Mº Cuatro Caminos; Mon–Sat 9.30am–2pm & 4.30–8pm; all cards). Trekking and mountain books, guides and survey (*topográfico*) maps.

Turner, c/Genova (Mº Alonso Martínez; Mon–Fri 10am–2pm & 5–8pm, Sat 10am–2pm; all cards). Specializes in English (and French) language books.

Fashion: clothes and shoes

Adolfo Domínguez, c/José Ortega y Gasset 4 and c/Serrano 96 (Mº Serrano; Mon–Sat 10am–2pm & 5–8.30pm; all cards). The classic modern Spanish look – subdued colours, free lines. Domínguez's designs are quite pricey but he has a cheaper *Basico* range. Both branches have men's clothes, women's are only at the Ortega y Gasset branch.

Alpargatería Lobo, c/Toledo 30 (Mº Tirso de Molina; Mon–Fri 9.30am–1.30pm & 5–8.30pm, Sat 9.30am–1.30pm; no cards). This shoeshop stocks *alpargatas* – espadrilles – in just about every imaginable colour.

Ararat, c/Conde Xiquena 10, 11 and 13 (Mº Colón; Mon–Sat 11am–2pm & 5–8.30pm; all cards). A trio of shops with clubby Spanish and foreign designs at reasonably modest prices. Men's clothes are at no. 13, women's at no. 10, both at no. 11.

Berlín, c/Almirante 10 (Mº Colón; Mon–Sat 11am–2pm & 5–8.30pm; all cards). Women's clothes from vanguard European designers.

Blackmarket, c/Colón 3 (Mº Chueca; Mon–Sat 10.30am–2pm & 5–8.30pm; all cards). Adventurous clothes for women.

Camper, c/Gran Vía 54 (Mº Gran Vía; Mon–Sat 10am–2pm & 5–8.30pm; *Visa*). Spain's best shoeshop chain, with covetable designs at modest prices. There are lots of other branches around the city. Men and women.

Carácol Cuadrado, c/Justiniano 6 (Mº Serrano; Mon–Sat 10.30am–2.30pm & 5–8.30pm; *Visa*). Bargain store selling last season's designs from big names, including Sybilla – Spain's trendiest designer. Men and women.

Contra Dos, c/Galileo 78 (Mº Quevedo; Mon–Fri 10am–2pm & 5–8pm; no cards). This is a second-hand clothes shop – a rarity in Madrid – with low prices and good quality designs, both for women and men.

Ekseption, c/Velázquez 28 (Mº Velázquez; Mon–Sat 10.30am–2.30pm & 5–8.30pm; all cards). A dramatic walkway gives onto some of the most *moderno* clothes in Madrid, from Sybilla and Antoni Miró, among others. Expensive. Men and women.

Excrupulus Net, c/Almirante 7 (Mº Chueca; Mon–Sat 11am–2pm & 5–8.30pm; all cards). Groovy shoes from Spanish designers, Muxart and Looky. Men and women.

Josep Font-Luz Díaz, c/Serrano 58 – patio (Mº Serrano; Mon–Sat 10am–2pm & 5–8.30pm; all cards). A beautiful, minimalist shop, selling original and expensive women's designs by this young and *muy moda* Catalan duo. Women only.

Sybilla, c/Jorge Juan 12 (Mº Retiro; Mon–Sat 10am–2pm & 4.30–8.30pm; all cards). Sybilla was Spain's top designer of the 80s – a Vivian Westwood of Madrid, if you will. She remains at the forefront of the scene, and the prices show it. Women only.

Food and drink

Baco – La Boutique del Vino, c/San Bernardo 117 (Mº Quevedo; Mon–Fri 11am–2pm & 5–8pm, Sat 10am–2pm; no cards). A good value range of quality Spanish wines, *cavas*, brandies and even Asturian cider (*sidra*).

Casa Mira, Carrera de San Jerónimo 30 (Mº Sol; daily 10am–2pm & 5–9pm; no cards). An old established *pastelaria*, selling delicious *turron, mazapan, frutas glaseadas*, and the like.

Lafuente, c/Luchana 28 (Mº Bilbao; Mon–Sat 10am–2pm & 5–8.30pm; *Visa*). Wines from Spain and abroad, including lots from Rioja, Ribera del Duero and Galicia, plus *cavas*.

Lhardy, Carrera de San Jerónimo 8 (Mº Sol; Mon–Sat 9.30am–3pm & 5–9pm, Sun 9am–2pm; all cards). This bar and deli is attached to one of Madrid's top restaurants – and a lot more affordable. You can put together wonderful and elaborate picnics (the *croquetas* and *empanadillas* are legendary), assuming you can resist consuming on the spot.

Mallorca, c/Serrano 6 (Mº Serrano; Mon–Sun 9.30am–9pm; all cards). The main branch of Madrid's best deli chain – like *Lhardy*, a pricey but fabulous treasure trove for picnics, or cakes or chocs for presents. All branches have small bars for drinks and canapés.

Mariano Aguado, c/Echegaray 19 (Mº Sevilla; Mon–Sat 9.30am–2pm & 5.30–8.30pm; no cards). Fine selection of Spanish wines and, especially, sherries (*vinos de Jerez*).

Records and CDs

Discos El Corte Inglés, Puerta del Sol (Mº Sol; Mon–Sat 9.30am–9.30pm; all cards). This annexe to the Sol *El Corte Inglés* store has the best general selection of CDs in Madrid – and a bit of vinyl tucked away, too. There is a decent flamenco section upstairs.

Madrid Rock, Gran Vía 25 – underground (Mº Callao; daily 10am–10pm; all cards). A big, slightly chaotic store, good for rock CDs and concert tickets.

Toni Martín, c/Martín de los Heros 18 (Mº Plaza de España; Mon–Sat 10.30am–2pm & 5.30–8.15pm; all cards). Rock CDs and discs, new and secondhand.

Listings

Airlines Most airlines have their offices along the Gran Vía or on c/de la Princesa, its continuation beyond the Plaza de España. Addresses include: *Avianca*, Gran Vía 88(☎205 43 20; Mº Plaza de España); *British Airways*, c/Serrano 60 5° (☎205 43 17; Mº Serrano); *Iberia*, Plaza Canovas del Castillo 4 (☎563 99 66; Mº Banco de España); and *KLM*, Gran Vía 59 (☎247 81 00; Mº Santo Domingo). The *Iberojet* counter at the airport sells discounted seats on scheduled flights if you're prepared to queue up and take the risk of not getting on.

Airport information ☎305 83 43. See p.53 for details of transport to the airport.

American Express Plaza de las Cortes 2 – entrance on Marqués de Cubas (☎322 55 00; Mon–Fri 9am–5.30pm & Sat 9am–noon for mail and transactions; Mº Sevilla).

Banks The main Spanish banks are concentrated on c/Alcalá and Gran Vía. International banks include: *Bank of America*, c/Capitan Haya 1 (☎555 50 00; Mº Lima); *Barclays*, Plaza de Colón 2 (☎410 28 00; Mº Colón); *Citibank*, c/José Ortega y Gassett 29 (☎435 51 90; Mº Nuñez de Balboa); *Lloyds*, c/Serrano 90 (☎276 70 00; Mº Nuñez de Balboa); and *National Westminster*, c/Miguel Angel 21 (☎419 39 56; Mº Rúben Darío).

Bicycle repairs Try *Bicicletas Chapinal*, c/Alcalá 242 (Mº El Carmen; Mon–Fri 10am–1.30pm & 4.30–8pm, Sat 10am–2pm; ☎404 50 12), or *Calmera*, c/Atocha 98 (Mº Antón Martín; Mon–Sat 9.30am–1.30pm & 4.30–8pm; ☎527 75 74).

Bullfights Madrid's main Plaza de Toros, the monumental *Las Ventas* (c/Alcalá 237; Mº Ventas) hosts some of the year's most prestigious events, especially during the June San Isidro festivities. Tickets are available at a couple of stalls on c/Victoria, just south of Sol, or at *Localidades de Galicia* (see "Ticket agencies", below); at any of these you pay around 50 percent more than the printed prices, which are for season tickets sold en bloc. There is a second bullring in the suburb of *Carabanchel* (Avda. Matilde Hernández; Mº Vista Alegre), about 4km to the southwest of the centre.

Buses A rough guide to times and frequencies follows in the "Travel Details", below. Note that companies and services change with great frequency and it's always worth checking schedules with the Turismo.

Car rental Major operators include: *Atesa*, c/Rosario Pino 18; ☎572 01 59; Mº Cuzco); *Avis*, Gran Vía 60 (☎247 20 48; Mº Santo Domingo); *Europcar*, c/Orense 29 (☎555 99 31; Mº Lima); *Hertz*,

Gran Vía 88 (☎542 58 05; Mº Plaza de España); all of these have branches at Barajas airport. *Rent Me*, Plaza de Herradores 6, just off Plaza Mayor (☎559 08 22; Mº Sol), is a good value local company.

Condoms They're sold at every *farmacia*, but Madrid also boasts a specialist condom shop: *La Discreta* at c/Jardines 19 (Mº Gran Vía).

Currency exchange In addition to the banks, branches of *El Corte Inglés* department store all have exchange offices with long hours and highly competitive rates and commissions; the most central is on Puerta del Sol.

Doctors English-speaking doctors are available at the *Anglo-American Medical Centre*, c/Conde de Aranda 1 (☎435 18 23; Mº Retiro).

Embassies include: *Australia*, Paseo de la Castellana 143 (☎579 04 28; Mº Cuzco); *Britain*, c/ Fernando el Santo 16 (☎319 02 00; Mº Alonso Martínez); *Canada*, c/Nuñez de Balboa 35 (☎431 43 00; Mº Nuñez de Balboa); *Ireland*, c/Claudio Coello 73 (☎576 35 00; Mº Serrano); *Netherlands*, Paseo Castellana 178 (☎458 21 00; Mº Cuzco); *New Zealand*, c/o Britain; *Norway*, Paseo Castellana 31 (☎410 68 63; Mº Rúben Darío); *Sweden*, c/Zurbano 27 (☎308 15 35); *USA*, c/Serrano 75 (☎577 40 00; Mº Serrano).

Emergency For an **ambulance** dial ☎734 47 94 or ☎252 32 64 – or get a taxi, which will be quicker, if no paramedics are neccessary; for the **police** dial ☎091 or ☎092.

Football The big teams are **Real Madrid**, who, for the past two seasons have lost the championship on the last day of the season to Barcelona, and **Atlético Madrid**. Tickets can be bought in advance (and usually on the day) at the stadium for most matches, though derbies between Real and Atlético, or visits to either by Barcelona, are always sell-outs. Real and the Spanish national team play at the 90,000-seat *Estadio Bernabeu* in the north of the city (bus #5 or #M12 from the centre); Atlético's home is the more modest, 70,000-seat *Estadio Vicente Calderón* in the southwest (bus #34, #35, or #23 from downtown). See also "Ticket agencies", below.

Fitness/gyms If you want to work out, try the *Holiday Gym* in the *Hotel Husa*, c/Princesa 40(☎564 15 50; Mº Plaza de España), or *Gimnasio Los Piramides*, c/del Limón 20 (☎547 53 36; Mº Plaza de España). There are council-sponsored **exercise tracks** in El Retiro, the Casa de Campo and at the Complutense University campus.

Hospitals The most central are: *El Clínico*, Plaza de Cristo Rey (☎544 15 00; Mº Moncloa); *Hospital Gregorio Marañon*, c/Dr. Esquerdo 46 (☎734 26 00; Mº O'Donnell); and *Hospital de la Princesa*, c/ Diego de León 62 (☎402 80 00; Mº Diego de León).

Language courses Madrid has numerous language schools, offering intensive courses in Spanish language (and culture). Two excellent choices are *Tandem*, c/Luís Vélez de Guevara 8 (☎369 09 32), and *International House*, c/Zurbano 8 (☎310 13 14).

Laundry Central *lavanderías* include: c/Barco 26 (Mº Gran Vía); c/Donoso Cortés 17 (Mº Quevedo); c/Hermosilla 121 (Mº Goya); c/Palma 2 (Mº Tribunal).

Left luggage If you want to leave your bags there are *consignas* at the *Estación Sur*, *Auto-Res* and *Continental Auto* bus stations; at the airport bus terminal beneath Plaza Colón; and lockers at Atocha and Chamartín train stations.

Pharmacies *Farmácias* are distinguished by a green cross; each district has a rota with one staying open through the night – for details ☎098 or check the notice on the door of your nearest pharmacy or the listings magazines. Madrid also has quite a number of traditional **herbalists**, best known of which is *Maurice Mességue*, c/Goya 64 (Mº Goya; Mon–Fri 10am–2pm & 5–8pm, Sat 10am–2pm).

Post office The main one is the *Palacio de Comunicaciones* in the Plaza de las Cibeles (Mon–Fri 9am–10pm, Sat 9am–2pm, Sun 10am–1pm for stamps and telegrams; Mon–Fri 9am–8pm, Sat 9am–2pm for *Lista de Correos* – poste restante). Branch offices, for example on c/Cruz Verde on the edge of Malasaña, are open Mon–Sat 9am–2pm.

Swimming pools and aquaparks The *Piscina Canal Isabel II*, Plaza Juan Zorrila – entrance on Avda. de Filipinas (daily 8am–8pm; Mº Rios Rosas), is a large and well-maintained outdoor swimming pool, and the best central option. Alternatively, try the open-air *piscina* in the Casa de Campo (daily 8am–8pm; Mº El Lago); this is an older pool and best (or at least, cleanest) earlier in the day. Both these pools have café-bars attached. There are also a number of aquaparks around Madrid. The closest – a 20-minute taxi ride from the centre, across the Puente de Segovia – is the *Aquapalace*, Paseo de la Ermita del Santo 48, which at night becomes an extension of the *Aqualung Universal* disco; it is open all year.

Telephones International calls can be made from any phone box or from any *telefónica*. The main *telefónica* at Gran Vía 28 (Mº Gran Vía) is open 24 hours.

Thefts If you've had something stolen ☎900 100 333 (English spoken).

Ticket agency *Localidades Galicia*, Plaza del Carmen 1 (☎431 37 32/☎531 91 31; Mº Sol) sells tickets for football games, bullfights, theatres and concerts.

Trains Information ☎563 02 02; reservations ☎562 33 33. Tickets can be bought at the individual stations (see "Travel Details", following, for services), or at the city centre *RENFE* office, c/de Alcalá 44 (Mon–Fri 8am–2.30pm & 4–7pm, Sat 8am–1.30pm; Mº Banco de España).

Travel agencies *Víajes Zeppelin*, Plaza Santo Domingo 2 (☎547 79 03), are English-speaking, very efficient and offer some excellent deals on flights and holidays. *Nuevas Fronteras* (c/Luisa Fernanda 2; Mº Ventura Rodríguez; ☎542 39 90; and in the Torre de Madrid, Plaza de España, ☎247 42 00) can be good for flights, too, as can the student agency, *TIVE* (Fernando el Católico 88; Mº Quevedo; ☎401 90 11). Many other travel agents are concentrated on and around the Gran Vía.

Women's groups The best place to make contact is Madrid's feminist bookshop, the *Librería de Mujeres*, c/San Cristóbal 17 (☎521 70 43), just east of Plaza Mayor.

travel details

Trains

All Madrid trains run through one or more of the three stations below. **Chamartín**, in the north, has the most services and includes through trains to **Atocha**. If you arrive at (or are leaving from) Chamartín, you can always use a *cercanía* train to/from Atocha. Some through trains also stop at the Recoletos and Nuevos Ministerios stations.

Note that the new **high-speed AVE trains** to Córdoba and Sevilla run from Atocha. These must be booked in advance, either in person at Atocha, or the RENFE office at c/Alcalá 44 Mon–Fri 9.30am–8pm, or by phone (☎534 05 05).

From Atocha Station (Mº Atocha): Algeciras (1 daily; 11hr); Almería (2 daily; 8–11hr); Badajoz via Ciudad Real (3 daily; 7–10 hr); Cáceres (5 daily; 4–6hr); Cádiz (3 daily; 8–11hr); Córdoba (6 daily; 5–7hr; *AVE* 2hr); Cuenca (8 daily; 5hr); Granada (2 daily; 7–10hr); Jaén (3 daily; 6hr); Lisbon (5 daily; 13hr); Málaga (2 daily; 7–9hr); Porto (5 daily; 11hr); Segovia via Chamartín (9 daily; 2–3hr); Sevilla (12 daily; 6–9hr; *AVE* 2hr30); Valencia (8 daily; 8hr). Plus most destinations in the south and west.

From Chamartín (Mº Chamartín): Alicante (4 daily; 9hr); Barcelona via Tarragona (4 daily; 10–12hr); Bilbao (3 daily; 7–8hr); Burgos (14 daily; 4hr); Caceres (1 daily; 5hr); Pamplona (1 daily; 6hr); Paris (8 daily; 14hr); San Sebastián (14 daily; 8hr); Santander (3 daily; 8–10hr); Sevilla (8 daily; 8hr); Zaragoza (4 daily; 5–7hr). Plus most other destinations in the east and northeast.

From Príncipe Pío (Mº Norte): Astorga (2 daily; 5hr 30min); El Ferrol (2 daily; 12hr); La Coruña (2 daily; 11hr); León (5 daily; 4–6hr); Lugo (2 daily; 10hr); Oviedo (3 daily; 7–9hr); Pontevedra (2 daily; 9–11hr); Salamanca via Ávila (4 daily; 3hr 30min–4hr), Santiago (2 daily; 9hr); Vigo (2 daily; 8–10hr); Zamora/Orense via Ávila (4 daily; 6–8hr); and all other points in the northwest.

Buses

A bewildering number of companies operate buses from (and into) Madrid, each from their own garage or terminus. Many of the services, however, run through the **Estación Sur de Autobuses** (☎468 45 11), to the south of Atocha, and just three stops from Mº Sol on the yellow #3 metro line.

Estación Sur de Autobuses (c/Canarias 17; Mº Palos de la Frontera): Albacete (3 daily; 4hr); Alicante (3 daily; 6hr); Barcelona (4 daily; 5hr); Ciudad Real (4 daily; 4hr); Córdoba (1 daily; 8hr); Gijón (3 daily; 7hr); Granada (1 daily; 8hr); Jaén (3 daily; 6hr); León (2 daily; 5hr 30min); Málaga (1 daily; 8hr); Sevilla (1 daily; 10hr); Teruel (4 daily; 5hr 30min); Toledo (24 daily; 1hr 30min); Zaragoza (4 daily; 10hr); and international services to France and Portugal. Additional services to Córdoba are operated by *Sepulcrano*, 300m west of the Sur bus station, at c/Palos de la Frontera 16.

Auto-Res (Fernández Shaw 1; Mº Conde Casal): Ávila (3 daily; 1hr 30min); Badajoz (7 daily; 6hr); Cáceres (8 daily; 4–5hr); Cuenca (6 daily; 3hr);

Mérida (7 daily; 5hr); Palencia (4 daily; 3hr 30min); Salamanca (12 daily; 2hr 30min–3hr 30min); Trujillo (7 daily; 4–5hr); Valencia (14 daily; 5–6hr); Valladolid (12 daily; 2hr 30min); Zamora (5 daily; 4hr).

Continental Auto (c/Alenza 20; Mº Ríos Rosas) to Aranda (5 daily; 3hr); Bilbao (4 daily; 7hr); Burgos (4 daily; 4hr), El Burgo de Osma (2 daily; 4hr); Guadalajara (3 daily; 1hr 30min); Logroño (2

daily; 5hr 30min); Pamplona (2 daily; 6hr); San Sebastián (3 daily; 8hr), Santander (2 daily; 7hr); Soria (6 daily; 3–4hr).

La Sepulvedana (Paseo de la Florida 11, Mº Norte) to Ávila (3 daily; 2hr); Segovia (15 daily; 1hr 30min); and other points in Old Castile.

Herranz (c/Isaac Peral 10, Mº Moncloa): to El Escorial (hourly; 1hr), continuing to El Valle de los Caídos.

CHAPTER TWO

AROUND MADRID

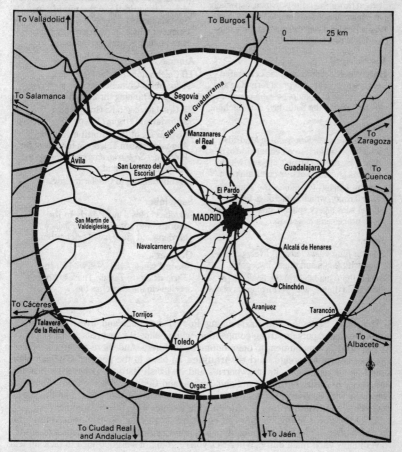

The lack of historic monuments in Madrid is more than compensated for by the region around the capital. Within a radius of 100km – and within an hour's travel by bus or train – are some of the greatest cities of Spain. Above all, there is **Toledo**, which preceded Madrid as the Spanish capital. Immortalized by El Greco, who lived and worked there for most of his later career, the city is a living museum to the many cultures – Visigothic, Moorish, Jewish and Christian – which have shaped the destiny of Spain. If you have time for just one trip from Madrid, there is really no other choice.

FIESTAS

February

Second weekend *Santa Agueda* women's festival in Segovia, when women take over city administration and parade and celebrate in traditional costume. Occurs to an extent throughout the province, especially in Zamarramala just outside the city.

Week before Lent *Carnival* is the excuse for lively fiestas all over the place.

March/April

Holy Week *Semana Santa* is celebrated everywhere, but with great formality and processions in Toledo, passion plays (especially on the Saturday) in Chinchón.

May

15 The *Fiestas de San Isidro* in Madrid – which spread for a week either side of this date – are among Spain's biggest. Music, parades and loads of free entertainment.

Corpus Christi (variable – the Thursday after Trinity, which sometimes falls in June) sees a very solemn, costumed religious procession in Toledo.

June

24 *San Juan y San Pablo*. A lively procession with floats and music in Segovia.

30 In Hita (Guadalajara) the fiesta has a medieval theme, with performances of old theatre, feasts, dances, and sporting events including falconry and bull-lancing.

July

Both Segovia and Ávila have big festivals around the **middle of the month:** in Segovia there's a week-long festival of chamber music, in Ávila a rowdy affair with bullfights, music and dances.

August

15 Celebrations for the *Virgen de la Asunción* in Chinchón include an *encierro*, with bulls running through the street.

25 Good fiestas in La Granja (near Segovia) and Orgaz (Toledo).

Third week of the month marks the August fiestas in Toledo, in honour of the *Virgen del Sagrario*; amazing fireworks on the final weekend.

28 Bull running in Cuéllar (Segovia).

September

Aranjuez holds a fiesta **early in the month**, with concerts in the palace gardens and more usual celebration.

October

Second week Ávila goes wild for the *Feria de Santa Teresa*. There are organ recitals in the churches too.

That said, **Segovia**, with its stunning Roman aqueduct and irresistible, Disney-prototype castle, puts up strong competition, while Felipe II's vast palace-mausoleum of **El Escorial** is a monument to out-monument all others. And there are smaller places too, less known to foreign tourists: **Aranjuez**, an oasis in the parched Castilian plain, famed for its asparagus, its strawberries and its lavish Baroque palace; the beautiful walled city of **Ávila**, birthplace of Saint Teresa; and Cervantes' home town, **Alcalá de Henares**, with its sixteenth-century university. For walkers, too, trails amid the sierras of **Gredos** and **Guadarrama** provide enticing escapes from the midsummer heat.

All of the towns in this chapter can be visited as an easy day trip from Madrid, but they also offer interesting jumping-off points into Castile and beyond; details of onward travel follow each main entry. Wherever you're going, it's a good idea to pick up leaflets in advance from one of the tourist offices in Madrid.

Toledo

By anyone's reckoning **TOLEDO** is one of the greatest cities in Spain, and for sheer concentration of attractions it ranks with anywhere in Europe. It's not a big place – the harsh craggy surroundings allow no room for expansion – but at every twist of the tangled streets there's a new source of wonder. Capital of medieval Spain until 1560, it remains the seat of the Catholic Primate and a city redolent of past glories. The **setting** has much to do with it. In a landscape of abrasive desolation, Toledo sits on a rocky mound isolated on three sides by a looping gorge of the Río Tajo (Tagus). Every available inch of this outcrop has been built upon: houses, synagogues, churches and mosques are heaped upon one another in a haphazard spiral which the cobbled lanes infiltrate as best they can.

Despite encroaching modernity, the extraordinary number of day trippers and intense summer heat, Toledo should be one of the most extravagant of Spanish experiences. To see it at its best, however, you'll need to stay at least a night: a daytrip can't possibly do justice, and even two will leave you hard pressed to see everything. And more importantly, in the evening, with the crowds gone and the skyline illuminated by floodlights, Toledo is a different city entirely.

Toledo also hosts one of the most extravagant celebrations of **Corpus Christi** in the country, with street processions and all the works. Other local festivals take place on May 25 and August 15 and 20.

Some history

Toledo was known to the Romans, who captured it in 193 BC, as *Toletum*, a small but well-defended town. Taken by the Visigoths, who made it their capital, it was already an important cultural and trading centre by the time the Moors arrived in 712. The period which followed, with Mozarabic (Arabized) Christians, Jews and Moors living together in relative equality, was one of rapid growth and prosperity and Toledo became the most important northern outpost of the Muslim emirates. Though there are few physical remains of this period, except the miniature mosque of **El Cristo de la Luz**, the long domination has left a clear mark on the atmosphere and shape of the whole city.

When the Christian king Alfonso VI "reconquered" the town in 1085, with the assistance of El Cid, Moorish influence scarcely weakened. Although Toledo became capital of Castile and the base for campaigns against the Moors in the south, the city itself was a haven of cultural tolerance. Not only was there a school of translators revealing the scientific and philosophical achievements of the East, but Arab craftsmen and techniques remained responsible for many of the finest buildings of the period: look, for example, at the churches of **San Román** or **Santiago del Arrabal** or at any of the old **city gates**.

At the same time Jewish culture remained powerful. There were, at one time, at least seven **synagogues** – of which two, **Santa María la Blanca** and **El Tránsito**, survive – and Jews occupied many positions of power. The most famous was Samuel Levi, treasurer and right-hand man of Pedro the Cruel until the king lived up to his name by murdering him and stealing his wealth. From this period, too, dates the most important purely Christian monument, Toledo's awesome **cathedral**.

This golden age ended abruptly in the sixteenth century with the transfer of the capital to Madrid, following hard on the heels of the Inquisition's mass expulsion of Jews and Moors. The city played little part in subsequent Spanish history until the Civil War (see the entry on the **Alcázar**) and it remains, despite the droves of tourists, essentially the medieval city so often painted by El Greco. Sadly, however, the Tajo, the city's old lifeblood, is now highly polluted, and its waters greatly depleted by industry and agriculture.

Arrival and accommodation

Orientation is pretty straightforward in Toledo, with the compact old city looped by the Tajo, and the new quarters across the bridges. **Getting to the city**, too, is easy, with eight direct trains a day from Madrid Atocha (6am–10pm), plus buses every half-hour (6.30am–10pm); either way the journey takes around seventy-five minutes.

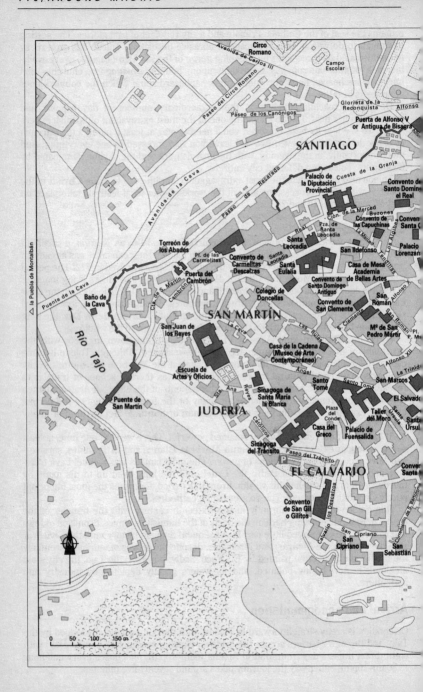

△ Madrid △ Aranjuez

△ Aranjuez

Perala

Río Llano

Bus Station

Puente de Azarquiel

La Carrera

Plaza Solar de la Antequeruela

ueva

ga

Pza. de la Virgen

LA ANTEQUERUELA

go

al

Pra. de la Antequeruela

Pza. de los Alfares

Azacanas

Train Station

Paseo de la Rosa

P

Gerardo

Lobo

Puerta del Sol

Puerta de los Alarcones

Carretas

l

a de rdón

Mezquita del Cristo de la Luz

Cuesta de Arce

Paseo del Miradero

Castillo San Servando (Youth Hostel)

Convento de San Pablo & convento de la Purísima Concepción

Puerta Rey Wamba

Convento de Santa Fe

Dos Codos

Los Alfileritos

La Sillería

Puente & puerta de Alcántara

Palacios de Galiana y huerta del Rey

Acueducto Romano

Cjón. de Menores

te

La Plata

Hospital y Museo de Santa Cruz

Plaza de Zocodover

Santa Fe

Pl. de la Concepción

Cervantes

Paseo del Carmen

o de tines as

n Ginés

Comercio

Pza. de la Magdalena

Alféreces Provisionales

Cervantes

Mezquita de Tornerías

Corral de San Diego

El Alcázar

Hombre de Palo

Arco del Palto

Plaza Mayor

Posada de la Hermandad

Pte. Nuevo de Alcántara

Puerta de Doce Cantos

La Catedral

Cardenal Cisneros

Pl. del Seco

Cabestreros

Río Tajo

untamiento

Vicario

Barco

Pl. de S. Justo

LA CANDELARIA

spo Ayo María

Pobo

San Justo

Cta. de S. Justo

Paseo de la Candelaria

Carretera de Circunvalación

San drés

San Pablo

Bldg. del Barco

Amargo

Convento de San Juan de la Penitencia

Paseo de la Candelaria

Piedrabota

San Lucas

Sebastián

Casa del Diamantista

TOLEDO

Toledo's **train station**, a marvellous mock-Mudéjar creation, is some way out on the Paseo de la Rosa, a beautiful twenty-minute walk – take the left-hand fork off the dual carriageway and cross the Puente de Alcántara – or a bus ride (#5 or #6) to the heart of town. The new **bus station** is on Avenida de Castilla la Mancha in the modern, lower part of the city; buses run frequently to Zocódover, though if you take shortcuts through the barrio at the bottom of the hill just inside the walls, it's a mere ten minutes to the Puerta de Bisagra.

If you're **driving** – and from Madrid there's little point if you're not going on – beware that parking in Toledo is a problem: the only 24-hour car park is the one at Miradero, below the Plaza de Zocódover, and it's expensive (1450ptas per day). If your hotel hasn't got its own parking facilities then leave your vehicle out of harm's way below the historic centre — the city tow truck is very active.

Information

Toledo's main **Turismo** is outside the city walls between the Puerta de Bisagra and the Hospital de Tavera (Mon–Fri 9am–2pm & 4–6pm; Sat 9am–3pm & 4–7pm; Sun 9am–3pm; ☎925/220843); it has full lists of places to stay, maps and a useful information board outside when it's closed.

There's also a smaller but more central branch office in the Plaza de Zocódover (Mon–Sat 10am–6pm, Sun 10am–3pm; ☎925/221400).

Accommodation

Booking a **room** in advance is important, especially at the weekend, or in summer, or both. If you're on a limited budget, hotel choice is complemented by private rooms, but you'll need to arrive early in the day. At slow times of the year guides hover in the Zocódover, pouncing on those arriving with baggage and offering to find a room for a small fee. Since places are scattered all over town, and the guides will know which have space, this can save time and trouble.

In summer, there are sometimes rooms available in **university** accommodation; ask at the *Oficina de Información Juvenil* in c/Trinidad, by the cathedral.

BUDGET OPTIONS

Hostal Las Armas, c/Armas 7 (☎925/221668). Tiny rooms in an old house. Easy to find – right next to Plaza de Zocódover – but open April to October only. ③.

Fonda La Belviseña, Cuesta del Can 7 (☎925/220067). South of the Alcázar; basic but as cheap as they come. ①.

Pensión Descalzos, c/Descalzos 32 (☎925/222888). Near El Greco's house and other major sights. A pricey *pensión* but with a few cheaper, bath-less rooms. ②–④.

Posada del Estudiante, Callejón de San Pedro 2 (☎925/214734). As the name suggests, a student residence, but great value and well worth trying in the summer university holidays. Well sited, directly behind the cathedral. ②.

Residencia Juvenil San Servando (☎925/224554). Toledo's youth hostel is on the outskirts of town in a wing of the fourteenth-century Castillo San Servando; a YHA card is generally required, but you might be able to talk your way in without one. It's a good option, with a free swimming pool and decent value meals. In summer, however, you need to book several days ahead.

ACCOMMODATION PRICE SYMBOLS

The symbols used in our hotel listings denote the following price ranges:

① Under 2000ptas	③ 3000–4500ptas	⑤ 7500–12,500ptas
② 2000–3000ptas	④ 4500–7500ptas	⑥ Over12,500ptas

See p.30 for more details.

Hostal-Residencia Labrador, c/Juan Labrador 16 (☎925/222620). This *hostal* is a bit dark and dingy but it has more rooms than most, so is worth a call. ②.

Pensión Lumbreras, c/Juan Labrador 9 (☎925/221571). Recently renovated, simple rooms; the top floor ones have fine rooftop views, although the water supply can be a little erratic. ②.

Pensión Madrid, c/Marqués de Mendigorría 7 (☎925/221114). Comfortable but located a bit of a way from the old town. ③.

Fonda María Soledad, c/Soledad 1 (☎925/223287). Basic rooms; located down an alley alongside the *Hotel Alfonso VI*. ①.

Fonda Segovia, c/Recoletos 2 (☎925/221124). Inexpensive rooms with washbasins only – and you pay extra for showers. ①.

Pensión Virgen de la Estrella, c/Real del Arrabal 18 (☎925/211234). A good option, handily placed on the main road up to the old town, near Puerta de Bisagra; ask at the bar of the same name across the road. ③.

HOTELS

Hotel Alfonso VI, c/General Moscardó 2 (☎925/222600). A pleasant old hotel behind the Alcázar; rooms at the rear have great sunny balconies. ⑤.

Hotel Carlos V, c/Trastamara 1 (☎925/222100). Comfortable hotel, close to the Alcázar and with some fine views, but very noisy at weekends due to the nearby disco. ⑤.

Hotel Imperio, c/Cadenas 7 (☎925/227650). Handy location near Plaza de Zocódover. ④.

Hotel Maravilla, c/Barrio Rey 7 (☎925/223304). Another prime location just off Plaza de Zocódover. ④.

Hotel Martín, c/Covachuelas 12 (☎925/221733). Excellent new mid-price hotel, located in a residential area close to the bus station. ④.

Parador Conde de Orgaz, Cerro del Emperador (☎925/221850). Superb views of the city from the terrace of Toledo's top hotel. ⑥.

Hotel Santa Isabel, c/Santa Isabel 24 (☎925/253136). Best of the mid-range hotels, right in the centre; garage space available. ④.

Hotel Sol, c/Azacanes 15 (☎925/213650). Good value, just off the main road up to the Plaza de Zocódover before the Puerta del Sol. ④.

CAMPING

Camping El Greco (☎925/220090; open all year). This is much the best campsite and only a ten-minute walk from the Puerta de Bisagra: cross the Puente de la Cava towards Puebla de Montalbán, then follow the signs. There are great views of the city from here, and a bar to enjoy them from.

Camping Circo Romano, Avda. Carlos III 19 (☎925/220442; open all year). A rundown site, worth considering only if the *El Greco* is full.

The city

You're bound to get lost in Toledo, but that's part of the charm: the city, above all other towns in Spain, is a place to wander and absorb. It's a veritable museum of art and architecture and you shouldn't leave without seeing at least the El Grecos, the cathedral, the synagogues and Alcázar, but give it all time . . . stumble upon things and don't overdose only on "sights". Enter any inviting doorway and you may find stunning patios, rooms and ceilings, often of Mudéjar workmanship, which can be as rewarding as anything listed in this or any other guidebook.

The cathedral

In a country so overflowing with massive religious institutions, the chief **Cathedral** has to be something special – and it is. A robust Gothic construction which took over 250 years (1227–1493) to complete, it has a richness of internal decoration in almost every conceivable style, with masterpieces of the Gothic, Renaissance and Baroque periods. The exterior is best appreciated from outside the city, where the 100-metre spire and the weighty buttressing can be seen to advantage. From the street it's less impressive, so hemmed in by surrounding houses that you can't really sense the scale or grandeur of the whole.

There are eight doorways, but the main entrance is through the **Puerta de Mollete** beside the main tower, which leads into the **cloister**. Here tickets are sold for the various chapels, chapter houses and treasuries which require them. The main body of the cathedral is closed from 1–3.30pm; the parts which need tickets – 350ptas – can be visited from 10.30am–1pm and 3.30–7pm, winter 3.30–6pm. On Sunday mornings the *coro* cannot be visited, and on Monday the New Museums are closed.

THE CORO AND CAPILLA MAYOR

Inside the cathedral, the central nave is divided from four aisles by a series of clustered pillars supporting the vaults, 88 in all, the aisles continuing around behind the main altar to form an apse. There is magnificent **stained glass** throughout, mostly dating from the fifteenth and sixteenth centuries, particularly beautiful in two rose windows above the north and south doors. Beside the south door (*Puerta de los Leones*) is a huge, ancient **fresco of Saint Christopher**.

At the physical heart of the church, blocking the nave, is the **Coro** (Choir), itself a panoply of sculpture. The carved wooden stalls are in two tiers. The lower level, by Rodrigo Alemán, depicts the conquest of Granada, with each seat showing a different village being taken by the Christians. The portraits of Old Testament characters on the stalls above were done in the following century, on the north side by Philippe Vigarni and on the south by Alonso Berruguete, whose superior technique is evident. He also carved the large **Transfiguration** here from a single block of alabaster. The *reja* (grille) which encloses the *coro* is said to be plated with gold, but it was covered in iron to disguise its value from Napoleon's troops and has since proved impossible to renovate.

The **Capilla Mayor** stands directly opposite. Its gargantuan altarpiece, stretching clear to the roof, is one of the triumphs of Gothic art, overflowing with intricate detail and fanciful embellishments. It contains a synopsis of the entire New Testament, culminating in a Calvary at the summit. On either side are the tombs of the mighty, including (on the left) those of kings Alfonso VII and Sancho III and the powerful Cardinal Mendoza and (on the right) that of Sancho II.

Directly behind the main altar is an extraordinary piece of fantasy – the Baroque **Transparente**. Wonderfully and wildly extravagant, with its marble cherubs sitting on fluffy marble clouds, it's especially magnificent when the sun reaches through the hole punched in the roof for that purpose. You'll notice a cardinal's hat hanging from the vaulting just in front of this. Spanish primates are buried where they choose, with the epitaph they choose, and with their hat hanging above them, where it stays until it rots. One of them chose to be buried here, and there are other pieces of headgear dotted around the cathedral.

CHAPELS AND TREASURES

There are well over twenty **chapels** around the walls, all of which are of some interest. Many of them house fine tombs, particularly the **Capilla de Santiago**, the octagonal **Capilla de San Idelfonso** and the gilded **Capilla de los Reyes**.

In the **Capilla Mozárabe** mass is still celebrated daily according to the ancient Visigothic rites. When the church tried to ban the old ritual in 1086 the people of Toledo were outraged. The dispute was put to a combat, which the Mozárabe champion won, but the church demanded further proof: trial by fire. The Roman prayer book was blown to safety, while the Mozárabe version remained, unburned, in the flames. Both sides claimed victory, and in the end the two rituals were allowed to coexist. If you want to attend mass, be there at 9.30am and look out for the priest – you may well be the only celebrant.

CATEDRAL DE TOLEDO

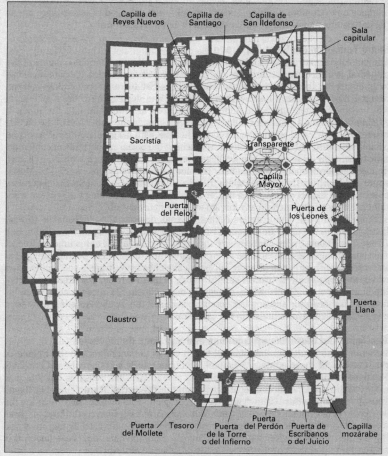

Capilla de Reyes Nuevos
Capilla de Santiago
Capilla de San Ildefonso
Sala capitular
Sacristía
Transparente
Capilla Mayor
Puerta del Reloj
Puerta de los Leones
Coro
Puerta Llana
Claustro
Puerta del Mollete
Tesoro
Puerta de la Torre o del Infierno
Puerta del Perdón
Puerta de Escribanos o del Juicio
Capilla mozárabe

The **Capilla de San Juan** houses the riches of the cathedral **Treasury**, above all a solid silver *custodia* (repository for eucharist wafers) ten-foot high and weighing over 200 kilos. It was made by German-born silversmith Enrique de Arfe in the sixteenth century, and gilded seventy years later. An even more impressive accumulation of wealth is displayed in the **Sacristía**, where paintings include a *Disrobing of Christ* and portraits of the Apostles by El Greco, Velázquez's portrait of Cardinal Borja and Goya's *Christ Taken by the Soldiers*.

In the adjoining rooms, the so-called **New Museums** house works of art that were previously locked away or poorly displayed. Among them are paintings by Caravaggio, Gerard David and Morales, and El Greco's most important piece of sculpture (only a few pieces survive), a polychromed wooden group of San Ildefonso and the Virgin. The **Sala Capitular** (Chapter House) has a magnificent sixteenth-century *artesonado* ceiling and portraits of all Spain's archbishops to the present day.

Lastly, you might try and gain access to the cathedral's **tower**, which has an entrance on c/Hombre de Palo. If you're in luck – you will need to ask as there are no regular visiting hours – the rewards are superb views across the city.

Santo Tomé and the Casa del Greco

The outstanding attraction of Toledo, outshining even the multifarious delights of the cathedral, is El Greco's masterpiece, *The Burial of the Count of Orgaz*. It's housed, alone, in an annexe to the church of **Santo Tomé** (Tues–Sat 10am–1.45pm & 3.30–6.45pm, winter 3.30–5.45pm, Sun 10am–1.45pm; 100ptas) and depicts the count's funeral, at which Saint Stephen and Saint Augustine appeared to lower him into the tomb. It combines El Greco's genius for the mystic, exemplified in the upper half of the picture where the count's soul is being received into heaven, with his great powers as a portrait painter and master of colour. The figures watching the burial are portraits of contemporaries, including (it is said) Lope de Vega, Cervantes and El Greco himself. Felipe II, though still alive when it was painted, is among the heavenly onlookers. Jan Morris wrote of this picture that "it epitomises the alliance between God and the Spanish ruling classes (who) expect miracles as a matter of policy, and are watching the saints at work rather as they might watch . . . any foreign expert sent to do a job".

From Santo Tomé the c/de los Amarillos leads down to the old **Judería** (Jewish quarter) and to the **Casa del Greco** (Tues–Sat 10am–2pm & 4–7pm, winter 6pm, Sun 10am–2pm; 200ptas), the house where the artist lived for much of his time in Toledo. The apartments themselves have been restored in a completely bogus fashion but there are some interesting pictures, including sketches by Velázquez and, in the room which was supposedly El Greco's studio, a study of his own hand. The **museum** part of the house is far more worthwhile, displaying many classic El Grecos, among them his famous *View of Toledo* and another complete series of the Twelve Apostles, done later and subtly different from the set in the cathedral.

The Taller del Moro, the synagogues and San Juan de los Reyes

Between Santo Tomé and the Casa del Greco you pass the entrance to the **Palace of the Counts of Fuensalida**, a beautiful fifteenth-century mansion where Carlos V's Portuguese wife Isabel died. You used to be able to visit her treasures but it is now closed to the public. A garden separates it from the **Taller del Moro** (Tues–Sat 10am–2pm & 4–6.30pm, Sun 10am–2pm; 100ptas. A joint ticket which also includes the Museo de Arte Contemporaneo and the Museo de Arte Visigótico costs 150ptas), three fourteenth-century rooms of a Mudéjar palace which were later used by masons working on the cathedral, with magnificent Mudéjar decoration and doorways intact. It is approached through its own entrance in the c/Taller de Moro.

Almost next door to the El Greco house, on c/Reyes Católicos, is the synagogue of **El Tránsito**, built along Moorish lines by Samuel Levi in 1366. It became a church after the expulsion of the Jews, but is being restored to its original form. The interior is a simple galleried hall, brilliantly decorated with polychromed stucco-work and superb filigree windows. Hebrew inscriptions praising God, King Pedro and Samuel Levi surround the walls. Nowadays it houses a small **Sephardic Museum** (Tues–Sat 10am–1.45pm & 4–5.45pm, Sun 10am–1.45pm), tracing the distinct traditions and development of Jewish culture in Spain. During restoration, however, there are restrictions on the number of visitors allowed in at any one time, and the museum may even be closed temporarily though admission is free until works are completed.

The only other surviving synagogue – **Santa María la Blanca** (10am–2pm & 3.30–7pm, winter 6pm; 100ptas) – is a short way down the same street. Like El Tránsito, which it predates by over a century, it has been both church and synagogue, though it looks more like a mosque. Four rows of octagonal pillars each support seven horseshoe arches, all of them with elaborate and individual designs moulded in plaster,

EL GRECO – AND A VIEW OF TOLEDO

Even if you've never seen Toledo – and even if you've no idea what to expect – there's an uncanny familiarity about your first view of it, with the Alcázar and the cathedral spire towering above the tawny mass of the town. This is due to **El Greco**, whose constant depiction of the city (as background, even, for the Crucifixion) seems to have stuck, albeit unwittingly, somewhere in everyone's consciousness. Domenico Theotocopoulos, "the Greek", was born in Crete in 1541 and settled in Toledo in about 1577 after failing to get work on the decoration of the Escorial. His paintings – the most individual, most intensely spiritual visions of all Spanish art – are extraordinary; however often he repeats the same subject, they always offer some surprise or insight.

For thrilling, uncluttered **views** of Toledo, walk along the Carretera de Circunvalación which runs along the south bank of the Tajo – the opposite bank from the city – from one of the medieval fortified bridges to the other. This takes about an hour, and will show to advantage the skyline so familiar from various El Grecos (though several other bridges have disappeared in the intervening centuries). For the panorama most resembling *Storm Over Toledo*, you have to climb the hill above the westerly bridge of San Martín.

Midway between the bridges, there is access to a little landing stage, by an old chain ferry, where for most of the year a **boatman** shuttles passengers across the river. This is an informal service and the boatman responds to waves or shouts from one or other bank; you tip whatever you feel is appropriate.

while it has preserved from its time as a church a fine sixteenth-century *retablo*. The whole effect is quite stunning, accentuated by a deep red floor tiled with decorative *azulejos*.

Continuing down c/Reyes Católicos, you come to the superb church of **San Juan de los Reyes** (10am–1.45pm & 3.30–7pm; winter 3.30–6pm; 100ptas), its exterior bizarrely festooned with the chains worn by Christian prisoners from Granada released on the reconquest of their city. It was originally a Franciscan convent founded by the "Catholic Kings", Fernando and Isabella, to celebrate their victory at the Battle of Toro and in which, until the fall of Granada, they had planned to be buried. Designed by Juan Gras in the decorative late-Gothic style known as Isabelline (after the queen), its double-storeyed cloister is quite outstanding: the upper floor has an elaborate Mudéjar ceiling, and the crests of Castile and Aragón, seven arrows and a yoke, are carved everywhere in assertion of the new unity brought by the royal marriage. This theme is continued in the airy church where imperious eagles support the royal shields.

From the Puerta del Cambrón to Santo Cristo de la Luz

If you leave the city by the **Puerta del Cambrón** you can follow the Paseo de Recaredo, which runs alongside a stretch of Moorish walls to the **Hospital de Tavera** (10.30am–1.30pm & 3.30–6pm; 300ptas museum, 200ptas church). This, a Renaissance palace with beautiful twin patios, houses the private collection of the Duchess of Lerma. The gloomy interior is a reconstruction of a sixteenth-century mansion scattered with fine paintings, including a *Day of Judgement* by Bassano; the portrait of Carlos V by Titian is a copy of the original in the Prado. The hospital's archives are kept here too: thousands of densely hand-written pages chronicling the illnesses treated. The museum contains several works by El Greco and Ribera's gruesome portrait of a freak "bearded woman". Also here is the death mask of Cardinal Tavera, the hospital's founder, and in the church of the hospital is his ornate marble tomb – the last work of Alonso Berruguete.

Toledo's main gate, the **Puerta Nueva de Bisagra**, is marooned in a constant swirl of traffic, but it still seems a formidable obstacle for any invader to overcome. Its patterned tile roofs bear the coat of arms of Carlos V. Alongside is the gateway that it replaced, the ninth-century Moorish portal through which Alfonso VI and El Cid led their triumphant armies in 1085. The main road bears to the left, but on foot you can climb towards the centre of town by a series of stepped alleyways, after a glance at the intriguing exterior of the Mudéjar church of **Santiago del Arrabal**.

The Cuesta del Cristo de la Luz leads up here past the tiny mosque of **Santo Cristo de la Luz**. Built by Musa Ibn Ali in the tenth century on the foundations of a Visigothic church, this is one of the oldest Moorish monuments surviving anywhere in Spain. Only the nave, however, with its nine different cupolas, is the original Arab construction; the apse was added when the building was converted into a church, and is claimed to be the first product of the Mudéjar style. The head of a Visigoth peering out from one of the capitals is proof, if any were needed, of Moorish tolerance. According to legend, as King Alfonso rode into the town in triumph, his horse stopped and knelt before the mosque. Excavations revealed a figure of Christ, still illuminated by a lamp which had burned throughout three and a half centuries of Muslim rule – hence the name *Cristo de la Luz*.

The mosque itself, set in a small park and open on all sides to the elements, is so small that it seems more like a miniature summer pavilion, but with an elegant simplicity of design that few of the great monuments can match. It has recently been fenced in and there are no set hours for visiting, but the caretaker lives across the street at c/ Cristo de la Luz 11 (☎925/223081) and will usually let visitors in; occasionally you'll see the mosque used for prayer by visiting Muslims. He'll also show you through the garden where you can climb to the battlements of the **Puerta del Sol**, a great fourteenth-century Mudéjar gateway.

The Alcázar

At the heart of modern Toledo is the **Plaza de Zocódover** (its name derives from the Arabic word *souk*), where everyone converges for an afternoon *copa*. Dominating this square, indeed all Toledo, is the bluff, imposing **Alcázar** (Tues–Sun 9.30am–1.30pm & 4–6.30pm; winter 5.30pm; 125ptas), entrance off Cuesta del Alcázar. There has probably always been a fortress at this commanding location, but the present building was originated by Carlos V, though it has been burned and bombarded so often that almost

---

THE SIEGE OF THE ALCÁZAR

At the outset of the Spanish Civil War, in July 1936, Colonel Moscardó and a group of Nationalist rebels under his command were driven into the Alcázar. They barricaded themselves in with a large group that included 600 women and children – and up to a hundred left-wing hostages (who were never seen again).

After many phone calls from Madrid to persuade them to surrender, a Toledo attorney phoned Moscardó with an ultimatum: within ten minutes the Republicans would shoot his son, captured that morning. Moscardó declared that he would never surrender and told his son, "If it be true, commend your soul to God, shout *Viva España*, and die like a hero". (His son was actually shot with others a month later in reprisal for an air raid.) Inside, though not short of ammunition, the defenders had so little food they had to eat their horses.

The number of Republican attackers varied from 1000 to 5000, with people coming from Madrid to take potshots from below. Two of the three mines they planted under the towers exploded but nothing could disturb the solid rock foundations. The besiegers tried spraying petrol all over the walls then setting fire to it, but with no effect. Finally, Franco decided to relieve Moscardó and diverted an army that was heading for Madrid. At the end of September Varela commanded the successful attack on the town, which was followed by the usual bloodbath – not one prisoner being taken.

nothing is original. The most recent destruction was in 1936 during one of the most symbolic and extraordinary episodes of the Civil War, involving a two-month siege of the Nationalist-occupied Alcázar by the Republican town (see box).

After the war, Franco's regime completely rebuilt the fortress as a monument to the glorification of its defenders – the fascist newspaper *El Alcázar* also commemorates the siege – and their propaganda models and photos are still displayed. Objectionable exercise though this is, it's a fascinating story, and the Alcázar also offers the best views of the town, its upper windows level with the top of the cathedral spire (though in recent years access has been restricted – part of the building is still occupied by the military). Across the river the ancient **Castillo de San Servando** stands next to a modern military academy.

Other museums

The **Hospital de Santa Cruz** (Tues–Sat 10am–6.30pm, Sun 10am–2pm; Mon 10am–2pm & 4.30–6.30pm but limited access), a superlative Renaissance building in itself, houses some of the greatest El Grecos in Toledo, including *The Assumption*, a daringly unorthodox work of feverish spiritual intensity, and a *Crucifixion* with the town as backdrop. As well as outstanding works by Goya and Ribera, the museum also contains a huge collection of ancient carpets and faded tapestries (including a magnificent fifteenth-century Flemish tapestry called *The Astrolabe*), a military display (note the flags borne by Don Juan of Austria at the Battle of Lepanto), sculpture and a small archaeological collection. Don't miss the patio with its ornate staircase – the entrance is beside the ticket office.

The **Museo de Arte Visigótico** (Tues–Sat 10am–2pm & 4–6.30pm; Sun 10am–2pm; 100ptas) can be found in a very different, though equally impressive building, the church of **San Román**. Moorish and Christian elements – horseshoe arches, early murals and a splendid Renaissance dome – combine to make it the most interesting church in Toledo. Its twelfth-century Mudéjar tower originally stood apart from the main body of the church, in the manner of Muslim minarets. Visigothic jewellery (though the best is in the *Museo Arqueológico* in Madrid), documents and archaeological fragments make up the bulk of the collection.

A few new museums have opened in Toledo recently. Not far from the Visigothic museum, in the **Convento de Santo Domingo el Antiguo**, the nuns display their art treasures in the old choir (11am–1.30pm & 4–7pm). More interesting is the high altarpiece of the church, El Greco's first major commission in Toledo. Unfortunately, most of the canvases have gone to museums and are here replaced by copies, leaving only two *St. John*s and a *Resurrection* in situ. The **Posada de la Hermandad**, near the market square at the back of the cathedral, is a recently restored building now the home of temporary exhibitions. Other exhibitions are staged at the **Museo de Arte Contemporáneo** (Tues–Sat 10am–2pm & 4–6.30pm, Sun 10am–2pm; 100ptas) in a refurbished sixteenth-century house near Santo Tomé. In the Mezquita de las Tornerias on c/de las Tornerias, the **Centro de Promoción de la Artesaní** (Tues–Sat 10am–2pm & 5–8pm, Sun 10am–2pm; free), houses good displays of beautiful local crafts, mainly pottery. The renovated eleventh-century mosque deconsecrated by the *Reyes Católicos* around 1500, is worth a visit in itself.

Eating, drinking and nightlife

Toledo is a major tourist centre and inevitably many of its bars and restaurants are geared to passing trade. However, the city is as popular with Spanish as foreign visitors, so decent, authentic places do exist – and there's a bit of nightlife, too, for the local population.

Eating out

Most **restaurants** in town do a good value lunchtime *menú*, with game such as partridge, pheasant or quail appearing on the more upmarket options, and everyone offering a tasty local meat-stew speciality, *carcamusa*. In the evenings, on a budget, you need to be selective: this can be an expensive town.

INEXPENSIVE

Bar Alcázar, c/Sierpe 5. Good range of *tapas* and *raciones*.

Alex, on the unnamed square at the top end of c/Nuncio Viejo. This combines a reasonable value restaurant and, at the side, a much cheaper café. Nice location.

La Cepa Andaluza, Méjico 11. A bar with dependable Andalucian cooking – fried fish and the like.

Bar Ludeña, Corral de Don Diego, off Plaza Magdalena. One of many places around this square, offering a cheap *menú* and the best *carcamusa* in town.

Bar Pastucci, c/Sinagoga 10. A small bar serving up slices of pizzas and other snacks.

Posada del Estudiante, Callejón de San Pedro 2. Unmarked workers café only open for very cheap lunchtime *menú* – well worth finding.

Restaurante Palacios, c/Alfonso X El Sabio. A popular and good local restaurant, whose *menú* always has an impressive choice.

MODERATE TO EXPENSIVE

Asador Adolfo, c/Granada 6 (closed Sun pm). One of the best restaurants in town, housed in an attractive old cavern and with a highly imaginative chef. Expensive.

Restaurante Los Cuatro Tiempos, c/Puerta Llana at southeast corner of the cathedral. Excellent mid-price restaurant with local specialities and good *tapas*.

Mesón La Hiedra, c/Nuncio Viejo 23. Atmospheric bistro with reasonable prices.

Restaurante Los Monteros, Plaza del Padre Juan de Mariana, opposite San Ildefonso. Reasonable food served on an open terrace – a rarity in Toledo's narrow streets.

Venta de Aires, c/Circo Romano 25. A little way out, this nineteenth-century restaurant is popular with locals.

Late bars and entertainment

Nightlife is not lively by the standards of other Spanish cities. Most late night bars line c/de la Sillería and its extension c/de los Alfileritos, west of Plaza de Zocódover, but the clientele tends to be a bit young. *La Abadía*, a fashionable but civilized bar with a large range of foreign beers, attracts an older crowd than most along here.

Two alternative places are *Broadway Jazz Club*, on Plaza Marrón near the Taller del Moro, and *La Boite de Garcilaso*, a similar place very nearby at the corner of c/ Alfonso XII and c/Rojas; both have occasional live jazz.

On from Toledo

The train line comes to a halt at Toledo but there are **bus** connections south to **Ciudad Real** (see p.154), west to **Talavera de la Reina** (a dull industrial town but a junction of routes on into Extremadura), and east to **Cuenca** (see p.148). If you have transport of your own, or fancy slow progress by bus and on foot, the **Montes de Toledo**, southwest of the city, are an interesting rural backwater. For details on all these places, see the "New Castile and Extremadura" chapter.

More local excursions, to the south of Toledo, could include **Guadamur** (served by three buses daily), whose outstanding castle graces the local tourist pamphlet, and **Orgaz**, where the Count came from, now a quiet village with a beautiful plaza and small castle on the main road to Ciudad Real.

Aranjuez and Chinchon

The Madrid–Toledo trains run via **Aranjuez**, a little oasis in the beginnings of New Castile, where the eighteenth-century Bourbon rulers set up a spring and autumn retreat. Their palaces and luxuriant gardens, and the summer strawberries (served with cream – *fresas con nata* – at roadside stalls) make an enjoyable stop. Nearby, too, connected by sporadic buses from Aranjuez and more regular services from Madrid, is **Chinchon**, a picturesque village that is home to Spain's best known *anís* – a mainstay of breakfast drinkers across Spain.

In summer (May 15–Oct 31, Sat & holidays), an old wooden **steam train**, *El Tren de la Fresa*, makes runs between Madrid and Aranjuez, leaving Estación de Atocha at 10am. Train enthusiasts won't begrudge the extra cost; tickets can be booked through most travel agents. If you are simply using Aranjuez as a connection on the rail line south, be sure to book seats ahead, as many of the **Madrid–Sevilla trains** are full at the Aranjuez stage.

Aranjuez

The beauty of **ARANJUEZ** is its greenery – it's easy to forget just how dry and dusty most of central Spain is until you come upon this town, with lush palaces and luxuriant gardens. In summer, Aranjuez functions principally as a weekend escape from Madrid and most people come out for the day, or stop en route to or from Toledo. If you wanted to break your journey, you'd need to book a room, or camp, as there's very little accommodation available.

The palace and gardens

The eighteenth-century **Palacio Real** (May–Sept Tues–Sun 10am–1pm & 3.30–6.30pm; joint ticket with gardens 400ptas) and its **gardens** (open all day) were an attempt by the Spanish Bourbon monarchs to create a Versailles in Spain; Aranjuez clearly isn't in the same league but it's a pleasant place to while away a few hours.

The palace is more remarkable for the ornamental fantasies inside than for any virtues of architecture. There seem to be hundreds of rooms, all exotically furnished, most amazingly so the **Porcelain Room**, entirely covered in decorative ware from the factory which used to stand in Madrid's Retiro park. The **Smoking Room** is a copy of one of the finest halls of the Alhambra in Granada, though executed with less subtlety. Most of the palace dates from the reign of the "nymphomaniac" Queen Isabel II, and many of the scandals and intrigues which led to her eventual abdication were played out here.

Outside on a small island, are the fountains of the **Jardín de la Isla**. The **Jardín del Príncipe**, on the other side of the main road, is more attractive, with shaded walks along the river and plenty of spots for a siesta. At its far end is the **Casa del Labrador** (Peasant's House), which is anything but what the name implies. Richard Ford described it well over a century ago as "another plaything of that silly Charles IV, a foolish toy for the spoiled children of fortune, in which great expense and little taste are combined to produce a thing which is perfectly useless". Great expense is right, for the house contains more silk, marble, crystal and gold than would seem possible in so small a place, as well as a huge collection of fancy clocks. The guided tour goes into great detail about the weight and value of every item.

Also in the gardens, by the river, is a small **boating museum** with the brightly coloured launches in which royalty would take to the river. A bus service occasionally connects the various sites, but all are within easy walking distance of each other, and it's a very pleasant place to stroll around.

Practicalities

The best **hostal** choice is the *Rusiñol*, c/San Antonio 76 (☎918/910155; ②), in the centre of town. The **campsite**, *Camping Soto del Castillo*, (☎918/911395; May–Sept), is on the far side of the river, easiest reached by the footbridge near the museum; it's crowded and rocky, but equipped with a swimming pool. The **Turismo** is in a little concrete kiosk just before the bridge on the way into town.

With plenty of fresh produce around, the *Mercado de San Antonio* near the Jardines Isabel II is a good place to buy your own food for a picnic. If you're after a memorable restaurant meal, *La Rana Verde* on the banks of the Tajo, is renowned but expensive. You can eat much more cheaply, if in rather less elegant surroundings, in the middle of town; *Casa Pablete*, on c/Stuart, is good for *tapas*.

Chinchón

CHINCHÓN, 45km southeast of Madrid, is an elegant little town, with a fifteenth-century castle and a fine Plaza Mayor, in which plays are sometimes performed, and in which stands the **Iglesia de la Asunción**, with a panel by Goya of *The Assumption of the Virgin*. It is as the home of **anís**, however, that the town is known, and most visitors come to visit the three distilleries – a couple of which are actually housed in the castle. To follow a few tastings with a meal try the *Mesón del Duende* or *Mesón del Comendador*, both modestly priced.

El Escorial, El Valle de los Caídos and the Sierra de Guadarrama

Northwest of Madrid, in the foothills of the Sierra de Guadarrama, is one of Spain's best-known and most visited sights – Felipe II's vast monastery-palace of **El Escorial**. Travel writers tend to go into frenzies about the symbolism of this building – "a stone image of the mind of its founder" was how the nineteenth-century writer Augustus Hare described it – and it is indeed a key historic sight. The town around the monastery, **San Lorenzo del Escorial**, is an easy daytrip from Madrid, or if you plan to travel on, rail and road routes continue to Ávila and Segovia (see sections following). The heart of the **Sierra de Guadarrama**, too, lies just to the north, offering Madrid's easiest mountain escape.

Tours from Madrid to El Escorial often take in **El Valle de los Caídos** (The Valley of the Fallen), 9km north. This is an equally megalomaniac yet far more chilling monument: an underground basilica hewn under Franco's orders, ostensibly as a monument to the Civil War dead of both sides, though in reality as a memorial to the Generalissimo and his regime.

El Escorial

The monastery of **El Escorial** was the largest Spanish building of the Renaissance: rectangular, overbearing and severe, from the outside it resembles more a prison than a palace. Built between 1563 and 1584, it was originally the creation of Juan Bautista de Toledo, though his one-time assistant, **Juan de Herrera**, took over and is normally given credit for the design. **Felipe II** planned the complex as both monastery and mausoleum, where he would live the life of a monk and "rule the world with two inches of paper". Later monarchs had less ascetic lifestyles, enlarging and richly decorating the palace quarters, but Felipe's simple rooms, with the chair that supported his gouty

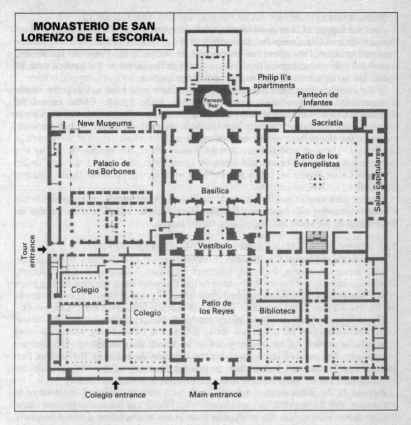

MONASTERIO DE SAN LORENZO DE EL ESCORIAL

Philip II's apartments

Pantéon de Infantes

Pantéon Real

New Museums

Sacristía

Palacio de los Borbones

Patio de los Evangelistas

Basílica

Salas Capitulares

Tour entrance

Vestíbulo

Colegio

Colegio

Patio de los Reyes

Biblioteca

Colegio entrance

Main entrance

leg and the deathbed from which he could look down into the church where mass was constantly celebrated, remain the most fascinating.

There's more to see than you can fit into a single day without total exhaustion, and you're liable to end up agreeing with Augustus Hare that while the Escorial "is so profoundly curious that it must of necessity be visited, it is so utterly dreary and so hopelessly fatiguing a sight that it requires the utmost patience to endure it".

The monastery

Visits to **El Real Monasterio del Escorial** (summer Tues–Sun 10am–1.30pm & 3.30–6pm; winter Tues–Sun 10am–1.30pm & 3–6pm; 500ptas, Wed free to EC citizens) used to be deeply regulated, with guided tours to each section. Recently, they've become more relaxed and you can use your ticket to enter, in whatever sequence you like, the Monastery, Palace, Royal Apartments, Pantheon and Library; the outlying **Casas de Aribe and Infante** now charge separate admission. To avoid the worst of the crowds, try visiting just before lunch, or pick that time for the royal apartments, which are the focus of all the coachtours.

For sustenance or relief, you'll find a **cafetería** and **toilets** near the ticket office; drinks are okay but meals a bit of a rip-off.

THE PATIO DE LOS REYES, BASILICA, CLOISTERS AND GARDENS

A good starting point is to head for the **west gateway**, facing the mountains, and go through the traditional main entrance. Above it is a gargantuan statue of San Lourenço holding a gridiron, the emblem of his martyrdom. Within is the **Patio de los Reyes**, named after the six statues of the kings of Israel on the facade of the basilica straight ahead. Off to the left is a school, to the right the monastery, both of them still in use.

In the **Basilica**, notice the flat vault of the *coro* above your head as you enter, which is apparently entirely without support, and the white marble Christ carved by Benvenuto Cellini – and carried here from Barcelona on workmen's shoulders. This is one of the few things permanently illuminated in the cold, dark interior, but put some money in the slot to light up the main altarpiece and the whole aspect of the church is brightened. The east end is decorated by Italian artists: the sculptures are by the father-and-son team of Leone and Pompeo Leoni, who also carved the two facing groups of Carlos V with his family and Felipe II with three of his wives (Mary Tudor is excluded).

You can also wander at will in some of the Escorial's courtyards, most notable is the **Claustro Grande**, with frescoes of the life of the Virgin by Tibaldi, and the **Jardín de los Frailes** on the south side (open only during lunch).

THE TREASURIES, MAUSOLEUM AND ROYAL APARTMENTS

The **Sacristía** and **Salas Capitulares** (Chapter Houses) contain many of the monastery's religious treasures, including paintings by Titian, Velázquez and José Ribera. Beside the sacristy a staircase leads down to the **Panteón Real**, the final resting place of all Spanish monarchs since Carlos V, with the exception of Felipe V and Fernando VI. Alfonso XIII, who died in exile in Rome, was recently brought to join his ancestors.

The deceased monarchs lie in gilded marble tombs: kings (and Isabel II) on one side, their spouses on the other. Just above the entry is the *Pudrería*, a separate room in which the bodies rot for twenty years or so before the cleaned-up skeletons are moved here. The royal children are laid in the **Panteón de Infantes**; the tomb of Don Juan, Felipe II's bastard half-brother, is grander than any of the kings', while the wedding-cake babies' tomb with room for sixty infants is more than half-full.

Beyond is the **Biblioteca**, a splendid hall, with shelves designed by Herrera to harmonize with the architecture, and frescoes by Tibaldi and his assistants, and showing the seven Liberal Arts. Its collections include the tenth-century *Codex Albeldensis*, Saint Teresa's personal diary, some gorgeously executed Arabic manuscripts, and a Florentine planetarium of 1572 demonstrating the movement of the planets according to the Ptolemaic and Copernican systems. What remains of the Escorial's art collection – works by Bosch, Gerard David, Dürer, Titian, Zurbarán and many others, which escaped transfer to the Prado – is kept in the elegant suite of rooms known as the **New Museums**.

Finally, there are the treasure-crammed **Royal Apartments**, for which you have to join the official convoys. On no account miss the **quarters of Felipe II**, but unless you're profoundly interested in inlaid wood it's not worth paying extra to see the **Maderas Finas** rooms. The craftsmanship is magnificent, but the entrance charge exorbitant – deliberately so, since too many visitors would damage the delicate decorations.

OUTLYING LODGES

The Escorial ticket also covers entry to the **Casita del Príncipe** and the **Casita del Arriba**. These two eighteenth-century royal lodges, both full of decorative riches, lie 400m uphill on the Ávila road (turn left outside the entrance to the Library). They were built by Juan de Villanueva, Spain's most accomplished Neoclassical architect, and are thus worth seeing in themselves as well as for their formal gardens.

The Casita del Arriba, which served as present King Juan Carlos's student digs, is a short way up into the hills and affords a good view of the Escorial complex; follow the road to the left from the main entrance and then stick to the contours of the mountain around to the right – it's well signposted. The Casita del Príncipe, in the Jardines del Príncipe below the monastery, is larger and more worthwhile, with an important collection of Giordano paintings and four pictures made from rice paste.

Lastly, 7km out of town, is El Sillon de Felipe – "Phillip's Seat" – a chair carved into a rocky outcrop with a view out towards the palace. His Majesty is supposed to have sat here to watch the construction going on. If you have a car, it still offers a great view; take the Ávila road and turn off after three kilometres.

Practicalities

There are well over twenty trains a day **from Madrid** (7am–11pm; Atocha or Chamartín stations) and fifteen buses. The bus is faster, slightly cheaper, and takes you right to the monastery. If you arrive by train get straight on the local bus which shuttles you up to the centre of town – they leave promptly and it's a long uphill walk. The **Turismo** (Mon–Fri 10am–2pm & 3–6pm, Sat 10am–1.30pm) is at c/Floridablanca 10.

If you want to stay in the town, San Lorenzo del Escorial, there's a range of **accommodation**, but in summer it's essential to book in advance. Among the cheaper *hostales*, try *Jardín*, c/Leandro Rubio 2 (☎918/961007; ②) or *Malagón*, San Francisco 2 (☎918/901576; ③). Slightly more upmarket places include the *Hotel Parrilla Príncipe*, c/Floridablanca 6 (☎918/901611; ④), *Hostal Cristina*, c/Juan de Toledo 6 (☎918/901961; ③) and *Hostal Vasco*, Plaza Santiago 11 (☎918/901619; ③). There's also a **campsite** 2km out on the road to Ávila, *Caravanning El Escorial* (☎918/902412) and a **youth hostel**, *Santa María del Buen Aire*, Finca de la Herreria (☎918/903640; ① members only), usually crowded with school groups. But it's preferable to arrive early, spend the day here, and continue in the evening to Ávila (11 trains daily, last at 10pm) or head back to Madrid.

For meals you'll need to head away from the monastery, up c/Reina Victoria into town. *Restaurante Cubero* on c/Don Juan Delegraz has reasonable *menús* as does the good restaurant at the *Hostal Vasco*. Alternatively, grab a *bocadillo* from a drinks stand on c/Floridablanca and save your appetite for later.

To visit **El Valle de los Caidos** from El Escorial, there is a local bus run by *Herranz*, which sells tickets at the *Bar Bolero*, opposite the Correos. The bus runs from El Escorial at 3.15pm, returning at 5.30pm (6.15pm from July to mid-Sept).

El Valle de los Caídos

The entrance to the **VALLE DE LOS CAÍDOS** (Valley of the Fallen) lies 9km north of El Escorial: from here a road (along which you are not allowed to stop) runs 6km into the underground basilica. Above it is a vast cross, reputedly the largest in the world, and visible for miles along the road to Segovia.

The **basilica complex** (10am–7pm; 400ptas) denies its claims of memorial "to the Civil War dead of both sides" almost at a glance: the debased and grandiose architectural forms employed, the constant inscriptions "Fallen for God and for Spain", and the proximity to El Escorial clue you in to its true function of the glorification of General Franco and his regime. The dictator himself lies buried behind the high altar, while the only other named tomb, marked simply "José Antonio", is that of his guru, the Falangist leader José Antonio Primo de Rivera, who was shot dead by Republicans at the beginning of the war. The "other side" is present only in the fact that the complex was built by the Republican army's survivors – political prisoners on quarrying duty.

From the church, a funicular (10.30am–2pm & 4–7.30pm) ascends to the base of the **cross**, offering, as you can imagine, a superlative view over the Sierra de Guadarrama.

The Sierra de Guadarrama

The road and rail routes from Madrid and El Escorial to Segovia strike through the heart of the **Sierra de Guadarrama** – a beautiful journey, worth taking for its own sake. The road is occasionally marred by suburban development, especially around **Navacerrada**, Madrid's main ski station, but from the train it's almost entirely unspoiled.

If you want to base yourself in the mountains for a while you'd do best to head for **Cercedilla**, ninety minutes by train on the Madrid–Segovia line – and a little way off the main road. Alternatively, over to the east, there is **Manzanares el Real**, with an odd medieval castle and a barrage-side setting.

Cercedilla and the Puerto de Navacerrada

CERCEDILLA is an Alpine-looking village and an excellent base for summer walking; it is much frequented by *Madrileños* at weekends. Accommodation is limited to the *Hostal Longinos*, near the station on Avda. Generalissimo 3 (☎918/521511; ③), and a pair of **youth hostels** (☎918/520334 & 918/520135; ①) up on the Dehesas road. However, there are a clutch of good restaurants and an information booth, 3km up the Dehesas road, which is helpful for trekking details. They also run free guided walks on summer weekends, while horse riding and bike rental is available in the village.

From Cercedilla, you can also embark on a wonderful little train ride to the **Puerto de Navacerrada**, the most important pass in the mountains and the heart of the ski area.

Manzanares el Real

Some 50km north of Madrid, on the shores of the Santillana reservoir (*embalse*), lies **MANZANARES EL REAL**, a town which in former times was disputed between the capital and Segovia. Nowadays it's a somewhat tatty resort, geared to Madrid weekenders, whose villas dot the landscape for miles. However, the ruggedly beautiful **La Pedriza**, a spur of the Sierra de Guadarrama, has been declared a national park, and has some enjoyable walks, as well as some much-revered technical climbs, notably the ascent to the jagged Peña del Diezmo.

In Manzanares itself, the one attraction is the **castle** (10am–2pm & 3–6pm; free), which despite its eccentric appearance is a perfectly genuine fifteenth-century construction, built around an earlier chapel. It was soon modified into a palace by the architect Juan Guas, who built an elegant gallery on the south side, false machicolations on the other, and studded the tower with stones resembling cannon balls. The interior has been heavily restored.

Oddly, there is just one **hostal** in Manzanares, El Tranco (☎918/530063; ④), plus an expensive **hotel**, the *Parque Real* (☎918/558512; ⑤). However, there is usually space at the campsite, *El Ortigal* (☎918/530120). **Buses** from Madrid are run by *Hermanos de Julia Colmenarejo* (c/Mateo Inurria 11; Metro *Plaza de Castilla*; three daily, five on Sundays). The train station is 6km out of town.

Ávila

Two things distinguish **ÁVILA**: its eleventh-century **walls**, two perfectly preserved kilometres of which surround the old town, and the mystic writer **Santa Teresa**, who was born here and whose shrines are a major focus of religious pilgrimage. Set on a high plain, with the peaks of the Sierra de Gredos behind, the town is quite a sight, especially if you time it right and approach with the evening sun highlighting the golden tone of the walls and the details of the eighty-eight towers.

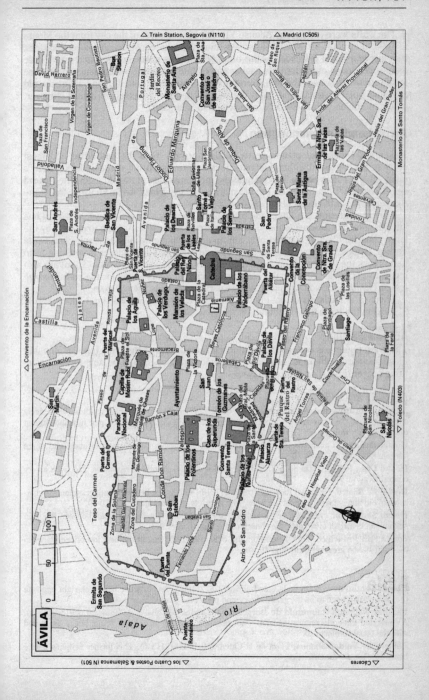

The **walls** were ordered by Alfonso VI, after his conquest of the city from the Moors in 1090; they took his Muslim prisoners nine years to construct. At closer quarters, they prove a bit of a facade, as the old city within is sparsely populated and a little dishevelled, most of modern life having moved into the new developments outside the fortifications. However, the fine **Romanesque churches** dotted in and about the old city, plus good walks around the walls, makes the town an excellent night's stopover, either combined with El Escorial, or en route to Salamanca.

Arrival and accommodation

Ávila's walls make orientation pretty straightforward, with the **cathedral** and most other sights contained within. Just outside the southeast corner of the walls is the city's main square, **Plaza Santa Teresa**, and the most imposing of the old gates, the **Puerta del Alcázar**. Within the walls, the old market square, **Plaza de la Victoria**, fronts the *Ayuntamiento* at the heart of the old city.

The **train station** is a fifteen-minute walk to the east of the old town, or a local bus into Plaza de la Victoria. On foot, follow the broad Avda. José Antonio to its end, by the large church of Santa Ana, and bear left up c/del Duque de Alba to reach Plaza Santa Teresa. **Buses** use a terminal on the Avda. de Madrid, a little closer in: walking from here, cross the small park opposite then turn right up c/Duque d'Alba. There are also buses to Plaza Victoria near the cathedral. **Driving**, follow signs for the walls (*murallas*) or *Parador* and you should be able to park just outside the old town.

There is a **Turismo** (Mon–Fri 9.30am–2pm & 4–7pm, Sat 9.30am–1.30pm; ☎918/211387) in the Plaza de la Catedral.

Accommodation

There are numerous *hostales* around the train station and along Avda. José Antonio, but these are hardly the most convenient locations and you should be able to find something nearer the walled centre of town.

BUDGET ROOMS

Albergue de Juventud, Avda. de Juventud (☎918/221716). The town's small youth hostel is nicely sited, out past the Convento de Santa Tomas by the local swimming pool. Open July and August only, however, with a strict 11pm curfew. ①.

Hostal Bellas, c/Caballeros 19 (☎918/212910). Excellent value for the great location, and offers bargain rates out of season. ③.

Hostal Casa Felipe, Plaza de la Victoria 12 (☎918/213924). Another reasonable place with a very central location. ③.

Hostal El Rastro, Plaza Del Rastro 1 (☎918/211218). This is the best mid-budget option – a characterful old inn, set right against the walls, with a variety of rooms and prices. ②–③.

Hostal Santa Ana, c/Alfonso de Montalvo 2 (☎918/220063). Good value *hostal* between the train station and centre of town, near the church of the same name. ③.

Fonda San Francisco, Trav. José Antonio 2 (☎918/220298). One of the best low-priced places in the train station area; very friendly. ②.

HOTELS

Hostal Continental, Plaza de la Catedral 6 (☎918/211502). An attractive old hotel, right opposite the cathedral; it used to be the grand choice and preserves a faded charm. ④.

Parador Nacional Raimundo de Borgoña, c/Marqués de Canales y Chozas 16 (☎918/211340). A converted fifteenth-century mansion – not the most exciting *parador* in Spain, but pleasant and with the usual comforts. ⑤.

Palacio de Valderrabanos, Plaza de la Catedral 9 (☎918/211340). This former bishop's palace beats the *Parador* for ambience. ⑤.

The town

The focus of Ávila's sights is, inevitably, **Santa Teresa**, with whom most of the numerous convents and churches claim some connection. On the secular front, a circuit outside the **walls** makes a fine walk, and from the Puerta del Alcázar you can climb up and stroll around a section.

Santa Teresa in Avila

The obvious place to start a tour of Teresa's Ávila is the **Convento de Santa Teresa** (9am–1pm & 3.30–8.30pm), built over the saint's birthplace just inside the south gate of the old town – entered off the Paseo del Rastro. Most of the convent remains *in clausura* but you can see the very spot where she was born, now a chapel in the Baroque church, which is decorated with scenes of the saint demonstrating her powers of levitation to various august bodies. In a small reliquary, beside the gift shop, are memorials of Teresa's life, including not only her rosary beads, but one of the fingers she used to count them with.

Heading through the old town, and exiting by the *Parador* gate, you can follow a lane, c/de la Encarnación, to the **Convento de la Encarnación** (Wed–Mon 9.30am–1pm & 4–7pm, winter 3.30–6pm; 75ptas). Each of the rooms here is labelled with the act Teresa performed, while everything she might have touched or looked at is on display. A small museum section also provides a reasonable introduction to the saint's life, with maps showing the convents, and a selection of her sayings – the pithiest, perhaps, "Life is a night in a bad hotel".

A third Teresan sight lies a couple of blocks east (away from the walls) of the Plaza de Santa Teresa. This is the **Convento de las Madres** (10am–1pm & 4–7pm), also known as San José, the first monastery that the saint founded, in 1562. Its museum contains relics and memorabilia, including the coffin in which Teresa once slept, and assorted personal possessions. The tomb of her brother Lorenzo is in the larger of the two churches.

Lastly, you might want to make your way up to **Las Cuatro Postes**, a little four-posted shrine, 1500m along the Salamanca road west of town. It was here, aged seven, that the infant Teresa was recaptured by her uncle, running away with her brother to seek Christian martyrdom from the Moors.

SANTA TERESA OF ÁVILA

Santa Teresa (1515–1582) was born to a noble family in Ávila and from childhood began to experience visions and religious raptures. At the age of seven she attempted to run away with her brother to be martyred by the Moors: the spot where they were recaptured and brought back, **Las Cuatro Postes**, is a fine vantage point from which to admire the walls of the town.

Teresa's religious career began at the Carmelite convent of La Encarnación, where she was a nun for twenty-seven years. From this base, she went on to reform the movement, and found convents, throughout Spain. She was an ascetic, but her appeal – and her importance to the Counter-Reformation – lay in the mystic sensuality of her experience of Christ, as revealed in her autobiography, for centuries a bestseller in Spain. As co-patron of Spain (together with Santiago), the saint remains a central pillar in Spanish catholicism and schoolgirls are brought into Ávila by the busload to experience first-hand the life of the woman they are supposed to emulate.

On a more bizarre note, one of Santa Teresa's mummified hands has now been returned to Ávila after spending the Franco years by the bedside of the great dictator.

The cathedral and other sights

The three most beautiful churches in Ávila – the cathedral, San Vicente, and the convent of Santo Tomás – are less directly associated with its most famous resident. Around the cathedral and Santo Tomás (just outside the northeast corner of the walls), there is also a scattering of impressive **Renaissance mansions** – none of them visitable but giving a glimpse of old Castilian wealth in their coats of arms and decorative facades.

Ávila's **Catedral** (10am–1pm & 3–6pm, winter 3–5pm, holidays 11am–7pm) was started in the twelfth century but has never been finished, as evidenced by the missing tower above the main entrance. The earliest Romanesque parts were as much fortress as church, and the apse actually forms an integral part of the city walls. Their defensive function was real, as the twelfth-century Bishop Sancho provided sanctuary here for the young Alfonso IX, prior to his accession.

Inside, the succeeding changes of style are immediately apparent; the Romanesque parts are made of a strange red-and-white mottled stone, then there's an abrupt break and the rest of the main structure is pure white stone and Gothic forms.

Although the proportions are exactly the same, this newer half of the cathedral seems infinitely more spacious. The *coro*, whose elaborate carved back you see as you come in, and two chapels in the left aisle, are Renaissance additions. A visitor's ticket (200 ptas) allows you to admire the carved stalls in the *coro*, carved by a Dutch sculptor, Cornelius, and the treasury-museum with its monstrous silver *custodia* and ancient religious images, and the tomb of a fifteenth-century bishop known as *El Tostado* (the "toasted" or "swarthy").

The basilica of **San Vicente** (Tues–Sun 10am–1pm & 4–7pm, winter 4–6pm; 50ptas), like the cathedral, is a mixture of architectural styles. Its twelfth-century doorways and the portico which protects them are magnificent examples of Romanesque art, while the church itself shows the influence of later trends. San Vicente was martyred on this site, and his tomb depicts a series of particularly gruesome deaths; in the crypt you can see the slab on which he and his sisters were executed by the Romans. The church shares with nearby **San Pedro** a warm pink glow from the sandstone of its construction – a characteristic aspect of Ávila but seen most clearly here.

El Real Monasterio de Santo Tomás (Mon–Sat 10am–1pm & 4–7pm, Sun 10am–1pm & 4–6pm; 100ptas for the museum parts) is a Dominican monastery founded in 1482, but greatly expanded over the following decade by Fernando and Isabella, whose summer palace it became. Inside are three exceptional cloisters, the largest of which contains an **oriental collection**, a strangely incongruous display built up by the monks over centuries of missionary work in the Orient. On every available surface is carved the yoke-and-arrows motif of the *Reyes Católicos*, surrounded by pomegranates, symbol of the newly conquered kingdom of Granada (*granada* means "pomegranate" in Spanish). In the **church** is the elaborate tomb of Prince Juan, Fernando and Isabella's only son, whose early death opened the way for Carlos V's succession and caused his parents so much grief that they abandoned their newly completed home here. It was subsequently damaged by Napoleon's troops, who stabled their horses in the church. Notice also the tomb of the prince's tutors, almost as elaborate as his own, and the thrones occupied by the king and queen during services. The notorious inquisitor Torquemada is buried in the sacristy. Santo Tomás is quite a walk downhill from the south part of town – you can get back up by the #1 bus, whose circular route takes in much of the old city.

A small **Museo Provincial**, Plaza Navillos 3 (Tues–Sat 10am–2pm & 5–8pm, Sun 10am–2pm) could occupy a little more of your time. Its exhibits include collections of archeological remains, ceramics, carpets and furnishings from around the Ávila province.

Eating and drinking

Ávila has a decent if unexceptional array of bars and restaurants, most of them sited just outside the walls. Local specialities include the Castilian standby *cordero asado* (roast lamb), *Judias del Barco con chorizo* (haricot beans with sausage), and candied egg-yolk *yemas de Santa Teresa* – the latter sold in confectioners all over town. One to avoid is *mollejas* – cow's stomach.

Recommended **bars and restaurants** include:

Casa Patas, c/San Millán 4 (closed Wed & Sept). A pleasant bar, with good *tapas*, and a little *comedor* (evenings only), near the church of San Pedro.

Gas, Vallespin 8, near the Plaza de la Constitución. This is Ávila's most fashionable drinking spot – a converted cinema with five bars and a summer *terraza*.

Cafetería Maspalomas. Inexpensive, simple meals, opposite the bus station.

El Molino de la Losa, Bajada de la Losa 12 (☎918/211101; closed Mon & 15 Oct–15 March). A converted fifteenth-century mill, with a deserved reputation. The *menú* is 3000ptas and you should reckon on a fair bit more with wine and service.

La Posada de la Fruta, Plaza de Pedro Davila. This attractive, sunny, covered courtyard is a nice place for a drink.

Mesón del Rastro, Plaza del Rastro 1. Attached to the hotel, this is an excellent bar, with a range of *tapas*. Behind it is a modest-priced restaurant, an old fashioned place with solid, traditional fare.

Bar El Rincón, Plaza Zurraquín 6. A generous three-course *menú* served here.

Vinos y Comidas, c/Carramolino 14. The name says it all; very cheap *menú* at side of San Juan church. Closed Sunday.

On from Ávila

Ávila is quite a nexus with road and rail routes to **Salamanca** and **Valladolid**, from where you can get to just about anywhere in northern Spain, while to the east **Segovia** (see p.133) is less than two hours away by bus. Within striking distance, too, to the south, is the beautiful Sierra de Gredos (see below).

On the **Salamanca route**, both road and rail lines pass through **PEÑARANDA DE BRACAMONTE**, a crumbling old town with a couple of large plazas and ancient churches. From here, if you have your own vehicle, you can continue to Salamanca on a slightly longer route through **ALBA DE TORMES**. Santa Teresa died here, and the Carmelite convent which contains the remains of her body (not much of it to judge by the number of relics scattered around Spain) is another major target of pilgrimage. There are the remains of a castle too, and several other interesting churches.

Heading north **towards Valladolid**, road and rail both pass through **Medina del Campo** with its beautiful castle (see the *Old Castile* chapter).

The Sierra de Gredos

The **Sierra de Gredos** continues the line of the Sierra de Guadarrama, enclosing Madrid to the north and west. A major mountain range, with peaks in excess of 2500m, Gredos offers the best trekking in central Spain, including high-level routes across the passes as well as more casual walks around the villages.

By bus, the easiest access is from Madrid to **Arenas de San Pedro**, from whence you can explore the range, and then move on west into the valley of La Vera in Extremadura (see p.159). If you have your own transport, you could head into the range south from Ávila along the C502, and you might prefer to base yourself in one of the villages on the north side of the range, along the **Tormes valley**, and do circular walks from there.

Arenas de San Pedro and Mombeltrán

ARENAS DE SAN PEDRO is a sizable town with a somewhat prettified **castle** and a good range of **accommodation**: pleasant options include the *Hostería Las Galayos* (☎918/371379; ④) and *Hostal El Castillo* (☎918/370091; ③). If you haven't already obtained **maps** of Gredos, you can pick up a functional pamphlet from the Turismo, or buy more detailed sheets from the bookshop *Librería Nava*.

MOMBELTRÁN, 12km north (an enjoyable, mainly downhill, walk from Arenas), is an attractive alternative stop, with its fourteenth-century **castle** of the dukes of Albuquerque set against a stunning mountain backdrop. The village has two further **hostales**, the *Albuquerque* (☎918/386032; ③) and *Prados Abiertos* (☎918/386061; ③), and a summer-only campsite (☎918/386061), 4km below.

El Arenal and El Hornillo

The main reason to stop in Arenas de San Pedro is to make your way up to the villages of El Hornillo and El Arenal, respectively 6km and 9km to the north, and trailheads for some excellent **mountain walks**. There are no buses but it's a pleasant walk up from Arenas to El Arenal on a track running between the road and the river – start out past the sports centre and swimming pool in Arenas.

EL ARENAL has the **accommodation**, including the *Hostal Isabel* (☎918/375148; ③), whose owner is knowledgeable about routes through the range, and a *fonda*; a **campsite** usually operates in summer, too, 4km above the village on the Mombeltrán road.

You can walk over the top of Gredos from El Arenal – the path via the pass at **Puerto de la Cabrilla** has been somewhat improved recently – and strike out along the ridge in either direction, to the main road at Puerto del Pico or back to El Arenal. **EL HORNILLO**, however, is the more common trailhead, and the beginning of the Circo de Gredos, one of the main recognized trekking routes over the Gredos watershed.

An alternative trek is to head due south from El Arenal, along a well-defined path over a broad pass to **Candeleda** (see below); this is a long day's walk but it's more or less all downhill.

Before setting out either way, make sure you have adequate supplies and know where you're going, as directions are not always clear.

The Circo de Gredos

The walk from El Hornillo **over the Gredos watershed** takes most of a day to accomplish, exchanging the pine and granite of the steep south slopes for the *matorral* (scrub thickets), cow pastures and wide horizons on the northern side. Over the top, you'll emerge on a twelve-kilometre stretch of paved road linking Hoyos del Espino, a village in the Tormes valley, and the so-called **Plataforma**, jumping-off point to the highest peaks of the Gredos. It's best to call it a day just above the Plataforma, where there's lots of camping space in the high Pozas meadows. From here, you can proceed up to the **Circo de Laguna Grande**, two hours' walk beyond Pozas on a well-defined path.

Circo de Laguna Grande and Circo de las Cinco Lagunas

The **Circo de Laguna Grande** is the centrepiece of the Gredos range, with its highest peak, **Almanzor** (2593m), looming above, surrounded by pinnacles sculpted into utterly improbable shapes. The valley with its huge lake is popular with day-trippers and weekenders, as you can drive up here from Hoyos del Espino, and its **refugio** (mountain hut) is often full, especially on weekends; camping out, however, is an accepted alternative.

The valley path, actually Alfonso XIII's old hunting route, continues west for a couple of hours before ending abruptly at the edge of a sharp, scree-laden descent into the **Circo de las Cinco Lagunas**. The drop is amply rewarded by virtual solitude, even in midsummer, and the sure sighting of *Capra pyrenaica gloriae*, the graceful (and almost tame) Gredos mountain goat. Protected by law since the 1920s, they now number several thousand and frequent the north slopes of Gredos in the warmer months.

The Tormes valley: Navarredonda
On the north side of Gredos is the Tormes valley, trailed by the C500 to the main N110 at El Barco de Ávila. There is accommodation at **NAVARREDONDA**, including a **youth hostel** (☎918/348005; ①) and Spain's first ever **parador** (☎920/348048; ⑤).

Candeleda and Madrigal de la Vera
The village of **CANDELEDA**, on the Arenas–Jarandilla road, is nothing special but it's amazingly popular with Spanish summer holidaymakers, who book its *hostales* weeks in advance. If you're planning ahead, the best value is *La Pastora* (☎920/380146; ②) and the fanciest the *Hostal Pedros* (☎920/380951; ③), where you might rub shoulders with John Major's bodyguards; the British Prime Minister spends his holidays each August in Candeleda as a guest of a local politician. Campers sometimes set up their tents alongside the river, west of town.

At **MADRIGAL DE LA VERA**, a more attractive village 12km to the west of Candeleda, there is an official campsite, and yet another **route across the Gredos**, this time leading to **Bohoyo**, a hamlet 4km southwest of El Barca de Ávila.

Segovia and around

After Toledo, **SEGOVIA** is the outstanding trip from Madrid. A small city, strategically sited on a rocky ridge, it is deeply and haughtily Castilian, with a panoply of squares and mansions from its days of Golden Age grandeur, when it was a royal resort and a base for the Cortes (parliament). It was in Segovia – in the unremarkable church of San Miguel, off the Plaza Mayor – that Isabella la Católica was proclaimed queen.

For a city of its size, there is a stunning number of outstanding architectural monuments. Most celebrated are the **Roman aqueduct**, the **cathedral** and the fairy-tale **Alcázar**, but the less obvious attractions – the cluster of ancient churches and the many mansions found in the lanes of the old town, all in a warm, honey-coloured stone – are what really make it worth visiting.

Just a few kilometres outside the city and easily accessible from Segovia are two Bourbon palaces, **La Granja** and **Riofrío**.

Arrival and accommodation

Well-connected by road and rail, Segovia is an easy trip from Madrid with ten trains daily from Atocha, as well as four buses (operated by *La Sepulvedana*, Paseo de la Florida 11; Metro Norte). The town's own **train station** is some distance out of town – take bus #3 to the central Plaza Mayor; the **bus station** is on the same route.

The **Turismo** (Mon–Fri 9.30am–2pm & 5–7pm, Sat 10am–2pm, summer Sat 5–7pm & Sun 10am–3pm), in the **Plaza Mayor**, offers full lists of local accommodation plus a *Guía Semanal* with transport timetables and current events; most significant facts are displayed in the window if it's closed. In summer, a second tourist office functions in the busy Plaza de Azoguejo.

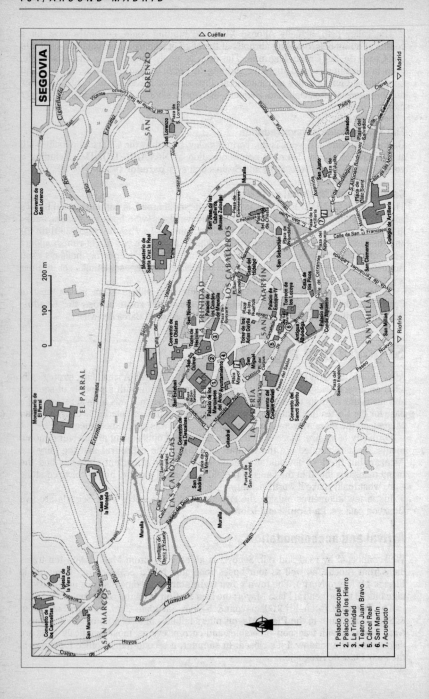

△ Cuéllar

SEGOVIA

▷ Madrid

SAN LORENZO

Convento de
San Lorenzo

Monasterio de
Santa Cruz la Real

LOS CABALLEROS

LA TRINIDAD

San Juan de los
Caballeros
(Museo Zuloaga)

San Sebastián

Cárcel de
los Picos

SAN MARTÍN

Plaza del
Azoguejo

Palacio de la
Audiencia de Medina

Palacio del
Conde Alpuente

Torreón de
los Lozoya

Antigua
Alhóndiga

Plaza de Artillería

Calle de San Francisco

El Salvador

Plaza del
Salvador

San Justo
Plaza de
San Justo

C.S.A.Alfonso Rodríguez
Plaza del
Díaz/Sanz

San Clemente

Colegio de Artillería

▷ Riofrío

San Millán

SAN MILLÁN

Plaza del
Seminario

Convento de las Oblatas

Torre de
Hércules

San Nicolás

Palacio de
Estación IV

Convento del
Corpus Christi

Convento del
Sancti Spíritu

San Esteban

ESTACIÓN

San
Quirce

Palacio del
Marqués
del Arco

Ayuntamiento

Plaza
Mayor

Catedral

LA JUDERÍA

Palacio de los
Marqueses de Moya

Convento
de las Descalzas

San Andrés

Puerta de
San Andrés

LAS CANONGÍAS

Plaza del
Conde

Plaza del
Mercado

Paseo del Salón

Monasterio de
El Parral

EL PARRAL

Casa de
la Moneda

Muralla

Convento de
las Carmelitas

Iglesia de
la Vera Cruz

San Marcos

Río Clamores

Río Hoyos

RÍO ERESMA

RÍO ERESMA

SAN MARCOS

Alcázar

0   100   200 m

1. Palacio Episcopal
2. Palacio de los Hierro
3. La Trinidad
5. Teatro Juan Bravo
6. San Martín
7. Acueducto

Accommodation

Most of the **accommodation** is to be found in the streets around the Plaza Mayor and Plaza de Azoguejo, but rooms can be hard to come by even out of season, so it's worth booking ahead if you're considering more than a day trip. Be warned that in winter, at over 1000m, the nights can be very cold here, and the more basic rooms aren't generally heated.

BUDGET OPTIONS

Albergue de Juventud, Paseo Conde de Sepúlveda (☎911/420226). This recently refurbished youth hostel has no curfew, is spacious and open throughout the day. ①.

Fonda Aragón (☎911/433527) and **Fonda Cubo** (☎911/436386), both Plaza Mayor 4. Rotten rooms but an ideal position and as cheap as they come. ①.

Hostal Residencia Don Jaime, c/Ochoa Ondategui 8 (☎911/444787). A new and excellent *hostal* near Plaza de Azoguejo. All doubles have their own bathroom. ③.

Hostal-Restaurante El Hidalgo, c/José Canalejas 3 (☎911/428190). A comfortable *hostal* with dreamlike views over San Millán from rooms 28, 29 and 30. ③.

Hostal Juan Bravo, c/Juan Bravo 12 (☎911/435521). Lots of big comfortable rooms and plant-festooned bathrooms. ③.

Hostal Postigo, c/Conde Gazzola Ceretto 2 (☎911/436840). A bargain if you can get in – it caters mainly to long-stay residents. Nice location near a viewpoint above the aqueduct. ②.

HOTELS

Hotel El Hidalgo, c/José Canalejas 3 (☎911/428190). Small, beautiful old building overlooking the church of San Martín, with a good restaurant. ④.

Hotel Infanta Isabel, c/Isabel la Católica 1 (☎911/443105). A brand new, luxury hotel in an ideal position on Plaza Mayor. ⑤.

Hotel Los Linajes, c/Dr.Velasco 9 (☎911/431201). Another comfortable, central three-star hotel. ⑤.

CAMPING

Camping Acueducto (☎911/425000; open July–Sept). The nearest campsite, a couple of kilometres out on the road to La Granja; take a #2 *Nueva Segovia* bus from the Plaza Mayor.

The city

Segovia has more than a full day's worth of sights. If you're on a flying visit from Madrid, obvious priorities are the **cathedral** and **Alcázar** in the old town, and the church of **Vera Cruz** and **aqueduct**, just outside the walls to west and east. Given more time, take a walk out of the city for the **views**, or just wander at will through the **old quarters** of the city, away from the centre: each has a village atmosphere of its own.

The Cathedral to the Alcázar

Segovia's **Catedral** (summer daily 9am–7pm; winter Mon–Fri 9.30am–1pm & 3–6pm, Sat & Sun 9.30am–6pm) was the last major Gothic building in Spain, and arguably the last in Europe. Accordingly it takes the style to its logical – or perhaps illogical – extreme, with pinnacles and flying buttresses tacked on at every conceivable point. Though impressive for its size alone, the interior is surprisingly bare for so florid a construction and its space cramped by a great green marble *coro* at its very centre. The treasures are almost all confined to the museum (200ptas) which opens off the cloisters.

Down beside the cathedral, c/de Daoiz leads past a line of souvenir shops to the church of San Andrés and on to a small park in front of the **Alcázar** (summer 10am–

7pm; winter 10am–6pm; 350ptas). An extraordinary fantasy of a castle, with its narrow towers and flurry of turrets, it will seem eerily familiar to just about every visitor, having served as the model for the original Disneyland castle in California. It is itself a bit of a sham. Although it dates from the fourteenth and fifteenth centuries, it was almost completely destroyed by a fire in 1862 and rebuilt as a deliberately hyperbolic version of the original. Still, it should be visited, if only for the magnificent panoramas from the tower.

Vera Cruz

The best of Segovia's ancient churches is undoubtedly **Vera Cruz** (Tues–Sun 10.30am–1.30pm & 3.30–7pm, winter 3.30–6pm and often closed throughout Nov; 125ptas), a remarkable twelve-sided building outside town in the valley facing the Alcázar. It was built by the Knights Templar in the early thirteenth century on the pattern of the church of the Holy Sepulchre in Jerusalem, and once housed part of the True Cross (hence its name; the sliver of wood itself is now in the nearby village church at Zamarramala). Inside, the nave is circular, and its heart is occupied by a strange two-storeyed chamber – again twelve-sided – in which the knights, as part of their initiation, stood vigil over the cross. Climb the tower for a highly photogenic vista of the city.

While you're over here you could take in the prodigiously walled monastery of **San Juan de la Cruz** (10am–1.30pm & 4–7pm), also referred to as the Convento de las Carmelitas, with the gaudy mausoleum of its founder-saint.

The synagogue and a tour of the churches

One of the lesser-known sights of Segovia is the **Synagogue**, which now serves as the convent church of **Corpus Cristi**, in a little courtyard at the end of c/Juan Bravo near the east end of the cathedral. You can see part of its exterior from the Paseo del Salón, near which are the streets of the old *Judería*. It's very similar in style to Santa María la Blanca in Toledo, though less refined. During the last century it was badly damaged by fire, so what you see now is a reconstruction, but historic synagogues are so rare in Spain that this is still of interest. Opening times are unpredictable.

Just east of the synagogue is the **Plaza Juan Bravo**, one of the city's grandest squares, whose ensemble of buildings include the **Torre de Lozoya** (open most evenings and Sun lunchtimes for exhibitions), and the church of **San Martín**, which demonstrates all the local stylistic peculiarities, though the best of none of them. It has the characteristic covered portico, a fine arched tower, and a typically Romanesque aspect; also, like most of Segovia's churches, it can only be visited when it's open for business, during early morning or evening services. In the middle of the plaza is a **statue of Juan Bravo**, a local folk hero who led the *comuneros* rebellion against Carlos V's attempts to take away their traditional rights. Around the square, notice the facades of the buildings, many of which display the local taste for plaster decoration (*esgrafado*) which is as common on new structures as it is on old.

North of here, the church of **La Trinidad** preserves the purest Romanesque style in Segovia: each span of its double-arched apse has intricately carved capitals, every one of them unique. Nearby – and making a good loop to or from the Alcázar – is the **Plaza San Esteban**, recently restored and worth seeing for its superb, five-storeyed, twelfth-century tower.

The aqueduct and other churches

The **Aqueduct**, over 800m long and at its highest point towering some 30m above the Plaza de Azoguejo, stands up without a drop of mortar or cement. No one knows exactly when it was built, but probably around the end of the first century AD under

WALKS AROUND SEGOVIA & THE MONASTERIO DE PARRAL

Segovia is an excellent city for walks. Follow the signposted bypass road outside the city, particularly to the south, and you get ever-changing views of the cathedral and the Alcázar from across the valley. The road then doubles back along the other side of the Alcázar, passing near San Juan de la Cruz and Vera Cruz.

From there you could continue to the **Monasterio del Parral** (Mon–Fri 10am–12.30pm & 3–6.30pm, Sat & Sun 9am–noon); or better still, follow the track which circles behind Vera Cruz. El Parral is a sizeable and partly ruined complex occupied by Hieronymites, an order found only in Spain. Ring the bell for admission and you will be shown the cloister and church; the latter is a late Gothic building with rich sculpture at the east end, but marred by damp and mould (this may be cured by current restorations, which may also mean unexpected closures).

For the **best view of all** of Segovia, however, take the main road north for 2km or so towards Cuéllar/Turégano. A panorama of the whole city, including the aqueduct, gradually unfolds.

the Emperor Trajan. Supposedly it's still in use, bringing water from the Río Frío to the city, but it's often dry, and in recent years traffic vibration and pollution have been threatening to undermine the entire structure. If you climb the stairs beside the aqueduct you can get a view looking down over it from a surviving fragment of the city walls.

Another fine Romanesque church in the typical Segovian style, with tower and open porticoes, is **San Millán**, which lies between the aqueduct and the bus station. Its interior has been restored to its original form. Also, beyond the aqueduct, you'll find **San Just** which has a wonderful Romanesque wall painting in the apse.

Museums

If you have time, check out the **Provincial Museum**, which should by now have reopened in a brand new setting in the Casa del Sol, the former town abattoir perched on the walls between the Puerta de San Andrés and the Alcázar. It has an enlarged collection of fine arts, sculpture and ceramics, and ethnological and archeological exhibits. There's also the **Casa-Museo de Antonio Machado** at c/Desamparados 5 (Tues–Sun 4–7pm, winter 4–6pm), one of Spain's greatest poets of the early twentieth century; he is more associated with Soria but spent the last years of his life teaching here.

Finally, kids might find the **Museo de Holográfica** (Tues–Sun 10.30am–2pm & 4–7.30pm; 200ptas), at c/Daoiz 9 near San Andrés, a welcome change from all the history; housed in a fifteenth-century cellar, it features gruesome 3D pictures of Dracula and others.

Eating and drinking

Segovia takes its cooking seriously, with restaurants of Madrid quality – and prices. Culinary specialities include roast suckling pig (*cochinillo asado*), displayed in the raw in the windows of many restaurants, and the rather healthier *judiones*, large white beans from La Granja.

Bars and restaurants

There is a concentration of cheaper bar-restaurants on c/de la Infanta Isabella, off the Plaza Mayor, and late-night bars on c/Escuderos and c/Judería Vieja, and along Avda. Fernández Ladreda.

INEXPENSIVE

El Abuelo, c/Juan Bravo. A good range of prices including a *menú economico* for 1000ptas including wine, beautifully served in a small, friendly, family-run restaurant.

Mesón del Campesino, c/Infanta Isabella. One of the best budget restaurants in town, serving decent value *menús* and *combinados* to a young crowd.

La Codorniz, c/Escultor Marinas 3. Features an inexpensive *menú* and lots of *combinados* involving *codorniz* (quail).

La Escuela, c/San Millán. Youthful bar with occasional live bands.

Bar-Mesón Cuevas de San Estebán, c/Valdelaguila, off the top end of Plaza San Estéban. A cavern-restaurant and bar, popular with locals and excellent value.

Bar José María, c/Cronista Lecea 11, just off Plaza Mayor. This bar-annex to one of Segovia's best restaurants (see below) has delicious and modest-priced *tapas*.

Narizotas, Plaza de San Martín. Bar-restaurant with a bright, relaxed atmosphere, good service and excellent value *menú*.

Café Once, c/San Agustín 11. An enjoyable bar to drink late-night *copas*.

Tasca La Posada, Juderia Vieja 1. Another fine *bar-mesón* for *tapas*, *raciones*, or a *menú*.

MODERATE–EXPENSIVE RESTAURANTS

Mesón de Cándido, Plaza Azoguejo(☎911/428102). The city's most famous restaurant, reopened in 1992 by the founder's son and still the place for *cochinillo* and the like. The menú is a relatively modest 2500ptas.

La Cocina de Sant Millán, c/Sant Millán 5 (☎911/436226; closed Sun night and Jan 7–31). A little out of the way but imaginative cooking and reasonable prices.

Mesón José María, c/Cronista Lecea 11, just off Plaza Mayor (☎911/434484; open daily). This is currently reckoned the city's best and most imaginative restaurant, with its modern variations on Castilian classics. The *menú* is a hefty 4000ptas but you could pay less.

Santa Bárbara, c/Ezequiel González 33. Extensive menu and excellent seafood.

OUT OF TOWN

La Posada de Javier, in the village of Torrecaballeros, 8km northeast on the N110 (☎911/401136; closed Sun night, Mon & July). Serious *Madrileño* – and Segoviano – gourmands eat out in the neighbouring villages, and this lovely old farmhouse is one of the most popular choices. It is pricey but has a good *menú* at 2500ptas. Booking is essential at weekends.

La Granja and Riofrío

Segovia has a major outlying attraction in the Bourbon summer palace and gardens of **La Granja**, 10km southeast of the town on the N601 Madrid road, and connected by regular bus services. True Bourbon afficionados, with time and transport, might also want to visit a second palace and hunting museum 12km west of La Granja at **Riofrío**.

La Granja

LA GRANJA (or San Ildefonso de la Granja, to give it its full title) was built by the first Bourbon king of Spain, Felipe V, no doubt homesick for the luxuries of Versailles. Its glories are the mountain setting and the extravagant wooded grounds and gardens, but it's worth casting a quick eye over the **palace** (Tues–Sat 10am–1.30pm & 3–5pm, Sun 10am–2pm; 400ptas, free to EC members on Wed). Though destroyed in parts and damaged throughout by a fire in 1918, much has been well restored. The most striking thing about the long series of rooms is their perfect symmetry – you get the uncanny feeling, as you stand looking through the open doorways, of gazing into a mirror endlessly reflecting the same room. Everything is furnished in plush French imperial style but it's almost all of Spanish origin; the huge chandeliers, for example, were made in the crystal factory (which still exists) in the village of San Ildefonso.

The highlight of the **gardens** (daily 10am–7pm) is its series of fountains, which culminate in the fifty-foot high jet of La Fama. They're really fantastic and on no account to be missed, which means timing your visit from 5.30pm, when they're all switched on.

The **village** of San Idelfonso de La Granja is a lively place, with several **bars** and **restaurants** where you can while away any spare time: try the *Bar La Villa* off the main square for *tapas*; *Bar Zaca*, also off the square, for lunch; or *Bar Madrid*, near the palace. There is a range of **accommodation**, too, if you prefer to stay here than Segovia: try the *Hostal Roma* (☎911/470369; ④), right outside the palace gates, or the inexpensive *Pensión El Parque* (☎911/470598; ②) on the Segovia road or *Pensión Engracia* (☎911/470154; ①), near the square. There is one **bus** a day direct to Madrid, which leaves at 8pm after the gardens close; otherwise connect via Segovia (last bus back at 9.30pm).

Riofrío

The palace at **RIOFRÍO** (Tues–Sat 10am–1.30pm & 3–5pm, Sun 10am–2pm; house and grounds 300ptas; grounds only 200ptas) was built by Isabel, the widow of Philip V, who feared she would be banished from La Granja itself by her stepson Fernando VI; however he died leaving the throne for Isabel's own son Carlos III and Riofrío was not occupied until the nineteenth-century when Alfonso XII moved in to mourn the death of his young queen Mercedes. He too died pretty soon after, which is perhaps why the palace has a spartan and slightly tatty feel.

The complex, painted in dusty pink with green shutters, is surrounded not by manicured gardens but by a deer park, which you can drive through but not wander into. Inside the palace, you have to join a guided tour, which winds through an endless sequence of rooms, none stunningly furnished. Around half the tour is devoted to a **museum of hunting**, whose most interesting items are reconstructions of cave paintings, including the famous Altamira drawings.

North from Segovia

Heading **north from Segovia**, you're faced with quite a variety of routes. The train line heads northwest towards Valladolid and León, past the castles of **Coca** and **Medina del Campo** – two of the very finest in Spain. If you have transport of your own, or time for convoluted local bus routes, you can take in further impressive castles in Segovia province at **Pedraza**, **Turégano** and **Cuéllar**, and still more by striking north again to **Peñafiel** and the chain of castles along the Duero river. If you are looking for a night's stop in a small town, Pedraza and Turégano, around 40km from Segovia, would fit the bill nicely.

For details on this area, see p.318–320 in the *Old Castile* chapter.

East of Madrid: Alcalá de Henares, Nuevo Baztán, Guadalajara and the Alcarria

East of the capital there's considerably less to detain you. The only tempting daytrips are to the old university town of **Alcalá de Henares**, Cervantes' birthplace, and for Baroque enthusiasts, **Nuevo Batzan**, an eighteenth-century new town planned by José de Churriguera. Further afield, the largely modern city of **Guadalajara** has little to recommend it although the region southwest of here, the **Alcarria**, has its charms, especially if you want to follow the footsteps of Spain's Nobel prizewinner, Camilo José Cela, who described his wanderings here in the 1940s in his book, *Viaje a la Alcarria*.

Alcalá de Henares

ALCALÁ DE HENARES, a little over 30km from Madrid, is one of Europe's most ancient university towns, and renowned as the birthplace of Miguel de Cervantes. In the sixteenth century the university was a rival to Salamanca's but in 1836 the faculties moved to Madrid and the town went into decline. Almost all the artistic heritage was lost in the Civil War and nowadays it's virtually a suburb of Madrid. It is not somewhere you'd want to stay longer than it takes to see the sights, but that's no problem with trains from Madrid (Chamartín or Atocha) every few minutes throughout the day.

The **Universidad Antigua** (11am–2pm & 6–8pm on Sun and holidays; daily in Aug) stands at the heart of the old town. It was endowed by Cardinal Cisneros (also known as Cardinal Jiménez) at the beginning of the sixteenth century and features a fabulous Plateresque facade and a Great Hall, the **Paraninfo** (entered through the *Hostería del Estudiante*, an expensive restaurant at the back), with a gloriously decorated Mudéjar *artesonado* ceiling. Next door, the **Capilla de San Ildefonso** has another superb ceiling, intricately stuccoed walls, and the Italian marble tomb of Cardinal Cisneros.

Two buildings lay claim to Cervantes' birthplace. The **Casa de Cervantes** on c/ Mayor (10am–2pm) is the more worthwhile: though the house itself is hardly thirty years old, it's authentic in style, furnished with genuine sixteenth-century objects, and contains a small museum with a few early editions and other curiosities related to the author.

The local **Turismo** (Mon–Fri 11am–2pm, Sat & Sun 11am–2pm & 4–6pm), just off the central Plaza de Cervantes, has maps and further information, and from here nothing of interest is more than a short walk away. You'll find no shortage of places to eat centrally and, if you wanted to stay, several *pensiones* on the Plaza de Cervantes itself.

Nuevo Baztán

Twenty kilometres southeast of Alcalá, or 45km from Madrid, **NUEVO BAZTÁN** should appeal to anyone interested in architecture, planning or the unusual. It was designed and built in 1709–13 by José de Churriguera in response to a commission from the royal treasurer, who aimed to develop a local decorative arts industry. Today it's semi-deserted, though brash modern villas are being built nearby for well-heeled commuters to the capital. As a focus, Churriguera built a **palace** and **church** as a single architectural unit. The latter has a massive twin-towered facade and a central dome and *retablos* by the architect within. Behind the palace, now fenced off, is the **Plaza de Fiestas**, with its balconies for watching celebrations. The houses of the workers comprise the rest of the settlement.

The best day to visit Nuevo Batzán is a Sunday. *Empresa Izquierdo* (c/Goya 80; Metro *Goya*) runs two buses daily from Madrid but only on Sunday do these allow you any time here, and this is the only day the church is sure to be open.

Guadalajara

GUADALAJARA, north from Alcalá de Henares, is not terribly exciting despite its famous name. Severely battered during the Civil War, it's now a small industrial city, provincial and scruffy. There are, however, one or two worthwhile buildings which survived bombardment, notably the **Palacio del Infantado** (Tues–Sat 10.15am–2pm & 4–7pm, Sun 10.15am–2pm; 100ptas). This, the former home of the Duke of Mendoza, boasts a wonderful decorative facade and cloister-like patio, and now houses a fairly average local art museum. It is to be found a few blocks to the northwest of the town's large park-like central square, Plaza Capitán Beixareu Rivera.

If you needed, or wanted, **to stay**, *Hostal España*, c/Teniente Figueroa 3 (☎911/211303; ②) is a decent budget option. **Bars** and **restaurants** are plentiful, too. *Can Vic* on Plaza Fernando Beladiez is a good low-priced place, or for a seafood and fish blow-out there's *Casa Victor* at c/Bardales 6. **Late-night** and **music bars** are mostly to be found along c/Sigüenza.

Moving on

The main road and rail lines from Madrid to Zaragoza and Barcelona both pass through Alcalá and Guadalajara, and continue more or less parallel throughout their journeys. Sigüenza (see p.146) and Medinaceli (see p.322) each make excellent resting points on your way. From Guadalajara you can also cut down to Cuenca, and from there continue towards Valencia and the coast. This is a very beautiful drive, past the great dams of the Embalse de Entrepeñas and Embalse de Buendía, and takes you through the heart of the **Alcarria region**.

The Alcarria

The **Alcarria** has few particular monuments but the wild scenery and sporadic settlements are eerily impressive, especially coming upon them so close to Madrid. Many of the high sierra villages, north of the N320, were deserted during the Nationalist advance on Madrid in the Civil War and have only a handful of permanent inhabitants, plus a few *Madrileño* weekenders who have inherited and are restoring the old cottages.

The largest town of the region, **PASTRANA**, 15km south of the N320, merits a diversion. The museum of its vast **Colegiata** church (10.30am–1pm & 4.30–6pm; 300ptas) contains some wonderful fifteenth-century tapestries depicting the conquest of Tangier by Alfonso V of Portugal, as well as richly decorated ebony and bronze altar pieces from the Phillipines. These were brought to Pastrana by the Princess of Eboli, duchess of the town, who after a court scandal was imprisoned in the palace overlooking the central square. Also of interest is the **Franciscan monastery**, a ten-minute walk out of town, originally founded by the Carmelites, where the Princess lived for a time. It houses a small museum of varied religious art (Sat & Sun noon–1pm & 4–5pm; 200ptas).

Pastrana's twisting streets, including its former **Jewish and Arab quarters**, offer endless rambling but not much diversion in the evening. If you want to **stay**, the only place is the *Pensión Moratín* (☎911/370116; ②), a clean and comfortable place on the main road through the village.

travel details

Buses
From Madrid

Estación Sur de Autobuses, c/Canarias 17 (M° Palos de la Frontera) to: Toledo (24 daily; 1hr 30min).

Auto-Res, Fernández Shaw 1 (M° Conde de Casal) to: Ávila (3 daily; 2hr).

Estación Herranz, c/Fernández de los Rios to: El Escorial (15 daily; 1hr).

La Sepulvedana, Paseo de la Florida 11 (M° Norte) to: Segovia (10 daily; 1hr 45min).

Ávila to: Madrid (3 daily; 2hr); Salamanca (5 daily; 1hr 30min); Segovia (1–5 daily; 1hr).

El Escorial to: Guadarrama (7 daily; 20min); Valle de los Caídos (1 daily; 15min).

Segovia to: Ávila (4 daily; 1hr 30min); La Granja (6–10 daily; 20min); Madrid 10–15 daily; 1hr 45min); Salamanca (4 daily; 3hr); Valladolid (3 daily; 2hr 30min).

Toledo to: Ciudad Real (for the south; 1 daily; 2hr); Talavera de la Reina (for Extremadura; 10 daily; 1hr 30min).

Trains

From Madrid

Atocha Station (M° Atocha) to: El Escorial via Chamartín (28 daily; 1hr); Segovia via Chamartín (9 daily; 2–3hr); Toledo via Aranjuez (8 daily; 1hr 30min).

Príncipe Pío (M° Norte) to: Ávila (28 daily; 2hr); Cercedilla (20 daily; 1hr 30min).

Aranjuez to: Cuenca (6 daily; 2hr); Madrid (8 daily; 45min); Toledo (9 daily; 30min–1hr 30min).

Ávila to: Madrid (28 daily; 2hr); Medina del Campo (16 daily; 1hr); Salamanca (13 daily; 2hr); Valladolid (14 daily; 1hr 45min).

Cercedilla to: Madrid (20 daily; 1hr 30min); Puerto de Navacerrada (11 daily; 30min); Segovia (10 daily; 45min).

El Escorial to: Ávila (11 daily; 1hr); Segovia (11 daily; 1hr).

Segovia to: Cercedilla (10 daily; 45min); Madrid (5–12 daily; 2hr); Valladolid (2 daily; 2hr).

Toledo to: Aranjuez (8 daily; 45min).

CHAPTER THREE

NEW CASTILE AND EXTREMADURA

T he vast area covered by this chapter is some of the most travelled, yet least visited, country in Spain. Once south of **Toledo** (which is covered in the previous chapter, "Around Madrid"), most tourists thunder non-stop across the plains of New Castile to Valencia and Andalucía, or follow the great rivers through Extremadura into Portugal. At first sight this is understandable. **New Castile** in particular is Spain at its least welcoming: a vast, bare plain, burning hot in summer, chillingly exposed in winter. But the first impression is not an entirely fair one – away from the main highways the villages of the plain are as welcoming as any in the coun-

---

FIESTAS

February

First weekend *La Endiablada* at Almonacid Marquesado (near Cuenca), a very old festival which sees all the boys dressing up as devils and parading through the streets.

Week before Lent *Carnival* everywhere.

March/April

Holy Week (*Semana Santa*) celebrated with magnificent ritual (floats, penitents, etc) in Cuenca.

Pascua (Passion of the Resurrection) major Easter fiesta in Trujillo.

April 23 *San Jorge.*. Celebrations characterized by tremendous enthusiasm continue for several days in Cáceres.

May

Late May fair at Cáceres. Also – again with no fixed date – *Cabalata*, muleteer races, at Atienza (on the road between Sigüenza and Aranda de Duero).

June

23–27 *San Juan.* Particularly manic festival in the picturesque town of Coria (50km west of Plasencia) with a bull let loose for a few hours a day, everyone dancing and drinking in the streets, and running for their lives when it appears.

Ancient Drama Festival in the Roman theatre at Mérida lasts through the summer.

July

14 July fiestas start in La Puebla de Montalbán, in the Montes de Toledo. Bulls are let loose in the streets.

September

First week *Vendimia* – grape harvest – celebrations at Valdepeñas; major fair at Trujillo also early in the month.

Week leading up to third Sunday Festivals in Jarandilla and Madrigal de la Vera with bullrunning in front of cows – which are served up on the final day's feast.

Spanish Classical Drama Festival at Almagro (Ciudad Real).

October

1 *San Miguel*. Fiestas at any town or church named after the saint – particularly at Badajoz.

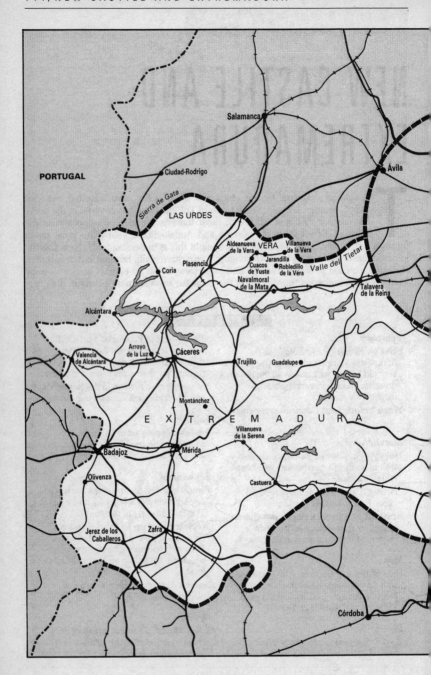

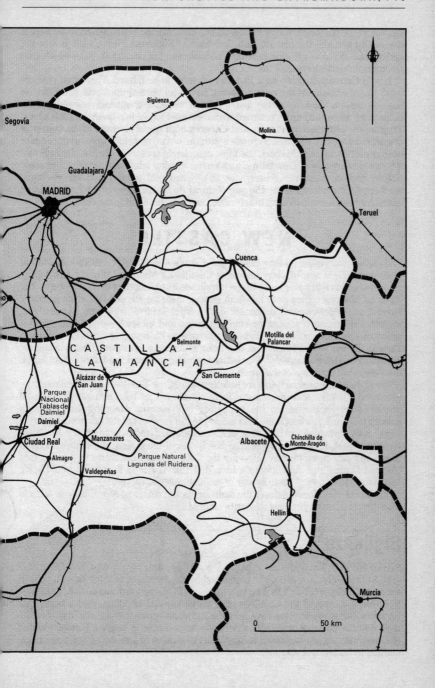

try, and in the northeast, where the mountains start, are the extraordinary cliff-hanging city of **Cuenca** and the historic cathedral town of **Sigüenza**. New Castile is also the agricultural and wine-growing heartland of Spain and the country through which Don Quixote cut his despairing swath.

It is in **Extremadura**, though, that there is most to be missed. This harsh environment was the cradle of the *conquistadores*, men who opened up a new world for the Spanish empire. Remote before and forgotten since, Extremadura enjoyed a brief golden age when the heroes returned with their gold to live in a flourish of splendour. **Trujillo**, the birthplace of Pizarro, and **Cáceres** both preserve entire towns built with *conquistador* wealth, the streets crowded with the ornate mansions of returning empire builders. Then there is **Mérida**, the most completely preserved Roman city in Spain, and the monasteries of **Guadalupe** and **Yuste**, the one fabulously wealthy, the other rich in imperial memories. Finally, for little-visited wild scenery and superb fauna, northern Extremadura has the **Parque Natural de Monfragüe**, where even the most casual birdwatcher can look up to see eagles and vultures circling the cliffs.

NEW CASTILE

The region that was for so long called **New Castile** – and until the 1980s held Madrid in its domain – is now officially known as **Castilla-La Mancha**. Although the heavily cultivated plains that cover much of the terrain are less bleak than they once were – the name La Mancha comes from the Arab *manxa*, meaning steppe – the main points of interest are widely spaced on an arc drawn from Madrid, with little between that rewards exploration. If you are travelling on **trains and buses** towards Aragón, there's little to justify a stop other than Sigüenza (en route to Zaragoza) or Cuenca (en route to Teruel). To the south, Toledo has bus links within its own province but heading for Andalucia or Extremadura you'd do better returning to Madrid and starting out again; the Toledo rail line stops at the town.

If you do have **transport**, and are **heading south**, the Toledo–Ciudad Real road, the Montes de Toledo, and the marshy Parque Nacional de las Tablas de Daimiel, all provide good alternatives to the sweltering NIV *autovia*. **Heading east**, through Cuenca to Teruel, the best route is to follow the Río Jucar out of the province, by way of weird rock formations in the Ciudad Encantada and the source of the Río Tajo. **Heading west**, into Estremadura, the NV is one of the dullest and hottest roads in Spain, and can be avoided by following the C501 through the Sierra de Gredos (see "Around Madrid") or cutting onto it from dull Talavera de la Reina; this would bring you to the Monastery of Yuste by way of the lush valley of La Vera.

The **sections following** cover the main sights and routes of New Castile in a clockwise direction, from northeast to southwest of Madrid.

Sigüenza

SIGÜENZA, 120km northeast of Madrid, is a sleepy little town with a beautiful cathedral. At first sight, it seems quite untouched by the twentieth century, though appearances are deceptive: taken by Franco's troops in 1936, the town was on the Nationalist front line for most of the Civil War, and its people and buildings paid a heavy toll. However, the post-war years have seen the cathedral restored, the Plaza Mayor recobbled, and the bishop's castle rebuilt virtually from rubble to house a *parador*, so that the only evidence of its troubled history is in the facades of unrestored buildings, pockmarked by bullets and shrapnel.

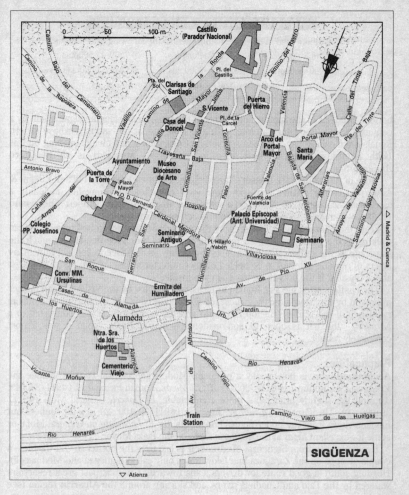

The cathedral, churches and castle

The main streets of the town lead you towards the hilltop **Cathedral** (11.30am–2.30pm & 4–6pm), built in the pinkish stone which characterizes the town. Started in 1150 by Sigüenza's first bishop, Bernardo of Toledo, it is essentially Gothic, with three rose windows, though it has been much altered over the years. Facing the main entrance is a huge marble *coro* with an altar to a thirteenth-century figure of the Virgin. Put a coin in the slot and it lights up like a pinball machine – a practice that sets a tone for the building, for this is one of those churches where every door is locked unless you buy the visitors' ticket (125ptas) inside. For once, it is well worth it.

The principal treasure is the alabaster tomb of Martín Vásquez de Arce, known as *El Doncel*; a favourite of Isabella la Católica, he was killed fighting the Moors in Granada. On the other side of the building is an extraordinary doorway: Plateresque at the bottom, Mudéjar in the middle and Gothic at the top – an amazing amalgam, built by a confused sixteenth-century architect. Take a look, too, at the sacristy, whose superb Renaissance ceiling has 304 heads carved by Covarrubias; in a chapel opening off this (with an unusual cupola, best seen in the mirror provided) is an El Greco *Annunciation*.

More of the cathedral's treasures are displayed in the **cloister** (11.30am–1.30pm & 4.30–7pm), while further artworks from local churches and convents, including a saccharine Zurbarán of *Mary as a child*, are displayed in a **Museu Diocesano** (11.30am–2pm & 3–7.30pm; winter 4–6pm) across the square.

From the **Plaza Mayor**, overseen by the cathedral's pencil-thin bell tower, you can walk up to the castle, passing en route the church of **San Vicente**. This is much the same age as the cathedral and is interesting mainly as a chance to see just how many layers of remodelling had to be peeled off by the restorers; an ancient figure of Christ above the altar is the only thing to detain you inside.

The **castle** started life as a Roman fortress, was adapted by the Visigoths and further improved by the Moors for their *Alcazaba*. Reconquered in 1124, it became the official residence of the warlike Bishop Bernardo and his successors. It was converted to a *parador* – the bar is open to non-residents – in the 1960s, when it was almost completely rebuilt.

Practicalities

Accommodation is not usually a problem. Modest and central *hostales* include the *Venancio*, San Roque 1 (☎911/390347; ③); *El Mesón*, Román Pascual 14 (☎911/390649; ③); and the slightly pricier but more comfortable, *El Doncel*, General Mola (☎911/391090; ③). The *Parador Castillo de Sigüenza* (☎911/390100; ⑤) is a bit soulless but has fine views from the upper floors. For **meals**, try *El Laberinto* on General Mola, or settle for excellent *tapas* at the *Cafetería Atrio* on the Plaza Mayor.

Heading north from Sigüenza, **Medinaceli** is just over the border in Old Castile – a couple of stops on the Zaragoza line (slow trains only call at Sigüenza and Medinaceli). Heading south, a good route for drivers leads **towards Cuenca**, past great reservoirs watered by the Tajo and Guadiela rivers, and skirting around the **Alcarria** region (see p.14).

Cuenca and around

The mountainous, craggy countryside around **CUENCA** is as dramatic as any in Spain, and all the more so in the context of New Castile. The city itself, too, the capital of a sparsely populated province, is an extraordinary-looking place, with balconied houses hanging over the clifftop – the finest of them converted to a Museum of Abstract Art – and a site enclosed on three sides by the deep gorges of the rivers Huécar and Júcar. No surprise, then, that this is a popular weekend outing from Madrid; to get the most from a visit, try to come on a weekday – and take the time to stay a night and absorb the atmosphere.

Arrival and accommodation

The old town of Cuenca – the **Ciudad Antigua** – stands on a high ridge, looped to the south by the Río Huécar and the **modern town** and its suburbs. If you're driving in, follow signs for the *Catedral* and try one of the car parks up in the old town. Arriving by **train** (be warned – the lines here are very slow) or **bus** you'll find yourself at the southern edge of the modern part of town: the bus station is just beyond the *RENFE* terminal. C/Ramón y Cajal leads from either to the Puerta Valencia, from whence it's a steep climb up to the old town; bus #1 or #2 will save you the walk.

Close by the bus and train stations, just left of c/Ramón y Cajal, at c/García Izcara 8, is a **Turismo** (Mon–Fri 9am–2pm & 4.30–6.30pm, Sat 10am–1pm), which has information and maps on the whole province and organizes summer trips to the Ciudad Encantada (see below).

Most **accommodation** is in the new town, with a concentration of *hostales* along c/Ramón y Cajal; if you want to stay in the old town there are just two options – the *Posada de San José* and the upmarket *Hotel Leonor de Aquitania*.

Hostal Avenida, Avda. Carretería 39 (☎966/214343). Functional but comfortable. ③.

Pensión Central, c/Alonso Chirino 9 (☎966/211511). Basic. ②.

Hotel Figón de Pedro, c/Cervantes 13 (☎966/224511). Well-run hotel at the heart of the modern town, with an excellent restaurant. ④.

Hotel Leonor de Aquitania, c/San Pedro 60 (☎966/231000). The town's prime hotel – beautifully sited in the old town, with superb views and prices to match. ⑤.

Pensión Marin, Ramón y Cajal 53 (☎966/221878). Good value *pensión*. ②.

Hostal San Isidro, Ramón y Cajal 33 (☎966/211163). Reasonable modern *hostal*. ③.

Posada de San José, c/Julián Romesco 4 (☎966/211300). A lovely old building in the old town near the cathedral. Only 25 rooms (16 with bath), so be sure to book ahead. ③.

Posada San Julian, c/de las Torres 1 (☎966/211704). Pleasant, no-frills rooms in an attractive former convent near the river. ②.

Fonda Tintes, c/de los Tintes. Worth a try in summer, when permanent guests are away. ②.

The Ciudad Antigua and the Abstract Art Museum

Cross one of the many bridges over the River Huécar and you start to climb steeply (most of the streets are stepped) towards the **Ciudad Antigua**, a narrow wedge of lanes, petering out in superb views to west and east.

More or less at the centre of the quarter is the Plaza Mayor, a fine space, entered through the arches of the Baroque *Ayuntamiento* and ringed by cafés. Occupying most of its east side is the **Catedral** (daily 9am–1.30pm & 4.30–7.30pm/6.30pm), whose ugly unfinished facade betrays a misguided attempt to beautify a simple Gothic building. The interior is much more attractive, especially the carved Plateresque arch at the end of the north aisle, and the chapel next to it, with distinctly unchristian carvings round its entrance. The east chapel, directly behind the high altar, has a superb *artesonado* ceiling, which can just about be glimpsed through the locked door.

Alongside is a small **Museo Catedralicio** (Tues–Fri 11am–2pm & 4–6pm, Sat 11am–2pm & 4–7pm, Sun 11am–2pm; 200ptas) which contains some beautiful gold and silver work as well as doors by Alonso Berruguete. The ceiling here, now a sea of Baroque icing sugar shades, was originally a beautiful Mudéjar work like the one in the east chapel. Further religious treasures are to be found down c/Obispo Valero in the **Museo Diocesano** (Tues–Sat 11am–2pm & 4–6pm, Sat till 8pm, Sun 11am–2pm; 200ptas), including two canvasses by El Greco, a magnificent *Crucifixion* by Gerard David, and a Byzantine diptych unique in Spain. Right opposite is a new and excellent **Museo Arqueológico** (Tues–Sat 10am–2pm & 4–7pm, Sun 10am–2pm; 200 ptas), showcasing local Roman finds.

The artistic highlight of Cuenca, however, has to be the **Museo de Arte Abstracto** (Tues–Fri 11am–2pm & 4–6pm, Sat 11am–2pm & 4–8pm, Sun 11am–2.30pm; 300ptas),

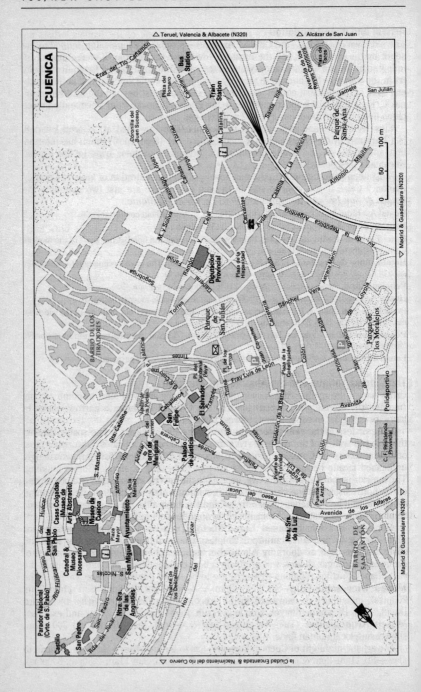

a gallery established in the 1960s by Fernando Zóbel, one of the leading artists in Spain's "abstract generation". It is now run by the prestigious Fundación Juan March, which displays works from a core collection of abstract painting and sculpture by, among many others, José Guerrero, Lucio Muñoz, Antonio Saura and Fernando Zobel, and hosts some of the best exhibitions to be found in provincial Spain. The museum itself is a stunning conversion from the extraordinary *Casas Colgadas* ("hanging houses"), a pair of fifteenth-century houses, with cantilevered balconies, literally hanging from the cliff face.

There are other monuments signposted in Cuenca, but the greatest attraction is the place itself. Have a drink in one of the bars opposite the cathedral in the Plaza Mayor and you get a sense of what it must feel like to live in one of the suspended houses, or walk along the gorge of the Huécar and look up at the *Casas Colgadas* and the other less secure-looking buildings high above the river. At night the effect is even more dramatic.

Eating, drinking and nightlife

The tourist heart of Cuenca is the Plaza Mayor, and for evening *copas*, there's no better place. You can have meals here, too, though you will eat better down at the **bars and restaurants** of the modern town. Cuenca isn't exactly full of **nightlife** – this is small town Castile – but there is a scattering of music and disco-bars in and around c/Doctor Galíndez, near the train and bus stations. Some of the best places to eat are listed below.

Figón de Pedro, c/Cervantes 13 (☎966/224511; closed Mon & Sun pm). A renowned restaurant, serving classic Castilian roasts, and a superb mero (fish) dish. Moderate to expensive.

Mesón Casas Colgada, c/Canónigos (☎966/223509; closed Thurs pm). A good restaurant up in the old town – housed in a fine hanging house. Features suckling pig and other Castilian specialities. Expensive.

La Ponderosa, c/San Francisco 20 (closed Sun). The best *tapas* selection in a street full of worthwhile *mesónes*.

Posada San Julian, c/de las Torres. A nice local with decent, inexpensive *menús*.

La Ciudad Encantada – and on towards Albarracín

The classic excursion from Cuenca is to the **Ciudad Encantada**, a 20-square-kilometre "park" of limestone outcrops, sculpted by erosion into a bizarre series of abstract, nature and animal-like forms. A few of the names – "fight between an elephant and a crocodile", for example – stretch the imagination a little, but the rocks are certainly amazing, and many of the creations really do look knocked into shape by human hands.

The most interesting area of sculptures is enclosed (admission daily 9.30am–8pm; 150ptas), and the extensive car park and restaurants outside testify to its popularity with weekending *Madrileños*. However, off season, or during the week, you can have the place almost to yourself. From Easter to October there are daily excursions from Cuenca for about 1000ptas; ask at the Turismo. Out of season, you'll need transport to get to the park, which is around 20km northeast, on signed backroads towards Albarracín. If you get stuck, there is a **hostal**, the *Ciudad Encantada* (③) opposite the entrance gate.

To the source of the Tajo

If you have transport, the route west from the Ciudad Encantada, towards Albarracín (see the Aragón chapter) is a delight, edging through the verdant **Júcar Gorge** and across the wild, scarcely populated Serrania de Cuenca. En route, still in Cuenca province, you might stop at **UÑA**, a village sited between a lagoon and barrage, where the *Hotel Agua Riscos* (☎966/281332; ③) has decent rooms, a panoramic restaurant and a garden bar.

Just over the provincial border, in Teruel province, the road **between Uña and Frías de Albarracín** runs past a point known as García, where a signpost directs you to the **source of the Río Tajo** (Tagus). Below a hideous 1960s sculpture, a trickle of muddy water seeps out, setting the course of one of Iberia's great rivers on its way to the Atlantic Ocean at Lisbon.

Belmonte and Alarcón

Travelling south from Cuenca – or west from Toledo – Cuenca province has a couple more places where you might consider breaking your journey: the castle villages of **Belmonte** (on the N420) and **Alarcón** (just off the NIII to Valencia).

Belmonte
The village of **BELMONTE** is encircled by a vast curtain wall, at the corner of which is a magnificent-looking fourteenth-century **castle** (daily 9am–2pm & 4–8pm; winter 3.30–6.30pm; 150ptas). Partially rebuilt in the last century, it is really little more than a shell, although belated restoration is revealing what must once have been stunning Muejar *artesanado* ceilings. The village, too, has seen better days, though it has a fine collegiate church, and a pleasant little **pensión**, *La Muralla* (☎967/171045; ③).

Continuing west from Belmonte, Cervantes enthusiasts might consider a detour to the village of **EL TOBOSO**, on a minor road south of the N301. This was the home of Dulcinea, whose "house" has of course been identified and turned into a small museum. West again from here, you could cut across country – and past the NIV – to **Consuegra**, with its trio of windmills.

Alarcón
ALARCÓN occupies a beautiful defensive site sculpted by the burrowings of the Júcar River. Almost completely encircled and walled, the village is accessible by a spit of land just wide enough to take a road which passes through a succession of **fortified gateways**. Unlike Belmonte, Alarcón has a bit of life about it, at least at weekends, as many of the old escutcheoned houses have been restored as retreats by *Madrileños*.

At the top of the village is an exquisite **castle**, eighth-century in origin and captured from the Moors in 1184 after a nine-month siege. This has been converted to house a **parador**, the *Parador Marqués de Villena* (☎966/331350; ⑥), one of the country's smallest and most characterful. More affordable accommodation is provided by the *Pensión El Infante* (☎966/331360; ③). Either option should be booked ahead in summer or at weekends.

Albacete province

Travelling between Madrid or Cuenca and Alicante or Murcia, you'll pass through **Albacete province**, one of Spain's more forgettable corners. Hot, arid plains, for the most part, this is very much the Spain of Castilla-La Mancha, with a dull provincial capital, **Albacete**, to match, known historically for its production of daggers and switchblades. Scenically, the only relief is in the hyperactive **Río Júcar**, which, in the north of the province, sinks almost without warning into the plain.

The Río Júcar: Alcalá del Júcar

If you are driving, it is worth a detour off the main roads east to cross the Júcar, cutting between **Casas-Ibáñez** (on the N322) and **Ayora** (on the N330) by way of the village of **ALCALÁ DEL JÚCAR**. Almost encircled by the river, this is an amazing sight, with its houses built one on top of the other and burrowed into the white cliff face. Several of these **cuevas** (caves) have been converted into bars and restaurants and they are well worth a stop, with rooms carved up to 170m through the cliff and windows overlooking the river on each side of the loop. They're open daily in summer but otherwise only at weekends. Alcalá also boasts a **castle**, adapted at intervals over the past 1500 years, though today just a shell – with views. If you want to stay, there are two **hostales** on the main road at the bottom of the village.

Albacete

ALBACETE was named *Al-Basit* – the plain – by the Moors, but save for a few old backstreets, it is basically a modern city. The underworked Turismo lists only two places of interest on its map. You could dispense with one of these, the **Catedral**, which is noted only for the presence of Ionic columns astride its nave instead of normal pillars. The **Museo de Albacete** (Tues–Sat 10am–2pm & 4.30–7pm, Sun 9am–2pm; 200ptas), however, has a more than respectable archeological and ethnographical collection, whose prize exhibits are five small Roman dolls, perfectly sculpted and jointed, and an array of local Roman mosaics.

Albacete has plenty of **accommodation**, but there's no reason to stay in this almost entirely modern city. Don't be tempted, either, by signs to Albacete's *parador*, a modern creation southeast of the town.

Chinchilla de Monte Aragón

Sixteen kilometres east of Albacete, **CHINCHILLA DE MONTE ARAGÓN** is a breezy hilltop village worth a look if you're passing by, though most of its grand mansions and churches are decayed or locked for restoration. The hilltop **fortress**, so impressive from the road below, is a windy ruin not really worth the climb, but the **Convento de Santo Domingo** in the lower part of the village has interesting four-teenth-century Mudejar work. There is also a small but nationally represented **Museo de Cerámica**, open on Saturday afternoons and Sundays.

Ciudad Real and the heartland of La Mancha

There is a huge gap in the middle of the tourist map of Spain between Toledo and the borders of Andalucía, and from Extremadura almost to the east coast. This, the province of Ciudad Real, comprises the heartland of **La Mancha**. The tourist authorities try hard to push their *Ruta de Don Quixote* across the plains, highlighting the windmills and other Quixotic sights, but unless you're completely enamoured of the book it's not of compelling interest. (See also El Toboso – p.152).

Nonetheless, there are a few places, even in this dreary plateau, which merit a visit if you've got time to spare, most notably **Consuegra**, for the best windmills, **Almagro**, for its arcaded square and medieval theatre, and **Calatrava**, for the castle ruins of its Order of Knights.

Consuegra

CONSUEGRA lies just to the west of the NIV *autovía*, roughly midway from Madrid to Andalucía, and has the most picturesque and typical of Manchegan settings, below a ridge of restored Quixotic windmills. The first of these is occupied by the town's **Turismo**, which is good for information on the *Ruta de Don Quixote*, while others house shops and workshops. They share their plateau with a ruined **castle** (daily

WET LA MANCHA: PARQUE NACIONAL DE LAS TABLAS DE DAIMIEL

A respite from the arid monotony of the Castilian landscape, and a treat for birdwatchers, is provided by the "oasis" of **La Mancha Húmeda** (Wet La Mancha). This is an area of lagoons and marshes, both brackish and fresh, along the high basin of the **Río Guadiana**. Although drainage for agriculture has severely reduced the amount of water, so that the lakes almost dry up in summer, there's still a good variety of interesting bird and plant life.

The area is best from April to July to see breeding water birds and flora, and from September through to midwinter for the inward migration. The best area, to the northeast of Ciudad Real, is designated the **Parque Nacional de las Tablas de Daimiel** (10am–5pm, summer 9am–8pm; closed Mon & Thur). There is a reception centre where two walking tracks begin, leading to good observation points. Also worthwhile is the **Parque Natural de las Lagunas de Ruidera**, northeast of Valdepeñas, which has plenty of water all year round, although here again there will obviously be fewer birds in midsummer.

There are buses from Ciudad Real to the Daimiel park, or you can take a taxi from **DAIMIEL**, 11km away. There are several **hostales** in this, the nearest town, including the basic *Madrid* which is dirt cheap and has no hot water (☎926/850200; ①); the *Hostal Las Brujas*, 1km along the Madrid road, which is good value (☎926/852289; ②); or the well-appointed *Las Tablas* (☎926/852107; ④).

10am–1.30pm & 5–9pm), headquarters of the order of St. John in the twelfth century. The town below, in spite of having perhaps the most potholed roads in Spain, is also attractive, with a lively Plaza Mayor and many Mudéjar churches.

If you want to **stay**, there's just one option, the busy and comfortable *Hotel Las Provincias* (☎925/480300; ④), on the main road north of town.

Ciudad Real

CIUDAD REAL, capital of the province at the heart of this flat country, makes a good base for excursions and has connections by bus with most villages in the area. It has a few odd sights of its own, too, including a Mudéjar gateway, the **Puerta de Toledo**, which fronts the only surviving fragment of its medieval walls, at the northern edge of the city on the Toledo road. Further in, take a look at fourteenth-century **San Pedro**, an airy, Gothic edifice, housing the alabaster tomb of its founder and a good Baroque altarpiece, and the **Museo Provincial** (10am–noon & 5–6.30pm; closed Mon & Sun pm), a modern building, opposite the cathedral, with two floors of local archaeology and a third devoted to artists of the region.

The local **Turismo** (Mon–Fri 9am–2pm) is at c/Alarcos 21 in the centre of town, and the **bus station** on c/Inmaculada Concepción. Ciudad Real's new **train station**, with high-speed *AVE* connections to Madrid, lies out of town on the Daimiel road, and has further turismo facilities; bus #5 connects with the central Plaza de Pilar.

Accommodation is not always easy to find, so it is worth booking ahead. Decent options include the *Hostal San Millán*, Ronda de Granada 23 (☎926/221579; ②), *Hostal Capri*, Plaza del Pilar 8 (☎926/214044; ③), and *Hotel Santa Cecilia*, c/Tinte 3 (☎926/228545; ④). An impressive range of **tapas bars** includes *Casa Lucio*, c/Gato 5; *Aldonza*, Plaza de la Provincia 4; and *Gran Mesón*, Ronda Ciruela 34, which also has a swankier restaurant, *Miami Park*, down the road at no 48. Nightlife includes a franchise of the Madrid/Ibiza **disco**, *Pácha*, a little out from the centre on the Carretera de Porzuna.

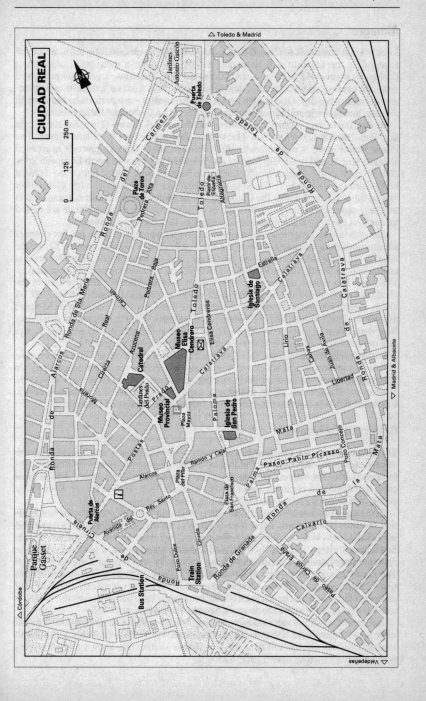

CIUDAD REAL

250 m
125
0

N

Toledo & Madrid

Córdoba

Valdepeñas

Madrid & Albacete

Parque Gasset

Bus Station

Train Station

Puerta de Alarcos

Museo Provincial

Catedral

Museo Elisa Cendrero

Iglesia de Santiago

Iglesia de San Pedro

Puerta de Toledo

Jardines Antonio Gascón

Plaza de Toros

Plaza Pedrera Alta

Jardines del Prado

Plaza Mayor

Plaza del Pilar

Plaza de San Francisco

Plaza de España

Ronda del Carmen
Ronda de Sta. María
Ronda de Alarcos
Ronda de Ciruela
Ronda de Granada
Ronda de Calatrava
Ronda de Mata

Pedrera Baja
Carmen
Real
Azucena
Cibiza
Morería
Postas
Alarcos
Rey. Santo
Avenida del Ciruela
Pozo Dulce
Ciruela
Ramón y Cajal
Paloma
Calatrava
Toledo
Elisa Cendreros
Estrella
Calatrava
Lirio
Cañas
Juan de Ávila
Libertad
Mata
Paseo Pablo Picasso
Palma
Pozo Concejo
Calvario
Paseo de Caños Eras
Atagracia

Almagro

Twenty kilometres east of Ciudad Real is **ALMAGRO**, an elegant little town, which for a period in the fifteenth and sixteenth century was quite a metropolis in southern Castile. Its main claim to fame is the **Corral de las Comedias**, a perfectly preserved sixteenth-century open-air theatre, unique in Spain. Plays from its sixteenth- and seventeenth-century heyday – the golden age of Spanish theatre – are performed regularly in the tiny, atmospheric auditorium and in July it hosts a fully-fledged theatre festival.

By day, the theatre is open to visitors of the **Museo del Teatro** (Tues–Sat 10am–2pm & 6–9pm, winter 4.30–7pm, Sun 11am–2pm; 225ptas), across the Plaza Mayor. The **Plaza Mayor** itself is magnificent: more of a wide street than a square, it is arcaded along its length, and lined with rows of green-framed windows – a north European influence brought by the Fugger family, Carlos V's bankers, who settled here. Also resident in Almagro for a while were the Knights of Calatrava (see below), though their power was on the wane by the time the **Convento de la Asunción de Calatrava** was built in the early sixteenth century. Further traces of Almagro's former importance are dotted throughout the town in the grandeur of numerous **Renaissance mansions**.

Almagro invites a stay more than anywhere in this region, and there is a fair range of **accommodation**. Cheapest options are the *Fonda Peña*, c/Emilio Pinuela 10 (☎926/860317; ②), near the church of San Bartolomé, and the more rustic *San Bartolomé* at c/Nra. Señora de las Nieves 5 (☎926/860988; ②), on the road north from Plaza Mayor. The *Hotel Don Diego*, on the Ronda de Calatrava (☎926/881287; ④), due east of the plaza, is a good mid-range hotel, and there is also a very good *parador* (☎926/860100; ⑤), in a former Franciscan convent. A number of **bars**, good for tapas, are to be found around the Plaza Mayor, and the *bodega* at the *parador* is worth a stop for a drink, too. Best **restaurant** in town is the *Meson El Corregidor* at Plaza Fray Fernando Fernández de Cordoba 7 (closed Mon & last week in July); it's moderately expensive.

Lastly, on the practical front, there's a small **Turismo** just south of Plaza Mayor on c/ Mayor de Carnicerías 5; if it's closed, the theatre museum is useful for information. On Wednesday mornings there's a lively **market** at the bottom of c/Mayor de Carnicerías. Moving on, Almagro has direct **trains** to Madrid, and five trains and six **buses** daily to Ciudad Real; buses stop near the *Hotel Don Diego* on the Ronda de Calatrava.

Calatrava La Nueva

The area known as the **Campo de Calatrava**, south of Almagro and Ciudad Real, was the domain of the **Knights of Calatrava**, a Cistercian order of soldier-monks at the forefront of the Reconquest of Spain from the Moors. So influential were they in these parts that Alfonso X created Ciudad Real as a royal check on their power. Even today, dozens of villages for miles around are suffixed with their name.

In the opening decades of the thirteenth century, the knights pushed their headquarters south, as land was won back, from Calatrava La Vieja, near Daimiel, to a commanding hilltop, 25km south of Almagro, protecting an important pass into Andalucía (Puerto de Calatrava). Here, in 1216, they founded **Calatrava La Nueva**, a settlement that was part monastery and part castle, and whose main glory was a great Cistercian church. The site (Tues–Sun 10am–2pm & 5–8pm, winter 4–7pm; 200ptas) is undergoing restoration, but you get a good idea of what must have been an enormously rich and well-protected fortress. The church itself is now completely bare but preserves the outline of a striking rose window and has an amazing stone vaulted entrance hall.

If you care about the vehicle you're driving, take the chance to stretch your legs and walk up – the track to the monastery from the C410 road is probably a thirteenth-century original. On the hill opposite is a further castle ruin, known as **Salvatierra**, which the Knights took over from the Moors.

Valdepeñas and beyond

The road from Ciudad Real through Almagro continues to **VALDEPEÑAS**, centre of the most prolific wine region in Spain and handily situated just off the main Madrid–Andalucía highway. You pass many of the largest **bodegas** on the main road into town, coming from Madrid; most of them offer free tastings, as does one in the centre, almost opposite the bus and train stations. Wine aside, the only "sight" is a **windmill**, again on the Madrid road, which is supposedly the biggest in Spain; it houses a museum of the works of local artist Gregorio Prieto. Behind it is the public swimming pool.

If you want or need to stay, there are numerous **hostales** and **hotels** along the main road: *Hostal Estación Autobuses* (☎926/325466; ③), by the bus station, is functional if you're stuck between connections, while in the centre, on c/6 Junio, is the reasonable *Hostal Cervantes* (☎926/323600; ③). The nearest **campsite**, *La Aguzadera* (☎926/323208), is 3km north along the main road; it has an excellent, if pricey, restaurant.

South from Valdepeñas

Heading south beyond Valdepeñas you enter Andalucía through the narrow mountain **Gorge of Despeñaperros** (literally, "throwing over of the dogs"), once a notorious spot for bandits and still a dramatic natural gateway which signals a change in both climate and vegetation, or as Richard Ford put it (travelling south to north), "exchanges an Eden for a desert".

The first towns of interest across the regional border, and more tempting places to break your journey than anywhere in this part of La Mancha, are **Úbeda** and **Baeza**. Both towns are connected by bus with the train station of **Linares-Baeza**, which is also where you'll change trains if you're heading for Córdoba. The provincial capital of **Jaén**, the first city on the main bus and train routes, is comparatively dull.

The Montes de Toledo and west into Extremadura

The **Montes de Toledo** cut a swathe through the upper reaches of La Mancha, between Toledo, Ciudad Real and Guadalupe. If you're heading into Extremadura, and have time and transport, the deserted little roads across these hills (they rise to just over 1400m) provide an interesting alternative to the main routes. This is an amazingly remote region to find so close to the centre of Spain: its people are so unused to visitors that in the smaller villages they may imagine you're an itinerant vendor. Covered below, too, is the main route west from Toledo into Extremadura, which runs just north of the hills.

Toledo to Navalmoral

The C502, west of Toledo, provides a direct approach into **Extremadura**, linking with the NV from Madrid to Trujillo, and with roads north into the valley of **La Vera** (see sections following). It follows the course of the **Río Tajo** virtually all the way to Talavera de la Reina, beyond which an attractive minor road, from Oropesa, with its castle *parador*, runs to El Puente del Arzobispo and south of the river to the Roman site of **Los Vascos**.

La Puebla de Montalbán – and Montalbán castle
LA PUEBLA DE MONTALBÁN, the first town west of Toledo, offers one of the best approaches into the Montes de Toledo. In itself, it is an unexceptional little place but it has a claim to fame as the birthplace of **Fernando de Rojas**, a precursor of the Golden

Age dramatists, whose play *La Celestina* was first published in 1500 and is still performed in Spain. He is remembered by a plaque on the *Ayuntamiento* in the Plaza Mayor, a building, like those surrounding it, endowed with an attractive facade of pillars and balconies. Across the square, the sixteenth-century **Palacio de los Condes de Montalbán** is an impressive, rambling affair, brooding behind small, barred windows.

There is a **hostal** on the Toledo side of town: the *Legázpiz* (☎925/750032; ①), though little reason to stay unless you happen to coincide with the atmospheric July fiestas, which include bull running through the streets.

South of La Puebla de Montalbán, the C403 leads into the foothills of the Montes de Toledo. At kilometre-stone 31 (15km south of La Puebla), a track leads 2km west to the **Castillo de Montalbán**. This is clearly visible from the road – a low, golden-brown edifice with central turrets – though close up you discover that only the walls actually survive. The interior is usually open for visits on Saturday mornings.

Talavera de la Reina, Oropesa and Navalmoral de la Mata

Continuing west from La Puebla de Montalbán you reach **TALAVERA DE LA REINA**, a dusty, unimpressive town at the junction of major road and rail routes. The town really is dusty – in addition to its arid New Castile locale, it has long been one of the most important centres of ceramic manufacture in Spain, and is covered in the fall-out from a score of porcelain factories. If you decide to stop, take a look round the many shops down the main street displaying the local products: much is the usual mass-produced tourist trash, but there are still a few real craftsmen working here.

There are hostales in Talavera but for a night's stop, **OROPESA**, 33km further west, although overlooking the busy NV, holds more promise – if you can afford the rates at the *Parador Virrey de Toledo* (☎925/430000; ⑥). This is installed in the village **castle**, a warm, stone building, rebuilt in the fifteenth century by Don Garica Álvarez de Toledo. Below it, stretches of the old town walls survive, along with a few noble mansions and a pair of Renaissance churches.

West again, **NAVALMORAL DE LA MATA** has nothing to offer other than its road, rail and bus connections to more engrossing places such as **Plasencia** and the **Monastery of Yuste** to the north, and Trujillo and Guadalupe to the south.

El Puente del Arzobispo and Los Vascos

EL PUENTE DEL ARZOBISPO, 14km south of Oropesa, is like Talavera, famed for the production of pottery and decorated tiles. It stands astride the Rio Tajo and if you were to approach from the south, you would drive in across the ancient **bridge** over the river which gives the place its name. According to legend this was built after the villagers appealed to a fourteenth-century archbishop to build them a bridge across the river. At first he refused, and when pressed pulled a ring from his finger and flung it into the Tajo, saying that he would build the bridge when the ring came back to him. Three days later he cut open his dinner of fish from the river, and there was the ring.

Today the ceramics industry dominates, with small factories and shops selling their products everywhere. The wares are not terribly exciting but the tiles do brighten up the Plaza Mayor, with its tile-covered benches, and the exuberantly ornate archbishop's house. The other local attraction is the ruined **Roman city of Los Vascos**, in beautiful country some 10km southeast of town, near the village of Navalmoralejo. There's little to see beyond a few walls, but it's an enjoyable excursion.

Into the hills

The most accessible route into the Montes de Toledo is the C410 south of La Puebla de Montalbán and its castle. This runs through **LAS VENTAS CON PEÑA AGUILERA**, a real backwater village, whose tobacconist's shop claimed to have just run out of postcards ordered twenty years ago, and had no plans to stock more. Rock-studded hills, including a curious outcrop shaped like three fat fingers, overlook the village – the name Peña Aguilera means Crag of Eagles – and to the south you reach the main pass over the Montes de Toledo, the **Puerto del Milagro**, with great views of the hills dipping down on either side to meet the plain.

Southwest of La Ventas, a tiny road leads to **San Pablo de los Montes**, a delightful village of fine stone houses nestling against the mountains. Beyond here, you could walk over the hills to the spa of **Baños del Robledillo**, a spectacular 5–6 hour walk (get directions locally).

Keeping to the C403, past the Puerto del Milagro, you can drive through lovely scenery towards Ciudad Real, or turn right at the El Molinillo junction to follow a road through the hills via Retuerta del Bullaque to **Navas de Estena**. Here the road curves round to the north again, passing a large crag with caves 5km beyond Navas, allowing you to loop round to Navahermosa and onto the C401 to Guadalupe.

The western villages

If isolated villages and obscure roads appeal, you could strike south from the C401, or west from the C403 (past the Puerto del Milagro), into the most remote part of the Montes de Toledo. The latter approach would take you some 54km, without a village, before you reached **Valdeazores**, itself scarcely inhabited with a population of just 35, and you could bypass this, if you wanted, following a road past the Cijara reservoir, and on to the N502 at Puerto Rey, passing nothing save the odd *finca*.

Coming from the C401, the first place you reach is **Roblado del Buey**, where there's a single bar. From here, a pine forest extends south to Los Alares. To the west, and the only place in these parts that gets any visitors, is **Piedraescrita**, a well-kept village with an incredibly spruce bar, and a squat, white church, allegedly sixteenth-century, and a miraculous image of the Virgin that pulls in the odd Spanish pilgrim. West again is the area's main administrative centre, **Robledo del Mazo**, with a doctor, chemist and bar.

EXTREMADURA

Extremadura is slowly getting on the tourist trail – and deservedly so. The grand old *conquistador* towns of **Trujillo** and **Cáceres** are excellent staging posts en route south from Madrid or Salamanca to Andalucía; **Mérida** has numerous Roman remains and an exemplary museum of local finds; and there is superb birdlife in the **Parque Natural de Monfragüe**. The only place that really pulls in the visitors, however, is the great **Monastery of Guadalupe**, whose revered icon of the Virgin has attracted pilgrims for the past five hundred years.

This section of the chapter is arranged north to south, starting with the lush hills and valley of **La Vera**, the first real patch of green if you have driven along the NV west from Madrid.

La Vera and the Monastery of Yuste

La Vera lies just south of the Sierra de Gredos (see the "Around Madrid" chapter), a range of hills tucked above the **Río Tiétar** valley. It is characterized by the streams or *gargantas* which descend from the mountains and in spring and summer attract increasing bands of weekenders from Madrid. At the heart of the region is the **Monastery of Yuste**, the retreat chosen by Carlos V (Emperor Charles V) to cast off the cares of empire.

Jarandilla and around

La Vera really comes into its element between Candeleda and Jarandilla de la Vera, along the C501, as the *gargantas* flow down from the hills. They are flanked in summer by some superb seasonal **campsites**. One is just outside **Villanueva de la Vera**, a village which gained British media notoriety in the 1980s due to its *Pero Palo* fiesta, in which donkeys are horribly mistreated. It seems strange to imagine, given the rural idyll hereabouts and the incredibly house-proud appearance of the villages, especially **Losar**, which has an almost surreal display of topiary.

The main village in these parts is **JARANDILLA DE LA VERA**, a good target if you want a room over your head, with a choice of three **hostales**, the *Marbella* (☎927/560218, ③), *Jaranda*, (☎927/560206, ④) and new *Posada de Pizarro*, (☎927/560727; ④), plus a fifteenth-century **castle-parador**, the *Parador Nacional Carlos V* (☎927/560117; ⑤), where the emperor stayed during the construction of Yuste. In the village there is a scattering of bars and a Roman bridge. Buses run through here, en route between Madrid and Plasencia; the stop is outside *Bar Charly* on the main road.

There is good walking around Jarandilla. A track into the hills leads to the village of **El Guijo de Santa Barbara** (4.5km) and then ends, leaving the ascent of the rocky valley beyond to walkers. An hour's trek away is a pool known as *El Trabuquete* and a high meadow with shepherds' huts known as *Pimesaíllo*. On the other side of the valley – a serious trek needing a night's camping and good area maps – is the *Garganta de Infierno* (Stream of Hell) and natural swimming pools known as *Los Pilones*.

The Monastery of Yuste

There is nothing especially dramatic about the **Monasterio de Yuste**, the retreat created by Carlos V after renouncing his empire: just a simple beauty and the rather gloomy accoutrements of the emperor's last years. The monastery had existed here for over a century before Carlos's retirement and he had earmarked the site for some years, planning his modest additions – which included a pleasure garden – while still reigning his empire from Flanders. He retired here with a retinue that included an Italian clockmaker, Juanuelo Turriano, whose inventions were his last passion.

The imperial apartments are draped throughout in black, and exhibits include the little sedan chair in which he was brought here, and another designed to support the old man's gouty legs. If you believe the guide, the bed and even the sheets are the very ones in which Carlos died, though since the place was sacked during the Peninsular War and deserted for years after the suppression of the monasteries it seems unlikely. A door by the emperor's bed opens out over the church and altar so that even in his final illness he never missed a service. Visiting hours are complex: summer Mon–Fri 9.30am–12.30pm & 3.30–6.30pm, Sat & Sun 9.30am–11.30pm, 1–1.30pm & 3.30–6.30pm; winter Mon–Fri 9.30am–12.30pm & 3–6pm, Sat & Sun 9.30am–11.30pm, 1–1.30pm & 3–6pm; admission is 100ptas (Thurs morning free).

Cuacos

The monastery is 2km into the wooded hills from **CUACOS**, an attractive village with a couple of squares, including the tiny Plaza de Don Juan de Austria, named after the house (its upper floor reconstructed) where Carlos's illegitimate son Don Juan lived when visiting his father. The surrounding houses, their overhanging upper floors supported on gnarled wooden pillars, are sixteenth-century originals, and from the beams under the overhang tobacco is hung out to dry after the harvest. There are several **bars**, a good **hotel**, *La Vera* (927/172178; ④), a **fonda**, *El Sol* (☎927/172241; ②) and a **campsite**, *Carlos I* (☎927/172222).

Jaraíz de la Vera and Garganta la Olla

West towards Plasencia, one last place you might be tempted to stop is **JARAÍZ DE LA VERA**. This has pleasant walking and a couple of reasonable places to stay: *Fonda Pili* (☎927/461083; ①), at the top of the main square, and the comfortable *Hotel Jefi* (☎927/461363; ③).

Just outside Jaraíz, a left turning leads to **GARGANTA LA OLLA**, a beautiful, ramshackle mountain village set among cherry orchards. There are several things to look out for: the **Museum of the Inquisition** (which has been closed but may soon be re-opening), the Casa de la Muñeca (House of the Doll), the Casa de Putas (a brothel for the soldiers of Carlos V's army, now a butcher's but still painted the traditional blue) and the **Casa de la Piedra** (House of Stone), a house whose balcony is secured by a three-pronged wooden support resting on a rock. The latter is hard to find; begin by taking the left-hand street up from the square and then ask.

From Garganta, there is a shortcut track to the Monasterio de Yuste.

El Valle de Jerte

Immediately north of La Vera, the main Plasencia–Avila road follows the valley of the **Río Jerte** to the pass of Puerto de Tornavacas, the boundary with Ávila province. The villages here are more developed than those of La Vera but the valley is renowned for its cherry trees, which for a ten-day period in spring cover the slopes with white blossom. If you're anywhere in the area at this time, it's a beautiful spectacle.

If you have transport, you can follow a minor road across the sierra to the north of the valley from **Cabezuela del Valle** to **Hervás**, where there's a fascinating former Jewish quarter. This is the highest road in Extremadura, rising to 1430m.

On the **southern side** of the valley, the main point of interest is the **Puerto del Piornal** pass, just behind the village of the same name. The best approach is via the villages of **Casas Del Castañar** and **Cabrero**. Once at the pass you can continue over to Garganta la Olla in La Vera.

Plasencia

Set in the shadow of the Sierra de Gredos, and surrounded on three sides by the Río Jerte (from the Greek *Xerte*, meaning "joyful"), **PLASENCIA** looks more impressive from afar than it actually is. Once you get up into the old city the walls are hard to find – for the most part they're propping up the back of houses – and the cathedral is barely half-built. However, Plasencia has some lively bars and a fine, arcaded **Plaza Mayor**, flanked by cafés and every Tuesday morning the scene of a farmers' **market**, held here since the twelfth century.

Around town

The **Catedral** (Mon–Sat 9am–1pm & 5–7pm, Sun 9am–1pm) is in fact two churches – old and new – built back-to-back. Work began on the second at the beginning of the sixteenth century and continued under two architects for almost forty years, but when neither managed to finish it, the open end was simply bricked up. The fact that the completed building would have been a particularly lofty Gothic construction only adds to the foreshortened feel of the interior. It does have some redeeming features, most notably the Renaissance choirstalls intricately carved by Rodrigo Alemán and described with some justice by the National Tourist Board as "the most Rabelaisian in Christendom". The older, Romanesque part now houses the obligatory **museum,** and the 100ptas entrance fee includes access to the similarly-aged **cloisters**.

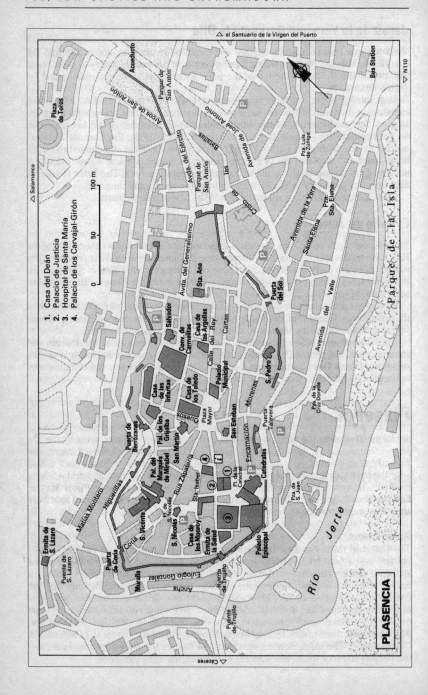

△ al Santuario de la Virgen del Puerto

△ Salamanca

Acueducto

Plaza de Toros

Arcos de San Antón

Parque de San Antón

Avda. del Ejército

Parque de San Antón

Avda. de José Antonio

Batallas

N110 ▽

Bus Station

Pza. Luis de Zúñiga

Parque de la Isla

Cristo de las

Avda. del Generalísimo

Sta. Ana

Puerta del Sol

Avenida de la Vera

Santa Elena

Pza. Sta. Elena

Avenida del Valle

1. Casa del Deán
2. Palacio de Justicia
3. Hospital de Santa María
4. Palacio de los Carvajal-Girón

100 m

50

0

Salvador

Conv. de Carmelitas

Casa de las Argollas

Calle. del. Rey

Casa de los Toledo

Casa de las Infantas

Rosario

Palacio Municipal

Cartas

S. Pedro

Morenas

Puerta de Berrozanas

Pal. de los Grijalba

San Martín

Queso

Plaza Mayor

San Esteban

Encarnación

Puerta Talavera

Pza. de la Cruz Dorada

Pal. del Marqués de Mirabel

Rúa Zapatería

Sta. Isabel

Catedrales

Matías Montero

Higuerillas

Pl. de S. Nicolás

Pl. de la Catedral

Pza. de S. Juan

S. Vicente

Coria

S. Nicolás

Casa de los Monroy

Ermita de la Salud

Palacio Episcopal

Puerta de Coria

Muralla

Puente de S. Lázaro

Ermita de S. Lázaro

Eulogio González

Ancha

Puerta de Trujillo

Puente de Trujillo

Río Jerte

Río

Rúa

△ Cáceres

PLASENCIA

Opposite the cathedral is the **Casa del Deán**, (Dean's House) with an interesting balcony like the prow of a ship. Continuing away from the cathedral along c/Blanca you come out at the **Plaza de San Nicolás**, where, according to local tradition, the church was built to prevent two local families from shooting arrows at each other from adjacent houses.

Nearby, on Plazuela del Marqués de la Puebla, the **Museo Etnográfico Textil Provincial** (Wed–Sat 11am–2pm & 5–8pm; Sun 11am–2pm; free) is worth a look for its colourful costumes and local crafts, excellently displayed in a fourteenth-century hospital. Many of the exhibits are still much in evidence in the remoter villages in the north of Plasencia province.

Practicalities

Plasencia's main **Turismo** is on c/del Rey 17 off the top of the Plaza Mayor (Tues–Fri 9am–2pm & 4–6pm, Sat & Sun 9.15am–2pm), with a secondary office (Mon–Fri 9am–2pm) on c/Trujillo. If you arrive by **bus**, you'll be about fifteen minutes' walk from the centre: the **train** station is much further out – take a taxi.

Good **places to stay** include two very cheap places near the Plaza Mayor: the *Fonda Salmantina*, c/Talavera 17 (☎927/414953; ①), perfectly adequate though in the noisiest nightlife area, and the clean and unpretentious *Pensión Santamaría*, c/Obispo Lazo 13 (☎927/412440; ①). For more comfort, try *Hostal La Muralla*, c/Berrozana 6 (☎927/413874; ②), the *Hotel Rincón Extremeño*, c/Vidrieras 6 (☎927/411150; ③), again just off the Plaza Mayor, or the upmarket *Hotel Alfonso VIII*, c/Alfonso VIII 32 (☎927/410250; ⑤), on the main road near the post office.

Bars are thick on the ground, with over fifty in the old town alone. This is the land of the *pincho*, a little sample of food provided free with your beer or wine – among which is the local *pitarra*. A high tally of promising bars is to be found in c/Maldonado (also known as c/Patalón; go down c/Talavera from the main square and it's the second turning on the left); the *Nuevo Pino* and *La Herradura* are good for *pinchos* and *pitarra*, and the *Asador el Refugio* for fish, squid and octopus *pinchos*. In the next street down, *Bar Media Luna* is famous for its ham – it's expensive, but if you're lucky you'll get a taste as a *pincho*, and the place is very atmospheric.

Finding good **restaurants** is less easy, but try the area between the cathedral and the Plaza Mayor. Easily the best budget option is that attached to the *Hostal La Muralla*. Another good, and rather fancier place is *El Acueducto*, c/Valentina Mirón 17, near the monument from which it takes its name.

Las Hurdes and the Sierra de Gata

Las Hurdes, the abrupt rocky lands north of Plasencia, have always been set apart and are a rich source of mysterious tales. According to legend, the region was unknown to the outside world until the time of Columbus, when two lovers fleeing from the Court of the Duke of Alba chanced upon it. The people who welcomed them were supposedly unaware of the existence of other people or other lands. Shields and other remnants belonging to the Goth Rodrigo and his court of seven centuries earlier were discovered by the couple, giving rise to the saying that the Hurdanos are descendants of kings.

Fifty years ago, the inhabitants of the remoter areas were still so unused to outsiders that they hid in their houses if anyone appeared. **Luis Buñuel** filmed an unflatteringly grotesque documentary, *Tierra Sin Pan* (Land Without Bread), here in the 1930s, in which it was hard to discern any royal descent in his subjects. Modernity has crept up on the villages these days, though they can still feel very remote. To explore the region, you really need transport of some kind and certainly a detailed local **map** – regular Spanish roadmaps tend to be pretty sketchy.

Las Hurdes villages

You could approach Las Hurdes from Plasencia, Salamanca or Ciudad Rodrigo (the region borders on the Sierrra Peña de Francia – see p.307). From Plasencia or Salamanca, the approach is along the C512. Turn off along this road at Vegas de Coria and you will reach **NUÑOMORAL**, a good base for excursions, with an excellent and inexpensive **hostal**, *El Hurdano* (☎927/433012; ①); this does big dinners, and there is a bank alongside – not a common sight in these parts. Nuñomoral is also the village best connected to the outside world, with early morning buses to both Ciudad Rodrigo and Plasencia.

In this rocky area, tiny terraces have been constructed on the riverbed as the only way of getting the stubborn land to produce anything. To the north of Nuñomoral, the tiny village of **La Huetre** is worth a visit; take a left fork just before the village of Casares de las Hurdes. The typical slate-roofed houses are in better than usual condition and it has an impressive situation, surrounded by steep rocky hills. The villages of **Avellanar**, **Horcajo**, **Fragosa** and **Erias** all have traditional houses. Walkers might also head for the remote and disarmingly primitive settlement of **El Gasco**, over to the west of Fragosa, where there is a huge waterfall beneath the Miacera Gorge.

The Sierra de Gata

The **Sierra de Gata** creates a westerly border to Las Hurdes, in a series of wooded hills and odd outcrops of higher ground. It is almost equally isolated – in some of the villages the old people still speak *maniego*, a mix of Castilian Spanish and Portuguese – and its wooded valleys are in parts stunningly beautiful. Unfortuately, much has been damaged in recent summers by forest fires, which, as with similar fires in Las Hurdes, are said to have been deliberately started to claim insurance money.

For a trip into the heart of the region, follow the C513 to the west of **Villanueva de la Sierra**. A couple of kilometres past the Río Arrago, a very minor road veers north towards **ROBLEDILLO DE GATA**, a village of old houses, packed tightly together. A shorter, easier detour, south of the C513, around 5km on, is provided by the hilltop village of **SANTIBÁÑEZ EL ALTO**, whose oldest houses are built entirely of stone, without windows. At the top of town, look out for a tiny bullring, castle remains and the old cemetery – there's a wonderful view over the Borbollón reservoir from here. Another 3km along the C513, a turn-off to the north takes you on a winding road up to **GATA**, a pretty village with rooms at the *Pensión Avenida* (☎927/441079; ②).

On to the west, keeping to the C513, is **HOYOS**, the largest village of the region, with some impressive mansions. There's no hostal but **rooms** are available in the house of the local photographer at c/Mayor 8 (☎927/514316; ②), or there's pleasant **camping** by a natural swimming pool, 3km below the village, created by the damming of the river. Lastly, further along the C513, another turning leads north to **SAN MARTÍN DE TREVEJO**, one of the nicest of the many lonely villages around; if you're here at mealtime there's good, cheap village fare in great abundance at the *Bar Avenida del 82* (also referred to as the *Casa de Julia*).

South to Cáceres: Coria and Palancar

Heading south from the Sierra de Gata, towards Cáceres along the C526, **CORIA** makes an interesting stop. It looks nothing much from the main road, but a visit reveals a cool and quiet old town with lots of stately whitewashed houses, enclosed within third- and fourth-century **Roman walls**.

For the most part the walls are built into and around the houses, but a good stretch is visible between the deserted tower of the fifteenth-century **Castillo**, built by the

Dukes of Alba, and the **Catedral**. The latter has beautifully carved west and north portals in the Plateresque style of Salamanca. Inside – it should be open in the mornings – the choir stalls and retablo are worth seeing. The building overlooks a striking medieval bridge across the fields, the river having changed course 300 years ago.

There's plenty of **accommodation** in Coria. The *Pensión Piro*, Plaza del Rollo 6 (☎927/500027; ①) is cheap and well-placed near the walls; *Hostal Los Kekes*, Avda. Sierra de Gata 49 (☎927/500900; ③), has more comforts and a decent restaurant.

Convento del Palancar

A detour off the C526, south of Coria, would take you to the **Convento del Palancar**, a monastery founded by San Pedro de Alcántara in the sixteenth century and said to be the smallest in the world at only seventy square metres. It's hard to imagine how a community of ten monks could have lived in these cubbyholes, though San Pedro set the example, sleeping upright in his cubicle. A small monastic community today occupies a more modern monastery alongside; ring the bell (daily except Wed 9.30am–1pm & 4–7.30pm) and a monk will come and show you around.

To reach Palancar, turn left off the C526 just after Torrejoncillo and follow the road to **Pedroso de Acim**; a left turn just before the village leads to the monastery.

The Parque Natural de Monfragüe

South of Plasencia a pair of dams, built in the 1960s, have turned the **Río Tajo** into a sequence of vast reservoirs. It's an impressive sight, driving across one of the half dozen bridges, and it's a tremendous area for wildlife. Almost at random here, you can look up to see storks, vultures and even eagles, circling the skies.

The best area for concerted wildlife viewing – and some very enjoyable walks – is the **Parque Natural de Monfragüe**, Extremadura's only protected area, which extends to either side of the Plasencia–Trujillo road, with its park headquarters at **Villareal de San Carlos**. The landscape is a wonderful diversity of rivers, woods, scrubland and pasture, and attracts an incredible range of flora and fauna. It has been spared the blights of much of the region hereabouts, which, after the completion of the dams, saw indiscriminate planting of eucalyptus by the rapidly expanding paper industry, and widescale destruction of wildlife habitats.

There are over 200 **species** in the park, including the ultra-rare Spanish lynx (which you are most unlikely to see). Most important is the **bird population**, especially the black stork – this is the only breeding population in western Europe – and birds of prey such as the black vulture (not averse to eating tortoises), the griffon vulture (partial to carrion intestine), the Egyptian vulture (not above eating human excrement), the Spanish imperial eagle (identifiable by its very obvious white shoulder patches), the golden eagle and the eagle owl (the largest owl in Europe).

Ornithologists should visit Monfragüe in May and June; botanists in March and April; and everybody should avoid July to September, when the heat is stifling.

Park practicalities

The easiest **approach to the park** is along the C524 from Plasencia to Trujillo, which runs past the park headquarters at Villareal de San Carlos. Transport of your own is an advantage unless you are prepared to do some walking. There is just one daily **bus** along the road, which runs between Plasencia and Torrejon El Rubio, 16km south of Villareal de San Carlos, and on Mondays and Fridays covers the whole distance to Trujillo. It's not a promising hitching route, though at weekends you should get a lift with Spanish birdwatchers.

Villareal de San Carlos has a couple of bars and a restaurant, plus an **information centre**, where you can pick up a colourful leaflet, with a map detailing three colour-coded walks from the village. There is also a seasonal shop, selling wildlife T-shirts and the like, and a useful guide to the park (in Spanish) by José Luis Rodríguez.

There's no **accommodation** in Villareal, and camping is prohibited in the park, but there are two friendly pensions in **Torrejón el Rubio**: the *Monfragüe* (☎927/455026; ②) and the *Avenida* (☎927/455050; ③). The nearest **campsite** is *Camping Monfragüe* (☎927/459220), a well-equipped, year-round site with a swimming pool and restaurant, 12km north of Villareal, on the Plasencia road. It is near the turning to the train station of Palazuelo-Empalme (a stop for slow trains on the Madrid–Cáceres line) and it also usually has **bikes for rent** to get to Monfragüe.

Into the park

Walking in Monfragüe, it is best to stick to the colour-coded **paths** leading from Villareal de San Carlos. Each of them is well paint-blobbed and leads to rewarding bird-watching locations. Elsewhere, it is not easy to tell where you are permitted to wander, and all too easy to find yourself out of the park area in a private hunting reserve.

The **Green Route**, to the Cerro Gimio, is especially good, looping through woods and across streams, in a landscape unimaginable from Villareal, to a dramatic cliff-top viewing station. The longer **Purple Route** heads south of Villareal, over a bridge across the Tajo, and past a fountain known as the *Fuente del Francés* after a young Frenchman who died there trying to save an eagle. Two kilometres further is a great crag known as the *Peñafalcón*, which houses a large colony of griffon vultures, and the Castillo de Monfragüe, a castle ruin high up on a rock, with a chapel next to it; there is an observation post nearby. These places are accessible from the C524 and if you're coming in on the bus, you could ask to get off here.

On the south side of the park, towards Trujillo, you pass through the **dehesas**, strange Africa-like plains which are among the oldest woodlands in Europe. The economy of the *dehesas* is based on grazing, and the casualties among these domestic animals provide the vultures of Monfragüe with their daily bread.

Trujillo

TRUJILLO is the most attractive town in Extremadura: a classic Conquistador stage-set of escutcheoned mansions, stork-topped towers and castle walls. Much of it looks virtually untouched since the sixteenth century, redolent above all of the exploits of the conquerors of the Americas; Pizarro was born here, as were many of the tiny band who with such extraordinary cruelty aided him in defeating the Incas.

The town

Trujillo is a very small place – still little more than its extent in Conquistador times. At the centre of a dense web of streets is the **Plaza Mayor** (also known as the Plaza de la Constitución), a grand square, overlooked by a trio of palaces and churches, and ringed by a half dozen cafés and restaurants, in which life for most visitors revolves. In the centre is a statue of Pizarro – oddly, the gift of an American sculptor, one Carlos Rumsey, in 1927. In the square's southwest corner is the **Palacio de la Conquista** (10.30am–2pm & 4.30–7pm), the grandest of Trujillo's mansions with its roof adorned by statues representing the twelve months. Just one of many built by the Pizarro clan, it was originally inhabited by Francisco's half-brother and son-in-law Hernando, who returned from the conquests to live here with his half-Inca bride (Francisco's daughter). Diagonally opposite, and with a skyline of storks, is the bulky church of **San Martín**. Its

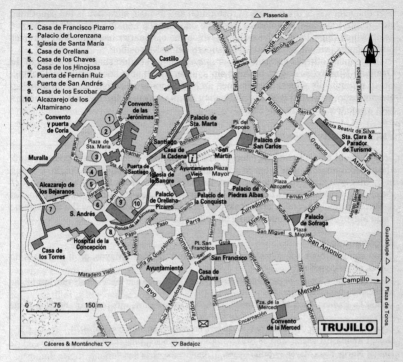

△ Plasencia

1. Casa de Francisco Pizarro
2. Palacio de Lorenzana
3. Iglesia de Santa María
4. Casa de Orellana
5. Casa de los Chaves
6. Casa de los Hinojosa
7. Puerta de Fernán Ruiz
8. Puerta de San Andrés
9. Casa de los Escobar
10. Alcazarejo de los Altamirano

Convento y puerta de Coria

Muralla

Alcazarejo de los Bejaranos

S. Andrés

Casa de los Torres

Hospital de la Concepción

Matadero Viejo

Castillo

Convento de las Jerónimas

Plaza de Sta. María

Palacio de Sta. Marta

Santiago

Casa de la Cadena

Puerta de Santiago

Iglesia de la Sangre

Palacio de Orellana-Pizarro

Ayuntamiento Viejo

Palacio de la Conquista

San Martín

Pl. del Reposo

Palacio de San Carlos

Plaza Mayor

Palacio de Piedras Albas

Palacio de Sofraga

Pza. S. Miguel

San Miguel

Pl. San Francisco

San Francisco

Ayuntamiento

Casa de Cultura

Pza. de la Merced

Convento de la Merced

Sta. Clara & Parador de Turismo

Sta. Beatriz de Silva

Atalaya

Campillo →

Plaza de Toros

0   75   150 m

Cáceres & Montánchez ▽   ▽ Badajoz

TRUJILLO

tombs include, among others, that of the Orellana family; Francisco de Orellana was the first explorer of the Amazon. Adjacent is the **Palacio de los Duques de San Carlos** (daily 9am–1pm & 4–6pm; 100ptas donation), home to a group of nuns who moved out of their delapidated convent up the hill and restored this palace in return for the lodgings. The chimneys on the roof boast aggressively of cultures conquered by Catholicism in the New World – they are shaped like the pyramids of Aztecs, Incas and others subjected to Spanish rule.

From the plaza, c/de Ballesteros leads up to the walled upper town, past the domed **Torre Del Alfiler** with its coats of arms and storks' nests, and through the gateway known as the Arco de Santiago. Here, to the left, is **Santa María Mayor** (daily 9am–2pm & 4.30–7pm), the most interesting of the town's many churches. The building is basically Gothic but contains a beautiful raised Renaissance *coro* noted for the technical mastery of its almost flat vaults. There is a fine Hispano-Flemish reredos by Fernando Gallego, and tombs including those of the Pizarros – Francisco was baptized here – and Diego García de Paredes, a man known as the "Extremeño Samson". Among other exploits, this giant of a man, armed only with his gargantuan sword, is said to have defended a bridge against an entire French army and to have picked up the font, now underneath the *coro*, to carry holy water to his mother.

Further up the hill, in the Pizarro's former residence, the **Casa Museu Pizarro** (Tues–Sun 11am–2pm & 4.30–6.30pm; 300ptas), is a small, dull and overpriced affair, with little beyond period furniture and a few panels on the conquest of Peru.

The **castle** is now virtually in open countryside; for the last hundred metres of the climb you see nothing but the occasional broken-down remnant of a wall clambered over by sheep and dogs. The fortress itself, Moorish in origin but much reinforced by later defenders, is in the process of restoration and its main attraction is the panoramic view of the town and its environs from the battlements. Looking out over the barren heath which rings Trujillo, the extent to which the old quarter has fallen into disrepair is abundantly evident, as is the castle's superb defensive position.

Of the many other town mansions, or *solares*, the most interesting is the **Palacio de Orellana-Pizarro**, just west of the main square, which now houses the local school. Go in through the superb Renaissance arched doorway to admire the courtyard: an elegant patio decorated with the alternating coats of arms of the Pizarros – two bears with a pine tree – and the Orellanas.

Practicalities

Trujillo could be visited easily enough as a daytrip from Cáceres, but if you can book ahead (accommodation is often in short supply), it is worth staying the night. Coming in by **bus**, you arrive in the lower town, just five minutes' walk from the Plaza Mayor/ Plaza de la Constitución, where there is a **Turismo** (Tues–Fri 9am–2pm & 5–7pm, Sat & Sun 9.15am–2pm) and a large-scale plan of the town. Driving, follow the signs to the Plaza Mayor, where, with luck, you'll be able to park.

Accommodation

If you can get them, the nicest rooms are around the Plaza Mayor, or, if money is no object, at the *parador*.

Pensión Boni, c/Domingo de Ramos 7 (☎927/321604). Cheap and meticulously run, just off the northeast corner of the Plaza. ②.

Hostal La Cadena, Plaza Mayor 8 (☎927/321463). Very attractive, with rooms overlooking all the action. ④.

Hotel Las Cigüeñas, (☎927/321250). A modern hotel down on the main road. ⑤.

Hostal Emilia, c/General Mola 28 (☎927/320083). Clean but slightly shabby. ③.

Hostal Nuria, Plaza Mayor 29 (☎927/320907). Another excellent *hostal*. ④.

Hotel-Pension Peru, Avda. de Calvo Sotelo (☎927/320745). A large, drab hotel above a bar, whose one virtue is that it may have rooms long after everywhere else is full. ②.

Parador Nacional de Trujillo, Plaza Santa Clara (☎927/321350). Luxurious accommodation in a former convent north of the Plaza Mayor. ⑤.

Pensión Trujillo, c/Francisco Pizarro 4 (☎927/322661). A pleasant *pensión* between the Plaza Mayor and the bus station. ③.

Bars and restaurants

There are plenty of bar-restaurants right in the Plaza Mayor. Perhaps the best of them is *Meson La Troya*, which offers huge *menús* – you'll probably find a giant salad and omelette on your plate before they've even asked what you want to order, and thereafter helpings are automatically replenished, should you somehow have room for them. The *Hostal Pizarro* has a rather more fancy restaurant, or there are excellent *raciones* and *tapas* at the *Bar Las Cigüeñas* and at the *Bar La Pata*, just round the corner.

Guadalupe

The small town of **GUADALUPE** is dominated in every way by the great **Monasterio de Nuestra Señora de Guadalupe**, which for five centuries has brought fame and pilrims to the area. It was established in 1340, on the spot where an ancient image of the Virgin, said to have been carved by Saint Luke, was discovered by a shepherd fifty or so years earlier. The delay was simply a question of waiting for the Reconquest to arrive in this remote sierra, with its lush countryside of forests and streams.

In the fifteenth and sixteenth centuries, Guadalupe was among the most important pilgrimage centres in Spain: Columbus named the Caribbean island in honour of the Virgin here, and a local version was adopted as the patron saint of Mexico. Much of the monastic wealth, in fact, came from returning *conquistadores*, whose successive endowments led to a fascinating mix of styles. The monastery was abandoned in the nineteenth century dissolution, but early this century was reoccupied by Franciscans, who continue to maintain it.

The town itself is a fitting complement to the monastery and countryside, a net of narrow cobbled streets and overhanging houses, around an arcaded plaza, the whole overshadowed by the monastery's bluff ramparts. There's a timeless feel only slightly diminished by modern development on the outskirts, and a brisk trade in plastic copies of religious treasures.

The church and monastery

The **monastery church** (summer 8.30am–8.30pm; winter 9am–6pm) opens onto the Plaza Mayor, with pilgrims constantly climbing up its steps. Its gloomy Gothic interior is, like the rest of the monastery, packed with treasures from generations of wealthy patrons. Note especially the incredibly orante *rejas* (grilles).

The entrance to the **monastery** proper (daily 9.30am–1pm & 3.30–7pm, 6pm in winter; 300ptas) is to the left of the church. The (compulsory) guided tour begins with a Mudéjar **cloister** – two brick storeys of horseshoe arches with a strange pavilion or tabernacle in the middle – and moves onto the **museum**, with an apparently endless collection of rich vestments, early illuminated manuscripts and religious paraphernalia, along with some fine artworks including a triptych by Isenbrandt and a small Goya. The **Sacristía**, beyond, is the finest room in the monastery. Unaltered since it was built in the seventeenth century, it contains eight paintings by Zurbarán, which, uniquely, can be seen in their original context – the frames match the window frames and the pictures themselves are a planned part of the decoration of the room.

Climbing higher into the heart of the monastery, you pass through various rooms filled with jewels and relics before the final ascent to the Holy of Holies. From a tiny room high above the main altar you can look down over the church while a panel is spun away to reveal the climax of the tour – the **image of the virgin** herself, bejewelled, richly dressed, and blackened by centuries of candle smoke.

On the way out, drop in at the **Hospedaria Real Monasterio**, around to the right. The bar in its Gothic cloister is one of the world's more unusual places to enjoy a *cuba libre*.

Practicalities

There are plenty of places to stay in Guadalupe and the only times you are likely to have difficulty finding a room are Easter Week or around September 8, the Virgin's festival day. If you need help, consult the **Turismo** (Tues–Fri 9am–2pm & 5–7pm, Sat & Sun 9.15am–2pm) in the Plaza Mayor. **Banks** and a **post office** are to be found close by this central square. **Buses** leave from either side of a street uphill from the *Ayuntamiento*: *Mirat* to Trujillo and Cáceres, *Doalde* to Madrid.

You can eat at most of the accommodation places listed below. The *Hostal Lujuan* has a particular good value *menú*, while the *Hospedaje del Real Monasterio* has a courtyard setting. Perhaps the best restaurant in town is the *Meson del Cordero* at c/Alfonso Onceno 27, a reasonably priced place with home cooking and grand views from the dining room. Recommended **accommodation** includes:

Hostal Cerezo, c/Gregorio López 12 (☎927/367379). A good mid-priced choice in the centre. ③.

Mesón Extremeño, Plaza Mayor (☎927/366360). A bar with basic rooms above. ①.

Hostal Lujuan, c/Gregorio López 21 (☎927/367170). Decent mid-priced rooms. ③.

Parador Nacional Zurbaran, Marqués de la Romana 10 (☎927/367075). A beautiful *parador*, housed in a fifteenth-century hospital, with a pool and immaculate patio gardens. ⑤.

Hospedaje del Real Monasterio (☎927/367000). This *hostal* is housed in a wing of the monastery and popular with Spanish pilgrims. ③.

Fonda Sánchez, c/El Chorro Gordo 2 (☎927/367301). One of several perfectly adequate *fondas* in the narrow streets leading down from the Plaza Mayor – a bit run down but cheap. It is owned by the *Restaurante Taruta* in the Plaza Mayor, through whom you should arrange rooms (there are a few more above the restaurant itself). ②.

Pensión Tena, Plaza Mayor (☎927/367104). Spotless, well-appointed and friendly. ②.

Mesón Típico Isabel, Plaza Mayor (☎927/367132). Another bar with rooms to let. ③.

The Sierra de Guadalupe: routes to Trujillo

A truly superb view of the town set in its sierra can also be enjoyed from the road north to Navalmoral. Five kilometres beyond, the **Capilla del Humilladero** marks the spot where pilgrims to the shrine traditionally caught their first glimpse of the monastery.

The surrounding **Sierra de Guadalupe** is a wild and beautiful region, with steep rocky crags abutting the valley sides. If you have your own transport, a good route is to strike northwest of the C410 at **Cañamero**, up to the village of **Cabañas del Castillo**, a handful of houses, most of them empty as only twelve inhabitants remain, nestling against a massive crag and ruined castle. Beyond here, you can reach the main **Navalmoral–Trujillo road** close to the **Puerto de Miravete**, a fabulous viewpoint, with vistas of Trujillo in the far distance. Another great drivers' route, again leaving the C410 at Cañamero, is to follow the narrow road **through Berzocana** to Trujillo.

Cáceres

CÁCERES is in many ways remarkably like Trujillo. At its centre is an almost perfectly preserved walled town, the *Cuidad Monumental*, packed with *solares* built on the proceeds of American exploration, while even more than Trujillo every available tower and spire is crowned by a clutch of storks' nests. As a provincial capital, however, Cáceres is a much larger and a much livelier place – especially in term-time, when the students of the University of Extremadura are in residence. With its Roman, Moorish and conquistador sights, and a lively bar and restaurant scene, it is an absorbing and highly enjoyable city.

The walled **old town** stands at the heart of Cáceres, with a picturesque **Plaza Mayor** just outside its walls. Almost everything of interest is contained within – or a short walk from – this area, and you would do well to base yourself as close to it as possible.

Practicalities

If you arrive by **train or bus**, you'll find yourself around 3km out from the old town, at the far end of the Avenida de Alemania. It's not an enjoyable walk, so take bus #1, which runs down the avenida to Plaza de San Juan, a square adjoining the Plaza Mayor; an irregular shuttle bus from the train station (free if you show a rail ticket) also runs into town, to the Plaza de América, a major traffic junction, west of the old town.

There is a helpful **Turismo** (Mon–Fri 9am–2pm & 5–7pm, winter 4–6pm, Sat & Sun 9am–2pm) in the Plaza Mayor; the main **Correos** is at c/Miguel Primo Rivera 2, near the Plaza de América; and numerous **banks** dot the central grid. If you wanted to **rent a car** to explore this region of Extremadura, try *Avis* in the *Hotel Extremadura*, Avenida Virgen de Guadalupe 5, or *Hertz*, next door at no. 3.

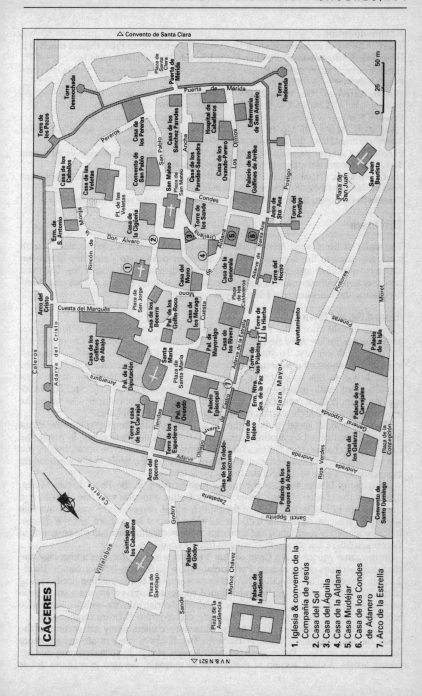

CÁCERES

1. Iglesia & convento de la Compañía de Jesús
2. Casa del Sol
3. Casa del Águila
4. Casa de la Aldana
5. Casa Mudéjar
6. Casa de los Condes de Adanero
7. Arco de la Estrella

Accommodation

There is plenty of **accommodation** to go round, even at fiesta time, though much of it is overpriced; the *pensiones* are often the better bets here. Options include:

Hotel Álvarez, c/Moret 22, off c/Pintores (☎927/246400). All the requisites for a place of its category, but showing its age. Still, a good location. ④.

Pensión Carretero, Plaza Mayor 23 (☎927/247482). Best value in town – large rooms, spotless bathrooms and a TV lounge. Elderly owners, however, may set a curfew. ②.

Pensión Márquez, c/Gabriel y Galán 2 (☎927/244969). Cheap and functional. ②.

Hotel Meliá, Plaza de San Juan (☎927/215800). Located in a sixteenth-century palace, just outside the walls of the old town, this is in many ways a nicer place than the *parador*. ⑤.

Parador de Cáceres, c/Ancha 6 (☎927/211759). The *parador* occupies a conquistador mansion in the Ciudad Monumental – the only hotel within the walls. ⑥.

Hostal Princesa, c/Camino Llano 34 (☎927/227000). Excellent value but a bit difficult to find; down the hill out of the gate shown at the left hand edge of our map. ②.

Pensión Soraya, Plaza Mayor 25 (☎927/244310). Good value double rooms (no singles). ②.

The town

The **walls** of the *Ciudad Monumental* are basically Moorish in construction, though parts date back to the Romans – notably the **Arco del Cristo** – and they have been added to, refortified and built against pretty much throughout the centuries. The most intact section, with several original adobe Moorish towers, runs in a clockwise direction, facing the walls from the Plaza Mayor.

Around the old town

Entering the old town – the **Parte Vieja**, as it's known – from the Plaza Mayor, you pass through the low **Arco de la Estrella**, an entrance built by Manuel Churriguera in the eighteenth century. To your left, at the corner of the walls, is one of the most imposing Conquistador *solares*, the **Casa de Toledo-Montezuma** with its domed tower. It was to this house that a follower of Cortés brought back one of the New World's more exotic prizes – a daughter of the Aztec emperor as his bride. The building has recently been restored – it was in imminent danger of collapse – to house the provincial historical archives, and it also stages occasional exhibitions.

Walking straight ahead, through the Arco de la Estrella, brings you into the **Plaza Santa María**, flanked by another major *solar*, the Casa de los Golfines de Abajo, the Palacio Episcopal, and the Gothic church of Santa María – Cáceres' finest. Inside, you can illuminate a fine sixteenth-century carved wood *retablo*, while in the surrounding gloom are the tombs of many of the town's great families.

A couple of blocks away, at the town's highest point, is the Plaza de San Mateo, flanked by the church of **San Mateo**, another Gothic structure with fine chapels, and the **Casa de la Cigüeña** (House of the Stork), whose narrow tower was the only one allowed to preserve its original battlements when the rest were shorn by royal decree. It is now a military installation and although the tower features on half the postcards in Cáceres, soldiers discourage the taking of further snapshots.

In the same square is the **Casa de las Veletas**, which houses the archeology and ethnology sections of the **Museo Provincial** (Tues–Sat 9.30am–2.30pm, Sun 10.15am–2.30pm; 200ptas). The collections here take second place to the building itself. Typical of the local style, its beautifully proportioned rooms are arrayed around a small patio and preserve the cistern (*aljibe*) of the original Moorish Alcázar with its horseshoe arches. It also has an extraordinary balustrade, created from Talavera ceramic jugs.

From here, a footbridge leads to the museum's contemporary art section in the **Casa de los Caballos** (House of Horses). Two floors of modern art and sculpture include works by Miró, Picasso and Eduardo Arroyo, alongside up and coming contemporary artists. A third section of the provincial museum, devoted to religious art, is displayed in the **Casa del Mono** (House of the Monkey), another beautiful *solar*, adorned with grotesque simian gargoyles. The exhibits include a minor El Greco.

Something could be said about almost every other building within the old walls, but notice above all the **family crests** – in particular on the **Casa del Sol** – and the magnificent facade of the **Palacio de los Golfines de Abajo**. It was in this latter Conquistador mansion that Franco had himself proclaimed generalísimo and head of state in October 1936.

Outside the walls

Outside the walls, wander up to the sixteenth-century church of **Santiago**, which fronts the plaza of the same name, opposite a more or less contemporary mansion, **Palacio de Godoy**, with its corner balcony. The church, only open for masses, has a fine altarpiece by Alonso Berruguete.

You might take time, too, for a visit to the **Casa Museo Arabe "Yusuf Al-Borch"** (daily 10.30am–1.30pm & 6–8pm; 100ptas), off Plaza San Jorge on Cuesta del Marques. The owner of this Moorish house has had the bright idea of decorating it more or less as it would have been when occupied by its original owner. The Alhambra it's not, and the red lights in the "harem" are a dubious touch, but it at least provides a context for all the horseshoe arches and curving brick ceilings.

If you want to enjoy a good **view** of the old town, go through the Arco del Cristo down to the main road and turn right on to c/de Fuente Concejo, following the signs for about five minutes or so and you have the whole town set out below you.

Eating and drinking

There is a good range of **bars, restaurants and bodegas** in and around the Plaza Mayor, while the old town offers a bit more style at not too inflated a price.

Restaurants

El Corral de las Cigüeñas, Cuesta de Aldana 6. A beautiful spot to enjoy a meal in the old town, with tables in a large, palm-shaded courtyard; reasonably-priced *platos combinados*.

El Figón de Eustaquio, Plaza San Juan 14. This features an extensive list of regional dishes, cooked with care and flare; it's moderately expensive, with a *menú* at 2500ptas.

Gran Muralla, Avda. Virgen de la Montaña 1. Chinese restaurant with friendly service and pleasant surroundings.

El Palacio del Vino, c/Ancha 4. A pleasant *mesón* near the *parador* in the old town.

El Pato Blanco, Plaza Mayor 24. A popular restaurant fronting the square – slightly more expensive than its neighbours but probably worth the extra.

El Puchero, Plaza Mayor 10. The cheapest restaurant on the plaza, with an ever-popular *terraza*.

La Taverna Marocantana, c/Donoso Cortés 2 – an extension of c/Pizarro. Excellent Moroccan-style cooking in an Arab setting; *tapas* at lunchtime, meals at night.

Bars

Bar del Jamón, Plaza San Juan 10. Small place to enjoy *pitarra* and a *pincho*.

El Extremeño, Plaza del Duque 10 – off the Plaza Mayor. A student favourite with Guinness on tap and beer sold by the metre.

Lancelot, Rincón de la Monja 2, off Cuesta del Marqués. A rather refined bar run by an Englishman – who parks his Jaguar outside.

La Machacona, c/Andrada 8 – down an alley under the arcades off the Plaza Mayor. A good place to hear Latin sounds and occasional live music.

El Torre de Babel, c/Pizarro 8. Laid-back café with occasional live music, plus clothes and jewellery stands downstairs.

La Traviata, c/Sergio Sánchez 7, off c/Pizarro. An arty joint with a wide range of music; everyone sips tea from little copper pots.

Northwest of Cáceres: Arroyo and Alcántara

Northwest of Cáceres is the vast **Embalse de Alcántara**, one of a series of reservoirs harnessing the power of the Río Tajo in the last few kilometres before it enters Portugal. The scheme swallowed up large tracts of land and you can see the old road and railway to Palencia disappearing into depths of the reservoir (their replacements cross the many inlets on double-decker bridges), along with the tower of a castle.

The C523 loops a way to the south of the reservoir, through **Arroyo de la Luz** and **Brozas**, each with fine churches, before reaching **Alcántara**, with its superb Roman bridge across the Tajo. The Portuguese border – and the road to Coimbra – is just a dozen kilometres beyond.

Arroyo de la Luz and Brozas

ARROYO DE LA LUZ (Stream of Light), despite its romantic name, is one of the least memorable Extremaduran towns. However, it does have one sight of note: the gaunt, late Gothic church of **La Asunción**, which houses a huge *retablo* of twenty panels by Luis Morales. This Extremaduran artist (1509–86) is known to the Spanish as "El Divino", though his heart-on-sleeve style has never found much favour with art historians. His work is certainly a lot more impressive seen here, in situ, than in a museum. To view it, ask for the keys from the local police at the side door of the *Ayuntamiento*, which faces the south side of the church, and bring a couple of 100pta coins for the meter.

Arroyo has a single **hostal**, inevitably the *Divino Morales* (☎927/270257; ③), at the edge of town where the buses stop, and a couple of basic restaurants. A more pleasant place to eat, drink, or stay, however, is the old *Hostal El Posada* (☎927/395019; ③) at **BROZAS**, 35km on towards Alántara. Brozas itself is an old conquistador town, centred on a seventeenth-century castle. Its Gothic church of Santa Maria La Mayor has a spectacular Baroque retablo.

Alcántara

The name **ALCÁNTARA** comes from the Arabic for "bridge" – in this case a beautiful six-arched **Puente Romano** spanning a gorge of the Río Tajo. Completed in 105 AD, and held together without mortar, it is reputed to be the loftiest bridge ever built in the Roman Empire. It is quite a distance from the town, which is built high above the river; if you're on foot, don't follow the signs via the road – instead, head to the far side of the village and down a steep cobbled path.

In the town there are further Roman remains, including a **triumphal arch** dedicated to Trajan and a tiny **classical temple**. The dominating landmark, however, is the recently restored **Convento San Benito**, erstwhile headquarters of the Knights of Alcántara, one of the great orders of the reconquest. For all its enormous bulk, the convent and its church is only a fragment; the nave of the church was never built. Outside, the main feature is the double-arcaded Renaissance gallery at the back; it serves as the backdrop for a season of classical plays which moves here from Mérida in August. Entry (Tues–Fri 9.30am–1.45pm & 4–6pm, Sat 10.30am–1.45pm) is through the adjacent *Fundación de San Benito*, who have been making attempts to restore the cloister and the Plateresque east end with its elaborate wall tombs.

Alcántara also contains the scanty remains of a **castle**, numerous **mansions** and street after street of humbler whitewashed houses. The place is marvellous for scenic walks, whether in the town, along the banks of the Tajo, or – best of all – in the hills on the opposite bank. Useful maps are available from the **Turismo** (Mon–Fri 10am–2pm) at the entrance to the town on the road to Cáceres.

JAMON SERRANO: A GASTRONOMIC NOTE

Extremadura, to many Spaniards, means **ham**. Along with the Sierra Morena in Andalucía, the Extremaduran sierra is the only place in the country which supports the pure-bred Iberian pig, source of the best *jamón serrano*. For its ham to be as highly flavoured as possible, the pig, a subspecies of the European wild boar exclusive to the Iberian peninsula, is allowed to roam wild and eat acorns for several months of the year. The undisputed kings of hams in this area, praised at length by Richard Ford in his *Handbook for Travellers*, are those that come from **MONTÁNCHEZ**, in the south of the region. The village is midway between **Cáceres** and **Mérida**, so if you're in the area try some in a bar, washed down with local red wine – but be warned that the authentic product is extremely expensive, a few thinly cut slices often costing as much as an entire meal. The local wine known as *pitarra* is an ideal accompaniment.

The town has only one actual **hotel**, the *Hostal Cruz de Alcántara* on the main street, c/General Franco 23 (☎927/390023; ②). However, the periodic influx of workers at the reservoir prompts bars, shops and private homes to let out rooms. If you have difficulty, ask in the bars, at the tourist office, or even the local police – the people are very hospitable. **Buses**, which run twice a day to and from Cáceres, stop at a little square ringed by cafés at the entrance to the historic part of the town. Here you can **eat** cheaply at *Restaurante Gurdín*, and *Restaurante Antonio*, by the Turismo, is also good.

Mérida

The former capital of the Roman province of Lusitania, **MÉRIDA** (the name is a corruption of *Augusta Emerita*) contains more **Roman remains** than any other city in Spain. Even for the most casually interested, the extent and variety of the remains here are compelling, with everything from engineering works to domestic villas, by way of cemeteries and places of worship, entertainment and culture. With a little imagination, and a trip to the superb new museum, the Roman city is not difficult to evoke – which is just as well, for the modern city, in which the sites are scattered, is no great shakes.

Each July and August, the Roman theatre in Mérida hosts a **theatre festival**, including performances of Classical Greek and classic Spanish plays.

The Roman sites

Built on the site of a Celto-Iberian settlement, Mérida was the tenth city of the Roman empire and the final stop on the *Vía de la Plata*, the Roman road which began in Astorga in northern Castile. The old city stretched as far as the modern bullring and Roman circus, covering only marginally less than the triangular area occupied by the modern town. **Visiting the sites**, a single 200ptas ticket covers the ancient theatre, amphitheatre, Roman villas and the Alcazaba.

The bridge, Alcazaba and around the centre

The obvious point to begin your tour is the magnificent **Puente Romano**, the bridge across the islet-strewn Guadiana. It is sixty arches long (the seven in the middle are fifteenth-century replacements) and was still in use until the 1990s, when the new **Puente de Lusitania** – itself a structure to admire – was constructed.

Defence of the old bridge is provided by a vast **Alcazaba**, built by the Moors to replace a Roman construction. The interior (Mon–Sat 9am–2pm & 5–7pm, Sun 9am–2pm) is a rather barren archaeological site, although in the middle there's an *aljibe* (cistern) to which you can descend by either of a pair of staircases.

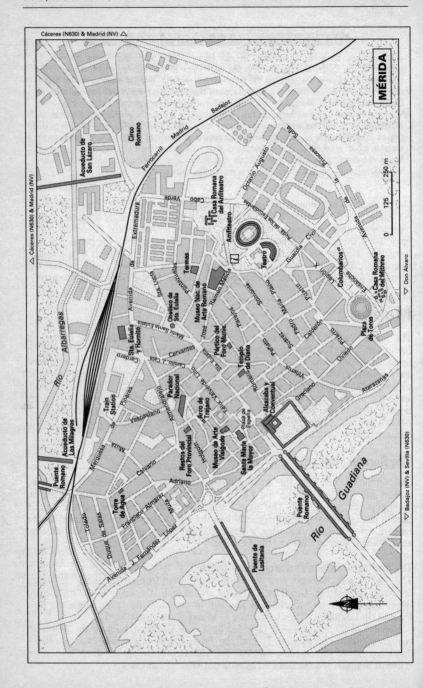

North of the Alcazaba, past the sixteenth-century Plaza de España, the heart of the modern town, is the so-called **Templo de Diana**, adapted into a Renaissance mansion, and further along are remains of the **Forum**, the heart of the Roman city. To the west of the plaza, a convent houses the **Museo de Arte Visigodo** (Tues–Sat 10am–2pm & 4–6pm, Sun 10am–2pm; free), with an unexciting collection of about a hundred lapidary items. Just behind here is the great **Arco Trajano**, an unadorned triumphal arch 15m high and 9m across.

The theatre and amphitheatre

A ten-minute walk northeast of the Plaza de España will take you to Mérida's main archeological site (daily from 8am–10pm), containing the theatre and amphitheatre, and a villa. Immediately adjacent is the new museum of Roman Art.

The elaborate and beautiful **Teatro Romano** is one of the best preserved anywhere in the Roman Empire. Constructed around 15BC, it was a present to the city from Agrippa, as indicated by the large inscription above the passageway to the left of the stage. The stage itself, a two-tier colonnaded affair, is in a particularly good state of repair, while many of the seats have been entirely rebuilt to offer more comfort to the audiences of the annual July season of classical plays.

Adjoining the theatre is the **Anfiteatro**, a slightly later and very much plainer construction. As many as 15,000 people – almost half the current population of Mérida – could be seated to watch gladiatorial combats and fights with wild animals.

The **Casa Romana del Anfiteatro** (Mon–Sat 9am–2pm & 5–7pm, Sun 9am–2pm), lies immediately below the museum, and offers an approach to it from the site. It has wonderful mosaics, including a vigorous depiction of grape-treading.

The Museo Nacional de Arte Romano

The **Museo Nacional de Arte Romano** (Oct–May Tues–Sat 10am–2pm & 4–6pm, Sun 10am–2pm; June–Sept Tues–Sat 10am–2pm & 5–7pm; Sun 10am–2pm; 200ptas) is one of the best new museums in Europe. Constructed in 1986 above the Roman walls, it is a wonderfully light, accessible building, using a free interpretation of classical forms to present the mosaics and sculpture as if emerging from the ruins. Rafael Moneo, its architect, and currently quite a star in Spain, achieved perfectly his aims here, to allow visitors "to see the entire collection almost in a glance".

The exhibits, displayed on three levels of the basilica-like hall, live up to their show-case. They include statues from the theatre, the Mithraeo villa (see below) and the vanished forum, and a number of mosaics – the largest being hung on the walls so that they can be examined at each level. There are frescoes, too, including a complete room, reconstructed. Individually, the finest exhibits are probably the three statues, displayed together, depicting Augustus, the first Roman emperor; his son Tiberius, the second emperor; and Drusus, Augustus's heir apparent until (it is alleged) he was murdered by Livia, Tiberius's mother.

Further out: the circus, aqueducts and Mithraeo villa

The remaining monuments are further out from the centre, on the other side of the rail-way tracks. From the museum, it's a ten minute walk out along the Avenida de Extremadura to the **Circo Romano**, essentially an outline, where horses and chariots once raced. Across the road from here, a stretch of the **Aqueducto de San Lázaro** leads off towards the Río Albarregas.

The more impressive aqueduct, however, is the **Aqueducto de los Milagros**, of which a satisfying portion survives in the midst of vegetable gardens, west of the train station. Its tall arches of granite, with brick courses, brought water to the city in its earliest days from the reservoir at Proserpina, 5km away (see below). The best view of the aqueduct is from a low and inconspicuous **Puente Romano** across the Albarregas; it was over this span that the *Vía de la Plata* entered the city.

Two further sights are the church of **Santa Eulalia**, by the train station, which has a porch made from fragments of a former Temple of Mars, and a second Roman villa, the **Mithraeo** (currently under restoration), in the shadow of the Plaza de Toros, south of the museum and theatres. The villa has a magnificent but damaged mosaic showing river gods. A short walk away is a Roman burial ground with two family sepulchres.

Proserpina and Cornalvo reservoirs

You can swim in the **Pantano de Proserpina**, a Roman-constructed reservoir, 5km north of town and a popular summer escape, with a line of holiday homes. Alternatively, if you have transport, head to the **Pantano de Cornalvo**, 18km east of Mérida (turn left after the village of Trujillanos). There's a Roman dyke here, and a small national park has recently been created in the area.

Practicalities

Mérida sees a lot of visitors and has plenty of places to stay, eat and drink. If you want maps or information on the region, look in at the **Turismo** (Mon–Fri 9am–2pm & 4–6pm, winter 5–7pm, Sat & Sun 9.15am–2pm), just outside the gates to the Theatre and Amphitheatre site.

The **train station** is pretty central, with the theatre site and Plaza de España no more than ten minutes' walk. The **bus station** is a grittier twenty minutes' walk from the centre, along Avenida de Libertad, which extends from the suspension bridge.

Accommodation

Pensión El Arco, c/Sta. Beatriz de Silva 4 (☎924/310107). The cheapest and friendliest pension in town. ②.

Hostal Bueno, c/Calvario 9 (☎924/311013). "Good" is pushing things a bit but this *hostal* is clean enough and all rooms have (tiny) bathrooms. ③.

Hotel Emperatriz, Plaza de España 19 (☎924/313111). An attractive and old-established hotel in a former palace, bang on the main square. ④–⑤.

Hostal Nueva España, Avda. de Extremadura 6 (☎924/313356). A good value *hostal* out towards the train station. ③.

Hostal Salud, c/Vespasiano 41 (☎924/312259). Again, decent value rooms. ③.

Hotel Vittoria, c/Calderón de la Barca 30 (☎924/311462). Comfortable small hotel with easy parking right outside. ③.

Parador Via de la Plata, Plaza Constitución 3, near the Arco Trajano (☎924/313800). Set in an eighteenth–century Baroque convent. ⑥.

CAMPING

Camping Mérida (☎924/303453). This is the nearest site, 2km out of town on the E90.

Camping Proserpina (☎924/313236). A much more pleasant site, by the reservoir (see above), 5km north of town.

Eating and drinking

The whole area between the train station and the Plaza de España is full of **bars and cheap restaurants** – fliers for many of which will be stuffed into your hands outside the theatre site entrance. Good choices might include:

El Antillano, c/Félix Valverde Lillo 15, west of Plaza de España (closed Sun night & second half of Sept). This is the town's best budget restauarant – an unpretentious meson attached to the classier **Restaurante Nicolas**, next door at no.15. Both are highly recommended.

Bar-Restaurante Briz, c/Félix Valverde Lillo 5, just off Plaza de España (closed Sun). Solid Extremeduran dishes and an inexpensive *menú*.

Casa Benito, c/San Francisco 3. Bullfighters' ephemera line the walls of this bar, which has local *pitarra* wine and local speciality *tapas*.

Restaurante Medea, c/Reyes Huertas 7, just behind the museum. Cheap and adequate if you want a quick snack near the Roman sites.

Restaurante Naya, c/Cardero 7, close to the train station. Offers a good, modest, four-course *menú*.

Badajoz

The valley of the Guadiana, followed by road and rail, waters rich farmland between Mérida and **BADAJOZ**. The main reason for visiting this provincial capital, traditional gateway to Portugal and the scene of innumerable sieges, is still to get across the border – it's not somewhere you'd want to stay long. Crude modern development has largely overrun what must once have been an attractive old centre, and few of the monuments have survived.

The town

At the heart of old Badajoz is the **Plaza de España** and the squat thirteenth-century **Catedral** (daily 11am–1pm), a fortress-like building, prettified a little during the Renaissance by the addition of a portal and embellishment of the tower.

Northeast of the square, c/de San Juan leads to **Plaza Alta**, once an elegant arcaded concourse, now seedy, and what remains of the town's fortress, the **Alcazaba**. This is largely in ruins but preserves Moorish entrance gates and fragments of a Renaissance palace inside. Part of it houses a **Museo Arqueológico** (Tues–Sun 10am–3pm), with local Roman and Visigothic finds. Defending the townward side is the octagonal Moorish Torre del Aprendiz, or *Torre Espantaperros* ("dog-scarer" – the dogs in question being Christians).

The Río Guadiana is the city's only other distinguished feature, and in particular the graceful **Puente de Palmas**, or Puente Viejo, spanning its course. The bridge was designed by Herrera (architect of the Escorial) as a fitting first impression of Spain, and leads into the city through the **Puerta de Palmas**, once a gate in the walls, now standing alone as a sort of triumphal arch.

From the plaza behind this arch, c/Sta. Lucía (formerly c/Coronel Yagüe) leads to the **Museo de Bellas Artes** (Mon–Fri 8.30am–2.30pm, Sat 9am–1pm), including works by local boy Luís Morales, and a couple of good panels by Zurbarán.

Practicalities

The town has two tourist offices. A municipal **Turismo** (Mon–Fri 8am–3pm, Sat 10am–2pm) is in c/de San Juan, just off Plaza de España, while the **Junta de Extremadura** (Mon–Fri 9am–2pm & 5–7pm, Sat & Sun 9am–2pm), good for information on the whole region, is down the hill on Plaza de la Libertad – follow the signs from any approach to the town.

The **bus station** is awkwardly located in wasteland beyond the ring road at the southern edge of the city. It's a 15 minute-plus walk from the centre, and better to take buses #3 or #4. The **train station** is still further from the action, on the far side of the river, up the road which crosses the Puente de Palmas. Any bus crossing the bridge will take you there, or it's a cheap taxi ride. If you're looking for **parking**, follow the signs to the Turismo from the Puerto de Palmas and turn right along Avenida de Huelva straight after you've passed it; there's a big attended lot at the end of this street.

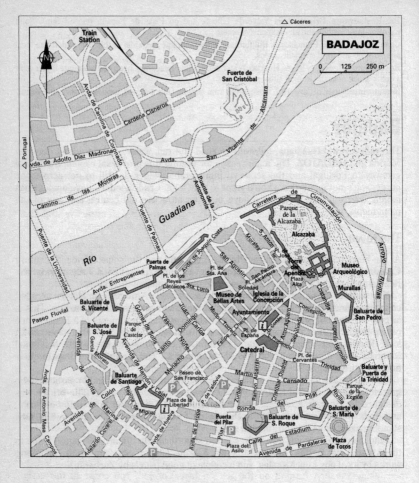

Accommodation

There's plenty of **accommodation** available in Badajoz, much of it inexpensive, if not terribly desirable. The best location is around the Plaza de España.

Albergue de Juventud, Ronda del Pilar 10 (☎924/235400). The town youth hostel is open in July and August only – and even then summer schools often fill the place up.

Hostal Conde Duque, Muñoz Torrero 27 (☎924/224641). A comfortable _hostal_. ④.

Hostal Menacho, c/Abril 12 (☎924/221853). The rooms aren't bad here and prices are more than reasonable. ②.

Pensión Orrego, Arco Agüero 41 (☎924/220832). Best of several _pensiones_ on this street just south of the cathedral. ②.

Hotel Río, Avda. Díaz Ambrona, by the new bridge (☎924/272600). Reasonable hotel with a swimming pool. ④.

Hotel Zurbarán, Paseo Castelar, by the Puerta de Palmas (☎924/223741). The best hotel in town, with a swimming pool. ⑤.

Eating and Drinking

The area around c/Conde Duque, a couple of blocks below the Plaza de España, is the most promising site for reasonably-priced food and lively bars.

Bar-Restaurante El Tronco, c/Muñoz Torrero. Perhaps the best reason to stay in town – this has a vast range of superb value bar snacks and excellent, fiery regional food in the restaurant.

Los Gabrieles, c/Vicente Barrantes 21 (closed Sun). Classic local cuisine, served in huge portions and at very reasonable cost.

La Toja, Av Díaz Ambrona – the Portugal road. This is the class restaurant in Badajoz, run by a Gallego and serving exclusively food from that region. Moderately pricey.

Southern Extremadura

The routes **south from Mérida or Badajoz** cross territory that is mostly harsh and unrewarding, fit only for sheep and the odd cork or olive tree, until you come upon the foothills of the Sierra Morena, on the borders of Andalucía. En route, **Olivenza**, a town that has spent more time in Portugal than Spain, is perhaps the most attractive stop, and offers a road approach to Évora, the most interesting city of southern Portugal.

Olivenza

Twenty-five kilometres southwest of Badajoz, whitewashed **OLIVENZA** seems to have landed in the wrong country; long disputed between Spain and Portugal, it has been Spanish since 1801. Yet not only are the character of the town and its buildings clearly Portuguese, the oldest inhabitants still cling to this language – you may overhear them chatting as they relax in the main square where the buses stop.

Inevitably, the town has long been strongly fortified, and traces of the **walls and gates** can still be seen, even though houses have been built up against them. They extend up to the **castle**, which has three surviving towers, and an ethnographic museum (Tues–Sun 11am–2pm & 4.30–6pm, summer 7–9pm) within.

Right beside the castle is the church of **Santa María del Castillo**, and around the corner is **Santa María Magdalena**. Both have sturdy bell towers and light, airy interiors adorned with *azulejo* tiles and ornate Baroque altars. The latter is in the distinctive Portuguese Manueline style, with arcades of twisted columns; the former is a more sober Renaissance affair with three aisles of equal height and a notable work of art in the huge "Tree of Jesse" *retablo*. Both are only open in the morning.

Just across the street from Santa María Magdalena is a former **palace**, now the public library, with a spectacular Manueline doorway. Continuing down this street, then taking the first turning on the left on to c/Coridad, you come to the early sixteenth-century **Hospital**, which still serves its original purpose. Its chapel (staff will open it up for you on request) is covered with early eighteenth-century *azulejos*.

Should you want to stay in Olivenza, there's a **hotel** on the fringes of town, *Heredero* (☎924/490835; ④) with a restaurant directly facing it, and a cheaper **pensión**, the *Puente Ayuda* (☎924/490298; ②), nearby.

Towards Portugal

Twelve kilometres northwest of Olivenza, a road heading towards Portugal stops abruptly at the ruined bridge of **Puente Ayuda**, where the Río Guadiana forms the border between the two countries. There's no way on other than to swim but it's a picturesque picnic spot; the river runs across many exposed rock beds giving good fishing and it's also an ideal spot for some discreet camping. To **enter Portugal**, you need to follow the C436 south from Olivenza for 39km to the Spanish border of **Villanueva del Franco**. From here it's 16km to **Mourao**, the first Portuguese town, which is on the main road (and bus route) to Évora.

South to Jerez de los Caballeros

The road from **Badajoz to Jerez de los Caballeros** is typical of southern Extremadura, striking across a parched landscape whose hamlets – low huts and a whitewashed church strung out along the road – look as if they have been dumped from some low-budget Western set of a Mexican frontier town. It's cruel country which bred cruel people, if we are to believe the names of places like Valle de Matamoros (Valley of the Moorslayers), and one can easily understand the attraction which the New World and the promise of the lush Indies must have held for its inhabitants.

It is hardly surprising, then, that **JEREZ DE LOS CABALLEROS** produced a whole crop of *conquistadores*. The two most celebrated are Vasco Núñez de Balboa, discoverer of the Pacific, and Hernando de Soto, who in exploring the Mississippi became one of the first Europeans to set foot in North America. You're not allowed to forget it – the bus station is in the Plaza de Vasco Núñez de Balboa, complete with a statue of Vasco in the very act of discovery, and from it the Calle Hernando de Soto (also known as the Hero of Florida) leads up into the middle of town.

It's a quiet, friendly place, where many tourists pass through but few stay. Grass grows up through most of the cobbled streets and there's no hurry about anything. From a distance it is the church towers that dominate the walled old town: a passion for building spires gripped the place in the eighteenth century, when three churches erected new ones. The silhouette of each is clearly based on that of the Giralda at Sevilla, but they are all distinctively decorated: the first is **San Miguel**, in the central Plaza de España, made of carved brick; the second is the unmistakable red-, blue-, and ochre-glazed tower of **San Bartolomé**, on the hill above it, with a striking tiled facade; and the third, rather dilapidated, belongs to **Santa Catalina**, outside the walls.

Above the Plaza de España the streets climb up to the restored remains of a **castle** of the Knights Templar (this was once an embattled frontier town), mostly fourteenth-century but with obvious Moorish influences. Adjoining the castle, and predating it by over a century (as do the town walls), is the church of **Santa María**. Built on a Visigothic site, it's more interesting seen from the battlements above than it is from the inside. The clock tower is a further embellishment to the skyline, and keeps remarkably good time as well. In the small park below the castle walls, a café commands fine views of the surrounding countryside, including the magnificent sunsets.

Places to stay are few. By far the cheapest is the *Pensión El Gordito*, Avda. de Portugal 104 (☎924/731452; ①), which is good for the price. The more upmarket alternatives are the *Hotel Oasis* (☎924/731244; ④) and *Hostal Las Torres* (☎924/731168; ③). The *Oasis* has the only real **restaurant** in town; for *tapas* and *pitarra* wine, try *La Ermita*, an old chapel on c/Dr. Benitez.

Zafra

If you plan to stick to the main routes or are heading south from Mérida, **ZAFRA** is rather less of a detour, though it's also much more frequented by tourists. It's famed mainly for its **castle** – now converted into a *parador* – which is remarkable for the white marble Renaissance patio designed by Juan de Herrera. Two beautiful arcaded plazas, the Plaza Grande and the Plaza Chica, adjoin each other in the town centre.

The most attractive of several interesting churches is **Nuestra Señora de la Candelaria** (daily 10am–1pm & 7–8pm), with nine panels by Zurbarán in the *retablo* and a chapel by Churriguera; the entrance is on c/José through a small gateway, around the side of the church. The tombs of the Figueroa family (original inhabitants of the castle) in the **Convento de Santa Clara** (closed 2–4pm & 7–8pm) just off the main shopping street, c/Sevilla are worth a look; ring the bell to get in. Zafra has a well-stocked **Turismo** (Mon–Fri 11.15am–2pm & 6.15–8pm, Sat 11.15am–1.30pm) in the

Plaza de España. Accommodation options include the *Parador* (☎924/550200; ⑤); *Hotel El Ancla* (☎924/552062; ⑤, but less expensive off-season); and *Hostal Rafael*, c/ Virgén de Guadalupe 7 (☎924/552052; ④ also cheaper off-season). Cheapest are the rooms at the *Bar Rogelio* (☎924/551439; ②), at the bottom of the kilometre-long avenue that leads to the train station.

South of Zafra: the Sierra Morena
Beyond Zafra the main road and the railway head straight down through the **Sierra Morena** towards **Sevilla**. By **road** it's more interesting – though bus services are less frequent – to go through **Fregenal de La Sierra** (where the road from Jerez de los Caballeros joins up) into the heart of the sierra around Aracena. On the **train** you can reach another interesting region by getting off at the station of Cazalla-Constantina; while if you're heading for **Córdoba** and eastern Andalucía, you should change at Los Rosales before reaching Sevilla.

travel details

Buses

Albacete to: Alicante (6 daily; 2hr 30min); Madrid (9 daily; 3hr); Murcia (6 daily; 2hr 15min); Valencia (9 daily; 3hr).

Badajoz to: Cáceres (4 daily; 2hr); Caya (Portuguese frontier – 4 daily; 30min); Córdoba (3 daily; 5hr); Lisbon (at least 1 each day; 7hr); Madrid (7 daily; 6hr); Mérida (6 daily; 1hr); Olivenza (7 daily; 30min); Sevilla (7 daily; 3hr); Valencia de Alcántara (3 daily; 1hr 30min); Zafra (7 daily; 1hr 30min).

Cáceres to: Alcántara (2 daily; 1hr 30min); Arroyo de la Luz (Mon–Sat 8 daily; 30min); Badajoz (4 daily; 2hr); Caminomorisco (1 daily; 2hr 30min); Coria (3 daily; 1hr 30min); Guadalupe (1 daily; 4hr); Madrid (7 daily; 4–5hr); Mérida (3 daily; 1hr); Plasencia (6 daily; 1hr 30min); Salamanca (3 daily; 3hr 30min); Sevilla (5 daily; 4hr); Trujillo (7 daily; 1hr); Valencia de Alcántara (4 daily; 2hr 15min).

Ciudad Real to: Almagro (5 daily; 1hr); Córdoba (1 daily; 4hr 30min); Jaén (2 daily; 4hr); Madrid (4 daily; 4hr); Toledo (1 daily; 3hr), Valdepeñas (3 daily; 2hr).

Cuenca to: Albaceta (2 daily; 3hr); Barcelona (1 daily; 9 hr); Madrid (8 daily; 2hr 30min); Tereul (1 daily; 3hr); Valencia (2 daily; 4hr).

Mérida to: Cáceres (2 daily; 1hr); Jerez de los Caballeros (1 daily; 2hr); Madrid (6 daily; 5hr); Sevilla (12 daily; 3hr 30min, some stopping in Zafra); Trujillo (1 daily; 1hr 30min); Zafra (5 daily; 1hr).

Navalmoral to: Jarandilla (2 daily; 3hr) Plasencia (2 daily; 2–4hr).

Plasencia to: Jarandilla (1 daily; 2hr); Salamanca (5 daily; 2hr).

Talavera to: Guadalupe (2 daily; 2hr 30min); Madrid (frequently; 3hr); Toledo (10 daily; 1hr 30min).

Trujillo to: Cáceres (5 daily; 1hr 30min); Guadalupe (2 daily; 3hr); Mérida (4 daily; 2hr).

Trains

Albacete to: Alicante (8 daily; 1hr 45min); Valencia (10 daily; 1hr 45min–2hr 15min).

Badajoz to: Cáceres (2 daily; 2hr); Lisbon (3 daily; 5hr); Mérida (5 daily; 1hr); Plasencia (1 daily; 4hr); Sevilla (3 daily; 5–7hr via Mérida (1hr) and Zafra (2–3hr).

Cáceres to: Lisbon (2 daily; 4hr 30min); Madrid (5 daily; 4hr 30min–6hr); Mérida (1 daily; 1hr); Plasencia (3 daily; 1hr 30min); Sevilla 1 daily; 5hr); Valencia de Alcántara (2 daily; 2hr 30min) Zafra (1 daily; 2hr).

Cuenca to: Valencia (3 daily; 3hr).

Madrid to: Albacete (15 daily; 2hr 10min); Badajoz (3 daily; 5hr 30min–7hr 30min); Cáceres (5 daily 3hr 30min–4hr 30min); Ciudad Real (7 daily AVE high speed service; 55min & 2 daily; 3hr); Cuenca (4 daily; 2hr 30min); Navalmoral (5 daily; 2hr 30min); Plasencia (4 daily; 3hr 30min); Sigüenza (10 daily; 1hr 30min–2hr 30min); Talavera (5 daily; 2hr).

Mérida to: Cáceres (4 daily; 1hr); Madrid (4 daily; 6hr); Plasencia (2 daily; 2hr 30min); Sevilla (1 daily; 4hr).

Sigüenza to: Barcelona (3 daily; at least 8hr), via Zaragoza (3–4hr).

CHAPTER FOUR

ANDALUCÍA

A bove all else – and there is plenty – it's the great **Moorish monuments** that compete for your attention in **Andalucía**. The Moors, a mixed race of Berbers and Arabs who crossed into Spain from Morocco and North Africa, occupied *al-Andalus* for over seven centuries. Their first forces landed at Tarifa in 710 AD and within four years they had conquered virtually the entire country; their last kingdom, Granada, fell to the Christian Reconquest in 1492. Between these dates they developed the most sophisticated civilization of the Middle Ages, centred in turn on the three major cities of **Córdoba**, **Sevilla** and **Granada**. Each one preserves extraordinarily brilliant and beautiful monuments, of which the most perfect is Granada's **Alhambra palace**, arguably the most sensual building in all of Europe. **Sevilla**, not to be outdone in the Christian era, has the greatest of all Gothic cathedrals, and is today the Andaluz city par excellence: a vibrant contemporary city that's impossible to resist.

These three cities have, of course, become major tourist destinations, but the smaller **inland towns** of Andalucía are often totally unspoiled. These offer amazing

---

FIESTAS

January

1–2 *La Toma* – celebration of the entry of the *Reyes Católicos* into the city – at Granada.

6 *Romería de la Virgen del Mar* pilgrimage procession from Almería.

17 *Romería del Ermita del Santo*. Similar event at Gaudix.

February

1 *San Cecilio* fiesta in Granada's traditionally gypsy quarter of Sacromonte.

February/March: *Carnival* is an extravagant week-long event (leading up to Lent) in all the Andalucian cities. Cádiz, above all, celebrates, with fancy dress, *flamenco* and camp-comic competitions.

April

Holy Week (*Semana Santa*), too, has its most elaborate and dramatic celebrations in Andalucía. You'll find memorable processions of floats and penitents at Sevilla, Málaga, Granada and to a lesser extent in smaller towns like Arcos, Baeza and Úbeda. All culminate on *Good Friday*, with *Easter Day* itself more of a family occasion.

Last week (or 1–2 weeks after Easter) Week-long *Feria de Abril* at Sevilla: the largest fair in Spain, a little refined in the way of the city, but an extraordinary event nonetheless. A small April fair – featuring bull-running – is held in Vejer.

Late April/early May *Festival of the Patios* in Córdoba includes a competition for decorations and numerous events and concerts organized by the local city council.

May

Early May (usually the week after Sevilla's fair) Somewhat aristocratic *Horse Fair* at Jerez de la Frontera.

3 *Moros y Cristianos* carnival at Pampaneira (Alpujarras).

15 *San Isidro Romería* at Setenil (Cádiz).

Pentecost (7 weeks after Easter) *Romería del Rocío*, when horse-drawn carriages and processions converge from all over the south on El Rocío (Huelva).

Corpus Christi (variable – Thursday after Trinity). Bullfights and festivities at Granada, Sevilla, Ronda, Vejer and Zahara De La Sierra.

potential; Renaissance towns like Úbeda, Baeza and Osuna, Guadix with its cave suburb, Moorish Carmona and the stark white hill towns around Ronda, are all easily accessible by local buses. Travelling for some time here you'll also get a feel for the landscape of Andalucía: occasionally spectacularly beautiful but more often impressive on a huge, unyielding scale, distinguished by a patchwork of colours and the interaction of land and buildings, or the gradual appearance of villages grouped beneath a castle and church.

The province also takes in mountains – including the Sierra Nevada, Spain's highest range. You can ski here in February, and then drive down to the coast to swim the same day. Perhaps more compelling, though, are the opportunities for walking in the lower slopes, Las Alpujarras. Alternatively, there's good trekking amongst the gentler (and much less-known) slopes of the Sierra Morena, north of Sevilla.

On the coast it's easy to despair. Extending to either side of Málaga is the Costa del Sol, Europe's most heavily developed resort area, with its beaches hidden behind a remorseless density of concrete hotels and apartment complexes. However, the province takes in two alternatives, much less developed and with some of the best beaches in all Spain. These are the villages between Tarifa and Cádiz on the Atlantic, and those around Almería on the southeast corner of the Mediterranean. The Almerian beaches allow warm swimming through all but the winter months; those near Cádiz, more easily accessible, are fine from about June to September. Near Cádiz, too, is the Coto Doñana, Spain's largest and most important nature reserve, whose remarkable bird- and wildlife can be observed on short prearranged tours.

June

Second week *Feria de San Bernabé* at Marbella, often spectacular since this is the richest town in Andalucía.

13 *San Antonio Fiesta* at Trevélez (Alpujarras) with mock battles between Moors and Christians.

Third week The Algeciras fair and fiesta, another major event of the south.

23–24 *Candelas de San Juan* – bonfires and effigies at Vejer and elsewhere.

30 Conil *feria*.

End June/early July *International Festival of Music and Dance*: major dance groups and chamber orchestras perform in Granada's Alhambra palace, Generalife and Carlos V palace.

July

Early July The *International Guitar Festival* at Córdoba brings together top international acts from classical, *flamenco* and Latin American music.

August

5 Trevélez observes a midnight *romería* to Mulhacén.

15 *Ascension of the Virgin* Fair with *casetas* (dance tents) at Vejer and elsewhere.

27 Grape harvest fiesta at Montilla (Córdoba).

Some time in August *Guadalquivir festival* at Sanlúcar de Barrameda with bullfights and an important *flamenco* competition.

August 17–20 The first cycle of horse races along Sanlúcar's beach, with heavy official and unofficial betting; the second tournament takes place a week later.

Late July/early August Almería's festival generally involves a handful of major jazz and rock concerts in its Plaza Vieja.

September

1–3 Celebration of the *Virgen de la Luz* in Tarifa: processions and horseback riding.

First/second week *Vendimia* (celebration of the vintage) at Jerez.

Early in the month Ronda bursts into life with a *feria*, *flamenco* contests and the *Corrida Goyesca*, bullfights in eighteenth-century dress.

29–Oct 2 *Feria* in Órjiva (Alpujarras).

October

1 *San Miguel* fiesta in Granada's Albaicín quarter and dozens of other towns, even at Torremolinos.

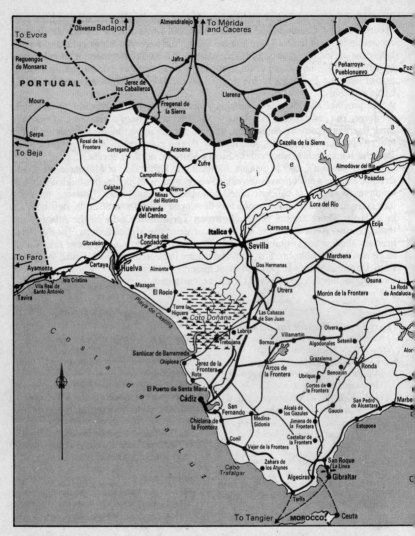

The realities of life in **contemporary Andalucía** can be stark. **Unemployment** in the province is the highest in Spain – well over twenty percent – and an even larger proportion of the population is still engaged in agriculture. Rural life is bleak; you soon begin to notice the appalling economic structure, at its most extreme in this part of Spain, of vast absentee-landlord estates and landless peasants. The Andaluz villages, bastions of anarchist and socialist groups before and during the Civil War, saw little economic aid or change during the Franco years – or indeed since, even though the Socialist party has its principal power base in Andalucía. The day labourers, *jornaleros*, earn a precarious living from seasonal work, and as recently as 1986 the regional government instituted land reform in an effort to head off a peasants' revolt. Numerous

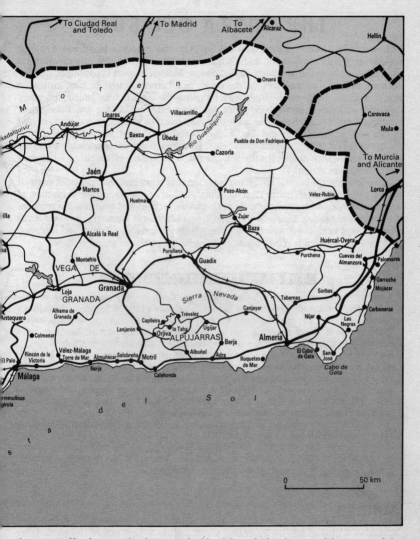

instances of land occupation have resulted in violent clashes between labourers and the Civil Guard. Tourism, and *Expo 92* in Sevilla, have brought some changes, however, with radical improvements in the infrastructure, and above all new road and rail projects aimed at providing faster connections within the region and with Madrid and Barcelona.

For all its poverty, Andalucía is also Spain at its most exuberant: the home of *flamenco* and the bullfight, and those wild and extravagant clichés of the Great Spanish Dream. These really do exist and can be absorbed at one of the hundreds of annual **fiestas, ferias** and **romerías**. The best of them include the giant **April Feria** in Sevilla, the ageless pilgrimage to **El Rocío** near Huelva in late May, and the **Semana Santa** (Easter) celebrations at Málaga, Granda and Sevilla.

THE COSTA DEL SOL

The outstanding feature of the **Costa del Sol** is its ease of access. Hundreds of charter flights arrive here every week, and it's often possible to get an absurdly cheap ticket from other cities in Europe, particularly London. **Málaga airport** is positioned midway between Málaga, the main city on the coast, and **Torremolinos**, its most grotesque resort. You can easily reach either town by taking the electric train which runs every half-hour (6.30am–11.30pm daily) along the coast between Málaga and **Fuengirola**. Granada, Córdoba and Sevilla are all within easy reach of Málaga; so too, and covered in this section, are **Ronda** and the "White Towns" to the west, and a handful of relatively restrained coastal resorts to the east. **Beaches** along this stretch are generally grit-grey rather than golden but the sea, at least, is reasonably clean, after a lot of work on the sewerage system.

Economically, the coastal hinterland is undergoing a gradual resurgence, in contrast to the general decline in the rest of Andalucía. In recent years the cultivation of subtropical fruits such as mangos, papayas, guavas, lychees and avocados has replaced the traditional orange, lemon and almond trees. Most farm labourers, however, can't afford coastal land; those who buy are often former migrants to France and Germany who have been forced to return because of the (un)employment situation there.

THE CARRETERA NACIONAL N340

A special note of warning has to be made about the Costa del Sol's main highway, which is one of the most dangerous roads in Europe. Nominally a national highway, it's really a 100-kilometre-long city street, passing through the middle of towns and *urbanizaciones*. Drivers treat it like a motorway, yet pedestrians have to get across, and cars are constantly turning off or into the road – hence the terrifying number of accidents, with over a hundred fatalities a year on average. A large number of these involve inebriated British package tourists who are further handicapped by lack of familiarity with left-hand-drive vehicles and traffic patterns. The first few kilometres, between the airport with its various car hire offices and Torremolinos, are among the most treacherous of the entire N340. The worst stretch is heading west from Marbella: around thirty accidents a year occur on each kilometre between Marbella and San Pedro.

Plans have been approved for a new motorway which will link the Costa del Sol with Madrid and Sevilla, and so reduce traffic on the N340. In the meantime, don't make dangerous (and illegal) left turns from the fast lane; be particularly careful after a heavy rain, when the hot, oily road surface sends you easily into a skid; and pedestrians should cross at traffic lights, a bridge or an underpass if possible.

Málaga

MÁLAGA seems at first an uninviting place. It's the second city of the south (after Sevilla) and also one of the poorest: official unemployment figures for the area estimate the jobless at one in four of the workforce. Yet though many people get no further than the train or bus stations, and though the clusters of high rises look pretty grim as you approach, it has its attractions. Around the old fishing villages of **El Palo** and **Pedregalejo**, now absorbed into the suburbs, are a series of small beaches and a *paseo* lined with some of the best **fish and seafood cafés** in the province. And overlooking the town and port are the Moorish citadels of the **Alcazaba** and **Gibralfaro** – excellent introductions to the architecture before pressing on to the main sites at Córdoba and Granada.

Arrival and accommodation

Arriving in Málaga from the **airport**, the **electric train** provides the easiest approach (every 20–30min). From the arrivals lounge, follow the *Ferrocarril* signs through the car park, cross via the pedestrian underpass and stay on the train right to the end of the line, the Guadalmedina stop. The stop before this is *RENFE*, the main **train station**, a slightly longer walk into the heart of town (bus #3 runs from here to the centre every 10min or so).

The **bus station** is just behind the *RENFE* station, a bit to the right as you face the *RENFE* logo from the esplanade. All buses (run by a number of different companies) operate from this same terminal. There's a useful machine in the station which saves queuing up at the information desk: indicate your destination and it details the connections and departure time of the next bus. In midsummer it's best to arrive an hour or so early for the bus to Granada, since tickets can sell out.

Málaga also has the remnants of a **passenger ferry** port, though these days there's a service only to the Spanish enclave of Melilla in Morocco. If you're heading for Fes and eastern Morocco, this is a useful connection – particularly so for taking a car over – though most people go for the quicker services at Algeciras and Tarifa to the west. Sailings are daily except Sunday, generally leaving around 1pm; the crossing takes ten hours. Tickets are from *Compañía Aucona* at c/Juan Díaz 1.

The **Turismo**, Pasaje de Chinitas 4 (Mon–Fri 9am–2pm, Sat 9am–1pm), can provide full accommodation lists and a large, detailed map of the city. There's also a helpful branch at the bus station.

Accommodation

Málaga boasts dozens of **fondas** and **hostales**, so budget rooms are rarely hard to come by, and there are some real bargains available in winter. You may well get offers at the train (or possibly the bus) station, and so long as the rooms are fairly central these will probably be as good as any. Numerous possibilities are to be found in the grid of streets just north of the *Centro/Alameda* station, which is probably the best place to start looking.

BUDGET OPTIONS

Albergue Juvenil Málaga, Plaza de Pio XII (☎952/308500). A modern youth hostel on the eastern outskirts of town, with its own sun terrace. The #18 bus from the Alameda will drop you nearby. ①.

Hostal Alameda, c/Casas de Campos 3 (☎952/222099). Friendly place, some rooms with bath. ③.

Hostal Avenida, Alameda Principal 5 (☎952/217729). Right on the Alameda but not too noisy. ③.

Casa Huéspedes Bolivia, c/Casas de Campos 24 (☎952/218826). Clean and simple with a friendly proprietor. ③.

Hostal El Cenachero, c/Barroso 5 (☎952/224088). A clean, quiet and reasonably priced place; left off the seafront end of c/Córdoba. ③.

Hostal Córdoba, c/Bolsa 9–11 (☎952/214469). Inexpensive, simple rooms in a family-run establishment near the cathedral. ②.

ACCOMMODATION PRICE SYMBOLS

The symbols used in our hotel listings denote the following price ranges:

① Under 2000ptas	③ 3000–4500ptas	⑤ 7500–12,500ptas
② 2000–3000ptas	④ 4500–7500ptas	⑥ Over 12,500ptas

See p.30 for more details.

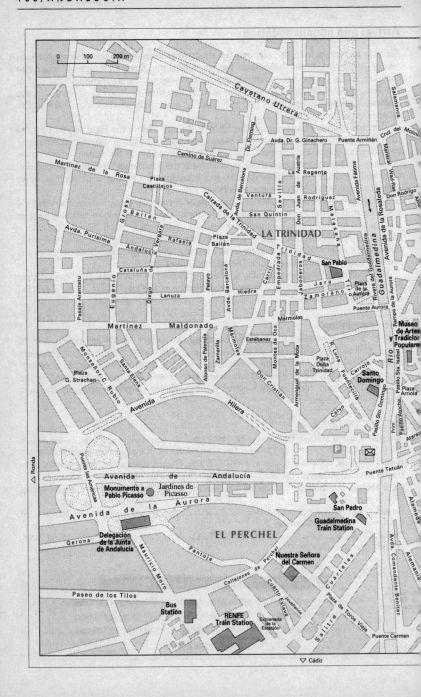

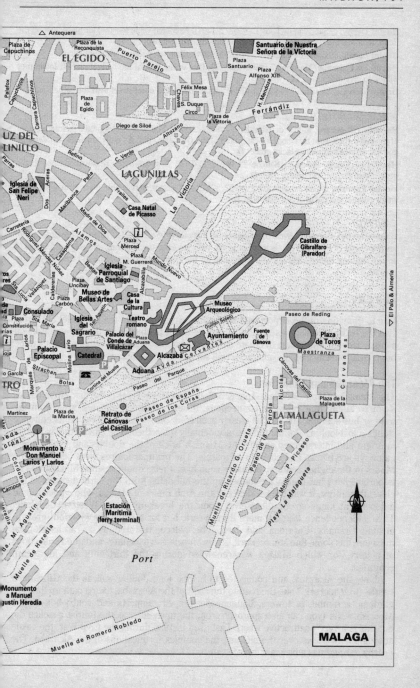

△ Antequera

Plaza de Capuchinos

EL EGIDO

Plaza de la Reconquista

Puerto Parejo

Palafox

Carrera Capuchinos

Plaza de Egido

Félix Mesa Chaves

S. Duque

Circo

Plaza de la Victoria

Santuario de Nuestra Señora de la Victoria

Plaza Santuario

Plaza Alfonso XIII

H. Mendoza

Ferrándiz

Diego de Siloé

Alhozano

C. Verde

UZ DEL LINILLO

Refino

Parras

Aceras

Dos

Iglesia de San Felipe Neri

LAGUNILLAS

La Victoria

Maribланca

Peña

Frailes

Carretera

Rodríguez Méndez Núñez

Casapalma

Álamos

Madre de Dios

Casa Natal de Picasso

Plaza Merced

M. Guerrero

Mundo Nuevo

Castillo de Gibralfaro (Parador)

Beatas

Iglesia Parroquial de Santiago

Alcazabilla

Plaza Uncibay

Museo de Bellas Artes

Plaza Carbón

Casa de la Cultura

Museo Arqueológico

El Palo & Almería ▷

Consulado

Sta. María

Iglesia del Sagrario

Teatro romano

Guillén Solato

Paseo de Reding

Plaza de Toros

Plaza Constitución

Larios

Palacio del Conde de Villalcázar

Plaza Aduana

Ayuntamiento

Fuente de Génova

Maestranza

Palacio Episcopal

Molina Lario

Catedral

Alcazaba

Cervantes

Cánovas del Castillo

Cervantes

Bolsa

Marqués

Strachan

Aduana

Avda.

Plaza de la Malagueta

TRO

Cortina del Muelle

Aduana

Paseo del Parque

San Nicolás

Martínez

Plaza de la Marina

Retrato de Cánovas del Castillo

Paseo de España

Paseo de los Curas

LA MALAGUETA

Paseo de la Farola

Monumento a Don Manuel Larios y Larios

Campos

M. Agustín Heredia

Estación Marítima (ferry terminal)

Muelle de Ricardo G. Orueta

P. Marítimo P. Picasso

Playa La Malagueta

Muelle de Heredia

Monumento a Manuel Agustín Heredia

Port

Muelle de Romero Robledo

MALAGA

Hostal Derby, c/San Juan de Dios 1 (☎952/221301). Excellent value fourth-floor place, just off the Plaza de la Marina, with some rooms overlooking the harbour. ③.

Hostal Indalo, c/Casas de Campos 5 (☎952/211974). Clean, airy rooms without bath. ③.

Hostal La Palma, c/Martínez 7 (☎952/226772). One of the best of the budget places; sometimes willing to give discounts. ③.

Hostal Viena, c/Strachan 3 (☎952/224095). Simple rooms in a quiet street near the cathedral. ②.

UPMARKET HOTELS

Parador Gibralfaro, Monte de Gibralfaro (☎952/221902). You won't get a better panoramic view of the coast than from this eagle's nest on top of the Gibralfaro hill; it's quite small as *paradores* go and the service sometimes lacks grace. ⑤.

Hotel Las Vegas, Paseo de Sancha 22 (☎952/217712). A smart hotel, reasonably close to the beach, with its own swimming pool. ⑤.

Hostal Victoria, c/Sancha de Lara 3 (☎952/224223). Pleasant, serviceable place with good value single rooms, just north of the Alameda. ④.

CAMPING

Balneario del Carmen, Avda. Juan Sebastián Elcano (☎952/290021). Three kilometres out of town towards El Palo, this site is a rather gritty affair set amid the decaying and elegant remains of an old "bathing station", but it's well positioned for the Pedregalejo *paseo*. Bus #11 from the centre of town.

The city

Due to the siting of the airport well west of the city, visitors to the Costa del Sol rarely visit the heart of Málaga itself. All this may be about to change, as the city embarks on a costly face-lift, with plans to create an enormous hotel-lined promenade, but it's to be hoped that the city's unique character will survive the development.

The Alcazaba and Gibralfaro

The **Alcazaba** (Mon–Sat 10am–1pm & 5–8pm, Sun 10am–2pm) is the place to make for if you're killing time between connections. It lies just fifteen minutes' walk from the train or bus stations, and can be clearly seen from most central points. At its entrance stands a lost-looking Roman theatre, accidentally unearthed. The citadel too, is Roman in origin and interspersed among the Moorish brick of the double- and triple-arched gateways are blocks and columns of marble. The main structures were begun by the Moors in the eighth century, probably soon after their conquest since Málaga was an important port, but the palace higher up the hill dates from the early decades of the eleventh century. It was the residence of the Arab Emirs of Málaga, who carved out an independent kingdom for themselves upon the break-up of the Western Caliphate. Their independence lasted a mere thirty years, but for a while the kingdom grew to include Granada, Carmona and Jaén. The palace, restored as an archaeological museum, has some fine stucco work, 1920s Moorish-style ceilings and good collections of pottery, for which Málaga was renowned during the thirteenth and fourteenth centuries.

Above the Alcazaba, and connected to it by a long double wall, is the **Gibralfaro castle** (free access). Take the road to the right of the Alcazaba, then a path up through gardens, a ramble of towers, bougainvillea-draped ramparts and sentry-box-shaped Moorish wells (you can also approach from the town side, as the tourist coaches do, but this is a very unattractive walk). Last used in 1936 during the Civil War, the castle affords terrific views over the city and the complex fortifications of the Alcazaba. The nearby *parador* has a pleasant terrace café.

The Cathedral and fine art museum

Most conspicuous from the heights is Málaga's peculiar, unfinished **Catedral** (Tues–Sun 10am–1pm & 4–5.30pm). It lacks a tower on the west front as a radical Malagueño bishop donated the earmarked money to the American War of Independence against the British. Unfortunately it also lacks any real inspiration and is distinguished only by an intricately carved and ultrarealistic seventeenth-century *sillería* (choirstall).

The **Museo de Bellas Artes** (Tues–Fri 10am–1.30pm & 5–8pm; 250ptas), just round the corner on c/San Agustín, is more interesting. It retains a few childhood drawings by **Picasso**, the city's most famous native. He was born a hundred yards away in the Plaza de la Merced (there are plans to create a museum in his birthplace) and it was in Málaga that his prodigious talent for drawing was first noticed. "When I was a child I could draw like Raphael," he later wrote, "it took me all my life to learn to draw like a child." It was here too that young Picasso saw the first solid shape that he wanted to draw: *churros*, those oil-steeped fritters that Spaniards dip into their breakfast chocolate.

Eating, drinking and nightlife

Málaga's food and nightlife can hardly be said to be outstanding, but there's more than enough to keep you entertained, and the city has a justified reputation for its seafood.

Food

Málaga's greatest claim to fame is undoubtedly its **fried fish**, acknowledged as the best in Spain. You'll find many fish restaurants grouped around the Alameda, although for the very best you need to head out to the suburbs of Pedregalejo and El Palo, served by bus #11 (from the Paseo del Parque). On the seafront paseo at **Pedregalejo**, almost any of the cafés and restaurants will serve you up terrific fish. Further on, after the *paseo* disappears, you find yourself amid fishing shacks and smaller, sometimes quite ramshackle, cafés. This is **El Palo**, an earthier sort of area for the most part, with a beach and fishing huts, and in summer or at weekends, an even better place to eat.

INEXPENSIVE RESTAURANTS

Los Culitos, c/Circo 1, just above Plaza Victoria at the end of c/Victoria (closed Thurs). An exceptional fish bar that's inexpensive and very popular.

Mesón de Jamon, Plaza María Guerrero 5. Good value *menú* and a selection of *jamón* and cheese *tapas*.

Bar Los Pueblos, c/Ataranzas. Serves satisfying, inexpensive food all day – bean soups and *estofados* are its specialities; *gazpacho* is served in half-pint glasses.

Bar El Puerto, c/Comisario. A good *marisquería* in a narrow alley on the northern side of the Alameda.

Bar San Agustín, c/San Agustín. A central place for *tapas* and *raciones*, near the cathedral.

La Tarantela, c/Granada 67. Tasty pizzas and salads.

El Tintero II, El Palo. Right at the far end of the seafront, just before the *Club Náutico* (stay on bus #11 and ask for "Tintero Dos"), this is a huge beach restaurant where the waiters charge round with plates of fish (all costing the same for a plate) and you shout for, or grab, anything you like. The fish to go for are, above all, *mero* (a kind of gastronomically evolved cod) and *rosada* (equally indefinable), along with Andalucian regulars like *boquerones* (fresh anchovies), *gambas* (shrimp), *calamares, chopos, jibia* (different kinds of squid) and *sepia* (cuttlefish).

Casa Vicente, c/Comisario. Another lively *marisquería* a few doors from the *El Puerto*.

MODERATE TO EXPENSIVE

Al-Yamal, c/Blasco de Garay 3. A good Arab restaurant serving up meat in spicy sauces, couscous and other typical Arab food.

Antonio Martín, Paseo Maritimo. One of Málaga's renowned fish restaurants and the traditional haunt of matadors celebrating their successes in the nearby bullring. Expensive.

Parador Gilbralfaro, Monte Gilbralfaro. Superior dining on the terrace with spectacular views over the coast and town. The *menú* (around 3000ptas) is excellent value.

Bars

A number of **traditional bars** serve the sweet **Málaga wine** (Falstaff's "sack"), made from muscatel grapes and dispensed from huge barrels; try it with shellfish at *Antigua Casa Guardia,* a great old ninteenth-century bar at the corner of c/Pastora, on the Alameda. The new season wine, *Pedriot,* is incredibly sweet; much more palatable is *Seco Añejo,* which has matured for a year.

Málaga has plenty of good **tapas bars** including *Terral,* on c/Cister, which also hosts occasional exhibitions. The *Antigua Reja* on Plaza de Uncibay off c/de Méndez Núñez is always lively and does excellent food in the evenings. If you're looking for a really low-priced place to drink, try the *Bar Los Pueblos,* opposite the *mercado*.

Nightlife

In summer, the streets just behind the **Pedregalejo** seafront host most of the action. Along and off the main street, Juan Sebastián Elcano, there are dozens of **discos** and smaller **bars**. Look out for *Bobby Logan,* a disco in a beautiful building but with lousy music; *S.A. Company,* a small, lively bar; *Duna,* a big, overdecorated and pricey place with dancing; and the pseudo-Moroccan *Safi.* In the streets parallel, closer to the seafront, more nightspots can be found on the Carretera del Palo and on c/Bolivia (try *Whizz* and the trendy *Zona Málaga*). Recently, all-night bars have opened on the beach itself: *La Chancla* bursts forth at midnight and continues until very late.

The **centre** of Málaga is comparatively quiet in the evenings, though there's a lively disco-bar scene, particularly at weekends, in the streets around c/Beatas and c/Granada north of the cathedral. *El Pimpi,* c/Granada 62, a cavernous place with TV screens and varied music is one of the saner places. *Salsa,* c/Denis Belgrano, plays samba and mambo and holds Karaoke evenings too.

El Chorro Gorge and Antequera

North of Málaga are two impressive sights, the magnificent limestone **gorge** near **El Chorro** and the prehistoric **dolmen caves** at **Antequera**. They lie close to the junction of roads inland to Sevilla, Córdoba and Granada and on direct train lines, and both are possible as day trips from Málaga. Approaching Antequera along the old road from Málaga via Almogía and Villeneuva de la Concepción, you also pass the entrance to the popular national park, **El Torcal**.

El Chorro Gorge

Fifty kilometres north of Málaga, **Garganta del Chorro** is an amazing place – an immense cleft in a vast limestone massif – but the real attraction is a concrete catwalk, *El Camino del Rey,* which threads the length of the gorge hanging precipitously halfway up its side. Built in the 1920s as part of a burgeoning hydroelectric scheme, it used to figure in all the guidebooks as one of the wonders of Spain; today it's largely fallen into disrepair, and will probably collapse completely unless (unlikely) renovation takes place. At present, despite a few wobbly – and decidedly dangerous – sections, with random holes in the concrete through which you can see the gorge hundreds of feet below, it's still possible to walk much of its length. You will, however, need a very good head for heights, and at least a full day starting from Málaga. If you've neither, it's possible to get a glimpse of both gorge and *camino* from any of the trains going north from Málaga – the line, slipping in and out of tunnels, follows the river for a considerable distance along the gorge, before plunging into a last long tunnel just before its head.

To explore the gorge, and walk the *camino*, head for **EL CHORRO**, served by direct trains from Málaga. In the village, *Bar-Restaurante Garganta del Chorro* (☎952/ 497219; ③) has pleasant rooms inside a converted mill. From here it's a beautiful 12km to the start of the path and the gorge, and to some magnificent lakes and reservoirs for swimming. You can camp along the rocky shore of the *Embalse del Guadalhorce*; alternatively, the tiny village of **ARDALES**, 4km beyond the lake, has shops, bars, a lone *fonda* on the main square and two daily buses to and from Ronda.

Into the gorge

From the train station at El Chorro, take the road signposted *Pantano de Guadalhorce*, which crosses over the dam, turns to the right and leads towards the hydroelectric plant. After 10km you'll come upon the bar-restaurant *El Mirador*, poised above the various lakes and reservoirs of the Guadalhorce scheme. From the bar a dirt track on the right (just manageable by car) covers the 2km to an abandoned power plant at the mouth of the gorge. The footpath to the left of this will take you into the chasm and to the beginning of **El Camino**.

Although it is marked "No Entry", you'll probably come upon a number of young Spaniards exploring the catwalk. The first section, at least, seems reasonably safe – despite places where it is only a metre wide and where parts of the handrail are missing – and this is in fact the most dramatic part of the canyon. Towards the end, where the passageway gets really dangerous, the gorge widens and it's possible to climb down and follow the riverbank or have a swim.

Bobastro

A few kilometres beyond El Chorro lies **BOBASTRO**, the remains of a Mozarabic (Arabized Christian) settlement on top of a mountain. The castle was said to be the most impregnable in the whole of Andalucía, but only a church, carved into an enormous boulder, remains of the once-great fortress. A couple of kilometres beyond the bar *Mirador*, close to the gorge, a series of signs point the way to the *Iglesia Mozárabe*. The last 400m to the site have to be completed on foot through pine woods.

Antequera and around

ANTEQUERA, on the main rail line to Granada, is an ordinary, modern town but it does have peripheral attractions in an outrageous Baroque church, **El Carmen**, which houses one of the finest *retablos* in Andalucía, and a group of three prehistoric **dolmen caves**. The most impressive and famous of these is the **Cueva de Menga** (Tues–Fri 10am–2pm & 3–5.30pm, Sat & Sun 10am–2pm), its roof formed by an immense 180-ton monolith. To reach this, and the nearby **Cueva de Viera** (same hours), take the Granada road out of town – the turning, rather insignificantly signposted, is after about 1km on the left. A third cave, **El Romeral**, is rather different (and later) in its structure with a domed ceiling of flat stones; it is again to the left of the Granada road, 2km further on, past a sugar factory with a chimney.

If you want to stay in Antequera there's a good **pensión**, Madrona, c/Calzada 25 (☎952/840014; ③) near the market, which serves excellent food. Antequera also has a rather unattractive modern *parador* and several *hostales* on the roads in and out of town.

El Torcal, 13km south of Antequera, is the most geologically arresting of Spain's national parks. A massive high plateau of glaciated limestone tempered by a lush growth of hawthorn, ivy, wild rose and fauna, it's painlessly explored using the **walking routes** that radiate from the centre of the park. The best designed and most exciting is picked out in yellow arrows (3km) and ends with suitable drama on a cliff edge with magnificent views over a valley. This is also the most popular walk, and in the summer you may find yourself competing with gangs of schoolkids who arrive en masse on vaguely educational trips. More peaceful is the red route (5km; allow 5hr), great for strolling and taking in the looming limestone formations, eroded into vast, surreal sculptures. Five daily buses (Mon–Fri) run from Málaga (one on Sun) and it's quite acceptable to **camp** in the park – but take plenty of provisions.

East from Málaga: the coast to Almería

The eastern stretch of the **Costa del Sol**, from Málaga to Almería, is uninspiring. Though far less developed than the wall-to-wall concrete from Torremolinos to Marbella in the west, it's not exactly unspoiled. If you're looking for a village and a beach and not much else, then you'll probably want to keep going at least to Almería.

Málaga to Nerja

There's certainly little to tempt anyone before Nerja. **RINCÓN DE LA VICTORIA**, a no-nonsense, scruffy sort of place, is a local resort for *Malagueño* families. It's a functional spot to swim if you've a day to fill before catching a plane home, but nothing more. **TORRE DEL MAR**, 32km further on, is a line of concrete tower blocks on a grey, gritty beach – Torremolinos without the money or fun. But at least it's quiet, and recent improvements include a paved promenade in an attempt to take the place upmarket.

Just inland from Torre, **VÉLEZ MÁLAGA** was an important centre in Moorish times (and possibly much earlier – Phoenician tombs have been found in the area), long since declined. The castle, though, has attractive gardens and fine views of the coast. There's a **campsite** up here, *Valle Niza* (☎952/513181) which is more pleasant than the one down in Torre.

Nerja and around

NERJA, at least, was a village before it was a resort, so it has some character, and development (more villas, fewer tower blocks) has been shaped around it. The beaches are reasonably attractive, too, with a series of coves within walking distance if you want to escape the main mass of crowds. Nerja has lots of English-run pubs and shops, including a couple of **bookshops**: in c/Granada *The Book Centre* buys and sells secondhand books, mainly paperbacks; whilst *WH Smiffs* on Puerta del Mar has new books. *Bici Nerja* at Pasaje Cantereo 1, near the bus station, and *Mountain Bike Holidays*, c/Cristo 10, **rent bikes** if you want a little more freedom about where you go off to swim. There are plenty of great **walks** around Nerja, well-documented in a locally available guide, *Twelve Walks Around Nerja* by Elma and Denis Thompson. Elma also leads guided walks from November to May (☎952/530782).

The drawback, and a thorny problem through most of the summer, is scarce **accommodation**. There are a dozen or so *hostales*, most reserved well in advance, although some have arrangements with *casas particulares*. In the centre of town try *Hostal Atambeni*, c/Disputación 12 (☎952/521341; ③), or *Hotel Cala-Bella*, c/Puerta del Mar 10 (☎952/520700; ③), with superb sea views and its own restaurant. Overlooking one of Nerja's most popular beaches, Playa de Burriana, is the *Parador Nacional*, c/

Almuñécar 8 (☎952/520050; ⑤), with a lift down the cliff, and sharing the same views is the *Hotel Berlin*, c/Carabeo 22 (☎952/521621; ④). The **campsite**, *Nerja Camping* (☎952/656896), with pool, bar and restaurant is 4km east of town. Full accommodation lists are available from the helpful **Turismo**, Puerta del Mar 2 (Mon–Fri 10am–9pm, Sat 10am–1pm; winter Mon–Fri 10am–3pm, Sat 10am–1pm; ☎952/521531). The **bus station** is on c/San Miguel, close to Plaza Ermita and there are hourly buses from here to Nerja's chief tourist attraction.

The **Cuevas de Nerja** (10.30am–2pm & 3.30–6pm; 400ptas), 3km from the town, are a heavily commercialized series of caverns, impressive in size though otherwise not tremendously interesting. They contain a number of prehistoric paintings, but these are not presently on public view.

Almuñécar

Beyond Nerja the road climbs inland, running high above the coast until it surfaces at **La Herradura**, a fishing village-resort suburb of Almuñécar, and a good place to stop off and swim; there's also a summer campsite, *La Herradura* (☎958/640056).

ALMUÑÉCAR itself is marred by a number of towering holiday apartments, though if you've been unable to find a room in Nerja you might want to stay here for a night. The rocky beaches are rather cramped and have grey sand, but the esplanade behind them, with palm-roofed bars (many offer free *tapas*) and restaurants, is fun, and the old town, attractive.

Half a dozen good value **fondas** and **hostales** ring the central Plaza de la Rosa in the old part of town; the cosy *Hostal Plaza Damasco*, c/Cerrajos 8 (☎958/630165; ②) and *Fonda Heredia*, c/San Jose 15 (☎958/630321; ②), are two of the best. If you want to be right by the beach, try *Hostal Tropical*, Avda. de Europa (☎958/631152; ④), comfortable and good value considering its position. The **campsite** here, *El Paraiso* (☎958/632370), is a hell-hole in summer and it's definitely worth carrying on to Salobreña if you want to camp.

The **Turismo** (summer Mon–Sat 10am–2pm & 4–9.30pm) is located in an imposing neo-Moorish mansion with a delightful garden on Avda. de Europa, and you'll find the **bus station**, with frequent connections to Málaga and Granada at the junction of Avda. Juan Carlos I and Avda. Fenicia, northeast of the centre.

Salobreña and beyond

SALOBREÑA, 10km further east on the coast road, is infinitely preferable to Almuñécar. A white hilltop town gathered beneath the shell of a Moorish castle, it's set back 2km from the sea, and thus comparatively little developed. On its beach – a black sandy strip, only partially flanked by hotels – is a good **campsite**, *El Peñón* (April–Oct; ☎958/610207). Along and off c/de Hortensia, the main avenue that winds down from the town to the beach, are a few **pensiones** and **hostales**; *Pensión Arneda*, c/Nueva 15 (☎958/610257; ②) has the least expensive rooms. *Pensión Mari Carmen* (☎958/610906; ②), over the road, is equally good with fans in the rooms. Buses arrive and leave from Plaza de Goya, close to the **Turismo**.

Just before **Motril**, the N323 heads north to Granada, a great route, skirting the Sierra Nevada. The coast road continues towards Almería through an unremarkable sprawl of resorts of which the most worthwhile is **CASTELL DE FERRO**. It's quite sheltered, still preserving remnants of its former existence as a small fishing village, with good, wide beaches to the east and west. Avoid the small town beach which is dirty and uninspiring. If you want to stay, head for the centre of town where there are numerous possibilities: *Hostal Bahía*, Plaza de España 12 (☎958/656060; ③) is worth trying. The closest **campsite** to town is *El Sotillo* (☎958/646078; summer only), near the beach. For the coast further east, see p.290.

The Costa del Sol resorts

West of Málaga – or more correctly, west of Málaga airport – the real **Costa del Sol** gets going, and if you've never seen this level of touristic development it's quite a shock. These are certainly not the kind of resorts you could envisage in Greece or even Portugal, with their 1960's and 70's hotel and apartment tower blocks. In recent years, there has been a second wave of property development, this time villa homes and leisure complexes, funded by massive international investment. It's estimated that 300,000 foreigners now live on the Costa del Sol, the majority of them British and other northern Europeans, though custom marina developments like Puerto Banús have also attracted Arab money.

Approached in the right kind of spirit it is possible to have fun in **Torremolinos** and, at a price, in **Marbella**. But if you've come to Spain to be in Spain, or even just to forget what inner-city housing looks like, put on the shades and keep going at least until you reach **Estepona**.

Torremolinos and Fuengirola

The approach to Torremolinos – easily done on the electric train from Málaga – is a rather depressing business. There are half a dozen beaches and stops, but it's a drab, soulless landscape of kitchenette apartments and half-finished developments.

TORREMOLINOS, to its enduring credit, is certainly different: a vast, grotesque parody of a seaside resort which in its own kitschy way is fascinating. This bizarre place, lined with sweeping (but crowded) beaches and infinite shopping arcades, crammed with (genuine) Irish pubs and (probably less genuine) real estate agents, has a large permanent expatriate population of British, Germans and Scandinavians. It's a weird mix, which, in addition to thousands of retired people, has attracted – due to a previous lack of extradition arrangements between Britain and Spain – an extraordinary concentration of British crooks. Torremolinos's social scene is strange too, including, among the middle-of-the-road family discos, a thriving, pram-pushing, gay transvestite scene. All in all it's an intriguing blend of the smart and the squalid, bargains and rip-offs.

If any of these possibilities attracts you – or you're simply curious about the awfulness of the place – it's easy enough **to stay**. There are few *hostales* but you can walk into almost any travel agent and, for remarkably little, get them to book you into one of the concrete monster hotels. The **Turismo** at c/Casablanca 25 (Mon–Fri 9.30am–2pm, Sat 9.30am–1.30pm; ☎952/371159) can provide more information on what's available. There is also a **youth hostel** (☎952/380882; ①) at Avda. Carlota Alessandri 127, a couple of blocks in from the beach; be wary of accepting free accommodation from the Torremolinos evangelists (who often invite hitchhikers to their villa), as it's not always so easy to leave their community after a week or two of heavy, "religious" mind games.

The sheer competition between Torremolinos's **restaurants**, **clubs** and **bars** is so intense that if you're prepared to walk round and check a few prices you can have a pretty good night out on remarkably little. The more elegant part of the resort lies to the east at **La Carihuela**, where there's a decent beach, good seafood restaurants along the seafront and a pleasant hostal, *Prudencia*, Paseo Carmen 41 (☎952/2381452; ④). If you need to escape altogether, there are **hydrofoils to Tangier** (summer only) from Benalmádena, halfway to Fuengirola. Lastly, if you're looking to replenish your stock of reading material, *George's Secondhand Bookshop*, at c/San Miguel 26 1°– the main shopping street in the middle of town, close to the train station – is an excellent source of used paperbacks.

Fuengirola

FUENGIROLA, half an hour along the train line from Torremolinos, is very slightly less developed and infinitely more staid. It's not so conspicuously ugly, but it is distinctly middle-aged and family-oriented. The huge, long beach has been divided up into restaurant-beach strips, each renting out lounge chairs and pedal-boats. At the far end is a windsurfing school.

Rooms are difficult to find in August, but at other times you could try the basic *Hostal Coca*, c/de Cruz 3 (☎952/474189; ③) or *Hostal Italia* (☎952/474193; ③), next door, which has rooms with balcony and room-safe for not much more. For excellent **seafood**, try the mid-priced *Bar La Paz Garrido* on the Avda. de Mijas just north of the Plaza de la Constitución; alternatively, quantity is the gimmick at two "as much as you can eat for 600ptas" places on the seafront, *Versalles*, Paseo Maritimo 3, and *Las Plameras* nearby.

Marbella

MARBELLA stands in considerable contrast, after another sequence of apartment-villa *urbanizaciones*, to most of what's come before. It is undisputedly the "quality resort" of the Costa del Sol. Everything costs considerably more, the restaurants and bars are more stylish, and phones are handily installed on the beach. It has the highest per capita income in Europe and more Rolls Royces than any European city apart from London (although many of the classy cars here are rumoured to have been stolen elsewhere and re-registered in Spain). In an ironic twist of history, there's been a massive return of Arabs to the area, especially since King Fahd of Saudi Arabia built a White House lookalike, complete with adjacent mosque, on the town's outskirts.

To be fair, it's all decidedly tasteful and the town has been spared the worst excesses of concrete architecture inflicted upon Torremolinos. Marbella also retains the greater part of its **old village** – set back a little from the sea and the new development. Slowly, this original quarter is being bought up and turned into "quaint" clothes boutiques and restaurants, but this process isn't that far advanced. You can still sit in an ordinary bar in a small old square and look up beyond the whitewashed alleyways to the mountains of Ronda.

It's in the old town, too, that you"ll find Marbella's only budget **pensiones** – of which the lowest priced is *Pensión Luisa* (they have roof space, often the only possibility in this hugely popular resort) in c/San Francisco, near the church of the same name. Further up the road is the *Africa Youth Hostel*, c/Trapiche; while at no. 18 there's a friendly (though small) family-run place. Budget places near the main road on the way in to town include *Hostal Juan*, c/Luna 18 (☎952/779475; ③) and the less expensive *Hostal Isabel*, c/Luna 24 (☎952/771978; ②), both good. There are plenty of more expensive places, too: *Hostal Enriqueta* (c/los Caballeros 18; ☎952/827552; ③) is comfortable and quiet, as is the charming *Hostal La Pilarica*, c/San Cristobal 31 (☎952/774252; ③), in a street lined with potted plants, the work of the enthusiastic residents. The old village, still partially walled, is hidden from the main road and easy to miss; to get there, turn left out of the bus station, walk straight for about 500m and then turn left again.

If you need help in finding a room it is probably worth calling in at the **Turismo** (Mon–Fri 9.50am–1pm & 5–7.30pm, Sat 10am–1pm; ☎952/771442), Avda. Miguel Cano 1, by the Alameda park, if only for their town plan and list of addresses.

Puerto Banús

The truly rich don't stay in Marbella itself. They lie around on phenomenally large and luxurious yachts at the marina and casino complex of **PUERTO BANÚS**, 6km out of town towards San Pedro. If you're impoverished, this fact is worth noting as it's sometimes possible to find work scrubbing and repairing said yachts – and the pay can be very reasonable. As you'd expect, Puerto Banús has more than its complement of cocktail bars and seafood restaurants, most of them very good.

West to Estepona

The coast continues to be upmarket (or "money-raddled" as Laurie Lee put it) until you reach Estepona, about 30km west. About the only place on this strip which isn't purely a holiday *urbanización* is the small town of **SAN PEDRO DE ALCÁNTARA**, an uninspiring resort striving to go the way of Marbella but hindered by the fact that it's set back from the sea. It has a Thursday morning flea market – trashy in all senses of the word – and that's about it. Not a place for a holiday.

Estepona

If you feel an irresistible urge to stop along this part of the Mediterranean coast, **ESTEPONA** is a more or less Spanish resort – inasmuch as that's possible round here. It lacks the enclosed hills that give Marbella character, but the hotel and apartment blocks which sprawl along the front are restrained in size, and there's space to breathe. The fine sand beach has been enlivened a little by a promenade studded with flowers and palms, and, away from the seafront, the old town is very pretty, with cobbled alleyways and two delightful plazas. The efficient **Turismo** is centrally sited on the seafront and has a good town map.

The **fish market** is definitely worth seeing: Estepona has the biggest fishing fleet west of Málaga, and the daily dawn ritual in the port, where the returning fleets auction off the fish they've just caught, is worth getting up early for – be there at 6am, since by 7am it's all over.

Estepona has a **campsite**, *La Chimenea* (☎952/800437), and a number of **hostales**. *Hostal El Pilar* (☎952/800018; ③), on the pretty Plaza Las Flores, and the friendly *Pensión San Miguel*, c/Terraza 16 (☎952/802616; ②), a little to the west, with its own bar, are both good bets. The town is well-provided with places **to eat**, among them a bunch of excellent *freidurías* and *marisquerías* along c/Terraza, the main street which cuts through the centre. There's an excellent *churrería* towards the southern end of c/ Mayor (one block back from, and parallel to, the promenade) – get there before 11am as they sell out early. Another good place for buying food is the covered **market** in the mornings. If you're sufficiently motivated, you could also head out of town to eat. South along the coast past the new Puerto de la Duquesa marina, is the tiny fishing village of **La Duquesa**, which has two excellent restaurants, *Restaurante Antonio* being the better of the two, with an excellent value *tapas* bar attached.

From May onward, Estepona's **bullfighting** season gets underway in a modern bullring reminiscent of a Henry Moore sculpture. At the beginning of July, the *Fiesta y Feria* week transforms the place, bringing out whole families in *flamenco*-style garb. The town also has a **flamenco** bar, *Ría-Pitá*, c/Caridad 3, east of c/Terraza, which, whilst it may not be the most authentic, has free entry, reasonably priced drinks and a good atmosphere.

Beyond Estepona

Eight kilometres along the coast from Estepona there's a minor road leading into the hills to **CASARES**, one of the classic Andaluz "White Towns" (see p.208). In keeping with the genre, it clings tenaciously to a steep hillside below a castle, and has attracted its fair share of arty types and expatriates. But it remains comparatively little known; bus connections are feasible for a day trip.

Further west, 3km inland from the village of Manilva, are some remarkably well-preserved **Roman sulphur baths**. If you want to partake of these health-giving waters you'll have to put up with the overpowering stench of sulphur, which clings to your swimwear for weeks, and be prepared to dive into a subterranean cavern.

The beaches beyond Estepona have greyish sands (a trademark of the Costa del Sol that always seems surprising – you have to round the corner at Tarifa before you meet yellow sand) and there are more greyish developments, before the road turns inland towards San Roque and Gibraltar.

San Roque and La Línea

SAN ROQUE was founded by the people of Gibraltar fleeing the British, who had captured the Rock and looted their homes and churches in 1704. They expected to return within months, since the troops had taken the garrison in the name of the Archduke Carlos of Austria, whose rights Britain had been promoting in the War of the Spanish Succession. But it was the British flag that was raised on the conquered territory – and so it has remained.

The **"Spanish-British frontier"** is 8km away at **LA LÍNEA**, obscured by San Roque's huge oil refinery. After sixteen years of (Spanish-imposed) isolation, the gates were finally reopened in February 1985, and crossing is now a routine affair of passport stamping. Be warned that, if you're planning on a stay in Gibraltar, accommodation there is very expensive and in summer the few budget places available are in tremendous demand; La Línea is more realistic although even here prices have risen and it's now more expensive than neighbouring towns. There are no sights as such; it's just a fishing village which has exploded in size due to the jobs in Gibraltar and Algeciras.

At the heart of La Linea is the Plaza de la Constitución, a large modern square. The **Turismo** is on the left, just off the square, and has town maps with *hostales* indicated; the **bus station** is on the right. The *Correos* is also in the main square: opposite the *Salon Monaco*, beside which an archway leads to a smaller, pedestrianized plaza with lots of reasonably priced **bars** and **restaurants**. Indeed there are countless bars and cafés throughout the centre. C/Real, the main pedestrianized shopping street again leading off the main square, has plenty of possibilities – try the *Bar Jerez* for a good range of *tapas*; *Blanco y Negro*, a couple of streets north near Plaza de Iglesia; *Okay Café* or *Jamaica Inn* (which opens early for breakfast). *El Económico*, an inconspicuous *comedor* with a *menú del día*, is almost directly opposite *Blanco y Negro*. C/Clavel, signposted from the main plaza to the Plaza de Toros, has more options: *Bar Almendra* at the far end is basic and excellent value. The **market**, north of c/Real, is also worth a visit for food.

The same areas have most of the budget **hostales**. In the Plaza de Iglesia, at the end of c/Real, *La Giralda* (②) has a friendly owner, free, hot showers and a hotplate in the kitchen for preparing simple meals. Almost directly opposite is the *Hostal Sevilla*, c/ Duque de Tetuán (☎956/764796; ②), and there are three or four others in the area: *La Esteponera*, c/Carteya 12 (☎956/106668; ③), just off the plaza between c/Cervantes and c/Aurora, has very low-priced rooms; the *Hostal Bahía*, c/Granada 54 (☎956/ 101725; ③), is more modern and extremely clean. Also worth trying is the *Pensión La Perla*, c/Clavel 10 (②).

Local **buses** from La Línea to Algeciras take forty minutes, with departures every half-hour. The closest main-line **train station** is San Roque-La Línea, 12km away, from where you can pick up a train to Ronda and beyond. Buses link La Línea with Sevilla, the journey taking four hours, and others go as far as Ayamonte on the Portuguese border, a seven-hour trip.

Gibraltar

GIBRALTAR's interest is essentially its novelty: the genuine appeal of the strange, looming physical presence of its rock, and the dubious one of its preservation as one of Britain's last remaining colonies. It's a curious place to visit, not least to witness the bizarre process of its opening to mass tourism from the Costa del Sol. Ironically, this threatens both to destroy Gibraltar's highly individual society and at the same time to make it much more British, after the fashion of the expatriate communities and huge resorts of the Costa. The frontier opening, however, has benefited most people: locals can buy cheaper goods in Spain and stretch their legs, and the boom the Rock is witnessing (after a long recession) should benefit the whole surrounding Campo area.

Arrival and orientation

The town and rock have a necessarily simple layout. **Main Street** (La Calle Real) runs for most of the town's length, a couple of blocks back from the port; from the frontier it's a short bus ride or about a fifteen-minute walk. If you have a **car**, don't attempt to bring it to Gibraltar – the queues at the border are always atrocious, and parking is a nightmare. Use the underground car parks in La Línea, 8km away, instead (it's worth paying for the extra security) and catch the **bus**. If you do join the queue to drive in, ignore the people who will attempt to sell you a "visa" – it's usually an old bus ticket.

In and around Main Street are most of the shops, including *The Gibraltar Bookshop* at no. 300 which sells good paperbacks. However, it's duty-free whisky that's the major attraction. This is also where most of the British-style pubs and hotels are. For information, the main **tourist office** is in Cathedral Square, and there are also offices at the airport, the Gibraltar Museum, Market Place and the Waterport coach park. The John Mackintosh Hall at the south end of Main Street is a useful resource – it's the cultural centre, with exhibitions and a library. The local paper is the *Gibraltar Chronicle*, a stultifyingly parochial daily with little of interest to visitors. Much of Gibraltar – with the exception of the cut-price booze shops – closes down on Saturday afternoon, but the tourist sites remain open. This can be a quiet time to visit. Virtually everything is shut on Sunday.

Around the Rock

From near the end of Main Street you can hop on a **cable car** (Mon–Sat 9.30am–7.15pm, last trip down 7.45pm; £3.50 return) which will carry you up to the summit – **The Top of the Rock** as it's logically known – via **Apes' Den** halfway up, a fairly reliable viewing point to see the tailless monkeys and hear the guides explain their legend. From The Top you can look over to the Atlas Mountains and down to the town, its elaborate water catchment system cut into the side of the rock, and ponder whether it's worth heading for one of the beaches. From the Apes' Den it's an easy walk south along Queens Road to **Saint Michael's Cave**, an immense natural cavern which led

---

GIBRALTAR'S CURRENCY

The **currency** used here is the Gibraltar pound (the same value as the British pound, but different notes and coins); if you pay in pesetas while in Gibraltar, you generally fork out about five percent more.

It's best to change your money once you arrive in Gibraltar, since the **exchange rate** is slightly higher than in Spain and there's no commission charged. Gibraltar pounds can be hard to change in Spain.

BRITISH SOVEREIGNTY OF GIBRALTAR

Sovereignty of the Rock (a land area smaller than the city of Algeciras across the water) will doubtless eventually return to Spain, but at present neither side is in much of a hurry. For Britain it's a question of precedent – Gibraltar is in too similar a situation to the Falklands/Malvinas, which conflict pushed the Spanish into postponing an initial frontier-opening date in 1982. For Spain too, there are unsettling parallels with the *presidios* (Spanish enclaves) on the Moroccan coast at Ceuta and Melilla – both at present part of Andalucía. Nonetheless, the British presence is in practice waning and the British foreign office clearly wants to steer Gibraltar towards a new, harmonious relationship with Spain. To this end they seem to be running down the significance of the military base on the Rock, and reduced the number of British troops by half in 1990. The Royal Naval Dockyard has now been replaced with *Gibrepair*, a commercial ship repair yard which, in the long term, should lead to diversification of the Gibraltar economy and reduce dependence on Britain.

The Gibraltarians, however, are firmly opposed to a return to **Spanish control** of the Rock. In 1967, just before Franco closed the border in the hope of forcing a quick agreement, the colony voted on the issue – rejecting it by 12,138 votes to 44. Most people would probably sympathize with that vote – against a Spain that was then still a dictatorship – but more than twenty years have gone by, Spanish democracy is now secure, and the arguments are becoming increasingly tenuous. Despite its impressive claims to law and order, Gibraltar is no model society either; its dirty jobs, for instance, are nearly all done by Moroccans on one-year contracts, who are housed in old army barracks.

March 1988 saw a change in the trend of internal **politics** when the first-ever Socialist government was elected, but the leader, Joe Bossano, re-elected in 1992 with a huge seventy-three percent majority, continues to oppose back-room deals between Britain and Spain on the future of the colony. A wily ex-trade union leader, he is attempting to make the Rock more self-reliant, encouraging its status as an "offshore" base – a kind of "Hong Kong of the Mediterranean". Already, some 24,000 companies, many somewhat dubious, are registered in Gibraltar.

What most outsiders don't realize about the political situation is that the Gibraltarians feel very vulnerable, caught between the interests of two big states; they are well aware that both governments' concerns are primarily strategic and political rather than with the wishes of the people of Gibraltar. Until very recently people were sent over from Britain to fill all the top civil service and Ministry of Defence jobs, a practice which, to a lesser degree, still continues. Large parts of the Rock are no-go areas for "natives"; the South District in particular being taken up by facilities for the armed services.

Local people also protest about the Royal Navy nuclear-powered submarines which dock regularly at the naval base, and secrecy surrounds the issue of whether nuclear warheads and/or chemical and biological weapons are stored in the arsenal, probably deep inside the Rock itself.

Yet Gibraltarians still cling to British status – perhaps simply because they have known nothing other than British rule since the former population was displaced – and all their institutions are modelled on English lines. Contrary to popular belief, they are of neither mainly Spanish nor British blood, but an ethnic mix descended from Genoese, Portuguese, Spanish, Minorcan, Jewish, Maltese and British ancestors. English is the official **language**, but more commonly spoken is what sounds to an outsider like perfect Andalucian Spanish. It is in fact *yanito*, an Andalucian dialect with borrowed words which reflect its diverse origins – only a Spaniard from the south can tell a Gibraltarian from an Andalucian.

ancient people to believe the rock was hollow and gave rise to its old name of *Mons Calpe* (Hollow Mountain). The cave was used during the last war as a bomb-proof military hospital and nowadays hosts occasional concerts. If you're adventurous you can arrange at the tourist office for a guided visit to **Lower Saint Michael's Cave**, a series of chambers going deeper down and ending in an underground lake.

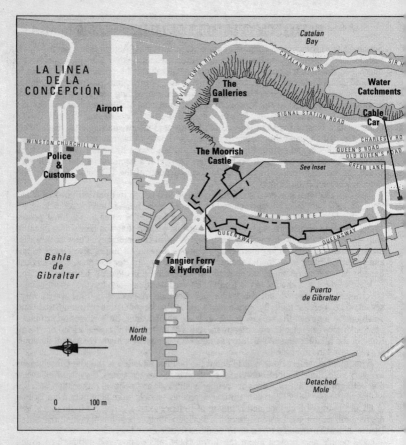

Although you can take the cable car both ways, it's an interesting walk up via Willis's Road to visit the **Tower of Homage**. Dating from the fourteenth century, this is the most visible surviving remnant of the old **Moorish Castle**. Further up you'll find the **Upper Galleries**, blasted out of the rock during the Great Siege of 1779–82, in order to point guns down at the Spanish lines. To walk down, take the **Mediterranean Steps** – they're not very well signposted and you have to climb over O'Hara's Battery, a very steep descent most of the way down the east side, turning the southern corner of the Rock. You'll pass through the Jews' Gate and into Engineer Road. From here, return to town through the Alameda Gardens and the **Trafalgar Cemetery**, overgrown and evocative, with a good line in epitaphs. The grand tour of the Rock takes a half to a full day, and all sites on it are open from 10am to 7pm in summer, 10am to 5.30pm in winter; if you visit all the attractions, buy a reduced-price ticket which includes the cave as well.

Back **in town**, incorporated into the **Gibraltar Museum** (Mon–Fri 10am–6pm), are two well-preserved and beautiful fourteenth-century **Moorish Baths**. This, along with the **casino**, and the **miniature golf**, is about the extent of it. Gibraltar has plans to reclaim an area equivalent to that of the present town from the sea, and is currently doing feasibility surveys on pumping up sand from the seabed. But at present there is

just the one tiny fishing village at **Catalan Bay**, which is where you'll find the **beach** with most character. The inhabitants of the village like to think of themselves as very distinct from the townies on the other side of the Rock. About 48km of recent tunnels, or **galleries**, have been bored through the Rock for military purposes – these are now being adapted to help solve the territory's traffic-flow crisis brought on by the extraordinary surplus of cars.

Practicalities

Shortage of space on the rock means that **accommodation** is at a premium, and you're much better off visiting on day trips from Algeciras (buses on the hour and half-hour, journey time 30min) or La Línea. The only remotely budget beds are at the *Toc H Hostel* on Line Wall Road (☎350/73431; about £11 a person) – and these are none too comfortable and almost always occupied by long-term residents – or the tiny *Seruya's Guest House* in Irish Town (☎350/73220; about £15 a double), which is also invariably full. Otherwise, you're going to have to pay normal British hotel prices: the next step up includes the *Queen's Hotel* on Boyd Street (☎350/74000) and the *Bristol* in Cathedral Square (☎350/76800) both of which charge over £40 for a double room.

If this tempts you to find a bit of sand to bed down on, forget it: **no camping** is allowed and if you're caught sleeping rough or inhabiting abandoned bunkers, you are more than likely to be arrested and fined. This law is enforced by Gibraltar and Ministry of Defence police, and raids of the beaches are regular.

Restaurants

Eating is less of a problem, though by Spanish standards still relatively expensive: pub snacks or fish and chips are reliable standbys. Main Street is crowded with touristy places, among which *Smiths Fish and Chip Shop*, near the Convent, is worth a try but avoid the curries. The *Café Capri* at no. 45 also caters to limited budgets. Other good choices are the *Penny Farthing* on King Street, always busy for home-cooked food at reasonable prices (take-away too); *Happy Eater* in Cornwalls Lane; *Corks Wine Bar*, Irish Town; and *La Cantina*, a slightly more expensive Mexican place. The *Market Café* in the public market and *Splendid Bar* in George's Lane both serve inexpensive meals and *tapas*. *Sacarrello's Coffee House* in Irish Town is more upmarket, but you can just have a drink here and they have a collection of old postcards upstairs showing the development of Gibraltar. Further afield, try *Biancas* in Marina Bay or *Piccolo* in Catalan Bay.

Pubs

Pubs all tend to mimic traditional English styles (and prices), the difference being that they are open all day and often into the wee hours. For pub food, the *Royal Calpe*, Main Street, *Calpe Hounds*, Cornwalls Lane and *Clipper*, Irish Town, are among the best. Of the obvious pubs grouped together on Main Street, the *Royal Calpe* has a beer garden, *The Horseshoe* has tables outside and shows videos, and the *Gibraltar Arms* also has outdoor seating: places on Main Street, however, tend to be rowdy – full of squaddies and visiting sailors at night. For a quieter alternative try the *Prince of Wales* in John Mackintosh Square or the *Canon Bar* in Canon Lane.

Working in Gibraltar

If you're staying around a while, Gibraltar is not a bad place to look for **work**, although competition abounds, so be persistent, and if you're working officially, taxes are high. For men, there are some labouring jobs (on the docks); for women the best possibilities are bar jobs. Gibraltar Radio broadcasts vacancies on Tuesday at about noon, but door-to-door (or site-to-site) footslogging is vital. Another possibility is crewing work on a yacht – look at the noticeboard in the chandler's store on Marina Bay, or put an ad there yourself; at the end of summer the yacht marina fills up with boats heading for the **Canaries**, **Madeira** and the **West Indies** and many take on crew to work in exchange for passage.

Onward travel

Two decidedly functional attractions of Gibraltar are its opportunities for reasonably cheap **flights** to England (standby one-way fares are about £70; call *GB Airways* ☎350/79200), and its role as a **port for Morocco**. The timetable is erratically subject to weather conditions even at the best of times (the trip is invariably very rough), and currently seems to change every few weeks. In season, though, there's a *Gibline* **catamaran** to Tangier daily: this takes just one hour, making day trips a possibility. There are occasional sailings also to **Mdiq**, near Tetouan on Morocco's Mediterranean coast, which gives a gentler introduction to the country. Tickets are available from *Beagle Travel*, 9B George's Lane – prices starting at around £30 with substantial reductions for day returns or fixed date tickets. There's also a new Moroccan **ferry**, currently running to Tangier on Friday evening and Monday morning: return fare from £28 for a two-hour trip; tickets from *Tourafrica* in the International Commercial Centre, Casemates

Square. By **plane**, *Gib Air* has services to Tangier (just 20 min away) and Marrakesh; tickets from any travel agent.

For travelling on through Spain, **RENFE** tickets can be bought from *Pegasus Travel* (☎350/72252).

Algeciras

ALGECIRAS occupies the far side of the bay to Gibraltar, spewing out smoke and pollution in the direction of the Rock. The last town of the Spanish Mediterranean, it must once have been an elegant resort; today it's unabashedly a port and industrial centre, its suburbs extending on all sides, and almost all construction is of modern vintage. When Franco closed the border with Gibraltar at La Línea it was Algeciras that he decided to develop to absorb the Spanish workers formerly employed in the British naval dockyards, thus breaking the area's dependence on the Rock.

Most travellers are scathing about the city's ugliness, and unless you're waiting for a bus or train, or heading for Morocco, there's admittedly little reason to stop. Yet some touch of colour is added by the groups of Moroccans in transit, dressed in flowing *djelabas* and yellow slippers, and lugging unbelievable amounts of possessions. Algeciras has a real port atmosphere, and even passing through it's hard to resist the urge to get on a boat south, if only for a couple of days in Tangier. Once you start to explore, you'll also discover that the old town has some very attractive corners which seem barely to have changed in fifty years, especially around the Plaza Alta. The number of people passing through also guarantees endless possibilities for food and drink.

Practicalities

If you're waiting for a morning ferry, or want to stay awhile, Algeciras has plenty of budget **hostales** and **pensiones** in the grid of streets between the port and the train station. There are several in c/Duque de Almodóvar, c/José Santacana and c/Rafael de Muro. Try *Levante*, c/Duque de Almodóvar 21 (☎956/651505; ③), *Vizcaíno* c/José Santacana 9 (☎956/655756; ②), or the more comfortable *González*, c/José Santacana 7 (☎956/652843; ③). The *Hotel Anglo-Hispano*, Avda. Villanueva 7 (☎956/572590; ④), has a marble-tiled lobby dripping with faded grandeur. If you have trouble finding space, pick up a town plan and check out the list in the **Turismo**, on c/Juan de la Cierva, towards the river and train line from the port. Prices tend to go up dramatically in midseason, but lots of simple *casas de huéspedes* cluster round the market.

The port/harbour area also has plenty of **places to eat**. Across the train line from the Turismo and invariably crowded is the good value *Casa Gil* at c/Sigismundo Moret 2. Fifty metres further along the same street, *Casa Sanchez*, at the corner of c/Río, is another good place with a *menú*, and they also have rooms. The **markets** are useful places to buy food, as well as vibrant and fascinating places to visit; the main one is

---

MOROCCANS IN ALGECIRAS

It's easy to take a romantic view of the exotic hustle and bustle in the port area, but there's a miserable story behind some of it. Algeciras is the main port for Moroccan migrant workers, who drive home every year during their holidays from the factories, farms and mines of France, Germany and the Low Countries. Half a million cross Spain in the six weeks from the end of June to the beginning of August, often becoming victims of all levels of racial discrimination (they are still referred to as *los moros*), from being ripped off to being violently attacked and robbed.

held on Plaza Palma, down by the port. In the centre, especially around the Plaza Baja and the food market, are plenty of excellent *tapas* bars. Plaza Alta is noticeably more expensive.

Onward Travel

If you are tempted by Morocco, it's easily enough done: there are three or four **crossings to Tangier** each day (a 2hr 30min-trip), and six or seven to the Spanish *presidio* of **Ceuta** (1hr 30min), little more than a Spanish Gibraltar with a brisk business in duty-free goods, but a relatively painless way to enter Morocco. Alternatively you can go by **hydrofoil** to Ceuta (daily, 1hr). Tickets are available at scores of travel agents all along the waterside and on most approach roads; there's no difference in price between them, though some may give you a better rate of exchange than others if you want to pay in foreign currency. Wait till Tangier – or if you're going via Ceuta, Tetouan – before buying any Moroccan currency; rates in the embarkation building kiosks are very poor. Make sure that your ticket is for the next ferry, and beware the ticket sellers who congregate near the dock entrance wearing official Ceuta/Tangier badges: they add a whopping "commission" to the normal price of a ticket. *InterRail/Eurail* card holders are entitled to a twenty percent discount on the standard ferry price: if you have trouble getting this, go to the official sales desk in the embarkation building.

At Algeciras the **train line** begins again, heading north to Ronda, Córdoba and Madrid. The route to Ronda – one of the best journeys in Andalucía – is detailed below; there are six departures a day. For Madrid (and Paris) there's a night express, currently leaving at 11pm, and also *Linebus/Iberbus* coaches to Paris and London. For Málaga, hourly **buses** leave from a bar on the main seafront avenue, just back from the port; from here too, there are less frequent, direct connections to Granada. Buses to Barcelona leave from in front of the harbour offices, but the journey is appallingly slow at 21 hours (versus a theoretical 20 on the train), with a change in Málaga. For Tarifa, Cádiz, Sevilla and most other destinations you'll need the **main bus station**, in c/San Bernardo, 250m or so behind the port, beside the *Hotel Octavio* and just short of the **train station**: to get there follow the train tracks. The bus to La Línea also goes every half-hour from here.

Ronda and the White Towns

Andalucía is dotted with small, brilliantly whitewashed settlements – the **Pueblos Blancos** or "White Towns" – most often straggling up hillsides towards a castle or towered church. Places like **Mijas**, up behind Fuengirola, are solidly on the tourist trail, but even here the natural beauty is undeniable. All of them look great from a distance, though many are rather less interesting on arrival. Perhaps the best lie in a roughly triangular area between Málaga, Algeciras and Sevilla; at its centre, in a region of wild mountainous beauty, is the spectacular town of **Ronda**.

To Ronda from the coast

Of several possible approaches to Ronda from the coast, the route up from Algeciras is the most rewarding – and worth going out of your way to experience. From Málaga, most of the buses to Ronda follow the coastal highway to San Pedro before turning into the mountains: dramatic enough, but rather a bleak route, with no villages and only limited views of the dark rock face of the Serrania (an alternative route, via Álora and Ardales, is far more attractive). The train ride up from Málaga is better, with three connecting services daily, including a convenient 6pm departure after the last bus leaves.

The **Algeciras route** – via Gaucín – is possible by either bus or train, or, if you've time and energy, can be walked in four or five days. En route, you're always within reach of a river and there's a series of hill towns, each one visible from the next, to provide targets for the day. Casares is almost on the route, but more easily reached from Estepona (see p.208).

Castellar de la Frontera

The first "White Town" on the route proper is **CASTELLAR DE LA FRONTERA**, a bizarre village within a castle, whose population, in accord with some grandiose scheme, was moved downriver in 1971 to the "new" town of La Almoraima. The relocation was subsequently dropped and a few villagers moved back to their old houses, but most of them were taken over by retired hippies (mainly German, mainly affluent). The result didn't entirely work, with suspicion from the locals and hostile exclusivity from some of the new arrivals, but it led to some strange juxtapositions – particularly as no one ever got round to moving the village school, so Spanish schoolchildren were in the midst of the setup. More changes seem afoot now, as ruined houses are restored and plans to create a *parador* revived. For the moment, perhaps, it's best to move on after a brief look around; there are a couple of bars and a solitary *hostal*, *El Pilar*, c/Leon Esquirel 4 (☎956/693022; ②), but nothing else.

Jimena de la Frontera and Gaucín

JIMENA DE LA FRONTERA lacks the traumas of Castellar. It's a far larger and more open hill town, rising to a grand Moorish castle with a triple-gateway entrance. There are several bars, a beautiful old **fonda** (which has no sign – ask for the *Casa María*; ①), and the more expensive *Hostal El Anon* (③) on c/Consuelo, as well as another *hostal* at the train station, a little way out of town. The best place for **food** is *Restaurante-Bar Cuenca*, Avda. de los Departes, on the way into town, which does wonderful *tapas* and meals.

Beyond Jimena it's a sixteen-kilometre climb through woods and olive groves to reach **GAUCÍN**, though there are bars halfway at the hamlet of San Pablo. Gaucín, almost a mountain village, commands tremendous views (to Gibraltar and the Moroccan coast on a very clear day) and makes a great place to stop over. It has a charming **fonda**, the *Nacional*, c/San Juan de Dios 8 (①), and food is available from the *Venta El Soccorro* on the main highway. You can reach the village by bus, but far more rewarding is the thirteen-kilometre walk from its train station. Though it's now known as Gaucín, this station is actually at El Colmenar, on the fringes of the Cortes nature reserve: if you need to rest up before the trek (getting on for 3hr, mostly uphill) there's a *hostal* and several bars here.

The train line between Gaucín and Ronda passes through a handful of tiny villages. En route, you can stop off at the station of Benaoján-Montejaque: from here it's an hour's trek to the prehistoric **Cueva de la Pileta** (see p.212). From Benaoján, Ronda is just three stops (and half an hour) down the line.

Ronda

Rising amid a ring of dark, angular mountains, the full natural drama of **RONDA** is best appreciated as you enter the town. Built on an isolated ridge of the sierra, it's split in half by a gaping river gorge, **El Tajo**, which drops sheer for 130m on three sides. Still more spectacular, the gorge is spanned by a stupendous eighteenth-century arched bridge, while tall whitewashed houses lean from its precipitous edges.

Much of the attraction of Ronda lies in this extraordinary view, or in walking down by the Río Guadalévin, following one of the donkey tracks through the rich green valley. Bird-watchers should look out for the lesser kestrels, rare in northern Europe, nesting in and launching themselves from the cliffs beneath the Alameda park. Lower down you can spot crag martins. The town itself is also of interest and, surprisingly, has sacrificed little of its character to the flow of day-trippers from the Costa del Sol.

The town

Ronda divides into three parts: on the near (northwest) side of the gorge, where you'll arrive, is the largely modern **Mercadillo** quarter. Across the bridge is the old Moorish town, the **Ciudad**, and its **San Francisco** suburb.

The **Ciudad** retains intact its Moorish plan and a great many of its houses, interspersed with a number of fine Renaissance mansions. It is so intricate a maze that you can do little else but wander at random. However, at some stage, make your way across the bridge and along the c/Santo Domingo, also known as c/Marqués de Parada, which winds round to the left. At no. 17 is the somewhat arbitrarily named **Casa del Rey Moro**, an early eighteenth-century mansion built on Moorish foundations. The house is not open to the public, but from its garden a remarkable underground stairway, the *Mina*, descends to the river; these 365 steps, guaranteeing a water supply in times of siege, were cut by Christian slaves in the fourteenth century.

Further down the same street is the **Palacio del Marqués de Salvatierra**, a splendid Renaissance mansion with an oddly primitive, half-grotesque frieze of Adam and Eve on its portal; the house is still used by the family but can usually be visited (daily except Thurs 11am–2pm & 4–7pm, Sun 11am–2pm; mildly interesting guided tour for 150ptas). Just down the hill you reach the two old town bridges – the **Puente Viejo** of 1616 and the single-span Moorish **Puente de San Miguel** – and nearby, on the southeast bank of the river, are the distinctive hump-shaped cupolas and bizarre glass roof-windows of the old **Baños Árabes** (Tues–Sat 10am–2pm & 4–7pm, Sun 10am–2pm). Dating from the thirteenth century, and wonderfully preserved, the barrel-vaulted ceiling and brickwork octagonal pillars supporting horseshoe arches, underline the sophistication of the period.

At the centre of the Ciudad quarter stands the cathedral church of **Santa María Mayor**, originally the Arab town's Friday mosque. Externally it's a graceful combination of Moorish, Gothic and Renaissance styles with the belfry built on top of the old minaret. Inside (by the ticket desk – 100ptas charge) you can see an arch covered with Arabic calligraphy, and just in front of the current street door a part of the old Arab *mihrab*, or prayer niche, has been exposed. Across the square – perhaps the finest in Ronda – is the **Casa de Mondragón**, probably the real palace of the Moorish kings (daily 10am–2pm). Inside, three of the patios preserve original stuccowork and there's a magnificent carved ceiling.

Near the end of the Ciudad are the ruins of the **Alcázar**, destroyed by the French in 1809 ("from sheer love of destruction", according to Richard Ford), and now partially occupied by a school. Once it was virtually impregnable – as indeed was this whole fortress capital, which ruled an independent and isolated Moorish kingdom until 1485, just seven years before the fall of Granada – now it's full of litter and stray sheep.

The principal gate of the town, through which passed the Christian conquerors (led personally by Fernando), stands to the southeast of the Alcázar at the entrance to the suburb of San Francisco.

The **Mercadillo** quarter, which grew up in the wake of the Christian conquest, is of comparatively little interest, with just a couple of buildings worth a quick look. The first is a remarkably preserved inn where Miguel Cervantes once slept, the sixteenth-century **Posada de las Ánimas** in c/Cecilia (also known as the Hogar del Pensionista), the oldest building in the quarter. The other is the **bullring** (10am–6.30pm; 150ptas), close by the Plaza de España and the beautiful clifftop *paseo* from which you get good views of the old and new bridges. Ronda played a leading part in the development of bullfighting and was the birthplace of the modern *corridas* (tournaments). The ring, built in 1781, is one of the earliest in Spain; at its September *feria*, *corridas* take place in eighteenth-century costume, and the fight season here is one of the country's most important. You can visit the bullring to wander around the arena, and there's a museum inside.

Lastly, don't leave without having a drink at the **bar** in the middle of the bridge – reached by a stairway in Plaza de España, operating only seasonally (there is another, always open, on the northwest edge of the chasm). The bridge bar was originally the town prison and last saw use during the Civil War, when Ronda was the site of some of the south's most vicious massacres. Hemingway, in *For Whom the Bell Tolls*, recorded how prisoners were thrown alive into the gorge. These days, Ronda remains a major military garrison post and houses much of the Spanish Africa Legion, Franco's old crack regiment, who can be seen wandering around town in their tropical green coats and tasselled fezes. They have a mean reputation.

Practicalities

Ronda's **train** and **bus stations** are both in the Mercadillo quarter. Trains arrive on Avda. Andalucía, and all the bus companies use the terminal close by on Avda. Concepción García Redondo.

All the **places to stay** are also in the Mercadillo quarter, though two of the least expensive are very close to the Plaza de España: *Hostal Virgen del Rocio*, c/Nueva 18 (☎952/877425; ②), just off the east side of the plaza is a clean, no frills place, and *Huéspedes La Española*, c/José Aparicio 3 (☎952/871052; ②), where some rooms have amazing views, is in the alleyway behind the **Turismo** (Mon–Fri 10am–2.30pm). Another low-priced *hostal* is the *Ronda Sol*, c/Cristo (☎952/874497; ②), near the intersection with c/Sevilla, and there are more round the corner on c/Sevilla itself, including the friendly *Pensión La Purisima*, c/Sevilla 10 (☎952/871050; ②). At the end of c/Sevilla and just off Plaza Carmen Abela, the *Hostal San Francisco*, c/Cabrera-Prim 18 (☎952/873299; ②), where all rooms have bath, is excellent value. Also worth trying is the three-star *Hostal Royal*, c/Virgen de la Paz 42 (☎952/871141; ③) opposite the Alameda. If you're feeling extravagant, try the *Hotel Polo*, Mariano Soubirón 8 (☎952/872447; ⑤, less out of season).

As for **eating**, most of the bargain options are grouped round the far end of the Plaza del Socorro. Right on the plaza, *Doña Pepa* is a decent family-run restaurant with a separate cafeteria-bar serving *bocadillos* and freshly squeezed orange juice. On the Pasaje Correos you'll find *Todo Natural*, a health food shop with a vegetarian restaurant (lunchtimes only). At the end of a central arcade next to *Bar Bananas*, *La Cancela* serves a medium priced *menú* as well as *tapas*. The best place for *tapas*, without question, is the *Marisquería Paco*, at no.8, fronting the plaza. The seafood is fresh and the *tapas*, washed down with a beer at tables on the square, is excellent. *La Rosalejo*, c/Borrego 7, off the northeast corner of the plaza is another good bar with a wide range of *tapas*. The *Hotel Polo*'s restaurant is expensive but well worth it. Moving towards the Plaza de España, there's reasonably priced Chinese food at *Peking*, c/Los Remedios 14, or traditional *tapas* in a great setting at the *Bodega La Giralda*, Avda. Nueva 19. The Plaza de España itself, has only one restaurant of note, *Don Miguel*, which serves up *rondeño* specialities and has a *menú*. However, the main attraction here is a terrace with a marvellous view of the Tajo.

Around Ronda

Ronda makes an excellent base for exploring the superb countryside in the immediate vicinity or for visiting more of the white towns; **Setenil**, one of the most unusual, is 15km away.

Walks around Ronda

Good walking routes from Ronda are pretty limitless. One of the best, and a good way to get a sense of the town as a rural market centre set among farmland, is to take the path down to the gorge from the Mondragón palace terrace. In the fields below there's a network of paths and some stupendous views, although unfortunately there are also several ferocious dogs. A couple of hours' walk will bring you to the main road to the northwest where you can hitch or walk back the 4–5km into the Mercadillo. Another excursion is to an old, unused **aqueduct** set in rocky pasture – from the market square just outside the Ciudad in the San Francisco area, take the straight residential street which leads up and out of town. After about an hour this ends in olive groves, by a stream and a large water trough. A path through the groves leads to the aqueduct.

Further afield, if you're mobile or energetic, are the ruins of a **Roman theatre** at a site known as **Ronda la Vieja**, 12km from the town and reached by turning right 6km down the main road to Arcos/Sevilla. At the site a friendly farmer, who is also the guardian, will present you with a plan (Spanish only) and record your nationality for statistical purposes. Entry to the site which sprawls away up the hill to the west, is free.

Based on Neolithic foundations, note the recently discovered prehistoric stone huts beside the entrance, it was as a Roman town in the first century AD that Acinipo (the town's Roman name), reached its zenith. Immediately west of the theatre, the ground falls away in a startlingly steep escarpment, and from here there are fine views all around, taking in the hill village of Olvera to the north. From here a track leads off towards the strange "cave village" of Setenil (see below).

The Cueva de la Pileta

West from Ronda, is the prehistoric **Cueva de la Pileta** (daily 9am–2pm & 4–7pm; 500ptas), a fabulous series of caverns with some remarkable paintings of animals (mainly bison), fish and what are apparently magic symbols. These etchings and the occupation of the cave date from about 25,000 BC – hence predating the famous caves at Altamira – to the end of the Bronze Age. The tour lasts one hour on average, but can be longer, and is in Spanish – though the guide does speak a little English. There are hundreds of bats in the cave, and no artificial lighting, so visitors carry lanterns with them. You may also want to take a jumper.

To reach the caves take an Algeciras-bound local train (4 daily) to the Estación Benaoján-Montejaque (35min; departures times vary with season); or a bus, which drops you a little closer, in Benaoján. There's a bar at the train station if you want to stock up on drink before the hour-long walk to the caves. Follow the farm track from the right bank of the river until you reach the farmhouse (approximately 30min). From here a track goes straight uphill to the main road just before the signposted turning for the caves. If you're driving, follow the road to Benaoján, and take the turn-off, from where its about 4km.

Setenil, Olvera and Teba

North of Ronda, and feasible as a day trip from the town, are Setenil and Olvera. **SETENIL**, on a very minor road to Olvera, is the strangest of all the white towns, its cave-like streets formed from the overhanging ledge of a gorge. Many of the houses – sometimes two or three storeys high – have natural roofs in the rock. There are a couple of bars, and a *pensión*, *El Almendral* (☎956/134029; ③) on the road just outside town. Four buses a day run from Ronda, or it's a possible walk from Ronda La Vieja. The train station is a good 8km from the village itself.

OLVERA, 15km beyond, is dominated by a fine Moorish castle. There's just one bus a day from Ronda, but there are a couple of *pensiones* if you want to stay and explore the region: *Maqueda* (☎956/130733; ②), and *Olid* (☎956/130102; ②), beautifully situated on the river, with olive groves and the stark backdrop of the Sierra de Lijar.

TEBA is a small community situated in the mountains five or six kilometres south of the N342 between Campillos and Olvera, or straight up on the C341 from Ronda. It's easily seen from the N342 and is approached by way of a single, clearly marked road which winds its way up to the town. The lower square has all the places to stay: three clean, friendly and relatively inexpensive **fondas**. Progressing up the hill to the heart of the town you are left in no doubt as to Teba's political persuasions – there's an enormous hammer and sickle painted on the tarmac in the middle of the crossroads. Higher up are the remains of a Moorish castle, constructed on Roman ruins, which has a superb keep. The views from here over the surrounding countryside are spectacular and the whole village has a calm and prosperous air.

Towards Cádiz and Sevilla

Ronda has good transport connections in most directions (see "Travel details" at the end of this chapter). Almost any route to the north or west is rewarding, taking you past a whole series of white towns, many of them fortified since the days of the Reconquest from the Moors – hence the mass of "de la Frontera" suffixes.

Grazalema, Ubrique and Medina Sidonia

Perhaps the best of all the routes, though a roundabout one, and tricky without your own transport, is **to Cádiz** via Grazalema, Ubrique, and Medina Sidonia. This skirts the nature reserve of **Cortes de la Frontera** (which you can drive through by following the road beyond Benaoján) and, towards Alcalá de los Gazules, runs through forests of cork oaks.

Twenty-three kilometres from Ronda, **GRAZALEMA** is a striking place, now the centre of the Sierra de Grazalana Natural Park, with the **Puerto de las Palomas** (Pass of the Doves, at 1350m the highest pass in Andalucía), rearing up behind. Cross this, and you descend to Zahara and the main road west (see below).

UBRIQUE, twenty kilometres southwest, is a natural mountain fortress which was one of the last Republican strongholds in the Civil War. According to Nicholas Luard's book, *Andalucía*:

> *It proved so difficult for the besieging nationalists to take they eventually called up a plane from Sevilla to fly over the town and drop leaflets carrying the message: "Ubrique, if in five minutes from now all your arms are not piled in front of the Guardia Civil post and the roofs and terraces of your houses are not covered in white sheets, the town will be devastated by the bombs in this plane". The threat was effective, although not quite in the way the nationalists had intended. Without spreading a single white sheet or leaving a gun behind them Ubrique's citizens promptly abandoned the town and took to the hills behind.*

This is a Civil War story typical of these parts. More unusual, however, is that the town today is relatively prosperous, surviving very largely on its medieval guild craft of leather making.

MEDINA SIDONIA, further west on the minor roads, is the old ducal seat of the Guzmán's, one of Spain's most famous families. Depopulated and now somewhat ramshackle, it nevertheless offers glimpses of sixteenth-century grandeur.

Zahara and Arcos de la Frontera

Heading directly to Jerez or Sevilla from Ronda, a beautiful rural drive, you pass below **ZAHARA DE LA SIERRA** (or *de los Membrillos* – "of the Quinces"), perhaps the most perfect example of these fortified hill *pueblos*. Set in beautiful country, a landmark for miles around, its red-tiled houses huddle round a church and castle on a stark outcrop of rock. Once an important Moorish town, its capture by the Christians in 1483 opened the way for the conquest of Ronda – and ultimately Granada. Again there are a couple of **places to stay** – a *fonda* and a *casa de huéspedes* as well as the excellent *Hostal Marqués de Zahara* (☎956/137261; ③) with a good restaurant.

Of more substantial interest, and serving as a better place to break the journey, is **ARCOS DE LA FRONTERA**. This was taken from the Moors in 1264, over two centuries before Zahara fell – an impressive feat, for it stands high above the Río Guadalete on a double crag and must have been a wretchedly impregnable fortress. This dramatic location, enhanced by low, white houses and fine sandstone churches, gives the town a similar feel and appearance to Ronda – only Arcos is poorer and, quite unjustifiably, far less visited. The streets of the town, despite particularly manic packs of local bikers, are if anything more interesting, with their mix of Moorish and Renaissance buildings. At the heart is the Plaza de España, easily reached by following the signs for the *parador*, which occupies one side of it. Flanking another two sides are the castle walls and the large Gothic-Mudéjar church of **Santa María de la Asunción**; the last side is left open, offering plunging views to the river valley.

The only budget **accommodation** in the old town is at the tiny *Mesón Las Callejas*, c/Callejas 19 (☎956/701773; ③), with its own restaurant and great views. Otherwise you're restricted to the *parador* (☎956/700500; ⑤), perched on a rock pedestal, or the new *Hotel Marqués de Torresoto*, c/Marqués de Torresoto 4; (☎956/700517; ④), housed in a converted seventeenth-century mansion complete with colonnaded patio and Baroque chapel. In the new town you'll find a couple of basic places on either side of the main street, c/Corredera: *Fonda del Comercio* (☎956/700057; ②) and *Pensión Galvín* (☎956/700554; ②). Alternatively, try the *Fonda de las Cuevas* at c/Alta 1 (☎956/701654; ②), the more upmarket *Hostal Voy-Voy*, Ponce de León 9 (☎956/701320; ⑤), or *Hotel El Convento* (☎956/702333; ④).

Eating and drinking tends to be expensive in the old quarter, where most of the hotels have their own restaurants. A good value option is *La Terraza* in the gardens of the Paseo de Andalucía, which serves a wide variety of *platos combinados* at outdoor tables.

Just out of town, towards Ronda, a road leads down to a couple of sandy **beaches** on the riverbank (buses every half-hour), a rather swanky two-star *hostal* and a **campsite**, *Arcos de la Frontera* (☎956/700514). If you swim in the Bornos reservoir, or further along toward the namesake village, take care – there are said to be whirlpools in some parts.

SEVILLA, THE WEST AND CÓRDOBA

With the major exception of **Sevilla** – and to a slightly lesser extent **Córdoba** – the west and centre of Andalucía are not greatly visited. The coast here, certainly the Atlantic **Costa de la Luz**, is a world apart from the Mediterranean resorts, with the entire stretch between Algeciras and Tarifa designated a "potential military zone". This probably sounds grim – and in parts, marked off by *Paso Prohibido* signs, it is – but the ruling has also had happier effects, preventing foreigners from buying up land and placing strict controls even on Spanish developments. So, for a hundred or more kilometres, there are scarcely any villa developments and only a modest number of hotels and campsites – small, easy-going and low-key even at the one growing resort of **Conil**. On the coast, too, there is the attraction of **Cádiz**, one of the oldest and, though it's now in decline, most elegant ports in Europe.

Inland rewards include the smaller towns between Sevilla and Córdoba, Moorish **Carmona** particularly. But the most beautiful, and neglected, parts of this region are the dark, ilex-covered hills and poor rural villages of the **Sierra Morena** north of

Sevilla. Perfect walking country with its network of streams and reservoirs between modest peaks, this is also a botanist's dream, brilliant with a mass of spring flowers.

On a more organized level, though equally compelling if you're into bird-watching or wildlife, is the huge nature reserve of the **Coto Doñana**, spreading back from Huelva in vast expanses of *marismas* – sand dunes, salt flats and marshes. The most important of the Spanish reserves, Doñana is vital to scores of migratory birds and to endangered mammals like the Iberian lynx. It can be visited by Land Rover tour from the new beach resort complex of **Matalascañas/Torre de Higuera**, accessible from Huelva or Sevilla.

Sevilla

"Seville," wrote Byron, "is a pleasant city, famous for oranges and women". And for its heat, he might perhaps have added, since **SEVILLA**'s summers are intense and start early, in April. But the spirit, for all its nineteenth-century chauvinism, is about right. Sevilla has three important monuments and an illustrious history, but what it's essentially famous for is its own living self – the greatest city of the Spanish south, of Carmen, Don Juan and Figaro, and the archetype of Andalucian promise. This reputation for gaiety and brilliance, for theatricality and intensity of life, does seem deserved. It's expressed on a phenomenally grand scale at the city's two great festivals – the **Semana Santa** (during the week before Easter) and the **April Feria** (which lasts a week at the end of the month). Either is worth considerable effort to get to. Sevilla is also Spain's second most important centre for **bullfighting**, after Madrid.

Despite its considerable elegance and charm, the underlying conditions in the city have been bleak in recent years. Sevilla has definite modern wealth, having cornered the Spanish arms industry and its lucrative export trade to Latin America, but it also lies at the centre of a depressed agricultural area and has an unemployment rate of nearly forty percent – the highest in Spain, along with Málaga. The total refurbishment of the infrastructure, including impressive new roads and bridges, a high-speed rail link and a revamped airport may help – but the long-term effects will take a while to assess.

Meantime, **petty crime** is a big problem, and the motive for stealing is usually cash for heroin. Bag snatching is common (often Italian-style, from passing *motos*) as is breaking into cars. There's even a special breed called *semaforazos* who break the windows of cars stopped at traffic lights and grab what they can. Western-style amateur bank robberies also seem to be in fashion. Be careful, but don't be put off. As one of the consuls in Sevilla put it: "This is not a dangerous city. No one gets mugged. I know of no town where the streets are safer at night." For violence against persons, at least, this is probably true.

Sevilla's most famous present-day native son is Prime Minister **Felipe González**; his deputy Alfonso Guerra also hails from here. Another, more bizarre *Sevillano* is one **Gregorio XVII**, who calls himself the true Pope – in defiance of his excommunication by the Vatican, "Pope Greg" is leader of a large ultra-reactionary order which has made the dead Franco a saint, and which gives out free beer and *churros* to all who call at its headquarters. He himself conspicuously enjoys the good life and stalks the city's bars, dressed in full silken regalia, along with his "papal" entourage.

The connection with Felipe González may have had something to do with Sevilla sharing the world stage with Barcelona in 1992, to celebrate the 500th anniversary of Columbus's discovery of the New World. Vast investment and the participation of over 100 countries went some way to justifying the billing of **Expo 92** as the "event of the century". What remains of the exhibition ground is at La Isla de la Cartuja, northwest of the centre across the river, where Columbus's remains are said to have rested before finally being moved to the Dominican Republic.

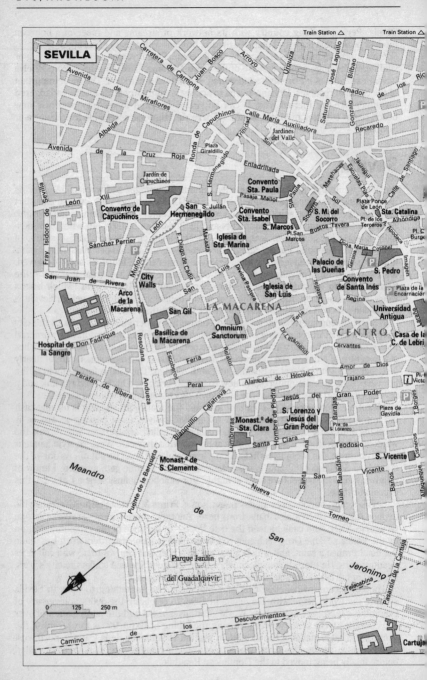

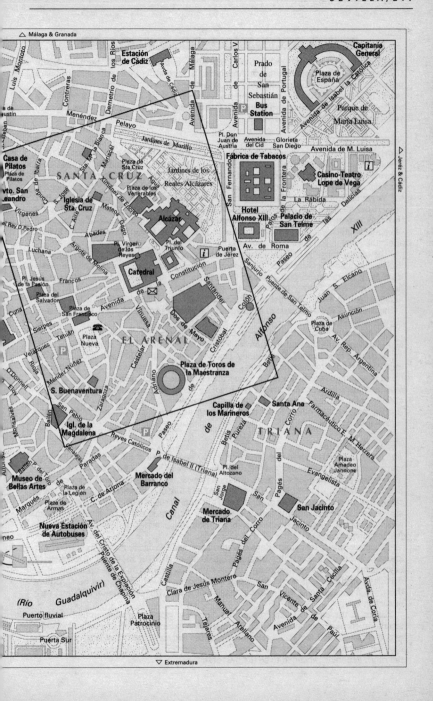

△ Málaga & Granada

△ Jerez & Cadiz

▽ Extremadura

Capitanía General

Estación de Cádiz

Plaza de España

Parque de María Luisa

Prado de San Sebastián

Bus Station

Pl. Don Juan de Austria

Avenida del Cid

Glorieta San Diego

Avenida de M. Luisa

Jardines de Murillo

Fábrica de Tabacos

Casa de Pilatos

Plaza de Pilatos

SANTA CRUZ

Plaza de Sta Cruz

Jardines de los Reales Alcázares

vto. San Leandro

Iglesia de Sta. Cruz

Plaza de los Venerables

Casino-Teatro Lope de Vega

La Rábida

Alcázar

Hotel Alfonso XIII

Palacio de San Telme

Pl. del Triunfo

Av. de Roma

Pl Virgen de los Reyes

Puerta de Jérez

Pl. Jesús de la Pasión

Catedral

Puente de San Telmo

Plaza de Cuba

Plaza del Salvador

Plaza de San Francisco

EL ARENAL

Plaza de Toros de la Maestranza

Plaza Nueva

S. Buenaventura

Capilla de los Marineros

Santa Ana

TRIANA

Igl. de la Magdalena

Plaza Amadeo Jannone

San Jacinto

Museo de Bellas Artes

Mercado del Barranco

P. de Isabel II (Triana)

Pl. del Altozano

Plaza de la Legión

Plaza de Armas

Nueva Estación de Autobuses

Mercado de Triana

(Río Guadalquivir)

Puerto fluvial

Plaza Patrocinio

Puerta Sur

Clara de Jesús Montero

SEMANA SANTA AND THE FERIA DE ABRIL

Sevilla boasts two of the largest festival celebrations in Spain. The first, **Semana Santa** (Holy Week), always spectacular in Andalucía, is here at its peak with extraordinary processions of masked penitents and carnival-style floats. The second, the **Feria de Abril**, is unique to the city: a one-time market festival, long converted to a week-long party of drink, food and *flamenco*. The *feria* follows hard on the heels of *Semana Santa*. If you have the energy, experience both.

SEMANA SANTA

Semana Santa may be a religious festival, but for most of the week solemnity isn't the keynote – there's lots of carousing and frivolity, and bars are full day and night. In essence, it involves the marching in procession of brotherhoods of the church (*cofradías*) and penitents, followed by *pasos*, elaborate platforms or floats on which sit 17th-century images of the Virgin or Jesus. For weeks beforehand the *cofradías* painstakingly adorn the hundred or so *pasos*, spending vast amounts on costumes and precious stones. The bearers (*costaleros*) walk in time to stirring, traditional dirges and drumbeats from the bands, which are often punctuated by impromptu street-corner *saetas* – short, fervent, *flamenco*-style hymns about the Passion and the Virgin's sorrows.

The official **route** goes from Plaza de la Campaña along c/Sierpes through the cathedral, and around the Giralda and the Bishop's Palace. *Pasos* leave churches all over town from early afternoon onward, snaking through the city and back to their resting place hours later. **Good Friday** morning is the climax, when the *pasos* leave the churches at midnight and move through the town for much of the night. The highlight is the viewing in the cathedral of *La Macarena*, an image of the patroness of bullfighters, and by extension, of Sevilla itself.

The pattern of events changes every day; a loose **timetable** is issued with local papers and is essential if you want to know which events are where – the ultra-Catholic *ABC* paper has the best listings. On Maundy Thursday women dress in black and it's considered respectful for tourists not to dress in shorts or T-shirts. Triana is a good location on this day, and there's always a crush of spectators outside the cathedral and c/Sierpes, the most awe-inspiring venue. Plaza de la Virgen de los Reyes under the Giralda is a good viewing point, but the best way of all to see the processions is to pick them up near their starting and finishing points in the respective barrios; here you'll see the true *teatro de la calle* – theatre of the streets.

FERIA DE ABRIL

The *Feria de Abril* lasts non-stop for a week in the second half of the month. For its duration a vast area on the far bank of the river, the *Real de la Feria*, is totally covered in rows of *casetas*, canvas pavilions or tents of varying sizes. Some of these belong to eminent Sevillana families, some to groups of friends, others to clubs, trade associations or political parties. In each one – from around 9 at night until perhaps 6 or 7 the following morning – there is *flamenco* singing and dancing. Many of the men and virtually all the women wear traditional costume, the latter in an astonishing array of brilliantly coloured, flounced gypsy dresses.

The sheer size of this spectacle is extraordinary, and the dancing, with its intense and knowing sexuality, a revelation. But most infectious of all is the universal spontaneity of enjoyment; after wandering around staring with the crowds you wind up a part of it, drinking and dancing in one of the "open" *casetas* which have commercial bars. Among these you'll usually find lively *casetas* erected by the anarchist trade union *CNT* and various leftist groups.

Earlier in the day, from 1pm until 5pm, Sevillana society **parades** around the fairground in carriages or on horseback. An incredible extravaganza of display and voyeurism, this has subtle but distinct gradations of dress and style; catch it at least once. Each day, too, there are **bullfights** (at around 5.30pm; very expensive tickets in advance from the ring), generally reckoned to be the best of the season.

Arrival and accommodation

Split in two by the Río Guadalquivir, Sevilla is fairly easy to find your way about (though hell if you're driving). The **old city** – where you'll want to spend most of your time – takes up the east bank. At its heart, side by side, stand the three great monuments: the **Giralda tower**, the **Cathedral** and the **Alcázar**, with the cramped alleyways of the **Barrio Santa Cruz**, the medieval Jewish quarter and now the heart of tourist life, extending north of them. West of the Barrio is the main shopping and commercial district, its most obvious landmarks the **Plaza Nueva** and **Campaña**, and the smart pedestrianized **c/Sierpes** which runs between them. Across the river – where the great April *feria* takes place – are the very much earthier, traditionally working-class districts of **Los Remedios** and **Triana**.

Points of arrival, too, are straightforward though the **train station, Santa Justa**, is a long way out on Avda. Kansas City, the airport road. Bus #70 will take you from outside here to the Prado de San Sebastián, in front of the main bus station. The airport bus, #EA, terminates in the centre at the Puerta de Jerez, at the top of Avda. Roma between the Turismo and the Fábrica de Tabacos.

The **main bus station** is at the Prado de San Sebastián. Most companies and destinations go from here: exceptions include buses for **Badajoz**, **Extremadura** and **Huelva** which are served by *La Estrella* and *Empresa Damas*, operating out of the new station at Plaza de Armas by the Puente del Cachaorro on the river.

If you arrive by **plane**, the aforementioned bus #EA will take you in to the Puerta de Jerez or *Iberia* buses go to their office, very nearby on c/Almirante Lobo.

The **Turismo** is at Avda. de la Constitución 21 (Mon–Sat 9.30am–7.30pm; ☎954/221404). You can get good city maps and the listings magazine, *El Giraldillo*, from here.

Accommodation

The most attractive **area to stay** is undoubtedly the **Barrio Santa Cruz**, though this is reflected in the prices. In mid-season or during the big festivals you can find yourself paying ridiculous amounts for what is little more than a cell (and not just in the Barrio); rooms are relatively expensive everywhere, in fact. Nonetheless there are reasonable places to be found in the Barrio and on its periphery (especially immediately north, and southeast towards the bus station) and they're at least worth a try before heading elsewhere. Slightly further out, another promising area is to the north of the Plaza Nueva, and especially over towards the river and the old Córdoba station. It's always worth trying to bargain the price down a little, though you may not always succeed.

At peak times you may face quite a walk. The list below is no more than a start, and it's worth checking at the places you'll pass between all these.

CHEAPER OPTIONS

Hostal Águilas, c/Águilas 15 (☎954/213177). Small and quiet, near the Casa de Pilatos. ④.

Albergue Juvenil Sevilla, c/Isaac Peral 2 (☎954/613150). Crowded youth hostel some way out in the university district; take bus #34 from Puerta de Jerez or Plaza Nueva. ③.

Pensión Alcázar, c/Deán Miranda 12 (☎954/228457). Tiny place in a tiny street beside the Alcázar; good value if they have space. ④.

Hostal Alvertos, c/Cervantes 4 (☎954/385710). Engagingly eccentric *hostal* near the Plaza Duque de la Victoria – the ramshackle patio crammed with plants, leather armchairs and a piano is a work of art. ③.

Hostal Bienvenido, c/Archeros 17 (☎954/413655). East of c/Santa María la Blanca; small rooms but nice roof terrace. ④.

Casa de Huéspedes Buen Dormir, c/Farnesio 8 (☎954/217492). Off c/Santa María la Blanca on the cathedral side; friendly but scruffy; check the room. ③.

Córdoba, c/Farnesio 12 (954/227498). Of a good standard, but more expensive than many the same facilities. ④.

Hostal Galatea, c/San Juan de la Palma 4 (☎954/563564). Friendly, new *hostal* in a restored town house situated on a charming square in the heart of the atmospheric Macarena quarter. ④.

Hostal Gravina, c/Gravina 46 (☎954/216414). Pleasant, family-run place close to the Museo de Bellas Artes. ③.

Hostal Marco de la Giralda, c/Abades 30 (☎954/228324). Good value for somewhere so close to the cathedral. ④.

Hostal Santa María, c/Hernando Colón 19 (☎954/228505). Small place on a noisy street, but in the Giralda's shadow. ③.

Hostal Unión, c/Tarifa 4 (☎954/211790). Slightly east of the Plaza Duque de la Victoria and one of the best value places in this area. Clean, economical rooms with bath. ③.

MORE EXPENSIVE HOSTALES AND HOTELS

Hotel Álvarez Quintero, c/Álvarez Quintero 12 (☎954/221298). Near the cathedral, this converted former *bodega* has a delightful seventeenth-century patio and great views from some rooms, especially nos. 201–206. ⑤.

Hotel Murillo, c/Lope de Rueda 7 (☎954/216095). Traditional hotel in restored mansion with all facilities plus amusingly kitsch features such as suits of armour and paint palette key rings. Close to the Plaza Santa Cruz. ⑤.

Hotel San Andrés, c/Angostillo 6 (☎954/562856). South of the Alameda de Hercules, an atttractively refurbished mansion on a pleasant and quiet *plazuela* facing the crumbling church of San Andrés. ⑤.

Hotel Simón, c/García de Vinuesa 19 (☎954/226660). Well-restored mansion with attractive patio and excellent position across Avda. de la Constitución from the cathedral. Can be a bargain out of season. ⑤.

Pensión Zahira, c/San Eloy 43 (☎954/221061). Comfortable rooms with bath. ⑤.

CAMPING

Camping Sevilla (☎954/514379). Right by the airport, so very noisy but otherwise not a bad site. The airport bus will get you there.

Club de Campo (☎954/720520). 12km out in Dos Hermanas, a pleasant shady site with a pool. Better than *Villsom*, nearby on the main Cádiz road. Half-hourly buses from the bus station.

Moorish Sevilla

Sevilla was one of the earliest **Moorish conquests** (in 712) and, as part of the Caliphate of Córdoba, became the second city of *al-Andalus*. When the Caliphate broke up in the early eleventh century it was by far the most powerful of the independent states (or *taifas*) to emerge, extending its power over the Algarve and eventually over Jaén, Murcia and Córdoba itself. This period, under a series of three Arabic rulers from the Abbadid dynasty (1023–91), was something of a golden age. The city's court was unrivalled in wealth and luxury and was sophisticated too, developing a strong chivalric element and a flair for poetry – one of the most skilled exponents being the last ruler, al Mu'tamid, the "poet-king". But with sophistication came decadence and in 1091 Abbadid rule was usurped by a new force, the **Almoravids**, a tribe of fanatical Berber Muslims from North Africa, to whom the Andalucians had appealed for help against the rising threat from the northern Christian kingdoms.

Despite initial military successes, the Almoravids failed to consolidate their gains in al-Andalus and attempted to rule through military governors from Marrakesh. In the middle of the twelfth century they were in turn supplanted by a new Berber incursion, the **Almohads**, who by about 1170 had recaptured virtually all the former territories. Sevilla had accepted Almohad rule in 1147 and became the capital of this last real empire of the Moors in Spain. Almohad power was sustained until their disastrous

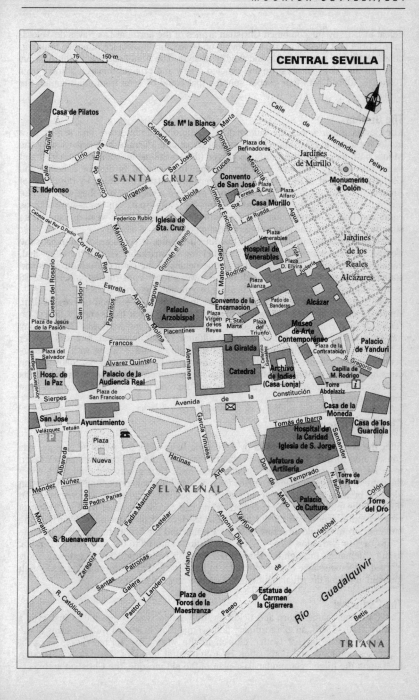

CENTRAL SEVILLA

0   75   150 m

Calle de Menéndez Pelayo

Casa de Pilatos

Sta. Mª la Blanca

Calle María
Céspedes
Sta. Doncella
Cruces
Mezquita

Plaza de Refinadores

Jardines de Murillo

Monumento e Colón

S. Ildefonso

SANTA CRUZ

Conde de Ibarra
Lirio
Calle Aguilas

San José
Virgenes
Fabiola

Convento de San José

Casa Murillo

Plaza S.Cruz
Teresa

Plaza Alfaro

Jardines de los Reales Alcázares

Cabeza del Rey D.Pedro
Federico Rubio

Iglesia de Sta. Cruz

Mármoles
Guzman el Bueno
Sta. Ximénez Enciso
L. de Rueda

Plaza Venerables

Hospital de Venerables

Corral del Rey
Cuesta del Rosario
San Isidoro
Estrella
Pajaritos
Argote de Molina
Segovia
C. Mateos Gago
Rodrigo

Plaza D. Elvira

Lentería

Vida
Agua

Plaza Alianza

Patio de Banderas

Plaza de Jesús de la Pasión
Plaza del Salvador
Jovellanos Sagasta

Palacio Arzobispal

Placentines
Francos
Álvarez Quintero

Convento de la Encarnación

Plaza Virgen de los Reyes
Pl. Sta. Marta

Plaza del Triunfo

Alcázar

Museo de Arte Contemporáneo

Plaza de la Contratación

Palacio de Yanduri

Hosp. de la Paz

Sierpes

San José
Velázquez Tetuán

Palacio de la Audiencia Real

Plaza de San Francisco

Alemanes

La Giralda

Catedral

Catedral
Fernández

Archivo de Indias (Casa Lonja)

Constitución

S. Gregorio
Capilla de M. Rodrigo
Torre Abdelaziz

Casa de la Moneda

Ayuntamiento

Avenida de la

García Vinuesa

Tomás de Ibarra

Casa de los Guardiola

Albareda
Méndez Núñez
Bilbao
Pedro Parias

Plaza Nueva

Harinas

Hospital de la Caridad
Iglesia de S. Jorge

Santander

Jefatura de Artillería

Torre de la Plata

S. Buenaventura

Moratín
Zaragoza

Castelar
Padre Marchena

EL ARENAL

Arfe
Dos de Mayo

Temprado

N.Balboa

Palacio de Cultura

Colón
Torre del Oro

R. Católicos
Santas
Galera

Patronas
Pastor y Landero

Adriano
Antonia Díez

Varflora

Cristóbal

Betis

Plaza de Toros de la Maestranza

Paseo

Estatua de Carmen la Cigarrera

Río Guadalquivir

TRIANA

defeat in 1212 by the combined Christian armies of the north, at Las Navas de Tolosa. In this brief and precarious period Sevilla underwent a renaissance of public building, characterized by a new vigour and fluidity of style. The Almohads rebuilt the Alcázar, enlarged the principal **mosque** and erected a new and brilliant minaret, a tower over 100m tall, topped with four copper spheres that could be seen from miles round: the Giralda.

The Giralda

The Sevilla minaret was the culmination of Almohad architecture and served as a model for those at their imperial capitals of Rabat and Marrakesh. It was used by the Moors both for calling the faithful to prayer (the traditional function of a minaret) and as an observatory, and was so venerated that they wanted to destroy it before the Christian conquest of the city. This they were prevented from doing by the threat of Alfonso (later King Alfonso X) that "if they removed a single stone, they would all be put to the sword". Instead the **Giralda** (Mon–Sat 11am–5pm, Sun 10am–4pm; 500ptas combined ticket), named after the sixteenth-century *giraldillo* or weather vane on its summit, became the bell tower of the Christian cathedral.

Beyond doubt the most beautiful building in Sevilla, it continues to dominate the skyline. You can ascend to the bell chamber for a remarkable view of the city – and, equally remarkable, a glimpse of the Gothic details of the cathedral's buttresses and statuary. But most impressive of all is the tower's inner construction, a series of 35 gently inclined ramps wide enough to allow two mounted guards to pass.

The Moorish structure took twelve years to build (1184–96) and derives its firm, simple beauty from the shadows formed by blocks of brick trelliswork, different on each side, and relieved by a succession of arched niches and windows. The harmony has been spoiled by the Renaissance-era addition of balconies and, to a still greater extent, by the four diminishing storeys of the belfry – added, along with the Italian-sculpted bronze figure of "Faith" which surmounts them, in 1560–68, following the demolition by an earthquake of the original copper spheres. Even so, it remains in its perfect synthesis of form and decoration one of the most important and beautiful monuments of the Islamic world.

Christian Reconquest

After the **Reconquest of Sevilla** by Ferdinand III in 1248, the Almohad mosque was consecrated to the Virgin Mary, as was the practice with all Spanish mosques taken from Islam, and it became the Christian cathedral. Thus it survived until 1402, when the cathedral chapter dreamt up plans for a new and unrivalled monument to Christian glory: "a building on so magnificent a scale that posterity will believe we were mad". To this end the mosque was demolished, while the canons, inspired by their vision of future repute, renounced all but a subsistence level of their incomes to further the building. From the old structure only the Giralda and the Moorish entrance court, the **Patio de los Naranjos**, were spared. The patio is entered to the north of the Giralda, from c/Alemanes, through the **Puerta del Perdón** – the original main gateway, sadly marred by Renaissance embellishments. In the centre of the patio remains a Moorish fountain, used for the ritual ablutions before entering the mosque.

The Cathedral

The **Catedral** (same hours and ticket as the Giralda) was completed in just over a century (1402–1506), an extraordinary achievement for, in accord with the plans of the chapter, it is the largest Gothic church in the world. As Norman Lewis says, "it expresses conquest and domination in architectural terms of sheer mass". Though built upon the huge, rectangular base-plan of the old mosque, the Christian architects

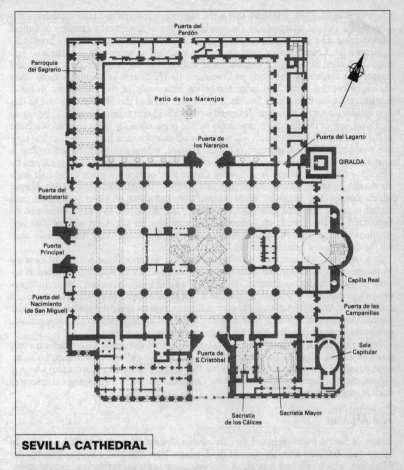

SEVILLA CATHEDRAL

(probably under the direction of the French master architect of Rouen Cathedral) added the extra dimension of height. Its central nave rises to 42 metres, and even the side chapels seem tall enough to contain an ordinary church. The total area covers 11,520 square metres, and new calculations based on cubic measurement, have now pushed it in front of Saint Paul's in London and Saint Peter's in Rome as the largest church in the world, verified by the Guinness Book of Records.

Sheer size and grandeur are, inevitably, the chief characteristics of the cathedral. But as you grow accustomed to the gloom, two other qualities stand out with equal force: the rhythmic balance and interplay between the parts, and an impressive overall simplicity and restraint in decoration. All successive ages have left monuments of their own wealth and style, but these have been limited to the two rows of side chapels. In the main body of the cathedral only the great box-like structure of the **coro** (choir) stands out, filling the central portion of the nave.

The *coro* extends and opens on to the **Capilla Mayor,** dominated by a vast Gothic **retablo** composed of 45 carved scenes from the life of Christ. The lifetime's work of a single craftsman, Pierre Dancart, this is the supreme masterpiece of the cathedral – the largest and richest altarpiece in the world and one of the finest examples of Gothic woodcarving. The guides provide staggering statistics on the amount of gold involved.

Behind the Capilla Mayor (and directly to your left on entering the cathedral) you pass the domed Renaissance **Capilla Real**, built on the site of the original royal burial chapel and containing the body of Ferdinand III (*El Santo*) in a suitably rich, silver shrine before the altar. The large tombs on either side of the chapel are those of Ferdinand's wife, Beatrice of Swabia, and his son, Alfonso the Wise. At the end of this first aisle are a series of rooms designed in the rich Plateresque style in 1530 by Diego de Riano, one of the foremost exponents of this predominantly decorative architecture of the late Spanish Renaissance. Through a small antechamber here you enter the curious oval-shaped **Sala Capitular** (Chapter House), whose elaborate domed ceiling is mirrored in the marble decoration of the floor. It contains a number of paintings by Murillo – the finest of which, a flowing *Conception*, occupies a place of honour high above the bishop's throne. Alongside this room is the grandiose **Sacristía Mayor** which houses the treasury. Amid a confused collection of silver reliquaries and monstrances – dull and prodigious wealth – are displayed the keys presented to Ferdinand by the Jewish and Moorish communities on the surrender of the city; sculpted into the latter in stylized Arabic script are the words "May Allah render eternal the dominion of Islam in this city."

Just beyond the entrance to the sacristy is an enormous nineteenth-century **Monument to Christopher Columbus** (*Cristóbal Colón* in Spanish), erected originally in the cathedral of Havana. By a wry stroke of irony, however, Cuban independence was declared seven years later and it had to be shipped to Sevilla. The mariner's coffin is held aloft by four huge allegorical figures, representing the kingdoms of León, Castile, Aragón and Navarra; note how the lance of Castile is piercing a pomegranate, symbol of Granada, the last Moorish kingdom to be reconquered.

If the monument inspires you, or you have a fervent interest in Columbus's travels, visit the **Lonja**, opposite the cathedral. This, the city's old stock exchange building, now houses the remarkable **Archives of the Indies** (Mon–Sat 10am–1pm). Among the selection of documents on display are Columbus's log and a changing exhibition of ancient maps and curiosities.

The Alcázar

Rulers of Sevilla have occupied the site of the **Alcázar** (Tues–Sat 10.30am–6pm, Sun 10am–2pm; 600ptas) from the time of the Romans. Here was built the great court of the Abbadids, which reached a peak of sophistication and exaggerated sensuality under the cruel and ruthless al-Mu'tadid – a ruler who enlarged the palace in order to house a harem of 800 women, and who decorated the terraces with flowers planted in the skulls of his decapitated enemies. Later, under the **Almohads**, the complex was turned into a citadel, forming the heart of the town's fortifications. Its extent was enormous, stretching to the Torre del Oro on the bank of the Guadalquivir.

Parts of the Almohad walls survive, but the present structure of the palace dates almost entirely from the Christian period. Sevilla was a favoured residence of the Spanish kings for some four centuries after the reconquest – most particularly of **Pedro the Cruel** (1350–69) who, with his mistress María de Padilla, lived in and ruled from the Alcázar. Pedro embarked upon a complete rebuilding of the palace, employing workmen from Granada and utilising fragments of earlier Moorish buildings in Sevilla, Córdoba and Valencia. Pedro's works form the nucleus of the Alcázar as it is today and despite numerous restorations necessitated by fires and earth tremors it offers some of the best surviving examples of **Mudéjar architecture** – the style devel-

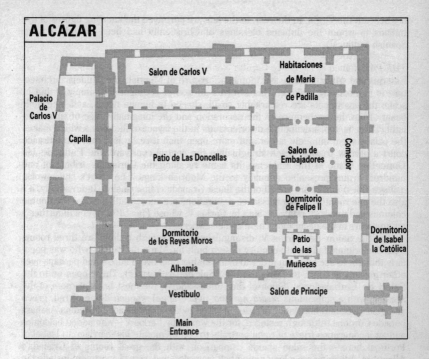

ALCÁZAR

Palacio de Carlos V

Capilla

Salon de Carlos V

Habitaciones de Maria de Padilla

Patio de Las Doncellas

Salon de Embajadores

Comedor

Dormitorio de Felipe II

Dormitorio de los Reyes Moros

Alhamia

Patio de las Muñecas

Dormitorio de Isabel la Católica

Vestibulo

Salón de Principe

Main Entrance

oped by Moors working under Christian rule. Later monarchs, however, have left all too many traces and additions. Isabella built a new wing in which to organize expeditions to the Americas and control the new territories; Carlos V married a Portuguese princess in the palace, adding huge apartments for the occasion; and under Felipe IV (c.1624) extensive renovations were carried out to the existing rooms. On a more mundane level, kitchens were installed to provide for General Franco, who stayed in the royal apartments whenever he visited Sevilla.

ENTRANCE – THE CASA DEL OCÉANO

The Alcázar is entered from the Plaza del Triunfo, adjacent to the cathedral. The gateway, flanked by original Almohad walls, opens on to a courtyard where Pedro (who was known as "the Just" as well as "the Cruel", depending on one's fortunes) used to give judgement; to the left is his **Sala de Justicia.** The main facade of the palace stands at the end of an inner court, the **Patio de la Montería**; on either side are galleried buildings erected by Isabella. This principal facade is pure fourteenth-century Mudéjar and, with its delicate, marble-columned windows, stalactite frieze and overhanging roof, is one of the finest things in the whole Alcázar. But it's probably better to look round the **Casa del Océano** (or *de las Américas*), the sixteenth-century building on the right, before entering the main palace. Founded by Isabella in 1503, this gives you a standard against which to assess the Moorish forms. Here most of the rooms seem too heavy, their decoration ceasing to be an integral part of the design. The only notable exception is the chapel with its magnificent *artesonado* ceiling inlaid with golden stars; within is a fine altarpiece depicting Columbus (in gold) and Carlos V (in a red cloak) sheltering beneath the Virgin. In the rear, to the left, are portrayed the kneeling figures of the Indians to whom the dubious blessings of Christianity had been brought by the Spanish conquest.

THE PALACE

Entering the **Main Palace** the "domestic" nature of Moorish and Mudéjar architecture is immediately striking. This involves no loss of grandeur but simply a shift in scale: the apartments are remarkably small, shaped to human needs, and take their beauty from the exuberance of the decoration and the imaginative use of space and light. There is, too, a deliberate disorientation in the layout of the rooms which makes the palace seem infinitely larger and more open than it really is. From the entrance court a narrow passage leads straight into the central courtyard, the **Patio de las Doncellas** (Patio of the Maidens), its name recalling the Christians' tribute of one hundred virgins presented annually to the Moorish kings. The court's stuccowork, *azulejos* (tiles) and doors are all of the finest Granada craftsmanship. Interestingly, it's also the one room where Renaissance restorations are successfully fused – the double columns and upper storey were built by Carlos V, whose *Plus Ultra* ("yet still further") motto recurs in the decorations here and elsewhere.

Past the **Salon de Carlos V**, distinguished by a superb ceiling, are three rooms from the original fourteenth-century design built for María de Padilla (who was popularly thought to use magic in order to maintain her hold over Pedro – and perhaps over other gallants at court, too, who used to drink her bath water). These open on to the **Salon de Embajadores** (Salon of the Ambassadors), the most brilliant room of the Alcázar, with a stupendous *media naranja* (half-orange) wooden dome of red, green and gold cells, and horseshoe arcades inspired by the great palace of Medina Azahara outside Córdoba. Although restored, for the worse, by Carlos V – who added balconies and an incongruous frieze of royal portraits to commemorate his marriage to Isabel of Portugal here – the salon stands comparison with the great rooms of Granada's Alhambra. Adjoining are a long dining hall (*comedor*) and a small apartment installed in the late sixteenth century for Felipe II.

Beyond is the last great room of the palace – the **Patio de las Muñecas** (Patio of the Dolls), which takes its curious name from two tiny faces decorating the inner side of one of the smaller arches. It's thought to be the site of the harem in the original palace. In this room Pedro is reputed to have murdered his brother Don Fadrique in 1358; another of his royal guests, Abu Said of Granada, was murdered here for his jewels (one of which, an immense ruby which King Pedro later gave to Edward, the "Black Prince", now figures in the British crown jewels). The upper storey of the court is a much later, nineteenth-century restoration. On the other sides of the patio are the **bedrooms** of Isabella and of her son Don Juan, and the arbitrarily named *Dormitorio del los Reyes Moros* (Bedroom of the Moorish Kings).

PALACIO DE CARLOS V AND THE GARDENS

To the left of the main palace loom the large and soulless apartments of the **Palacio de Carlos V**. Something of an endurance test, with endless tapestries and pink-orange or yellow paintwork, their classical style asserts a different and inferior mood. Best to hurry through to the beautiful and rambling **Alcázar gardens**, the confused but enticing product of several eras, where you can take a well-earned rest from your exertions. Here are the vaulted baths in which María de Padilla is supposed to have bathed (in reality, an auxilliary water supply for the palace), and the tank specially built for Felipe V in 1733, who whiled away two solitary years at the Alcázar fishing in this pool and preparing himself for death through religious flagellation. Also here is an unusual maze of myrtle bushes and the **pavilion of Carlos V**, the only survivor of several he built in the gardens.

The Plaza de España and María Luisa Park

Laid out in 1929 for an abortive "Fair of the Americas", the Plaza de España and adjoining María Luisa Park are among the most pleasant – and impressive – public spaces in Spain. They are an ideal place to spend the middle part of the day, just ten minutes' walk to the east of the cathedral.

En route you pass by the **Fábrica de Tabacos**, the city's old tobacco factory and the setting for Bizet's *Carmen*. Now part of the university, this massive structure was built in the 1750s and for a time was the largest building in Spain after El Escorial. At its peak in the following century it was also the country's largest single employer, with a workforce of some 4000 women *cigarreras* – "a class in themselves" according to Richard Ford, who were forced to undergo "an ingeniously minute search on leaving their work, for they sometimes carry off the filthy weed in a manner her most Catholic majesty never dreamt of."

The **Plaza de España**, beyond, was designed as the centrepiece of the Spanish Americas Fair, which was somewhat scuppered by the Wall Street crash. A vast semicircular complex, with its fountains, monumental stairways and mass of tilework, it would seem strange in most Spanish cities but here it looks entirely natural, carrying on the tradition of civic display. At the fair, the Plaza de España was used for the Spanish exhibit of industry and crafts, and around the crescent are *azulejo* scenes and maps of each of the provinces – an interesting record of the country at the tail end of a moneyed era.

Spaniards and tourists alike come out to the plaza – slightly shabby now – to potter about in the little boats hired out on its tiny strip of canal, or to hide from the sun and crowds amid the ornamental pools and walkways of the **Parque de María Luisa**. The park is designed like the plaza in a mix of 1920s Art Deco and mock-Mudéjar. Scattered about, and round its edge, are more buildings from the fair, some of them amazingly opulent, built in the last months before the Wall Street crash undercut the scheme's impetus – look out, in particular, for the stylish **Guatemala building**, off the Paseo de la Palmera.

Towards the end of the park, the grandest mansions from the fair have been adapted as **museums**. The furthest contains the city's **archaeology** collections (Tues–Sun 10am–2pm; 250ptas). The main exhibits are Roman mosaics and artefacts from nearby Italica, along with a unique Phoenician statuette of Astarte-Tanit, the virgin goddess once worshipped throughout the Mediterranean. Opposite is the fabulous-looking **Popular Arts Museum** (same hours), generally besieged by schoolkids but with interesting displays relating to the April *feria*.

Barrio Santa Cruz, the river and Triana

After the park, perhaps the two best areas of Sevilla in which to wander – stopping for the occasional drink – are the Barrio Santa Cruz and the banks of the Guadalquivir.

Santa Cruz is very much in character with the city's romantic image, its streets narrow and tortuous to keep out the sun, the houses brilliantly whitewashed and barricaded with *rejas* (iron grilles) behind which girls once kept chaste evening rendezvous with their *novios*. Almost all of the houses have patios, often surprisingly large, and in summer these become the principal family living room. One of the most beautiful is within the Baroque **Hospicio de los Venerables Sacerdotes** (Tues–Sun 10am–2pm & 4–8pm; 500ptas), near the centre in a plaza of the same name – one of the few buildings in the Barrio worth actively seeking out.

Of numerous mansions, by far the finest is the so-called **Casa de Pilatos** (daily 9am–6pm; 500ptas), built by the Marqués de Tarifa on his return from a pilgrimage to Jerusalem in 1519 and popularly thought to have been in imitation of the house of

Pontius Pilate. In fact it's an interesting and harmonious mixture of Mudéjar, Gothic and Renaissance styles, featuring brilliant *azulejos*, a tremendous sixteenth-century stairway and the best domestic patios in the city.

Down by the **Guadalquivir** are more pedal-boats for idling away the afternoons, and at night a surprising density of local couples. The main riverside landmark here is the twelve-sided **Torre del Oro**, built by the Almohads in 1220 as part of the Alcázar fortifications. It was connected to another small fort across the river by a chain which had to be broken by the Castilian fleet before their conquest of the city in 1248. The tower was later used as a repository for the gold brought back to Sevilla from the Americas – hence its name. It now houses a small **naval museum** (Tues–Sat 10am–2pm, Sun 10am–1pm).

One block away is the **Hospital de la Caridad** (Mon–Sat 10am–1pm & 3–6pm; 200ptas) founded in 1676 by Don Miguel de Manara, the inspiration for Byron's Don Juan. According to the testimony of one of Don Miguel's friends, "there was no folly which he did not commit, no youthful indulgence into which he did not plunge . . . (until) what occurred to him in the street of the coffin." What occurred was that Don Miguel, returning from a reckless orgy, had a vision in which he was confronted by a funeral procession carrying his own corpse. He repented his past life, joined the Brotherhood of Charity (whose task was to bury the bodies of tramps and criminals), and later set up this hospital for the relief of the dying and destitute, for which purpose it is still used. Don Miguel commissioned a series of eleven paintings by Murillo for the chapel, six of which remain. Alongside them hang two *Triumph of Death* pictures by Valdés Leal. One, depicting a decomposing bishop being eaten by worms (beneath the scales of justice labelled *Ni más, Ni menos* – No More, No Less), is so powerfully repulsive that Murillo declared that "you have to hold your nose to look at it".

Further along, past the Plaza de Armas station, lies the **Museo de Bellas Artes** (Tues–Sun 10am–2pm; 250ptas, free with EC passport). Housed in recently modernized galleries in a beautiful former convent, this is certainly worth a visit; outstanding

---

SEVILLA'S PARISH CHURCHES

Sevilla's parish **churches** display a fascinating variety of architectural styles. Several are converted mosques with belfries built over their minarets, others range through Mudéjar and Gothic (sometimes in combination), Renaissance and Baroque. Most are kept locked except early in the morning, or in the evenings from about 7 until 10pm – a promising time for a church crawl, especially as they're regularly interspersed with bars.

For a good circuit make first towards Gothic **San Pedro**, where a marble tablet records Velázquez's baptism, and **San Marcos**, with a fine minaret tower. Nearby, in this old cobbled part of town, is the fifteenth-century **Convento de Santa Paula** (Mon–Sat 9.30am–1pm & 4.30–6.30pm), its church decorated with a vivid ceramic facade and superb *azulejos*. Further on you meet the last remaining stretch of Moorish **city walls** – remains of the Almoravid fortifications which once spanned twelve gates and 166 towers. Now there's only one gate, the **Puerta Macarena**; beside it a basilica houses the city's cult image and patroness of matadors, *La Esperanza Macarena*, a tearful Virgin seated in the midst of gaudy magnificence.

Looping down towards the river, you reach the **Monasterio de Santa Clara** (entered from c/Santa Clara no. 40) – once part of the palace of Don Fadrique, brother of Alfonso X, and with a Romanesque-Gothic tower dating from 1252. A couple of blocks away are the distinctive columns (two at the far end are Roman) of the **Alameda de Hércules**. This leads back towards the town centre, with two more churches worth a look on the way: the Renaissance chapel of the **Universidad Antigua** and Baroque **San Salvador**, the latter built on the site of Sevilla's first Friday mosque (part of whose minaret is incorporated in its tower).

are the paintings by Zurbarán of Carthusian monks at supper and El Greco's portrait of his son.

You'll find more modern art in the **Museo del Arte Contemporáneo**, c/San Tomás 5, by the Turismo (Tues–Fri 10am–7pm, Sat & Sun 10am–2pm; 250ptas) and at the privately run **Galería Juana de Aizpara**, c/Canalejos 10, Santa Cruz. Also in the Barrio, at the far end of the Jardines de Murillo, is the **Museo de Murillo**, c/Santa Teresa 8 (Tues–Fri 10am–2pm & 4–7pm, Sat 10am–2pm, Sun 10am–2pm & 4–7pm). The artist's former home, it's furnished with contemporaneous artworks, craftsmanship and furniture.

Triana

Over the river is the **Triana** *barrio*, scruffy, lively and well away from the tourist trails. This was once the heart of the city's gypsy community and, more specifically, home of the great *flamenco* dynasties of Sevilla who were kicked out by developers earlier this century and are now scattered throughout the city. The gypsies lived in extended families in tiny, immaculate communal houses called *corrales* around courtyards glutted with flowers; today only one remains intact. Triana is still, however, the starting point for the annual pilgrimage to El Rocío (at the end of May), when a myriad of painted wagons leave town, drawn by elephantine oxen. It houses, too, the city's oldest working ceramics factory, *Santa Ana*, where the tiles, many still in the traditional, geometric Arabic designs, are painted by hand. Otherwise, specific "sights" are scant, but the quarter is a good place for an evening's drinking.

Outside the city: Roman Italica

The Roman ruins and remarkable mosaics of **ITALICA** (Tues–Sat 9am–5.30pm, Sun 10am–4pm; 250ptas) lie some 9km to the north of Sevilla, just outside the village of Santiponce. There's also a well-preserved **Roman theatre** in Santiponce itself, signposted from the main road.

Italica was the birthplace of three emperors (Trajan, Hadrian and perhaps Theodosius) and was one of the earliest Roman settlements in Spain, founded in 206 BC by Scipio Africanus as a home for his veterans. It rose to considerable military importance in the second and third centuries AD, was richly endowed during the reign of Hadrian (117–138), and declined as an urban centre only under the Visigoths, who preferred Sevilla, then known as Hispalis. Eventually the city was deserted by the Moors after the river changed its course, disrupting the surrounding terrain.

Throughout the Middle Ages the ruins were used as a source of stone for Sevilla, but somehow the shell of its enormous **amphitheatre** – the third largest in the Roman world – has survived. Today it's crumbling perilously, but you can clearly detect the rows of seats, the corridors and the dens for wild beasts. Beyond, within a rambling and unkempt grid of **streets** and **villas**, about twenty **mosaics** have been uncovered. Most are complete, including excellent coloured floors with birds, Neptune and the Seasons, and several fine black-and-white geometric patterns.

Italica is easily reached from Sevilla by bus departing every half-hour from the c/ Reyes Catolicos at the end of c/Marqués de Paradas. Santiponce is not well-endowed with facilities but the restaurant opposite the Italica site entrance does reasonable *platos combinados*.

Eating, drinking and nightlife

Sevilla is packed with lively and enjoyable bars. It's a wonderfully late-night city, too, and you can eat and drink at just about any hour. In summer and during fiestas, the streets are often packed out at 2am.

Restaurants and bar meals

With few exceptions, bars and restaurants around the sights and the **Barrio Santa Cruz** are expensive. The two most promising central areas are down **towards the bullring** and north of here towards the former Plaza de Armas station. The **Plaza de Armas** area is. slightly seedier but has the cheapest *comidas* this side of the river. Wander down c/Marqués de Paradas, and up c/Canalejas and c/San Eloy, and find out what's available. Avda. Menéndez Pelayo is also a good hunting ground, with lots of cheap local cafés.

INEXPENSIVE RESTAURANTS

Alboronía, c/Alhondigia 51. Pleasant place in Macareno barrio with a cheap *menú*.

El Arenal, c/Vinuesa. Good *freiduría* (fried fish shop) in the rewarding area between the bullring and the cathedral.

Bar-Pizzeria El Artesano, Mateus Gago 11. Very reasonably priced, in the Barrio Santa Cruz and popular with young locals.

Buffet Libre, c/Mateus Gagos, about 100m into the Barrio Santa Cruz with another branch at Avda. de la Constitución 10. Cheap, self-service *platos combinados*.

Don Camillo e Peppone, c/Salado 11, near the Plaza de Cuba. Authentic Italian pizzas over in Triana.

Bar Las Gadas, c/Álvarez Quintero. An excellent place for *tapas* .

Restaurante de los Gallegos, c/Capataz Franco, a tiny alleyway off c/Martin Villa not far from the Plaza del Duque. So good and low-priced that locals queue up to eat here.

Jalea Real, c/Sor Angela de la Cruz 37 (closed Mon). Excellent vegetarian restaurant run by a friendly and enthusiastic *sevillana*.

Jerez en Sevilla, San Eloy s/n. Bar serving excellent *churros* and *chocolate*.

Kiosko de las Flores, (closed Mon). Just across the Puente de Triana (Isabel II bridge), tucked into the side of the bridge. One of Sevilla's best-loved fried fish emporia serving *tapas* in the bar and *raciones* at outdoor tables near the river – just the place on a summer night.

La Mandragora, c/Albuera 11. Sevilla's second vegetarian restaurant with a wide range of dishes and a *menú*.

Bodegón Pez Espada, c/Hernando Colón 8, near the cathedral. One of the few inexpensive places to eat in the Barrio Santa Cruz. Excellent seafood and *paella* with a buffet where you can refill your plate as many times as you like.

Bodeguita San Eloy, San Eloy s/n. Has a certain local fame for its *pringa bocadillos* – tasty, if best unspecified, grilled meats.

MODERATE TO EXPENSIVE

La Albahaca, Plaza Santa Cruz 29 (closed Sun). Charming traditional restaurant with outdoor tables in the one of the city's prettiest squares. Expensive.

Hotel Alfonso XIII, c/San Fernando 2 (☎954/222850). Swankiest place in town – worth a look at this beautiful building even if you're not eating. Expensive.

Río Grande, c/Betis 70. Over in Triana with the best views in town from its terrace on the river. Medium-priced *menú*.

Mesón San Andrés, Plaza San Andrés. Andalucian restaurant with its own *terraza*.

Restaurante San Francisco, Plaza San Francisco. A stylish place just down from the cathedral.

Bars for drinking and tapas

For straight drinking and occasional *tapas* you can be much less selective. There are **bars** all over town – a high concentration of them with barrelled sherries from nearby Jerez and Sanlúcar (the locals drink the cold, dry *fino* with their *tapas*, especially shrimp); a *tinto de verano* is the local version of *sangría* – wine with lemonade, a summer drink.

One of the liveliest places in **Santa Cruz** is *La Gitanilla* in c/Ximénez de Enciso (inexpensive drinks, but pricey *tapas*), though perhaps the best *tapas* bar in the city, with just about every imaginable snack, is *Bar Modesto* (up at the north corner of the quarter by Avda. Menéndez Pelayo – ask for it by name, it's well known). *Bar Giralda* in c/Mateus Gagos is also excellent, with a wide selection of *tapas*. *La Moneda* is a lively student bar off the Avda. de la Constitución and off that street in c/García de Vinuesa is a very good traditional bar with barrelled wine. Plaza Santa Teresa also has a couple of bars worth searching out. *Las Teresas* is a "ham gallery" with cured hams lining the beautiful, tiled walls and it serves good beer. It's also worth trying for breakfast the morning after. Try too *El Rinconcillo*, c/Gerona by the church of Santa Catalina, one of the oldest bars in the city. C/San Eloy has several good bars including the unamed ones at no. 5 (with wine straight from the barrel) and no. 9. Also *El Refugio*, c/Heulva 5, slightly west of Plaza del Salvador serves a wide variety of snacks including vegetarian *tapas*.

Up around the **Alfalfa** area near the Alameda de Hércules is another lively, young area with loud music in many of the bars: *Sopa de Ganso* and *El Lamentable* in c/Pérez Galdos, *Alcaicería* in c/Empinado and *Trama* in c/Siete Revueltas are all worth a look. Try, too, some of the places across the river in **Triana** – particularly in c/Castilla, c/Betis (*Metro* and *La Tertulia*) and in and around c/Salado.

Flamenco

Flamenco – or more accurately *sevillanas* – music and dance are offered at dozens of places in the city, some of them extremely tacky and expensive. Unless you've heard otherwise, avoid the fixed "shows" or *tablaos* (many of which are a travesty, even using recorded music). The spontaneous nature of flamenco makes it almost impossible to timetable into the two-shows-a-night cabaret demanded by impresarios. The nearest you'll get to the real thing is at *Los Gallos* in the Plaza Santa Cruz which has a professional cast. However, it is pricey (3000ptas including one drink), and you'd probably enjoy the floorshow just as much at Puerto de Triana, c/Castilla 137, just across the bridge; there's no entry charge, but your first drink (which you must have) will cost 1200ptas.

An excellent **bar** which often has spontaneous *flamenco* is *La Carbonería*, c/Levies 18, just to the northeast of the church of Santa Cruz. It used to be the coal merchant's building (hence the name) and is a large, simple and welcoming place. *La Garrocha*, c/Salado in Triana, has an interior like a combination youth hostel/milk bar, and a horrendous amplification system, but good *flamenco* when all is said and done. *Quita Pesares* in the Plaza Jerónimo de Córdoba near the church of Santa Catalina is run by a *flamenco* singer, a chaotic place where there's often impromptu music when things get lively around midnight.

Live music and clubs

For **rock music** the bars in c/Tarifa, at the end of c/Sierpes can be a good bet. So too can c/Trastamara, near Plaza de Armas, though the main places here (*Trastamara 24* at no. 24, *DOK* at no. 22) are essentially **gay clubs**. In c/Marqués de Paradas near the Puente Isabel II is the **disco-pub** *Poseidon*: free entrance, drinks not too expensive, open till 3am. Over in Triana, *Druida*, c/Rodrigo de Triana, often has live music and *RRIO* at c/Betis 67 and *B60* at no. 60, are in competition for an energetic younger crowd. Live jazz can be found at *El Sol*, c/Sol 40 (closed Aug) and *Bluemoon*, c/JA Cavestany.

Major **concerts**, whether touring British and American bands or big Spanish acts like Paco de Lucía or Miguel Ríos, usually take place in one or other of the football stadiums. Check the local press, or in term the university noticeboard, for possibilities.

Through the summer there are occasional **free concerts**, held in the Plaza San Francisco, by Plaza Nueva, and in other squares.

Listings

Airport Mainly internal flights run by *Iberia* (c/Almirante Lobo; ☎954/229639, 516111 for airport flight information). *Iberia* buses leave from the bar opposite their office, and the municipal airport-bus, #EA, departs from the Puerta de Jerez.

Banks Numerous places on the Avda. de la Constitución. *American Express* is represented by *Viajes Alhambra* (c/Coronel Segui 3, off Plaza Nueva; ☎954/212923). *El Corte Inglés* stores offer good exchange rates, low commission and long hours.

Bike Rental Motorcycles available from *Alkimoto*, c/Recaredo 28 (☎954/441115), east of the Casa de Pilatos.

Books/newspapers Reasonable selection of English books – mainly on Spain – at *Librería Pascuallazaro* (c/Sierpes 4), and in the *El Corte Inglés* department store on the Campaña. There's a good newspaper stand at the Campaña end of c/Sierpes. British newspapers and the *International Herald Tribune* are also sold in the international bookshop on c/Reyes Católicos.

Bullfights Details and tickets from the Plaza de Toros or (with commission) from the kiosks in c/Sierpes.

Buses/trains See "Arrival" for details and addresses of the various terminals. For train tickets/info go to the *RENFE* office, off the Plaza Nueva at c/Zaragoza 29, which saves the long trek out to the station for tickets or information (☎954/414111 for information, ☎954/21562 for reservations). Several of the travel agents round the cathedral and on Avda. de la Constitución sell bus tickets direct to the Algarve (daily in summer and good value).

Car rental Most agents are along the Avda. de la Constitución. One of the lowest priced operators, represented in the foyer of the *Hotel Alfonso XIII* (by the tobacco factory), is *Atesa*.

Cinema Most movies showing are listed in *El Giraldillo* the Turismo's listings magazine. "VO" indicates a screening in the original language.

Consulates UK, Plaza Nueva 8 (☎954/228875); USA, Paseo de las Delicias 7 (☎954/231884); Canada, Avda. de la Constitución 30, 2° 4 (☎954/229413).

Coto Doñana Details on the procedures for visiting this nature reserve are given under the section on the park (see "Huelva" p.246). If you want to do anything out of the ordinary the office responsible for its administration is the *Estación Biológica de Doñana* (c/Paraguay 1). To book Land Rover tours contact *Centro de Recepción del Acebuche*, Avda. de la Constitución 21 (☎954/221440).

Feminism Best contact is the *Librería Feminista* at c/Zaragoza 36.

Flea market A *rastro* takes place on Thursday mornings along the c/Feria past the Plaza Encarnación, and a bigger one on Sunday at the Alameda de Hércules.

Food market A cheap and cheerful one takes place daily in Triana – immediately on the right as you cross Puente Isabel II.

Hiking maps 1:50,000, 1:100,000 and 1:200,000 military maps from the *Servicio Geográfico del Ejército* (Plaza de España building, Sector Norte). Maps may also be purchased from *CNIG*, Edificio Sevillas, c/San Francisco Javier 9 (☎954/644256).

Hospital English-speaking doctors available at the *Hospital Universidad* (Avda. Dr. Fedriani; ☎954/378400). Dial ☎091 for emergency treatment.

Police Bag snatching is big business. If you lose something get the theft documented at the Plaza de la Gavidia station (☎954/228840), near Plaza de la Victoria. Dial ☎092 in emergency.

Post Office Avda. de la Constitución 32, by the cathedral; *Lista de Correos* (poste restante) stays open Mon–Fri 9am–8pm, Sat 9am–1pm.

Rock concerts Official agents for many concerts, in Sevilla and elsewhere in Spain, are *Viajes Meliá*, Avda. de la Constitución 30, opposite the cathedral.

Soccer Sevilla has two major teams – *Sevilla CF* (currently the better one, play at the Sánchez Pizjuan stadium) and *Real Betis* (Estadio Benito Villamarín). Match schedules are in the local or national press.

Telephones Plaza de la Gavidia 7, near Plaza Concordia (Mon–Sat 9am–1pm & 5.30–9pm).

The Sierra Morena

The longest of Spain's mountain ranges, the **Sierra Morena** extends almost the whole way across Andalucía – from Rosal on the Portuguese frontier to the dramatic pass of Despeñaperros, north of Linares. Its hill towns marked the northern boundary of the old Moorish Caliphate of Córdoba and in many ways the region still signals a break, with a shift from the climate and mentality of the south to the bleak plains and villages of Extremadura and New Castile. The range is not widely known – with its highest point a mere 1110m, it's not a dramatic sierra – and even Andalucians can have trouble placing it.

Climate, flora and fauna

The Morena's climate is mild – sunny in spring, hot but fresh in summer – but it can be very cold in the evenings and mornings. Tracks are still more common than roads, and tourism, which the government of Andalucía is keen to encourage, has so far meant little more than a handful of new signs indicating areas of special interest.

A good time **to visit** is between March and June, when the flowers, perhaps the most varied in the country, are at their best. You may get caught in the odd thunderstorm but it's usually bright and hot enough to swim in the reservoirs or splash about in the clear springs and streams, all of which are good to drink. If your way takes you along a river, you'll be entertained by armies of frogs and turtles plopping into the water as you approach, by lizards, dragonflies, bees, hares and foxes peering discreetly from their holes – and, usually, no humans present for miles round.

The locals maintain that, while the last bears disappeared only a short time ago, there are still a few wolves in remoter parts. Of more concern to anyone trekking in the Sierra Morena, however, are the **toros bravos** (fighting bulls), since you are quite likely to come across them. The black ones are the only dangerous ones; the red ones, although equipped with some daunting headgear, are said not to be aggressive. Apparently, too, a group of bulls is less to be feared than a single one, and a single one only if he directly bars your way and looks mean. The thing to do, according to expert advice, is to stay calm, and without attracting the bull's attention, go round. If you even get a whiff of a fighting bull, though, it might well be best to adopt the time-honoured technique – drop everything and run.

Transport

East–west **transport** in the sierra is very limited. Most of the bus services are radial and north–south, with Sevilla as the hub, and this leads to ridiculous situations where, for instance, to travel from Santa Olalla to Cazalla, a distance of some 53km, you must take a bus to Sevilla, 70km away, and then another up to Cazalla – a full day's journey of nearly 150km just to get from one town to the next. The best solution if you want to spend any amount of time in Morena is to organize your routes round **treks**. A bicycle too could be useful, but your own car much less so – this is not Michelin car-window-view territory. If you have a **bike**, you'll need plenty of gears, especially for the road between El Real de la Jara and El Pintado (Santa Olalla–Cazalla), while the roads round Almonaster, and between Cazalla and Constantina, are very bad for cycling.

Buses from Sevilla to the sierra leave from the main bus station. If you just want to make a quick foray into the hills, **Aracena** is probably the best target (and the most regularly served town). If you're planning on some walking it's also a good starting point: before you leave Sevilla, however, be sure to get yourself a good **map** from the military *Servicio Geográfico* in the Plaza de España – these are well-produced and cheap, and though crammed with misleading information they do point you in the right direction to get lost somewhere interesting.

Aracena – and its sierra

The highest town in the Sierra Morena – guarded to its south by a small offshoot of the range – **ARACENA** has sharp, clear air, all the more noticeable after Sevilla. Capital of the western end of the sierra with 10,000 inhabitants, it's a substantial but pretty town, rambling up the side of a hill topped by the **Iglesia del Castillo**, a Gothic-Mudéjar church built by the Knights Templar around the remains of a Moorish castle.

Although the church is certainly worth the climb, Aracena's principal attraction is the **Gruta de las Maravillas** (daily 10am–1pm & 2.30–6pm), the largest and arguably the most impressive cave in Spain. Supposedly discovered by a local boy in search of a lost pig, the cave is now illuminated and there are guided tours as soon as a dozen or so people have assembled; on Sunday there is a constant procession, but usually plenty of time to gaze and wonder. The cave is astonishingly beautiful, and funny too – the last chamber of the tour is known as the *Sala de los Culos* (Room of Buttocks), its walls and ceiling an outrageous, naturally sculpted exhibition, tinged in a pinkish orange light. Close by the cave's entrance are a couple of excellent restaurants, open lunchtime only.

There are numerous **places to stay** – the most enticing of which, at the bottom end of the scale, is the *Carmen*, c/Mesones (☎955/110764; ②), a homely place with a good restaurant. *Hostal Sierpes* (☎955/110147; ③), on the same street, is not much more expensive, but has some better rooms with bath, while the *Hotel Sierra de Aracena*, Gran Vía 21 (☎955/110775; ④), offers relative luxury. There's also a **campsite**, about 5km out on the Sevilla road, then left towards Corteconcepción; the site is about 500m along this road. It has been closed for renovation, so check with the **Turismo** (at the Gruta). If you intend to do some **walking in the sierra**, ask the Turismo for a pamphlet entitled *Senderismo* (paths) which details waymarked trails between the local villages.

Aracena is at the heart of a prestigious *jamón*-producing area, so try to sample some, and, when they're available, the delicious wild asparagus and local snails – rooted out from the roadside and in the fields in spring and summer respectively. The medium-priced *Restaurante Sierra*, Avda. Andalucía 51, specializes in *jamón* and pork dishes including a mouthwatering *solomillo* (pork loin).

Villages around Aracena

Surrounding Aracena you'll find a scattering of attractive but economically depressed villages, most of them dependent on the **jamón industry** and its curing factory at Jabugo. *Jamón serrano* (mountain ham) is a *bocadillo* standard throughout Spain and some of the best, *jamón de bellotas* (acorn-fed ham), comes from the Morena. Herds of sleek grey pigs grazing beneath the trees are a constant feature here. In October the acorns drop and the pigs, waiting patiently below, gorge themselves, become fat and are promptly whisked off to be slaughtered and then cured in the dry mountain air.

The **sierra villages** – Jabugo, Aguafría, Almonaster La Real – all make rewarding bases for walks, though all are equally ill-served by public transport. The most interesting is **ALMONASTER LA REAL**, whose castle encloses a tiny ninth-century mosque, **La Mezquita** (daily 10am–sunset), and a bullring. The village also has a couple of **places to stay**: the very hospitable *Pensión La Cruz* (☎955/143135; ③), in the centre, and *Hostal Casa Garcia* (☎955/130409; ③), by the main road. *La Cruz* also has a fine restaurant, with great *jamón* and *ensaladilla*. There are some superb paint-splashed waymarked walks northwest of the village, off the Cartegana road.

Zufre and east to Cazalla and Constantina

From Aracena a single daily **bus** – currently at 5.45pm, connecting with the bus from Sevilla – covers the 25km southeast to Zufre (for those going further afield, there's also a direct bus to Lisbon). Ten kilometres out of Aracena you come upon the **Embalse de Aracena**, one of the huge reservoirs that supply Sevilla, dammed by a massive construction across the southern end of the valley. From here a lovely but circuitous route will take you down towards Zufre along the **Rivera de Huelva**. From Zufre east there are no buses directly linking the villages en route to Cazalla.

Zufre

ZUFRE must be one of the most spectacular villages in Spain, hanging like a miniature Ronda on a high palisade at the edge of a ridge. Below the crumbling Moorish walls, the cliff falls away hundreds of feet, terraced into deep green gardens of orange trees and vegetables. Within the town the **Ayuntamiento** and **church** are both interesting examples of Mudéjar style, the latter built in the sixteenth century on the foundations of a mosque. In the basement of the *Ayuntamiento*, too, are a gloomy line of stone seats, said to have been used by the Inquisition. The focus of town, however, is the **Paseo**, a little park with rose gardens, a balcony, a bar at one end and a *casino* (bar-club) at the other. Here the villagers gather for much of the day: there is little work either in Zufre or its surrounding countryside. Finding food and drink shouldn't be a problem, but there's no official **accommodation** in Zufre; ask around, however, and there's a fair chance of finding a private room.

Santa Olalla

SANTA OLALLA DEL CALA, the next village to the east, is a walkable 16km from Zufre – a flattish route through open country with pigs and fields of wheat and barley, and then a sudden view of the Moorish **castillo** above the town. There have been several half-hearted attempts to reconstruct the castle but they haven't been helped by its adaptation in the last century as the local cemetery – the holes for coffins in the walls rather spoil the effect. Below its walls is the fifteenth-century parish church, with a fine Renaissance interior.

Coming from Zufre it's a surprise to find **hostales** in Santa Olalla, but the town is actually on the main Sevilla–Badajoz road and sees a fair amount of traffic – and regular buses to both cities. These stop outside the *Bar Primitivo*, c/Marina 3 (☎955/190052; ②), an admirable place to sleep, eat or just drink, all for a very reasonable price; its name is that of the owner, and no judgement.

Real de la Jara

Eight kilometres further east is Real de la Jara. After 4km of winding through stone-walled olive groves, the road flattens out into a grassy little valley above the **Río Calla** – a spot where the villages of Real and Olalla hold their joint *romería* at the end of April. These country *romerías* are always good to stumble upon, and if you happen on one in the Sierra Morena you should be well looked after. Proceedings start with a formal parade to the local *ermita* but they're very soon given over to feasting and dancing, the young men wobbling about on donkeys and mules in a wonderful parody of the grand *hidalgo* doings of Jerez and Sevilla, children shrieking and splashing in the river, and everyone dancing *sevillanas* to scratchy cassettes.

REAL DE LA JARA is in much the same mould as Santa Olalla: two Moorish *castillos* (both in ruins), an over-priced and eccentrically run *casa de huéspedes* at c/Real 66 (②), and a very welcome public swimming pool. Cazalla de la Sierra, the next village, is some 45km along a mountainous route which sees few cars. The one relief, 30km on, is the **Embalse del Pintado**, another huge reservoir.

Cazalla and the Central Sierra

Another regional sierra "capital", **CAZALLA DE LA SIERRA** seems quite a metropolis. Not only does it have four **fondas** (the best is in Plaza Iglesia, the rest in the main street, c/Llana) but there's a hotel (*Posada del Moro*; ☎954/884326; ⑤), numerous bars and even a pub – pronounced "pa" in Andaluz – where the locals go to drink cocktails and listen to jazz and rock music. If this is all too much of a shock, a more traditional bar and restaurant, but still lively, is the *Boleras* in Plaza Manuel Nosea – right next to the *Guardia Civil*, who are themselves ensconced in a beautiful former nunnery.

The place to make for, however, is **La Plazuela**, where you'll find the local *casino*. This is essentially a place to drink and relax – quieter and more comfortable than most of the bars – and serves as a kind of club, with locals paying a nominal monthly membership charge. Most towns of Cazalla's size have one, and tourists and visitors are always welcome to use the facilities free of charge – worth doing since the membership rule means everybody drinks at reduced prices.

The main sight is the church of **Nuestra Señora de la Consolación** at the southern end of town, an outstanding example of Andalucian architecture which was begun in the fourteenth century, continued with some nice Renaissance touches and finally completed in the eighteenth century.

Within easy wandering distance of Cazalla are some fine spots: a walk of just 5km will take you east to the **Ermita del Monte**, a little eighteenth-century church on a wooded hill above the Rivera de Huesna.

Cazalla is well-served by public transport. **Buses** run to the Estación de Cazalla y Constantina, twenty minutes to the east, at 6.45am or 1pm. From here there are three or four **trains** a day northwest to Zafra and Extremadura, and a similar number follow the river down towards El Pedroso and ultimately Sevilla. Daily buses also connect Cazalla with Sevilla. If you're making for El Pedroso, though, you might consider walking from the station – a lovely route, with great river swimming and a fabulous variety of valley flora and fauna; it takes about five hours.

El Pedroso and Constantina

EL PEDROSO, a pretty little town with a notable Mudéjar church, is somewhat less depressed than most towns in the sierra due to the local factory, the *fábrica*, one stop up on the train line, which seems to employ most of the locals. Accommodation is limited and basic; the woman who runs the station *cantina* supplies **rooms**. Across the road is an excellent **tapas bar**, the *Serranía*, which serves up local specialities such as venison, hare, pheasant and partridge.

Eighteen kilometres further to the east – and perhaps as good a place as any to cut back to Sevilla if you're not counting on trekking the whole length of the range – lies **CONSTANTINA**, a lively and beautiful mountain town with a population of almost 15,000. High above the town is the **Castillo de la Armada**, particularly impressive and surrounded by shady gardens descending in terraces to the old quarters. At the base is the parish **church**, once again with a Mudéjar tower, Moorish influence having died hard in these parts.

There are two **fondas** in the main street, c/Mesones, and one dubious *comidas y camas* place in the Alameda; try the *fondas*. There's also a summer **youth hostel**, c/ Cuesta Blanca. Travelling to Sevilla, there are two buses a day, at 6.45am & 3pm.

The Costa de la Luz

Stumbling on the villages along the **Costa de la Luz**, between Algeciras and Cádiz, is like entering a new land after the dreadfulness of the Costa del Sol. The journey west from Algeciras seems in itself a relief, the road climbing almost immediately into rolling green hills, offering fantastic views down to Gibraltar and across the straits to the just-discernible white houses and tapering mosques of Moroccan villages. Beyond, the Rif Mountains hover mysteriously in the background and on a clear day, as you approach Tarifa, you can distinguish Tangier on the edge of its crescent-shaped bay.

Tarifa

TARIFA, spreading out beyond its Moorish walls, was until the mid-1980s a quiet village, known in Spain, if at all, for its abnormally high suicide rate – a result of the unremitting winds that blow across the town and its environs. Today it's a prosperous, popular and at times very crowded, resort, following its discovery as Europe's prime **windsurfing** spot. There are equipment rental shops along the length of the main street, and in peak season crowds of windsurfers pack out every available bar and *hostal*. Even in winter, there are windsurfers to be seen – drawn by regular competitions held year-round. Development is fast as a result of this new-found popularity, but for the time being it remains a fairly attractive place.

If windsurfing is not your motive, there can still be an appeal in wandering the crumbling ramparts, gazing out to sea or down into the network of lanes that surround the fifteenth-century, Baroque-fronted church of **San Mateo**. The **castle** was the site of many a struggle for this strategic foothold into Spain. It is named after Guzmán el Bueno (the Good), Tarifa's infamous commander during the Moorish siege of 1292, who earned his tag for a superlative piece of tragic drama. Guzmán's nine-year-old son had been taken hostage by a Spanish traitor and surrender of the garrison was demanded as the price of the boy's life. Choosing "honour without a son, to a son with dishonour", Guzmán threw down his own dagger for the execution. The story – a famous piece of heroic resistance in Spain – had echoes in the Civil War siege of the Alcázar at Toledo, when the Nationalist commander refused similar threats, an echo much exploited for propaganda purposes.

Practicalities

Tarifa has plenty of **places to stay**, though finding a bed in summer can be a struggle. The *Hostal Tarik* in the western part of town, at c/San Sebastián 32–36 (☎956/685240; ④), is very clean and has helpful owners. In the same area are more *hostales* and an attractive hotel with sea views, *La Mirada* (☎956/684427; ④). Built into the west wall of the old quarter is an excellent *fonda-restaurante* called the *Villanueva* (②). The newly remodelled and excellent *Hostal La Calzada*, c/Justina Pertiñes 7 (☎956/680366; ④), by San Mateo church, and the charming *Pensión Correo*, c/Coronel Móscardo 8 (☎956/680206; ②), located in the old post office, just south of the cathedral entrance are both good places. Finally, there are two reasonable *casa de huéspedes*: *Casa Concha*, c/Rosendo (②), around the corner from *La Calzada*, and *Facundo* (②), 200m out on the main road to Cádiz. Just off the highway on c/Amador de los Ríos, *Hostal las Fuserías* (③) is better than it looks, with a laundry area and a shady courtyard, and preferable to the overpriced *Hostería Tarifa* (☎956/684076; ④) on the same street.

You'll find the **bus station**, a supermarket, a **laundry**, adjacent fried fish and *churro* stalls and many of the larger hotels on the main Cádiz–Algeciras road.

For **meals**, the *Chan*, *Villanueva* and *Agobio*, all within a few hundred metres of each other just outside the western wall, have cheap *menús*; most pleasant for lunch is the *Bar Alameda* on the Alameda, which does reasonable *platos combinados*. Of the dozen other **bars**, **pubs** and **discos**, the German-run *Bistro Point* is a windsurfers' hangout and a good place for finding long-term accommodation as well as secondhand windsurfing gear. In the centre and down the side of San Mateo's church, *Mesón El Cartijo*, c/General Copons, is a bit more upmarket with a good value *menú*.

Tarifa offers the tempting opportunity of a quick approach **to Morocco**, with Tangier feasible as a day trip on the seasonal hydrofoil. However, this is presently suspended, so check with the **Turismo** (Mon–Fri 11am–1pm & 6–8pm), located in a kiosk at the junction of Batalla del Salado and Avda. Andalucía, or with local travel agents. Normally it goes at 9.30am, returning at 4.30 or 6pm (Spanish time – which is 1hr ahead of Moroccan). The trip takes just half an hour; tickets are available from the embarkation office on the quay or in advance from travel agents. If you're planning a day trip, it's wise to book a few days ahead, as tour companies often take over the whole boat. This crossing is a lot more expensive than going from Algeciras, but might be a better bet if the latter is chock-a-block in summer or when Moroccans are returning home for the two major Islamic festivals (which rotate between January, February and March). There's also a car ferry from Tarifa to Tangier (Mon–Sat 10am, returning at 3pm).

Tarifa Beach

Heading northwest from Tarifa, you find the most spectacular **beaches** along the whole Costa de la Luz – wide stretches of yellow or silvery-white sand, washed by some magical rollers. The same winds – the eastern *Levantera* and western *Poniente* – that have created such perfect conditions for windsurfing can, however, be a problem for more casual enjoyment, sandblasting those attempting to relax on towels or mats and whipping the water into whitecaps.

The beaches lie immediately west of the town. They get better as you move past the tidal flats and the mosquito-ridden estuary – until the dunes start, and the first camper vans lurk among the bushes. At **TARIFA BEACH**, a little bay 9km from town, there are restaurants, campsites and a *hostal* at the base of a tree-tufted bluff. The German-owned windsurfing school here acts as the centre for the sport. For more seclusion head for one of the numerous **beach-campsites** on either side, signposted from the main road or accessible by walking along the coast. All of these – the main ones are *Río Jara* (☎956/643570), *Tarifa* (☎956/684778), *Torre de la Peña* (☎956/684903) and *Paloma* (☎956/684203) – are well-equipped and inexpensive.

The coast west of Tarifa

Around the coast from Paloma are extensive ruins of the Roman town of **BOLONIA**, or *Baelo Claudia*, where you can make out the remains of three temples and a theatre, as well as numerous houses (guided tours at 10am, 11am, noon, 1.15pm, 4pm, 5pm & 6.15pm; 100ptas, free with EC passport). The site lies sheltered by the cape known as Punta Camarinal and can be reached down a small side road which turns off the main Cádiz road 15km after Tarifa. There's also a fine beach here with bars and eating places. Alternatively it's a good walk along the coast from either Paloma or, from the west, Zahara de los Atunes (3–4hr).

ZAHARA, a small fishing village beginning to show signs of development, has a fabulous eight-kilometre-long beach There's a smallish plush hotel and three *hostales*, all fairly expensive and usually full until at least the end of September; *Nicolás*, by the lagoon, is probably the best value (☎956/431174; ④). Camping is also feasible, but don't forget the insect repellent. **BARBATE DE FRANCO**, 15km along the coast and linked by daily bus (except Sun), is less enticing – a sizeable town dominated by its

---

TUNA FISHING

The catch of the bluefin tuna is a ritual which has gone on along the Costa de la Luz for a thousand years and, today, still employs many of the age-old methods. The bluefin is the largest of the tuna family weighing in at around 200 kilos each, and the season lasts from April to June as the fish migrate south towards the Mediterranean, and from early July to mid-August when they return, to be herded and caught by huge nets. The biggest market is Japan, where tuna is eaten raw as sushi. Tuna numbers, however, are declining and the season shortening – probably the result of overfishing – much to the concern of the people of Barbate, Conil de la Frontera and Zahara de los Atunes, for whom the catch represents an important source of income.

harbour and tuna canning industry. **LOS CAÑOS DE MECA**, a very small village connected to Barbate by a tiny road that loops round by the sea, has a long, beautiful beach, and encroaching development. Just west, towards Cape Trafalgar, is a **campsite**, *Caños de Meca* (☎956/450405).

Vejer de la Frontera

While you're on the Costa de la Luz, be sure to take time to visit **VEJER DE LA FRONTERA**, a classically white, Moorish-looking hill town set in a cleft between great protective hills that rear high above the road from Tarifa to Cádiz. If you arrive by bus, it's likely to drop you at two *hostal-restaurantes* well below the town; *La Barca de Vejer* (☎956/450369; ③) does superb *bocadillos de lomo*. The road winds up for another 4km but just by one of the bus-stop cafés there's a donkey path that takes only about twenty minutes. This is a perfect approach – for the drama of Vejer is in its isolation and its position, which gradually unfold before you. If you don't fancy the walk, though, taxis are usually available.

Until the last decade, the women of Vejer wore long, dark cloaks that veiled their faces like nuns' habits; this custom seems now to be virtually extinct, but the town has a remoteness and Moorish feel as explicit as anywhere in Spain. There's a castle and a church of curiously mixed styles (mainly Gothic and Mudéjar) but the main fascination lies in exploring the brilliant white and labyrinthine alleyways, wandering past iron-grilled windows, balconies and patios, and slipping into a succession of bars. At one of these, *Peña Flamenca Aguilar de Vejer*, you can sample *manzanilla* from the barrel and take in weekend *flamenco* performances. Try, too, the *Bar Chirino* on Plaza España, which contains a photographic history of the town. The only **accommodation** in town is at the slightly pricey but excellent *Hostal la Janda* (☎956/450142; ③) or the delightful, upmarket *Hotel Convento San Francisco* (☎956/643570; ⑤) – both rather hidden away, so ask for directions.

Conil

Back on the coast, a dozen or so kilometres on, **CONIL** is an increasingly popular resort. Outside July and August, though, it's still a good place to relax, and in mid-season the only real drawback is trying to find a room. Conil town, once a poor fishing village, now seems entirely modern as you look back from the beach, though when you're actually in the streets you find many older buildings too. The majority of the tourists are Spanish (with a lesser number of Germans), so there's an enjoyable atmosphere, and if you are here in mid-season, a very lively nightlife.

The **beach**, Conil's *raison d'être*, is a wide bay of brilliant yellow stretching for miles to either side of town and lapped by an amazingly, not to say disarmingly, gentle Atlantic – you have to walk halfway to Panama before it reaches waist height. The area immediately in front of town is the family beach: up to the northwest you can walk to some more sheltered coves; across the river to the southeast is a topless and nudist area. Walking along the coast in this direction – back towards Barbate – the beach is virtually unbroken until it reaches the cape, the familiar-sounding **Trafalgar**, off which Lord Nelson achieved victory and met his death on October 21, 1805. If the winds are blowing, this is one of the most sheltered beaches in the area. It can be reached by road, save for the last 400 metres across the sands to the rock.

Most **buses** use the *Transportes Comes* station: walk towards the sea and you'll find yourself in the centre of town. There's a very helpful **Turismo** at Alameda Cristina 7. **Accommodation** needs are served by numerous hotels and hostales. *Mesón de las Quince Letras*, Plaza de España 6 (☎956/441053; ②), is one of the most reasonable. Conil also has private rooms for rent. The easiest way to find one of these is to go to the first "supermarket" on the right-hand side of the road to Playa Fontanilla (the road opposite the *Rinkon Way* open-air disco), where they have a complete list; there are good ones at c/Velásquez 1. Nearby **campsites** include *Fuente del Gallo* in the nearby *urbanización*, Fuente del Gallo (☎956/440137; March–Oct), a three-kilometre walk despite all signs to the contrary.

Conil has lots of good seafood **restaurants** along the front; try the *ortiguillas* – deep-fried sea anemones – which you only see in the Cádiz area. For a really excellent, modest-priced meal, search out the *Bar-Restaurante Peña Federata de Caza*, on the road uphill towards Barbate.

Towards Cádiz

Beyond Conil's beaches there's little else on the coast to attract you before you reach Cádiz. **Chiclana De La Frontera** is nothing special, but it's a useful road junction with sporadic buses to Medina Sidonia (see p.213). Beyond Chiclana you emerge into a weird landscape of marshes, dotted with drying salt pyramids, in the midst of which lies the town of **San Fernando** – once an elegant place (and still so at its centre) but quickly being swallowed up by industrial suburbs. These extend until you reach the long causeway that leads to Cádiz, an unromantic approach to what is one of the most extraordinarily sited and moody towns of the south.

Cádiz

CÁDIZ is among the oldest settlements in Spain, founded about 1100 BC by the Phoenicians and one of the country's principal ports ever since. Its greatest period, however, and the era from which the central part of town takes most of its present appearance, was the eighteenth century. Then, with the silting up of the river to Sevilla, the port enjoyed a virtual monopoly on the Spanish-American trade in gold and silver, and on its proceeds were built the cathedral – itself golden-domed (in colour at least) and almost Oriental when seen from the sea – the public halls and offices, and the smaller churches.

Inner Cádiz, built on a peninsula-island, remains much as it must have looked in those days, with its grand open squares, sailors' alleyways and high, turreted houses. Literally crumbling from the effect of the sea air on its soft limestone, it has a tremendous atmosphere – slightly seedy, definitely in decline, but still full of mystique.

Unlike most other ports of its size, Cádiz seems immediately relaxed, easy-going, and not at all threatening, even at night. Perhaps this is due to its reassuring shape and compactness, the presence of the sea making it impossible to get lost for more than a few blocks. But it probably owes this tone as much to the town's tradition of liberalism and tolerance – one maintained all through the years of Franco's dictatorship even though this was one of the first towns to fall to his forces, and was the port through which the Nationalist armies launched their invasion. In particular Cádiz has always accepted its substantial gay community, who are much in evidence at the city's brilliant *carnaval* celebrations.

The town

Cádiz is more interesting in its general ambience – its blind alleys, cafés and back-streets – than for any particular buildings. As you wander, you'll find the **Museo de Bellas Artes**, at Plaza de Mina 5 (Tues–Sun 9.30am–2pm; 250ptas, free with EC passport), just across from the **Turismo**. This contains an impressive local archaeological display and a quite exceptional series of saints painted by **Zurbarán**, brought here from the Carthusian monastery at Jerez and one of only three such sets in the country (the others are at Sevilla and Guadalupe) preserved intact, or nearly so. With their sharply defined shadows and intense, introspective air, Zurbarán's saints are at once powerful and very Spanish – even the English figures such as Hugh of Lincoln, or the Carthusian John Houghton, martyred by Henry VIII when he refused to accept him as head of the English Church. Perhaps this is not surprising, for the artist spent much of his life travelling round the Carthusian monasteries of Spain and many of his saints are in fact portraits of the monks whom he met.

The **sea fortifications** and waterside **alamedas** are very striking and give direction to walks around the town. Even if you don't normally go for High Baroque it's hard to resist the attraction of the huge eighteenth-century **Catedral Nueva** (Mon–Sat 10am– 1pm; 250ptas including museum), decorated entirely in stone, with no gold or white in sight, and absolutely perfect proportions. In the crypt is buried Manuel de Falla, the great *gaditano* composer of such Andalucía-inspired works as *Nights in the Gardens of Spain* and *El Amor Brujo*.

Over on the seaward side of the mammoth complex, the "Old" Cathedral, **Santa Cruz**, is also worth a look, its interior liberally studded with coin-in-the-slot votive candles. And, lastly, there are two churches of note for the paintings they contain. Foremost of these is the chapel of the **Hospital de Mujeres** (daily 9am–6pm) – ask the porter for admission – which has a brilliant El Greco of *St Francis in Ecstasy*. The other, an oval, eighteenth-century chapel, **Santa Cueva** (Mon–Sat 10am–1pm; 50ptas), entered by ringing at c/San Francisco 11, one block north, has three frescoes on Eucharistic themes by Goya.

Practicalities

Arriving by **train** you'll find yourself on the periphery of the old town, close to the Plaza de San Juan de Dios, busiest of the many squares. By **bus** you'll be a few blocks further north, along the water – either at the *Los Amarillos* terminal (which serves Rota, Chipiona and the resorts west of Cádiz) or just beyond in the Plaza de Independencia at the *Estación de Comes* (used by buses from Sevilla, Tarifa and most other destinations toward Algeciras). *Los Amarillos* also runs a twice-daily service through Arcos to Ubrique, with a connection there to Ronda – by far the best route.

Radiating around the **Plaza de San Juan de Dios** is a dense network of alleyways crammed with **hostales**, **fondas** and straightforward dosshouses or brothels. *Hostal La Isleña* (☎956/287064; ②), is a reasonable place to stay, as is *La Aurora* at c/ Sopranis 8 (☎956/253352; ②). In general, though, the more salubrious *pensiones* and *hostales* are to be found a couple of blocks away, towards the cathedral or **Plaza de Candelaria**. Near the latter, try *Hostal Barcelona*, c/Montañes 10 ☎956/213949; ③), basic despite credit card stickers, but clean and friendly. One block over, *Pensión Nacional*, c/Feduchy 20; ②) is another good possibility. Mid-priced *hostales* here seem no better than the budget ones – for more luxurious alternatives try the *Hotel Francia y París*, Plaza San Francisco 2 (☎956/222348; ⑤), which is quiet and central, or the modern *Hotel Atlántico*, Parque Genovés 9 (☎956/226905; ⑥), a *parador* with Atlantic views and an outdoor pool.

Fried fish is excellent everywhere, especially from stands around the beach, while in the **bars**, *tortilla de camarones* (shrimp omelette), is a superb local speciality. The Plaza de San Juan de Dios, protruding across the neck of the peninsula from the port and the first long stretch of Cádiz's naval dockyards, has several cafés and inexpensive **restaurants**. *La Caleta*, whose interior is built like the bow of a ship, serves wonderful *champiñones al Jerez* (mushrooms in sherry), *chipirones en su tinta* (squid in ink) and other hearty *raciones*; it also has a *comedor* with excellent value *menús*. In the square's top right-hand corner, *El 9*, *Pasaje Andaluz* and *La Económica* are also good. Also try the tiny Plaza Tío de la Tiza, in the old quarter near the beach, which has outdoor tables in summer, or the more upmarket *El Faro*, c/San Felix 15, nearby, one of the best fish restaurants in Andalucía.

△ Punta de San Felipe

Bahía de Cádiz

Estación Marítima
Plaza de Filipinas
Plaza de las Tres Carabelas
Autobuses Comes S.A.
Plaza de la Hispanidad
Plaza de Argüelles
Plaza de España
Palacio de la Diputación Provincial
Museo de Belles Artes y Arqueológico
Iglesia y claustro de San Francisco
Santa Cueva
Baluarte de Candelaria
Alameda de Apodaca
Plaza de San Francisco
Plaza de Mina
Iglesia del Carmen
Plaza de San Antonio
Ancha
Pza. Gral. Var (del Palilleri)
Iglesia de San Antonio
Torre Tavira
Plaza de M. Núñez (del Mentidero)
Plaza de Viudas
Museo Histórico Municipal
Iglesia oratorio de San Felipe Neri
Parque Genovés
Plaza Manuel de Falla
Hospital de las Mujeres
Plaza de la Cruz Verde
Gran Teatro Falla
Plaza del Tío de la Tiza
Parroquia de la Palma
BARRIO DE LA VIÑA
Baluarte del Bonete
Castillo de Santa Catalina
Balneario de la Palma y del Real
Playa de la Caleta

CÁDIZ

▽ Castillo de San Sebastián

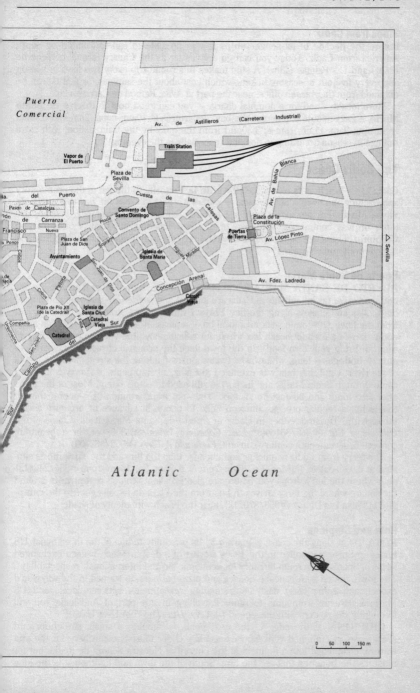

Puerto Comercial

Av. de Astilleros (Carretera Industrial)

Train Station

Vapor de El Puerto

Plaza de Sevilla

a. del Puerto

Paseo de Canalejas

Cuesta de las Caleias

ón de Carranza

Nueva

Francisco

a Ponce

Plaza de San Juan de Dios

Ayuntamiento

Av. de Bahía Blanca

Av. López Pinto

Plaza de la Constitución

Puertas de Tierra

Convento de Santo Domingo

Plocia

Corralón

Iglesia de Santa María

S. Juan de Dios

Higuera Mirador

△ Sevilla

de acia

Cocos

Pelota

Concepción Arenal

Av. Fdez. Ladreda

Plaza de Pío XII (de la Catedral)

Iglesia de Santa Cruz

Catedral Vieja

Compañía

San Juan

F. Fola

Sur

Catedral

Sopranis

del

Campo

Sur

Cárcel Vieja

Atlantic Ocean

0   50   100   150 m

Ships from Cádiz

Before the decline of passenger **ships** it was possible to sail to London or South America from Cádiz. Today you can go only as far as the Canary Islands of Tenerife (36hr) and Las Palmas (43hr). A ship makes this round trip every two days in season and every five out of season; tickets, which cost about the same as for flights, can be obtained from the *Ancona* office, near the port at Avda. Ramón de Carranza 26.

More locally – and for a nominal charge – you can get a boat to **Puerto de Santa María**, a forty-minute trip across the bay; departures at 10am, noon, 2pm and 6.30pm (returning 9am, 11am, 1pm & 3.30pm) from the quay by the train station, with extra sailings in season according to demand (especially in the evening).

The Cádiz Coast

Cádiz has a beach of its own – the **Playa de la Victoria**, to the left of the promontory approaching the town – but for clearer waters it's best to cross the bay to **Puerto de Santa María**. Further along the coast towards Sanlúcar de Barremeda, beaches are more or less continuous, with two of the best flanking the resorts of **Rota** and **Chipiona**. These are both popular weekend retreats from Cádiz, and during July and August pretty much packed.

Puerto de Santa María

PUERTO DE SANTA MARÍA is the obvious choice, a traditional family resort for both *gaditanos* (as inhabitants of Cádiz are known) and *sevillanos* – many of whom have built villas and chalets along the fine **Playa Puntillo**. This strand is a little way out from the town (10–15min walk or a local bus), a pleasant place to while away an afternoon; there's a friendly beach bar where for ridiculously little you can nurse a litre of sangría (bring your own food). In the town itself the principal attraction is a series of **sherry bodegas** – long, whitewashed warehouses flanking the streets and the banks of the river. Until the train was extended to Cádiz, all shipments of sherry from Jerez came through Santa María, and its port is still used to some extent. Most of the firms offer free tours and tastings to visitors (Tues–Sat from around 10am–noon), though this is not a regular process and you need to phone in advance or organize a visit through the Turismo, either in Cádiz or Puerto de Santa María itself. Choose from *Osborne y Cía* (☎956/861600), *Luis Caballero* (☎956/861300) or, in a beautiful, converted, seventeenth-century convent, *Fernando A Terry* (☎956/862700).

The **ferry** from Cádiz is quicker and cheaper than the bus and the **Turismo** is situated at c/Guadalete 1 (Mon–Fri 10am–2pm & 6–8pm, Sat 10am–1pm; ☎956/542413) near where the ferry drops you. There are also excellent seafood **restaurants** around the square where the ferry arrives. A bus from the Plaza de España goes to the **campsite** at Playa Las Dunas (☎956/870112), near the beach with plenty of shade.

Rota and Chipiona

ROTA, 16km along the coast, is marred by its proximity to one of the three major **US bases** in Spain – installed in the 1950s as part of a deal in which Franco exchanged strips of Spanish sovereign territory for economic aid and international "respectability". The town, dotted with pancake houses and pizza parlours, is warped in the way you'd expect, and some fairly nasty long-standing resentments between locals and US Marines flare up from time to time. Travelling in this part of Andalucía you will frequently see posters with the legend *USA Nos Usa* (The USA Uses Us).

CHIPIONA, at the edge of the next point, is simpler: a small, straightforward seaside resort crammed with family *pensiones*. Older tourists come here for the **spa waters**, channelled into a fountain at the church of Nuestra Señora de Regla, but for most it's the **beaches** that are the lure. South of the town and lighthouse is the long

Playa de Regla, where, outside July and August, it's easy enough to leave the crowds behind; northeast, towards Sanlúcar, are sand bars and rocks. If you're planning on staying in the town, the **hostales** along the beach are the most attractive; in mid-season you'll need help getting a room from the women who meet new arrivals at the bus station. The **campsite**, *Pinar de Chipiona*, (☎956/372321), is 3km out of town towards Rota.

Sanlúcar de Barrameda
Like Puerto Santa María, **SANLÚCAR DE BARRAMEDA** also has its sherry connections. Set at the mouth of the Guadalquivir, it's the main depot for **Manzanilla** wine, a pale, dry variety much in evidence in the bars, which you can also sample during visits to the town's **bodegas**: *Bodega Hijos de A. Pérez Mejía*, at c/Farina 56 (Tues–Sat 11am–1pm), and *Bodega Antonio Barbadillo*, c/Eguilaz 11 (Mon–Fri 7.30am–3pm; ☎956/365103. Sanlúcar is also the setting for some exciting **horse races** along the beach in the last two weeks of August, the best time to be here.

There's not a great deal to see, although the attractive old quarter in the upper town or *barrio alto* is worth taking time to explore. The port was the scene of a number of important maritime exploits: Columbus sailed from here on his third voyage; Magellan set out to circumnavigate the globe; and it was from Sanlúcar that Pizarro embarked to conquer Peru. The few buildings of interest – the **ducal palaces** of Montpensier and Medina Sidonia (the former with wild Gothic decoration), and parts of a Moorish castle – are perched above the main part of town on the Cuesta de Belén.

The best thing about Sanlúcar is its shell-encrusted **river beach** and warm waters, a couple of kilometres' walk from the town centre and usually quite deserted. This is flanked, on the opposite shore, by the beginnings of the **Coto Doñana National Park** (see below), whose vast marshy expanses (strictly regulated access) signal the end of the coast road to the west. Visits to the park are now possible with a new boat cruise which, while it doesn't allow for serious exploration, is nevertheless a wonderful introduction to this remarkable area. The trip lasts approximately four hours and allows two short guided walks inside the park. The *Real Fernando Sanlúcar* leaves daily from the Bajo de Guia quay (summer 8.30am & 4.30pm, winter 10am; 2000ptas, 1000ptas children and senior citizens; ☎956/363813).

Accommodation isn't easy to find in summer, but try *Pensión Blanca Paloma*, Plaza San Roque 9 (☎956/363644; ③), with a magnificent position or otherwise seek assistance from the **Turismo** (Mon–Fri 10am–2pm & 6–8pm, Sat 10am–1pm), Calzada del Ejército, on the road up to the *barrio alto*.

Jerez de la Frontera

JEREZ DE LA FRONTERA, inland towards Sevilla, is the home and heartland of sherry (itself an English corruption of the town's Moorish name – *Xerez*) and also, less known but equally important, of Spanish brandy. It seems a tempting place to stop, arrayed as it is round the scores of wine *bodegas*. But you're unlikely to want to make more than a quick visit (and tasting) between buses; the town itself is hardly distinctive unless you happen to arrive during one of the two big **festivals** – the May Horse Fair (perhaps the most refined of the Andalucian *ferias*), or the celebration of the vintage towards the end of September.

The **tours of the sherry and brandy processes**, however, can be interesting – almost as much as the sampling that follows – and provided you don't arrive in August when much of the industry closes down, there are a great many firms and *bodegas* to choose from. The most central, next to the large but derelict ruins of a Moorish *alcázar*, is **González Byass** (open all year). Tours are given here, as with most other firms, from Monday to Saturday, 9am to 1pm, and are conducted in English – very much the second language in Jerez's sherry fraternities. Many of the firms were founded by British Catholic refugees, barred from careers at home by the sixteenth-century Supremacy Act, and even now they form a kind of Anglo-Andalucian aristocracy (on display, most conspicuously, at the Horse Fair). The *González* cellars – the *soleras* – are perhaps the oldest in Jerez, and though it's no longer used, preserve an old circular chamber designed by Eiffel (of the tower fame).

If you feel you need comparisons, most of the other *bodegas* are on the outskirts of town; pick up a **plan** of them and the town from any travel agent in the centre or from **Turismo** (Mon–Fri 8am–3pm & 5.30–8pm, Sat 10am–1.30pm; ☎956/331159) at Alameda Cristina 7. For **accommodation**, the best budget beds are at *Pensión Los Amarillos*, c/Melina 39 (②), which you reach by turning left from the bus station and walking three blocks; or try *Hotel Trujillo*, c/Medina 36 (☎956/342438; ③) or *Las Palomas*, c/Higueras, off c/Medina (☎956/343773; ④), for rather more class. *Hostal Torres*, c/Arcos 29 (☎956/323400; ③), north of the bus station, is friendly and has two charming patios.

The **train** and the **bus stations** are more or less next door to each other, eight blocks east of the *González bodega* and the central Plaza de los Reyes Católicos. The most attractive of the town's buildings, including an imposing Gothic-Renaissance **Catedral** and a substantial eleventh-century Moorish **Alcázar** (10.30am–2pm & 5–7pm; August, 10.30am–2pm) are within a couple of minutes' walk of the central Plaza del Arenal.

Huelva Province

The **province of Huelva** stretches between Sevilla and Portugal, but aside from its section of the Sierra Morena (see p.233) it's a pretty dull part of Andalucía, laced with large areas of swamp – the *marismas* – and notorious for mosquitoes. This dismal habitat is, however, particularly suited to a great variety of wildlife, especially birds, and over 60,000 acres of the delta of the Río Guadalquivir (the largest roadless area in western Europe) have been fenced off to form the **national park of the Coto Doñana**. Here, amid sand dunes, pine woods, marshes and freshwater lagoons, live scores of flamingos, along with rare birds of prey, lynx, mongooses and a startling variety of migratory birds.

Coto Doñana National Park

The seasonal pattern of its delta waters, which flood in winter and then drop in the spring, leaving rich deposits of silt, raised sandbanks and islands, give **Coto Doñana** its special interest. Conditions are perfect in winter for ducks and geese, but spring is more exciting: the exposed mud draws hundreds of flocks of breeding birds. In the marshes and amid the cork oak forests behind you've a good chance of seeing squacco herons, black-winged stilt, whiskered tern, pratincole and sand grouse, as well as flamingos, egrets and vultures. There are, too, occasional sightings of the Spanish imperial eagle, now reduced to fourteen breeding pairs. In late summer and early autumn, the *marismas* dry out and then support far less bird life. The park is also home to some 25 pairs of lynx.

Inevitably, it seems, the park is under threat from development. Even at current levels the drain on the water supply is severe, and made worse by pollution of the Guadalquivir by pesticides and Sevilla's industry. Several lynx have also been killed by traffic on the road to Matalascañas. More serious are the proposals for a huge new tourist centre to be known as the **Costa Doñana**, on the very fringes of the park.

Pressure by national and international environmental bodies has resulted in this project being shelved, but the threat remains, much of it stemming from local people who see much-needed jobs in the venture. In the ensuing row large demonstrations were organized by both sides, and there have been mysterious outbreaks of vandalism against park property.

Visiting the park

To visit the Doñana involves a certain amount of frustration. At present it's only open to brief, organized **tours** (spring & summer daily 8.30am & 5pm; 2400ptas a seat) by Land Rover – four hours at a time along one of five charted, seventy-kilometre routes. The starting point for these, and the only place to book them (essential), is at the *Centro de Recepción del Acebuche* (☎959/245092 or 430432; English spoken), 5km north of Matalascañas towards El Rocío and Almonte. The tours are quite tourist-oriented, and point out only spectacular species like flamingos, imperial eagles, deer and wild boar. If you're a serious ornithologist and are equally interested in variations on little brown birds, the tour isn't for you. Instead, enquire at the *Centro* – or at the Sevilla office at Avda. de la Constitución 21 (☎954/221440) – about the adjacent Doñana **hides** and the new hides that have been opened at La Rocina and El Acebron, 9km to the north. You'll need to bring your own binoculars. The natural history exhibition at the *Centro* is in itself worthy of a visit.

Matalascañas

Birds and other wildlife apart, the settlement of **MATALASCAÑAS** inside the park is unlikely to excite; with five large hotel complexes and a concrete shopping centre, it looks like it's only recently been built (as it has), and it would be difficult to imagine a more complete lack of character. In summer, too, the few **hostal rooms** are generally booked solid and unless you plan in advance (any Sevilla travel agent will try to reserve you a room) you'll probably end up **camping** – either unofficially at the resort itself, or at the vast *Camping Rocío Playa* (☎959/430238), down the road towards Huelva. This site is a little inconvenient without your own transport if you're planning to take regular trips into the Doñana. If you just want a **beach**, though, it's not a bad option. Playa Doñana and its continuation Playa Mazagón (with another campsite, *Doñana Playa*; ☎959/376281) stretch the whole distance to Huelva, and with hardly another foreign tourist in sight. This route is covered at present by just one daily bus.

El Rocío

The other and more usual approach to Matalascañas is via Almonte, a small, unmemorable town, and **EL ROCÍO**, a tiny village of white cottages and a church stockade where perhaps the most famous pilgrimage-fair of the south takes place annually at Pentecost. This, the **Romería del Rocío**, is an extraordinary spectacle, with whole village communities and local "brotherhoods" from Huelva, Sevilla and even Málaga converging on horseback and in lavishly decorated ox carts. Throughout the procession, which climaxes on the Saturday evening, there is dancing and partying, while by the time the carts arrive at El Rocío they've been joined by dozens of busloads of pilgrims. What they have all come for – apart from the fair itself – is the commemoration of the miracle of *Nuestra Señora del Rocío* (Our Lady of the Dew) a statue found, so it is said, on this spot and resistant to all attempts to move it elsewhere. The image, credited with all kinds of magic and fertility powers, is paraded before the faithful early on the Sunday morning.

El Rocío is a nice place to stay, with wide, sandy streets and a frontier-like feeling. There are two good **hostales**; the *Hostal Vélez*, c/Algaida 2 (☎959/442117; ④), and *Hostal Cristina*, c/Real 32 (☎959/442413; ③). In the spring, as far as **bird-watching** goes, the town is probably the best base in the area. The *marismas* and pine woods adjacent to the town are teeming with birds, and following tracks east and southeast of El Rocío, along the edge of the reserve, you'll see many species (up to a hundred if you're lucky).

Huelva and the coast down to Portugal

Large, sprawling and industrialized, **HUELVA** is the least attractive and least interesting city of Andalucía. It has claims as a *"flamenco* capital", but unless you're really devoted it's unlikely you'll want to stop long enough to verify this. By day – and in the evening as well – the most enticing thing to do is to take the hourly ferry (summer only) across the bay to **Punta Umbría**, the local resort, also linked by a new road bridge spanning the marshlands of the Río Odiele estuary. This is hardly an inspiring place either, but it does at least have some life, a fair beach, numerous *hostales* and a campsite.

Columbus
Nearby, across the Río Tinto estuary, the monastery of La Rábida and the villages of Palos and Moguer are all places connected with the voyages of Columbus (Cristóbal Colón in Spanish) to the New World.

La Rábida, 8km from Huelva and easily reached by bus, is a charming and tranquil fourteenth-century Franciscan monastery whose abbot was instrumental in securing funds for the voyage from Ferdinand and Isabella. At **Palos**, 4km to the north, is the church of **San Jorge** where Columbus and his crew heard mass before setting sail from the now silted-up harbour. A further 8km north, at **MOGUER** is the fourteenth-century **Convent of Santa Clara** in whose church Columbus spent a whole night in prayer as thanksgiving for his safe return. The small town is a beautiful place, the birthplace of the poet Juan Ramón Jiménez, and boasts a scaled down, whiter version of Sevilla's Giralda attached to the church of **Nuestra Señora de la Granada**.

West to Portugal
From Huelva it's best either to press on inland to the Sierra Morena or straight **along the coast to Portugal**. You're unlikely to attain nirvana anywhere along the drab stretch of coastline between Huelva and the frontier town of **Ayamonte**, but there's a good bus service along this route and a new road suspension bridge across the Rio Guadiana estuary and border linking Ayamonte and **Vila Real de Santo Antonio**. From here, a good first night's target in Portugal is Tavira, on the Algarve train line.

Sevilla to Córdoba

The direct route from **Sevilla to Córdoba**, 135km along the valley of Guadalquivir, followed by the train and some of the buses, is a flat and rather unexciting journey. There's far more to see following the route just to the south of this, via **Carmona** and **Écija**, both interesting towns, and even more if you detour further south to take in **Osuna** as well. There are plenty of buses along these roads so there's no real need to stay – **Carmona** in particular is an easy day trip from Sevilla.

Carmona

CARMONA is a small, picturesque town with a fifteenth-century tower built in imitation of the Giralda. This is the first thing you catch sight of and it sets a tone for the place – an appropriate one, since the town shares a similar history to Sevilla, less than 30km distant. It was an important Roman city (from which era it preserves a fascinating subterranean necropolis) and under the Moors was often governed by a brother of the Sevillan ruler. Later, Pedro the Cruel built a palace within its castle, which he used as a "provincial" royal residence.

The buses stop right by the old Moorish **Alcázar de Abajo**, a grand and ruinous fortified gateway to the old town. Inside the walls, narrow streets wind up past Mudéjar churches and Renaissance mansions. There's a map of the town pinned up in the porch of **San Pedro** (the church with the Giralda-type tower): get your bearings and head uphill to the **Plaza San Fernando** (or Plaza Mayor), modest in size but dominated by splendid Moorish-style buildings. Behind it there's a bustling fruit and vegetable market most mornings. The **Turismo** (Mon–Fri 10am–2pm & 5–7pm; ☎954/142200) is located in the *Casa del Cultura* on the Plaza de Descalzas, in the centre of the old town.

Close by is **Santa María**, a fine Gothic church built over the former main mosque, whose elegant patio it retains; like many of Carmona's churches it is capped by a Mudéjar tower, possibly utilizing part of the old minaret. Dominating the ridge of the town are the massive ruins of **Pedro's palace**, destroyed by an earthquake in 1504 and now taken over by a remarkably tasteful but very expensive *parador* (see below). To the left, beyond and below, the town comes to an abrupt and romantic halt at the Roman **Puerta de Córdoba**, from where the old Córdoba road (now a dirt track) drops down to a vast and fertile plain.

The extraordinary **Roman necropolis** (June–Sept Tues–Sat 9am–2pm, Sun 10am–2pm; Oct–May Tues–Fri 10am–2pm & 4–6pm, Sat & Sun 10am–2pm) lies on a low hill at the opposite end of Carmona; walking out of town from San Pedro take c/Enmedio, the middle street (parallel to the main Sevilla road) for about 450m. Here amid the cypress trees, more than 900 family tombs dating from the second century BC to the fourth century AD can be found. Enclosed in subterranean chambers hewn from the rock, the tombs are often frescoed and contain a series of niches in which many of the funeral urns remain intact. Some of the larger tombs have vestibules with stone benches for funeral banquets, and several retain carved family emblems (one is of an elephant, perhaps symbolic of long life). Most spectacular is the *Tumba de Servilia* – a huge colonnaded temple with vaulted side chambers. Opposite is a partly-excavated **amphitheatre**, though as yet it isn't included in the tour.

Practicalities

Budget **accommodation** is limited: the best bet is *Pensión El Comercio* (☎954/140018; ③), built into the town's gateway; or try the seedy, but clean, *El Potro*, c/Sevilla 78 (☎954/141465; ②), 100m back along the Sevilla road. The *Parador Alcázar del Rey Don Pedro* (☎954/141010; ⑥), in the ruins of the palace, is Carmona's only upmarket hotel.

The old town is an expensive place for **food**; try the *tapas* bars on c/Fuente which descends to the right before **San Pedro**. Beyond the church, the *Gamero* restaurant serves reasonably priced *platos combinados* and has a *menú*. *El Potro* also has a decent and economical, if soulless restaurant.

Écija

Sevilla and Córdoba are reputedly the hottest cities of Spain; **ÉCIJA** lies midway between them in a basin of low sandy hills. It's known, with no hint of exaggeration, as *la sartenilla de Andalucía* (the frying pan of Andalucía). In mid-August the only possible strategy is to slink from one tiny shaded plaza to another, or with a burst of energy to make for the riverbank.

The effort is worth it, since this is one of the most distinctive and individual towns of the south, with eleven superb, decaying church towers, each glistening with brilliantly coloured tiles. It has a unique domestic architecture, too – a flamboyant style of twisted and florid forms, best displayed in the **Calle de los Caballeros**, a whole street full of mansions and palaces, a block or two south of the Plaza Mayor (where the bus stops). Most interesting of the churches is **Santa Cruz**, the old mosque.

A couple of **hostales** are located near the centre; try *Pensión Santa Cruz*, c/Romero Gordillo 8 (☎954/83022; ③), off the eastern end of the Plaza Mayor. Others are to be found on the outskirts, off the Sevilla–Córdoba road.

Osuna

OSUNA (like Carmona and Écija) is one of those small Andalucian towns which are great to explore in the early evening: slow in pace and quietly enjoyable, with elegant streets of tiled, whitewashed houses interspersed by fine **Renaissance mansions**. The best of these are in c/Carrera, running down from the Plaza Mayor, and in c/San Pedro which intersects it (no. 16 has a superb geometric relief round a carving of the Giralda). The Plaza Mayor has a marvellous **casino** – with 1920s Mudéjar-style decor and a grandly bizarre ceiling – which is open to all visitors and makes an excellent place to drink.

Two huge stone buildings stand on the hilltop: the old university (suppressed by reactionary Fernando VII in 1820) and the lavish sixteenth-century **Colegiata** (guided tours Mon–Fri 10.30am–1.30pm & 3.30–7pm, Sat & Sun 10.30am–1.30pm; 200ptas), which contains the gloomy pantheon and chapel of the dukes of Osuna, descendants of the kings of León and once "the Lords of Andalucía".

Opposite the entrance to the Colegiata, is the Baroque convent of **La Encarnación** (daily 10am–1.30pm & 4.30–7.30pm), which has a fine plinth of ninth-century Sevillan *azulejos* round its cloister and gallery.

Osuna has a reasonable range of **accommodation**. *Casa Paco*, c/Asistento Arjona 35 (☎954/810218; ②), is a very friendly *fonda*, reached through the double arch beside the casino. There are also several bars that offer noisy rooms along c/Carrera: better alternatives are *Hostal Cinco Puertas*, c/Carrera 79 (☎954/811243; ③) or, opposite, the *Hostal Caballo Blanco*, c/Granada 1 (☎954/810184; ④), which has some better rooms with bath. Both of these also serve decent meals.

Córdoba

CÓRDOBA stands upstream from Sevilla beside a loop of the Guadalquivir, which was once navigable as far as here. It is today a minor provincial capital, prosperous in a modest sort of way. Once, however, it was the largest city of Roman Spain, and for three centuries it formed the heart of the Western Islamic Empire, the great medieval Caliphate of the Moors.

It is from this era that the city's great sight dates: the **Mezquita**, the grandest and most beautiful mosque ever constructed by the Moors in Spain. It stands right in the centre of the city, surrounded by the old Jewish and Moorish quarters, and is a building of extraordinary mystical and aesthetic power. Make for it on arrival and keep returning as long as you stay; you'll find its beauty and power increase with each visit, as of course is proper, since the mosque was intended for daily and regular attendance.

The Mezquita apart, Córdoba itself is a place of considerable charm. It has few grand squares or mansions, tending instead to introverted architecture, calling your attention to the tremendous and often wildly extravagant **patios**. These have long been acclaimed, and they are actively encouraged and maintained by the local council, which runs a "Festival of the Patios" in May. Just 7km outside the town are the ruins of the extravagant palace complex of **Medina Azahara** which is undergoing fascinating reconstruction.

Arrival and accommodation

Finding your way around Córdoba is no problem. From the **train station** on Avda. de America, the broad Avda. del Gran Capitán leads down to the old quarters and the Mezquita. **Bus terminals** are numerous and scattered around the city. The main company, *Alsina Graells*, is at Avda. de Medina Azahara 29 (the continuation of c/ Gondomar), two or three blocks to the west of the Paseo de la Victoria gardens; it runs services to and from Sevilla, Granada and Málaga.

The **Turismo** (Mon–Fri 9.30am–2.30pm & 5–7pm, Sat 9.30am–1.30pm; ☎957/ 471235) is at the Palacio de Congresos y Exposiciones in c/Torrijos alongside the Mezquita. There's also a small municipal office in Plaza Judá Leví, west of the Mezquita (mornings only) which gives out an illustrated brochure on places to visit, with a town plan. For information on fringe theatre and music, the **Casa del Cultura** is at Plaza del Potro 10. You'll find the main **Correos** (for *poste restante*) at c/Cruz Conde 15, parallel to the Avda. del Gran Capitán, and the **Telefónica** office is on Plaza de las Tendillas at the end of this avenue.

Accommodation

Places to stay can be found all over Córdoba, but the best are concentrated in the narrow maze of streets above the Mezquita. Less obvious, less savoury, but likely to have room, are very run-down *fondas* in the **Plaza de la Corredera**. This is a wonderful, ramshackle square, like a decayed version of Madrid's Plaza Mayor, and worth a look whether you stay or not; it hosts a small morning market.

BUDGET OPTIONS

Albergue Juvenil, Plaza Judá Leví (☎957/290166). Córdoba's brand new youth hostel which also serves meals. ①.

Hostal Los Arcos, c/Romero Barros 14 (☎957/485643). This *hostal* has its own superb patio. ③.

Hostal Mari, c/Pimentera 6 (☎957/479575), off c/Calderos to the east of the Mezquita. This clean and pleasant *hostal* is one of the lowest priced in town. ②.

Hostal Mari II, c/Horno de Porras 6 (☎957/486004). A friendly, simple place with some excellent bargains. ②.

Hostal Plaza Corredera, corner of Plaza Corredera and c/Rodríguez Marin. Clean and friendly, with great views over the plaza from some of the rooms. ②.

Hostal El Portillo, c/Cabezas 2 (☎957/472091). A beautiful old place offering both singles and doubles. ②.

Fonda Rey Heredia, c/Rey Heredia 26 (☎957/474182). One of three very reasonable *fondas* on this street. ③.

Hostal Seneca, c/Conde y Luque 7 (☎957/473234), just north of the Mezquita. Breakfast also available at this attractive and good value *hostal*. ③.

MORE EXPENSIVE PLACES

Hotel Amistad de Córdoba, Plaza de Maimónides 3 (☎957/420305). A wonderful hotel incorporating two eighteenth-century mansions, near the old wall in the Judería. ⑤.

Parador La Arruzafa, Avda. de la Arruzafa (☎957/275900). Córdoba's modern *parador* is located on the outskirts of the city, but it does have a pool and every other amenity to justify the price. ⑥.

Hostal Maestre, c/Romero Barros 6 (☎957/475395). An excellent if overpriced place between c/ San Fernando and the Plaza del Potro. ④.

Hotel Maimónides, c/Torrijos 4 (☎957/471500). This hotel has a particularly central and attractive location, near to the Turismo. ⑤.

Hotel Marisa, c/Cardenal Herrero 6 (☎957/473142). A two-star hotel with a superb position immediately outside the Mezquita. ④.

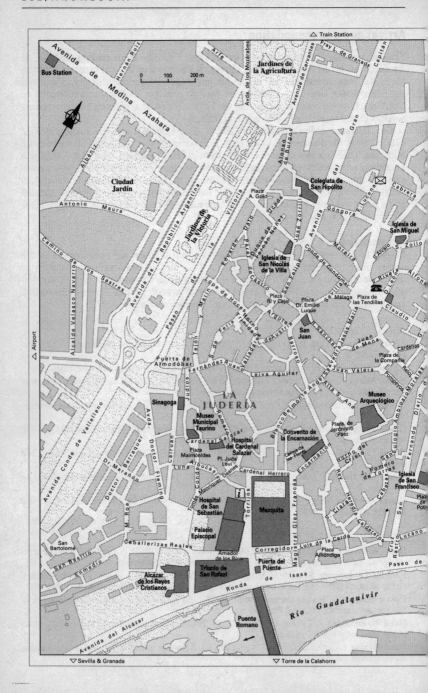

CÓRDOBA

CAMPING

Campamento Municipal (☎957/472000). The local campsite is 2km north on the road to Villaviciosa, served by a regular bus.

Moorish Córdoba and the Mezquita

Córdoba's **domination of Moorish Spain** began thirty years after its conquest – in 756, when the city was placed under the control of **Abd ar-Rahman I**, the sole survivor of the Umayyad dynasty which had been bloodily expelled from the eastern Caliphate of Damascus. He proved a firm but moderate ruler, and a remarkable military campaigner, establishing control over all but the north of Spain and proclaiming himself *Emir*, a title meaning both "King" and "Son of the Caliph". It was Abd ar-Rahman who commenced the building of the Great Mosque (*La Mezquita*, in Spanish), purchasing from the Christians the site of the Cathedral of Saint Vincent (which, divided by a partition wall, had previously served both communities). This original mosque was completed by his son **Hisham** in 796 and comprises about one-fifth of the present building, the first dozen aisles adjacent to the Patio de los Naranjos.

The **Cordoban Emirate**, maintaining independence from the eastern caliphate, soon began to rival Damascus both in power and in the brilliance of its civilization. **Abd ar-Rahman II** (822–52) initiated sophisticated irrigation programmes, minted his own coinage and received embassies from Byzantium. He in turn substantially enlarged the mosque. A focal point within the culture of al-Andalus, this was by now being consciously directed and enriched as an alternative to Mecca; it possessed an original script of the Koran and a bone from the arm of Muhammad, and, for the Spanish Muslim who could not go to Mecca, it became the most sacred place of **pilgrimage**. In the broader Islamic world it ranked third in sanctity after the Kaaba of Mecca and the Al Aksa mosque of Jerusalem.

In the tenth century Córdoba reached its zenith under a new emir, **Abd ar-Rahman III** (912–67), one of the great rulers of Islamic history. He assumed power after a period of internal strife and, according to a contemporary historian, "subdued rebels, built palaces, gave impetus to agriculture, immortalised ancient deeds and monuments, and inflicted great damage on infidels to a point where no opponent or contender remained in al-Andalus. People obeyed en masse and wished to live with him in peace." In 929, with Muslim Spain and part of North Africa firmly under his control, Abd ar-Rahman III adopted the title of "Caliph". It was a supremely confident move and was reflected in the growing splendour of Córdoba, which had become the largest, most prosperous city of Europe, outshining Byzantium and Baghdad (the new capital of the eastern caliphate) in science, culture and scholarship. At the turn of the tenth century it had 27 schools, 50 hospitals (with the first separate clinics for the leprous and insane), 900 public baths, 60,300 noble mansions, 213,077 houses and 80,455 shops.

The **development of the Great Mosque** paralleled these new heights of confidence and splendour. Abd ar-Rahman III provided it with a new minaret (which has not survived), 80m high, topped by three pomegranate-shaped spheres, two of silver and one of gold and each weighing a ton. But it was his son **al-Hakam II** (961–76), to whom he passed on a peaceful and stable empire, who was responsible for the most brilliant expansion. He virtually doubled its extent, demolishing the south wall to add fourteen extra rows of columns, and employed Byzantine craftsmen to construct a new *mihrab* or prayer niche; this remains complete and is perhaps the most beautiful example of all Moorish religious architecture.

Al-Hakam had extended the mosque as far to the south as was possible. The final enlargement of the building, under the chamberlain-usurper **al-Mansur** (977–1002), involved adding seven rows of columns to the whole east side. This spoiled the symme-

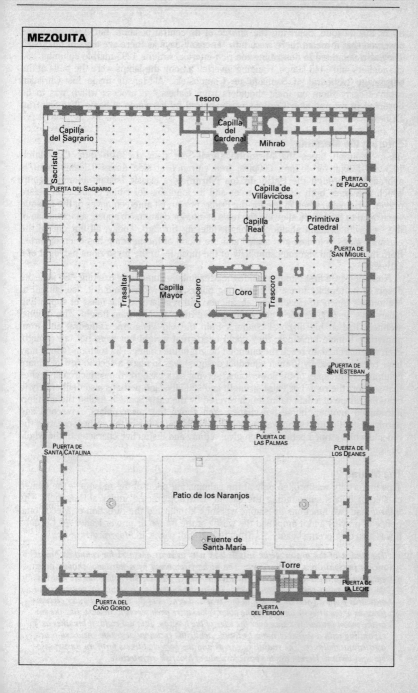

MEZQUITA

Tesoro

Capilla del Sagrario

Sacristía

Capilla del Cardenal

Mihrab

PUERTA DEL SAGRARIO

PUERTA DE PALACIO

Capilla de Villaviciosa

Capilla Real

Primitiva Catedral

PUERTA DE SAN MIGUEL

Trasaltar

Capilla Mayor

Crucero

Coro

Trascoro

PUERTA DE SAN ESTEBAN

PUERTA DE LAS PALMAS

PUERTA DE SANTA CATALINA

PUERTA DE LOS DEANES

Patio de los Naranjos

Fuente de Santa María

Torre

PUERTA DE LA LECHE

PUERTA DEL CAÑO GORDO

PUERTA DEL PERDÓN

try of the mosque, depriving the *mihrab* of its central position, but Arab historians observed that it meant there were now "as many bays as there are days of the year". They also delighted in describing the rich interior, with its 1293 marble columns, 280 chandeliers and 1445 lamps. Hanging inverted among the lamps were the bells of the pilgrimage cathedral of Santiago de Compostela. Al-Mansur made his Christian captives carry them on their shoulders from Galicia – a process which was to be observed in reverse after Córdoba was captured by Fernando el Santo (the Saint) in 1236.

Entering the Mezquita

As in Moorish times the **Mezquita** (April–Sept daily 10.30am–7pm; Oct–March 10.30am–1.30pm & 4–7pm; 600ptas; free entrance at side doors 8.30am–10am) is approached through the **Patio de los Naranjos**, a classic Islamic ablutions court which preserves both its orange trees and its fountains for ritual purification before prayer. Originally, when in use for the Friday prayer, all nineteen naves of the mosque were open to this court, allowing the rows of interior columns to appear an extension of the tree with brilliant shafts of sunlight filtering through. Today, all but one of the entrance gates is locked and sealed and the mood of the building has been distorted from the open and vigorous simplicity of the mosque, to the mysterious half-light of a cathedral.

Nonetheless, a first glimpse inside the Mezquita is immensely exciting. "So near the desert in its tentlike forest of supporting pillars," Jan Morris found it, "so faithful to Mahomet's tenets of cleanliness, abstinence and regularity". The mass of supporting pillars was, in fact, an early and sophisticated innovation to gain height. The original architect had at his disposal columns from the old Visigothic cathedral and from numerous Roman buildings; they could bear great weight but were not tall enough, even when arched, to reach the intended height of the ceiling. His solution (which may have been inspired by Roman aqueduct designs) was to place a second row of square columns on the apex of the lower ones, serving as a base for the semicircular arches that support the roof. For extra strength and stability (and perhaps also deliberately to echo the shape of a date palm, much revered by the early Spanish Arabs) the architect introduced another, horseshoe-shaped arch above the lower pillars. A second and purely aesthetic innovation was to alternate brick and stone in the arches, creating the red-and-white striped pattern which gives a unity and distinctive character to the whole design.

The Mihrab

This uniformity was broken only at the culminating point of the mosque – the domed cluster of pillars surrounding the sacred **Mihrab**, erected under al-Hakam II. The *mihrab* had two functions in Islamic worship: it indicated the direction of Mecca (and hence of prayer) and it amplified the words of the *imam*, or prayer leader. At Córdoba it was also of supreme beauty. As Titus Burckhardt wrote, in *Moorish Art in Spain*:

> The design of the prayer niche in Córdoba was used as a model for countless prayer niches in Spain and North Africa. The niche is crowned by a horseshoe-shaped arch, enclosed by a rectangular frame. The arch derives a peculiar strength from the fact that its central point shifts up from below. The wedge-shaped arch stones or voussoirs fan outwards from a point at the foot of the arch and centres of the inner and outer circumferences of the arch lie one above the other. The entire arch seems to radiate, like the sun or the moon gradually rising over the edge of the horizon. It is not rigid; it breathes as if expanding with a surfeit of inner beatitude, while the rectangular frame enclosing it acts as a counterbalance. The radiating energy and the perfect stillness form an unsurpassable equilibrium. Herein lies the basic formula of Moorish architecture.

The inner vestibule of the niche (which is roped off – forcing you to risk the wrath of the attendants in getting a glimpse; if you don't want to pay yourself, wait for it to be lit up for someone else) is quite simple in comparison, with a shell-shaped ceiling carved from a single block of marble. The chambers to either side – decorated with exquisite Byzantine mosaics of gold, rust-red, turquoise and green – constitute the *maksura*, where the caliph and his retinue would pray.

The Cathedral and other additions

Originally the whole design of the mosque would have directed worshippers naturally towards the *mihrab*. Today, though, you almost stumble upon it, for in the centre of the mosque squats a Renaissance **cathedral coro**. This was built in 1523 – nearly three centuries of enlightened restraint after the Christian conquest – and in spite of fierce opposition from the town council. The erection of a *coro* and *capilla mayor*, however, had long been the "Christianizing" dream of the cathedral chapter and at last they had found a monarch – predictably Carlos V – who was willing to sanction the work. Carlos, to his credit, realized the mistake (though it did not stop him from destroying parts of the Alhambra and Sevilla's Alcázar); on seeing the work completed he told the chapter, "You have built what you or others might have built anywhere, but you have destroyed something that was unique in the world." To the left of the *coro* stands an earlier and happier Christian addition – the Mudéjar **Capilla de Villaviciosa**, built by Moorish craftsmen in 1371 (and now partly sealed up). Beside it are the dome and pillars of the **earlier mihrab**, constructed under Abd ar-Rahman II.

The **belfry**, at the corner of the Patio de los Naranjos, is contemporary with the cathedral addition. If it's open after restoration, the climb is a dizzying experience. Close by, the **Puerta del Perdón**, the main entrance to the patio, was rebuilt in Moorish style in 1377. Original "caliphal" decoration (in particular some superb lattice-work), however, can still be made out in the gates along the east and west sides of the mosque.

The town

After the Mezquita, Córdoba's other remnants of Moorish – and indeed Christian – rule are not individually very striking. The river, though, with its great **Arab water-wheels** and its **bridge** built on Roman foundations, is an attractive area in which to wander. The wheels, and the ruined mills on the riverbank, were in use for several centuries after the fall of the Muslim city, grinding flour and pumping water up to the fountains of the Alcázar, or Palace Fortress. This originally stood beside the Mezquita, on the site now occupied by the **Episcopal Palace**. After the Christian conquest it was rebuilt a little to the west by Fernando and Isabella, hence its name, **Alcázar de los Reyes**. The buildings (daily 9.30am–1.30pm & 4–7pm) are a bit dreary, having served as the residence of the Inquisition from 1428–1821. They display a few miscellaneous Roman mosaics, unearthed nearby. The gardens, though, are attractive.

Judería

Between the Mezquita and the beginning of the Avda. del Gran Capitán lies the **Judería**, Córdoba's old Jewish quarter and a fascinating network of lanes – more atmospheric and less commercialized than Sevilla's, though souvenir shops are beginning to gain ground. Near the heart of the quarter, at c/Maimonides 18, is a **synagogue** (Tues–Sat 10am–2pm & 3.30–5.30pm, Sun 10am–1.30pm; 50ptas), one of only three in Spain – the other two are in Toledo – that survived the Jewish expulsion of 1492. This one, built in 1316, is minute, particularly in comparison to the great Santa María in Toledo, but it has some fine stucco work elaborating on a Solomon's-seal motif and retains its women's gallery. Outside is a statue of Maimónides.

Nearby is a rather bogus **Zoco** – an Arab *souk* turned into a crafts arcade – and, adjoining this, a small **Museo Taurino** (Tues–Sat 9.30am–1.30pm & 4–7.30pm, Sun 9.30am–1.30pm; 200ptas, free Tues). The latter warrants a look, if only for the kitschy nature of its exhibits: row upon row of bulls' heads, two of them given this "honour" for having killed matadors. Beside a copy of the tomb of Manolete – most famous of the city's fighters – is exhibited the hide of his taurine nemesis, Islero. If bullfighting is your thing, it's possible to go on a guided tour of the city's **bullring** (tours on the hour, 10am–1pm & 4–7pm); complete with distastefully reverential commentary, this includes even the high-tech emergency room. Ask at the Turismo for further details.

Museums and mansions

More interesting, perhaps, and really more rewarding, is the **Museo Arqueológico** (Tues–Sat 10am–2pm & 5–7pm, Sun 10am–1.30pm; 250ptas, free to EC passport holders). During its original conversion, this small Renaissance mansion was revealed as the unlikely site of a genuine Roman patio. As a result it is one of the most imaginative and enjoyable small museums in the country, with good local collections from the Iberian, Roman and Moorish periods. Outstanding is an inlaid tenth-century bronze stag found at the Moorish palace of Medina Azahara (see below) where it was used as the spout of a fountain.

A couple of blocks below the Archaeological Museum, back towards the river, you'll come upon the **Plaza del Potro**, a fine old square named after the colt (*potro*) which adorns its fountain. This, as local guides proudly point out, is mentioned in *Don Quixote*, and indeed Cervantes himself is reputed to have stayed at the inn opposite, the **Mesón del Potro**, which is now used for *artesanía* displays. On the other side of the square is the **Museo de Bellas Artes** (Tues–Sat 10am–2pm & 6–8pm; Sun 10am–1.30pm; 250ptas) with paintings by Ribera, Valdés Leal and Zurbarán. Across its courtyard is a small museum (free) devoted to the Cordoban artist **Julio Romero de Torres** (1885–1930), painter of some sublimely dreadful canvases, most of which depict reclining female nudes with furtive male guitar players.

In the north of town, towards the train station, are numerous Renaissance churches – some converted from mosques, others showing obvious influence in their minarets – and a handful of convents and palaces. The best of these, still privately owned, is the **Palacio del Marqués de Viana** (guided tours daily except Wed summer 9am–2pm , winter 10am–1pm & 4–6pm; 200ptas).

Eating and drinking

Bars and **restaurants** are on the whole reasonably priced – you need only to avoid the touristy places round the Mezquita. There are lots of good places to eat not too far away in the Judería and in the old quarters off to the east, above the Paseo de la Ribera.

Restaurants

Restaurante Cafetín Halal, c/Rey Heredia 28. An Islamic cultural centre serving excellent inexpensive food with vegetarian options. No alcohol.

El Churrasco, c/Romero 16 (not c/Romero Barros). Has a long-standing reputation for its *churrasco* (a kind of grilled pork dish, served with pepper sauces) and *salmorejo*, a thick Cordoban version of *gazpacho* with hunks of ham and egg. Expensive.

El Extremeño, Plaza Benavente 1. Excellent evening meals and an enthusiastic owner who will guide your choice.

Restaurante La-La-La, c/Cruz del Rastro. Situated on the river by the Paseo de la Ribera and serving inexpensive set menus.

Casa Paco Acedo, beneath the ancient Torre de Malmuerta at the northen end of town. The house speciality is a memorable *rabodetoro* – a very superior oxtail stew and Córdoba's traditional dish.

Bodega Taberna Rafaé, c/Deanes. A bar full of bullfighting posters, with good inexpensive food.

Taberna Salinas, c/Tundidores 3 just off the Plaza Corredera. An excellent place serving great *salmorejo*.

Taberna Santa Clara, c/Oslo 2, corner of c/Rey Heredia. Very friendly, with good value *menús*.

Mesón El Tablón, c/Cardenal González. One place close to the Mezquita that is reasonable; the other places on this street are best avoided.

Bars

For drinking and *tapas*, try *Bar La Mezquita,* a tiny place near the top corner of the mosque. The local barrelled **wine** is mainly *Montilla* or *Moriles* – both are magnificent, vaguely resembling mellow, dry sherries. The *Solar Plateros* opposite the *Hostal Maestre* specializes in *Montilla* and also has great *tapas*. Good *tapas* and *bocadillos* can be found at the tiny *Casa Elisa*, c/Almanzor near Puerto del Almo, northwest of the Mezquita. One bar not to be missed is the Taberna San Miguel behind the church of the same name to the north of Plaza Tendillas. An ancient old place hung with guitars and faded *corrida* posters, the *tapas*, especially *callos* (tripe) and *manitas* (trotters) in sauce, are excellent.

Flamenco performances take place at *La Buleria*, c/Pedro López 3, near Plaza de la Corredera, from 10pm every night; being a café-bar there's no entrance fee, but your first drink will cost 1000ptas. After that food and drink are slightly more expensive than usual, but it all costs a great deal less (for as good a show) as the more touristy *tablaos*.

Medina Azahara

Seven kilometres to the northwest of Córdoba lie the vast and rambling ruins of **Medina Azahara**, a palace complex built on a dream scale by **Caliph Abd ar-Rahman III**. Naming it after a favourite, az-Zahra (the Radiant), he spent one-third of the annual state budget on its construction each year from 936 until his death in 961. Ten thousand workers and 1500 mules and camels were employed on the project and the site, almost 2000m long by 900m wide, stretched over three descending terraces. In addition to the palace buildings, it contained a zoo, an aviary, four fish ponds, 300 baths, 400 houses, weapons factories and two barracks for the royal guard. Visitors, so the chronicles record, were stunned by its wealth and brilliance: one conference room was provided with pure crystals, creating a rainbow when lit by the sun; another was built round a huge pool of mercury.

Medina Azahara was a perfect symbol of the western caliphate's extent and greatness, but it was to last for less than a century. **Al-Hakam II**, who succeeded Abd ar-Rahman, lived in the palace, continued to endow it, and enjoyed a stable reign. However, distanced from the city, he delegated more and more authority, particularly to his vizier Ibn Abi Amir, later known as **al-Mansur** (the Victor). In 976 al-Hakam was succeeded by his eleven-year-old son Hisham II and after a series of sharp moves al-Mansur assumed the full powers of government, keeping Hisham virtually imprisoned at Medina Azahara, to the extent of blocking up connecting passageways between the palace buildings.

Al-Mansur was equally skilful and manipulative in his wider dealings as a dictator, retaking large tracts of central Spain and raiding as far afield as Galicia and Catalunya; consequently Córdoba rose to new heights of prosperity. But with his death in 1002 came swift decline as his role and function were assumed in turn by his two sons. The first died in 1008; the second, Sanchol, showed open disrespect for the caliphate by forcing Hisham to appoint him as his successor. At this a popular revolt broke out and the caliphate disintegrated into Civil War and a series of feudal kingdoms. Medina Azahara was looted by a mob at the outset and in 1010 was plundered and burned by retreating Berber mercenaries.

The site

For centuries **the site** (Tues–Sat 10am–2pm & 4–6.30pm, Sun 10am–2pm; 250ptas, free entry with EC passport) continued to be looted for building materials; parts, for instance, were used in the Sevilla Alcázar. But in 1944 excavations unearthed the remains of a crucial part of the palace – the **Royal House**, where guests were received and meetings of ministers held. This has been meticulously reconstructed, and though still fragmentary, its main hall must rank among the greatest of all Moorish rooms. It has a different kind of stuccowork from that at Granada or Sevilla – closer to natural and animal forms in its intricate Syrian *Hom* (Tree of Life) motifs. Unlike the later Spanish Arab dynasties, the Berber Almoravids and the Almohads of Sevilla, the caliphal Andalucians were little worried by Islamic strictures on the portrayal of nature, animals or even men – the beautiful hind in the Córdoba museum is a good example – and it may well have been this aspect of the palace that led to such zealous destruction during the Civil War.

The reconstruction of the palace gives a scale and focus to the site. Elsewhere you have little more than foundations to fuel your imaginings, amid an awesome area of ruins, hidden beneath bougainvillea and rustling with cicadas. Perhaps the most obvious of the outbuildings yet excavated is the **mosque**, just beyond the Royal House, which sits at an angle to the rest of the buildings in order to face Mecca.

To reach Medina Azahara, follow the Avda. de Medina Azahara out of town, on to the road to Villarubia and Posadas. About 4km down this road, make a right turn, after which it's another two or three kilometres. Alternatively, take a bus from the Calle de la Bodega station and ask the driver to drop you off at the intersection for the final three-kilometre walk.

EASTERN ANDALUCÍA

There is no more convincing proof of the diversity of Andalucía than its eastern provinces: **Jaén**, with its rolling, olive-covered hills; **Granada**, dominated by Spain's highest peaks, the Sierra Nevada; and **Almería**, waterless and in part semi-desert.

Jaén is slightly isolated from the main routes around Andalucía, but if you're coming down to Granada from Madrid you might want to consider stopping over in the small towns of **Úbeda** or **Baeza**, served on the main train line by their shared station of Linares-Baeza. Úbeda serves as the gateway to **Cazorla** and its neighbouring natural park.

Granada, a prime target of any Spanish travels, is easily reached from Sevilla, Córdoba, Ronda, Málaga or Madrid. When you've exhausted the city, there are dozens of nearby possibilities, perhaps most enticing being the walks in the **Sierra Nevada** and its lower southern slopes, **Las Alpujarras**. The **Almería beaches**, least developed of the Spanish Mediterranean, are also within striking distance of Granada and Málaga.

Jaén province

There are said to be over 150 million olive trees in the **province of Jaén**. They dominate the landscape as infinite rows of green against the orange-red earth, occasionally interspersed with stark white farm buildings. It's beautiful on a grand, sweeping scale, though concealing a bitter and entrenched economic reality. The majority of the olive groves are owned by a mere handful of families, and for most residents this is a very poor area.

Jaén

JAÉN, the provincial capital and by far the largest town, is an uneventful sort of place with traces of its Moorish past in its ruined castle and in the largest surviving Moorish baths in Spain. The town is centred around the Plaza de la Constitución and its two arterial streets, Paseo de la Estación and Avda. de Madrid. The **Turismo** (Mon–Fri 8.15am–2.15pm) c/Arquitecto Bergés 1, with good town maps, is just off Paseo de la Estación, and the **train station** is further north along the same street. Jaén's bus station is off Avda. de Madrid on Pio XII.

West of the main plaza is the imposing Renaissance **Catedral** (daily 8.30am–1pm & 4.30–7pm), and to the north, between the churches of San Andrés and Santo Domingo, you'll find the Moorish **hamam** (Tues–Fri 10am–2pm & 5–8pm, Sat & Sun 10am–2pm; 200ptas; free with EC passport).The baths were originally part of an eleventh-century Moorish palace, over which was constructed the Palacio de Villadompardo. Jaén's **Museo Provincial**, Paseo de la Estación 29 (Tues–Sat 10am–2pm & 4–7pm), has a large archeological collection including some fine fifth-century BC Iberian sculptures.

If you **stay**, there are some budget options around the Plaza de la Constitución – try *Hostal La Española*, c/Bernardo Lopez 9 (☎953/230254; ③), or the more basic *Hostal Martín*, c/Cuatro Torres 5 (☎953/220633; ②). There are more expensive options on the Paseo de la Estación and Avda. de Madrid, including *Hostal Europa*, Plaza de Belen 1, just off Avda. Madrid (☎953/222704; ④). Overlooking the town, with superb views, is the *Parador Castillo de Santa Catalina*, built in the shell of a Moorish castle (☎953/264411; ⑤).

Calle Nueva immediately east of Plaza de la Constitución has a whole crowd of **bars** and **places to eat** – *La Gamba de Oro* and *Bodegón de Pep*e are good.

Baeza and Úbeda

Less than an hour from Jaén are the rarely visited, elegant towns of **Baeza** and **Úbeda**. Each has an extraordinary density of exuberant Renaissance palaces and richly endowed churches, plus fine public squares. Both towns were captured from the Moors by Fernando el Santo and, repopulated with his knights, stood for two centuries at the frontiers of the reconquered lands facing the Moorish kingdom of Granada.

Baeza

BAEZA is tiny, compact and provincial, with a perpetual Sunday air about it. At its heart is a combined Plaza Mayor and *paseo*, flanked by cafés and very much the hub of the town's limited animation.

The **Plaza de Leones**, an appealing cobbled square enclosed by Renaissance buildings, stands slightly back at the far end. Here, on a rounded balcony, the first Mass of the Reconquest is reputed to have been celebrated; the mansion beneath it houses the **Turismo** (Mon–Sat 8am–2.30pm), where you can pick up an English-language walking-tour brochure of the town.

Finest of Baeza's mansions, is the **Palacio de Marqueses de Jabalquinto**, now a seminary, with an elaborate "Isabelline" front (showing marked Moorish influence in its stalactite decoration). Close by, the sixteenth-century **Catedral**, like many of Baeza and Úbeda's churches, has brilliant painted *rejas* (iron screens) by Maestro Bartolomé, a local craftsman. In the cloister, part of the old mosque has been uncovered, but the cathedral's real novelty is a huge silver *custodia* – cunningly hidden behind a painting of Saint Peter which whirls aside for a 25-ptas coin.

There are some good walks around town: wandering up through the Puerta de Jaén on the Plaza de los Leones and along the Paseo Murallas/Paseo de Don Antonio

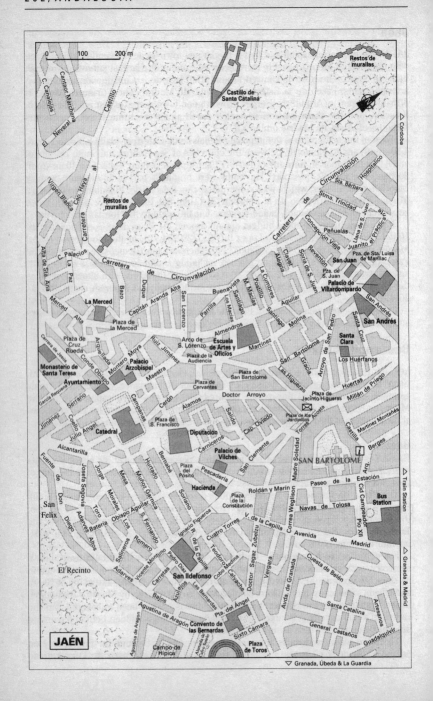

JAÉN

Machado takes you round the edge of Baeza with good views over the surrounding plains. You can cut back to the Plaza Mayor via the network of narrow stone-walled alleys – with the occasional arch – that lie behind the cathedral.

Accommodation is scarce: try the *Fonda Adriano*, c/Conde Ramones 13, near the Plaza de Leones (☎953/740200; ②), an old Renaissance mansion set around an enclosed courtyard with a wood-beamed dining hall; or the *Hostal Comercio* (☎953/740100; ②) at c/San Pablo 21, a main road at the end of the central square. The latter serves evening meals – which is handy as the town has few restaurants.

The nearest **train station** is Linares-Baeza on the direct line from Madrid and 13km from Baeza (there is a connecting bus for most trains, except on Sun). Most bus connections are via Úbeda.

Úbeda

ÚBEDA, 9km east of Baeza, is a larger town with modern suburbs. Follow the signs to the *Zona Monumental* and you'll eventually reach the **Plaza de Vázquez de Molina**, a tremendous Renaissance square which overshadows anything in Baeza.

Most of the buildings round this square were the late sixteenth-century work of Andrés de Vandaelvira, the architect of Baeza's cathedral and numerous churches in both towns. The *Ayuntamiento*, originally a palace for Felipe II's secretary now houses the **Turismo** (Mon–Fri 8.15am–2.15pm). At the opposite end of the plaza is the church of **El Salvador**, erected by Vandaelvira, though actually designed by Diego de Siloé (architect of the Málaga and Granada cathedrals). This is the finest church in Úbeda, its highlight a gilded, brilliantly animated *retablo* of the Transfiguration; to enter you have to go through the sacristy at the side – ring for the caretaker at the fine doorway in the white wall. Across town, the idiosyncratic church of **San Pablo**, Plaza del Generalísimo has a thirteenth-century balcony (a popular feature in Úbeda) and various Renaissance additions.

Most of the **accommodation** options are grouped around the main **bus station** in Avda. de Ramón y Cajal, in the modern part of town. The *Hostal Castillo* at no. 16 (☎953/750430; ③), and the *Sevilla* at no. 9 (☎953/750612; ③) are both reasonable, and both have better rooms with bath. For some of the least expensive rooms in town, try *Hostal San Miguel*, Avda. Libertad 69 (☎953/752049; ②), a five-minute walk from the bus station. In the centre of town, the only option is the *Parador Condestable Dávalos*, Plaza de Vázquez de Molina 1 (☎953/750345; ⑤), in a fabulous sixteenth-century Renaissance mansion.

There are plenty of **places to eat** around Avda. Ramón y Cajal. *El Gallo Rojo*, c/Torrenueva 3 has outdoor tables in the evening, *El Olivo*, Avda. Ramón y Cajal 6 serves good *platos combinados*, and *Hostal Castillo* has its own excellent restaurant.

Cazorla and the Parque Natural

During the reconquest of Andalucía, **CAZORLA**, linked by bus to Úbeda, Jaén and Granada, acted as an outpost for Christian troops. The two castles which dominate the town testify to its turbulent past – both were originally Moorish but later altered and restored by their Christian conquerors. Today it's the main base for visits to the **Parque Natural de las Sierras de Segura y Cazorla**, a vast protected area of magnificent river gorges and forests. Cazorla also hosts the **fiesta de Cristo del Consuelo**, with fairgrounds, fireworks and religious processions on September 16–21.

The town

The town is constructed around three main squares. Buses arrive in the busy, commercial Plaza de la Constitución, where there's a privately run **tourist information**

centre, offering Land Rover trips into the park. The main c/de Muñoz connects with the second square, the Plaza de la Corredera (or *del Huevo*, "of the Egg," because of its shape). The seat of the administration, the *Ayuntamiento*, is here, a fine Moorish-style palace at the far end of the plaza.

Beyond, a labyrinth of narrow, twisting streets, leads to Cazorla's liveliest square, the **Plaza Santa María**. This takes its name from the old cathedral which, damaged by floods in the seventeenth century, was later torched by Napoleonic troops. Its ruins, now preserved, and the fine open square form a natural amphitheatre for concerts and local events as well as being a popular meeting place. The square is dominated by **La Yedra**, an austere, reconstructed castle tower, home of the town's museum.

Practicalities

There is a surprising range of **accommodation** in Cazorla. *Pensión Taxi* (①) in Plaza de la Constitución, is at the bottom end; as a resident, you can also eat for very little in their *comedor*. Better rooms are available at the *Hostal Guadalquivir*, c/Nueva 6 (☎953/720268; ③), off Plaza de la Corredera – it's spotlessly clean and very friendly, though disconcertingly close to the municipal slaughterhouse for those with sensitive ears. In the square itself, try *Hostal Betis* (☎953/720540; ②) which has some rooms overlooking the plaza. There are plenty of more upmarket hotels, of which the *Andalucía*, c/Martínez Falero 42 (☎953/721268; ④), is typical. If you have a car there are some very attractive alternatives out in the Sierra, including the *Sierra de Cazorla II* (☎953/720015; ④), 2km outside the village, with a pool, and the *Parador el Adelantado* (☎953/721075; ⑤), a dull modern building also with pool in a wonderful setting 25km away in the park. Cazorla also has a **youth hostel**, at Mauricio Martínez 2 (☎953/720329), open summer, Christmas and Easter. Ask at the *Mesón la Cueva* (see below) if you want to **rent an apartment** for a longer stay.

Several spit-and-sawdust **bars** with good *tapas* cluster round the Plaza Santa María, along with the rustic *Mesón la Cueva* which offers authentic local food cooked on a wood-fired range but reheated, discreetly, in a microwave. Other places where you can **eat** well are the two *mesones* on Plaza de la Corredera; the one next to the church is excellent value and the other prepares exquisite fish – both serve *tapas* and *raciones* rather than full meals. The only other restaurant in town – avoid the one attached to the *Hotel Cazorla* – is the expensive *La Sarga*, opposite the market. There are two discos (weekends only) and several "pubs" with loud music.

The Parque Natural

Even casual visitors to the park are likely to see a good variety of wildlife, including *Capra hispanica* (Spanish mountain goat), deer, wild pig, birds and butterflies. Ironically, though, much of the best viewing will be at the periphery, or even outside the park, since the wildlife is most successfully stalked on foot and walking opportunities within the park itself are surprisingly limited.

INFORMATION

The official **information office** for the Parque Natural is located in Cazorla at c/ Martínez Falero 11, just off Plaza de la Constitución. It's worth getting a good map from here, either the 1:100,000 map, *Parque Natural de las Sierras de Cazorla y Segura*, or the 1:50,000 version called "Cazorla".

TRANSPORT AND ACCOMMODATION

Public transport into the park is sparse; two daily **buses** link Cazorla with **Coto Ríos** in the middle of the park: one at 6.30am, the other at 2pm, returning from Coto at 5.30pm. Distances between points are enormous, so to explore the park well you'll need a car or be prepared for long treks. Such problems are complicated by the fact that most of the *camping libre* (free camping) areas shown on the 1:100,000 map have been closed recently; one still functioning is to be found beyond El Tranco on the dam. There is more accommodation at Coto Ríos, with three privately run **campsites** and a succession of *hostales*.

WALKS

There are only three signposted **tracks** in the park, all pitifully short. One leads from the Empalme de Vadillo to the Puente de la Herrera via the Fuente del Oso (2km eachway); another of about 1700m curls round the Cerrada (narrows) de Utrero near Vadillo-Castril village; and the best marked segment, through the lower Barossa gorge (see below), is also a mere 1700m long.

The classic walk along the **Río Barrosa** can be done as a day trek even if you are relying on public transport. The early morning bus to Coto Ríos can drop you at the visitors' centre at Torre de Vinagre where the route begins. Cross the Guadalquivir on a low causeway which is a bridge or a ford, depending on the season; 2km later you pass a trout hatchery, and just beyond this is a car park where all private vehicles must be left.

From here follow the rough track along the northwest (right) bank of the Barrosa, swift and cold even in summer. Within a few minutes a signposted footpath diverges to the right; this also marks the beginning of the **gorge**. Two or three wooden bridges now take the path back and forth across the river, which is increasingly confined by sheer rock walls. At the narrowest points the path is routed along planked catwalks secured to the limestone cliff. The walk from Torre de Vinagre to the end of the narrows takes about two hours.

There the footpath rejoins the track; after another half-hour's walk you'll see a turbine and a long metal pipe bringing water from **two lakes** – one natural, one a small dam – up the mountain. The road crosses one last bridge over the Barrosa and stops at the turbine house. When you get to a gate, beyond which there's a steeply rising gully, count on another full hour up to the lakes. Cross a footbridge and start the steep climb up a narrow track over the rocks below the cliff (at one point the path passes close to the base of the palisade – beware falling stones). At the top of the path is a cavernous amphitheatre, with a waterfall in winter. The path ends about halfway up the cliff, where an artificial tunnel has been bored through rock; walk through it to get to the lake.

Allow three and a half hours' walking time from Torre del Vinagre, slightly less going down. It's a very full day's excursion but you should have plenty of time to catch the afternoon bus back, which passes the visitors' centre at 5pm.

Granada

If you see only one town in Spain it should be **GRANADA**. For here, extraordinarily well preserved and in a tremendous natural setting, stands the **Alhambra** – the most exciting, sensual and romantic of all European monuments. It was the palace-fortress of the Nasrid Sultans, rulers of the last Spanish Moorish kingdom, and in its construction Moorish art reached a spectacular and serene climax. But the building seems to go further than this, revealing something of the whole brilliance and spirit of Moorish life and culture. There's a haunting passage in Jan Morris's book, *Spain*, which the palace embodies: "Life itself, which was seen elsewhere in Europe as a kind of probationary preparation for death, was interpreted [by the Moors] as something glorious in itself, to be ennobled by learning and enlivened by every kind of pleasure."

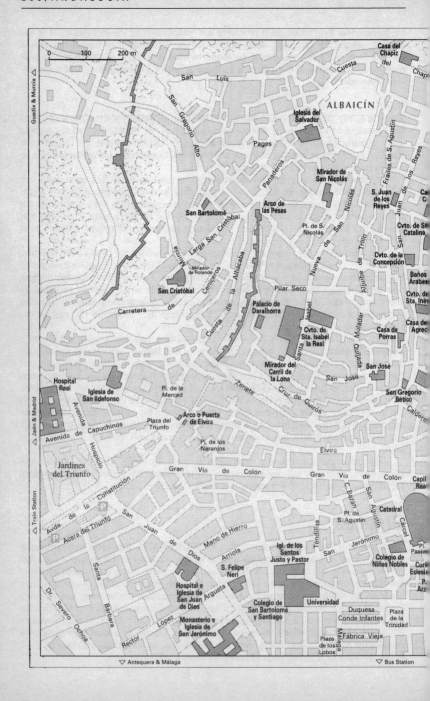

0   100   200 m

Guadix & Murcia ◁

Casa del Chapiz

Cuesta   del

Chap

San   Luis

ALBAICÍN

Iglesia del Salvador

Frailes de S. Agustín

San Gregorio Alto

Pages

Mirador de San Nicolás

S. Juan de los Reyes

Juan de los Reyes

Cas C

Arco de las Pesas

San Bartolomé

Larga San Cristóbal

Pl. de S. Nicolás

San Nicolás

Nueva de San Nicolás

Cvto. de St Catalina

Murcia

Mirador de Rolando

Nueva de la Albacaba

Cvto. de la Concepción

Aljube

Trillo

Baños Árabes

San Cristóbal

Cenceros

Pilar Seco

Cvto. de Sta. Inés

Carretera   de

Cuesta de la Albacaba

Palacio de Daralhorra

Santa Isabel

Muladar

Casa de Agreg

Cvto. de Sta. Isabel la Real

Quinto

Casa de Porras

Mirador del Carril de la Lona

San José

San José

Hospital Real

Zenete

Cruz de Quirós

San Gregorio Bético

Jaén & Madrid ◁

Iglesia de San Ildefonso

Pl. de la Merced

Caldere

Avenida

Avenida de Capuchinos

Arco o Puerta de Elvira

Hospicio

Plaza del Triunfo

Pl. de los Naranjos

Elvira

Jardines del Triunfo

Gran   Via   de   Colón

Gran   Via   de   Colón

Capil Rea

Train Station ◁

Avda. de la Constitución

C. Bajan

San Agustín

Catedral

Acera del Triunfo

San   Juan   de   Dios

Pl. de S. Agustín

Mano de Hierro

Tendillas

Cárcel

Arriola

Igl. de los Santos Justo y Pastor

San

Jerónimo

Pl Paele

Santa

S. Felipe Neri

Colegio de Niñas Nobles

Curi Eclesia

Bárbara

Hospital e Iglesia de San Juan de Dios

Arguta

P. Arz

Dr. Severo Ochoa

López

Monasterio e Iglesia de San Jerónimo

Colegio de San Bartolomé y Santiago

Universidad

Duquesa Conde Infantes

Plaza de la Trinidad

Rector

Plaza de los Lobos

Málaga

Fábrica Vieja

▽ Antequera & Málaga

▽ Bus Station

SACROMONTE

GRANADA

Río Darro

Chico

del Rey

Cuesta

Paseo de
los Tristes

Palacio de
los Leones
Patio de los
Leones
Jardines
del
Partal

Baños de Comares
Palacio de
Comares

Carmen
de los
Mártires

rimias

Cuarto
Dorado
Palacio del
Mexuar
Sta. María de
la Alhambra

San Pedro
San Pablo
Palacios
Reales
Palacio de
Carlos V

Paseo Central

nte
Cadí
La Alcazaba
(Entrada)

Antequeruela Alta
Campo de los Mártires

Antequeruela Baja
Cuesta del
Caldero

ana
Peña Partida
Vargas

San Cecilio
Belén

Cuesta de Gomérez
Molinos

Cuesta
Los Alamillos
Campo del
Príncipe

Cuesta del Realejo

Molinos

Santiago

Casa del
Padre Suárez
Santiago
Solares
Pº de la Bomba

Casa de
los Tiros
Pavaneras
Pl. Santo
Domingo
Santo
Domingo
P. S. de Lucena

Basílios

Mon. a las
Capitulaciones
Cvto. de
S. Francisco
Cuesta del Pescado

o
abe
Pl. Isabel
la Católica
San Matías
Plaza de
los Campos
Cuarto Real

△ Sierra Nevada

Palacio de
Abrantes
Corral de
Carbón
Paseo del Salón

Alcaicería
Reyes Católicos
Ayuntamiento
Plaza de
Mariana
Pineda
Ancha de la Virgen
Río Genil

Plaza del
Carmen
Angel
Ganivet
Palacio de
Bibataubín
(Dip. Prov.)
Carrera del Genil
Humilladero
Puente
Genil

Puerta
Real
Acera
del
Casino
Virgen de
las Angustias

Carretera

Acera
del
Darro
Plaza de
las Arenas

Recogidas
San
Antón
Rejas de la Virgen
San
Isidro

▽ Purchil & Motril

MOORISH GRANADA

Granada's glory was always precarious. It was established as an **independent kingdom** in 1238 by **Ibn Ahmar**, a prince of the Arab Nasrid tribe which had been driven south from Zaragoza. He proved a just and capable ruler but all over Spain the Christian kingdoms were in the ascendant. The Moors of Granada survived only through paying tribute and allegiance to Fernando III of Castile – whom they were forced to assist in the conquest of Muslim Sevilla – and by the time of Ibn Ahmar's death in 1275 theirs was the only surviving Spanish Muslim kingdom. It had, however, consolidated its territory (stretching from just north of the city down to a coastal strip between Tarifa and Almería) and, stimulated by refugees, developed a flourishing commerce, industry and culture.

By a series of shrewd manoeuvres Granada maintained its autonomy for two and a half centuries, its rulers turning for protection, in turn as it suited them, to the Christian kingdoms of Aragón and Castile and to the Merinid Muslims of Morocco. The city-state enjoyed a particularly confident and prosperous period under **Yusuf** I (1334–54) and **Mohammed V** (1354–91), the sultans responsible for much of the existing Alhambra palace. But by the mid-fifteenth century a pattern of coups and internal strife became established and a rapid succession of rulers did little to stem Christian inroads. In 1479 the kingdoms of Aragón and Castile were united by the marriage of Fernando and Isabella and within ten years had conquered Ronda, Málaga and Almería. The city of Granada now stood completely alone, tragically preoccupied in a **civil war** between supporters of the sultan's two favourite wives. The *Reyes Católicos* made escalating and finally untenable demands upon it, and in 1490 war broke out. **Boabdil**, the last Moorish king, appealed in vain for help from his fellow Muslims in Morocco, Egypt and Ottoman Turkey, and in the following year **Fernando and Isabella** marched on Granada with an army said to total 150,000 troops. For seven months, through the winter of 1491, they laid siege to the city. On January 2, 1492, Boabdil formally surrendered its keys. The Christian Reconquest of Spain was complete.

Arrival and accommodation

Virtually everything of interest in Granada – including the hills of **Alhambra** (to the east) and **Sacromonte** (to the north) – is within easy walking distance of the centre.

The **train station** is a kilometre or so out on the Avda. de Andaluces, off Avda. de la Constitución (Avda. Calvo Sotelo); to get into town take bus #11 which runs a circular route: inbound on the Gran Vía de Colón and back out via the Puerta Real and Camino de Ronda. The most central stop is by the cathedral on the Gran Vía (take it from across the road heading out). Bus #4 also runs between the train station and Gran Vía.

Alsina Graells, on the Camino de Ronda, runs **bus services** to and from Jaén, Úbeda, Córdoba, Sevilla, Málaga, Alpujarras (high and low), Motril, Almería and the coast. Other bus companies and possible arrival points are: *Empresa Bonal*, Avda. Calvo Sotelo 19, for the north side of Sierra Nevada; *Empresa Autedia*, c/Rector Martín 10, off Avda. Calvo Sotelo for Guadix; and *Empresa Bacoma* near the train station for Valencia/Alicante. All terminals are on the #11 bus route.

Information

Full details and timetables – and much else besides – are posted on the walls of the **Turismo** (Mon–Fri 9am–2pm & 4.30–7pm, Sat 10am–1pm; ☎958/226688), c/Mariana Pineda, in the Corral del Carbón near the cathedral, just off the eastern side of c/Reyes Católicos. You can buy **maps and guides** for the Sierra Nevada there also, though for a wider selection try the *Librería Dauro* at c/Zacatín 3 (a pedestrian street between the cathedral and c/Reyes Católicos). There's also a municipal tourist office at Plaza Mariana Pineda 10.

Accommodation

Finding a **place to stay** in the centre of town, along the Gran Vía, c/Reyes Católicos or in the Plaza Nueva and Puerta Real is easy enough except at the very height of season (Semana Santa is impossible), and prices are no higher than elsewhere in Spain. Otherwise, try the streets to either side of the Gran Vía, at the back of the Plaza Nueva, round the Puerta Real and Plaza de Carmen (particularly c/de Navas), the Plaza de la Trinidad in the university area (and east of there), or along the Cuesta de Gomérez, which leads up from the Plaza Nueva towards the Alhambra. **Hostales** and **pensiones** are so plentiful round here – and turnaround of guests so regular – that individual places are hard to recommend. Those below are no more than an indication of some that have proved good: the main problem, almost anywhere, is noise. However, a new road to the Alhambra, diverting traffic away from the centre should transform the Cuesta de Gomérez, which is planned to become a pedestrianized street. Don't bother trying to find "interesting" accommodation in the Albaicín area – there are no *hostales* there.

BASIC OPTIONS

Albergue Juvenil, Camino de Ronda 171, not far from the *Alsina Graells* bus station (☎958/272638). If you arrive late in the day, Granada's youth hostel is conveniently close to the train or bus stations (from *RENFE*, turn left onto Avda. de la Constitución, left again onto Camino de Ronda); it's the large white building by the sports stadium. Lots of facilities including a pool (in summer), and good beds, but it's rather institutional.

Hostal Britz, Cuesta de Gomérez 1 (☎958/223652). Noisy, but otherwise very comfortable and well placed. Some rooms with bath. ③.

Hostal Europa, c/de la Cruz. Friendly and small, with plenty of other *hostales* nearby. ②.

Hostal Fabiola, c/Angel Gavinet 5 (☎958/223572). Close to the Puerta Real; on the third floor and relatively quiet. All rooms with bath and many with sun balcony. ③.

Casa de Huéspedes Gomérez, Cuesta de Gomérez 2 (☎958/226398). Simple but convenient. ②.

Casa de Huéspedes González, c/Buensuceso, between Plaza de Trinidad and Plaza de Gracia, east of the cathedral. Perfectly good rooms, very good value. ②.

Hostal Lisboa, Plaza del Carmen 27 (☎958/221413). Can be noisy at the front, but clean and comfortable. ③.

Pensión Olympia, off Gran Vía de Colón opposite *Banco de Jeréz*. Central, good value, nice people. ②.

Hotel La Perla, c/Reyes Católicos 2 (☎958/223415). Simple hotel right in the centre, near the cathedral, but this is a noisy street. ③.

Hostal San Joaquin, c/Manode de Hierro 14, close to the church of San Juan (☎958/282879). Great rambling old place with simple rooms and charming patios. ③.

Casa de Huéspedes Santa Ana, c/Puente de Espinosa, over the Darro river across the first bridge after the church at the east end of Plaza Nueva and at the top of the steps. Brilliant location, but not the cleanest or friendliest of places. ②.

Hostal Terminus, Avda. de Andaluces 10, on the right outside the train station (☎958/201424). Absolutely no frills, but rock bottom prices and right by the station if you arrive late. ②.

Hostal Turin, Ancha de Capuchinos 16 (☎958/200311). Another near the train station, off the Jardines del Triunfo: inexpensive and well run. ②.

Hostal Viena, c/Hospital de Santa Ana 2, first left off Cuesta de Gomérezs (☎958/221859). Friendly Austrian-run *hostal* in a quiet street. Some rooms with bath. ③.

Women Only, c/San Juan de Dios 14, press buzzer for 4th floor. Nameless private accommodation for women only in student area. Clean, friendly and helpful. ①.

HOTELS

Hotel América, Real de la Alhambra 53 (☎958/227471). Simple one-star hotel, in the Alhambra grounds: you pay for the location, but it's worth it. Booking is essential. ⑤.

Hotel Kenia, c/Molinos 65 (☎958/227506). Quiet position on slopes below Alhambra, south of the centre. Well-converted old mansion. ⑤.

Hotel Macía, Plaza Nueva 4 (☎958/227536). Central position, comfortable rooms overlooking the square. ④.

Hotel Montecarlo, c/Acera de Darro 44 (☎958/257900). Again central, with facilties including video and air-conditioning. ⑤.

Parador San Francisco, Real de la Alhambra (☎958/221441). Without question the best place to stay in Granada, a converted monastery in the Alhambra grounds. Also the most expensive. ⑥.

Hotel Los Tilos, Plaza de Bib-Rambla 4 (☎958/266712). Good position near the cathedral – a plain two-star hotel. ④.

CAMPING

Camping Sierra Nevada, Avda. de Madrid 107 (☎958/150062; March–Oct), easiest reached from the centre on #3 bus. The closest site to the centre, and probably the best too.

El Último, Camino Huetor Vega 22 (☎958/123069). Not much further out, via Avda. de Cervantes, and with a pool.

The Alhambra

There are three distinct groups of buildings on the Alhambra hill: the **Casa Real** (Royal Palace), the palace gardens of the **Generalife**, and the **Alcazaba**. This latter, the fortress of the eleventh-century Ziridian rulers, was all that existed when Ibn Ahmar made Granada his capital, but from its reddish walls the hilltop had already taken its name; *al-Hamra* in Arabic means literally "the red". Ibn Ahmar rebuilt the Alcazaba and added to it the huge circuit of walls and towers which forms one's first view of the castle. Within the walls he began a palace, which he supplied with running water by diverting the river Darro nearly 8km to the foot of the hill; water is an integral part of the Alhambra and this engineering feat was Ibn Ahmar's greatest contribution. The Royal Palace was essentially the product of his fourteenth-century successors, particularly Mohammed V, who built and redecorated many of its rooms in celebration of his accession to the throne (in 1354) and conquest of Algeciras (in 1369).

After their conquest of the city, **Fernando and Isabella** lived for a while in the Alhambra. They restored some rooms and converted the mosque but left the palace structure unaltered. As at Córdoba and Sevilla, it was **Emperor Carlos V**, their grandson, who wreaked the most insensitive destruction, demolishing a whole wing of rooms in order to build a Renaissance palace. This and the Alhambra itself were simply ignored by his successors and by the eighteenth century the Royal Palace was in use as a prison. In 1812 it was taken and occupied by **Napoleon's forces**, who looted and damaged whole sections of the palace, and on their retreat from the city tried to blow up the entire complex. Their attempt was thwarted only by the action of a crippled soldier who remained behind and removed the fuses.

Two decades later the Alhambra's "rediscovery" began, given impetus by the American writer **Washington Irving**, who set up his study in the empty palace rooms and began to write his marvellously romantic *Tales of the Alhambra* (on sale all over Granada – and good reading amid the gardens and courts). Shortly after its publication the Spaniards made the Alhambra a **national monument** and set aside funds for its restoration. This continues to the present and is now a highly sophisticated project, scientifically removing the accretions of later ages in order to expose and meticulously restore the Moorish creations.

Approaches to the Alhambra

The standard **approach** to the Alhambra is along the Cuesta de Gomérez, the road which climbs uphill from Granada's central Plaza Nueva. After a few hundred metres you reach the **Puerta de las Granadas**, a massive Renaissance gateway erected by Carlos V. Here two paths diverge to either side of the road: the one on the right climbs up towards a group of fortified towers, the **Torres Bermejas**, which may date from as early as the eighth century. The left-hand path leads through the woods past a huge terrace-fountain (again courtesy of Carlos V) to the main entrance of the Alhambra. This is the **Puerta de la Justicia**, a magnificent tower gateway which forced three changes of direction, making intruders hopelessly vulnerable. It was built by Yusuf I in 1340 and preserves above its outer arch the Koranic symbol of a key (for Allah the Opener) and an outstretched hand whose five fingers represent the five Islamic precepts: prayer, fasting, alms-giving, pilgrimage to Mecca and the oneness of God.

Within the citadel stood a complete "government city" of mansions, smaller houses, baths, schools, mosques, barracks and gardens. Of this only the **Alcazaba fortress** and the **Royal Palace** remain; they face each other across a broad terrace (constructed in the sixteenth century over a dividing gully), flanked by the majestic though incongruous **Palace of Carlos V**.

Within the walls of the citadel, too, are a fairly expensive buffet **restaurant-bar**, the beautiful *Parador San Francisco* (a converted monastery, where Isabella was originally buried – bar open to anyone), and the *Hotel América*. There are a handful of drinks stalls around as well, including one, very welcome, in the Portal gardens (towards the Carlos V Palace after you leave the Casa Real). No one, however, seems to mind if you take a bottle of wine into the Generalife and cool it in one of the fountains – and this is perhaps the best way to enjoy and appreciate the luxuriance. See "Eating, drinking and entertainment" for shops to fix up a picnic.

Admission

Tickets to the complex (summer daily 9am–7.45pm; winter daily 9am–5.45pm; 600ptas, free on Sunday afternoons after 3pm). The tickets have tear-off slips for each part (Alcazaba, Casa Real, Portal and Torres, Generalife) and these must be used on the same day. The two museums in the Palace of Carlos V have separate admission fees of 250ptas; free with EC passport. The Alhambra is also open for limited floodlit visits (600ptas) from 10pm until midnight on Tuesday, Thursday and Saturday nights in season (out of season; Sat only, 8–10pm), and occasional concerts are held in its courts.

In an attempt to cope with the drastic overcrowding of recent years, tickets are stamped with a half-hour time slot during which you must enter the Casa Real section. You will not be allowed to enter before or after this time, but once inside you can stay as long as you like. Once you've got your ticket, any waiting time, usually up to an hour, can be spent in the Alcazaba (see below) or at one of the cafés. A reservation system (☎958/220912) allows you to book a time for your visit prior to arrival.

The Alcazaba

Ideally you should start with the earliest, though most ruined, part of the fortress – the **Alcazaba** – where you can get a grip on the whole site. At its summit is the **Torre de la Vela**, named after a huge bell on its turret which until recent years was rung to mark the irrigation hours for workers on Granada's vast and fertile plain. It was here, at 3pm on January 2, 1492, that the Cross was first displayed above the city, alongside the royal standards of Aragón and Castile and the banner of Saint James. Boabdil, leaving Granada for exile in the Alpujarras, turned and wept at the sight, earning from his mother Aisha the famous rebuke: "Do not weep like a woman for what you could not defend like a man".

The **Aljibe**, a cistern beneath the area between the Alcazaba and Casa Real, is open for viewing on Monday, Wednesday and Friday from 9.30am to 1.30pm.

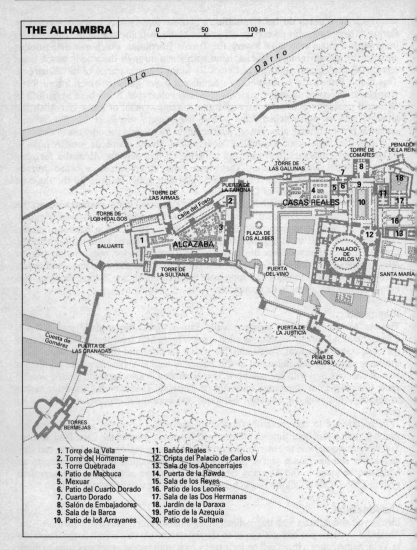

THE ALHAMBRA

0   50   100 m

1. Torre de la Vela
2. Torre del Homenaje
3. Torre Quebrada
4. Patio de Machuca
5. Mexuar
6. Patio del Cuarto Dorado
7. Cuarto Dorado
8. Salón de Embajadores
9. Sala de la Barca
10. Patio de los Arrayanes
11. Baños Reales
12. Cripta del Palacio de Carlos V
13. Sala de los Abencerrajes
14. Puerta de la Rawda
15. Sala de los Reyes
16. Patio de los Leones
17. Sala de las Dos Hermanas
18. Jardín de la Daraxa
19. Patio de la Azequia
20. Patio de la Sultana

The Casa Real (Royal Palace)

It is amazing that the **Casa Real** has survived, for it stands in utter contrast to the strength of the Alcazaba and the encircling walls and towers. It was built lightly and often crudely from wood, brick and adobe, and was designed not to last but to be renewed and redecorated by succeeding rulers. Its buildings show a brilliant use of light and space but they are principally a vehicle for ornamental stucco decoration. This, as Titus Burckhardt explains in *Moorish Culture in Spain*, was both an intricate science and a philosophy of abstract art in direct contrast to pictorial representation:

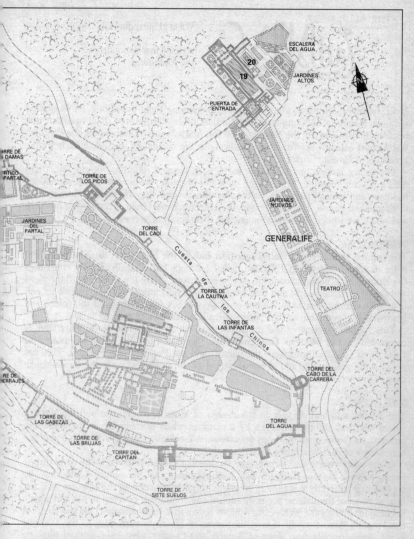

With its rhythmic repetition, [it] does not seek to capture the eye to lead it into an imagined world, but, on the contrary, liberates it from all pre-occupations of the mind. It does not transmit any specific ideas, but a state of being, which is at once repose and inner rhythm.

Burckhardt adds that the way in which patterns are woven from a single band, or radiate from many identical centres, served as a pure simile for Islamic belief in the oneness of God, manifested at the centre of every form and being.

Arabic inscriptions feature prominently in the ornamentation. Some are poetic eulogies of the buildings and builders, others of various sultans (notably Mohammed V).

Wa-la-ghaliba illa-Llah

stylized inscription from the Alhambra

Most, however, are taken from the Koran, and among them the phrase *Wa-la ghaliba illa-Llah* (There is no Conqueror but God) is tirelessly repeated. It is said that this became the battle cry of the Nasrids upon Ibn Ahmar's return from aiding the Castilian war against Muslim Sevilla; it was his reply to the customary, though bitterly ironic, greetings of *Mansur* (Victor).

The palace is structured in three parts, each arrayed round an interior court and with a specific function. The sultans used the **Mexuar**, the first series of rooms, for business and judicial purposes. In the **Serallo**, beyond, they received embassies and distinguished guests. The last section, the **Harem**, formed their private living quarters and would have been entered by no one but their family or servants.

THE MEXUAR

The council chamber, the main **reception hall** of the Mexuar, is the first room you enter. It was completed in 1365 and hailed (perhaps formulaically) by the court poet Ibn Zamrak as a "haven of counsel, mercy, and favour". Here the sultan heard the pleas and petitions of the people and held meetings with his ministers. At the room's far end is a small oratory, one of a number of prayer niches scattered round the palace and immediately identifiable by their distinctive alignment (to face Mecca).

This "public" section of the palace, beyond which few would have penetrated, is completed by the Mudéjar **Golden Room** (decorated under Carlos V, whose *Plus Ultra* motif appears throughout the palace) and the **Patio of the Mexuar**. This has perhaps the grandest facade of the whole palace, for it admits you to the formal splendour of the Serallo.

THE SERALLO

The Serallo was built largely to the design of Yusuf I, a romantic and enlightened sultan who was stabbed to death by a madman while worshipping in the Alhambra mosque. Its rooms open out from delicate marble-columned arcades at each end of the long **Court of the Arrayanes** (Myrtles).

At the court's north end, occupying two floors of a fortified tower, is the royal throne room, known as the **Hall of the Ambassadors**. As the sultan could only be approached indirectly it stands at an angle to the entrance from the Mexuar. It is the largest room of the palace, perfectly square and completely covered in tile and stucco decoration. Among the web of inscriptions is one that states simply "I am the Heart of the Palace". Here Boabdil signed the terms of his city's surrender to the Catholic kings, whose motifs (the arms of Aragón and Castile) were later worked into the room's stunning wooden dome, a superb example of *lacería*, the rigidly geometric "carpentry of knots". Here too, so it is said, Fernando met with Columbus to discuss his plans for finding a new sea route to India – which led to the discovery of the Americas. The dome itself, in line with the mystical-mathematical pursuit of medieval Moorish architecture, has a complex symbolism representing the seven heavens. Carlos V tore down the rooms at the southern end of the court; from the arcade there is access to the gloomy **Chapel Crypt** of his palace which has a curious "whispering gallery" effect.

THE HAREM

The **Court of the Lions**, which has become the archetypal image of Granada, constitutes the heart of the harem section of the palace. The stylized and archaic-looking
lions beneath its fountain probably date, like the patio itself, from the reign of
Mohammed V, Yusuf's successor; a poem inscribed on the bowl tells how much fiercer
they would look if they weren't so restrained by respect for the sultan. The court was
designed as an interior garden and planted with shrubs and aromatic herbs; it opens on
to three of the finest rooms in the palace, each of which looks directly on to the
fountain.

At the far end is the **Hall of the Kings**, whose dormitory alcoves preserve a series
of unique paintings on leather. These, in defiance of Koranic law, represent human
scenes; it's believed that they were painted by a Christian artist in the last decades of
Moorish rule. However, the most sophisticated rooms, apparently designed to give a
sense of the rotary movement of the stars, are the two facing each other across the
court. The largest of these, the **Hall of the Abencerrajes**, has the most startlingly
beautiful ceiling in the Alhambra: sixteen-sided, supported by niches of stalactite vaulting, lit by windows in the dome and reflected in a fountain on the floor. This light and
airy quality stands at odds with its name and history, for here Abu'l-Hasan (Boabdil's
father) murdered sixteen princes of the Abencerraje family, whose chief had fallen in
love with his favourite, Zoraya; the rust stains in the fountain are popularly supposed to
be the indelible traces of their blood.

The **Hall of the Two Sisters**, across the patio, is more mundanely named – from
two huge slabs of marble in its floor – but just as spectacularly decorated, with a dome
of over 5000 "honeycomb cells". It was the principal room of the sultan's favourite,
opening on to an inner apartment and balcony, the **Mirador de Daraxa** (known in
English as the "Eyes of the Sultana"); the romantic garden patio below was added after
the Reconquest.

Beyond, you are directed along a circuitous route through **apartments** redecorated
by Carlos V (as at Sevilla, the northern-reared emperor installed fireplaces) and later
used by Washington Irving. Eventually you emerge at the **Peinador**, or Queen's
Tower, a pavilion that served as an oratory for the sultanas and as a dressing room for
the wife of Carlos V; perfumes were burned beneath its floor and wafted up through a
marble slab in one corner.

From there, passing the **Patio de la Reja** (Patio of the Grille) added in the seventeenth century, you reach the **Royal Baths**. These are tremendous, decorated in rich
tile mosaics and lit by pierced stars and rosettes once covered by coloured glass. The
central chamber was used for reclining and retains the balconies where singers and
musicians – reputedly blind to keep the royal women from being seen – would entertain the bathers.

TOWERS AND THE PALACIO DE CARLOS V

Before leaving the palace compound a number of the **towers** are worth a look. Most
are richly decorated – particularly the first, the **Torre de las Damas** – which stands in
front of its own patio (restored to the original design). The usual exit is through the
courtyard of **Carlos V's palace**, where bullfights were once held. The palace itself
(begun in 1526 but never finished) seems totally out of place here, but is in fact a distinguished piece of Renaissance design in its own right – the only surviving work of Pedro
Machuca, a former pupil of Michelangelo. On its upper floors is a forgettable *Museo de
Bellas Artes*; on the lower, currently closed for repairs but otherwise open from
10.30am to 3pm, is a small collection of Hispano-Moorish art, its highlight the beautiful
fifteenth-century "Alhambra vase". These museums are officially closed on Monday,
but frequently fail to open on other days.

The Generalife

Paradise is described in the Koran as a shaded, leafy garden refreshed by running water where the "fortunate ones" may take their rest under tall canopies. It is an image which perfectly describes the **Generalife**, the gardens and summer palace of the sultans. Its name means literally "garden of the architect" and the grounds consist of a luxuriantly imaginative series of patios, enclosed gardens and walkways.

By chance an account of the gardens during Moorish times, written rather poetically by a Moorish historian called Ibn Zamrak, survives. The descriptions that he gives aren't all entirely believable, but they are a wonderful basis for musing as you lie around by the patios and fountains. There were, he wrote, celebrations with horses darting about in the dusk at speeds that made the spectators rub their eyes (a form of festival still indulged in at Moroccan *fantasías*); rockets shot into the air to be attacked by the stars for their audacity; tightrope walkers flying through the air like birds; men bowled along in a great wooden hoop, shaped like an astronomical sphere . . .

Today, devoid of such amusements, the gardens are still evocative – above all, perhaps, the **Patio de los Cipreses**, a dark and secretive walled garden of sculpted junipers where the Sultana Zoraya was suspected of meeting her lover Hamet, chief of the unfortunate Abencerrajes. Nearby, too, is the inspired flight of fantasy of the **Camino de las Cascadas**, a staircase with water flowing down its stone balustrades. This is just above the wonderful little **Summer Palace**, with its various decorated belvederes. From just below the entrance to the Generalife the **Cuesta del Rey Chino** – an alternative route back to the city – winds down towards the river Darro and the old Arab quarter of the Albaicín (see below).

The Albaicín and around the town

If you're spending just a couple of days in Granada it's hard to resist spending both of them in the Alhambra. There are, however, a handful of minor Moorish sites and, climbing up from the Darro, the run-down medieval streets of the **Albaicín**, the largest and most characteristic Moorish quarter that survives in Spain. In addition, it's worth the distinct readjustment and effort of will to appreciate the city's later Christian monuments.

The Albaicín and other Moorish remains

The Albaicín stretches across a fist-shaped area bordered by the river, the Sacromonte hill, the old town walls and the winding Calle de Elvira (parallel to the Gran Vía de Colón, the main avenue which bisects central Granada). The best approach is along the Corredera del Darro, beside the river. At no. 31 in this street are the remains of the **Baños Árabes** (Tues-Sat 10am–2pm), marvellous and very little-visited Moorish public baths. At no. 43 is the **Casa de Castril** (Tues–Sun 10am–2pm; 200ptas), a Renaissance mansion which houses the town's **Archaeological Museum**. Of particular note here are some remarkable finds from the Neolithic **Cueva de los Murciliegos** (cave of the bats) in the Alpujarras, including grass sandals, baskets and jewellery. Beside the museum a road ascends to the church of San Juan (with an intact thirteenth-century minaret) and to **San Nicolás**, whose square offers a view of the Alhambra considered to be the best in town.

Outside the Albaicín are the two most interesting Moorish mansions: the **Corral del Carbón**, a fourteenth-century *caravanserai* (an inn where merchants would lodge and, on the upper floors, store their goods), now home of the Turismo; and the **Casa de los Tiros**, actually built just after the Reconquest. The Corral del Carbón is a little tricky to find; it's down an alleyway off the c/de los Reyes Católicos, opposite the **Alcaicería**, the old Arab silk bazaar, burned down in the nineteenth century and poorly restored as an arcade of souvenir shops.

Perhaps the most interesting Moorish building in the lower town, though, and oddly one of the least well known, is the so-called **Palacio Madraza**, a strangely painted building opposite the Capilla Real. Built in the early fourteenth century, this is a former Islamic college (*medressa* in Arabic) and retains part of its old prayer hall, including a magnificently decorated *mihrab*. It is open somewhat sporadically for exhibitions; you may have to knock for admission.

The Capilla Real, Cathedral and churches

The **Capilla Real** (daily March–Sept 10.30am–1pm & 4–7pm; Oct–Feb 11am–1pm & 3.30–6pm; 200ptas) itself is an impressive building, flamboyant late Gothic in style and built ad hoc in the first decades of Christian rule as a mausoleum for *Los Reyes Católicos*, the city's "liberators". The actual tombs are as simple as could be imagined: Fernando and Isabella, flanked by their daughter Joana ("the Mad") and her husband Felipe ("the Handsome"), resting in lead coffins placed in a plain crypt. But above them – the response of their grandson Carlos V to what he found "too small a room for so great a glory" – is a fabulously elaborate monument, with sculpted Renaissance effigies of all four monarchs. In front is an equally magnificent *reja*, the work of Maestro Bartolomé of Baeza, and an altarpiece which depicts Boabdil surrendering the keys of Granada.

Isabella, in accordance with her will, was originally buried on the Alhambra hill (in the church of San Francisco, now part of the *parador*) but her wealth and power proved no safeguard of her wishes; recently the candle that she asked should perpetually illuminate her tomb was replaced by an electric bulb. In the capilla's **Sacristy** is displayed the sword of Fernando, the crown of Isabella and an outstanding collection of medieval Flemish paintings – including important works by Memling, Bouts and van der Weyden – and various Italian paintings, including works by Botticelli and Pedro Berruguete.

For all its stark Renaissance bulk, Granada's **Catedral**, adjoining the Capilla Real and entered from the door beside it (same hours as Capilla Real; 200ptas), is a disappointment. It was begun in 1521, just as the chapel was finished, but was then left incomplete well into the eighteenth century. At least it's light and airy inside, though, and it's fun to go round putting coins in the slots to light the chapels up.

Other churches have more to offer, and with sufficient interest you could easily fill a day of visits. North of the catedral, ten minutes' walk along c/San Jerónimo, the Baroque **San Juan de Dios**, with a spectacular *retablo*, is attached to a majestically portalled hospital (which is still in use). Close by is the elegant Renaissance **Convento de San Jerónimo** (10am–1.30pm & 4–7pm; 200ptas), founded by the Catholic kings though built after their death.

Lastly, on the northern outskirts of town, is the **Cartuja** (Mon–Sat 10am–1pm & 4–7pm; Sun 10am–noon & 4–7pm; 150ptas), perhaps the grandest and most outrageously decorated of all the country's lavish Carthusian monasteries. It was constructed at the height of Baroque extravagance – some say to rival the Alhambra – and has a chapel of staggering wealth, surmounted by an altar of twisted and coloured marble. It's a further ten- to fifteen-minute walk beyond San Juan de Dios (or take bus #8 from the centre going north along Gran Vía de Colón).

Fuente Vaqueros Lorca Museum

To the west of the city in the village of Fuente Vaqueros, the birthplace of Frederico Garcia Lorca has been transformed into a **museum** (Tues–Sun 10am–1pm & 5–7pm; guided visits on the hour; 200ptas). The house contains a superb and highly evocative collection of Lorca memorabilia.

Buses operated by *Ureña* run to the village from Avda. de Andaluces, fronting the train station.

Eating, drinking and entertainment

You don't come to Granada for food and nightlife, and it's certainly not one of the gastronomic centres of Spain. On the other hand, like so many Spanish cities, the centre has plenty of animated bars serving good, inexpensive food and staying open late. All along c/Calderería Nueva you'll find health-food stores, and Moroccan and traditional Spanish groceries. Its an ideal place to assemble picnics for Alhambra visits. Alternatively, try the Mercado Municipal at the southern end of c/Agustín.

Restaurants and tapas bars

Relatively **inexpensive** food is to be found all over Granada, though there are inevitably plenty of tourist traps too. The warren of streets between Plaza Nueva and Gran Vía has plenty of good value places, particularly *tapas* bars, as does the area around Plaza del Carmen (near the *Ayuntamiento*) and along c/Navas leading away from it. Another good location is the Campo del Principe, a pleasant square below the southside of the Alhambra hill, with a line of open-air restaurants serving inexpensive *menús*.

IN THE CITY CENTRE

Cepillo, c/Pescadería. Very popular with locals for its great value filling *menús* – fish and squid are the specialities.

Cunini, c/Pescadería 9, off c/Príncipe behind the Alcaicería. One of Granada's established upmarket restaurants, mainly fish with a cheaper *tapas* bar attached. Expensive.

Bar Gambino, Plaza Mariana Pineda, next door to the Sampedro. Has a *comedor* which serves good roast chicken.

Gargantua, Placeta Sillería 7 near c/Reyes Católicos. Excellent atmosphere and food.

Restaurante León, c/Pan 3. A good place to linger, serving *menús* at all prices. *Tapas* is served at the bar during the week.

El Mesón, Plaza Gamboa 2, behind the *Ayuntamiento*. Serves classic Granada food like *habas y jamón*. Medium to Expensive.

Nueva Bodega, c/Cettimeriem 3. A traditional place, with a crowd of locals at the bar where the prices are cheaper.

Patio Andaluz, Escudo del Carmen 10. Very lively with one of the lowest-priced *menús* in town.

Cafetería-Restaurante La Riviera, c/ Cettimeriem 5. Popular café with a good *menú económico*, including a vegetarian option.

Café-Bar Sampedro, in Plaza Mariana Pineda, southwest of c/Navas. Good *tapas*.

Mesón Yunque, Plaza San Miguel Bajo in Albaicín. Great atmosphere; mainly student clientele.

AROUND TOWN

El Amir, General Narváez 3, in the south of the city near the the Plaza de Gracia. Superb Arab restaurant with delicious hummus and falafel, wonderful dishes of rice and ground meat with pine nuts and cinnamon, and meatballs in a spicy sauce. Expensive.

La Estancia, c/Pedro Antonio de Alarcón. A medium-priced French restaurant on the eastern edge of the university area.

Hindi, c/de la Cruz 2, near the Plaza de Gracia. An Indian vegetarian restaurant – quite a rarity for Spain.

El Mesón, **La Esquina**, **La Gotera** and **Sol**, c/Pedro Antonio de Alarcón. A string of good *tapas* bars along this street.

Café-bar Ochando, Avda. de los Andaluces. Situated right by the train station and open 24 hours. Very handy for late or early travellers; serves a good breakfast.

Nightlife

Enjoyable central **bars** include *Bodegas Castañeda* on the corner of c/Elvira and c/Almireceros, near the top of the Gran Vía, a traditional *bodega*, though recently modernized; *La Buhardilla*, unsigned, on nearby c/Sillería; and *Bar Sabanilla*, c/San

Sebastian 14, which claims to be the oldest in Granada, and serves free *tapas* with every drink. All these stay open until around midnight.

If you want to go on drinking through the early hours, head out to the student areas round the university. Gran Capitán, c/San Juan de Dios and c/Pedro Antonio de Alarcón are all extremely lively: try *Los Girasoles*, San Juan de Dios 25. In term time, students also gather in **pubs** near the bus station round the Campo del Príncipe, a square on the eastern slopes of the Alhambra.

Good **disco-bars** include *Entresuelo*, c/Azacallas, a popular meeting place for English-language teachers; *Patapalo*, c/Naranjos 2; *Berlín* and *Espacio Abierto*, both in c/Obispo Hurtado; *La Estrella*, c/Cuchilleros near Plaza Nueva; the long-established *Planta Baja*, Carril del Picón; and *Camborio*, a newly fashionable place in Sacromonte. Two **women's bars** are *La Sal*, c/Marqués de Falces and *Pie de la Vela*, Paseo Tristes just off Plaza Nueva. The city's liveliest discos are in Sacromonte (see below).

For the city's most authentic **flamenco**, try the *Peña Platería* at Patio de los Aljibes 13, near San Nicholas in Sacromonte; this is a members' club, but visitors are allowed in most evenings – turn up at around 9pm.

Sacromonte

Like many cities of Andalucía, Granada has an ancient and still considerable gypsy population, from whose clans many of Spain's best *flamenco* guitarists, dancers and singers have emerged. Traditionally the gypsies inhabit cave homes on the **Sacromonte hill**, and many still do, giving displays of *zambras* to the tourists. These can occasionally be good, though more often they're straight-faced and fabulously shameless rip-offs: you're hauled into a cave, leered at if you're female, and systematically extorted of all the money you've brought along (for dance, the music, the castanets, the watered-down sherry . . .). The simple solution is to take only as much money as you want to part with. Turn up mid-evening; the lines of caves begin off the Camino de Sacramonte, just above the Casa del Chapiz.

One of the most touristy and heavily promoted of the *flamenco* shows is *Los Jardines Neptuno*, which in summer you should avoid: in winter, however, it's better, with an intimate atmosphere and a log fire in the bar. When the university is in session, several of the cave dwellings are turned into **discos**, packed with students at weekends.

The Sierra Nevada

The mountains of the **Sierra Nevada** rise to the south of Granada, a startling backdrop to the city, snowcapped for much of the year and offering good trekking and also skiing from November until late May. The ski slopes are at **Solynieve**, an unimaginative, developed resort just 28km away. From here, you can make the two- to three-hour trek up to **Veleta** (3470m), the second highest peak of the range. This is a perfectly feasible day trip from Granada by bus. For more serious enthusiasts, the renowned trek across the Sierra is the **Ruta de los Tres Mil**.

The best **map** of the Sierra Nevada and of the lower slopes of the Alpujarras (see p.281) is the one coproduced by the *Instituto Geográfico Nacional* and the *Federación Española de Montañismo* (1:50,000), which is generally available in Granada.

Flora and fauna

The Sierra Nevada is particularly rich in **wild flowers**. Some fifty varieties are unique to these mountains, among them five gentians, including *Gentiana bory*, the pansy *Viola nevadensis*, a shrubby mallow *Lavatera oblongifolia*, and a spectacular honeysuckle, the seven- to ten-metre-high *Lonicera arborea*. **Wildlife** abounds away from the roads; one of the most exciting sights is the *Cabra hispanica*, a wild horned goat which you'll see standing on pinnacles, silhouetted against the sky. They roam the mountains in herds and jump up the steepest slopes with amazing agility. Bird-watching is also superb, with the colourful hoopoe – a bird with a stark, haunting cry – a common sight.

The Veleta/Mulhacén ascent

The Sierra Nevada is easily accessible from Granada. Throughout the year, *Autocares Bonal* runs a bus to the Solynieve resort, southeast of the city and, just above this, to the *Parador de Sierra Nevada* (see below). The bus leaves from the Fuente de las Batallas, by the *Hotel Zaida* (top of Avda. José Antonio, above the Puerta Real) at 9am, returning from the *parador* at 5pm (and passing Solynieve 10 minutes later).

From the *parador* the Capileira road continues to climb and actually runs past the **peak of Veleta**; the dirt surface is perfectly walkable even when it's closed to cars. Allow two to three hours up to Veleta and two hours down.

During the summer, you can drive all the way to Capileira (see p.285). With a great deal of energy you could conceivably walk the route, though it's a good 25km, there's nothing along the way, and this being the highest motorable pass in Europe, temperatures drop pretty low by late afternoon. An hour beyond Veleta you pass just under **Mulhacén** (the tallest peak at 3481m), two hours of exposed and windy ridge-crawling from the road.

Solynieve

SOLYNIEVE is a hideous-looking ski resort and regarded by serious Alpine skiers as something of a joke. But with snow lingering so late in the year, it does have obvious attractions. At least you can have fun. From the middle of the resort a lift takes you straight up to the main ski lift, which provides access to most of the higher **slopes**, and when the snow is right you can ski a few kilometres back down to the *zona hotelera* (the lifts run only when there's skiing).

The Turismo in Granada can advise on snow conditions, and accommodation at the resort, or contact the *Federación Andaluz de Esquí*, Paseo de Ronda 78 (☎958/250706). There are plenty of places to rent ski equipment in Solynieve. For budget **accommodation** try the *Albergue Universitario* (☎958/480122; ③ half board) at Peñones de San Francisco, just off the main road, up towards the *parador*. The *Parador Sierra Nevada* is more modern, less elaborate and less expensive than many (☎958/480200; ⑤).

Ruta Integral de los Tres Mil (High Peaks Traverse)

The classic **Ruta Integral de los Tres Mil**, a complete traverse of all the Sierra's peaks over 3000m high, starts in Jeres del Marquesado on the north side of the Sierra Nevada (due south of Guadix) and finishes in Lanjarón, in the Alpujarras; an exhausting three- to four day itinerary. A slower pace entails overnight stays near Puntal de Vacares, in the Siete Lagunas valley, at the Félix Méndez shelter and at the Cerro Caballo hut. Slightly shorter, and more practicable variations involve a start from the Vadillo refuge in the Estrella valley (northwest of Vacares), or from Trevélez in the Alpujarras, and a first overnight at Siete Lagunas.

Whichever way you choose, be aware that the section between Veleta and Elorrieta calls for rope, an ice axe (and crampons before June) and good scrambling skills. There is another difficult section between Peñón Colorado and Cerro de Caballo. If you're not up to this, it is possible to **detour** round the Veleta–Elorrieta section, but you will end up on the ridge flanking the Lanjarón river valley on the east rather than on the west; here there is a single cement hut (the *Refugio Forestal*), well-placed for the final day's walk to Lanjarón.

For **any exploration of the Sierra Nevada**, do take a tent and ample food. If you cannot reach or find the huts (which are marked correctly on the 1:50,000 map), and the weather turns nasty, you will need to be able to fend for yourself.

An easier alternative

The full *Ruta* is probably more than most people – even hardy trekkers– would want to attempt. A modified version, starting in **Trevélez** and ending in **Lanjarón** (with the detour noted above), is more realistic though still strenuous.

Ascending Mulhacén from Trevélez is a full six hours up, four hours down – assuming that you do not get lost or rest (both unlikely) and that there is no snowpack on Mulhacén's east face (equally unlikely until July). If you decide to try, be prepared for an overnight stop. Heading out of Trevélez, make sure that you begin on the higher track over the Crestón de Posteros, to link up with *acequias* (irrigation channels) coming down from the top of the Río Culo Perro (Dog's Arse River) valley; if you take the main, tempting trail which goes toward Jeres del Marquesado, and then turn into the mouth of the Río Culo Perro, you face unbelievable quagmires and thorn patches. The usual place to **camp** is in the Siete Lagunas valley below the peak, allowing an early-morning ascent to the summit before the mists come up.

Continuing the traverse, you can drop down the west side of Mulhacén (take care on this awkward descent) to the dirt road coming from Veleta. Follow this toward Veleta, and you can turn off the road to spend a second night at Félix Méndez hut (main area not open until after spring snow melt, meal service thereafter; the hut's annexe with four bunks should always be open). Moving on, to the west, plan on a third night spent at either Cerro Caballo or the *Refugio Forestal*, depending on your capabilities.

Las Alpujarras

Beyond the mountains, further south from Granada, lie the great **valleys of the Alpujarras**, first settled in the twelfth century by Berber refugees from Sevilla, and later the Moors' last stronghold in Spain.

The valleys are bounded to the north by the Sierra Nevada, and to the south by the lesser sierras of Lujar, La Contraviesa and Gador. The eternal snows of the high sierras keep the valleys and their seventy or so villages well watered all summer long. Rivers have cut deep gorges in the soft mica and shale of the upper mountains, and over the centuries have deposited silt and fertile soil on the lower hills and in the valleys; here the villages have grown, for the soil is rich and easily worked. The intricate terracing that today preserves these deposits was begun as long as 2000 years ago by Visigoths or Ibero-Celts, whose remains have been found at Capileira.

The **Moors** carried on the tradition, and modified the terracing and irrigation in their inimitable way. They transformed the Alpujarras into an earthly paradise, and here they retired to bewail the loss of their beloved lands in *al-Andalus*, resisting a series of royal edicts demanding their forced conversion to Christianity. In 1568 they rose up in a final, short-lived revolt, which led to the expulsion of all Spanish Moors. Even then, however, two Moorish families were required to stay in each village to show the new Christian peasants, who had been marched down from Galicia and Asturias to repopulate the valleys, how to operate the intricate irrigation systems.

Through the following centuries, the valley settled into an impoverished existence, with the land falling into the hands of a few wealthy families, and the general population becoming impoverished labourers. The Civil War passed lightly over the Alpujarras; the occasional truckload of Nationalist youth trundled in from Granada, rounded up a few bewildered locals, and shot them for "crimes" of which they were wholly ignorant; Republican youths came up in their trucks from Almería and did the same thing. Under Franco the stranglehold of the landlords increased and there was real hardship and suffering. Today, the population has one of the lowest per capita incomes in Andalucía, with – as a recent report put it – "a level of literacy bordering on that of the Third World, alarming problems of desertification, poor communications and a high degree of under-employment".

Ironically, the land itself is still very fertile – oranges, chestnuts, bananas, apples and avocados grow here – while the recent influx of **tourism** is bringing limited wealth to the region. The so-called "High" Alpujarras have become popular with Spanish tourists; Pampaneira, Bubión and Capileira, all within half an hour's drive from Lanjarón, have been scrubbed and whitewashed. Though a little over-prettified, they're far from spoiled, and have acquired shops, lively bars, good unpretentious restaurants and small, family-run *pensiones*. Other villages, less picturesque, or less accessible, have little employment, and are sustained only by farming.

Approaches: Lanjarón and Órjiva

The road **south from Granada to Motril** climbs steeply after leaving the city, until at 860m above sea level it reaches the **Puerto del Suspiro del Moro** – the Pass of the Sigh of the Moor. Boabdil, last Moorish king of Granada, came this way, having just handed over the keys of his city to the *Reyes Católicos* (see "The Alhambra"). From the pass you catch your last glimpse of the city and the Alhambra. Just beyond Béznar, is the turning to **Lanjarón** and **Órjiva**, the market town of the region. There are several buses a day from both Granada and Motril to Lanjarón and Órjiva, and one a day from Almería in the east.

There's also a bus which goes to Ugíjar, in the "Low" Alpujarras, from Granada, via a less scenic route through Lanjarón, Orjiva, Torvizcón, Cadiar, Yegen and Valor; about four hours to the end of the line. A bus direct to the High Alpujarras leaves the main Granada bus station at 1.30pm daily. It goes via Trevélez as far as Murtas; in the other direction it passes Berchules at 7.15am, Trevélez at 8am, arriving in Granada at noon.

Lanjarón

LANJARÓN has been subject to tourism and the influence of the outside world for longer than anywhere else in the valley, good enough reason perhaps for passing straight through to the higher villages. Its attraction is the curative powers of its waters, sold in bottled form throughout Spain. Between June and October the spa baths are open, and the town fills with the aged and infirm. The place itself is little more than a ribbon of buildings, mostly modern, along the road. Below, marking Lanjarón's medieval status as the gateway to the Alpujarras, is a Moorish castle, now dilapidated and barely visible. A ten-minute stroll reveals its dramatic setting – follow the signs down the hill from the main street and out onto the terraces and meadows below the town.

The countryside and mountains within a day's walk of Lanjarón, however, are beyond compare. Walk up through the backstreets behind the town and you'll come across a track that takes you steeply up to the vast spaces of the **Reserva Nacional de la Sierra Nevada**. For a somewhat easier day's walk out of Lanjarón, go to the bridge over the river just east of town and take the sharply climbing, cobbled track which parallels the **river**. After two to two-and-a-half hours through small farms, with magnificent views and scenery, a downturn to a small stone bridge permits return to Lanjarón on the opposite bank. Allow a minimum of six hours, including snack stops and contingencies.

There's no shortage of **hotels** and **pensiones** in the town. The grand-looking *Hotel España*, c/Generalísimo Franco 44 (☎958/770187; ③) is very good and friendly, and the *Bar Galvez* offers inexpensive accommodation (②) and excellent meals. More upmarket, the *Hotel Miramar*, Avda. Andalucía 10 (☎958/770161; ④) has a pool, garden and garage, whilst 1km east of town, there's peace, tranquillity and excellent *tapas* at the *Pensión El Mirador* (☎958/770181; ②).

Lanjarón has plenty of **restaurants** and *tapas* bars too. The *Manolete*, c/Queipo de Llano 107, is much esteemed by the locals for its *tapas*, while *Los Mariscos* in the square off Avda. Andalucía is the place to go for seafood. *Bar Suizo* looks like a Swiss tearoom but the food here is excellent. More expensive, *El Club*, Avda. Andalucía 18, serves Alpujarran dishes and is reckoned to be the best restaurant in town.

There's even a nightclub, *Noche Azul*, on the corner of the main square, with two Italian ice cream parlours opposite.

Órjiva

Eleven kilometres east of Lanjarón is **ÓRJIVA** (also spelled Órgiva), the "capital" of the western Alpujarras. It is closer to the heart of the valley but still really a starting point; if the bus goes on to Capileira, you may want to stay on it. If you're **driving** it's worth noting that this is the last stop for petrol before Cadiar or Ugíjar.

Órjiva is a lively enough town, though, with a local produce market on Thursdays, and a number of good bars and hotels. On the main street is a sixteenth-century Moorish palace which today houses various shops; in its proportions and design it still has a certain beauty. A yoga centre, *Cortijo Romero*, just 1km east of Órjiva, often has programmes of shiatsu and other activities besides yoga – a sign of the times hereabouts; Órjiva, and surrounding farms and villages, are attracting a growing band of expatriate "New Age" Europeans. The **mercado** building in town is now full of wholefood stalls and jugglers.

For budget **accommodation**, choose from the *Alma Alpujarra* and the *Pensión Nemesis* facing each other across the road; a *fonda* above the *Bar Ortega*; and a *comidas/camas* next to the *Alsina Graells* office (all ①–②). More luxurious, and recently refurbished, is the *Hostal Mirasol* (☎958/785159; ③), which also does good *tapas* and reasonable *menús* inside or on their terrace. The best *tapas*, though, are at the *Semaforo* by the traffic lights, particularly the *calamares*. For good meals at reasonable prices try the quiet family-run *Mirasierra* at the bottom of town.

The mountains behind Órjiva form the **Sierra de Lujar**, running into the **Sierra la Contraviesa**. The whole range of hills on the south side of the valley was once densely forested, indeed many years ago the whole of the Alpujarras was well covered with trees. But in 1980 a great forest fire swept for miles along the hillsides, scorching the life from the trees but leaving the wood undamaged; tens of thousands of acres of forest were ruined overnight. It's alleged that a pulp paper company paid hoodlums to start the fire – the next day they were buying up the dead trees at a fraction of the real price.

The High (Western) Alpujarras

The best way to experience the **High Alpujarras** is to walk and there are a number of paths between Órjiva and Cadiar, at the furthest reaches of the western valleys (see box). Equip yourself with the *Instituto Geográfico Nacional/Federación Española de Montañismo* 1:50,000 map, which covers all the territory from Órjiva up to Berja, and a compass. Alternatively, a bus leaves daily from Lanjarón at 2.30pm and winds through all the upper Alpujarran villages; hitching, too, is generally good in these rural areas, though cars are few and far between.

Trekking in the Alpujarras

Half a century ago the **Camino Real** (Royal Way), a mule track that threaded through all the high villages, was the only access into the Alpujarras. Today the little that's left is quiet, used only by the occasional local mule or foreign walker. At their best, Alpujarran paths follow mountain streams, penetrate thick woods of oak, chestnut and poplar, or cross flower-spangled meadows; in their bad moments they deteriorate to incredibly dusty firebreaks, forestry roads or tractor tracks, or (worse) dead-end in impenetrable thickets of bramble and nettle. Progress is slow, grades are sharp and the heat (between mid-June and Sept) is taxing. A reasonable knowledge of Spanish is a big help.

Cañar, Soportújar and Carataunas

Heading on from Órjiva, the first settlements you reach, almost directly above the town, are **CAÑAR** and **SOPORTÚJAR**. Like many of the High Alpujarran villages, they congregate on the neatly terraced mountainside, planted with poplars and laced with irrigation channels. Both have bars where you can get a **meal and a bed** for the night; both are perched precariously on the steep hillside with a rather sombre view of Órjiva in the valley below, and the mountains of Africa over the ranges to the south. Just below the two villages, the tiny hamlet of **CARATAUNAS** is particularly pretty, though it has nowhere to stay.

The Poqueira Gorge and up to Capileira

Shortly after Carataunas the road swings to the north, and you have your first view of the **Poqueira Gorge**, a huge sheer gash into the heights of the Sierra Nevada. Trickling deep in the bed of the cleft is the Río Poqueira, which has its source near the peak of Mulhacén. The steep walls of the gorge are terraced and wooded from top to bottom, and dotted with little stone farmhouses. Much of the surrounding country looks barren from a distance, but close up you'll find that it's rich with flowers, woods, springs and streams.

A trio of villages – three of the most spectacular and popular in the Alpujarras – teeters on the steep edge of the gorge among their terraces. The first is **PAMPANEIRA**, neat, prosperous and pretty. Around its main square are a number of bars, restaurants and **pensiones**; try *Casa Diego* by the fountain (②). A weaving workshop just down the hill specializes in traditional *Alpujarreño* designs. On the very peak of the western flank of the Poqueira Gorge is the **Tibetan Buddhist Monastery of Al Atalaya**. The Spanish reincarnation of the head lama – one Yeshé – is currently undergoing training under the Dalai Lama in the Himalayas. Lectures on Buddhism are held regularly and facilities exist for those who want to visit the monastery for periods of retreat.

HIGH ALPUJARRAS TREKS: THE HIGHLIGHTS

For the determined, the most rewarding **sections of treks** include:

Pitres to Mecina Fondales: Twenty minutes' trek, and then a good hour-plus from neighbouring Ferreirola to Busquistar.

Busquistar toward Trevélez: One hour's trek, and then two-plus hours of road walking.

Pórtugos toward Trevélez: Two hours' trek, meeting the tarmac a little beyond the end of the Busquistar route.

Trevélez to Berchules: Four hours' trek, but the middle two hours is dirt track.

Trevélez to Juviles: Three hours' trek, including some sections of firebreak.

HOUSES IN THE ALPUJARRAS

Houses in the valleys are built of grey stone, flat-roofed and low; whitewashing them is a recent innovation. The coarse walls are about 750cm thick, for summer coolness and protection from winter storms. Stout beams of chestnut, or ash in the lower valleys, are laid from wall to wall; on top of these is a mat of canes or split chestnut; upon this flat stones are piled, and on the stones is spread a layer of *launa*, the crumbly grey mica found on the tops of the Sierra Nevada. It must, and this maxim is still observed today, be laid during the waning of the moon for the *launa* to settle properly and thus keep rain out. Gerald Brenan wrote in *South from Granada* of a particularly ferocious storm: "As I peered through the darkness of the stormy night, I could make out a dark figure on every roof in the village, dimly lit by an esparto torch, stamping clay into the holes in the roof."

BUBIÓN is next up the hill: there's a fancy hotel, *Villa Turística del Poqueira* (☎958/763111; ⑤), a comfortable *pensión*, *Las Terrazas* (☎958/763034; ③), and a bar where you can ask for rooms in private houses. There is also a ranch which will arrange **horseback riding** ; trips of from one to five days are offered in groups with a guide (☎958/763135, 763034 or 763038). The new **Turismo** can also book horse-riding tours and help with accommodation.

Capileira

CAPILEIRA is the highest of the three villages (the seasonal road across the heart of the Sierra Nevada, "Europe's highest road", ends here), with many **bars, hostales and restaurants** – the *Casa Ibero* (aka the *Mesón Alpujarreón*) serves excellent food; and the *Mesón-Hostal Poqueira* is good value (☎958/763048; ③, with heating), and also offers one of the best *menús* in the province. One of the quietest places in town, well away from the main road, is the *Fonda Restaurante El Tilo* (②) on Plaza Calvario, while one of the houses in the village, the *Residencia de Artistas*, is reserved for the use of visiting artists; a part of it is set aside as a **museum** containing various bits and pieces belonging to, or produced by, Pedro Alarcón, the nineteenth-century Spanish writer who visited the Alpujarras and wrote a book about it.

In addition to the direct daily afternoon **bus** from Granada, continuing to Murtas and Bérchules, anything going to Ugíjar and Berja will come very close to Capileira; the bus out to Granada passes by at 9am.

Capileira is a handy base for easy **day walks** in the Poqueira Gorge. For a not too strenuous example, take the northernmost of three paths below the village, each with bridges across the river. This sets off from alongside the *Pueblo Alpujarreño* villa complex. The path winds through the huts and terraced fields of the river valley above Capileira, ending after about an hour and a half at a dirt track within sight of a power plant at the head of the valley. You can either retrace your steps or cross the stream over a bridge to follow a dirt track back to the village. In May and June, the fields are tended – laboriously and by hand, as the steep slopes dictate. Reasonably clear paths or tracks also lead **to Pampaneira** (2–3hr, follow lower path to the bridge below Capileira), continuing to Carataunas (1hr, mostly road) and Órjiva (45min, easy path) from where you can get a bus back. In the other direction, taking the Sierra Nevada road and then the first major path to the right, by a ruined stone house, you can reach **Pitres** (2hr), Pórtugos (30min more) and Busquístar (45min). Going in the same direction but taking the second decent-sized path (by a sign encouraging you to "conserve and respect nature"), **Trevélez** is some five hours away – you can also get to Pórtugos this way.

Along the High Route to Trevélez

PITRES and **PÓRTUGOS**, the next two villages on the High Route are perhaps more "authentic" and less polished. You're more likely to find **rooms** here during high season, while all around spreads some of the best Alpujarran walking country. In Pitres try the *Fonda Sierra Nevada* (②) on the main square or there's a campsite, *Balcón de Pitres* (☎958/766111), with pool, in a stunning position just out of town. Pórtugos has the *Hostal Mirador* (☎958/766014; ④) on the main square and a *fonda* at Los Castaños, 1km east.

Down below the main road are the three villages of Mecina Fondales, Ferreirola and Busquistar; along with Pitres, these formed a league of villages known as the *Taha* under the Moors. **FERREIROLA** and **BUSQUISTAR** are especially attractive, as is the path between the two, clinging to the north side of the valley of the Río Trevélez. You're out of tourist country here and the villages display their genuine characteristics to better effect; there's an unmarked **inn** just uphill from the church in Busquistar but no real restaurant. A walking circuit of the three from either Pitres or Pórtugos need take no more than two hours, though in practice you'll probably want to linger along the way.

TREVÉLEZ, at the end of an austere ravine carved by the Río Trevélez , is purportedly Spain's highest permanent settlement. In traditional Alpujarran style it has upper and lower *barrios*, overlooking a grassy, poplar-lined valley where the river starts its long descent. The village is also well provided with **hostales**, located in both the lower and upper squares, and with *camas* advertised over a few bars. Try *Pensión Regina*, Plaza Francisco Abellán (☎958/858564; ③), or *Hostal Fernando* (☎958/858565; ②), on the road into town. There's also a **campsite**, *Trevélez* (☎958/765075), just outside the village. Among **restaurants**, the *Río Grande*, down near the bridge, has good, solid food and is often the only place open in the evening; one to avoid is the unnamed joint near the upper plaza advertising roast chicken and rabbit – an absolute rip-off. *Jamón serrano* is a local speciality and obsession, and a good place to try it is *Mesón del Jamón* in the *barrio medio* above the Plaza de la Iglesia.

Although Capileira is probably the more pleasant base, Trevélez is traditionally the jump-off point for the **high sierra peaks** (to which there is a bona fide path) and for treks across the range (on a lower, more conspicuous track). The latter is still used, and begins down by the bridge on the eastern side of the village. After skirting the bleak *Horcajo de Trevélez* (3182m), and negotiating the Puerto de Trevélez (2800m), the path drops gradually down along the north flank of the Sierra Nevada to Jeres del Marquesado (see the *Ruta de los Tres Mil*, p.280).

East from Trevélez

Heading east from Trevélez, you come to **JUVILES**, an attractive town straddling the road. At its centre is an unwhitewashed, peanut-brittle-finish church with a clock that's slightly slow (like most things round here). In the evening people promenade in the road, knowing that there will be no traffic, although there's a perfectly good plaza by the church. A single all-in-one *fonda-restaurante*-store (meals on demand; ②) is reasonable, with great views from the second floor east over the valley to Cadiar.

BÉRCHULES, a high village of grassy streams and chestnut woods, lies only 4km beyond Juviles, but a greater contrast can hardly be imagined. It is a large, abruptly demarcated settlement, three streets wide, on a sharp slope overlooking yet another canyon. The *Fonda-Restaurante Carvol* has decent **rooms** (②), and next door there's an excellent grocery – a godsend if you're planning on doing any walking out of here, since most village shops in the Alpujarras are primitive.

Just below Bérchules, **CADIAR**, the central town of the Alpujarras, is more attractive than it seems from a distance, and there are a handful of **hostales** and *camas* if you want to stay; *Hostal Montaro*, c/San Isidro 20 (☎958/750068; ①) near the central plaza, has heated rooms. There's a colourful **produce market** on the 3rd and 18th of every month, sometimes including livestock. And from October 5–9 a **Wine Fair** takes place, turning the waters of the fountain literally to wine.

Cadiar and Bérchules mark the end of the western Alpujarras, and a striking change in the landscape; the dramatic, severe, but relatively green terrain of the Guadalfeo and Cadiar valleys gives way to open rolling land that's much more arid.

Eastern Alpujarras

The villages of the eastern Alpujarras display many of the characteristics of those to the west but as a rule they are poorer and much less visited by tourists. There are vineyards on the hills in the south of this region and the good dry red wine is available in most of the Alpujarran villages, west or east, and is always worth asking for.

Yegen and Ugíjar

In **YEGEN**, some 7km northeast of Cadiar, there's a plaque on the house where **Gerald Brenan** lived during his ten or so years of Alpujarran residence. His autobiography of these times, *South from Granada*, is the best account of rural life in Spain between the wars, and describes the visits made here by Virginia Woolf, Bertrand Russell and the arch-complainer Lytton Strachey. Disillusioned with the strictures of middle-class life in England after World War I, Brenan rented a house in Yegen and shipped out a library of 2000 books, from which he was to spend the next eight years educating himself. He later moved to the hills behind Torremolinos, where he died in 1987, a writer better known and respected in Spain (he made an important study of Saint John of the Cross) than in his native England.

Brenan connections aside, Yegen is still one of the most characteristic Alpujarran villages, with its two distinct quarters, cobbled paths and cold-water springs. It has a **fonda**, *Bar La Fuente* (①), opposite the fountain in the square.

UGÍJAR, 12km on from Yegen, is the largest community of this eastern part, and an attractive, quiet, market town. There are easy and enjoyable walks to the nearest villages (up the valley to Mecina-al-Fahar, for example), and plenty of places to stay: try the relatively luxurious *Pensión Pedro* (☎958/767149; ②) which also serves midday meals, or the very cheap *camas* opposite the bus stop in the central plaza. *Seis Estrellas*, on the corner of the plaza by the church, serves excellent food. There is a bus service on to Almería (3hr).

The Southern Ranges

The tiny hamlets of the southern Alpujarras have an unrivalled view of the Mediterranean, the convexity of the hills obscuring the awful development that mars the coast. There are few villages of any size, but the hills host the principal **wine-growing district** of the Alpujarras. For a taste of the best of its wine, try the *venta* (wine shop) at Haza del Lino (Plain of Linen); the house brew is a full-bodied rosé.

Inland towards Almería: Guadix

An alternative **route from Granada to Almería** runs via **GUADIX**, a crumbling old Moorish town with a vast and extraordinary cave district. This, the **Barrio Santiago**, still houses some 10,000 people and it's well worth a stop .

The quarter extends over a square mile or so in area, just beyond the ruined **Alcazaba (**daily 9am–1pm & 4–6pm; 100ptas), which is signposted as you come into the old walled part of town and is entered from the adjoining theological school. The entrance to the Barrio is behind the whitewashed church of Santiago. The lower caves, on the outskirts, are really proper cottages with upper storeys, electricity, television and running water. But as you walk deeper into the suburb, the design quickly becomes simpler – just a whitewashed front, a door, a tiny window and a chimney. Penetrating right to the back you'll come upon a few caves which are no longer used: too squalid, too unhealthy, their long-unrepainted whitewash a dull brown. Yet right next door there may be a similar, occupied hovel, with a family sitting outside and other figures following dirt tracks still deeper into the hills.

Guadix itself is a pleasant, modest old place with a grand Plaza Mayor and some good-looking mansions. If you want **to stay**, try the *Fonda García* (☎958/660596; ②), just inside the walls by a prominent Moorish gateway, the Puerta San Turcuato, or either of the *hostales* on the main Carretera de Murcia at the edge of town; *Hostal Río Verde* (☎958/660729; ③) and *Pensión Mulhacén* (☎958/660750; ③). For **food**, the *Mesón Cato*, Pasajede la Purisina 6, just off the Plaza Mayor, has a *menú*, and the *Restaurante El Albergue*, Avda. Medina Olmos 48, next to the bus station is also a reasonable place.

Buses run direct from Granada to Guadix (*Empresa Autodia* from c/Rector Marín). The bus station in Guadix is a five-minute walk outside the walls.

On from Guadix

En route towards Almería you pass through more of the strange, tufa-pocked landscape from which the Guadix caves are hewn. The main landmark is a magnificent sixteenth-century castle high above **La Calahorra** (keys from c/de los Claveles 2 if you find it closed). Guadix–Almería buses normally follow the train line, along the minor N324 over the last section. If you're driving, you might want to keep going straight on the main road, meeting the Almería–Sorbas road at what has become known as **Mini Hollywood** (see p.29), the preserved film set of *A Fistful of Dollars*.

Almería Province

The **province of Almería** is a strange corner of Spain. Inland it has an almost lunar landscape of desert, sandstone cones and dried-up riverbeds. On the coast it's still largely unspoiled; lack of water and roads frustrated development in the 1960s and 1970s and it is only now beginning to take off. A number of **good beaches** are accessible by bus, and in this hottest province of Spain they're worth considering during what would be the "off-season" elsewhere, since Almería's summers start well before Easter and last into November. In midsummer it's incredibly hot (frequently touching 100°F/38°C in the shade), while all year round there's an intense, almost luminous, sunlight. This and the weird scenery have made Almería one of the most popular film locations in Europe – much of *Lawrence of Arabia* was shot here, along with scores of spaghetti westerns.

Almería

ALMERÍA is a pleasant modern city, spread at the foot of a stark grey mountain. At the summit is a tremendous **Alcazaba** (daily 10am–2pm & 5.30–8pm; 250ptas, free with EC passport), probably the best surviving example of Moorish military fortification, with three huge walled enclosures, in the second of which are the remains of a mosque, converted to a chapel by the *Reyes Católicos*. In the eleventh century, when Almería was an independent kingdom and the wealthiest, most commercially active city of Spain, this citadel contained immense gardens and palaces and some 20,000 people. Its grandeur was reputed to rival the court of Granada but comparisons are impossible since little beyond the walls and towers remains, the last remnants of stuccowork having been sold off by the locals in the eighteenth century.

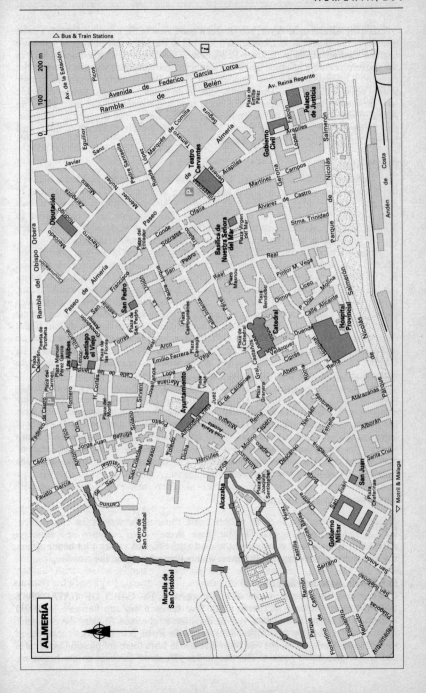

△ Bus & Train Stations

ALMERÍA

From the Alcazaba, however, you do get a good view of the coast, of Almería's **cave quarter** – the *Barrio de la Chanca* on a low hill to the left – and of the city's strange fortified **Cathedral** (daily 10.30am–12.30pm & 5.30–6.30pm & service hours), built in the sixteenth century at a time when the southern Mediterranean was terrorized by the raids of Barbarossa and other Turkish and North African pirate forces; its corner towers once held cannons. There's little else to do in town, and your time is probably best devoted to strolling between the cafés, bars and *terrazas* on the main Paseo de Almería, which runs from the central Puerta de Purchena down towards the harbour, and taking day trips out to the beach. The city's own **beach**, southeast of the centre beyond the train lines, is long but dismal.

Practicalities

The **Turismo** (Mon–Fri 10am–2pm & 5–7pm) is on c/Hermanos Machado, between the harbour and the train and bus stations; they have a list of most buses out of Almería in all directions, as well as train schedules. Almería **airport** is 8km out of town with a connecting bus service every half-hour. The city also has a **daily boat to Melilla** on the Moroccan coast throughout the summer – an eight-hour journey which can pay dividends in both time and money over Algeciras if you're driving.

Rooms are not normally difficult to come by at any time of the year, and a good place to start looking is around the Puerta de Purchena, the hub of the modern town. Just off this intersection, *Hostal Andalucía*, c/Granada 9 (☎950/237733; ②), is a charming old hotel with good value rooms. One street along on the west side, *Hostal Nixar*, c/Antonio Vico 24 (☎950/237255; ③), is another good value place; ask for a high airy room. To the east of Puerta de Purchena, the friendly *Hostal Maribel*, Avda. García Lorca 153 (☎950/235173; ②), is another budget option. Close to the bus station, *Hostal Americano*, Avda. de la Estación 6 (☎258011; ③), is handily placed if you're arriving on a late bus. The nearest **campsite**, *La Garrofa* (☎951/235770) is on the coast at La Garrofa, some 5km west, easily reached by the buses to Aguadulce and Roquetas de Mar (where there's another, giant site; ☎950/235770).

When it comes to **eating** and **drinking**, the Puerta de Purchena is a great place to head for, particularly at night. On the north side, in a small street, *Restaurante Alfareros*, c/Marcos 6, has an excellent value *menú*. On the opposite side of the junction, there's a popular *marisquería*, *Bar El Alcázar*, Paseo de Almería 4, with plenty of *tapas* possibilities. Just in from here, you'll find an alley, c/Tenor Iribarne, filled with tables from many other *tapas* establishments, and close by, *Bodegas Las Botas*, c/Fructuoso Perez 3 is well worth seeking out. For **bars**, try the streets around Plaza Masna off the southern end of the Alameda.

The beaches and inland

Almería's best **beaches** lie on its eastern coast; those to the west of the city, particularly Aguadulce and Roquetas de Mar, have already been exploited and although they're not quite as bad as many on the Costa del Sol, they're not a lot better either. Either place is an easy day trip, however, with hourly buses along the coast.

El Cabo de Gata and San José

Heading east, the closest resort with any appeal is **EL CABO DE GATA**, where there's a lovely expanse of coarse sand. Five buses a day run between here and Almería, making an intermediate stop at Retamar, a retirement/holiday development. Arriving at El Cabo, you pass a lake, the **Laguna de Rosa**, protected by a conservation society and home to flamingos and other waders. In town there are plentiful bars, cafés and shops, plus a fish market. The two *fondas* (③) above the bars on the beach are both quite expensive; **rooms** at the *Pizzería Pedro* (②) are cheaper and self-contained. The beach gets windy in the afternoons, and it's a deceptively long walk eastwards to **Las Salinas** (The Salt Pans – exactly that) for a bar and café.

Beyond lies **SAN JOSÉ**, also reached by bus from Almería. This is an established and popular resort, set back from a sandy beach in a small cove, with shallow water, and fine beaches within walking distance. **Accommodation**, however, can be hard to come by in summer. *Casa de Huéspedes Costa Rica* (②), on the main road a little way out, is one of the most inexpensive and also serves a reasonable *menú*. *Hostal Bahia* (☎950/380307; ③) is a comfortable modern hotel in the centre. A good **campsite** (April–Oct) on the beach offers hope if everywhere seems full. There are again numerous excellent bars and cafés, and a well-stocked supermarket.

Next along the coast is **LOS ESCULLOS**, with a reasonable beach and a pleasant, if slightly overpriced, beachfront hotel-restaurant, *Casa Emilio* (☎950/389761; ④). **LA ISLETA** is another fishing town, with a sleepy atmosphere, a sandy beach and a **hostal** overlooking the harbour, *Hostal Isleta de Moro* (☎951/366313; ③); this is reasonably priced and has a popular bar for *tapas*, often full (or choosy about its customers). At **LAS NEGRAS**, further on, there's a cove with a pebbly beach and a few bars; you might strike lucky with a room in a private house but there's no other accommodation.

Inland: Mini Hollywood

Rather livelier than the eastern resorts is the strip of coast between Carboneras and La Garrucha, centred on the town of Mojácar. This is some way up the coast and to get there you'll have to travel through some of Almería's distinctive desert scenery. There are two possible routes: via Níjar to Carboneras, or via Tabernas and Sorbas to Mojácar.

NÍJAR is a neat, white and typically Almerían town, with narrow streets designed to give maximum shade and it makes a good base from which to explore the coast. There are two or three small **hostales**; try *Montes* (☎951/360157; ②), with a *comedor*, on the main road into town. There's also a pizzeria on this road, one of very few places to eat here. Níjar's **pottery** is attractive, traditional patterns and mineral dyes giving the ware an archaic quality. Blankets and rugs made at the local textile mills are on sale too.

The most dramatic landscapes, however, lie further north, between **TABERNAS** and **SORBAS**. Both towns look extraordinary, especially Sorbas, whose houses overhang an ashen gorge, but neither is really a place to linger – this is the middle of a desert. Just outside Tabernas, in a particularly gulch-riven landscape, is **MINI HOLLYWOOD**, the set of the spaghetti western *A Fistful of Dollars* and various other movies. This has been preserved and opened up as a tourist attraction: you can wander into the saloon for a drink, and on Saturday (in season) the fantasy is carried a step further with a mock bank raid.

Mojácar

MOJÁCAR, Almería's main and growing resort, lies a couple of kilometres back from the sea, a striking town of white cubist houses wrapped round a harsh outcrop of rock. In the 1960s, when the main Spanish *costas* were being developed, this was virtually a ghost town, its inhabitants – among them the infant Walt Disney – having long since taken the only logical step, and emigrated. The town's fortunes suddenly revived, however, when the local mayor, using the popularity of other equally barren spots on the Spanish islands and mainland as an example, offered free land to anyone willing to build within a year. The bid was a modest success, attracting one of the decade's multifarious "artist colonies", and now, twenty years later, they are quickly being joined by package holiday firms and second-home professionals. A plush new 280-room hotel has opened in the town, as well as a *parador* on the beach and a burgeoning foreign jet-set now lives here for half the year and migrates in summer.

PALOMARES AND SOME BOMBS

Near the border of Andalucía and Murcia province is the village of **Palomares**. Here, on January 17, 1966, an American B-52 bomber collided with a tanker aircraft during a mid-air refuelling operation. Following the collision, three ten-megaton **H-bombs** fell on land and a fourth into the sea, just off the village. Those that fell in the fields were recovered quickly, though one had been damaged, causing radioactive contamination nearby. Fifteen US warships and two submarines searched for many weeks before the fourth bomb was recovered. On March 19 thousands of barrels of plutonium-contaminated soil were transported by the USAF for disposal in South Carolina. Nobody has ever convincingly explained how the incident happened, nor is it known why the bombs didn't explode, for the damaged bomb had actually lost its safety catch.

If you want to stay in the town there are a handful of small **hostales**; try *Casa Justa*, c/Morote 5 (☎950/478372; ③). Down at the beach, there's a good **campsite**, *El Cantal de Mojácar* (☎951/478204), lots of fine beach bars (currently a little overwhelmed by Spanish heavy metal), rooms to **let** and several **hostales**. Among the *hostales*, try either the *Puntazo* (☎951/478229; ③) or the *Africano* (③); the latter has a fine seafood restaurant. The modern *Parador Reyes Católicos* (☎951/478250; ⑤) is set in a palm-tree landscape right by the beach. The **beach** itself is excellent and the waters (like all in Almería) are warm and brilliantly clear.

Bus services, incidentally, reflect Mojácar's popularity with Catalans; you can arrange a ticket to Barcelona, from the beach, at the *Viajes Solar* travel agent at the La Gaviota complex.

Carboneras and La Garrucha

South of Mojácar beach lie a succession of small, isolated coves, the most accessible of them reached down a rough coastal track that turns off towards the sea just under 4km down the road to Carboneras. The scenic Mojácar–Carboneras road itself winds perilously through the hills some way inland, and offers only occasional access to some tempting beaches. There's no bus either, and you'd need to be very intent on escaping the crowds to want to drive this way.

CARBONERAS has an average beach and a couple of **hostales**: *San Antonio*, c/Castillo (☎951/130019; ③), is reasonable, slightly marred by the shadow of a massive cement factory around the bay. Beyond, a small road extends to the isolated fishing hamlet of **AGUA AMARGA**, a more attractive spot with a tasteful crop of villas.

North from Mojácar there's easier access, with occasional buses and reasonably easy hitching to **LA GARRUCHA**, a lively, if unattractive, town and fishing harbour. This is in the process of development, with villas now thick on the ground and many more in the offing, but it does have a life of its own besides tourism. There are several expensive **hostales** and a summer-only **youth hostel**, but you're more likely to visit its reasonable beach as a good afternoon's break from Mojácar. There are also some fine seafront fish restaurants; try *Los Porrones* at the south end of the promenade.

travel details

Trains

Algeciras to Córdoba (4 daily; 5–6hr); Granada (2 daily; 5hr 30min–6hr); Madrid (2 daily; 12hr 30min–15hr). All Algeciras trains via Ronda and Bobadilla.

Córdoba to Madrid (5 daily; 4hr 30min–8hr; via Linares-Baeza 2hr 30min–3hr).

Granada to Almería (2 daily; 3hr 45min–4hr 15min); Guadix (2 daily; 2hr); Linares-Baeza (2 daily; 3–4hr); Madrid (2 daily; 6–8hr); Ronda (1 daily; 5hr); Valencia (3 daily; 8–12hr, 1 via Linares-Baeza).

Huelva to Zafra (2 daily; 4hr 30min).

Jaén to Madrid (2 daily; 4–5hr).

Málaga to Córdoba (8 daily; 2hr 30min–3hr 30min); Fuengirola (every 30min; 50min); Granada (2 daily; 3hr 30min); Madrid (5 daily; 7–10hr); Ronda (3 daily; 3hr); Sevilla (5 daily; 3hr 30min–4hr); Torremolinos (every 30min; 28min).

Sevilla to Badajoz (4 daily; 5–7hr); Cádiz (8 daily; 1hr 30min–2hr); Córdoba (10 daily; 1hr 30min–2hr); Huelva (2 daily; 1hr 30min); Madrid (12 daily; AVE 3hr 15min or 6–9hr); Mérida (4 daily; 3hr 30min).

Buses

Algeciras to Cádiz (9 daily; 3hr); La Línea (for Gibraltar: hourly; 30min); Madrid (1 daily; 10hr); Sevilla (6 daily; 3hr 30min); Tarifa (11 daily; 30min).

Almería to Alicante (2 daily; 7hr); Granada (2 daily; 4hr); Guadix (2 daily; 2hr 30min); Mojácar (4 daily; 2hr).

Cádiz to Chipiona (9 daily; 1hr 30min); Conil (6 daily; 1hr); Jerez de la Frontera (8 daily; 45min).

Córdoba to Badajoz (1 daily; 6hr 30min); Écija (4 daily; 1hr 15min); Granada (5 daily; 4hr); Jaén (5 daily; 2hr); Madrid (1 daily; 6hr); Sevilla (5 daily; 2hr 30min).

Granada to Alicante (5 daily; 5hr 30min); Almería (7 daily; 4hr); Guadix (4 daily; 1hr); Madrid (4 daily; 6hr); Motril (7 daily; 2hr); Sierra Nevada/Alpujarras (4 daily to Lanjarón and Órjiva in 2hr 15min; 1 daily to most of the other villages along most of the routes); Valencia (5 daily; 7hr 30min).

Huelva to Ayamonte/Portuguese frontier (8 daily; 1hr).

Jaén to Baeza (8 daily; 1hr 15min); Granada (10 daily; 2hr); Madrid (1 daily; 5hr 30min); Úbeda (8 daily; 1hr 30min).

Málaga to Algeciras (10 daily; 3hr 30min); Almería (5 daily; 5hr); Córdoba (2 daily; 4hr); Granada (14 daily; 2hr 30min); Madrid (5 daily; 7–9hr); Marbella (every 30min; 1hr 30min); Motril (10 daily; 2hr 30min); Nerja (10 daily; 1hr 30min); Ronda (4 daily; 3hr 30min); Sevilla (2 daily; 3hr–4hr 30min); Torremolinos (every 30min; 30min).

Ronda to Arcos de la Frontera (3daily; 1hr 45min); Cádiz (2 daily, 3hr 30min); Jerez (3 daily, 2hr 30min); Olvera (1 daily; 30min); San Pedro de Alcántara (6 daily; 2hr, continuing to Málaga); Setenil (1 daily; 15min); Sevilla (4 daily; 3hr 15min); Ubrique (2 daily; 45min).

Sevilla to Aracena (2 daily; 2hr); Ayamonte (access to Portugal's Algarve – 3 daily); Badajoz (2 daily via Zafra, 2 daily via Jerez de los Caballeros; 5hr); Cádiz (8 daily; 1hr 30min–2hr 30min); Carmona (10 daily; 45min); Córdoba (3 daily; 3hr 15 min); Écija (3 daily; 2hr); El Rocío (5 daily; 2hr 30min); Huelva (7 daily; 2hr 30min); Madrid (3 daily; 6–10hr); Matalascañas (5 daily; 3hr); Mérida (6 daily; 3hr 30min).

Ferries

Algeciras to Ceuta (12 boats daily; 1hr 30min); Tangier (5 or 6 ferryboats daily; 2hr 30min); seasonal hydrofoil (daily; 1hr).

Almería to Melilla seasonal boat (daily, except Sun; 8hr).

Benalmádena to Tangier seasonal hydrofoil .

Cádiz to the Canary Islands of Tenerife (36hr) and Las Palmas (43hr); every two days in season, every five out; Puerto Santa María (4 daily; 20min).

Gibraltar to Tangier seasonal hydrofoil (daily; 1hr). Twice weekly ferry (Fri & Mon; 3hr).

Málaga to Melilla (daily, except Sun; 7hr 30min).

Tarifa to Tangier seasonal hydrofoil (daily; 30min); does not run in bad weather (temporarily suspended). Ferry (daily; except Sun; 2hr).

CHAPTER FIVE

OLD CASTILE AND LEÓN

The foundations of modern Spain were laid in the kingdom of **Castile**. A land of frontier fortresses – the *castillos* from which it takes its name – it became the most powerful and centralizing force of the Reconquest, extending its domination through military gains and marriage alliances. By the eleventh century it had merged with and swallowed **León**; through Isabella's marriage to Fernando in 1469 it encompassed Aragón, Catalunya and eventually the entire peninsula. The monarchs of this triumphant and expansionist age were enthusiastic patrons of the arts, endowing their cities with superlative monuments, above which, quite literally, tower the great Gothic cathedrals of Salamanca, León and Burgos.

Salamanca and **León** are the two outstanding highlights – ranking in interest and beauty with the greatest cities of Spain: with Toledo, Sevilla and Santiago. Try to take in some of the lesser towns, too, like **Ciudad Rodrigo**, **El Burgo de Osma**, **Zamora** or the village of **Covarrubias**. In all of them you'll be struck by a wealth of mansions and churches incongruous with present, or even imagined past, circumstances and status. In the people, too, you may notice something of the classic Castilian *hidalgo* archetype – a certain haughty solemnity of manner and a dignified assumption, however straitened present circumstances, of past nobility.

Over the past decade, the historic cities have grown to dominate the region more than ever. Although the Castilian soil is fertile, the harsh extremes of land and climate don't encourage rural settlement, and the vast central plateau – the 700- to 1000-metre-high *meseta* – is given over almost entirely to grain. Huge areas stretch into the horizon without a single landmark, not even a tree. Surprisingly, however, the Duero river, which has the most extensive basin in Spain, runs right across the province and into Portugal. And despite being characterized by *meseta* landscape, there are enclaves of varied scenery – in particular, the **valley of Las Batuecas** and the lakeland of the **Sierra de Urbión**, where the Duero begins its course.

The sporadic and depopulated villages, bitterly cold in winter, burning hot in summer, are rarely of interest – travel consists of getting as quickly as you can from one grand town to the next. The problem with many of the smaller places, and even some of the larger ones, is that they have little appeal beyond their monuments: **Toro**, **Tordesillas** and **Valladolid**, for example, are important historically, but their "sights" lack a stimulating setting. The most impressive of the castles are at **Coca**, **Gormaz** and **Berlanga de Duero**. The other architectural feature of the region is the host of Romanesque churches, monasteries and hermitages, a legacy of the **Camino de Santiago** (pilgrim route) which cut across the top of the province.

ACCOMMODATION PRICE SYMBOLS

The symbols used in our hotel listings denote the following price ranges:

① Under 2000ptas	③ 3000–4500ptas	⑤ 7500–12,500ptas
② 2000–3000ptas	④ 4500–7500ptas	⑥ Over 12,500ptas

See p.30 for more details.

FIESTAS

January
30 Processions in Burgos to honour *San Lesmes*.

February
3 *Romería* to Ciudad Rodrigo (Salamanca).

Week before Lent *Carnival* is also particularly lively in Ciudad Rodrigo (Salamanca).

March/April
Holy Week is if anything even more fanatically observed than in most areas – processions in all the big cities, particularly Valladolid, León, Salamanca and Zamora. The one at Medina De Rioseco (Valladolid) is also worth aiming for. Good Friday in Bercanos De Aliste (Zamora) is almost chillingly solemn, participants dressed in white gowns which will later become their shrouds. The **week after Easter** is marked by the *Fiesta del Angel* in Aranda de Duero (Burgos) and Peñafiel (Valladolid).

May
12 *Día de Santo Domingo* celebrated with a traditional fiesta in Santo Domingo de la Calzada (Rioja).

Pentecost (variable) is marked by the week-long *Feria Chica* in Palencia and with more religious celebrations in Miranda de Ebro (Burgos).

Corpus Christi (variable) sees celebrations in Palencia and Valladolid; in Benavente (Zamora) the *Toro Enmaromado* runs through the streets in the evening, endangering the lives of everyone. The following day sees the festival of *El Curpillos* in Burgos.

June
11 Logroño's *Fiestas Bernabeas* run around this date.

12 *Día de San Juan de Sahagún* celebrated in Salamanca (of which he is patron) and his birthplace, Sahagún (Leon).

24 *Día de San Juan* sees a secular fiesta with bullfights and dance in León and more religious observances in Palencia.

The following week sees a big fiesta in Soria.

23–26 *Fiesta de San Juan* at San Pedro de Manrique (Soria) – the first night opens with the famous barefoot firewalking of the *Paseo del Fuego*, described in Norman Lewis's *Voices of the Old Sea*.

29 *Día de San Pedro*. In Burgos the start of a 2-week-long *feria;* lesser events in León, and in Haro (Rioja) there's the drunken *Batalla del Vino* celebrating local wine production.

July
22 In Anguiano (Rioja) performance of the famous stilt dance – *danza de los zancos*.

August
15 Colourful festivals for the Assumption in La Alberca (Salamanca), Coca (Segovia) and Peñafiel (Valladolid).

16 *Día de San Roque* fiesta in El Burgo de Osma (Soria).

Last week *Fiesta de San Agustin* in Toro (Zamora), with the "fountain of wine" and *encierros*, and in Medinaceli (Soria) musical evenings with medieval and Renaissance music.

September
8 A big day everywhere – the first day of Salamanca's major fiesta, beginning the evening before and lasting two weeks, as well as a famous bull running in Tordesillas (Valladolid).

21 *Día de San Mateo*. Major *ferias* in Valladolid and especially Logroño, where the Rioja harvest is celebrated.

October
First Sun *Fiesta de las Cantaderas* in León.

Valladolid's *International Film Week* also falls in Oct.

November
13 The *Toro Júbilo* runs through the streets of Medinaceli on the night of the nearest Saturday, suffering agonies best not described here.

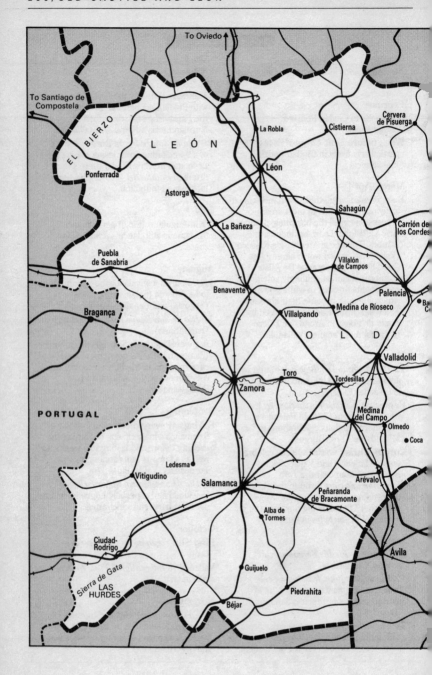

To Oviedo↑

To Santiago de
Compostela

EL BIERZO

L E Ó N

La Robla

Cistierna

Cervera
de Pisuerga

Léon

Ponferrada

Astorga

Sahagún

Carrión de
los Cordes

La Bañeza

Puebla
de Sanabria

Villalón
de Campos

Benavente

Palencia

Bragança

Villalpando

Medina de Ríoseco

Ba
C

O   L   D

Valladolid

Toro

Tordesillas

PORTUGAL

Zamora

Medina
del Campo

Olmedo

Coca

Ledesma

Vitigudino

Salamanca

Arévalo

Peñaranda
de Bracamonte

Alba de
Tormes

Ciudad-
Rodrigo

Ávila

Sierra de Gata

LAS
HURDES

Guijuelo

Piedrahita

Béjar

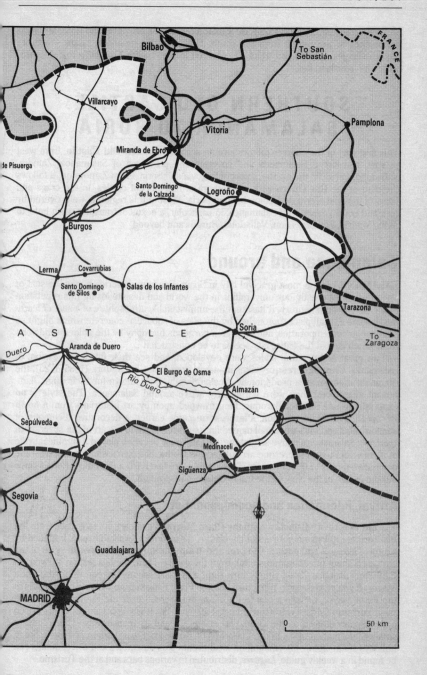

Technically, parts of the **Picos de Europa** lie in León province, and there are good approaches to the region from the south. However, this mountain range – with its superb villages, wildlife and treks – is covered in the chapter *Cantabria and Asturias*, where its heartland lies.

SOUTHERN OLD CASTILE: SALAMANCA TO SORIA

This first part of the chapter follows a route across **Southern Old Castile**, from west to east, starting at Salamanca and covering the provinces of Salamanca, Zamora, Valladolid, Palencia, the northern part of Segovia and Soria. From Zamora on, it follows the path of the **Río Duero** with its plethora of magnificent castles, to the crags and lakes of the wild Sierra de Urbíon beyond Soria. Most of this region is well-covered by **bus** and **train** routes, with Salamanca, in particular, a nexus of transport, with links to Ávila/Madrid, Zamora/León, Valladolid/Burgos and beyond.

Salamanca and around

SALAMANCA is the most graceful city in Spain. For four centuries it was the seat of one of the most prestigious universities in the world and despite losing this reputation in the seventeenth century, it has kept the unmistakable atmosphere of a seat of learning. It's still a small place, untouched by the piles of suburban concrete which blight so many of its contemporaries, and is given a gorgeous harmony by the golden sandstone from which almost the entire city seems to be constructed.

Two great architectural styles were developed, and see their finest expression, in Salamanca. **Churrigueresque** takes its name from José Churriguera (1665–1723), the dominant member of a prodigiously creative family. Best known for their huge, flamboyant altarpieces, they were particularly active around Salamanca. The style is an especially ornate form of Baroque, long frowned upon by art historians from a north European, Protestant tradition. **Plateresque** came earlier, a decorative technique of shallow relief and intricate detail named for its resemblance to the art of the silversmith (*platero*); Salamanca's native sandstone, soft and easy to carve, played a significant role in its development. Plateresque art cuts across Gothic and Renaissance frontiers – the decorative motifs of the university, for example, are taken from the Italian Renaissance but the facade of the New Cathedral is Gothic in inspiration.

Arrival, information and accommodation

The **old centre** of Salamanca, with the **Plaza Mayor** at its heart, spreads back from the Rio Tormes, still spanned by a Roman bridge. It's a compact walkable area, bounded by a loop of avenues and *paseos*. The **bus and train stations** are on opposite sides of the city, each about fifteen minutes' walk from the centre. From the bus station at Avda. de Filiberto Villalobos 73–83 simply turn right and you'll eventually end up in the Plaza Mayor. If you've arrived by train, turn left into Plaza España from where c/Toro leads to the Plaza Mayor, or take a bus to the Plaza del Merced near the Roman bridge. The main **Turismo** (Mon–Fri 9.30am–2pm & 4.30–7pm, Sat 10am–2pm) and **Correos** are on c/de España (known as the Gran Vía) at nos. 39 and 25 respectively. There's also a smaller information office in the Plaza Mayor (Mon–Fri 10am–1.30pm & 4–6pm, Sat & holidays 10am–2pm). Information on local events plus timetables and travel details can be found in a weekly guide, *Lugares*, distributed in various bars and at the Turismo.

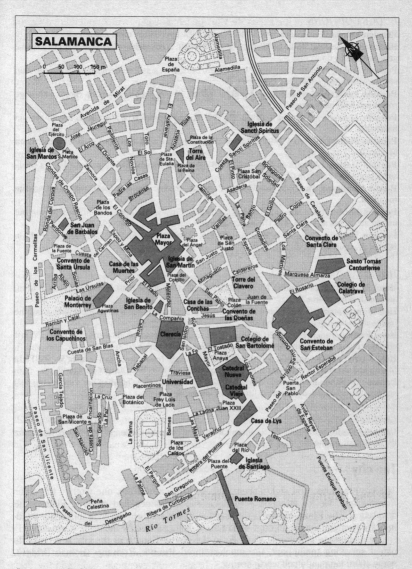

Accommodation

Prices for **accommodation** in Salamanca are reasonable, but it can be hard to find a room in high season – especially at fiesta time in September. During the summer months you may well be approached at the train station and offered *casa particulares* (private rooms). These are often the lowest priced options available as many of the *pensiones* are more or less permanently occupied by students during the academic year.

BUDGET OPTIONS

Pensión Estefania, c/Jesus 3 (☎923/217372). No frills, but reliable, clean and tidy. ②.

Hostal Internacional, Avda. de Mirat 15 (☎923/262799). A convenient place near Plaza de España; good value. ③.

Pensión Isabel, Plaza de Barcelona 24–25 (☎923/249254). A small, modern *pensión*, near the train station, with three doubles and two triples. ③.

Pensión Las Vegas, c/Meléndez 13 (☎923/218749). A very popular low-price choice with large rooms and frilly bathrooms. ②.

Pensión Lisboa, c/Meléndez 1 (☎923/214333). The best *pensión* on the street, maybe even in Salamanca. ②.

Pensión Madrid, c/Toro 1 (☎923/214296). The rooms are a bit tired, but some overlook Plaza Mayor. ②.

Pensión Marina, c/Doctrinos 4, 3° (☎923/216569). A very friendly and clean place, but it's small, so try to get there early in the day. ②.

Hostal Mindonao, Paseo de San Vicente 2 (☎923/263080). Pleasant *hostal* with good ensuite rooms. ③.

Pensión Robles, Plaza Mayor 20, 2° (☎923/213197). This central *pensión* is on Plaza Mayor, but unfortunately has no views of it. The rooms have new but small bathrooms. ③.

Pensión Virginia, Paseo de la Estación 109–115, 2° (☎923/241016). A well-run *pensión*, right in front of the train station. ③.

HOTELS

Hotel Amefa, c/Pozo Amarillo 18–20 (☎923/218189). One of the most luxurious hotels in town, and worth every peseta. ⑤.

Hotel Emperatriz, c/Compañías 44 (☎923/219200). A central hotel in a historic building, but the rooms are in need of a lick of paint. ④.

Hotel Paris, c/Padilla 1–5 (☎923/262970). Great value with ensuite bathrooms and colour TV; just off Paseo de Canalejas within walking distance of the city centre. ④.

Hostal Orly, c/Pozo Amarillo 3 (☎923/216225). Recently refurbished, this is bang on the Plaza Mayor, and as central as they come; rooms are on the small side. With its own garage. ④.

Parador de Salamanca, Toso de Feria 2 (☎923/228700). This new building has a swimming pool and great views, situated just across the Roman bridge. ⑥.

CAMPING

Camping Regio (☎923/200250). Salamanca's excellent campsite is open all year round, 4km along the Ávila road behind the *Hotel Regio*.

The city

The city's architectural sights seem endless: two **cathedrals**, one Gothic, the other Romanesque, vie for attention with Renaissance **palaces** and gems of Plateresque decoration. The **Plaza Mayor** is the finest in Spain; and the surviving university buildings are tremendous throughout – all of them distinguished by the same warm stone.

For a stunning panoramic view, go to the extreme south of the city and cross its oldest surviving monument, the much-restored **Puente Romano** (Roman Bridge), some 400m long and itself worth seeing.

Around the Plaza Mayor

The grand **Plaza Mayor** is the hub of Salamantine life. You get the impression that everyone passes through its cafés and arcaded walks at least ten times a day. Its bare central expanse, in which bullfights were staged as late as 1863, is enclosed by one continuous four-storey building decorated with iron balconies and medallion portraits. It was the work of Andrea García Quiñones and Alberto Churriguera, younger brother of José, and nowhere is the Churrigueras' inspired variation of Baroque so refined as here.

From the south side of the plaza (facing the *Ayuntamiento*), Rua Mayor leads to the vast Baroque church of **La Clerecía**, seat of the Pontifical University. At present you can only visit the patio (Mon–Fri 9am–1.30pm & 4.30–8.30pm, Sat 9am–1pm) as the church is opened just for Mass. Opposite stands the city's most distinctive (and reproduced) building, the early sixteenth-century mansion, **Casa de las Conchas** (House of Shells), so-called because its facades are decorated with rows of carved scallop shells, symbol of the pilgrimage to Santiago.

The University

From the Casa de las Conchas, c/Libreros leads to the **Patio de las Escuelas** and the Renaissance entrance to the **University** (Mon–Sat 9.30am–1.30pm & 4–6.30pm, Sun 10am–1pm; 200ptas). The ultimate expression of Plateresque, this building symbolizes the tremendous reputation of Salamanca in the early sixteenth century.

The **facade** of the university is covered with medallions, heraldic emblems and a profusion of floral decorations, amid which lurks a hidden frog said to bring good luck and marriage within the year to anyone who spots it unaided. The centre is occupied by a portrait of Isabella and Fernando, surrounded by a Greek inscription commemorating their devotion to the university; above them is the coat of arms of Carlos V, grandson and successor of Isabella.

Inside, the old **lecture rooms**, surprisingly small for a seat of learning that once boasted over 7000 students, are arranged round a courtyard. The **Sala de Fray Luís de León** preserves the original benches and the pulpit where this celebrated professor lectured. In 1573, the Inquisition muscled its way into the room and arrested Fray Luís for alleged subversion of the faith; five years of torture and imprisonment followed, but upon his release he calmly resumed his lecture with the words *"Dicebamus hesterna die . . ."* ("As we were saying yesterday . . .").

THE UNIVERSITY AT SALAMANCA

Salamanca University was founded by Alfonso IX in the 1220s, and after the union of León and Castile swallowed up the University of Palencia to become the most important in Spain. Its rise to international stature was phenomenal and within thirty years Pope Alexander IV proclaimed it equal to the greatest universities of the day. As at Oxford, Paris and Bologna, theories formulated here were later accepted as fact throughout Europe. It made major contributions to the development of international law, and Columbus sought support for his voyages of discovery from the enlightened faculty of astronomy.

The university continued to flourish under the *Reyes Católicos*, even employing a pioneering woman professor, Beatriz de Galindo, who tutored Queen Isabella in Latin. In the sixteenth century it was powerful enough to resist the orthodoxy of Philip II's Inquisition but, eventually, freedom of thought was stifled by the extreme clericalism of the seventeenth and eighteenth centuries. Books were banned for being a threat to the Catholic faith, and mathematics and medicine disappeared from the curriculum. Decline was hastened during the Peninsular War when the French demolished 20 of the 25 colleges, and by the end of the nineteenth century there were no more than 300 students.

In recent decades, numbers have been replenished (the present size is about 12,000), though, like so many of Spain's universities, it still suffers an intellectual hangover from the appointments and backward operation of Franco's regime. Although socially prestigious, it officially ranks only seventh academically, well below Madrid, Barcelona and Sevilla. It does, however, run a highly successful language school – nowhere in Spain will you see so many young Americans.

In similar tradition, one of the most spirited confrontations of the Civil War took place here when Professor Miguel de Unamuno openly challenged the Fascist General Millán Astray, who could only retort with his motto, "Long Live Death!" The **Casa-Museo Unamuno** (Tues–Fri 11am–1.30pm & 4.30–6.30pm, Sat & Sun 10am–2pm; free), next to the university's main entrance, celebrates the work of this writer and university rector. He didn't live here but in the best tradition of Spanish casa-museos, his bedroom can be seen as well as personal effects, letters, poems and an impressive array of folded paper figures no doubt constructed in moments of writer's block.

The Patio de las Escuelas is surrounded by other university buildings including the **Escuelas Menores**, which served as a kind of preparatory school for the university proper (same hours and admission as university). It has a fine zodiacal ceiling, formerly in the chapel, moved here after two-thirds of it was destroyed by tremors from the 1755 Lisbon earthquake. Again lecture rooms open off a beautiful Renaissance cloister, whose walls are inscribed with records of academic successes (*vitores*).

Adjacent is a mildly interesting **Museo de Bellas Artes** (Tues–Sun 9am–2pm), installed in the house once occupied by the doctors of Queen Isabella.

The Cathedrals

The **Catedral Nueva** (June–Sept Mon–Sat 10am–2pm & 4–8pm, Sun 10am–2pm & 4–7pm; Oct–May daily 10am–1pm & 4–6pm) was begun in 1512 as a declaration of Salamanca's prestige, and in a glorious last-minute assertion of Gothic architecture. It was built within a few yards of the university and acted as a buttress for the Old Cathedral which was in danger of collapsing. The main Gothic-Plateresque facade is contemporary with that of the university and equally dazzling in its wealth of ornamental detail. For financial reasons, construction spanned two centuries and thus the building incorporates a range of styles, with some Renaissance and Baroque elements and a tower modelled on that of the cathedral at Toledo. Alberto Churriguera and his brother José both worked here – the former on the choirstalls, the latter on the dome.

The Romanesque **Catedral Vieja** (same opening hours; 200ptas) is dwarfed by its neighbour. Its most striking feature is the massive fifteenth-century *retablo* by Nicolás Florentino. Fifty-three paintings of the lives of the Virgin and Christ are surmounted by a powerfully apocalyptic portrayal of the Last Judgement; a thirteenth-century fresco on the same theme is hidden away in the **Capilla de San Martín** at the back of the building. The cathedral's distinctive *media naranja* dome, shaped like the segments of an orange, derives from Byzantine models and is similar to those at Zamora and Toro. The exterior is known as the **Torre de Gallo** (Cock Tower) and can be seen from the Patio Chico next to the New University's south entrance.

The chapels opening off the cloisters were used as university lecture rooms until the sixteenth century. One, the **Capilla de Obispo Diego de Anaya**, contains the oldest organ in Europe (mid-fourteenth-century); the instrument shows Moorish influence and, in the words of Sacheverell Sitwell, "is one of the most romantic, poetical objects imaginable". In the Chapter House there's a small **museum** with a fine collection of works by Fernando Gallego, Salamanca's most famous painter. Active in the late fifteenth century, he was a brilliant and conscious imitator of early northern Renaissance artists such as Rogier van der Weyden.

San Esteban, Santa Clara and around

Churriguera's work is again evident in Salamanca's magnificent monastic buildings. The **Convento de San Esteban** (9am–1pm & 4–8pm), whose facade is another fault-less example of Plateresque art, is a short walk down c/del Tostado from the large Plaza de Anaya at the side of the New Cathedral. Its facade is divided into three hori-zontal sections and covered in a tapestry of sculpture, the central panel of which depicts the stoning of its patron saint, St Stephen. The east end of the church is occupied by a huge Baroque *retablo* by José Churriguera, a lavish concoction of columns, statuary and floral decoration. The monastery's cloisters, through which you enter, are magnificent too.

The most beautiful cloisters in the city, however, stand across the road in the **Convento de las Dueñas** (10am–1pm & 4–7pm). Built on an irregular pentagonal plan in the Renaissance-Plateresque style of the early sixteenth century, the imaginative upper-storey capitals are wildly carved with human heads and skulls. On the opposite side of San Esteban stands the monumental Churrigueresque **Palacio de Calatrava**.

Nearby, on Plaza San Román, is the newly restored **Convento de Santa Clara** (Mon–Fri 9am–2pm & 4–7pm, Sat & Sun 9.30am–2pm; 100ptas), a thirteenth-century building, outwardly plain but with beautiful interior features which encompass virtually every important feature of Spanish architecture and design. In 1976 the walls of the chapel, whitewashed during a long-forgotten cholera epidemic, were found to be covered with an important series of frescoes from the thirteenth to the eighteenth century, while further probing of the ceiling revealed medallions similar to those in the Plaza Mayor. Romanesque and Gothic columns, and a stunning sixteenth-century polychrome ceiling, were also uncovered in the cloister. But the most incredible discovery was made in the church, where the Baroque ceiling constructed by Churriguera was found to be false; rising above this, you can see the original fourteenth-century beams, decorated with heraldic motifs of the kingdoms of Castille and León. The prize-winning restoration is fascinating, and the icing on the cake is perhaps the city's best view of the bulk of the Catedral Nueva.

The final monument in this quarter worthy of special note is the **Torre del Clavero**, a fifteenth-century turreted octagon. It's at the far end of the Plaza de Colón, behind the convent of Las Dueñas.

West of the Plaza Mayor

Salamanca's remaining buildings of interest are situated in the **western part of the city**. If you follow c/de la Compañía from the Casa de las Conchas, you pass the Plaza San Benito, which has some fine houses, and come to the Plaza Agustinas. In front is the large **Palacio de Monterrey**, a sixteenth-century construction with end towers, unfortunately not seen to best advantage in the narrow street. Across from it is the seventeenth-century Augustinian monastery usually called **La Purísima**, for which Ribera painted several fine altarpieces, including the main *Immaculate Conception*.

Behind the Palacio de Monterrey is another interesting convent, **Las Ursulinas** (9.30am–1pm & 4.30–7.30pm). In its church, is the marble tomb of Archbishop Alonso Fonseca, a superb piece of Renaissance sculpture by Diego de Siloé. Facing the east wall of this church is the impressive facade of the **Casa de las Muertes** (House of the Dead).

Diagonally opposite the park from Las Ursulinas, c/de Fonseca leads to the magnificent Plateresque palace still commonly known as the **Colegio de los Irlandeses**. For centuries this served as the Irish seminary, until in the 1950s it was decided to concentrate resources at home. It is a corporate work by many of the leading figures of Spanish architecture in the early sixteenth century, led by Juan de Álava. The Renaissance patio, is a particular delight, with beautifully carved portrait medallions, each distinctly characterized. In the chapel there's an altarpiece with paintings and sculptures by Alonso Berruguete. Now a teacher-training college, the patio and chapel can in theory be visited from 9am to 2pm and from 4 to 7pm, although in practice whether you're allowed in or not seems to depend on the whim of the caretaker. There is also some extensive renovation taking place at present.

Eating, drinking and nightlife

Salamanca is a great place for hanging out in bars and cafés. Those in the Plaza Mayor are nearly twice the usual price but worth every peseta. Close at hand in the Plaza del Merced (by the **market**, itself a good source of provisions), there's a row of lively *tapas* bars, while the university area offers loads of good value **bars and restaurants** catering to student budgets.

Restaurants

El Bardo, c/Compañía 8. Very good value restaurant with a vegetarian *menú*.

Chez Victor, Espoz y Mina 26 (☎923/213123; closed Sun night, Mon & Aug). Upmarket French-influenced restaurant specializing in game. Reckoned to be Salamanca's finest.

La Covachuela, Plaza del Merced. Worth a drink and *tapas* in this small bar to see the waiter and his coin-flipping exploits – a Salmantine tourist attraction in his own right.

Bar Marín, c/del Prado. Good reputation for its summer speciality, frogs' legs fried in batter.

Restaurante Río de la Plata, Plaza Peso 1 (closed Mon & July). Quality Castilian home cooking; the *menú* is a reasonable 2200 ptas.

Restaurante Roma, c/Rúiz Aguilera. Inexpensive place to try *chanfaina* – a rice-based dish with meats cooked in spicy juices and the nearest Spanish cuisine gets to a curry.

El Trigal, c/de Serranos, near the University entrance. Genuine vegetarian restaurant with no alcohol and no smoking. Good value meals and a wide range of fruit juices.

Bars

For simple drinking with a chance to sample some *pinchos* (a selection of *tapas*), head for the cluster of **bars** round the *Cine Van Dyck*; there is another good selection round Plaza de la Fuente. Salamanca also has many laid-back **cafés** where you can hear live music – try *El Corrillo* in the plaza of the same name for jazz, or *El Callejón* at c/ España 68, for folk. *El Savor*, c/San Justo 34, has good latin music.

There's a whole host of **clubs** and disco bars, many along Gran Vía; *El Gran Café Moderno* at no. 65 has an excellent DJ in between sets of live music. *Camelot*, c/ Bordadores, and *El Puerto de Chus*, Plaza de San Julian, are much frequented by foreign students. *De Laval Genovés*, c/San Justo 27 has good sounds and three bars.

Around Salamanca

The countryside around Salamanca is an attractive swathe of New Castile, especially along the Río Tormes, which flows into the Duero to the northwest.

Alba de Tormes

The small hillside town of **ALBA DE TORMES**, 20km southeast of the city, makes an interesting day's excursion. The main attraction here is the **Convento de Carmelitas** (9am–1.30pm & 4–6.30pm, winter till 7.30pm), founded by Saint Teresa in 1571, with its ornate Renaissance facade and a rather dubious reconstruction of the cell in which Teresa died. Alba is a centre for making traditional Castilian **pottery**, and you can watch its manufacture at *Bernardo Pérez Correas* on c/Matadero near the river. If you want to **stay the night**, the lowest priced rooms are at the *Hostal Trébol* at c/Pizarro 1 (☎923/300089; ②). For spacious accommodation with bath try the *Hotel Alameda*, Avda. Juan Pablo II (☎923/300985; ③), which also has a good resturant. The town is served by local buses from Salamanca.

North to Zamora: Ledesma

Heading northwest from Salamanca, a delightful minor road via Ledesma makes an excellent alternative route to **Zamora**. For most of the way this route trails the beautiful

Río Tormes, where there's excellent fishing (for giant carp), herons and storks in the trees, enormous, delicious mushrooms (*setas*) in autumn and a variety of meadow flowers in spring. **LEDESMA** itself – little more than a large village these days – retains its ancient walls, the remains of a Roman bridge and baths, and a couple of attractive churches. If you're staying overnight, the *Fonda Mercado* (no phone; ②) is good. The greenery round here seems atypical of Castile – it's created in large part by the **Embalse de Almendra**, a dam almost at the Portuguese border, whose reservoir stretches all the way back to Ledesma.

Ciudad Rodrigo and the Sierra Peña de Francia

In the far southwest corner of Salamanca province, the unspoiled frontier town of **Ciudad Rodrigo** – astride the road and rail line to Portugal – is worth a detour even if you don't plan to cross the border. East of the town lies the **Sierra Peña de Francia**, with good walking and a stunning village, **La Alberca**, the whole of which has been declared a national monument.

Ciudad Rodrigo

CIUDAD RODRIGO is a quiet old place which, despite an orgy of destruction during the Peninsular War, preserves streets full of **Renaissance mansions**. If you follow the walls round – a pleasant walk – you'll pass an austere castle (now a *parador*), which overlooks a Roman bridge on the Río Agueda and commands an enticing view across into Portugal.

Focal point of the town is the **Catedral**, built in a mixture of styles but originally Transitional Gothic: take a look at the highly unusual eight-part vaults, dome-like in shape. You'll need to find the sexton to see the building's other interesting features: the *coro*, with wonderfully grotesque stalls carved by Rodrigo Alemán, who also created those at Toledo and Plasencia; the narthex, with statues of Apostles; and the cloisters (guided tours 11.30am–1.30pm & 4–7pm; 200ptas), half of which are fourteenth-century and half sixteenth-century with grotesque carvings of biblical scenes.

A pagoda-like monument to **General Herrasti** and his men (see box) stands in the little square beside the cathedral. A plaque in the corner of the walls near this marks the site of the Great Breach through which the British entered Ciudad Rodrigo; from outside, the gaping hole is clearly visible. The British guns were on the two ridges opposite (the lower one with the block of the flats, the other higher up beyond the rail line). This side of the cathedral is thus covered with cannonball dents; half the railing is smashed from the top of the dome and the tympanum above the door is wrecked.

CIUDAD RODRIGO IN THE PENINSULAR WAR

Along with Badajoz, Ciudad Rodrigo was a crucial border point in the Peninsular War. No army could cross safely between Spain and Portugal unless these two towns to its rear were secured. Ciudad Rodrigo fell to the French in 1810, despite valiant resistance from General Herrasti's Spanish garrison – in admiration for whose bravery, the French permitted them to march away from the devastated city.

Britain's Duke of Wellington re-took Ciudad Rodrigo with a devastatingly rapid siege in 1812. Aware that French reinforcements were approaching, Wellington had announced "Ciudad Rodrigo must be stormed this evening" – his soldiers duly did so, embarking on a triumphant rampage of looting and vandalism. When order was restored, the troops paraded out dressed in a ragbag of stolen French finery. A bemused Wellington muttered to his staff, "Who the devil *are* those fellows?"

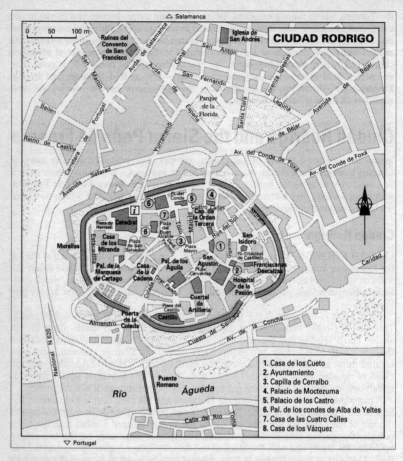

CIUDAD RODRIGO

1. Casa de los Cueto
2. Ayuntamiento
3. Capilla de Cerralbo
4. Palacio de Moctezuma
5. Palacio de los Castro
6. Pal. de los condes de Alba de Yeltes
7. Casa de las Cuatro Calles
8. Casa de los Vázquez

Ciudad Rodrigo's empty streets are ideal for wandering with no particular purpose, though if you're curious, the local tourist pamphlets provide great detail on the churches and palaces. Two of the most imposing are the **Palacio de los Castro** and **Palacio de Moctezuma**, both on Plaza Conde; the latter is now the town *Casa de la Cultura* and may be open to visits.

Practicalities

Ciudad Rodrigo has a **Turismo** (Mon–Fri 9.30am–2pm & 4.30–7pm, Sat 9.30am–2pm), facing the cathedral at the entrance to the town.

For budget **rooms**, try the *Pensión Moderno Francés* (②), opposite the bus station, which is impeccable; or, within the walls, *Pensión Madrid* (☎923/462467; ②) on c/ Madrid or *Pensión El Alamo* (☎923/460025; ②), just round the corner on c/Cadimus. Moving considerably upmarket, *Hotel Conde Rodrigo* (☎923/461404; ④), on Plaza San Salvador (and with a riverside annexe) is more luxurious, while the superb *Parador Enrique II* (☎923/460404; ⑤), in the castle, has an unrivalled location.

There are two good outdoor **cafés** on the Plaza Mayor, and several *tapas* bars in the roads radiating away on all sides. *El Kiosco* on c/San Martín is a good, inexpensive place for dinner; you'll also find plenty of substantial *menús* if you head down to the **restaurants** along the main Salamanca–Portugal road. The restaurant at the *parador* is the best and most expensive in town.

Ciudad Rodrigo's **train station** is about ten minutes' walk along the road to Lumbreras. There are two trains a day **into Portugal**, but one of these is in the dead of night.

The Sierra Peña de Francia

The village of **La Alberca** is a good place to head for, both in its own right, and as a starting point for walks in the **Sierra Peña de Francia**. There are daily buses from Salamanca, but only on Sunday does the timetable make a day trip possible.

La Alberca
LA ALBERCA has an extraordinary collection of houses, constructed from diverse materials: wood, pebbles, stone and rubble built in amongst the rocks. Due to its national monument status, plenty of tidying-up is going on, and "local craft" shops have sprung up all over, but the character of a rural community remains; horses still take precedence over cars, the restorers use donkeys instead of vans, and goats, sheep and poultry often block the streets.

The most elegant houses are in the **Plaza Mayor**, which is dominated by a Calvary. Look into the church in the square behind for its elaborate polychromed pulpit, carved in a popular style. Most of the houses in the Plaza Mayor seem to serve as cafés these days, for the tourist trade, but there is an air of timelessness to the place. Many age-old customs, including costume, have survived, and the local celebration of the Feast of Assumption on August 15 is considered to be the best in Spain.

Accommodation can be unpredictable. The two **pensiónes** are over-priced and not always open: they are *Pensión Hernandez* just off the Plaza Mayor (☎923/415039; ③), and the large, modern *Las Eras* up the hill on the Butuecas road (☎923/415040; ③). The two-star *Hostal El Castillo* (☎923/437481; ③), at the far end of the village, is the next best bet. There are also two **campsites**, (mid-June to mid-Sept), 3km and 5km north on the Salamanca road.

La Peña de Francia
A very circuitous route road behind La Alberca climbs to the summit of the **Peña de Francia**. There's no short cut on foot, except at the beginning, where you can save a couple of kilometres by cutting across the campsite furthest from town (you can ask for a route plan here). The road emerges from the trees half way up to give fine panoramas not only of the mountain itself (disfigured by a television tower serving the whole province and beyond) and the plains below, but also out over the wild hills of Las Hurdes to the south and the Sierra de Gredos to the east. At the top you can have lunch or refreshments at the *Hospedería* of the **Monasterio Peña de Francia**, which is occupied during the summer by Dominicans from San Esteban in Salamanca.

Valle de Las Batuecas
Another excellent trip from La Alberca is south to the **Valle de Las Batuecas**, a national reserve bordering Las Hurdes (see p.163). This makes an impressive day-long walk or a beautiful drive; you'll need to take a picnic, for although fresh water abounds, there isn't a bar, restaurant or even house in sight until you reach the village of Las Mestas, just over the Extremaduran border, some 19km away.

From La Alberca, take the minor road south out of the village. After 2km you'll come to the pass of **El Portillo**, surrounded by solemn, rugged hills. From here, the road dips and loops spectacularly, offering a different vista at every turn. You reach the valley floor at the 12km point, and a short road leads to the gate of the **Carmelite Monastery**, founded at the beginning of the seventeenth century for a community of hermits. One of the first tasks of the monastery was to exorcize the demons and evil spirits which supposedly inhabited the nearby valleys of Las Hurdes. In 1933, the great film-maker **Luis Buñuel** stayed in the monastery – then a hotel – while shooting his early masterpiece, *Land Without Bread*, about the extremely primitive lifestyle of the people of these valleys. Today, two superannuated monks pass their last years in this most beautiful of locations.

A footpath skirts the outside of the monastery's perimeter wall and follows the course of the river, which forms a gorge with splendid rock formations. There are **caves** with prehistoric rock paintings here, but unfortunately the most important ones have had to be closed in order to preserve them from deterioration and vandalism.

If you're walking back to La Alberca after exploring the valley, you're faced with a daunting climb; there is little traffic, although the chances of a lift from cars that do pass are good. By car, it makes a good round trip to keep going beyond **Las Mestas**, turning east at the T-junction and crossing back into Salamanca province via **Miranda Del Castañar**, with its pretty views and romantic, crumbling castle.

Zamora to Valladolid

Zamora is the quietest of the great Castilian cities, with a population of just 60,000. Its province is pretty low-key, too, though with a cluster of historic names. The road east from Zamora follows the **Río Duero** into the heartland of Old Castile, taking in **Toro**, the site of the battle which established Fernando and Isabella on the Spanish throne in 1476, and **Tordesillas** where the treaty which ratified the division of lands discovered in the New World was signed in 1494.

Zamora

In medieval romances, **ZAMORA** was known as *la bien cercada* (the closed one) on account of its strong fortifications; one siege here lasted seven months. Its old quarters, still walled and medieval in appearance, are spread out along the sloping banks of the Río Duero (known as the Douro once it crosses into Portugal). In and around the old centre are a dozen Romanesque churches whose unassumingly beautiful architecture is the city's greatest distinctive feature. Most of them date from the twelfth century and reflect Old Castile's sense of security following the victorious campaigns against the Moors by Alfonso VI and El Cid – notably the recapture of Toledo in 1085.

The **Catedral**, enclosed within the ruined citadel at the far end of town, is a fitting climax to the series. Begun in 1151, it is again Romanesque overall, though the grandiose north entrance is in the classical style of the High Renaissance. A Byzantine-inspired dome, looking quite out of place, is its most striking feature, showing the same turrets and "fish-scale" tiles as the Old Cathedral at Salamanca. The carved choir-stalls, which depict lusty carryings-on between monks and nuns, were closed for a long time at the orders of a particularly sanctimonious bishop, but are now on view again. The cathedral museum (Mon 5–8pm, Tues–Sat 11am–2pm & 4–8pm, Sun 11am–2pm; 200ptas), houses the city's celebrated and unsurpassed "Black Tapestries". The patrons who commissioned these fifteenth-century Flemish masterpieces clearly demanded their money's worth, since every inch is woven in stunning detail. Traditional Greek and Roman themes were chosen but often contemporary dress and

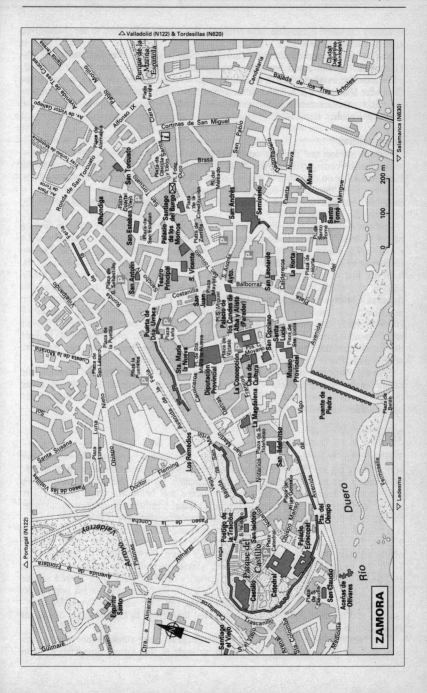

△ Valladolid (N122) & Tordesillas (N620)

△ Portugal (N122)

▽ Salamanca (N630)

▽ Ledesma

Río Duero

ZAMORA

weaponry intruded, illustrating how nobles in the Middle Ages liked to see themselves as heroes from the past.

Among the other Romanesque churches, **San Juan de Puerta Nueva** (10.30–11.30am & 7–8.30pm) and **Santiago del Burgo** (12–1.30pm) are the most rewarding, while attached to **Santa María la Nueva** is an unusual **Museo de la Semana Santa** (Mon–Sat 10am–2pm & 4–8pm, winter 4–6pm, Sun 10am–2pm; 200ptas). This contains the *pasos* – statues depicting the Passion of Christ – which are paraded through the streets at Easter.

Practicalities

The **train station** and the **bus terminal** are adjacent to each other, fifteen mintues' walk from the centre; to reach the Plaza Mayor, follow Avda. de las Tres Cruces to the Plaza Alemania on the edge of the old town. The **Turismo** (summer Mon 8am–3pm, Tues–Sat 8am–3pm & 4.30–8.30pm, Sun 10am–2pm & 4.30–8.30pm; winter Mon–Fri 8am–3pm, Sat 9am–2pm) is at c/Santa Clara 20 – take c/Pelayo, the second road to the left, from the Plaza Alemania.

Zamora suffers no more than a trickle of tourism and there's no problem finding places to stay. The best budget **accommodation** is at the modern, clean *Hostal La Reina*, c/La Reina 1 (☎988/533939; ②), with an excellent view, and at *Pensión Balborraz*, c/Balborraz 25–29 (☎988515519; ①) which has large well-furnished rooms; both are just off the Plaza Mayor. There's also a prison-like **youth hostel** (☎988/526536; ①), which is best avoided. For modern mid-priced rooms, try the *Hotel Dos Infantas*, Cortinas de San Miguel 3 (☎988/512875; ④). The very best accommodation in Zamora is at the atmospheric *Parador Condes de Alba de Aliste*, Plaza de Viriato 1 (☎988/514497; ⑥), situated in the fifteenth-century ducal palace; it's one of Spain's most beautiful *paradores* and its restaurant is superb. Popular local restaurants include the *España* and the *Pozo* on c/Ramón Alvárez north of the Plaza Mayor, and there are several inexpensive bars serving *tapas* on c/Herreros nearby.

Leaving town, you can continue north easily enough to **León** by road. The rail line heads northwest into **Galicia** – to Orense and Santiago. If you're heading east along the Duero, the minor road to Toro (along the south bank of the river) offers good opportunities for bird-watching or fishing.

Toro

TORO, 30km from Zamora, looks dramatic: "an ancient, eroded, red-walled town spread along the top of a huge flat boulder," as Laurie Lee described it when he arrived here with a group of travelling German musicians. Its raw, red, hillside site is best contemplated from the rail line several hundred feet below the town in the Duero valley. At closer quarters it turns out to be a pleasant, rather ordinary provincial town, though embellished with one outstanding Romanesque reminder of past glory.

Toro did, however, play a role of vital significance in both Spanish and Portuguese history. The **Battle of Toro** in 1476 effectively ended Portugal's interest in Spanish affairs and laid the basis for the unification of Spain. On the death of Enrique IV in 1474, the Castilian throne was disputed: almost certainly his daughter Juana *La Beltraneja* was the rightful heiress, but rumours of illegitimacy were stirred up and Enrique's sister Isabella seized the throne. Alfonso V of Portugal saw his opportunity and suported Juana. At Toro the armies clashed in 1476 and the *Reyes Católicos* – Isabella and her husband Fernando – defeated their rivals to embark upon one of the most glorious periods in Spanish history.

Toro had long been a major military stronghold enjoying considerable royal patronage, and the monument that hints most strongly at this former importance is the

Colegiata Santa María la Mayor (11am–1.45pm & 5.30–7.30pm). The West Portal (c.1240) is one of the best preserved and most beautiful examples of Romanesque art: its seven recessed arches carved with royal and biblical themes. All such portals were originally painted in a variety of colours, and this one remains close to its pristine decorative state (though in 1993 it was under restoration). If locked, enquire at the **Turismo** in the *Ayuntamiento* on the plaza for the keys.

The Dominican **Convent of Sancti Spiritus** on the western edge of town (10.30am–12.30pm & 4–6.30pm, closed last Sun in the month, Lent and Advent; 300ptas) is worth a visit, too. It's a rambling fourteenth-century building containing some genuine treasures in amongst the mass of exhibits; chiefly a series of sixteenth-century Flemish tapestries depicting the betrayal and crucifixion of Christ. In the church is the tomb of Beatriz of Portugal (wife of Juan I of Castile, died 1410), who lived here for various periods after she was widowed at the age of eighteen.

Toro's **train station** is a steep twenty-minute walk below the town and there's a *hostal*, *La Estación* (☎988/690928; ②) alongside. The only **accommodation** in the town itself is the *Hostal Juan II*, Plaza Espolon 1 (☎988/690300; ④).

Tordesillas

TORDESILLAS, like Toro, can boast of an important place in Spain's history. It was here, under the eye of the Borgia Pope Alexander VI, that the **Treaty of Tordesillas** (1494) divided "All Lands Discovered, or Hereafter to be Discovered in the West, towards the Indies or the Ocean Seas" between Spain and Portugal, along a line 370 leagues west of the Cape Verde Islands. Brazil, allegedly discovered six years later, went to Portugal – though it was claimed that the Portuguese already knew of its existence but had kept silent to gain better terms. The rest of the New World, including Mexico and Peru, became Spanish.

Further fame was brought to Tordesillas by the unfortunate **Juana la Loca** (Joanna the Mad), who spent 46 years in a windowless cell here. She had ruled Castile jointly with her husband Felipe I (the Handsome) from 1504–6 but was devastated by his early death and for three years toured the monasteries of Spain, keeping the coffin perpetually by her side, stopping from time to time to inspect the corpse. In 1509 she reached the Convent of Santa Clara, here, where first Fernando (her father) and later Carlos V (her son) declared Juana insane, imprisoning her for half a century and assuming the throne of Castile for themselves.

Juana's place of confinement could have been worse. The **Real Monasterio de Santa Clara** (Tues–Sat 10.30am–1.30pm & 3.30–7pm, Sun 10.30am–1.30pm; 350ptas, 100ptas for Arab baths) overlooks the Duero and is known as "The Alhambra of Castile" for its delightful Mudéjar architecture. It was built as a royal palace by Alfonso el Sabio (the Wise) in 1340 and its prettiest features are the tiny "Arab Patio" with horseshoe arches and Moorish decoration and the superb *artesonado* ceiling of the main chapel, described by Sacheverell Sitwell as "a ceiling of indescribable splendour, as brilliant in effect as if it had panes or slats of mother-of-pearl in it".

Elsewhere in Tordesillas, the long medieval **bridge** over the Duero, the arcaded **Plaza Mayor** and the church of **San Antolín**, now a museum with an impressive collection of sculpture, are all of interest.

If you intend **staying** in Tordesillas be warned that it stands on a major crossroads (of the Madrid–Galicia road and the direct Salamanca–Valladolid route) and *hostales* tend to be expensive. The lowest priced is the *Lorenzo* (☎983/770228; ②). Upmarket options are the modern *Parador Nacional* (☎983/770051; ⑤) and *El Montico* (☎983/770751; ⑤), an old farmhouse with a good restaurant. All these places are on the Salamanca road.

Medina del Campo

MEDINA DEL CAMPO, 24km south of Tordesillas, and the major rail junction before Valladolid, stands below one of the region's great castles. The Moorish design of the brick-built **Castillo La Mota**, is similar to that at Coca further east, but less exotic and more robust. It was intended as another stronghold for the same family, the Fonsecas, but they were thrown out by the townsfolk in 1473. Queen Isabella lived here for several years (and died, in 1504, in a room overlooking the town's Plaza Mayor) after which the castle was reincarnated as a prison, then as a girls' boarding school, and more recently as a cultural centre. You can go inside the castle walls any day except Sunday, but there are no rooms to see, and it is the exterior which is impressive.

In the fifteenth and sixteenth centuries, Medina del Campo (Market of the Field) was one of the most important market towns in the whole of Europe, with merchants converging from as far afield as Italy and Germany to attend its fairs. The largest sheep market in Spain is still held here and the beautifully ramshackle **Plaza Mayor** is evocative of the days when its bankers determined the value of European currencies.

Budget **rooms** are offered by a couple of bars on c/de Almirante just off the plaza and there's a single mid-range *hostal*, *La Mota*, c/Fernando el Católico 4 (☎983/800450; ③). For **meals**, try *Restaurante Monaco* on the Plaza de España, a splendid place with a bargain *menú*.

Valladolid

VALLADOLID, at the centre of the *meseta*, ought to be exciting. Many of the greatest figures of Spain's Golden Age – Fernando and Isabella, Columbus, Cervantes, Felipe II – lived in the city at some point and for many years it vied with Madrid as the royal capital. In reality its old quarter is today an oppressive labyrinth of dingy streets, and those of its palaces that survive do so in a woeful state of decline. Many of the finest have been swept away on a tide of speculation and official incompetence – to be replaced by a dull sprawl of high-rise concrete. Modern Valladolid may be an expanding industrial city of 400,000 inhabitants but it has lost much that was irreplaceable.

The one time you might actively seek to be in Valladolid is **Semana Santa** – Easter week – when it is host to some of the most extravagant and solemn processions in Spain.

The city

Despite the despoliation of many of the city's finest monuments, there are a couple of terrific examples of late Gothic architecture, an excellent Oriental museum and – above all – the finest collection of sculpture assembled anywhere in Spain. Aside from the national museum, almost all of the city's historic churches contain further examples of Valladolid's passionate religious sculpture.

The Cathedral and sculpture museum

At the centre of things, as ever, is the **Catedral**, designed but not completed by Juan de Herrera (architect of El Escorial) and later worked on by Alberto Churriguera; only half of it was ever built, but the model in the museum shows how classically grand the original design was. What stands is a disappointment: the vast dimensions and sweeping arches do have something of Herrera's grandeur, but the overall effect is one of plainness and severity. Inside, the highlight is the *retablo mayor* by Juan de Juni, which was actually made for **Santa María la Antigua**, in the large plaza behind: a Gothic church with modest flying buttresses and a Romanesque bell-tower which culminates in a pyramidal roof.

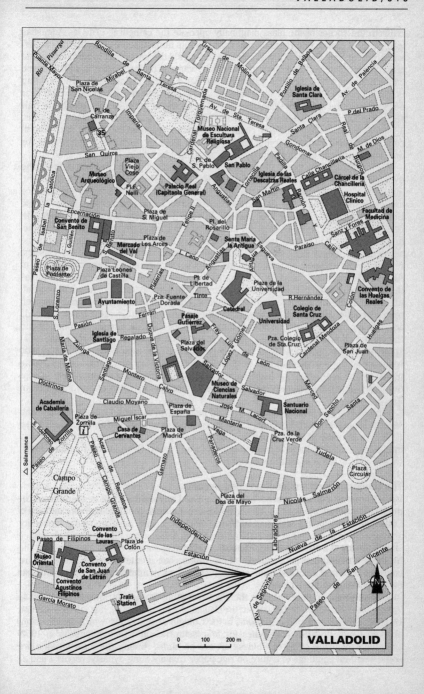

VALLADOLID

From the corner of the plaza diagonally opposite the cathedral, c/de las Angustias leads a short distance to Plaza de San Pablo and its unmistakable church. The exuberant facade of **San Pablo** is a wild mixture of styles – the lower part is a product of the lavish form of late Gothic known as Isabelline, whereas the upper part is a Platersque confection, similar to the New Cathedral and San Esteban at Salamanca. The building is treated purely as a surface for whimsical and highly decorative carvings which bear no relation to the structure that supports it. The facade of the adjacent **Colegio de San Gregorio**, a purer example of the Isabelline style, is adorned with coats of arms, sculpted twigs, naked children clambering in the branches of a tree and several comical long-haired men carrying maces. It's a lot like icing on a cake – Jan Morris, for one, was convinced that the flamboyant facades must be edible.

Behind the gaudy front, there's serious business, for San Gregorio houses the dynamic **Museo Nacional de Escultura Religiosa** (Tues–Sat 10am–2pm & 4–6pm, Sun 10am–2pm; 200ptas), where the most brilliant works of the Spanish Renaissance are on display. Much the most important figures in this movement were Alonso Berruguete, Diego de Siloé and Juan de Juni: all three were active in the sixteenth century and spent several years in Florence where they perfected the realistic depiction of anatomy, fell heavily under the influence of Michelangelo and immersed themselves in the Italian Renaissance. Their genius lies in the adaptation of the classical revival to the religious intensity of the Spanish temperament. The masterpiece of **Alonso Berruguete** (1486–1561) is a massive dismantled altarpiece which occupies the first three rooms of the museum – a remarkable demonstration of his skills in painting, relief sculpture and free-standing statuary. **Diego de Siloé** (1495–1565) was even more versatile. He created a classical building from the Gothic cathedral at Granada and was an equally accomplished sculptor – see his *Sagrada Familia* in room 10 and the carved choirstalls in room 11. Works of the Frenchman **Juan de Juni** (1507–77) show an almost theatrical streak and foreshadowed the emotional and naturalistic sculpture of the seventeenth and eighteenth centuries. This later period is best exemplified by the agonizingly realistic work of **Gregorio Fernández** (rooms 4 and 5, near the ticket desk) and **Alonso de Villabrille** (especially his *Head of San Pablo*, room 27).

While here, you should also take in the beautiful **patio** with lace-like tracery, and several Moorish-inspired ceilings taken from other buildings in the city. The chapel (entrance is immediately left of the main door, opposite the ticket booth) has many interesting exhibits, including another *retablo* by Alonso Berruguete, this time intact (hours are the same as for the museum).

The University and a miscellany of museums

Valladolid is also a famous academic centre. The **Universidad**, just beyond the cathedral, has a portal by Narciso Tomé, the man who built the *Transparente* in Toledo Cathedral – one of his very few surviving works. Further on, part of the university administration is housed in the **Colegio de Santa Cruz**, a late fifteenth-century edifice which signals the introduction of Renaissance architecture to Spain. You can visit the beautiful three-storey patio during office hours, but in the morning there's more chance of being able to visit other rooms including an exhibition room with a Mudéjar ceiling and the Baroque library.

In a surprisingly different vein there's a delightful **Museo Oriental** (Tues–Sat 4–7pm, Sun 10am–1pm; 200ptas) on the Paseo de los Filipinos, just off the Campo Grande. This occupies a dozen rooms in the Colegio de Agustinos, which sent missionaries to China and the Philippines for four centuries until their expulsion in 1952. Countless exquisite gems of Chinese art are on show. Among the most striking are some beautiful paintings of nature on rice paper (mainly Sung dynasty; rooms 1 and 2) and three gorgeous porcelain pieces entitled *The Three Happy Chinamen: Fu, Shou and Lou* (Qing epoch; room 2). On the way out you can look at the lavishly decorated interior of the church, a good example of the academic style of Ventura Rodríguez, fashionable in the late eighteenth century.

Other museums include the **Museo Arqueológico** (Tues–Fri 10am–2pm & 4–7pm, Sat & Sun 10am–2pm), just up from Plaza San Miguel in a Renaissance mansion; it has medieval and prehistoric sections. The **Museo de San Joaquín y Santa Ana** (Tues–Sat 10.30am–1pm & 4.30–7pm, Sun 10.30am–noon & 4.30–7pm) is filled mostly with religious dust-collectors but has a few good statues, plus three Goya paintings in the chapel.

Practicalities

Arrival points and information are centred around the Campo Grande, a large triangular park where Napoleon once reviewed his troops. The **train station** is on Paseo de Campo Grande; the **bus station** is a ten-minute walk west at Puente Lodgante 2. The **Turismo** is actually in a corner of the Campo, at Plaza de Zorilla 3 (Mon–Fri 9am–2pm & 4–6pm, Sat 9am–2pm; ☎983/351801). A good **travel bookshop**, *Beagle* at c/Cascajares 2, stocks a wide range of maps.

Accommodation

If you want to stay in Valladolid, there's a reasonable choice of **rooms**, but they're spread all over town. You'll find several budget possibilities near the train station and also in the seedy area around the cathedral.

BUDGET OPTIONS

Pensión Dani, c/Perú 11, 1° (☎983/300249). Excellent value, clean rooms with scrubbed wooden floors just off the road leading to Plaza de Zorilla. ①.

Pensión Dos Rosas, c/Perú 11, 2° (☎983/207439). The second of two superb value *pensiónes* owned by sisters in the same building. ①.

Hostal Residencia Paris, c/Especería 2 (☎983/358301). Centrally located with its own car park and good quality rooms. ③.

Residencia Juvenil Río Esgueva, c/Cementerio 2 (☎983/251550, 340044). Advance booking is essential at this youth hostel. ①.

Hostal Val VI, Plaza del Val 6 (☎983/352512). Reasonable rooms in the market area, north of Plaza Mayor. ②.

HOTELS

La Enara, Plaza España 5 (☎983/300311). A good central place with plenty of character. ④.

El Nogal, c/Conde Ansurez 10 (☎983/340233). Beautifully situated with comfortable rooms and its own restaurant. ④.

Restaurants and bars

The central area is the best place for eating and drinking. Near Santa María la Antigua, c/Marqués de Duero, c/Paraíso and c/Esgueva are full of good *tapas* bars, and the Plaza Mayor is also a popular place to linger.

Caballa de Troya, c/Correos 1. Pleasant *taberna* with an outdoor patio.

La Criolla, c/Correos. This is one of many restaurants in town serving the Valladolid speciality, *lechazo asado* (roast lamb).

Casa de Glaicia, opposite the Colegio de Santa Cruz. Excellent, inexpensive dishes.

Café León d'Or, Plaza Mayor. This relaxed central café is a good place to watch the world go by.

La Mina, c/Correos. An enjoyable bar behind the plaza, near the post office.

Núñez de Arce, c/Núñez de Arce. This extremely popular bar-restaurant offers interesting house specialities, such as rabbit, which can also be eaten as a *tapa ración*.

Taberna Pan con Tomate, Plaza Mayor 18. Good *tapas* bar with a modest restaurant attached.

Mesón Panero, c/Marina Escobar 1 (☎983/301673; closed Sun night). The city's gastronomic temple – pricey, but not horribly so, with a *menú* at 1900ptas.

La Pedriza, c/Marina Escobar. A good place to enjoy traditional Castilian *menús* including roast lamb.

Nightlife

Valladolid's youth congregate at night in the modern **bars** of the Paco Suárez area, around Plaza Coca and c/San Lorenzo. For something a little different try the ancient *El Penicilino* on Plaza de la Libertad, with an atmosphere more like an apothecary than a bar; its speciality is a lurid pink concoction. There's also **live jazz** in the *Café España*.

Palencia

PALENCIA is Castile's least known and least impressive province and its capital city is no exception. Despite a rich past, it has no great sights. There are numerous plazas, usually dominated by Romanesque churches built in a rather gaunt white stone, but while all are pleasant, none is outstanding.

The **Catedral**, a fourteenth- to fifteenth-century Gothic building is plain by Spanish standards, except for the two south portals. Inside, most of the decoration is contemporary with, or only slightly later than, the architecture, thanks to the patronage of Bishop Fonseca. Soon after it was completed, Palencia fell into decline – hence the almost complete absence of Baroque trappings. Buy a ticket in the sacristy to see the artistic treasures; one of the staff will take you to the crypt (part Visigothic, part Romanesque) and the museum in the cloisters, which includes a very early *San Sebastián* by El Greco and Flemish tapestries. In addition, lights are switched on so you can see the various altars, and the chapel doors opened – a facility not always available in Spain. The highlight is probably the *retablo mayor*, which contains twelve beautiful little panels, ten of them painted by Juan de Flandes, court painter to Isabella la Católica – it's the best collection of his work anywhere.

Not far from the cathedral is the Río Carrión, spanned by a picturesque old bridge known as **Puentecillas**, which contrasts well with the sturdier and later **Puente Mayor**. If you have time to kill, you could also search out one of Spain's more personal and idiosyncratic museums, the **Museo Historia del Calzado** (Mon–Wed, Fri & Sat noon–2pm & 7–9pm), above the shop of the master shoemaker, Julio Vibot Tristán at c/Barrio y Mier 10, off c/Mayor. Señor Vibot is cobbler to the royal family and this is your chance to find out about Juan Carlos's taste in footwear: there's a well-marked display of beautifully crafted shoes, the fruits of sixty years in the trade, as well as shoes from different ages belonging to various historical figures.

Practicalities

Palencia's **bus and train stations** are both on the Plaza Calvo Sotelo; at its far corner, the long c/Mayor opens out, and the **Turismo** is near the end of it. On the way, *Pensión Comercio*, c/Mayor 26 (☎988/745074; ②) is an adequate place to stay, and on the other side of the Turismo, is the friendly and spotless *El Salón*, Avda. República Argentina 10 (☎988/726442; ③). *Hostal Monchas*, c/Menéndez Pelayo 3 (☎988/744300; ④) is more luxurious but good value. For good *tapas* and *raciones* try *La Taberna Plaza Mayor* in the southeast corner of the plaza, or *Don Jamón* off its northeast corner. *Lorenzo*, Avda. Casado del Alisal 10 (closed Sept 10–Oct 10), is the top restaurant and quite modestly priced.

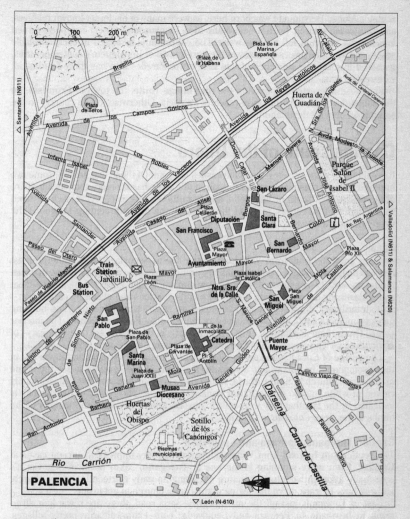

Around Palencia

South of Palencia, at the ugly, modern town of **Venta de Baños** is an important train junction. If you are changing trains here, it's well worth following the signs to the village of **BAÑOS DE CERRATO** 2km out of town. This has the oldest church in the peninsula – *Monumento Nacional 1* in the catalogue: a seventh-century basilica (Tues–Sun 10am–1pm & 4–7pm) dedicated to **San Juan** by the Ostrogoth King Recesvinto. It has tiny lattice windows, horseshoe arches and incorporates materials from Roman buildings. The caretaker, Patrizio, lives opposite. Across the road is a spring with delicious water.

PAREDES DE NAVA, on the train line to León, has another church of interest, **Santa Eulalia** (summer 11am–2pm & 4–7pm; winter 11am–2pm & 4–6pm). The great sculptor Alonso Berruguete was born here, as were many of his lesser-known relatives, and the parish church (with a beautifully tiled Romanesque tower) has been turned into a small museum full of their work. The collection is arranged in every available space, and includes pieces by many of the best-known of Berruguete's contemporaries, gathered from all the churches of this little town. Paredes also has three **fondas**, all with restaurants.

For those interested in pursuing the **pilgrimage route**, the town of **Frómista**, on the Santander road, is within easy reach of Palencia. Otherwise, castle country to the south is an obvious destination.

Castles south of the Duero

It is said there were once ten thousand castles in Spain. Of those that are left, some five hundred are in a reasonable state of repair, and Castile has far more than its fair share of them. The area south of Valladolid, and towards Segovia, is especially rich – ringed with a series of fortresses, many of them built in the fifteenth century to protect the royal headquarters.

Coca

An hour south by train from Valladolid on the line to Segovia, **COCA** is the prettiest fortress imaginable. Less a piece of military architecture than a country house masquerading as one, it's constructed from narrow pinkish bricks, encircled by a deep moat and fantastically decorated with octagonal turrets, merlons and elaborate castellation – an extraordinary design strongly influenced by Moorish architecture. The building dates from about 1400, and was the base of the powerful **Fonseca family**. The interior (Mon–Thurs 8am–8.30pm & Fri 8.30am–3pm) is used by by the Ministry of Agriculture so it's advisable to phone ahead to check opening hours (☎911/586062).

The village of Coca itself is pretty lifeless, but there are a few bars and if you ask in these you should be able to find a room for the night. While here, try to see the inside of the parish church of **Santa María**, where there are four tombs of the Fonseca family carved in white marble in the Italian Renaissance style. The power of the dynasty is indicated by the fact that they were able to hire Bartolomé Ordóñez, the sculptor of the tombs of the *Reyes Católicos* in Granada.

Cuéllar, Turégano, Pedraza and Sepúlvada

The route south by road from Valladolid, passes another impressive ancient castle at **Cuéllar**. Even more stunning is the one at **Turégano**, 28km north of Segovia; it's essentially a fifteenth-century structure enclosing an early thirteenth-century church, and you have to track down the sexton of the parish church to get inside.

East of Turégano, just off the main Segovia-Soria road, there are rewarding diversions to be made to Pedraza and Sepúlveda, both extraordinarily pretty villages. **PEDRAZA** is almost perfectly preserved from the sixteenth century, a homogeneity enhanced by the uniformity of the rich brown stone in which it's constructed. Protected on three sides by a steep valley, the only entrance to the village is the single original gateway (which used to be the town prison) from where the narrow lanes spiral gently up towards a large **Plaza Mayor**, still used for a **bull fighting festival** in the first week in September. Pedraza also has a **castle** (privately owned), where the eight-year-old Dauphin of France and his younger brother were imprisoned in 1526, given up by their father François I who swapped his freedom for theirs after he was captured at the battle of Pavia.

SEPÚLVEDA is less of a harmonious whole, but has a more dramatic setting, strung out high on a narrow spit of land between the Castilla and Duratón river valleys.

Its physical and architectural highpoint is the distinctive Romanesque church of **El Salvador** (open third Sun in month), below which is a ruined castle out of which the town hall protrudes.

Both villages are best avoided at weekends, when every young *Madrileño* with a Mercedes seems to descend on them for the local speciality, roast lamb, but otherwise you can have the places to yourself. Sepúlveda is the better bet for **accommodation** with two *hostales*; *Hernanz* (☎ 911/540378; ④), and *Postigo* (☎ 911/540172; ④), while Pedraza has only the luxurious *Posada de Don Mariana* (☎911/509886; ⑤).

The Pantano de Burgomillodo and Riaza

In addition to its castles, this area of Old Castile is rich in **wildlife**.The **Pantano De Burgomillodo**, a reservoir just to the west of Sepúlveda, is a particularly exciting spot for bird-watchers, surrounded by heaths of wild lavender which are the haunt of griffon vultures and other exotic species. From here you can head towards El Burgo de Osma on the road through **RIAZA**, skirting the foothills of the Sierra de Guadarrama. It's a lovely route, and Riaza itself is a pleasant place to stop with several good bars (try *El Museo*) and restaurants, and a couple of places offering rooms. There's also a station here on the main line from Madrid to Burgos.

Along the Duero: Valladolid to Soria

The **Duero**, east from Valladolid to Soria, is trailed by by a further panoply of castles and old market towns; the river long marked the frontier between Christian and Arab territory. Road (and bus) routes follow the river, allowing leisurely and rewarding small town stops.

Peñafiel

The reason for stopping at **PEÑAFIEL**, 60km east of Valladolid, is to see its fabulous elongated **castle** (Tues–Sun 11am–2.30pm & 4–8pm, winter 4–6pm; 150ptas), which bears an astonishing resemblance to a huge ship run aground: it is 210m long but only 23m across, with its central tower playing the role of the ship's bridge. Built in 1466 out of the region's distinctive white stone, the castle was designed around the narrow ridge upon which it stands, a location best appreciated from the top of the tower.

From the "prow" of the castle there's a tremendous view of Peñafiel, and good views too from the hill at the foot of the castle particularly from the **Plaza del Cosa**. This large square is extraordinary in itself; its buildings are wooden, with several tiers of loggias, and it makes the most spectacular bullring in Spain when bullfights are held in August. Nearby is **San Pablo**, now a college, with a superb brick Gothic-Mudéjar apse, to which a Plateresque chapel was later added.

If you want to stay, try the *Hostal Linares* at Mercado Viejo 11 (☎983/880942; ②–③), which has a few basic **rooms**, and several that are considerably more comfortable. *Bar Plata*, at c/Franco 22, does good *tapas* and is a bit of a nightspot. There's a **bus** each way to and from Valladolid in the morning, at lunchtime and in the evening.

Aranda de Duero

Another 35km east, and at a junction with the Madrid-Burgos *autopista*, is **ARANDA DE DUERO**, a busy commercial town which has managed to retain the feel of a grace-ful and picturesque village, and is at its liveliest for the Saturday morning market. If you're passing through, take a look at the south facade of **Santa María**, an ornate Isabelline work in which even the doors are carved.

Restaurants vie with each other in Aranda to tempt you with the local treat of roast lamb (*cordero* or *lechazo asado*); the *comedor* upstairs in the *Bar El Cordobés* next to Santa María is particularly good. For **accommodation**, try the *Hostal Sole*, c/Puerta Nueva 16 (☎947/500607; ③); the *Nati* at Pio XII 1 (☎947/501976; ②); or the *Julia* at c/San Gregorio 2 (☎947/501200; ②–④). There is a very well-equipped **campsite**, with pool, *Costaján* (April–Sept; ☎947/502070) on the main N1 heading north of town. The thrice-daily buses from Valladolid to Peñafiel continue to Aranda then eastwards on to El Burgo de Osma.

El Burgo de Osma and around

EL BURGO DE OSMA, the episcopal centre of Soria province, is a wonderfully picturesque place, with crumbling town walls and ancient colonnaded streets overhung by houses supported on precarious wooden props. In the relaxed village atmosphere of the Plaza Mayor, its **Catedral** (10am–1.30pm & 4–7pm), one of the richest in Spain, seems more than usually over the top. Basically Gothic in style, it has had many embellishments over the years, notably the superb Baroque tower decorated with pinnacles and gables which dominates the town. If you buy a visitor's ticket, lights will be switched on for you to see the theatrical *retablo mayor* by Juan de Juni and his pupils, and a series of dark chapels, one of which contains a powerful Romanesque carving of the Crucifixion. You will also be escorted to the cloisters and the museum. Most impressive of all is the thirteenth-century painted stone tomb of San Pedro de Osma – a uniquely naturalist treatment for its age.

You can get some idea of Osma's former importance from the fact that it was once the seat of a university. The sixteenth-century building, now a school, is at the edge of town, near where the buses stop. This is also where you'll find the budget-priced **accommodation**: *Hostal La Perdiz*, c/Universidad 33 (☎975/340309; ②); *Hostal Casa Agapito*, c/Universidad 1 (☎975/340212; ②); and *Hotel Virrey Palafox*, c/Universidad 7 (☎975/340222; ③). If money is no object, the town's best hotel is *Il Virrey* (☎975/341311; ⑤) on the Plaza Mayor. There's also a **campsite**, *La Pedriza* (June–Sept; ☎975/340806); take the first left off c/Mayor and then turn right along c/Rodrigo Yusto. For meals, the *Virrey Palafox* restaurant is good and resonably priced.

El Burgo de Osma can be reached by bus from Valladolid or from Soria to the east.

San Esteban de Gormaz and Gormaz

Thirteen kilometres to the west of El Burgo de Osma, **SAN ESTEBAN DE GORMAZ** has a ruined castle and a pair of Romanesque churches. There's also a pleasant *hostal*, *El Moreno* (☎975/320217; ③), which could be useful if you find everything full in Osma.

GORMAZ, 15km south of El Burgo de Osma, is a particularly intriguing fortification since it was originally built in the Caliphate style, and two Moorish doorways dating from the tenth century have survived. Later captured and modified by Christians, it was one of the largest fortified buildings in the West – there are 28 towers in all, ruined but impressive. The inside is a shell, but there are good panoramas from here, and the wonderful views as you approach make the long walk up less daunting. Gormaz itself is little more than a hamlet, without any accommodation.

Calatañazor

Just off the main El Burgo–Soria road lies **CALATAÑAZOR**, a severely depopulated medieval village with walls and the ruins of a castle, chiefly remarkable for its **houses**, with their distinctive conical chimneys, decorative coats of arms and wooden balconies. A village guide is based at the *mesón*, where good simple meals are served. The only available **accommodation** is the *Hostal Calatañazor*, c/Real 10 (☎975/340570; ④) on the main road where the bus stops, but the place makes a good half-day excursion from either El Burgo de Osma or Soria, 30km east.

Berlanga de Duero

BERLANGA DE DUERO east again along the Duero, stands just off the main road between El Burgo de Osma and Almazán; it can also be reached from Soria by daily bus (departure 6pm, return 9am).

Once again, the main attraction is a **castle**, whose massive cylindrical towers and older double curtain wall, reminiscent of Ávila, loom above the town. The way up is through a doorway in a ruined Renaissance palace at the edge of town; entrance is free at all times. The other dominant monument is the **Colegiata** (usually open), one of the last flowerings of the Gothic style. Its unusually uniform design is a consequence of rapid construction – it was built in just four years. Berlanga also has an old-world **Plaza Mayor** (where markets are held regularly), several fine mansions, arcaded streets, an impressive entrance gateway and the unique **La Picota** – a pillar of justice to which offenders were tied (it's on a wasteground outside the old town, where the buses stop).

Not far from the pillar is the only **place to stay** in Berlanga that can be relied upon to be open, the two-star *Hostal La Hoz* at c/Postigo 42 (☎975/343136; ③) – quite luxurious and a remarkable bargain. It doubles as the town's disco at the weekend, and also has a good restaurant. One of the bars opposite the Colegiata lets rooms at the height of summer.

Ermita de San Baudelio de Berlanga

Eight kilometres south of Berlanga, the tiny **Ermita de San Baudelio de Berlanga** (Nov–March Wed–Sun 10.30am–2pm & 4–6pm, April–June & Sept–Oct 10.30am–2pm & 4–7pm, July & August 10.30am–2pm & 5–9pm) is the best-preserved and (with San Miguel de Escalada, see p.340) most important example of Mozarabic style in Spain. It was even better before the 1920s: five years after being declared a national monument, its marvellous cycle of frescoes was acquired by an international art dealer and exported to the USA . After much fuss, the Spanish government got some of them back on indefinite loan, but they are now kept in the Prado.

In spite of this loss, the hermitage remains a beauty. Its eight-ribbed interior vault springs from a central pillar, while much of the space is taken up by the tribune gallery of horseshoe arches. Some original frescoes do remain, including two bulls from the great sequence of animals and hunting scenes of the nave. You can also see the entrance to the cave below, which the hermit, San Baudelio, made his home.

Almazán

Some 35km due south of Soria lies **ALMAZÁN**, which despite a lot of ugly modern development still possesses complete **medieval walls**, pierced by three gateways. On the Plaza Mayor stands the fine Renaissance **Palacio Hurtado de Mendoza**, with a Gothic loggia at the rear, visible from the road around the walls. The church of **San Miguel**, across from the palace, has a memorable interior, with Romanesque and early Gothic features, and a remarkable dome in the Cordoban style; the altar has a relief of the martyrdom of Saint Thomas à Becket. To gain access, try the parish offices in the adjacent Plaza Santa María, opposite the church of the same name.

Places to stay include *Hostal El Arco*, c/San Andrés 7 (☎975/300433; ③) and *Hostal Mateos*, c/San Lázaro (☎975/301400; ③), across the river. The latter is also one of the few places to eat in town along with *Restaurante Toma*, c/Manuel Cartel 11. However, you are not likely to want to stay long, and there are regular bus and train connections to Soria.

Medinaceli

MEDINACELI, perched in an exhilarating breezy position above the Río Jalón, is something of a ghost town – steeped in history and highly evocative of its former glory as a Roman and Moorish stronghold. It's 76km south of Almazán and positioned on the main Madrid-Barcelona rail line. If you arrive this way, it's a 3km climb by road up from the station to the village, though you can take a shortcut straight up the hill to a distinctive Roman arch. The **Roman arch** – a triple arch in fact – is worn but impressive, and unique in Spain. Its presence is something of a mystery as such monuments were usually built to commemorate military triumphs but the cause of celebration at Medinaceli is unknown. Nearby stands the dilapidated Moorish **castle**, now a mere facade sheltering a Christian cemetery.

The quiet streets are full of ancient mansions with proud coats of arms, the grandest of which is the **Palacio de los Duques de Medinaceli** on the dusty and desolate Plaza Mayor, a square that looks like a disused film set. The palace was the seat of the family regarded as rightful heirs to the Castilian throne until, in 1275, Fernando, eldest son of Alfonso El Sabio (the Wise), died before he could assume his inheritance. His two sons were dispossessed by Fernando's brother Sancho El Valiente (the Brave) and their descendants, the Dukes of Medinaceli, long continued to lay claim to the throne. Today Medinaceli is a declining village with no more than 1200 inhabitants, though its *duquesa* remains the most betitled woman in Spain.

There are several *hostales* near Medinaceli's station, such as the *Catalán* (☎975/326001; ②), while if you prefer to stay up near the castle the tiny *Hostería de Medinaceli* (☎975/326264; ③) is a good bet. *Los Llaves* (closed Sun night & Mon), on the Plaza Mayor, is an attractive restaurant, stuffed with antiques.

Santa María de Huerta

On the Aragonese border, 25km and just half an hour by train or bus from Medinaceli, lies **SANTA MARÍA DE HUERTA**. This tiny community is dominated by a Cistercian **monastery** (9am–1pm & 3.30–7pm), whose story of royal and noble patronage was brought to a sudden end by the First Carlist War in 1835. The buildings were repopulated in 1930, and the main church has recently been restored. The highlight of the complex is the French-Gothic refectory (1215–23), whose superb sexpartite vaulting and narrow pointed windows are worthy of the best church, let alone a dining room. Adjacent stands the kitchen with a mammoth chimney protruding above Plateresque upper cloisters. The village has a single **pensión**, *Santa María* (☎975/327218; ②), and on the Zaragoza road, a former *parador*, now privately run, the *Hotel Santa María de Huerta* (☎975/327011; ⑤). Southwest of Medinaceli, Sigüenza (see p.146) is just 20km away across the border in New Castile, a couple of stops on any Madrid-bound train.

Soria and around

SORIA is a modest little provincial capital – an attractive place, despite encroaching suburbs. It stands between a ridgeback of hills on the banks of the Duero, with a castle ruin above, a medieval centre dotted with mansions and Romanesque churches, and one of the country's greatest cloisters.

The town

The centre of town is marked by the **Concatedral de San Pedro**, a rather stolid Plateresque building, whose interior (open only for church services) takes the Spanish penchant for darkness to a ridiculous extreme. To the side are three bays of a superb

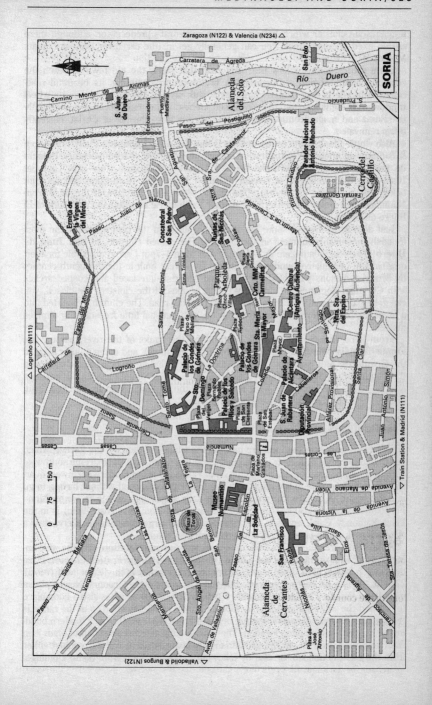

SORIA

Zaragoza (N122) & Valencia (N234) △

Carretera de Ágreda

San Pdo

Río Duero

Alameda del Soto

S. Prudencia

Camino Monte de las Ánimas

Paseo del Postiguillo

S. Juan de Duero

Puente Medieval

Embarcadero

△ Logroño (N111)

Ermita de la Virgen del Mirón

Paseo S. Juan de Pedro

Paseo S. Juan de Narros

Concatedral de San Pedro

Ruínas de San Nicolás

Parador Nacional Antonio Machado

Cerro del Castillo

Fernán González

Paseo del Mirón

Santa Apolonia

Sma. Trinidad

Parque Vinuo Aboleda

Plaza Sta Catalina

Nra. Sra. de Calatañazor

Posdas

Martín de S. Clemente

Principe Cautivo

Forum

Plaza Torso de Molina

Plaza Aylon

Cnto. MM. Carmelitas

Centro Cultural Antigua Audiencia

Nra. Sra. del Espino

Carretera de

Clemente Saenz

Santa

Logroño

Palacio de los Condes de Gómera

La Doctrina

Plaza Bernardo Robles

Santo Domingo

Palacio de los Condes de Gómara

Sta. María la Mayor

Colegio

Pr Santiago

Santa Clara

Santa

Simon

Sta. Tomé

Palac. de los Pilar y Salcedo

Plaza del Vergel

Plaza de San Clemente

Plaza Mayor

Palacio de Alcántara

Ayuntamiento

Plaza de San Esteban

S. Juan de Rabanera

Diputación Provincial

Caballeros

Alférez Provisional

Juan Antonio Simón

Casas

Casas

Numancia

Plaza de Mariano Granados

Las Cortes

△ Train Station & Madrid (N111)

Avenida de la Victoria

Avenida de Mariano Vicen

0 75 150 m

Rota de Catalañazor

Plaza de Toros

Museo Numantino

Escolón

La Soledad

San Francisco

Rebal

Sanz Vila

Eloy

Sta. Teresa de Jesus

Paseo de las Pardas

Paseo de Valladolid

San Benito

San Ángel de la Guarda

Avda. de

Sto.

Paseo del

Alameda de Cervantes

Nicolás

Plaza de José Antonio

Francisco Acosta

Carretera de Ágreda

Malecon

Santa Bárbara

Verguilla

Paseo de

△ Valladolid & Burgos (N122)

Romanesque cloister which belonged to the cathedral's predecessor: although there are no fixed opening times, you can generally get in (the caretaker lives at c/Santa Monica 16, 1° izda).

From the cathedral, follow the main road that skirts the old town to reach the convent church of **Santo Domingo**. A twelfth-century building, its beautiful rose-coloured facade is decorated symmetrically with sixteen "blind" arches and a wheel window with eight "spokes". The recessed arches of the main portal are excellently preserved and magnificently sculpted with scenes from the life of Christ, currently being renovated.

Also worth a look in the centre of town is **San Juan de Rabanera** (daily 11am–1pm & 3–5pm), another fine Romanesque church, the massive sixteenth-century **Palacio de los Condes de Gomara** and the new **Museo Numantino** (July–Sept Tues–Sat 10am–2pm & 5–9pm, out of season 9.30am–7.30pm, Sun 10am–2pm; 200ptas joint ticket with San Juan de Duero). This features excellent displays of the finds from Numancia (see below) and Tiermes, another Celto-Iberic and Roman city, south of El Burgo de Osma.

Just across the Duero, some ten minutes' walk from the centre, stands the most freakish medieval monument in the country. The ruined cloisters of **San Juan de Duero** (Tues–Sat 10am–2pm & 4–7pm, Sun & Mon 4–7pm) are remarkable for their original and imaginative synthesis of styles. They were built in the thirteenth century by Mudéjar masons who playfully combined Moorish interlaced and cusped arches with Christian Romanesque and early Gothic shapes. If the cloisters are closed, you can get a partial aerial view from a low hill across the road. The church, converted into a museum, is more orthodox in style, but has two unusual little freestanding temples inside.

From here, there's a good walk south along the banks of the river, passing the former Templar church of **San Polo** (now a private home), and coming, after 2km, to the **Ermita de San Saturio**, a two-tiered complex including an octagonal chapel with thirteenth-century frescoes (May–Sept 10am–2pm & 3.30–6pm; Oct–April 10am–2pm & 4.30–8pm). The landscape here is typical of the province, with its parched, livid, orange earth and the solemn river lined by poplars.

Practicalities

Soria's **train and bus stations** are both on the fringes of the city; the former, which has had its services ruthlessly pruned in the last few years, is at the extreme southwest corner. A new bus station has been built on c/Valladolid in the modern northwest quarters; to walk from one to the other, you can follow the ring road without having to go into the centre. A helpful **Turismo** (summer daily 10am–2pm & 5–9pm; winter Mon–Fri 10am–2.30pm & 4.30pm–7pm, Sat 10am–2pm & 4–8pm, Sun 10am–2pm) is in the Plaza Ramón y Cajal, opposite the entrance to the large Alameda de Cervantes, a spacious park which is one of Soria's most attractive features.

Around this area there's a wealth of inexpensive **accommodation** – try the welcoming *Fonda Ferial* on Plaza del Salvador 6 (☎975/221244; ②), or *Pensión Carmen*, Plaza del Olivo 2 (☎975/211555; ②). *Las Heras* at no. 5 on Plaza Ramón y Cajal itself (☎975/223346; ③) is a bit more upmarket, but still has a few budget rooms. Newer places include *La Posada*, Plaza San Clemente 6 (☎975/223603; ④) which is also a good place to eat, and the well-equipped *Alvi*, c/Alberca 2 (☎975/228112; ④). Top of the range is the *Parador António Machado*, Parque del Castillo (☎975/214345; ⑤), a modern building with a panoramic hilltop location. The most mouth-watering selection of *tapas* is in the Plaza San Clemente, in the pedestrian-only central area; it can be reached either from the main c/Collado, or else by following c/Aduana Vieja from Santo Domingo.

You'll find a good local *menú* at the *Capri*, c/San Benito 8, and more adventurous and pricey food at *Maroto*, Paseo del Espolon (closed Thurs).

Moving on

Moving on from Soria there's a rich choice of destinations: west to Burgos, east into Aragón or north to Logroño and the Basque country. If you're heading into the immediate countryside around Soria, *Ociotur* at c/Sagunto 4 (☎975/228923) organizes climbing, mountaineering, cross-country skiing and other **outdoor activities**.

Numancia

The barren site of Roman **NUMANCIA** (winter 10.30am–1.30pm & 4.30–6pm, summer 10am–2pm & 4–7pm; 200ptas) stands on a hill above the village of **Garray**, 8km north of Soria. The Celto-Iberian town which originally occupied this site resisted Scipio and his legions for over a year, and when finally defeated, the inhabitants destroyed the town rather than surrender it. What survives are some excavated remains of the Roman city that replaced it, with the outline of the streets clearly visible. They're not exciting unless you're an archeologist.

Río Lobos Canyon and the Sierra de Urbión

Some of Castile's loveliest and least-visited countryside lies northwest of Soria, on either side of the N234 to Burgos. South of this road a **Parque Natural** has been created around the canyon of the Río Lobos. To the north rises the **Sierra de Urbión**, a lakeland region much loved by the Sorian-born poet, António Machado. The Cañon Río Lobos can also be approached on minor roads from El Burgo de Osma, to the south.

Río Lobos Canyon

The whole area of the **Parque Natural del Cañón del Río Lobos** is impressive, with fantastically shaped rocks on both sides of the canyon. The most interesting part lies 1km from the park's car lot, southeast of San Leonardo de Yague. Here as well as some of the prettiest rock formations, there's a **Romanesque chapel** founded by the Templars (kept locked) and, behind this, a beautiful natural **cave**. From here, the path continues through the Lobos gorge; at times the river is a mere trickle – its tributaries have dried up completely, providing ready-made walking tracks. For this, or more adventurous treks into the high ground, you really need proper walking boots, but any shoes will do on the main paths. The park will appeal to bird-watchers; eagles and vultures are often seen, even though they are not protected here.

SAN LEONARDO DE YAGUE makes a convenient base, with a good *hostal*, the *Torres* (☎975/376156; ③). Alternatively, you can camp in the officially designated areas around the entrance to the park.

Vinuesa and the Sierra de Urbión

For the **Sierra de Urbión**, the most obvious base is **VINUESA**, situated just north of an enormous man-made reservoir, **Pantano de la Cuerda del Pozo**. It's on a slow country bus route between Soria and Burgos, and is a spaciously laid-out village with many fine old houses. There's a choice of the two-star *Hostal Visontium* (☎975/378354; ③), or the *Urbión* (☎975/378055), and a **campsite** 2km along the Montenegro road (mid-April–mid-Sept; ☎975/378331),which has bikes for hire.

Nineteen kilometres north of Vinuesa lies the most famous of the lakes, the beautiful **Laguna Negra**. There's no public transport to it, but a good road leads through thickly wooded country before climbing steeply up the green mountainside. For the last couple of kilometres, by the side of a ravine, the road is much rougher then; finally a path leads to the lagoon. Ice Age in origin, set in an amphitheatre of mountains from which great boulders have fallen, it presents a primeval picture – Machado was inspired to write some of his most purple verse here. The area remains delightfully unspoiled though, and the bar (June–Sept only) and picnic area are out of sight, 3km down the mountain.

Serious hikers can make a tortuous ascent from the Laguna Negra to the **Laguna de Urbión**, just over the border in Logroño province – a route that takes in a couple of other tiny, glacially formed lakes. A less taxing version of the same excursion is to take the long way round, from the village of **Duruelo de La Sierra**, some 20km west of Vinuesa.

THE CAMINO DE SANTIAGO:
FROM LOGROÑO TO LEÓN

This part of the chapter is laid out in an east-west direction, following, more or less, the **Camino de Santiago**, the great pilgrim route to the shrine of Saint James at Compostela (see p.448). The route had many variants but its most popular point of entry to Spain was – indeed is – at the pass of Roncesvalles in the Pyrenees. From there, the old paths strike south through Navarra to Logroño and then west across Castile through the great cathedral cities of **Burgos** and **León**. These are major architectural sights but each of the smaller towns along the *camino* has some treasure or reminder – a bridge, a Romanesque church, or a statue of the saint. For uncommitted pilgrims, the highlights of the route can be taken in by car, bus, or sometimes train.

Old Castile, in this section, is used in a loose, historical sense, for this region actually takes in two other provinces. In the east is **La Rioja**, Spain's premier wine-producing region, with its capital in **Logroño** and wine trade centre in nearby **Haro**. Over to the west is the old kingdom of **León**, whose northern reaches merge with Asturias in the Picos de Europa mountains (see p.414).

Logroño

LOGROÑO is a modern, prosperous city, lacking in great monuments, but pleasant enough with its broad, elegant streets and open squares. It has a lively old section, too, stretching down towards the Río Ebro from the twin-towered **Catedral de Santa María la Redonda**. Here the city becomes more than just an extended parade of shop-lined avenues and modern parks, and the narrow streets bustle with unexpected energy.

Whether you stay or not, you're likely to pass through Logroño at some point since it lies on the borders of Old Castile, the Basque provinces and Navarra, a position that has stimulated commerce and light industry. Most importantly, however, this is the very heart of the **Rioja wine region** (see below).

The town
Before the wine trade and industry brought prosperity to Logroño, it owed its importance for some six centuries to the **Camino de Santiago**. In almost every town on the route you can still find a church dedicated to the saint; in Logroño it stands close to the iron bridge over the Ebro – the lofty sixteenth-century Gothic structure of **Santiago el Real**. High on its north side, above the main entrance, is a magnificent eighteenth-

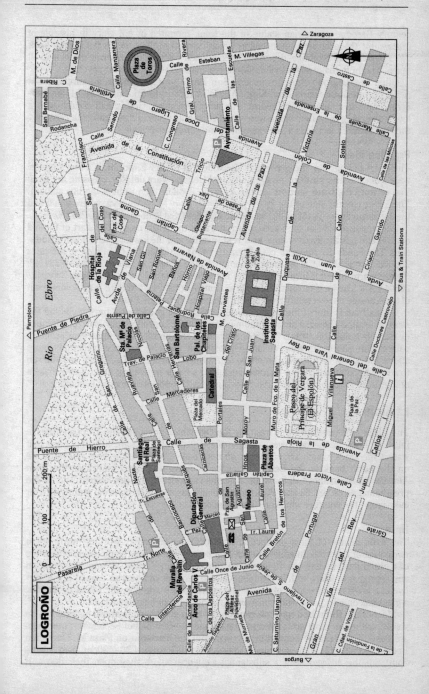

LOGROÑO

century Baroque equestrian statue of the saint, mounted in full glory in his role of *Matamoros* (Moorslayer), on a stallion which Edward Mullins, in his fascinating book *The Pilgrimage to Santiago*, describes as "equipped with the most heroic genitals in all Spain, a sight to make any surviving Moor feel inadequate and run for cover".

Other fine Logroño churches include **San Bartolomé**, which has an unrefined but richly carved Gothic portal, and **Santa María la Redonda** (mornings until 11am & 6–8pm. The latter, now the cathedral, was originally a late Gothic hall church with a lovely sweeping elevation which was extended at both ends in the eighteenth century – the twin-towered facade is a fine example of the Churrigueresque style.

Practicalities

The heart of Logroño, the gardens of the wide **Paseo del Espolón**, is a few minutes' walk from the **bus station** (straight up c/del General Vara del Rey, crossing the Gran Vía) or from the **train station** (up the Avda. de España, then right at the bus station). The lower (south) side of the Paseo is bordered by c/M. Villanueva, where you'll find the **Turismo** at no. 10 (Mon–Fri 9am–2pm & 5–8pm, Sat 9am–2pm; ☎941/291260).

The opposite side of the Paseo, down towards the river, marks the start of the old quarter and has the liveliest **bars and restaurants** and the lowest-priced **accommodation**. The *Fonda La Bilbaéna* c/Gallarza 10 (☎941/254226; ②), *CH Villar*, c/Martínez Zaporta 7 (☎941/220228; ②) and the homely *Fonda Blanca*, c/Laurel 24 (☎941/224148; ③) are worth trying. More modern and upmarket is *Hostal Niza*, c/Gallarza 3 (☎941/206044; ④). The local **campsite**, *La Playa* (June–Sept; ☎941/252253), is a kilometre out of town beside its own sandy river beach, signposted from the Paseo.

C/San Juan is one of the best areas for eating with good **tapas bars** including the *Beronés* and *La Cueva*. The gastronomic highlight of Logroño is *La Merced*, Marqués de San Nicholás 109 (☎941/221166), a fabulous restaurant in an eighteeenth-century palace with enormous wine cellars. Opposite, at no. 136, is the considerably more affordable *Mesón del Camino*, an old *bodega* formerly owned by *La Merced* and still run to a very good standard. For snacks – including superb *empanados* and cakes – make a detour to *El Paraiso*, a **bakery** at c/San Augustin 27, opposite the main post office.

La Rioja

The **Rioja** area takes its name from the Río Oja, which flows into the Tirón and thence into the Ebro to the northwest of Logroño. Effectively, though, it is the Ebro that waters the vines, which are cultivated on both banks. Many of the best vineyards are on the north bank in the Basque province of Alava – an area known as the *Rioja Alavesa*. Look out above all for wines described as *Reserva* or *Gran Reserva*, and for the great vintages of '68, '69 and '70 – though many say that with controls getting stricter every year, the younger wines are the better ones.

Haro

The main centre of Rioja production is **HARO**, an attractive, working town, 40km northwest of Logroño. In addition to tasting possibilities, it has some lovely reminders of a grand past, notably the Renaissance church of **San Tomás**, an imposing sight on any approach to town, with its wedding-cake tower. The old quarter around it is attractive in a low-key, faded kind of way, its lower margins marked by the **Plaza de la Paz**, a glass-balconied square whose mansions overlook an archaic bandstand.

Most of the **Rioja bodegas** are close to the train station, and several of them can be visited (although most are closed in August and the first half of September; mornings are best). Tours can be booked in advance from the **Turismo** on Plaza M. Florentino Rodrígue (☎941/312726; summer Mon–Sat 10am–2pm & 4.30–7.30pm, Sun 10am–2pm) but the *bodegas* seek a substantial audience before they open their doors. If you're not with a group, ask at the campsite (see below) about getting one together, or simply hang around the gates looking interested but not too thirsty. A good first try is *Bodegas Bilbainas* (opposite the station) where they make sparkling wines as well as red and white Riojas. Nearby is *Bodegas Tondoria*, perhaps the most interesting as it is the oldest and still uses oak vats instead of stainless steel. The new and hi-tech **Museo del Vino** (Tues-Sat 10am–2pm; free) in the Estación Erológica on c/Breton de los Herreros, behind the bus station, has detailed and highly complicated displays of the processes involved, but no tastings.

The only budget **accommodation** in town is at *Hostal Aragón*, c/La Vega 9 (☎941/ 310004; ②), though there's an excellent **campsite** (☎941/312737; open all year) down by the river below town, with a bar and swimming (in the river or the pool) nearby. If you're after luxury, Haro also has a superb hotel in a converted Augustinian monastery, *Los Agustinos*, San Agustín 2 (☎941/311308; ⑥).

Even the humblest *menú del día* in town is transformed by a bottle of Rioja, and you'll get more – and very cheaply – in the many good **bars** that lie between the *Ayuntamiento* and the church of San Tomás. Best of the restaurants are *Beethoven*, c/ San Tomás 5 (☎941/311181; closed Mon night, Thurs, July 1–15 & Dec), and *Terete*, c/ Lucrecia Arana 17 (☎941/310023; closed Sun night & Mon); prices at both are mid-range and the cooking is serious.

Haro's **train station** is some distance out of town; from it, walk down the hill to the main road, turn right and when you reach the bridge (campsite off to the right), cross it and head straight uphill. **Buses** stop in Plaza Castañares, a 10–minute walk from the centre (follow signs for *centro* straight up c/la Ventilla).

The pilgrim route west from Logroño

From Logroño, the **Camino de Santiago** heads through Santo Domingo de la Calzada and out across northern Castile – a long, straight trek to Burgos, León and Astorga – before heading over the mountains into Galicia.

Najera

The first town of note west of Logroño is **NAJERA**, which is sited dramatically situated below a pink rock formation, and has an interesting Gothic monastery, **Santa María la Real** (10am–12.30pm & 4–6.30pm; 100ptas). This contains a royal pantheon of ancient monarchs of Castile, León and Navarra – a host of sarcophagi and statues, some of which seem to have been made long after the death of the sitter. Best of all is the cloister of rose-coloured stone and elaborate tracery, closer to the Manueline style of Portugal than anything in Spain. There is nothing more to detain you but the town caters for modern pilgrims with several cheap restaurants, a *hostal*, *San Fernando* (☎941/363700; ④), and a *fonda*.

Santo Domingo de la Calzada

SANTO DOMINGO DE LA CALZADA, 46km west of Logroño, owes its very existence to the pilgrimage. It takes its name from a saint who settled here in the eleventh century and devoted his life to assisting travellers by paving roads, tending the sick, and engineering bridges (hence *Calzada*, or causeway).

These days it's a dull, unattractive place for the most part, though the saint's **causeway** survives at the end of town, on the Burgos road. His tomb lies in the crypt of the **Catedral** (summer 10am–2pm & 3.30–7pm with guide; winter 8.30am–8pm without guide; 150ptas), whose detached Baroque tower looms above everything in the centre of town. Santo Domingo was once a fortified town (fragments of the walls can still be seen) and the cathedral's massive west porch used to serve as a fortress. The interior is strongly evocative of what a medieval cathedral must have looked like, with a *coro*, tombs, *rejas* – and a pair of caged chickens.

These are kept in celebration of the local version of a legend popular throughout Spain and Portugal. A young German pilgrim is said to have resisted the advances of an innkeeper's daughter who "wolde have had hym to medyll with her carnally". She retaliated by falsely accusing him of theft, for which offence he was summarily strung up on the gallows. There he was kept alive by the miraculous intervention of Santo Domingo, to the disbelief of the local judge who was busily munching on a roast. "He's as dead as those chickens," claimed the judge, whereupon the birds crowed their disagreement and flew off the table.

Beside the cathedral stands a **pilgrims' hospice**, now converted to a *parador* (see below), and a handful of fine Renaissance **mansions**.

Practicalities

By far the best budget **accommodation** is offered by *Bar Albert*, Plaza Harmosilla 6, behind the bus stop (☎941/340827; ②). Alternatives include *Hostal Río* at c/ Etchegoyen 2 (☎941/340085; ②); the large and comfortable *Hostál Santa Teresita* at c/ General Mola 2 (☎941/340700; ③), and the newly modernized *parador* on Plaza del Santo (☎941/340300; ⑤). For **meals**, *Bar Albert*, and *El Vasco* at Avda. Rey Juan Carlos 17, offer good inexpensive *menús*. *Mumm* at c/Madrid 5, is a pleasant *mesón* with a summer terraza; *Zeta*, next door, is a late-night bar, open every evening in summer, otherwise weekends only.

Buses run to Burgos four times a day, timetables are posted in *Bar Bilbao* on Plaza de San Jerónimo Hermosilla, or you can head north to the Basque provinces and the coast.

Burgos

BURGOS was for some five hundred years the capital of Old Castile and with its dark-stone old town and castle it remains redolent of these years of power and military strength. It has historic associations as the home of El Cid, in the eleventh century, and as the base two centuries later of Fernando El Santo (Fernando III), the recon-queror of Murcia, Córdoba and Sevilla. It was Fernando who began the city's famous Gothic **cathedral**, one of the greatest in all Spain, though it too seems to share in the solemnity and severity of the city's history.

To Spaniards, the city has more modern military connotations. A large military garrison has been stationed here virtually since the Civil War, when Franco temporarily installed his fascist government in the city. Burgos, in addition, owes much of its modern industry and expansion to Franco's "Industrial Development Plan", a strategy to shift the country's wealth away from Catalunya and the Basque country and into Castile. Even now, such connotations linger.

The most exciting time to be in Burgos, is at the end of June for the two-week **Fiesta de San Pedro**. *Gigantillos* parade in the streets and bullfights and all-night parties take place.

Arrival, orientation and accommodation

Orientation in Burgos could not be simpler, since wherever you are the cathedral makes its presence felt. The Río Arlanzón bisects the city and neatly delimits the old quarters. The main pedestrian bridge is the **Puente de Santa María**, nearest the cathedral and facing the gateway of the same name. On the "new side" of the river this bridge opens out into Plaza de Vega and c/de Madrid, which is the main area for bars, restaurants and *hostales*.

The **bus station** is right in the centre of the city at c/ Mirandor 4; the **train station** a short walk away at the bottom of Avda. Conde Guadalhorre. The **Turismo** (Mon–Fri 9am–2pm & 4.30–6.30pm, Sat 10am–1.30pm; ☎947/203125) is at Plaza de Alonso Martínez 7, around the side of the cathedral and up c/Lain Calvo; there's another equally good office quite nearby on c/San Carlos, off c/San Lorenzo (Mon–Sat 10am–2pm & 5.30–8.30pm; Sun noon–2pm).

Accommodation

Rooms can often be difficult to come by; they're at a premium in late June and July, while during the university year many of the cheaper *pensiones* are brim-full of students, so it's worth calling ahead to check. The best place to try for inexpensive accommodation is around the Plaza de Vega, and any road off towards the bus station as far as c/ de San Pablo. There are plenty of smart, upmarket hotels in town, as well as one of the region's most luxurious and memorable places to stay just out of town on the road to Madrid.

BUDGET OPTIONS

Pensión Arribas, c/Defensores de Oviedo 6 (☎947/266292). One of the city's lowest-priced *pensiones*, situated near the bus station; reliable. ②.

Pensión Dallas, Plaza Vega 6 (☎947/205457). This *pensión* is right on the river front. Double rooms are very good value here. ③.

Residencia Juvenil Gil de Siloe, Avda. de General Vigón (☎947/220362; July–Sept). Meals are available at this youth hostel. ①.

Hostal Hidalgo, Almirante Bonifaz 14 (☎947/203481). Large, airy rooms with very friendly atmosphere. ③.

Hostal Manjón, c/Conde Jornada 1–7 (☎947/208689). Clean and comfortable, near the river. ③.

Hostal Niza, c/General Mola 12 (☎947/261917). A low-priced *hostal* and always reliable. ③.

Pensión Paloma, c/Paloma 39 (☎947/276574). Warm and clean, bang next to the cathedral. ③.

HOTELS

Mesón del Cid, Plaza Santa María 8 (☎947/208715). Facing the cathedral, this rustic-looking hotel has on-site parking and a stylish basement bar. ④.

Hotel Conde de Miranda, c/Miranda 4 (☎947/265267). Smart and comfortable rooms, located conveniently above the bus station. ④.

Hotel Condestable, c/Vitoria 8 (☎947/267125). The top hotel in the centre of town, in a beautiful old building. ⑥.

Hotel Cordón, La Puebla 6 (☎947/265000). A modern city-centre hotel close to the cathedral, with public parking nearby. ④.

Landa Palace, Carretera Madrid-Irún. (☎947/206343). A stunning and fabulously expensive hotel in a medieval tower, complete with antique furnishings and a renowned restaurant. This hotel is just out of town on the road to Madrid. ⑥.

CAMPING

The local **campsite**, *Camping Fuentes Blancas* (April–Sept; ☎947/221016) is out by the *Cartuja* (see "Monasteries" for directions), 45 minutes' walk or a bus ride from the centre (buses once an hour between 11am and 9pm, leaving from the Cid statue) – it's a very good site with excellent facilities, including free hot showers.

PILGRIMS REFUGE

Genuine pilgrims who can prove their status can obtain exceptionally good value rooms at a new **refuge**, the *Albergue Municipal de Peregrino*, in the Colegio San Lorenzo on Paseo Fuentecillas near the river to the west of town. Ideally, you should report to the Turismo first, before 8pm. Bed and board cost 350ptas.

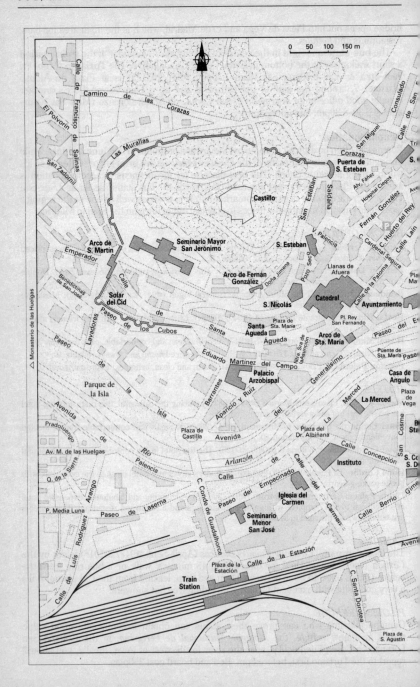

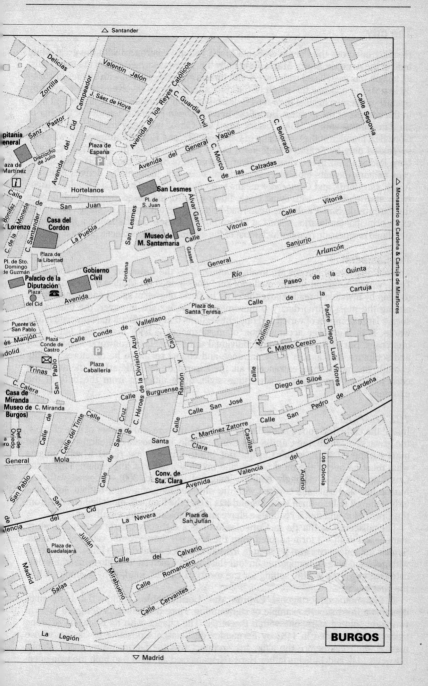

△ Santander

Delicias

Zorrilla

Valentín Jalón

J. Sáez de Hoya

Sanz Pastor

Campeador

C. Guardia Civil

Avenida de los Reyes Católicos

C. Reyes Católicos

pitanía eneral

aza de Martínez

Dieciocho de Julio

Avenida del Cid

Plaza de España

Avenida del General

Yagüe

C. Moreo

C. de las Calzadas

C. Belorado

Calle Segovia

i

Calle

de

Benitez

C. de la Moneda

San Juan

Hortelanos

Casa del Cordón

Pl. de S. Juan

San Lesmes

San Lesmes

Alvar García

Calle

Vitoria

Calle

Vitoria

Lorenzo

C. Santander

La Puebla

Museo de M. Santamaria

Gasset

Vitoria

Sanjurjo

Arlanzón

Pl. de Sto. Domingo de Guzmán

Plaza de la Libertad

Gobierno Civil

Jordana

General

Río

del

Paseo de la Quinta

Cartuja

Palacio de la Diputación

Plaza del Cid

Avenida

Plaza de Santa Teresa

Calle

de

la

Padre Diego Luis Vitores

Puente de San Pablo

és Manjón

dolid

Plaza Conde de Castro

Calle Conde de Vallejano

División Azul

Cajal

Molinillo

C. Mateo Cerezo

Trinas

San Pablo

Plaza Caballería

C. Héroes de la

Burguense

Ramón y

Calle

Diego de Siloé

Cardeña

Casa de Miranda Museo de Burgos)

C. Miranda

Calle

Cruz

Santa

de

Calle San José

Calle

San

Pedro

de

Def. de Oviedo

ra

Calle del Tinte

Calle

Santa

C. Martínez Zatorre

Casillas

Cid

General

Mola

San Pablo

San

del

Cid

de

lencia

Santa Clara

Conv. de Sta. Clara

Avenida

Valencia

del

Andino

Los Colonia

La Nevera

Plaza de San Julián

Plaza de Guadalajara

Julián

Calle

del

Calvario

Madrid

Salas

Mirabueno

Calle

Romancero

Calle Cervantes

La Legión

BURGOS

▷ Monasterio de Cardeña & Cartuja de Miraflores

▽ Madrid

The city

Heading in across the Puente de Santa María you are confronted with the great white bulk of the **Arco de Santa María**. Originally this gateway formed part of the town walls; its facade was castellated with towers and turrets and embellished with statues in 1534–36 in order to appease the wrath of Carlos V after Burgos's involvement in a revolt by Spanish noblemen against their new Belgian-born king. Carlos's statue is glorified here in the context of the greatest Burgalese heroes: Diego Porcelos, founder of the city in the late ninth century; Nuño Rasura and Lain Calvo, two early magistrates; Fernán González, founder of the Countship of Castile in 932; and **El Cid Campeador**, who was surpassed only by *Santiago Matamoros* in his exploits against the Moors. El Cid was born Rodrigo Díaz in the village of Vivar, just north of Burgos, though his most significant military exploits took place around Valencia; *Cid*, incidentally, derives from the Arabic *sidi* (lord), and *Campeador* means supreme in valour. There's a splendid **equestrian statue** of him – with flying cloak, flowing beard and raised sword – lording over the **Puente de San Pablo**, the main road-bridge to the old town. The statue, one of the city's principal landmarks, stands at the end of the **Paseo del Espolón**, a fashionable tree-lined promenade round which most of the evening life takes place.

The Cathedral

The old quarters of Burgos are totally dominated by the **Catedral** (9.30am–1pm & 4–7pm), whose "wild and slightly mad roof-line" does indeed (as Mullins observed) "seem to hang by invisible threads above the city". Its florid filigree of spires and pinnacles are among the most extraordinary achievements of Gothic art; however, the building is such a large complex of varied and opulent sections that it's difficult to appreciate it as a whole. It is the sheer accumulation of masterpieces – both inside and out – that impresses. Burgos has outstanding individual achievements in ironwork, wood carving and sculpture, and almost every entrance and chapel seems to be of interest. Oddly enough, the most ornate entrance of all, the **Puerta de la Pellejería** at the northeast corner, is in a Renaissance-Plateresque style, quite different from the bulk of the exterior.

THE CHAPELS

Inside the cathedral you're immediately struck by the size and number of side chapels, the greatest of which, the **Capilla del Condestable**, is almost a cathedral in itself. The most curious, though, is the **Capilla del Santo Cristo** (first right) which contains what must be one of the most bizarre and mystical icons in Christendom. This is the *Cristo de Burgos*, a cloyingly realistic image of Christ (c.1300), endowed with real human hair and nails and covered with the withered hide of a water buffalo, still popularly believed to be human skin. Legend has it that the icon was modelled directly from the Crucifixion and that it requires a shave and a manicure every eighth day.

The adjacent **Capilla de la Consolación** has a distinctive, early sixteenth-century star-shaped vault – a form adapted from the Moorish "honeycomb" vaults of Granada. Similar influences can also be seen in the cathedral's central dome (1568), highlighted with gold and blue and supported on four thick piers which fan out into remarkably delicate buttresses – a worthy setting for the **tomb of El Cid**, marked by a simple slab in the floor below.

The sumptuous, octagonal **Capilla del Condestable**, behind the high altar, contains a third superb example of star-vaulting. Here the ceiling is designed to form two eight-pointed stars, one within the other. The chapel, with its profusion of stone tracery, was founded in 1482 by Fernández de Velasco, Constable of Castile, whose marble tomb lies before the altar; the architect was the German Simón de Colonia. Between 1442 and 1458 his father Hans (Hispanicized as Juan) had built the twin openwork spires of the west facade, possibly modelling them on the spires planned for the cathedral in his home city of Cologne. In the third generation, Francisco de Colonia built the central dome and the Puerta de la Pellejería. Another father-and-son combination of artists was that of Gil and Diego de Siloé, the former from Flanders but his son born and raised in Spain. Gil worked on the *retablo* in the Capilla de Santa Ana (second left), while Diego's masterpiece, one of the crowning achievements of the cathedral, is the glorious **Escalera Dorada**, a double stairway in the north transept. To get into some of these smaller chapels you'll have to buy a Treasury ticket (350ptas), which also admits you to the cloisters, the Diocesan museum inside them, and the **Coro** at the heart of the cathedral, which affords the best view into the dome.

San Nicholás and San Esteban

Overlooking the plaza in front of the cathedral stands the fifteenth-century church of **San Nicolás**. Unassuming from the outside, it has an altarpiece within by Francisco de Colonia, which is as rich as anything in the city. At the side of San Nicolás, c/Pozo Seco ascends to the early Gothic church of **San Esteban**, which is now being refitted as a museum.

Monasterio de las Huelgas and the Cartuja de Miraflores

Inevitably the lesser churches of Burgos tend to be eclipsed by the cathedral, but on the outskirts are two monasteries which are by no means overshadowed. The closest, the Cistercian **Monasterio de las Huelgas** (Mon–Sat 11am–1.15pm & 4–5.15pm, Sun 11am–1.15pm; 400ptas including guided tour in Spanish) is remarkable for its wealth of Mudéjar craftsmanship. It lies on the "new side" of the river, a twenty-minute walk from the city centre: cross Puente de Santa María, turn right and follow the signs along the riverbank. Founded in 1187 as the future mausoleum of Alfonso VIII and Eleanor of Aquitaine, daughter of Henry II of England, it became one of the most highbrow and powerful convents in Spain. It was popularly observed that "if the Pope were to marry, only the Abbess of Las Huelgas would be eligible!" The main **church**, with its typically excessive Churrigueresque *retablo*, contains the tombs of no less than sixteen Castilian monarchs and nobles. That of the Infanta Blanca (d. 1325), daughter of Afonso III of Portugal, is vigorously carved with heraldic insignia surrounded by Moorish borders. Priceless embroidery, jewellery and weaponry of a suitably regal splendour were discovered inside the tombs and are exhibited in a small museum.

The highlight of the convent is its Mudéjar-Gothic **cloister**. Here again are the familiar eight-pointed stars, along with rare peacock designs – a bird holy to the Moors. The **Capilla de Santiago**, an obvious reminder that Las Huelgas stood on the pilgrim route, also has a fine Mudéjar ceiling and pointed horseshoe archway. Its cult statue of Saint James has an articulated right arm, which enabled him to dub Knights of the Order of Santiago (motto: "The Sword is Red with the Blood of Islam") and on occasion even to crown kings. At the other end of the pilgrim scale the convent was responsible for the nearby *Hospital del Rey* where food and shelter were provided free for two nights. It is presently in a very bad state of neglect, although the portals merit a visit.

The **Cartuja de Miraflores** (Mon–Sat 10.15am–3pm & 4–7pm, Sun 11.20am–12.45pm) is famous for three dazzling masterpieces by Gil de Siloé. The buildings are still in use as a monastery and most are closed – you can, however, visit the **church**, built between 1454 and 1488 by Juan and Simón de Colonia. In accordance with Carthusian practice, it is divided into three sections for the public, the lay brothers and the monks. In front of the high altar lies the star-shaped joint tomb of Juan II and Isabel of Portugal, of such perfection in design and execution that it forced Felipe II and Juan de Herrera to admit "we did not achieve very much with our Escorial". Isabella la Catolica, a great patron of the arts, commissioned it from Gil de Siloé in 1489 as a memorial to her parents. The same sculptor carved the magnificent altarpiece, which was plated with the first gold shipped back from America. His third masterpiece is the tomb of the Infante Alfonso, through whose untimely death in 1468 Isabella had succeeded to the throne of Castile.

Miraflores lies in a secluded spot about 4km from the centre: turn left from the Puente de Santa María; the *Cartuja* is well signposted along c/de Valladolid. There's a good restaurant in the nearby park. A bus runs on Sunday but returns right after the well-attended mass; there's also a bus to the nearby campsite (see above).

Eating, drinking and nightlife

You'll find plenty of restuarants in Burgos serving the traditional dishes, *cordero asado* (roast lamb) and *morcilla* (a kind of black pudding with rice) but there's also a wide choice of other food, and due to the large student population, a lively bar scene.

Restaurants and bars

There are several excellent bars serving **tapas** along c/Avellanos off Plaza Alonso Martinéz; *Mesón Astorga* and *La Flor* are two of the best. More formal Spanish **restaurants** include the *Rincón de España* between the river and the cathedral, and *Gaona* on c/Virgen de la Paloma next to the cathedral, while the *Prega* on c/Huerta del Rey serves Italian dishes. *Casa Ojeda*, c/Vitoria 5, is a good choice however deep your pocket, with a smart restaurant upstairs, a less expensive *comedor* downstairs, or *tapas* at the bar. If you're fed up with *asados* and the rest of Castilian cuisine, *Marisquería Bringas*, Laín Calvo 50, is a good fish restaurant. In the *Café-bar Luz*, Plaza de Vega 3, you can sample *chocolate con bizcochos*, light sponge fingers with hot chocolate, an alternative to *churros*.

Nightlife

There's a lively atmosphere in the city's bars and cafés, particularly at weekends. Nightlife depends on the time of night – the action progresses from the **bars** on c/San Juan, c/Laín Calvo, c/Huerta del Rey and c/San Lorenzo in the early evening, to c/Llanes from around 10pm onwards. This is a pedestrianized area of bars at the foot of the cathedral; try *Espadena, Rincón, La Nuit, Trastos, La Pécora, El Oliver* or *El Casco Viejo* which also serves great *tapas*. After 3am, head for the **clubs** in the new district of Bernardos round c/Las Calzadas and Avda. General Yagüe. Most places play loud rock and dated heavy metal, but two places with a more relaxed atmosphere and soothing jazz music are *Café de España*, c/Laín Calvo 12, and *Café La Cabala*, c/Puebla 7.

Southeast of Burgos

Southeast of Burgos, off the road to Soria, are a trio of sights: the town of **Covarrubias**, a medieval treasure on the Río Arlanza; the great monastery of **Santo Domingo De Silos**; and, at **Quintanilla de las Viñas**, a tiny Visigothic church and hermitage.

These are easy excursions if you have transport. If you don't, you'll need commitment and time to get the daily (5pm) bus from Burgos to Silos, via Lerma. Pilgrims, of course, used to (and still do) walk to Silos as a detour from the *camino*.

Santo Domingo de Silos

The Benedictine abbey of **SANTO DOMINGO DE SILOS** is one of Spain's greatest Christian monuments. Its main feature is a great double-storey eleventh-century

Romanesque cloister (Mon–Sat 10am–1pm & 4–7pm, Sun noon–1pm & 4–7pm) whose beautiful sculptural decoration is in many ways unique. The most remarkable features of the cloister are eight almost life-sized **reliefs** on the corner pillars. They include *Christ on the Road to Emmaus*, dressed as a pilgrim to Santiago (complete with scallop shell), a detail that shows that pilgrims made a detour from the route to see the tomb of Santo Domingo, the eleventh-century abbot after whom the monastery is named.

The same sculptor was responsible for about half of the **capitals.** Besides a famous bestiary, these include many Moorish motifs, giving rise to speculation that he may even have been a Moor. Whatever the case, it is an early example of the effective mix of Arab and Christian cultures, which was continued in the fourteenth century with the painted Mudéjar vault showing scenes of everyday pastimes. A quite different sculptor carved many of the remaining capitals, including the two that ingeniously tell the stories of the Nativity and the Passion in a very restricted space. A third master was responsible for the pillar with the Annunciation and Tree of Jesse, which is almost Gothic in spirit.

Visits to the monastery also include the eighteenth-century **pharmacy**, which has been reconstructed in a room off the cloister, and the **museum**, which houses the tympanum from the destroyed Romanesque church.

The **church** itself is an anticlimax, a rather nondescript construction designed by the eighteenth-century academic architect Ventura Rodríguez. Its Romanesque predecessor was too dark for the taste of the times; fortunately, the cloister's size and spaciousness saved it from a similar fate. The monks are famous for their **Gregorian chants**, in which they are considered one of the two or three best choirs in the world. It's particularly worth attending the morning Mass (9am) or even better, vespers, which currently start at 7pm.

Staying at Silos

Men can **stay** in the monastery itself (☎947/380768; ②), if they contact the Guest Master (*Padre Hospedería*) in advance; he prefers people to stay a few days. This is a wonderful bargain, with comfortable single rooms and good food at a ridiculously low cost. There are also some excellent places to stay in the village: the recently upgraded *Hotel Arco de San Juan* in the Pradera de San Juan (☎947/380794; ④), very near the cloister entrance, which has a lovely garden; the new, clean and well-furnished *Hostal Cruces* in the Plaza Mayor (☎947/380864; ③), which serves a good value evening meal; and the *Hotel Tres Coronas de Silos*, Plaza Mayor 6 (☎947/38072; ④), an imposing stone house which dominates the square.

The gorges of Yecla

The landscape around Silos is some of the most varied in Castile. A short walk up the hill gives a superb bird's-eye view of the village and the surrounding countryside and a couple of kilometres away are the impressive **gorges of Yecla**.

To reach these, take the road to Burgos, heading west of Silos, and turn left at the first village. You cross two rivers in quick succession, the Mataviejas and the Yecla. A few hundred metres later, a path off to the left leads through an incredibly narrow rocky gorge – the **Desfiladero de la Yecla** – which was impassable until a series of wooden walkways and plank bridges was built in the 1930s. It makes a spectacular hike, with the birds of prey circling high in the thin strip of visible sky.

If you continue west from the gorge rather than heading straight back to Silos, you can climb to the picturesque hilltop village of **Hinojar de Cervera**, and descend on the far side, after a couple of kilometres, to the **Cueva de San García**. This is a small cave containing various faded and rudimentary specimens of prehistoric art.

Covarrubias

The superbly preserved small town of **COVARRUBIAS** is just under 20km north of
Silos, on the C110 between Lerma and the Burgos–Soria road. The main sight is the
town itself: many of its white houses are half-timbered, with shady arcades, and
remnants of the fortifications are still standing, including a tenth-century tower. The
Colegiata looks plain from the outside, but a visit to the interior is a must; to do so, call
at the priests' houses left of the entrance. Four adults are needed for a tour group,
which shouldn't present a problem in summer, but be insistent if necessary. Inside
you'll find a late Gothic hall church crammed with tombs, giving an idea of the grandeur of the town in earlier times. The organ is an amazing seventeenth-century instrument still in good working order; you'll probably have to be content with hearing a
recording. There are several good paintings in the museum, but the chief attraction is a
triptych whose central section, a polychromed carving of the Adoration of the Magi, is
attributed to Gil de Siloé.

Public **transport** is limited: there's no bus service between Covarrubias and Silos,
although it is just possible to see both towns in a day on foot; the alternative is to come
direct on the single daily bus from Burgos. If you plan to stay in Covarrubias, bear in
mind that apart from the expensive *Parador Arlanza*, Plaza Mayor 11 (☎947/403025;
⑥), there's just one small **fonda**.

Quintanilla

An equally important monument, this time a rare Visigothic survival, is to be found at
QUINTANILLA DE LAS VIÑAS, which lies 4km north of Mazanriegos on the main
Burgos–Soria road, about 40km southeast of Burgos. Signs labelled *Turismo* lead to a
house where the caretaker of the **Ermita de Santa María** lives; if he isn't there, he'll
probably be at the hermitage itself, 1km further north. It's a simple building, of which
only the transept and the chancel survive. Dating from about 700, it's remarkable for its
unique series of sculptures: the outside bears delicately carved friezes, and inside
there's a triumphal arch with capitals representing the sun and moon, and a block
which is believed to be the earliest representation of Christ in Spanish art.

Burgos to León

The pilgrim route west from Burgos to León is one of the most rewarding sections in
terms of art and architecture. The N120 between the two cities passes through
Carrión de los Condes and **Sahagún**, and the other stops on the *camino* are only a
short detour off the main road.

Frómista

FRÓMISTA was the next important pilgrimage stop after Burgos. The present-day
town is much decayed, with a fraction of the population it once had. There's only one
sight of any note – the extremely beautiful church of **San Martín**, originally part of an
abbey which no longer exists, and is now deconsecrated (daily 10am–2pm & 4.30–8pm,
winter 3–6.30pm; free). Carved representations of monsters, human figures and
animals run right around the church, which was built in 1066 in a Romanesque style
unusually pure for Spain, with no traces of later additions. In fact, what you can see
now is a result of a turn-of-the-century restoration which was perhaps rather too thorough, although it is pleasing to the eye. Its beauty is enhanced by being completely
devoid of furnishings; there's nothing to detract from the architecture, and the only

colour is provided by twin wooden statues of San Martín and Santiago. The other church associated with the pilgrimage, **Santa María**, is near the train station, but it is also redundant and kept locked.

If you want to **stay** there are two comfortable places, *Pensión Camino de Santiago* (☎988/810053; ③) on the square on the road north to Santander, and *Fonda Marisa* (☎988/810023; ②), behind San Martín. The latter does a discreet and very popular lunchtime *menú*. The *Hostería de Los Palmeros*, Plaza Mayor (☎988/810067; ⑤) is a former medieval pilgrims's *hostal* now converted into a superbly furnished hotel with an excellent restaurant. The **Turismo** (daily in summer 11am–2pm & 5–8pm) is at the crossroads in the centre of town where the buses stop. Frómista is connected with Burgos by a daily bus, although it's reached more easily from Palencia since it lies on the Palencia–Santander rail line.

Villalcázar de Sirga

Thirteen kilometres from Frómista lies **VILLALCÁZAR DE SIRGA**, notable for a **church** built by the Knights Templar: from a distance it seems to crush the little village by its sheer mass, and originally its fortified aspect was even more marked. The Gothic style here begins to assert itself over the Romanesque, as witnessed by the figure sculpture on the two portals and the elegant pointed arches inside. The **Capilla de Santiago** has three polychromed tombs, among the finest of their kind and contemporary with the building. If the church is closed, as it usually is, take the street to the left in front of it and turn left at the corner; the sexton's house is the first brick building on the right.

In the square itself are a few medieval houses, one of which has been converted into the excellent **restaurant**, *El Mesón de Villasirga*. There is no accommodation, however, and Villalcázar is probably best seen as a day's excursion from Carrión de los Condes, 5km away.

Carrión de los Condes

The dusty, quiet atmosphere of **CARRIÓN DE LOS CONDES** belies its sensational past. It's reputed to be the place where, before the Reconquest, Christians had to surrender one hundred virgins annually to the Moorish overlords – a scene depicted on the portal of **Santa María** (situated at the edge of town, where the buses stop). For fine sculpture, however, look at the doorway of **Santiago**'s own church in the centre of town, overlooking the Plaza Mayor. Time has not treated this kindly – burned out during the last century, the church was rebuilt but now stands disused and neglected. The upper frieze reveals a debt to classical art, but the extraordinarily delicate covings above the door, which depict the trades and professions of the Middle Ages, are finer. The town's third main monument is the Plateresque cloister of **San Zoilo**, located over the sixteenth-century bridge; a side room off the cloister contains the tombs of the counts of Carrión, from whom the town's name comes. The nuns of **Santa Clara** have recently opened a small **museum** (summer Tues–Sun 10.30am–12.30pm & 5–7pm; winter 10.30am–12.30pm & 4–6pm) with a moderately interesting collection, including one of Spain's oldest organs. Their main work of art, however, is the theatrical *Pietà* by Gregorio Fernández, is kept in the church, which is only open for the early morning Mass.

The *Hostal La Corte* at c/Santa María 34 (☎988/880138; ②) in Carrión is very good value, and boasts an excellent cheap **restaurant**. Two other restaurants in town also sometimes offer rooms, the *Méson Pisarros* and *El Resbalón*, though the food in the latter is not so good. There's plenty of room for unofficial **camping** down by the river, or in the shady and modern official campsite, *El Edén* (☎988/880185), also by the river and back from the main road. Carrión is linked by bus to both Burgos and Palencia.

Sahagún and San Miguel de Escalada

From Carrión the route west continues to **Sahagún**. No other town so clearly illustrates the effect of the decline from the heyday of the pilgrimage. Once the seat of the most powerful monastery in all Spain, it's now a largely modern town, above which the towers of the remaining old buildings rear up like dinosaurs in a zoo. The nearby monastery at **San Miguel de Escalada**, has similarly slipped into insignificance.

Sahagún

SAHAGÚN is generally thought to be the birthplace of the brick churches built by the Moorish craftsmen who stayed on to work for the Christians after the Reconquest. Unfortunately, the great monastery these days is little more than a memory, and its main surviving sections – the gateway and belfry – date from a period of reconstruction in the seventeenth century. However, the twelfth-century parish churches of **San Tirso** and **San Lorenzo** remain, each with a noble tower. The town's guide is based at the former, where work has begun on the long-term project of removing the whitewash and returning the place to its original form (summer Tues–Sat 10.30am–1.30pm & 5–8pm, Sun 10am–3pm; winter 10.30am–1.30pm & 4–7pm, Sun 10.30am–1.30pm). The guide will also show you **La Peregrina**, up the hill from San Tirso, a thirteenth-century monastery built by Mudéjars – it's in a shocking state of disrepair, but a beautiful little chapel with stuccowork has been restored. San Lorenzo has the most imposing exterior, but the inside has been completely transformed, and is only open for Masses at the weekend.

Finally, you should see the little **museum** in the **Monasterio Santa Cruz** (Sun–Thur 10am–2.30pm & 4.30–6.30pm), through the archway from San Tirso; the nuns here have inherited the great *custodia* made by Enrique de Arfe, founder of a dynasty of silversmiths. Its big sister is the famous one at Toledo; like that one, the only airing it gets is during the Corpus Christi celebrations. The nuns prefer to open up to groups but try anyway if you're on your own – many pilgrims pass by here to get the official stamp for their *Camino de Santiago* card.

Sahagún has plentiful low-priced **accommodation**. The friendly proprietors of *La Bilbaina* (☎987/780754; ②), near the train station, speak English, while near San Tirso the *Fonda Asturiana* (☎987/780073; ②), is a building that would look more at home in Biarritz. The Alfonso VI (☎987/781144); ③) and *La Codorniz* (☎987/780276; ③) are smarter. *Fonda Asturiana* also has great home cooking, and bar-restaurant *Pacho* in town does good **food**.

Sahagún lies on the Palencia–León rail line. Buses leave from the Plaza Mayor but are very infrequent and many services have limited stops along this section of the pilgrim route. Buses from León to Carrión pass through Sahagún, but do not stop, nor issue tickets to here, so you will have to ask the driver specifically to drop you off.

San Miguel de Escalada

Although León is just a short distance further on from Sahagún, the medieval pilgrim would probably first have made a slight detour to see the **monastery of SAN MIGUEL DE ESCALADA**, a precious Mozarabic survival from the tenth century. Founded by refugee monks from Córdoba, it's a touching little building, with a simple interior of horseshoe arches, and a later portico, again Moorish in style. At the moment it's the subject of a heavy restoration programme, and you can't go inside; it's best to check the current situation with the tourist office in León before setting out. Getting there by public transport also presents a problem; although there are two buses a day to and from León, one turns back thirty minutes after it arrives, while the other requires spending the night – and there's nowhere to stay.

León

Even if they stood alone, the stained glass in the cathedral of **LEÓN** and the Romanesque wall paintings in its Royal Pantheon would merit a very considerable journey, but there's much more to the city than this. For León is as attractive – and enjoyable – in its modern quarters as it is in those parts that remain from its heyday: a prosperous provincial capital and lively university town.

Arrival, orientation and accommodation

León's modern sectors have been imaginatively laid out with wide, straight streets radiating like spokes from three focal plazas. The first of these is the **Glorieta de Guzmán el Bueno** near the river and the **train station**. Just south of here, León has a brandnew **bus station** on Paseo Ingeniero Miera.

From the Glorieta one can see straight down the Avenida de Ordoño II and across the **Plaza de Santo Domingo** to the towers of the cathedral. Just off the Plaza de Santo Domingo stands the **Casa de Botines**, an uncharacteristically restrained work by Antoni Gaudí (see "Astorga", below, and "Barcelona"). The third key square is the **Plaza de Calvo Sotelo**, connected to the Glorieta by the Avenida de Roma.

Head straight up from Plaza de Santo Domingo to the cathedral and you'll arrive in the Plaza Regia; here, directly opposite the cathedral's great west facade, stands the main **Turismo** (Mon–Fri 9am–2pm & 4–6pm, Sat 10am–1pm; ☎987/237082) and the **Correos**.

Accommodation

Budget accommodation is scattered all over León; there's no particular concentration and you don't have to leave the main streets. Handiest for the train station are the places along the Avenida de Roma, just before the bridge in front of it. Rooms round the Plaza Mayor are less expensive but dingy and noisy, and often full of permanent residents – certainly not worth a long trail with heavy bags.

BUDGET OPTIONS

Hostal Americana, Avda. Ordoño II 25 (☎987/251654). Inexpensive, clean rooms, with very low prices out of season. ②.

Hostal Covadonga, Avda. de Palencia 2 1° (☎987/222601). An adequate *hostal* in a lovely location, with parking opposite by the river. ③.

Hostal Guzmán el Buero, c/López Castrillón 6 (☎987/236412). Quiet rooms and handily placed near Palacio de los Guzmanes. ③.

Residencia Juvenil Infanta Doña Sancha, c/de la Corredera 4 (☎987/202201). León's youth hostel has a swimming pool. Follow Avda. de Independencia from Plaza de Santo Domingo. ①.

Hostal Residencia Londres, Avda. de Roma 1 (☎987/222274). One of several budget places on this street, which leads to the new town on the other side of the river. Good views, nice rooms and good value. ③.

Hostal Oviedo, Avda. de Roma 26 (☎987/222236). Good budget place near the train station. ②.

Pensión Roma, Avda. de Roma 4 (☎987/224663). Dark, old and inexpensive, run by a delightful old woman. ①.

HOTELS

Hostal Orejar, c/Villafranca 8 (☎987/252909). Comfortable rooms with bath and TV. ④.

Hotel Paris, c/Generalísimo 20 (☎987/271572). Modern rooms in a former palace close to the cathedral. ④.

Parador San Marcos, Plaza San Marcos 7 (☎987/237300). Has been described as the best hotel in the world, with antiques in the rooms and a superb restaurant. ⑥.

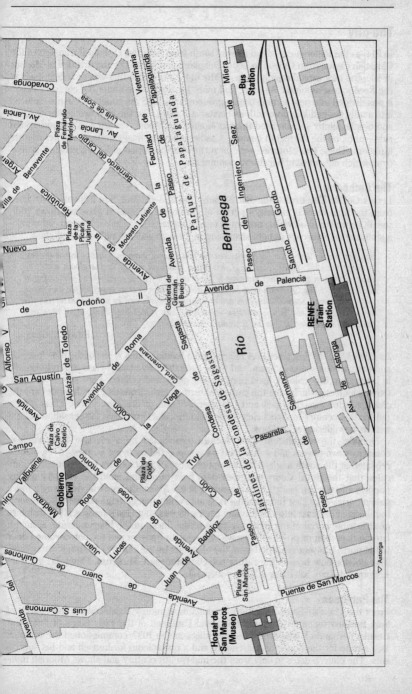

The city

In 914, as the Reconquest edged its way south from Asturias, Ordoño II transferred the Christian capital from Oviedo to León. Despite being sacked by the dreaded al-Mansur in 996, the new capital rapidly eclipsed the old – a scenario that was to repeat itself as the Reconquest unfolded. As more and more territory came under the control of León it was divided into new administrative groupings: in 1035 the county of Castile matured into a fully fledged kingdom with its capital at Burgos. For the next two centuries León and Castile jointly spearheaded the war against the Moors – as often as not under joint rule – until, by the thirteenth century, Castile had come finally to dominate her mother kingdom. These two centuries were nevertheless the period of León's greatest power, from which date most of her finest monuments.

The Cathedral

León's Gothic **Catedral** (Mon–Sat 9.30am–1pm & 4–6.30pm, Sun 9.30am–1pm) dates from the final years of the city's period of greatness. Its stained glass **windows** (thirteenth century and onwards) are equal to any masterpiece in any European cathedral – a stunning kaleidoscope of light streaming in through walls of multicoloured glass.

> *It is not simply that León Cathedral has the best stained glass in Spain – which it does: to enter the chill, twilit interior of this place and look round in the gloom until, by chance, the sun chooses that moment to come out is, I felt, to comprehend something of the hold which the Christian faith has been able to retain over so many people and for so long. In general, Spanish churches are exceptionally dark, and in my view exceptionally oppressive; and León is no exception – until the sun comes out. Then, more than any building I have ever set eyes on, it seems to burst into fire.*
>
> Edwin Mullins

As Edwin Mullins describes in *A Pilgrimage to Santiago*, this is one of the most magical and harmonious sights in Spain, and while such extensive use of glass is purely French in inspiration, the colours used here – reds, golds and yellows – are strictly Spanish. Other elements which take the cathedral further away from its French model are the cloister (admission 100ptas) and the later addition of the *coro*, whose glass screen (added this century to give a clear view up to the altar) enhances the sensation of light with its bewildering refractions.

Outside, the magnificent **west facade**, dominated by a massive rose window, comprises two towers and a detached nave supported by flying buttresses – a pattern repeated at the south angle. The inscription *locus appelationis* on the main porch indicates that the Royal Court of Appeal was held here, and amid the statuary a king ponders his verdict, seated on a throne of lions. Above the **central doorway** a more sublime trial – the Last Judgement – is in full swing: angels weigh souls in the balance, the damned are cast into the fire and the righteous sing God's praises. The sculpture on this triple portal of the facade is some of the finest on the Pilgrim Route, although later in date than most. The doorways of the south transept and the polychromed door to the north transept (shielded from the elements by the cloister) are other attractions. The cloister now houses the rather eclectic **Diocesan Museum**. (Mon–Fri 9.30am–1.30pm & 4–7pm, Sat 10am–1.30pm ; 300ptas).

The Pantheon

From the Plaza de Santo Domingo, Avenida de Ramón y Cajal leads to the church of **San Isidoro** (open all day) and the Royal Pantheon of the early kings of León and Castile. Fernando I, who united the two kingdoms in 1037, commissioned the complex as a shrine for the bones of San Isidoro and a mausoleum for himself and his successors. The church dates mainly from the mid-twelfth century and shows Moorish influence in the horseshoe arch at the west end of the nave and the fanciful arches in the transepts. The bones of the patron saint lie in a reliquary on the high altar.

The **Panteón** (July & Aug Mon–Sat 9am–2pm & 3–8pm, Sun 9am–2pm; Sept–June Tues–Sat 10am–1.30pm & 4–6.30pm, Sun 10am–1.30pm; 300ptas), comprising two surprisingly small crypt-like chambers, was constructed between 1054 and 1063 as a narthex or portico preceding the west facade of the church. It's one of the earliest Romanesque buildings in Spain, and the carvings on the portal which links the Pantheon and church herald the introduction of figure sculpture into the peninsula. In contrast, the capitals of the side piers and the two squat columns in the middle of the Panteón are carved with thick foliage which is still rooted in Visigothic tradition. Towards the end of the twelfth century, the vaults were vividly covered in some of the most significant, imaginative and impressive paintings of Romanesque art. They are extraordinarily well preserved and their biblical and everyday themes are perfectly adapted to the architecture of the vaults. The central dome is occupied by Christ Pantocrator surrounded by the four Evangelists depicted with animal heads – allegorical portraits which stem from the apocalyptic visions in the Bible's Book of Revelation. One of the arches bordering the dome is decorated with quaint rustic scenes which represent the months of the year. Eleven kings and twelve queens were laid to rest here but the chapel was desecrated during the Peninsular War and the remaining tombs command little attention in such a marvellous setting.

With a guide you can also visit the treasury and library – the former contains magnificent reliquaries, caskets and chalices from the early Middle Ages, but only reproductions of the manuscripts are on view.

San Marcos

If the Pantheon is a perfect illustration of the way Romanesque art worked its way into Spain along the Pilgrim Route from France, the opulent **Monasterio de San Marcos** (reached from the Plaza de Calvo Sotelo via Avenida de José Antonio) stands as a more direct reminder that León was a station on this route. Here, on presentation of the relevant documents, pilgrims were allowed to regain their strength before the gruelling Bierzo mountains west of León. The original monastery was built in 1168 for the Knights of Santiago, one of several chivalric orders founded in the twelfth century to protect pilgrims and lead the Reconquest. Eventually these powerful, ambitious and semi-autonomous Knights posed a political threat to the authority of the Spanish throne, until in 1493 Isabella la Católica subtly tackled the problem by "suggesting" that her husband Fernando be "elected" Grand Master. Thus the wealth and power of this order was assimilated to that of the throne.

In time, the order degenerated to little more than a men's club – Velázquez, for instance, depicts himself in its robes in *Las Meninas* – and in the sixteenth century the monastery was rebuilt as a kind of palatial headquarters. Its massive facade is lavishly embellished with Plateresque appliqué designs: over the main entrance Santiago is once again depicted in his battling role of *Matamoros*; more pertinently, protruding above the ornate balustrade of the roofline, are the arms of Carlos V, who inherited the grand mastership from Fernando in 1516. The monastery is now a government-owned five-star hotel, and is off limits to non-residents beyond its foyer and (modern) bar and restaurant. You can, however, ask specifically to see the *coro alto* of the church (access only from the hotel), which has a fine set of stalls by Juan de Juni.

Adjacent to the main facade stands the **Iglesia San Marcos**, vigorously speckled with the scallop shell motif of the Pilgrimage. Its sacristy houses a small **museum** (Tues–Sat 10am–2pm & 5–7.30pm, Sun 10am–2pm), whose most beautiful and priceless exhibits are grouped together in a room separated from the lobby of the hotel by an oddly symbolic thick pane of glass. Foremost among them are a thirteenth-century processional cross made of rock crystal and an eleventh-century ivory crucifix – a tiny piece of Romanesque sculpture, primitive and strangely proportioned, but with the peculiar mark of faith about it.

Eating, drinking and nightlife

The time of year to be in León is for the **fiestas** of Saint Peter in the last week of June. The celebrations, concentrated around the Plaza Mayor, get pretty riotous, with an enjoyable blend of medieval pageantry and buffoonery. For the rest of the year, the liveliest **bars and restaurants** tend to be those in the small square of San Martín and the dark narrow streets which surround it; an area known as **Barrio Húmedo** for the amount of liquid sloshing around all weekend. All the bars here will give you a *pincho* with every drink, so you can eat pretty well if you drink enough, especially hopping from bar to bar ordering *cortos* – small tumblers of beer for about 60–70ptas. The garlic-smothered potatoes dished up in *El Rincón del Gaucho* are particularly delicious.

Café Carmela, c/de Serradores 7. Lively café specializing in liqueur coffees, with magazines to browse through.

Casa Pozo, Plaza San Marcelo 15 (☎987/223039; closed Sun & July 1–15). Excellent *bodega* for traditional Leónese dishes; *menú* is 2500ptas.

Restaurante Fornos, c/Cid 8. Great food and atmosphere. Closed Sunday night and Monday.

Mesón Leones del Racimo de Oro, Caño Badillo 2 (closed Sun night and Tues). An authentic and modest-priced *mesón*, with a good 1200ptas *menú*.

Nuevo Racimo de Oro, Plaza San Martín 8. Slightly more formal and expensive than usual, but worth it. Closed on Sunday in summer and Wednesday in winter.

Bar Restaurante Real, c/Mariano D. Berrueta 7. Good lunch place near the cathedral.

Astorga and beyond

For the fittest of the pilgrims it was one day's walk of 29 miles from León to the next major stop at Astorga. On the way – at **Puente de Orbigo** – you pass the most ancient of the bridges along the route (probably the oldest in all Spain), now bypassed by the new road and offering a delightful and popular spot for a riverside stroll or picnic. As you get closer to Galicia, the terrain becomes mountainous and offers spectacular views. Beyond the valley town of **Ponferrada**, weary pilgrims confronted the mountains of **El Bierzo**, a region linked historically with León though distinct in more than just geography; in remoter villages you'll hear *gallego* spoken and see rather hopeful graffiti demanding independence for the area.

Astorga

ASTORGA resembles many of the smaller cities along the way: sacked by the Moors in the eleventh century, it was rebuilt and endowed with the usual hospices and monasteries, but as the Pilgrimage lost popularity in the late Middle Ages the place fell into decline. Many of its buildings were ravaged during the Peninsular War and today it seems to be crumbling gently into a peaceful old age.

Not without the odd flurry, though, for the bizarre **Palacio Episcopal** – commissioned by a Catalan bishop from his countryman Antoni Gaudí – injects some real vitality. Its appearance will not surprise anyone who has seen Gaudí's work in Barcelona. Surrounded by a moat and built of light grey granite, it resembles some horror-movie Gothic castle from the mountains of Transylvania with an equally striking, remarkably spacious interior. For half a century it stood empty and was considered a scandalous and expensive white elephant, but nowadays it houses the unique and excellent **Museo de los Caminos** (daily 11am–2pm & 3.30–6.30pm; 200ptas or 325ptas inclusive ticket

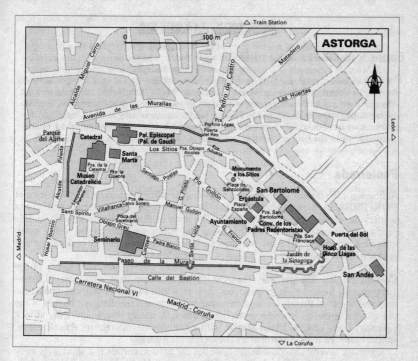

with Diocesan Museum). A host of knick-knacks throws interesting sidelights on the story of the Pilgrimage: hanging on the wall are examples of the documents issued at Santiago to certify that pilgrims had "travelled, confessed and obtained absolution", and there are photographs of the myriad villages and buildings along the way, and charts to show the precise roads taken through the towns.

Nearby – though stylistically worlds apart – stands the **Catedral**. Built between 1471 and 1693, it combines numerous architectural styles, but without any notable success. The **Diocesan Museum** (10am–2pm & 4–8pm; entrance to the left of the main facade) is interesting, however, especially for its beautiful twelfth-century wooden tomb painted with scenes from the lives of Christ and the Apostles.

Practicalities

Astorga connects with León by train but the **train station** is a long way from the centre of town. It makes far more sense to arrive and depart by **bus** as the station is very conveniently placed opposite the Palacio Episcopal. If you're coming from Santiago, there's an *Intercar* bus at 10.30am that is cheaper than most of the trains.

Astorga has a small **Turismo** (☎987/615947; June–Oct Mon–Sat 10am–2pm & 4–8pm), outside the Palacio Episcopal. There is a shortage of good inexpensive **accommodation** in the town. The *Coruña* (☎987/615009; ③) and the *Gallego* (☎987/615450; ③) close together on the main road to Ponferrada, are about the most convenient. Two good places to eat also let rooms; *Restaurante García* near the town hall and the pricier *Restaurante La Peseta*, Plaza San Bartolomé 3. *Hotel Gaudí*, Eduardo de Castro 6 (☎987/615654; ⑤), near the cathedral, is Astorga's top hotel and its restaurant has a *menú* which changes daily.

Ponferrada

At first sight the heavily industrialized bowl-shaped valley, centred on the large town of **PONFERRADA**, seems to have little to offer, but the mountainous terrain around has scenery as picturesque as any in Spain. The town of Ponferrada itself sums up this dichotomy, dominated by a huge slagheap and spreading suburbs yet with a quiet, unspoiled old quarter. The two are separated by a river blackened by coal mining and spanned by the iron bridge that has given Ponferrada its name.

Above the sharp valley the fancy twelfth-century turrets and battlements of the **Castillo de los Templarios** (Tues–Sat 10.30am–1.30pm & 4–7pm, Sun 10.30am–1.30pm), may look like gingerbread, but they were built to protect pilgrims against the very real threat of the Moors, and the arcaded streets and overhanging houses of the old quarter grew up in their protective shadow. A quaint *Puerta del Reloj* (Clock Gateway) leads into the **Plaza Mayor**, with a late seventeenth-century *Ayuntamiento*, similar in design to its contemporary counterpart at Astorga.

There are several churches in the town but the most important is a short walk away in the outskirts: **Santo Tomás de las Ollas**, a small Mozarabic church dating from the tenth century with nine round Moorish horseshoe arches and Visigothic elements.

Bus and **train** stations, and most **accommodation**, are in the new part of town which can be quite difficult to find your way around – Avda. de la Puebla is the main road which leads to the river; after crossing the bridge head right up the hill to reach the centre of the old town. The **Turismo** is on the road next to the castle (Mon–Sat 10am–2pm & 5–7pm). The only rooms up here are at the adequate *Pensión Mondelo*, c/ Flores Osorio 3 (☎987/416351; ②) just off c/del Reloj. In the new town, the best low-price places to try are *Hostal Santa Cruz*, c/Marcelo Macias 4 (☎987/416351; ②) and *Hostal Marán*, c/A. López Pelaez 29 (☎987/411800; ②). The *Hotel de Madrid*, Avda. de la Puebla 44 (☎987/411550; ③), also has a good restaurant, and for real luxury, Ponferrada has its own palace hotel, *Del Temple*, Avda. de Portugal (☎987/410058; ⑥). The *Bar/Restaurante Gundin*, near the *Santa Cruz* offers good value *menús*.

Las Médulas

Twenty kilometres southwest of Ponferrada lies **LAS MÉDULAS**, the jagged remains of Roman stripmining for gold. Nine hundred thousand tonnes of the precious metal were ripped from the hillsides using carefully constructed canals, leaving an eerie scene reminiscent of Arizona, peppered with caves and needles of red rock. From **Carucedo**, a road leads for 4km up to the village of Las Médulas; from here you can walk right through the zone. It's a good idea to make for the ridge overlooking the whole desolation; the quarry visible in the background from here is a reminder of how nature can turn man's devastation into beauty given a few thousand years. Another road leads from this viewpoint back down to Carucedo; the round trip takes about 4 or 5 hours.

Villafranca del Bierzo

The last halt before the climb into Galicia, **VILLAFRANCA DEL BIERZO,** was where pilgrims on their last legs could chicken out of the final trudge. Those who arrived at the Puerta del Perdón (Door of Forgiveness) at the church of **Santiago** could receive the same benefits as in Santiago de Compostela itself. The simple Romanesque church is of little interest, and the impressive castle opposite is in private hands and unvisitable, but the town is a pleasant enough spot to spend a few hours, with slate roofed houses, cool mountain air and the clear Burbia river providing a setting reminiscent of the English Lake District. Of the other churches the most rewarding is **San Francisco** just off the Plaza Mayor; it has a beautiful Mudéjar ceiling, a *retablo* so warped that it makes you dizzy to contemplate it, and an unusual well. If either church is locked, the bookshop on the plaza has the keys.

There's a range of places to stay including the modern *Parador de Villafranca del Bierzo*, Avda. Calvo Sotelo (☎987/540175; ⑥) and the *Ponterrey*, c/Dr. Arén 17 (☎987/540075; ③). *Restaurante Eurbia*, c/La Granja, is an excellent place to eat, specializing in fish. Regular buses from Ponferrada stop right outside the *parador*.

travel details

Buses

Burgos to: Aranda (6 daily; 1hr 15min); Bilbao (2 daily; 3hr); Carrión de los Condes (2 daily; 1hr 30min); Covarrubias (1 daily; 1hr); Frómista (1 daily; 1hr); León (2 daily; 3hr 30min; Logroño (7 daily; 2hr 30min); Madrid (4 daily; 4hr); Palencia (4 daily; 1hr 15min); Sahagún (2 daily; 2hr 30min); Salamanca (1 daily; 3hr 30min); Santo Domingo de la Calzada (4 daily; 1hr 30min); Santo Domingo de Silos (1 daily; 1hr 30min); San Sebastián (2 daily; 3hr 30min); Santander (2 daily; 3hr); Soria (2 daily on each route via San Leonardo 3hr, or via Vinuesa; 3hr 30min); Valladolid (2 daily; 1hr 45min).

Ciudad Rodrigo to: Fuentes de Oñoro (1 daily except Sun; 35min).

León to: Astorga (7 daily; 45min); Lugo (1 daily; 4hr 30min); Madrid (4 daily; 4hr 30min); Oviedo (4 daily; 2hr); Ponferrada (7 daily; 2hr); Salamanca (5 daily; 3hr 30min); San Miguel de Escalada (2 daily; 1hr 15min); Santander (1 daily; 3hr); Zamora (5 daily; 2hr 30min).

Logroño to: Barcelona (4 daily; 6hr); Bilbao (4 daily; 2hr 30min); Burgos (5 daily; 2hr); Pamplona (4 daily; 2hr); Santo Domingo de la Calzada (5 daily; 45min); Vitoria (8 daily; 1hr); Zaragoza (8 daily; 2–3hr).

Palencia to: Carrión de los Condes (3 daily; 1hr); Valladolid (2 daily; 1hr).

Salamanca to: Alba de Tormes (11 daily; 30min); La Alberca (1 daily; 1hr 30min); Ávila (5 daily; 1hr 30min); Badajoz (2 daily; 4hr 30min); El Burgo de Osma (1 daily; 4hr); Cáceres (4 daily; 3hr 30min); Ciudad Rodrigo (7 daily; 1hr 30min); Ledesma (2; 45min); León (4 daily; 2hr 30min–4hr); Madrid (13 daily, 11 on Sun; 2hr 30min–3hr 30min); Mérida (3 daily; 4 hr); Peñafiel (1 daily; 2hr 30min); Plasencia (4 daily; 2hr); Santander (1; 5hr 30min); Sevilla (3 daily; 7hr); Soria (1 daily; 5hr); Tordesillas (4 daily; 1hr 15min); Toro (3 daily; 1hr 30min); Valladolid (4 daily; 1hr 45min); Zamora (13 daily; 1hr 15min).

Soria to: Agreda (4 daily; 1hr 30min); Almazán (4 daily; 30min); Aranda (2 daily; 2hr); Berlanga de Duero (1 daily; 1hr 30min); El Burgo de Osma (3 daily; 1hr 15min); Guadalajara (2 daily; 3hr); Logroño (5 daily; 2hr); Madrid (4 daily; 3–4hr); Pamplona (3 daily; 3hr 30min); Tarazona (4 daily; 2hr); Valladolid (2 daily; 3hr 30min); Vinuesa (3 daily; 45min); Zaragoza (4 daily; 3hr 15min).

Valladolid to: El Burgo de Osma (1 daily; 3hr); Burgos (2 daily; 3hr); León (4 daily; 2hr 15min); Peñafiel (3 daily; 1hr); Segovia (3 daily; 2hr 30min); Soria (1 daily; 4hr).

Zamora to: Toro (4 daily; 30min); Valladolid (4 daily; 1hr 30min).

Trains

Burgos to: Ávila (1 daily; 2hr 30min); Barcelona (3 daily; 8hr); Bilbao (6 daily; 3–3hr 30min); Irún (10 daily; 3hr 30min–4hr); Madrid (3 daily; 3hr); San Sebastián (10 daily; 3–4hr); Vitoria (10 daily; 1hr 30min–2hr).

Salamanca to: Ávila (5 daily; 1hr 45min); Ciudad Rodrigo (5 daily; 1hr 30min); Fuentes de Oñoro with onward connections to Coimbra and Lisbon (5 daily; 2hr); Guarda (Portugal) (5 daily; 3hr); Madrid (5 daily; 3hr); Medina del Campo (8 daily; 1hr); Valladolid (7 daily; 2hr); Vila Formosa (Portuguese frontier) (4 daily; 2hr).

León to: Astorga (7 daily; 45min); Barcelona (4 daily; 9hr 30min–11hr); Becerril (3 daily; 1hr 30min); Burgos (7daily; 2–3hr); Lugo (4 daily; 5hr) Madrid (8 daily 4–6hr); Medina del Campo (11 daily; 2–3hr); Orense (6 daily; 4hr 30min); Oviedo (9 daily; 2hr 30min); Palencia (17 daily; 1–1hr 45min); Paredes de Nava (7 daily; 1–1hr 15min); Ponferrada (7 daily; 2hr); Sahagún (9 daily; 30–45min); Valladolid (13 daily; 1hr 30min–2hr 30min).

Logroño to: Bilbao (2 daily; 3–3hr 30min); Burgos (3 daily; 2 hr 15min); León (3 daily; 4hr 30min); Madrid (1 daily; 5hr 30min); Palencia (3 daily; 3hr); Zaragoza (2 daily; 2–3hr).

Medina del Campo to: Ávila (9 daily; 1hr); Burgos (5 daily; 2hr 30min); Coca (5 daily; 30min, 2 trains; 1hr, 3 trains); León (6 daily; 1hr 30min–3hr); Madrid (9 daily; 2hr 30min–3hr); Palencia (6 daily; 1hr 15min); Segovia (3 daily; 2hr 15min); Toro (3 daily; 1hr); Valladolid (11 daily; 1hr, 5 trains; 1hr 45min, 6 trains); Zamora (3 daily; 1hr 15min).

Ponferrada to: Lugo (4 daily; 3hr 30min).

Soria to: Almazán (4 daily; 30min); Madrid (4 daily; 3hr); Pamplona (1 daily; 3hr).

All **other lines** are now closed.

CHAPTER SIX

EUSKADI: THE BASQUE PROVINCES & NAVARRA

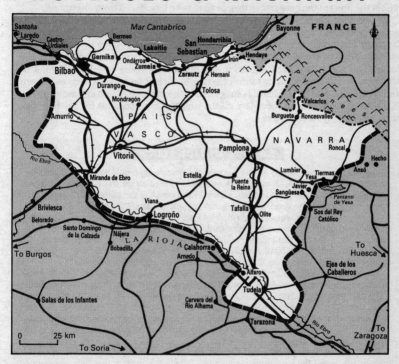

Euskadi is the name the Basque people give to their own land, an area that covers the three Basque provinces, **Gipuzkoa**, **Bizkaia** and **Araba**, much of **Navarra**, and part of southwestern France. It's an immensely beautiful region – mountainous, green and thickly forested. It rains often, and much of the time the countryside is shrouded in a fine mist. But the summers, if you don't mind the occasional shower, are a glorious escape from the unrelenting heat of the south.

Despite the heaviest industrialization on the peninsula, Euskadi is remarkably unspoiled – neat and quiet inland, rugged and enclosed along the coast – and transport everywhere is easy and efficient. **San Sebastián** is the big draw on the coast, a major resort with superb but crowded beaches, but there are any number of lesser known, equally attractive villages along the coast all the way to **Bilbão** and beyond into

Asturias and Galicia. Inland, there's the exuberant **Fiesta de San Fermín** in **Pamplona**, as well as many other destinations with charms of their own, from the drama of the **Pyrenees** to the quiet elegance of **Vitoria**.

The Basques

No one knows much about the origin of **the Basques**. They are a distinct people, generally with a different build from the French and Spanish and a different blood group distribution from the rest of Europe. Certainly their language, the complex *Euskara*, is one of the most ancient spoken in Europe, predating the migrations from the east which brought the Indo-European languages some 3000 years ago. It is now considered to go back in time as far as the Basque race itself and to have evolved within the present territory rather than to have been introduced from elsewhere.

Establishing concrete data has been complicated by the fact that *Euskara* did not appear in written form until the sixteenth century (in the French Basque Country). The language has largely been maintained and has even evolved through the oral traditions of *bertsolariak* or popular poets specializing in improvized verse, a tradition still alive today. The vocabulary itself implies a way of thinking going well back beyond the Christian era, as evidenced by terms referring to ancient burial sites such as dolmens and cromlechs. Further evidence is suggested in the strong tradition of Basque mythology relating to *gentiles*, or legendary giants, supposedly responsible for building these sites, ancient ways and bridges.

BASQUE NATIONALISM

Though highlighted recently by the horrors of Franco's attempted suppression and the counter-activities of **ETA** (*Euskadi ta Askatasuna* – Freedom for the Basques), **Basque nationalism** is no new phenomenon. Richard Ford wrote in the nineteenth century that "these highlanders, bred on metal-pregnant mountains, and nursed amid storms in a cradle indomitable as themselves, have always known how to forge their iron into arms, and to wield them in defence of their own independence". The Visigoths perceived the *Vascones* as being a "dangerous rural population emerging from the mountains to threaten the settled inhabitants of the valleys". The Visigoth king, Recared, unable to subdue the region, used to send his troops out here just to keep them fit.

For almost the entire history of Spain, the Basques jealously defended their *fueros* – the ancient rights under which they ruled themselves almost as an independent republic – against constant pressure from Madrid, and guarded the wealth brought by seafaring skills, mineral riches and industrial enterprise. It was not until 1876 and the second and final defeat of the Carlists, whom the Basques supported as upholding their own traditionalist values, that the victorious liberals finally abolished the *fueros* altogether as an act of vengeance on the Basques.

Although the conservative, traditionalist **Basque National Party** (PNV) emerged towards the end of the nineteenth century, it is only in this century that Basque nationalism has become associated with the political left, mostly in reaction to the terrors of Franco's regime. Cut off from their Republican allies by Navarra, which sided with the Nationalists, the Basque provinces were conquered in a vicious campaign that included the infamous German bombing of **Gernika** in 1937. Franco's vengeful boot went in hard, and as many as 21,000 people died in his attempts to tame the Basques after the war. Public use of the language was forbidden, and central control was asserted with the gun. But the state violence signally failed, succeeding only in nurturing a new resistance based on ETA, whose violent activities included many bombings, and whose most spectacular success was the assassination in Madrid of Franco's right-hand man and probable successor, Admiral Carrero Blanco. Even now the military and the *Guardia Civil* are regarded – and behave – as an army of occupation, and the more radically-minded Basques of the *Abertzale* (nationalist) movement continue to support ETA's aims, if not their methods.

Some think that the Basque people are the last surviving representatives of Europe's aboriginal population, a theory borne out by archeological finds earlier this century. Skull fragments of late Cro-Magnon man believed to date from the Paleolithic era, around 9000 BC, have been shown to be identical to present day Basque cranial formation. Much anthropological work, above all by the revered Joxe Miguel Barandiaran (who died in December 1991, aged 101), lends itself to the view that the Basques have continuously inhabited the western Pyrenees, largely in isolation, for thousands of years. Indeed, over the centuries they have had very little contact with the peoples who originally migrated into Europe, partly due to being surrounded by impenetrable mountains and partly because they were considered to be barbarians by potential invaders.

Food

Basque cuisine is accepted as Spain's finest, and the people here are compulsive eaters: try *bacalao* (cod) *a la vizcaina*, *merluza* (hake) *a la vasca*, *chipirones en su tinta* (squid cooked in its ink) or *txangurro* (spider crab), which you'll find in very reasonably priced roadside *caseríos* (*baserri* in Basque), on the outskirts of towns throughout the region. You'll also come across traditional Basque food in the form of *tapas* (known in Basque Country as *pinchos*) in virtually every bar, freshly cooked and always excellent.

The tradition of **gastronomic societies**, unique to the Basque Country, deserves special mention: first founded in the mid-nineteenth century, they came about origi-

Following the **return to democracy**, however, things *have* changed. The Basque parliament has been granted a fair degree of autonomy in its own affairs (it's the only autonomous community allowed to collect its own taxes), and there's a Basque police force, the *ertzaintza* (distinguished by its red berets) much in evidence in the streets. The Basque **language** is flourishing again and is taught in at least half of all primary schools in the region. The Basque flag (the *Ikurriña*) flies everywhere – the exterior design of Euskadi's pavilion at Expo'92 in Sevilla was of a giant illuminated *ikurriña*.

Since gaining home rule, Euskadi has, like Catalunya and Galicia, been controlled by the right. The government has offered an amnesty to activists who publicly renounce ETA's methods, and has been engaged in secret negotiations with ETA leaders to end the violence. But the government continues to wield a big stick while granting these concessions: an ultra-right group known as GAL (formed some years ago to liquidate ETA members by persons considering government anti-terrorist policies to be inadequate), although not recognized by the government, has been proved to consist largely of certain members of the *Guardia Civil*. Their operations have been principally confined to the French Basque Country where an extradition treaty with the French has also denied gunmen their former safe refuges across the border. In early 1992 the French police arrested several of the top *etarras* in one swoop on a house near Biarritz.

None of this has put an end to ETA activity, but it has marginalized it. Their political wing, *Herri Batasuna* (Popular Unity), has little influence in a Basque parliament dominated by the PNV and the Socialists (just over 10 percent voted for them in the last election, although the proportion is considerably higher in the Basque heartland of Gipuzkoa and parts of Bizkaia). Polls show that while wanting increased autonomy, many Basques oppose forming a breakaway state. The economic recession no doubt has much to do with this – the *País Vasco*'s former industrial glories are now reduced to rusty, outdated factories and closed-down steel foundries and shipyards.

Terrorism keeps away new investment and unemployment is extremely high. In January 1988 a historic pact was signed by all the Basque parties except *Herri Batasuna*, condemning ETA's tactics while upholding their goals. There's little doubt that a substantial portion of the Basque population now feels that more will be achieved through the new channels than by the old ETA methods.

nally as socializing places for different craftsmen. Controversy has surrounded them due to the fact that women have traditionally not been allowed to enter (although this is changing) and all cooking is done by men who pay a token membership fee for the facilities. Members prepare elaborate dishes to perfection as a hobby and it can be said that true Basque cookery has largely retreated to these societies. The so-called *Nueva Cocina Vasca* (New Basque Cookery), heavily influenced by French cuisine, is becoming increasingly evident on menus.

Sport

The **Basque sport** of *jai alai*, or *pelota*, is played all over Spain, but in Euskadi even the smallest village has a *fronton* or pelota court and betting on the sport is rife among Basques. Other unique Basque sports include *aizkolaritza* (log-chopping), *harri-jasotzea* (stone-lifting), *soka-tira* (tug-of-war) and *segalaritza* (grass-cutting). The finest exponents of the first two in particular are popular local heroes (the world champion stone-lifter Iñaki Perurena's visit to Japan resulted in the sport being introduced there –

FIESTAS

January

19–20 *Tamborrada* – march with pipes and drums – in San Sebastián, with more festive action in the evenings.

March

4–12 A series of pilgrimages to the castle at Javier, birthplace of San Francisco Javier.

June

21 *Fiesta de la Magdalena* in Bermeo, with torch-lit processions of fishing boats and the usual races and Basque sports.

End of the month Similar events in Lekeitio, spilling over into early July.

July

First week sees the great fiesta at Zumaia, with dancing, Basque sports and an *encierro* on the beach.

7–14 *Fiestas de San Fermín* in Pamplona.

22 Basque sports and boat races take place all along the coast, especially at Bermeo and Mutriku.

Third week Jazz festival in Vitoria.

24–29 *Fiesta de Santa Ana* in Tudela, with bands, marches and *encierros*.

Ten days in July The International Jazz Festival in San Sebastián – one ticket covers all the gigs.

August

First weekend Patron saint's celebrations in Estella.

First week *Fiesta de la Virgen Blanca* in Vitoria, with bullfights, fireworks and *gigantones*.

15 The middle of the month witnesses an explosion of celebration. Notably in Bilbao, with Basque games and races; Zarautz, with rowing regattas; Gernika and Tafalla, with an *encierro;* and San Sebastián, where the highlight is an International Fireworks Competition.

31 *Dia de San Ignacio Loyola* is big everywhere above all, in his birthplace, Loyola.

September

First week *Euskal Jaiak* (Basque Feasts) in San Sebastián, and the *Fiesta de San Antolín* in Lekeitio where the local youth attempt to knock the head off a goose – a sort of living *piñata*.

8 Fiestas at Vitoria, Bermeo, Viana, Eibar and Hondarribia among others.

9 In Zarautz the start of a week-long Basque festival.

12 Sangüesa holds its own *encierros*.

14 Patron saint's day in Olite, with more bulls.

Middle of the month The San Sebastián film festival.

December

Christmas Celebrations are particularly exuberant in Pamplona. At midnight on Christmas Eve there's an open-air mass by firelight in Labastida (Araba).

he remains the only lifter to surpass the legendary 315-kilo barrier). All form an important part of the many local fiestas.

Accommodation

The main drawback to travelling in the region is that prices (apart from for food) are
higher than in much of the country, particularly for accommodation, although there is
a considerable difference between prices on the Cantabrian coast and inland (with the
exception of Pamplona). Accommodation in smaller towns has had a recent substantial
boost with the introduction of the Basque Government's **agroturismo**, or homestay,
programme, which offers the opportunity to stay in traditional Basque farmhouses and
private homes, usually in areas of outstanding beauty, at very reasonable cost. They are
identified by a red and green circular sign with the word *nekazalturismoa*. In Navarra
these are known as **casas rurales**, and lists showing facilities and prices may be
obtained from regional tourist offices (who also handle bookings). Except in the very
small villages, there is usually a *fonda* or *hostal*, or entering any bar and asking for a
room will generally produce results.

ACCOMMODATION PRICE SYMBOLS

The symbols used in our hotel listings denote the following price ranges:

① Under 2000ptas   ③ 3000–4500ptas   ⑤ 7500–12,500ptas

② 2000–3000ptas   ④ 4500–7500ptas   ⑥ Over 12,500ptas

See p.30 for more details.

Irún and around

The Basque province of Gipuzkoa ajoins the French frontier, and its border town, **Irún**,
is one of the major road and rail entry points into Spain. There are fast connections on
to San Sebastián, although if you're travelling more slowly, the fishing ports of
Hondarribia and **Pasajes** are worth a stop. The main route to the south crosses into
Navarra and leads via the beautiful Valle de Bidasoa to Pamplona.

Irún

Like most border towns, **IRÚN**'s chief concern is how to make a quick buck from passing travellers, and the main point in its favour is the ease with which you can leave;
there are trains to **Hendaye** in France and to San Sebastián throughout the day, and
regular long-distance and international connections. If arriving by train from Paris (or
elsewhere in France) at Hendaye, note that it is far quicker to take the *topo* (mole train,
so-called because of all the tunnels it goes through) from the separate platform on the
right outside Hendaye main station; it runs every thirty minutes to Irún (to the station
at Avda. de Colón 52) and San Sebastián.

If you do need to spend the night, there are plenty of bars and places to eat, and
prices are markedly lower than in France or San Sebastián (which is no place to arrive
late at night with nowhere to stay). In the vicinity of Irún's main train station are
several small, reasonably priced **hostales** and **restaurants** specializing in good local
food. *Fonda Algorta* (③) and *Bar Pensión los Fronterizos* (③), both along c/Estación
leading from the main station, have some of the lowest priced rooms; for more comfort
try the nearby *Hostal Irún*, c/Zubiaurre 5 (☎943/612283; ③), *Lizaso*, c/Aduana 5–7
(☎943/611600; ③) or *Madrinventa*, Avda. de Colón 23 (☎943/621384; ③).

Hondarribia

The fishing port of **HONDARRIBIA** (Fuenterrabía), 6km north of Irún and overlooking Hendaye, is a more attractive place. Calle San Pedro, the tamarisk-lined main street, is flanked with traditional, wood-beamed Basque houses interspersed with bars offering some of the best seafood and *pinchos* around. In summer, the fine **beaches** just beyond the town are an escape from the ultra-crowded *Concha* in San Sebastián.

Hondarribia has a picturesque, walled old town entered through the fifteenth-century **Puerta de Santa María**. Calle Mayor, leading up to the Plaza de Armas, has further fine examples of wood-beamed houses, some displaying the family coats of arms above doorways, and the square itself is dominated by the **Palacio de Carlos Quinto**, started originally in the tenth century by Sancho the Strong of Navarra and subsequently extended by Carlos V in the sixteenth. It is now a luxurious *parador* (see below), and it's worth at least having a drink at the bar inside.

Practicalities

There are several good **hostales** in town; try *Hostal Alvarez Quinto*, c/Bernat Etxepare, in the *Edificio Miramar* (☎943/642299; ④), or *Txoko-Goxoa*, c/Miguel Maria Ayestaran 19 (☎943/644658; ③), in the old town. The **youth hostel**, *Juan Sebastián Elcano*, is on Carretera Faro (☎943/641550; ①); fork left beyond c/San Pedro on the way to the beaches. The three-star *Río Bidasoa*, c/Nafarroa Behera (☎943/645408; ⑤), has its own pool, while the *Parador Nacional El Emperador* (☎943/642140; ⑥) is stunningly located in the town's fortified *palacio*. The closest **campsite**, *Camping Jaizkibel* (☎943/641679; open year round), is 2km out of town along Carretera Guadalupe towards Pasajes. Also outside town, just by the chapel of Nuestra Señora de Guadalupe, is a signposted turn-off to an **agroturismo**, *Montaña Artzu* (☎943/640530; ③), offering accommodation in an old restored farmhouse.

The bars along c/San Pedro are the best hunting ground for **food** and **drink**. In the old town, tucked away in a narrow cobbled alley two streets behind c/Mayor, the *Mamutzar* restaurant serves a good value *menú del día*, and next door is the tiny

Hamlet bar, a popular haunt for Basque radical punks and skins (of the left wing variety) from Irún and other towns in the area.

Frequent **buses** leave from c/San Pedro to San Sebastián. The stretch of coastline from here as far as the port of Pasajes is particularly rugged and has long been a haven for smugglers.

Pasajes San Juan

The one place you might consider stopping for any length of time en route between Irún and San Sebastián is the port of Pasajes. While much of the town is highly industrialized, the old town, **PASAJES SAN JUAN** (Pasaia Donibane) retains its charm. The narrow cobbled c/San Juan (Victor Hugo once lived at no. 65, the house built over the tunnel) leads to the plaza with its colourful houses. Pasajes San Juan is famous for its waterside **fish restaurants**, many of which offer good value *menús del día* and even choosing from the evening menus here works out considerably less expensive than those in San Sebastían's old quarter. A **launch** (*txalupa*) runs throughout the day until 10.30pm across the harbour to Pasajes San Pedro, from where frequent buses run to San Sebastián's Boulevard.

Towards Pamplona

If you're heading straight down to Pamplona, you'll pass through the **Bidasoa valley** with its string of beautifully-preserved towns, the best of which are Vera de Bidasoa, Lesaka and Etxalar. South from Etxalar, the road forks right and the N121 leads over the Velate Pass to Pamplona. The left fork takes you up to the Baztan valley (see p.392). Both valleys are on direct bus routes from San Sebastián/Irún and Pamplona.

Vera de Bidasoa
VERA DE BIDASOA offers some of the finest examples of old wood-beamed and traditional stone houses in the region; the brightly painted buildings along c/Altzarte and the main square are particularly attractive. About 100 metres off the square, just past the old border crossing, is the former house (no. 24) of the Basque writer Pio Baroja, which is now a small ethnographic museum with the old library still intact. You can arrange a visit through the **Turismo** (summer only) in c/Altzarte or by phoning ☎948/630020.

If you want to **stay,** there's the small *Fonda Chantre*, c/San Esteban 13 (☎948/ 630239; ②) or the better standard *Euskalduna*, c/Bidasoa 5 (☎948/630392; ④), with a good restaurant offering a *menú del día* and local specialities. Alternatively, there's a **casa rural** just outside town, *Casa Etxebertea*, Barrio de Zelain (☎948/630272; ③) which also has bicycles to rent.

Five kilometres east of Vera at the top of Luzuniaga Pass right on the French border, **Monte Larrun** is an easy climb: from the top you'll get spectacular views across the Pyrenees and the French Basque coast. There's a bar/restaurant at the top which serves tourists taking the funicular from the French side.

Lesaka
South of Vera along the Bidasoa valley, a right turn leads to **LESAKA**. Despite the eyesore of a large factory on the outskirts of town, it's a beautiful place dominated by the hilltop parish church in which the pews bear family names of the local farms and mansions. On the banks of the irrigation channel which flows through town is one of the best remaining examples of a *casa torre* (fortified private house) of a design peculiar to the Basque Country, dating back to the days when north Navarra was in the hands of a few powerful and constantly feuding families.

For **accommodation** try *Hostal Juan Gosenea*, Plaza Zaharra 20 (☎948/637077; ③) or *Pensión Tolareta*, Plaza Nueva 2 (☎948/637106; ②), in a new building just off the main square.

Etxalar

ETXALAR is a tiny place, 4km off the main road, but is perhaps the best preserved town of the valley, famous for the impressive array of Basque funerary steles in the churchyard. There's a lovely *casa rural*, *Casa Domekenea* (☎948/635031; ③), otherwise try the *Hotel Venta de Etxalar*, on the main road (☎948/635000; ④).

San Sebastián

The undisputed queen of the Basque resorts, **SAN SEBASTIÁN** (DONOSTIA) is a picturesque – though expensive – seaside town with good beaches. Along with Santander, it has always been the most fashionable place to escape the heat of the southern summers, and in July and August it's always packed. Though it tries hard to be chic, San Sebastián is still too much of a family resort to compete in those terms with the South of France, which is all to its good. Set around the deep, still bay of La Concha and enclosed by rolling low hills, it's beautifully situated; the old town sits on the eastern promontory, its back to the wooded slopes of Monte Urgull, while newer development has spread along the banks of the Urumea, around the edge of the bay to the foot of Monte Igüeldo and on the hills overlooking the bay.

Arrival, information and accommodation

Most **buses** arrive at Plaza Pio XII, fifteen minutes' walk along the river from the centre of town, but from Pasajes and Astigarraga they arrive on the Alameda del Boulevard, and from Hondarribia on c/Oquendo near the Turismo. The main-line **train station** is across the Río Urumea on the Paseo de Francia, although local lines from Hendaye and Bilbão via Zarauz and Zumaya (which do not accept *InterRail* passes) have their terminus on c/Easo.

The **Turismo** (Mon–Sat 9am–2pm & 3.30–7pm, closed Sat afternoon out of season) is on c/Reina Regente in the *Teatro Victoria Eugenia*. For a greater selection of pamphlets there is the very useful Basque Government tourist office (Mon–Thurs 9.30am–1.30pm & 3.30–6pm, Fri & Sat 9.30am–1.30pm) at Paseo de los Fueros 1, just off the main Avenida de la Libertad .

San Sebastián is something of a travel hub for the region. *Viajes TIVE*, c/Tomas Gros 3 (☎943/276934) is a youth/student **travel agency** that sells tickets for international buses and discount plane tickets. They also issue *ISIC* cards with no fuss at all (any vaguely official-looking letter will do, plus a couple of photos). Another good travel agency is *Viajes Aran*, c/Elkano 1 (☎943/429009 or 429011). For travel books and maps (both local and elsewhere), and for books on all things related to the Basque Country, the best is *Graphos* on the corner of Alameda del Boulevard and c/Mayor. Also recommended are *Bilintx*, c/Esterlines 10, and *Dr. Camino*, c/31 de Agosto 32–36, which has a small reading room.

Accommodation

Accommodation, though plentiful, is not particularly low in price and can be hard to come by in season – if you arrive in July or especially August or during the film festival in September, you'll have to start looking early in the day. There is no great difference in rates between the cheapest places in the *parte vieja* (old quarter), and elsewhere, although *hostales* along the Alameda del Boulevard do tend to be slightly higher-priced.

There is often more chance of finding space in the cathedral (*centro*) area around c/ Easo, c/San Martin, c/Fuenterrabia and the lively c/San Bartolomé, or on the other side of the river in **Gros**, behind the main train station in **Egia** or in the new part of town, **Amara Nuevo** on the way to the Anoeta sports complex. Asking in bars in any of the above-mentioned areas about unofficial private rooms will also often produce results.

THE PARTE VIEJA

Albergue Juvenil, Paseo de Igüeldo (☎943/310256). The new youth hostel, known as *La Sirena*, is just a few minutes' walk from the end of Ondarreta beach. ①.

Pensión Amaiur, c/31 de Agosto 44, 2° (☎943/429654). A pleasant and friendly place with carpeted doubles and a few triples. The owner serves breakfast in the kitchen for 200ptas outside the summer period and always tries to arrange a room elsewhere when full. ③.

Pensión Arsuaga, c/Narrica 3, 3° (☎943/420681). Simple, spacious doubles; can be chilly in winter but has its own restaurant and offers good full board deals. ③.

Pensión La Estrella, Plaza de Sarriegui 1 (☎943/420997). Attractive old place. Rooms with or without shower; either overlooking the plaza or Alameda del Boulevard. ④.

Pensión Kaia, c/Puerto 12, 2° (☎943/431342). Recently refurbished rooms with bath. ④.

Pensión Larrea, c/Narrica 21, 1° (☎943/422694). Clean, new rooms but on a busy street corner and a bit cramped and noisy. ③.

Hostel Parma, c/General Jauregui 11 (☎943/428893). Comfortable rooms with all amenities, the best ones overlooking the sea. A good location between *parte vieja* and Paseo Nuevo. ⑤.

Pensión San Jeronimo, c/San Jeronimo 25, 2° (☎943/286434, 281689). Adequate though spartan rooms with crumbling hallway and stairs. ③.

Pensión San Lorenzo, c/San Lorenzo 2, 1° (☎943/425516). A small place where guests can use the kitchen to prepare food. ③.

Pensión Urgull, c/Esterlines 10, 3° (☎943/430007). No lift, but spotless and tastefully furnished, airy rooms with constant hot water. Only five rooms, so arrive early or book. ③.

ALAMEDA DEL BOULEVARD

Hostal Alameda, Alameda del Boulevard 23 (☎943/421687). An old building with a bit of character, but rooms are without bath and not great value. Only open May 1–Oct 15 as it is used as student accommodation during the rest of the year. ④.

Pensión Boulevard, Alameda del Boulevard 24, 1° (☎943/429405). Big, comfortable modern rooms, but only one with bath. ④.

Hostal Eder II, Alameda del Boulevard 16, 2° (☎943/426449). Spacious rooms some with bath. Has a an elegant hallway with fine wood panelling. ④.

CENTRO

Pensión Alemana, c/San Martin 53, 1° (☎943/464881). An excellent central location on the street by the cathedral. ④.

Pensión Añorga, c/Easo 12, 1° (☎943/467945). A large *pensión* on two floors; fairly plain, but clean rooms some with bath. ③.

Hostal Comercio, c/Urdaneta 24 (☎943/464414). Simply furnished but reasonable rooms with washbasin and fan heaters. ④.

Hostal Easo, c/San Bartolomé 24 (☎943/466892). Offers one of the best accommodation deals in town; low-priced rooms with washbasin or shower. ③.

Hostal Eder, and **Hostal Ederra**, c/San Bartolomé 33 and 25 (☎943/424696). Two smart *hostals* run by the same management as the *Eder II* in Alameda del Boulevard. ④.

Pensión Josefina, c/Easo 12, 3° (☎943/461956). Has a couple of large rooms facing the street, otherwise offers only cramped singles and doubles with little or no natural light. ④.

Pensión La Perla, c/Loiola 10 (☎943/428123). Very good value, spotless rooms with bath. Close to Buen Pastor cathedral and the food market. ③.

Pensión Urkia, c/Urbieta 12, 3°(☎943/424436). Run by the sister of *La Perla's* owner, and has equally good rooms with bath. ③.

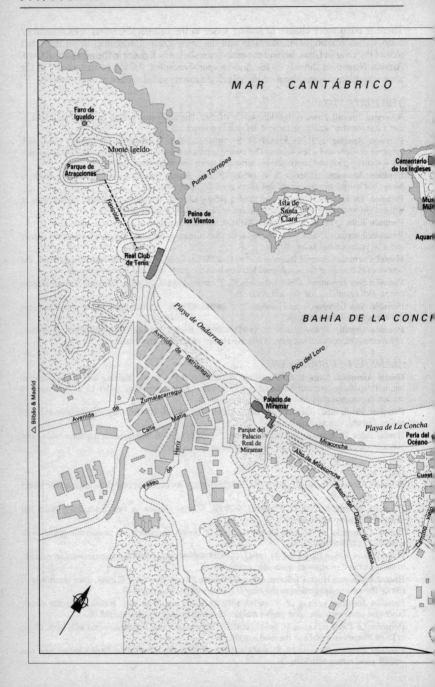

MAR CANTÁBRICO

Faro de
Igueldo

Monte Igeldo

Parque de
Atracciones

Punta Torrepea

Cementerio
de los ingleses

Peine de
los Vientos

Isla de
Santa
Clara

Mus
Mili

Aquari

Real Club
de Tenis

Playa de Ondarreta

BAHÍA DE LA CONCH

Avenida de Satrústegui

Pico del Loro

△ Bilbao & Madrid

Zumalacarregui

Palacio de
Miramar

Avenida de

Calle Matia

Parque del
Palacio
Real de
Miramar

Playa de La Concha

Miraconcha

Perla del
Océano

Paseo de Heriz

Alto de Miraconcha

Cuest

Paseo

Paseo del Duque de Baena

Camino viejo

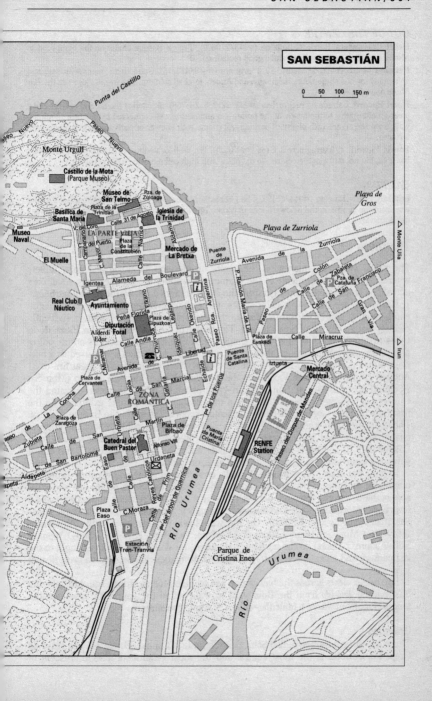

SAN SEBASTIÁN

0   50   100   150 m

Punta del Castillo

Paseo Nuevo

Monte Urgull

Castillo de la Mota
(Parque Museo)

Museo de
San Telmo

Pza. de
Zuloaga

Playa de
Gros

Basílica de
Santa María

Plaza de la
Trinidad

Iglesia de
la Trinidad

Calle 31 de Agosto

V. del Coro

Museo
Naval

LA PARTE VIEJA

C. del Puerto

Playa de Zurriola

Plaza
de la
Constitución

Mercado de
La Bretxa

Puente
de
Zurriola

Zurriola

Avenida   de   la

El Muelle

Colón

Pza. de
Cataluña Francisco

Igentea

Alameda   del   Boulevard

Calle   de   San

Gran Vía

Real Club
Náutico

Ayuntamiento

Peña Florida

Plaza de
Gipuzkoa

Plaza de
Euskadi

Calle   Miracruz

Diputación   Foral

Alderdi
Eder

Calle Andía

Libertad

Puente
de Santa
Catalina

Iztueta

Mercado
Central

Plaza de
Cervantes

Avenida

Santa   Marcial

Plaza de
Zaragoza

ZONA
ROMÁNTICA

RENFE
Station

La Concha

Plaza de
Bilbao

Puente
de María
Cristina

Catedral del
Buen Pastor

Alfonso VIII

Zubieta

Calle   de   San

Urdaneta

Río   Urumea

C. de San Bartolomé

Aldapeta

Plaza
Easo

C. Moraza

Estación
Tren-Tranvía

Parque de
Cristina Enea

Río   Urumea

Monte Ulía

Monte Ulía

Irun

OUT OF THE CENTRE

Hotel Buenavista, Barrio de Igüeldo (☎943/210600). Typical Basque chalet on the main road to Monte Igüeldo. Great sea views and a good restaurant. ④.

Pensión Maite, Avda. de Madrid 19, 1°, Amara (☎943/470715). Good clean rooms with bath and TV; handy for bus station, Astoria cinema and Anoeta football stadium. The owners also run the *Bar Maite* opposite. ④.

Hotel Record, Calzada de Ategorrieta (☎943/271255, 285768). Situated at the far end of Gros and a pleasant alternative to the bustle of the *parte vieja* and *centro*; well-connected by bus or a 15-minute walk from the centre with plenty of parking. All rooms with shower or bath and larger rooms with terraces. ④.

Fonda Vicandi, c/Iparraguirre 3, Gros (☎943/270795). Well-located just across the river in a lively bar area, but not far from the centre. An old place with high ceilings and basic rooms. ③.

CAMPING

Igüeldo, Barrio Igüeldo (☎943/214502). San Sebastián's campsite is excellent, although it's a long way from the centre on the landward side of Monte Igüeldo, reached by bus #16 from the Alameda del Boulevard.

The town

The **parte vieja** (old quarter) is the centre of interest – cramped and noisy streets where the crowds congregate in the evenings to wander among the many small bars and shops or sample the shellfish from the street traders down by the fishing harbour.

Here, too, are the town's chief sights: the elaborate Baroque facade of the eighteenth-century church of **Santa María**, and the more elegantly restrained sixteenth-century Gothic church of **San Vicente**. The centre of the old quarter is **La Plaza de la Constitución** (known by the locals simply as *La Consti*) – the numbers on the balconies of the apartments around the square refer to the days when it was used as a bullring. Situated just off c/31 de Agosto (the only street to survive the great fire of 31 August, 1813), behind San Vicente, is the excellent **Museo de San Telmo** (Mon–Sat 9.30am–1.30pm & 4–7pm, Sun 10.15am–2pm; 350ptas), whose displays – around the cloisters of a former convent – include a fine Basque ethnographic exhibition on the first floor and the largest collection of discoidal funerary steles in the Basque Country. There are regular exhibitions of work by modern Basque painters and the convent chapel is decorated with a series of frescoes by José Sert, depicting scenes from Basque life. In the same square as the side entrance to the museum is the oldest surviving gastronomic society in the city, the **Kainoneta**.

Behind the plaza, rises **Monte Urgull**, crisscrossed by winding paths. From the mammoth figure of Christ on its summit there are great views out to sea and back across the bay to the town; up here too are the dilapidated remains of the castle and a few relics of forgotten sieges on display in the military museum (Mon 3.30–5pm, Tues–Sat 10am–1pm & 3.30–5.30pm). On the way down you can stop at the **Aquarium** (May–Sept Mon–Sat 10am–1.30pm & 3.30–8pm; Oct–April Tues–Sat 10am–1.30pm & 3.30–7.30pm; 200ptas) on the harbour; it contains the skeleton of a whale caught in the last century and an extensive history of Basque navigation, although not a great deal of fish.

Still better views across the bay can be had from the top of **Monte Igüeldo**: take the bus marked *Igüeldo* from the Boulevard or walk round the bay to its base near the tennis club, from where a funicular will carry you to the summit.

Beaches

There are three **beaches** in San Sebastián: Playa de la Concha, Ondarreta and Playa de Gros. **La Concha** is the most central and the most celebrated, a wide crescent of yellow sand stretching round the bay from the town. Despite the almost impenetrable mass of flesh here during most of the summer, this is the best of the beaches, enlivened by sellers of peeled prawns and cold cokes and with great swimming out to the sand bars and boats moored in the bay. Out in La Concha bay is a small island, **Isla de Santa Clara**, which makes a good spot for picnics; a boat leaves from the port every half-hour in the summer (daily, until 8.30pm).

Ondarreta, the best beach for swimming and even in summer somewhat less crowded than La Concha, is a continuation of the same strand beyond the rocky outcrop which supports the **Palacio de Miramar**, once a summer home of Spain's royal family. Set back from Ondarreta beach are large villas, some of the most expensive properties in Spain, and usually owned by wealthy families from Madrid who vacation here – the area is known as *La Diplomática* for this reason and has a reputation for being rather more staid than the central area, although the lively district of **El Antiguo** with its many bars is only a few minutes' walk beyond.

Though it's far less crowded, the aptly named **Playa de Gros** is to be avoided, as the currents can be dangerous and it's the repository for all the filth that comes floating down the river. Nonetheless, one of the best views of the whole town and bay may be had by climbing up the steps to the cider house on the side of **Monte Ulia** from the far end of the beach. This walk can easily be extended for about 5km along the coast to the lighthouse overlooking the entrance to Pasajes harbour

Eating, drinking and entertainment

Centred around the *parte vieja*, San Sebastián has plenty of lively bars and good places to eat offering international and local cuisine at all prices. Prices tend to reflect the popularity of the old quarter, especially in the waterside restaurants, but it's no hardship to survive on the delicious *pinchos* which are laid out in all but the fanciest bars.

Restaurants and tapas bars

If you're in the mood for a gastronomic treat, San Sebastián has some of the best **restaurants** in Spain – most are closed Sunday evening and Monday. On a less exalted level, the lunchtime *menús del día* in the *parte vieja* are generally good value, and the *pinchos* and *raciones* in the bars are a great way to eat cheaply in the evenings.

Akelarre, Paseo de Padre Orcolaga in Barrio Igüeldo (☎943/212052). One of the city's top restaurants with wonderful sea views. Expensive.

Arzak, Alto de Miracruz 21 (☎943/278465). A shrine of Basque cuisine, this restaurant has three Michelin rosettes and a superb *menú* for nearly 7000ptas.

Casa Maruxa, Paseo de Bizkaia 14, Amara. Specializes in food from Galicia and attracts the crowd on their way to the *Astoria* cinema complex just around the corner.

Casa Nicolasa, c/Aldamar 4 (☎943/421762). Specializes in classic Basque cookery. Expensive.

Casa Senra, c/San Francisco. A good value restaurant in Gros.

Domenico's, c/Zubieta 3. Upmarket Italian restuarant, very popular with the locals.

Bar Etxadi, c/Reyes Católicos 9. A lively place for *raciones* and inexpensive *menús*.

Gaztelu, c/31 de Agosto 22. A good bar in the *parte vieja* where you can choose from a selection of reasonably priced *raciones*.

Mama Mia's, c/Triunfo 8. Good, inexpensive Italian restaurant serving vegetarian dishes.

Morgan Jatetxea, c/Narrica 7. Specializes in the French-influenced new Basque school of cookery and also has dishes suitable for vegetarians – especially tasty first courses. It's quite normal to order two of these instead of the more meat- and fish-orientated main courses.

Oriental, c/Reyes Católicos 6. One of seven Chinese restaurants in town and the best of the bunch in terms of quality food, price and extremely friendly atmosphere.

Cafetaria Ubarrechenea, c/San Martin 42. Excellent and economical *menús*.

SIDRERÍAS

If you're in San Sebastián between late January and early May, a visit to one of the many **sidrerías** (*sagardotegiak* in Basque, or cider houses) in the area around **Astigarraga**, about 6km from town is a must – take the red Hernani-bound bus from the Alameda del Boulevard or a taxi for about 1000ptas.

Cider production is one of the oldest traditions in the Basque Country – until the Civil War and the subsequent move towards industrialization, practically every farmhouse in Gipuzkoa used to a lesser extent the other provinces produced cider, which was a valuable commodity used as barter. Barter remained the main form of exchange in rural communities here until comparatively recently, and the farms were practically open houses where local people socialized – the *bertsolariak* tradition of oral poetry originated in these places – and drank cider. Cider houses are again flourishing, and for 1500–2500ptas you can feast on enormous steaks, grilled fish and codfish omelette followed by local cheese and walnuts, drink unlimited quantities of cider and in general enjoy the raucous atmosphere. Of the fifty or so *sidrerías*, some of the most accesible include *Petritegi* and *Gartziategi*, just a few kilometres out of town, while many of the more rustic (ie authentic) ones, such as *Sarasola* and *Oiarbide*, are on the so-called *ruta de las sidrerías* (the cider trail) beyond Astigarraga. Check in the local Yellow Pages for a full list with phone numbers.

Bars and clubs

In the evenings, you'll find no shortage of action, with clubs and bars everywhere. The two main areas are the **parte vieja**, where you'll find most of the punk and heavy metal bars, including *Akerbeltz* or *Iguana*, and the area around **c/Reyes Católicos**, where a large number of the city's more expensive music pubs are located; try *Pokhara*, *Kalima*, *La Bodeguilla* or *El Nido*, which plays a wide selection of music. C/San Bartolomé, a few streets back from the Concha promenade, attracts a very young crowd and here you'll find San Sebastián's only karaoke bar. For **jazz**, try *BeBop* or *Etxekalte*, both on the edge of the *parte vieja*. In Gros there are also a couple of excellent German-style pubs, *El Chofre* and *Bidea*, with a range of imported beers.

Once the pubs close, usually by about 3.30am, the night continues at the *Komplot* in c/Pedro Egaña and at *La Piscina* and *Tenis*, both at the far end of Ondarreta beach, where there is often live music (especially *salsa*) well into the small hours.

Festivals

Throughout the summer there are constant **festivals**, many involving Basque sports including the annual rowing (*trainera*) races between the villages along the coast. The International Jazz Festival, at different locations throughout the town for ten days in July, invariably attracts top performers as well as hordes of people on their way home from the fiesta in Pamplona. There is also the Film Festival during the last two weeks in September and frequent theatrical and musical performances throughout the year at both the *Victoria Eugenia* and the *Teatro Principal*. The Turismo produces a monthly guide to what's on.

Listings

Banks Most banks have their main branches along Avda. de la Libertad including *Banco Central Hispano* at no.17 and *Banco Bilbão Bizkaia* on the corner with c/Hernani.

Bike rental You can rent mountain bikes from *Mini*, c/Escolta Real 10 (☎943/211758) in the *parte vieja*.

Car rental *Avis* c/Triunfo (☎943/461527, 261556); *Hertz* c/Marina 2 (☎943/461084); and *Europcar* c/San Martín 60 (☎943/461717).

Hiking information Contact *Club de Montaña de Kresala*, c/Euskalerría 9 (☎943/420905). *Noresta*, Pg. Ramón (☎943/293520). A travel and map bookstore that also rents skis and trekking gear.

Post office The *Correos* is at c/Urdaneta, just south of the cathedral (Mon–Fri 8am–9pm, Sat 9am–2pm).

Swimming pool The sports centre in Anoeta, Polideportivo de Anoeta (☎943/458797), has an open-air pool, track, tennis courts and a gym.

Telephones There is a *telefónica* on c/San Marcial 29, one block from Avda. de la Libertad (Mon–Sat 9.30am–11pm).

Inland from San Sebastián: a circuit through Gipuzkoa

Gipuzkoa is the smallest province in Spain and public transport is good, meaning that most places of interest can be visited comfortably as a day trip from San Sebastián: alternatively, try the circuit set out below which can also act as a stepping stone to Vitoria and places further south.

Tolosa and Ordizia

Twenty-four kilometres south of San Sebastián is **TOLOSA**, famous for its **carnival** in February, celebrated here with fervour and considered by Basques to be superior to San Sebastián's (it was the only one whose tradition was maintained throughout the Franco era). In October, the town hosts an international choir festival. Although fairly industrialized, Tolosa has an extensive old quarter with an impressive old town square and is a lively place for a weekend night out. Make sure you sample a plate of *alubias* (kidney beans) in one of the many eating places – they're considered the best in Euskadi. If you want to **stay**, try *Hostal Oyarbide*, Plaza Gorriti 1 (☎943/670017; ④).

A further 20km south, on the main railway line to Vitoria, is **ORDIZIA**, the fastest growing town in the Oria valley. If your visit coincides with a Wednesday, don't miss the weekly **market** of farm products when all the farmers in the region converge on the town to buy and sell livestock, cheese and the like.

Walks around Ordizia

Ordizia is backed by the impressive peak of **Txindoki**, rising above the town like a mini-Matterhorn. You can climb it in about three hours from Larraitz, the highest village, and the whole thing can be done as a day-trip from San Sebastián or Tolosa.

The **Sierra de Aralar** stretching beyond Txindoki is a great place for a few days' walking – one possibility is to walk all the way from Larraitz to the **monastery of San Miguel** in Navarra, where it's possible to stay and eat cheaply (7–8 hours in all, largely on the flat over the plateau), and from where a road leads down the escarpment to **Huarte** on the main Vitoria–Pamplona rail line. In winter the range becomes a popular centre for cross-country skiing.

Segura and the monastery of Aranzazu

One of the most attractive inland villages in Gipuzkoa is **SEGURA**, southeast of Ordizia. An original seignorial village from where the powerful Guevara family once wielded power, there are various old mansions once belonging to the Guevaras and other families of note along its long, winding main street. Today, it's a sleepy backwater which comes alive during the **Easter processions** (not otherwise much celebrated in Euskadi) and which hosts one of the best village fiestas in Euskadi in mid-June.

Segura, and Zegama further south, were important stops on the ancient **Pilgrim Route** to Santiago, which joined up with the main route in Santo Domingo de la

Calzada (La Rioja). The old Roman way the pilgrims once followed is still partly in evidence and you can walk a section of it as an easy day-trip, even without your own transport. Take the 9.54am Vitoria-bound train from San Sebastián to **OTZAURTE**, a small halt south of Zegama. From here it's an hour's walk to the refuge of **San Adrian** (open weekends throughout the year and daily in summer; meals available). The best-preserved section of Roman road on the mountain is just beyond the natural tunnel of San Adrian above the refuge, from where it's downhill (2 hours) to **Araia**, the first town in Araba just off the Vitoria–Pamplona road; from here, a bus departs at 3.15pm for Vitoria and trains leave from the station 2km beyond town.

Alternatively, head west across the plateau or along the spectacular ridge of Aitzkorri to the refuge of **Urbia** (same hours as San Adrian) and the monastery of **Aranzazu** (3–4 hours), where there are several *hostales* and hotels, best value of which is *Hospedería de Aranzazu* (☎943/781313; ③). This is the prime place of pilgrimage for Basques, **Our Lady of Aranzazu** being the patron saint of Gipuzkoa, and is located in a particularly spectacular setting clinging to the mountainside above a gorge. Although a monastery on this site dates back to the fifteenth century, the present futuristic-looking building was built in 1950 and features contemporary work by the sculptors Chillida (the doors) and Oteiza (part of the facade). It gets packed out on Sundays when worshippers come from all over the province and elsewhere.

Oñati

OÑATI, 8km below Aranzazu, is without doubt the most interesting inland town in Gipuzkoa, with some fine examples of Baroque architecture among its many historic buildings; indeed the Basque painter Zuloaga described it as the "Basque Toledo".

The old **university** dominates the town, built in 1548 and the only functioning university in Euskadi for hundreds of years. The facade with its four pilasters adorned with figures, and the serene courtyard, are particularly impressive. The Baroque town hall and parish church of **San Miguel** are at opposite ends of the arcaded Plaza de los Fueros. In the church crypt are buried all the Counts of Oñati from 988 to 1890; the cloister is unusual in that it is actually built over the river. Other fine buildings around the town include various *casas torres* of the type also found in north Navarra, private family mansions and the Plateresque-style monastery of **Bidaurreta**. A very helpful **Turismo** at Plaza de los Fueros 11 (open daily year round) can arrange visits to the university and parish church. They also stock plenty of leaflets detailing walking and motoring routes to places of interest in the vicinity.

The *Bar-Restaurante Echeverria*, c/Kalebarria 19 (☎943/780460; ③), is the only **hostal** in the town centre and the best bet if you want to stay – the **restaurant** below also offers a reasonable *menú del día*. Enquire at the Turismo about an **agroturismo** which may now be open on the outskirts of town, or the possibility of a private room.

Oñati is well-served by **buses** to San Sebastián, Vitoria and Bilbão and at weekends there is a service to and from Aranzazu.

The Costa Vasca

Heading west from San Sebastián, both road and rail run inland, following the Río Oria, towards the coast at Zarautz. Along the way, the pretty fishing village of **Orio** on the estuary makes an enjoyable break in the journey. From **Zarautz** onwards, the coastline of the **Costa Vasca** is glorious – rocky and wild, with long stretches of road hugging the edge of the cliffs – all the way to Bilbão. There are buses that take the motorway along this route, but even if you're not planning to stop (and there are plenty of picturesque villages to tempt you to do so) it's worth taking the old road for the scenery. The further you go, the less developed the resorts are.

Zarautz

ZARAUTZ itself is certainly not the most attractive spot along the coast. Developed as a fashionable overspill of San Sebastián, the old village has been swamped by a line of hotels and pricey cafés sandwiched between the busy road and the busier beach, a popular place for surfers. The town and surrounding area (and, to a lesser extent, towns further along the coast towards Bizkaia) are famous for the production of *txakoli*, a strong, dry white wine – the vineyards cling to hillsides along the coast from here to Guetaria.

The well-stocked **Turismo** is on c/Nafarroa, the busy main road through town and they can advise on **accommodation**. One if the best places to stay is large and well-situated *agroturismo*, *Agerre-Goikoa* (☎943/833248; ③), just before the turn-off to the main campsite. The **youth hostel**, *Monte Albertia* (☎943/132910; ①), on the Meagas road out of town, is open all year round. Zarautz has two **campsites**, *Gran Camping Zarautz* (☎943/831238) on the clifftops overlooking the beach, reached from town on the old San Sebastián road, with a marked turning on the left up the hill, and the cheaper *Talai-Mendi* (☎943/830042), a short walk from the beach but only open July–September.

Getaria

Five kilometres on is **GETARIA**, a tiny fishing port sheltered by the hump-backed islet of **El Ratón** (The Mouse). It's a historic little place, one of the earliest towns on the coast, preserving the magnificent fourteenth-century church of San Salvador, whose altar is raised theatrically above the heads of the congregation. The first man to sail around the world, Juan Sebastián Elcano, was born here and his ship was the only one of Magellan's fleet to make it back home. Every four years on August 6, during the village's **fiestas**, Elcano's landing is re-enacted on the beach. The *Mayflower* bar overlooking the harbour is worth a visit for the round-the-wall nautical map of the entire Basque coast and there's a small but interesting art gallery of oil reliefs by local painter Elorza. Check the prices at the tempting fish **restaurants** before you eat; many are expensive. **Accommodation** options include *Pensión Getariano*, c/Herrerieta 3 (☎943/830657; ④) and three somewhat cheaper *agroturismos* a few kilometres up the hillside on the way to Meagas (check with the Turismo in Zarautz or the small summer-only **Turismo** in Getaria for details).

Zumaia and Azpeitia

The coast becomes still more rugged on the way to **ZUMAIA** – an industrial-looking place at first sight, but with an attractive centre and pleasant waterfront along the estuary of the Río Urola. Zumaia's local **fiesta** in the first days of July is one of the most exuberant, with Basque sports, dancing and bullocks let loose on the beach to test the mettle of the local youth.

Zumaia has two very different **beaches** – one of these, over the hill behind the town, is a large splash of grey sand enclosed by extraordinary sheer cliffs of layered slate-like rock which channel the waves in to produce some of the best surfing on the coast. There are spectacular walks along the clifftops to the west. The other beach, across the river from the port, is yellow and flat, sheltered by a little pine forest. On the road behind this you'll find the **Villa Zuloaga** (June 6–Sept 15 Weds–Sun 4–8pm; 400ptas), a small art museum in the former home of the Basque painter Ignacio Zuloaga.

The only **accommodation** in town is at *Bar Tomas* in the square; if the rooms here are full, the owner should be able to organize a private room elsewhere without much trouble.

Inland from Zumaia, near the town of **AZPEITIA** is the imposing eighteenth-century Baroque **Basilica of Loyola** (birthplace of San Ignacio de Loyola, the founder of the Society of Jesus) with its impressive rotunda and marble decor – this is a major pilgrimage spot.

Mutriku

Beyond Deva (Deba), itself an unprepossessing place, the main road veers inland and the coastal route becomes still wilder as it enters the province of Bizkaia. The road is narrow and slow, but there are a fair number of buses from San Sebastián and hitching is surprisingly easy.

MUTRIKU, despite some ugly recent construction above the town, has some attractive narrow streets leading down steeply to the fishing harbour. It's the centre of another *txakoli* producing area. Admiral Churruca, the "Hero of Trafalgar" to locals, was born here; his imposing statue faces the incongruous church of Nuestra Señora de Asunción, built along the lines of a Greek temple. Mutriku boasts no less than five **campsites** around several small beaches, and there is also an **agroturismo**, *Casa Matzuri* (☎943/603001; ③), just beyond town on the road to Ondarroa. Beyond Mutriku, the road temporarily turns inland and reaches the coast once more at the beach of **Saturrarán** (very popular and crowded in summer when there's a **campsite**; ☎943/603847).

Ondarroa

Around the headland from Saturrarán, **ONDARROA**, the first coastal town in Bizkaia, presents a very different aspect from the other small resorts further east. Here,the usual town beach and attractive tree-lined rambla end at a no-nonsense **fishing port** filled with an eclectic set of trawlers. In the early morning, an endless succession of trucks files in from the coastal road to fill up with fish – the traffic is so great that a large bridge is under construction across the bay to channel the fishing trucks directly to the port. On the quayside, burly fishermen haul up skips of quivering fish from the bowels of their vessels and hurl them into the back of the waiting trucks.

The **bars** at the harbour stay open late (some 24hr) as deckhands come and go, and – recently modernized and stuffed with a tempting array of seafood *pinchos* – they're accommodating enough to keep the promenading locals and occasional stray tourist happy. If you want to stay, try the *Hostal Vega*, c/Antiguako Ama 8 (☎943/683 00 02; ④), right by the fishing port and overlooking the water. The rooms are spacious and clean, some with massive picture windows, and the terrace restuarant serves a good 1100ptas *menú*, incorporating whatever's been landed that day. You're unlikely to want to stay more than one night, but Ondarroa is an interesting place to stop over, particularly in August when the town hosts its **fiestas**.

Lekeitio

LEKEITIO is another good bet along this stretch. Still an active fishing port, it has two fine beaches – one beside the harbour, the other, much better, across the river to the east of town. There's little **accommodation**, the choice being between the *Hotel Beitia*, Avda. Pascual Abaroa 25 (☎94/684 01 11; ④), and the *Hostal Piñupe*, Avda. Pascual Abaroa 10 (☎94/684 29 84; ④), both of which are very popular in summer, when the town becomes a prime destination for the masses from Bilbão. You could, however, always sleep on the beach, where there are showers and, in season at least, a couple of restaurants. Lekeitio is literally teeming with **bars**, many offering food. An official **campsite**, *Endai* (☎94/684 24 46; Easter and summer only) can be found on

Playa Mendexa, a few kilometres east and there is a summer-only **agroturismo**, *Mendexakua* (☎94/624 31 08; ③) in the village of Mendexa, 3km inland.

Elantxobe

The road turns inland from Leikeitio, but the fishing village of **ELANTXOBE** (Elanchove) is worth a detour back to the coast. The village, almost entirely in its original condition, is perched high above a small harbour, connected to it by an incredibly steep cobbled street lined with attractive fishermen's houses. C/Mayor continues up to the cemetery from where a signposted track leads to **Mount Ogoño** – the highest cliff on the Basque coast at 280m.

Elantxobe has a small **restaurant** in c/Mayor but no accommodation – make it a day trip or stay at either *Pensión Arboliz* (☎94/627 62 83; ④) or the **agroturismo** (☎94/627 63 37; ③), both located 500m from the crossroads in the direction of Lekeitio.

Direct **buses** run between Elantxobe and Gernika (depart Gernika 9.45am & 3.40pm) or, from Lekeitio, take the Gernika bus to the crossroads at Ibarrangelua and walk 1km down to the village.

Gernika

Immortalized by Picasso's nightmare picture (finally brought home to Spain after the fall of Franco, and now exhibited in the Centro de Arte Reina Sofia, Madrid), **GERNIKA**, inland and west of Lekeitio, is the traditional heart of Basque nationalism. It was here that the Basque parliament used to meet, and here, under the **Tree of Gernika** (the *Gernikako Arbola*), that their rights were reconfirmed by successive rulers. Sadly it was also Gernika's fate to be chosen for the first-ever saturation bombing raid on a civilian centre – an attempt to blast the soul out of Basque resistance in the Civil War. In only four hours on April 27, 1937 more than 1600 people were killed and the town centre destroyed.

The parliament building, the **Casa de las Juntas** (Mon–Sat 10am–2pm & 4–7pm, Sun 10am–1.30pm), is well worth a visit for the stained glass window depicting the tree and important scenes and monuments from the region. The adjacent church of **Santa María la Antigua**, adorned with portraits of the various nobles of Bizkaia who pledged allegiance to to the *fueros*, has traditionally served as a kind of church/parliament, used for Assemblies. The parliament, church and tree remained miraculously unscathed by the bombing, but the rest of the town was rebuilt and is now nondescript. For a Basque, at least, a visit here is more pilgrimage than tourist trip. A walk through Europa Park with its ornamental gardens, fast-flowing stream and peace sculptures by Henry Moore and Eduardo Chillida captures something of the elegiac atmosphere.

There's a helpful **Turismo**, at c/Artekale 8 (summer daily 10am–2pm & 4–8pm; rest of the year Mon–Sat 10am–1pm & 4.30–8pm) in the arcaded main street, with one of the best selections of pamphlets in English on all areas of Euskadi and details of rooms if you want to **stay**. Otherwise, try *Hostal Iratxe*, c/Juan Grandarias 6 (☎94/625 64 63; ③), or *Pensión Agirre*, c/Pedro Elejalde 10 4° (☎94/625 12 64; ①). If you have your own transport, the Turismo can make bookings at any one of four **agroturismos** within a ten-kilometre radius of town. There's a good, inexpensive *menú* at *Jatetxea Madariaga*, c/Juan Madariaga 10.

The Cueva de Santimamiñe

Five kilometres from Gernika, on the Lekeitio road, lies the **Cueva de Santimamiñe** (guided tours Mon–Fri at 10am, 11.15am, 4.30pm & 6pm; 1 hr). Inside are extraordinary rock formations and some Paleolithic cave paintings of bison. See them now, since the long-term plan for the cave may eventually result in permanent closure, due to deterioration brought about by rising temperatures.

Without your own transport, it may be worth coming on an organized tour (details from tourist offices in Gernika or Bilbāo), as there is no public transport to the cave. The thrice daily Gernika–Lekeitio bus can, however, drop you at Kortezubi from where it's a 2km walk. It's a steep climb up to the entrance and you may have to wait as numbers are limited to fifteen at one time – a good **bar-restaurant** in the car park helps pass the time. If you do have to wait, or wish to spend longer, the area is very scenic and walking trails from the cave are well signposted. Opposite the *Lekiza* restaurant (look out for *agroturismo* signs), a road leads to the farmhouse *Bizketxe* (☎94/625 49 06; ③) situated in a tiny unspoilt Basque village tucked away in a beautiful green valley and highly recommended (this *agroturismo* may be booked at the Gernika Turismo).

Mundaka and Bermeo

Continuing the route west, the Río Mundaka flows from Gernika into a narrow estuary fringed by hilly pine woods and dotted with islets. There's a succession of sandy coves to swim in, but the best spots are at **PEDERNALES** and especially **MUNDAKA**, where there's a **campsite**, *Portuondo* (☎94/687 63 68), high above the water with steps leading down to a rocky beach, and magnificent surfing. A passenger ferry plies across the bay (twice daily; summer only) to an excellent stretch of white sand, **Playa de Laìda**, on the far side of the estuary at the base of Monte Ogoño. There is a group of holiday villas here and another campsite, *Camping Arketa* (☎94/627 63 02; it's a rather small site, so phone beforehand if possible).

The local train line from Gernika gives good access to the estuary beaches and continues beyond Mundaka to **BERMEO**, whose fishing fleet is the largest remaining in these waters, a riot of red, green and blue boats in the harbour. The beach isn't the best, but try some of the fish in the restaurants around the port – the local standards *merluza* (hake) and *bacalao* (cod) are particularly good. Also worth checking out while you're here is the **Fisherman's Museum** (Tues–Sat 10am–1.30pm & 4–7.30pm, Sun 10am–1.30pm), a three-storey converted building near the harbour, full of local interest and more general maritime displays. The **Turismo** (Mon & Tues 5–8pm, Wed–Sun 10am–1pm & 5–8pm), just opposite the train station at Askatasea Bidea 2, has a good pamphlet detailing a walk through the narrow streets and can arrange **accommodation** in one of two small *pensiones* in town (space is limited in the summer).

Westwards, on the way to Baquio, the hermitage of **San Juan de Gaztelugatxe** stands on a rocky islet, connected by a long and winding flight of steps to the shore at one of the most rugged parts of the Bizkaian coast. If you're travelling by bus, ask the driver to let you off at the clifftop crossroads and walk down. Near Baquio, the road passes **Lemóniz**, infamous for the government's attempt to build a nuclear power station and the Basques' fierce resistance to it. The half-finished project has been shelved since two of its directors were assassinated by ETA, and the area is now controlled by the military.

Bilbāo

Stretching for some 14km along the narrow valley of the heavily polluted Río Nervión, **BILBÃO** (Bilbo) is a large city that rarely feels like one, its urban sprawl having gradually engulfed a series of once-separate communities. Even in the city centre you can always see the green slopes of the surrounding mountains beyond the high-rise buildings. A prosperous, modern city, animated in its busy centre and surrounded by grim graffiti-covered slums and smoke-belching factories, Bilbāo isn't a place of grand sights or glamorous tourism. But it has an unmistakable feel to it, incredibly friendly inhabitants, and some of the best places to eat and drink in the whole of Euskadi.

Arrival and information

Arriving in Bilbāo can be confusing, since there's a welter of different bus and train stations. Most of them, however, are near the bridge which links the Plaza de España, in the new part of town, with the Plaza Arriaga and the *casco viejo* (old quarter).

The main *RENFE* train station is the **Estación de Abando** on Plaza de España, but local services to San Sebastián, Gernika and Durango use the **Estación Atxuri** (Achuri), on the other side of the river, to the south of the *casco viejo*. *FEVE* services along the coast to Santander and beyond, stop at the highly decorative **Estación Concordia**, on the riverbank right below the Estación de Abando. Local trains to Algorta and the beaches at Plencia use the small *ET/FV* **Estación Las Arenas**, up behind the church of San Nicolás in the Casco Viejo.

Most long-distance and international **bus** routes are covered by *ANSA*, c/Autonomía 17, whose entrance is round the corner at Alameda de Recalde 73 (☎94/444 31 00), south of the centre in the new town – turn right on Autonomía to a roundabout, then follow Hurtado de Amézaga to the Plaza de España, about ten long blocks. *Turytrans* and *ALSA*, with buses to Santander, Gijón and Oviedo, as well as certain international destinations such as Paris and Brussels, depart from around the corner on Plaza Amezola and there's a combined booking office for *Turytrans* and *ALSA*, at *VIACA*, Alameda de Recalde 68 (☎94/421 03 63 or 421 20 49, 444 48 58). Services along the coast to San Sebastián and Irún, Durango, Ondarroa, Markina, Oñati (Gipuzkoa) and a direct service to Biarritz and Bayonne are handled by *PESA* (☎94/424 88 99), located just up from Abando station on Hurtado de Amézaga. The hourly San Sebastián-bound buses depart from outside the office on the main road, while other routes depart from either c/Luchana (first street up the road on the right) or from behind the Teatro de Arriaga. *Vascongadas* runs local services to Gernika and Lekeitio, and is also situated in Hurtado de Amézaga, with buses departing from the tunnel under Abando station (☎94/423 78 60). For additional international services other than those by *ANSA* and *VIACA*, try *SAIA*, Plaza Martínez Artola 4 (☎94/444 17 08 or 444 56 12).

From Bilbāo **airport**, buses run to the bus station on c/Sendeja alongside the river next to the Puente del Ayuntamiento (town hall bridge). You can get off the bus on its way through the town, either on the Plaza de España or at the bridge by the museum.

The **P&O ferry** from Portsmouth in the UK docks at **Santurtzi** across the river from Algorta. An unusual way to cross the Río Nervión is by the hundred-year old *puente colgante* (hanging bridge) which transports both passengers and cars every 10– 30 minutes day and night between Portugalete and Las Arenas.

Information and orientation

The **Turismo** (Mon–Fri 9am–1.30pm & 4–8pm; ☎94/416 00 22) is located adjacent to the *Teatro Arriaga*. A new and very helpful Turismo on Algorta's seafront at Muelle de Areaga (☎944/693800) is handy for those arriving off the ferry who don't wish to head straight into Bilbāo.

Most facilities are along the city's main thoroughfare, the **Gran Vía**, where you'll find all the major **banks**, public buildings, expensive shops and *El Corte Inglés*. It leads through the heart of the modern city to the huge stadium of **San Mames**, the "cathedral of Spanish football" as the Basques would have it.

Accommodation

The best **places to stay** are almost all in the *casco viejo* – especially along c/ Bidebarrieta, which leads from Plaza Arriaga to the cathedral, and in the streets around it; c/Loferia, c/Santa María and c/Barrencalle Barrena, which is off c/Barrencalle. C/ Barrencalle itself is best avoided for accommodation, due to excessive noise at night from the bars in this hyper-active street. The very cheapest options (rather grim *fondas*

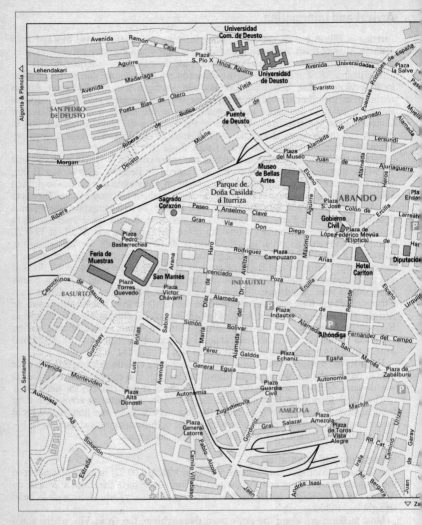

and *casas de huéspedes* in something of a red light district) are on the east bank around the Estación de Abando, particularly round the back on c/San Francisco. The parallel c/de las Cortes has become somewhat dangerous and is best avoided. Another area to try for accommodation is in the streets leading down from Plaza España around c/ Buenos Aires. Staying in **Algorta** is a good alternative to city centre accommodation and can be particularly useful the night before catching the ferry.

BUDGET OPTIONS

Hostal La Estrella, c/María Muñoz 6, off Plaza Miguel Unamuno (☎94/416 40 66). Good clean rooms with and without bath; has a bar serving breakfast and a lounge with TV. ③.

Hostal de la Fuente, c/Sombrería 2, 2° (☎94/416 99 89). Excellent value with large and well-furnished rooms in an extremely popular *hostal*. ②.

Hostal Gurea, c/Bidebarrieta 14, 4° (☎94/416 32 99). Spacious double rooms with faded furniture; good value but it's up four flights of stairs (no lift). ③.

Hostal Ibarra, c/Ribera 6 (☎94/41 82 68). A reasonable place along the river by the *Teatro Arriaga* but with a very gloomy entrance hall. ③.

Pensión Josean, c/Esperanza 20, 4° (☎94/415 92 83). A few minutes's walk from the *casco viejo* and near Estación Las Arenas. Very clean, small and friendly. ②.

Hostal Ladero, c/Loteria 1, 4° (☎94/415 09 32). Recently renovated, good value *hostal* with modern furnishings. There is a fifth-floor annexe reached by a curious, narrow spiral staircase. ②.

Hostal Manoli, c/Libertad 2, 4° (☎94/415 56 36). Just off Plaza Nueva with simple, clean and spacious rooms. ②.

Pensión Mardones, c/Jardines 4, 3° (☎94/415 31 05). Entered by the side of a newspaper kiosk, this *pensión* has been recently renovated and has rooms with and without bath. Preferable to the annexe on the second floor. ③.

Hostal Roquefor, c/Loferia 2, 2° and 4° (☎94/415 07 55). Situated on the second and fourth floors of a rather dark and musty building. Ask for a room overlooking the cathedral square to get as much light as possible. ②.

MORE EXPENSIVE HOTELS

Hotel Arriaga, c/Ribera 3 (☎94/479 00 01). The best of the medium-range hotels, in a good position just along from the *Teatro*, by the river; modern, comfortable rooms with bath and TV; garage available. ④.

Hostal Buenos Aires, Plaza de Venezuela 1 3° (☎94/424 07 65). A very comfortable and well-run *hostal* with a pleasant lounge and small bar. ④.

Hotel Ripa, c/Ripa 3 (☎94/423 96 77). Just over Puente del Arenal from the *casco viejo*, on the street by the waterfront; good value rooms with bath and TV. ④.

Hotel Zabalburu, Plaza Martínez Artola 8 (☎94/443 71 00). Good, clean doubles and handy for the major bus terminals. ④.

ALGORTA

Pensión Basagoiti, Avda. Basagoiti 72 (☎94/446 79 75). Good value, comfortable *pensión*. ③.

Hotel Igeretxe Agustin, Playa de Areaga (☎94/470 70 00). Upmarket hotel right on the Algorta seafront with a bar where you can watch the ships coming in to port. ⑥.

Pensión Salsidu, c/Salsidu 21 (☎94/469 86 52). Very friendly with good rooms. ③.

Camping

The nearest **campsites** are to the east on the beaches at Sopelana, *Sopelana* (☎94/676 21 20; bus or train towards Plencia) or Gorliz, *Gorliz* (☎94/677 19 11; just beyond Plencia). You can also camp to the west at the beach of Somorrostra (bus there or train to San Julián de Musques). The latter is just behind a huge oil refinery, however, and the beach seems polluted (with strange reddish sand that stains, and a heavy undertow).

The city

Although the city suffered severely from flooding at the end of 1983, there has been little permanent damage and many of the older areas have been dazzlingly refurbished. The main point of interest is the **casco viejo**, the old quarter on the east bank of the river. It's here that you'll find the best bars and restaurants among the thronged narrow streets and antiquated shops contained in the *siete calles* (seven streets) area borderd by c/de la Ronda and c/Pelota.

In the *casco viejo* are the sights that Bilbão does have to offer: the beautiful **Teatro Arriaga**, the elegantly arcaded **Plaza Nueva** (or *de los Mártires*), the Gothic **Catedral de Santiago** and the **Museo Arqueológico, Ethnográfico e Histórico Vasco** in Plaza Miguel Unamuno (Tues–Sat 10.30am–1.30pm & 4–7pm, Sun 10.30am–1.30pm; free) housed in the former School of San Andrés with its beautiful cloister and large selection of coats of arms of the former Bizkaian nobility – a very pleasant retreat from the city bustle. The one sight not in this part of town is the **Museo de Bellas Artes** (Tues–Sat 10.30am–1.30pm & 4–7.30pm, Sun 10am–2pm; free), in the Parque de Doña Casilda de Iturriza on the northern edge of the new town off the Gran Vía. This is considered one of Spain's most important collections, and it's a shame that the handful of fine canvases it does have (including works by El Greco, Zurbarán and Goya) are swamped by a host of mediocre ones. Much attention is currently being drawn to the ambitious and costly project of the new Guggenheim Museum, to be located in the quayside area next to the Puente de la Salve and which, it is hoped, will put Bilbão firmly on the cultural map.

Beaches

The city is well-served with **beaches** along the mouth of the estuary and around both headlands. For day trips you should go either to **Playa las Arenas**, an established city outing with lots of bars, cafés and opportunities for walking around and window-shopping, or to **Sopelana** and the other beaches around **Plencia** north of the city. The pretty old quarter of **Algorta** (known locally as Getxo) with its white houses and green-painted doors has an impressive waterfront promenade fringed with private mansions belonging to Bilbão's millionaire set.

The easiest way of getting to Algorta and the northern beaches is by **train** from Estación Las Arenas.

Eating, drinking and nightlife

Bilbão is definitely one of those cities where the most enjoyable way to eat is to move from bar to bar, snacking on *tapas*. The city can be very lively at night – and totally wild during the August **fiesta**, with scores of open-air bars, live music and impromptu dancing everywhere, and an incredible atmosphere. The *casco viejo* has all the most interesting places to **eat and drink**, with almost wall-to-wall places on c/Santa María and c/Barrencalle Barrena.

If you want to get together something of your own, the attractive **Mercado de la Ribera** on c/de la Ribera towards the Estación Atxuri offers a dazzling array of produce.

Restaurants and tapas bars

Taberna Aitor, c/Barrencalle Barrena. Excellent *tapas* bar and one for football fans, with the bonus of a beautiful wooden interior.

Café Gargantua, c/Barrencalle Barrena. A simple place serving sandwiches, and a selection of excellent different priced *menús* and *platos combinados*.

Garibolo, c/Fernandez del Campo 7 and Alameda de Urquijo 33 (both in the centre just north of the Gran Vía). A good vegetarian restaurant, with two sites and few surprises.

Herriko Taberna, c/de la Ronda 20. An excellent place for a straightforward, inexpensive meal; a strong Basque nationalist atmosphere and a great *menú*.

Café-Restaurante Kalean, c/Santa María. A new and highly popular café-bar offering excellent economical *nueva cocina vasca*. After midnight, there's a resident pianist and great atmosphere here.

Taberna Txiriboga, c/Santa María. Lively *tapas* bar in the heart of the *casco vieja*.

Taberna Txomin Barullo, c/Barrencalle. A great café-bar with nationalist murals specializing in more experimental *nueva cocina vasca* (lunch *menú* only Thurs–Sun) at reasonable prices.

Bars and entertainment

Bars can be found all through the **casco viejo**, but they are particularly lively around c/Pelota, c/Barrencalle, c/Santa María, c/de la Ronda and c/Torre. *Lamiak* on c/Pelota is a café-bar full of students, with good music and a notice-board worth checking for events, women's groups, work, flatshares and the like. *Txokolanda* is a **gay** bar, upstairs from *Solokuetxe*, reached via steps from c/de la Ronda, and, along with the *Lasaí* bar on c/de la Ronda itself, is one of the last places to close. For a relaxed drink in the early evening, head for the outdoor tables in the beautiful Plaza Nueva, not as pricey as you might expect.

Over in the **new town**, lively areas with a slightly smarter atmosphere are near the Plaza de España, between the Alameda de Mazarredo and c/de Buenos Aires, especially on c/Ledesma, a street teeming with bars and especially popular during early evening. *Bar Iruña*, on Colón de Larreategui, parallel to c/Ledesma, is marvellously atmospheric.

Bilbāo's other **historic cafés** include the *Boulevard* on c/Riberia near the *Teatro Arriaga*; the *Granja* in Plaza de España; and *Concordía* on c/Jose María Olavatti, a small side street just off Plaza de España – this bar has long been a haunt of poets, writers and workers at the Stock Exchange, and retains its atmosphere despite being rather run down.

Further east, south of the Gran Vía, around the junction of c/de Licenciado Poza and Gregorio de Revilla, an area known as **Pozas** is highly popular before lunch and in the early evening; *Ziripot* is a bar worth trying here. For action well into the night, one of the in-places is the cluster of bars known as the **Ripa** on the modern city side of the riverbank between Puentes del Arenal and Ayuntamiento, with a mixed crowd ranging from Basque yuppies to rockabillies.

Finding **live music** can be tricky, as the posters which advertise bands seem to be covered by others within hours of going up. The local paper *El Correo* probably has the best listings, and also details movies, few of which are in English: one place you do regularly see films in their original language is the *Filmoteca* at the Museo de Bellas Artes, which is free – programmes generally start around 5pm.

Listings

Airport information ☎94/453 08 51.

American Express c/o *Viajes Cafranga*, Alameda de Recalde 68 (☎94/444 48 58).

Bookshops *Libropolis*, c/General Concha 10, is a large travel bookshop with the most complete range of maps and guides in the city. *Borda*, c/Cueva de Santimamiñe at Plaza Nueva, stocks a wide range of local guides as well as some English-language publications; *Mendiko Etxea*, c/Autonomía 9, specializes in local trekking and cycling guides. The best place to buy English and other foreign newspapers (one day late) is *Librería Cámara* on c/Euskalduna 10, four streets up on the right from Plaza de España along Hurtado de Amézaga.

Car rental *Avis* is at Alameda Dr. Areilza 34 (☎94/427 57 60) and *Europcar* (☎94/442 28 49) is at c/Rodríguez Arias.

Consulates The British consulate is at Alameda Urquijo 2 (☎94/415 77 22), and the US at Avda. de Ejército 11 (☎94/475 83 00).

Hospital The general hospital is Hospital Civil de Basurto, Avda. de Montevideo 18 (☎94/441 88 00, 442 40 51. Call ambulances on ☎94/441 00 81).

Post office The main *Correos* is at Alameda Urquijo 15 (Mon–Fri 8am–9pm, Sat 9am–2pm).

Telephones There is a *telefónica* at c/Baroeta Aldamar 7, close to the Plaza de España.

Travel agents *TIVE*, Gran Vía 50 (☎94/441 42 77), specialize in student/youth travel and international buses; and *Banoa*, Alameda de Mazarredo 4 deals in "active" tourism, unusual excursions, trekking, etc, throughout Spain.

Inland routes from Bilbão

Inland Bizkaia is well off the beaten track yet has much to offer, with spectacular walking and climbing country, particularly around Durango, and remarkable limestone caves, accessible as a day trip from Bilbão.

Around Durango

The otherwise uninspiring factory town of **DURANGO** (easily accessible by train from Atxuri station) is the gateway to the impressive **Duranguesado Massif**. To explore this area of rocky peaks, the best access point is the Urkiola Pass (on the Durango–Vitoria road and bus route) from where it's about three hours to the highest peak, **Anboto**. This summit is a favourite with Basque walkers and climbers – the final scramble to the top can be a bit vertigo-inducing. Alternatively, head for the beautiful Atxondo valley off the Durango–Elorrio road. If you don't have your own transport, take the hourly buses as far as the signposted crossroads and then walk 2.5km to the village of **Axpe-Marzana**, nestling at the base of Anboto – a good base for a couple of days' walking. There is an **agroturismo**, *Imitte-Etxebarria* (☎94/623 16 59; ③), 500m before the village.

Markina and Bolibar

Also east of Bilbão, on the bus route to Ondarroa, the attractive town of **MARKINA** is famous for producing many of the finest *pelota* players – the *fronton* here is known as *La Universidad de la Pelota*. If you want to stay, try *Hostal Vega* in the main square (☎94/686 60 15; ③). From Markina you can visit the tiny village of **BOLIBAR**, ancestral home of the South American liberator, where there is a small museum depicting the great man's feats (Tues–Fri 10am–1pm, Sat & Sun 12–2pm; July & Aug also daily 5–7pm). From the village a short, restored stretch of a coastal branch of the *Camino de Santiago* leads up to the **Colegiata de Zenarruza**, a former pilgrims' *hostal* and hospital containing a beautiful sixteenth-century cloister and Romanesque church.

Orduña

Thirty-five kilometres south of Bilbão is **ORDUÑA**, a curious enclave of Bizkaia in Alaba province (served by several trains a day from Abando station). The Plaza de los Fueros boasts a collection of fine old buildings including the Neoclassical former customs house and a belfry where a pair of storks have taken up residence – apparently one of only three such nests in Euskadi. In the plaza is an old shop selling the local speciality, *mantecades de badillo*, a kind of sweet spongecake, sold straight from the oven by the old woman who runs it. You can walk up to **Fraileburu** (monk's head), a peculiarly shaped rock at the top of the escarpment immediately south of the town which is regarded as one of the prime hang-gliding and paragliding spots in Spain.

West to the limestone caves

The little-known area of **ENCARTACIONES**, west of Bilbã, makes another rewarding day trip, with places to stay if you want to extend your visit. Head for the village of **KARRANTZA** on the Bilbão–Ramales road (one hour by train on the Santander line out of Abando station; no public transport onwards to the caves). In the village square is an *agroturismo* office which can make bookings for three places in the area. Four kilometres west of Karrantza on the main road, just past a curious thermal spa resort run by German monks at **Molinar**, where you can stay and eat (☎94/680 60 02), a road heads up the mountain to the tiny village of **RANERO** and the **caves of Pozalagua** (3km). Half the enjoyment is the trip up through the craggy limestone outcrops of the mountainside which take on an almost lunar appearance, but the caves themselves (Sat & Sun 11am–2pm & 4–7pm; 500ptas) are equally remarkable for their eccentric coral-like stalactites. Unfortunately, some of the formations have been damaged by previous dynamiting in local quarries, but there are many other opportunities for speleology in the area, including visits to the **Torca de Carlista**, further into the mountain, one of the world's largest cave chambers.

Vitoria and around

VITORIA (Vitoria-Gasteiz), the capital of Áraba, crowns a slight rise in the heart of a fertile plain. Founded by Sancho el Sabio, King of Navarra, it was already a prosperous place by the time of its capture by the Castilian Alfonso VIII in 1200. Later, as the centre of a flourishing wool and iron trade, Vitoria became seriously rich, and the town still boasts an unusual concentration of Renaissance palaces and fine churches. It's off the tourist circuit but is by no means dull. The university here – or rather, its students – have made Vitoria one of northern Spain's "in" cities, and the old town is full of rowdy bars and *tabernas,* not to mention an abundance of excellent Basque eateries, making it as pleasant a place to pass a few days away from the crowds as you'll find.

The streets of the Gothic old town spread out like a spider's web down the sides of the hill, surrounded on level ground by a neater grid of later development. You'll get the feel of the town simply by wandering through this old quarter – a harmonious place, the graceful mansions and churches all built from the same greyish/gold stone. The porticoed **Plaza de España**, especially, is a gem, a popular location for early evening strolling and drinking.

Take time to visit the church of **San Miguel**, just above the Plaza de España, which marks the southern end of the old town. Outside its door stands the fourteenth-century stone image of the Virgen Blanca, revered patron of the city. The streets below hold any number of interesting buildings, one of the finest being the **Escoriaza-Esquivel Palace** with its sixteenth-century Plateresque portal, at the opposite end of town on c/ Fray Zacarías. A little closer, the old Gothic cathedral of **Santa María** (daily 9am–1pm & 4–6pm) has a superb west doorway, intricately and lovingly carved, whilst inside a delicate stone gallery runs around most of the higher sections of the naves. Unfortunately the building has now been closed indefinitely due to serious structural problems in the foundations.

Behind the cathedral, down the hill on the left, the **Portalón** is the most impressive of the surviving trading houses of Renaissance Vitoria, its dusty red brick and wooden beams and balconies in marked contrast to the golden stone of the rest of the town. Over the road you'll find the province's **Museo Arqueológico** (Tues–Sat 11am–2pm & 5–7pm, Sun 11am–2pm; free). Southwest of the centre on the attractive, pedestrianized, tree-lined Paseo de Fray Francisco is the **Museo de Bellas Artes** (Tues–Fri 11am– 2pm & 5–7 pm, Sat & Sun 11am–2pm; free), which has a substantial collection of works by Spanish and Basque contemporary artists. An annexe of this museum houses the unusual **Fournier card museum** with over 6000 exhibits from all corners of the globe .

Practicalities

There's a useful **Turismo** (Mon–Thurs 9am–1.30pm & 3–6pm, Fri 8am–3pm), on c/Ramón y Cajal (in the corner of the park), close to the **train station**, with lots of colourful brochures and a good free map. A second Turismo, open longer hours but a bit further away from the centre, is on the corner of Avda. de Gasteiz and c/de Chile (Mon–Sat 10am–7pm, Sun 11am–2pm; ☎945/161598, 161599). The **bus station** is across town on c/Francia, a two-minute walk (straight up the cobbled Cantón de San Francisco Javier Colegio) from the old town.

Accommodation

The only time you might have trouble locating a room is during Vitoria's annual **jazz festival** in the third week of July, or during the town **fiesta** at the beginning of August. There are several budget **places to stay** near the train station, around the junction of c/de los Fueros and Ortiz de Zarate, and near the bus station, but it's far nicer to stay in the old quarter near the action.

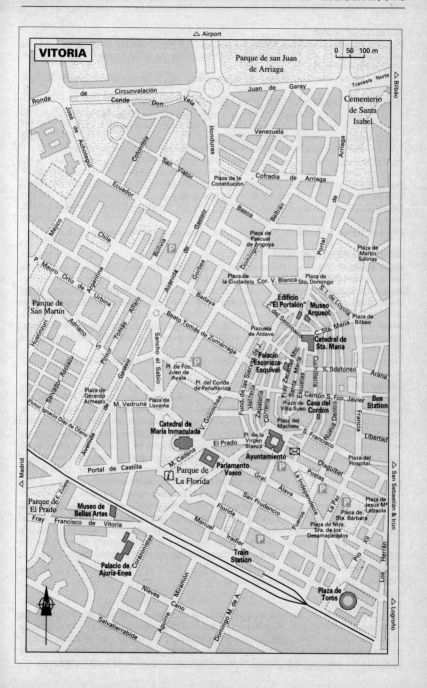

BUDGET OPTIONS

Pensión Balzola, c/Prudencio María de Verástegui 6 2° (☎945/256279). In the street beside the bus station; ring the bell by the unnamed *CH* sign on the left of the doorway. Simple, but clean doubles and singles. ②.

Casa de Huéspedes, c/de Francia 23. Simple rooms with an annexe at c/Prudencio María de Verástegui 6. ③.

Hotel Dato, c/Dato 28 (☎945/232320). Well equipped and comfortable. ④.

Fonda Económica, c/Pintorería 72. Only one triple room and two singles, but worth trying as the owner will wash your clothes at no extra charge and will reduce the price if you stay a few days. ②.

Hostal Eguíleta, c/Nueva Fuera 32 (☎945/258082). The cheaper annexe of the *Hotel Desidorio* opposite, where you need to ask for rooms at the *hostal*; reasonable doubles with washbasin. ③.

Hostal Florida, c/Manuel Iradier 33 (☎945/260675). Comfortable, well-furnished rooms on the first street down from the station towards the bullring. Has more expensive rooms with bath. ③.

Bar La Riojana, at the corner of c/San Francisco Javier and c/Cuchillería (☎945/268795). Pick up keys here for *camas* at c/Cuchillería 66. It's the best of the bunch in the old quarter. ②.

Hostal Savoy, c/Prudencio María de Verástegui 4 (☎ 945/250056). Belongs to the *cafetería* of the same name. ④.

Pensión Zurine, c/Florida 24, 2° (☎945/142240). Clean rooms with cork-tiled floors. ③.

MORE EXPENSIVE PLACES

Hotel Amarica, c/Florida 11(☎945/130506, 130548). New hotel which has become very popular; two singles and eight doubles with bath and satellite TV. ④.

Hostal La Bilbaina, c/Prudencio María de Verástegui 2 (☎945/254400). Comfortable rooms above a large cafetería; all with bath and cable TV showing English football on Saturday afternoon and films in original language. ④.

Hotel Dato, c/Dato 28 (☎945/147230, 147307). Excellent value place on main pedestrian mall down from the station. A different colour scheme in every room, colourful batik bedspreads and all rooms with bath and some with enclosed balcony. ④.

Hotel Desiderio, Colegio San Prudencio 2 (☎945/251700). Spacious rooms with bath and TV. ④.

Eating and drinking

The streets of the old town – in particular c/Cuchillería, c/Pintorería, c/Hurrería and c/Zapatería – are lined with **bars**, **tabernas** and **bodegas** differentiated only by the music they play, each spilling out on to the narrow pavements at night. At c/Zapatería 36, just off Virgen Blanca, *Bar-Restaurante Néstor* has a good *comedor*; *Bailarín 8*, on the next street over, c/Herrería, is popular with the locals; and for solid Basque cooking, try *Amboto Oleagarena* at c/Cuchillería 29. *Kirol* next door has an amazing selection of different *raciones*, and *Bar Rosi* on the corner of c/Hurrería and Canton de la Soledad by the church of San Pedro serves inexpensive *cazuélitas*. *Restaurante Casablanca 3*, just down from the train station on c/Dato, has one of the best *menús* in Vitoria.

There is a superb vegetarian restaurant (Mon–Sat 1–4pm) at c/Manuel Iradier 80, opposite the bullring with a *menú* for 900ptas. Further down, on the pedestrianized section of c/Dato, there are various other bars and cafés with chairs and tables outside which offer quieter, classier surroundings than the old town. Equally pleasant are the outdoor cafés of Plaza de España and those on the other pedestrian thoroughfares in the lower new town.

Around Vitoria

Attractive though the town is, a significant part of Vitoria's charm is the beauty of the surrounding **countryside**. Almost every hamlet of mountainous Euskadi has something of interest: an old stone mansion proudly displaying the family coat of arms, a richly decorated church, or a farmhouse raised Swiss-style on stilts. In the immediate vicinity of Vitoria are many notable places, most at which are accessible by public transport.

The nearby **Pantanos de Zadorra** is a large scenic reservoir very popular with the locals; the waterside villages of Gamboa-Ullibarri and Landa (both served by bus three times daily), make a pleasant retreat on a hot summer's day. A few kilometres to the west of Vitoria, another popular day trip is to the village of **MENDOZA**, dominated by a fortified tower-house now established as the **Heraldry Museum of Araba** (summer Tues–Fri 11am–2pm & 4–7.30pm, Sat & Sun 10am–2.30pm; winter Tues–Sun 11am–2.30pm; free), which contains a fascinating collection of coats of arms of the Basque nobility through the ages and an exhibition of the history of the principal clans and their often bloody feuds.

To the east, on the **Llanada Alavesa** (Plain of Araba) are some of the best-preserved villages of inland Euskadi. Take the side road off the main N1 *autovia* via **NARVAJA**, where there is an *agroturismo*, *Koipe-Enea* (☎945/300298; ③), **ZALDUONDO** and **ARAÍA** (served by a twice daily bus from Vitoria). From the latter two it's possible to walk on a branch of the *Camino de Santiago* to the San Adrian tunnel and its refuge (see p.366).

The main town on the plain, **SALVATIERRA**, makes a good base for exploration. The old walled quarter rises above the countryside offering splendid views, and the Gothic church of Santa María is visible for miles around. Situated on the main Vitoria–Pamplona/Irún rail line, the town has a couple of small *fondas*; one attached to the *Bar Merino* opposite the church of San Juan in Plaza Mayor (③), and the other at c/Mayor 53 (②).

South of Vitoria lies the wine-growing district of **Rioja Alavesa** and its town of **LAGUARDIA**, where the useful **Turismo** c/Sancho Abarca (Mon–Fri 10am–2pm & 4–6.30pm, Sat 10am–2pm, Sun 10.45am–2pm; ☎941/100845) has information on the many *bodegas* in the area – visits usually require a phone call beforehand. Laguardia itself is an interesting old walled town of cobbled streets and historic buildings, entered through the Puerta de San Juan. The Turismo has keys to the church of Santa María de los Reyes with its ornately carved Gothic doorway. The two best places to **stay** are a small *agroturismo* in the old town at c/Paganos 96 (☎941/100191; ③), or *Restaurante Begoña*, c/Mayor 17 (☎941/100114; ②), run by a charismatic woman who (rumour has it) was once a nun. She serves the best *menú* in town in her restaurant downstairs. There are two more *hostales* on the main road; *Pachico Martinez*, c/Sancho Abarca 20 (☎941/100009; ④), and *Marixa*, c/Sancho Abarca (☎941/100165, 100202; ④).

Pamplona

PAMPLONA (IRUÑA) has been the capital of Navarra since the ninth century, and long before that was a powerful fortress town defending the northern approaches to Spain at the foothills of the Pyrenees. Even now it has something of the appearance of a garrison city, with its hefty walls and elaborate pentagonal citadel. With a long history as capital of an often semi-autonomous state, Pamplona has plenty to offer around its old centre, the *casco antiguo* – enticing churches, a beautiful park, the massive citadel – and it's an enjoyable place to be throughout the year. But for anyone who has been here during the thrilling week of the **Fiestas de San Fermín**, a visit at any other time can only be an anticlimax.

San Fermín

From midday on July 6 until midnight on July 14 the city gives itself up entirely to riotous non-stop celebration. The centre of the festivities is the **encierro**, or the running of the bulls, which draws tourists from all over the world, but this has become just one aspect of a massive fair along with bands, parades and dancing in the streets 24 hours a day. You could have a great time here for a week without ever seeing a bull, and even if you are violently opposed to bullfighting, the *encierro* – in which the animals decisively have the upper hand – is a spectacle not to miss.

Six bulls are released each morning at eight (traditionally it was an hour earlier, so that the festival started on the seventh hour of the seventh day of the seventh month) to run from their corral near the Plaza San Domingo to the bullring. In front, around, and occasionally under them run the hundreds of locals and tourists who are foolish or drunk enough to test their daring against the horns. It was Hemingway's *The Sun Also Rises* that really put "Los San Fermines" on the map and the area in front of the Plaza de Toros has been renamed Plaza Hemingway by a grateful council. His description of it as "a damned fine show" still attracts Americans by the thousands. No amount of outsiders, though, could outdo the locals in their determination to have a good time, and it's an indescribably exhilarating event in which to take part.

Arrival, information and accommodation

Although Pamplona is a sizable city, the old centre is remarkably compact – nothing you're likely to want to see is more than five minutes from the main **Plaza del Castillo**. The **train station** is on Avda. San Jorge; bus #9 runs every ten minutes from here to the citadel end of the Paseo de Sarasate, a few minutes' walk from the Plaza del Castillo. There's a handy central *RENFE* ticket office at c/Estella 8 (Mon–Fri 9.30am–2pm & 4.30–7.30pm, Sat 9.30am–1pm; ☎948/227282). The **bus station** is more central, on c/Conde Oliveto just in front of the citadel: schedules are confusing, given the number of companies operating from here – check the timetable posted at the station.

The **Turismo** (daily in summer 10am–7pm; winter Mon–Fri 10am–2pm & 4–7pm, Sat 10am–2pm; ☎948/220741) is at c/Duque de Ahumada 3, just off Plaza del Castillo. A municipal information bus (June–Sept 10am–2pm & 5–8pm; longer hours at San Fermín) also parks in Plaza del Castillo over the summer.

Banks are scattered throughout the central area, with much restricted, morning-only hours during the festival – one that also opens in the afternoons (4–6pm) is the *Caja de Ahorros de Navarra* in c/Roncesvalles. There's a central **post office** at Paseo Sarasate 9 (Mon–Fri 8am–9pm, Sat 9am–7pm). A **laundry** (in case your clothes have borne the brunt of the festivities) can be found at c/de Descalzos, a couple of minutes' walk from the Plaza de San Francisco.

Accommodation

Most of the budget *fondas* and *hostales* are in c/San Nicolás and c/San Gregorio, off the Plaza del Castillo. Even outside San Fermín, when prices can double or triple, rooms fill up quickly in summer, and it might be easier to accept that you'll have to pay a little more to avoid the hassle of trudging around. If you want to continue looking, the streets around the cathedral, across the Plaza del Castillo, yield other possibilities. Further away from the Plaza del Castillo and the old town, there are several *hostales* in the more modern, yet not so interesting, central area.

CHEAPER OPTIONS
Fonda La Aragonesa, c/San Nicolás 32 (☎948/223428). Reasonable doubles with washbasin; ask at *Hostal Bearán* across the street (this hostal may also be taking guests, but has been closed for some time for upgrading). ②.

Hostal Artazcoz, c/Tudela 9, 2° (☎948/225164). A well-established *hostal* going back forty years; has recently undergone renovation to give all rooms en suite facilities. ③.

Camas, c/Neuva 24, 1° (☎948/227825). Next to the upmarket *Hotel Maisonnave*; well-furnished doubles and singles. ③.

Camas, c/del Pozo Blanco 16, 4° (☎948/220798). A cluster of over-priced rooms at the top of the building, including bunk beds at 1500ptas. ②–③.

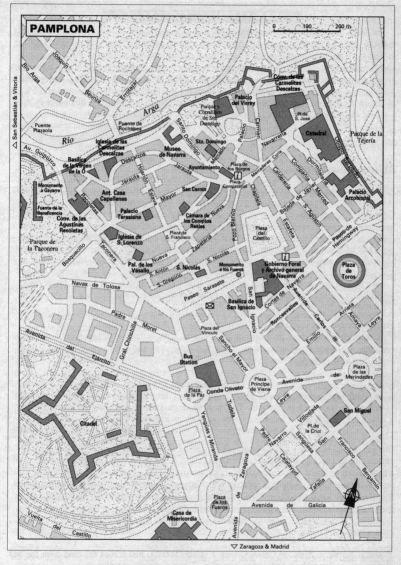

Casa García, c/San Gregorio 12 (☎948/223893). Double rooms without bath above a restaurant; it's worth considering their reasonable full-board rate. ③.

Casa de Huéspedes Santa Cecilia, c/Navarrería 17, 1° (☎948/222230). Spacious rooms in a former palace right by the fountain much splashed in during San Fermín. The place looks foreboding with a massive heavy door and grey facade, but the owner is extremely welcoming. ③.

Fonda La Montañesa, c/San Gregorio 2 (☎948/224380). Doubles and singles; nothing very special. ③.

SAN FERMÍN – THE FACTS

Accommodation and security

Don't expect to find **accommodation** during the fiesta unless you have booked well in advance – the town is packed to the gills. However, the Turismo opposite the bullring fills with old women willing to let **rooms** for the night at exorbitant prices. If you have no luck, accept that you're going to sleep on the ramparts, in the park or plaza (along with hundreds of others), and deposit your valuables and luggage at the bus station on c/ Conde Oliveto – it's inexpensive, and you can have daily access (this fills early in the week, too – hang around and be insistent). There are also free cold showers here.

Probably the **best plan**, though, is not to stay here at all: find a room somewhere else (Vitoria or Estella for instance), get plenty of sleep, leave your luggage there, and arrive in Pamplona by bus, staying as long as you can survive on naps in the park before escaping for some rest and a clean-up. You can always come back again. The first few days are best – by the end the place is getting pretty filthy.

Alternatively, there's a **campsite**, *Ezcaba* (✆948/330315), 7km out of town on the road to France. You have to be there a couple of days before the fiesta to get a place. Facilities include good toilets and showers but they can't really handle the numbers during San Fermín – be prepared for long queues or for going "primitive", and bear in mind that the shop is only really well stocked in the drinks department. The main bonus is that security is tight – admission is by pass only and there's a guard who patrols all night. For the period of the fiesta there are also two **free campsites**, one by the river just below *Ezcaba*, and another nearer the centre of town along the France road – turn off near the *Restaurante Ezcabarte*. Security at these is doubtful, however. The bus service, which goes to all the campsites, is poor (about five a day, first at 9am, last at 10pm), but it's easy to hitch or, more expensively, get a lift on one of the tour buses that stay at the official campsite (they leave in time to see the *encierro*).

Wherever you sleep, keep an eye on everything you have with you – there's a very high rate of **petty crime** during the festival; cars and vans are broken into with alarming frequency and people are often robbed as they sleep, occasionally with violence. Several **banks** and a **post office** are open mornings during the festival, so changing travellers' cheques is no problem.

El Encierro

To watch the *encierro* it's essential to arrive early (about 6am) – crowds have already formed an hour before it starts. The best **vantage points** are near the starting point around the Plaza Santo Domingo or on the wall leading to the bullring. If possible, get a spot on the outer of the two barriers – don't worry when the one in front fills up and blocks your view, as all these people will be moved on by the police before the run. The event divides into two parts: there's the actual running of the bulls, when the object is to run with the bull or whack it with a rolled-up newspaper. It can be difficult to see the bulls amid all the runners but you'll sense the sheer terror and excitement down on the ground; just occasionally this spreads to the watching crowd if a bull manages to breach the wooden safety barriers. Then there's a separate event after the bulls have been through the streets, when bullocks with padded horns are let loose on the crowd in the bullring. If you watch the actual running, you won't be able to get into the bullring (too

Pensión Navarra, Avda. de Conde Oliveto 3 (✆948/249321), Just across the road from the bus station; nice rooms without bath but with satellite TV and plenty of hot water. ③.

Hostal Otano, c/San Nicolás 5 (✆948/225095). Very well-run and popular *hostal* above bar and restaurant which have been in the family since 1929. The bar originally served as a watering hole for those working in the cattle yard once on this site. ③.

Bar-Restaurante Redin, c/del Mercado 5 (✆948/222182). Well-located in the street by the market and within a stone's throw of the start of the *encierro*. Mostly double rooms with a bar/restaurant downstairs; full board available. ③.

many people), so go on two separate mornings to see both things. For the bullring you have to arrive at about 6am to get the free lower seats. If you want to pay for a seat higher up buy from the ticket office outside, not from the touts inside, who will rip you off.

We advise against it, but if you do decide to **run**, remember that although it's probably less dangerous than it looks, at least one person gets seriously injured (sometimes killed) every year. Find someone who knows the ropes to guide you through the first time, and don't try any heroics; bulls are weighed in tons and have very sharp horns. Don't get trapped hiding in a doorway and don't get between a scared bull and the rest of the pack. Traditionally women don't take part, though more and more are doing so; if you do, it's probably best to avoid any officials, who may try to remove them. A glass of *Pacharrán*, the powerful local liqueur, is ideal for a dose of courage.

The only official way in is at the starting point, Plaza Santo Domingo, entered via Plaza San Saturnino: shortly before the start the rest of the course is cleared, and then at a few minutes before eight you're allowed to make your way along the course to your own preferred starting point (you should walk the course beforehand to get familiar with it). To mark the start, two rockets are fired, one when the bulls are released, a second when they are all out (it's best if these are close together, since the bulls are far safer if they're running as a herd rather than getting scared individually). As soon as the first goes you can start to run, though if you do this you'll probably arrive in the ring well before the bulls and be booed for your trouble: if you wait awhile you're more likely to get close to the bulls. Although there are plenty of escape points, these are only for use in emergency – if you try to get out prematurely you'll be shoved back.

Other events

There are plenty of other hazardous things to do in Pamplona, especially once the atmosphere has got the better of a few people's judgement. Many people have fun hurling themselves from the fountain in the centre of town and from surrounding buildings (notably the mussel bar), hoping their friends will catch them below. Needless to say, several people each year are not caught by their drunken pals.

Other events include **music** from local bands nightly from midnight in the Plaza de Castillo, continuing until about 4am in the fairground on the Avda. de Bayona, which is where local political groupings and other organizations have their stands. There are **fireworks** every evening in the citadel (about 9pm), and a **funfair** on the open ground beside it. Competing **bands** stagger through the streets all day playing to anyone who'll listen. If things calm down a bit you can sunbathe, take a shower, catch up on sleep and even swim at the public **swimming pool** outside the walls below the Portal de Zumalacàrregui.

Bullfights take place daily at 6.30pm, with the bulls that ran that morning. Tickets are expensive (about 2000–3500ptas), and if you have no choice but to buy from the touts, wait until the bullfight has begun, when you can insist on paying less (the price drops with each successive killing). At the end of the week (midnight, July 14) there's a mournful candlelit procession, the **Pobre De**, at which the festivities are officially wound up for another year.

If you're hooked on danger, many **other Basque towns** have fiestas which involve some form of *encierro*. Among the best are Tudela (July 24–28), Estella (last week of July and one of the few which has no official ban on women participants), Tafalla (mid-Aug) and Ampuero in Santander province (Sept 7–8).

MORE EXPENSIVE HOTELS

Hotel Eslava, Plaza Virgen de la O 7 (☎948/222270, 225157). Very cosy and comfortable hotel run by the Eslava family in a quiet corner of the old city – views from balconies overlooking the plaza stretch out to the plain beyond. Singles and doubles with all facilities and a bar in the basement. ⑤.

Hotel Europa, c/Espoz y Mina 11 (☎948/221800). Just off Plaza del Castillo before the Turismo; a good three-star hotel with restaurant of the same repute. ⑤.

Hotel La Perla, Plaza del Castillo 1 (☎948/227706). Great character with a few rooms with balcony overlooking the street (price triples during San Fermín). Hemingway stayed in Room 217. ④–⑤.

Hotel Yoldi, Avda. de San Ignacio 11 (☎948/224800). The hotel where the bullfighters and VIPs from the *taurino* world stay during San Fermín, when there's no chance of a room. Garage parking. ⑤.

The town

The **Plaza del Castillo**, a tree-lined square ringed with fashionable cafés, is the centre of the town and much of its activity. The narrow streets of the former *Judería* fill the area to the south and west, towards the city walls by the cathedral; virtually the only trace of a large Jewish community that thrived here before the persecutions and expulsions of the Inquisition. From the opposite side of the square, c/San Nicolás runs down towards the citadel and the more modern area of the city to the east. It's in c/San Nicolás and its continuation, c/San Gregorio, that you'll find most of the *hostales* and *fondas,* a number of excellent small restaurants and loads of raucous little bars.

The **Cathedral** is basically Gothic, built over a period of 130 years from the late fourteenth to the early sixteenth century but with an unattractive facade added in the eighteenth. It doesn't look promising, but the interior, containing the tomb of Carlos III and Eleanor in the centre of the nave, and the ancient *Virgen de los Reyes* above the high altar, is fine, and the cloister is magnificent. The **Museo Diocesano** (May 16–October 15 daily 9am–2pm; 100ptas) is entered via the cloisters and is housed in two superb buildings, the refectory and the kitchen – both are worth seeing in their own right. Don't miss the many sculpted doorways in the cloister, particularly the *Puerta de la Preciosa* and the chapel with a lovely star vault, built by a fourteenth-century bishop to house his own tomb.

Behind the cathedral is one of the oldest parts of the city, an area known as **La Navarrería**. Here you'll find the best section of the remaining **city walls** with the Baluarte de Redín and Portal de Zumalacárregui (or de Francia) looking down over a loop of the Río Arga. If you head out through the gate, paths lead down to the river from where you get the full force of the impregnability of these defences. Follow the inside of the walls and you'll come to the **Museo de Navarra** (Tues–Sat 10am–2pm & 5–7pm, Sun 11am–2pm; 200ptas) in the magnificent old hospital building on c/Santo Domingo. Inside is displayed material on the archeology and history of the old kingdom of Navarra, along with some good mosaics and an art collection that includes a portrait of the Marqués de San Adrián by Goya. Heading back to the plaza via c/Santo Domingo and the Plaza Consistorial you'll pass the **market** and the fine Baroque **Ayuntamiento**.

There's much more to be seen along the streets of the old town, with ancient churches and elegant buildings on almost every street. In particular, though, take time to wander around the parks and gardens that surround and include the ruinous **Citadel**, with its views over the new part of town. From here you can follow the line of the old walls through the **Jardines de la Taconera** and down to the river by an alternative route.

Eating and drinking

For good inexpensive **menús**, and a wide range of **tapas** and *bocadillos*, head for the streets around c/Major, in particular c/San Lorenzo – try *Bar La Cepa, Bar Piskolaris* and *Restaurante Lanzale*. On c/Jarauta *Club Deportivo Navarro* is worth a visit. The popular *Bar La Campana*, c/de Campana 12, near the church of San Saturnino has one of the best *menús* in town, while *Café Roch* on c/de las Comedías (perpendicular to c/San Nicholás) is very good for *pinchos*. A place with real character and surprisingly inexpensive food, is the *Mesón del Caballo Blanco*, a beautiful old building up by the city walls to the left of the cathedral at the end of c/Redin, where you can choose from a good selection of *raciones* and traditional fare from Navarra (evenings only).

The elegant *Café Iruña*, on Plaza del Castillo is the place to sit over a leisurely coffee and take in the action, or try the more modern yet equally enjoyable *Café Niza* opposite the Turismo on c/Duque de Ahumada. The best and rowdiest **bars** are on and around c/San Nicolás.

For **breakfast** in peaceful surroundings and a chance to read the paper, there's no better place than *Café Alt Wien*, known to the locals as *El Vienés*, in the Jardines de la Taconera – it can get crowded with families in the afternoon.

Southern Navarra

South of Pamplona, the country changes rapidly; the mountains are left behind and the monotonous plain so characteristic of central Spain begins to open out. The people are different, too – more akin to their southern neighbours than to the Basques of the north. There are regular bus and train services south to **Tudela**, the second city of Navarra, passing through **Tafalla** and **Olite**, once known as the "Flowers of Navarra", though little remains of their former glory.

Tafalla

TAFALLA, 35km south of Pamplona, is a shabby provincial town apparently left behind by modern Spain. If you find yourself here, it's worth going to the parish church of **Santa María**, where there's a huge *retablo,* one of the finest in Spain. It was carved by Juan de Ancheta, among the most recognized of the Basque Country's artists.

There are a couple of overpriced places to **stay***: Pensión Arotza*, Plaza de Navarra 3 (☎948/700716; ⑤), and *Hotel Tafalla* (☎948/700300; ④), on the main Pamplona–Zaragoza road.

Olite

OLITE, also rather neglected, is more attractive. Now hardly more than a village, it boasts a magnificent **castle** (April–Sept Mon–Sat 10am–2pm & 6–8pm, Sun 10am–2pm; Oct–March Mon–Sat 10am–2pm & 4–5pm, Sun 10am–2pm; 100ptas) which was once the residence of the kings of Navarra. An amazing ramshackle ramble of turrets, keeps and dungeons, it is slowly being restored, and part of the building already houses a *parador*. There are also two gorgeous old churches, Romanesque **San Pedro** and Gothic **Santa María**, the latter with a superb carved *retablo*.

Accommodation in Olite is expensive. Apart from the *Parador Príncipe de Viana* (☎948/74000; ⑤), there are a couple of other pricey hotels: *Casa Zanito* (☎948/740002; ⑤), among the old streets, is the more atmospheric, but is frequently full during the summer; *Hotel Carlos III el Noble*, Rua de Medios 1 (☎948/740644; ④), is slightly less expensive.

Ujué

East of Tafalla and Olite in the direction of Sangüesa, a winding road branches off to the right at San Martín de Unx (a good place to stock up on wine from the local *bodega*), to the hilltop village of **UJUÉ** – one of the real jewels of Navarra. It's a perfect medieval defensive village perched up on the terraced hillside above the harsh, arid landscape and dominated by the thirteenth-century Romanesque church of **Santa María**, where the heart of King Charles II of Navarra is supposedly preserved inside the altar. The church has Gothic additions dating from the fourteenth century and, from its balconied exterior, the view extends over the whole southern Navarra region of La Ribera. The main doorway contains some intricate sculptures depicting the Last Supper and the Three Kings.

From the main square, where you can eat *migas de pastor* and other dishes from the region, a couple of pedestrianized cobbled streets plunge down to another beautiful little square and a *casa rural, Casa Isolina Jurio* (☎948/738184; ③); a second smaller one in the village, *Casa El Chofer* (☎948/738097; ③), also has a couple of rooms.

Tudela

The route south continues to **TUDELA** on the banks of the Ebro. On arrival, it seems as ugly a town as you could ever come across, but don't despair – a short walk down the main street takes you into the old town and an entirely different atmosphere. Around the richly decorated **Plaza de los Fueros** are a jumble of narrow lanes apparently little-changed since the Moorish occupation of the city was ended by Alfonso I of Aragón in 1114. The twelfth-century **Colegiata de Santa Ana** is a fine, strong, Gothic construction. It has a rose window above the intricately carved alabaster west doorway which portrays a chilling vision of the Last Judgement. Inside there's an unusual *retablo* and some beautiful old tombs, while the Romanesque cloister has some deft primitive carvings, many badly damaged. The bizarre thirteenth-century **bridge** over the Ebro looks as if it could never have carried the weight of an ox cart, let alone seven centuries of traffic on the main road to Zaragoza.

There are a couple of pricey **hostales** in the main street through the new part of town: best value is *Hostal Remigio*, c/Gaztambide 4 (☎948/820850; ③), which also has more expensive rooms with bath; *Delta*, Avda. Zaragoza 29 (☎948/821400; ④) is reasonable; or try the *casa de huéspedes* at c/de Carniceras 13 (②), above the *Restaurante La Estrella*. You'll find many other places to **eat and drink** around the Plaza de los Fueros.

The Pilgrim Route

The ancient **Pilgrim Route** to Santiago passed through Aragón (see p.499) and into Navarra just before Leyre, travelling through the province via **Sangüesa**, **Puente la Reina** (where it met an alternative route crossing the Pyrenees at Roncesvalles) and **Estella**, before crossing into Old Castile at Logroño.

Yesa and the Monasterio de Leyre

The first stop for the pilgrims in Navarra, the **Monasterio de San Salvador de Leyre**, stands amid mountainous country 4km from Yesa, on the main Pamplona–Jaca road, connected with both places by a daily bus in either direction. **YESA** has several **hostales**, the best being *El Jabali* (☎948/884042; ③), on the main road, with a pool and restaurant. A daily **bus** links Pamplona, Yesa and Jaca.

From the village a good road leads up to Leyre, arriving at the east end of the monastery. Although the convent buildings are sixteenth- to eighteenth-century, the church is largely Romanesque; its tall, severe apses are particularly impressive. After languishing in ruins for over a century, it was restored and reoccupied by the Benedictines in the 1950s and now looks in immaculate condition. The leaflet available in English at the porter's lodge is useful to shed light on the complicated sculptured facade of the church. Inside, the crypt, with its sturdy little columns, can be illuminated by putting a coin in the slot. Try to catch a service if you can; the Benedictines here employ the Gregorian chant in their Masses and are well worth hearing.

The former pilgrims' guest house here is now run as a two-star **hotel**, the *Hospedería de Leyre* (☎948/884100; ④), and although far more expensive than staying in Yesa, it is still a remarkable bargain. Men can stay at the monastery itself for a nominal fee, but anyone wanting to do this should write or phone ahead.

THE CAMINO DE SANTIAGO IN NAVARRA

Following the European Parliament's decision to designate the *camino* Europe's first "cultural itinerary", Navarra has invested considerably in improving facilities along the route. There are a total of eleven pilgrims' *hostales* within Navarra which *bona fide* pilgrims can use – to qualify you must show a letter of introduction from your parish church or town hall at the place where you plan to start the route (in Spain this is usually Roncesvalles or Somport, or the church of San Cernino or the Archbishop's palace in Pamplona). You'll be given a "passport" as an accredited pilgrim which is then stamped at each *hostal* along the route. Most of the *hostales* have hot showers, some have kitchens and are either free or charge only a nominal 500ptas fee. A few of the *hostales* may only be open during the summer months, but regional Turismos in Navarra can provide up-to-date details.

The route itself is clearly marked as long-distance footpath GR65. Long stretches do run alongside the main Pamplona–Estrella–Logroño road, but wherever possible the official walking route avoids major highways.

Javier

From Yesa it's only a few kilometres south to **JAVIER**, birthplace of San Francisco Xavier – one of the first Jesuits – and home to a fine **castle** (daily 10am–1pm & 4–7pm). Javier had nothing to do with the Pilgrim Route, but it is something of a place of pilgrimage in its own right, with a museum of the saint's life in the restored keep. The elderly guide takes great glee in describing the horrors that the castle has seen, and in particular, a set of extraordinary demonic murals – recently discovered – depicting the dance of death.

It's a popular picnic spot and there's a **hostal** in the grounds, *Hostal Xavier* (☎948/ 884006; ④), alongside two churches dedicated to the saint. Alternatively, try the cheaper *Mesón*, Plaza de Javier (☎948/884035; ④ with bath). Javier is served by one daily **bus**, at 5pm, from Pamplona.

Sangüesa

The Pilgrim Route proper stops next at **SANGÜESA**, a delightful small town preserving many outstanding monuments, including several churches from the fourteenth century and earlier. See above all the south facade of the church of **Santa María Real** (at the far end of town beside the river), which has an incredibly richly carved doorway and sculpted buttresses; God, the Virgin and the Apostles are depicted amid a chaotic company of warriors, musicians, craftsmen, wrestlers and animals. The entrance is flanked by two groups of three statues, one of which is signed by the artist Leodagarius (c. 1200); the other sculptor known to have worked on the doorway was the Master of San Juan de la Peña.

Sangüesa is an enjoyable place simply to wander around. Many of its streets have changed little in centuries and aside from the churches – Romanesque Santiago is also lovely – there are some handsome mansions, the remains of a royal palace and a medieval hospital; the last two are currently under restoration.

Unfortunately, there's not much in the way of **accommodation**: the *Pensión Las Navas*, c/Alfonso el Batallador 7 (☎948/870077; ③), opposite the main bus stop, is the only convenient place to stay, though there's also a fairly fancy hotel, *Yamaguchi* (☎948/870127; ⑤), on the road to Javier. Three **buses** daily run to and from Pamplona and one (leaving Sangüesa very early) goes to the Aragonese town of Sos del Rey Católico, 12km away.

Puente La Reina

Perhaps no town is more perfectly evocative of the days of the medieval pilgrimage than **PUENTE LA REINA**, 200km southwest of Pamplona. This is the meeting place of the two main Spanish routes: the Navarrese trail, via Roncesvalles and Pamplona, and the Aragonese one, via Jaca, Leyre and Sangüesa. From here onward, all the pilgrims followed the same path to Santiago.

At the eastern edge of town, the **Iglesia del Crucifijo** was originally a twelfth-century foundation of the Knights Templar, its porch decorated with scallop shells (the badge of the Santiago pilgrims). To one side is the former pilgrims' hospice, later in date, but still one of the oldest extant. In town, the tall buildings along c/Mayor display their original coats of arms, and there's another pilgrim church, Santiago, whose portal is sadly worn, but which has a notable statue of Saint James inside. The **bridge** at the end of the street gives the town its name. The finest medieval bridge in Spain, it was built at the end of the eleventh century by royal command and is still used by pedestrians and animals only – an ugly modern bridge has been constructed for vehicular traffic.

Practicalities

There are two places to **stay** in town: *Hostal Puente*, Paseo de los Fueros (☎948/340146; ⑤ in July and August, ④ out of season), is friendly, clean and serves good food, though it can be noisy; and *Fonda Lorca* (☎948/340127; ②), is basic but again serves meals – however, most of the rooms are semi-permanently filled with construction workers. *Mesón del Peregrino* (☎948/740002; ⑤), an ancient building with a modern pool, just out of town on the main road towards Pamplona offers more luxury, or try next door at the *Hotel Jakue* (☎948/341017; ⑤) for rooms of a similar standard. There's a good **campsite**, *El Molino*, (☎948/740002) at **Mendigorria**, 5km south. There are several places to **eat**, most near the main road which, thankfully, skirts the town.

Estella

Twenty kilometres west lies **ESTELLA**, a beautiful town rich in monuments and high in interest. During the nineteenth century this was the headquarters of the Carlists in the Civil Wars, and each May there is still a pilgrimage up a nearby mountain to honour the dead. **Plaza de los Fueros** marks the centre of town, but most of the more interesting buildings are on the opposite side of the river in the Barrio San Pedro de la Rúa.

Immediately after crossing the bridge, you'll find the well-stocked **Turismo** (Mar–Dec 10am–2pm & 4–7pm; ☎948/554011). Next door is the twelfth-century **Palacio de los Reyes de Navarra**, a rare example of large-scale Romanesque civil architecture, part of which is now open as an art gallery (Tues–Sun 11am–1pm & Tues–Sat 5–7pm; free) devoted to the painter Gustave de Maeztu.

Estella has a wealth of churches. You can also visit the fortified pilgrimage church of **San Pedro de la Rúa** (Mon–Sat noon–1pm & 5–6pm, Sun 10am–2pm), whose main doorway shows unmistakable Moorish influence – staff from the turismo are usually on call to show poeple around the church and cloister. From the former *Ayuntamiento*, an elegant sixteenth-century building opposite the *palacio*, c/de la Rúa leads past many old merchants' mansions. Further along, past a stud farm, you reach the abandoned church of Santo Sepulcro with a carved fourteenth-century Gothic doorway. Cross the hump-backed bridge, take the first left, then right uphill, and you come to the church of **San Miguel**: not a terribly inspiring building in itself but with a north doorway that is one of the gems of the Pilgrim Route. Its delicate capitals are marvellous, as are the modelled reliefs of the *Three Marys at the Sepulchre* and *St Michael Fighting the Dragon*. The dingy interior is a letdown after this, and in any case, may only be visited just before or just after Mass (Mon–Fri 7pm, Sun 8.30am, 11.30am & 1pm).

If you want to **stay** in Estella, many of the budget places are located round the Plaza de los Fueros. On the corner of the plaza is the *Fonda San Andrés* (☎948/550448; ③) and in the streets nearby are several cheaper places including *El Volante*, c/ Merkatondoa 2 (☎948/553975; ③), and *Fonda Izarra*, c/Calderería (☎948/550678; ③). For more comfort, try the *Hostal Cristina*, Baja Navarra 1 (☎948/550772; ④). There's also a **casa rural** (☎948/520203; ②), 8km north in the village of Abarzuza, and a **campsite**, *Camping Lizarra* (☎948/551733).

Estella has plenty of bars, many serving good *platos combinados*; the **restaurants**, on the other hand (except those attached to the *fondas*), are expensive, although most offer a lunchtime *menú* for 800-1200ptas.

Estella to Logroño

From Estella, the Pilgrim Route follows the main road to Logroño and there are a number of interesting stops. At **IRACHE**, near the village of Ayegui, there's a Cistercian monastery (Tues–Fri 10am–2pm & 5–7pm except Tues pm, Sat & Sun 9am–2pm & 4–7pm) which is currently being restored: inside it boasts an ornate Plateresque cloister. Beside the adjacent Museo de Vino (principally a showroom for *Bodega Irache*), are two taps in the wall, ostensibly for use by pilgrims – out of one comes water and from the other, red wine. Seventeen kilometres further on is **LOS ARCOS**, whose handsome church of Santa María (9am–2pm) has a Gothic cloister. The *Hostal Ezequiel* (☎948/640296; ③) here is good, and has a special pilgrim rate, or try the *Hostal Monaco*, Plaza del Coso (☎948/640000; ③ with bath).

Of more direct interest is **TORRES DEL RÍO**, 7km further still. This unpretentious village is built round the church of the **Holy Sepulchre**, a little octagonal building whose function is uncertain – it may have been a Knights Templar foundation or a funeral chapel. The names of the three local women who look after the monument are posted on the door of the church, and anyone of them may be found to show visitors around (access at any reasonable time), for a small charge. Inside it's a surprise to find that the dome is of Moorish inspiration.

VIANA, the last stop before the border and where Cesare Borgia died, is an attractive place with many beautiful Renaissance and Baroque palatial houses, in addition to the Gothic church of Santa María with its outstanding Renaissance carved porch. Logroño is only 10km away, but if you want to stay, *Pensión Granjo*, c/Navarro Villoslada 19 (☎948/645078; ④), has comfortable rooms with bath.

The Pyrenees

The mountains of Navarra may not be as high as their neighbours to the east, but they're every bit as dramatic and far less developed. And there's not – as yet – a single ski lift in the province. The historic **pass of Roncesvalles** is the major route through the mountains from Pamplona, and always has been – celebrated in the *Song of Roland* and more recently, when Jan Morris called it "one of the classic passes of Europe and a properly sombre gateway into Spain". It was the route taken by countless pilgrims throughout the Middle Ages; Charlemagne's retreating army was decimated here by Basque guerrillas avenging the sacking of Pamplona; Napoleon's defeated armies fought a running battle along the pass as they fled Spain; and thousands of refugees from the Civil War made their escape into France along this narrow way.

The beautiful Pyrenean valleys, particularly the **Valle de Baztán** north of Pamplona, and the **Valle de Salazar** to the southeast, are a perfect place to relax, and they offer inexpensive and plentiful accommodation with the the largest number of **casas rurales** in the province.

Burguete and Roncesvalles

Northeast of Pamplona, the N135 winds upwards until it reaches the neighbouring villages of Burguete and Roncesvalles, about half an hour's walk apart. The surrounding country is superb for walking, or simply to sit back and admire. Beyond these villages, the road continues into France via the border town of Valcarlos.

Burguete

BURGUETE has more of a village atmosphere than Roncesvalles. If you've come on the daily bus from Pamplona you've little choice but to **stay** in Burguete, as it doesn't arrive here till 8pm. The best place is the wonderfully ramshackle, yet strangely formal, *Hostal Loizu* (☎948/760008; ③) on the main road. Others on the main road include the *Burguete* (☎948/760005; ③) and the *Juandeaburre* (☎948/760078; ③). Better still, try one of the two *casa rurales* for a more family atmosphere; *Casa Loigorri* (☎948/760016; ②) or Casa Vergara (☎948/760044; ③), which has more expensive rooms with bath. Food is available at all of these places. There's also a **campsite**, *Urrobi* (☎948/760200), 3km south of the village at **Espinal-Auzperri** on the Pamplona road.

Roncesvalles

The few buildings at **RONCESVALLES** are clustered around the **Colegiata** with its beautiful Gothic cloister. A side chapel houses a prostrate statue of Sancho VII el Fuerte (The Strong); measuring 2.25m long, it is supposedly life-size. Here also are the chains that Sancho broke in 1212 at the battle of Navas de Tolosa against the Moors – a symbol which found its way into the Navarrese coat of arms. A small museum next to the monastery has relics of centuries of pilgrimage and a great deal of (mainly bogus) exhibits relating to the ambush of Charlemagne. A beautiful half-hour walk from the back of the monastery (on the marked path) will take you up to the pass of the **Puerto de Ibañeta** – this is said to be the very route taken by Charlemagne.

Accommodation is fairly limited: there's the *Casa Sabina*, right next to the monastery (☎948/760012; ③), or the newer *La Posada* (☎948/760225; ④), run by the monastery. If you're a walker or cyclist following the Pilgrim Route, you might be able to stay in a dormitory at the monastery; ask for Father Javier Navarro.

Valcarlos

If you're continuing into France – a journey redolent with history – you'll come to the border village, **VALCARLOS**, 18km on. There's no bus on this road but hitching is easy. Valcarlos is a typical border town full of souvenirs and booze – though the views are better than usual – with the *Hostal Maitena* (☎948/790210; ③) conveniently on the main road should you need to **stay**. On the Frenchward side of the village, the excellent *Casa Etxezuria* (☎948/790011; ③), has a couple of beautifully furnished rooms and offers luxury at a bargain price – this place has become a big success with pilgrims following the *Camino de Santiago*, so phone in advance if possible. There are also houses with rooms to let – ask in the bars.

Valle de Baztán

Due north of Pamplona, the N121 climbs over the Velate pass at **Mugaire** near the **Senori de Bértiz gardens**, a former private estate now designated as a Parque Natural and recreation area. At Oronoz, a left fork heads up the scenic Valle de Bidasoa with its interesting old towns (see p357) to Irún and San Sebastián. Continuing along the right fork, you enter the **Valle de Baztán** with its string of tiny villages, beautiful countryside and cave formations.

Elizondo

The centre of this most typically Basque of Navarran valleys is **ELIZONDO**. The town is full of fine Basque Pyrenean architecture, especially alongside the river, but above all, it serves as a good base for exploring the beautiful villages and countryside in the area.

There are several places to **stay** in Elizondo. The best option is *Casa Jaén* (☎948/580487; ③), but it has only two rooms; *Pensión Esquisaroy*, c/Jaime Urrutia 40 (☎948/580013; ③), is a good second choice. There are also two considerably more expensive places: the three-star *Hotel Baztán* (☎948/580050; ④) on the Pamplona road south of town, complete with garden and pool; and in the town itself, *Hostal Saskaitz*, c/Azpilikueta 10 (☎948/580488; ④). Three **buses** run daily from both Pamplona and San Sebastián, but there is no public transport to the smaller villages beyond.

Around Elizondo

In nearby **ARIZCUN** is the seventeenth-century Convent of Our Lady of the Angels with its striking Baroque facade and, just beyond the village, is a typical example of a fortified house (very common in the valley) where Pedro de Ursua, the leader of the Marañones expedition up the Amazon in 1560 in search of El Dorado, was born. You can stay in Arizcun at the friendly and well-run *Fonda Etxevarria* (②), which also serves good lunches and dinners.

Just before the spectacular, narrow **Izpegui Pass** is **ERRAZU**, another gem, with a couple of well-preserved *casas rurales*: one is a fourteenth-century palatial home, *Casa Etxebeltzea* (☎948/453157; ③), and the other, *Casa Marimartinenea*, (☎948/453117; ③), still has livestock on the ground floor.

MAIA, a few kilometres to the north, where the last battle for the independence of Navarra took place, is another unspoilt village worth a stop. The gateway to its single street displays the village shield depicting a red bell – most houses still proudly show off the shield above their doorways.

The caves of Zugarramurdi

North of Elizondo, the main road climbs over the **Otxondo Pass** to the villages of Urdax and Zugarramurdi, a good stopover between Pamplona and the French Basque coastal towns of Biarritz and Bayonne. The only public transport on this stretch is the noon post bus from Elizondo – check in town first.

ZUGARRAMURDI is famous for its **caves** whose centrepiece is the giant natural arch through which the *regata de infierno* (hell's stream) flows. It was a major centre for witchcraft in the Middle Ages and consequently the area bore the brunt of persecution at the time of the Inquisition. Underneath the arch, *akelarres* or witches' sabbaths allegedly took place and have passed into Basque legend. The village itself is very pretty and a good place to base yourself for excursions into the surrounding countryside – one possibility is to walk on the track beyond the caves into France to another set of caves at **Sara**.

Zugarramurdi is well-served with **casa rurales**, although they often get booked out at weekends; *Casa Sueldeguía* (☎948/599088; ③) and *Casa Teltxegu* (☎948/599167; ②) are both in the centre of the village, or there is a **campsite**, *Camping Josenea* (☎948/599011) by the main road near Urdax.

Valle de Salazar

Southeast of Pamplona, 10km before Yesa, the road to Lumbier leads into the beautiful Salazar valley, the most spectacular part of which is the **Foz de Arbayún** – a deep gorge, visible from a viewing platform by the road, which may be descended by the intrepid. One kilometre from **LUMBIER** is the entrance to the Foz de Lumbier, a major nesting place for **eagles** which can usually be spotted high up in the walls of the gorge or circling overhead. There's a **campsite** at Lumbier, *Camping Iturbero* (☎948/880405), open all year round.

Forty kilometres further on you reach the unspoilt Pyrenean town of **OCHAGAVÍA**, served by one bus daily from Pamplona, except Sunday. The most attractive parts of town are the tree-lined streets on both sides of the river, which is crossed by a series of low stone bridges. There are no less than nine **casas rurales** (②) here offering accommodation in attractive traditional stone houses for which the town is famous (consult the *guía de alojamientos*: *turismo rural* for a full list – free from the Turismo in Pamplona). A good place to eat is *Aunamenu* on the east side of the river; it also has rooms to let.

The **forest of Irati** to the north is one of the most extensive pine and beech forests in Europe, and **Monte Ori**, the first 2000m peak in the Pyrenees rising from the Atlantic side, offers some excellent walking and climbing options with views every bit as spectacular as the highest peaks.

Valle de Roncal – the Parque Natural Pirenaico

If you're really serious about exploring the mountains, the **Valle de Roncal** further east, is considerably more rewarding although very popular in July and August. The bus route from Pamplona passes north of Sangüesa, and briefly into Aragón by the huge reservoir, *Embalse de Yesa*, before heading north up the valley of the Esca and back into Navarra. It's a lovely route, crisscrossing the river all the way up through Burgui and Roncal to Isaba. There is a *hostal* in **RONCAL**, the *Zaltua* (☎948/895008; ③), and also a couple of *casa rurales*, best of which is *Casa Pepita* (☎948/475133; ③), a large private mansion which also provides good meals at very reasonable cost. If you want to stay round here, though, you're much better off continuing to Isaba.

Isaba and around

ISABA has plenty of rooms available in private houses, the majority of which are now grouped as **casa rurales**, although expect to have to try several places at weekends as Isaba (along with Ochagavía) is a major touring centre for the Western Pyrenees and gets invaded by the hordes from Pamplona, Bilbāo and elsewhere. There's also the *Albergue Oxanea* (①), a sort of private **youth hostel** where you sleep in dormitories; the *Hostal Lola* (☎948/893012; ③), and *Pensión Txabalkua* (☎948/893101; ②), both offering good food; *Pensión Txiki* (☎948/893118; ④), above the bar-restaurant of the same name; as well as a fairly luxurious hotel, the *Isaba* (☎948/893000; ④–⑤). The **campsite**, *Asolaze* (☎948/893034), is at the edge of the Parque Natural, 6km up the road towards the border, or with discretion you can camp freelance along the banks of the river beyond the village.

Despite its convenience, there's too much new building in Isaba for it to be really attractive. For the best walking and magnificent views, continue up the valley of the Río Belagua to the *Refugio de Belagua*, a mountain refuge (popular in July & August) almost on the border, in the middle of the **Parque Natural**, high among the peaks in a landscape of extraordinary beauty. In summer the bus from Pamplona continues this far, or there's an 8am service up from Isaba. There's a restaurant and bar, and if you bring a sleeping bag you can hire a basic bed for the night – bring your own food if you plan to stay long. There are many **walks** you can undertake from here – some very ambitious – to make the most of which you need a proper **map** (*Editorial Alpina* 1:40,000 *Ansó-Hecho* covers the park) and a compass. There are also plenty of easy strolls; details in the *Refugio*.

travel details

Trains

Bilbão Estación de Abando to: Barcelona (2 daily; 10–12hr); Logroño (4 daily; 2hr 30min); Madrid (3 daily; 8hr); Orduña (hourly; 1hr); Salamanca (2 daily; 9hr).

Estación Atxuri to: Durango (10–12 daily; 1 hr); Gernika (15 daily; 2hr).

Estación Concordia to: Karranza (4 daily; 1hr); Santander (5 daily; 2hr).

Estación Las Arenas to: Algorta (every 30min; 25 min); Larrabesterra (every 30min; 35min); Plencia (every 30min; 45min).

Irún to: Hendaye, France (every 30min 7am–10pm; 5 min); Paris (2 daily; 8hr); San Sebastián (every 30min 5am–11pm; 30min).

Pamplona to: Madrid (1 daily; 6hr); Zaragoza (7 daily; 2hr 30min).

San Sebastián to: Bilbão (9 daily; 2hr 30min–3hr); Burgos (12 daily; 4hr); Madrid (4 daily; 6hr 30min–8hr 30min); Pamplona (6 daily; 2–3hr); Salamanca (2 daily; 9hr); Valencia (1 daily; 12hr); Vitoria (15 daily; 2–3hr); Zaragoza (4 daily; 4–5hr).

Buses

Bilbão to: Burgos (4 daily; 2hr); Elantxobe (3 daily; 1hr 30min); Gernika (9 daily; 1hr); Lekeitio (4 daily; 1hr 30min); Logroño (1 daily; 2hr 15min); Ondarroa, via Markina (2 daily; 1hr 30min); Pamplona (3 daily; 4hr); Santander (5 daily; 2hr 30min); Vitoria (8 daily; 1hr 30min); Zaragoza (3 daily; 5hr).

Irún to: Pamplona (3 daily; 2hr); San Sebastián (constantly; 30min).

Pamplona to: Burguete (1 daily; 1hr 30min); Elizondo (3 daily; 2hr); Estella (10 daily; 1hr); Isaba (1 daily; 2hr); Jaca (2 daily in summer, 1 in winter, except Sun; 2hr); Logroño (4 daily; 2hr); Madrid (2 daily; 6hr); Ochagavía (1 daily, except Sun; 2hr); Puenta la Reina (hourly; 30min); Tafalla (10 daily; 1hr); Tudela (4 daily; 1hr 30min); Vitoria (9 daily, fewer Sun; 1hr 30min); Yesa (1 daily; 1hr); Zaragoza (2–3 daily; 4hr).

San Sebastián to: Bilbão (13 daily; 2hr); Elizondo (3 daily; 2hr); Hondarribia (every 15min; 30min); Lekeitio (3–5 daily; 2hr); Lesaka (2 daily; 1hr 15min); Oñate (4 daily; 1hr 30min); Pamplona (6 daily; 3hr); Vera de Bidasoa (2 daily; 1hr); Vitoria (7 daily; 2hr 30min); Zarautz (hourly; 30–40min); Zumaia (4 daily; 1hr).

Vitoria to: Araía (via villages of Llanada Alavesa; 2 daily; 1hr); Durango (4 daily; 1hr); Estella (4 daily; 1hr 15min); Laguardia (4 daily; 1hr); Logroño (8 daily; 1hr) Pantanos de Zadorra (3 daily; 30min); Santander via Castro Urdiales (3 daily; 2hr).

CHAPTER SEVEN

CANTABRIA AND ASTURIAS

The northern provinces of **Cantabria** and **Asturias** are popular holiday terrain for Spaniards and French but surprisingly little known by other foreign tourists. Their climate, of course, is distinctly un-Mediterranean, with modest sunshine, and all-too-common sea mists washing over the coastline. But the sea is warm enough for swimming through the summer months; there are old and elegant seaside towns, and tiny, isolated coves; and, inland, rear the fabulous **Picos de Europa** – a gorgeous mountain range, with peaks, gorges, flora and fauna, to satisfy walkers and trekkers of any level of expertise.

Cantabria, centred on the city of Santander, was formerly a part of Old Castile, and was long a conservative bastion amid the separatist leanings of its coastal neighbours.

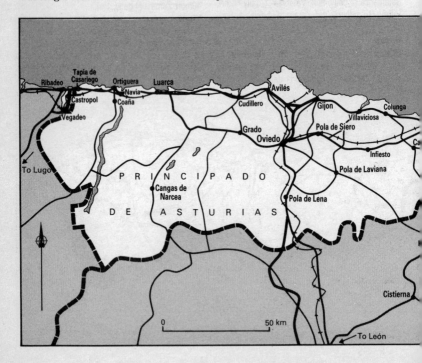

Santander, its capital, is an elegant, if highly conventional, resort, with one of Spain's few remaining ferry links with Britain – to Plymouth. Attractive, low-key resorts lie to either side, crowded in the Spanish and French holiday season – August especially – but generally enjoyable; the best are **Castro Urdiales**, to the east, and **Comillas** and **San Vicente** to the west. Inland, there are a series of **prehistoric caves**, several of which can be seen at **Puente Viesgo**, near Santander, though the most famous, **Altamira**, cannot now be visited.

To the west is mountain-locked **Asturias**, an idiosyncratic, Celtic land that was the one part of Spain never to be conquered by the Moors. It is a little like Wales, both in its scenery – harsh mountains and rugged coves – and in its idiosyncratic traditions, which include status as a principality (the heir to the Spanish throne is known as the *Príncipe de Asturias*) and a culture that includes such things as bagpipes and cider (*sidra* – served from shoulder height to add fizz). The Welsh comparisons extend, too, to Asturia's base of heavy industry, especially mining and steelworks, and a long-time radical and maverick workforce. Having conducted wildcat strikes during the early days of the Republic, Asturian miners were among its staunchest defenders of the Republic against Franco.

The coastline is a delight, so long as you steer clear of the steel mills of Avilés and the factories of Gijón, with wide, rolling meadows leading down to the sea. Tourism here is largely local, with a succession of old-fashioned and very enjoyable **seaside towns**: small places such as **Ribadesella**, **La Isla** and **Luarca**. Inland, everything is dominated by the **Picos de Europa**, though a quiet pleasure on the peripheries of the mountains, as in Cantabria, is the wealth of Romanesque – and even Visigothic – churches, scattered on the hillsides. These reflect the history of the old Asturian king-

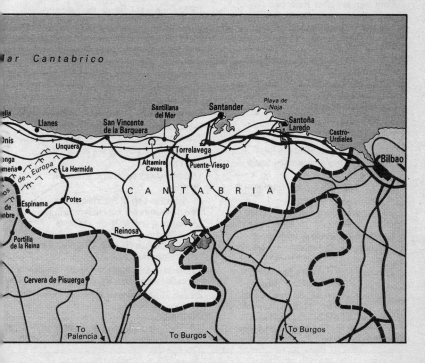

dom – the embryonic kingdom of Christian Spain – which had its first stronghold in the mountain fastness of **Covadonga**, and was slowly to spread south with the Reconquest. The churches are often at their best when you come upon them by accident, rounding a corner in the countryside, though **Santa María del Naranco**, just outside Oviedo, is worth a special effort to see.

The Picos de Europa, as noted earlier, take in parts of León, as well as Cantabria and Asturias, though for simplicity the whole region is covered in this chapter.

FIESTAS

January

22 Saint's day fiesta at San Vicente De La Barquera.

February/March

Start of Lent Week-long *carnaval* festivities in Avilés, Gijón, Oviedo, Mieres, Santoña – fireworks, fancy dress and live music.

April

Holy Week Celebrations include the *bollo* (cake) festival on Easter Sunday and Monday at Avilés.

First Sunday after Easter *La Folia*, torch-lit maritime procession at San Vicente De La Barquera.

June

28 *Coso Blanco* nocturnal parade at Castro Urdiales.

29 Cudillero enacts *La Amuravela* – an ironic review of the year – and then proceeds to obliterate memories.

July

10 Fiesta at Aliva.

15 Good solid festival at Comillas with greased-pole climbs, goose chases and other such events.

16, 17 & 18 Fiestas in Tapia de Casariego.

25 Festival of Saint James at Cangas De Onis.

Last Sunday *Fiesta de los Vaqueros* – cowboys – at La Brana de Aristebano near Luarca.

Through July there is a Jazz Festival at Santander, which towards **August** expands into an International Music Festival. This being one of the wealthiest cities of the north, you can usually depend on the festival featuring some prestigious acts.

Weekly fiestas in Llanes, with Asturian dancers balancing pine trees on their shoulders and swerving through the streets. Also, tightrope walking and live bands down at the harbour.

August

First or second weekend Canoe races between Arriondas and Ribadesella on the Río Sella, with fairs and festivities in both towns.

First Sunday Asturias Day, celebrated above all at Gijón.

12 Fiesta at Llanes.

15 *El Rosario* at Luarca – the fishermen's fiesta when the Virgin is taken to the sea.

31 Battle of the Flowers at Laredo.

Last week Fairly riotous festivities for San Timoteo at Luarca: best on the final weekend of the month, with fireworks over the sea, people being thrown into the river, and a Sunday *romería*.

September

7–8 Running of the bulls at Ampuero (Santander).

14 Bull-running by the sea at Carreñón (Oviedo).

16 Llanes folklore festival, strong on dancing.

19 Americas Day in Asturias, celebrating the thousands of local emigrants in Latin America; at Oviedo there are floats, bands and groups representing every Latin American country. The exact date for this can vary.

21 *Fiesta de San Mateo* at Oviedo, usually a continuation of the above festival.

29 San Miguel *romería* at Puente Viesgo.

November

30 Small regatta for San Andrés day at Castro Urdiales.

The FEVE railway

Communications in this region are generally slow, with the one decent road in Asturias following the coast through the foothills to the north of the Picos de Europa. Using public transport, you may want to make use of the **FEVE rail line**, which is unmarked on many maps and independent of the main *RENFE* system. This begins at Bilbao in the Basque country and follows the length of the Cantabrian coast (with an inland branch to Oviedo) to El Ferrol in Galicia: a terrific route, skirting beaches, crossing *rías* and snaking through a succession of limestone gorges.

Santander

Long a favourite summer resort of *Madrileños*, **SANTANDER** is an elegant, rather refined resort, much in the same vein as its Basque neighbours to the east, Biarritz and San Sebastián. Some people find the city a clean and restful base – indeed it's a popular centre for summer Spanish language courses – while others (especially younger Spaniards) will tell you it's dull and snobbish. On a brief visit, the balance is probably tipped in its favour by its variety of excellent beaches and the sheer style of its setting. The narrow Bahía de Santander is dramatic, with the city and port on one side in clear view of open countryside and high mountains on the other – a great first view of Spain if you're arriving on the ferry from Plymouth.

In July and August, the city hosts a **Jazz and International Music Festival** and is host to an **international university**. You'll need to book accommodation well ahead if you plan to stay at these times.

Orientation and accommodation

The **centre** of Santander is a compact grid of streets, set between the city's two ports, the **Puerto Grande** (where the ferries arrive) and the **Puerto Chico** (which serves pleasure boats). Its main square is **Plaza de Velarde**, where there's a very good and informative **Turismo** (Mon–Fri 9am–1.30pm & 4–7pm, Sat 9am–1.30pm; ☎942/310708), with a 24-hour VDU outside. Around the waterfront to the east, **La Magdalena**, a wooded headland, shelters **Playa Magdalena**, on its near side, and, beyond, the 2km-long sands of **El Sardinero**, with its beachside suburb.

The **RENFE** and **FEVE** train stations are side by side on the Plaza Estaciones, just back from the waterside, under an escarpment which hides the main roads. A largely subterranean **bus station** faces them directly across the square. The **Aeropuerto de Santander** is 4km out of town – an inexpensive taxi ride.

City buses #4, #5, #6 and #7 shuttle daily between the centre and El Sardinero.

Accommodation

July and August aside (see above), Santander usually has enough accommodation to go round. There is a choice of locations between the **centre** or **El Sardinero**, though many of the *pensiones* and *hostal* at the latter don't open until July. *TIVE*, the Spanish student travel agency, can help locate rooms in private houses (*casas particulares*).

ACCOMMODATION PRICE SYMBOLS

The symbols used in our hotel listings denote the following price ranges:

① Under 2000ptas ③ 3000–4500ptas ⑤ 7500–12,500ptas
② 2000–3000ptas ④ 4500–7500ptas ⑥ Over 12,500ptas

See p.30 for more details.

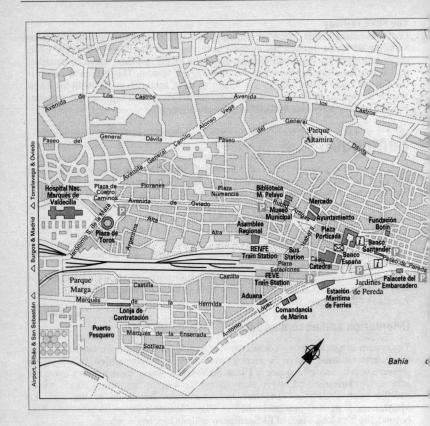

IN THE CENTRE

Pensión Angelines (☎942/312584) and **Pensión San Miguel** (☎942/210881), both at c/de Atilano Rodríguez 9. Two excellent pensiones, close by the train station. ③.

Los Caracoles, Marina 1 (☎942/212697). A central budget option. ②.

La Corza, c/de Hernán Cortés 25 (☎942/212950). Clean, friendly and very central. ③–④.

Hostal Gran Antilla,c/Isabel II 8 (☎942/213100). Good mid-price *hostal*. ③.

Hostal Mexicana, Juan de Herrera 3 (☎942/222350). Pleasant clean rooms with bath and an excellent position; very friendly. ③–④.

Fonda Perla de Cuba, c/de Hernán Cortés 8 (☎942/210041). The city's best budget accommodation – located in a wonderful old building with ornate wrought-iron balconies. ①.

EL SARDINERO

Hostal-Residencial Luisito, Avda. de los Castros 11 (☎942/271971). A pleasant *hostal* just back from the beach. Open July–Sept only. ③.

Hotel Roma, Avda. de los Hoteles 5 (☎942/272700). A traditional, turn-of-the-century hotel on the beach. This is the place to splash out on if you can afford it. ⑤.

Hostal La Torre, Avda. de los Castros 53 (☎942/275071). One of the few Sardinero *hostales* that stays open all year round. ③.

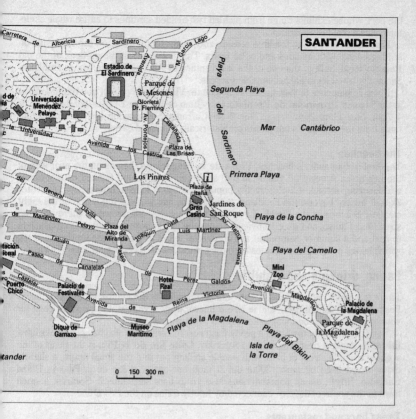

CAMPING

Camping Bellavista (☎942/274873) and **Camping Cabo Mayor** (☎942/273566). Well-equipped sites, flanking the Sardinero beach, 2km north of the Casino, on a bluff known as Cabo Mayor.

The town and its beaches

Santander was severely damaged by fire in 1941, losing most of its former pretensions along with its medieval buildings. What was left of the old city was reconstructed on the grid around the cathedral, but, while the avenues are pleasant enough, and some of the shops impressively unaware of the recession, there is little of interest beyond a couple of museums. The appeal of Santander lies firmly in its beaches.

Around the centre

Santander's **Catedral** is a dull building, almost uniquely bereft of treasures, save for its Gothic-Romanesque crypt (separate entrance). The **Museo de Bellas Artes**, nearby, is not much more promising, overburdened with nineteenth-century portraits. If you have time to fill, better to look in at the **Museo Marítimo** (summer Tues–Sat 11am–1pm, Sun 11am–2pm; winter Mon–Sat 10am–1pm & 4–6pm, Sun 11am–2pm; free), near the port, whose exhibits range from pickled two-headed sardines to entire whale skeletons, plus a real life aquarium.

Kids might also enjoy the little seaside **zoo** (9am–10pm; free), on the Peninsula de la Magdalena, with its lions and polar bears. This is housed in the gardens of the old **Palacio Real**, built at the end of the last century by Alfonso XIII, to whose residence Santander owed its initial fashionable success.

If you're planning to visit the caves at Puente Viesgo (see p.407), you might look in at the **Museo Provincial de Prehistoria**, c/Juan de la Costa 1 (Tues–Sat 9am–1pm & 4–7pm, Sun 11am–2pm; free). This is well arranged, displaying and reconstructing finds from the province's numerous prehistorically inhabited caves.

The beaches

The first of Santander's beaches, **Playa de la Magdalena**, begins on the near side of the headland. A beautiful yellow strand, sheltered by cliffs and flanked by a summer **windsurfing** school, it is deservedly popular. So too is **El Sardinero** itself: a further 2km of beach, beyond the headland, with its own flag announcing it one of the eight cleanest beaches in the world. If you find both beaches too crowded, there are long stretches of dunes and excellent views across the bay at **Somo** (which has windsurfers to rent and a summer **campsite**) and **Pedreña**; to get to them, jump on the taxi-ferry which leaves every fifteen minutes from the central *Muelle de Ferrys* (225ptas return).

Eating, drinking and nightlife

There is a huge choice of cafés, bars and restaurants in the centre, around the Barrio Pesquero (the fishing port), and at El Sardinero, while if you want to picnic or cook for yourself, there's a good foodmarket behind the *Ayuntamiento*.

Being a university town and a pretty flash resort, Santander also has plenty of **nightlife**, at its liveliest from Thursday to Saturday. **Calle Rio de la Pila** is the heart of the scene – a whole street of bars, with people spilling out into the small hours; a slightly older crowd is to be found 300m uphill (and left out of c/Rio de la Pila) in **Plaza Cañadio**. Bright young Santanderians also go to bars and clubs in **Solares**, a small town to the south of the city, connected by hourly trains on the *FEVE* line.

Tapas bars and restaurants

Bodegas Bringas and **Bodegas Mazon**, c/de Hernán Cortés 47 and 57. These *bodegas* serve tasty local food, wine and *sidra*, amidst vast wine vats. *Bringas* is open evenings only and reputed for its *anchoas* and *pimientos*; *Mazon* is good for *chipirones* and *tortilla*.

Bar Brumas, c/Eduardo Benot. Good *platos combinados* and Voll Damm beer.

Restaurante Cañadio and **Bar Cañadio**, c/Gómez Oreña 15 (☎942/314149; closed Sun). The Cañadio is the city's best restaurant, known far and wide for the sublime fish and regional cooking of its chef, Paco Quirós. If you can't spare 4000ptas and up, don't despair – just join the foodies snacking on a fabulous spread of canapés at the much more modest bar.

Bar Cantabria, c/Rio de la Pila 12. *Tapas* bar (wonderful *empanadas* and *pinchos*) with a little dining room at the back.

La Conveniente, c/Gómez Oreña 19. Nineteenth-century *bodega* with live music, fried fish and other delicious snacks.

La Cueva, **Las Peñucas** and **Vivero**, c/Marqués de la Ensanada, Barrio Pesquero. A trio of popular and unpretentious seafood and fish restaurants down by the fishing port. You can spend almost anything, from a few hundred pesetas for a *menú del dia* or plate of sardines, to a small fortune for fishy exotica, so order with care!

Cerveceria Lisboa, Plaza Italia, Sardinero. An ever-popular place behind the casino, with a summer *terraza*, and a good choice of *platos combinados*.

Picón, c/Santa Lucía 36. Excellent little *tapas* bar specializing in cheese and sausage.

Bar El Solórzano, c/Peña Herbosa 17. A great neighbourhood bar with traditional music, *vermut* on tap, and the whole array of Cantabrian seafood.

Bar and clubs

Agua de Valencia, c/Perinas. A very popular place to start the evening, with a killer house cocktail at 800ptas a jug.

Balneario-Oliver, Avda. El Stadium 7b, Sardinero. More exotic cocktails. Run by the same people as the *Balneario* bar in Madrid.

Blues, Plaza Cañadio. Blues and jazz music bar, with a connecting restaurant.

Castelar-5, c/Castelar 5. A pleasant music bar with a summer *terraza*.

Cuic, El Sardinero. The clubbers' last port of call, playing hardcore *bakalao* (a kind of housed-up Spanish traditional dance music) till 9am.

El Grifo, Plaza Cervezas. Youthful bar with a choice of fifteen beers.

Escena, Plaza Rubén Dario. Old-time danceclub still frequented for *rumbas* and *sevillanas*.

Maria's and **Swing**, both on c/Casmiro Saiuz and both open for dancing till dawn.

Rocambole, c/de Hernán Cortés 36. Late night club attracting a young and trendy crowd from 3am on; motown music and expensive drinks.

Tienduca, c/Rio de la Pila. One of the best bars on this street.

Listings

Airport The Aeropuerto de Santander is 4km out of town at Parayas, Santander–Bilbao road (☎942/251004).

American Express c/o Viajes Altair, c/Lealtad 24 (☎942/311700).

Car rental *Avis*, c/Nicolas Salmerón 3 (☎942/227025); *Europcar*, c/Rodríguez 9 (☎942/214706).

Consulates British Consulate, Paseo Pereda 27 (☎942/220000).

Ferry tickets Tickets for the Brittany Ferries crossing to Plymouth are sold by *Modesto Piñeiro* at their office at the ferry dock (☎942/214500). Advance reservations are essential in summer, both for cars and passengers.

Hospital The General Hospital is on Avda. Valdecilla (☎942/330000).

Post office The city's main *correos* is on Avda Alfonso XIII; open Mon–Fri 8am–9pm, Sat 9am–2pm.

Skiing/Travel agency *TIVE*, the Spanish student travel agency, is useful for most travel plans – and arranges good value packages to the ski resort of Alto Campoo; their office is just off Plaza de Velarde at c/Canarias 2 (Mon– Fri 8am–3pm, Sat 9am–1pm).

Telephones The *Telefónica* is at c/de Hernán Cortes 37.

Trekking The *Federacíon Cantabria de Montaña*, c/Rubio 2 (☎942/373378) provides information and organizes treks in the Picos de Europa.

East along the coast to Castro Urdiales

The coast east of Santander has been heavily developed, with villas and apartment complexes swamping most of the coves. **Noja**, until recently remarkable only for the strange-shaped rocks along its shore, now has seven campsites, while **Laredo** has become one of the north's major holiday resorts. Things improve as you move east, however, to the beach at **Islarés**, or to the old town of **Castro Urdiales**.

Laredo and around

LAREDO is very popular with French tourists and has a summer profusion of pubs, clubs and discos. In parts, though, it's still an attractive place though. For a spell in the last century it was Cantabria's provincial capital, and the village-like core of the old town, **El Rastrillar**, rambles back from the harbour, with occasional traces of its former walls and gates, climbing up towards a splendid thirteenth-century parish church, **La Ascunción** (open afternoons only). Beyond the church you can climb quickly out of town to the cliffs and to grand open countryside, while below lies the best **beach** this side of San Sebastián, a gently shelving crescent of sand, 5km long and well protected from the wind.

There isn't much inexpensive **accommodation** in Laredo. If you're arriving by bus, strike across the park to the main road and the *Hostal Tucan*, corner of c/Lopez Seña and c/Gutierrez Rada (☎942/607053; ③), a clean place, 100m from the beach, with a café downstairs serving good *menús*. *Hostal Salomon* c/Melendez Pelayo 11 (☎942/605081; ④), two blocks further east, is friendly and efficient and has good rooms with bath. There's a cluster of slightly more expensive places on the west side of town in the residential district, but still only 10 minutes' walk from the bus station and close to the beach. Try the superbly located *Hotel Montecristo*, c/Calvo Sotelo 2 (☎942/605700, 605034; ④), *El Cortijo*, Gonzalez Gallego 3 (☎942/605600; ④), or *El Ancla*, Gonzalez Gallego 10 (☎942/605500; ⑤). There are two **campsites** (June–Sept) close to the beach: *Laredo* (☎942/605035) and *Costa Esmeralda* (☎942/603250).

There are bars and *cafeterías* on the beach, while in town Rua de San Marcial has a good selection of **restaurants**. If you want the town's best, it is the *Meson del Marinero* (☎942/606008) on c/Zamanillo, a creative, though pricey, shellfish specialist.

Santona

Just across the bay from the west end of Playa de Laredo lies the resort of **SANTONA**. Ferries run across the water to the small beach, or it's a half an hour by road. Santona is, remarkably, still a working fishing port; you can watch the catch being unloaded and sample it in the tiny bars grouped around the streets leading up from the port, particularly c/General Salinas. There are grand views across the bay to Laredo from the hilltop castle **Fuente de San Martin**.

Islares

If you're looking for somewhere more peaceful, the village of **ISLARES**, east from Laredo, beyond the headland, is as yet little developed. There's a beach a short walk past the houses, well sheltered by cliffs, a very modest-sized **campsite**, and just a handful of *hostales* and *pensiones*. *El Langostero* (☎942/862212; ④), just off the main highway is far enough from the road that you don't hear the traffic and is virtually on the beach; clean with nice views and has its own restaurant. Closer to the main road, *Pensión Playamonte* (☎942/862696; ③) is a cheaper, but noisier option. *Hostal Arenillas*, Carretera Irún-La Coruña (☎942/860766; ③), Islares' original *hostal*, is still a good bet.

Castro Urdiales

CASTRO URDIALES is a congenial and good-looking resort, less developed than Laredo, though rooms and space on the beaches are still at a premium in high season, and at weekends, when everyone descends from Santander and Bilbao. At such times, the main "town beach", **Playa del Brazomar**, a small strip of sand, hemmed in by a cement esplanade used for sunbathing, and bordered by two large hotels, is pretty unattractive. However, the crowds can be left behind by heading east to more secluded coves, or west to **Playa Ostende**, with its dark sand. From this latter beach, there's an unusual walk back to town along the cliffs, most of which seem to be hollow – you can hear the sea pounding beneath you. Along the route is a tiny bay where the sea comes in under a spectacular overhang.

As well as its tourist functions, the town retains a considerable fishing fleet, gathered around a beautiful natural harbour. Above this looms a massively buttressed Gothic church, **Santa María**, and a lighthouse, built within the shell of a Knights Templar castle. The old quarter, the **Mediavilla**, is relatively unspoiled, with arcaded streets and tall glass-balconied houses.

Practicalities

The town's best budget accommodation is in the old town. Ask here at *Bar Rincon*, c/La Mar, which has big clean and airy rooms (②), or *Astor*, c/Javier Echevarrai 12

(☎942/861116, 860555), an electronics shop whose owner rents rooms (①) and will negotiate prices of 1000ptas a day for long-term stays. Other possibilities include *Fonda La Marina* (③) on the waterfront and *Fonda Baracaldo* (②) at c/Ardigales 14. More upmarket options include the smart *Hostal La Mar*, c/La Mar 27 (☎942/870524; ④) and *Hostal Catamaran*, c/Victoria Gainza 1 (☎942/870066; ③), a friendly place next to the bus stop. Hotels in the new part of town are expensive, and heavily booked at weekends, but are very close to the beach: two of the best are *Hotel Las Rocas*, Avda. de la Playa (☎942/860400, 861382; ⑤) and the superior *Hotel Miramar*, Avda. de la Playa 1 (☎942/860200, 860204; ⑤).

There is no shortage of places to **eat**. Many of the less expensive places are around the *Ayuntamiento* at the castle end of the harbour, with some excellent fish/seafood bars on c/El Carrerias. The lively c/Ardigales is packed with *mesónes* and *tabernas: Bar Agora* at no. 7 is a very reasonable Basque-run establishment with outdoor tables, while *Restaurante Baracaldo*, across the street, features huge all-seafood *menús* for under 800ptas. *Mesón Marinero* is Castro's renowned fish restaurant located in a huge building near the *Ayuntamiento* with windows displaying the dishes swimming around; it can be pricey, but if you sit at the bar and choose from the *tapas* on display, you can eat very well for under 1000ptas. You'll find **disco-bars** and **clubs** mostly around the Paseo de Alvaro Villota, though *Mambo*, c/Ardigales 14, is also worth trying.

The **bus station**, shared by the companies *Turytrans* and *La Burundesa*, is in the *Bar Cerámica*, c/Victorina Gainza, five blocks from the front. There are through services to towns between Irún and Gijón from here although buses to Bilbao leave from *Cafe/Bar Ronda* on the main N634.

Santillana and the prehistoric caves

If you see a postcard in Santander depicting gorgeous sandstone churches and mansions, it is **Santillana del Mar**: an outrageously picturesque village, 26km west of Santander, which has been prettified beyond belief for tourism. It remains beautiful, by the skin of its teeth, but in season it's a major tourist spot. The crowds would be worse were the caves at **Altamira**, on the edge of the village, still open to visitors, for these contain Spain's most dramatic prehistoric drawings. Two other caves, less well known, but still preserving Altamira-epoch paintings, are accessible, and located at **Punte Viesgo**, 24km south of Santander on the N623 Burgos road.

Santillana del Mar

Jean Paul Sartre (in *Nausea*) describes **SANTILLANA DEL MAR** as "*le plus joli village d'Espagne*" – an unlikely source, but none the less accurate for that. The village (once you reach it past the coach and car parks) is all ochre-coloured stone houses, mansions, and farms. Despite the name – *del Mar* – Santillana actually stands some three or four kilometres back from the sea, and while its fine houses flaunt their aristocratic origins the village itself has long been completely rural. Its single street, with one loop and two plazas, saunters back from the access road towards a wonderful Romanesque collegiate church and then stops abruptly amidst farms and fields.

The village
Santillana's fifteenth- to eighteenth-century **mansions**, vying with each other in the extravagance of their coats of arms, are as splendid as they are anomalous. One of the best is the **Casa de los Hombrones**, named after two moustachioed figures, flanking its grandly sculpted escutcheon. Another, the **Casa de Bustamentes**, established its credentials with a simple motto: "The Bustamentes marry their daughters to kings".

Although many of the mansions still belong to the original families, their noble owners rarely visited in this century or the last; indeed up until the 1970s, villagers kept their cattle in some of the less-used mansions.

The village church, **La Colegiata**, is dedicated to Santa Juliana, an early martyr whose tomb it contains; she is legendarily supposed to have captured the devil and is depicted with him in tow in various scenes around the building. Its most outstanding feature, however, is the twelfth-century **Romanesque cloister**, one of the best preserved in the whole country, with its squat paired columns and lively capitals carved with animals and hunting scenes. It can be visited, with the church, only on a tour (10am–1.30pm & 3–6pm; 200ptas), and to join you need "decent" clothing: no shorts, no singlets, and skirts for women.

Also worth a look is the seventeenth-century **Convento de Regina Coeli** (same hours and tickets as the Colegiata cloisters), across the main road near the entrance to the village. This houses an exceptional museum of painted wooden figures and other religious art: pieces brilliantly restored by the nuns and displayed with great imagination to show the stylistic development of certain images, particularly of San Roque, a healing saint always depicted with his companion, a dog who licks the wound in his thigh. There is a resident ghost, too, on the first floor.

Practicalities

Santillana is an attractive overnight stop if you are travelling out of season, and it has rooms to suit most budgets. Least expensive are the **casas particulares** (private rooms) next to the post office in the Plaza de Ramón Pelayo (opposite the *parador*); up a track behind these; and by the *Ayuntamiento;* followed by *Pensión Angelica* at c/Los Holnos 3 (☎942/818238; ③). Only if you find these all full should you settle for the modern **hostales** on the main road, best value of which is *Hospedaje Fernando* (☎942/818018; ②), a little way out towards Altamira. The two tempting **upmarket options**, both in the heart of the village, are the *Parador Gil Blas* (☎942/818000; ⑤), in one of the finest mansions, and the grand old *Hotel Altamira* at Cantón 1 (☎942/818025; ④). There is also a **campsite**, *Camping Santillana* (☎942/818250), large and a bit soulless, but with a pool and other good facilities, 1km out along the Altamira road.

Restaurants are decent if unexceptional. *Mesón de Los Villa*, c/Santo Domingo 5, is pleasant, serving meals outside in a little orchard in summer. *La Vega* is a late-night bar, serving excellent *tortillas*. *Los Infantes*, a disco-pub opposite the convent, also stays open late. You don't come to Santillana, however, for the nightlife.

The village has a **post office** and **Turismo** (Mon–Sat 9.30am–1pm & 4–7pm; ☎942/818251), both in the Plaza de Ramón Pelayo – the square opposite the *parador*. There are several direct **buses** daily to Santillana from Santander run by *SA Continental* from the main station (first bus 10.30am); the bus drops you outside the convent with the town straight ahead. You can also get to the village by regular buses from Torrelavega, which is on the *FEVE* railway line. Leaving Santillana, buses go to Comillas and San Vicente de la Barquera at 10.30am and 1.30pm.

Altamira

The prehistoric **Caves of Altamira** lie 2km west of Santillana, off the San Vicente road. Dating from around 12,000 BC, they consist of an extraordinary series of caverns, covered in paintings of bulls, bison, boars and other animals etched in red and black with a few confident and impressionistic strokes. When discovered in the 1870s they were in near-perfect condition, with striking and vigorous colours, but in the 1950s and 60s the state of the murals seriously deteriorated, and they are now **closed** to all but twenty visitors a day, a limit intended to prevent the build-up of surplus moisture (from breathing) in the cavern's atmosphere.

Unless you have an academic interest in cave paintings, and write months in advance to the *Centro de Investigación de Altamira* (Santillana, Santander), you stand little chance of getting inside. You can, however, look around a couple of lesser grottoes at the site and a small **museum** (Mon–Sat 10am–1pm & 4–6pm, Sun 10am–1pm; free), introduced to humour the still considerable flow of tourists.

Puente Viesgo

A more rewarding cave visit is to hand at **PUENTE VIESGO**, 29km out of Santander on the N623 road to Burgos (*SA Continental* bus from the main station in Santander). Around the village, set amid magnificent rolling green countryside, are four separate **prehistoric caves**, one of which, **Castillo**, is open to tours (Tues–Sun 10am–1pm, last entry 12.15pm). This is a magnificent sight, with stalactites and stalagmites in the weirdest shapes, in addition to the remarkable paintings – clear precursors to the later developments at Altamira.

If you want to stay, the village has a luxurious four-star hotel, *Gran Hotel Puente Viesgo*, (☎942/598061; ⑥), and a few budget places: *Hostal La Terraza* (☎942/598102; ③), rooms without bath; and *La Troncal* (☎942/598117; ②), set back a bit from the bus stop. A couple of other places open up for the summer season.

South of Santander: Reinosa and the Ebro

South of Santander lies a large area of quiet Cantabrian countryside, dominated by the extensive **Pantano del Ebro**. The N611 to Palencia brushes the shores of this reservoir and passes through **Reinosa**, a transport hub for the region and a pleasant old town if you want to break your journey. To the west, the high Sierra de Peña Labra has **skiing** opportunities, with a small resort at **Alto Campoo**, 24km from Reinosa. To the east, the **Río Ebro** trails a lovely valley, past a succession of unspoilt villages, Romanesque architecture sand cave churches.

Reinosa

REINOSA is a pretty, characteristically Cantabrian town with lots of glass-fronted balconies and *casonas* – seventeenth century townhouses – displaying the coat of arms of their original owners. The **Turismo** occupies one of these, midway down the main street, Avda. de la Puente, near the distinctive Baroque church of **San Sebastián**.

Two inexpensive places to stay are *Fonda Los Tilos* (②), small, warm and family-run, and the *Pensión Sema* (☎942/750047; ③), at c/Juliobriga 6 and 12, respectively. For a bit more comfort, try the *Hotel Ruben*, c/Abrego 12 (☎942/754914; ④), or, across the bridge, *Hostal Tajahierro*, c/Pellila 8 (☎942/753524; ③). For a small place, there's an amazing range of traditional *bodegas* and *mesónes*. On the main street, *Pepe de los Vinos* is a good place for a glass of wine and a snack, and the restaurants *Avenida* and *Los Angeles* offer more substantial fare; the latter is open late.

If you are pressing on deeper into the countryside, two local buses daily go south to Polientes at 9.50am and 6pm, and another two travel east around the reservoir to **Cabanas** and **Arija** at 10.45am and 6pm.

Skiing: Alto Campoo

Twenty-four kilometres to the west of Reinosa lies the ski resort of **Alto Campoo**, served by regular buses in season. It's a tiny resort, with a ski school, 17km of pistes and a three-star **hotel**, *La Corza Blanca* (☎942/779250).

Along the Ebro: Polientes

East of Reinosa, a network of tiny, winding roads trail the Ebro river, passing through villages of no more than a few houses. The largest of these is **POLIENTES**, a lovely place, totally rural, though with a couple of places to stay: a **pensión** (③), by the bus stop, and a **hostal** just down the road (☎942/776053; ③); in season, be sure to ring before you arrive. The café/bar in the main square serves good food (it's run by the mayor) and the *hostal* does a good value *menú*, too.

East of Polientes, you'll need your own transport to continue along the valley and on to the Santander–Burgos road. Twelve kilometres from Polientes is the village of **San Martin de Elines**, with a twelfth-century Romanesque **Colegiata** containing medieval sarcophagi, and a church set into rock. At nearby **Cadalso**, you'll find another smaller rock church.

The coast: Comillas to Gijon

The coastline **west of Santillana** and **into Asturias**, is dotted with a succession of enticing resorts. Most of them are popular in a small-scale, local sort of way, and have been spared the tower-block hotel and apartment treatment, and amid the villages and river valleys, there are coves which see only the occasional weekender from Santander. The coast is tracked, most of the way, by the **FEVE rail line**, and the countryside, with a massed backdrop of hills rolling into the Picos de Europa, is invariably magnificent.

Comillas

COMILLAS, the first resort west of Santillana del Mar, is actually skirted by the *FEVE* line, though it has good bus connections with both Santillana and (to the west) San Vicente de la Barquera. A curious little town with cobbled streets and unwieldy mansions, it's set just back from the sea and a pair of superb beaches: the **Playa de Comillas**, the closest, with a little anchorage for pleasure boats and makeshift beach cafés, and the longer **Playa de Oyambre**, out towards the cape to the west.

The town also has a trio of sights, including a Gaudí-designed villa, **El Capricho**, a short (and signposted) walk uphill from the centre. This is now a restaurant but its gardens are open to visitors, and it is enough on the tourist trail to maintain a souvenir shop. It is certainly worth a look, even if you're not staying in Comillas, with its circular gestures, optical tricks, and a dome half-suspended in the air.

Next door to El Capricho, is another nineteenth-century *modernista* flourish, the **Palácio de Marqués de Comillas**, designed by Gaudí's associate, Juan Martorell. It is closed to visitors but can be glimpsed through the gates of El Capricho. The Marqués, an industrialist friend of Alfonso XII, also commissioned the huge **Seminario Pontífico**, on the hillside above, from Domenech y Montaner, another of the Barcelona *modernista* group.

Practicalities

Accommodation is pretty limited in Comillas and in season you will need to book ahead, or arrange a private room through the **Turismo** (Mon-Sat 10am–1pm & 4–7pm; ☎942/720768), centrally located (and signposted) at c/La Aldea 2.

The best budget rooms are those at *Pensión Bolingos*, c/Guzo de la Torre (☎942/720841; ②), clean, friendly and just off the main square, and above *Restaurante Casa La Aldea*, c/La Aldea (☎942/720300; ②). More upmarket choices include the *Hostal Esmeralda*, Antonio López 7 (☎942/720097; ④), a beautifully furnished place at the top of the town, the *Fuente Real*, c/Fuente Real (☎942/720155; ③), right beside El

Capricho, and the Casal de Castro, c/San Jerónimo (☎942/720036; ④). Two expensive fallbacks are the modern and characterless *Hotel Paraiso*, Padres Páramo y Nieto, just off the main square (☎942/720030, or winter 720270); ④), and *Hotel Josein*, Santa Lucía 27 (☎942/720225; ④), which is better value and has excellent coastal views.

There are **campsites** at both beaches (see above), with the *Comillas* (☎942/720074; July–Aug) significantly better than *El Rodero* at Oyambre (June–Oct).

Comillas has good food to offer. At the bottom end of the scale, try *Picoteo*, just down from the *Esmeralda*, which does generous meals at rock bottom prices; or for *tapas* try the bars around Plaza Ruiz de la Rabia. For a blow-out, credit cards can pay for Gaudí decor and Spanish nouvelle cuisine at *El Capricho de Gaudí* (☎942/720365), in the villa.

San Vicente de la Barquera

The approach to **SAN VICENTE DE LA BARQUERA** is dramatic, with the town, marooned on both sides by the sea, entered across a long causeway. From the hill above, an impressive **ducal palace** and Romanesque-Gothic church, **Santa María de los Angeles** (the latter with restored, gilded altarpieces) look on. The town itself, a thriving fishing port with a string of locally famed but expensive seafood restaurants, has had its old core encroached upon, and is split by the main coast road with its thundering lorries, but it still makes a good overnight stop. There's a good sweep of sand on the near side of the causeway (opposite the town), flanked by a small forest.

Accommodation is a little easier to find than at Comillas. The central *Hostal la Paz*, c/Mercado 2 (☎942/710180; ③) is clean and spacious, while the cheapest rooms in town are at the *Fonda Liebana* (☎942/710211; ②), at the top of the stairs leading from the back of the main square. More expensive options include Hostal *Boga-Boga*, Plaza José Antonio 9 (☎942/710135; ④) and *Hotel Luzón*, Carretera Santander-Oviedo (☎942/710050; ④). There is a pleasant **campsite** (☎942/711461) on the beach. Among the seafood **restaurants**, try *El Pescador*, a reasonably-priced place, on the right as you head westwards out of town. *Bar Colón*, further down on the left, does good *raciones*.

Using public transport, San Vicente is best left or approached by **bus** (*Turytrans* serves the coast and *Palomera* covers inland routes), as the *FEVE* station is about 4km south at **La Alcebasa**. Buses leave from the stop near the bridge; details of timetables are available at *Fotos Noly* opposite the bus stop. The local **Turismo** (July–Sept Mon–Sat 9am–9pm; ☎942/810280) is on the main road, at Avda. Generalisimo 20.

Into Asturias: Unquera to Ribadesella

Asturias begins 9km west of San Vicente, at **UNQUERA**. Here buses for the Picos turn south towards **Potes**, and here too the *FEVE* railway comes into its own after the inland stretch from Santander. Unquera itself is a pretty dire place, with its only bright spots in the restaurants *Ríomar* and *Granja*; the latter also serves as the local bus stop and is just across from the *FEVE* station.

If you're on the train or bus, you'll do much better staying on until **Llanes**, Asturia's easternmost resort – and one of its most attractive.

Llanes

LLANES, a stop for both buses and *FEVE* trains between Oviedo and Santander, is a delightful seaside town with a little harbour at the mouth of the river and a lovely *rambla* along the sea wall. Its crenellated towers and little squares are undergoing a face lift at present, with huge sums of money being invested in widening the entrance to the port and restoring the crumbling monuments. Nonetheless, it's a fine place to rest up for a few days, with several cafés by the river in town, an excellent beach, **Playa Ballota**, 2km to the east, with its own supply of spring water down on the sand (and a nudist stretch), and to the west a whole series of beautiful **coves**, yours for the walking.

The cheapest **rooms** are at the *Bar Colón* (☎98/540 08 83; ②), overlooking the river, and at *Fonda La Guía*, Plaza Parres Sobrino 1 (☎98/540 25 77; ②), which is a bit old and decaying but good value. For excellent accommodation near the beach, try *Hostal de Rio*, Avda. de San Pedro 3 (☎98/540 11 91; ③). *La Paz*, Avda. de la Paz (☎98/540 29 11; ③) is another possibility, slightly out of town. There are two large **camp-sites**: *Las Baracenas* (☎98/540 28 87; June–Sept), five minutes from town; and *El Brao* (☎98/540 00 14; April–Sept), just off the main road.

For good **seafood** – and Asturian cider (*sidra*) – head for *La Marina*, a restaurant shaped like a boat at the end of the harbour, where you can sit outside and tuck into swordfish steaks and sardines. At the end of the lunchtime rush, the fish bones and scraps are dumped on the habourside providing photo-opportunities of a raucous mass scrap by the local seagulls. At night, the best place to eat is along a lane, down the steps from the bridge over the river. Here, three or four simple open-air café-restaurants under corrugated iron roofs serve up above-average platters of seafood – fried prawns, great *chipirones*, and tuna steaks the size of a house. At the *El Campanu*, and others, you'll pay between 600ptas and 2000ptas a dish; drink the cider or the local white wine.

Villahormes and Nueva

Following the coast (and FEVE line), the next tempting stop to the west of Llanes is **VILLAHORMES**. This is an unprepossessing-looking place: no more than a train station, a handful of houses, a café-bar and a **pensión**, the *Residencia-Albergue Verdemar* (☎98/540 81 44; ①; basic but very cheap, with full board at under 2000ptas). Follow the rusty signpost to **Playa de la Huelga**, however, and, after 1500m of driva-ble track, you reach one of the best swimming coves imaginable, with a rock arch in the bay and an enclosed sea pool for kids to splash around in safety. It is flanked by a pleasant bar-restaurant.

A thirty-minute walk west of Villahormes, or five minutes more on the train, will get you to another hamlet, **NUEVA**, tucked into a fold of the hills, 3km inland from another gorgeous little cove.

Ribadesella

RIBADESELLA, 18km west of Llanes, is an unaffected old port, sprawled at the mouth of the Sella river, and with dozens of excellent little bars and *comedores* on the streets parallel to the **fishing harbour**. Freshly caught fish is still unloaded most nights (after midnight) at the **Lonja**, so it's fun to hang out until then in the bars. The town **beach** is a beauty, too, with very limited development on either side of its old grand hotel. It is reached across a long causeway from the town.

On the beach side of the causeway, too, is the **Cueva Tito Bustillo** (Mon–Sat 10am–1pm & 3.30–5.15pm; closed Mon except July–Aug; 235ptas), an Altamira-style cave more impressive for its stalactites than its paintings, though it has a museum of prehistoric finds from the area. Only 400 visitors are allowed into the caves each day, so in summer try to arrive early in the day.

Practicalities

Arriving by train, you'll emerge at the **FEVE station**, at the top end of town; the **bus station** is out on the Oviedo road. There is a **Turismo** (☎98/586 00 38; summer-only) in an original *hórreo* (granary), just over the causeway.

Accommodation is a bit more expensive than usual, although the impecunious may be able to find *camas*, and there's a **youth hostel** on c/Ricardo Cangas (☎98/586

13 80; ①) in an old house on the east side of the estuary. Among the *hostales*, try the *Apolo* (☎98/586 04 42; ③) and *Varadero* (☎98/586 03 39; ③), at Gran Via 31 and 32, respectively, or – better than both of them – the *Covadonga* (☎98/586 02 22; ③), at the end of Gran Via at c/Manuel Caso de la Villa 7. Ribadesella's top hotel, the old-fashioned *Gran Hotel del Sella* (☎98/586 01 50; ⑤), fronts the beach and the newly-built promenade. Also recommended is the *Hostal El Pilar* (☎98/586 04 46; ③), 2km out of town at Puente del Pilar, which has a restaurant serving traditional Asturian food.

There are two beachside **campsites**: *Los Sauces*, Carretera San Pedro la Playa (☎98/586 13 12; March–Sept) and *Playa de Vega* (June–Sept).

For **meals**, try *Rompoelas*, a classic if slightly pricey *marisqueria* in the old town, with piles of seafood lining its long wooden counter.

Lastres and Villaviciosa

Beyond Ribadesella the railway turns inland, as do most tourists, heading for Cangas de Onis and the western flanks of the Picos de Europa. The route into the mountains – the N634 and M625 – is a superb one, following the valley and gorge of the Río Sella. The coast itself deteriorates the closer you get to Gijón, Asturias's main industrial port, though there are a few last highlights, including the small resort of **La Isla** and the town of **Colunga**, both of which are noted for their seafood and cider; and the fishing villages of **Lastres** and **Villaviciosa**.

Lastres

LASTRES, a couple of kilometres north of Colunga, off the Santander–Gijón highway, is a tiny fishing village built on the cliffside with a port and a couple of good beaches on its outskirts. It has escaped much tourist attention so far and if you've just come from a few strenuous days' trekking in the Picos would be as good a spot as any to recuperate.

There are several **seafood restaurants** – *Casa Eutimio*, near the port, is a good one – and an excellent **hostal**, the *Miramar*, Bajada al Puerto (☎98/585 01 20; ③; be sure to ask for a room with a sea view). If you don't get in, the *Hostal Mary Paz* (☎98/585 02 61; ③), at the top of town, is a last resort, while if you've money to spare, there's also a luxury **hotel**, the *Palacio de los Vallados*, Pedro Villarta (☎98/585 04 44; ⑤).

Villaviciosa

VILLAVICIOSA, 30km from Gijón, is set in beautiful Asturian countryside, on the shores of the Río Villaviciosa, and with green rolling hills behind. There's a market on Wednesday and an atmospheric old town where you'll find the thirteenth-century church of Santa María and the best restaurants.

If you want to stay, *Pensión Sol*, c/Sol 27 (☎98/589 11 30; ②) is very friendly and has large airy rooms. The *Hotel Montse*, c/Arguero (☎98/589 15 16; ③) is a good mid-price choice. The **Turismo** (☎98/589 17 59) is in Parque Vallina.

Gijón and Avilés

Gijón and **Avilés** are Asturias' major industrial cities: daunting places, with their smoking factory chimneys, and best passed by if you are looking for a seaside holiday on this coast. However, each of the cities has something going for it: Gijón in its big-city "feel", nightlife and summer **film festival** (late June/early July); Avilés in its well-preserved old centre. In addition, both cities know how to party, especially during **Carnaval** (see box) and during **Semana Santa** (Easter week), when Avilés hosts some of the country's most spectacular parades.

Gijón

GIJÓN, the largest city in Asturias, was completely rebuilt after its destruction in the Civil War. It was the scene of one of the most intensive bombardments of the war, when in August 1936, miners armed with sticks of dynamite stormed the barracks of the Nationalist-declared army. The beleaguered colonel asked ships from his own side, anchored offshore, to bomb his men rather than let them be captured.

Once past the industrial outskirts, the city has quite a breezy, open feel about it, with a grid of streets backing onto the sands of the **Playa de San Lorenzo**, a surprisingly unpolluted beach. In winter, you'll find the occasional hardy surfer out here, while in the summer the whole city seems to descend for the afternoons and weekends. The old part of town, **Cimadevilla**, occupies a headland west of the beach. Its chief monument is the eighteenth–century **Palacio de Revillagigedo**, built in a splendid mix of neo-Baroque and neo-Renaissance styles; it houses occasional exhibitions. Facing the palace, in the centre of the square, is a statue of Pelayo, the seventh-century king who began the Reconquest.

West again from Cimadevilla is a pretty **harbour** area, a focus for the city's evening and weekend *paseo*. This apart, there's little more in the way of sights – though Gijón offers serious shopping, if that's of interest – other than a few scattered museums. The most interesting of these is the bagpipe museum, the **Museo de Gaita**, Paseo Dr Fleming (daily 10am–8pm), an amazing array of instruments from all over the Celtic world and beyond.

Practicalities

Gijón's city centre is a fairly small area, just south of the old town and headland. Its three main squares, separated by a couple of blocks each, are, from north to south, Plaza del Humedal, Plaza del Carmen and Plaza del Marques (flanked by the palace described above). Two of the **train stations** (FEVE and RENFE local services) and the **bus station** (a wonderful piece of art deco) are just off Plaza del Humedal. Long distance *RENFE* services use a third train station on Avda. de Juan Carlos I. The **Turismo** (☎98/534 60 46) is off the Plaza del Marques.

Finding **accommodation** is rarely a problem. There are plenty of good *pensiones* including *Pensión Argentina*, c/San Bernardo 30 (☎98/533 44 81; ②), *Pensión Gonzalez*, in the same building (☎98/535 58 63; ②), and *La Posada de Morgan*, c/Pedro Duro 4 (☎98/535 60 36; ③). In the mid-price category try *La Botica*, c/San Bernardo 2 (☎98/534 50 33; ④), a comfortable *hostal* in the old town, or *Hostal-Residencia Manjon*, Plaza Marqués 1 (☎98/535 23 78; ③), which has a great location – ask for a room overlooking the harbour. Gijón's most luxurious hotel is the *Parador Molino Viejo*, Parque de Isabel la Católica (☎98/537 05 11; ⑤), sited in a park at the east end of the beach.

The streets around the seafront and immediately behind contain a mass of little **café-restaurants**, all reasonably priced and most with a *menú*. Fish is a speciality here particularly at *Pulperia a Caldevra*, c/Campa Torres and *Casa Justo*, Avda. del Hermanos Felgueroso 50, a superb *sidrerira* (cider house) with a seafood restaurant behind. *El Cartero*, c/Cienfugos 30 serves *sidra* to drink and *sidra*-cooked dishes. For traditional Asturian fare including *fabada*, a rich sausage and bean stew, try *Casa Zabala*, c/Viz Compgrade (☎98/534 17 31; closed Sun & Feb). One of Gijón's more renowned and upmarket restaurants is the century-old *La Pondala*, Avda. Dionisio Cifuentes, Somio area (☎98/536 11 60; closed Thurs & Nov), famous for its rice and seafood dishes.

Nightlife centres around the area known as **La Ruta**, a grid enclosed by c/ Santa Lucia, c/Buen Suceso and c/Rosa, five minutes' walk from the harbour. *Chevis* is a good place to start; *Bulevar*, down towards the harbour, plays good music and serves *carijillos*. Later on, the **club and disco** scene is focused on an area to the west of the beach: *Amnesia*, c/Jacobo Olaneta, plays up-to-date dance music and has a wild atmosphere; *Quimica*, further down the road, is similar but smaller. For insomniacs there are some all-nighters: *Tik*, in the Somio area, and *La Fabrica*, south of town; they play *bakalao* till 8am and noon.

Lastly, Gijón is home to one of the country's premier **football** clubs, **Sporting Gijón**; they play at a stadium just east of the beach.

Avilés

AVILÉS, 20km from Gijón and inland, has most of the Asturian steel industry, and the unwelcome honour of being one of Europe's most polluted cities. As you approach, from any direction, it's not hard to see why: line upon line of grim factories ring the town, putting off even the hardiest of travellers. But press on to the tiny, arcaded old centre of town and you can forget they exist.

This **old district**, strewn with fourteenth- and fifteenth-century churches and palaces, is about five minutes' walk from the bus station and not difficult to find. Most of the shops, bars and places to stay are here, too, and there's also a large and very pretty park, the Parque Muelle. Among several churches worth a closer look are **San Nicholas** in c/Ferreria, which contains the tomb of Don Pedro de Avilé, erstwhile governor of Florida, and **San Francisco**, in the street of the same name, with its Renaissance cloister and thirteenth-century fresco. There are three superb palaces too, notably Baroque **Camposagrado**, on c/de la Fruta; the **Palacio de Marqués de Ferrera** in Plaza de España; and the **Palacio de Llano Ponte**, now a cinema.

Practicalities

Avilés is a good transport junction and you may well find yourself here changing buses or trains. The main **bus station** is opposite the Parque Muelle, although *Autobuses Hernandez* (☎98/575 06 89) are based in Parque de las Meanas. The **FEVE station** is on

---

CARNAVÁL IN ASTURIAS

Carnavál, the *mardi gras* week of drinking, dancing and excess, takes place in early March. In Spain, the celebrations are reckoned to be at their wildest in Tenerife, Cadiz and Asturias – and in particular, **Avilés**.

Events begin in **Avilés** on the **Saturday** before Ash Wednesday, when virtually the entire city dons fancy dress and takes to the streets. Many costumes are bizarre works of art ranging from toothbrushes to mattresses and packets of sweets. By nightfall, anyone without a costume is likely to be drenched in some form of liquid, as gangs of nuns, Red Indians and pirates roam the streets. Calle Galiana is central to the action, and the local fire brigade traditionally hoses down the street, and any passing revellers, with foam. A parade of floats also makes its way down this street, amid the frenzy.

The festivities, which include live music, fireworks and fancy dress competitions, last till dawn. It's virtually impossible to find accommodation but the celebrations continue throughout Asturias during the following week, so after a full night night of revelling you can just head on to the next venue. The first buses leave town at 6.45am.

Sunday is, in fact, a rest day before *Carnavál* continues in **Gijón** on the **Monday** night. Much the same ensues and fancy dress is again essential; La Ruta is the place to be for the start of the night, with people and events shifting between Plaza Mayor and the harbour area till dawn. On **Tuesday** night, the scene shifts to **Oviedo**: the crowds are smaller here and events are less frantic again, but a fair part of the city again dons costume. There's a parade along Calle Uria, a midnight fireworks display in the Plaza Escandelera, and live bands in the Plaza Mayor.

Finally, on the Friday after Ash Wednesday, **Mieres**, a mining town, just east of Oviedo, plays host to *Carnavál*. Events take place in an area known as Calle del Vicio, which locals claim contains the highest concentration of bars in the province.

c/Muelle and **RENFE** on c/de los Telares, both a short walk from the centre of town. The **Turismo** (☎98/554 43 52) is in the centre, off Plaza de España, at c/Ruiz Gomez 21.

Staying in the city is surprisingly tricky as **accommodation** is scarce, and the few reasonably priced *hostales* are invariably full of businesspeople. At the bottom end of the scale try *Hostal Rivero*, c/Rivero 39 (☎98/554 23 19; ①), just off Plaza de España or *Pensión Villablanca*, c/El Acero 5 (☎98/554 51 70). More expensive, the *Pensión Conde*, c/del Doctor Graino, third left off c/de la Camara (③), is clean and friendly. The upmarket *Hotel San Felix*, Avda. de Lugo 48 (☎98/556 51 46; ④) is slightly out of town.

The streets around Plaza de España are full of promising **bars and restaurants**, in particular c/del Ferreria, c/Rivero and c/Galiana: *Cataguyo* is a good *sidreria* at the end of c/Galiana with inexpensive food at the bar and a restaurant at the back. Elsewhere, *Casa Lin*, Avda. Telares 3, is a beautiful *sidreria* with excellent seafood, and *Casa Tataguyo*, Plaza Carbayedo 6, is a beautiful 1870s *mesón,* serving Asturian specialities; both are moderately priced. Late night, there are music bars on c/Galiana, and an all-nighter, *La Real*, at c/González Albarca 6, off Plaza de la Merced.

The Picos de Europa

The **PICOS DE EUROPA**, although not the highest mountains in Spain, are the favourite of many walkers, trekkers and climbers. The range is a miniature masterpiece: a mere forty kilometres across in either direction, shoehorned in between three great **river gorges**, and straddling the provinces of Asturias, León and Cantabria. Asturians see the mountains as a symbol of their national identity, and celebrate a cave-church at **Covadonga**, in the west of the range, as the birthplace of Christian Spain.

Walks in the Picos de Europa are amazingly diverse, considering the size of the region, and they include trails for all levels of activity – from a casual morning's walk to two- and three-day treks. The most spectacular and popular walks are along the twelve-kilometre **Cares Gorge** – a route you can take in whole or part – and around the high peaks reached from a cablecar (*teleférico*) at **Fuente Dé**. But there are dozens of other paths and trails, both along the river valleys and woodlands, and up in the mountains. Take care if you go off the marked trails: the slowly undulating plateaus you appreciate from a distance can too easily turn out to be a series of chasms and gorges that entail backtracking, winding around and scrambling up to points you never wished to be at.

In addition to the walking, the Picos **wildlife** is a major attraction. In the Cares Gorge you're likely to see griffon vultures, kestrels, black redstarts, rock thrushes, and, most exciting of all for the initiated, wallcreepers. Wild and domestic goats abound, with some unbelievably inaccessible high mountain pastures. Wolves are easy to imagine in the grey boulders of the passes, but bears, despite local gossip, and their picturesque appearances on the tourist board maps, are not a likely sight. An inbred population of about sixty specimens of *Ursus ibericus* remains in the eastern mountains, most of them tagged with radio transmitters.

The Picos has long been on the map for trekkers and, over the last few years, as road access has opened up the gorges and peaks, has been brought increasingly into the mainstream of tourism. The most popular areas can get very crowded in July or August, as can the narrow roads, and the *teleférico* at Fuente Dé. If you have the choice, and you are content with lower-level walks, spring is best, when the valleys are gorgeous and the peaks still snowcapped.

Approaches

You can approach – and leave – the Picos along half a dozen roads: from León, to the south; Santander and the coast, to the northeast; Oviedo and Cangas de Onis, to the northwest. Our accounts of the regions and routes are arranged in six sections:

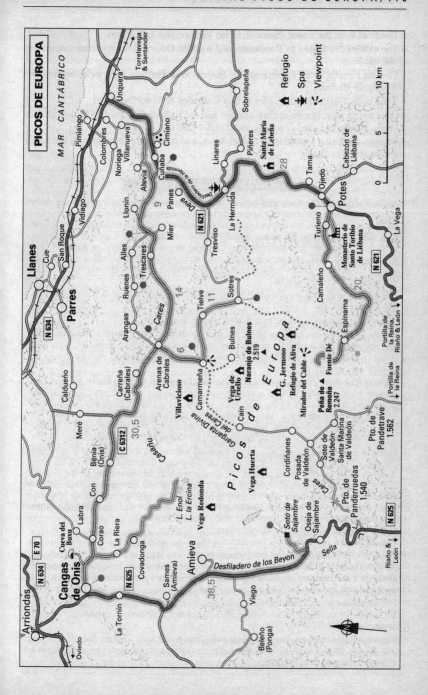

PICOS DE EUROPA

Refugio
Spa
Viewpoint

MAR CANTÁBRICO

Torrelavega & Santander
Unquera
Cabezón de Liébana
Sobrelapeña
Pimiango
Colombres
Villanueva
Noriega
Cuñaba
Cimiano
Santa María de Lebeña
Piñeres
Linares
Tama
Ojedo
Vidiago
San Roque
Cue
Mier
Alles
Llonín
Deva
Panes
N 621
La Hermida
Tresviso
Turieno
Potes
La Vega
Llanes
Parres
N 634
Ruenes
Trescares
Cares
Tielve
Sotres
Monasterio de Santo Toribio de Liébana
Camaleño
N 621
Calabero
Arangas
Arenas de Cabrales
Carreña (Cabrales)
Camarmeña
Villavicioso
Bulnes
Naranjo de Bulnes 2.519
G. Jermoso
Refugio de Aliva
Fuente Dé
Espinama
Vega de Urriello
Mirador del Cable
Peña de Remoña 2.247
Portilla de la Reina, Riaño & León
Meré
Benia (Onís)
C 6312
30,5
Casaño
Cain
Garganta Divina del Cares
Vega Huerta
Cordiñanes
Posada de Valdeón
Soto de Valdeón
Santa Marina de Valdeón
Pto. de Pandetrave 1.562
Portilla de la Reina
Labra
Con
L. Enol
L. la Ercina
Vega Redonda
Cares
Pto. de Panderruedas 1.540
N 625
Corao
La Riera
Cangas de Onís
N 634
E 70
Cueva del Buxu
Covadonga
Sames (Amieva)
Amieva
Soto de Sajambre
Oseja de Sajambre
Sella
Riaño & León
Arriondas
La Tornín
Desfiladero de los Beyon
38,5
Viego
Beleño (Ponga)
Oviedo

0 5 10 km

28
20
9
14
11
6

● The road from the coast (Santander/San Vicente; N621) to **Potes**.

● The valley from **Potes to Espinama** and **Fuente Dé** – and the mountains at the top of the *teleférico*.

● The trail north from **Espinama to Sotres and Bulnes**, and treks around the **Naranjo de Bulnes**.

● The **Cares Gorge** and the valley of **Las Cabrales** at its northern end.

● Over to the west: the **Sajambre** villages and the **Sella valley** road (N625) to Cangas de Onis; **Riaño** and the León road, south of the Picos.

● **Cangas de Onis**, **Covadonga** and its lakes, and treks from there up into the northern sierras of the Picos.

PICOS PRACTICALITIES

Accommodation *Pensiones* and *hostales* have proliferated in recent years in the more popular villages, but whenever you can it is worth phoning ahead to book a room – especially in summer or at weekends. Up in the mountains there are a number of alpine *refugios*, which range from organized hostels to free, unstaffed huts where you'll need to bring your own food and sleeping bag. Camping beside the *refugios* is accepted, and there are about half a dozen campsites, too, scattered around the villages. Camping outside these sites, you are subject to on-the-spot fines of 6000ptas if you're found in the wrong place at the wrong time.

Banks are located on the periphery of the region: at Potes, Arenas de Cabrales, Riaño and Cangas de Onis.

Bikes Mountain bikes can be rented at various outlets in Potes.

Buses There are bus services along the main roads but they're limited to one or two a day and very sketchy out of season. You can complement these, however, with bike rental, and hitching – which is easy enough with fellow tourists, and can often be arranged at campsites.

Climate There are good days even in the depths of winter for walking below the snowline, though high altitudes dictate a spring–summer walking season, from late June to September, for mountain treks. At all times of year, be warned that clouds can build up very fast and Asturian rain is cold and heavy; alternatively, or in tandem, sudden mists can blot out visibility. Accordingly, rain gear and a compass are virtually mandatory. Reliable water sources are sporadic along the trails and it's always worth carrying a bottle.

Equipment Walking in summer, or on low-level routes, you don't necessarily need any experience or special equipment, at least on the routes described in this guide; all of these treks are practicable as long as you're reasonably fit. If you wander off the marked routes or attempt any actual climbing, proper equipment and experience are essential – otherwise you may quickly find yourself in trouble. What with the abundance of sharp, loose stones, and stiff gradients, **walking boots** are a distinct plus, and **sunglasses** are useful to combat the glare.

Maps Best are those printed by the *Federación Española de Montañismo* (entitled "Los Tres Macizos", single sheet at 1:50,000), and in cooperation with the *IGN* ("Macizo del Cornión"). *Editorial Alpina* covers the western and central massifs in two 1:25,000 sheets. All these maps are old but still fairly accurate, despite recent road building, and most are available in the Picos at Cangas de Onis, Potes, Sotres, Bulnes or Arenas de Cabrales.

Mountain Federations You can get further information on trekking and climbing in the Picos from these organizations: *Federacíon Asturiana de Montaña*, c/Melquiades Alvarez 16, Oviedo (☎98/521 10 99; Mon–Fri 6.30–7.30pm) and *Federacíon Cantabria*, c/Rubio 2, Santander (☎942/373378).

Potholing Federations For details on potholing in the area, contact Apt. de Correos 540, Oviedo (☎98/521 17 90; Fri 7–9pm), Apt. de Correos 51, Santander or at c/Alfonso X el Sabio 1, Burgos (☎947/222427).

Note that the "road" shown on some maps linking **Fuente Dé** with the **Portilla de la Reina–Posada de Valdeon road** is a jeep track, practicable only in summer and only to those who know exactly where they're going.

From the coast to Potes

The N621 heads inland from the coast at **UNQUERA**, right on the Cantabria–Asturias border, between San Vicente de la Barquera and Llanes. From there, it follows the twisting course of the Río Deva, past **PANES**, where the C6312 forks west, along the upper reaches of the Rio Cares to Arenas de Cabrales (see p.422) and Cangas de Onis. There are buses along this latter route (currently 8am and 5.30pm) from **Colombres**, just west of Unquera; you can also pick them up in Panes, around half an hour later, from the *Bar de la Cortina* across the bridge.

Panes to Potes: the Deva Gorge

Continuing from Panes towards Potes, you enter the eerily impressive gorge of the Río Deva, the **Desfiladero de La Hermida**, whose sheer sides are so high that they deny the village of **LA HERMIDA** any sunlight from November to April. There are one or two places to stay here if you want to break your journey; the *Hostal Marisa* (②), on the road out towards Potes, is clean and modern. From nearby **Urdón**, a rough road leads west to Sotres (see p.419); it's a pleasant walk, with mountains looming up around you.

Around 10km beyond La Hermida, the village of **LEBEÑA** lies just east of the main road. It is worth a detour to see the church of **Santa María**, built in the early tenth century by "Arabized" Christian craftsmen and considered the supreme example of Mozarabic architecture. It makes an interesting visit with its thoroughly Islamic geometric motifs and repetition of abstract forms, and is set in beautiful countryside – the Hermida gorge having by now opened out into sheltered vineyards and orchards.

Potes

POTES is the main base on the east side of the Picos, still not all that high above sea level at 500m but beautifully situated in the shadow of tall white peaks. It is a small town and market centre (there's an open-air **flea market** on Monday mornings), and although devoted largely to tourism retains some identity beyond it.

It is a useful place to change money, with the last banks before the mountains, and, if you haven't already done so, to buy **trekking maps**. The latter are available from the **Turismo** (June–Sept Mon–Fri 10am–1pm & 4–8pm, Sat 10am–1pm; ☎942/730820), just behind the *Ayuntamiento* in Plaza Jesús del Monasterio, or from *Fotos Bustamente*, in the same square. You can rent **mountain bikes** at *Wences* (1500ptas a day plus your passport as deposit) next to the *Ayuntamiento*.

There is a good choice of places to **stay** in and immediately around Potes. If you want a room in town, *Casa Cayo*, c/Cántabra 6 (☎942/730150; ③) is very pleasant, with a lively bar and good-value restaurant downstairs; *Casa Cuba* (☎942/730064; ①), at the end of the same road, is much more basic. For a bit more comfort, try the modern *Picos de Europa*, San Roque 16 (☎942/730005; ③), the first hotel on the left coming into town from Panes; the *Rubio* (☎942/730015; ④), next door, which has its own garage; or the *Casa de Labranza* (☎942/732122; ③), 2km out of town in an idyllic setting.

If you're unsure just how to tackle the Picos and don't speak much Spanish, the *Casa Gustavo Guesthouse* (☎942/732010; ③) is ideal. It is owned by two English people, who operate **mountain-biking, skiing and canoeing trips** for residents (and allcomers), and can arrange nights in the nearby *refugio* at Tama. Another good place for activities is *El Portalon*, 6km south of Potes at La Vega de Liebana (☎942/730548; ②). This is a hostel, with dormitory rooms, and an "Escuela del aire libre", offering **paragliding**, mountain biking, climbing and trekking.

There are two **buses** daily from Potes to Espinama (1pm and 8pm; returning from Espinama at 9am and 2.10pm). *Palomera* services run to Unquera three times a day (7am, 9.45am and 5.45pm).

Turieno, Liebana and Piasca

Turieno, 3km west of Potes along the road to Espinama, is a quiet village, in sight of some tall peaks and well placed for acclimatizing to the mountains, with lots of short walks along narrow mule tracks to villages where the locals don't see many tourists and may well open up the bar just for you. The walk to the hamlets of **Lon** and **Brez** is especially worthwhile, through a profusion of wild flowers and butterflies. In Turieno, there's an attractive campsite, *La Isla* (☎942/730896; open April–Oct), situated behind an orchard, and with **pony-trekking** on offer. If they're full the *San Pelayo* campsite (☎942/730597; April–Oct), a little further up the road towards Espinama, is just as good and has its own pool.

Close by Turieno, but reached on a different road from Potes, is the eighth-century **Monasterio de Santo Toribio de Liebana**, one of the earliest and most influential of medieval Spain. Although much-reconstructed, it preserves fine Romanesque and Gothic details, the largest claimed piece of the True Cross, and some extraordinary Mozarabic paintings (now replaced by reproductions) of the Visions of the Apocalypse.

Architecturally more important is the church of **Santa Maria Piasca**, 6km south of Potes. This is pure Romanesque in style, beautifully proportioned, and with some terrific exterior sculpture. Like Santo Toribio it was once a Cluniac monastery, and is flanked by the ruins of monastic and conventual buildings.

Potes to Espinama and Fuente Dé

The road from **Potes to Espinama and Fuente Dé** runs below a grand sierra of peaks – the Macizo Oriental – and past a handful of villages, built on the slopes. In summer, and at weekends, there is near constant traffic towards the *teleférico* at Funte Dé, which has spoilt the villages on the road. However, all have attractive walking, with woodland and streams, and from Espinama you can cut across the range to Sotres.

Cosgaya

COSGAYA, midway between Potes and Espinama, can be an attractive base. If you feel like a little luxury before or after trekking, the Alpine-looking *Hotel del Oso* (☎942/730418; ④) is the place, set in neat paddocks beside a tidy stream, and with a swimming pool in summer. The *Hostal La Casona* (③), a seventeenth-century farmhouse, and hidden away in the woods off the side of the road is equally relaxing. Inexpensive rooms are provided by the *Mesón de Cosgaya* (☎942/730147; ①), which also does excellent meals.

Espinama

Twenty kilometres from Potes, **ESPINAMA** is really into the mountains. Like Cosgaya, its position and one-time isolation is marred by the road running through, but below it a stream bubbles its way between sagging farmhouses, crossed by unsteady wooden footbridges, and stray animals wander along the pathways and around the locked, tumbledown church.

There is comfortable accommodation at any of the four **hostales**: the *Vicente Campo* and its annexe, *Mesón Máximo* (☎942/730119; ③); the *Remoña* (☎942/730495; ③); the *Puente Deva* (☎942/730119; ③); and the *Nevandi* (☎942/730872; ③). All of these serve meals, with the *Vicente Campo* having the edge, if only for its feel of a wayfarers' inn, and a crackling fire in winter. The village also has a grocery store which provides for picnics and trekking snacks.

Fuente Dé and the teleférico

The road comes to a halt 4km past Espinama, in a steep-sided cul-de-sac of rock. This is the source of the Río Deva; debate as to whether its name should be Fuente de Deva or Fuente de Eva has left it called simply **Fuente Dé**. There is no settlement here, save for a modern **parador** (April–Oct only; ☎942/730001; ④), a **campsite**, *El Redondo*, and a *teleférico* or cable car, with ticket office and café attached.

The **teleférico** lurches alarmingly up 900m of sheer cliff. It's an extremely popular excursion throughout the year, and in summer a wait to ascend of between two and five hours is by no means uncommon. A system of numbered tickets (500ptas each way) means that you can wait in the shelter of the **café-bar** at the bottom, as long as your Spanish is up to interpreting the garbled announcements of the PA. Remember that you may well have to queue again for an hour or two before coming down, which is not nearly so congenial in the mountain chill.

At the top is an extraordinary mountainscape, in which Spanish day-trippers wander around in bathing suits. However, within a few minutes' walk there is hardly a soul. If you are on for a walk, you can follow a bulldozer track 4km to the **Refugio de Aliva** (open June 1–Sept 30, with its own *fiesta* on July 10) which has *hostal*-like rooms and prices, and a restaurant. From there, you can wind your way back down to Espinama on another rough track. It is also possible to arrange a lift in a **jeep** from the top of the *teleférico*, either to Aliva or to Sotres (see below).

Espinama to Sotres – and beyond

The **trek from Espinama to Sotres** is an enjoyable day's outing. A dirt track runs the whole length, practicable by jeep, or around five hours on foot. If you are walking, set out north from the *Bodega Peña Vieja* in Espinama, under an arching balcony, and on to the twisting track behind. This, climbing stiffly, winds past hand-cut hay fields and through groups of barns, until tall cliffs on either side rise to form a natural gateway. Through this you enter a different landscape of bare summer pasture, streams running through rocky beds and close-cropped grass nibbled by flocks of sheep.

Over the divide the scenery changes again, into a mass of crumbling limestone. In spring or winter, the downhill stretch of track here is slippery and treacherous to all but goats – and perhaps jeeps. The hamlet of **Vegas de Sotres**, at the bottom of the hill, has a seasonal bar selling drinks; from there you need to climb again slightly to reach Sotres, which, when it appears, has a grim, almost fortified feel, clinging to a cliff edge above a stark green valley.

Sotres

SOTRES is an established walkers' base – it is a trailhead for some superb treks – and has three, fairly basic **places to stay**. The best of these is the *Pensión Cipriano* (①), which also has a *comedor* with a 750ptas *menú*; an unmarked *fonda* next door has dormitory bunks (*literas*) but is often taken up by school groups. A third *pensión* (②), across the way, offers similar rooms to the *Cipriano* at higher prices.

Casa Gallega, the village **store**, has provisions, and will do good meals with an hour or two's notice; they sell cured sheep's and cow's milk cheeses, as well as the five-month-fermented *cabrales*, a local speciality similar to Roquefort.

East to Tresviso and Urdón

Until the late 1980s, only a mulepath led east from Sotres to **Tresviso** and **Urdón** on the Panes–Potes road. This is now a paved road, though still a beautiful route. If you prefer your walking a bit rougher, you can cut down a footpath from this road, 4km out of Sotres, which leads through the **Valle de Sobra** to **La Hermida**; the final stretch is a spectacular switchback.

In **Tresviso** there are a couple of places to stay. The local bar has clean modern rooms (③), as does the restaurant, *La Taberna* (**☎**942/730160; ③).

West to Bulnes

Most walkers head west from **Sotres to Bulnes**, using a combination of the old, steep cobbled path and a new dirt road, which cuts from Sotres to **Invernales de Cabao** and up the broad, windy pass of **Pandébano**, tufted with heather, rocks, and endowed with the welcome *Bar de los Picos*. At present, the dirt road ends here, leaving just the old path, but it looks only a matter of time before it is extended all the way to Bulnes – whose cheesemakers, reasonably enough, have been agitating for a road to get their products out.

BULNES is actually a double village: Castillos and La Villa. All facilities are in La Villa, including a decent *albergue* (①), with a restaurant next door, and the *Bar Guillermina*, which sells T-shirts proclaiming the village a "friend to all mountaineers". Camping here is tolerated, too.

The Naranjo de Bulnes – and across the massif

From the pass at Pandébano and from Bulnes village there are well-used paths up to the **Vega de Urriello**, high pasture at the base of the **Naranjo de Bulnes**, a sugarloaf peak which is one of the "sights" of the Picos. The approach from Pandébano is easier, along a newly regraded track, taking between two and three hours. The direct path up from Bulnes is heavy-going, and could take up to six hours, with a slippery scree surface which can prove very difficult and at times dangerous. Once up on the plateau you'll find a *refugio*, and (a rarity in the Picos) a permanent spring, as well as large numbers of campers and rock-climbers, for whom the Naranjo is a popular target.

Seasoned trekkers equipped for an overnight stop can continue across the central massif to the top of the **Fuente Dé** funicular, through a roller-coaster landscape unforgiving of mistakes – go in a group and with proper gear. Alternatively, you can bypass Fuente Dé and instead make a slow lap around the highest peaks. This involves a night's camp at **Vega de Liordes** and a descent down the ravine of **Asotín**, ending at **Cordiñanes** at the top of the Cares Gorge.

The Cares Gorge

The **Cares Gorge** is the classic walk in the Picos, and deservedly so. A massive cleft, more than 1000m deep and some 12km long, it separates the central massif from the western one of Cornión. The most enclosed section **between Caín and Poncebos** bores through awesome terrain along an amazing footpath hacked out of the cliff face. It's maintained in excellent condition by the water authorities (it was built to service a hydroelectric scheme) and is perfectly safe. With reasonable energy you can walk it in well under a day – or you could, like many Spanish daytrippers, get a taste of it by just walking a section from Caín.

The usual **starting point** is from the southern trailheads, **Posada de Valdeón** and **Caín**, which can be reached from Potes via Portilla de la Reina, from Cangas de Onis via Oseja de Sajambre, or from León via Riaño. There is a daily bus/Land Rover to Posada de Valdeón from **Portilla de la Reina**, an odd little hamlet at the bottom of a lichen-covered chasm of limestone; Portilla itself is on the León–Potes bus line. On foot, you can reach Posada de Valdeón from Fuente Dé in about four hours, over a mix of dirt tracks and footpaths; the occasional Land Rover makes the trip in summer.

Access from the north is, if anything, easier with a Land Rover bus connecting **Poncebos**, the northern trailhead, with Arenas de Cabrales – which has a regular bus service to Cangas de Onis, Llanes and Panes. Poncebos can also be reached on foot from Bulnes – see below.

Santa Marina and Posada de Valdeón, Cordiñanes and Caín

The bus from Portilla de la Reina gives out at **SANTA MARINA DE VALDEÓN**, transferring its passengers to a Land Rover for the final 3km ride on the narrow lane leading down to Posada. Santa Marina is a lovely village – quite unspoilt, still – with a bar and a **campsite**, *El Cares* (☎987/270476), and as yet no other accommodation.

POSADA DE VALDEÓN is very much on the tourist trail, these days, with building sites everywhere, though nothing can detract from the views of the huge mountains that hem in the valley to the south and above Posada. The most characterful **accommodation** is at the *Pensión Begoña* (☎987/740516; ③), an old *fonda* given a recent splash of paint. For meals, forget the *Begoña*, and follow signs to the *Sidreria La Asturiana*, at the edge of the village; it does excellent grills. There is a campsite, *El Valdeón* (☎987/742605), 3km east of the village at the hamlet of Soto de Valdeón.

The **Río Cares** runs through Posada and its gorge begins just north of the village. Over this first section – to Caín – it is relatively wide and is trailed by a road. However, it's still pretty delightful, with odd pockets of brilliant green meadows at the base of the cliffs. If you're pushed for time (or energy) there is a **Land Rover** service from Posada to the trailhead – 3000ptas per carload – and hitching is easy enough. Most people will prefer to walk the distance, though, and some of the tarmac can be bypassed by taking a dirt track from the lower end of Posada to the **Mirador del Tombo**, just past the village of Cordiñanes. From there to Caín it's around 6km, along a downhill road.

CORDIÑANES makes for a pleasant night's stop – a better, or at least quieter, base than Posada or Caín – and has a couple of small **pensiones**: *El Tombo* (☎987/740526; ③) and *El Rojo* (☎987/740523; ③). In summer, **CAÍN** itself is quite a honeypot, full of cars, groups, daytrippers and trekkers. It has a handful of bars and a new supermarket, plying the trade, and a **hostal**, *La Ruta* (☎987/740501; ③), right at the opening of the gorge path. Alternatively, you can camp in the meadow nearby for the princely sum of 200ptas (no amenities whatsoever).

Into the gorge

Just beyond Caín the valley opens out, then, following the river downstream, suddenly seems to disappear as a solid mountain wall blocks all but a thin vertical cleft. This is where **the gorge** really begins, the path along its course dramatically tunnelled within the rock in the early stages before emerging on to a broad, well-constructed and well-maintained catwalk.

The path owes its existence to a long-established hydroelectric scheme, for which a canal was constructed (often buried inside the mountain) all the way from Caín to Poncebos, and into which the river can be diverted in varying quantities. The footpath is still used for maintenance and each morning a power plant worker walks the entire length, checking water volume in the canal and waking up those who have elected to spend a night out in the mountains. If you feel like camping, but with more privacy, there is a side valley leading off to the east about 1km into the gorge.

The first stretch of the path is more of an engineering spectacle than anything else and in midsummer or at weekends is thronged with daytrippers strolling through the Gaudiesque tunnels and walkways. Once you get 4km or so from Caín, you're down to more committed walkers, and the mountains, freed of most waterworks paraphernalia, command your total attention. They rise pale and jagged on either side, with griffon vultures and other birds of prey circling the crags. The river drops steeply, some 150m below you at the first bridge but closer to 300m down by the end.

A little over halfway along, the canyon bends to the right and gradually widens along the **descent to Poncebos**. About 9km into the gorge an enterprising individual has cornered the market with a makeshift refreshments stand, handy as there's a final ascent before the end. From this uphill section another side path leads up to the bar, *hostal* and *mirador* at the cliffside village of **Camarmeña**, which has tremendous perspectives on the Naranjo de Bulnes peak. However, most people stick to the main route and finish at Poncebos.

Poncebos – and a trail to Bulnes

At **PONCEBOS** you'll find the *Fonda/Bar El Garganta del Cares* (②) and, a bit further down past the bridge (coming from Caín), next to the power plant, the modern *Hostal Poncebos* (☎98/584 50 47; ③). Either of these might be welcome facilities at the end of a long day, but they're a bit institutional and somewhat gloomy due to blocked sunlight. They are, incidentally, the only buildings at Poncebos – in no sense is the place a village. The hostal runs a Land Rover taxi service down to Arenas de Cabrales (see below), 6km north. If daylight permits, you might prefer to make the superb hour-and-a-half trek up the gorge of the Tejo stream to **Bulnes** (see p.420) and stay overnight there. The path begins over the photogenic medieval bridge of Jaya, located just to the right (south) at the end of the marked Cares path – there's no need to descend to the *fonda*.

Arenas de Cabrales

The foothill area to the north of the Picos is known as **Cabrales**, as is the delicious and exceptionally strong fermented sheep's cheese made in a dozen-odd villages here. The C6312 runs through the valley; there are buses four times a day (Mon–Sat) between Cangas de Onis and Arenas de Cabrales, two of which run through to Panes and on to the coast. If you're driving, the minor roads to the coast are pleasant, allowing you to bypass traffic on the Cangas road.

ARENAS DE CABRALES (Las Arenas on some maps) is the main village of this region: a friendly place, and an excellent first or last stop in the Picos. There are two good **hotels**, the *Naranjo de Bulnes* (☎98/845119; ③) and luxurious *Los Picos de Europa*, (☎98/584 54 91; ⑤), a pair of **fondas**, and a **campsite** (☎98/584 51 78), 1km to the east. If you find all of the accommodation full, there are two further *hostales* a couple of kilometres down the road in Carreña de Cabrales, and another, *El Ermitage* (②), on the road to Poncebos. Back in Arenas, the *Mesón Castaneu* has outstanding à la carte food at *menú* prices, while *Bar Palma* is a lively spot for an evening's drinking – they serve *queimadas* if you're in a large enough group.

Arenas also has a helpful **Turismo** (☎98/584 52 84), to fill you in on mountain or transport details, two **banks** and various stores. On the last Sunday in August it is host to the **Asturian Cheese Festival**, an excuse for plenty of dancing and music but, oddly enough, not all that much cheese.

Over to the west: the Sella valley and Riaño

The road running along the western end of the Picos, the N625 between Cangas de Onis and Riaño, is spectacular in its own right. Mountains rear to all sides and for much of the way the road traces the gorge of the **Río Sella**. The central section of this, the **Desfiladero de los Beyos**, is said to be the narrowest motorable gorge in Europe – a feat of engineering far surpassing anything in the Alps.

There are *EASA* **buses** (Mon–Fri) in each direction between Cangas and Oseja de Sajambre; from Cangas, twice weekly services run through Oseja to Riaño.

The Sajambre villages

Coming from Posada de Valdeón, you turn onto the N625 right by the 1290m **Puerto del Pontón**, a pass almost continually fogged in since the reservoir was built at Riaño to the south (see below). Heading north, the road passes through **OSEJA DE SAJAMBRE**, a very pretty village, high on the steep slope of a broad and twisting valley. Comfortable rooms and good **meals** are available at *Hostal de Pontón* (③), and cheaper beds at *Bar Minerv* (①), up on the hill.

Six kilometres beyond Oseja, to the east of the road, is **SOTO DE SAJAMBRE**, an excellent base for walkers, with a single **hostal**, the *Peña Santa* (②). This is a possible starting point for a south-to-north traverse of the western Picos massif to the Lakes of Covadonga, as well as for treks in the valley of the Río Dobra.

Riaño and south towards León

South from the **Puerto del Pontón**, you descend to the spectacular **Pantano de Riaño** (see box). The creation of this reservoir flooded half a dozen villages and a swathe of farmland – leaving just the odd tree top above water.

The main village of the valley, **Riaño**, was relocated just above the reservoir, and has a hotel and a few bars. There are plans to turn it into a winter- and water-sports resort, though little has come of this so far.

RIAÑO: THE MAKING OF A RESERVOIR

Travelling in Asturias, you often see posters with the slogan "Don't let them destroy our Picos". The threat to the mountains is real: the Picos is a small range, and every year the despoliation of previously pristine areas seems to increase. The Asturians are doing what they can, but if you enter the Picos from the south, from León through Riaño, you'll see the worst that can (and has) happened – the loss of a whole valley.

In 1966 the Franco regime claimed right of eminent domain over the entire valley of **Riaño**, prior to turning it into a reservoir. Compensation of sorts was paid at that time, and then plans stalled until the 1980s, when the project was revived by the PSOE government. The inhabitants of Riaño, most of them children of those who had accepted the "settlement" in the 1960s, were forcibly evicted, with no further compensation offered. The newer generation erected a tent village overlooking their destroyed homes, but that too was bulldozed, after demonstrations broken up by riot police. On December 31, 1987, the dam was suddenly sealed, and flooding commenced. The authorities claimed that conditions were optimal – there was a storm in progress – but the reality was that the government had imposed a deadline and wanted no more protests.

The dam, clearly, has a value for the Spanish agricultural economy, irrigating the plains of León and Palencia to the south. But the investment came from outside corporations, and that's where the profits will go. The water from the reservoir will benefit no one locally.

Cangas de Onis, Covadonga and the lakes

The main routes between the Picos and central Asturias meet at **Cangas de Onis**, a busy market town, and a bit of a traffic bottleneck, especially so in summer and at weekends. If you're not intent on a visit to **Covadonga**, with its pilgrim shrine and **mountain lakes** beyond, you may prefer to make a detour.

Cangas de Onis

The distant peaks around **CANGAS DE ONIS** provide a magnificent backdrop to its big sight – a **Roman bridge**, festooned with ivy, which you'll see splashed across the front of many Asturian tourist brochures. The town's other attraction, less photogenic but perhaps more curious, is the **Capilla de Santa Cruz**, a fifteenth-century rebuilding of an eighth-century chapel founded over a Celtic dolmen stone. This, like the Liebana monastery at Potes, is among the earliest Christian sites in Spain, and Cangas, as an early residence of the fugitive Asturian-Visigothic kings, lays claim to the title of "First Capital of Christian Spain". Today, however, it belies such history: a functional town, muscled-in upon by new developments, though good for a comfortable night and a solid meal after a spell in the mountains.

Most facilities lie within a few hundred metres of the **bus station** (next to the *Café Colón*). A **Turismo** kiosk (summer Mon 10am–2pm, Tues–Sat 10am–2pm & 4–10pm, winter Mon 10am–2pm, Tues–Sat 10am–2pm & 4–7pm) is on Avda. Covadonga, outside the *Ayuntamiento*. More comprehensive information for trekkers and mountaineers is available from *Compañia de Guías de Montaña*, c/Emilio Laria 2 (☎98/584 87 16).

There's a wide range of **accommodation**. Good choices include the *Hostal El Sella* (☎98/584 80 11; ②), by the old bridge; an unmarked *pensión* (☎98/584 90 78; ②), right opposite; *Pensión Audelina* (☎98/584 83 50; ②) and *Fonda/Bar El Chófer* (☎98/584 83 05; ③), just off the main street; or, for more comfort, *Hotel Ventura* (☎98/584 82 01; ④) on the Avda. Covadonga. The best **campsite** in the area is *La Mata* (☎98/584 42 30; summer only) at Monte Oscuro, 12km out of town along the Arenas de Cabrales road; this is also a fine restaurant (meals include veggie options), and has bicycles, canoes and horses for hire.

Freshwater fish and *sidra* are the specialities in Cangas **bars and restaurants**. The *Sidrería/Mesón Puente Romano* by the bridge has a grand outdoor setting, with good value *menús*. *Restaurante Los Arco*s, on Avda. Covadonga, has a less romantic site but excellent, if slightly pricey, cooking.

Covadonga and the lakes

The **Reconquista** is said to have begun at **COVADONGA**, 11km southeast of Cangas in a northerly sierra of the Picos. Here in 718 the Visigothic King Pelayo and a small group of followers repulsed the Moorish armies – at odds, according to Christian chronicles, of 31 to 400,000. In reality the Moors can hardly have been more than an isolated expeditionary force and their sights were already turned to the more lucrative lands beyond the Pyrenees, where in 732 they were defeated at Poitiers by Charles Martel. But the symbolism of the event is at the heart of Asturian, and Spanish, national history, and the defeat probably did allow the Visigoths to regroup, slowly expanding Christian influence over the northern mountains of Spain and Portugal.

Certainly, Covadonga is a serious religious shrine, with huge signs in the streets proclaiming: "Remember – you have come to pray". The focus of the pilgrimage is the **cave** (8am–10pm; free) said to have been used by Pelayo. This shrine, containing the hero's sarcophagus, is now a chapel, sited impressively on the side of a mountain above a waterfall and lake. Below is a grandiose nineteenth-century pink basilica, and, opposite this, a **Museo del Tesoro** (11.30am–2pm & 4–6pm; 50ptas) displaying various religious artefacts.

There are a few **fondas** and **hostales** on the road into town. Good choices include the *Hospedería del Peregrino* (☎98/584 60 47; ③), which has an excellent restaurant, and the *Casa Prieno* (③).

Lakes Enol and Ercina

Beyond Covadonga the road begins to climb sharply, and after 12km you reach the **mountain lakes** of **Enol** and **Ercina**. These are connected by a daily bus service from June 15 to September 15 (passing Cangas at 11.15am, Covadonga at 12.15pm and returning from the lakes at 4.45pm), but it's not difficult to hitch if you miss out. The **Mirador de la Reina**, a short way before the lakes, gives an inspiring view of the assembled peaks.

The **lakes** themselves are placid and swimmable, and subject to quirky weather. Even if it is misty at Cangas or Covadonga, you may find that the cloud cover disperses abruptly just before the lakes; conversely, sunny weather down below is no guarantee of the same higher up, so come prepared. There is a **refugio** and a **campsite** at the southwest corner of Lake Enol.

The Cornión Massif

From the lakes a good path leads east-southeast within three hours to the **Vega de Ario**, where there's a newly refurbished **refugio**, lots of campers on the meadow, and unsurpassed **views** across the Cares Gorge to the highest peaks in the central Picos. Unless you have good mountaineering skills for the steep descent to the Cares, this is something of a dead end, since to cross the bulk of the western peaks you'll need to backtrack at least to Lake Ercina to resume progress south.

Most walkers, however, trek south from the lakes to the **Vega Redonda refugio**. This popular route initially follows a dirt track but later becomes an actual path through a curious landscape of stunted oaks and turf. Vega Redonda, about three hours' walk, overlooks the very last patches of green on the Asturias side of the Cornión massif.

Beyond the Vega Redonda refugio, walks are in a different category of difficulty altogether. Nerve and skill are required to cross the barren land to **Llago Huerta**, the next feasible overnight spot – and like Redonda popular with pot-holers who disappear down various chasms in the area. From Llago Huerta it's possible to descend to Cordiñanes, Santa Marina de Valdeón or Oseja de Sajambre.

Oviedo

The principal reason for visiting **OVIEDO**, the Asturian capital, is to see three small **churches**. They are among the most remarkable in Spain, built in a style unique to Asturias which emerged in the wake of the Visigoths and before the Romanesque style had spread south from France. All of them date from the first half of the ninth century, a period of almost total isolation for the Asturian Kingdom, which was then just 65km by 50km in area and the only part of Spain under Christian rule. Oviedo became the centre of this outpost in 810 with the residence of King Alfonso II, son of the victorious Pelayo (see Covadonga, above).

Churches aside, modern Oviedo has little to hold visitors. Like its fellow Asturian cities, it has a fair bit of heavy industry, while much of the centre is devoted to local government offices and the like. The university, however, adds a bit of youthful life; and there are some excellent restaurants, dozens of bars, and, of course, *sidrerias*. The city has excellent transport links, too, with buses to just about everywhere in the province, and trains on both the FEVE and RENFE lines.

Orientation and accommodation

Central Oviedo is bounded by a loop of roads. At its heart is the extensive **Campo de San Francisco**; the **cathedral** is a couple of blocks to the east of this, with the **Plaza Mayor** and **Ayuntamiento** to its south. There is a **Turismo** (Mon–Fri 9am–2pm & 4–6pm, Sat 10am–2pm; ☎98/521 33 85) in Plaza Alfonso II, the cathedral square.

Coming in by public transport, points of arrival can be a little confusing. There are two separate **FEVE train stations** in addition to the regular **RENFE** one on c/Uría (which serves León). The *FEVE Asturias*, next to the *RENFE*, is for the line towards Santander; the so-called *FEVE Basque*, on c/Victor Chavarri, oddly enough serves stations west to El Ferrol; they're a good fifteen minutes' apart, so don't try to make too tight a connection.

Most long distance **buses** run from an underground station in the Plaza Primo de Rivera, with the important exception of *Turytrans* services, to inland Asturias and the smaller coastal towns, which run from opposite the *FEVE Asturias*, just above the plaza; its ticket office is on c/Jeronimo Ibran.

Accommodation

Accommodation is fairly plentiful, with a concentration of **hostales** on c/de Uría, opposite the *RENFE* train station, and along c/9 de Mayo and c/de Caveda, parallel. Some recommendations:

Pensión Arco Iris, c/de Uría 39 (no phone). Clean and friendly with large rooms. ③.

Pensión Arcos, just off Plaza Mayor (☎98/521 47 73). Nice site in the heart of old Oviedo; friendly and good value. ③.

Hostal Asturias, c/de Uría 16 (☎98/521 46 95). Central location in a grand old building. ③.

Hostal Belmonte, c/de Uría 31 (☎98/524 10 20). Pleasant and recently refurbished. ③.

Hotel Favila, c/de Uría 37 (☎98/525 38 77). A comfortable business hotel. ④.

Pensión Fidalgo, c/Jovellanos 5–3° (☎98/521 32 87). A pretty, well-kept *pensión*, just north of the cathedral. Ask for the range of (negotiable) room prices. ③–④.

Gran Hotel España, c/Jovellanos 2 (☎98/522 05 96). A grand (and expensive) hotel, as the name claims, close by the cathedral. ⑥.

Hostal México, c/de Uría 25 (☎98/524 04 04). A good mid-priced option with its own bar. ③.

Pensión Riesgo, c/9 de Mayo 16 1° (☎98/521 89 45). A pleasant, tiny *pensión*. ②.

The town and churches

Around the cathedral, enclosed by scattered sections of the medieval town walls, is what remains of **Old Oviedo**: a compact, attractive quarter in what, it has to be said, is a fairly bleak industrial city. The cathedral aside – and the churches on the periphery – monuments are thin on the ground. As at Gijón, much was destroyed in the Civil War when Republican Asturian miners laid siege to the Nationalist garrison; the defenders were relieved by a Gallego detachment when on the brink of surrender.

The Cathedral and around

In the ninth century, King Alfonso II built a chapel, the **Cámara Santa**, to house the holy relics rescued from Toledo when it fell to the Moors. Remodelled in the twelfth century, this now forms the inner sanctuary of Oviedo's **Catedral** (daily 9am–1pm & 3.30–6pm; 250ptas combined ticket to *Cámara Santa* and cloister), a Gothic structure at the heart of the modern city. The *Cámara Santa* (Holy Chamber) is in fact a pair of interconnecting chapels. The innermost, with its primitive capitals, is thought to be Alfonso's original building. The antechapel, rebuilt in 1109, is a quiet little triumph of Spanish Romanesque; each of the six columns supporting the vault is sculpted with a pair of superbly humanized apostles.

Around the cathedral, some of the city's ancient **palaces** – not least the archbishop's, opposite – are worth a look, though most are in government use and none are open to visitors. Of interest, too, is the **Museo Archeologico** (Mon–Sat 10am–1.30pm & 4.30–6.30pm, Sun 11am–1pm), immediately behind the cathedral in the former convent of San Vicente. This displays various pieces of sculpture from the "Asturian-Visigoth" churches.

The nearest of these churches, **Santullano**, is ten minutes' walk to the northeast along the c/de Gijón and by some unfortunate quirk of local city planning stands right next to a highway. However, it's well worth seeing. Built around 830, it is considerably larger and more spacious than the other Asturian churches, with an unusual "secret chamber" built into the outer wall. It is kept locked but the keys are available at the priest's house to the left; there are original frescoes inside, executed in similar style to those of Roman villas.

Santa María del Naranco

The greatest of the Asturian churches, indeed the architectural gem of the principality, is **Santa María del Naranco** (summer Mon–Sat 10am–1pm & 3–7pm, Sun 10am–1pm; winter Mon–Sat 10am–1pm & 3–5pm; 150ptas, free on Mon), majestically located

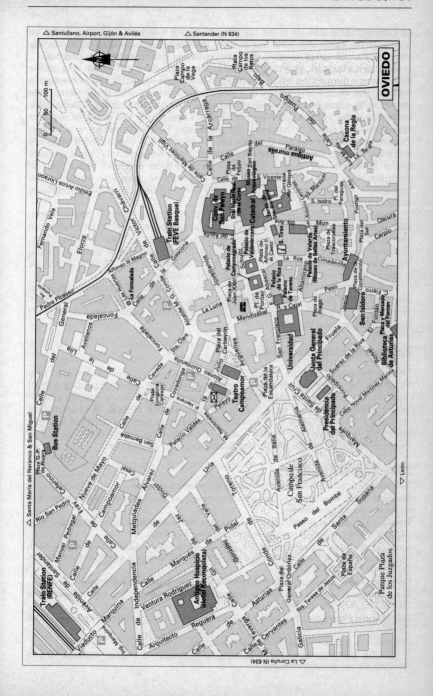

OVIEDO

on a wooded slope 3km above the city. It's a 45-minute walk from the centre, or half an hour from the station; the local tourist office has marked out a walking route, starting on one of the pedestrian streets in the town centre and leading on to a beautiful trail.

Perhaps it's the walk, providing glimpses of the warm stone and simple bold outline of the church through the trees, that makes Santa María so special, almost mystical, a building. But when you've arrived and gazed upon it from all sides it still seems quite perfect in its harmony of form, decoration, and natural surroundings – "formidable beyond its scale", to use Jan Morris's phrase. Curiously, it was designed not as a church but as a palace or hunting lodge for Ramiro I (842–52), Alfonso's successor. The present structure was just the main hall of a complex that once included baths and stairways, features which the caretaker may point out. Architecturally, the open porticos at both ends are most interesting – an innovation developed much later in Byzantine churches – as well as the thirty or so decorative medallions which give the appearance of being suspended from the roof. The crypt bears a notable resemblance to the *Cámara Santa* back in town.

A couple of hundred metres beyond Santa María is King Ramiro's palace chapel, **San Miguel de Lillo** (same hours as Santa María), built with soft golden sandstone and red tiles. This is generally assumed to be by the same architect as Santa María, Tiodo (whom some scholars credit also with the *Cámara Santa* and Santullano), though its design, the Byzantine cross-in-square, is quite different. Much of its interior sculpture has been removed to the archeological museum.

Further up from the two little churches is a Rio-style **figure of Christ** that looks out over the city and is spectacularly illuminated at night. It was built by Republican prisoners of war and although ugly close up (it's constructed from concrete blocks), there are wonderful views from the site.

Eating, drinking and nightlife

Head to the area around the cathedral for the best eating and drinking. You can't help but notice the **sidrerias**, spit-and-sawdust places with a lot of people pouring a lot of drink from a great height. These will baffle the newcomer, but just order a bottle (about 200ptas), and you'll soon pick up the right drinking method. Most of the best are along c/Gascona, down from the cathedral. There are plenty of cafés and bars too, most with remarkable value *menús* – anything over 800ptas is expensive – as well as more pricey traditional *mesónes* serving *fabada* and other Asturian fare.

Restaurants and tapas bars

Babilonia, c/Asturias 16. *Tapas* bar specializing in cheese and sausages.

Bocamar, Plaza Trascorrales 14. A terrific *marisqueria*: try the *fabas con almejas* (beans with clams) and delicious rice dishes.

Canela, c/Campoamor 20 (☎98/522 00 45; closed Sun, Feb 15–28 & Aug 1–15). A great little restaurant with quality cooking at a remarkable price; the *menú* is 1500ptas.

Casa Fermín, c/San Francisco 8 (☎98/521 64 52; closed Sun). A classic, much written about restaurant, serving imaginatively recreated Asturian dishes. The *menú* is a hefty 3000ptas and you could easily spend a lot more.

Casa Manolo, c/Altamirano 9. A superior *sidreria* known for its game and other *tapas*.

Gran Muralla, c/Asturias and **Joya de Oriente**, c/Jeronimo Ibran. If you want a change from Spanish food, these are acceptable Chinese restaurants.

Labrador and **Pinera Sanchez**, both c/de Arguelles. Two fine and modest-priced *mesónes*, just off the cathedral square.

Los Italianos, Avda. de Galicia. Reliable pasta and pizza.

El Mirador, midway up the road to Naranco. A good restaurant with a terrace that looks out over the whole city and mountains beyond.

Nightlife and entertainment

There's a strong Celtic tradition in the **pubs** and **bars** of Oviedo. You'll find Guinness on tap and loud Irish music playing at the extremely popular *Ca Beleño*, c/Martinez Vigil 4, *Cicero*, c/San José 2–4 or any of the pubs on c/Carta Puebla, all of which serve a vast variety of beers and the highly potent *carajillo*, an Irish whiskey with cream on top. For more of a variation in music, try any of the places on c/Mon, particularly *Diario Roma*, loud and crowded with a great atmosphere and *Montañes* which is a quieter refuge with cheaper drinks. *Monster* on Plaza de Sol plays heavy metal while *Berlin*, c/Postigo Alto, plays more alternative sound. *Salsipuedes*, c/Salsipuedes 3, is a relaxed place with a trio of bars and a great summer *terraza*.

If you're looking for **discos**, there's a row of good places on c/Canoniga behind the cathedral; *Equilíbrio* plays mainly Spanish pop, with mainstream chart music at *Danzeteria* and house/*bakalao* at *Be Bop*. Places on c/Altamarino stay open a bit later: *La Botica* has a good selection of dance music and *La Tamara* wonderful decor. If you want to dance all night, head to the new part of town, where *Almacen*, c/Gil de Jaz, an underground disco-complex, only really gets going from about 5am. In the same area, *La Real*, c/Cervantes and *Whipoorwhil*, c/Marqués de Tevera, stay open till 7am.

Listings

American Express c/o *Viajes Cafranga*, c/Uria 26 (☎98/525 56 66).

Books *Libreria Cervantes*, c/Dr. Casal 3/9 has a good stock, including walking and wildlife guides to Asturias, and English-language novels.

Car rental *Avis*, c/Ventura Rodriguez 12 (☎98/524 13 83); *Europcar*, c/Independencia 24 (☎98/524 46 16).

Classical music Oviedo is home to the *Orquestra de Asturias*, who perform mainly in the *Teatro Campoamor*. There are usually a couple of concerts each week.

Post office The *Correos Principal* is at c/Alonso Quintanilla 1 (Mon–Fri 8am–9pm, Sat 9am–7pm).

Telephones The *Telefónica* is at c/Foncalada 6 (Mon–Sat 10am–2pm & 4–10.30pm).

Trekking The *Federacion Asturiana de Montaña*, c/Melquiades Alvarez 16 (☎98/521 10 99) provides information and organizes treks in the Picos. The student agency, *TIVE*, c/Calvo Sotelo 5 (☎98/523 60 58), also offers good value trekking trips.

Avilés and Oviedo to Galicia

The **coast west of Avilés**, as far as the Río Navia, is pretty rugged, with scarcely more than a handful of resorts carved out from the cliffs; most attractive of them – by some way – is the old port and resort of **Luarca**. West again from the Río Navia, the coast becomes marshy and, save for an honorary mention to the unspoilt fishing village of **Tapia de Casariego**, unexceptional. Again, the *FEVE* line trails the coast, with some spectacular sections, though some of the stations (including Cudillero and Luarca) are inconveniently sited some way out of town.

Inland from Oviedo, the N634 and C630 offer a winding approach over the hills to Lugo in Galicia. The old town of **Salas**, with its castle, is of passing interest, but the main appeal of the route is the mountainous wildness of this area, which sees hardly a tourist from one year to the next.

Cudillero

CUDILLERO is a small, active and picturesque fishing port, with arcaded houses rising one upon each other over a steep horseshoe of cliffs around the port. The town retains its charm, though tourism has recently caught on, with souvenir shops and the like. As there's no beach as such here – the nearest is **Playa Aguilar**, 3km to the east –

the most obvious appeal is the fish tavernas in its narrow, seaside plaza; at weekends these are packed out, and prices are geared to tourist rather than local trade.

In the village proper, there is a single **hotel**, the pricey *San Pablo*, c/Suarez Inclan 36–38 (☎98/559 11 55; ⑤). The **hostales** listed as Cudillero are along the main highway, a good twenty minutes' walk out of town; closest is the *Casa Fernando II* (☎98/ 559 02 92; ③), on the road out to Luarca on the right. There are also two **campsites** on the road out to Playa Aguilar: *Cudillero* (☎98/559 06 63; June–Sept) and *L'Amuravela* (☎98/559 09 95; June–Sept). Another campsite, *San Pedro de Brocamar* (☎98/559 72 58; April–Sept), is located at Soto de Luiña, 5km west, near the beach at San Pedro de la Rivera.

Cudillero can be reached by **FEVE trains** from Avilés or Oviedo; the station is at the top of town, a fifteen minute walk from the centre. The **bus station**, with regular connections to Avilés and sporadic ones to Oviedo, is midway between here and the town centre. There is a **Turismo** (☎98/559 00 20) on Plaza de San Pedro, by the port.

Luarca

Beyond San Pedro the coast is rocky and the road winds through dark hills before dipping down through thick woods to the port of **LUARCA**. This is one of the most attractive towns along the whole northern coastline, a mellow sort of place, built around an S-shaped cove amid sheer cliffs. Down below, the town is bisected by a small, winding river, and knitted together by numerous narrow bridges.

This is a seaside resort in a very modest sort of way, with a slim beach of slightly murky sand, a scattering of accommodation, and some excellent bars and restaurants. In contrast to Cudillero, Luarca has defiantly retained its traditional character, including a few *chigres* – old-fashioned Asturian taverns – where you can be initiated into the art of *sidra* drinking. The fishing harbour area is the best place for meals, too: cross the bridge from the plaza, follow the river, and pick from a line of good value restaurants here, among them the huge and popular *Mesón de la Mar*.

On the way into town, there are some good budget places to **stay**: *El Redondel* (☎98/ 564 07 33; ②), on the main highway, and *California* (☎98/564 10 83; ②), just before the roundabout on the left. In town, *El Cocinero* (②) is a fine ramshackle old **fonda** in the main plaza; next door is *Rico* (☎98/547 05 59; ③), recently refurbished and good value; and there are further modest rooms at *Bar Oviedo* (☎98/564 09 06; ②) on c/del Crucero, a pedestrianized street behind the plaza. The upmarket choice is the *Hotel Gayoso*, Plaza Gómez 4 (☎98/564 00 54; ⑤), an old "grand hotel". The **Turismo** (☎98/ 564 00 83), in the *Ayuntamiento*, on the main plaza, provides lists of private rooms and apartments.

The town **beach** is divided in two. The closer strip is narrower but more protected, the other broad one beyond the jetty is subject to seaweed litter. On the clifftop above, a fair climb but well-marked from the town centre, is a **campsite**, *Los Cantiles* (☎98/ 564 09 38; summer only), with facilities to match its superb setting.

Luarca has good **bus** connections to Oviedo, Gijón, Avilés and into Galicia; the bus station is just off c/del Crucero. The *FEVE* station is 3km out of town.

Luarca to Ribadeo

West from Luarca, you cross the wide Río Navia – a foretaste of Galicia's *rias* or estuaries – at **NAVIA**, a pleasant little port, though lacking the style and life of Luarca. If you have transport, the inland route from here to Lugo is fascinating. At **COAÑA**, 5km south of Navia, there's a Celtic *citania*, and beyond that the road winds above the reservoirs of the Navia river before twisting into Galicia and the remote mountainous region around Fonsagrada.

The best beach along this stretch is the last in Asturias, the **Playa de Represas**, which flanks the unspoilt fishing village of **TAPIA DE CASARIEGO**. This is a lively little place, with an entertaining "alternative" *Teatro Popular*, and a very helpful **Turismo** in a small kiosk in the plaza. There are three reasonably priced **hostales**, including *La Ruta* (☎98/562 81 38; ③) which is great value, and opposite, *Puente de los Santos* (☎98/562 81 55; ③), slightly more expensive. Just outside town are two **campsites**, about 1km towards Ribadeo; *Playa de Tapia* (☎98/547 27 21; June–Sept) and *El Carbayin* (☎98/554 26 06; open all year). The port area is again the place to eat and drink; walk down to the beaches and turn left.

CASTROPOL, set back from the coast on the Río Eo – the border with Galicia – is a tiny, pretty place with a pair of *hostales*. However, you're better off staying across the border in Ribadeo. There's a **Turismo** on the main highway, if you're entering from Galicia and want pamphlets and information on Asturias.

Salas

SALAS, 35km west of Oviedo, was the home of the Marqués de Valdés-Salas, founder of Oviedo university and one of the prime movers of the Inquisition. The town **castle** is actually the Marqués's old palace; you can climb an adjoining tower from the **Turismo** (☎98/589 09 88) for fine views of the town and surrounding countryside. Among the other monuments are a sixteenth-century **Colegiata** and, in the main square, the tenth-century church of **San Martín**.

If you want to **stay**, there are two options: the *Hotel Castillo de Valdés-Salas* (☎98/583 10 37; ④), in the castle, with an out-of-the-ordinary restaurant; and the *Pensión Soto* (☎98/583 00 37; ②), which has big clean rooms. Buses to Oviedo leave on the hour from outside the *Café Berlín*.

travel details

Buses

Castro Urdiales to: Bilbao (7 daily; 1hr); Vitoria (3 daily; 1hr 15min).

Comillas to: San Vicente (3 daily; 30min); Santillana (4 daily; 35min).

Gijón to: Irún via Oviedo (4 daily; 5hr 30min); Léon via Oviedo (8 daily; 2hr 30min); Madrid via Oviedo (7 daily; 6hr); Ribadeo via Luarca, Navia, La Caridad, Tapia, Castropol, Vegadeo (4 daily; 4hr); Sevilla (2 daily; 13 hr 30min).

Llanes to: Arenas (2 daily; 1hr); Oviedo via Ribadesella (9 daily; 2hr).

Oviedo to Avilés: (every 30min; 35min); Betanzos/La Coruña (2 daily; 4hr 30min/5hr); Covadonga (5 daily; 1hr 45min); Cudillero (10 daily – but 3 more by changing at Avilés); Gijón (every 30min; 30min); León (8 daily, 2hr); Luarca/Ribadeo (5 daily; 3hr 20min/4hr 30min); Lugo (3 daily; 5hr); Madrid (8 daily; 5hr 30min); Pontevedra (2 daily; 10hr); Ribadesella (10 daily; 1hr 40min); Santiago (2 daily; 7 hr); Sevilla (2 daily; 13hr); Valladolid (4 daily; 3hr 30min); Vigo (2 daily; 10hr).

Picos buses Potes–Espinama–Fuente Dé (3 daily; 1hr), Arenas de Cabrales–Cangas de Onis (4 daily; 1hr 30min), Colombres/Panes–Arenas (2 daily; 45/30min), Cangas de Onis–Covadonga (4 daily, 1 continuing to lakes; 45min/1hr 30min), Cangas de Onis–Sajambre (1 daily; 2hr), León–Posada de Valdeón (1 daily via Riaño and Portilla de la Reina; 4hr 30min). Also **Land Rover service** between Valdeón and Caín, and Poncebos and Arenas.

Ribadesella to: Arriondas (change for Cangas)/Oviedo (5 daily; 20min/2hr); Villaviciosa/Oviedo (3 daily; 1hr/2hr 30min).

San Vicente to: Potes via Unquera (2 daily; 1hr 30min); Ribadesella (3 daily; 2hr).

Santander to: Barcelona (1 daily; 10hr, change at Bilbao); Bilbao (9 daily; 4 of which continue to French border; 2hr 30min); Burgos (3 daily; 4hr); Castro Urdiales (3 daily; 1hr 30min); Comillas (6 daily; 1hr – usually change in Torrelavega); Laredo (7 daily; 1hr); Madrid (4 daily; 8hr); Oviedo (6 daily; 3hr 30min); Potes (3 daily; 3hr – possible to pick up in San Vicente or Unquera); Puente Viesgo (4 daily; 1hr); Santiago, Vigo, and Portuguese border (2 daily; 10–12hr); Santillana (5 daily; 45min); San Vicente la Barquera (4 daily; 1hr 15min);Vitoria via Castro Urdiales, skips Bilbao (3 daily; 2hr).

Trains
RENFE

Santander to: Madrid (4 daily; 6hr 30min), change at PALENCIA for east–west routes including León.

Oviedo to: Alicante (1 daily; 11hr); Barcelona (2 daily; 12hr); León (9 daily; 2hr 45min); Madrid (4 daily; 7hr 30min).

FEVE

This independent service runs along the north coast between **Bilbao, Santander and El Ferrol**. The narrow-gauge railway has a poor record for safety, let alone efficiency, but is at present being modernized, with new cars and extensive right-of-way renovation. Currently only one train per day covers the whole distance in either direction from Santander, and even on that you have to change at Oviedo. Two trains connect Santander with Oveiedo; three, Santander with Bilbão. Shorter journeys vary widely. Main stops in Cantabria and Asturias, from east to west, are: Santander, Torrelavega, Llanes, Ribadesella, Noreña, Oviedo, Gijón, Avilés, Pravia, Cudillero, Luarca, Navia, and, in Galicia, Ribadeo, Foz, Viv and El Ferrol. The full journey takes nearly 13hr, best split over two or more days, with an obligatory change of trains (and stations) at Oviedo.

Ferries

Car/passenger ferry from **Santander** to **Plymouth,** (Tue & Thur except from mid-Dec to mid-Jan; 24hr).

CHAPTER EIGHT

GALICIA

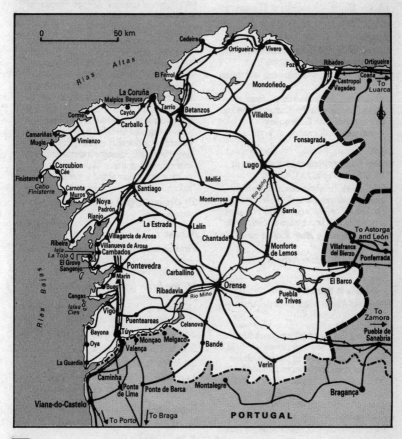

Remote, rural, and battered by the Atlantic, **Galicia** is a far cry from the popular image of Spain. It not only looks like Ireland; there are further parallels in the climate, culture, and music, as well as the ever-visible traces of its Celtic past. Above all, despite its green and fertile appearance, Galicia has a similar history of famine and poverty, with a continuing decline in population owing to forced emigration.

Galicia is lush and heavily wooded, with a landscape dominated by water. The coast-line is shaped by fjord-like *rías*, source of some of the best seafood in Europe and shel-tering unspoiled old villages and fine beaches. As you enter Galicia from the east, the rolling meadows of Asturías are replaced by a patchwork of tiny fields, with terraces of

FIESTAS

January

1 Livestock fair at Betanzos.

6 Horseback procession of *Los Reyes* (the Three Kings) in Bayona.

15 *San Mauro* – fireworks at Villanueva de Arosa.

March

1 Celanova's big festival, of *San Rosendo*, at the monastery above town.

28 Wine festival, with partying and music, at Ribadavia.

Pre-Lenten *carnavales* throughout the region, along with the *Lazaro* festival, a gathering of both Gallego and Portuguese folk groups, at Verín.

April

Palm Sunday Stations of the Cross at Monte San Tecla, La Guardia.

Holy Week Celebrations include a symbolic *descendimiento* (descent from the Cross) at Vivero on Good Friday and a resurrection procession at Finisterre.

Second Monday after Easter *San Telmo* festival at Tuy.

25 *San Marcos* observance at Noya.

May

1 *Romería* at Pontevedra.

22 *Santa Rita* at Villagarcía de Arosa.

June

Sundays Country fairs and roundups of wild horses, known as *curros*, are held on successive Sundays in the hills above Bayona and Oya; villages include La Valga, Torroña, Mougas and Pinzas.

Corpus Christi Flower festival, with flower "carpets" in the streets, in Ponteareas.

24–25 Two days of celebration for *San Juan* in many places, with processions of bigheads and *gigantones* on the 24th and spectacular parades with fireworks and bands through the following evening.

July

First weekend *Rapa das Bestas* – capture and breaking in of wild mountain horses – at Vivero and San Lorenz (Pontevedra). At the latter the horses are raced before being let loose.

11 *San Benito* fiesta at Pontevedra, with river processions and competitions, and folk groups, and a smaller *romería* at Cambados.

16 *Virgen del Carmen*. Sea processions at Muros and Corcubión.

25 Galicia's major fiesta, in honour of Saint James, at Santiago de Compostela. It's worth attending mass to see the National Offering to the Shrine (of the country and government) as well as the swinging of the *botafumeiro*. The evening before, there's a fireworks display and symbolic burning of a cardboard effigy of the mosque at Córdoba. The festival – also designated Galicia Day – has become a nationalist event with traditional separatist demonstrations and an extensive programme of political and cultural events for about a week on either side.

29 Octopus festival at Villanueva de Arosa.

August

First Sunday Wine festival at Cambados; bagpipe festival at Ribadeo; *Virgen de la Roca* observances outside Bayona.

16 *San Roque* festivals at all churches that bear his name: at Betanzos there's a Battle of the Flowers on the river; at Sada there are boat races and feasts.

24 Fiesta (and bullfights) at Noya.

25 *San Ginés* at Sangenjo.

28 *Romería del Naseiro* outside Vivero.

Last Sunday *Romería* sets out from Sangenjo to the Praia de La Lanzada.

September

6–10 *Fiestas del Portal* at Ribadavia.

8 *San Andreu* at Cervo.

14 Seafood festival at El Grove; *romería* with bigheads at Vivero.

November

11 *Fiesta de San Martín* at Bueu.

Last Sunday Oyster festival at Arcade.

December

Last week Crafts fair, *O Feitoman* at Vigo.

vines supported on granite props and allotments full of turnip-tops and cabbages growing on stalks. Archaic inheritance laws have meant a constant division and redivision of the land into little plots too small for machinery and worked with the most primitive agricultural methods; ox carts with solid wooden wheels are still a common sight on the backroads. Everywhere you see *horreos*, granaries made here of granite rather than wood, with saints and sculpted air-vents, standing on pillars away from rodents and the damp.

While it is a poor, "backward" part of the country, unlike the south it never seems oppressively so. Food is plentiful, most people being involved in its production, and there's a strength and solidity in the culture, run, uniquely for Spain, by the women. In the countryside, women and children frequently work the land while the men work at sea, whether as merchant seamen or fishermen, catching octopus and lobster from rowing boats, and minding the *mejilloneiras* (the mussel rafts anchored in the *rías*). Others, undoubtedly, are engaged in the old standby of smuggling – which, these days, means drugs as well as more traditional contraband. For centuries men have also sought their fortunes abroad, traditionally in Argentina (there are said to be more Gallegos in Buenos Aires than in Galicia), though more often these days as migrant labourers in northern Europe.

With so many men absent, and almost no heavy industry, there is little of the radicalism of Asturías. Galicia has always been deeply conservative and since 1875 has provided Spain with a gallery of prominent right-wing leaders; it was the birthplace of General Franco, and is today dominated by the right-wing Alianza Popular, whose founder Manuel Fraga, is another local boy. Nonetheless, there is a strong and proud Gallego Nationalist movement, which may not approach the scale – or political intensity – of the Catalans and the Basques, but has formed links with Brittany and Ireland, and championed the revival of the long-banned local language.

Gallego today sounds like a fusion of Castilian and Portuguese, but has existed every bit as long as either, and is still spoken by an estimated 85 percent of the population. In the smaller communities few people speak anything else. It is definitely a living language, taught in schools and with its own literary heroes such as the poet Rosalia de Castro and the essayist and caricaturist Castelao. Road signs and maps these days tend to be in **Gallego**; we've given Gallego place names in parentheses after the Castilian version, since you may see either form. The most obvious characteristic is the large number of *X*s, which in Castilian might be *G*s, *J*s or *S*s; these are pronounced as a soft *sh*. You will also find that the Castilian *plaza* becomes *praza* and *playa* becomes *praia*.

The obvious highlight of the region is **Santiago de Compostela**, the greatest goal for pilgrims in medieval Europe and once again a flourishing centre for tourists. The cathedral, and the unified architecture of the whole city, with its granite colonnades and mossy facades, together make Santiago quite unforgettable. But there are smaller and equally charming old stone towns throughout Galicia, and those that have retained a vibrant sense of life and atmosphere, such as **Pontevedra** and **Betanzos**, are enjoyable bases for a touring holiday. The coastal countryside is always spectacular, but the best and safest swimming beaches are along the **Rías Bajas** towards Portugal, with **El Grove** and **Bayona** the most popular resorts. Far fewer visitors come here than to the Mediterranean, and while the sea is never as warm, the pine-fringed coves are delight-

---

ful. Inland, Galicia can be bleak and empty; the most rewarding route is to follow the Miño (Minho) river upstream from the Portuguese border to towns such as **Ribadavia** and **Celanova**, and then up to the Roman walls of **Lugo**.

THE RÍAS ALTAS AND SANTIAGO

It's not nearly as difficult as it once was to move around the north coast of Galicia, where the **Rías Altas** (High Estuaries) include both the northernmost and western-most points of Spain. Roads, which until recently were poorly surfaced and barely frequented, are now reliable and safe, and the facilities for visitors have improved with the increasing importance of the revenues from tourism. The savagery of the ocean has created a wild and dramatic coastline that slows down travel, and even if you have a car it's advisable to choose just a couple of targets. **Vivero** (Viveiro), to the east, and the stretch between **Finisterre** and **Muros** to the west, are particularly good to explore. With the grand exception of **Santiago de Compostela**, the cities of this area are best avoided; neither **El Ferrol** nor **La Coruña** is particularly exciting. No words of praise could be too extravagant for Santiago, and if you really want to appreciate this pilgrimage centre to the fullest it makes sense to approach it by the ancient Pilgrim Route from León. Its one drawback, often exaggerated, is the weather; Santiago must be one of the few cities in the world which actually boasts about its excessive rainfall.

The north coast

The closing stretch of the *FEVE* **railway** (see p.399), from Luarca to El Ferrol, is perhaps the best, as long as you're in no hurry to arrive. It clings to every nuance of the coastline, looping around a succession of *rías* and rambling through the pine forests and wild-looking hills which buffer the villages from the harsh Atlantic. Settlements are concentrated at the sides of the estuaries, with the occasional beach tacked beside or below them. By **road**, too, it's a slow route. Most buses to La Coruña and Ferrol detour inland as far as Lugo rather than tackle the endless bends of the C642 (at their most severe around Ortigueira) – this stretch, though, is currently being improved.

Along the FEVE

RIBADEO, the first Gallego town and *ría*, makes a poor introduction to the region. It does have a certain crumbling charm, and the overgrown main praza features a few decent bars and a **hostal** or two – such as the *Costa Verde*, Praza de España 13 (☎982/110113; ③), which drops its prices in winter – but overall it's drab. The nearest **beach**, the Praia del Castro, is a few kilometres further west, with **campsites** at Benquerencia and Reinante, but by now you're getting a bit too close to the industrial port of **FOZ**. Beyond that, **CERVO** has little more to boast of than a huge rust-red aluminium factory, although **MONDOÑEDO**, 20km up the valley of the Río Masma, is an attractive old riverside town.

Vivero

VIVERO (Viveiro) is something special. Too remote to make its living as a resort, it's an elegant port with a self-confident presence all its own. High glass-fronted houses line the streets, with white wooden frames as delicate as lacework (modelled on those of La Coruña), while the whole ensemble is protected inside an imposing circuit of Renaissance walls and gates. These, in fact, conspire to make initial impressions rather misleading: until you penetrate the walls, through one of the gateways, Vivero appears less than attractive; once inside, it's lovely and its central squares and streets are largely closed to traffic.

The sloping main drag down to the harbour is crammed with lively bars full of the local youth, and the bay shelters several peaceful **beaches**, particularly the Praia de Faro up towards the open sea. Just off the Praia de Covas, the delightful semi-fortified rock, **San Roque**, is not far from the *Viveiro* **campsite** (☎982/560004).

Buses stop on Travesia de la Marina, the waterfront road below the old town. Through the gates, several **hostales** and inexpensive **fondas** can be found in the alleyways of the pedestrianized *ramblas* which run parallel to the main road between the *FEVE* **station** (on c/Verxeles) and the harbour. The *Serra* at c/Antonio Bas 2 (☎982/560374; ②), at the northern end of Avda. Cervantes, is a real bargain; the more central *Nuevo Mundo*, just up from the main square at c/Teodoro de Quirós 14 (☎982/560025; ③), is also good value, a beautiful old building with attractive balconied rooms (though those at the front are within ear-splitting distance of the bells of Santa María church, opposite).

GALLEGO FOOD AND DRINK

One of the most compelling attractions of Galicia is the local **food**. Gourmets claim the quality of the **seafood** here is to be equalled only in Newfoundland, and with a few exceptions it is not expensive, at least when eaten as *tapas* in bars. Local wonders to look out for include *vieiras* (the scallops whose shells became the symbol of St. James), *mejillones* (the rich orange mussels from the *rías*), *cigallas* (a kind of crayfish usually and inadequately translated as shrimp), *anguilas* (little eels from the river Miño), and *choquitos* and *chipirones* (different kinds of small squid best served in their own ink). *Pulpo* (octopus) is so much a part of Gallego eating that there are special *pulperías* which serve it, and it is a mainstay of local country fiestas. In the province of Pontevedra alone, Villanueva de Arosa has its own octopus festival, Arcade one devoted to oysters, and El Grove goes all the way with a generalized seafood fiesta. One word of warning, however; although a wide variety of crab and lobster are always on display in the restaurants, make sure to have a price quoted in advance – the cost of these specialities is often exorbitant, and the demand so great that certain items such as *necoras* (spider crab) even have to be imported from England to keep up the supply.

Throughout Galicia there are superb **markets**; the coastal towns have their rows of seafront stalls with supremely fresh fish, while cities such as Santiago and Pontevedra have grand old arcaded market halls, piled high with farm produce from the surrounding countryside. Most enjoyable of all are the ports (such as Cambados and Marin), with *lonjas* open to the public, where you can wait for the fishing boats to come home (usually around midnight, but more like 6am in La Coruña) and take part in the auctioning of their catch – much of which will have left Galicia well before dawn for the restaurants of Madrid, on the nightly special train.

Another speciality, imported from the second Gallego homeland of Argentina, is the **churrasquería** (grill house). Often unmarked and needing local assistance to find, these serve up immense *churrascos* – what we inadequately call "spare ribs" (it's more like a steak with bones in it). The Gallegos don't normally like their food highly spiced, but *churrascos* are traditionally served with a devastating garlic-based *salsa picante*. Other common dishes are *caldo Gallego*, a thick stew of cabbage and potatoes in a meat-based broth, and *lacon con grelos*, ham boiled with turnip greens.

The local **wines** can be great, both the whites and the thick port-like reds (some bars even serve a "black" wine), and are still usually drunk from *tazas*, handleless ceramic cups. Local **beer** is *Estrella Galicia*, good and strong. **Liqueurs** tend to be fiery, based on the clear *aguardiente* (which is elsewhere known as *eau de vie* or *aquavit*); one much-loved Gallego custom is the *queimada*, when a large bowl of *aguardiente* with fruit and sugar is set alight and then drunk hot.

The *Nuevo Mundo* has a good **restaurant** downstairs – 1000ptas for a four-course feast. As you might expect, seafood is a local speciality: the excellent *Laurel*, c/Melitón Cortiñas 26 – three streets east of the main square – is a busy *bodega* with wooden barrels and tables, and the cooks on view, battling away to fill the orders; around 3000ptas for two, including the fine local wine. There's a swankier *marisquería* down the same street, the *Vivero*, with higher prices and a more refined setting.

El Barqueiro, Ortigueira and Porto de Vares

The next two *ría* villages (and *FEVE* stops) are **PORTO DO BARQUEIRO** (O Barqueiro), a tiny fishing port of slate-roofed houses near Spain's northernmost point, and the larger **ORTIGUEIRA**, set amid a dark mass of pines. The former has at least three places to stay dotted around its tiny harbour, their rooms facing the water and outdoor café seating prompting you to pull up a chair and go no further. Ortigueira, too, has a couple of decent *hostales*, such as the *Monterrey*, at Avda. Franco 105 (☎981/ 400135; ②). Ortigueira was for a few years the home of a particularly raucous Celtic festival, but that seems now to have been discontinued in view of its tendency to degenerate into violence (dark mutterings hold *agents provocateurs* responsible). Public transport being so infrequent, you may rapidly feel trapped in either place if you do decide to visit.

Drivers, though, should take the opportunity to head the 7km north of Barqueiro up to the headland, through pine and eucalyptus forest, to straggly Vila de Vares. Two kilometres beyond, **PORTO DE VARES** is a highly attractive clump of fishermen's houses overlooking the bay, flanked to the south by a superb, wide, sandy beach. You can camp here; back in the hamlet, there's one restaurant, the terrific *Marina*, with outdoor tables and window seats overlooking bay and beach. Fresh seafood meals – including great octopus and an *especial paella* – start from 1500ptas a head (though the *paella* will set you back considerably more than that).

El Ferrol

The city of **EL FERROL** is one of Spain's principal naval bases and dockyards. Unfortunately the navy, and what's left of the shipbuilding industry, have usurped the best of the coastline, leaving a provincial centre dominated by a status-conscious, navy-orientated community and a large statue of *El Caudillo* (the Chief), Francisco Franco, who was born here in 1892. Although frequently considered a bastion of conservatism, El Ferrol was also the birthplace of Pablo Isglesias, founder of the Spanish Socialist Party, which has now ruled Spain for over a decade.

Getting out shouldn't be too difficult; the **FEVE** and **RENFE** stations are housed in the same building, and the **bus station** is just outside: exit and make two quick lefts, and you'll see it some 50m ahead of you. If you need **accommodation**, one of the more reasonable places is the spartan *Noray* on c/Barbeito (☎981/310079; ②), and there are plenty of other choices along c/Pardo Bajo – the *Aloya* is at no. 28 (☎981/351231; ③) – or c/del Sol and c/María, all within a few minutes' walk of the station and the central Praza de España. If you're driving, beware of outrageous traffic jams out of Ferrol on Friday and in again on Sunday nights, when the entire community heads out of the city for the weekend, blocking local roads solid.

The Ría de Betanzos

El Ferrol stands more or less opposite La Coruña, only 20km away across the mouth of the **Ría de Betanzos**, but a seventy-kilometre trip by road or rail. The coast in between is considerably more appealing than either of the two cities, with the contours of the *ría* speckled with forests and secluded beaches.

Puentedeume, Perbes and Sada

Heading south from Ferrol, you cross the Río Eume by a vast medieval bridge at **PUENTEDEUME** (Pontedeume). The stones on either side of the bridge as you enter town are, in fact, boars from the arms of the once-powerful overlords, the counts of Andrade. Their tower overlooks the river at Puentedeume, and the Castelo de Andrade is perched on a hill over the town.

Just beyond, *Camping Perbes* (☎981/783104) is sandwiched between woods and water on the **Praia Perbes** near Miño (Minho). At **SADA**, opposite, you'll find the *Marina Española* **youth hostel** (☎981/620118; ①), and there are also several **campsites** in the area.

Betanzos

The town of **BETANZOS** is a really enjoyable place to stay. The site it's built on is so old, dating back from before the Romans, that what was once a steep seaside hill is now set well back from the coast, at the spot where the rivers Mendo and Mandeo meet. The base of the hill is surrounded by still-discernible medieval walls composed largely of houses, above which rises a mass of twisting and tunneling narrow streets. Follow these, and you'll come to the twelfth-century church of **Santa María de Azogue**, reconstructed by the Andrade lords in the fourteenth century; Andrade influence probably explains the unlikely stone pig with a cross on its back over the adjacent and contemporary church of San Francisco.

The focus of Betanzos is the large, attractive main square, **Praza de Garcia Hermanos**, to the right of the town walls as you approach from the *RENFE* station (see below). The **Turismo** here (actually a green kiosk below the bandstand with erratic opening hours) can supply a map, though you won't need one to find the the the *Hostal Barreiros* (☎981/772259; ②), Betanzos' best bet for **accommodation** – it's across the main square at c/Argentina 6, directly behind the statue of the Garciá brothers, and has pleasant, if basic rooms, which fill quickly in summer. Failing this, *Hotel Los Angeles*, c/ de los Angeles 11 (☎981/771511; ③), also off the main square and professionally run, if a bit anonymous, and the unnamed pension at no. 17, 3° (②) on one of the alleys off the east side of the square (see below), just about round up the accommodation options.

Eating and drinking centres around the row of bars on the main square – with outdoor seating – and the tiny, unnamed alleys leading off it, to the left of the *Café-Bar Avenida*. The popular *O Pote* on the second alley has a great range of *tapas* at 250ptas a serving, though you may have to stand. Further down, whole families spend their nights at the *Café-Bar As Vegas*, which provides good-quality budget meals. The owner of the *Hostal Barreiros* also runs the rather classy, wood-panelled *Mesón dos Arcos* below the *hostal*, whose dining room serves an excellent 800ptas *menú del día* and great grills.

It's a ten-minute walk to the town from the *Betanzos Ciudad RENFE* **station** (across the park and over the bridge to the town walls), but it's only used by trains to and from El Ferrol. Other trains use instead *Betanzos Infesta*, 2.5km away at the top of a steep climb – or wait for an El Ferrol-bound connection. *ALSA* **buses** drop off in the main square around four times a day from La Coruña, a twenty-minute journey; buses also run from Lugo and El Ferrol.

La Coruña

Despite its long history, the port of **LA CORUÑA** (A Coruña) is surprisingly modern, focused more on the office blocks and apartments of its rising middle class than on what's left of the old town. Quaint it isn't, but it is a major transport nexus, with a more cosmopolitan range of shops and services than in most other places in Galicia, and a vibrant nightlife that ends with 5am chocolate and *churros*, watching the fishing boats come in.

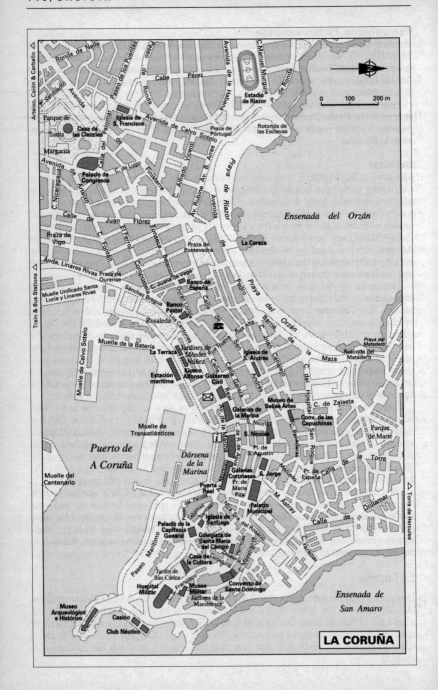

LA CORUÑA

The newly-constructed **Paseo Marítimo** walkway edges the city's extensive coastline, bending around the port and marina, where it's overlooked by an elegant lacework of glassed-in balconies – a practical innovation against La Coruña's wind and showers. The **Turismo** is here at the Darsena de la Marina (Mon–Fri 9am–2pm & 4.30–6.30pm, Sat 10am–1pm), a good half-hour's walk across the city from the **bus** and **train** stations, which are 200m apart opposite *El Corte Inglés* department store; take buses #1 or #1a.

The city

Departure point of the doomed 1588 Armada, and veteran of the Peninsular Wars, Coruña has a lengthy history of naval combat. The restored Castelo San Antón, an easy walk along the Paseo Marítimo from the marina, was once a garrison and, until the 1960s, a military and political prison. It now houses the **Museo Arqueológico e Histórico** (daily 10am–2pm & 4–7.30pm; 150ptas), worth the entrance fee alone for the view across the bay from the top and the medieval stone carvings at the back. Inland from here are the walled **Jardines de San Carlos** and, inside, the **tomb of Sir John Moore**, killed in 1809 during the British retreat from the French in the Peninsular Wars, and immortalised in the jingoistic rhythms of Reverend Charles Wolfe ("Not a drum was heard, not a funeral note . . .") which you will find here inscribed. Across the road, a new military museum contains relics from the city's various miltary adventures. Keep going and you'll find yourself in the narrow streets of the old town, which wind around the Romanesque churches of **Santiago** and **Santa María del Campo**. To the west of the old town, directly behind the café-terraces of the Darsena de la Marina, the huge, colonnaded **Praza de María Pita** is the city's grandest square, with a thriving café scene that continues into the early hours.

From outside the Jardines de San Carlos, bus #3 or #3a runs out to the rocky outcrop where the much-trumpeted lighthouse, the **Torre de Hercules**, the city's symbol, has been warning ships off the treacherous Costa da Morte since Roman times. It was entirely recased in the eighteenth century and there's not a trace of ancient stone to be seen. The latest victim of the coast was the oil tanker that went down in 1993; only a typically vicious storm saved the region from absolute ecological disaster, by breaking up the slick.

Accommodation, eating, drinking and nightlife

Accommodation shouldn't be too much of a problem. The Turismo has up-to-date listings, or try *Centro Gallego*, c/Estrella 2 (☎981/222236; ①), *Hostal Residencia Merche*, c/Estrella 12 (☎981/228010; ③), or the *Roma*, Rua Nueva 3 (☎981/228075; ①), all an easy walk from the Turismo.

The small streets to the west of Praza de María Pita, particularly c/Franja, following into calles La Galera, Los Olmos and Estrella, are crowded with **bars** that, at their best, offer some of Spain's finest seafood, and excellent *tapas*. The **late-night** scene moves to the other side of the isthmus around the two beaches of Praia de Ríazor and Praia de Orzán; try the bars *La Latina*, *Zix* or *Agua Mineral*, and the *discoteca*, *Praia Club*. Inland, the more yuppified c/de Juan Florez has jazz, salsa and the perennial *Pirámide* nightclub. Five kilometres out of town, the bars and clubs at **Praia Santa Cristina** are lively and fun throughout the summer.

Inland to Santiago

The **Camino de Santiago**, the pilgrims' route, is the longest-established "tourist" route in Europe, and its final section through Galicia provides a fair representation of the medieval pilgrimage to the thousands who walk it every year, armed with the traditional staff and the shell emblem of St James. Hundreds more cycle the route, and it's possible to drive, too, although this is the least satisfying way of making the journey, offering tantalizing glimpses of ancient footpaths winding through woods as the road and footpath intertwine and then separate. Both routes are well-signposted with yellow scallop shell symbols, and local buses cover much of the road route, a boon to the footsore. Basic hostels for pilgrims are set up along the way, with priority given to walkers. Walking or cycling, the *camino* is a tough but unforgettable experience. Local Turismo offices have lists of the hostels and special pilgrim facilities (there are phone lines for medical emergencies); you'll also need a hat to guard against the hot sun, rainwear against Gallego deluges, and a big stick to keep the dogs at bay.

The pilgrim route branches off the main Ponferrada-to-Lugo road at the **Pedrafita do Cebreiro** pass which marks the Gallego frontier. This is a desolate spot, where hundreds of English soldiers froze or starved to death during Sir John Moore's retreat towards La Coruña in 1809. In such a forbidding landscape, you can only be impressed by the sheer scale of work that medieval builders put into providing spiritual and material amenities for the pilgrims. Crumbling castles, convents and humble inns line the road, and it's not hard to imagine what a welcome sight each must have been.

Cebreiro

The village of **CEBREIRO** itself is quite appallingly situated to catch the worst of the Gallego wind and snow – not that you would realize that on one of the rare fine days of summer. It's highly picturesque, an undulating settlement of thatched stone huts (*pallozas*) surrounding a stark ninth-century church. No one actually lives in the *pallozas* any more, which are maintained as a national monument, with a guide on site to answer visitors' questions. In high season up to 1000 people per day pass this way; at other times it feels as remote as it ever did, and it's even possible to take refuge for the night in the former monastery next to the church. There are similar villages in the vicinity, where a few farmers still choose to live in the ancient dwellings; their children, however, seem to be unanimous in the desire to move away in pursuit of creature comforts, and the old way of life must surely be coming to an end.

Following the Pilgrim Route

Many of the places along the pilgrim route that medieval travellers stopped at are now little more than ruins, but some survive. The **Monasterio de Samos** (daily 10.30am–1pm & 4.30–7pm), for example, famous for its library in the Middle Ages, and badly damaged by fire in 1951, has been restored. Its moss-covered exterior, pierced only by two small barred windows, leads to two sunny and peaceful cloisters.

The once-great monastery of **Sobrado de los Monjes** (daily 10.15am–1.30pm & 4.15–6.45pm) was also allowed to decay for a long time, but the provincial government is beginning to repair and restore it, and with your own transport this remains a highly worthwhile detour. After the empty approach road, the huge cathedral church with its strong west towers comes as a dramatic shock. The range of the abbey buildings proclaims past royal patronage, their scale emphasized by the tiny village below. The church itself sprouts flowers and foliage from every niche and crevice, its honey-coloured stone blossoming with lichens and mosses. Within, all is immensely grand – long, uncluttered vistas, mannerist Baroque, and romantic gloom; there are superb, worm-endangered choirstalls (once in Santiago cathedral), and, through a small arch in the north transept, a small, ruinous Romanesque chapel. These are the highlights, but take time to explore the outbuildings, too, including a magnificent thirteenth-century kitchen, in good condition and imaginatively lit, with a massive chimney flue. A small community of monks maintain the monastery as well as they can, and operate a small shop.

Equipped with a handful of *hostales* and cafés, **SARRIA** makes a logical stopover on this part of the *camino*; try the *Londres*, Calvo Sotelo 153 (☎982/532456; ②). The lower part of town is unimpressive, but old Sarria straggles gloriously uphill, topped by a (privately owned) castle. Further along the route, the whole town of **PORTOMARÍN** was flooded by the damming of the Miño, but its Templar castle and church were carried stone by stone to a new site further up the hillside.

Lugo

The *Camino de Santiago* bypassed **LUGO**, although it was already an ancient city even a thousand years ago. Built on a Celtic site above the Miño (and named after the Celtic sun god Lug), it is the only Spanish town to remain completely enclosed within superb **Roman walls**. These are ten to fifteen metres high, with 85 circular towers along a circuit of almost three kilometres, and are broad enough to provide a pleasant thoroughfare for walks around the city. Sadly, insensitive building has blocked out most of the views of the surrounding countryside – and a busy loop road makes it impossible to appreciate the walls from any distance outside. But the road does at least keep the traffic out of the centre, which itself maintains an enjoyable if neglected medley of cultivated patches and medieval and eighteenth-century buildings.

The town

Lugo is more of a place to walk around, savouring the granite staircases, narrow arcades and relaxed open spaces, than one with any great sights. The largest and best of the city's gardens, the **Parque Rosalía de Castro**, has a fine little café and weekend performances by the local brass band. It's a popular destination for the evening *paseo*, positioned a little way out of the Puerta de Santiago, with good views over the Miño valley.

The large mossy **Cathedral**, flanked by three distinctive towers, was, like so many Gallego churches, modelled after the one at Santiago de Compostela, with imitation here perpetuated by the eighteenth-century Baroque additions to the facade. Inside, choirstalls cramp the central space, forcing you around a ring of chapels, in one of which an Imperial soldier in cherubic posture tramples a dying Moor. Walk down Rua Nova and you'll come to Lugo's exceptionally good **Museo Provincial** (Mon–Fri 10am–1pm & 4–7pm, Sat 10am–2pm; free to EC passport holders), partly housed in the old Convento de San Francisco – you'll see the stone kitchen, complete with a fireplace big enough to sit in (and people did). Well laid out, the museum features Gallego art, including a wonderful statue of a kneeling peasant woman, staff in one hand, priest in the other; Spanish contemporary work swiped from the Prado; an early collection of Galicia's Sargadelos china; alongside more predictable displays of Roman remains and ecclesiastical clutter.

Of the two squares, the graceful colonnades of the **Praza España** (Praza Maior on some maps) shelter some good cafés and a couple of reasonable restaurants (as well as the Turismo in the Galerías); the Praza Santo Domingo is less inviting, watched over by a black statue of a Roman Imperial eagle, commemorating the 2000th anniversary of Caesar Augustus' entry to the city.

Practicalities

The **train station** (to the east) and **bus terminal** (to the south) are immediately outside the walls, a fair distance apart. If you enter the town at the **Puerto de Santiago**, the best of its old gates, you can then climb up onto the most impressive stretch of wall, leading past the cathedral.

The **Turismo** is in the *Galerías* of the Praza España (Mon–Fri 9am–2pm & 4–8pm, Sat 10am–2pm). Most of the budget **hostales** are outside the walls, around the train and bus stations, but it's more fun to be inside. *Hostal Parames*, Rua do Progreso 28 (☎982/

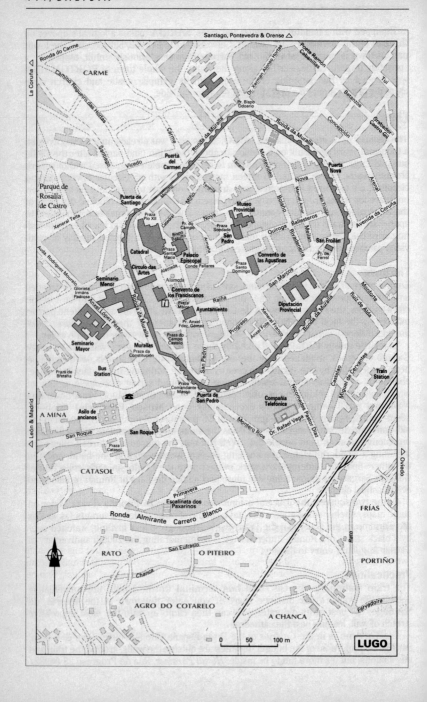

LUGO

226251; ②) is comfortable and good value, and the *Alba* at Calvo Sotelo 31 (☎982/ 226056; ②), is perfectly adequate, too. For **bars**, explore those along the very long straight **Rua Nova** leading north, most of these establishments also serve *pinchos*.

Santiago de Compostela

Built in a warm golden granite, **SANTIAGO DE COMPOSTELA** is one of the most beautiful of all Spanish cities, rivalled in the north only by León and Salamanca. The medieval city has been declared in its entirety to be a national monument, and remains a remarkably integrated whole, all the better for being almost completely pedestrianized. The buildings and the squares, the long stone arcades and the statues, are hewn from the same granite blocks and blend imperceptibly one into the other, often making it impossible to distinguish ground level from raised terrace.

The **pilgrimage** to Santiago captured the imagination of Christian Europe on an unprecedented scale. At the height of its popularity, in the eleventh and twelfth centuries, the city was receiving over half a million pilgrims each year. People of all classes came to visit the supposed shrine of Saint James the Apostle (Santiago to the Spanish, Saint Jacques to the French), making this the third holiest site in Christendom, after Jerusalem and Rome.

The atmosphere of the place is much as it must have been in the days of the pilgrims, with tourists now as likely to be attracted by Santiago's art and history as by religion. Not that the function of pilgrimage here is dead. It fell into decline with the Reformation – or as the local chronicler Molina reported, "the damned doctrines of the accursed Luther diminished the number of Germans and *wealthy* English" – but fortunes have revived of late. Each year on July 25, the Festival of St. James, there is a ceremony dedicating the country and government to the saint at his shrine, and recent pilgrims have included Generals de Gaulle and Franco, and, to put his seal on the myth, Pope John Paul II (in 1982). Years in which the saint's day falls on a Sunday are designated "Holy Years", and the activity becomes even more intense.

With its large population of students, most of whom live in the less appealing modern city slightly downhill, Santiago is always a lively place to visit, far more than a mere historical curiosity. Uniquely, it's also a city that's at its best in the rain; in fact it's situated in the wettest fold of the Gallego hills, and suffers brief but constant showers. Water glistens on the facades, gushes from the innumerable gargoyles, and flows down the streets. As a result vegetation sprouts everywhere, with the cathedral coated in orange and yellow mosses, and grass poking up from the tiles and cobbles. It's also a manageable size – you can wander fifteen minutes out of town and reach wide open countryside. You may well find yourself staying longer than you'd planned, particularly if you arrive when the great **July 25 Festival** is in full swing (see p.434).

Arrival, information and accommodation

Arriving at the **bus station** you are 1km or so north of the town centre; bus #10, onto which everyone climbs, will take you in to Praza de Galicia. Santiago is a major nexus for buses; as well as comprehensive local services, buses run to Portugal, France, Switzerland and England. The **train station** is a long walk to the south, along c/del Morreo, which also leads to Praza de Galicia. The **Turismo** in town is at Rua del Vilar 43 (Mon–Fri 9am–2pm & 4–7pm, Sat 9am–1pm; ☎981/584081), and can provide complete lists of accommodation and facilities.

Labacolla **airport** (☎981/597400) is some 13km out east on the road to Lugo. Eight buses a day run into the centre via the train and bus stations; the *Iberia* office in town is at c/General Pardiñas 24.

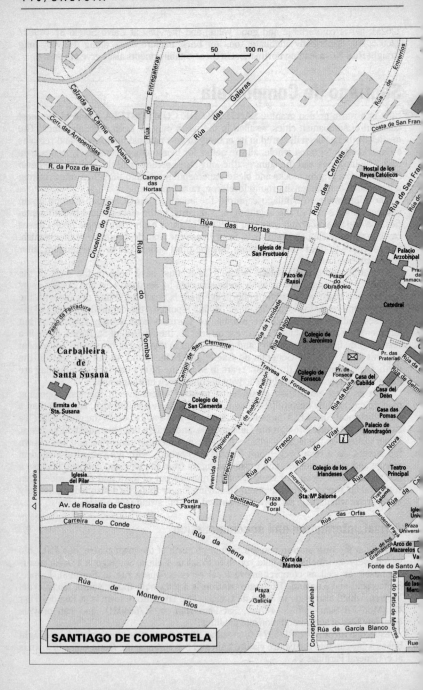

SANTIAGO DE COMPOSTELA

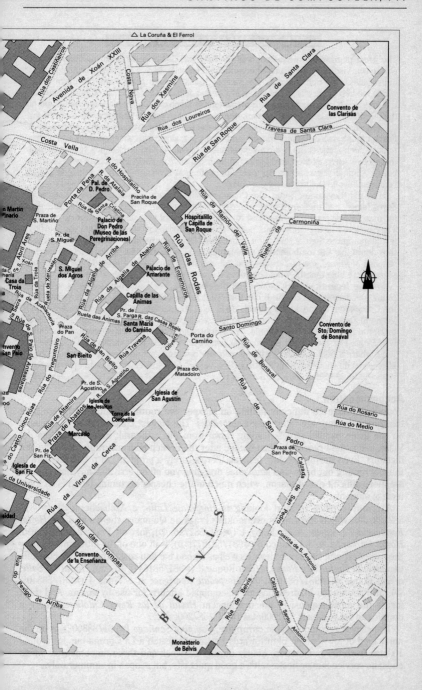

△ La Coruña & El Ferrol

THE PILGRIMAGE TO SANTIAGO

The great pilgrimage to Santiago was the first exercise in mass tourism. Although the shrine was visited by the great – Fernando and Isabella, Carlos V, Francis of Assisi – you didn't have to be rich to come. The various roads through France and Northern Spain which led here, collectively known as *El Camino de Santiago* (The Way of Saint James, or the Pilgrim Route), were lined with monasteries and charitable hospices for the benefit of the pilgrims. Villages sprang up along the route, and an order of knights was founded for the pilgrims' protection. There was even a guidebook, the world's first – written by a French monk called Aymery Picaud, and recording, along with water sources and places to stay, such facts as the bizarre sexual habits of the Navarrese Basques (who exposed themselves when excited, and protected their mules from their neighbours with chastity belts). All in all it was an extraordinary phenomenon in an age when most people never ventured beyond their own town or village.

Why did they come? Some, like Chaucer's Wife of Bath, who had "been in Galicia at Seynt Jame", had their own private reasons: social fashion, adventure, the opportunities for marriage or even for crime. But for most pilgrims, it was simply a question of faith. They believed in the miraculous power of Saint James, and were told that the journey would guarantee them a remission of half their time in purgatory. Not for a moment did they doubt that the tomb beneath the high altar at Compostela Cathedral held the mortal remains of James, son of Zebedee and Salome and first cousin of Jesus Christ. It seems scarcely credible that the whole business was an immense ecclesiastical fraud.

Yet **the legend**, at each point of its development, bears this out. It begins with the claim, unsubstantiated by the Bible, that Saint James came to Spain, at some point after the Crucifixion, to spread the gospel. He is said, for example, to have had a vision of the Virgin in Zaragoza. He then returned to Jerusalem, where he was undoubtedly beheaded by Herod Agrippa. His body should, by all rights and reason, be buried somewhere in the Nile Delta. But the legend records that two of James's disciples removed his corpse to Jaffa, where a boat appeared, without sails or crew, and carried them to Padrón, twenty kilometres downstream from Santiago. The voyage took just seven days, at once proving

Accommodation

You should have no difficulty finding an inexpensive **room** in Santiago, though note that *pensiones* here are often called *hospedajes*. The biggest concentration of places is on the three parallel streets leading down from the cathedral: Rua Nueva, Rua del Villar, and c/del Franco (this last named after the French pilgrims, rather than the late dictator). Even during the July festival, there's rarely a problem, with half the bars in the city renting out beds, and landladies dragging you off on arrival; if anything, things are more difficult out of season, when much of the cheaper accommodation is let long-term to students.

A favourite place to start looking is *Hospedaje Lalin*, c/Azabachería 31 (☎981/582123; ①), which has rooms overlooking Praza de Quintana; there's also the *Hostal Residencia La Estela*, Avda. Rajoy 1 (☎981/582796; ②), just off Praza de Obradoiro. *Hostal Barbantes*, c/del Franco 6 (☎981/581077; ③), is in one of the little squares near the cathedral, and has great views as well as a good bar and restaurant. Other possibilities include *Hostal San Roque*, c/San Roque 8 (☎981/581647; ②), and *Hostal La Salle*, c/San Roque 6 (☎981/584611; ③). *Hospedaje Rodriguez* at c/Pinos 4 (☎981/588408; ②), off Patio de los Madres, has a well-equipped kitchen for use by guests. And don't forget the most expensive, the magnificent *Hostal de los Reyes Católico*s, where a double can set you back 238,000ptas (☎981/582200; ⑥).

The closest recommendable **campsite**, *Camping Santiago* (☎981/888002), is on the north side of town, about 5km towards La Coruña (catch a La Coruña bus for around 100ptas from the bus station, hourly during the week and three times daily at weekends; no service Sun or fiestas). It's a good quiet site, but is open in summer only.

the miracle "since", as Ford wrote in 1845, "the Oriental Steam Company can do nothing like it".

At this stage the body was buried, lost and forgotten for the next 750 years. It was redis-covered at Compostela in 813, at a time of great significance for the Spanish church. Over the preceding century, the Moors had swept across the Iberian peninsula, gaining control over all but the northern mountain kingdom of Asturías, and in their campaigns they had introduced a concept entirely new to the west: *jihad*, or holy war. They also drew great strength from the inspiration of their champion, the Prophet Muhammad, whose death (in 632) was still within popular memory and a bone from whose body was preserved in the Great Mosque of Córdoba. Thus the discovery of the bones of Saint James, under a buried altar on a site traditionally linked with his name, was singularly opportune. It occurred after a hermit was attracted to a particular spot on a hillside by visions of stars, and the hill was known thereafter as Compostela, from the Latin *campus stellae*, meaning "field of stars". Alfonso II, King of Asturías, came to pay his respects, built a chapel, and the saint was adopted as the champion of Christian Spain against the Infidel.

Within decades the saint had appeared on the battlefield. Ramiro I, Alfonso's succes-sor, swore that he had fought alongside him at the Battle of Clavijo (844), and that the saint had personally slaughtered 60,000 Moors. Over the next six centuries *Santiago Matamoros* (Moor-killer) manifested himself at some forty battles, even assisting in the massacre of American Indians in the New World. It may seem an odd role for the fisher-man-evangelist, but presented no problems to the Christian propagandists who portrayed him most frequently as a knight on horseback in the act of dispatching whole clutches of swarthy, bearded Arabs with a single thrust of his long sword. (With consummate irony, when Franco brought his expert Moroccan troops to Compostela to dedicate themselves to the overthrow of the Spanish Republic, all such statues were discreetly hidden under sheets.)

The cult of Santiago was strongest during the age of the First Crusade (1085) and the Reconquest; people wanted to believe, and so it gained a kind of truth. In any case, as Ford acidly observed, "if people can once believe that Santiago ever came to Spain at all, all the rest is plain sailing".

The Cathedral

All roads to Santiago lead to the **Catedral**. And this, as Jan Morris asserts, "is still, as it was for those ancient pilgrims, one of the great moments of travel". Traditionally the first member of a party of pilgrims to catch sight of their goal would cry "Mon Joie!" and become "king" of the group; the hill on the eastern side of Santiago thus became known as "Mountjoy". But you first appreciate the sheer grandeur of the cathedral upon venturing into the vast expanse of the Praza de Obradoiro. Directly ahead stands a fantastic Baroque pyramid of granite, flanked by immense bell towers and every-where adorned with statues of Saint James in his familiar pilgrim guise with staff, broad hat, and scallop-shell badge. This is the famous **Obradoiro facade**, built in the mid-eighteenth century by an obscure Santiago-born architect, Fernando Casas y Novoa. No other work of Spanish Baroque can compare with it, nor with what Edwin Mullins (in *The Road To Compostela*) sublimely calls its "hat-in-the-air exuberance".

The main body of the cathedral is Romanesque, rebuilt in the eleventh and twelfth centuries after a devastating raid by the Muslim vizier of Córdoba, al-Mansur in 977. He failed to find the body of the saint (perhaps not surprisingly), but forced the citizens to carry the bells of the tower to the mosque at Córdoba – a coup which was later dramatically reversed (see "Córdoba", p.250). The building's highlight – indeed one of the great triumphs of medieval art – is the **Pórtico de Gloría**, the original west front, which now stands inside the cathedral behind the Obradoiro. Completed in 1188 under the supervision of one Maestro Mateo, this was both the culmination of all Romanesque sculpture and a precursor of the new Gothic realism, each of its host of figures being strikingly relaxed and quietly humanised. They were originally painted, and still bear traces of a seventeenth-century renovation.

The real mastery, however, is in the assured marshaling of the ensemble. Above the side doors are representations of Purgatory and the Last Judgment, while over the main door Christ presides in glory, flanked by his *Apostles* (Saint John with his eagle, Saint Mark with his lion, etc) and surrounded by the 24 *Elders of the Apocalypse* playing celestial music. *Saint James* sits on the central column, beneath Christ and just above eye level in the classic symbolic position of intercessor, since it was through him that pilgrims could gain assurance of their destiny. The pilgrims would give thanks at journey's end by praying with the fingers of one hand pressed into the roots of the *Tree of Jesse* below the saint. So many millions have performed this act of supplication that five deep and shiny holes have been worn into the solid marble. Finally, for wisdom, they would lower their heads to touch the brow of Maestro Mateo, the humble squatting figure on the other side.

The spiritual climax of the pilgrimage, however, was the approach to the **High Altar**. This remains a peculiar experience. You climb steps behind the altar, embrace the Most Sacred Image of Santiago, kiss his bejewelled cape, and are handed, by way of certification, a document in Latin called a *Compostela*. The altar is a riotous creation of eighteenth-century Churrigueresque, but the statue has stood there for seven centuries and the procedure is quite unchanged. (You also get a God's-eye view from up there, during services, of the priest and congregation.) The pilgrims would then make confession and attend a High Mass. You should try to do the latter at least, as a means of understanding Santiago's mystique.

You'll notice an elaborate pulley system in front of the altar. This is for moving the immense incense-burner, "Botafumeiro", which, operated by eight priests, is swung in a vast 25–30-metre ceiling-to-ceiling arc across the transept. It is stunning to watch, but takes place only at certain services; it's unusual outside Holy Years, but the Turismo shows a video if you're curious. The saint's bones are kept in a **crypt** beneath the altar. They were lost for a second time in 1700, having been hidden before an English invasion, but were rediscovered during building work in 1879. In fact they found three skeletons, which were naturally held to be those of Saint James and his two disciples. The only problem was identifying which one was the Apostle. This was fortuitously resolved as a church in Tuscany possessed a piece of Santiago's skull which exactly fitted a gap in one of those here. Its identity was confirmed in 1884 by Pope Leo XIII, and John Paul II's visit presumably reaffirmed official sanction.

The cathedral is full of collecting boxes; there are two on either side if you wish to kneel before the bones. But to visit the **Treasury, Cloister, Archaeological Museum,** and Mateo's beautiful **Crypt of the Portico**, you need to buy a collective ticket for 300ptas. The late Gothic cloisters in particular are well worth seeing; from the plain, mosque-like courtyard you get a wonderful view of the riotous mixture of the exterior, crawling with pagodas, pawns, domes, obelisks, battlements, scallop shells and cornucopias. The museum is behind the balconies overlooking the great cathedral square. These parts of the building – unlike the cathedral itself, which stays open throughout the day – are limited to set openings hours of 10.30am–1.30pm and 4–6.30pm (Sun 10.30am–1.30pm).

The rest of the city

The whole city, with its flagstone streets and arcades, is quietly enchanting, but if you want to add direction to your wanderings, perhaps the best plan is first to examine the buildings around the cathedral – the Archbishop's palace and Hostal de los Reyes Católicos – and then head for some of the other monasteries and convents. Finally, to get an overall impression of the whole architectural ensemble of Santiago, take a walk along the promenade of the **Paseo de la Herradura**, in the spacious public gardens just southwest of the old part, at the end of c/del Franco.

Around the cathedral

The **Palacio Arzobispal Gelmirez** (10am–1.30pm & 4–7.30pm) occupies the north side of the cathedral, balancing the cloister, with its entrance just to the left of the main stairs. Gelmirez was one of the seminal figures in Santiago's development. He rebuilt the cathedral in the twelfth century, raised the see to an archbishopric, and "discovered" a ninth-century deed which gave annual dues to St. James's shrine of one bushel of corn from each acre of Spain reconquered from the Moors. It was enforced for four centuries, and repealed only in 1834. In his palace, suitably luxuriant, are a vaulted twelfth-century kitchen and some fine Romanesque chambers.

As late as the thirteenth century the cathedral was used to accommodate pilgrims (the *Botafumeiro* was used at least in part as a fumigator), but slowly its place was taken by convents founded around the city. Fernando and Isabella, in gratitude for their conquest of Granada, added to these facilities by building a hostel for the poor and sick. This, the elegant Renaissance **Hostal de los Reyes Católicos**, fills the northern side of the Praza de Obradoiro in front of the cathedral. It is now a *parador* – a five-star hotel – which means that unless you're staying here, it's not all that easy to get in to see the four superb patios, the chapel with magnificent Gothic stone carving, and the vaulted crypt-bar (where the bodies of the dead were once stored). However, although do-it-yourself tours are frowned on, you can always stop in for a drink in the bar (which isn't that expensive, unlike the restaurant).

You could easily spend half an afternoon just getting to know the squares around the cathedral. Each of these is distinct. The largest is the **Praza de Quintana**, where a flight of broad steps joins the back of the cathedral to the high walls of a convent. It is unreachable by road, and thus takes on the character of a stage, successively peopled by whoever stumbles upon it. The "Puerta Santa" doorway in this square is only opened during those "Holy Years" in which the Feast of Santiago falls on a Sunday. To the south is the **Praza de las Platerías**, the silversmiths' square, dominated by an extravagantly ornate fountain, and to the north is the **Praza de la Azabachería**, which at one time was the financial centre of Spain.

Central churches

The enormous Benedictine **San Martín** stands close to the cathedral, the vast altarpiece in its church ("a fricassee of gilt gingerbread", according to Ford) depicting its patron riding alongside Saint James. Nearby is **San Francisco**, reputedly founded by the saint himself during his pilgrimage to Santiago.

In the north of the city you'll find two more: Baroque **Santa Clara**, with a unique curving facade, and a little beyond it, **Santo Domingo**. This last is perhaps the most interesting of the buildings, featuring a magnificent seventeenth-century triple stairway, each spiral leading to different storeys of a single tower, and the fascinating **Museo do Pobo Gallego** (Mon–Sat 10am–1pm & 4–7pm; free), featuring Gallego crafts and traditions. Many aspects of the way of life displayed haven't yet entirely disappeared, though you're today unlikely to see *corozas*, straw overcoats worn until recent decades by mountain shepherds. The exhibits are labelled in Gallego, but guides are available in major European languages.

Santa María del Sar

Outside the main circuit of the city, the one really worthwhile visit is the curious Romanesque church of **Santa María del Sar**. This lies about a kilometre down the c/ de Sar, which begins at the Patio de las Madres. Due to the subsidence of its foundations Santa María has developed an extraordinary slant of about fifteen degrees, though it remains utterly symmetrical. It also has a wonderfully sculpted cloister, reputedly the work of Maestro Mateo. The church is supposed to stay open all day, but you may have to ask around in the buildings at the back.

Eating, drinking and nightlife

Many of the most attractive buildings in old Santiago are still used by the university, and the presence of so many students guarantees that the city has a healthy animation to go with its past. There are excellent **bars**, with prices rarely above normal; it's the best place in Galicia to hear the local Celtic music, played on *gaitas* (bagpipes), often by student groups known as *Tunas* – they'll probably try and sell you a tape in Praza de Obradorio. Gallego food – and drink – are also plentiful and excellent in Santiago, with a plethora of good, solid **places to eat**.

If you're shopping for your own food, or if you just like to browse around, don't miss the large covered **market** held daily in the old halls of the Praza de San Félix. The excellence of the fresh produce does much to explain the shortage of food shops elsewhere in Santiago. Also look out for *La Casa de los Quesos* on Rua del Villar, where they sell the traditional breast-shaped **cheese**, *queso de tetilla*.

Restaurants

Among the most famous of the **restaurants** is the lovely *El Asesino* at Praza Universidad 16, where three sisters serve lunches so cheap and popular that they don't bother with a sign – just ask to be directed. Another student haunt is the *Casa Manolo* at Rua Traviesa 27, while the c/del Franco is full of bar-restaurants such as *El Bombero* with reliable *tazas* and *tapas*. *Bodegón de Xulio* here is a really good seafood restaurant. If money's no object the city's best restaurant is either *Don Gaiferos* in Rua Nueva – superb seafood in highly attractive cellar-like surroundings – or *Anexo Vilas* at Avda. Villagarcía 21, on the road south out of town. Count on 3000ptas a head and upwards.

Bars

Bars change a bit too often, and are in any case too plentiful, for it to be worth offering more than a few suggestions, but on a long night out try and call in at the *Bar Ourense* and *O'Barril* on c/del Franco, *O Gato Negro* on Rua Raiña, and *O'Galo d'Ouro*, in a cellar on the Cuesta Conga (indicated by a Portuguese cock symbol), which has a superbly cosmopolitan jukebox. For a somewhat narrower focus, recorded Celtic music can be heard at *Casa de Crechas* near the Praza Immaculada.

The Rías Altas

The wild indented coastline to the west of La Coruña and Santiago – known as the **Rías Altas**, and consistently harsher than the Rías Bajas further south – is nonetheless beautiful, with pine forests covering the mountain slopes, and villages only occasionally interrupting the line of the shore. The sun setting over the ocean, with mighty Atlantic waves battering the bleak rocky headlands, is as powerful a sight as you could wish for. For the medieval pilgrims this was the **end of the world**, and it remains inaccessible and somewhat forbidding. Irregular buses do run to the larger towns, along slow, winding roads, but there are no trains. If you have your own car, it's well worth following the length of the coastal road from La Coruña down to **Finisterre** and around to **Muros** and **Noya**.

You should be warned, however, that even where the isolated coves do shelter fine beaches, you will rarely find resort facilities. While the beaches may look splendid, braving the water is recommended only to the hardiest of swimmers, and the weather is significantly wetter and windier here than it is a mere hundred kilometres further south.

Carballo to Corme

There are few potential stopping points immediately west of La Coruña; you should first cover the 35km to the inland road junction of **CARBALLO**. *Hostal Puñal* here, at c/Poniente 13 (☎981/700915; ②), is the only budget place to stay and has a good restaurant. From the sizeable and badly signposted bus station (at the corner of Rua Poniente and c/del Peru you'll see an arrow) you can catch *Transportes Finisterre* **buses** to a succession of tiny seaside harbours.

Heading northwest out of Carballo, **BUÑO** has a long tradition of pottery-making, particularly gorgeous tortilla plates and wine jugs, with their distinctive brown-and-yellow designs. *La Cacharrera*, on the main road, has a good selection, made behind the shop. From Buño, a road leads north to **MALPICA**, where an attractive, stone-walled harbour backed by modern buildings shelters a fishing fleet. Three desolate islands just off the coast make up a seabird sanctuary; walk to the very end of the sea wall and you'll see them, though access is only possible if you come to some informal arrangement with a fisherman. The *Panchito* at Praza Villar Amigo 6 (☎981/720307; ③) makes a reasonable overnight stop, and there's a friendly seafood **restaurant**, the *San Francisco* on Rua Eduardo Pondal.

Across the headland from Malpica, **CORME** is set back above a deep, round bay, its cramped streets leading to a minute praza. The beach is split by a freshwater stream, and, should you require even greater privacy, deserted sand dunes and forgotten inlets hide within easy walking distance. Even by the standards of local villages whose social structures are still clan-based, Corme is fiercely insular. In the 1940s and 1950s, it was the stamping-ground of Gallego guerillas, who swooped down from the hills to beat up the Civil Guard. In August 1993, 650 kilos of hashish appeared in the nets of a local fishing boat – to the amazement of no-one. **CORME ALDEA**, an agricultural settlement on the hill above the port, has perhaps more charm than its sea-based sister, but back in Corme the view across the harbour from the back of *O Biscoiteiro* bar-restaurant, on Avda. Remedios, is lovely, and the food's good, too. There are **beds** available above the restaurant *Miramar*, if you wanted to stay.

Spanish people set up tents around small fires on the sheltered **Praia de Niños**, midway between Malpica and Corme. The turning is signposted, then turn left at the granite cross and follow the road between fields of maize to the sea. There's a *fuente* beneath the granite church that overlooks the beach, and a solitary bar that closes at night; otherwise, you'll need to bring your own supplies. Another great, though illegal, campsite is at **Praia de Balarés**, below Corme and approaching Ponteceso; a lovely sheltered inlet with a couple of high-season bars, where the swimming is relatively safe.

Ponteceso to Traba

An ancient bridge crosses the river Anllóns at **PONTECESO**, just beyond the stone mansion that was the home of the Gallego poet, Eduardo Pondal (1835–1917) – you'll see roads names after him all over Galicia. A long sweep of fine, clean sand is backed by café-lined streets at **LAXE** (pronounced "Lashay"), which offers the area's safest swimming, thanks to a formidable sea wall which also protects a small harbour. *Bar Mirador*, off the square, is owned by the descendant of a family of photographers who began work here in the 1870s – there's a pictorial history of the area up on the bar walls.

Following the coast road out of Laxe, the sign for **PEDREIRA** (too small to be marked on most maps) points you to a tiny, untouched stone hamlet; turn left where three narrow roads meet for the beach, or sharp right for a gravel road around the coastline. There's a perfect cove a couple of kilometres along here, between two stone fishing huts (a hippy comune until a large storm came along), beyond which the road is unsafe. This massively long beach is the **Praia de Traba**, remote as anything, and backed by sand dunes and the jigsaw mini-fields of what is still basically strip-farming, although newly collectivized. On a hill above, the ancient village of **TRABA** (unsign-posted; turn right just before the *Costa Dorada* bar on the main road) is made up of stone houses and exceptionally well-laden fruit trees, guarded by vociferous dogs. This is prime smuggling territory, with a long and lawless history. In Traba's shop/bar, *Casa de Parages*, look for the picture on the wall of a hapless American fighter plane that crashed here in the 1930s – villagers rushed to throw sand in the eyes of the emerging pilot so he couldn't prevent them from stripping the plane. You can walk along the sand from Traba all the way to Camelle, this place now a bit worn beyond its pleasant harbour.

The Costa da Morte

The most exposed and westerly stretch of all, from Camariñas to Finisterre, has long been famed as the **Costa da Morte** (Coast of Death), and Celtic legends, here as at the Breton Finisterre, tell of doomed cities drowned beneath the sea. Even scavenging for shellfish along the rocks can be lethal. One of Galicia's most popular delicacies are *percebes* (barnacles) – you'll see them on sale in the markets at vastly inflated prices, repulsive shrivelled little things which look for all the world like mummified toes). This coast is prime territory for hunting *percebes*, which have to be scooped up from the very waterline. Old women have been known to be swept away by the dreaded "seventh wave", which can appear out of nowhere from a calm sea.

Camariñas

Picturesque **CAMARIÑAS** is back off the beaten track and the bus route: if you're planning a night's stay it has a definite edge over Finisterre. Stretching around an attractive harbour containing a fishing fleet and the yachts of well-heeled visitors, Camariñas' buildings have white-painted, glassed-in balconies while the town sports a tradition in lace-making – you'll see old women, with lace-making pillows and extensive experience in markets, strategically placed to corner tourists.

For **accommodation**, *La Marina* (☎981/736030; ②), c/Miguel Freijo 4, at the beginning of the harbour wall, has clean rooms, great views and a good restaurant (if a rather obstreperous owner). *Triñanes II*, Area de Vila (☎981/736108; ①), is a good bet, and inexpensive without bath, as is the *Hostal Praza* (☎981/736103; ②), in the old market square. There are several more *hostales* around the waterfront.

You can trek out from Camariñas to **Cabo Vilán**, five kilometres away, where a light-house rising out of a parador-sized mansion guards a rocky shore; climb the adjacent rocks for a stunning sea view. Winds whip viciously around the cape, which is why it was chosen for the site of the towering experimental windmill park next door to the lighthouse. Huge, sci-fi propellors spin in the wind – dramatic and, in the evening when lit by the seachlight beam of the lighhouse, eerie.

On to Finisterre

The inland road (C552) from Carballo to Finisterre is surprisingly good, a result of the unprecedented burst of 1990s' road-building that is changing Galicia forever. **VIMIANZO** has spent years restoring its mostly sixteenth-century castle (Tues–Fri 10am–1pm & 4–7pm, Sat 10am–2pm & 4–8.30pm; free), which now makes a wonderful setting for a new cultural centre, with paintings, photographs and costumes.

Heading west, 2km past the small but industrialized port of Cée, **CORCUBIÓN**, 14km shy of Finisterre, retains some elegance, though decay has set in behind its brave seafront facade. However, there's some evidence of restoration – the thirteenth-century church has a new roof – and the views from town are lovely. Try the small *La Sirena*, c/Antonio Porrua 15 (☎981/745036; ②), for a **room** or continue on to the white sand beach at **SARDIÑEIRO**, halfway between Finisterre and Corcubión, though there's nothing to do there in the evenings. In a curve of the road nestle the **campsite** *Ruta Finisterre* (☎981/745585; open June–Sept) and the **hostal** *Praia de Estorde* (☎981/745585; ②), open all year.

Finisterre

The town of **FINISTERRE** (Fisterra) still feels as if it's ready to drop off the end of the world. Other than its symbolic significance, there's no great reason to come here – particularly since the public transport is so minimal. It's no more than a grey clump of houses wedged into the rocks on the side of a headland away from the open ocean; but it does have a number of inexpensive **hostales**, such as the *Rivas* (☎981/740027; ③) and the *Cabo Finisterre* (☎981/740000; ②) on c/Santa Catalina. The terrace of the *Café Tearrón* looks over the harbour, while the *marisquería* across the street has fresh seafood crawling around in tanks.

The actual tip of the **headland** is a two-kilometre walk beyond, along a heathered mountainside, through a newly-planted pine forest. A lighthouse perches high above the waves and when, as so often, the whole place is shrouded in thick mist and the mournful foghorn wails across the sea, it's an eerie spot. When the sun shines, you're better steering clear of the ice cream kiosks and shell-necklace sellers, and turning right up the zig-zag road that climbs to the **Vista Monte do Facho**, high above the lighthouse, for stupendous views.

Ezaro and Carnota

Around **EZARO**, where the Río Xallas meets the sea, the scenery is marvellous. The rocks of the sheer escarpments above the road are so rich in minerals that they are multicoloured, and glisten beneath innumerable tiny waterfalls. At Ezaro itself, a hydro-electric power plant on the bleak hillside manages to look awesomely appropriate, while further upstream there are warm natural lagoons and more cascades.

The *hostal* above the *Bar Stop* (☎981/747015; ①) has inexpensive **rooms**, or you could continue another couple of kilometres to the charming little port of **PINDO**. Beneath a stony but thickly wooded hill dotted with old houses, there's the *Hospedaje La Morada* (②) for sleeping and, next door, the *Marisquería La Revolta* for eating seafood.

Towards **CARNOTA** the series of short beaches finally join together into a long unbroken line of dunes, swept by the Atlantic winds. The village of Carnota is 1km from the shore, but its palm trees and old church are still thoroughly caked in salt. The *Hostal Miramar* (☎981/857016; ③) is large and comfortable. Carnota also boasts the longest *horreo* (granite grainstore) in Galicia, and presumably therefore in the world. *Horreos* can be attractive and interesting, but this one – originally eighteenth-century – is a triumph of form over function, moved here and extended in 1966 for the sake of sheer size.

Muros and Noya

Some of the best traditional Gallego architecture outside Pontevedra can be found in the grand old town of **MUROS**. It rises in tiers of narrow streets from the curve of the seafront to a Romanesque church; almost everywhere you look are squat granite columns and arches, flights of wide steps, and benches and stone porches built into the housefronts. The old market building in particular is almost a miniature Versailles.

Buses stop along the seafront, and a sea-facing room in any of the several **hostales** along here is a pleasure: *Hostal Ría de Muros*, Avda. Calvo Sotelo 53 (☎981/826056; ③), has excellent double rooms with views and balconies; *La Muradana,* Avda. de la Marina 107 (☎981/826700; ④), is also recommended; while *As Gaviotas*, c/Serres 124 (☎981/826266; ①), is probably the least expensive. Weather permitting, there's also a **campsite**, *A Bouga* (☎981/826025), beside the beach 2km out at Louro. For **dinner**, *El Bodegon*, also on the main road along the front, has a stone-vaulted interior, fresh seafood and grilled meats – around 2000ptas a head.

The larger town of **NOYA** (Noia), near the head of the first of the Rías Bajas, is, according to a legend fanciful even by Gallego standards, named after Noah, whose Ark is supposed to have struck land nearby. Scarcely less absurd is Noya's claim to be a "Little Florence", principally on the strength of a couple of nice churches and an arcaded street, and if you're coming from Santiago or further south it makes more sense to pass straight through Noya and head for Muros and beyond. If you do want to halt, you'll be made welcome; the *Sol y Mar* (☎981/820900; ②) is the best value place to stay.

The southern side of the Ría da Noya, which is sometimes called the "Cockle Coast", is dauntingly exposed, although in good weather the dunes serve as excellent beaches. At **BAROÑA** (Basonas), a rocky outcrop juts from the sand into the sea, and built on top of it you can still see the ruins of an impregnable pre-Roman settlement, with round stone huts enclosed behind a fortified wall. From here you can follow the increasingly bleak coastal road around into the Ría de Arosa, or take a shortcut through the deep lush gorges along the LC301 to Padrón.

THE RÍAS BAJAS AND THE MIÑO

Only in the three lowest of the **Rías Bajas** – the Rías de **Arosa**, **Pontevedra** and **Vigo** – can Galicia be said to have much of a tourist industry. The summer sun is more dependable and the climate milder, avoiding the worst of the Atlantic storms, which tend just to brush the northwest corner. Each of these narrow inlets is sheltered by islands and sandbanks right offshore. They are deep and calm beneath mountains of dark pines, busy with bright fishing boats and mussel rafts, and fringed with little towns of whitewashed houses and safe bathing beaches. Most of the visitors are Spanish or Portuguese; there is none of the overexploitation of the Mediterranean resorts, and only in the areas around Vigo and Villagarcía is the coastline built up for any considerable distance.

To the south, the slow, wide, mist-filled Río Miño marks the border with Portugal, and can be followed inland in search of unspoiled towns and hilltop monasteries, but the chief pleasures of the region are to be found by the sea. The two most obvious places to base yourself are **Pontevedra** and **Vigo**, each dominating its own magnificent and spacious *ría*.

Ría de Arosa (Arousa)

Following the road and rail route south from Santiago, it will take you a while to realize that things are changing. **Padrón** and Catoira are not especially appealing, and in fact the train swings inland again at Villagarcía without reaching the main resorts of this first *ría*, **Cambados** and **El Grove**. The northern shore is pretty inaccessible, and is still not sufficiently far south for travellers in search of beaches to feel confident of favourable weather.

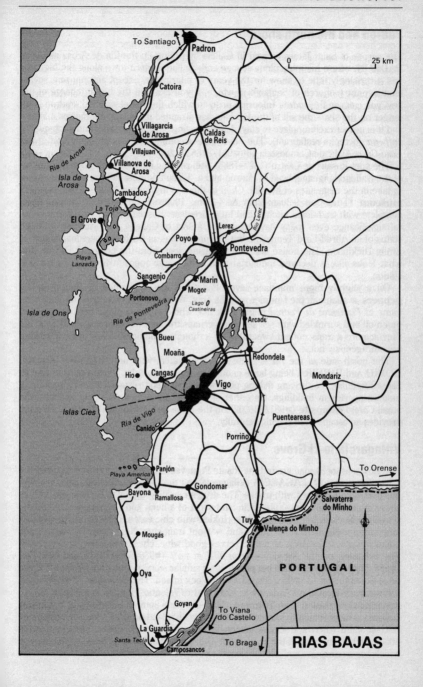

RIAS BAJAS

Padrón and the north shore

The corpse of Saint James arrived in Galicia by sailing up the Ría de Arosa as far as **PADRÓN**, where his miraculous voyage ended. The modern town along the highway has surprisingly little to show for the years of pilgrimage, except an imposing seventeenth-century church of Santiago in which, if you can find the boy in charge of the key, you can see the *padrón* (mooring post) to which the vessel was tied. Padrón is no longer on the sea – the silt of the Río Ulla has stranded it a dozen kilometres inland – and it is not an exciting place to stay, despite having several **hostales** and a top-quality *pulpería* (octopus restaurant). The best value accommodation is probably that at the *Casa Cuco*, Avda. de Compostela 16 (☎981/810511; ②).

The poet Rosalia de Castro (1837–1885), still revered as one of the great champions of the Gallego language, lived in Padrón and a "Circuit de Rosalia" has been organized to take in the main sites of her life. Chief of these is her former house, which is now a **museum** (Tues–Sun 9.30am–2pm & 4–8pm; 100ptas), furnished in period style, complete with traditional kitchen and huge fireplace. Rosalia's public image and cultural significance even today have made her a sort of Gallego poet laureate with the status of an Alfred Lord Tennyson; but her poetry was as fresh and personal as that of Emily Dickinson. The house is an unpromising walk from the centre of Padrón into what looks like a decayed industrial area – it's right opposite the Padrón *RENFE* station.

On a slightly more mundane level, Padrón is also renowned in Galicia for its **peppers**, available in the summer months only. What you get in a *tapas* bar under the name of *Pimientos de Padrón* might look like whole green peppers fried in a bit too much oil and sprinkled with sea salt, but perhaps through the intercession of Santiago they acquire a transcendent sweet flavour – though a memorable few in each serving are outrageously hot.

The north side of the *ría* is quite underpopulated, with only **RIANJO** (Rianxo), **BOIRO** and **RIBEIRA** being large enough to support *hostales*. Ribeira (also known as Santa Eugenia) is a thriving fishing port, which has good restaurants but also a lot of modern apartment buildings. On either side of the town there are long beaches; the small *Coroso* **campsite** (☎981/838002) on the Praia de Coroso, next to the C550 road, provides an escape from staying centrally.

Villagarcía to El Grove

The slow, cluttered road around the Ría de Pontevedra offers postcard views across the water. Sprawling **VILLAGARCÍA** (Vilagarcía), on the Coruña–Vigo main train line, is a serious port, its quays lined with trucks. The drug-smuggling capital of Galicia, and with its share of passing tourists, Villagarcia isn't short of a buck and Avenida de la Marina – actually a block in from the sea – is sprinkled with chic **cafés**. Look in on *Pub Museo*'s lofty stone walls, dark cane chairs and way-out trappings. Next door, the more traditional *Bodega de los Arcos* at no. 68 serves good wine, cheese and ham at fair prices. The **hostales** on the Avenida – *Leon XIII* at no.7 (☎986/506500; ③) and *San Luis* (☎986/507009; ③) – are nice but pricey; it's a similar story at attractive *Hostal 82*, Praza de la Constitución 13 (☎986/500383; ③), a block inland. The *Cortegada* (☎986/500383; ②), centrally located off Avda. de la Marina at c/Valentin Viqueira is cheaper, but it's exceptionally dreadful. The **Turismo** (Mon–Fri 9am–2pm & 4.30–6.30pm, Sat 10am–2.30pm) is inconveniently located a 20-minute walk inland on what's known as Praza de la Gasolinera (there's a service station in the middle of it). Buses leave (somewhat erratically) from outside the market for the wooded **Isla de Arosa** out in the *ría*, which has a **campsite** and a lot of pleasant beaches.

On the road towards **VILLAJUÁN** (Vilaxoan) about 1km out of Villagarcía (on the left) is what is popularly acknowledged to be the best restaurant in Galicia, **Chocolate's**. The walls are festooned with letters of praise from such sources as Juan Perón, *La Oficina del Presidente*, Buenos Aires, and Edward Heath, Westminster, London. The flamboyant owner personally serves clients with two-pound steaks impaled on pitchforks, and the fish is superb – though the prices are around 2500–4000ptas per head.

You enter **CAMBADOS** from the north via a remarkable paved stone square, the **Praza de Fefiñanes**. There are beautiful buildings on all sides, including a seventeenth-century church and a *bodega*, but it's normally deserted, probably because the road that cuts diagonally across it is not controlled in any way and pedestrians are therefore at constant risk of imminent death. The very helpful **Turismo** (daily 11am–1.30pm & 4.30–8.30pm), just off the square on Rua Novedades, is housed in the old stone house of the poet Ramon Cabanillas; they'll give you a map that shows every tree, though you don't really need one to wander the narrow streets to the pretty, café-lined seafront. Unless you can afford to stay at the **parador** – the *Albariño* (☎986/542250; ⑤) – try *El Duende*, c/Orense 10 (☎986/543075; ②), off the seafront just past the tree-lined promenade; or the nearby *Pazos*, c/Curros Enriquez 1 (☎986/542810; ②).

El Grove and La Toja

The coast road curves back on itself to the resort of **EL GROVE** (O Grove), one of the few towns in Galicia whose principal *raison d'être* is the tourist trade. El Grove is specifically a "family" resort, full of inexpensive, small-scale bars, restaurants and *hostales*, and not altogether without charm. There are dozens of **hostales**, most of them concentrated along Avda. González Besada, c/Teniente Domínguez, and Rua Castelao, including the *Casa Otero*, Avda. González Besada 133 (☎986/730110; ②) and *Concha*, c/Teniente Domínguez (☎986/730060; ③). As for **eating**, there are plenty of *tapas* bars around.

A **campsite** near the sea just west of Reboredo, *Camping Os Fieitas*, has superb facilities. All of the accommodation is packed throughout the summer, but there's room for everybody on the local beaches. The largest of these is *La Lanzada*, which is described on p.462.

It's also possible to walk across a bridge to the pine-covered islet of **LA TOJA** (A Toxa), much-loved by Galicia's nouveau-riche, who stay in the couple of upmarket hotels and play the casino. Heavily coated with expensive holiday homes, La Toja is

---

SMUGGLERS

Smuggling is a long-established tradition in Galicia. Not all the boats you see sailing into the picturesque fishing harbours are carrying fish; not all the lobster pots sunk offshore are used for holding crustaceans; not all those huts on the mussel-rafts are occupied by shellfish-growers. All along the coast you'll find beaches known locally as the "Praia de Winston", notorious for the late-night arrivals of shipments of foreign cigarettes.

Recently, however, it has become more difficult to laugh off the smugglers as latter-day Robin Hoods. Taking advantage of the infrastructure developed over the years by small-time tobacco smugglers, and of the endlessly corrugated coastline frequented by innumerable small boats, the big boys have moved in. At first, there were stories of large consignments of hashish brought in at night; now heroin abuse has become a major concern. At some point, the Medellín cartel of Colombia began to use Galicia as the European entrance point for large consignments of cocaine. Several major police crackdowns, particularly on the Isla de Arosa where certain segments of the population seemed all of a sudden to have become inexplicably rich, have yet to reverse the trend that has locals worrying that Galicia is heading towards becoming "another Sicily".

fast becoming horrible, its little shell-covered church shedding cockles among a throng of pushy souvenir sellers. La Toja actually owes much of its nationwide fame to to the soap that's made from the salts of the spa here; *Magno*, the original, is pitch black and available from the shops on the island (and most Spanish supermarkets).

The inland route: Caldas de Reyes

The motorway between Santiago and Pontevedra is expensive, though it does circumvent traffic jams around Padrón. If you take the inland road (the N550) you come, halfway between Padrón and Pontevedra, to the thermal spa town of **CALDAS DE REYES**. There's a Roman fountain, the waters of which guarantee you will be married within a year should you be so foolhardy as to drink them. At the exact point where the road crosses the Río Umia, there's a gorgeous bar/restaurant, **O Muiño**, down under the bridge next to a broad clear weir. The barbecues and the octopus are unbeatable; the one hazard is that a local fly-fisherman may land a trout on your plate.

Ría de Pontevedra

Of all the Rías Bajas, the long narrow **Ría de Pontevedra** is the archetype, closely resembling a Scandinavian fjord with its steep and forested sides. **Pontevedra** itself is a lovely old city, now slightly back from the sea at the point where the Río Lérez begins to widen out into the bay. It's a good base for expeditions along either shore of its *ría* – such expeditions made necessary by the fact that the town itself doesn't have a beach. The **north coast** of the *ría* is the more popular with tourists, **Sangenjo** being its best-known resort with well over fifty hotels, often full of British and German visitors. The **south coast** is thus the better choice for exploring, heading out past lovely beaches towards the rugged headland, ideal for camping in privacy.

Pontevedra

PONTEVEDRA is the definitive old Gallego town, a maze of cobbled alleyways and colonnaded squares, with granite crosses and squat stone houses with floral balconies. There are some "sights" to see – the museum is good, and there are several interesting churches – but the real joy of visiting Pontevedra is to spend time in an ancient town so lively and lived-in. It's perfect for a night out; the traditional local food and drink are both at their best. Pontevedra is very compact, despite being the administrative capital of a district which includes the much larger city of Vigo. The town's growth was curtailed by the silting up of its medieval port (from which one of Columbus's ships supposedly sailed; there is even a long-standing claim that Columbus was born a Gallego in Pontevedra). There are some slightly dismal industrial suburbs, but the old quarter, the *Zona Monumental*, remains distinct and unchanged, hard against the Río Lérez within the sweeping crescent of the main boulevards.

Both the **bus** and **train stations** are about 1km southeast of the centre, side by side, and served by intermittent buses which will drop you next to **La Peregrina**. This is a small pilgrim chapel built in the shape of a scallop shell, standing next to Praza la Peregrina, known locally as the **Herrería**. This paved praza, lined by arcades on one side and rose trees on the other, is the border between the old and new quarters of Pontevedra. To the east is the town's main church, **San Francisco**. All around there are fountains, gardens, and open-air cafés, old women playing cards and teenagers courting, and the daily rituals of life going on in a town small enough for everyone to know everyone else.

A selection of narrow lanes leads north from the Herrería into the **Zona Monumental**. Following c/Figueroa, you come to the small and shaded **Praza de**

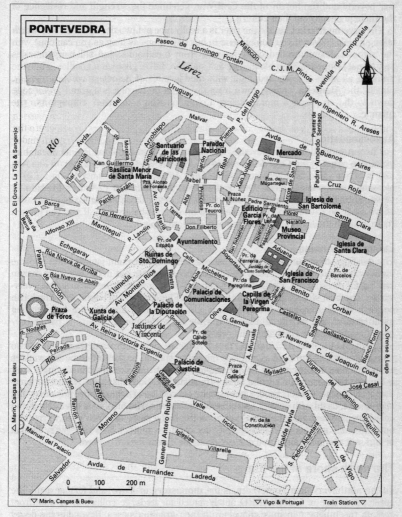

PONTEVEDRA

Leña: *the* postcard image of Pontevedra, a typical Gallego square complete with granite columns and a calvary. Two of its mansions have been joined to form an elegant and well-conceived **Museo Provincial** (Tues–Sat 10.30am–1.30pm & 4.30–8pm, Sun 11am–1pm; free to EC passport holders). Star exhibits include jet jewellery from Santiago de Compostela, which held a monopoly on the stone throughout the Middle Ages, the pre-Roman gold, and a fair – though badly lit – selection of Spanish masters; Ribera, Zubarán and Murillo. The museum's real draw is a top-floor room in the second building devoted to the twentieth-century artist, caricaturist and writer Alfonso Castelao, author of *Sempre en Galizia*, the Bible of Gallego nationalists and now a set text for the region's schools. His drawings, at their most moving when depicting prewar poverty and the horror of the Civil War, celebrate the strength and resilience of the Gallego people and their culture.

The covered **market** beside the river is a really nice old two-tier building, well worth taking a look at even if you don't intend to buy anything – as long as you can cope with the sight of disembowelled cows hanging from meathooks, and still-hairy muzzles poking out from buckets of blood. The fish stalls are full of glistening goodies, while the walls on all sides are stacked high with muddy piles of nameless edible greenery. Finally, the **Alameda** leading down from the Praza de España is a grand promenade down to the sea, with a monument to Columbus where the river empties into the Atlantic.

Accommodation

For **accommodation** in Pontevedra, the choicest spot in the *Zona* is – as usual – an expensive *parador*, the *Casa del Barón* (☎986/855800; ⑤–⑥). *Casa Maruja* on Rua Alta (②) is better value, and very neat, while *Casa Alicia*, Avda. da Santa María 5 (③) is pleasant and spotlessly clean. Out of the *Zona*, the *Madrid* at c/Andrés Mellado 11 (☎986/851006; ②) is a sizeable place that's seen better days; *Fonda La Lanzada* (①), above a bar on c/Charino, off c/Calles, is a bit on the shabby side. If you can't find a room, consult the lists at the **Turismo** at c/General Mola 3.

Eating and drinking

The twisting streets of the *Zona* are packed with tiny **bars** and jammed late into the night with drinkers and revellers. You'd probably do best to **eat** in the bars, rather than looking for a restaurant. Platters of fish and jugs of rich white wine are available everywhere. The best streets for which to head are c/Figueroa and c/Pasanteria, which run between the Herrería and Praza de Leña. On c/Figueroa, *Bar Ampara* has amazing garlic *gambas*, not for the fainthearted, while on c/Pasantería, *Rianxo* is particularly good for inexpensive *tapas* and white wine.

Try to end up at *Os Maristas*, in Praza I. Armesto, next to Praza de Leña, one of two unmarked bars on the right as you face the police station. Baskets of crabs and winkles are propped up on the counter, but the singular factor that makes the bar so sought after is the astonishing liqueur **Tumba Dios** – translated as "God falls down". It was the creation of the former owner, Paco; a home-made concoction of *aguardiente* (firewater) and *licor de café*, laced with sundry secret herbs and spices. The alcohol is devastating, the coffee invigorating, and the herbs verge on the hallucinogenic. Paco used to ration it out, two small glasses to a customer; if you asked for another he'd say "We're human beings, not animals!", and if you came in drunk he'd deny it even existed.

The north shore of the Ría

To the north, very near Pontevedra, is the **monastery of Poyo**, and further along the coast the village of **COMBARRO**, justly famed for its large collection of waterfront *horreos*, resembling miniature chapels with their granite crosses. Beyond is the resort of **SANGENJO** (Sanxenxo), the area's main venue for a serious summer night out. From 10pm onwards, the seafront bars and cafés are packed with revellers, the clubs playing Eurodance music to a lively crowd. You can judge the scale of things from the fact that there are over sixty hotels between here and the similar resort of **PORTONOVO**, but prices are high; you'd be lucky to find a room under 4000ptas.

A few kilometres beyond begins the vast **beach** of **La Lanzada**, a favourite with strong swimmers and **windsurfers**. In the summer there are temporary enclaves of cafés and restaurants, and **campsites** such as the recommended *Muiñeira* (☎986/731240), or the *O Revo* (☎986/743160) and *Espiño* (☎986/731248); during the rest of the year it's left to the wild ocean waves.

The south shore of the Ría

The southern side of the Ría de Pontevedra is less developed and has fewer visitors, although once past Marín (see below) it's quite superb. The first stretch, however, is off-putting in the extreme. Just outside (and upwind from) Pontevedra sits a monstrous paper factory, **La Cellulosa**, where a titanic yellow metal spider spouts mountains of sawdust and emits a staggering stench; on a bad day you can smell it fifty kilometres away. Plenty of orange buses run from Pontevedra's bus station, right around the headland to Marín.

Marín

Nearby **MARÍN** is not on first impression all that appealing. It's a very busy port, with the seafront cut off from the town by forbidding walls for most of its length, and is populated largely by bored cadets from the local naval academy. Even the wooded island in the middle of the *ría* belongs to the navy, and is inaccessible.

However, Marín does boast the best **churrasquería** in Spain, the *Cantaclara*, which is very cheap and almost impossible to find, housed in what looks like a deserted blue shed very near the harbour, about a mile back towards Pontevedra from the middle of town. The window display has been known to feature two completely skinned dead lambs, one wearing a pair of green plastic sunglasses and with its teeth firmly clamped into the throat of the other. Inside, there's a huge roaring flame from the wooden fire of the barbecue, and the restaurant itself is screened from the bar by stacked boxes of the Rioja house wine. The charcoal-grilled meat of all kinds is delicious.

Mogor, Bueu and beyond

Once past Marín, the scenery rapidly improves, the bay broadening into a whole series of breathtaking sandy coves. A narrow side road drops away from the main coast road immediately beyond the naval academy outside Marín, leading to three beaches. The second of these, the **Praia de Mogor** (on the bus route from Pontedvedra), is perfect, with fields of green corn as the backdrop to a crescent of fine, clean sand. There are a couple of bars overgrown with vines, and the villagers' rowboats are pulled up in the shade of the trees next to some weird, bald rocks. One side is shielded by a thick headland of dark green pines; at the other end you'll find the rocks are deeply carved with religious and fascist symbols and slogans.

In fact, rocks all over the surrounding hills were carved by the same man, a shoe-maker who spent the afternoons of his declining years glorifying God and Franco with a hammer and chisel on every available surface. In the late 1970s, when the carver was in his nineties, a professor found some carvings in Mogor and announced that they were prehistoric. The villagers said no, that's just the old shoemaker. So the professor and the shoemaker spent days combing the area, the shoemaker having to separate his carvings from those which had already been there. Some of the cruder stone spirals were duly authenticated as megalithic remains, and the professor wrote a book and made a TV documentary. The shoemaker died discredited.

BUEU (pronounced *bwayo*) is a quiet market town and port about 12km beyond Marín, and offers another pleasant strip of **beach** stretching away from its rambling waterfront. The two **hostales**, *A Centoleira* (☎986/320896; ③) and *Incamar* (☎986/320067; ②), are good value.

A smaller road turns away from the sea at Bueu, towards Cangas, but if you make your way along the coast, towards the village of **ALDAN** and the cape of **HIO**, you'll find an unspoiled expanse of pine trees and empty beaches – an ideal place to go **camping** if you stock up in advance. Particularly worth following is the unpaved road to the huge boulders at **CABO DE UDRA**, where wild horses roam the hillsides and the waves come crashing down in deserted coves. Hio itself has Galicia's best-known granite *cruceiro* (not a "passenger liner" as the official brochure translates it, but a crucifix), looking down on the spectacular *ría* of Vigo.

Ría de Vigo

Following the main road south from Bueu, you cross the steep ridge of the Morrazo peninsula to astonishing views on the far side over the **Ría de Vigo**, one of the most sublime natural harbours in the world. This region was once a hotbed of witchcraft, although Gallegos are careful to distinguish between *brujas* (malevolent witches) and *meigas* (wise women herbalists with healing powers). Tradition tells of a local woman who was accused of trafficking with the Devil by the Inquisition in the seventeenth century; she proved her claim to be a *meiga*, and was sentenced to stand outside Cangas church in her oldest clothes every Sunday for six months. Presumably she fell foul of the Holy Inquisition in one of its more lenient moods. Even today, you'll find charms against witches (in the shape of a clasped hand) on sale everywhere in Galicia, often next to crucifixes.

The *ría*'s narrowest point is spanned by a vast suspension bridge which carries the Vigo–Pontevedra highway; you'll see its twin towers from all around the bay. On the inland side is what amounts to a saltwater lake, the inlet of **San Martín**. The road and railway from Pontevedra run beside it to **REDONDELA**, separated from the sea by just a thin strip of green fields, and pass close to the tiny San Martín islands, once a leper colony and used during the Civil War as an internment centre for Republicans. The calm waters here are deceptive; somewhere under them lies a fleet of galleons lost in 1702. Seeking shelter from a storm, the ships foundered on hidden sandbanks and went down with the largest single shipment of silver ever sent from the New World.

The city of **Vigo** looks very appealing, spread along the waterfront, but apart from its possibilities for sleeping and eating, it's not a particularly interesting place to stay. If Vigo is your point of arrival in this region, one obvious alternative is to head down to the waterfront and get a **ferry** across to the little resort of **Cangas**; another would be to take a bus (the train doesn't follow the coast any further) out to **Bayona**, at the edge of the ocean. Wherever you end up staying, be sure not to miss the boat trip out to the wonderful **Islas Cíes**.

Cangas and Moaña; ferries across the Ría

CANGAS, where the road south from Bueu descends, is today a burgeoning resort, at its most lively during the Friday **market**, when the seafront gardens are filled with stalls. The town spreads perhaps 1km along the coast, though not up the hillside, to reach the **Praia de Rodeira**. There are **rooms** available at the far end, next to the beach in the *Praia* at Avda. de Orense 78 (☎986/301363; ③–④) or at the *Rodeiramar* bar (☎986/300011; ②), but both these fill quickly in summer. Closer to town try the *Jucamar* at Avda. de Marín 5 (☎986/300694; ④) – here, off-season discounts bring the price down considerably.

The main cluster of **bars and restaurants** is around the port. *O Pote* at Avda. Castelao 13, opposite the derelict former fish market, specializes in wonderful clams and baby squid, while the *Bar Celta* at c/A. Saralegui, up some steps slightly to the left of the jetty as you face the town, and looking out over the bay, is an excellent old-fashioned *tapas* bar whose *comedor* serves bargain, budget meals. You can monitor the ferries from here, and hurry down when the hooter announces a departure. The **ferry** (foot passengers only) leaves Cangas for Vigo every thirty minutes (Mon–Sat 6am–10pm, Sun 9am–10.30pm; 180ptas), a pleasant twenty-minute trip. There's a **Turismo** at the port, upstairs from the ticket office. One ferry a day also leaves for the Islas Cíes (see below), departing at 12.20pm and returning at 8pm; a return ticket costs 1600ptas.

Hourly boats to Vigo (same times as from Cangas) also leave from **MOAÑA**, 5km along the coast, which is similar to Cangas, including a fine long beach, but with fewer facilities. The **hostal** *Elec-Mar* (☎986/311742; ②) is a short steep climb up from the port, or there are plenty of other *hostales* back towards the port. The appeal of the Moaña trip is that you sail right alongside the *mejilloneiras* of the *ría*. These rope-rigged ramshackle rafts, perched on the sea like water-spiders and sometimes topped by little wooden huts, are used for cultivating mussels.

Vigo

VIGO is a large and superbly situated city, dominating the broad expanse of its *ría*. Seen from a ship entering the harbour, it is magnificent, though once ashore you may find the views back out to sea to be its most attractive feature. It is so well sheltered from the Atlantic that the wharves and quays which make it Spain's chief fishing port stretch along the shore for nearly 5km.

The declining passenger port has kept the prime spot in the middle of this stretch. This was where Laurie Lee disembarked "with the whole of Spain to walk through", a journey marvellously recorded in *As I Walked Out One Midsummer's Morning*. Here too generations of Gallego emigrants have embarked for and returned from South America, and Caribbean immigrants have had their first glimpse of Europe. Although these days, the only tourists who arrive at the **Estación Marítima de Ría** are those who have come on the ferry from Cangas and Moaña, the steep, winding streets of the old city remain crammed with tiny shops and bars catering for the still-plentiful sailors.

The cobbled streets around the **c/López Puigcerver** (or *Calle Real*, once the main street, and what Todman calls "the best drinking street in Christendom") remain a focal point for visitors. Along the seafront early in the morning, kiosks revive fishermen with strong coffee, while there and in the nearby **market** their catch is sold: all day long women stand at granite tables rooted in **Real Teófilo Llorente**, with plates of fresh oysters set out for passers-by. On **Rua Carral** shops sell pocket knives and exotic marine souvenirs, and in the evening the myríad bars on all the tiny streets come alive. A surprising old-fashioned red-light district still operates on the **Rua Abeleira Menéndez**, tucked away behind the town hall.

For the most part, the **beaches** adjacent to Vigo are crowded and not nearly as appealing as those further along, or across the ría – and certainly not a patch on the Islas Cíes (see below). Some, however, such as the one at **CANIDO**, are quite reasonable, and equipped with campsites and *hostales*.

Practicalities

As you cross the road from the port, you can't miss the **Turismo** (☎986/430577) whose free map has accommodation marked on it. The **RENFE station** has direct services to Santiago, Barcelona and Madrid, and down into Portugal. **Buses** to all major destinations, including Bayona, use the terminal, a little way out from the centre, at the junction of Avda. de Madrid and Avda. Gregorio Espiño just south of the Praza de España.

The choice is basically between staying down in the old streets, such as Rua Carral, or in the more modern areas where the trains and buses come in, further up the hill, where you get a bit more for your money. **Accommodation** possibilities on Rua Carral include the very friendly, family-run *Hostal Bienvenido* (☎986/228657; ②), opposite the Turismo; the neat and appealing *Hostal Savoy 2*, at no. 20 (☎986/432541; ③); and the *Carral* at no. 18 (☎986/224927; ②). The *Hostal Residencia Gravina*, c/Gravina 6 (☎986/484888; ②), is also a good bet. The best places near the station are the comfortable *Hostal Norte* right beside it (☎986/223805; ③) and *La Nueva* at c/Lepanto 26 (☎986/439311; ③).

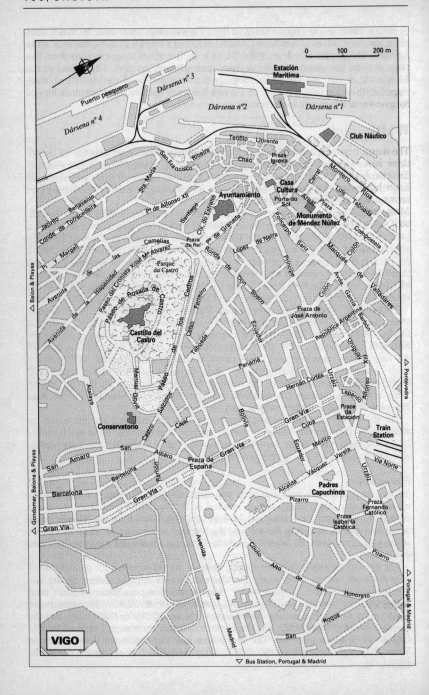

Puerto pesquero

Dársena nº 3

Dársena nº 4

Estación Marítima

Dársena nº2

Dársena nº1

Club Náutico

Teófilo Llorente

Praza Igrexa

San Francisco

Ribeira

Chão

Casa Cultura

Montero Ríos

Carral

Luis Taboada

Sta. María

Pº de Alfonso XII

Ayuntamiento

Porta do Sol

Área

Praza de Compostela

Jacinto

Benavente

Santiago

Cx. do Estreito

Pº de Granada

Policarpo

Sanz

Monumento de Méndez Núñez

Marqués Colón

Conde de Torrecedeira

Praza do Rei

Camelias

Ronda

López de Neira

Príncipe

Pi y Margall

Praza do Castro

Paseo del Cronista Xosé Mª Álvarez

Paseo de Rosalía de Castro

las

de

la

Hispanidad

de

Cedros

Ferreiro

Avda. Garcia Barbón

Avenida

de

los

Calton

de

Don Bosco

Colón

Avda. de Valladares

García Barbón

Praza de José Antonio

Castillo del Castro

Avenida

Paseo

de

Taboada

Ecuador

Manuel

Olivie

Panamá

Uruguay

República Argentina

Atalaya

Castro

Sagos

Cajal

Hernán Cortés

Bolivia

Urzáiz

Lepanto

Alfonso XIII

Conservatorio

Ramón

Amaro

Gran Vía

Cuba

Gran Vía

Praza da. Estación

San

Amaro

Praza de España

México

Ecuador

Varela

Train Station

San

Barcelona

Gran Vía

Alcalde

Vázquez

Urzáiz

Vía Norte

Barcelona

Pizarro

Padres Capuchinos

Gran Vía

Praza Fernando Católico

Gran Vía

Praza Isabel la Católica

Pizarro

Cauto

Alto

de

San

Honorato

Avenida

de

Roque

Madrid

San

◁ Baion & Playas

◁ Gondomar, Baiona & Playas

▷ Pontevedra

▷ Portugal & Madrid

0 100 200 m

VIGO

Among the budget **restaurants**, *O'Meu Lar* on Rua Fermín Penzal, off Rua Carral, offers a decent set menu for around 700ptas, while of the **bars** in the old streets, virtually all of which serve great *tapas*, *Chavalos* (for cuttlefish) and *Taberna Ramón* on Rua Cesteiros, the atmospheric *Bar Johnny's* at c/Real 15, and *La Parra* on Rua Alta (try the octopus) stand out. More expensive tastes will lead you to seek out the local delicacy, *angullas*, the baby eels which come swimming up the Río Miño fresh from the Sargasso Sea, all ready to be eaten.

The Islas Cíes

The most irresistible sands of the Ría de Vigo must be those of the **Islas Cíes**. These three islands protect the entrance to the *ría*, and can be reached by boats from the Estación Marítima in Vigo or from the harbours in Bayona and Cangas. One is an off-limits bird sanctuary; the other two are joined by a narrow causeway of sand, which forms a beach open on one side to the Atlantic and on the other to a placid lagoon. Most visitors stay on the beach, with its sprinkling of bars and a **campsite** in the trees, so it's easy to escape the crowds and find a deserted spot all your own – which can feel particularly remote on the Atlantic side of the islands. A long climb up a winding rocky path across desolate country leads to a lighthouse with a commanding ocean view.

The **campsite** (☎986/278501) is the only legal accommodation on the islands, so if you want to stay in midseason, phone ahead to make sure there's room. You have to buy a camping token before you get on the boat – this acts as a deposit (1000ptas per person), deducted from your camping bill; the difference is either made up or refunded when you leave the site. There is a small shop, as well as a couple of restaurants which aren't at all bad, but these are free to charge more or less what they choose, so you might prefer to take your own food and drink. In the summer there are six boats per day **from Vigo** (at 9am, 11am, 1pm, 3pm, 5pm and 7pm), the last one back leaving the islands at 8pm, with the return trip costing 1600ptas. In addition, six daily boats per day connect the islas with Bayona, and one daily with Cangas. Only a certain number of visitors are allowed to go to the Cíes on any one day; aim for an early boat to make sure. The season lasts from mid-June to mid-September, and during the rest of the year you can't get out there at all.

Bayona and around

BAYONA (Baiona) is situated just before the open sea at the head of a miniature *ría*, the last and the smallest in Galicia. It is arguably the region's best resort, not yet over-exploited for all its popularity with the Spanish. This small and colourful port was the first place in Europe to hear of the discovery of the New World, when Columbus's *Pinta* appeared on March 1, 1493. Nowadays the harbour contains at least as many pleasure yachts as fishing boats.

The medieval walls surrounding the wooded promontory which is Bayona's most prominent feature enclose an idyllic **parador**, partly hidden in a pine forest and with a reputation as Spain's best hotel. The hotel itself is a new but tasteful addition (*Parador Conde de Gondomar*, ☎986/355000; ⑥), which has a couple of bars including a nice one standing alone in the grounds.

It's definitely worth paying the 100ptas fee to walk around the parapet, with an unobstructed view in every direction, across the *ría* and along the chain of rocky islets which leads to the Islas Cíes. There's a footpath beneath the walls at sea level, barely used, which gives access to several diminutive beaches. These are not visible from the town proper, which has only a small patch of sand despite its fine esplanade.

The town is full of reasonably priced **hostales** such as the *Asturías* (Alférez Barreiro 17, ☎986/355591; ②) and the *Mesón del Burgo* (☎986/355309; ③), and it's a terrific place to stay. The hotel *Tres Carabelas* (☎986/355441; ④) in the cobbled alleyway just behind the seafront is very atmospheric. The bars along the alleyway are excellent, too; look for *tapas* at *Jalisco*, on the square behind the alley. All around Praza de Castro, **restaurants** such as *El Túnel* have enticing window displays of live lobsters and assorted shellfish. There's a **Turismo** (daily 10am–8pm) inside the *Concello de Baiona*, next door to *El Túnel*.

Praia de América, Ramallosa and Sabaris

There are two good **beaches** next to the road in from Vigo a couple of kilometres before Bayona. The first is the **Praia de América** (take the Vigo–Bayona bus via Panjón – Panxon – not Nigran), a superb long curve of clean sand backed by rows of vacation villas. This has its own **campsite** (☎986/365404); the *Baiona Praia Camping* (☎986/ 350035), however, is nearer the town (and accessible on both bus routes) on the shorter and scruffier *Praia Ladeira* at **SABARIS**. The inlet here is popular with **windsurfers**.

Look out for the wonderful Roman stone footbridge at **RAMALLOSA**, next to the road between the two beaches, and in Sabaris climb up the hill opposite the Ladeira beach road for good food at the very welcoming and gregarious *Churrasquería Franky*. If you keep going up this road, you'll reach the bleak plateau at the very top. It's a great place for long walks in the woods, and there's a scattering of old villages up there where life seems to go on as it always did, oblivious to the developments below.

Buses from Bayona run from c/Carabela la Pinta, just off the seafront, near the market building, except for the La Guardia buses which carry straight on around the headland; catch them opposite the *O Moscon* restaurant by the port.

The coastal route towards Portugal

The road between Bayona and La Guardia, which once threaded through a deserted, windswept wilderness, has recently been improved and is now scattered with *hostales* and hotels. There are no beaches (although the sight of the ocean foaming through the rocks is mightily impressive), or even shops, and only three buses per day.

Just outside Bayona on this road is the so-called **Virgen de la Roca**, a massive granite image overlooking the sea; it's possible to climb up inside it and on to the boat she holds in her right hand on appropriately solemn religious occasions. Halfway between Bayona and La Guardia is the town of **OYA** (Oia), no more than a very tight bend in the coast road, beneath which nestles a remarkable Baroque **monastery**, with its sheer stone facade surviving the constant battering of the Atlantic.

La Guardia

At the mouth of the great Río Miño stands the dishevelled and slightly disappointing port of **LA GUARDIA** (A Guarda), which is largely the modern creation of emigrants returned from Puerto Rico. In consolation you can **eat seafood** well and inexpensively (sometimes free, if it's *tapas*) and search out **rooms**, possibly with a harbour view. The *Hostal Martirrey* at José Antonio 8 (☎986/610349; ②) is recommended, as is the central *Hospedaje Celta*, c/Pontevedra 7 (☎986/611172; ②). There's also **camping** out towards the river – well-signposted from town. *ATSA* **buses** leave every 30 minutes to Tuy (Tui), and there are three services a day to Bayona.

Just above the town are the thick woods of **Monte Santa Tecla**, with extensive remains of a Celtic *citania* (pre-Roman fortified hill settlement), common in this part of Galicia, and even more so in northern Portugal. The ruins are about two-thirds of the way up the mountain, about half an hour's climb up a footpath-stairway cut through the forest; the way starts at the edge of La Guardia nearest Tuy.

The **citania** was probably occupied between around 600 and 200 BC, and abandoned when the Romans established control over the north. It consists of the foundations of

HORSES AND CURROS

The scrubby exposed hills around here are home to hundreds of **wild horses**, who sometimes venture down to graze by the sea. In May and June a series of day-long fiestas known as **curros** are held on successive Sundays on the hilltops further inland. At these absolutely unmissable events the horses are rounded up, counted and branded, and set free again. Wooden corrals are built at clearings in the pine woods, and surrounded by makeshift stalls and bars set up among the trees. The misty dawns see riders swathed in crude, poncho-like blankets scouring the countryside, standing in stirrups like solid wooden wedges as they chase and lasso the fleeing horses. Penned together the animals are magnificent, all sleek brown bodies and flashing eyes, tossing their unkempt manes and whinnying their disgust at being handled for the first time. It's very much a country festival, hugely enjoyed by the Gallegos you never see in the towns below, feasting on *pulpo* and picnicking in the woods, splashing dark wine from great barrels into chipped white bowls. Those villages currently holding *curros* include La Valga, Torroña, Mougas and Pinzas. Ask at local tourist offices or in the bars for details; they're not organised for tourists, and so may not be advertised.

well over a hundred circular dwellings, crammed tightly inside an encircling wall. A couple of them have been restored as full-size thatched huts; most are excavated to a few feet, though some are still buried. Set in a thick pine grove on the bleak, seaward hillside, the ancient village with its winding stone paths, wells or cisterns, and grand entranceways forms a striking contrast to the humdrum roofscape of La Guardia below. On the north slope of the *monte* there is also a large **cromlech**, or stone circle, while continuing upwards you pass along an avenue of much more recent construction, lined with the stations of the cross, and best seen looming out of a mountain mist.

At the top are a church, a small **museum** (Tues–Sun 11am–2pm & 4–7.30pm; free) of Celtic finds, a relatively inexpensive one-star **hotel** – the *Pazo Santa Tecla* (☎986/ 610002; ③) – and a café-restaurant. This last has a rhyming Gallego sign reading "Please don't go; stay and watch the television". With a view up and down the Portuguese and Spanish coasts and along the Miño, and a good selection of *tapas*, you shouldn't need much persuading.

Camposancos

La Guardia itself has only a small and rather shingly beach, but you can walk around the Monte Santa Tecla and down to the village of **CAMPOSANCOS** (about 3km) where, facing Portugal and a small islet capped by the ruins of a fortified Franciscan monastery, you'll find an adequate stretch of sand along the riverbank and a café. The council in La Guardia, along with promises to improve the look of the place, has pledged to revive a long-defunct ferry service linking Camposancos with Caminha in Portugal.

Along the Miño

The **RÍO MIÑO** (Minho in Portuguese and Gallego), the border between Spain and Portugal, so wide and beautiful upstream, is surprisingly narrow at its mouth. Only about 100m, mostly of sandbank, separate the two countries, and it's barely navigable. No large ships can make their way inland to Tuy or Valença; Viana is the first port of any size down the Portuguese coast. The miles of dunes that stretch down to Viana make for better beaches than those few around La Guardia on the Spanish side. At present, the first place you can cross the river is a few miles upstream at **GOYAN** (Goian), where a car ferry makes hourly journeys to the delightful walled village of Vila Nova da Cerveira.

Tuy

TUY (Tui, pronounced *twee*), 30km from La Guardia, is the main Gallego frontier town, staring across to the neat ramparts of Portuguese Valença and is worth a visit even if you don't plan to continue across the border. There is, of course, the usual border-crossing street of tacky wares, but old Tuy stands back, tiered amid trees and stretches of ancient walls above the fertile riverbank. Sloping lanes, paved with huge slabs of granite, climb to the imposing fortress-like **Catedral** dedicated to San Telmo, patron saint of fishermen; its military aspect is a distinctive mark of Tuy, scene of sporadic skirmishes with the Portuguese throughout the Middle Ages. There are other churches of interest too, like the Romanesque San Bartolomeo, or Gothic Santo Domingo with its ivy-shrouded cloisters. More memorable, though, is the lovely rambling quality of the place, coupled with a pair of enticing little river beaches. There's a **market** on Thursdays along the main road through town.

If you're looking to **stay**, there's the inexpensive *Habitaciones Otilia*, c/ Generalissimo 8 (☎986/601062; ②), on the edge of the old town, just up the steps from the main road – rickety and down-at-heel, but friendly enough. Other slightly more expensive places to stay include the *Hostal San Telmo*, Avda. de la Concordia 98 (☎986/603011; ②), towards the train station, or *Hostal La Generosa*, c/Calvo Sotelo 37 (☎986/600055; ②). Tuy's *parador* (☎986/600309; ⑥) is a splendid, high-class alternative, on the road to Portugal. There's a fine **pizzería** just around the corner from *Habitaciones Otilia*, which is surprisingly good and not at all expensive.

Tuy is well-connected with Vigo by **bus**; there's at least one departure every hour. If you're heading inland by rail towards Ribadavia and Orense, it's much quicker to catch your **train** from Guillarei station, 3km east of town, than to wait for a connection in Tuy itself.

Crossing the border

It's a twenty-minute walk to the Portuguese border, across an iron bridge designed by Eiffel; the little town of **VALENÇA**, dwarfed behind its mighty ramparts, lies a similar distance beyond. There's no border control at the bridge any more: just stroll (or drive) across and head up the hill to Valença, past a Turismo which can provide details about onwards Portuguese transport. A ferry, from Salvaterra do Minho further upstream, crosses to the similarly attractive old Portuguese town of Monção.

North of Tuy

There is a road from Tuy to **GONDOMAR**, and from there to Bayona, which avoids Vigo and makes a spectacular drive through thick virgin forests, but no buses run that way.

From **PORRIÑO**, halfway between Tuy and Vigo, the N120 is the most direct route to Orense, up very steep bleak mountains with not a habitation in sight. On the way, **PUNTEAREAS** has a **Corpus Christi** festival (in June) when the streets are spread out with gorgeous patterned "carpets" of bright flowers. Nearby, **MONDARIZ** is a pretty spa town with bathing beaches by a secluded river.

Upstream to Ribadavia and Celanova

Whether you follow the main inland highway or the train line parallel to the Miño, one of the best towns to end up in is **RIBADAVIA**. The trip there by train from Tuy or Vigo is a lovely riverside journey, although the valley of the Miño does tend to fill up with freezing mist until midday or so. The town stands among woods and vineyards above the river, looking grander than its size would promise, with several fine churches, including the Visigothic **San Ginés** and a sprawling **Dominican monastery** which was once the residence of the kings of Galicia. Several pleasant **bars** serve the region's excellent, port-like wine, and there are a couple of **hostales**.

The first hydroelectric dam blocks the Miño about 30km below Ribadavia, and it's from then on up that the flooding of the valley makes the river so broad and smooth-flowing, with forests right to the water's edge. The high and winding road along the south bank through **CORTEGADA** to the border at **SÃO GREGORIO** makes a good excursion, and can also be used as part of the route to **CELANOVA**. This is hardly more than a village, dominated by a vast and palatial **Benedictine monastery**. It was here that Felipe V retired into monastic life, having spent much of his reign securing the throne in the War of the Spanish Succession (1701–13). The monastery is now a school, but you can borrow the key to explore its two superb cloisters – one Renaissance, the other Baroque – and the cathedral-sized church. Most beautiful of all is the tiny Mozarabic chapel of **San Miguel** in the garden of the monastery. This dates from the tenth century, and is the work of "Arabicized" Christian refugees from al-Andalus. Buses also come in from Orense, and the **hotel** *Betanzos* on Castor Elices 12 (☎988/451036; ③) is excellent.

Orense

ORENSE (Ourense) is worse than disappointing, having lost most of its atmosphere (along with its old buildings) in a sprawl of anonymous modern suburbs. There are a few attractive small squares, and the approach is deceptively magnificent, across a seven-arched, thirteenth-century bridge. The Praza Maior is an attractive old arcaded square below the dark **Catedral**, an imitation of Compostela's, with a painted (but greatly inferior) copy of the Pórtico de Gloría, and a museum in the cloisters. From here, the old town disappears rapidly into the delapidated areas around Rua Dois de Mayo, while c/Calvo Sotelo takes you into c/del Paseo and the new town, a pleasant café-lined stroll. There's a **Turismo** kiosk in the new town at the corner of c/del Paseo at Paque San Lázaro.

There are several **fondas** around the long main street which leads from the centre to the train station, but Orense has a rather drab, soulless feel – astonishing when you consider that it was the birthplace of Julio Iglesias! (Fidel Castro's family was also from Orense.) It's a half-hour walk out to the **RENFE station** on the opposite side of the river, so you can't expect to be able to drop in and see anything between trains. You'd do better to stay the night in Ribadavia and just pass through.

Gorges of the Río Sil

The Miño is more spectacular the further you go upstream; it arrives at Orense having flowed south from Lugo through the harsh landscape traversed by the *Camino de Santiago*. Twenty kilometres northeast of Orense it meets the Río Sil at **LOS PEARES**, a crumbling old village on the main train line. You can walk from there along the **Gorges of the Sil**, with precarious farm terraces tumbling down to a chaos of rocks and foam. High above **SAN ESTEBAN** is another monastery, the three-cloistered **Monasterio de Ribas do Sil**. On the plain to the north, **MONFORTE DE LEMOS** is a major rail junction. Again, the station is a long way from the town centre, but Monforte is a satisfyingly unspoilt and ancient place. Its **Torre de Lemos** looks out across a featureless expanse from the top of a hillful of tumbledown old houses, and there's a strikingly elegant Renaissance **Colegio** lower down.

To the south of the Sil, **MANZANEDA** is the only Gallego ski resort, offering most of the necessary facilities but not always the snow, and on the other side of the mountains is **VERÍN**, where a fine castle above the fortified town, on a site occupied since prehistoric times, is now a *parador*. The town itself is quite modern, though a few tradi-

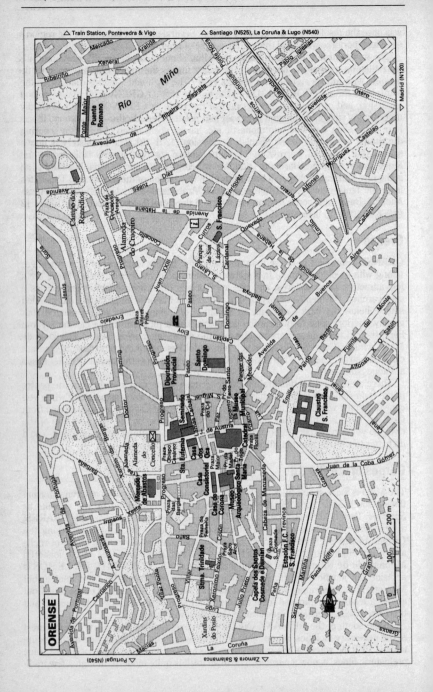

ORENSE

tional balconied houses remain around the main square, near which c/Mayor is a promising area for cheaper accommodation. There's a swimming area, with a few bars and a grassy bank for sunbathing, down beside the Tamega river. Here you're once more within a dozen kilometres of Portugal; buses run alongside the river to the rugged Portuguese frontier town of **CHAVES**.

travel details

Buses

La Coruña to Betanzos (12 daily; 45min); Camariñas (2 daily; 2hr); Corme (2 daily; 1hr 30min); El Ferrol (hourly; 40min); Finisterre (3 daily; 2hr 30min); Gijón (1 daily; 8hr); Lugo (4 daily; 3hr); Madrid (2 daily; 12hr); Orense (3 daily; 5hr); Oviedo (1 daily; 7hr); Ribadeo (2 daily; 4hr); Sobrado de los Monjes (1 daily; 2hr 30min), Vivero (2 daily; 2hr 30min).

Lugo to Foz (2 daily; 2hr 30min); Monforte (4 daily; 1hr 30min); Orense (5 daily; 2hr 30min); Oviedo (1 daily; 5hr); Ribadeo (3 daily; 2hr); San Sebastián (1 daily; 10hr); Vivero (2 daily; 2hr).

Orense to Celanova (1 daily; 1hr 30min); Oporto (1 daily; 8hr); Ponferrada (2 daily; 3hr); Verín (1 daily; 1hr 30min).

Pontevedra to Andorra (2 weekly; 18hr); Arbo (2 daily; 2hr); Bandeira (4 daily; 2hr); Bueu (16 daily; 45min); Cambados (10 daily; 1hr); Cangas (16 daily; 1hr); El Grove/La Toja (12 daily; 1hr); Isla de Arosa (6 daily; 1hr 30min), Lalín (6 daily; 1hr 30min); Lugo (6 daily; 2hr); Mondariz (2 daily; 1hr 30min); Monforte de Lemos (1 daily; 3hr 30min); Orense (4 daily; 2hr); Tuy (2 daily; 2hr); Vigo (12 daily by inland expressway, 30min; 12 by the coast, 1hr); Villagarcía (12 daily; 1hr).

Santiago de Compostela to Betanzos (4 daily; 1hr 30min); Camariñas (2 daily; 3hr); Cambados (5 daily; 2hr); La Coruña (hourly; 2hr); El Ferrol (4 daily; 2hr 30min); Finisterre (4 daily; 3hr); Lalín (9 daily; 1hr); Lugo (7 daily; 3hr); Madrid (2 daily; 10hr); Malpica (2 daily; 2hr); Muros (8 daily; 2hr 30min); Noya (8 daily; 1hr 30min); Orense (5 daily; 4hr); Padrón (12 daily; 1hr); Pontevedra (15 daily; 1hr 30min); Ribeira (12 daily; 2hr 30min); Vigo (15 daily; 2hr 30min); Villagarcía (5 daily; 1hr 30min).

Vigo to Barcelona (3 weekly; 14hr); Bayona (every 30min; 45min); Betanzos (4 daily; 4hr); El Ferrol (4 daily; 4hr 30min); La Coruña (5 daily; 4hr); La Guardia (hourly; 2hr); Lugo (6 daily; 3hr); Madrid (2 daily; 9hr); Noya (1 daily; 3hr); Orense (8 daily; 2hr); Oviedo (2 daily; 10hr); Oya (3 daily; 1hr); Santiago (10 daily; 2hr 30min); Tuy (hourly; 1hr); Villagarcía (2 daily; 2hr).

Trains

La Coruña to Betanzos (10 daily; 30min); El Ferrol (5 daily; 1hr–1hr 30min); Lugo/Monforte (2 daily; 2hr 30min/3hr 30min); Madrid (2 daily; 9–11hr).

Santiago to La Coruña (12 daily; 2hr); Madrid (2 daily; 8–10hr); Orense (3 daily; 4hr); Pontevedra (11 daily; 1hr 15min); Vigo (9 daily; 2hr).

Vigo to Barcelona (1 daily; 15hr); Madrid (2 daily; 8–11hr); Orense/Monforte (5 daily; 2hr 30min/3hr 15min); San Sebastián/Irún (2 daily; 12hr); Tuy/Oporto (3 daily; 1hr 30min/6hr).

El Ferrol to Lugo/Monforte (2 daily; 2hr 30min/3hr 30min). Also **FEVE** line to Oviedo via Vivero, Ribadeo, and Luarca; 6–7hr total run, with only two through trains per day.

Ferries

Goyan to Vilanova do Cerveira, Portugal (hourly; 5min).

Salvaterra do Miño to Monção, Portugal (hourly; 5min).

Vigo to Cangas (every 30min; 20min); Moaña (hourly; 20min); Islas Cíes (6 daily in summer only; 1hr); and Isla de Ons (daily in summer; 2hr).

CHAPTER NINE

ARAGÓN

olitically and historically **Aragón** has close links with Catalunya, with which it formed a powerful alliance in medieval times, exerting influence over the Mediterranean as far away as Athens. It is a Castilian rather than Catalan-speaking area, though, and, locked on all sides by mountains, has always had its own identity, with traditional *fueros* like the Basques. The modern *autonomia* – containing the provinces of Zaragoza, Teruel and Huesca – is well out of the Spanish political mainstream, especially in the rural south, where Teruel is the least populated region in Spain. Coming from Catalunya or the Basque country, you'll find the Aragonese pace, in general, noticeably slower.

It is the **Pyrenees** that draw most visitors to Aragón, with their stunning valleys, old farming villages, and trekking. The mountains are remarkably unspoilt – and much less commercialized than across the border France – and they have a stunning focus in the **Parque Nacional de Ordesa**, with its panoply of canyons, waterfalls and peaks. Aragón's Pyrenean villages are also renowned for their Romanesque architecture; **Jaca** has the country's oldest Romanesque cathedral.

The most interesting monuments of central and southern Aragón are, by contrast, **Mudéjar**: a series of churches, towers and mansions built by Muslim workers in the early decades of Christian rules. **Zaragoza**, the Aragonese capital, and the only place of any real size, sets the tone with its remarkable **Aljafería Palace**, the most spectacular Moorish monument outside Andalucía. Other examples are to be found in a string of smaller towns, in particular **Tarazona**, **Calatayud** and – above all – the southern provincial capital of **Teruel**.

In southern Aragón, two mountainous regions are also of interest. West of Teruel, the **Montes Universales**, a frontier with Cuenca province, offer some gorgeous routes and walking, especially around the massively walled village of **Albarracín**. To the east is the isolated region of **El Maestrazgo**, a wild countryside stamped with dark peaks and gorges, whose villages feel extraordinarily remote.

This chapter is arranged in two sections: **Zaragoza, Teruel and southern Aragón** (covering Zaragoza and Teruel provinces); and **The Aragonese Pyrenees** (covering Huesca province).

ZARAGOZA, TERUEL AND SOUTHERN ARAGÓN

Zaragoza houses over half of Aragón's one million population, and most of its industry. It's a big but enjoyable city, with a lively zone of bars and restaurants tucked in among remarkable monuments, and is a handy transport nexus, both for Aragón and beyond. Its province includes the Mudéjar towns of **Tarazona, Calatayud** and **Daroca**, and, along the border with Navarra, the old **Cinco Villas**, really just ennobled villages, of which the most interesting is **Sos del Rey Católico**. Wine enthusiasts may also want to follow the **ruta de los vinos**, south from Zaragoza through Cariñena to Daroca.

Teruel province is a lot more remote, and even the capital doesn't see too many passing visitors. It is unjustly neglected, considering its superb Mudejar monuments,

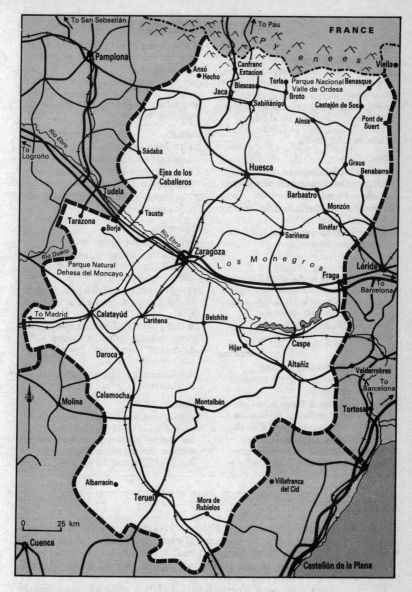

and if you have transport of your own there are some superb rural routes to explore: especially east, through **Albarracín** to Cuenca, or south through **Ademuz** to Valencia. The valleys and villages of the **Maestrazgo**, which border Valencia province, are the most remote of the lot: a region completely untouched by tourism, foreign or Spanish, and where transport of your own is a big help.

April

8–9 Pilgrimage to the Santuario de Nuestra Señora de la Alegría in Monzón, the journey made in decorated carriages.

Holy Week Small-scale but emotional celebrations at Calatayud and elsewhere. On Maundy Thursday/Good Friday there's the festival of *La Tamborrada* in Calanda, near Alcañiz.

May

First Friday Jaca commemorates the Battle of Vitoria against the Moors with processions and folkloric events.

25 More of the same at Jaca for the *Fiesta de Santa Orosia*.

Monday of Pentecost *Romería N.S. de Calentuñana* at Sos.

June

Nearest Sunday to the 19th Cantavieja celebrates the *Fiesta de los Mozos*: a serious religious event but with dancing and the usual fairground activities.

30 *Ball de Benas*: small festival at Benasque.

July

First Sunday *Romería del Quililay*, pilgrimage and picnic up the mountain above Tarazona.

First-second week Teruel bursts into 10 days of festivities for the *Vaquilla del Ángel*, one of Aragón's major festivals.

Late July/early Aug International Folklore Festival of the Pyrenees alternates between France and Spain: it's at Jaca in odd-numbered years, accompanied by a very full programme of traditional music and dance.

July and August Symposium of Modern Art and Sculpture at Hecho sees the hills around the village turned into an open-air sculpture museum.

August

14-15 *Fiestas del Barrio* in Jaca – street markets and mass parties.

16 Patron saint's festival at Biescas – "bigheads" and eats.

27 *Encierros* – crazy local bull-running – at Cantavieja and Tarazona.

September

Early September Teruel fair.

4–8 Fiesta at Barbastro includes *jota* dancing, bullfights and sports competitions (like pigeon-shooting contests).

8 Virgin's birthday signals fairs at Alcañiz, Hecho, Catalayud, Alacalá de la Selva and Villel.

12 Three days of Patron saint festivities at Graus including stylized traditional dances and "dawn songs". *Romería* at L'Iglesuela del Cid.

14 Bull-running and general celebrations at Albarracín.

October

Second week Aragón's most important festival in honour of the Virgen del Pilar. Much of the province closes down around October 12th and at Zaragoza there are floats, bullfights and *jota* dancing.

Zaragoza

ZARAGOZA is an interesting and inviting place, having managed to absorb its suburbs and rapid growth with a rare grace. Its centre, at least, reflects an air of prosperity in its wide, modern boulevards, stylish shops and bars. In addition, the city preserves the spectacular Moorish **Aljafería**, and an awesome basilica, devoted to one of Spain's most famous icons, **Nuestra Señora del Pilar**.

The city's **fiestas** in honour of Nuestra Señora del Pilar – which take place throughout the second week of October – are well worth planning a trip around, so long as you can find accommodation. In addition to the religious processions (whch focus on the 12th), the local council lays on a brilliant programme of cultural events, featuring top rock, jazz and folk bands, floats, bullfights and traditional *jota* dancing.

Orientation and accommodation

The **old centre** of Zaragoza is bordered to the north by the **Río Ebro**, and on the other sides by a loop of broad *paseos*; bisecting it is the **Avda. de César Augusto**, leading in from the old city gate, Puerta del Carmen. With the exception of the **Aljafería**, most other points of interest are within this loop. Backing onto the river are the two cathedrals, **La Seo** and the **Basílica de Nuestra Señora del Pilar**, flanked on their south side by **Plaza del Pilar**, a huge stone square which is in every sense the heart of the city. Just south of the square, between c/de Alfonso and c/de Don Jaime is a zone known as **El Tubo**, the hub of Zaragoza's bar and nightlife scene. This leads to the **Plaza de España**, a central terminus for local city buses.

Points of arrival are scattered. **Trains** use the *Estación del Portillo*, a 25-minute walk (or bus #21 clockwise around the Paseo María Agustín) to Plaza de España; a small Turismo booth at the station can supply you with a map if you decide to walk. By **bus**, you could arrive at various terminals. The principal one is at Paseo María Agustín 7, near the Puerta del Carmen; *Agreda* services for Madrid, Catalunya and the Basque provinces, and *Oscense* services to Huesca and Jaca, operate from here. Services south to Daroca, Cariñena and Muel, and some other local destinations, use a terminal across the railway tracks (south of the train station) at Avda. Valencia 20.

Leaving for elsewhere, best check with the **Turismo** opposite the basílica on Plaza del Pilar (Mon–Sat 10am–1.30pm & 4.30–8pm, Sun 10am–1.30pm, winter 10am–12.30pm). This caters for the city and province of Zaragoza. For pamphlets and maps on destinations and routes throughout Aragón, make your way to the **regional office** in the Torreón de la Zuda (same hours), the tower at the east end of Plaza del Pilar.

Accommodation

There are numerous places to stay close to the **train station**, along the side streets off the Paseo María Agustín. However, if you don't mind the noise and company of bars, there's more atmosphere in **El Tubo**, where you'll find upwards of a dozen *pensiones* located in airy mansion blocks; c/Méndez Núñez here, and the smaller streets off it, like c/Estabañes, are good locations. More upmarket hotels in Zaragoza are pricey and not very special, catering mainly to a business market.

Albergue Juvenil Baltázar Gracián, c/Franco y López 4, off Avda. de Valencia (☎976/551387). Zaragoza's refurbished youth hostel is open Jan–July & Oct–Dec. ①.

Posada de las Almas, c/San Pablo 22 (☎976/439700). A comfortable *hostal* with its own restaurant, in a rather downbeat area of the old town, west of Avda. César Augusta. ④.

Hostal César Augusta, Avda. Anselmo Clavé 45 (☎976/282727). Newly renovated hotel close by the train station. ④.

Hostal Cumbre, Avda. de Cataluña 24 (☎976/291148). This has mostly budget rooms, plus a few more expensive ones with bath. ②.

Hostal España, c/Estebañes 2 (☎976/298848). Big, old rooms – not very glamorous but the better ones have balconies and the location, in El Tubo, is excellent. ②.

Hostal Estrella, Avda. de Clave 27 (☎976/238053). Decent rooms with en-suite baths. ③.

Hostal Los Molinos, c/San Miguel 28 (☎976/224980). Good value place with its own café; central location. ④.

Hostal Plaza, Plaza del Pilar 14 (☎976/294830). Possibly the best budget choice: decent rooms with showers, and, of course, an excellent location. ②–③.

Pensión Rex, c/Méndez Núñez 31 (☎976/392633). Basic, large rooms, at the heart of El Tubo. ②.

Fonda Satué, c/Espoz y Mina 4, 3º (☎976/390709). Another pleasant cheapie in El Tubo. ②.

Hostal Las Torres, Plaza del Pilar 11 (☎976/394250). Comfortable en-suite rooms and, again, an unbeatable position, overlooking the square. ④.

Hostal Via Romana, c/Don Jaime I 54 (☎976/398215). A spruce new hotel on the edge of El Tubo. ④.

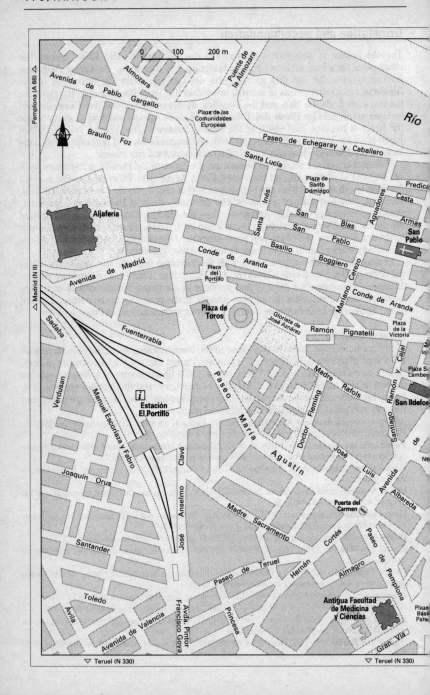

0   100   200 m

Pamplona (A 68)

Almozara

Avenida de Pablo Gargallo

Braulio Foz

Puente de la Almozara

Plaza de las Comunidades Europeas

Río

Paseo de Echegaray y Caballero

Santa Lucía

Plaza de Santo Domingo

Predica

Casta

Aljafería

Madrid (N II)

Avenida de Madrid

Santa Inés

San

San

San Basilio

Blas

Pablo

Boggiero

Aguadores

Armas

San Pablo

Conde de Aranda

Plaza del Portillo

Mariano Cerezo

Conde de Aranda

Plaza de Toros

Glorieta de José Aznárez

Ramón Pignatelli

Plaza de la Victoria

Sadaba

Fuenterrabía

Madre Rafols

Plaza S. Lamber

Cajal

Ramón

San Ildefon

Verdusan

Manuel Escoriaza y Fabro

ℹ️ Estación El Portillo

Paseo María Agustín

Madre Rafols

Doctor Fleming

José Luis

Santiago

de

Joaquín Orus

Clavé

José Anselmo

Madre Sacramento

Puerta del Carmen

Cortés

Avenida

Albareda

N

Santander

Paseo de Teruel

Hernán

Almagro

Paseo de Pamplona

Toledo

Avila

Avenida de Valencia

Princesa

Avda. Pintor Francisco Goya

Paseo de Teruel

Antigua Facultad de Medicina y Ciencias

Gran Vía

Plaza Bási Para

△ Huesca (N 330)

ida de Ranillas

Ricardo del Arco

Sobrarbe

Estación del Norte

▷ Lleida & Barcelona (A 2 & N II)

Avenida de Cataluña

Jesús

Paseo de la Ribera

Arboleda de Macanaz

Puente de Santiago

Sixto Celorrio

Glorieta de Pio XII

Ebro

Rambla

Puente de Piedra

Paseo

Abén-Aire

Augusto

Saldubi

Murallas Romanas

Plaza César Augusto

Basílica de Ntra. Sra. del Pilar

Echegaray

César

Plaza Lanuza

Avenida

Torre

Santa Isabel

Plaza Justicia

Plaza de Nuestra Señora del Pilar

y Lonja

Caballero

Santiago

Ayuntamiento

Plaza de la Seo

La Seo

Sepulcro

Paúl

Plaza de San Nicolás

Palacio de los Pardo

Casa de la Maestranza

Museo de Tapices y M. Capitular

Plaza de S. Felipe.

Alfonso

Espoz

Santa Cruz

Mina

Plaza de Santa Marta

aza e la ona

Callo Ponte

Mendez Núñez

Plaza Cruz

Plaza Ariño

Don Jaime

Museo Etnológico

Vicente de

Plaza de Asso

Plaza Tenerías

Plaza San Roque

Coso

San

Jorge

San Gil

Plaza de José Sinués

Mayor

La Magdalena

San

San

Lorenzo

Coso

Arcadas

San Agustín

Plaza Miguel alamero

Plaza de España

Teatro romano

Plaza de San Pedro Nolasco

Plaza de la Magdalena

ue

Cinco de Marzo

Verónica

San

Jorge

Romea

Francisco Cantín y Gamboa

Cádiz

Independencia

Coso

Casa de los Morlanes

San Carlos

Heroísmo

Alcalá

de

San

Miguel

Sta. Catalina

San Miguel

Cadena

Eras

Jerónimo

Zurita

Reconquista

Avenida

Isaac Peral

Plaza de Santa Engracia

Plaza de los Sitios

Gil

Plaza de San Miguel

San Miguel

Mina

Asalto

la

Joaquín Costa

Sancho

Paseo

de la

Río Miguel

Huerva

Santa Engracia

José Canalejas

Museo Provincial

Servet

de

la

Constitución

P

San Ignacio de Loyola

Andrés Gurpide

ZARAGOZA

▽ Alcañiz (N232)

CAMPING

Camping Casablanca, Valdefierro – 2km from the centre along the Avda. de Madrid (☎976/330322). A rather barren-looking site, but large and well equipped, with a swimming pool. Bus #36 from Plaza del Pilar or Plaza de España runs past. Open April 1–Oct 15.

The city

The **Plaza del Pilar** is the obvious point to start exploring Zaragoza. The square, paved in a brilliant, pale stone, was remodelled in 1991, creating a vast, airy expanse from the old cathedral, **La Seo**, past the great **Basilica del Pilar**, and over to the Avda. César Augusto. A look around the square spans the whole extent of the city's history: at one end a patch of Roman wall remains; between the churches is a Renaissance exchange house, **La Lonja**; while at the centre is some modern statuary and a waterfall shaped like a map of South America.

Even if you plan only to change trains or buses in Zaragoza, it is worth coming into the centre to see the square and basilica, and making your way over to **La Aljaifería**, either on foot (around 20 mins) or by taxi.

The Basilica de Nuestra Señora del Pilar

Majestically fronting the Río Ebro, the **Basilica de Nuestra Señora del Pilar** (daily 5.45am–9.30pm) is one of Spain's greatest and most revered religious buildings. It takes its name from a pillar – the centrepiece of the church – on which the Virgin is said to have descended from heaven in an apparition before Saint James the Apostle. The structure around this shrine is truely monumental with great corner towers and a central dome surrounded by ten brightly-tiled cupolas; it was designed in the late seventeenth-century by Fr. Herrera el Mozo and built by Ventura Rodríguez in the 1750s and 1760s.

The **pillar**, topped by a diminutive cult image of the Virgin, is constantly surrounded by pilgrims, who line up to touch an exposed (and thoroughly worn) section, encased in a marble surround. The main artistic treasure of the cathedral is a magnificent alabaster reredos on the high altar, a masterpiece sculpted by Damien Forment in the first decades of the sixteenth century.

Off the north aisle is the **Museo Pilarista** (daily 9am–2pm & 4–6pm; 100ptas), where you can inspect at close quarters the original sketches for the decoration of the domes by Francisco de Goya, González Velázquez, and Francisco and Ramon Bayeu. Your ticket also admits you to the **Sacristía Mayor**, off the opposite aisle, with a collection of religious paintings and tapestries.

Around the square

The old cathedral, **La Seo**, stands at the far end of the Plaza del Pilar, shrouded in scaffolding for an extensive restoration programme. It is at present (and, it seems, for some time to come) closed to visitors, though you can still admire the exterior, which is essentially Gothic-Mudéjar, with minor Baroque and Plateresque additions. To the left of the main entrance is a Mudéjar wall with elaborate geometric patterns. Inside, the superb *retablo mayor* contains some recognizably Teutonic figures executed by the German Renaissance sculptor, Hans of Swabia.

Midway between the two cathedrals stands the sixteenth-century **Lonja**, the old exchange building, a Florentine-influenced building, with an interior of elegant Ionic columns, open periodically for art exhibitions. Over to the other side of the basilica, and now housing one of the city's tourist offices, is the **Torreón de la Zuda**, part of Zaragoza's medieval fortifications, and the remains of **Roman walls**, insignificant ruins but a reminder of the city's Roman past. Zaragoza's name derives from that of Caesar Augustus (César Augusto in the Spanish form).

South of the Plaza del Pilar

A block south of the square, in the impeccably restored Palacio de los Pardo at c/ Espoz y Mina 23, is the **Museo Camón Aznar** (Tues–Fri 10am–2pm, Sat 10am–1pm, Sun 11am–2pm). This houses the private collections of José Camón Aznar, one of the most distinguished scholars of Spanish art, including a permanent display of most of Goya's prints. At the far end of the street, which becomes c/Mayor, is the church of **La Magdalena**, which has the finest of Zaragoza's several Mudejar towers.

A number of portraits by Goya – who was born at nearby Fuendetodos (see p.483) – are on display at the **Museo Provincial** (Tues–Sat 9am–2pm, Sun 10am–2pm; 200ptas, students free), in the Plaza de los Sitios. Other exhibits here span the city's Iberian, Roman and Moorish past.

Close by the museum are a pair of interesting churches: **San Miguel**, with a minor *retablo* by Forment, and a Mudejar tower, and **Santa Engracia**, with a splendid Plateresque portal and palaeo-Christian sarcophagi in its crypt. Two further Mudejar towers are to be seen at **San Pablo** (daily 8–10am & evenings), over to the west of Plaza del Pilar, with another *retablo* by Damien Forment, and **San Gil**, near the Plaza de España.

The Aljafería

Moorish Spain was never very unified, and from the tenth to the eleventh century Zaragoza was the centre of an independent dynasty, the Beni Kasim. Their palace, the **Aljafería** (Tues–Sat 10am–2pm & 4–8pm, winter 4.30–6.30pm, Sun 10am–2pm; free), was built in the heyday of their rule in the mid-eleventh century, and as such predates the Alhambra in Granada and Sevilla's Alcázar. Much, however, was added later, under twelfth- to fifteenth-century Christian rule, when the palace was adapted and used by the *Reconquista* kings of Aragón. Since 1987, the Aragonese parliament has met here; a move which adds prestige to both the building and the institution.

From the original design the foremost relic is a tiny and beautiful **mosque**, adjacent to the entrance. Further on is an original and intricately decorated court, the **Patio de Santa Isabella**. Crossing from here, the **Grand Staircase** (added in 1492) leads to a succession of mainly fourteenth-century rooms, remarkable for their carved *artesonado* ceilings; the most beautiful is in the Throne Room, currently under restoration.

Eating, drinking and nightlife

Zaragoza's **bars** – for both *tapas* and *copas* – are neatly concentrated on El Tubo, and many of the best value **restaurants** are to be found in this zone, too – no-nonsense *comedores*, often incorporated into the *fondas* and *pensiones*. As you'd expect in a city of this size, there are some very good, more upmarket restaurants, too, scattered about, plus all the **shops and services** you are likely to need.

Tapas bars and restaurants

Posada de las Almas, c/San Pablo 22. An attractive old inn with a cheap *menú*.

Casa Amadico, c/Jordán de Urriés 3 (closed Mon & Aug). A popular *cerveceria* with a large range of *tapas*, especially seafood.

Los Borrachos, c/Sagasta 64 (☎976/275036). A classic Zaragoza restaurant, just south of the Plaza de Aragón, whose specialities are mostly game dishes. It is fairly expensive: reckon on 3000ptas and up for a meal with wine.

Circo, c/Blancas 4. Serious *tapas*, including some terrific casserole dishes (*cazuelas*), line the bar at this *cerveceria*.

Costa Vasca, c/Teniente Coronel Valenzuela 13 (☎976/217339). This is an excellent Basque restaurant, worth a splurge if you're not going to be eating in the Basque country itself, for a taste of Spain's best cuisine. The *menú* is 3500ptas.

Dominó, Plaza Santa María. *Tapas* include a fine selection of local cheeses, hams and chorizo, and there's a good range of Aragón wines to accompany them.

Fonda La Peña, c/de Ciregio 3. The *comedor* here, open to allcomers, dishes up particularly vast quantities of simple home cooking.

El Lince, Plaza Santa Marta. *Tapas* bar specializing in all manner of sardines.

Marly, Gran Vía 50. A small bar with excellent fried *tapas*.

Café de Praga, Plaza Santa Cruz. Elegant bar in a quiet residential square, with good *tapas*.

La Zanahoria, c/Tarragona 4, near the train station. A good veggie restaurant.

Music bars and nightlife

In addition to El Tubo, Zaragoza has a concentration of nightclubs and music bars in two main quarters: Zona Bolivia La Paz and Zona Mercado Central. To get to them, just say the names to a taxi driver. The latter is perhaps the liveliest part of town, with a major concentration of bars in and around Plaza Vedruna.

Bars, clubs and dancehalls elsewhere in the city include:

Chastón, c/Plaza Ariño 4. A pleasant city centre bar with jazz sounds and a summer *terraza*.

Erzo, c/Santa Catalina 3. A beer specialist, with bottled (and a few draft) brews from all over Europe, plus basic *tapas*.

Malvaloca, c/Mayor 16. Dancehall bar with a tango orchestra.

El Monaguillo, c/Refugio 8. The street name is apt. This is a cavern-bar which plays classical music and Gregorian chants.

Oasis, c/Boggiero 28. A grand old concert hall transformed into a traditional cabaret – a kind of Aragonese equivalent of the Parisian *Moulin Rouge* and suchlike places.

El Plata, c/4 de Augusto 23 (El Tubo). This is a rare survivor: a traditional *café cantante* – a singing café – where they have three evening sessions of *boleros* and *pasodobles*.

La Radio, c/Lorente 46. A quiet bar which plays low-key jazz music.

La Taberna de Harry McNamara, c/Méndez Núñez 36. So you didn't expect to end the evening in a Scottish pub? Think again . . .

Vertical, c/Predicadores. A large bar in the old centre, for drinking and dancing.

Listings

American Express c/o *Viajes Turopa*, c/Sagasta 3, south of the Plaza de Aragón (☎976/383911).

Bike rental You can rent mountain bikes from the Parque Primo de Ribera, at the south end of Gran Vía (bus #30 or #40 from Plaza de España). From the park, paths lead out into forestland on the edge of the city.

Car rental *Hertz* (☎976/353462) are at the train station; *Avis* are at Paseo Fernando El Católico 9 (☎976/357863); *Atesa* are at Avda. Valencia 3 (☎976/352805).

Cinemas The *Filmoteca*, on c/Sagasta, opposite *El Corte Inglés*, is a beautiful old cinema, with an arts programme, including original language movies.

Flea market *El Rastrillo* takes place near the football stadium, La Romadera, every Sunday and Wednesday morning.

Post office The *Correos Central* is at Paseo de la Independencia 33 (Mon–Fri 8am–9pm, Sat 9am–7pm, Sun 9am–2pm). Poste restante (*Lista de Correos*) is downstairs at window 4.

Shops The big shopping street is Paseo de la Independencia, south of Plaza de España; it is full of fashion shops, and at the end is a large branch of *El Corte Inglés* – good for English-language books and newspapers, and everything department store-ish.

Skiing If you plan to go skiing in the Pyrenees you are probably better off buying a package deal from a travel agent in Zaragoza than turning up and going your own way. For the **Astún** resort, for instance, you could buy a weekend or week-long package that includes bed and breakfast in Jaca, bus transport daily to the slopes and ski equipment. One of the best agents to try is *Marsans*, Avda. de la Independencia 18; there are others on Paseo María Agustín.

Swimming pools There's a pleasant open-air pool in the Parque Primo de Ribera, at the south end of Gran Vía (bus #30 or #40 from Plaza de España). It is open 10.30am–10pm, from mid-June to mid-September.

Telephones There is a *telefónica* behind the main post office at c/Castellano Tomás 4 (Mon–Sat 9am–1.30pm & 6–10pm).

Around Zaragoza

Few tourists spend much time exploring the sights and towns around Zaragoza, and with the Pyrenees just a step to the north, it is perhaps no wonder. However, wine buffs heading south might want to follow the **ruta del vino** south through **Cariñena**, and for Goya enthusiasts there are murals at the monastery of **Aula Deli** (though entry is restricted to men only) and at **Muel**.

Further afield, northwest of the capital, the **Cinco Villas** stretch for some 90km along the border with Navarra. These are really little more than villages, set in delightful, scarcely-visited countryside; their title is owed to Felipe V, who awarded it for their services in the War of the Succession (1701–13). The most interesting of the five is the northernmost "town", **Sos Del Rey Católico**, on the C127 to Pamplona.

The Cartuja de Aula Dei

At the **Cartuja de Aula Dei**, 12km north of Zaragoza, Goya painted a series of eleven murals on the lives of Christ and the Virgin in 1774. They suffered badly after the Napoleonic suppression, when the buildings were more or less abandoned, but subsequent repainting and restoration have revealed enough to show the cycle to be one of the artist's early masterpieces. The monastery is today a strict Carthusian community – and thus open only to male visitors (Wed & Sat 10am–1pm & 3–7pm).

To reach Aula Dei, take the Montañana road out of the city, along the east bank of the Río Gállego. The *Agreda* bus to San Mateo de Gallego runs past the monastery. For times (and advice on how much you can see amid the ongoing restoration work) check at the Turismo in Zaragoza.

The wine route – and Goya

There are vineyards all over Aragón, but the best wines – strong, throaty reds and good whites – come from the region to the south of Zaragoza, whose towns and villages are accessible from both the road and rail line down to Teruel. The tourist authorities have marked out a **ruta del vino** through the area; an alternative route could take you on a brief **Goya trail**, to see further frescoes and his birthplace.

Muel

MUEL marks the northernmost point of the region and was once a renowned pottery centre. It has seen much better days, however, and few trains stop here anymore. Its interest lies in a Roman fountain and a hermitage, **La Ermida de Nuestra Señora del Fuente**, which has some early (1771) frescoes of saints by Goya. The artist, who became court painter to Carlos IV, was in fact born at the village of **FUENDETODOS**, 24km southeast, where a little **Casa Museu** has been done up with period furnishings (Tues–Sun 11am–2pm; 300ptas).

Cariñena

Continuing south from Muel, **CARIÑENA** is a larger, rather ramshackle old town, with a clutch of **wine bodegas**. Out on the main road behind the church, the *Bodega Morte* (open every day) welcomes visitors to sample its wines, and buy bottles, or fill their own for next to nothing from the huge barrels. If you wanted **to stay** – and Cariñena, with its open-air swimming pool, is a quiet alternative to Zaragoza – there are good, inexpensive rooms at the *Pensión Care*, c/Mayor 43 (☎976/620278; ①) and *Hostal Iliturgis*, on Plaza Ramón y Cajal (☎976/620492; ②). Both are near the church and a five-minute walk from the train station. The *Care* has a good *comedor*, and at the *Iliturgis* there's more wine tasting. The town also has a **Saturday market**.

Sos del Rey Católico and the Cinco Villas

Moving north from Zaragoza, the **Cinco Villas** comprise : **Tauste**, **Ejea de los Caballeros**, **Sádaba**, **Uncastillo** and **Sos del Rey Católico**. They make a pleasant rambling approach to the Pyrenees (the road past Sos continues to Roncal in Navarra) or to Pamplona, though you really need transport to explore more than one of them. Only one bus a day makes it up from Zaragoza to Sos.

Zaragoza to Sos

TAUSTE, closest of the "towns" to Zaragoza, has an interesting parish church built in the Mudéjar style – and accommodation at *Pensión Casa Pepe* (☎976/855832; ③). Nearby **EJEA DE LOS CABALLEROS** retains elements of Romanesque architecture in its churches, and rooms at the *Hostal Aragón* (☎976/660630; ③).

SÁDABA boasts an impressive medieval castle, thirteenth-century in origin, as well as the remains of an early synagogue. **UNCASTILLO**, on a minor road to Sos, through the Sierra de Santo Domingo, also has a castle, as its name suggests, this time dating from the twelfth-century, and the remains of an aqueduct.

Sos del Rey Católico

SOS DEL REY CATÓLICO is the most interesting town of the five and an excellent place to relax, especially if you're on your way to or from Navarra. The town derives its name from Fernando II, *El Rey Católico*, born here in 1452 and as powerful a local-boy-made-good as any Aragonese town could hope for. This connection inevitably lends its name to various aspects of the town – the *Fonda Fernandino*, for instance, which, with the bar close by, provides the only **rooms** apart from the (modern but very pleasant) *Parador Fernando de Aragón* (☎976/888011; ③). However, there's little exploitation and only a token amount of tidying and restoration.

The narrow cobbled streets, like so many in Aragón, are packed with marvellously grand mansions, including the **Palacio de Sada** where Fernando is reputed to have been born, and there's an unusually early parish **church**, with a curious crypt dedicated to the Virgen del Pilar. These are the real attractions of the place, but you could wander up too towards the **Castillo de la Peña Fernando** and into the **Ayuntamiento**, which displays – as ever – interesting tidbits of information about local government in a town whose population scarcely tops a thousand.

Tarazona and around

The Aragonese plains are dotted with reminders of the Moorish occupation, and nowhere more so than **TARAZONA**, which the local tourist authorities promote as "La Ciudad Mudejar" and even "the Aragonese Toledo". The latter is a bit of an an over-statement but Tarazona is a fine-looking place, and if you're en route to Soria or

Burgos, makes a good place to break the journey. Don't miss out, either, on the superb Cistercian monastery of **Veruela**, 15km southeast, off the N122 to Zaragoza.

The town

It is the **Barrios Altos**, the old "upper quarters" of Tarazona, that are of interest. They stand on a hilly site, overlooking the river, with medieval houses and mansions lining the *callejas* and *pasadizos* – the lanes and alleyways.

At the heart of the quarter, as ever, is a Plaza de España, which is flanked by a truely magnificent **Ayuntamiento**, a sixteenth-century town hall, with a facade of coats of arms, sculpted heads and figures in high relief. A one-foot-high frieze, representing the capture of Granada, runs the length of the building. From here, a *Ruta Turística* directs you up to the church of **Santa Magdalena**, whose Mudéjar tower dominates the town. The *mirador* here gives a good view of the town, and especially the eighteenth century **Plaza de Toros** – a circular terrace of houses, with balconies (now filled in) from which spectators could view the *corrida*. Further uphill lies another church, **La Concepción**, again with a slender brick tower.

In the lower town, the main sight is the **Catedral**, built mainly in the fourteenth and fifteenth centuries. It is a typical example of the decorative use of brick in the Gothic-Mudéjar style, with a dome built to the same design as that of the old cathedral in Zaragoza. The interior is closed for restoration, probably until 1996. If you are allowed in, be sure to see the Mudéjar inner cloister.

Practicalities

The **Turismo**, next door to the cathedral on c/de la Iglesia (Tues–Sat 9am–1.15pm & 4–7.30pm, Sun 11am–1pm; ☎976/640074), will arrange a guided tour of the town if you give them some notice. Going your own way, take a look at the **town plan**, showing the principal sights, outside the nearby church of San Francisco.

There are three **accommodation** choices: *Hostal María Cristina* (☎976/640084; ②), on the Soria road, across from the municipal swimming pool; *Hostal Brujas de Becquer* (☎976/640400; ③), just out of town on the Zaragoza road; and the upmarket *Hotel Ituri-Asso* (☎976/643196; ④), just across the road from the Turismo. The *Marisquería Galeón*, in the lower town at Avda. La Paz 1, is a reasonably priced **restaurant**, with good seafood.

Veruela

El Monasterio de Veruela (summer 10am–2pm & 4–7pm, winter 10am–1pm & 3–6pm, closed Mon; 200ptas) is one of Spain's greatest religious houses. Isolated in a fold of the hills, it stands within a massively fortified perimeter. It is uninhabited now but the great monastic church, built in the severe twelfth-century transitional style of the Carthusians, is kept open. The monastery admission ticket also gives access to the four-teenth-century cloisters and convent buildings, parts of which house a museum of modern Aragonese art. The monastery makes an easy excursion from Tarazona, or a break in the journey to Zaragoza. If you are travelling by bus, you need to get off at **Vera de Moncayo** and then walk uphill for 3km.

Calatayud, Piedra and Daroca

Like Tarazona, **Calatayud** is a town of Moorish foundation, with some stunning Mudéjar towers, and again it offers access to a Cistercian monastery, **Piedra**, set in lush parkland. The town itself, however, is an uninviting, impoverished place, where you wouldn't choose to be stranded, especially with the delightful old town of **Daroca** so close, on the train line and main road southeast to Teruel.

Calatayud

If you are passing, it's worth climbing up to the old upper town of **CALATAYUD**, where amid a maze of alleys are the churches of **San Andrés** and **Santa María**, both of which have ornate brickwork Mudéjar towers, reminiscent of Moroccan minarets. Santa María, the collegiate church, also has a beautifully decorative Plateresque door-way, while **San Juan**, towards the river, has frescoes attributed to the young Goya.

Ruins of the Moorish **castle** survive too, on high ground at the opposite end of town from the train station. The views from here are outstanding, though for a closer view of the towers you'd do best to climb the hill to the hermitage in the centre of the old town.

If you have to stay in Calatayud, there are a couple of *fondas* immediately across the square from the train station, at the edge of town, and more **accommodation** in the centre. None of it is too great. *Fonda El Comercio*, c/Dato 33 (☎976/881155; ②), close to the central Plaza España, is very basic but as good as any; for a step up, try the *Hostal Marivella*, out on the Madrid road (☎976/881237; ②), which has a range of rooms, with and without baths.

El Monasterio de Piedra

El Monasterio de Piedra – "The Stone Monastery" – lies 20km south of Calatayud, 4km from the village of **Nuévalos**. The monastic buildings, once part of a grand Cistercian complex, are a ruin, but they stand amid park-like gardens (775ptas), which seem all the more gorgeous in this otherwise harsh, dry landscape.

There are two **routes** through the park. The blue arrows lead around the cloister and shell of the church to the twelfth-century **Torre del Homenaje**, whose *mirador* gives a panoramic view over the park. The red ones take you past a series of romanti-cally-labelled waterfalls, grottoes and lakes. If there are crowds, it will be easy enough to escape them here, though be warned that you're not allowed to take food into the park; if you've brought a picnic you'll have to eat it before you enter the grounds.

The only accommodation nearby is at the luxurious *Hotel Monasterio de Piedra* (☎976/849011; ⑤), near the park entrance. Alternatively, there is a very well-equipped campsite, *Lago Park Camping* (☎976/849038; April–Sept), 3km from Nuévalos (in the other direction from the monastery) on a promontory by a reservoir. There are good fishing opportunities here, if you're an enthusiast.

Just one **bus** daily runs from Calatayud to Nuévalos, leaving at 11am and returning at 5pm. If you have your own transport, the **roads south** to Cuenca or Albarracín (see p.489) are enjoyable routes.

Daroca

DAROCA, southeast of Calatayud, is a lovely old place, set within an impressive run of **walls** that comprise no fewer than 114 towers and enclose an area far greater than that needed by the present population of 2700. The last major restoration of the walls was in the fifteenth century, but today, though largely in ruins, they are still magnificent.

You enter the town through its original gates, the **Puerta Alta** or stout **Puerta Baja**, the latter endowed with a gallery of arches and decorated with the coat of arms of Carlos I. Within, the Calle Mayor runs between the two gates, past ancient streets dotted with Romanesque, Gothic and Mudéjar churches. The principal church, the **Colegiata de Santa María**, is sixteenth-century Renaissance and has a small museum. But the interest of Daroca lies more in the whole ensemble rather than any specific monuments.

There are two choices of **accommodation**. The preferable one is *Bar-Pensión El Ruejo*, c/Major 88 (☎976/801190; ③), which has a range of rooms and a pleasant patio restaurant. The *Hostal Legido* (☎976/870190; ④) is a characterless modern fallback, on the main road, outside town. Daroca is on the Calatayud–Teruel **train line**, though the station is 2km outside town and **buses** are easier. There are a couple of daily services each to and from Calatayud, Teruel and Cariñena/Zaragoza.

Teruel

The little provincial capital of **TERUEL** is basically a market town, catering for its remote and sparsely populated rural hinterlands. It is hard to overestimate how much of a backwater this corner of Aragón is: a recent survey found that it was the only part of Spain where deaths outnumbered births. The land is very harsh, and very high, with the coldest winters in the country. If you like back-of-beyond villages, with medieval sights that haven't been prettified, it is a region that merits a fair bit of exploring.

Teruel itself is a likeable and impressively monumental place, with some of the finest Mudéjar work to be found. Like Zaragoza, it was an important Moorish city and it retained significant Muslim and Jewish communities after its Reconquest by Alfonso II in 1171. Approaching the town, the Mudéjar towers, built by Moorish craftsmen over the next three centuries, are immediately apparent. These – and the fabulous Mudéjar ceiling in the cathedral, should not be missed.

The town

The old part of Teruel, **El Casco Histórico**, stands on a hill above the Río Turia: a confusing lay-out, enclosed by the odd patch of wall, and with a viaduct linking it to the modern quarter to the south. Leading off to the north is a sixteenth-century aqueduct, **Los Arcos**, a slender and elegant piece of monumental engineering.

If you arrive by train, you will see straight ahead of you **La Escalinata**, a flight of steps decorated with bricks, tiles and turrets that is pure civic Mudéjar in style. From the top of the steps c/El Salvador leads to the **Torre del Salvador**, the finest of the town's four Mudéjar towers, covered with intricately patterned and proportioned coloured tiles. The effect is beautiful, and echoed closely in its more modest sister tower, **San Martín**, best reached via c/de los Amantes (third left off c/El Salvador just at the corner of Plaza Carlos Castell). A common feature of all the towers is that they stand separate from the main body of the church, a technique surely influenced by the freestanding minarets of the Muslim world.

The **Catedral**, built in the twelfth century, but gracefully adapted over subsequent years, boasts another fine Mudéjar tower, incorporating Romanesque windows, and a lantern that combines Renaissance and Mudéjar features. The interior follows a more standard Gothic-Mudéjar pattern and at first sight seems unremarkable, save for its brilliant Renaissance retablo. Climb the stairs by the door, however, and put money in the illuminations box, and the fabulous **artesonado ceiling** is revealed. This was completed between 1260 and 1314 by Moorish craftsmen, in a gorgeous and fascinating mix of geometric Islamic motifs and medieval painting of courtly life.

A couple of blocks from the cathedral is Plaza del Torico (aka Plaza Carlos Castell), the centre of the old quarter, and flanked by a trio of modernista houses. Just beyond here, in another attractive square, is the church of **San Pedro**, once again endowed with a Mudéjar tower. Its fame, however, realates to the adjacent **Mausoleo de los Amantes** (Tues–Sun 9am–1pm & 3–9pm), a chapel containing the alabaster tomb of the *Lovers of Teruel*, Isabel de Segura and Juan Diego Martínez de Marcilla. This pair are a legend througout Spain through their thirteenth-century tale of thwarted love. The story goes that Diego, ordered by his lover's family to go away and prove himself

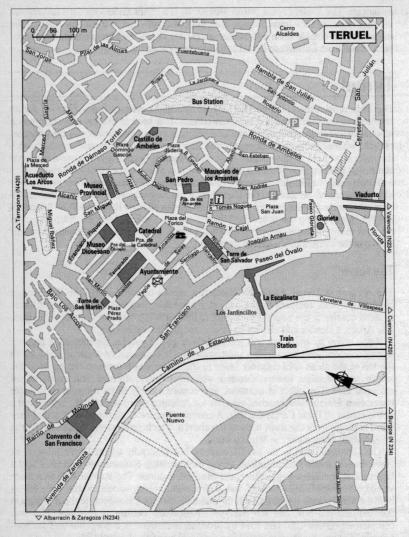

worthy, left Teruel for five years, returning only to find Isabel was to be married that same day. He asked for a last kiss, was refused, and expired, heartbroken; Isabel, not to be outdone, arranged his funeral, kissed the corpse, and died in its arms. The lovers' (reputed) bodies were exhumed in 1955 and now lie illuminated for all to see; it is a macabre and popular pilgrimage for newlyweds.

Lastly, if you intend heading out to the Teruel countryside, the **Museo Provincial** (Tues–Fri 10am–2pm & 5–7pm, Sat & Sun 10am–2pm), close by the cathedral, could be worthwhile. Its range of exhibits include objects of local folklore and traditional rural life.

Practicalities

Teruel doesn't feel quite like a city, despite its capital status, and the separation of the old town from the new reinforces this. Nonetheless, it has most facilities you might need, trains to Zaragoza and Valencia, and buses to most destinations in the province. If you need specifics on bus times or anything else, the **Turismo**, near San Salvador at c/Tomás Nogués 1, should be able to help.

Accommodation is rarely a problem, though be warned that if you're here for the raucous **Fiesta Vaquilla del Ángel** (at the beginning of July) every place in town will be booked solid, and you may have to join other exhausted revellers sleeping in the park down by the train station. For **food and drink**, the area around c/San Esteban (the first street into the old town, from the bus station) is the main *zona*.

Accommodation

Casa de Huespedes Alcodori, c/Temperado 15. Nice location by the San Martín tower. ②.
Hostal Aragón, c/Santa María 4 (☎974/601387). Small but comfortable rooms. ②.
Hostal Civiera, Avda. Sagunto 37 (☎974/602300). A modern hostal across the *viaducto* in the new part of town. ④.
Hostal Goya, c/Tomás Nogués 4 (☎974/601450). A pleasant and inexpensive *hostal* right by the Turismo. Range of rooms with and without baths. ②–③.
Fonda El Tozal, c/Rincón 5 (☎974/601022). A spotless if rather chilly old *fonda*. ①.
Parador de Teruel, 2km out on the Zaragoza road (☎974/601800). This is a modern building but its position is inspired, on a wooded hillside overlooking the town and towers. ⑤.

Food and drink

La Menta, c/Bartolomé Esteban – behind the Mausoleo de los Amantes (closed Sun, last week of July & Aug 1–14). The city's top restaurant – pricey, with dishes 1200ptas and up, but a good choice for a splurge in southern Aragón.
Meson Óvalo, Paseo del Óvalo 2 (closed Mon & Jan 8–28). A very popular *mesón* with quality cooking (the trout dishes are excellent) and a pretty good value, 1300ptas, *menú*. It is located on the street between the train station and San Salvador.
La Parilla, c/San Esteban 2. A good value grill restaurant.
Bar La Plata, c/Amantes 7. *Tapas* bar with lots of local treats. Located on the street leading from the Plaza del Torico to the *Ayuntamiento*.

Albarracín

ALBARRACÍN, 37km west of Teruel, is one of the more accessible targets in rural southern Aragón – and one of the most picturesque towns in the province, poised above the Río Guadalaviar and retaining, virtually intact, its medieval streets and tall, balconied houses. There's a historical curiosity here, too, in that from 1165 to 1333 the town formed the centre of a small independent state, the kingdom of the Azagras.

Over the last few years a small trickle of tourism has begun, and some of the houses have been prettified a bit too much. But Albarracín's dark, enclosed lanes and those buildings that remain unrestored, with their splendid coats of arms, still make for an intriguing wander – reminders of lost and now inexplicably prosperous eras. Approaching from Teruel, you may imagine that you're about to come upon a large town, for the **medieval walls** swoop back over the hillside – protecting, with the loop of the river, a far greater area than the current or past extent of the town.

The town follows the line of a ridge, above the river, and breaks into two main parts. On the Teruel side, you enter through a gate known as El Tunel, and shortly reach the **Plaza Mayor** and **Ayuntamiento**. Follow the Calle de Santiago, up towards the walls, and you reach Santiago church and a gateway, the Portal del Molina. If you take

EL RINCÓN DE ADEMUZ

El Rincón de Ademuz, due south of Teruel, is a strange little region: a Valencian province enclosed within Aragonese territory. It is a very remote corner of Spain, with a bleak kind of grandeur, and scarcely a tourist from one year to the next.

The place to head for – and if you are bussing it, the only realistic place to get to from Teruel – is **ADEMUZ** itself, without a doubt Spain's tiniest and least significant provincial capital. Strung along a craggy hill at the confluence of two long rivers, this could make a beautiful base for walking, and it has a fascination just in wandering the streets with their dark stone cottages and occasional Baroque towers. If you want to stay, there's a single **hostal**, *Casa Domingo* (☎96/782030; ③ rooms with bath).

For energetic trekking, **Torre Baja** lies to the north along the Río Turia, and beyond it the beautiful village of **Castielfabib**. The most interesting of these little Ademuz hamlets, **Puebla de San Miguel**, lies to the east, in the Sierra Tortajada, most easily accessible by road from Valencia, but also from a small route just out of Ademuz in the Teruel direction, east over the Río Turia bridge and signposted to Sabina, Sesga and Mas del Olmo.

instead the Calle de la Catedral, a quiet rural lane, you reach a small square (cars can access this from the other side) with the **Catedral** – a medieval building remodelled in the sixteenth and eighteenth centuries – and Palacio Episcopal.

Practicalities

If you want to stay – and you'll have to if you arrive on the daily bus from Teruel – there are a cluster of **hostales** at the foot of the hill, where the buses stop. These are all quite pleasant, housed in converted mansions, and there's not a great deal to choose between them. Choices include the *Hostal El Gallo* (☎974/710032; ③), the *Olimpia* (☎974/710083; ③) and the *Arabia* (☎974/710212; ③). There's also a **youth hostel**, the *Albergue Juventud Rosa Brios* (☎974/710005; closed Sept & Oct; ①), just past the cathedral at c/Santa María 1. The local **fiesta** takes place from September 8–17.

Moving on from Albarracín, if you have transport, there's a fabulous route west to Cuenca, through beautiful country, and by way of **Frías de Albarracín** and the **source of the Río Tajo** (see p.151).

El Maestrazgo

The mountains of **El Maestrazgo**, northeast of Teruel, are an area of great variety and striking, often wild, beauty, with their severe peaks, deep gorges and lush meadows. Tourism isn't a presence here, though you will find at least one simple *fonda* in most of the tiny, scattered villages. The places below are just a small selection and are geared to the more accessible; armed with a decent map, your own transport, or the will to do some walking, the choice is very much your own.

Inevitably **buses** are infrequent (often their main purpose is to deliver the mail) but most villages are connected once a day, with each other and/or Teruel; an alarm clock is useful since they have a nasty habit of leaving before dawn. The main approaches to the region are from Teruel (daily bus to Cantavieja/Villafranca del Cid) or from Morella in the province of Castellón (see "Valencia" chapter).

Southern Maestrazgo

Approaching the Maestrazgo from Teruel, you take a minor road off the N420, just a kilometre or so out of town. This passes **Cedrillas**, with its conspicuous, ridgetop castle ruin, and then starts climbing into the hills, over a sequence of *puertos* – gates, or passes. At the **Puerto de Villaroya** (1655m) you cross the highest point of the Maestrazgo, a hair-raising trip on the bus which twists its way down across the valleys, following dried-up rivers, and thundering over narrow, crumbling stone bridges. The first village of any size, beyond here, is **Cantavieja**.

Cantavieja and El Cid country

CANTAVIEJA is a little livelier and larger than most Maestrazgo villages, though its population is still under a thousand. The whitewashed and porticoed **Plaza Mayor** here is typical of the region, and the escutcheoned *Ayuntamiento* bears a Latin inscription with suitably lofty sentiments: "This House hates wrong-doing, loves peace, punishes crimes, upholds the laws and honours the upright". It is a useful base for exploring – or walking in – the region, with a pair of reasonable **fondas**, a modest **hotel**, the *Balfagón Alto Maestrazgo* (☎964/185076; ③ for rooms with bath), and an unexpectedly high class and imaginative **restaurant**, *Buj* (closed Feb), run by a woman and her two daughters.

MIRAMBEL, 15km northeast of Cantavieja and walkable in about four hours, has a population of a mere 200 and preserves a very ancient atmosphere, with its walls, gateways and stone houses. The main **bar** offers accommodation (though it has no sign to indicate it) and a good atmosphere, and there is also a good little **fonda**, recently renovated to *hostal* status, the *Guimera* (☎964/178269; ②).

A similar distance to the southeast of Cantavieja, and another fine walk along a rough country road, is **LA IGLESUELA DEL CID**. The village's name bears witness to the exploits of El Cid Campeador, who came charging through the Maestrazgo in his fight against the Infidel. Its ochre-red, dry stone walls, ubiquitous coats of arms and stream flowing right through the centre are striking enough in this remote countryside, though these features aside, it's a shabby sort of place. There is, however, a characterful **fonda**, *Casa Amada* (☎964/441155; ② for rooms with bath), which offers good and substantial country cooking.

Continuing east for 10km would bring you to **VILLAFRANCA DEL CID**, across the border in Castellon province – and at the end of the bus route from either Teruel or Morella. This is a more attractive village, straddling the hillside, and it has an excellent little hotel, *L'Hom de Llosar* (☎964/441325; ③ for comfortable rooms with bath), as well as cheaper rooms at the bar across the road. If you decide to turn around from here, the daily bus to Teruel departs at 5.45am.

Northwest from Cantavieja

Another dramatic, almost Alpine route is in store if you head northwest from Cantavieja, past Cañada de Benatanduz, to **VILLARLUENGO**, a beautiful village of ancient houses stacked on a terraced hillside. Just beyond here, you cross a pass, and the Río Pitarque, with a side valley leading to a hamlet of the same name. Here, by the riverside, in isolated and magnificent countryside, is a stylish **hotel**, the *Hostal de la Trucha* (☎974/773008; ③). Its restaurant serves trout caught a few yards away.

Over another, higher pass, the Puerto de Majalinos (1450m), the road drops down to **EJULVE**, a small village with two **fondas** and a bar decorated with the fearsome head of a boar – wild country indeed. Just a few more kilometres north, you reach the N420 between Montalbán and Alcañiz.

The **bus** runs this way once a day from Cantavieja, taking nearly four hours to cover the 90-kilometre journey to **Alcorisa** on the N420.

Northern Maestrazgo: Alcañiz and Valderrobres

The northern limits of the Maestrazgo edge into Tarragona province in Catalunya, and can be approached from Tarragona/Gandesa, or from Zaragoza through Alcañiz. This town also lies at the end of the N420, east of Alcorisa.

Alcañiz

The castle-topped town of ALCAÑIZ is quite a sight as you approach, though close up it's a bit of a disappointment. The **Castillo** has been unsympathetically modernized as a **parador**, *La Concordia* (☎974/830366; ⑤), and the best thing about the place is the panorama from its heights. These allow a grand bird's eye view of the huge Baroque church of **Santa María** which dominates the town below.

The town (and this is a big place in comparison to the Maestrazgo villages, with a population of some 11,000) gives access by bus to Valderrobres (see below), and, by bus or rail, east to Zaragoza and west to the coast at Tortosa or Viñaros via Morella. You probably won't need or want to stay but – in addition to the *parador* – there are several cheapish **hotels**; try the *Aragón* (☎974/831045; ②) or the *Guadalupe* (☎974/830750; ③).

Valderrobres

VALDERROBRES is one of the Maestrazgo's most accessible and most attractive towns. It stands 36km from Alcañiz, near the border with Catalunya and astride the Río Matarrana, whose crystal waters teem with trout. The old quarter is crowned by a **castle-palace** once occupied by the kings of Aragón, and a Gothic parish church – **Santa María** – which has a fine rose window. In the Plaza Mayor, the unassuming seventeenth-century **Ayuntamiento** was considered so characteristic of the region that it was reproduced in Barcelona's *Pueblo Español* in 1929.

Opposite the *Ayuntamiento* is a reasonable and very hospitable **hostal**, the *Querol* (☎974/850192; ③ for rooms with bath). It has a *comedor* which serves excellent Maestrazgo specialities.

THE ARAGONESE PYRENEES

Aragón has the best stretch of the **Pyrenees** on the Spanish side: a fabulous region, where you can enjoy anything from casual daywalks in the high valleys to long distance treks across the mountains. There are numerous trails, marked out by the Aragón mountain club as **GR** (*grande recorrido* – long-haul) or **PR** (*pequeño recorrido*) trails.

The most popular jumping-off point for the mountains is **Jaca**, an attractive town in its own right and with an important cathedral. From here, most walkers head to the **Parque Nacional de Ordesa** – the most spectacular mountainscape, with its canyons and waterfall valleys. Over to the east, the highest Pyrenean peaks, Anneto (3404m) and Posets (3371m) are accessible from **Benasque**, while to the west the valleys of **Ansó and Hecho** offer less serious rambles amid wonderful scenery. If you're here in winter, there is also **skiing** at the resorts of (from west to east) Astún-Candanchú, Sallen de Gallego and Cerler; they are reasonably inexpensive.

There are a number of possible **routes into the region**. For Jaca and Ordesa, the most obvious way is via **Huesca**, the provincial capital; this is no great shakes in itself but is poised for the great castle of **Loarre** and the sugarloaf **Los Mallos** mountains, that are among the country's most amazing landscapes. Alternatives might include a slow approach to Anso/Hecho or Jaca via the Cinco Villas (see p.484), or, if you're coming from Catalunya (or aiming for Benasque), the scenic route via **Fraga** and **Barbastro**.

You can **travel by rail** through Huesca, Jaca and up to the Spanish border at Canfranc – though there, sadly, the trains stop. Buses, however, continue **into France** over the **Puerto de Somport**, while drivers can also cross over the pass to the east, the **Puerto del Portalé**, or, over towards Benasque, take the **Biesca tunnel**. All of these are open year-round, except for periods of exceptionally heavy snow.

From the east: Fraga, Monzón and Barbastro

If you're approaching the Pyrenees from Catalunya, it's possible to approach either Huesca or Benasque via **Monzón** and **Barbastro**; both have regular bus connections with Lleida (Lérida), and interesting sights. If you have time and transport, you could approach more slowly from Lleida, following a little-used minor route along the Río Cinca valley from **Fraga**, a pleasant medieval town.

Fraga

It's worth taking a morning to visit **FRAGA**, 25km from Lleida, and just off the *autopista* to Zaragoza. An array of fine brick buildings help maintain the medieval air of the old town, which is perched high over the Río Cinca. If you're arriving by bus, cross back over the river from the bus station and strike uphill through the steep and convoluted streets of the old town. The tower of the twelfth-century (restored and restyled) church of San Pedro keeps disappearing and reappearing until you reach a tiny square, dominated entirely by the church. If you want to stay, the cheapest rooms are at *Hostal Trébol*, Avda. Aragón 9 (☎974/471533; ②).

North of Fraga, a tiny road follows the east bank of the Río Cinca to Monzón; it starts out immediately below Fraga's old town. If you have transport, it is a highly recommended route: great steppes fall away to the west beyond the river while coarse vegetation and red clay cliffs flank the road.

If you don't have transport, Fraga is still a good stop. It has bus connections with Lleida (5 daily) and Huesca (leaving at 6am & 7am, Mon–Sat).

Monzón

MONZÓN, 50km from Fraga, stands in a triangle between the rivers Cinca and Sosa (the latter now dry), a strategic position that explains its **Templar castle**, forgotten on the crumbling rock above. Originally a ninth-century Moorish fort, it was later endowed for the Templars by Ramón Berenguer IV and was the residence of Jaime I, in his youth. The ruins (daily: summer 10am–1pm & 5–8pm; winter 11.30am–1pm & 3–5pm) include a tenth-century Moorish tower and a group of Romanesque buildings, including a small chapel.

The town below is reasonably substantial – 15,000 population – and has old and new quarters, the former with many fine Aragonese mansions and a Romanesque Colegiata. There are three **places to stay**: *Hostal Rabal* (☎974/401277; ②) is the cheapest; *Hostal Bellomonte* (☎974/402004; ③) considerably more comfortable; and the modern *Hotel Vianetto*, Avda. de Lérida 25 (☎974/401900; ④), better still, and with an excellent restaurant. Two other very good **restaurants** are *Jairo* (closed Mon), c/Santa Barbara 10, and *Piscis*, Plaza de Aragón 1; both specialize in fish and are reasonably priced, with *menús*, respectively, at 1500ptas and 1000ptas.

Barbastro

BARBASTRO, 20km further along the Río Cinca, is a historic town of no small importance. It was here that the union of Aragón and Catalunya was declared in 1137, sealed by the marriage of the daughter of Ramiro of Aragón to Ramón Berenguer IV, Lord of Barcelona. Although it's now little more than a provincial market town, Barbastro retains an air of importance in its *casco viejo*, or old quarter. Up on the hill, the Gothic **Catedral**, on a site once occupied by a mosque, has a high altar whose construction was under the authority of Damien Forment: when he died in 1540 only part of the alabaster relief had been completed, and the remainder was finished by his pupils. The **Ayuntamiento**, a restored fifteenth-century edifice designed by the Moorish chief architect to Fernando el Católico, is also worth seeing. Elsewhere, there are some lovely fading **mansions** in the narrow, pedestrianized shopping streets which tumble down towards the river, while a central, tree-lined *paseo* at the top of the town is home to most of the town's bars and cafés.

Practicalities

The bus station is at the top of the *paseo*, and offers four departures daily for Huesca and one each to Benasque and Lleida. There's an English-speaking **Turismo** right next door, which can give you a map and help out with accommodation. Drivers will find parking in town a bit of a pain. The best place to head for is the small parking lot in front of the bus station, by the *paseo*, where meters are in operation 8am–6pm; free overnight.

There are several inexpensive **hostales** in town. On c/Argensola, one block back from the river, *La Sombra* (☎974/311352; ①) has cheap and cheerful rooms, and the *Roxi* (☎974/311064; ②) offers a bit more comfort and your own bathroom. Rooms at the *Goya* (②) come with bath but are noisy; ask at the *Bar La Sombra* next door. The best place to eat is at the *Fonda San Ramon* (rooms here, too), easily found on the pedestrianized street between the river and the *paseo*. The superbly decorated first-floor dining room features a chandelier, old tiling, glass cabinets and potted plants – an expertly cooked four-course *cubierto* costs around 1300ptas. Another good place to eat is the *Bar Stop Meriendas*, next door to the *Roxi*; it has no menu but a terrific range of dishes to choose from in the kitchen. Alternatively, try *Restaurante Flor* at c/Goya 3, for food at mid-range prices.

JOSEMARÍA ESCRIVA AND OPUS DEI

Barbastro was the birthplace of **Josemaría Escriva** (1902–75), the founder of **Opus Dei**. This fundamentalist and ultra-conservative Catholic movement has, today, a world-wide following of around 80,000, including sympathetic ears at the Vatican, where, in 1992, Pope John Paul II "beatified" Escriva, putting him on the first rung to sainthood. Its power, however, has been far greater. In the latter years of Franco's regime, three of the Generralissimo's cabinet were Opus Dei members, and the organization looked, for a while, set to control the government in the years to come.

Escriva launched the movement in 1928, while a young priest in Madrid. His followers were to be encouraged to dedicate their lives to God, following an ascetic spiritual programme, but to work within the world rather than withdrawing into monastic orders. The **members** were (and are) designated in one of three categories. At the top are the *numenaries*, who have pledged celibacy and live in Opus Dei houses; some of them become priests but the majority have professional jobs. Next are the *oblates*, lay people who choose celibacy but live with their family. Then there are the *supernumenaries*, who live regular lives, though, like the rest, follow the "norms" laid down by Escriva in his book, *El Camino*. These are the best-known and most controversial aspect of Opus Dei, for, as well as daily mass and a day's spiritual retreat each week, they include "mortifications": wearing a spiked bracelet for two hours a day and self-flagellation once each week.

The spiritual home of Opus Dei is at **Torreciudad**, 20km north of Barbastro. At the old hermitage here, the two-year-old Escriva was brought to be cured. On the slopes above, his followers have built the largest modern monastery in Spain, and they have elevated the Virgin of Torreciudad to the highest rank, on a par with those of Zaragoza and Lourdes.

Huesca and around

HUESCA is one of the least memorable Aragonese towns and if you're heading for the mountains, you could bypass it altogether, or stay on the train to Jaca or beyond. However, northwest of the town, the beautiful **Los Mallos** mountains and the castle at **Loarre** represent a very good reason for breaking a journey towards Jaca.

To say Huesca is unmemorable is perhaps a bit of a slight, for it has a reasonably well-preserved **Casco Viejo**, tucked into a loop of *paseos* and the Río Isuela. At the core of this is a late Gothic **Catedral**, whose unusual facade combines the thirteenth-century portal of an earlier church with a brick Mudéjar gallery, and a pinnacled uppermost section that's Isabelline in style. The great treasure inside is the retablo by Damián Forment, which is considered this Renaissance sculptor's masterpiece.

Next door, the **Museo Diocesano** (daily 11am–1pm & 4–6pm) contains a rather mixed collection, gathered from churches in the countryside. Across the way is a Renaissance **Ayuntamiento**. These apart, there's little to detain you.

Practicalities

Huesca isn't hard to find your way around. The train station is at the south end of c/ Zaragoza, a main thoroughfare, and the **bus station** is up the street at Plaza Navarra. There is a **Turismo**, with stacks of pamphlets on the mountains, at Coso Alto 35, on the ring road at the top of c/Zaragoza; the **Correos** is across the road at no. 14–16.

Huesca's big **fiesta**, in honour of San Lorenzo, is held over the week that includes August 10th.

Accommodation

Accommodation can be hard to find, and in summer, when trekkers from all over are passing through, it is well worth booking ahead. The fallback is a private room (*casa particular*), which you'll find advertised on c/Lizana and elsewhere.

Hotel choices include:

Pensión Augusto, c/Ainsa 16 (☎974/220079). A touch more comfort. ②.

Pensión Chaure, corner of Plaza Navarra and c/Zaragoza. Basic rooms but the cheapest in town. ①.

Hostal El Centro, c/Sancho Ramirez 3 (☎974/226823). Large, well renovated rooms. ③.

Hostal Lizana (☎974/221470) and **Hostal Lizana II** (☎974/220776), both on Plaza de Lizana. Nice situation, on a quiet square, just downhill from the cathedral. ③–④.

Hotel Pedro I de Aragón, Avda. de Parque 34 (☎974/220300). Huesca's top hotel, offering air-conditioned luxury and a swimming pool. ⑥.

Hostal Sancho Abarca, Plaza de Lizana 13 (☎974/220300). Another modern hotel on this well located square. ④.

Food, drink and nightlife

Restaurants are plentiful enough, with many places offering solid mountain fare, including lamb and freshwater fish specialities. For excellent **tapas bars** and the centre of the town's **nightlife** head for the *zona* around c/San Lorenzo, between the Coso Bajo and the Plaza de Santa Clara. The following restaurants are recommended:

Restaurante Ceres, c/Padre Huesca 37 (closed Sun). Quality veggie food and a new agey decor and clientele.

Restaurante Navas, c/San Lorenzo 15 (closed Mon, June 21–30 & Oct 18–27). The city's top restaurant has delicious fish dishes, exquisite desserts, and a choice of *menús* from a modest 200ptas up to 4000ptas for the chef's full works.

Restaurante Las Torres, c/María Auxiliadora 3 (closed Sun & Aug 20–Sept 3). A relaxed restaurant with French-influenced cooking; the *menú* is 1800ptas.

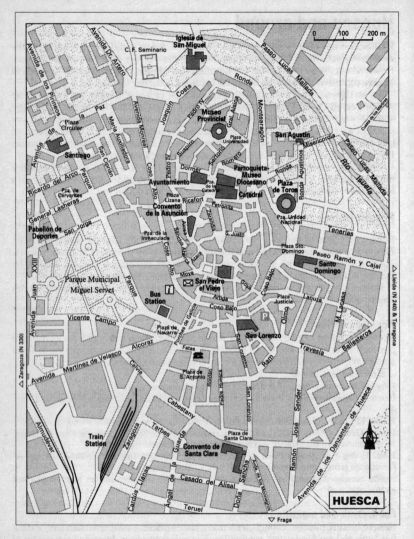

Map: HUESCA

Castillo de Loarre

The **Castillo de Loarre** (daily 9am–2pm & 4–7pm) is Aragón's most spectacular fortress – indeed, there are few that can rival it anywhere in Spain. As you approach, the castle at first seems to blend into the hillside but gradually assumes a breathtaking grandeur: superbly compact, it rises dizzily on a rocky outcrop, commanding the landscape for miles around.

Its builder was Sancho Ramírez, King of Navarra (1000–35), who used it as a base for his resistance to the Moorish occupation. Within the curtain walls is a delicately proportioned Romanesque church, with 84 individually carved capitals. There is access, also, to a pair of towers, the Torre de la Reina and the taller Torre del Homenaje, which can be climbed by iron rungs cemented into the wall. Be careful, though, as the rungs, especially those at the top, are not in the best state of repair.

The castle stands some 40km northwest of Huesca, 6km beyond the village of Loarre. By **public transport**, it's an awkard trip and you may decide that the views from the road or rail line are sufficient, as bus and train timetables do their best to conspire against a day trip, and there is nowhere to stay in either Ayerbe (the nearest train station) or Loarre. Loarre village has two buses daily from Huesca.

Los Mallos

The train line from Huesca to Jaca, and the N240 road from Huesca to Pamplona, give views not only of Loarre but of the fantastic, pink-tinged sugarloaf mountains known as **Los Mallos** – the ninepins.

If you're travelling by train and want a closer look, get off at **Riglos-Concilio** and walk along the road to **Riglos** village, tucked high up underneath the most impressive stretch of the peaks. Along the way, you'll be rewarded by a series of superb views not only of the Mallos, but also of the valley below. At Riglos there's another (unstaffed) station, below the village, from where you can resume your journey.

There's another group of Mallos mountains near **Agüero**, a completely isolated village, 5km off the main Huesca–Pamplona road and easily visible from Riglos. This would make a 7-km walk from Riglos–Concilio station, or a 5-km walk from Murillo (on the Huesca–Pamplona bus route). The reward, in addition to Mallos views, is an unspoilt village, and a gorgeous, unfinished Romanesque church, the **Iglesia de Santiago** (c.1200), with portal carvings by the Master of San Juan de la Peña (see p.501); it is reached up a dirt road above the main road – ask in the village for the key.

Jaca and around

JACA is approached through scruffy, traffic-choked suburbs: an unpromising introduction to this early capital and stronghold of Aragón – and the base from which the kingdom was recaptured from the Moors. The old centre, however, is a lot more characterful, overlooked by a huge star-shaped citadel, retaining patches of Roman and medieval walls, and endowed with a **cathedral** that is one of the highpoints of Romanesque architecture. This, together with the monastery of **San Juan de la Peña**, 20km southeast, are the major local sights, though in winter there is a bonus in the proximity of **Astún–Candanchu**, Aragón's best ski resort, while, year-round, rail enthusiasts may be tempted by the trip to **Canfranc**, almost at the French border.

After a spell in the mountains, Jaca's (relatively) "big town" feel and facilities may well be an equal attraction. It can be a lively place – the population is boosted by conscripts at the large military academy and a summer university – and it hosts a terrific week-long **fiesta** (last week of June) with live bands in the main square, lots of traditional costume, and partying in the streets.

The town

Jaca is an ancient city, founded by the Romans and occupied continuously since. It had a very brief period of Moorish rule, having been captured around 716, but in 760 the Christians reconquered the town and held it, save for a few years, from then on. The battle of **Las Tiendas**, in which the Moorish armies were repulsed, in large part by women, in 795, is still commemorated on the last Friday in May, in a mock all-women

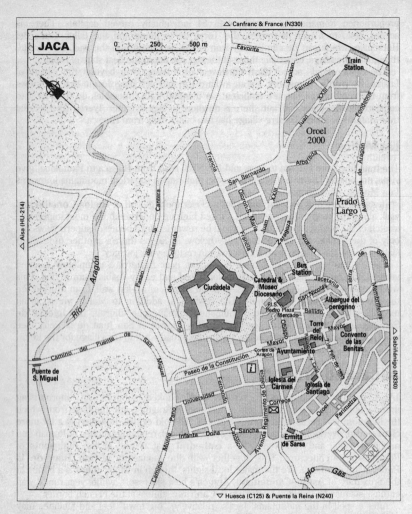

△ Canfranc & France (N330)

JACA

0   250   500 m

Favorita

Rapitán
Ferrocarril
XXIII
Train
Station
Fontanosa

Juan

Oroel
2000

Albeada
Autonomia de Aragón

San Bernardo
XXIII
Francia

Prado
Largo

Oloron-S. Maria
Zaragoza

Bus
Station

Jacetania
de

Catedral &
Museo
Diocesano

Membrilleras
Biescas

Ciudadela

San Nicolás

Albergue del
peregrino

Pico
de
San
Miguel

Pl.S.
Pedro Plaza
Mercado

Bellido

Torre
del
Reloj

Mayor

Convento
de las
Benitas

Río
Aragón
△ Aisa (HU-214)

Paseo
de
la
Collarada

Cantera

Francia

Laguna
Tierra

▷ Sabiñánigo (N330)

Camino del Puente de San

Cortes de
Aragón

Mayor
Ayuntamiento

Puente de
S. Miguel

Paseo de la Constitución

C. Feb. de 1959

Fermando

Universidad

el

Iglesia del
Cármen

i

Iglesia de
Santiago

Oroel
Perimetral

Infanta Doña Sancha

Avenida Regimiento de Galicia

Correos

Camino Monte Pano

C.
Católico

Ermita
de Sarsa

Río Gas

△ Huesca (C125) & Puente la Reina (N240)

battle between Christians and Moors. The town's greatest period, however, came after 1035, when **Ramiro I**, son of Sancho of Navarre, established a court here. It was in this era that the first parliament on record took place, and that cathedral was rebuilt.

The Cathedral and its museum

The **Catedral** is main legacy of Jaca's years as an early capital of the kingdom of Aragón, and one of Spain's most appealing and architecturally important monuments. Rebuilt on old foundations during the first half of the eleventh century, it was the first cathedral in Spain to adopt the French Romanesque architecture, and, as such, it became a huge influence on churches along the pilgrim routes of northern Spain; the new designs themselves having been carried along the route from France.

Ramiro's endowment of the cathedral was undoubtedly designed as a confirmation of Jaca's role as a Christian capital, in what was still almost exclusively a Moorish Iberian peninsula. Its design saw the introduction of the classic three-aisled basilica, though sadly the original Romanesque simplicity has been much adapted over the centuries. It retains some of the original sculpture, however, including realistic carving on the capitals and doorway; a sixteenth-century statue of Santiago looks down from the porch. Inside, the main treasure is the silver shrine of Santa Orosía, Jaca's patron saint; a Czech noble, married into the Aragón royal family, she was martyred by the Moors for refusing to renounce her faith.

Installed in the dark cathedral cloisters is an unusually good **Museo Diocesano** (summer 10am–2pm & 4–8.30pm; 200ptas). This features a beautiful collection of twelfth- to fifteenth-century Aragonese frescoes, gathered from village churches in the area and from higher up in the Pyrenees. If your interest is sparked, there is a comparable, though far more extensive, display of their Catalunyan equivalents in Barcelona.

The Ciudadela and Puente San Miguel

The **Ciudadela**, a redoubtable sixteenth-century fort, built in the French-style star design, is still part-occupied by the military. You can visit a part of the interior (daily 11am–12.30pm & 5–6.30pm), however, on a free guided tour. Its walls offers good views of the surrounding peaks, and of the wooded countryside around.

Below the citadel, reached along a rough track from the end of the Paseo de la Constitución, Jaca preserves a remarkable medieval bridge, the **Puente San Miguel**. It was across this bridge, over the Río Aragón, that pilgrims on the **Camino de Santiago** (see p.448) entered Jaca: a welcome sight, marking the end of the arduous Pyrenean stage for pilgrims following the *camino Aragonése*. This branch of the route, from Provence, crossed into Spain over the Puerto de Somport and, from Jaca, headed westwards, through Puente la Reina de Jaca, towards Navarra, where it met with the more popular route from Roncesvalles.

This Aragón section of the Camino de Santiago – like other branches of the route – has experienced quite a revival in recent years. In town, there is a **pilgrims' hostel** in the medieval hospital on Travesia Conde Don Aznar, and route maps and pilgrimage-related souvenirs are widely available.

Practicalities

Jaca has two characters: the northeast side is a little frowsy, and shelters all of the budget accommodation and bars; the southwest quarter, abutting Avda. Regimiento de Galicia, is flashier with a series of sidewalk cafes, restaurants and banks.

The **train station** (the ticket office is open 10am–noon & 5–7pm) is a fair walk from the centre, so look out for the shuttle bus (50ptas). Leaving, you can catch this by the **bus station** on Avda. Jacetania, around the back of the cathedral. Useful bus services include: Pamplona (7.25am & 4.45pm), Sabiñánigo (9am), Biescas (6pm) and Ansó/ Hecho (4.45pm); there are also more frequent services to Zaragoza and Huesca. Note that although the timetables don't say so, hardly any buses run on Sundays.

If you're heading for the mountains, look in at the **Turismo**, on Avda. Regimiento de Galicia (Mon–Fri 9am–2pm & 4.30–8pm, Sat 9am–1.30pm & 5–8pm, Sun 10am–1.30pm). This has a range of leaflets on trekking, skiing, mountain-biking, horseriding, and activities from yoga to weaving.

Accommodation

As a gateway to the peaks, Jaca has a lot of demands on its accommodation; it is not very good value and it is well worth booking in advance.

Albergue Juvenil, Avda. Perimetral 6 (☎974/360536). The local youth hostel has doubles, triples and five-bed rooms. It is located at the south end of the town by the skating rink. ①.

Hostal Ciudad de Jaca, c/Siete de Febrero 8 (☎974/364311). Central hostal with good en-suite rooms. ④.

Hotel Conde Aznar, Paseo de la Constitución 3 (☎974/361050). An attractive old family-run hotel, with well-renovated rooms. ④.

Hostal Residencia El Abeto, c/Bellido 15 (☎974/361642). A comfortable *hostal*, with en-suite facilities, although it's a bit noisy, with a lot of bars nearby. ③.

Habitaciónes Martínez, c/Mayor 53 (☎974/363374). Cheap rooms above the bar and better, new ones in an annexe alongside. ③.

Habitaciónes Morcillo, c/de la Población 5. Clean and pleasant rooms, near the bus station. There is no sign advertising the rooms – just ring the bell. ③.

Casa Paco, c/de la Salud 10 (☎974/361618). The address is the reception; the rooms themselves are at c/Mayor 57. They're functional. ③.

Hostal París, Plaza de San Pedro 5 (☎974/361020). Good value and central hostal, across from the cathedral. ③.

CAMPING

Camping Peña Oroel, 4km out on the Sabiñánigo road (☎974/360215). An attractive campsite, set amid woods, with excellent facilities. Open Easter week and mid-June to mid–Sept.

Camping Victoria, 1500m out of town on the Pamplona road (☎974/360323). A cheaper and more basic site, near the Río Aragón. Closed Oct 15–Dec 2.

Restaurants, bars and cafés

La Cabaña, c/del Pez 10. Inexpensive *menú* and cheerful surroundings.

Casa la Abuela Primera, c/de la Población 3. Another unpretentious place serving up cheap *menús*.

Chapeau, c/Terrenal 17. Music bar with a fine range of beers and *tapas*, and a summer *terraza*.

La Cocina Aragonesa, c/Cervantes 5 (closed Thurs). This is the restaurant of the hotel Conde Aznar and it is reckoned the best in town. The cooking is elaborate and Basque-influenced. Expect to pay 3000ptas.

Crepería El Breton, c/Ramiro I 10 (closed Sun & Mon). An authentic French-run *creperie*.

Croissanterie Demilune, Avda. Regimiento de Galicia 2. A wide variety of filled croissants and *batidos* (fruit shakes) make this a great place for snacks or breakfast.

Equiza, c/Primo de Rivera 3. This rather ritzy-looking bar has a big reputation for its *tapas* – especially its *gambas* and other *fritos*.

La Fragua, c/Gil Berges 4 (closed Wed). Excellent, reasonably priced grills.

Mesón El Rancho, c/Arco 2. Fairly expensive but very impressive Aragonese cooking – a good place for a blow-out.

Pizzeria La Fontana, corner of c/Ramiro I and Plaza del Marques de la Cadena. Dependable and substantial pizzas.

Tomás, c/Terrenal 8. No nonsense bar with a vast range of *tapas* and *raciones*.

Listings

Bike rental You can get a mountain bike at short notice from a number of outlets. The cheapest, at 2500ptas a day, is *Nuevo Jaca* Avda. Regimiento de Galicia 19 (☎974/362769) in the Nuevo Jaca apartment block at Avda. Regimiento de Galicia 15.

Car rental Good value outlets include *Aldecar* at the very end of Avda. Jacetania (☎974/360781), and *Viajes Abad*, Avda. Regimiento de Galicia 19 (☎974/361081). In high season all cars must be booked at least a day in advance. Rental for a car, including extras, is around 7000ptas a day; four by four vehicles cost around 13000ptas a day.

Post office The *Correos* – including poste restante (*lista de correos*) – is at c/Correos 13 (Mon–Fri 9am–2pm, Sat 9am–1pm).

Tours Trekking, rafting, climbing, skiing and other activity expeditions are organized by *Transpirineos*, Avda. Regimiento de Galicia 2 (☎974/364998) and *Nuevo Jaca* (see "bike rental", above).

Trekking maps are available from two book stores on c/Mayor and at a mountaineering shop, *Charli*, Avda. Regimiento de Galicia 3.

San Juan de la Peña

San Juan de la Peña, up in the hills to the southwest of Jaca, is the best known monastery in Aragón. In the middle ages, it was an important detour on the pilgrim route from Jaca to Pamplona, as it was reputed to hold the Holy Grail – a Roman era chalice which later found its way to Valencia cathedral. These days, most tourists (and there are a lot – including school parties) visit for the views and Romanesque cloister.

The most direct **route to the monastery** is from the Jaca–Pamplona (N240) road. A turning, 10km from Jaca, leads in 5km to the village of **Santa Cruz de los Serós**, and from here it's a further 7km up to San Juan. There is no public transport, although you could take a Puente la Reina/Pamplona bus from Jaca and walk from there. **Renting a bike** would be easier: reckon on one hour for Jaca to Santa Cruz, then a further hour up the steep road to San Juan. Descending, you could take the C125 via Bernues: a gradual descent to Bernues, a slight climb to Puerto de Oroel, then a fierce drop to Jaca; this is very scenic, and car-free, but not a leg to do uphill.

Santa Cruz de los Serós

SANTA CRUZ DE LOS SERÓS is a picturesque hamlet, dominated by a fine Romanesque **church** (11am–1pm & 4–6pm; 100ptas), that was once part of a large Benedictine monastery. Opposite, the *Santa Cruz* (③) is a **hostal** with a bar and grill-restaurant.

From Santa Cruz, walkers can take the **old path** up to San Juan in about an hour. The path is waymarked as a variant of GR65.3 and is signposted from near the church (where there is also a sign with a map). The road takes a more circuitous route around the mountainside, giving wonderful views over a vast panorama, with the peaks of the Pyrenees clearly visible to the north and the oddly-shaped Peña de Oroel to the east.

San Juan de la Peña

SAN JUAN DE LA PEÑA actually comprises two monasteries, 2km apart. Coming from Santa Cruz, you reach first the lower (and older) one.

Built into a hollow under the rocks, the **Lower Monastery** (Tues–Sun 10am–1.30pm & 4–7pm; free) is an unusual and evocative complex, even in its partial state of survival. It was here that the Latin Mass was introduced to the peninsula and here, too, that the Aragonese maintained a stronghold in the early years of the Reconquest. Entering, you pass first into a ninth–century Mozarabic chapel, which was adapted as the crypt of the main Romanesque **church**; it retains fragments of Romanesque frescoes. Upstairs, alongside the main church, is a **pantheon** for Aragonese nobles, while to the side is a pantheon for the kings of Aragón, remodelled in a cold, neoclassical style in the eighteenth century and sacked by Napoleon's troops. Reliefs on the Gothic nobles' tombs show events from the early history of Aragón.

The artistic highlight, however, is the twelfth-century Romanesque **cloisters**. Only two of the bays are complete – another is in a fragmentary state – but the surviving capitals are among the greatest examples of Romanesque carving. They were the work of an idiosyncratic master who made his mark on a number of churches in the region. He is now known as the Master of San Juan de la Peña and his work is easily recognizable by the unnaturally large eyes he gave his figures.

The **Upper Monastery**, a sizeable complex with a Baroque facade, can be seen from the outside only, but it is worth the climb, if only for the views of the Pyrenees from a nearby *mirador*. There's a small and rather institutional **hostal** here (②), in the former outbuildings, and a bar and restaurant with a 1500ptas *menú del día* – there are seats inside the *comedor*, or buy your drinks and sit outside underneath the monastery's facade. Facing the monastery is a huge meadow, enclosed by woods, which is a very popular picnic ground.

Canfranc-Estación

Ever since the French railways discontinued their part of the trans-Pyrenean line, **CANFRANC-ESTACIÓN**, 30km north of Jaca, has been a white elephant: a train station equipped with a hotel, post office and police station – but no onward traffic. The re-opening of the rail line is periodically mooted – and especially advocated by those opposed to the planned Somport car tunnel, but it won't happen unless the French and Spanish can work out a deal on sharing the proceeds of the ski resorts on each side. Spanish undercutting of French prices prompted the closure of the line in the first place in the 1970s, amid French mutterings about ostensible safety concerns over the Spanish track.

The village, such as it is, exists solely to catch the passing tourist trade (mostly French), and sports a few gift shops and hotels. It's just about worth the day's trip from Jaca, even if you don't continue into France, for the train ride up the valley. If you decide to **stay**, choose between the *Hostal Casa Marraco*, c/Fernando el Católico 31 (☎974/373005; ③) and the *Hotel Ara*, c/Fernando el Católico 1 (☎974/373028; ③). There is also a **campsite**, open during the summer only, 5km north on the road towards Candanchú. For meals, *Casa Flores*, next to *Casa Marraco*, is inexpensive and excellent.

Though there's no train, you can travel on into France by public transport. There are two daily **bus** departures, co-run by *La Oscense* and a French outfit. Coming from France, buses arrive in Canfranc from Oloron at 9.35am, 12.39pm and 4.18pm, thus allowing for train connections on to Jaca. More information, if you need it, can be had from the Canfranc **Turismo** (Mon–Fri 9am–2pm & 4–8pm, Sat 10am–2pm & 4–7pm, Sun 10am–2pm), on the Jaca road.

SKIING IN ARAGÓN

There are half a dozen **ski resorts** in Aragón's stretch of the Pyrenees and most of them – following the province's hosting of the 1982 University Winter Olympics – are well equipped. You may find that package deals, bought from any travel agent in northern Spain, work out cheaper than going your own way but there's nothing to prevent you from just turning up. The Spanish National Tourist Organization publishes a special pamphlet on skiing and there are piles of more detailed information at the tourist offices in Zaragoza, Huesca and Jaca. It's easy enough to go through these, decide where you feel like going, and phone ahead to check conditions and reserve a room (the latter vital around Christmas or the New Year).

Perhaps the best, and certainly the most varied, option is the twin resort of **ASTÚN-CANDANCHÚ**, north of Canfranc (buses from Jaca). The resorts – Astún is new, Candanchú established – are just 8km apart, and you can alternate between them. Astún is particularly well organized, rarely crowded and has plentiful (generally new) equipment for hire at reasonably modest rates. Accommodation in Cadanchú includes a pair of cheap *albergues*: the highly rated *El Aguila* (☎974/373291; ③) and *Valle del Aragón* (☎974/373222; ③), both open all year, and the *Hostal Somport*, Carretera Francia 198 (☎974/373009; ③ for a room without bath). The *Tobazo*, Carretera Francia (☎974/373125; ④–⑤) and *Candanchú* (☎974/373025; ⑤), reflect the more usual prices for this resort.

Other good winter resorts in Aragón include **Sallent De Gallego**, to the east of Jaca (buses from Sabiñánigo via Biescas) and **Cerler**, close to Benasque.

Hecho and Ansó

Hecho and **Ansó** are two of the most attractive valleys in the Pyrenees. Their rivers water the Río Aragón, to the west of Jaca, and, until very recently, both valleys felt extremely remote, with villagers wearing traditional dress and speaking a dialect, Cheso, descended from medieval Aragonese. These days, they're on the tourist map, for Spanish weekenders and summer walkers, though the rural life goes on pretty much unaffected.

If you don't have transport of your own, renting a **mountain bike** in Jaca would be a good investment for exploring the valleys, as there is only a single **daily bus** (calling first at Hecho and continuing to Ansó; it leaves Jaca late afternoon and begins the journey back from Ansó at 6.30am, passing Hecho 20mins later). By bike, reckon on around two-and-a-half-hours from Jaca to Hecho village, turning off the N240 at Puente la Reina de Jaca, or much the same to Ansó village, turning off at Berdún.

For **trekking in the region**, the Editorial Alpina booklet, *Guia Cartográfica de las Valles de Ansó y Hecho* (500ptas) is extremely useful.

Valle de Hecho

HECHO (the first H is silent) is a splendid old village, with stone and whitewash houses, and a claim to fame in Aragonese history as the seat of the embryonic Aragonese kingdom under Aznar Galindez in the ninth century, and the birthplace of the "warrior king", Alfonso I. It is today very much a farming community, although in July and August it takes on an extra dimension, hosting an annual **art festival**, the *Simposio de Escultura y Pintura Moderna*. The beginning of this coincides with the village *fiesta*, held in the first week of July.

The festival has left a permanent legacy in an open-air **gallery of sculpture**, on the hillside west of the village. Created by a group of artists led by Pedro Tramullas, these pieces are not too stunning individually but the location makes up for them; unfortunately, the venture does not enjoy wholehearted backing from the locals, who have resisted its expansion. Near the village church, there is also a more conventional museum, the **Museu Etnologico** (daily 11am–2pm & 6–9pm; 100ptas), with interesting collections on Pyrenean rural life and folklore.

In summer or at the weekend you would be well advised to book ahead at one of Hecho's three **hostales**. The clear first choice is *Casa Blasquico*, unmarked save for a P – *pensión* – sign at Plaza de la Fuente 1 (☎974/375007; closed Sept; ③); this is a wonderful six-bedroomed place, based on trust and disregarding locks and keys. Fallbacks are the modern *Hostal Lo Foratón* (☎974/375247; ③–④) and *Hostal de la Val* (☎974/375028; ④), both at the north end of the village. There is also a **campsite**, *Valle de Hecho* (☎974/375361), just south of the village.

For **meals**, don't miss the chance to try a *menú gastronomico* – or, if money's tight, the 1500ptas *menú turistica*, including great house wine – at *Casa Blasquico* (closed Sept). The owner-chef here, Gaby Coarasa, is brilliant and her tiny *comedor* is often singled out in Spanish magazines as the most creative restaurant in the Pyrenees. She starts serving at 2pm and 9pm; you can drink beforehand at the village bar next door.

Siresa and beyond

Two kilometres north of Hecho – a fine walk down the valley – is another beautiful village, **SIRESA**. Standing watch over the river is a remarkable ninth-century church, San Pedro, once the core of a monastery; it is kept locked. There is a pleasant hotel here, if you can't get into Hecho, the *Castillo d'Acher* (☎974/375011; ②–④, depending on season); this also operates the *fonda* (②), over the village bar, and a restaurant.

Walkers may be tempted to continue 10km up the valley from Siresa, to **Selva de Oza**, where there's a **campsite**, *Selva de Oza* (☎974/375168; June–Sept), with hot water and a restaurant, and a refuge, *Refugio Oza* (140 places; staffed all year). These are both excellent bases for following trails up the surrounding limestone peaks of **Bisaurin** (2669m), **Agüerri** (2449m) and **Castillo de Acher** (2390m). The finest of these is Agüerri, whose summit is a fairly strenous 6–7hr walk from the *refugio*.

North of Selva de Oza, the frontier peaks of **Lariste** (2168m) and **Laraille** (2147m) are classic trekking targets, again around 6–7hrs walking from the *refugio*. Walkers also have tempting routes in the long-distance **GR11 footpath**, which cuts across the valleys 2km north of Oza: west to Zuriza in the Ansó valley (see below) and east to Candanchú; either route will take you a full 7–9hr day's trekking.

On to Ansó

The daily **bus** from Jaca to Hecho continues to Ansó: a good route, along 12km of narrow, twisting road, up over the ridge and then, through two tunnels and a gorge, dropping into the **Valle de Ansó**, which is guarded by two strangely shaped rocks known locally as "the Monk and the Nun".

There's also a very enjoyable two-and-a-half-hour **trail** from **Siresa to Ansó**, shakily signposted by the stream below Siresa.

Valle de Ansó

Once a prosperous, large village, **ANSÓ** fell upon hard times during the depopulation of rural Aragón in the 1950's and 1960's. These days, though, there are signs of revival, with Jaca and Pamplona professionals keeping weekend residences here, as well as a growing stream of tourists. It's certainly an attractive weekend base, with a little river beach for splashing around in the Río Veral. Sights are slight, though; as at Hecho, there's a **Museo Etnologico** (daily 10.30am–1.30pm & 4–8pm; 200ptas), housed in an ancient church building.

Ansó's growing popularity is reflected in four places to **stay**, all of which fill quickly in summer. Best are the *Posada Magoria* (☎974/370049; ③), which serves communal vegetarian meals (preference is given to guests); *Hostal Estanes* (☎974/370146; ②–③) has good-value rooms with and without baths; and the Peruvian-run *La Posada Veral*, Cocorro 6 (☎974/370119; ③). *Hostal Aisa*, above the namesake bar and restaurant at Plaza Domingo Miral 2 (☎974/370009; ③), is a bit unwelcoming. There's no campsite but tents are tolerated on the grass down by the riverside municipal swimming pool, at the south end of the village.

In addition to the *hostal* **restaurants** affiliated with the *hostales*, there are two others, *Kimboa*, in the centre, and *Cubilarrola* at the swimming pool, plus a number of **bars**, the liveliest of which are *Zuriza* on the main street and the one in *La Posada Veral*.

Zuriza and beyond

Other than the path in from Siresa, the lower Ansó valley has little trekking potential; to start **walking** you really must go to **ZURIZA**, 14km north. There's no bus service, and the paved road up the valley is tedious, so try to arrange a lift if you don't have transport. At Zuriza, there is a combined **refugio/campsite** (☎974/370196; ① beds and a few ③ rooms), a general store and a restaurant. Equipped with the *Editorial Alpina* booklet, you're well poised here to tackle the popular day-trek up **Pico Sorbacal**, one of the highest in the area, or **Pico Chipeta**.

Other popular, longer outings from Zuriza include the traverses east to **Selva de Oza**, or west to **Isaba** in Navarra, along the GR11. Serious walkers might also continue north from Zuriza, along a track by the Petrachema stream, to the camping area at

Plano de la Casa (5km). From here, you could make a day walk to Tres Reyes, at the heart of the karst region around the French border, or reach the high-level HRP, near the *Refugio Belagos*.

Parque Nacional de Ordesa

The **Parque Nacional de Ordesa y Monte Perdido** was one of Spain's first protected national parks, and it is perhaps the most dramatic: a place – as the tourist leaflet poetically puts it – "where all the different elements of nature seem to have agreed that here was the perfect spot to offer an uninterrupted spectacle of enjoyable surprises". The reality almost lives up to this brief, with beech and poplar forests, mountain streams, dozens of spring and early summer waterfalls, and of course a startling backdrop of peaks. The **wildlife**, too, is impressive, including golden eagles, lammergeiers, griffon vultures and Egyptian vultures, and Pyrenean chamois – mountain goat – so common that at certain times hunters are allowed to cull the surplus.

The park is an increasingly popular destination for walkers, and its foothill villages are becoming more and more commercialized each year. In midsummer, you will need to book accommodation well in advance, unless you plan to camp. Nevertheless, this is the Pyrenees at its very best, and well worth a few days of anyone's time.

Trailheads and approaches

Heading for Ordesa from the south, the place to make for is the gateway village of **Torla**, whence the GR15 leads into the park.

From **Sabiñánigo** (east of Jaca) there is a daily **minibus** (10.50am; plus an extra service at 6.30pm between July 15–Aug 31) to Torla and on to Broto and Sarvise (the morning departure continues to Ainsa). Sabiñánigo can be reached by regular bus or train from Jaca and Huesca. Coming **from the east**, you can catch this same minibus, returning from Ainsa to Sabiñánigo. The regular service leaves Ainsa at 2.30pm and runs through Torla at around 3.30pm; the high season service turns around at Sarvise about 8pm, passing Torla around fifteen minutes later.

At present, it is tricky approaching Ordesa **from the Catalan Pyrenees**, unless you're walking or prepared to hitch. There is no bus between Ainsa and Barbastro, nor along the N260 between Ainsa and the Barbastro–Benasque (C139) road, leaving as your only option a roundabout route via Huesca.

Sabiñánigo and Biescas

There's not much to industrial **SABIÑÁNIGO** and you'll probably want to push straight on. The **train station** is 300m northwest of the **bus terminal**, on the same street. Should you need to stop over, there are a half-dozen mostly overpriced places **to stay** along this road, nicest and cheapest being the *Fonda Lagarta* (②), above the *Bar Lara*, just southeast of the bus station. During the evening this same street is surprisingly lively, the bar clientele – a mix of locals and walkers – spilling out onto the pavement.

If you miss the morning through service to Torla, there is a year-round evening service to **BIESCAS**, 17km north, from where you could try your luck hitching the remaining 25km to Torla. If you get stuck (likely), Biescas isn't unpleasant, and has a central campsite as well as several *hostales* and restaurants. **LINAS DE BROTO**, 17km east on the way to Torla, with two *hostales* and a fine position, would also be a reasonable spot to stop over.

Torla

The old stone village of **TORLA**, just 8km short of Ordesa, is fast being hidden away behind concrete blocks of rooms and apartments. It exists very much as a walkers' base and almost everything is geared to the trade. The **bus** from/to Sabiñánigo/Ainsa stops at the north end of town, by the pharmacy. There is a bank, and, alongside it, an **information office** for Ordesa National Park; this offers free **walking tours** in the park with an experienced mountain guide; they are graded according to difficulty and usually begin from the office here.

In July and August, you'll need to book **accommodation** in Torla at least a week ahead; at other times, it is rarely a problem. In addition to the places listed below, there are two **campsites** along the road out to Ordesa: the *Río Ara* (☎974/486248), on the riverside, 2km from Torla, and the remoter and pricier *Ordesa* (☎974/486146), intended mainly for cars and caravans, which has a pool, shop and decent restaurant.

Albergue L'Atalaya ☎(974/486022; ①). A rather elitist French-run walkers' hostel, with 21 bunks and – getting its priorities right – a classy and quite pricey restaurant. ①.

Albergue Lucien Briet (☎974/486221). A friendly thirty–bed hostel; it is run by the nearby *Bar Brecha*, which serves good and inexpensive meals. ①.

Hostal Alto Aragón (☎974/486172). Good value and friendly *hostal*. ③.

Casa Carpintero (☎974/486256). Pleasant rooms in a private house, behind the *Bar Brecha*; they may have space left when everyone else is full. ③.

Fonda Ballarín (☎974/486155). Very reasonably-priced, as is its *comedor*, owned by the same people as the Alto Aragón, across the road. ②.

Hotel Viñamala (☎974/486156). Located on the village square, this is the best of the more upmarket hotels. ④.

Broto, Oto, Sarvise and Ainsa

If you find Torla full, you may need or prefer to stop in one of the villages just to the east, along the road to Ainsa.

BROTO, 4km south of Torla, is a noisy, teeming place, its old quarter hemmed by traffic and new construction, a plight symbolized by the collapsed Roman bridge just upriver. Just beside this bridge is the quietest place to stay, and one of the last to fill: *Tabierna Bar O Puente* (no phone; ③). The **Turismo** (daily except Mon 10am–2pm & 4.30–8.30pm) can advise on vacancies in high season. If you are walking, you can follow a well-trodden *camino* to Torla in 45 minutes; it begins near the ruined bridge.

OTO, 2km south, is a more attractive village, with traditional architecture and a pair of medieval towers. It has two **casas rurales**: *Herrero* (☎974/486093; ③) and *Pueyo* (☎974/486075; ③), and a large **campsite**.

The lowest village of the Valle de Broto, a further 4km from Broto, is **SARVISE**. This again has a fair bit of accomodation, including the mid-range *Casa Frauca* (☎974/486353; ③) and *Casa Puyuelo* (☎974/486140; ③).

East of Sarvise, the landscape widens into a broad valley with evidence of large-scale depopulation; medieval villages just off the road are largely deserted, their fields gone to seed. Indeed, Aragón has the highest proportion of abandoned settlements in Spain, and life doesn't return to the countryside here until you're at **AINSA**, which has of late been prettified with walkways and boutiques in an attempt to cash in on some of the cross-border trade pouring over from the Bielsa tunnel to the north. Its **old quarter** up on the hill remains attractive, centred on an exceptional Romanesque church with a dark, primitive interior, and a vast, arcaded Plaza Mayor. Budget **accommodation** options include the bizarrely named *Hostal Apolo XI* (☎974/500281; ③); *Hostal Ordesa* (☎974/500009; ③), and *Hotel Sánchez* (☎974/500014; ③). The *Bodegas del Sobrarbe* (closed Nov to Easter), at Plaza Mayor 2, is an attractive, if somewhat pricey, **restaurant**, housed in a medieval cellar.

The Ordesa Canyon and central park treks

A tarmac road from Torla leads to the Ordesa Park information office, at the mouth of the **Ordesa Canyon**. It is from here – and the adjoining car park area – that most of the marked out treks in the park begin. If you're walking (there's no bus), you can bypass the tarmac by following the *camino* marked as GR15 variant II. This begins in Torla next to the *Hostal Bella*, crosses the river on a cement-and-masonry bridge, then turns sharply left (north) to join the *Camino de Turieto*. After that, it's an easy and beautiful two-hour walk, signposted all the way and taking you past some voluminous waterfalls, high above the river. The path, like the road, leads right to the Information Office, which adjoins a large car park and a restaurant, with an inexpensive daily *menú*; there is no shop, so bring provisions.

At the **information office** (*Casa de Recepción*; 10am–2pm & 4–7pm) you can buy a range of **maps** of the park; the clearest is the French 1:50,000 IGN sheet (which also covers Gavarnie, across the French border), though cheaper ones are perfectly adequate if you're going to stick to the popular, signed paths. All the maps mark the park's network of very basic, stone **refugios**, where you will need to stay on longer treks, as camping is prohibited in the park. The only exception to this is when the *refugios* are full, which happens in July and August, when you're allowed to camp alongside them.

Treks in the park

Most daytrippers to Ordesa aim no further than a loop to the *mirador* (viewing point) at the **Cascada del Abanico**, six easy and well waymarked kilometres from the information office, with a return path on the opposite bank of the Río Arazas. However, there are dozens of trails, encompassing most levels of enthusiasm and expertise. The following are just a selection.

Be aware that some of the "paths" marked on the maps are actually climbing routes and don't underestimate their time and difficulty.

CIRCO DE SOASO

This is one of the most popular and rewarding short-distance treks. It's not especially difficult: a steep, 7.5km-walk, along a signposted path, which brings you out at the **Cola de Caballo** (Horsetail Waterfall) in 3–4hrs (reckon on 6–7hrs, there and back). The path sets out through beech forest and then climbs past a mirador, to emerge into the upper reaches of a startling valley gorge.

The path is not usually crowded, except in July and August, but for more solitude you could take the steady, but steep, climb of nearly two hours up the south wall of the gorge, reaching the *mirador* after a long contouring section. From the top you get an aerial view of the canyon, while above loom a succession of remote peaks and features: Brecha de Rolando (a curious niche, also visible from the French side), Cilindro and Monte Perdido.

You descend on the **Senda de los Cazadores** (the Hunters' Path) by a long series of tight zigzags back to the car park by the information office.

COTATUERO FALLS AND BEYOND

A shorter and easier walk is to the impressive **Cotatuero Falls**. Starting from the top of the car park, the Cotatuero route takes you steeply but easily through the woods to a vantage point below the waterfall.

An exciting onward route takes over here, if you have a head for heights. With the help of iron pegs, you can climb above the falls on to the Brecha de Rolando and trek onwards to Gavarnie (see below).

CARRIATA FALLS AND BEYOND
Another waterfall route is signposted from the informaton office to the **Carriata Falls**. You head into the trees, fork left, and begin a steep zig-zag up to the falls, which are most impressive in late spring when melted snow keeps them flowing.

If you want to continue, the left-hand route (at a fork on the open mountainside) ascends to the top of the gorge walls via a series of thirteen iron pegs, not nearly as intimidating as those on the Cotatuero route and feasible for any reasonably fit, active walker. The right-hand fork contours spectacularly along the canyon's north wall to meet up with the path up to Cotatuero.

REFUGIO GORIZ AND MONTE PERDIDO
A path climbs up from the top of Circo de Soaso, in around an hour, to the **Refugio Góriz** (2169m; open year round), which is more elaborate than the other refuges, equipped with beds and sheets, and an overpriced restaurant. It can also be reached on a path from the car park, in around four hours' walk. In July and August, it is usually packed to the gills, but you can camp alongside.

For most walkers, the refuge is a starting point for the ascent of **Monte Perdido**. This is a scramble rather than a climb but a serious expedition nonetheless, for which you should be properly equipped and prepared; the Goriz guardian can advise. The summit takes around 5hrs and is reached via a mountain lake, Lago Helado.

TORLA TO GAVARNIE
The Ordesa park adjoins the French **Parc National des Pyrenees** and it is possible to trek across to the French border town of **Gavarnie**. This is a fair haul and most easily done from Torla; the routes from the Ordesa park office are longer and harder.

Leaving Torla, you follow the path to Ordesa, out beyond the campsites and as far as the signposted left fork for the Puente de los Navarros (around 45min), then climb down to the river and follow the GR11 markers up the valley. There's a campsite (*Camping Valle Bujaruelo*) after another 4km, and, further beyond, the hamlet of San Nicolás, from where the path, now mostly track, heads over the mountains and down to Gavarnie in six to eight hours.

The Southern Canyons: Escuaín and Añisclo

In the southeast corner of the Ordesa park yawn a pair of **canyons** – the *gargantas* of **Escuaín** and **Añisclo** – which are every bit the equal of the Ordesa gorge but with far fewer visitors. The lack of transport to the trailheads, and limited accommodation, contribute to this, but the extra effort is amply rewarded.

The Añisclo canyon
The **Garganta de Añisclo** is the most spectacular of the two canyons, and more frequently visited. If you have transport, you can reach this on a minor but paved road from Sarvise to Escalona (10km north of Ainsa). This road runs through a narrow gorge, the Desfiladero de las Cambras defile, at the west end of which knots of parked cars announce the mouth of Añisclo.

From here, two broad paths – each as good as the other – lead north into this marvellous, wild gorge; it's five hours' round trip through the most spectacular section to La Ripareta. Long-haul trekkers also use the canyon as an alternate approach to the Góriz hut, exiting the main gorge via the Fon Blanca ravine.

If you're doing a day-walk, the best place to stay locally is **Nerín**, 45 minutes' walk west of the canyon, via the deserted hamlet of Sercué, along a trail marked as part of the GR15. Nerín has a fine Romanesque church – typical of these settlements – and an *albergue* (☎974/486138; ①); this serves meals but requires reservations, or else you may end up camping. **Fanlo**, 6km west, is the biggest place hereabouts but as yet doesn't have any accommodation, just a snack-bar.

The Escuaín canyon

The **Garganta de Escuaín**, more properly the valley of the Río Yaga, is easiest reached from **Lafortunada**, 17km northwest of Ainsa and a convenient overnight base, with congenial rooms and filling *menús* at the *Casa Sebastian* (☎974/505120; ②) or the adjacent *Hotel Badain* (☎974/505134; ③).

From here, if you don't have transport, the quickest way into the canyon country is along the newly marked **GR15** trail; this climbs within two hours to the picturesque village of **Tella**, with a clutch of Romanesque churches and a park **information office** (daily July–Oct 8.30am–9pm), but no other facilities. Beyond, the trail drops to the river at Estaroniello hamlet before climbing through thick woods to **Escuaín**, an abandoned settlement taken over in summer by enthusiasts exploring **the gorge**, which lies just upstream. If you arrive early enough, you can lunch at the *albergue* (☎974/500939; ①) here, before continuing along paths into the water-sculpted ravine.

These routes through the gorge emerge at or near Revilla, a similarly desolate hamlet on the opposite bank. From there you can backtrack to Tella or follow a lovely and little-trodden *pequeño recorrido* path through Estaroniello to Hospital de Tella, 3km west of Lafortunada. You can complete this figure-of-eight itinerary in a single, long summer's day, taking in the best this limestone Shangri-La has to offer.

The Benasque area

Serious climbers and trekkers gravitate to **Benasque**, in the Valle del Ésera, for, above the town, just out of sight, loom the two highest peaks in the Pyrenees – Aneto (3404m) and Posets (3371m). The town can be reached most easily from Barbastro (see p.493), with which it is connected by a daily bus, via Castejon de Sos; to the north, in the shadow of Aneto is the ski resort of **Cerler**.

Over to the west of Benasque, and reachable from it on an HRP trail, or more easily on a road from Castejon de Sos, is the **Valle de Gistau**, a remote area which should appeal to walkers wanting to get away from the more established trekking areas.

Castejon de Sos, should you get stuck en route, has a trio of *hostales*, an **albergue**, the *Pajaro Loco* (☎974/553003; ①), and a **campsite** (☎974/553456; April–Sept), 2km out on the Benasque road.

Benasque and its peaks

Surrounded by hay fields in a wide stretch of the Valle del Ésera, **BENASQUE** might seem spoiled if you knew it a decade ago. But otherwise it's an agreeable place, combining modern amenities with old stone houses, some of them built as summer homes for the Aragonese nobility in the seventeenth century. It is a good place to rest up before or after the rigours of the nearby peaks. There is a good range of **accommodation**. Cheapest are *Fonda Barrabes*, c/Mayor 5 (☎974/551654; ① dorms, ② rooms), which is run by – and pitched at – outdoor types; the slightly run-down *Hostal Salvaguardia* (☎974/551039; ②–③), nicely sited by the church; and *Hostal Valero* (☎974/551079; ②), which is unmarked – enquire at adjacent *Hostal Aneto*. For a fair bit more comfort, try the *Hotel Avenida* on Avda. de los Tilos (☎974/551126; ④).

Competition for walkers' custom means that 900–1200ptas *menús* abound at the **bars and restaurants**. Try the *comedores* of the *Barrabes* or *Salvaguardia*; the *Bar Bardanca*; the excellent diner in the *Disco Ñaka*, across from the *Salvaguardia*; or the more ambitious *Restaurante La Parrilla* (closed Sept 15–30) on Avda. Luchon.

Climbs and treks around Benasque

Benasque attracts committed climbers and trekkers, and if you already count yourself among their number you'll probably be intent on bagging the **peaks of Aneto and Posets**. These are ascents for the experienced only, requiring crampons, ice-axe and a rope, and a helmet to guard against falling rocks.

For casual walkers, however, there are plenty of possibilities. The Aragón mountain club has marked out a number of blue-and-white- and yellow-and-white-painted **pequeño recorrido** (*PR*) paths, and they are documented in a locally available guide prepared by the club. The trails, to surrounding villages and also to all three local refuges, are routed so that you avoid roads as much as possible.

Further afield: Viados and the Valle de Gistau

With a full pack and the stamina for day-long traverses, Benasque is a jump-off point for some of the best parts of the Spanish Pyrenees. Moderate itineraries include following the GR11 east to **Aigües Tortes** in Catalunya (a day and a half, tent necessary until the refuge at Llausets is completed); or heading west on the same numbered trail, around the Posets massif, for a two-day trek. No tents are necessary there, since the **refugios** of **Estós** (4 hours from Benasque) and **Viadós** (9 hours from Benasque) are well placed. From Viadós you could walk in another day to **Bielsa**, an eastern gateway to Ordesa National Park, with a **parador** (*Parador de Monte Perdido*; ☎974/501011; ⑤), or descend by track to the villages of the **Valle de Gistau**.

Valle de Gistau

A mesh of trails link the villages of the Valle de Gistau. **PLAN** is the biggest place, with shops, a **Turismo** and two **casas rurales** (the norm for accommodation in this area), *Casa Mur* (☎974/506123; ②) and *Casa Ruche* (☎974/506072; ②). Heading west out of the valley, a new GR19 trail leads through **SIN**, with an *albergue* (☎974/506212; ①), and on to Salinas and Lafortunada (see "The Southern Canyons", p.508).

Alternatively, you can descend from Sin on another PR trail to **SARAVILLO**, near the mouth of the valley. This has a large **campsite**, *Los Vives* (☎974/506171; June–Sept), and a **casa rural**, *Casa Cazcarreta* (☎974/506073; ②). It is also the starting point for excursions into the evocatively shaped mountains to the south and the **lakes and refugios** of the Circo de Armeña.

travel details

Trains

Zaragoza to: Barcelona (14 daily, 7 of them via Tarragona; 4hr–4hr 30min); Canfranc (2 daily; 4hr); Huesca (3 daily; 1hr 20min); Jaca (3 daily; 3hr 30min); Lleida (12 daily; 1hr 30min–2hr); Madrid (13 daily; 3hr 30min–5hr 30min); Teruel (4 daily, 3 of them continuing on to Valencia; 4hr).

Buses

Alcañiz to: Cantavieja (daily at 11.30am, connecting with 1.30pm from Alcorisa; 3hr 30min–4hr 30min); Valderrobles (3 daily; 1hr).
Barbastro to: Benasque (2 daily at 10.30am &

5.30pm; 2hr 30min); Huesca (4 daily; 50 min); Lleida (2 daily; 1hr 20min).
Huesca to: Barbastro (2 daily; 50 min); Barcelona (2 daily; 4hr 15min); Fraga (1 daily, for Lleida; 1hr); Monzón (2 daily; 1hr 15min); Sabiñánigo (2 daily, at 9.45am for connection to Torla, and at 5.15pm; 1hr 30min); Zaragoza (3 daily; 1hr 30min).

Jaca to: Astún/Candanchú (at least daily in season; 1hr); Hecho/Ansó (1 daily except Sun, 1 with change in Puente la Reina at 4.45pm; 1 hr/ 1hr 15min); Huesca (3 daily; 1hr 30min–1hr 45min); Pamplona (1 or 2 daily via Puente la Reina;

7.25am summer only, 4.45pm year round; 2hr); Sabiñánigo (2 daily, 8am and 1.30pm; 30 min).

Sabiñánigo to: Biescas/Sallent de Gallego (1 daily at 10.50am, additional departures 15 July–31 Aug at 6.30pm except Sun; change in Biescas; 20min/45min); Biescas/Torla/Ainsa (1 daily at 10.50am; 20min/1hr 15min/2hr 30min); Huesca (3 daily, 2 on Sun; 1hr 30min); Jaca (5 daily, 2 on Sun, last at 6pm; 20min); Torla (1 daily at 11.30am; 1hr 30min); Torla/Sarvise (1 daily 15 July–31 Aug only, at 6.30pm; 1hr 15min/1hr 30min); Zaragoza (3 daily, 2 on Sun; 3hr).

Teruel to: Albarracín (daily at 3.30pm, return at 7am; 2 hr); Cantavieja/L'Iglesuela del Cid/ Villafranca del Cid (daily at 3.30pm, return at 5.45am; 2hr 30min/3 hr/3hr 30min).

Zaragoza to: Barcelona (1 direct; 7 hr); Huesca (5 daily; 1hr 45min); Lleida (4 daily; 3 hr); Sos (daily at 6.30pm, return at 7am; 2hr 15min); Tarazona (4 daily; 1hr 30min); Teruel (4 daily; 4hr); Valladolid (1 daily; 8hr).

International buses

Zaragoza to: Lourdes via Huesca, Jaca, Canfranc, Pau, Tarbes (2 daily at 7am & 2pm; 7hr for entire trip. Passes through Jaca at 9.30am & 4.30pm. Same departure times in opposite direction).

CHAPTER TEN

BARCELONA

Barcelona, the self-confident and progressive capital of Catalunya, is a tremendous place to be. A thriving port and the most prosperous commercial centre in Spain, it has a sophistication and cultural dynamism way ahead of the rest of the country. There's an awful lot to do here: the city boasts outstanding Gothic and *modernista* (Art Nouveau) buildings, and some superb **museums** – most notably the individual art museums dedicated to Picasso, Joan Miró and Antoni Tàpies. Barcelona has also evolved an individual and eclectic cultural identity, most perfectly and eccentrically expressed in the architecture of **Antoni Gaudí**, reason in itself for visiting the city. But there's also a multitude of very agreeable ways of doing very little. In part this reflects Barcelona's position, near France, whose influence is apparent in the parks, the elegant boulevards – most notably the famous **Ramblas** – and in the city's imaginative cooking.

The energy of Barcelona will impress you, too. It is channelled into its industry and business, art and music, political protest and merrymaking. Even on a brief visit you'll probably be aware of this – certainly if you stay during the city's main **fiestas**. There's a list on p.566, but the main ones of which to be aware are April 23 (*Dia de Sant Jordi*, or St George's Day), June 24 (*Dia de Sant Joan*) and September 24 (*Festa de la Mercè*). It doesn't take long to sense the city's pleasure and pride in being, indisputably, The Best: *Barcelona Mès Que Mai* – Barcelona More Than Ever – as the slogans put it.

Barcelona has long had the reputation of being the most cosmopolitan city in Spain, especially in design and architecture, though in the 1980s much of the real intellectual impetus passed to Madrid. Gaining the 1992 **Olympics** was an important boost, greeted with car-honking euphoria; 70,000 volunteers signed up to help the very next day. The enormous popular support for sports in Barcelona (especially for football, the chief focus of the incessant rivalry with Madrid) helped win the nomination in the first place, and the legacy of the games was an outstanding set of new facilities and a spruced up city centre. The Olympic Village and **Parc de Mar** development arose from the ruins of the old industrial area of Poble Nou, while the Olympic stadium on Montjuïc, built in 1929 and used for the alternative (anti-Nazi) games to the Berlin Olympics in 1936, was entirely refitted.

But there are darker sides to this new-found prosperity and confidence. As more money is poured into the sleek image, poorer areas are left behind. Indeed, despite the post-Olympic sheen and the high-tech edge to much of the city infrastructure, there is a great deal of poverty here and hard drugs are rapidly acquiring a high profile. This means that **petty crime** is rife and it's not unusual for tourists to feel threatened in their peregrinations around the seedier areas flanking the Ramblas. If you're *very* unlucky you'll be mugged, so take a few precautions; leave passports and tickets locked up in your hotel, don't be too conspicuous with expensive cameras and, if you are attacked, *never* offer any resistance. If you've brought your car, don't leave anything in view, and always remove the radio and tape deck.

The telephone code for Barcelona is ☎93.

Orientation

Despite a population of over three million, Barcelona is a surprisingly easy place to find your way around. Most things of historic interest are in the **old town** – or **La Ciutat Vella** – which despite its confused streets and alleys is small enough to master quickly on foot. This spreads northwest from the harbour for about 1.5km up to the southern borders of the city's nineteenth-century grid system. At its heart is the **Barri Gòtic** (*Barrio Gotico* in Castilian), the medieval nucleus of the city – around 500 square metres of gloomy, twisted streets and historic buildings. Bisecting the old town, at the western edge of the Barri Gòtic, are the famous **Ramblas**, Barcelona's main thorough-fare, its northern end marked by **Plaça de Catalunya**. At the southern end of the Ramblas lies the **harbour**, immediately below the old town district known as the **Barri Xines** (*Barrio Chino*, or China Town). Strictly speaking, the Barri Xines lies on the west side of the Ramblas, between the harbour and c/de l'Hospital, but in practice the lower streets east of the Ramblas are no different in character; ie, highly atmospheric and – often – fairly alarming, certainly late at night.

The medieval streets continue on either side of the Ramblas: reaching northeast through the Barri Gòtic – and past the celebrated **Museu Picasso** – to the **Parc de la Ciutadella** (*Parque de la Ciudadela*); and southwest to the fortress-topped hill of **Montjuïc** (*Montjuich*), where some of the city's best museums and the main Olympic stadium are sited. A cable car connects Montjuïc with **Barceloneta**, the waterfront district east of the harbour, below the Parc de la Ciutadella. Beyond here to the north-east, the old industrial suburb of **Poble Nou** has been thoroughly transformed over the last few years from grim decay into the Olympic **Parc de Mar** site.

Beyond Plaça de Catalunya stretches the modern city and commercial centre. Known as the **Eixample** (*Ensanche*), it was conceived in the last century as a breath-ing space for the congested old town, its simple grid plan split by two huge avenues that lead out of the city; the **Gran Via de les Corts Catalanes** and the **Avinguda Diagonal**. No visit to Barcelona is complete without at least a day spent in the Eixample, as it's here that some of Europe's most extraordinary architecture – includ-ing Gaudí's **Sagrada Família** – is located.

Beyond the Eixample lie suburbs which were until relatively recently separate villages. The nearest, and the one you're most likely to visit, is trendy **Gràcia**, with its small squares and lively bars. Gaudí left his mark in these areas, too, particularly in the splendid **Parc Güell**, but also in a series of embellished buildings and private subur-ban houses which the enthusiastic will find simple to track down. The good public transport links make it easy to head further **out of the city**, too. The mountain-top monastery of **Montserrat** is the most obvious day trip to make, though the **beaches** on either side of the city also beckon in the summer.

Arrival and information

Most **points of arrival** are fairly central, with the obvious exception of the airport. If you're aiming to stay on the Ramblas or in the Barri Gòtic – much the best idea – there are fast city transport connections right there from most termini.

By air

Barcelona's **airport** is 12km southwest of the city at El Prat de Llobregat. There's an information office (see below), as well as exchange facilities and car rental offices; for details of these and flight information numbers, see "Listings", p.568.

The airport is linked to the city by regular and direct train or bus services. The **train** (6am–11pm; 240ptas; journey time 30min; info on ☎379 00 24) runs every 30 minutes to

MAR MEDITERRÁNEO

0   250   500 m

BARCELONA

Estació-Sants and – more usefully if you're staying in the Barri Gòtic – continues to the station at Plaça de Catalunya. Buy your ticket from the automatic vending machine at the platform (you don't need the exact change) or at the ticket office. There's also a very useful **Aerobus** service (Mon–Fri 6.25am–11pm, Sat & Sun 6.45am–10.45pm; 400ptas) which leaves every 15 minutes (every 30min on Sat, Sun and bank holidays) from outside both terminals, stopping in the city at Plaça d'Espanya, Gran Via (at c/ Comte d'Urgell), Plaça Universitat, Plaça de Catalunya and Passeig de Gràcia (at c/de la Diputació) – this takes around 30 minutes to reach Plaça de Catalunya, though allow longer in rush hour. A **taxi** from the airport will cost roughly 1500–1800ptas to Estació-Sants, and about 2200–2500ptas to somewhere more central in the old town. There's a list of current prices posted inside the airport near the baggage reclamation area.

When leaving town, always allow yourself plenty of time to **get to the airport**, particularly if you're taking the bus. *Aerobus* departures (Mon–Fri 5.30am–10pm, Sat, Sun and bank holidays 6am–10pm) are from Plaça de Catalunya (corner of Passeig de Gràcia), Avda. de Roma (at c/Comte d'Urgell) or Estació-Sants. The principal advantage of the **train** is that it doesn't get stuck in traffic – services back to the airport leave every half an hour (6am–10.30pm), either from Plaça de Catalunya, or from Sants (Platform 3).

By train

The main station for national and some international arrivals is **Estació-Sants**, west of the centre. Again, there are exchange, information and car rental offices here, as well as a hotel booking service (see "Accommodation" below). From Sants, it's easiest to take the metro into the centre; line 3 runs direct to Liceu for the Ramblas.

Estació de França (also known as the Estació Terminal), next to the Parc de la Ciutadella, east of the centre, has now reopened and handles many of the long-distance arrivals and departures: essentially this means *Talgo* services from Madrid, Sevilla and Malaga, *Intercity* services from other major Spanish cities, and international trains from Paris, Zürich, Milan and Geneva. Some trains will stop at both Sants and França – check the timetable first. From França either take the metro (line 4) from nearby Barceloneta, or you can simply walk into the Barri Gòtic, up Via Laietana and into c/ Jaume I.

Other possible arrival points by train are the stations at **Plaça de Catalunya**, at the top of the Ramblas (for trains from coastal towns north of the city, the airport, Lleida, and towns on the Puigcerdà–Vic line); **Plaça d'Espanya** (FF.CC trains from Montserrat and Manresa); and **Passeig de Gràcia** (trains from Port Bou).

By bus

The main bus terminal, used by most long-distance and provincial buses, is the **Estació del Nord** on Avda. Vilanova, three blocks north of the Parc de la Ciutadella (nearest metro, Arc de Triomf). When **leaving**, it's a good idea to reserve a seat in advance on the popular long-distance routes; the day before is usually fine. There's a round-up of bus companies and their destinations in "Listings".

By ferry

Ferries from the Balearics dock at the **Estació Maritima** at the bottom of the Ramblas. There are daily services from Palma (Mallorca) and several times weekly from Ibiza and Menorca. From here you're only a short walk from Plaça Portal de la Pau at the bottom of the Ramblas; nearest metro, Drassanes. Schedules and tickets for **departures are** available from *Transmediterranea*, at the Estació Maritima; see "Listings", p.568.

FINDING AN ADDRESS

Addresses in Barcelona are all written in Catalan, though a lot of maps – including official ones – haven't yet caught up and still use Castilian spellings. In this book, the text and maps use Catalan names and addresses.

Addresses are written as: c/Picasso 2, 4° – which means Picasso street (*carrer*) no. 2, 4th floor. You may also see left- (*esquerra*) hand apartment or office; *dreta* is right; *centro* centre. C/Picasso s/n means the building has no number (*sin numero*). In the gridded streets of the Eixample, **building numbers** run from south to north (ie, lower numbers at the Plaça de Catalunya end) and from west to east (lower numbers at Plaça d'Espanya).

The main address **abbreviations** used in Barcelona are: Avda. (for *Avinguda*, avenue); c/ (for *carrer*, street); Pg. (for *Passeig*, more a boulevard than a street); Bxda. (for *Baixada*, alley); Ptge. (for *Passatge*, passage); and Pl. (for *Plaça*, square).

For a full rundown of the Catalan language – and a list of useful words – see the feature on p.574.

Information

It's a good idea to visit a **Turismo** as soon as possible after arrival, where you can pick up a free large-scale map of the city and a very useful public transport map – as well as more detailed pamphlets and brochures on aspects of the city's architecture, history and culture.

There are offices at the **airport** (Mon–Sat 9.30am–8pm, Sun and holidays 9.30am–3pm; ☎478 47 04), **Estació de França** (June–Sept daily 8am–8pm; Oct–May Mon–Fri 8am–2pm & 4–10pm, Sat & Sun 8am–2pm ☎319 57 58), **Estació-Sants** (June–Sept daily 8am–8pm; Oct–May Mon–Fri 8am–8pm, Sat & Sun 8am–2pm; ☎490 91 71), and **Gran Vía de les Corts Catalanes** 658 (Mon–Fri 9am–7pm, Sat 9am–2pm; ☎301 74 43). There's also a **Municipal Information Office in** Plaça de Sant Jaume, in the Ajuntament building (Mon–Fri 8am–8pm, Sat 8am–2pm; ☎318 25 25), which is not really for tourists, but is invariably helpful. For the 24-hour English-speaking **Generalitat Information Service**, call ☎010.

Getting around

Apart from the medieval Barri Gòtic where you'll want to (and have to) walk, you'll need to use the city's excellent transport system to make the most of what Barcelona has to offer. The system comprises the metro, buses, trains and a network of funicular railways and cable cars: to sort it all out, pick up a free **public transport map** (*Guía del Transport Públic de Barcelona*) at any of the tourist offices, or at the city information office in Plaça de Sant Jaume; the map is also posted at bus stops and metro stations.

On all the city's **public transport** you can buy a single **ticket** every time you ride (120ptas, night buses 140ptas), but even over only a couple of days it's cheaper to buy one of the available *targetes* – discounted ticket strips which you either pass through the box on top of the barrier or punch in the machine at the metro entrance or on the bus.

There are two **targetes**: the T1 (625ptas), valid for ten separate journeys on either the metro or the buses; or the T2 (600ptas), used for ten journeys just on the metro. These *targetes* are not valid on night buses, but you can buy a *Nitbus targeta* for 620ptas which is valid for ten rides. You can buy the *targetes* at metro station ticket offices; the T2 is also available at FF.CC stations (see below). You could also consider one of the **travel passes** available at station ticket offices and valid on the buses and metro: the *T-Dia* (1 day; 435ptas) or the *T-Mes* (1 month; 4200ptas) – for the latter you'll need a

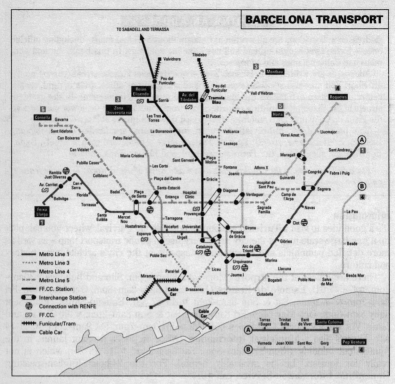

transport ID card, available from the *TMB* office at Plaça Universitat metro. Anyone caught without a valid ticket is liable to an **on-the-spot fine** of 5000ptas.

The Metro

The quickest way of getting around Barcelona is by the modern and efficient **metro**, which runs on four lines (numbered L1, L3, L4 and L5; line 2 is under long-term renovation); entrances are marked with a red diamond sign. Its **hours of operation** are Mon–Thurs 5am–11pm; Fri, Sat and the night before a holiday 5am–1am; Sun 6am–midnight; and holidays 6am–11pm. In other words, it shuts down just when most people in Barcelona are thinking of going out.

Buses

Bus routes are easy to master if you get hold of a copy of the transport map and remember that the routes are colour-coded: **city centre buses** are red and always stop at one of three central squares (Plaça Catalunya, Universitat or Urquinaona); **cross-city buses** are yellow; green buses run on all the **peripheral routes** outside the city centre; and **night buses** are blue (and always stop near or in Plaça de Catalunya). In addition, the route is marked at each bus stop, along with a timetable – where relevant, bus routes are detailed in the text.

Most buses **operate daily**, roughly from 4–5am until 10.30pm, though some lines run on until after midnight. The **night buses** fill in the gaps on all the main routes, with services every 30 minutes from around 10pm to 4am.

Between mid-June and mid-September, there's also a **tourist bus**, *Transports Turístics* (#100), which runs on a circular route (every 30min; daily 9am–7pm), starting at Plaça de Catalunya and linking all the main sights and tourist destinations, including the Sagrada Família, Parc Güell and the Poble Espanyol. Tickets cost 1000ptas and are valid for a day, allowing you to get on and off as you please; a half-day fare (valid 2–9.30pm) or a child's ticket is 700ptas.

Trains, funiculars and cable cars

The city has a commuter **train line**, the *Ferrocarrils de la Generalitat de Catalunya* (**FF.CC**), with its main stations at Plaça de Catalunya and Plaça d'Espanya. You'll use this going to Montserrat and Tibidabo.

You may also use the **funicular railway** (165ptas one-way, 275ptas return) and **cable car** (325ptas one-way, 525ptas return) when going to Montjuïc, and there's a tram (150ptas one-way, 225ptas return) and funicular service (250ptas one-way, 420ptas return) to Tibidabo, too – full details in those sections of the text. On these services, your *tarjeta* (the T1) is only valid for the Tibidabo tram. You also have to pay separately for the **cross-harbour cable car**, which is well worth taking at least once for the views. Expect to pay 700ptas one-way for the cross-harbour trip, 750ptas return.

Taxis

Black-and-yellow **taxis** (with a green roof-light on when available for hire) are inexpensive and plentiful and well worth utilizing, especially late at night. There's a minimum charge of 270ptas and after that it's 100ptas per kilometre. But taxis won't take more than four people and charge extra for baggage and on public holidays, or for picking up from Sants, or for a multitude of other things. Asking for a *recibo* should ensure that the price is fair. **Cabs** can be called on the following numbers: ☎490 22 22; ☎300 38 11; ☎330 08 04; ☎358 11 11; ☎212 22 22.

Accommodation

You can pick up a list of hotels and *hostales* at any Turismo, though these don't usually include the less expensive categories of accommodation. If you don't want to wander the streets when you first arrive, **hotel reservations offices** at the airport and at Sants station (daily 8am–10pm) will book you a place to stay on arrival – there's a fee of 100ptas – but they don't handle the very cheapest places and, of course, you won't get to see the room beforehand.

Hotels and *hostales*

Most of the **budget accommodation** in Barcelona is to be found in the **Barri Gòtic**, a convenient and atmospheric place in which to base yourself. However, what may be atmospheric by day can seem plain threatening after dark, and the further down towards the port you get, the less salubrious, and noisier, the surroundings. As a very general rule, anything above c/Escudellers tends to be acceptable (though not necessarily fancy or modern); anything right on the Ramblas or on the streets above c/Portaferrissa should be reliable and safe. The best hunting-ground is between the Ramblas and Plaça de Sant Jaume, in the area bordered by c/Escudellers and c/de la Boqueria, where there are loads of options, from *fondas* to three-star hotels. Beyond, in the wider streets of the **Eixample**, are found most of the city's more expensive places to stay, though you'll be able to find reasonably priced rooms here. There are more possibilities in the **Gràcia** district, which – though further out – is still easily reached by metro.

On (and just off) the Ramblas

The further up the Ramblas you go, towards Plaça de Catalunya, the quieter, more pleasant and more expensive the places become. Note that the places in the lower categories on the Ramblas tend to post prices at the top of the range for that category. Alternatively, there are several places on Plaça Reial, halfway down the Ramblas, a fine square dotted with palm trees and arcaded walks. It's been cleaned up considerably in recent years, and the permanent police post here means you don't have to worry too much about being hassled after dark – though be careful with money and valuables.

Pensión Colom 3, c/Colom 3 (☎318 06 31). The least expensive choice on the square. Adequate singles, doubles and triples, some with bath – book in advance if possible. Dorm beds available too (see *Youth Hostels*, below). ③.

Don Quijote, Ramblas 70 (☎302 55 99). Standard-looking doubles, and less pricey rooms without bath available. Its prime location means it tends to take advantage in July and August, when prices here can shoot through the roof. ④.

Hotel Internacional, Ramblas 78 (☎302 25 66). Comfortable, doubles with bath and breakfast, and a good central Ramblas location. ⑤.

Hotel Lloret, Ramblas 125 (☎317 33 66). A grand Ramblas building whose large rooms are better value than most in this category. Rooms with just washbasins are at the lower end of the scale. ④.

Hostal Maritima, Ramblas 4 (☎302 31 12). Popular – if noisy and occasionally unkempt – backpackers' choice next to the Wax Museum, offering basic doubles and triples with and without showers; there's a washing machine and luggage storage service too. ③.

Hostal Mayoral, Plaça Reial 2 (☎317 95 34). Longtime favourite on the plaça and a little better value than the *Roma* (below) if you take a room without shower. ③.

Pensión Noya, Ramblas 133 (☎301 48 31). The best choice in this block and a popular stop for young travellers. Nice rooms, separate showers; you might find prices in high season fall into the next category up. ③.

Hotel Oriente, Ramblas 45 (☎302 25 58). Appealing turn-of-the-century decor and smart modern rooms, some with Ramblas views, make this a popular choice. It's at the lower end of this category. ⑥.

Hostal Roma Reial, Plaça Reial 11 (☎302 03 66). Popular choice with airy rooms overlooking the square. Space here is at a premium in the summer. ③.

Between Carrer de Ferran and Carrer de la Boqueria

These two streets, and the alleys that run between them, are a good place to start for budget possibilities back from the Ramblas. Shop around, though, as not all are as clean and appealing as those listed below.

Pensión Bienestar, c/Quintana 3 (☎231 32 66). Not a lot of space and unpromising from the outside, but efficient and clean inside; separate bathrooms. ③.

Pensión Dalí, c/de la Boqueria 12 (☎ 318 55 80). Not terribly inspiring, but often with space. Rooms with bath nudge into the next category in July and August; a few hundred pesetas discount on all rooms during the rest of the year. ③.

Pensión Europa, c/de la Boqueria 18 (☎318 76 20). Try here first if you want a room with a balcony over the street. Fairly well-appointed, and budget rooms without bath available too. ③.

Pensión Fernando, c/Arc del Remei 4 (☎221 03 58). A dingy sidestreet off c/de Ferran, near Plaça Reial, but the *pension* is friendly enough, with basic rooms and separate showers. ②.

Hostal Palermo, c/de la Boqueria 21 (☎302 40 02). Friendly place with clean high-ceilinged rooms with bath. Probably the most attractive of the budget places on this street. ③.

Plaça de Sant Miquel, Plaça de Sant Jaume and c/Princesa

The streets between and around the Barri Gòtic's two central squares are rather more attractive than most in the area and contain several decent budget hotels.

Hostal Canadiense, Baixada de Sant Miquel (☎301 74 61). Down a quiet side street of Plaça de Sant Miquel, this is a friendly, labyrinthine *hostal* – all the doubles have a balcony, some onto the street, others onto the inner patio. A good, quiet, central location. ③.

Hostal Levante, Baixada Sant Miquel 2 (☎317 95 65). On the same street as the *Canadiense*, this welcoming wood-panelled *hostal* is a another good first choice. Nice, plain rooms (with and without shower) in a well-kept block; the bathrooms have just been renovated. Recommended. ③–④.

Hostal Lourdes, c/Princesa 14 (☎319 33 72). Good location for the Barri Gòtic, and very reasonable, too – with clean bathrooms, and a newly refurbished TV room. ②.

Pension Princesa, c/Princesa 7 (☎319 50 31). This *pensión* comes without frills but you'll not beat the price around here. Separate showers. ②.

Hostal Rey Don Jaime I, c/Jaume I 11 (☎315 41 61). Fine location (next to Plaça de Sant Jaume), approachable management, and an elevator up to comfortable rooms with bath, some with balconies overlooking the busy main street below. ④.

Near the Cathedral: Plaça Sant Josep Oriol and Carrer Portaferrissa

Around and beyond the cathedral, from Plaça Sant Josep Oriol northwards, the price and quality of accommodation takes a general step up. Carrer Portaferrissa in particular is a good street to aim for with several decent choices.

Pensión Fina, c/Portaferrissa 11 (☎317 97 87). The *Fina* is an exception along this street – dull rooms which are overpriced to boot. It's included here because there's often room when others are full. ③–④.

Hotel Jardi, Plaça Sant Josep Oriol 1 (☎301 59 00). Very popular by virtue of its extremely attractive position and pleasant rooms. Overlooking the square, and above a trendy café. Try and book ahead. ⑤.

Hostal Layetana, Plaça Ramón Berenguer el Gran 2 (☎319 20 12). Close to the cathedral, and with airy rooms, some without showers, for which you'll pay around 1500ptas less. ④.

Hostal-Residencia Rembrandt, c/Portaferrissa 23 (☎318 10 11). An excellent place, run by accommodating people. Spotless rooms with shower and balcony at the bottom of this category; less expensive rooms without too. ④.

West of the Ramblas

There are lots of places to stay on the west side of the Ramblas – a district rich in budget restaurants, too – though the proximity of the Barri Xines red-light district may not make it the most enticing part of Barcelona. Look especially on c/de Sant Pau and c/Hospital, and c/Junta del Comerç, which runs between these two streets.

Hotel España, c/de Sant Pau 9–11 (☎318 17 58). Designed by Domenech i Montaner, the highlight of this elegant hotel is the splendid *modernista* dining room, though the rooms are attractive enough too. ⑤.

Hostal Opera, c/de Sant Pau 20 (☎318 82 01). Close enough to the Ramblas to make you overlook the rather unkempt rooms. Other rooms without shower too, in the next category down. ④.

Hostal Segura, c/Junta del Comerç 11 (☎302 51 74). Large, reliable *hostal* with plain singles, doubles and triples, with and without shower. ③.

Pensión Venecia, c/Junta del Comerç 13 (☎302 61 34). A spacious place that's a cut above most of the budget choices on this street. Rooms without shower available too. ③.

Around Plaça de Catalunya and the Eixample

The top end of the Ramblas, around Plaça de Catalunya, is a safe and central place to stay – with the added advantage of being reached directly from the airport by train. The choice of budget places outside the medieval streets, in the Eixample, isn't so wide. On the whole, the extra money it costs to stay in this part of town is well spent if you're concerned about looks and safety, less so if you're after character and a central position.

Hostal-Residencia Alicante, Ronda Universitat 4 (☎318 34 70). A useful standby if you can't get into the *Australia* (see below), though at a few hundred pesetas more, a bit pricey for what you get – and noisy too. ④.

Residencia Australia, Ronda Universitat 11, 4th floor (☎317 41 77). Good rooms (some with bath) well cared for by a pleasant English-speaking management. You'll need to reserve ahead – try at least a fortnight in advance in summer. ③.

Hotel Claris, c/de Pau Claris 150 (☎487 62 62, fax 215 79 70). Recently renovated Eixample house featuring stylish, modern accommodation and up-to-the-minute facilities. ⑥.

Hostal Colón, c/d'Aragó 281 (☎318 06 31); Metro Passeig de Gràcia. Fairly shabby, but well-sited for the most interesting parts of the Eixample. Even more reasonably priced rooms without bath available too. ③.

Hostal Goya, c/Pau Claris 74 (☎302 25 65); Metro Urquinaona. Longstanding budget Eixample choice. Rooms with and without bath. ③.

Pensión Maria, c/Consell de Cent 470 (☎231 41 10); Metro Passeig de Gràcia. As inexpensive as you'll find in the Eixample, but only a few rooms so ring ahead. ③.

Hostal-Residencia Oliva, Passeig de Gràcia 32 (☎317 50 87 or ☎488 01 62); Metro Passeig de Gràcia. Nice old building, fine rooms on the 4th floor, and a bit of a bargain if you can do without an en-suite shower. ④.

Hostal-Residencia Palacios, Gran Vía de les Corts Catalanes 629 (☎301 37 92); Metro Catalunya. Close to the main Turismo and with a full range of decent rooms; singles and doubles, with and without shower or bath. ③.

Hostal Windsor, Rambla de Catalunya 84 (☎215 11 98); Metro Passeig de Gràcia. Small, recently renovated *hostal* in a lovely building on the Eixample's nicest avenue. There are only 15 rooms (some without shower) so book ahead. ④.

Gràcia

Staying in Gràcia, you're further away from the old town sights but the trade-off is the pleasant local neighbourhood atmosphere and the proximity to some excellent bars, restaurants and clubs.

Hotel Abate, c/Gran de Gràcia 67 (☎218 55 24); Metro Fontana. Friendly, 14-roomed family-run hotel, whose pleasant if somewhat basic rooms have shower. Triples are available at a good rate, too. ④.

Hostal La Cartuja, c/Tordera 43 (☎213 33 12); Metro Joanic. Not far from Plaça Reus i Taulet, this small *hostal* marks a step up in quality. Good rooms (though only 10, so book ahead in summer), good plumbing. ③–④.

Pensión Norma, c/Gran de Gràcia 87 (☎237 44 78); Metro Fontana. Pleasant place with keenly-priced, spotless rooms, with and without shower. ④.

Youth Hostels

There are several official (*IYHF*) and not-so-official **youth hostels** in Barcelona, where accommodation is in multi-bedded dorm rooms; you'll need a membership card only for the *IYHF* hostels. Prices are around 850–1000ptas per person, more in an *IYHF* hostel if you're over 26 or a non-member. Most get full in the summer, so if you really need to secure a budget bed, ring ahead.

Albergue Pere Tarrés, c/Numancia 149 (☎410 23 09); Metro Les Corts. Near Sants station, but otherwise inconvenient for most things. There's a maximum three-night stay, and a midnight curfew; breakfast included. Open 4–10pm.

Albergue Studio, Avda. Duquesa d'Orleans 58 (☎205 09 61); Metro Sarria or FF.CC Reina Elisenda. Small summer-only hostel (July–Sept); essential to book in advance.

Albergue (Verge) de Montserrat, Passeig de la Mare de Déu del Coll 41–51 (☎210 51 51); Metro Vallcarca and follow the signs, or bus #28 from Plaça de Catalunya to the hostel. An *IYHF* hostel (membership essential) a long way out of the city – near Parc de la Creueta del Coll. Open 7.30am–midnight with breaks in mid-morning and afternoon. Maximum three-night stay; breakfast is included, and there's an optional dinner.

Pensión Colom 3, c/Colom 3 (☎318 06 31); Metro Liceu. With an entrance inside Plaça Reial, this is the better hostel choice in the square; open 24 hours. Small balconied rooms stuffed with bunk beds; laundry facilities available.

Hostal de Joves, Passeig de Pujades 29 (☎300 31 04); Metro Arc de Triomf. An *IYHF* hostel right by the Parc de la Ciutadella that usually has space. You can stay one night without a card, five nights with. Open 7.30–10am & 3pm–midnight.

Hotel Kabul, Plaça Reial 17 (☎318 51 90); Metro Liceu. An eminently avoidable and noisy private hostel, open 24 hours (July–Sept). It's slightly cheaper than the *Colom*; you pay a key deposit on top of the overnight fee; breakfast included.

Campsites

Although there are hundreds of **campsites** on the coast in either direction, there are none less than 7km from the city. The prices – around 500–600ptas per person, often the same again per tent – do you no favours either, and you'd be better saving your camping for later. For the record, the four sites closest to the city are listed below.

Albatros, Gavá (☎662 20 31; May–Sept). Bus #L90 or #L93 from Plaça d'Espanya or Plaça de Universitat.

Cala-Gogo-El Prat, Prat de Llobregat (☎379 46 00; Feb–Nov). Bus from Plaça d'Espanya.

Don Quijote, Montgat (☎389 10 16; mid-June–mid-Sept). Train from Plaça de Catalunya to Monsolis.

Hispano, Masnou (☎555 08 75; April–Oct). Train from Plaça de Catalunya.

The Ramblas and the Old Town

It is a telling comment on Barcelona's character that one can recommend a single street – **the Ramblas** – as a highlight. No day in the city seems complete without a stroll down at least part of what, for Lorca, was "the only street in the world which I wish would never end". Littered with cafés, shops, restaurants and newspaper stalls, it's at the heart of Barcelona's life and self-image – a focal point for locals every bit as much as for tourists, and one to which you'll return again and again.

The Ramblas bisect Barcelona's **old town** (*La Ciutat Vella*), which spreads north from the harbour in an uneven wedge, and is bordered by the Parc de la Ciutadella to the east, Plaça de Catalunya to the north and the slopes of Montjuïc to the west. Contained within this jumble of streets is a series of neighbourhoods – originally separate medieval parishes and settlements – that retain certain distinct characteristics today. Some of these old town neighbourhoods are accessible by diving off the Ramblas into the side streets as you go – like the **Barri Xines**, the city's notorious red-light district, and the area back from the **harbour** around c/de la Mercè; both, incidentally, are excellent places to eat. But by far the greatest concentration of interest is in the cramped **Barri Gòtic**, which curls out from around the cathedral. Here you'll find the city's finest medieval buildings and churches tucked into unkempt streets and alleys, along with several museums (a couple decidedly offbeat), and the surviving portions of walls and buildings dating back as far as Roman times. East of here, across the broad **Via Laietana**, the old town streets continue, encompassing two of Barcelona's most favoured sights: the graceful church of **Santa María del Mar** and the showpiece **Museu Picasso**.

You could see most of the places and buildings described in this section in a long day's outing. You'll have to **walk around the old town**, but the distances aren't great and pounding the medieval streets is half of the appeal anyway; to start your tour, the nearest **metro** stops are Catalunya, Liceu or Drassanes (top, middle and bottom of the Ramblas respectively), or Jaume I for the Barri Gòtic.

Along the Ramblas

Everyone starts with the **RAMBLAS**, no bad thing since they're the city's most famous feature – and deservedly so. The name, derived from the Arabic *ramla* (or "torrent"), is a reminder that in earlier times the Ramblas marked the course of a seasonal river. In the dry season, the channel created by the water was used as a road, and by the fourteenth century this had been paved over in recognition of its use as a link between the harbour and the old town. In the nineteenth century, benches and decorative trees were added, overlooked by stately, balconied buildings, and today – in a city choked with traffic – this wide swathe is still given over to pedestrians, with cars forced up the narrow strip of road on either side.

For the visitor, the first eccentricity is that the tree-lined Ramblas is (or rather are) **five separate streets** strung head to tail – from north to south, Rambla Canaletes, Estudis, Sant Josep, Caputxins and Santa Monica – though this plurality of names doesn't amount to much more than a subtle change in what's being sold from the kiosks as you head down the street. Here, under the plane trees, you'll find pet canaries, rabbits, tropical fish, flowers, plants, postcards and books. You can buy jewellery from a blanket stretched out on the ground, cigarettes from itinerant salespeople, have your palm read and your portrait painted, or just listen to the buskers and watch the pavement and performance artists. If you're around when *Barça* wins an important match you'll catch the Ramblas at its best: the street erupts with instant and infectious excitement, fans driving up and down with their hands on the horn, cars bedecked with Catalan flags, pedestrians waving champagne bottles.

The following account of the Ramblas runs from **north to south**, from Plaça de Catalunya at the top down to the Columbus monument.

From Plaça de Catalunya to Palau de la Virreina

The huge **Plaça de Catalunya** is many people's first real view of Barcelona. If you've emerged blinking from the metro and train station here, the first few minutes can be a bit bewildering as you try to figure out which way to go for the Ramblas. The square, with its central gardens, seats and fountains, is right at the heart of the city, with the old town and port below it, the planned Eixample above and beyond. An initial orientation point is the massive **El Corte Inglés** department store in the northern corner. It's a good idea to fix the plaça in your mind early on, since you'll probably pass through on several subsequent occasions as you go about the city.

There are a couple of traditional spots to rest up and take stock of your surroundings: the ninth-floor cafeteria of *El Corte Inglés* has some stupendous views of the city, while the *Café Zurich*, at the junction of the plaça with the Ramblas, is ideally placed for starting or finishing a stroll to the port.

Heading down the Ramblas, the first two stretches are **Rambla Canaletes**, with its iron fountain (a drink from which supposedly means you'll never leave Barcelona), and **Rambla Estudis**, named for the university (*L'Estudi General*) that was sited here until the beginning of the eighteenth century. This part is also known locally as *Rambla dels Ocells* as it contains a bird market, the little captives squawking away from a line of cages on either side of the street. Over on the right, the **Església de Betlem** was begun in 1681, built in Baroque style for the Jesuits, but destroyed inside during the Civil War. Opposite, the arcaded **Palau Moja** dates from the late-eighteenth century and still retains a fine exterior staircase and elegant great hall. The ground floor of the building, restored by the Generalitat, is now a cultural bookshop; try also at the entrance around the corner in c/Portaferrissa as the interior is occasionally open for exhibitions.

Another restored palace on the opposite side of the Ramblas is definitely open for visits: the graceful eighteenth-century Baroque **Palau de la Virreina** (Tues–Sat 9am–2pm & 4.30–9pm, Sun 9am–2pm), at no. 99, on the corner of c/del Carme. The ground floor of the palace is a walk-in **information centre** and ticket office for cultural events run by the *Ajuntament*; it's always worth dropping in to pick up a programme.

Rambla Sant Josep

Beyond the Palau de la Virreina starts **Rambla Sant Josep**, the switch in names marked by the sudden profusion of flower stalls at this point of the Ramblas. The city's main food market – the glorious **Mercat Sant Josep** (Mon–Sat 8am–8pm) – is over to the right, a cavernous hall stretching back from the high wrought-iron entrance arch facing the Ramblas. Built between 1836 and 1840 – though the arch was added 30 years later – and known locally as the *Boqueria*, it's a riot of noise and colour with great piles of fruit, vegetables, herbs and spices, mounds of cheese and sausage, fish so fresh it's alive, and bloody meat counters.

Past the market, c/Hospital leads off to the right to the interesting Hospital de la Santa Creu (see "Barri Xines", below). This part of the Ramblas is known as **Plaça de la Boqueria**, and is marked (in the middle of the pavement) by a large round **mosaic** by Joan Miró, just one of a number of the artist's city works (fans should visit the Fundació Miró; p.541). Here, too, are a couple of *modernista*-decorated buildings, rare enough in this part of town to be worth a second glance. On the left, at no. 82, Josep Vilaseca's **Casa Bruno Quadros** was built in the 1890s to house an umbrella shop, while on the other side of the Ramblas a *farmacia* and a cake shop get the treatment: the *Genové* at no. 77 (from 1911) and more impressively the **Antiga Casa Figueras** at no. 83.

By now you've reached the handy Liceu metro station, a little way beyond which is what remains of the **Gran Teatre del Liceu**, Barcelona's celebrated opera house, which burned down for the third time in January 1994, when a worker's blowtorch set fire to the scenery during last-minute alterations to an opera set. The building has had an unfortunate history, to say the least. Founded in 1847, it was first rebuilt after a fire in 1861 to become Spain's grandest opera house. Regarded as a bastion of the city's late nineteenth-century commercial and intellectual classes, the Liceu was devastated again in 1893 when an Anarchist threw two bombs into the stalls during a production of *William Tell*. He was acting in revenge for the recent execution of a fellow Anarchist assassin – twenty people died in the bombing. The latest devastation came as a severe blow to the city: Spain's king and queen offered their sympathy, while opera stars like Montserrat Caballé immediately pledged support to raise funds to rebuild it – something destined to take at least three years.

In the meantime you can ponder the destruction from across the way, at Rambla 74, where the famous **Café de l'Opera** remains a very fashionable meeting place, as it has been for a century or so. Inside, it's not as pricey as you might imagine from the period furnishings and white-coated waiters, though if you're lucky enough to secure an outside table on the Ramblas you can expect to pay a little more than usual.

Plaça Reial

A hundred metres or so further down the Ramblas, now the **Rambla de Caputxins**, the elegant nineteenth-century **Plaça Reial** is another good place to call a halt – it's hidden behind an archway on the left and is easy to miss. Laid out in around 1850, the Italianate square is studded with tall palm trees and decorated iron lamps (by the young Gaudí), bordered by graceful arcaded buildings, and centred on a fountain depicting the Three Graces. Once there was a real danger in loitering aimlessly here, but now the heavier night-time atmosphere is more imagined than real and the conspicuous police post established in the square has had its desired effect. Stop for a drink at one of the terrace cafés, and before you leave take at look in the shop at no. 8 on the square, the so-called **Museo Pedagogico**, which is full of stuffed and preserved animals (including an ape in a glass case). The other diversion here is on Sunday morning (10am–2pm) when there's a **coin and stamp market**, attended by serious dealers but with enough lightweight exhibits and frenetic bargaining to be entertaining.

Rambla de Santa Monica

Continuing down the Ramblas, Gaudí's magnificent Palau Güell stands on c/Nou de la Rambla (see "Barri Xines" below), just over the way from Plaça Reial, beyond which you're on the final stretch, the **Rambla de Santa Monica**. There's little to see until you reach the bottom of the Ramblas, though you can derive some diversion from the pavement artists and palm readers who occasionally set up stall here, augmented in the afternoons at the weekend by a small street market selling jewellery, ornaments and clothes. There's a wax museum here, too, the **Museu de Cera**, on the left-hand side at nos. 4–6 (Mon–Fri 10am–2pm & 4–8pm, Sat & Sun 10am–8pm; 450ptas, 380ptas for 5–11 year-olds), though it's of little relevance to Barcelona, or even Spain; the usual trawl through the international famous and infamous.

The Ramblas end at **Plaça Portal de la Pau**, coming up hard against the teeming traffic that runs along the harbourside road. In the centre stands Columbus, pointing out to sea at the top of a tall grandiose, iron column built for the Universal Exhibition in 1888: the **Monument a Colom**. You can get inside (June–Sept daily 9am–9pm; rest of the year Tues–Sat 10am–2pm & 3.30–6.30pm, Sun 10am–7pm; 200ptas, children 100ptas) and take the lift to his head 52m up for aerial views of the city.

The harbour

Columbus is the most obvious landmark down at Barcelona's **harbour**, an area spruced up considerably over recent years. A harbourside *passeig*, the **Moll de la Fusta** – the city's old timber wharf – has been landscaped with benches and trees from the Colom monument as far as the Post Office building. You cross to this on little bridges which span the new ring road built to link Montjuïc with the Olympic Village away to the east. Once across, there are seats from where you can look out over the docks, while a couple of fancy bar-restaurants along the promenade provide meals with pricey views, particularly *Gambrinus* whose giant crayfish-top was designed by Xavier Mariscal, the man behind the Olympic mascot.

If you're down here at lunchtime or later, it's worth knowing that Barcelona's best **tapas bars** are found in the old harbour neighbourhood (see p.558). The streets leading off Plaça Duc de Medinaceli – c/de la Mercè particularly – are lined with likely-looking places.

The Drassanes: Museu Maritim

Opposite Columbus, set back from the road on the western side of the Ramblas, are the **Drassanes**, unique medieval shipyards dating from the thirteenth century. Originally used to fit and arm Catalunya's war fleet, in the days when the Catalan kingdom was vying with Venice for control of the Mediterranean, the shipyards were in continous use (and frequently refurbished) until well into the eighteenth century. The basic structure – long parallel halls facing the sea – has changed little, however; its size and position couldn't be bettered, whether the shipbuilders were fitting out medieval warships or eighteenth-century trading vessels destined for South America.

Nowadays the huge, stone-vaulted buildings make a fitting home for an excellent **Museu Marítim** (Tues–Sat 9.30am–1pm & 4–7pm, Sun 10am–2pm; 200ptas), whose centrepiece is a copy of the sixteenth-century Royal Galley (*Galeria Reial*), a red-and-gold barge rowed by enormous oars. It's surrounded by smaller models, fishing skiffs, sailing boats, old maps and charts, and other nautical bits and pieces – none of which, worthy though they are, can really compete with the soaring building itself.

Harbour rides and views

From a couple of points along the Moll de la Fusta, regular sightseeing boats, **Los Golondrinas** (April–Oct Mon–Fri 11am–5pm, Sat & Sun 11am–8pm, or 9pm July–Sept; Nov–March Mon–Fri 11am–4pm, Sat & Sun 11am–8pm; 330ptas, children 180ptas), make the half-hour ride across the harbour through the modern docks to the breakwater. There's also a two-hour ride east to the Port Olímpic (daily at 11am, 1pm & 4pm; 1100ptas, children 500ptas), including a twenty-minute stop at the port.

A more dramatic view of the city is offered by the **cable car** (daily noon–7pm; 700ptas one-way, 750ptas return), which sweeps right across the water from the base of Montjuïc to the middle of the new docks and on to Barceloneta – film buffs may remember Jack Nicholson riding it in Antonioni's film, *The Passenger*. The central **cable car tower**, *Jaume I*, is just a few minutes' walk up the Moll de Barcelona from the Columbus monument, and even if you're saving the ride for a full trip from either Barceloneta or Montjuïc, you might consider taking the lift (250ptas) to the top of the tower, as at this point the views over the city are supreme.

The Barri Xines

West of the Ramblas, from the harbour roughly as far north as c/de Hospital, the triangular **BARRI XINES** is not the most obvious area of Barcelona in which to sightsee, but – during the day at least – you'll find it's an interesting place to wander around. First and foremost, it's known as a red-light area (the name is misleading; there are no Chinese here). Like any port, Barcelona has a long history of prostitution: Orwell relates how after the 1936 Workers' Uprising "in the streets were coloured posters appealing to prostitutes to stop being prostitutes". Franco, for rather different reasons, was equally keen to clear the streets. Neither succeeded, though measuring by its former reputation, the Barri Xines is pretty tame these days.

It may be rather hard to credit given the often shabby surroundings, but the quarter also contains several sights firmly on the tourist map. During the day little will happen to you here that wouldn't happen elsewhere in the city, so don't be unduly concerned as you make your way to the destinations below – which include one of Gaudí's early works. At night, sensible precautions (like not carrying large wallets down unlit side streets) should see you right: certainly, it would be a shame not to patronize some of the excellent **restaurants** that thrive in the area.

Architecturally, most of the *barri* is fairly undistinguished, though in among the down-at-heel surroundings is a splash of **modernista** colour worth keeping an eye out for: the **Hotel España** at c/de Sant Pau 9–11 is perhaps the best-known of the buildings, with a hugely attractive tiled dining room designed by Domenèch i Montaner.

The Palau Güell

Much of Antoni Gaudí's early career was spent constructing elaborate follies for wealthy patrons. The most important was Don Eusebio Güell, a shipowner and industrialist, who in 1885 commissioned the **Palau Güell**, at c/Nou de la Rambla 3, just off the Ramblas (Mon–Fri 10am–1pm & 5–7pm, public holidays 10am–1pm). It's now used as a theatre museum, so, unusually, you can see the interior: most of the Gaudí houses are still privately owned. Here, Gaudí's feel for different materials is remarkable. At a time when architects sought to conceal the iron supports within buildings, Gaudí turned them to his advantage, displaying them as attractive decorative features. The roof terrace, too, makes a virtue of its functionalism, since the chimneys and other outlets are decorated with glazed tiles, while inside, columns, arches and ceilings are all shaped and twisted in an elaborate style that was to become the hallmark of Gaudí's later works.

Sant Pau del Camp

Behind the Liceu on the Ramblas, c/de Sant Pau leads down through the heart of the Barri Xines to the church of **Sant Pau del Camp** (St Paul of the Plain), its name a reminder that it once stood in open fields beyond the city walls. The oldest and one of the most interesting churches in Barcelona, Sant Pau was a Benedictine foundation of the tenth century, built on a Greek Cross plan. Sitting in a small courtyard studded with trees it has been well restored, and if you can't get in there's plenty to interest you on the outside (the church is open for services on weekdays at 8am, Sundays at 10am, noon, 1pm and 7pm). Above the main entrance are curious, primitive (and faded) thirteenth-century carvings of fish, birds and faces, while other animal forms adorn the capitals of the twelfth-century cloister; at the back of the church the delicately curved apses are worth a detour, too.

Hospital de la Santa Creu

On the northern fringes of the Barri Xines – you'll probably divert to see it on your way down the Ramblas – the **Hospital de la Santa Creu** is the district's most substantial relic. The attractive complex of Gothic buildings here, reached down c/de Hospital (from where you get the best views of the building's facade), was built in the fifteenth century on the site of a tenth-century refuge, later transformed into a hospital for pilgrims. The hospital itself shifted site earlier this century (to Domènech i Montaner's new creation in the Eixample; see p.542), and most of the remaining buildings have been converted to educational use, leaving you free to wander among the spacious cloisters and courtyards. Just inside the entrance are some superb seventeenth-century *azulejos* of various religious scenes; note the figure on the right with the word *Iesus* written in mirror image – a formula signifying death. You can also go into the eighteenth-century *Academia de Medicina* whose lecture theatre is decked out in red velvet and chandeliers, complete with revolving marble dissection table.

The Barri Gòtic

A remarkable concentration of beautiful medieval Gothic buildings just a couple of blocks northeast of the Ramblas, the **Barri Gòtic** forms the very heart of the old town. Once it was entirely enclosed by fourth-century AD Roman walls, but what you see now dates principally from the fourteenth and fifteenth centuries, when Barcelona reached the height of her commercial prosperity before being absorbed into the burgeoning kingdom of Castile. Parts of the ancient walls can still be seen incorporated into later structures, especially around the cathedral.

Plaça de Sant Jaume and around

The quarter is centred on the **Plaça de Sant Jaume**, a spacious square at the end of the main c/de Ferran. Once the site of Barcelona's Roman forum and marketplace, it's now one venue for the weekly dancing by local people of the Catalan folk dance, the *sardana*, and is also the traditional site of demonstrations and gatherings.

The square contains two of the city's most significant buildings. On the south side stands the restored town hall, the **Ajuntament**, from where the Spanish Republic was proclaimed in April 1931. The most interesting part, the restored fourteenth-century

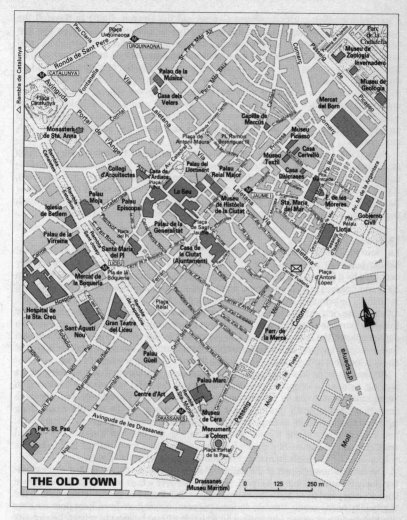

council chamber, the *Saló de Cent*, is on the first floor; sadly it is currently closed to the public, though if you're in a group you may be able to organize a visit. Otherwise, you get a much better idea of the grandeur of the original structure by nipping around the corner, down c/de la Ciutat, for a view of the former main entrance. It's a typically exuberant Catalan-Gothic facade, but was badly damaged during renovations in the nineteenth century – a move which led the city council to commission the much less pleasing Neoclassical facade on Plaça de Sant Jaume.

Right across the square rises the **Palau de la Generalitat**, traditional home of the Catalan government, which since 1977 has once again been operating from this address. Begun in 1418, this presents its best – or at least its oldest – aspect around the side, on c/del Bisbe, where the early fifteenth-century facade by Marc Safont contains a spirited medallion portraying Saint George and the Dragon. Going in through the Renaissance main entrance facing the square, there's a beautiful cloister on the first floor with superb coffered ceilings, while opening off this gallery are the chapel and salon of **Sant Jordi** (St George, patron saint of Catalunya as well as England), also by Safont, and other chambers of the former law courts. Sadly, the only time you can visit the interior is each year on Sant Jordi's Day, 23 April (expect a two-hour wait), when the whole square is festooned with book stalls and flower sellers. Celebrated as a nationalist holiday in Catalunya, St George's Day is also a kind of local Valentine's Day – tradition has it that you give a man a book and a woman a rose, and the stalls set up on Plaça de Sant Jaume and the Ramblas to sell them are mobbed all day with customers.

Behind the *Ajuntament* is the **Església dels Sants Just i Pastor**, whose very plain stone facade belies the rich stained glass and elaborate chapel decoration inside – enter from the back, at c/Ciutat; the main doors on Plaça Sant Just are open less often. It's claimed (though there's no real evidence) that this is the oldest church site in Barcelona, held to have first supported a foundation at the beginning of the ninth century; the restored interior, though, dates from the mid-fourteenth century.

La Seu

La Seu (daily 8am–1.30pm & 4–7.30pm), Barcelona's cathedral, is one of the great Gothic buildings of Spain. Located just behind the Generalitat, on a site previously occupied by a Roman temple and Moorish mosque (a familiar pattern), it was begun in 1298 and finished in 1448, with one notable exception commented on by Richard Ford in 1845: "The principal facade is unfinished, with a bold front poorly painted in stucco, although the rich chapter have for three centuries received a fee on every marriage for this very purpose of completing it." Perhaps goaded into action, the authorities set to and completed the facade within a ten-year period in the 1880s. Some critics complain that this delay cost the cathedral its architectural harmony, though the facade is Gothic enough for most tastes – and is seen to startling effect at night when it's lit up.

Artificial lighting has transformed the **interior**, replacing the dank mystery with a soaring airiness to echo the grandeur of the exterior. The cathedral is dedicated to Santa Eulàlia, martyred by the Romans for daring to prefer Christianity, and her tomb rests in a crypt beneath the high altar; if you put money in the slot the whole thing lights up to show off its exemplary Catholic kitschiness. See, too, the rich altarpieces, and carved tombs of the 29 side chapels. Among the finest of these is the painted wooden tomb of Ramon Berenguer I, Count of Barcelona from 1018 to 1025, who was responsible for establishing many of the *usatges*, ancient Catalan rights.

The most renowned part of the cathedral is its magnificent fourteenth-century **cloister** (daily 8.45am–1.30pm & 4–7pm), which looks over a lush tropical garden complete with soaring palm trees and – more unusually – honking white geese. If they disturb the tranquillity of the scene, they do so for a purpose: geese have been kept here for over five hundred years either (depending on which story you believe) to reflect the virginity of Santa Eulàlia or as a reminder of the erstwhile Roman splendour of Barcelona.

The cloister opens onto various small chapels and church offices, as well as a small **Museu de la Catedral** (Mon–Fri 11am–1pm). This incorporates the *Sala Capitular*, with its ageing leather seats and assorted fifteenth-century religious paintings.

Plaça de la Seu and Plaça Nova

Flanking the cathedral, to the west of the **Plaça de la Seu**, are two fifteenth-century buildings closely associated with it. The **Casa de l'Ardiaca** (once the Archdeacon's residence, now the city archives) boasts a tiny cloistered and tiled courtyard with a small fountain, while the **Palau Episcopal**, just beyond on c/del Bisbe, was the

Bishop's palace. This is on a grander scale altogether. Though you're not allowed inside either building, you can go as far as both courtyards to see their fine outdoor stairways, a frequent local feature; there's a patio at the top of the Palau Episcopal's stairway with Romanesque wall paintings.

The large **Plaça Nova**, facing the cathedral, marks one of the medieval entrances to the old town – beyond it, you're fast entering the wider streets and more regular contours of the modern city. Even if you're sticking with the Barri Gòtic for now, walk over to study the frieze surmounting the modern **Collegi d'Arquitectes** building (College of Architects) on the other side of the square. Designed in 1960 by Picasso, it has a crude, almost graffiti-like quality at odds with the more stately buildings to the side.

Plaça del Rei and around

The cathedral and its associated buildings aside, the most concentrated batch of historic monuments in the Barri Gòtic is the grouping around the neat **Plaça del Rei**, behind the cathedral apse. The square was once the courtyard of the rambling palace of the Counts of Barcelona, and across it stairs climb to the great fourteenth-century **Saló del Tinell** (Mon–Sat 10am–8pm, Sun 10am–2pm; 250ptas), the palace's main hall and a fine, spacious example of secular Gothic architecture; the interior arches span seventeen metres. At one time the Spanish Inquisition met here, taking full advantage of the popular belief that the walls would move if a lie was spoken; nowadays it hosts various exhibitions, while concerts are occasionally held in the hall, or outside in the square. It was on the steps leading from the Saló del Tinell into the Plaça del Rei that Ferdinand and Isabella stood to receive Columbus on his triumphant return from America.

The palace buildings also include the late-medieval five-storeyed **watchtower** which rises above one corner of the square, as well as the beautiful fourteenth-century **Capella de Santa Àgata**, with its tall single nave and unusual stained glass. This is entered through the building that closes off the rest of the square, the Casa Clariana-Padellás, a fifteenth-century mansion moved here brick by brick from nearby c/de Mercaders earlier this century to house the splendid **Museu d'Historia de la Ciutat** (Tues–Sat 10am–2pm & 4–8pm, Sun 10am–2pm; 300ptas, 150ptas on Wed, free Sun); the entrance is on c/del Veguer. Underground, extensive Roman and Visigothic remains (including whole streets and a fourth-century Christian basilica) have been preserved where they were discovered during works in the 1930s.

The surrounding streets, between Plaça del Rei and the cathedral, reveal a similar kind of historical cross-section. The mid-sixteenth-century **Palau del Lloctinent**, the Viceroy's palace, has a facade facing the Plaça del Rei: the building contains the enormous medieval archives of the kingdom of Aragón, which you won't be allowed in to see, and another fine courtyard with staircase and coffered ceiling, which you will (enter on c/dels Comtes).

Perhaps the most engaging sight in the area, however, is the extraordinary **Museu Marès** (Tues–Sat 10am–5pm, Sun 10am–2pm; 300ptas, 150ptas Wed, free first Sun of month), which occupies another wing of the old royal palace, behind Plaça del Rei (entrance on c/dels Comtes), and whose large arcaded courtyard is the most impressive so far. The bulk of this museum consists of an important body of religious sculpture, including a vast number of wooden crucifixes showing the stylistic development of this form from the twelfth to the fifteenth centuries. This is infinitely more interesting than it might sound, but in case boredom should set in, the upper floors house the **Museu Sentimental** of local sculptor Frederico Marès (not always open), an incredible retrospective jumble gathered during fifty years of travel, with everything from tarot cards to walking sticks by way of cigarette papers.

Plaça Sant Felip Neri to Plaça Sant Josep Oriol

Heading east, back towards the Ramblas from the cathedral, you snake through a series of interconnecting squares and dark streets. Behind the Palau Episcopal, **Plaça Sant Felip Neri** is wholly enclosed by buildings and used as a playground by the kids at the square's school. Beyond are three more delightful little squares, with the four-teenth-century **Església de Santa María del Pi** at their heart. Burned down in 1936, and restored in the 1960s, the church boasts a Romanesque door but is mainly Catalan Gothic in style, with just a single nave with chapels between the buttresses. The rather plain interior only serves to set off some marvellous stained glass, the most impressive of which is contained within a huge rose window, often claimed (rather boldly) as the largest in the world.

The church stands on the middle square, **Plaça Sant Josep Oriol**, the prettiest of the three, overhung with balconies and scattered with seats from the excellent *Bar del Pi*, a fine place for a drink in the evening. This whole area becomes an artists' market at the weekend, while buskers and street performers often appear here, too. The squares on either side – Plaça del Pi and Placeta del Pi – are named, like the church, for the pine tree that once stood here.

North towards Plaça de Catalunya

Beyond Plaça Sant Josep Oriol, two or three diversions on the way north to Plaça de Catalunya make it worthwhile to stick to the back streets, avoiding the Ramblas. Much of the area is devoted to antique shops and art galleries: one of the most famous is at c/Petritxol 5, where the **Sala Pares** was already well-established when Picasso and Miró were young; it still deals exclusively in nineteenth- and twentieth-century Catalan art.

The large **Plaça Vila de Madrid** features some well-preserved Roman tombs in its sunken garden, and here you're close to c/Montsió and **Els Quatre Gats** (The Four Cats; no. 3), the bar opened by Pere Romeu and other *modernista* artists in 1897 as a gathering place for their contemporaries. Also known as the Casa Marti, the building itself is gloriously decorated inside – it was the architect Puig i Cadafalch's first commission – and *Els Quatre Gats* soon thrived as the birthplace of *modernista* maga-zines, the scene of poetry readings and shadow-puppet theatre and, in 1901, the setting for Picasso's first public exhibition. Today you can sit inside and soak up the atmos-phere, by having a beer or a meal.

JEWISH BARCELONA

Barcelona's medieval **Jewish quarter**, *El Call*, was just to the south of Plaça Sant Josep Oriol, centred on today's c/Sant Domingo del Call (*Call* is the Catalan word for a narrow passage). In the narrow, dark alleys on either side of the street, a closed ghetto survived and even prospered for some 300 years before the Jews were expelled from Spain in the fifteenth century. Excavations have proved that the main synagogue was on the site of the building that now stands at c/Sant Domingo del Call 7, but today little except the street name survives as a reminder of the Jewish presence – after their expulsion, the buildings used by the Jews were torn down and used for construction elsewhere in the city, a pattern repeated throughout Catalunya. There are still some echoes of the Jewish presence in Barcelona, however: on the eastern side of Montjuïc (Mountain of the Jews) was the Jewish cemetery, already a long-established burial place by the eleventh century; while the Palau del Lloctinent (off the Plaça del Rei) preserves many records of medieval Jewish life in its archives of the Aragón crown. You won't get to see these unless some are transferred to the Museu d'Historia de la Ciutat in the future, as is planned, but the castle at Montjuïc does display around thirty tombstones recovered from the cemetery earlier this century.

A small diversion across the nearby Via Laietana takes you to another *modernista* classic, Domènech i Montaner's **Palau de la Música Catalana**, which doesn't seem to have enough breathing space in the tiny c/Sant Pere Mes Alt. Built in 1908 for the *Orfeó Català* choral group, its bare brick structure is smothered in tiles and mosaics, the highly elaborate facade resting on three great columns, like elephant's legs; the corner sculpture, by Miquel Blay, supposedly represents Catalan song. If you can get a ticket for one of the many fine concerts here do so, since the building is as fantastic acoustically as it is visually. There are hour-long **guided tours** of the interior on Tuesdays and Thursdays at 3pm, and Saturdays at 10am and 11am, which cost 200ptas per person.

Via Laietana to Parc de la Ciutadella

In 1859, as the plans for the Eixample took shape, a wide, new avenue was also constructed to the south, cutting through the old town. This was the **Via Laietana**, running roughly parallel to the Ramblas. Nowadays it delineates the eastern extent of the Barri Gòtic, but not to push on over the road into the equally dense network of medieval streets beyond would be a mistake. True, there isn't the same concentration of preserved buildings here as in the Barri Gòtic, but there is the major attraction of the **Museu Picasso**, while the street on which it lies (c/de Montcada) and the church at the end of it (Santa María del Mar) encapsulate some of Barcelona's most perfect Catalan-Gothic features.

Carrer de Montcada and the Passeig del Born

Everyone makes the trip to **c/de Montcada** sooner or later, and the narrow street lined with leaning late-medieval mansions has been spruced and paved (and signposted from the c/de la Princesa) in response to the growing number of tourists. The draw is the Museu Picasso (see below), housed in one of the grander buildings, but the street itself is one of the best-looking in the city. Laid out in the fourteenth century, until the Eixample was planned almost 500 years later it was home to most of the city's leading citizens who occupied spacious mansions built around central courtyards, from which external staircases climbed to the living rooms on the first floor. The Picasso Museum aside, several of the other mansions are also used as exhibition space today.

Almost opposite the Picasso Museum, at no. 12, the fourteenth-century Palau de Llió and its next door neighbour contain the extensive collections of the **Museu Textil i d'Indumentaria** (Tues–Sat 10am–5pm, Sun 10am–2pm; 300ptas) – 4000 items altogether including textiles from the fourth century onwards and costumes from the sixteenth, dolls, shoes, fans and other accessories. Close by there's the *Caixa de Pensións* art gallery at no. 14, housed in a sixteenth-century building, and another private gallery at no. 25, the *Galeria Maeght*, spread across two floors of the former Palau dels Cervelló. C/de Montcada ends at the church of Santa María del Mar (see below), fronting which is the fashionable **Passeig del Born**, once the site of medieval fairs and tournaments and now, perhaps fittingly, lined with trendy bars.

The Museu Picasso

The **Museu Picasso** (Tues–Sat 10am–8pm, Sun 10am–3pm; 500ptas, 250ptas Wed, free first Sun of month), at c/de Montcada 15–19, is Barcelona's biggest tourist attraction, housed in a strikingly beautiful medieval palace converted specifically for the museum. It's one of the most important collections of Picasso's work in the world and certainly the only one of any significance in his native country. Even so, some visitors are disappointed: the museum isn't thoroughly representative, it contains none of his best-known works, and few in the Cubist style. But what *is* here provides a unique opportunity to trace Picasso's development from his early paintings as a young boy to the major works of later years.

PICASSO IN BARCELONA

Although born in Málaga, Pablo Picasso (1881–1973) spent much of his youth – from the age of 14 to 23 – in Barcelona. He maintained close links with Barcelona and his Catalan friends even when he left for Paris in 1904, and is said to have always thought of himself as Catalan rather than Andaluz. The time Picasso spent in Barcelona contained the whole of his "Blue Period" (1901–04) and many of the formative influences on his art.

Apart from the Museu Picasso, there are echoes of the great artist at various sites throughout the old town. Not too far from the museum, you can still see many of the buildings in which Picasso lived and worked, notably the **Escola de Belles Arts de Llotja** (c/ Consolat del Mar, near Estació de França), where his father taught drawing and where Picasso himself absorbed an academic training. The **apartments** where the family lived when they first arrived in Barcelona – Passeig d'Isabel II 4 and c/Cristina 3, both opposite the Escola – can also be seen, though only from the outside. His first public exhibition was in 1901 at *Els Quatre Gats* bar/restaurant (c/Montsió 3). Less tangible is to take a walk down **c/d'Avinyó**, which cuts south from c/de Ferran to c/ Ample. Large houses along here were converted into brothels at the turn of this century, and Picasso used to haunt the street sketching what he saw; women at one of the brothels inspired his seminal Cubist work, *Les Demoiselles d'Avignon*.

The museum opened in 1963 with a collection based largely on the donations of Jaime Sabartes, friend and former secretay to the artist. The **early drawings** in which Picasso – still signing with his full name, Pablo Ruiz Picasso – attempted to copy the nature paintings in which his father specialized, and the many studies from his art school days, are fascinating. Even at the age of fifteen and sixteen (by which time he was living in Barcelona) he was painting major works – a self-portrait and a portrait of his mother from 1896, copies of paintings in the Prado from the following year. Indeed, it's the early periods that are the best represented: some works in the style of Toulouse-Lautrec, like the menu Picasso did for *Els Quatre Gats* restaurant in 1900, reflect his interest in Parisian art at the turn of the century; other selected works show graphically Picasso's development of his own style – there are paintings here from the famous **Blue Period** (1901–04), the Pink Period (1904–6), and from his Cubist (1907–20) and Neoclassical (1920–25) stages.

The large gaps in the main collection (for example, nothing from 1905 until the celebrated *Harlequin* of 1917) only underline Picasso's extraordinary changes of style and mood. This is best illustrated by the large jump after 1917 – to 1957, a year represented by two rooms on the first floor which contain the fascinating works Picasso himself donated to the museum, his fifty-odd interpretations of Velázquez's masterpiece *Las Meninas*.

Santa María del Mar

At the bottom of c/de Montcada sits the graceful church of **Santa María del Mar** (daily 9am–12.30pm & 5–8.15pm; Sun choral mass at 1pm), built on what was the seashore in the fourteenth century. The church was at the heart of the medieval city's maritime and trading district (c/Argentería, named after the silversmiths who worked there, still runs from the church square to the city walls of the Barri Gòtic), and its soaring lines were the symbol of Catalan supremacy in Mediterranean commerce, much of it sponsored by the church. Built quickly, and therefore largely pure in style, it's an exquisite example of Catalan-Gothic architecture, with a wide nave and high, narrow aisles, and for all its restrained exterior decoration is still much dearer to the heart of the average local than the cathedral, the only other church in the city with which it compares.

Ciutadella to Montjuïc

Recreational space has always been high up the list with every re-design of the city. Recently, peripheral bits of industrial wasteland have benefited from the drive to provide some greenery and relative peace, but the late-nineteenth-century expansion of Barcelona relied instead on transforming previously fortified, and very central, sections of the city. The quickest respite from the centre is still in the **Parc de la Ciutadella**, east of the old town and easy walking distance from the Barri Gòtic. Once the site of a Bourbon fortress, this is a formal park, with several museums and other attractions spread about its attractive paths and gardens. To the south lies the fishing (and seafood-eating) district of **Barceloneta**, jutting out into Barcelona's central harbour, while a short walk from here, the newly built **Parc de Mar** has totally transformed a previously redundant section of the city's coastline.

You'll probably want to reserve most of a day for the more substantial attraction of **Montjuïc**, the hill that rises over on the other side of the harbour, to the west of the Barri Xines. This still retains its castle, while the museums, monuments and gardens are connected by an extensive series of paths and viewpoints; some of the attractions are also linked by cable car – a method of transport that also connects Montjuïc with Barceloneta, enabling you to jump fairly swiftly between all the areas described in this chapter. For **transport details**, see the information boxes.

Parc de la Ciutadella

The **PARC DE LA CIUTADELLA** seems to have a peculiar ability to take in far more than would seem possible from its outward dimensions. As well as a lake, Gaudí's monumental fountain and the city zoo, you'll find here the meeting place of the Catalan parliament and a modern art museum. The last two occupy parts of a fortress-like structure right at the centre of the park, the surviving portion of the star-shaped **citadel** from which the park takes its name. It was erected by Felipe V in 1715, to subdue Barcelona after its spirited resistance to the Bourbons in the War of the Spanish Succession, and a whole city neighbourhood had to be destroyed to make room for the citadel. The Bourbon symbol of authority survived uneasily, until it too was destroyed in 1869 and the surrounding area made into a park. It seems a fitting irony that the main palace structure is once again home to the autonomous Catalan parliament, which first sat here between 1932 and 1939.

Perhaps the most notable of the park's sights is the **Cascada**, the monumental Baroque fountain in the northeast corner. Designed by Josep Fontseré, the architect chosen to oversee the conversion of the former citadel grounds into a park, this was the first of the major projects undertaken here. Fontseré's assistant in the work was the young Antoni Gaudí, then a student, who was also thought to have had a hand in the design of the Ciutadella's iron park gates, at the entrance on Avda. Marqués de l'Argentera

The Park and the 1888 Exhibition

In 1888, barely twenty years after it was first created, the park was chosen as the site of the **Universal Exhibition**, which helped start the cultural regeneration of Barcelona. Many of the *modernista* giants called upon to help left their mark here, beginning with Josep Vilaseca i Casanoves' giant brick **Arc de Triomf**, outside the main gates at the top of Passeig Lluís Companys, studded with ceramic figures and motifs, and topped by two pairs of bulbous domes.

Just inside the main entrance, Domènech i Montaner designed a castle-like building intended for use as the exhibition's café-restaurant. Dubbed the *Castell dels Tres*

Dragons, it became a centre for *modernista* arts and crafts, and many of Domènech's contemporaries spent time here experimenting with new materials and refining their techniques. It's now the **Museu de Zoologia** (Tues–Sun 10am–2pm; 300ptas, 150ptas Wed, free first Sun of month), which – given that it contains the usual parade of stuffed birds and animals – is better avoided unless you're a fan. In any case, the decorated red-brick exterior knocks spots off the rather more mundane interior.

The Museu d'Art Modern de Catalunya

In the centre of the park, the surviving parts of Felipe's citadel – the governor's palace and old arsenal – stand on the Plaça d'Armes. They are now shared by the Catalan parliament and the **Museu d'Art Modern de Catalunya** (daily except Tues 9am–9pm; 300ptas). The museum has often been seen as a sort of collection of also-rans – Barcelona has separate galleries for Picasso, Miró and Tapiès, and Dalí gets his own place in Figueres – but there's enough fine work here to dispel the charge effectively.

Following renovations, and wrangling between various artisitic bodies, the attractively laid out museum is now devoted to Catalan art dating from the mid-nineteenth century until around 1930 and, as you might expect, it's particularly good on *modernista* and *noucentista* painting and sculpture, the two dominant schools of the period. There are fine examples of the work of Ramon Casas (whose work once hung on the walls of *Els Quatre Gats*) and Santiago Rusiñol, the latter particularly interesting if you've seen some of the lesser works at his house, now a museum, in Sitges (see p.562). Later *modernista* works include the landscapes of Joaquim Mir and the astonishingly varied output of Isidre Nonell. The museum's latter rooms cover *noucentista* works, a style at once more classical and less consciously flamboyant than *modernisme* – perhaps the best known *noucentista* artist, Joaquim Sunyer, is among those displayed here, though there are works by a host of others, too, including Xavier Nogués and the sculptor Pau Gargallo.

The Parc Zoològic

For all Ciutadella's cultural appeal, the most popular attraction – apart from the green spaces of the park itself – is the city's zoo, the **Parc Zoològic** (daily 10am–6pm, July–Sept until 7pm; 850ptas), taking up most of the southeast of the park. There's an entrance on c/de Wellington if you've arrived at Metro Ciutadella, as well as one inside the park. Here the star exhibit is *Snowflake*, a unique (in captivity at least) and much-gawped-at, pure-white albino gorilla. The zoo is another casualty of the city's endless reorganisation drive, and is due to be moved in time to a new site further to the east – at which point the space it now occupies in Ciutadella will be landscaped and returned to the city's strollers and sunbathers.

Barceloneta and Parc de Mar

South of the park, and across the tracks of the Estació de França, the port district of **Barceloneta** is the closest to the centre of the self-contained village suburbs that used to ring the city and are now part of greater Barcelona. The triangular wedge of development was laid out in 1755 – a classic eighteenth-century grid of streets where previously there had been mud-flats – to replace the neighbourhood destroyed to make way for the Ciutadella fortress. The long, narrow streets are still very much as they were planned, broken at intervals by small squares and lined with low-built, multi-windowed houses designed to give the sailors and fishing folk who lived here plenty of sun and fresh air.

Barceloneta is still a working fishing district, the large quayside taken up by the repair yards, boats and nets of the local fleet. Indeed, the main reason most people – city inhabitants included – come to Barceloneta is to eat in one of the district's many **fish and seafood restaurants**. Despite redevelopment, which closed down many of

BARCELONETA TRANSPORT

• **Metro**: line 4 to Barceloneta, from where it's a short stroll down to the Passeig Nacional.

• **Buses**: #17 and #45 from Via Laietana, #39 from Arc de Triomf, and #57 and #64 from Avda. Paralell and Passeig de Colom, all dropping on Passeig Nacional. Stay on any bus (except the #45) until the end of the line in Barceloneta, at the top of

Passeig Nacional, and you're very close to the cable car station.

• **Cable car**: connects Montjuïc (*Miramar*) and the Moll de Barcelona (*Jaume I*), in the centre of the docks, to Barceloneta (*Sant Sebastià*: daily noon–7pm; 700ptas one-way, 750ptas return for the whole trip, 650ptas and 700ptas respectively for the ride to *Jaume I* only).

the restaurants that once faced the beach on the southeast side of Barceloneta, those on the main **Passeig de Bourbó** (still Passeig Nacional on some maps), facing the harbour, haven't been affected and they remain lively throughout the day and night; you can sit outside at most, for good views back over to the city centre.

After your meal, you can cut through the Barceloneta streets to the **beach**, much cleaned up recently, furnished with outdoor showers, and backed by the long promenade of the Passeig Maritim.

Parc de Mar: the Vila Olímpica

On the beach at Barceloneta you're within walking distance of perhaps the most adventurous urban development project undertaken by the city since the nineteenth-century extension to the north. The old industrial suburb of Poble Nou and its waterfront have been torn apart to make way for the **Parc De Mar**, a huge seafront development that incorporates the **Vila Olímpica** (Olympic Village), home to the athletes and administrators during the 1992 Games. The project was the brainchild of a specialist firm of urban architects led by Josep Martorell, Oriol Bohigas and an Englishman, David Mackay, which planned to turn the 5km of shoreline from Barceloneta to the Río Besòs to the east into a hi-tech but user-friendly corridor of apartment blocks, conference and shopping centres, hotels, offices, parks and transport links. The Olympic Village itself was built to house 15,000 competitors and support staff, the idea being to convert it into permanent housing for around 7000 people after the Games.

Not everyone, of course, supported the redevelopment, and the promise of new housing, particularly, had a hollow ring in Barceloneta and Poble Nou, two of the poorer areas of the city, since it was soon clear that the apartment blocks and residential complexes were not exactly being built on low-cost lines. In a way, the protestors have been vindicated, for with the Olympics now long over, parts of the Vila Olímpica still look like a building site. Despite assertions that 80 percent of the apartments have been sold, the area often looks suspiciously deserted, and shops and businesses have been slow to move in, put off by the high prices and poor location.

Montjuïc

Easily visible from Barcelona's harbourside, the steep hill of **MONTJUÏC** is much the largest green area in the city and contains the most of interest. It took its name from the Jewish community that once settled on its slopes, and there's been a castle on the heights since the mid-seventeenth century, which says much about the hill's obvious historical defensive role. But since landscaping at the beginning of this century, and more pertinently since the erection of buildings for the International Exhibition of 1929, Montjuïc has been the city's greatest cultural draw – it takes a full day at least to sample its varied attractions, which include five museums, an amusement park, various

MONTJUÏC TRAVEL DETAILS

• From **Plaça d'Espanya Metro**, you can **walk** (or take the escalators) up to the Palau Nacional, or take one of three **buses** – #61, which runs past most of the sights (last bus 8.30pm); the free bus (half-hourly 10am–3pm, 4–9pm and 10pm–midnight) that links the Plaça to the Poble Espanyol; or the #100, which runs past the Poble Espanyol (see p.540 for full details of this route).

• Starting at the eastern end of the hill, there's a dramatic **cable car** ride from Barceloneta or from the Moll de Barcelona, near the Columbus statue, to Jardins de Miramar (daily noon–7pm; 700ptas one-way, 750ptas return). Just beyond, you can then pick up a second cable car to the amusement park and the castle; or simply walk to the nearby museums.

• There's also a **funicular railway** which runs from Parallel Metro station to the cable car station for the castle (daily in summer, every 15min, 11am–9.30pm; winter Sat, Sun and holidays only; 150ptas one-way, 250ptas return). From here, you're only a few minutes' walk from the Fundació Miró.

gardens and the famous "Spanish Village". The architecture on Montjuïc is disappointing if you've been inspired by the remnants from 1888 in the Ciutadella park; *modernisme* was a spent force by 1929 and the bland, monumental designs here seem purely functional. However, spurred on by the Olympics, a new spate of building and improvement work produced some rather more unorthodox designs. With these set alongside the few unusual relics from 1929, Montjuïc has never looked so spruce as it does now.

From Plaça d'Espanya to the Palau Nacional

Although it's a stiff climb from the Plaça d'Espanya, through the forty-seven-metre-high twin towers and up the imposing Avda. de la Reina Maria Cristina, it's worth doing at least once for the rewarding views as you go. Central position is given over to the illuminated fountains (the *Font Màgica*) in front of the Palau Nacional. For years the fountains formed part of a spectacular light and music show, though they currently require millions of pesetas to get them back into working order, and their future is unclear. More likely to be working are the giant outdoor escalators, part of the improvements sponsored by the 1992 Olympics; they start when you step on them and save you the legwork up the steps.

The towering **Palau Nacional**, set back at the top of the flight of steps, was the centrepiece of Barcelona's 1929 International Exhibition. It was due to be demolished once the exhibition was over but gained a reprieve and later became home to one of Spain's great museums, devoted to Catalan art.

The **Museu d'Art de Catalunya** (daily 9am–9pm; 500ptas) inside the Palau Nacional is by far the best art museum in Barcelona. Sadly, much of the collection has been off-limits for several years now in order to facilitate an extensive refit and reorganisation, which should, but may not, be concluded by the time you read this book. At the time of writing, just three rooms of selected works were open to the public, enough to give a frustrating taste of the museum's enormous medieval collection.

The medieval collection has two main sections, one dedicated to Romanesque art and the other to Gothic – periods in which Catalunya's artists were pre-eminent in Spain. Medieval Catalan studios concentrated on decorating churches with murals, but they also produced painted altar frontals, often based on a figure of a saint surrounded by scenes from his life. In time, these grew in scale into the large *retablos* over the high altar – a key feature of Spanish churches for centuries.

The **Gothic** collection is fascinating, ranging over the whole of Spain and particularly good on Catalunya, Valencia and Aragón. The Catalan and Valencian schools in

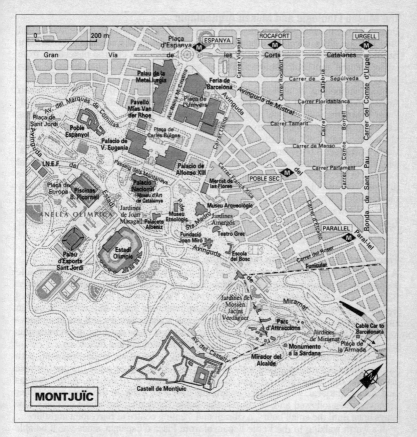

particular were influenced by contemporary Italian styles and you'll find some outstanding altarpieces (including three by the famous Serra brothers), tombs and church decoration as well as colourful, if less refined, paintings.

The **Romanesque** section is even more remarkable, perhaps the best collection of its kind in the world. Thirty-five rooms are filled with eleventh- and twelfth-century frescoes, meticulously removed from a series of small Catalan Pyrenean churches to prevent them being stripped and sold off. For the most part, these churches and their decorative frescoes were either ruined by later renovations or lay abandoned – prone to theft and damage – until a concerted effort from 1919 onwards to remove the murals to the museum for preservation.

The frescoes are beautifully displayed, and while you're unlikely to be familiar with such art (surviving examples are rare and invariably remote) you're equally unlikely not to be converted to its charms. For the most part, they have a vibrant, raw quality, best exemplified by those taken from churches in the Boí valley – like the work of the so-called Master of Taüll, whose decoration of the apse of the church of Sant Climent in Taüll (see p.649) combines a Byzantine hierarchical composition with the imposing colours and strong outlines of the contemporary manuscript illuminators.

The Museu Etnologic and Museu Arqueològic

Downhill from the Palau Nacional, just to the east, are a couple more collections to find time for; the city's excellent ethnological and archeological museums. The **Museu Etnologic** (Tues–Sun 10am–2pm; 200ptas) boasts extensive cultural collections from Japan, Central and South America, Turkey and Senegal, housed in a series of glass hexagons.

More compelling, or at least more relevant to Catalunya, is the important **Museu Arqueològic** (Tues–Sat 9.30am–1pm & 4–7pm, Sun 9.30am–2pm; 200ptas, free Sun), lower down the hill. Mostly devoted to the Roman period, the museum also has Carthaginian relics (especially from the Balearics), Etruscan bits and pieces and lots of prehistoric objects: it's of particular interest if you're planning to visit Empúries on the Costa Brava (see p.587), since most of the important finds from that impressive coastal site, and some good maps and photographs, are housed here. Among the more unusual exhibits in the museum is a reconstructed Roman funeral chamber whose walls are divided into small niches for funeral urns; a type of burial known as *columbaria* (literally pigeon-holes), which may be seen in situ in the south of Spain, at Carmona in Andalucía.

Over the way, cut into the hillside, is a reproduction of a Greek theatre, the **Teatre Grec**, again built for the 1929 Exhibition and now used during Barcelona's summer cultural festival, the *Grec* season.

From the Poble Espanyol to the Olympic area

A short walk over to the western side of the Palau Nacional brings you to the **Poble Espanyol** or "Spanish Village" (Mon 9am–8pm, Tues–Sun 9am–3am; 650ptas, children 325ptas). This was designed for the International Exhibition and its streets and squares consist of famous or characteristic buildings from all over Spain. At the time, it was an inspired concept and as a crash-course in Spanish architecture it's still not at all bad – everything is well labelled and reasonably accurate and there are a couple of museums on site (both open daily 9am–2pm), displaying ethnographical and folk items.

Until 1992, however, the village was becoming a bit of an embarrassment, with tawdry shops catering exclusively for tourist trade. At this stage, amid the pre-Olympic frenzy, the city authorities brought in Barcelona's hippest designers, Alfred Arribas and Xavier Mariscal, who installed a club, the *Torres de Ávila*, in the Avila gate. Other trendy venues followed and, of course, this being Barcelona, the whole complex now stays open until the small hours, a vibrant and exciting centre of Barcelona nightlife.

It's worth walking to the Poble Espanyol from Plaça d'Espanya, since you'll be able to stop off at a couple of restful spots on the way. Just down the road from the village, the 1986 reconstruction by Catalan architects of the **Pavelló Mies van der Rohe** (daily 10am–6pm; free) recalls part of the German contribution to the 1929 Exhibition. Originally designed by Mies van der Rohe, the pavilion has a startlingly beautiful conjunction of hard straight lines with watery surfaces, its dark green polished onyx alternating with shining glass. Close by, Montjuïc's **Botanical Gardens** (*Jardí Botànic*: summer 9am–2pm & 3–7pm; winter 9am–2pm & 3–5pm) are another possible retreat between museums, though these are currently closed for restoration.

The Olympics on Montjuïc

From the Poble Espanyol, the main road through Montjuïc climbs around the hill and up to the city's principal **Olympic area**. It's a superb spot, sporting some amazing views of the city and its suburbs, and the road leads you right past some of Barcelona's most celebrated new buildings – like Ricardo Bofill's **Sports University** (the *Institut Nacional d'Educacio Fisica de Catalunya*), the **Complex Esportiu Bernat Picornell** (swimming pools – see p.569 – and sports complex), and the low-slung, Japanese-designed, steel-and-glass **Palau Sant Jordi**, a sports and concert hall seating 17,000 people, and opened in 1990 with Pavarotti in attendance.

Even this, however, is overshadowed by the **Estadi Olímpic** (visits daily 10am–6pm; free), which comfortably holds 65,000. Built originally for the 1929 Exhibition, and completely refitted by Catalan architects to accommodate the 1992 opening and closing ceremonies, it's a marvellously spacious arena. Remarkably, the only part not touched in the rebuilding was the original Neoclassical facade – everything else is new. The **Galeria Olímpica** (Tues–Sat 10am–2pm & 4–8pm, Sun 10am–2pm; 300ptas) exhibits items from the opening and closing ceremonies, and displays videos of the Games themselves.

The 1992 Olympics were the second planned for Montjuïc's stadium. The first, in 1936 – the so-called "People's Olympics" – were organised as an alternative to the Nazis' infamous Berlin games of that year, but the day before the official opening Franco's army revolt triggered the civil war and scuppered the Barcelona games. Some of the 25,000 athletes and spectators who had turned up stayed on to join the Republican forces.

Fundació Joan Miró

Continuing down the main Avda. l'Estadi, heading towards the cable car station, you pass possibly Barcelona's most adventurous museum, the **Fundació Joan Miró** (Tues–Sat 11am–7pm, Thurs until 9pm, Sun 10.30am–2.30pm; 500ptas, students 250ptas) – an impressive white structure, opened in 1975, and set in gardens overlooking the city. Joan Miró (1893–1983) was one of the greatest of Catalan artists, establishing an international reputation whilst never severing his links with his homeland. He had his first exhibition in 1918 and after that spent his summers in Catalunya (and the rest of the time in France) before moving to Mallorca in 1956, where he died. His friend, the architect Josep-Luis Sert, designed the beautiful building that now houses the museum, a permanent collection of paintings, graphics, tapestries and sculptures donated by Miró himself and covering the period from 1914 to 1978.

The **paintings and drawings**, regarded as one of the chief links between surrealism and abstract art, are instantly recognisable. Miró showed a childlike delight in colours and shapes and developed a free, highly decorative style – one of his favourite early techniques was to spill paint on the canvas and move his brush around in it. But for all that, perhaps the most affecting pieces in the museum are those of the *Barcelona Series* (1939–44), a set of fifty black-and-white lithographs executed in the immediate post-Civil War period. Other exhibits include his enormous bright **tapestries** (he donated nine to the museum), pencil drawings (particularly of mis-shapen women and gawky ballerinas) and **sculpture** outside in the gardens.

As well as the permanent exhibits, excellent temporary exhibitions, which may or may not be to do with aspects of Miró's own work, are a regular feature. There is work by other artists, too, on permanent display, including pieces conceived in **homage to Miró** by the likes of Henri Matisse, Henry Moore, Robert Motherwell and the Basque sculptor Eduardo Chillida. The single most compelling exhibit, however, has to be Alexander Calder's **Mercury Fountain**, which he built for the Republican pavilion at the Paris Universal Exhibition of 1936 – the same exhibition for which Picasso painted Guernica. It is housed in a corridor on the ground floor.

The Parc d'Atraccions and the Castell de Montjuïc

Over in the eastern corner of Montjuïc, in a huddle above the port, are the hill's final set of attractions. From a point on the main road by the **Jardins de Mossen Jacint Verdaguer**, a second cable car system climbs to Montjuïc's amusement park, the **Parc d'Atraccions** (mid-June to mid-Sept Tues–Sat 6pm–midnight, Sun noon–11.15pm; rest of the year Sat & Sun only noon–8pm), which has forty or so rides, some of them fairly scary (though none as unnerving as the white-knuckle cable-car ride across the harbour).

From the amusement park, the cable car tacks up the hillside, offering magnificent views across the city, before coming to rest close to the eighteenth-century **Castell de Montjuïc**. Built on seventeenth-century ruins, the castle has been the scene of much bloodshed – the first president of the *Generalitat*, Lluís Companys, was executed here by the Franco regime on 15 October, 1940 – and perhaps appropriately now houses a remarkably good **Museu Militar** (Mon–Sat 9.30am–1.30pm & 3.30–7.30pm; free). Inside are models of the most famous Catalan castles and an excellent collection of swords and guns, medals, uniforms, maps and photographs, capped by a collection of suits of armour down in the dungeons.

The Eixample

As Barcelona grew more prosperous throughout the nineteenth century, the Barri Gòtic was filled to bursting with an energetic, commercial population. By the 1850s it was clear that the city had to expand beyond the Plaça de Catalunya. The plan that was accepted was that of an engineer, Ildefons Cerdà, who drew up a grid-shaped new town marching off to the north, intersected by long, straight streets and cut by broad, angled avenues. Work started in 1859 on what became known as the *Ensanche* in Spanish – in Catalan, the **EIXAMPLE**, or "Extension".

It was a fashionable area in which to live, and the monied classes soon started moving from their cramped quarters by the port in the old town to spacious new apartments and business addresses. As the money in the city moved north, so did a new class of *modernista* architects who began to pepper the Eixample with ever more striking examples of their work, which were eagerly snapped up by status-conscious merchants and businessmen. These buildings – most notably the work of **Antoni Gaudí, Lluís Domènech i Montaner** and **Josep Puig i Cadafalch**, but others too (see "*Modernisme*" below) – are still often in private hands, restricting your viewing to the outside, but turning the Eixample into a huge urban museum around which it's a pleasure to wander.

The Eixample is still the city's main shopping and business district, spreading out on either side of the two principal (and parallel) thoroughfares, **Passeig de Gràcia** and **Rambla de Catalunya**, both of which cut northwest from the Plaça de Catalunya. The former features several of the best-known examples of Barcelona's *modernista* architecture, including the famous **Manzana de la Discòrdia** and Gaudí's **La Pedrera**. The latter is the district's most attractive avenue, largely pedestrianised and sporting benches and open-air cafés. Almost all the things you're likely to want to see are on the eastern side of the Rambla de Catalunya – an area known as *Dreta de l'Eixample* – and south of the wide **Avda. Diagonal**, which slices across the entire Eixample. There's less to get excited about on the west side of Rambla de Catalunya – the so-called *Esquerra de l'Eixample* – which housed many of the public buildings contained within Cerdà's nineteenth-century plan. Nevertheless, certain areas provide an interesting contrast with the *modernista* excesses over the way, particularly those urban park projects close to the **Estació-Sants** which heralded a movement known here as *nou urbanisme*.

If you're not interested in shopping or architecture, it's not immediately clear why you might spend time in the Eixample, though one bonus is that many of the buildings also contain noteworthy exhibitions and museums; the newest, the **Fundació Antoni Tàpies**, is Barcelona's latest gallery dedicated to the work of just a single artist. Moreover, the Eixample contains the one building in the city to which a visit is virtually obligatory: Gaudí's extraordinary **Sagrada Família** church, beyond the Diagonal, in the northeast of the district.

Along Passeig de Gràcia

If you want to walk in the Eixample, the stretch you'll get most out of is the wide **Passeig de Gràcia** which runs northwest from the *El Corte Inglés* store on the corner of Plaça de Catalunya. Laid out in its present form in 1827, it's a splendid, showy avenue, bisected by the other two main city boulevards, the Gran Via and Avda. Diagonal, and continues as far as the former village (now a suburb) of Gràcia – but you're probably not going to walk that far. Stick with it, though, as far as Metro Diagonal for a view of some of the best of the city's *modernista* architecture, flaunted in a series of remarkable buildings on and just off the avenue.

Manzana de la Discòrdia

The most famous grouping of buildings, the so-called **Manzana de la Discòrdia** or "Block of Discord", is just four blocks up from Plaça de Catalunya. It gets its name because the adjacent buildings – built by three different architects – are completely different in style and feeling. (The nearest metro stop is Passeig de Gràcia.)

On the corner with c/de Consell de Cent, at Passeig de Gràcia 35, the six-storey **Casa Lleó Morera** is by Domènech i Montaner, completed in 1906. It's the least appealing of the buildings in the block (in that it has the least extravagant exterior), and has suffered more than the others from "improvements" wrought by subsequent owners, which included removing the ground-floor arches and sculptures. But it's still got a rich Art Nouveau interior – flush with ceramics and wood – and its semi-circular, jutting balconies are quite distinctive.

A few doors up at no. 41, Puig i Cadafalch's **Casa Amatller** is more striking, an apartment block from 1900 created largely from the bones of an existing building and paid for by Antoni Amatller, a Catalan chocolate manufacturer. The facade rises in steps to a point, studded with coloured ceramic decoration and with heraldic sculptures over the doors and windows. The block contains an Hispanic art institute, the *Institute Amatller d'Art Hispanic* (library open Mon–Fri 10am–1.30pm, also Tues & Thurs 3.30–7pm), located inside the old Amatller family apartments, so you may be granted a look at Puig's interior designs, too, including some of the furniture.

Perhaps the most extraordinary creation on the Block of Discord is next door, at no. 43, where Gaudí's **Casa Batlló** (finished in 1907) – designed for the industrialist Josep Batlló – was similarly wrought from an apartment building already in place but considered dull by contemporaries. Gaudí was hired to give it a facelift and contrived to create a facade which Dalí later compared to "the tranquil waters of a lake". There's an animal aspect at work here, too: the stone facade hangs in folds, like skin, and from below, the twisted balcony railings resemble malevolent eyes.

Casa Montaner i Simon: the Fundació Antoni Tàpies

Turn the corner onto c/d'Aragó and at no. 255 (just past Rambla de Catalunya) you'll find Domènech i Montaner's first important building, the **Casa Montaner i Simon**, finished in 1880. The building originally served the publishing firm of *Montaner i Simon*, but as the enormous aluminium tubular structure on the roof now announces, it's recently been converted to house the **Fundació Antoni Tàpies** (Tues–Sat 11am–8pm, Sun 11am–3pm; 400ptas, students 200ptas).

The third of Barcelona's showpiece single-artist collections is devoted to the life and work of Antoni Tàpies, born in the city in 1923. His first major paintings date from 1945, at which time Tàpies was interested in collage (using newspaper, cardboard, silver wrapping, string and wire) and engraving techniques. Later, coming into contact with Miró among others, he underwent a brief surreal period (the fruits of which are displayed in the basement). After a stay in Paris he found his feet with an abstract style that matured

MODERNISME

Modernisme, the Catalan offshoot of Art Nouveau, was the expression of a renewed upsurge in Catalan nationalism in the 1870s. The early nineteenth-century economic recovery in Catalunya had provided the initial impetus, and the ensuing cultural renaissance in the region – the *Renaixença* – led to the fresh stirrings of a new Catalan awareness and identity after the dark years of Bourbon rule.

Lluís Domènech i Montaner (1850–1923) – perhaps the greatest *modernista* architect – was responsible for giving Catalan aspirations a definite direction with his appeal, in 1878, for a national style of architecture, drawing particularly on the rich Catalan Romanesque and Gothic traditions. The timing was perfect, since Barcelona was undergoing a huge expansion: the medieval walls had been pulled down and the gridded Eixample was giving the city a new shape, with a rather French feel to it, and plenty of new space to work in. By 1874 **Antoni Gaudí** (1852–1926) had begun his architectural career. Born in Reus to a family of artisans, his work was never strictly modernist in style (it was never strictly anything in style), but the imaginative impetus he provided to the movement was incalculable. Fourteen years later the young **Josep Puig i Cadafalch** (1867–1957) would be inspired to become an architect (and later a reforming politician) as he watched the spectacularly rapid round-the-clock construction of Domènech's *Grand Hotel* on the Passeig de Colom. It was in another building by Domènech (the café-restaurant of the Parc de la Ciutadella) that a craft workshop was set up after the Exhibition of 1888, giving Barcelona's *modernista* architects the opportunity to experiment with traditional crafts like ceramic tiles, ironwork, stained glass and decorative stone carving. This combination of traditional crafts with modern technology was to become the hallmark of *modernisme* – a combination which produced some of the most fantastic and exciting modern architecture to be found anywhere in the world.

Most attention is usually focused on the three main protagonists mentioned above; certainly they provide the bulk of the most extraordinary buildings that Barcelona has to offer. But keep an eye out for lesser known architects who also worked in the Eixample; **Josep Maria Jujol**, renowned as Gaudí's collaborator on several of his most famous projects, can also boast a few complete constructions of his own; or there's the hardworking **Jeroni Granell** (1867–1931), and **Josep Vilaseca i Casanoves** (1848–1910), who was responsible for the brick Arc de Triomf outside the Ciutadella park.

It's Antoni Gaudí, though, that most have heard of – by training a metalworker, by inclination a fervent Catalan nationalist. His buildings are the most daring creations of all Art Nouveau, apparently lunatic flights of fantasy which at the same time are perfectly functional. His architectural influences were Moorish and Gothic, while he embellished his work with elements from the natural world. Yet Gaudí rarely wrote a word about the theory of his art, preferring its products to speak for themselves. Like all the *modernista* buildings in the city, they demand reaction.

during the 1950s, during which time he held his first major exhibitions, including a show in New York. His large works – splashed across the main gallery – are deceptively simple, though underlying messages and themes are signalled by the inclusion of everyday objects and symbols on the canvas, while he has also experimented with unusual materials, like oil paint mixed with crushed marble. His work became increasingly political, too, during the 1960s and 1970s: the harsh colours of *In Memory of Salvador Puig Antich* commemorate a Catalan Anarchist executed by Franco's regime.

La Pedrera and Vinçon

Gaudí's weird apartment block, the Casa Milà, at Passeig de Gràcia 92 (Metro Diagonal) is another building not to be missed, worked on between 1905 and 1911. Its rippled facade, curving around the street corner in one smooth sweep, is said to have been inspired by the mountain of Montserrat, and the apartments themselves, whose balconies of tangled metal drip over the facade, resemble eroded cave dwellings. The building – still split into private apartments – is more popularly known as **La Pedrera**, the "rock pile" or "stone quarry". This was one of Gaudí's last secular commissions – and one of his best – but even here he was injecting religious motifs and sculptures into the building until told to remove them by the building's owners. Gaudí, by now working full-time on the Sagrada Família, determined in future to use his skills only for purely religious purposes (for more, see the "Sagrada Família", below). You can visit the roof, to see at close quarters the enigmatic chimneys, from Tuesday to Saturday at 10am, 11am, noon and 1pm. However, it's essential to book at least a day in advance to reserve a place on the free **tour**: call ☎487 36 13 (English-speaking) or go to the *Caixa* office at La Pedrera itself (closed Mon).

Right next to La Pedrera, in the same block, the **Casa Casas** dates from 1899, a huge building designed for the artist Ramon Casas who maintained a home here. In 1941, the **Vinçon** store was established in the building, which emerged in the 1960s as the country's pre-eminent purveyor of furniture and design, a position today's department store (Mon–Sat 10am–2pm & 4.30–8.30pm) still maintains. There are several entrances – at Passeig de Grácia 96, c/de Provemça 273 and c/Pau Claris 175 – and apart from checking out the furniture floor, which gives access to a terrace with views of the interior of La Pedrera, make time, too, for *La Sala Vinçon* (open same hours as the store), the store's exhibition hall and art gallery.

East: Between Passeig de Gràcia and Avda. Diagonal

The buildings along Passeig de Gràcia are perhaps the best-known in the Eixample, but the blocks contained within the triangle to the east, formed by the Passeig and **Avda. Diagonal**, sport their own important, often extraordinary structures. Several are by the two hardest working architects in the Eixample, Domènech i Montaner and Puig i Cadafalch, while Gaudí's first apartment building, the Casa Calvet, is also here. Apart from the Casa Calvet, all the buildings are within a few blocks of each other between the Passeig de Gràcia and Diagonal Metro stops.

Just a few blocks from the Plaça de Catalunya, Gaudí's **Casa Calvet** (c/de Casp 48) dates from 1899. This was his first apartment block and though fairly conventional in style, the Baroque inspiration on display in the main facade was to surface again in his later, more elaborate buildings on the main Passeig de Gràcia. Follow any of the long streets north – particularly c/de Roger de Llúria or c/del Bruc – and you'll pass a number of other splendid, unsung modernist buildings, all dating from within thirty years of each other. If you need a target, aim for the church and market of **La Concepció**, in between c/de Valencia and c/d'Aragó. The early fifteenth-century Gothic church and cloister once stood in the old town, part of a convent abandoned in the early nineteenth century and then transferred here brick-by-brick in the 1870s by Jeroni Granell. The market was added in 1888, its iron-and-glass tramshed structure reminiscent of others in the city. One block north, the neo-Gothic **Casa Thomas** at c/de Mallorca 291, with its understated pale ceramic tiles, has a ground floor that welcomes visitors into its furniture design showroom. A little way along, set back from the crossroads in a little garden, the **Palau Montaner** (c/de Mallorca 278) was finished a few years later, in 1893. In comparison, it's rather a plain, low structure, though enlivened by rich mosaic pictures on the facade and a fine interior staircase.

From here you can head up Avda. Diagonal to finish at the Metro stop. On the right, at nos. 416–420, is Puig i Cadafalch's largest work, the soaring Casa Terrades, more usually known as the **Casa de les Punxes** (House of Spikes) because of its red-tiled turrets and steep gables. Built in 1903 for three sisters, and converted from three separate houses spreading around an entire corner of a block, it's a satisfying, almost northern European, castellated block.

Further up, on the other side of the road at no. 373, Puig's almost Gothic **Palau Quadras** from 1904 now houses the **Museu de la Música** (Tues–Sun 10am–2pm; 300ptas, free first Sun of month). The collection of instruments from all over the world, dating from the sixteenth to the twentieth century, gives an excuse to see inside.

La Sagrada Família

While diverting, and occasionally provocative, the pockets of architectural interest throughout the Eixample hardly command mass appeal. The same is not true, however, of the new town's most famous monument, Antoni Gaudí's great **Templo Expiatiorio de la Sagrada Família** (daily 9am–8pm, 600ptas; *Metro* line 5 to Sagrada Família), a good way northeast of the Plaça de Catalunya and just north of the Diagonal. It's an essential stop on any visit to Barcelona, for more than any building in the Barri Gòtic it speaks volumes about the Catalan urge to glorify uniqueness and endeavour.

Begun in 1882 by public subscription, the Sagrada Família was conceived originally by its progenitor, the Catalan publisher Josep Bocabella, as an expiatory building which would atone for the city's increasingly revolutionary ideas. Bocabella appointed the architect Francesc de Paula Villar to the work, and his plan was for a modest church in an orthodox neo-Gothic style. After arguments between the two men, **Gaudí** took charge two years later and changed the direction and scale of the project almost immediately, seeing in the Sagrada Família an opportunity to reflect his own deepening spiritual and nationalist feelings. Indeed, after he finished the Parc Güell in 1911, Gaudí vowed never to work again on secular art, but to devote himself solely to the Sagrada Família (where, by now, he lived in a workshop on site), and he was adapting the plans ceaselessly right up to his death. (He was run over by a tram on the Gran Via in June 1926 and died in hospital two days later – initially unrecognised, for he had become a virtual recluse, rarely leaving his small studio. His death was treated as a Catalan national disaster, and all of Barcelona turned out for his funeral procession.)

Today the church remains unfinished, though amid great controversy **work restarted** in the late 1950s and still continues. Although the church building survived the Civil War, Gaudí's plans and models were destroyed in 1936 by the Anarchists, who regarded Gaudí and his church as conservative religious relics that the new Barcelona could do without: George Orwell – whose sympathies were very much with the Anarchists during the Civil War – remarked that the Sagrada Família had been spared because of its supposed artistic value, but added that it was "one of the most hideous buildings in the world" and that "the Anarchists showed bad taste in not blowing it up when they had the chance". However, since they didn't, and as no one now knows what Gaudí intended, the political arguments continue. Some maintain that the Sagrada Família should be left incomplete as a memorial to Gaudí's untimely death, others that he intended it to be the work of several generations, each continuing in their own style.

The building

The size alone is startling. Eight **spires** rise to over 100 metres. They have been likened to everything from perforated cigars to celestial billiard cues, both of which are good descriptions. For Gaudí they were symbolic of the Twelve Apostles; he planned to build four more above the main facade and to add a 180-metre tower topped with a lamb (representing Jesus) over the transept, itself to be surrounded by four smaller towers symbolising the Evangelists.

A precise **symbolism** also pervades the facades, each of which is divided into three porches devoted to Faith, Hope and Charity. The east facade further represents the Nativity and the Mysteries of Joy; the west (currently the main entrance and nearing completion) depicts the Passion and the Mysteries of Affliction. Gaudí meant the south facade to be the culmination of the *Templo* – the Gloria, designed, he said, to show "the religious realities of present and future life ... man's origin, his end and the ways he has to follow to achieve it". Everything from the Creation to Heaven and Hell, in short, was to be included in one magnificent ensemble.

Use the **elevator** (95ptas) which runs up one of the towers around the rose window, or face the long, steep climb to the top (a twisting 400 steps). Either route will reward you with partial views of the city through an extraordinary jumble of latticed stonework, ceramic decoration, carved buttresses and sculpture. You're free to climb still further around the walls and into the other towers, a dizzy experience to say the least.

On site, there's the small **Museu de la Sagrada Família** (daily except Sat 10am–2pm & 4–7pm; 150ptas), which traces the career of the architect and the history of the Sagrada Família. Models, sketches and photographs help to make some sense of the work going on around you.

Around the Sagrada Família: Hospital de Sant Pau

While you're in the neighbourhood, it would be a shame not to stroll out from the Sagrada Família to Domènech i Montaner's innovative **Hospital de la Santa Creu i de Sant Pau**, possibly the one building that can touch the church for size and invention within the limits defined by Cerdà's street plan. The building has its own metro stop, but it's far better to walk up the four-block-long diagonal Avinguda de Gaudí, which gives terrific views back over the spires of the Sagrada Família.

Work started on the hospital in 1902, the brief being to replace the ageing hospital buildings in the old town with a large, modern and planned series of hospital departments and wards. Domènech i Montaner spent ten years working on the building and left his trademarks everywhere: cocking a snook at Cerdà, the buildings are aligned diagonally to the Eixample, surrounded by gardens; and everywhere, turrets and towers sport bright ceramic tiles and little domes.

Esquerra de l'Eixample: Plaça de Catalunya to Estació-Sants

The long streets **west of the Passeig de Gràcia** – making up the *Esquerra de l'Eixample* – are no competition when it comes to planning a route around the Eixample, and most visitors only ever travel this part of the city underground – on their way into the centre by metro. This was the part of the Eixample meant by Cerdà for public buildings, and many of these still stand: the grand **Universitat** building, at Plaça de la Universitat; the local **Hospital Clínic** (1904); the prison – the **Preso Model** – with its star-shaped cell blocks; and **Les Arenes** bullring, the last a beautiful structure from 1900 with fine Moorish decoration. It's not suggested that you make a special effort to visit any of these buildings. Indeed, probably your only venture into this part of the Eixample will be a window-shopping stroll along the **Gran Via de les Corts Catalanes** (usually shortened to just the Gran Via), which links Plaça d'Espanya with Plaça de les Glòries Catalanes to the east.

However, there is one part of the *Esquerra de l'Eixample* that it is possible to justify a short walk around, starting at the Plaça d'Espanya. Between here and **Sants** station, several public spaces have been created over the last decade or so in a style known as **nou urbanisme** – typified by a wish to transform former industrial sites into urban parks accessible to local people.

Parc Joan Miró and around Sants station

Built on the site of the nineteenth-century municipal slaughterhouse, the **Parc Joan Miró** (Metro Tarragona) features a raised piazza whose main feature is Miró's gigantic mosaic sculpture *Dona i Ocell* (Woman and Bird), towering above a small lake. It's a familiar symbol if you've studied Miró's other works, and was originally entitled "The Cock", until the city authorities suggested otherwise.

Even more controversial are the open park areas created around Sants station, just up the road. Directly in front of the station, the **Plaça dels Països Catalans** features a series of walls, raised meshed roofs and coverings designed by Helio Piñon – a rather comfortless "park" in most people's eyes, more intimidating than welcoming. It's easier to see the attraction of Basque architect Luis Peña Ganchegui's **Parc de l'Espanya Industrial**, two minutes' walk away around the side of the station. Built on an old textile factory site, it has a line of red-and-yellow striped lighthouses at the top of glaring white steps with an incongruously classical Neptune in the water below, seen to best effect at night.

The suburbs

Until the Eixample stretched out across the plain to meet them, a string of small towns ringed the city to the north. Today, they're firmly entrenched as **SUBURBS** of Barcelona, but most still retain an individual identity worth investigating even on a short visit to the city. **Gràcia**, particularly – the closest to the centre – is still very much the liberal, almost bohemian stronghold it was in the nineteenth century, with an active cultural life and night scene of its own. Apart from mere curiosity, each of the other suburbs also has a specific sight or two that makes it a worthwhile target. Some, like Gaudí's **Parc Güell**, between Gràcia and Horta, and the Gothic monastery at **Pedralbes**, are included in most people's tours of the city, and for good reason. Other sights are more specialised – like the football museum at FC Barcelona's superb **Camp Nou** stadium or the ceramics collection in the **Palau Reial** – but taken together they do help to counter the notion that Barcelona begins and ends in the Barri Gòtic. Finally, if you're saving yourself for just one aerial view of Barcelona, wait for a clear day and head for **Tibidabo**, way to the northwest; a mountain with an amusement park and a couple of bars with the best views in the city.

Gràcia

GRÀCIA is the most satisfying of Barcelona's peripheral districts, and given its concentration of bars, clubs and restaurants, the one you're most likely to visit. Beginning at the top of the Passeig de Gràcia, and bordered roughly by c/de Balmes to the west and the streets above the Sagrada Família to the east, it has been a fully fledged suburb of the city since late last century – traditionally home to arty and political types, students and the intelligentsia, but also still supporting a very real local population which lends Gràcia an attractive, no-frills, small-town atmosphere. Come here to eat and drink by all means, but also take time to stroll the streets and squares, and get the feel of a neighbourhood that – unlike most of the city – still feels like a neighbourhood. **Getting there** by public transport means taking the FF.CC railway from Plaça de Catalunya to Gràcia station; or taking the metro to either Diagonal, to the south, or Fontana, to the north.

Plaça del Sol is an enjoyable place to sit out during the day at one of the cafés, admiring the solid nineteenth-century buildings that surround the square and the more recent architectural additions by Gabriel Mora and Jaume Bach. At night, especially at the weekend, the square becomes an outdoor meeting-place, a base from which to launch yourself at the bars, clubs and restaurants in the vicinity. A couple of blocks down is another pleasant stop, **Plaça Rius i Taulet**, whose most obvious feature is a thirty-metre-high bell tower.

Gaudí's first major private commission, the **Casa Vicens** (which he finished in 1885), is at c/de les Carolines 24 (Metro Fontana is the closest station). Here he took inspiration from the Mudejar style, covering the facade in linear green-and-white tiles with a flower motif. However, Casa Vicens is really only a minor distraction, and for one of Gaudí's more extraordinary projects, you should continue to Parc Güell, twenty to thirty minutes' walk from Gràcia.

Parc Güell

From 1900–1914 Gaudí worked for Don Eusebio Güell (patron of his Palau Güell, off the Ramblas) on the **Parc Güell** (July–Sept daily 9am–8pm; Oct–June daily 10am–6pm; free), on the outskirts of Gràcia. This was Gaudí's most ambitious project after the Sagrada Família – which he was engaged on at the same time – commissioned as a private housing estate of sixty dwellings and furnished with paths, recreational areas and decorative monuments. In the end, only two houses were actually built, and the park was opened to the public instead in 1922.

Laid out on a hill which provides fabulous views back across the city, the park is an almost hallucinatory expression of the imagination. Pavilions of contorted stone, giant decorative lizards, a vast Hall of Columns (intended to be the estate's market), the meanderings of a huge ceramic bench – all combine in one manic swirl of ideas and excesses. The immediate and obvious comparison is with an amusement park, something not lost on a variety of literary visitors. The Hall of Columns was described by Sacheverell Sitwell (in *Spain*) as "at once a fun fair, a petrified forest, and the great temple of Amun at Karnak, itself drunk, and reeling in an eccentric earthquake".

The ceramic mosaics and decorations found throughout the park were mostly executed by J.M. Jujol, who assisted on several of Gaudí's projects, while one of Gaudí's other collaborators, Francesc Berenguer, designed and built a house in the park in 1904, in which Gaudí was persuaded to live until he left to camp out at the Sagrada Família for good. The house is now the **Casa Museu Gaudí** (Mon–Fri 10am–2pm & 4–7pm, Sun 10am–2pm; 150ptas), a diverting collection of some of the furniture he designed for other projects – a typical mixture of wild originality and brilliant engineering – as well as plans and objects related to the park and to Gaudí's life.

To get to the park, take **bus** #24 from Plaça de Catalunya right to the side gate by the car park, or the **metro** to Vallcarca, from where you walk down Avda. de l'Hospital until you see the mechanical escalators on your left, then follow the path right to the park entrance. **Walking from Gràcia**, head straight up the main c/Gran de Gràcia and you'll pass Metro Lesseps, where you should turn right on to the Travessera de Dalt.

Pedralbes and around

Northwest of the city, **PEDRALBES** is a well-to-do, residential neighbourhood of wide avenues and fancy apartment blocks. Allow yourself the best part of a day and you can include the Gothic monastery here in a longer route that takes in the Camp Nou stadium, an early Gaudí creation and the ceramics museum recently installed in the Palau Reial.

Camp Nou: the Museu del Futbol Club Barcelona

Within the city's Diagonal area, behind the university buildings, the magnificent **Camp Nou** football stadium of FC Barcelona (Metro Collblanc or Maria Cristina) will be high on the visiting list of any sports fan. Built in 1957, and enlarged to accommodate the 1982 World Cup semi-final, the comfortable stadium seats a staggering 120,000 people in steep tiers that provide one of the best football-watching experiences in the world – on a par with the famous Maracaña stadium in Brazil. The club is Spain's most successful in recent years, domestic league and cup winners on a regular basis, and European Cup winners in 1992. But it's more than just a football club to most people in Barcelona. During the Franco era, it stood as a Catalan symbol, around which people could rally, and perhaps as a consequence FC Barcelona has the world's largest football club membership – currently 106,000 – including the planet's most celebrated clerical goal-keeper, the Pope, who was persuaded to join on his visit to Spain in 1982.

If you can't get to a game, a visit to the club's **Museu del Futbol** (April–Oct Mon–Fri 10am–1pm & 3–6pm, Sat & Sun 10am–8pm; Nov–March Tues–Fri 10am–1pm & 4–6pm; 300ptas), is a good second-best: a splendid celebration of Spain's national sport. There are team and match photos dating back to 1901, and a gallery of foreign players who have graced Barça's books: in 1911, there were five British players in the team, though the first in modern times was Steve Archibald (1984), since when Mark Hughes and Gary Lineker (both in 1986) have followed. Current England coach, Terry Venables, became an honorary Catalan when he managed the team to League championship and the European Cup Final; Maradona made his name here in 1982; Johann Cruyff played for Barça in 1973, and later became the manager; while recent European stars to turn out for the team include Bulgaria's Christo Stoichkov, Holland's Ronald Koeman and Denmark's Michael Laudrup.

Palau Reial de Pedralbes and the Finca Güell

Opposite the university, on the other side of Avda. Diagonal, the **Palau Reial de Pedralbes** (Metro Palau Reial) is an Italianate palace set in pleasant, formal grounds (open winter daily 10am–6pm; summer daily 10am–8pm). Open to the public as the **Museu de Ceràmica** (Tues–Sun 10am–2pm; 300ptas), the many exhibits range from the thirteenth to the nineteenth centuries, and include fine Mudéjar-influenced tiles and plates from the Aragonese town of Teruel, as well as whole rooms of Catalan water stoups (some from the seventeenth century), jars, dishes and bowls. In the modern section, Picasso, Miró and the *modernista* Antoni Serra i Fiter are all represented.

From the palace, it's a walk of fifteen minutes or so up Avda. Pedralbes to the monastery. Just a couple of minutes along the way, you'll pass Gaudí's **Finca Güell** on your left. Built as a stables and riding school for the family of Gaudí's old patron, Don Eusebio Güell, and now a private residence, you can see no further than its extraordinary metal dragon gateway, with razor teeth snarling at the passers-by.

Monestir de Pedralbes

At the end of Avda. Pedralbes, the Gothic **Monestir de Pedralbes** (Tues–Sat 10am–5pm, Sun 10am–2pm; 300ptas, 150ptas Wed, free first Sun of month) is reached up a cobbled street that passes through a small archway set back from the road. If you're coming from the city centre, the monastery is about a half-hour journey by **bus** (#22 from the Passeig de Gràcia, just north of Plaça de Catalunya, to the end of the line), or take the metro to Palau Reial (see above).

Founded in 1326 for the nuns of the Order of St Clare, this is in effect an entire monastic village, preserved on the outskirts of the city. Parts, particularly the original dormitories, are undergoing long-term restoration, but there's still plenty to see inside the superb medieval walls and gateways. The harmonious **cloisters** are perhaps the finest in the city, built on three levels and adorned by the slenderest of columns. Rooms opening off the cloisters give the clearest impression of monastic life you're likely to see in Catalunya (much more than at, say, Poblet): there's a large refectory, a fully equipped kitchen, infirmary (complete with beds and water jugs), separate infirmary kitchen, and windows overlooking a well-tended kitchen garden. The adjacent **church**, a simple, single-naved structure which retains some of its original stained glass, is also well worth looking in on. In the chancel, to the right of the altar, the foundation's sponsor, Elisenda de Montcada, wife of Jaume II, lies in a superb, carved marble tomb.

After years of negotiations, the mainly Italian religious paintings of the controversial Thyssen-Bornemisza art collection are now on permanent view in one of the monastery's old dormitories. The immense private art collection of Baron Heinrich Thyssen-Bornemisza came to Spain in 1989, and the bulk of it is displayed in Madrid's

Villahermosa palace, but the promptings of the Baron's Catalan wife ensured a cachê of paintings found its way to Barcelona. This now forms the **Colleccio Thyssen-Bornemisza** (Tues–Fri & Sun 10am–2pm, Sat 10am–5pm; 300ptas, students 175ptas), a superb body of work encompassing such artists as Titian, Rubens and Tintoretto, as well as representative pieces by Cranach the Elder and Velázquez.

Tibidabo

If the views from the Castell de Montjuïc are good, those from the 550-metre heights of **Mount Tibidabo** – which forms the northwestern boundary of the city – are legendary. On one of those mythical clear days you can see across to Montserrat and the Pyrenees, and out to sea even as far as Mallorca. The very name is based on this view, taken from the Temptations of Christ in the wilderness, when Satan led him to a high place and offered him everything which could be seen: *Haec omnia tibi dabo si cadens adoraberis me* (All these things will I give thee, if thou wilt fall down and worship me).

At the summit there's a modern **church** topped with a huge statue of Christ, and – immediately adjacent – a wonderful **Parc d'Atraccions** (summer Mon–Thurs 5pm–2am, Fri & Sat 5pm–3am, Sun noon–11pm; reduced hours off-season, and winter Sat, Sun and public holidays only noon–8pm), where the amusements are scattered around several levels of the mountain-top, connected by landscaped paths and gardens. It's a good mix of traditional rides and hi-tech attractions, at all of which large queues form at peak times. There are various **admission** charges depending on what you want to do: entry is 950ptas and the ticket allows you on twelve designated rides and attractions (none of which are much good); 1700ptas gets you a ride on everything, but if you don't want to splash out before seeing what's on offer you can always convert your 950ptas ticket by paying the difference once inside.

Take the FF.CC **railway** (Sarrià line) or **bus** #17 (both from Plaça de Catalunya) to Avda. Tibidabo. From there a regular **tram** service (the *Tramvia Blau*; every 30min 7am–9.30pm; 125ptas one-way, 200ptas return) runs you up to Plaça Doctor Andreu (there's a bus service instead if the tram's not running). Here, there are a couple of café-bars, and a **funicular railway station** with regular connections to the top – departures are daily from 7.15am–9.45pm (later from July–Sept) and funicular tickets cost 225ptas one-way, 400ptas return.

Out of the city

Day trips out of the city are easy and popular, particularly up or down **the coast** to one of the beach-resorts that city-dwellers have appropriated for themselves. The best coastal destination is Sitges, forty minutes away along the Costa Daurada, dealt with in *Catalunya*. However, there are plenty of other beaches closer to the city that are worth considering, like **Castelldefels** to the south, and those of the **Costa Maresme** to the north – all of them are connected to Barcelona by very frequent train services that run throughout the summer. Otherwise, the one essential excursion is to **Montserrat**, the extraordinary mountain and monastery 40km northwest of the city: few visitors are disappointed.

The coast: Castelldefels and the Costa Maresme

All **trains** to the beaches below depart from Estació-Sants, which is where you should go for current timetables. Those heading south to Castelldefels also stop at the station at Passeig de Gràcia; north to the Costa Maresme, you can pick the train up at Plaça de Catalunya.

South, the first coastal stop is at **CASTELLDEFELS**, 20km from Barcelona. Don't get off at the earlier town stop; you want Castelldefels-Platja, where vast numbers alight in summer to descend upon the extremely long beach, which starts just a couple of blocks from the station. **GARRAF**, another five minutes or so south on the train, has a much smaller beach, and more of a family atmosphere, but the town itself is far prettier, with a small port to take up some of your time as well.

Immediately **north** of Barcelona, before you reach the Costa Brava, is a stretch of coast known as the **Costa Maresme**. On the whole it's far more industrial and less attractive than the Costa Brava, but its proximity to the city means clogged-up roads and packed trains in the summer, as people head out of in search of a change of scenery. The first 40km of coastline is dominated by the grim industrial towns of Badalona and Mataró, and if you're after a town with a bit more to it than interesting chemical smells, you should continue at least as far as **ARENYS DE MAR**, an hour from Barcelona. It's the largest fishing port hereabouts and consequently has a harbour that bears investigation and a beach that's serviceable. **CALDETES**, a couple of kilometres south from here, is visited for its thermal baths, first exploited by the Romans; while **CANET DE MAR**, just to the north, also has a decent beach.

SANT POL DE MAR, 45km from Barcelona, is probably your best bet if you're heading for just one spot on the coast. Small, and as unspoiled as these coastal villages get, it offers rocky coves and crowd-free swimming around fifteen minutes' walk from the station, and several restaurants along the main street. From the train station, cross the tracks and walk to the left, around the corner.

The Mountain and Monastery of Montserrat

The **MOUNTAIN OF MONTSERRAT**, with its weirdly shaped crags of rock, its monastery and its ruined hermitage caves, stands just 40km northwest of Barcelona, off the road to Lleida. It is one of the most spectacular of all Spain's natural sights, a saw-toothed outcrop left exposed to erosion when the inland sea that covered this area around 25 million years ago was drained by progressive uplifts of the earth's crust. Legends hang easily upon it. Fifty years after the birth of Christ, Saint Peter is said to have deposited an image of the Virgin carved by Saint Luke in one of the mountain caves, and another tale makes this the spot in which the knight Parsifal discovered the Holy Grail. Inevitably the monastery and mountain are no longer remote; in fact they're ruthlessly exploited as a tourist trip from the Costa Brava. But don't be put off – the place itself is still magical and you can avoid the crowds by striking out onto the moutainside, along well-signposted paths, to potent and deserted hermitages. The main **pilgrimages** to Montserrat take place on April 27 and September 8.

Practicalities

The most thrilling approach is by train and cable car from Barcelona. **FF.CC trains** leave from beneath Plaça d'Espanya (daily from 9.11am–5.11pm at two-hourly intervals); their destination is Manresa, but you get off at Montserrat Aeri, just over an hour away. From here, a **cable car** (the *Teleferic de Montserrat Aeri*; every 15min Mon–Sat 10am–5.45pm, Sun and holidays 10am–6pm) makes a five-minute swoop up the sheer mountainside to a spot just below the monastery – probably the most exhilarating ride in Catalunya. A return ticket, including train and cable car, costs 1400ptas: if you drive here, the cable car journey alone costs around 750ptas return. **Returning to Barcelona**, the trains back from Montserrat Aeri station, are again two-hourly, this time from 11.26am to 7.26pm.

Otherwise, daily **buses** run from Barcelona (by *Julia Tours*, Plaça Universitat 12 (☎317 64 54) usually leaving at 9am and returning at around 5pm. These cost around 1200ptas per person, tickets from *Julia Tours* or any travel agent. **Drivers** should take the A2 motorway as far as Martorell, and then follow the N11 and C1411 before zig-zagging up to the monastery.

The area immediately outside the monastery gates is thoroughly touristy these days, with the result that the **food** at the couple of self-service restaurants is pricey and uninspiring – and the restaurants themselves are crammed at peak times. There's a lot to be said for taking your own picnic and striking off up the mountainside. If you need to supplement your provisions, the *Bar de la Plaça*, on the square just outside the gates, has normal priced drinks and good sandwiches.

Staying over at Montserrat can be an attractive option: it's a very different place once the tour groups have departed. To the left of the basilica, the three-star *Hotel Abat Cisneros* (☎835 02 01; ⑨) has double rooms with or without shower or bath; while the *Hotel Residencia Monestir* (same telephone) is slightly cheaper. The only other option is to **camp**. The site (☎835 02 51), signposted *Camping*, is up beyond the Sant Joan funicular, overlooking monastery and mountains, with a clean shower and toilet block and excellent views; 300ptas per person and 300ptas per tent.

The Monastery

It is the "Black Virgin" (*La Moreneta*), the icon supposedly hidden by Saint Peter (and curiously reflecting the style of sixth-century Byzantine carving), which is responsible for the existence of the **MONASTERY OF MONTSERRAT**. The legend is loosely wrought, but it appears the icon was lost in the early eighth century after being hidden during the Moorish invasion. It reappeared in 880, accompanied by the customary visions and celestial music and, in the first of its miracles, would not budge when the Bishop of Vic attempted to remove it. A chapel was built to house it, and in 976 this was superseded by a Benedictine monastery, set about three-quarters of the way up the mountain at an altitude of nearly 1000m.

Miracles abounded and the Virgin of Montserrat soon became the chief cult-image of Catalunya and a pilgrimage centre second in Spain only to Santiago de Compostela. Over 150 churches were dedicated to her in Italy alone, as were the first chapels of Mexico, Chile and Peru; even a Caribbean island bears her name. For centuries, the monastery enjoyed outrageous prosperity, having its own flag and a form of extraterritorial independence along the lines of the Vatican City, and its fortunes declined only in the nineteenth century. In 1835 the monastery was suppressed for its Carlist sympathies. Monks were allowed to return nine years later but by 1882 their numbers had fallen to nineteen. In recent decades Montserrat's popularity has again become established; there are over 300 brothers and, in addition to the tourists, tens of thousands of newly married couples come here to seek *La Moreneta*'s blessing on their union.

Quite apart from its spiritual significance, Montserrat has become an important **nationalist symbol** for Catalans. At the beginning of this century Montserrat's Abbot Marcel was a vigorous promoter of the Catalan language, creating a printing press in 1918 which published the Montserrat Bible in Catalan. During Franco's dictatorship books continued to be secretly and illegally printed here, and it was then and afterwards the site of massive Catalan nationalist demonstrations.

The monastery itself is of no particular architectural interest, save perhaps in its monstrous bulk. Only the Renaissance **Basilica** (dating largely from 1560–92) is open to the public. **La Moreneta**, blackened by the smoke of countless candles, stands above the high altar – reached from behind, by way of an entrance to the right of the basilica's main entrance. The best time to be here is at the chanting of Ave Maria, around 1pm, when Montserrat's world-famous **boys' choir** sings. The boys belong to the *Escolania*, a choral school established in the thirteenth century and unchanged in musical style since its foundation.

Near the entrance to the basilica, the **Museu de Montserrat** (300ptas) is split into two parts: the section adjoining the cloister (10.30am–1.30pm) contains paintings by

Caravaggio and El Greco and a few archeological finds; while under the plaça in front of the basilica (3–5.30pm) are Catalan paintings from the nineteenth century.

Walks on the mountain

After you've poked around the monastery grounds, it's the **walks** around the woods and mountainside of Montserrat which are the real attraction. Following the tracks to various caves and the thirteen different hermitages you can contemplate what Goethe wrote in 1816: "Nowhere but in his own Montserrat will a man find happiness and peace".

Two separate **funicular railways** run from points close to the cable car station. One drops to the **Santa Cova** (Holy Grotto), a seventeenth-century chapel built where the icon is said to have originally been found. The other rises to the hermitage of **Sant Joan**, from where it's another hour or so's walk to the **Sant Jeroni** hermitage, near the summit of the mountain at 1300m. The funiculars run every fifteen to twenty minutes (10am–7pm) and cost 700ptas return for a ticket valid for both.

Eating

There is a great variety of **food** available in Barcelona and even low-budget travellers can do well for themselves, either by using the excellent markets and filling up on sandwiches and snacks, or eating cheap meals in bars and cafés. Good **restaurants** are easily found all over the city, though you'll probably do most of your eating where you do most of your sightseeing, in the **old town**, particularly around the **Ramblas** and in the Barri Gòtic. Don't be afraid to venture into the Barri Xines, though, which hides some excellent restaurants, some surprisingly expensive, others little more than hole-in-the-wall cafés. In the **Eixample** prices tend to be higher, though you'll find plenty of lunchtime bargains around; **Gràcia**, further out, is a nice place to spend the evening, with plenty of good mid-range restaurants. For the food which Barcelona is really proud of – elaborate *sarsuelas* (fish stews), and all kinds of fish and seafood – you're best off in the **Barceloneta** district (bus #64 or #17, final stop, or Metro Barceloneta), down by the harbour. Sitting down here for a huge plateful of prawns or mussels and a beer, you'll get away for around 1200ptas. A full seafood dinner will be considerably more expensive, even the *paellas* starting at around 1200ptas a head.

If you can find a place serving a *menú del día* – usually three or four courses and wine – it's nearly always great value. There's one available at most restaurants and cafés, and at some bars, too, though it's generally a lunchtime affair; indeed, some of the smaller places only open at lunchtime. Otherwise you can put together a full meal by eating *tapas* in bars and restaurants, and these small dishes are available right through the day and night.

Breakfast, snacks and sandwiches

For breakfast, you can get coffee and bread or croissants almost anywhere, but a few café-bars and specialist places – *granjas* and *orxaterias* especially – are worth looking out for. Snacks and sandwiches abound, too, and you'll be tempted by *ensaimadas* (turnovers), pizza slices and cakes at any bakery or pastry shop – which, incidentally, are among the few shops to open on Sundays.

Antiga Casa Figueres, Ramblas 83. Wonderful *modernista*-designed pastry shop. Open Mon–Sat 9am–3pm & 5–8.30pm.

Can Conesa, c/Llibretaria 1. Sandwiches and pizza slices, just off Plaça de Sant Jaume. Open Mon–Sat 8am–9.30pm; closed first two weeks in Aug.

Forn de Sant Jaume, Rambla de Catalunya 50; Metro Passeig de Gràcia. A croissant and sweet specialist, either to take away or eat at the adjacent café. Open Mon–Sat 9am–9pm.

Granja La Pallaresa, c/Petritxol 11. Bow-tied waiters glide around this specialist snack and break-fast stop, dispensing superb *xurros*, pastries, *crema catalana*, croissants, milkshakes and whipped-cream hot chocolates. Open Mon–Sat 9am–1.30pm & 4–9pm, Sun 5–9pm.

Horchateria El Carmen, c/del Carme 39. Authentic *orxata* and real ice cream, served from the depths of the marble counter. Open May–Sept 9am–9pm.

Mesón del Cafe c/Llibreteria 16. Tiny, off-beat bar where you'll probably have to stand to sample the pastries and the excellent coffee, including a "capuccino" laden with fresh cream. Open Mon–Sat 7am–12.30am.

Santa Clara, Plaça de Sant Jaume (corner of c/de la Llibreteria). Marvellous coffee and cakes, right on the square; especially busy on Sunday mornings. Open daily 8am–9.30pm.

Café Viena, Rambla Estudis 115. Turn-of-the-century decor, and splendid croissants and coffee for breakfast. Open 8am–2am.

La Xicra, Plaça Sant Josep Oriol. A decorative *xocolateria* with a touch of "ye olde-worlde" about it but lovely cakes and coffee. Open Mon–Sat 9am–9pm, Sun 9am–2pm & 5–9.30pm; closed two weeks in Aug.

Tapas bars

For a more substantial snack, you can't beat Barcelona's **tapas bars**. The best (and most famous) concentration in the Barri Gòtic is down by the port, between the Columbus monument and the post office – along c/Ample, c/de la Mercè, c/del Regomir and their offshoots. Of course, you don't have to treat the *tapas* as snacks at all: jumping from bar to bar, with a bite to eat in each, is as good a way as any to fill up on some of the best food that the city has to offer. Done this way, your evening needn't cost more than a meal in a medium-priced restaurant – say 1200–1600ptas a head for enormous amounts to eat and drink.

Ramblas and the old town

Ambos Mundos, Plaça Reial 10. Popular tourist choice; certainly one of the best places to sit outside in the old town and have a snack and a drink, though it will cost more than usual. Open 9.30am–2am; closed Tues.

Bar Celta, c/de la Mercè 16. Galician *tapas* specialities, including excellent fried *calamares*, and heady Galician wine. Very popular. Open Mon–Sat 10am–1am, Sun 10am–midnight; closed Aug.

La Bodega, c/del Regomir 11. A great barn of a place with long wooden benches, delicious food and jugs of wine as rough as a rat-catcher's glove. Open Tues–Sun 1.30–3pm & 6pm–1am; closed Aug.

Casa del Molinero, c/de la Mercè 13. Huge doors open into a wood-panelled bar with small tables and benches. The speciality is cooked and cured meats, including spicy *chorizo* which hangs from the ceiling. Open Mon–Fri 6.30pm–1.30am, Sat & Sun 6.30pm–2.30am.

Pla de la Garsa, c/Assaonadors 13. One of Barcelona's hidden delights, this beautifully restored stone and beam house is a relaxed place to sip wine, eat paté and cheese, and enjoy the classical music. Open daily 7pm–1am.

La Socarrena, c/de la Mercè 21. Asturian bar serving strong goat's cheese, cured meats and fine Asturian cider (*sidra*). Open Mon–Fri & Sun 1.30–4pm & 6pm–1am, Sat 1.30–4pm & 6pm–2.30am.

El Xampanyet, c/de Montcada 22. Terrific, bustling, blue-tiled champagne bar with fine seafood tapas, *cava* by the glass or bottle, and local *sidra*. There's no sign, it's opposite *La Nostra Pizza* restaurant. Open noon–4pm & 6.30–11pm; closed Sun evening and Mon; closed Aug.

Eixample and Gràcia

Els Barrils, c/de Aribau 89; Metro Hospital Clinic. Lavish, expensive *tapas* bar specialising in seafood and cured meat.

Bodega Sepúlveda, c/Sepúlveda 173; Metro Universitat. An anchovy specialist, which boasts more than a hundred different types of *tapas* and *torradas*. Open 9.30am–1am; closed Sun.

La Bodegueta, Rambla Catalunya 98; Metro Passeig de Gràcia. Long-established basement *bodega* with *cava* and a serious range of other wines by the glass or bottle, and cheese and cured meat to soak it all up. It gets very crowded – you may have to stand to snack. Open 7am–2am, closed Sun and third week in Aug.

Taberna Marcelino, Plaça del Sol 1; Metro Fontana. *Tapas* and fish specialities in Gràcia's trendiest square. Come more for the location than the food.

O'Nabo de Lugo, c/Pau Claris 169; Metro Passeig de Gràcia. Galician restaurant with a separate, excellent *tapas* bar. Pricey. Open 1–4pm & 8.30pm–midnight; closed Sun and August.

Restaurants

The most common **restaurants** in Barcelona are those serving local **Catalan** food, though more mainstream Spanish dishes are generally available too. There are several speciality **regional Spanish and colonial Spanish** restaurants as well, which are nearly always worth investigating, while the fancier places tend towards a refined Catalan-French style of cooking that's as elegant as it's expensive. The range of **international cuisine** is not as wide as in other European capitals, but if you've been in Catalunya (or other parts of Spain) for any length of time, you may be grateful that there's a choice at all – pizzas, Chinese and Indian/Pakistani food provide the main choices, though the cuisines of Mexico, North Africa, the Middle East and Japan are represented, too.

Restaurants are generally **open** approximately 1–4pm and 8–11pm. A lot of restaurants also **close on Sundays, on public holidays and throughout August** – check the listings for specific details but expect changes since many places imaginatively interpret their own posted opening days and times. At the more expensive restaurants, it's recommended that you **reserve a table** in advance; either ring the number provided, or call in earlier in the day.

Ramblas and the Barri Gòtic

Amaya, Rambla Santa Mónica 20–24 (☎302 10 37). Famous Basque restaurant that gets packed out, especially on Sunday. Expect to pay around 3000ptas a head; more if you have the excellent fish, less if you have the *menú del día* (2000ptas) or *tapas* in the adjacent bar. Open daily 1pm–12.30am. Moderate.

Bar Cal Kiko, c/del Palau (junction with c/Cervantes). Local workers' dining room where the 675ptas *menú del día* is filling and the atmosphere jovial if hurried. Meals 1–4pm only, *tapas* at the bar at other times. Open 7am–10pm. Inexpensive.

Can Culleretes, c/Quintana 5 (☎317 30 22). Supposedly Barcelona's oldest restaurant, located in a dark side street between c/de Ferran and c/de la Boqueria. Good-value Catalan food in pleasant traditional surroundings. Open 1.30–4pm & 9–11pm; closed Sun night. Expensive.

Los Caracoles, c/Escudellers 14 (☎302 31 85). A cavernous Barcelona landmark whose name means "snails", so it would be churlish not to have them, or the fine spit-roast chicken on display in the street outside. Around 3500ptas a head if you include both as part of a big meal. Either phone or call in earlier in the day to reserve. Open daily 1–11pm. Moderate.

Casa Jesus, c/dels Cecs de la Boqueria 4 (off c/de la Boqueria). Come here for the extremely good 900ptas *menú del día;* otherwise you'll eat for around 1500ptas. Open Mon–Fri 1–4pm & 8–11pm; closed Aug. Inexpensive.

Gallo Kirico, c/d'Avinyó 19. Pakistani-run joint with bargain rice and couscous combinations (around 500ptas a plate) served at the long bar or at tables in a dining room hacked out of the old Roman wall. Open noon–12.30am. Inexpensive.

RESTAURANT PRICES

As a rough guide, you'll be able to get a three-course meal with drinks for:

Inexpensive	Moderate	Expensive
under 1500ptas a head	1500–3500ptas a head	3500ptas and upwards

But bear in mind that the lunchtime *menú del día* often allows you to eat for much less than the price category might lead you to expect; check the listings for details.

Cafe Moka, Ramblas 126 (☎302 68 86). Less fancy than its glossy appearance and old-fashioned, formal service would suggest; in 1937 this was occupied by civil guards who were fired on by George Orwell and his *POUM* colleagues from across the street. Pizzas, pasta and salads alongside mainstream Spanish food. Open 1pm–1am, Sat until 1.30am. Moderate.

La Parilla, c/Escudellers 8 (more prominently labelled *Grill Room*). A more economic version of *Los Caracoles*, owned by the same people and serving much the same kind of filling food. Open 1–4pm & 8–11.30pm; closed Wed & Thurs mid-June–mid-July. Moderate.

Restaurant Pitarra, c/d'Avinyó 58 (☎301 16 47). A renowned Catalan cookery in operation since 1890, lined with paintings and serving good, reasonably priced local food from around 2500ptas a head. Closed Sun. Open 1.15–4pm & 8.30pm–1am. Moderate.

La Rioja, c/Duran i Bas 5 (off Avda. Portal de l'Angel). Bright, welcoming, white-tiled Riojan restaurant with a fine selection of Riojan dishes and wines. Open 1–4pm & 8–11pm; closed Aug. Moderate.

Self Naturista, c/Santa Ana 15; Metro Catalunya. Popular self-service vegetarian restaurant with a 725ptas *menú del día*, dishes that change daily and a long list of desserts. Open Mon–Sat 11.30am–10.30pm. Inexpensive.

Set Portes *(Las Siete Puertas)*, Passeig d'Isabel II 14 (☎319 30 46 or 319 30 33); Metro Barceloneta. The wood-paneled decor in the "Seven Doors" has barely changed in 150 years, and while very elegant, it's not exclusive – you will need to book ahead, though. The seafood is excellent, particularly the *paella*. Around 4000ptas a head and up. Open daily 1pm–1am. Expensive.

Tut Ankh Amon, c/Rauric 18 (off c/de Ferran). Middle Eastern food, with great falafels and kebabs served in tacky ethnic surroundings. Set meals (including vegetarian) available from around 1000ptas upwards. Open 1–4pm & 7pm–midnight; closed Tues. Inexpensive.

C/de Montcada and the Born

Bunga Raya, c/Assaonadors 7 (off c/de Montcada, on north side of c/de la Princesa). Good-value Malaysian and Indonesian restaurant. The menu is short, but the food is highly spiced and filling – the house set-meal at 1700ptas is a bumper spread. Open 1–4pm & 7pm–midnight, closed Mon. Inexpensive.

Bar-Restaurant Can-Busto, c/de Rera Palau (off Plaça de les Olles, behind Passeig del Born). Basic dining room with a limited menu, open lunch and dinner. Quick service, budget-priced food. Open 12.30–4pm & 7.30–11.30pm. Inexpensive.

Restaurante Carpanta, c/Sombrerers 13 (☎319 99 99). An intimate restaurant housed in a candlelit Gothic house around the back of Santa Maria del Mar, this is a great place to sample *arros negre* (1000ptas) or *paella* (1300ptas), though other meals will set you back 3500–4000ptas. Reserve a table in advance. Open 1–5pm & 8.30pm–midnight; closed Sun and Mon. Expensive.

La Cuina, c/Sombrerers 7. A friendly joint down the side of the church of Santa María del Mar, with a whole range of competently cooked *platos combinados*. Closed Mon. Inexpensive.

Lluna Plena, c/de Montcada 2 (☎310 54 29). Catalan restaurant making good use of its mansion surroundings: fresh flowers, candles and reasonable food for 2500–3000ptas a head. Open 1–4pm & 9–11.30pm; closed Sun night, Mon, and Aug. Moderate.

West of the Ramblas: Barri Xines

Egipte, c/Jerusalem 12, off c/del Carme (☎317 74 80). Well-known, popular restaurant, with an extensive Catalan menu. Eat well for 2500–3000ptas, and book in advance in the evening. Open 1–4pm & 8pm–1am, until 2am Fri & Sat; closed Sun. Moderate.

Restaurant España, c/de Sant Pau 9–11 (☎318 17 58). Eat fine food in *modernista* splendor in a building designed by Domènech i Montaner. The *menú del día* is good value at 1300ptas, but it's not available at night when a full meal will cost 3500–4000ptas a head. Open 1–4pm & 8.30pm–midnight.

Restaurant Garduña, c/Morera 17–19. Tucked away at the back of La Boqueria market, off the Ramblas, this recommended restaurant (busiest at lunch, when there's a 1000ptas *menú del día*) offers excellent *paellas* and good, fresh market produce. Around 2500ptas. Closed Sun. Moderate.

Pollo Rico, c/de Sant Pau 31. Great spit-roast chicken, french fries and glass of *cava* for under 550ptas makes this one of the area's most popular budget joints. A Barcelona institution, and always busy. Open 10am–1am; closed Wed. Inexpensive.

Restaurant Tallers, c/dels Tallers 6–8; Metro Catalunya. A 750ptas *menú del día* (900ptas if you opt for the fine baked chicken) served from 1–3pm and 8–10pm only. Closed Mon, and Aug. Inexpensive.

Els Tres Nebots, c/de Sant Pau 42. An extensive list of Catalan favourites served quickly and efficiently at tables at the back of the bar. The *menú del día* is great value at 800ptas, otherwise put
together a nourishing meal for well under 1500ptas. Open 12.30pm–midnight. Inexpensive.

The harbour and Barceloneta

Can Ganassa, Plaça de Barceloneta 4–6. An extensive range of *tapas*, snacks and *torrades* on
Barceloneta's central square, a filling 900ptas *menú del día* at lunchtime, and more expensive
seafood if you want it. Open 9am–11pm; closed Wed and Nov. Moderate.

Gambrinus, Moll de la Fusta (☎310 55 77). Designer café-restaurant with a terrace, part of the new
harbour development, picked out by Mariscal's big crayfish on the roof. Seafood *tapas* a speciality.
Open 8am–2am. Expensive.

Restaurant Perú, Passeig de Bourbó 10. Elegantly served, with Montjuïc views accompanying the
competently cooked, if unexciting, food. Open 1–4.15pm & 8pm–midnight. Moderate.

El Rey de la Gamba, Passeig de Bourbó 46–48 & 53 (☎319 30 14). Much promoted restaurant,
whose various extensions now occupy half the street and whose outdoor tables are always busy. It's
popular for its prawns and dried meats, but the food is overpriced. Open noon–midnight. Expensive.

Eixample

Alsham, c/de Mallorca 202; Metro Passeig de Gràcia. Between c/d'Enric Granados and c/d'Aribau,
the highly recommended *Alsham* is Syrian, with great food, presentation and service at reasonable
prices; *cuscus* comes in at 850ptas. Open 1–4pm & 8pm–midnight; closed Mon. Moderate.

Campechano Merendero, c/de Valencia 286; Metro Passeig de Gràcia. This specialist grilled
meat restaurant is hidden away in a dark entrance hall, but inside the rustic theme runs wild. Open
10.30am–4pm & 8pm–midnight; closed Mon. Moderate.

Can Segarra, Ronda Sant Antoni 102; Metro Universitat. Fairly ordinary restaurant enlivened by an
interesting list of daily Catalan specials. There's an 800ptas *menú del día* at lunchtime. Open 8am–
1am; closed Thurs. Moderate.

Les Corts Catalanes, Gran Vía de les Corts Catalanes 603 (corner Rambla de Catalunya); Metro
Catalunya. Licensed vegetarian restaurant that doubles as a health food store. There's an 950ptas
menú del día (Mon–Fri lunch only), otherwise around 2000–2500ptas a head, filling up on Catalan
vegetarian dishes, pizzas and salads. Open 1–4.30pm & 8–11pm. Moderate.

Drugstore, Passeig de Gràcia 71; Metro Passeig de Gràcia. The Mon–Fri lunch *menú* for 750ptas is
a good buy, or there are salads and *platos combinados* for around the same price. The bar-restaurant
and shopping complex itself is open 24hrs. Inexpensive.

Madrid-Barcelona, c/Aragó 282 (junction with Passeig de Gràcia); Metro Passeig de Gràcia.
Fashionable turn-of-the-century interior, attentive service and a standard Catalan menu. Open 1–
4pm & 8–11pm; closed Sat night, Sun, and Aug. Moderate.

Pastafiore: Plaça Urquinaona 10; Rambla Catalunya at c/de la Disputació; c/Provença 278 at
Rambla Catalunya; Trav. de Gràcia 60 at c/d'Aribau. Trendy fast-food pasta joint with several
outlets, serving a good 950ptas *menú del día* (evenings, too) and meals from around 700ptas. Open
Sun–Thurs noon–midnight, Fri & Sat noon–1am. Inexpensive.

Taj Mahal, c/Londres 89 (between c/Muntaner and c/Casanova); Metro Hospital Clinic. The city's
first Indian restaurant and one of the best. Open 1.30–3.30pm & 9–11.30pm; closed Mon lunch.
Moderate.

Gràcia

Ca l'Augusti, c/Verdi 28; Metro Fontana. A popular local choice, with reasonably priced *torradas*,
grilled meats, omelettes, and *paella* on Sunday. There's a very reasonably priced lunchtime *menú
del día*, though other meals run to 1500ptas and upwards. Open noon–4.30pm & 8.30pm–midnight;
closed Tues night and Wed. Inexpensive.

Bar-Restaurante Candanchu, Plaça Rius i Taulet 9; Metro Fontana. Sit beneath the clock-tower
in summer and enjoy a sandwich; or choose from the wide selection of local dishes. The *menú del
día* is 1000ptas and it's usually splendid. Open 1–5pm & 8pm–midnight; closed Tues. Inexpensive.

Cantina Mexicana, c/Encarnació 51 (☎210 68 05); Metro Fontana. Head-shrinking cocktails, to go
with the Mexican snacks and meals, and live Mexican music – all for around 2000ptas a head. Open
8pm–1am; closed Sun. Moderate.

Flash, Flash, c/de la Granada del Penedés 25; Metro Diagonal. Very 1970s, with white leatherette booths in which to eat one of around fifty different types of *tortilla*, priced from 4–800ptas. Open 1.30–5pm & 8.30pm–1.30am. Moderate.

El Glop, c/Sant Lluís 24; Metro Joanic. An authentic Catalan taverna, with enough *torradas* and salads to satisfy vegetarians, as well as grilled meats. Lively and popular; around 2000ptas a head, less if you're careful. Open 1–4pm & 7–10pm; closed Mon. Moderate.

Illa de Gràcia, c/Sant Domenec 19; Metro Fontana. Bright vegetarian restaurant with a pine-tabled interior, serving decent salads, pasta, rice dishes, omelettes and crêpes – all around 500ptas. Open Mon–Fri 1–4pm & 9pm–midnight, Sat & Sun 2pm–midnight; closed mid-Aug–mid-Sept. Inexpensive.

El Tastavins, c/Ramon y Cajal 12; Metro Fontana. Good local cooking in attractive, down-to-earth surroundings (try the chicken stuffed with prunes or the steak in anchovy sauce), and with a 600ptas lunch *menú*; otherwise around 1500–2500ptas a head. Highly recommended. Open 9am–5pm & 8.30pm–1.30am; closed Sun. Moderate.

Buying your own food: markets, supermarkets, delis

If you want to buy fresh food, or make up your own snacks and meals, use the city's **markets**. There's less choice in the **supermarkets**, though they're worth trying for tinned products, as are the **delicatessens** and small central shops which specialize in tinned fish and meat, cheeses and cooked meats. The best-value food and provisions shops are those in the Barri Xines, particularly down c/de Sant Pau.

Centre Comercial Simago, Rambla 113. Department store with food department in the basement. Open Mon–Thurs 9am–8pm, Fri & Sat 9am–9pm.

Dia, c/del Carme; and at c/Comtessa de Sobradiel. Fairly basic supermarket, with the first branch just around the corner from the much pricier *Simago* (see above).

Drugstore, Passeig de Gràcia 71; Metro Passeig de Gràcia. Expensive supermarket, coffee bar and snacks. Open 24hrs.

La Fuente, c/de Ferran 20; Metro Liceu. A *xarcuteria*, but better visited for its wide selection of tinned and preserved food, wines and cheeses. Open Mon–Fri 9am–1pm & 4–8pm, Sat 9am–1pm; closed Aug.

Mauri, Rambla de Catalunya 100; Metro Passeig de Gràcia. A superb deli specializing in cakes and pastries, with an attached café. Open Mon–Sat 9am–9pm, Sun 9am–3pm.

Mercat Sant Antoni, Ronda de Sant Pau (junction with c/del Comte). Food stalls in the middle of this large market – though most are shut in August. Open Mon–Sat 8am–3pm & 5–8pm.

Mercat Sant Josep/La Boqueria, Rambla Sant Josep 89; Metro Liceu. The best place in the city for fresh fruit, vegetables, meat, fish and dried foods. Open Mon–Sat 8am–8pm.

Drinking and nightlife

There are lively **bars and cafés** throughout the centre – in the Barri Gòtic as well as the Eixample and Gràcia – catering for all types and styles. One of the city's great pleasures is to pull up a pavement seat outside a bar, sip a coffee or a beer, and watch the world go by). There's little difference between a bar and café (indeed, many places incorporate both words in their name), but some of the other names you'll see do actually mean something – a *bodega* specializes in wine; a *cervesería* in beer; and a *xampanyería* in champagne and *cava*. Alongside the regular bars and cafés, Barcelona also has a range of **designer bars** geared towards late-night drinking, and there's a disco and club **nightlife** that, at present, is one of Europe's most enjoyable.

For **listings** of bars and clubs, get the weekly *Guía del Ocio* from news-stands, or *SexTienda*'s map of **gay** Barcelona with a list of bars, clubs, and contacts (see p.569 for *SexTienda*'s address). It's worth noting, that – unlike restaurants – most bars and cafés stay open throughout August.

Bars and cafés

Generally, the choice of bars in the **old town** is fairly mainstream, with most drinking places either traditional tourist haunts or firmly local. The in-crowd don't spend much time in the Barri Gòtic, though the area around the Museu Picasso does have its quota of trendy bars – **Passeig del Born**, the square at the end of c/de Montcada behind Santa María del Mar, is the main focus. Otherwise, *bars modernos* or *bars musicals* are the fashionable choice, hi-tech, music-filled places concentrated mainly (though not exclusively) in the **Eixample** and the streets in the western part of **Gràcia**. For more low-key, lateish drinking (though still pricey), the centre of Gràcia itself is the place, full of little squares bordered by busy café-terraces.

The Ramblas, Barri Gòtic and Barri Xines

L'Antiquari, c/Veguer 13. A former antique shop, this late-opening old town bar attracts a decent mix of locals. There's terrace seating in Plaça del Rei, but you can end up waiting ages for your drinks here. Open June–Oct 3pm–1am, Nov–May 3pm–midnight.

L'Ascensor, c/Bellafila 3 (bottom of c/de la Ciutat). Old lift doors and control panel signal the entrance to this popular local bar. Open 6pm–2.30am.

El Born, Passeig del Born 26. Comfortable bar that uses its old shop interior to good effect. Turn up after 11.30pm for the best action. Open 7pm–3am, closed Sun.

Bar London, c/Nou de la Rambla 34. Opened in 1910, this well-known *modernista* bar these days attracts a mostly tourist clientele, puts on live jazz and hosts fortune-telling sessions. Open 7pm–midnight; closed Mon & Tues.

El Nus, c/Mirallers 5. Chic bar with split-level drinking, good taped music and the local, arty hair-cuts as clientele. It's a bit tricky to find, in a back street behind Santa María del Mar, but persevere. Open 7pm–2am, closed Wed.

Café de l'Opera, Rambla Caputxins 74. Morning coffee, afternoon tea or late-night brandies in this fashionable, turn-of-the-century bar. Always busy. Open until 3am.

La Palma, c/Palma de Sant Just. 7. Comfortable, traditional *bodega*, with large wooden tables and antiques on display. Open 8am–4pm & 7–10pm; closed Sun.

El Paraigua, c/Pas de l'Ensenyança 2 (by Plaça de Sant Miquel). Impressive, if dark, *modernista* interior, just the place for early evening drinks, cocktails and a burst of classical music. Open Mon–Fri 6pm–2am, Sat 5pm–2am.

Bar Pastis, c/Santa Monica 4 (just behind Centre d'Art S. Monica). Tiny, dark French bar, right in the red-light district, awash with artistic and theatrical memorabilia, and soothed by wheezy French music. Open 7.30pm–2.30am, closed Tues.

Bar del Pi, Plaça de Sant Josep Oriel. In a lovely location, this tiny bar attracts a mixed tourist and local crowd, which spills out into the square at the drop of a hat. Open Mon–Sat 9am–11pm, Sun 10am–10pm; closed third week in Aug.

Els Quatre Gats, c/Montsío 5. *Modernista*-designed haunt of Picasso and his contemporaries (see p.532.), and still an interesting, arty place for a drink or meal. Open 1–4pm & 8.30pm–midnight; closed Sun lunch, and usually in Aug.

Café Zurich, Plaça de Catalunya 1. Right at the top of the Ramblas, this is the traditional meeting place for trendies and foreigners, its position making it *the* place to sit and watch passing crowds. Open 9am–midnight, 10.30pm on Sun (when it's self-service).

Eixample

Boliche, Avda. Diagonal 508. Big designer bar, refashioned from an earlier hangout in the early 1980s, and sporting a popular ten-pin bowling alley at the back. Open 6pm–3am.

La Fira, c/de Provença 171 (between c/Muntaner and c/Aribau; Metro Provença). One of the city's most bizarre – and fun – bars, complete with turn-of-the-century fairground rides, and deco-rated with circus papaphernalia. Open 7pm–3am, Sun until midnight.

La Gasolinera, c/Aribau 97 (Metro Passeig de Gràcia). Petrol pumps outside, the young and trendy inside. Open from 6pm–2/3am.

Metropol, Ptge. Domingo 3 (Metro Passeig de Gràcia). One of the first *bars modernos*, in a tiny street running parallel between Rambla Catalunya and Passeig de Gràcia, behind the all-night *Drugstore*. Open until 3am.

Nick Havanna, c/del Rosselló 208 (Metro Diagonal). One of the most futuristic bars in town, the 1986 brainchild of Eduard Samnsó. The cool crowd have deserted it of late, but it's still worth a look at what's been dubbed the "ultimate bar". Open 8pm–4am.

Punto BCN, c/Muntaner 63–65. Stylish gay bar, with good music – a popular metting place. Open 6pm–3am.

SiSiSi, Avda. Diagonal 442 (Metro Diagonal). One of the first and still one of the most style-conscious but laid-back modern bars. Live music at night too. Open 7pm–3/4am.

El Velòdrom, c/Muntaner 213 (Metro Diagonal). Old-style bar and pool hall, resembling an airy student beer cellar – and none the worse for all that. Open 6pm–1.30am, closed Sun, and Aug.

Velvet, c/Balmes 161 (Metro Diagonal). The creation of designer Alfredo Arribas, this was inspired by the velveteen excesses of film-maker David Lynch. Slightly cosier and smoother than others, with an older clientele which appreciates the mainly 60s' and 70s' sounds. Open until 5am.

La Xampanyería, c/de Provença 236 (corner of c/Enric Granados; Metro Provença). Smart, stylish champagne bar, boasting a huge list of *cavas* washed down with pricey nibbles. Open until 3am, closed Sun.

Zsa Zsa, c/del Rosselló 156 (between c/Muntaner and c/Aribau). A newish joint showing off its fashionable wall hangings, and handing out loud music and pricey cocktails to the trendy set. Open until 3am.

Gràcia

ARS Studio, c/Atenas 27 (near Ronda del General Mitre). A large modern bar, with a young, rich-kid clientele. A former cinema, it still shows old films and videos; later on, there's loud music and dancing. Open 9pm–4am.

Bahia, c/Séneca 12. The latest addition to the street, this is a relaxed and attractive bar with gay, lesbian and straight punters. Open 7pm–2.30am.

Bella Bestia, c/Riera de Sant Miquel 6. A stuffed lion welcomes you in to smooth lighting, good cocktails, and African music. Open 8pm–3am.

Café del Sol, Plaça del Sol 9. Popular, split-level neighbourhood bar attracting the local cool types. Seats outside in the square make this pleasant at any time of the day or night. Open until 2am.

Network, Avda. Diagonal 616 (just beyond Plaça Francesc Macia). More *moderno* madness from Alfredo Arribas (with Eduardo Samsó), the slick design is a cross between *Brazil* and *Blade Runner*. Banks of videos, and food and music. Open 8pm–2am.

Triptic, c/Mozart 4 (Metro Diagonal). Lively, hippyish locals' bar, with marble-topped tables, mirrors and loud music. Open 6.30pm–2am.

Universal, c/de María Cubí 184 (Metro Fontana). A classic designer bar that's been at the cutting edge of Barcelona style since 1985; severe surroundings, stylish haircuts. Open 11pm–3am.

Yabba Dabba Club, c/Avenir 63. The haunt of the spiky-haired crowd, with Gothic decor including candelabras and a sculpted torso protruding from the wall. Open 7pm–3am, closed Sun.

Zig Zag, c/de Plató 13 (a side street near the top of c/de Muntaner). This long-established place (open since 1980) was designed by Alicia Nuñez and Guillem Bonet (creators of *Otto Zutz*; see "Discos and Clubs" below). It has all the minimalist designer accoutrements – chrome and video – but better, quieter music than usual, and a young, rich clientele. Open until 2am.

XAMPANYERIAS

If you've acquired a taste for *cava*, the Catalan champagne, you could plan a very enjoyable bar crawl around the city's specialist champagne bars. Here's a quick checklist.

La Cava del Palau
c/Verdaguer i Callis 10, Barri Gòtic.

El Xampanyet,
c/de Montcada 22, Barri Gòtic.

La Xampanyería,
c/de Provença 236, Eixample.

Xampu Xampany
Gran Via 702, Eixample

Elsewhere

Gambrinus, Moll de la Fusta. The first joint project by ace designers Xavier Mariscal and Alfredo Arribas, *Gambrinus* is the one with a giant crayfish on top, down on Barcelona's waterfront. A seafaring theme, fish and seafood snacks and meals, and an outdoor café-terrace. Open 8am–2am.

Mirablau, Plaça del Funicular, Avda. Tibidabo (at the top of the Tibidabo tram line, opposite the funicular station). Unbelievable city views from a chic, expensive bar, that fills to bursting at times. Open noon–5am (Mon from 5pm).

Torres de Avila, Avda. Marqués de Comillas, Poble Espanyol, Montjuïc. The creation of Mariscal and Arribas, located inside the mock twelfth-century gateway in the "Spanish Village" built for the 1929 fair. It's a stunning fantasy, with a fabulous panoramic terrace. Beware that the dress code is strict (no sports shoes) and drinks are very expensive. Open 11pm–4am.

Discos and clubs

Quite why Barcelona is one of Europe's hippest nightspots is something of a mystery to everyone except the Catalans, who knew all along. There aren't, in fact, too many places which are *that* good – but gripped by Friday and Saturday night fever it's eminently possible to suspend disbelief.

Be warned that clubbing in Barcelona is extremely expensive and that in the most exclusive places a beer is going to cost you roughly ten times what it costs in the bar next door. If there is free entry, don't be surprised to find that there's a minimum drinks charge of anything from 500–800ptas – if you're given a card as you go in and it's punched at the bar, be prepared to pay a minimum charge. Also note that the distinction between a music-bar and a disco is between a closing time of 2 or 3am and 5am – with a corresponding price rise. Barcelona stays open **very late** at the weekends, if you can take it; some of the places listed below feature a second session of action some time between 5am and 9am.

Area Beethoven, c/Beethoven 15, just above Plaça Francesc Macia (Metro Hospital Clinic). One of the chief rivals to *Otto Zutz* (see below) and with the same entry criteria. The café here is open 6pm–4am; otherwise disco open 11pm–6am, Thurs & Sun 6–9pm, too.

Centro Ciudad, c/de Consell de Cent 294 (at Rambla Catalunya). Massive, hi-tech club with a decent sound system and a mixed music policy. There's live music on Thursdays. Open 11pm–4am.

Daniel's, Plaça Cardona 7–8 (Metro Fontana, FF.CC Gràcia). Reputedly the first lesbian club in Spain, a small place with a dance floor, pool table and free entry (though there's a minimum drinks charge of around 500ptas). Open until 2am.

Distrito Distinto, Avda. Meridiana 104 (Metro Clot). A gay club with a selective door policy, this is a lively weekend sweatbox and in summer has a splendid "urban patio" and very good dance music. It's quite a long way out, east of the Sagrada Família, on the main road out of the city. Open midnight–5am.

Enfants, c/Guàrdia 3 (off c/Nou de la Rambla). Student-dominated disco. Open Wed, Thurs & Sun 11pm–4.30am, Fri & Sat 11pm–5am.

Karma, Plaça Reial 10. A good, studenty basement place with homegrown rock and pop sounds, and a lively local crowd milling around the square outside. Open 11.30pm–4/5am.

KGB, c/Alegre de Dalt 55 (Metro Joanic). No frills, and as cool as they come, *KGB* is the last on the club-crawl list – aim to finish up here. The warehouse bar/club was designed in 1984 by Alfredo Vidal with a "spy" theme. Live music Wed–Sat, and open 10pm–4am and then again from 5.30–8am.

Members, c/Sèneca 3 (Metro Diagonal). A young gay and lesbian crowd packs into this very popular club, which resembles an L-shaped box. Free entry but high bar prices. Open until 3am.

Monumental, c/Gran de Gràcia 25. Large multi-space venue with a policy of putting on live local bands and playing soul, funk and dance; Tuesdays is Latin night, Wednesdays reggae. Open midnight–5/6am.

Otto Zutz, c/de Lincoln 15. Still the most fashionable place in the city, a three-storey warehouse converted by architects Nuñez and Bonet into a nocturnal shop window for everything that's for sale or hire in Barcelona. With the right clothes and face you're in (you may or may not have to pay – around 2000ptas – depending on how impressive you are, the day of the week, etc); the serious dancing is from 2–4.30am.

Paolo Bonner, c/de Bruniquer 59–61 (Metro Joanic). A popular techno club, with a mainly gay clientele; don't turn up before 2am. Open until 5am.

Qué ! te dise, c/Riera de Sant Miquel 55–57 (Metro Diagonal). House music, fashion victims, and a very mixed scene. Open 11pm–3am.

Salsa Latina, c/Bori i Fontestà 25. No musical surprises – the name says it all. Open until 4am.

Satanassa, c/Aribau 27. A mural-covered interior and a friendly, funky gay and straight crowd. There's no admission charge, but it gets very busy at the wekends. Open 11pm–4am.

Soweto, c/Socrates 68 (Metro Fabra i Puig). Reggae and African sounds, but a good way out of the centre. Open Fri and Sat 11pm–3am.

Zeleste, c/dels Almogavers 122 (Metro Llacuna). A huge former warehouse on whose various levels gigs and lower key events are held, in addition to a disco floor and several bars. Best when there's a band on, otherwise you rattle around the spacious interior a bit. Open 11pm–5/6am.

Music, the arts and festivals

Quite apart from the city's countless bars, restaurants and clubs, there's a full **cultural life** worth sampling. Barcelona hosts a wide range of **live music** events throughout the year and **film** and **theatre** are also well represented, as you'd expect in a city this size. Even if you don't speak Catalan or Spanish there's no need to miss out, since several cinemas show films in their original language, while Barcelona also boasts a series of old-time music hall/**cabaret** venues putting on largely visual shows, appealing in any language. Catalan performers have always steered away from the classics and gone for the innovative, and so the city also boasts a long tradition of **street and performance art.** Finally, if you're lucky (or you've planned ahead) you'll coincide with one of the city's excellent **festivals** and open air events in which case you'll be able to immerse yourself in what Barcelona does best: enjoying itself.

The most important ticket office is the **Centre d'Informació** in the Palau de la Virreina, Rambla Sant Josep 99 (Metro Liceu; Mon–Fri 10am–2pm & 4–8pm, Sat and Aug 10am–2pm; ☎301 77 75), which dispenses programmes, advance information and tickets for all the *Ajuntament*-sponsored productions, performances and exhibitions, including the *Grec* season events. Otherwise, the booth on the corner of c/Aribau and the Gran Via, close to Plaça Universitat (daily 10.30am–1.30pm & 4–7.30pm) sells tickets for major rock and pop concerts and for most theatre productions; record shops also carry concert tickets; or go straight to the relevant box office at the venue.

For **listings** of almost anything you could want in the way of culture and entertainment, buy a copy of the weekly *Guía del Ocio* (95ptas) from any newspaper stand. This has full details of film, theatre and musical events (free and otherwise), as well as extensive sections on bars, restaurants and nightlife. It's in Spanish but easy enough to decipher.

Live Music

Many major bands now include Barcelona on their tours at a variety of big venues (including the Camp Nou stadium, Olympic stadium, and Palau d'Esports), and tickets for these are every bit as pricey as they are elsewhere in the world. However, lots of the city's clubs and discos regularly feature bands too – the more reliable places are listed below, and entrance to these is a lot less expensive than to a stadium gig. June sees the **Festival de Jazz Ciutat Vella**, and a **European jazz festival**; and there's also the annual **jazz festival** in October/November, which highlights visiting bands in the clubs and hosts street concerts and events. Most of Barcelona's **classical music** concerts take place in Domènech i Montaner's Palau de la Música Catalana, a splendid turn-of-the-century *modernista* creation (for more on which see p.533). **Opera** (and to a lesser extent, **ballet**) used to be confined to the *Gran Teatre del Liceu* on the Ramblas, though since this burned down at the beginning of 1994 (see p.524 for more details), the current situation is unclear – the opera house in Sabadell has offered to host the Liceu's future programmes; the Turismo should be able to fill you in on what's happening.

Rock, pop, folk and jazz

La Cova del Drac, c/Vallmajor 33, Gràcia (☎200 70 32); FF.CC Muntaner. The best of the city's jazz clubs has settled into its new home, serving up live music Tues–Sat 11pm–2am. Closed in August. Cover charge from 2000–4000ptas depending on the act. Closed Aug.

Estandard, Trav. de Gràcia 39, Gràcia (☎202 23 22). One of the newest music clubs which seems to be catching all the big Spanish and Catalan bands, and attracting a fair few foreign ones, too.

Garatge Club, c/Pallars 195, Poble Nou. Local rock and pop bands, never on much before midnight.

Harlem Jazz Club, c/Comtessa de Sobradiel 8, Barri Gòtic ☎310 07 55. A small, central venue for mixed jazz styles; live music most nights from around 9–10pm. Usually no cover charge, and reasonably priced drinks. Closed Aug.

Humedad Relativa, Plaça Mañé i Flaquer 9, Gràcia (☎238 18 99); Metro Lesseps. Regular Spanish rock and pop gigs in this music club.

Sala Communique, c/Hostafrancs 18 (☎329 40 73); Metro Hostafrancs. Mainly Catalan and Spanish rock and pop in this very small club, though with the odd European act too.

Savannah, c/Muntanya 16; Metro Clot. East of the Sagrada Família, this rock venue is open Wed–Sat only; bands on after midnight.

Zeleste, c/Almogavers 122 (☎309 12 04); Metro Llacuna. Foreign rock and pop bands play regularly at the warehouse-style club.

Classical music and opera

Centre Cultural Caixa de Pensions, Passeig Sant Joan 108 (☎245 89 07). Regular concerts and recitals.

L'Espai, Trav. de Gràcia 63 (☎201 29 06). Performances by a variety of soloists and groups.

Mercat de les Flors, c/Lleida 59 (☎426 18 75); Metro Poble Sec. Occasional concerts throughout the year at this theatre – a beatifully restored flower market – and a regular programme during the *Grec* season.

Palau de la Música Catalana, c/Sant Francesc de Paula 2, off c/Sant Pere Més Alt (☎268 10 00); Metro Urquinaona. Home of the *Orfeó Català* choral group, and venue for concerts by the *Orquestra Ciutat de Barcelona* among others. Concert season runs from October to June. Box office open Mon–Fri 5–8pm.

Sala Cultural Caixa de Madrid, Plaça de Catalunya 9 (☎301 44 94). Regular, free concerts and recitals.

Saló del Tinell, Plaça del Rei ☎200 39 26. Choral music in the Gothic hall of the Palau Reial; usually free entry.

Teatre Grec, Passeig de Santa Madrona, Montjuïc (☎325 10 93); Metro Espanya. Impressive open-air summer venue for concerts and recitals. The amphitheatre is used extensively during the summer *Grec* season.

Theatre and cabaret

Barcelona has nothing like the **theatrical life** of Madrid, but it does have some worthy venues and happenings. Ninety-nine percent of the regular theatre productions, however, are in Catalan and you'll rarely see a Spanish classic. The centre for commercial theatre is on Avda. Parallel and the streets immediately around. Some theatres draw on the city's strong **cabaret** tradition – more music-hall entertainment than stand-up comedy, and thus a little more accessible to non-Catalan/Spanish speakers.

Tickets for most theatres are available from the kiosk on the corner of c/Aribau and the Gran Via, or from the *Centro de Localidades* at Rambla Catalunya 2. For advance

---

CATALAN THEATRE COMPANIES

In Barcelona, check for forthcoming appearances of the following theatre companies.

Els Comediants use Catalan popular theatre tradition in a modern context; they've just set up their own theatre at Canet de Mar, north of Barcelona on the coast

La Cubana is a highly original and popular company that started life as a street theatre group. It still hits the streets occasionally, taking on the role of market traders in the Boqueria or cleaning cars in the street in full evening dress.

Els Fura del Baus (Vermin of the Sewer) are performance artists who aim to shock and lend a new meaning to audience participation.

Els Joglars is a political theatre company, particularly critical of the church.

El Tricicle – a three-man mime group.

---

tickets for the *Mercat de les Flors* productions, you have to go to the Palau de la Virreina (Ramblas 99).

Bodega Bohemia, c/Lancaster 2 (☎302 50 61); Metro Drassanes. Old performers doing old turns in a decrepit cabaret venue. Somehow the faded decor and jaded routines gel into an entertaining night out. Nightly performances until late. Sunday afternoons too; closed Wed.

Café Concert Llantiol, c/Riereta 7 (☎329 90 09); Metro Parallel. Daily cabaret featuring curious bits of mime, song, clowns and magic, as well as children's theatre on Sundays at 12.30pm. Closed Mon.

Mercat de les Flors, c/de Lleida 59 (☎318 85 99 or 425 18 75); Metro Poble Sec. A nineteenth-century building worth going to for the architecture alone. Hosts visiting fringe theatre and dance companies.

El Molino, c/de Vila Vilá 99 (☎441 63 83); Metro Parallel. Best-known of the cabaret venues. Old-style music hall turns and sketches in a *modernista* building dating from 1913. Two performances a night (closed Mon); the 6pm performance is around half the price of the 11pm show.

Teatre Lliure, c/Montseny 47, Gràcia (☎218 92 51); Metro Fontana. The "Free Theatre" is the home of a progressive Catalan company. Also hosts visiting dance companies, concerts and recitals.

Teatre Poliorama, Rambla Estudis 115 (☎317 75 99). Home of the distinguished Josep Maria Flotats theatre company, which puts on Catalan translations of all sorts of material, as well as original work.

Teatre Romea, c/Hospital 51 (☎301 55 04). Built in 1863, the theatre was forced to use Castilian under Franco, but has now come back as the *Centre Dramàtic de la Generalitat de Catalunya* with exclusively Catalan productions.

Film

All the latest international films reach Barcelona fairly quickly (though they're usually shown dubbed into Spanish) – central **main screens** include those at Rambla de Canaletes 138, Rambla Catalunya 90, Plaça de Catalunya 3 and Passeig de Gràcia 13. More accessibly, the **cinemas** listed below show mostly original-language ("V.O") foreign films. **Tickets** cost from 550–650ptas, and most cinemas have one night (usually Mon or Wed) – a *Día del espectador* – when entry is discounted, usually to around 350ptas.

Casablanca, Passeig de Gràcia 115, Eixample (☎218 43 45); Metro Diagonal. Discount night Mon. Late-night film on Fri and Sat.

Filmoteca, Avda. de Sarrià 33, Gràcia (☎430 50 07). Run by the Generalitat, the *Filmoteca* has an excellent programme, showing three or four different films (often foreign, dubbed or sub-titled) every night except Monday. 400ptas per film, or buy a pass for 2500ptas allowing entry to ten films.

Lauren, c/Girona 175, Eixample (☎457 76 41). Discount night Wed. Late-night films on Fri and Sat.

Verdi, c/Verdi 32, Gràcia (☎237 05 16); Metro Fontana. Discount night Mon. Now has five screens showing quality "V.O" movies. Late-night films on Fri and Sat.

Arts festivals, open-air events, and the sardana

Best of the annual arts events is the *Generalitat*'s summer *Grec* season, when theatre, music and dance can be seen at various venues around the city, including the Teatre Grec at Montjuïc. But there are plenty of other times when Barcelona lets its hair down: the main arts-orientated events are listed below. Catalunya's national **folk dance**, the *sardana*, can be seen for free at several places in the city: in front of the cathedral (Sun 10am–12.30pm, Wed 7–9pm); Plaça Sant Jaume (Sun 6–8pm); and Plaça de Catalunya (Sun mornings). Mocked in the rest of Spain, the Catalans claim theirs is a very democratic dance. Participants (there's no limit on numbers) all hold hands in a circle, each puts something in the middle as a sign of community and sharing, and since it is not overly-energetic (hence the jibes) old and young can join in equally.

April/May *Tamborinada* is a day of children's entertainment in Ciutadella – theatre, dancing giants and music.

May The *Marató de l'Espectacle* (Entertainment Marathon) takes place at the Mercat de les Flors theatre, a non-stop two days' worth of local theatre, dance, cabaret, music and children's shows.

June. The *Grec* season starts in the last week (and runs throughout July and into August), a summer festival incorporating a wide variety of events, some of which are free. Information and booking is at the Palau de la Virreina. Also, the *Día de Sant Joan* celebrations on the 23rd involve fireworks, dancing and music throughout the city. The *Caixa Flamenco Festival* takes place in the same month; while the *Barcelona Film Festival* starts at the end of the month and continues throughout July.

August. The *Festa Major* in mid-August is in Gràcia; bands and events in the streets and squares.

September. *Festa de la Mercè* at the end of the month: parades, free concerts, fireworks and general mayhem.

Shopping and markets

While not on a par with Paris or the world's other style capitals, Barcelona is head and shoulders above the rest of Spain when it comes to **shopping**. It's the country's fashion and publishing capital, and there's a long tradition of innovative design which is perhaps expressed best in the city's fabulous architecture but which is also revealed in a series of shops and malls selling the very latest in designer clothes and household accompaniments.

Shops

Shop **opening hours** are typically Monday–Friday 10am–1.30/2pm and 4.30–7.30/8pm, Saturday 10am–1.30/2pm, although various markets, department stores and shopping centres open right through lunch.

As well as the places picked out below, visit one of the city's **department stores and shopping arcades**: *Bulevard Rosa*, at Passeig de Gràcia 55, and Avda. Diagonal 609–615, Barcelona's first shopping mall, both arcades featuring around 100 shops; *El Corte Inglés*, Plaça de Catalunya 14, and Avda. Diagonal 617, the city's biggest department store; and *Drugstore*, Passeig de Gràcia, a small complex of shops, supermarket, and café-bar which stays open 24hr.

Antiques, arts and crafts

La Bola, c/Sepulveda 184 (Metro Universitat). Old things, bric-a-brac and antique clothing.

La Caixa de Fang, c/Freneria 1. Off Baixada de la Llibretaria, behind the cathedral, this has very good value ceramics and recycled glass.

La Manual Alpargatera, c/Avinyó 7. Workshop making and selling *alpargatas* (espadrilles) to order, as well as other straw and rope work.

Populart, c/de Montcada 22. Delightful shop filled with antiques and crafts.

1748, Plaça de Montcada 2. Good ceramic shop with one of the widest selections.

Books

You'll find English-language books, newspapers and magazines at the stalls along the Ramblas, and a good selection of English-language books (novels and general unless otherwise stated) at the following shops.

BCN, c/Aragó 277, Eixample. Good selection of English language novels.

The Book Store, c/la Granja 13, Gràcia (closed Aug). Second-hand English language books.

Llibreria Prolèg, c/Dagueria 13, Barri Gòtic (closed Aug). A women's/feminist bookshop.

Llibreria Quera, c/Petritxol 2, Barri Gòtic. Maps and trekking guides.

Clothes, shoes and accessories

Adolfo Domínguez, Passeig de Gràcia 89 (Metro Passeig de Gràcia). Men and women's designs from the well-known Gallego designer.

Artesanía Eva, c/Conde de Salvatierra 10. Hand-painted shoes, shirts, trousers and much more.

Joaquín Berao, c/Roselló 277 (Metro Diagonal). *Avant garde* jewellery in a stunningly designed shop.

Jean Pierre Bua, Diagonal 469 (Metro Diagonal). The city's temple for fashion victims: a postmodern shrine for Yamamoto, Gaultier, Miyake, Westwood, Miró and other international stars.

Camper, c/Muntaner 248; c/València 249; Avda. Pau Casals 5; Bd. Rosa Pedralbes. These are the four branches of Spain's most stylish value-for-money shoeshop chain.

Groc, Rambla Catalunya 100 bis; Muntaner 385. The shops of Barcelona's most innovative designer, Antoni Miró; the first is for men, the second for women.

Lailo, c/Riera Baixa 20. Off the west side of the Ramblas, this second-hand clothes shop and bar is usually worth a look.

La Manual Alpargatera, Avinyó 7. This old, characterful shop sells nothing but *alpargatas*, or *espardenyes*, the Catalan versions of espadrilles, available in every style and colour.

Pedro Morago, Diagonal 520 (Metro Diagonal). Morago is a classic Barcelona designer, producing everything from suits to sports shirts for men and women.

Sara Navarro, Avda. Diagonal 598 (Metro Maria Cristina). Original leather clothes and shoes.

Design and decorative art

BD Ediciones de Diseño, c/Mallorca 291 (Metro Diagonal). The building's by Domènech i Montaner, the interior is filled with the very latest in furniture and household design.

D.Barcelona, Avda. Diagonal 367 (Metro Diagonal). Up the road from *Dos i Una*, and with a similar but much bigger selection.

Dos i Una, c/Rosselló 275 (Metro Diagonal). Contemporary, imaginative household and personal items.

Vinçon, Passeig de Gràcia 96 (Metro Passeig de Gràcia). This palace of design houses stylish and original items, pioneered since the 1960s by Fernando Amat, and with logo and carrier bags by the uniquitous Mariscal. Temporary art and design exhibitions are held here too.

Markets

Barcelona's **daily food markets**, all in covered halls, are open Monday–Saturday 8am–3pm and 5–8pm, though the most famous, *La Boqueria* on the Ramblas, opens right through the day. Other **specialist markets** are open only on certain days.

Good ones to try include:

Antiques: every Thurs in Plaça del Pi from 9am (not Aug; Metro Liceu).

Coins, books and postcards: every Sun outside Mercat Sant Antoni from 10am–2pm.

Crafts: first Sun of the month at Avda. Pau Casals, Gràcia from 10am – ceramics, textiles, glassware, wrought iron (Metro Hospital Clinic).

Flea market: *Els Encants,* every Mon, Wed, Fri and Sat in Plaça de les Glòries from 8am – clothes, jewellery, junk and furniture (Metro Glòries).

Food: *Mercat Abaceria Central,* c/de Puigmartí, Gràcia (Metro Diagonal); *Mercat Sant Antoni,* Ronda de Sant Pau (Metro Sant Antoni); *Mercat Sant Josep/La Boqueria,* Ramblas (Metro Liceu); *Mercat Santa Catarina,* Avda. Francesc Cambó 16 (Metro Jaume I).

Listings

Airlines Almost all are located on Passeig de Gràcia or around the corner on the Gran Via. The main ones include: *Air France,* Passeig de Gràcia 63 (☎487 25 26), and also at c/Mallorca 277 and Plaça d'Espanya; *British Airways,* Passeig de Gràcia 85 (☎487 21 12); *Iberia,* Passeig de Gràcia 30 (☎301 39 93) and Rambla de Catalunya 18 (☎215 70 3); *TWA,* Passeig de Gràcia 55 (☎215 23 82).

Airport *El Prat de Llobregat* (☎478 50 32 or 478 50 00); flight information on ☎301 39 93 or 317 01 78.

American Express The offfice is at c/Rosselló 259 (Mon–Fri 9.30am–6pm, Sat 10am–noon; Metro Diagonal; ☎217 00 70). There's also an Amex cash machine at the airport.

Banks and exchange Main bank branches are in Plaça de Catalunya and Passeig de Gràcia. *El Corte Inglés* department store, in Plaça de Catalunya, and *American Express* (see above) also have efficient exchange facilities which offer competitive rates. *Banco de Santander* on c/de Ferran (corner Plaça de Sant Jaume), and *Caja de Madrid* on Plaça de Catalunya both have automatic money exchanges, which accept British, French and German paper currency. Exchange offices include: Airport (daily 7.30am–10.45pm); Estació-Sants (daily 8am–10pm); *Viajes Marsans,* Ramblas 134 (Mon–Fri 9am–1.30pm & 4–7.30pm).

Buses For buses to all destinations, go to the Estació del Nord (☎265 65 08 or 265 78 45) on Avda. Vilanova (metro Arc de Triomf). Companies represented include: *Alsina Graells* (☎302 40 86; to Lleida, Vall d'Aran, Andorra and La Pobla de Segur); *Ansa-Viacarsa* (☎419 86 72; Bilbao and Teruel); *Autocares Julia* (☎490 40 00; London and Europe, and to Montserrat and Zaragoza); *Bacoma* (☎231 38 01; Còrdoba, Granada, Sevilla); *Barcelona Bus* (☎237 04 59; Girona); *Empresa Sarfa* (☎318 93 92; Costa Brava); *Enatcar* (☎245 25 28; Vigo, Madrid, Valencia, Palencia); *Iberbus* (☎441 54 94; London, Rome, Paris and Amsterdam); *Zatrans* (☎231 04 01; Logroño, Burgos, Valladolid, Zamora).

Car rental *Atesa,* c/Balmes 141 (☎237 81 40) and airport (☎302 28 32); *Avis,* c/Casanova 209 (☎209 95 33), c/Aragó 235 (☎487 87 54) and airport (☎379 40 26); *Budget,* Avda. Roma 15 (☎322 90 12); *Europcar,* c/Consell de Cent 363 (☎488 19 53) and Estació-França (☎488 19 53); *Hertz,* c/Tuset 10 (☎217 32 48) and Estació-Sants (☎490 86 62); *Ital,* Trav. de Gràcia 71 (☎201 21 99); *Vanguard* c/ Londres 31 (☎439 38 80).

Consulates *Australia,* Gran Via Carles III 98 (☎330 94 96); *Britain,* Avda. Diagonal 477 (☎419 90 44); *Canada,* Via Augusta 125 (☎209 06 34); *Denmark,* c/Comte d'Urgell 240 (☎419 04 28); *France,* Passeig de Gràcia 11 (☎317 81 50); *Germany,* Passeig de Gràcia 111 (☎415 36 96); *Ireland,* Gran Via Carles III 94 (☎330 96 52); *Italy,* c/Mallorca 270 (☎488 02 70); *Netherlands,* Passeig de Gràcia 111 (☎217 37 00); *New Zealand,* Trav. de Gràcia 64 (☎209 03 99); *Norway,* c/Provença 284 (☎215 00 94); *Portugal,* Ronda Sant Pere 7 (☎318 81 50); *Sweden,* Avda. Diagonal 601 (☎ 410 11 08); *USA,* Passeig de la Reina Elisenda 23 (☎280 22 27).

Credit cards To cancel lost or stolen credit cards, call the following numbers: *American Express* (☎217 00 70 or 572 03 03); *Diners Club* (☎302 13 49 or 247 40 00); *Mastercard* (☎315 25 12); *Visa* (☎315 25 12 or 435 24 45).

Cultural institutes The *British Council* at c/Amigó 83 (☎209 63 88 or 200 45 38) has an English-language library, lists of language schools and a good noticeboard advertising lessons and accommodation. The *American Institute,* Via Augusta 123; FF.CC Plaça Molina (☎209 27 11 or 200 75 51) has newspapers, magazines and a reference library.

Emergencies For an ambulance or emergency doctor, dial ☎061. Or go to the accident and emergency departments of the *Hospital Clinic* or *Hospital Sant Pau* (see below).

Ferries Departures to the Balearics are from the Estació Maritima (☎302 16 98), at the bottom of the Ramblas; metro Drassanes. Buy tickets here at the *Transmediterranea office* (☎412 25 24). The ferries get very crowded in July and August – book ahead.

Football See p.549 for full details of the Camp Nou stadium and FC Barcelona.

Gay and lesbian Barcelona There's a lesbian and gay city telephone hotline on ☎237 70 70 (7–9pm only). For a map of gay Barcelona, detailing bars, clubs, hotels and restaurants, contact *SexTienda*, c/Rauric 11, Barri Gòtic (near Plaça Reial), or *Zeus*, c/Riera Alta 11 (Metro Liceu). Most of the city's lesbian groups meet at *Ca la Dona* (see "Women's Barcelona", below): these include the *Grup de Lesbianes Feministes de Barcelona,* which meets on Thursdays at 8pm, and *L'Eix Violeta*, a young lesbian group. The city's annual lesbian and gay pride march is on 28 June, starting in the evening at Plaça Universitat.

Hospitals *Hospital de la Creu Roja,* c/Dos de Maig 301 (☎235 92 85; outpatients ☎348 11 33); *Hospital Clínic,* c/Casanovas 143, Metro Hospital-Clinic (☎454 60 00); *Hospital de Sant Pau*, c/Sant Antoni Mari Claret, Metro Hospital Sant Pau; *Centro Diagnostic Malaltiès Sexuales* (Sexually Transmitted Disease Clinic), Avda. Drassanes 17–19 (☎329 44 95).

Language schools The cheapest Spanish/Catalan classes in Barcelona are at the *Escuela Oficial de Idiomas*, Avda. Drassanes (☎329 34 12), where a lottery system is in force – queue up for a ticket, then see if you've won a place to sit the exam that day. Expect big queues at the start of term. Or try *International House*, c/Trafalgar 14 (☎268 45 11).

Laundries Self-service launderettes (*lavanderías automáticas*) are rare – you normally have to leave your clothes for the full works. Try *Lava Super*, c/Carme 63 (off the Ramblas). Note that you're not allowed by law to leave laundry hanging out of windows over a street, and some *hostales* can get shirty if you're found doing excessive washing in your bedroom sink. A dry cleaner is a *tintorería*.

Library *Biblioteca Central* at c/del Carme 47, next to the Hospital de la Santa Creu (Mon–Fri 9am–8pm, Sat 9am–2pm). The university public library is at Gran Via 585 (Mon–Fri 8am–9.30pm, Sat 9am–2pm; closed July–Sept).

Lost property If you lose anything, try the *Ajuntament* (*objetos perdidos*) in Plaça de Sant Jaume (Mon–Fri 9.30am–1.30pm; ☎402 70 00), but you'll be lucky to get it back.

Luggage At Estació-Sants the *consigna* is open daily from 6.30am–midnight and costs 200ptas a day; at the Estació Marítima the hours are daily 9am–1pm & 4–10pm.

Newspapers You can buy foreign newspapers at the stalls down the Ramblas, around Plaça de Catalunya and at Estació-Sants. The same stalls also sell an impressive array of international newspapers, magazines and trade papers.

Noticeboards For flat-sharing, lifts, lessons and other services check the noticeboards at the cultural institutes (see above); at *International House* (c/Trafalgar 14); at the university (in the main building; take door on far left and, inside, bear left and then right); at *Escuela Oficial de Idiomas* (see "Language Schools"), and at *Llibreria Prolèg* (see "Bookshops").

Police Main police stations are at c/Ample 23 (☎318 36 89), and Via Laietana 49 (☎290 30 00). The tourist police – the *Centro Atencíon Policial* – are at Rambla 43 (open summer 24hr). There's English-speaking help for women who've suffered violent crime at *Informacions i Urgencies de les Dones*, c/d'Avinyó 7 (☎402 78 00); as well as a special police section for women, the *Comisaria de la Dona*, in Plaça d'Espanya.

Post office The main post office (*Correos*) is at Plaça d'Antoni López, facing the water at the end of Passeig de Colom. It's open Monday–Saturday 8.30am–10pm, Sunday 10am–noon. Poste restante is at Window 17 (Mon–Fri 9am–9pm, Sat 9am–2pm).

Residence permits In Barcelona, residence permits are issued by the *Servicio de Extranjeros* at c/ de Balmes 192 (Mon–Fri 9am–2pm; ☎290 30 00). It's advisable to apply a few weeks before your time runs out, and to have proof that you're going to be able to support yourself without working (easiest done by keeping bank exchange forms every time you change money).

Swimming pools To swim at one of Barcelona's pools, take your passport along; you may need to show it at some of the pools before being allowed in. Central pools include *Club Natació* at Passeig Marítim, Metro Ciutadella (daily 8am–9pm; 350ptas) and, best of all, the Olympic *Piscines Bernat Picornell*, Avda. de l'Estadi 30–40, Montjuïc, Metro Espanya (Mon–Fri 9am–9pm, Sat & Sun 9am–8pm; 500ptas, 6–15yr-olds 350ptas).

Telephone offices There are *Telefónica* offices at c/Fontanella 4, off Plaça de Catalunya (Mon–Sat 8.30am–9pm) and at Estació-Sants (daily 8am–10pm).

Trains For train information, call *RENFE* (☎379 00 24). You can buy train tickets at the *Renfe* office in the underground foyer at Passeig de Gràcia (corner of c/Aragó). Otherwise, at Estació-Sants there's both a *RENFE* information office (daily 6.30am–10.30pm; English-speaking) and an International Train Information Office (daily 7am–10pm), where you can reserve seats and couchettes on international trains. This is recommended in high season, compulsory on some trains, and should be done in advance – at least a couple of hours before departure, the day before if possible.

Travel agencies General travel agencies are found on the Gran Via, Passeig de Gràcia, Via Laietana and the Ramblas. For specific deals try: *Julia Tours,* Plaça Universitat 12 (☎317 64 54 or 317 62 09) for city tours, Catalunya holidays and trips; *TIVE* c/Gravina 1, between Ramblas and Pl. Universitat off c/Pelai (☎302 06 82) for discounted youth and student bus, train and flight deals; *Viajes Marsans,* Rambla 134 (☎318 72 16), for discounted train tickets, flights and holidays; and *Wasteels* inside Estació-Sants, for youth train tickets.

Women's Barcelona The most useful contact address in the city is *Ca la Dona,* Gran Via de les Corts Catalanes 549, 4th floor, #1 (☎323 33 07), a women's centre used for meetings of various feminist and lesbian organizations; information available to callers; open evenings. There's also *Dones Joves,* c/d'Avinyo 16, Barri Gòtic (☎317 00 16), an organization for young women; and *La Nostra Illa,* c/Reig i Bonet 3, Gràcia (Metro Joanic; ☎210 00 72), a women's bar and cultural centre (open 7.30pm–1am, 2am at weekends; closed Tues).

Youth information There's a youth information office at c/d'Avinyó 7, Barri Gòtic (☎402 78 00 or 402 78 01), with city information and advice, a library and English-speakers (Mon–Fri 10am–2pm and 4–8pm).

travel details

Buses

Barcelona to Alicante (5 daily; 9hr); Andorra (2 daily; 4hr 30min); Banyoles (2–3 daily; 1hr 30min); Besalú (2–3 daily; 1hr 45min); Cadaqués (2–4 daily; 2hr 20min); Girona (Mon–Sat 6–8 daily, Sun 3; 1hr 30min); Lleida (5 daily; 3hr); Lloret de Mar (July–mid-Sept 10 daily; 1hr 15min); Madrid (4 daily; 10hr); Olot (2–3 daily; 2hr 10min); Palafrugell (6 daily; 4 hr); Perpignan, France (2 daily; 4hr); La Pobla de Segur (1 daily; 3hr 30min); La Seu d'Urgell (2 daily; 4hr); Tarragona (18 daily; 1hr 30min); Torroella (3 daily; 4hr 30min); Tossa de Mar (July to mid-Sept 10 daily; 1hr 35min); Valencia (7 daily; 6hr); Vall d'Aran (1 daily; 7hr); Viella (June–Nov 1 daily; 7hr); Zaragoza (4 daily; 5hr).

Trains

Barcelona to Cérbére, France (18 daily; 2hr 55min); Girona (hourly; 1hr 20min); Figueres (19 daily; 1hr 30min–2hr); Lleida via Manresa (3 daily; 3hr 30min); Lleida via Valls or Tarragona/Reus (13 daily; 2–3hr 30min); Madrid (4 daily; 12hr); Paris (7 daily; 11–15hr); Port Bou (18 daily; 2hr 50min); Puigcerdà (6 daily; 3hr 30min); Ripoll (6 daily; 2hr); Sitges (every 10–15min; 25–40min); Tarragona (every 30min; 1hr 30min); Valencia (7 daily; 4–5 hr); Vic (6 daily; 1hr); Zaragoza (13 daily; 4hr 30min–6hr 30min).

Ferries

Barcelona to Palma, Mallorca (10 weekly; 8hr); Ibiza (daily in summer, 4 weekly winter; 9hr); to Mahón, Menorca (3–5 weekly).

CHAPTER ELEVEN

CATALUNYA

Y ou can't think of visiting Barcelona without seeing something of its surroundings. Although the city is fast becoming international, the wider area of
Catalunya (*Cataluña* in Castilian Spanish, traditionally Catalonia in English)
retains a distinct regional identity that borrows little from the rest of Spain, let
alone from the world at large. Out of the city – and especially in rural areas – you'll
hear Catalan spoken more often and be confronted with better Catalan food, which is
often highly specialised, varying even from village to village. Towns and villages are
surprisingly prosperous, a relic of the early industrial era, when Catalunya developed
far more rapidly than most of Spain; and the people are enterprising and open, celebrating a unique range of **festivals** (see the list on p.579) in almost obsessive fashion.
There's a confidence in being Catalan that traces right back to the fourteenth-century
Golden Age, when what was then a kingom ruled the Balearics, Valencia, the French
border regions, Sardinia and Corsica, too. Today, Catalunya is officially a semi-
autonomous province, but it can still feel like a separate country – cross the borders
into Valencia or Aragón and you soon pick up the differences.

Catalunya is also a very satisfying region to tour, since two or three hours in any
direction puts you in the midst of varying landscapes of great beauty; from rocky coast-
lines to long, flat beaches, from the mountains to the plain, and from marshlands to
forest. There are some considerable distances to cover, especially in the interior, but
on the whole everything is easily reached from Barcelona, which is linked to most
main centres by excellent bus and train services. The easiest targets are the **coasts**
north and south of the city, and the various **provincial capitals** – Girona, Tarragona
and Lleida – all destinations that make a series of day trips or can be linked together in
a loop through the region.

The best of the beach towns lie on the famous **Costa Brava**, which runs up to the
French border. This was one of the first stretches of Spanish coast to be developed for
mass tourism, and though that's no great recommendation, the large, brash resorts to
the south are tempered by some more isolated beaches and lower-key holiday and fishing villages further north. Just inland from the coast, the small town of **Figueres**
contains another reason to visit the area: the Museu Dalí, Catalunya's biggest tourist
attraction. **South** of Barcelona, the **Costa Daurada** is less enticing, though it has at
least one fine beach at **Sitges** and the attractive coastal town of **Tarragona** to recommend it; inland, the romantic monastery of Poblet figures as one approach to the enjoyable provincial capital of **Lleida**.

Travels in inland Catalunya depend on the time available, but even on a short trip
you can take in the medieval city of **Girona** and the surrounding area, which includes
the isolated Montseny hills and the extraordinary volcanic **Garrotxa** region. With
more time you can head for the **Catalan Pyrenees**, with their magnificent and relatively isolated hiking territory, particularly in and around the **Parc Nacional de
Aigües Tortes**. East of here is **Andorra**, a combination tax-free hellhole and mountain
retreat set amidst quieter, generally neglected border towns, all offering great hiking
and, in winter, good skiing.

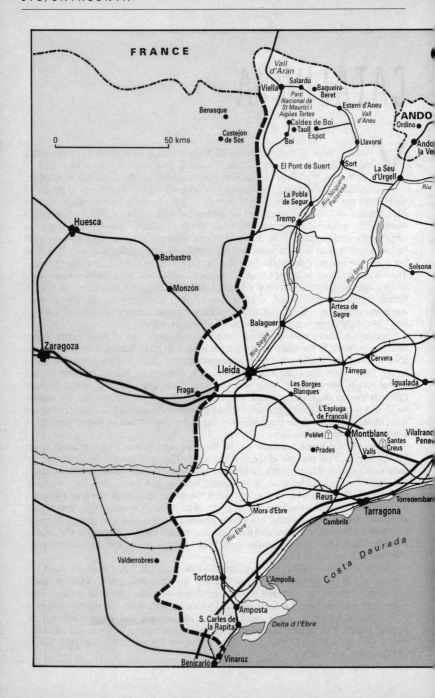

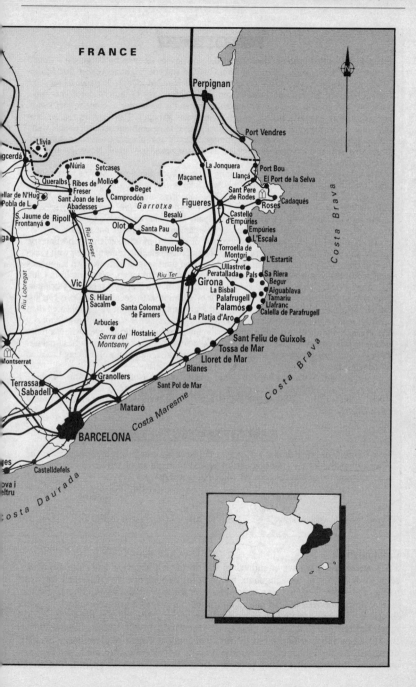

CATALÀ

The traveller's main problem throughout the province is likely to be **language** – *Català* (Catalan) has more or less taken over from Castilian and you might not realise that *Dilluns Tancat*, for example, is the same as *Cerrado Lunes* (closed Monday). On paper it looks like a cross between French and Spanish and is generally easy to understand if you know those two but, spoken, it has a very harsh sound and is far harder to come to grips with, especially away from Barcelona where accents are stronger. Few visitors realise how ingrained and widespread *Català* is, and this can lead to resentment because people won't "speak Spanish" for you. Increasingly, though, *Català* is replacing Castilian rather than cohabiting with it, a phenomenon known as the *venganza* (revenge). Never commit the error of calling it a dialect!

When Franco came to power, publishing houses, bookshops and libraries were raided and *Català* books destroyed. While this was followed by a letup in the mid-1940s, the language was still banned from the radio, TV, daily press and, most importantly, schools, which is why many older people today cannot read or write *Català* (even if they speak it all the time). Conversely, in the capital virtually everyone *can* speak Castilian, even if they don't, while in country areas, many people can only understand, not speak it.

Català is spoken in Catalunya proper, part of Aragón, most of Valencia, the Balearic islands, the Principality of Andorra, and in parts of the French Pyrenees, albeit with variations of dialect (it is thus much more widely spoken than several better-known languages such as Danish, Finnish and Norwegian). It is a Romance language, stemming from Latin and more directly from medieval Provençal and *lemosí*, the literary French of Occitania. Spaniards in the rest of the country belittle it by saying that to get a *Català* word you just cut a Castilian one in half. In fact, though, the grammar is much more complicated than Castilian and it has eight vowel sounds (three diphthongs). There is a deliberate tendency at present in the media to dig up old words not used for centuries, even when a more common, Castilian-sounding one exists. In Barcelona, because of the mixture of people, there is much bad *Català* and much bad Castilian spoken, mongrel words being invented unconsciously.

In the text we've tried to keep to *Català* names (with Castilian in parentheses where necessary) – not least because street signs and Turismo maps are in *Català*. Either way, you're unlikely to get confused as the difference is usually only slight; ie Girona (Gerona) and Lleida (Lérida).

CATALÀ GLOSSARY

Most **Català** words are similar to Castilian, but some are completely unrecognizable. The criteria therefore for the following entries which you might encounter are either that they are very common or that they are very different from Castilian.

One	*Un(a)*	Four	*Quatre*
Two	*Dos (dues)*	Five	*Cinc*
Three	*Tres*	Six	*Sis*

Catalanisme

The **Catalan people** have an individual and deeply felt historical and cultural identity, seen most clearly in the language, which takes precedence over Castilian on street names and signs. Despite being banned for over thirty years during the Franco dictatorship, Catalan survived behind closed doors and has staged a dramatic comeback since the Generalissimo's death. As in the Basque country, though, regionalism goes back much further than this. On the expulsion of the Moors in 874, Guifré el Pilós (Wilfred the Hairy) established himself as the first independent **Count of Barcelona**; his kingdom flourished and the region became famous for its seafaring, mercantile and commercial skills, characteristics which to some extent still set the region apart. In the twelfth

Seven	Set	In	Dins
Eight	Vuit	With	Amb
Nine	Nou	Still/yet/even	Encara
Ten	Deu	A lot, very	Força
Eleven	Onze	A little	Una mica
Twelve	Dotze	Near	(a) Prop
		Far	Lluny
Monday	Dilluns	(Six) years ago	Fa (sis) anys
Tuesday	Dimarts	Self/same	Mateix
Wednesday	Dimecres	Half/middle	Mig/mitja
Thursday	Dijous	Stop, enough!	Prou!
Friday	Divendres	Too much/too	Massa
Saturday	Dissabte	many	
Sunday	Diumenge		
		To work	Treballar
Day before	Abans d'ahir	To go	Anar
yesterday		To call, phone	Trucar
Yesterday	Ahir	To have dinner	Sopar
Today	Avui	(evening)	
Tomorrow	Demà	To eat	Menjar
Day after tomorrow	Demà passat		
		Girl	Una noia
Left, Right	Esquerre (a),	Boy	Un noi
	Dret(a)	Child/term of	Nen(a)
Ladies, Gents (WC)	Dones, Homes	affection	
	(Toaleta)	Dog	Gosso
Open, Closed	Obert(a), Tancat		
Good morning/	Bon dia	Place	Lloc
Hello		Light	Llum
Good evening/	Bona nit/Adéu	Chief, head	Cap
Goodbye		Time, occasion	Vegada
Very well	Molt bé		
Bad	Malament	Drinking glass	Got
Got a light?	Tens foc?	Table	Taula
I like	M'agrada	Milk	Llet
Well, then	Sisplau	Egg	Ou
What do you want?	Que vols?	Strawberry	Maduixa
Where is?	On és?	Orange	Taronge
Sometimes	A vegades	Carrot	Pastanaga
Never, ever	Mai	Lettuce	Enciam
More	Més	Salad	Amanida
Nothing	Res	Apple	Poma
None, some, any,	Cap		
towards			

century came union with Aragón, though the Catalans kept many of their traditional, hard-won rights (*usatges*) and from then until the fourteenth century marked Catalunya's **golden age**. By the end of that time the kingdom ruled the Balearic islands, the city and region of Valencia, Sardinia, Corsica and much of present-day Greece. In 1359 the Catalan *Generalitat* formed Europe's first parliamentary government.

In 1469, through the marriage of Fernando V (of Aragón) to Isabella I (of Castile), the region was added on to the rest of the emergent Spanish state. Throughout the following centuries the Catalans made various attempts to secede and to escape from the stifling grasp of the central bureaucracy, which saw Catalan enterprize as merely another means of filling the state coffers. Early industrialization, which was centred here and in the Basque country, only intensified political disaffection. In the 1920s and 1930s, anarchist, communist and socialist parties all established major power bases in Catalunya. In 1931, after the fall of the dictator General Primo de Rivera, a **Catalan Republic** was proclaimed and its autonomous powers guaranteed by the new Republican government. Any incipient separatism collapsed, however, with the outbreak of the Civil War, during which Catalunya was a bastion of the Republican cause, Barcelona holding out until January 1939.

In return, Franco pursued a policy of harsh suppression, attempting to wipe out all evidence of the Catalan cultural and economic setup and finally to establish the dominance of Madrid. Among his more subtle methods – employed also in Euskadi – was the encouragement of immigration from other parts of Spain in order to dilute regional identity. Even so, Catalunya remained obstinate, the scene of protests and demonstrations throughout the dictatorship. After Franco's death there was massive and immediate pressure – not long in paying dividends – for the reinstatement of a **Catalan government**. This, the semi-autonomous *Generalitat*, enjoys a very high profile, whatever the complaints about its lack of real power. It controls education, health and social security, with a budget based on taxes collected by central government and then returned proportionally. The province's official title is the *Comunitat Autonoma de Catalunya* and it is also known internally as the *Principalitat*. Since autonomy was granted, the state has consistently elected right-wing governments, which may be difficult to understand in view of the recent past, but which might be explained by the fact that such regimes are seen to be better able to protect Catalan business interests.

THE COSTA BRAVA

The **Costa Brava** (Rugged Coast), stretching from Blanes, 60km north of Barcelona, to Port Bou and the French border, was once the most beautiful part of the Spanish coast with its wooded coves, high cliffs, pretty beaches and deep blue water. In parts it's still like this: the very northern section of the coast retains its handsome natural attractions and boasts a string of small towns and villages, which – while hardly undiscovered – are at least only frequented by locals and passing French motorists. The rest of the coast, however, to the south, is an almost total scenic disaster: thirty years of package-holiday saturation have taken their inevitable toll, and the concrete development has been ruthless. In places, there's a density of hotel and apartment blocks worse even than on the Costa del Sol.

Although the development appears all-encompassing at first glance, the Costa Brava splits into two distinct parts. The southern string of resorts, beginning at **Blanes**, *is* fairly horrible, though it's redeemed in a couple of places: the old town and medieval walls of **Tossa de Mar** are as attractive as anything you'll see in Catalunya, and **Sant Feliu de Guixols** further north has more going for it than most towns along the coast. Even the area's most notorious resort, **Lloret de Mar**, is a matter of taste: a brash, tacky concrete pile it may be, but if you like your nightlife loud, late and libidinous you'll have few complaints.

ACCOMMODATION PRICE SYMBOLS

The symbols used in our hotel listings denote the following price ranges:

① Under 2000ptas	③ 3000–4500ptas	⑤ 7500–12,500ptas
② 2000–3000ptas	④ 4500–7500ptas	⑥ Over 12,500ptas

See p.30 for more details.

GETTING AROUND THE COSTA BRAVA

Driving is the easiest way to get around, though you can expect the smaller coastal roads to be very busy in summer and parking to be tricky in the major resorts. **Buses** in the region are almost all operated by the *SARFA* company, but although they are reasonably efficient, it can be a frustrating business trying to get to some of the smaller coastal villages. Consider using Figueres, or even Girona, as a base for lateral trips to the coast; both are big bus termini and within an hour of the beach. The **train** from Barcelona to Port Bou and the French border runs inland most of the time, serving Blanes, Girona and Figueres, but only emerging on the coast itself at Llançà.

There's also a daily **boat service** (*Cruceros*) in the summer – June to September – from Calella (south of Blanes and not to be confused with the one near Palafrugell) to Palamós, calling chiefly at Blanes, Lloret, Tossa, Sant Feliu and Platja d'Aro. The Lloret–Tossa trip, for example, costs around 900ptas return, and it's worth taking at least once as the rugged coastline makes for an extremely beautiful ride.

Beyond **Palamós** the main road runs inland and the coastal development here is relatively low-key; the beaches and villages close to the small inland town of **Palafrugell**, in particular, are still wonderfully scenic. An added attraction is the ancient Greek site of **Empúries**, within walking distance of **L'Escala**, itself a resort on an eminently reasonable scale. Beyond here, the hinterland of the large bay, the **Golfo de Roses**, is rural and fairly isolated, crossed by only a few minor roads and encompassing a nature reserve, the Parc Natural dels Aiguamolls de la Empordá. Around the bay, **Roses** is the last of the Costa Brava's massive tourist developments; nearby **Cadaqués** is becoming more popular by the year, though you can find quieter coastal fishing villages right the way up to the French border, including the likeable small resort of **Port Bou**, last stop before France. Inland the region's largest town, **Figueres**, is the birthplace of Salvador Dalí and home to his superb, surreal museum.

There's more accommodation along the Costa Brava than anywhere else in Catalunya, but that doesn't necessarily make **rooms** any easier to find. In the large resorts block-booking by tour operators reduces the supply considerably and if you're heading independently to Lloret or Tossa, for example, in the summer, you'd be wise to book well in advance. You *will* generally find something if you arrive on spec, but you'll almost certainly pay over the odds for it. There are few problems with **camping,** provided you can put up with enormous, crowded sites often some way out of the towns and villages.

Blanes

Just over an hour from Barcelona, **BLANES** is the first town of the Costa Brava, though this apart there's little to distinguish it from the other resort towns back down the coast towards the city. With its industrial base and heavy-duty fishing port, it's an uninspiring stop. If you rose to the challenge you could doubtless derive some satisfaction from the town's botanical garden, which covers five hectares, the remains of a tenth-century castle keep and the surviving fourteenth-century church, but the main interest – inevitably – is provided by the pine-sheltered, sandy **beach**, one of the coast's longest. With Lloret de Mar only 8km away, and Tossa another 13km beyond, there's little incentive to do much more than dip a toe in the sea and then press on.

Blanes at least has the advantage over many similar places of being a real town rather than just a tourist settlement. There are dozens of **hotels and hostales** here, and no fewer than thirteen local **campsites** as well. If you booked in advance, one reason to stop would be a night at the seafront *Hostal Patacano*, Passeig del Mar 12 (☎972/330002; ⑤), which has what is widely recognized to be one of the best Catalan **restaurants** on the coast, with excellent seafood-laden meals weighing in at about 3000ptas a head. The *hostal* is open all year, and is much cheaper out of season, but only has six rooms. The locals also eat at *Unic Parrilla*, c/Porta Nova 7 (closed Tues and Dec), an old fisherman's cottage serving good meat and fish dishes; it's one block back on a street leading away from the seafront.

The **train** station is inland, a little way out of town – there's a half-hourly service to Barcelona and several trains daily to Girona and Figueres. Regular buses run from the station to the beach, and **buses** also connect Blanes with Lloret. The **Turismo** in Plaça de Catalunya (June–Sept Mon–Sat 9am–8pm, July & Aug also Sun 9am–2pm; May & Oct Mon–Fri 9am–2pm & 4–7pm; Nov–April Mon–Fri 9am–3pm; ☎972/330348) can help you find a room should you decide to stay.

Lloret de Mar

Despite the increasingly developed character of the coast as you head north, nothing will prepare you for **LLORET DE MAR**, one of the most extreme resorts in Spain. It's the one place on the Costa Brava that most people have heard of, with a sky-high tourist profile that puts many off and attracts countless others for roughly the same reasons – the bars, the discos, bastardized European cuisine, English pubs, German beer, and visitors who, on the whole, do their best to ignore the fact that they're in Spain at all.

On the surface, Lloret is a mess: high rise concrete tower blocks, a tawdry mile or so of sand and alongside it the most prosaic, unimaginative display of cafés, restaurants and bars you'll ever see. Looking for cultural distraction is a waste of effort, and only a tiny portion of the town – around Plaça de l'Esglesia and the sixteenth-century parish church – hints at what Lloret once was. But to see the town in this way is misguided, since Lloret makes no pretence that it's anything other than an out-and-out holiday resort. And as out-and-out holiday resorts go, Lloret de Mar is as accommodating as they come, excelling in giving its guests what they want. During the day, the central **beach** is packed with oily bodies, but it's flanked by attractive little coves and lookout points which you can either reach by footpath or view from the coastal boat service that calls at Lloret. Budget meals abound – in Dutch and German bars, overly convivial cafés, pizzerias and Chinese restaurants – while there are plenty of more expensive, and more impressive, Catalan and Spanish **restaurants** too. Beer and sangria flow ceaselessly, mopped up in the loud bars, pubs and discos along c/de la Riera and the surrounding streets.

Practicalities

Cruceros coastal **boats** dock at the beach, which is where the ticket office is, too (info on ☎972/364499); there are services 11 times daily to Tossa de Mar, 45min away. The **bus station** is north of the town centre, on Carretera de Blanes, in front of the football ground. As well as regular services from nearby Blanes and Tossa, there are daily buses from Barcelona, too. There's a **Turismo** (Mon–Sat 9am–1pm & 4–8pm; winter closes at 7pm; ☎972/365788) at the bus station if you want to pick up a map and hotel listings, and another one in the centre close to the seafront at Plaça de la Vila 1 (July & Aug Mon–Sat 9am–9pm, Sun 9am–2pm; rest of the year Mon–Sat 9am–2pm & 4–8pm; ☎972/364735).

If you're intending **to stay**, arm yourself with a list of hotels and *hostales* and start looking early in the day. Among the more reasonable places close to the sea are *Roca y Mar*, c/Venecia 51 (☎972/365013; ④), *Reina Isabel*, c/Venecia 12 (☎972/364121; ③), and the new *Tropicana*, c/Joan Llaverias 19 (☎972/364130; ③) – this last has sea views.

Further back, in the quieter parts of Lloret, the *Montserrat*, c/Carmen 54 (☎972/364493; June–Sept only; ③), the *Valls*, c/Santa Teresa 11 (☎972/364389; ③), and the extremely inexpensive *El Cuarto Escalón* on c/Santa Catarina (☎972/368643; ①), are all good bets.

If you're determined to eat Spanish **food** – an heretical choice in Lloret – then the heavily Catalan *El Tunel*, on c/Felicia Serramont, up the hill from the seafront, serves excellent, pricey dishes in a modern setting.

FIESTAS

January
20–22 Traditional pilgrimage in Tossa de Mar, the *Pelegri de Tossa*, followed by a lively *fiesta*. Annual festival at Llança.

February/March
Carnaval Sitges has Catalunya's best celebrations (see p.650). Celebrations also at Solsona, Sort, Rialp and La Molina.

Easter
The *Patum* festival in Berga (see p.623) is the biggest and best festival in Catalunya; Holy Week celebrations at Besalú and La Pobla de Segur.

April
23 *Semana Medieval de Sant Jordi* in Montblanc – a week of exhibitions, games, dances and medieval music to celebrate the legend of St George.

May
11–12 Annual *Festival* in Lleida; and the annual wool fair, *Festa de la Lana*, in Ripoll.

Festa de Corpus Christi in Sitges – big processions and streets decorated with flowers.

Third week *Fires i Festes de la Santa Creu* in Figueres; processions and music.

June
21–23 *Festival* in Camprodon.

24 *Día de Sant Joan* celebrated everywhere; watch out for things shutting down for a day on either side.

29 Annual *Festival* at Tossa de Mar.

Last week The *Raiers* (rafters) *Festival* and river racing in Sort.

July
First Sunday Annual *Festival* at Puigcerdà.

10 *Sant Cristobal* festival in Olot, with traditional dances and processions.

Third week *Festa de Santa Cristina* at Lloret de Mar. Also, annual *Festival* at Palafrugell.

25 *Festival* at Port Bou in honour of St James.

26 Annual *Festival* at Blanes.

August
First week *Festa Major* at Andorra la Vella; annual festival at Sant Feliu de Guixols.

10–12 Annual festival at Castelló d'Empúries.

15 *Festival* at La Bisbal and Palafrugell.

19 *Festa de Sant Magi* in Tarragona.

Last week *Festa Major* in Sitges, to honour the town's patron saint, Sant Bartolomeu.

September
First week *Festival* at Cadaqués and at L'Escala.

8 Religious celebrations in Cadaqué, Núria and Queralbs. Processions of *gigantes* at Solsona. *Festivals* at Sort and Esterri d'Àneu.

22 Annual *Festival* at Espot.

23 *Festa de Sant Tecla* in Tarragona, with processions of *gigantes* and human castles.

24 Annual *Festival* at Besalú.

October
8 Annual fair at Viella.

Last week *Ferias de Sant Narcis* in Girona, and *Festa de Sant Martiriano* in Banyoles.

November
1 *Sant Ermengol* celebrations in La Seu d'Urgell.

December
18 *Festival* at Cadaqués.

Tossa de Mar

Arriving by boat at **TOSSA DE MAR**, 13km north of Lloret, is one of the Costa Brava's highlights, the medieval walls and turrets pale and shimmering on the hill above the modern town. Although an unashamed resort, Tossa is still very attractive and – if you have the choice – infinitely preferable to Lloret as a base. Founded originally by the Romans, Tossa has twelfth-century walls surrounding an old quarter, the **Vila Vela**, which is all cobbled streets, whitewashed houses and flower boxes, offering terrific views over beach and bay. Within the quarter you'll eventually happen upon the **Museu de la Vila Vela** (Mon–Sat 10am–1pm & 3–6pm, Sun 10am–1pm; 175ptas), which features some Chagall paintings, a Roman mosaic and remnants from a nearby excavated Roman villa.

Tossa's best **beach** (there are three) is the Mar Menuda, around the headland away from the old town. The main central beach, though pleasant and clean enough, gets crowded even on the gloomiest of days. Booths here sell tickets for **boat trips** around the surrounding coastline, a reasonable way to blow 1000ptas or so if you're not going to take the *Cruceros* coastline service beyond Tossa.

Out of season Tossa's attraction is even greater, simply because there are fewer people to disturb the tranquil old town streets. It's in the winter, too, that you'll see something of the Costa Brava's previous, more traditional, life. This is best represented by the annual *Pelegri de Tossa*, on January 20, a **pilgrimage** from Tossa to the inland town of Santa Coloma in honour of Saint Sebastian, followed by a winter fair.

Practicalities

There are plenty of day-trippers in Tossa, which is linked to Lloret by half-hourly buses. If you're going to stay, pick up a free map and accommodation lists from the **Turismo** (June–Aug Mon–Sat 9am–9pm, Sun 10am–1pm & 4–8pm; Sept–May Mon–Fri 10am–1pm & 4–7pm, Sat 10am–1pm; ☎972/340108), in the same building as the **bus station**. To reach the centre, and the beaches, head straight down the road in front of you and turn right at the roundabout. The *Cruceros* **boats** dock at the main beach, where there's a ticket office (info on ☎972/340319).

Accommodation

There is plenty of **accommodation** to be had in the warren of tiny streets around the church and below the old city walls; in summer, the more obscure streets away from the front are the ones to check. The following are usually worth trying for inexpensive rooms: *Pensión Moré*, c/Sant Telmo 9 (☎972/340339; ②), *Pensión Can Tort*, c/Pescadores 1 (☎972/341185; ③) and *Fonda Lluna*, c/Roqueta 20 (☎972/340365; March–Nov only; ③). A couple of more expensive, very pleasant, options are *Diana*, Plaça d'Espanya 10 (☎972/341886; ⑤), which is much better value in winter, and the *Mar Blau*, at Avda. de la Costa Brava 16 (☎972/340282; ④).

There are five local **campsites**, all within a two-to-four-kilometre walk of the centre. *Cala Llevado* (☎972/340314; May–Sept) is 3km out, off the road to Lloret; around 650ptas per person and per tent. The bus to Lloret should drop you close by if you ask.

Eating

Most of Tossa's **restaurants** feature *menús del día* of varying quality, while there are endless "Full English Breakfast" bargains offered in places on the way out to the bus station. More atmospherically, there is a whole host of excellent restaurants up in the old quarter and just outside the walls, where you'll require big money or a credit card. For local specialities, two well-known places are *Bahía*, Passeig del Mar (☎972/340322; closed Nov–Jan), whose swish interior is the setting for pricey seafood meals, and *Es*

Molí, c/Trull 3 (Oct–April closed Tues), also expensive but with a garden patio and fine local cooking. A less exclusive place, with reliable Catalan food and a reasonable *menú del día* is *Tito's*, at c/Sant Telmo 6. The *Roqueta Mar*, c/de la Roqueta 2, is similarly inexpensive and has a lovely setting – with a creeper-shaded terrace in a rambling corner of the old town.

Sant Feliu to Palamós

Tossa is something of an aberration and the coast immediately to the north is again heavily developed and often thoroughly spoiled. Fairly regular buses ply the route, though, and the ride isn't bad in parts, particularly the winding section between Tossa and Sant Feliu. Even nicer is to use the boat service, which continues up the coast via Sant Feliu to Palamós – another lovely ride, and really the only reason to be stopping in most of the towns below. Incidentally, many of the buses on this coastal route originate in Girona or Palafrugell, so it's easy enough to see the various towns on day trips from either of those places, too.

Sant Feliu de Guixols

SANT FELIU DE GUIXOLS is probably the best stop between Tossa and the beaches of Palafrugell. It's another full-blown resort, but at least a reasonably pleasant one with only low-rise hotels, a decent sweep of coarse sand, a yacht harbour, and an attractive seafront Passeig del Mar decked out with pavement cafés and plane trees. Back from the beach, the narrow streets of the old town – thick with café-bars – are commercial but undeniably appealing, while a weekly market in the central Plaça de Mercat (formerly Plaça d'Espanya) adds a bit of local colour. Sant Feliu owes its handsome buildings and air of prosperity to the nineteenth-century cork industry which was based here, but the origins of the town go back as far as the tenth century, when a town grew up around the Benedictine **monastery**, whose ruins still stand in Plaça Monestir. The squat round tower and tenth-century arched gateway, the *Porta Ferrada*, sit back from the square, and if you want to look inside, the complex is usually open from 8am mass until noon, and again at 8pm mass. A **museum** around the back is currently being expanded to house a permanent display of work by local artist Josep Albertí, who died in April 1993.

Practicalities

Cruceros **boats** dock on the main beach, where there's a ticket office (☎972/320026). There are two **bus terminals**: *Teisa* services to and from Girona stop opposite the monastery, next to which you'll also find the **Turismo**, at Plaça Monestir 54 (Mon–Fri 8am–8pm, Sat 9am–1pm & 4–8pm, Sun 10am–1pm & 4–8pm; Oct–June closed Sat afternoon & Sun; ☎972/820051); the *SARFA* bus station (for buses to and from Palafrugell, Girona and Barcelona) is five minutes' walk north of the centre on the main Carretera de Girona, at the junction with c/Llibertat.

A score of family-run **pensions and hotels** can be found in the old town streets, all within a five-minute walk of each other and the sea; pick up a list and current prices from the Turismo. The most obvious is the *Hostal Zürich*, Avda. Juli Garreta 43–45 (☎972/321054; ④), just off Plaça Monestir, opposite the Turismo; while a favourite budget choice is the *Gas Vell*, c/Santa Magdalena 29 (☎972/321024; ②), though it's a long way from the sea.

There are **restaurants** everywhere, although those on the Passeig del Mar are overpriced, certainly if you're eating fish. Probably the best-value *menú del día* is at *La Plaça*, which has tables outside in Plaça de Mercat. Otherwise, try the *Club Nautic*, at the far end of the harbour in among the yachts, less for the food than for the unimpeded sea views; *La Cava*, c/Maragall 11 (closed Wed), a good place in the old town; and *Segura*, c/Sant Pere 11–13, or *Amura*, Plaça Sant Pere 7, for fish.

The *modernista*-influenced *Nou Casino de la Constancia*, which faces the water on Passeig dels Guixols, is also worth a visit at some point. It's open daily from 9am to 1am, and you can get a beer here and watch the old-timers fleecing each other at cards.

La Platja d'Aro, Calonge and around

There's another immense concrete concentration a few kilometres to the north, in the area around **LA PLATJA D'ARO** (Playa de Aro in Castilian), whose only recommendation is its three-kilometre beach – though as it recommends itself to thousands of others, too, you may as well give it a miss.

Beyond Platja d'Aro, buildings are still going up, and around **SANT ANTONI DE CALONGE** the main road traffic kicks up swirls of concrete dust. Four times daily the Palafrugell bus detours to **CALONGE** itself, just 2km inland but hardly visited by the beach hordes. It has a closely packed medieval centre with a church and castle, and there's a **restaurant**, *Can Muni*, at c/Major 5, whose speciality mussel recipes and 850ptas *menú del día* are alone worth the trip. The village also has several upmarket *hostales,* though you'd be better off moving back to the coast for the night.

Eleven kilometres west of Calonge along a minor road (no public transport), the ancient, megalithic stone of **Cova d'en Dayna** at **ROMANYÁ DE LA SELVA** is one of the very few surviving examples in Catalunya. If you're driving, the diversion is warranted, though under your own steam getting there involves taking the bus between Sant Feliu and Girona and asking to be put off at the turning outside Llagostera, from where it's a tiring seven-kilometre walk.

Palamós

Heading for Palafrugell, the only other realistic stop is at **PALAMÓS**, a modern looking resort set around a harbour full of yachts, and last stop on the *Cruceros* boat run (information on ☎972/314969). The town was originally founded in 1277, and the old part is set apart from the new, on a promontory at the eastern end of the bay. Palamós still retains its fishing industry, the day's catch being auctioned off on the busy quayside in the late afternoon. You can kill time until then on the town's good beach. Don't bother with the small Museu de la Pesca, signposted from various points in the town; you'll spend more time finding it than you will inside it.

The **bus station** (for services to and from Sant Feliu, Palafrugell and Girona) is one block back from the **Turismo** (June–Sept daily 9.30am–10pm; Oct–May daily 9.30am–1.30pm & 3.30–7.30pm) on the seafront.

Palafrugell and around

The small town of **PALAFRUGELL**, 4km inland from a delightful coastline, has managed somehow to remain almost oblivious to its tourist-dominated surroundings. An old town at its liveliest during the morning market, Palafrugell maintains a cluster of old streets and shops around its sixteenth-century church that aren't entirely devoted to the whims and wants of foreigners. The central square, it's true, is ringed with pavement cafés, but you're as likely to fetch up next to a local as a tourist, and elsewhere in town there are only five or six hotels, and a similar number of restaurants. All of which means that Palafrugell is still a very pleasant place to visit, while it's also a convenient place to base yourself if you're aiming for the nearby coastline – and considerably less expensive than staying at the beach.

The coast, too, makes a marked change from what's gone before. With no true coastal road, this stretch boasts quiet, pine-covered slopes backing the little coves of Calella, Llafranc and Tamariu, all with scintillatingly turquoise waters. The beach development here has been generally mild – low-rise, whitewashed apartments and hotels – and although a fair number of foreign visitors come in season, it's also where many of the better-off Barcelonans have a villa for weekend and August escapes. All this makes for one of the nicest (though hardly undiscovered) stretches of the Costa Brava.

Practicalities

Buses arrive at Palafrugell's *SARFA* **bus terminal** at c/Torres Jonama 67: the town centre is a ten-minute walk away to the right; while you turn left from the terminal and left again at the roundabout to find the **Turismo** at c/Carrilet 2 (June–Sept Mon–Sat 10am–1pm & 5–8pm, Sun 10am–1pm; Oct–May Mon–Sat 10am–1pm & 5–7pm; ☎972/300228). It hands out a map (including a useful plan of the local coastline) and accommodation lists. **Drivers** should be warned that finding a metered parking space in the narrow central streets can take hours.

Accommodation

Accommodation is available at any of the nearby beaches (see "Around Palafrugell" below), though it is expensive and zealously sought after. It's easier, and cheaper, to stay in Palafrugell itself and get the bus to the beach with everyone else: in summer it's wise to try and book ahead.

Quite the best budget choice is the friendly *Fonda L'Estrella*, c/de les Quatre Cases 13 (☎972/300005; ②), on a little street very near to the main Plaça Nova. It has simple, cool rooms ranged around a secluded, cloistered courtyard, which is scattered with tables and potted plants. Similarly priced is the more mainstream *Pensión Familar*, c/ Sant Sebastiá 29, over the other side of the square (☎972/300043; ②). Both places have separate bathrooms and showers.

On the same street as the *Familiar,* and slightly pricier, are the comfortable *Hostal Plaja*, c/Sant Sebastiá 34 (☎972/300526; ④), and the welcoming, family-run *Hotel Costa Brava*, c/Sant Sebastiá 10 (☎972/300558; ③), which has its own garden. Or try the small *Hostal Cypsele*, c/Ample 30 (☎972/300192; ③), which only has eight rooms.

Eating, drinking and entertainment

If you stay in Palafrugell, you'll have to **eat** there as well since the last bus back from the beaches is at around 9.15pm. There's not a great deal of choice, but what there is is generally good value. The biggest and best *menú del día* is at the *comedor* at the back of the *Pensión Familiar*, where gangs of locals pile in for the good-value meals – the almost exclusively male atmosphere can be a bit off-putting, though to be fair most diners are eating and not ogling. The *Hostal Cypsele* has its own reasonably priced Catalan restaurant, too, specializing in grilled meats (and with very few other dishes). Up a few steps from Plaça Nova, *Restaurant d'Arc* is recommended for pizzas and other main dishes for well under 1000ptas. Pricier is *Reig*, c/Torres Jonama 53, close to the bus terminal, a very pleasant Catalan restaurant where a meal will run to 3000ptas a head; here, too, there's a good *menú del día*, served from 1–3pm and 8–10pm. The town **market** runs daily (not Mon) from 7am onwards; it's on c/Pi i Margall, leading north from Plaça Nova.

Drinking and entertainment revolve entirely around Plaça Nova, where the café-bars are reasonably priced and well-placed for idling the time away. In July and August, on Tuesday and Thursday nights from around 10pm, there's dancing to a piano-and-drum-machine combo, while Friday nights at the same time see a more traditional *sardana* in the square.

Around Palafrugell

Such is the popularity of the **nearby beaches** that a new highway has been built from Palafrugell and, in the summer, an almost non-stop shuttle service runs from the bus terminal to Calella and then on to Llafranc. You might as well get off at Calella, the first stop, since Llafranc is only a twenty-minute coastal walk away and you can get a return bus from there. Other less frequent services run to the more distant beach at Tamariu, and **inland** to Begur.

All **bus services** are drastically reduced before June and after October. Basically, buses from Palafrugell run to Calella and Llafranc (8am–9pm, July and Aug every 30min, June & Sept roughly hourly), to Tamariu (June–Sept 3–4 daily), and to Begur (June–Sept 3–4 daily). However, it's also reasonably inexpensive to make the trip to the coast from Palafrugell by **taxi** – around 700ptas to Calella.

Calella and Llafranc

CALELLA is still (just) a fishing port. Its gloriously rocky coastline is punctuated by several tiny sand beaches which are always packed, but the water is inviting and the village's whitewashed villas and narrow streets very attractive. If you want to do more than lounge about, a 45-minute walk south leads to the **Castell i Jardins de Cap Roig** (daily 8am–8pm; 200ptas), a clifftop botanical garden which took fifty years to lay out. There are bars and restaurants lining the coastline at Calella, or one less obvious place to look out for is the *Bar Bacus* in the Plaça Sant Pere, back from the beach, with a fair choice of dishes served at its outdoor tables.

A gentle, hilly twenty-minute walk high above the rocks brings you to **LLAFRANC**, tucked into the next bay, with one goodish stretch of beach and a glittering marina. Llafranc seems a little more upmarket, its hillside villas glinting in the sun, its beach-side restaurants expensive, but essentially the development in both places remains on a human scale. While you're here, try *cremat*, a typical drink of the fishing villages in this region, reputedly brought over by sailors from the Antilles. The concoction contains rum, sugar, lemon peel, coffee grounds and sometimes a cinnamon stick; it will be brought out in an earthenware bowl and you have to set fire to it, occasionally stirring until (after a few minutes) it's ready to drink.

The **bus back to Palafrugell** leaves from the roundabout on the main road outside Llafranc. If you want to stay in either village, pick up a **hotel** list in Palafrugell and ring from there: a good place in Calella is the *Hostería Plankton* at Plaça de l'Esglesia (☎972/615081; ③), open in the summer only. In Llafranc, the *Hotel Casamar*, c/d'el Nero 3 (☎972/300104; ④), is up 113 steps from the seafront, a climb well worth making for the view of the bay from the hotel's balconies. There's probably more chance of a space at one of the villages' **campsites**, which are only open from April to September: *Moby Dick* (☎972/304807) and the less good *La Siesta* (☎972/300258) in Calella; or *Kim's Camping* (☎972/301156) in Llafranc.

Tamariu

TAMARIU, 4km north of Llafranc, is even lovelier, and although it has a smaller beach than either of the other two villages, there are fewer buses and consequently fewer people. You could just about walk through the woods from Llafranc (around 90min), although the last part of the winding road, with its speeding traffic, is rather dangerous. In any case, walk at least as far as the **lighthouse** above Llafranc, with grand views over the beach villages and Palafrugell set in the plain behind. There's a **campsite** in Tamariu, 200 metres from the beach (☎972/300422; May–Sept), and several *hostales* and **hotels**, though nothing that costs less than 6000ptas a night in July and August. The *Hotel Tamariu* (☎972/300108; ④) is small and friendly, and has a restaurant that faces the sea.

Begur, Aiguablava and other nearby beaches

For something other than just beaches, and for fewer people, head instead for **BEGUR**, about 8km from Palafrugell and slightly inland. It's a crumbling hill town, and the remnants of its seventeenth-century castle command extensive views of the central Costa Brava. The peeling medieval streets harbour a squat church and a couple of empty restaurants – and nothing but peace and quiet in the heat of the day. *Hotel Plaja* (☎972/622197; ④), opposite the church, has decent rooms, and serves a remarkably good-value *menú del día*.

With a little energetic walking from Begur, you can reach the beaches at **AIGUAFREDA** and **FORNELLS** or, if you have transport, the tranquil hamlets of **SA RIERA** and **SA TUNA** to the north. There are *hostales* at several of these beaches, only open in summer, and Sa Riera in particular has a selection of bars and restaurants for lunch. Drivers can also detour to **AIGUABLAVA** where the views are even more scenic than from Begur. The magnificent *Parador Nacional de la Costa Brava* (☎972/622162; ⑥) is the best place to soak up the scenery: non-guests can fork out for a couple of drinks at the bar just for the sheer luxury of enjoying the pool and getting a look at the marble and mosaic opulence within. If you're thinking of staying, book in advance and expect to pay up to 20,000ptas a night in high season.

Inland: La Bisbal, Pals and Torroella

Inland from Palafrugell there are several towns and villages that can provide an afternoon's escape from the beaches. A couple would even serve as overnight stops if you prefer tranquil medieval streets to the teeming coastal promenades.

La Bisbal and around

LA BISBAL, 12km northwest of Palafrugell and on the bus route to Girona, is a medieval market town in an attractive river setting. Since the seventeenth century, La Bisbal has specialized in the production of **ceramics**, and pottery shops line the main road through town, where – with a bit of browsing – you can pick up some terrific local pieces. Ceramics apart, La Bisbal makes a pleasant stop anyway as its handsome old centre retains many impressive mansions, the architectural remnants of a once thriving Jewish quarter, and parts of a medieval castle built for the bishops of Girona.

From La Bisbal, a couple of tiny medieval villages to the northeast – now rather desolate – are worth visiting, though you'll need to have your own transport. At **ULLASTRET** there was an Iberian settlement, whose ruins can be seen a little way outside the village. Nearby **PERATALLADA** is especially beautiful, with a ruined castle whose origins have been dated back to pre-Roman times, a fortified church and a number of houses embellished with coats of arms and arches. There's good local food and wine at *Can Nau*, c/d'en Bas 12 (closed Wed).

Pals

The bus north to L'Escala passes through a couple more relaxed places where you could break the journey. **PALS**, 8km north of Palafrugell, is a fortified, medieval village being rescued from long years of neglect by skillful restoration. This is inevitably attracting an increasing number of day-trippers, and ceramic and pottery shops are proliferating in its old quarter, whose buildings date largely from the fourteenth century. However, this commercialization doesn't really detract from the beauty of Pals' quiet hilltop setting: golden-brown buildings cluster around a stark tower, all that remains of the town's Romanesque castle. Below is the beautifully vaulted Gothic parish church, while you could also look into the town **museum** (100ptas), an eclectic collection housed in a restored mansion. Exhibits here include odds and ends retrieved from an English warship sunk in the siege of Roses in the 1808 War of Independence, and there's a steady turnover of art exhibitions, too.

Pals has a regular programme of dances and concerts throughout the summer, including a **wine festival** in mid-August, for which you might be tempted to stay. The only **accommodation** is at the *Hostal Barris* at c/Enginyer Algarra 51 (☎972/636 02; ④), in the non-descript new quarter of town, which also does meals. **Buses** stop right opposite the *hostal*, while the **Turismo** (June–Sept Mon–Sat 10am–2pm & 5–8pm, Sun 10am–1pm) is on the road out to Torroella de Montgrí.

Torroella de Montgrí and L'Estartit

TORROELLA DE MONTGRÍ, 9km beyond Pals on the Ter river, was once an important medieval port which has been left high and dry by a receding Mediterranean. It now stands 5km inland, beneath the shell of a huge, battlemented thirteenth-century castle (a stiff 30min walk away), and remains distinctly medieval in appearance with its narrow streets, fine mansions and fourteenth-century parish church. Oddly, only a couple of coachloads of tourists a day come to look round, and hardly anyone stays. The *Fonda Mitja*, at c/d'Esglesia 14 (☎972/756003; ③) just off the arcaded Plaça de la Vila, is excellent should you decide to do so, and there are several other *hostales* scattered about town.

The nearest beach is 6km to the east at **L'ESTARTIT**, a typical Costa Brava resort, though one with a quieter, more family-oriented atmosphere than many. There's a wide, though not particularly stunning, beach, and boat services to the nearby **Illes Medes**, Catalunya's only offshore islands. These form a protected nature reserve, hosting the most important colony of herring gulls in the Mediterranean, numbering some 8000 pairs. There are hourly **buses** from Torroella to L'Estartit.

L'Escala and Empúries

From either Palafrugell or Figueres you're only 45 minutes by bus from **L'ESCALA**, a small holiday resort at the southern end of the Golfo de Roses. On nothing like the same scale as the resorts to the south, it caters mainly for local tourists, which means that the steeply sloping streets and rocky coastline are genuinely appealing. L'Escala's proximity to the archeological site of **Empúries** (Ampurias), which lies just a couple of kilometres out of town, is a considerable further attraction. One of Spain's most interesting sites, Empúries' fascination derives from the fact that it was occupied continuously for nearly 1500 years. You can see the ruins in a leisurely afternoon, spending the rest of your time either on the crowded little sandy **beach** in L'Escala or on the more pleasant duned stretch in front of the ruins. The wooded shores around here hide a series of lovely cove-beaches with terrific, shallow water and soft sand. At weekends the woods are full of picnicking families, setting up tables, fridges and gas stoves from the backs of their cars. L'Escala is also widely known for its canning factories where Catalunya's best **anchovies** are packaged. You can sample them in any bar or restaurant, or buy small jars to take home from shops around town.

Practicalities

Buses all stop on Avda. Ave María, just down the road from the **Turismo** at the top of town (July & Aug Mon–Sat 8.30am–8.30pm, Sun 9.30am–1.30pm; Sept to June Mon–Wed and Fri–Sat 10am–1pm & 4–7pm, Thurs 10am–1pm; ☎972/770603). Here, you can pick up a map, local bus timetables – for Figueres, Palafrugell, Girona and Barcelona – and an up-to-date list of hotels. Drivers can find **free parking** at the football stadium on Cami Ample, around the corner from the bus stop, near the campsite.

Accommodation

L'Escala usually has plenty of **rooms** available, mostly in the streets sloping back from the sea, around the central Plaça Victor Català. Carrer de Gràcia has several choices, including the *Hostal Poch* at no. 10 (☎972/770092; ④). *Hotel Mediterráneo*, c/Riera 22–24 (☎972/770028; ③) is a nice place whose prices drop outside July and August, and *Torrent*, just up the road at c/Riera 28 (☎972/770278; ②), is also friendly and clean. The other alternative is to stay close to the beaches and woods around the archaeological site (see below), where there's little development save the one-star hotel *Ampurias* (☎972/770207; ④), overlooking the sea.

There's a **youth hostel** (☎972/771200; ①), open all year except mid-December to mid-January, right on the beach by the ruins, though it's often full; breakfast is included, meals are available, and a campsite is attached. Other **campsites** are found at each of the little bays that surround L'Escala, or – in the centre of town – at Cami Ample (☎972/770084; April–Sept), which is down the hill and right from the bus stop.

Eating, drinking and entertainment

The best deals for food are in the **restaurants** attached to the small hotels and *hostales*. Both the *Poch* and *Mediterráneo* have decent menus, while the shabby *Hostal Riera* at the top of c/de Gracia (no. 22) is a bit hit-and-miss but at best serves very tasty meals for around 1000ptas. The restaurant at the *Hostal Garbi*, just back from the beach at c/ Sant Maxima 7, is more formal, but still affordable, while if you're missing *tapas*, you can get into a wide choice at the *Taberna Gallego*, c/del Port 60.

Otherwise, there are sea views with the food at any of the bars and restaurants overlooking the town beach, but bear in mind that you'll often pay through the nose for the privilege, particularly if you occupy one of the appealing clifftop seats. As for **entertainments** other than beach-going, a *sardana* is held on the seafront every Wednesday night in summer.

Empúries: the site

Empúries was the ancient Greek *Emporion* (literally "Trading Station"), founded in 550 BC by merchants who, for three centuries, conducted a vigorous trade throughout the Mediterranean. In the early third century BC, their settlement was taken by Scipio, and a Roman city – more splendid than the Greek, with an amphitheatre, fine villas and a broad marketplace – grew up above the old Greek town. The Romans were replaced in turn by the Visigoths, who built several basilicas, and *Emporion* only disappears from the records in the ninth century when, it is assumed, it was wrecked by either Saracen or Norman pirates.

The **site** (June–Sept Tues–Sun 10am–2pm & 3–8pm, Oct–May closes at 5pm; 400ptas) lies behind a sandy bay about 2km north of L'Escala. The remains of the original **Greek colony**, destroyed by a Frankish raid in the third century AD – at which stage all moved to the Roman city – occupy the lower part of the site. Among the ruins of several temples, to the left on raised ground is one dedicated to *Asklepios*, the Greek healing god whose cult was centred on Epidavros and the island of Kos. The temple is marked by a replica of a fine third-century BC statue of the god, the original of which (along with many finds from the site) is in the Museu Arqueologic in Barcelona. Nearby are several large cisterns: *Emporion* had no aqueduct so water was stored here, to be filtered and purified and then supplied to the town by means of long pipes, one of which has been reconstructed. Remains of the town gate, the **agora** (or marketplace, in the centre) and several streets can easily be made out, along with a mass of house foundations, some with mosaics, and the ruins of Visigoth basilicas. A small **museum** (entry included in the site ticket) stands above, with helpful models and diagrams of the excavations as well as some of the lesser finds. Beyond this stretches the vast but

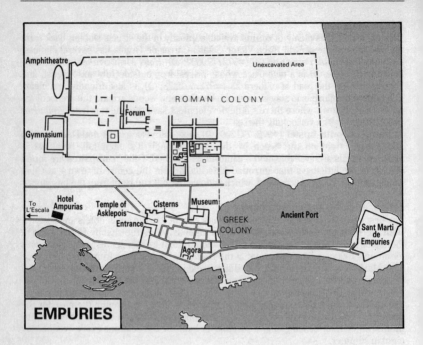

only partially excavated **Roman town**. Here, two luxurious villas have been uncovered, and you can see their entrance halls, porticoed gardens and magnificent mosaic floors. Further on are the remains of the **forum**, **amphitheatre** and outer walls.

Sant Marti d'Empúries

A short walk along the shore from the site brings you to the tiny walled hamlet of **SANT MARTI D'EMPÚRIES**. What was once a lovely, decaying place has been entirely taken over by visiting tourists who descend upon the shaded bar-restaurants in the square for lengthy lunches. Though it's still undeniably pretty, there are usually too many people around for comfort – generally, it's less oppressive in the evenings, when Sant Marti can still be perfect for a drink amid the light-strung trees. From the walls outside the village you can see the whole of the Golfo de Roses, with kilometre after kilometre of beach stretching right the way round to Roses itself, glinting in the distance. There are a couple of places to stay, one right on the square, the *Fonda Can Roura* (☎972/770305; ③–④), which owes its price more to its location than to any special facilities.

Figueres and around

The northernmost resorts of the Costa Brava are reached via **FIGUERES**, a provincial town with a population of some 30,000. Although it's capital of Alt Empordà – the upper part of the massive alluvial plain formed by the Muga and Fluvià rivers – it would pass almost unnoticed were it not for the **Museu Dalí**, installed by Salvador Dalí in a building as surreal as the exhibits within. As it is, Figueres itself tends to be overshadowed by the museum, which is the only reason most people come here. Stay longer and you'll find a pleasing town with a lively central *rambla* and plenty of cheap food and accommodation. It's also a decent starting point for excursions into the little-visited **Albères mountains**, to the north, which form part of the border with France.

The Museu Dalí

The **Museu Dalí** (July–Sept daily 9am–8pm; Oct–June Tues–Sun 10.30am–5.15pm; 900ptas) is the most visited museum in Spain after the Prado, a real treat, appealing to everyone's innate love of fantasy, absurdity and participation. Dalí was born in Figueres in 1904 and gave his first exhibition here when he was just fourteen. In 1974, in a reconstruction of the town's old municipal theatre, the artist inaugurated his Museu Dalí, which he then set about fashioning into an inspired repository for some of his most bizarre works. Having moved back to Figueres at the end of his life, Dalí died here on January 23, 1989; his body now lies behind a simple granite slab inside the museum.

Although it does contain paintings (some by other artists) and sculpture, the thematically arranged display is not a collection of Dalí's "greatest hits" – those are scattered far and wide. Nonetheless, what you do get beggars description and is not to be missed.

The very building (signposted from just about everywhere, on Plaça Gala i Salvador Dalí, a couple of minutes' walk off the Rambla) is an exhibit in itself, as it was designed to be. Topped by a huge metallic dome and decorated with luminous egg shapes, it gets even crazier inside. Here, the walls of the circular central well are adorned with stylized figures preparing to dive from the heights, while you can water the snail-infested occupants of a steamy Cadillac by feeding it with coins. There's also a soaring totem pole of car tyres topped with a boat and an umbrella. Climb inside to the main building and one of the rooms contains an unnerving portrait of Mae West, viewed by peering through a mirror at giant nostrils, red lips and hanging tresses. Other galleries on various levels contain such things as a complete life-sized orchestra, skeletal figures, adapted furniture (a bed with fish tails), sculpture and ranks of surreal paintings.

DALÍ: WHOSE LIFE IS IT ANYWAY?

Controversy surrounds Dalí's final years, with some observers believing that he didn't so much choose to live as a recluse as find himself imprisoned by his three guardians. Dalí suffered severe burns in a fire in 1984, after which he moved into the Torre Galatea, the tower adjacent to the museum. Fitted with a pacemaker and suffering psychological problems, Dalí became increasingly depressed, and several Spanish government officals and friends fear that, in his senile condition, he was being manipulated. In particular, it's alleged that he was made to sign blank canvases – and this has inevitably led to the questioning of the authenticity of some of his later works. Since the mid-1980s, there has been a series of trials in the US based on charges that various individuals have exploited bogus prints and lithographs. In 1990, two Americans, William Mett and Marvin Wiseman, were found guilty of art fraud – in particular of promoting spurious Dalí reproductions – and were fined nearly $2 million and sentenced to three years in prison.

The divison of his legacy of (genuine or otherwise) paintings is made yet more complicated by the fact that Dalí, by the terms of his last will made in 1982, left his entire estate, valued at $130 million, to the Spanish state, with the works of art to be divided between Madrid and Figueres. The Catalan art world was outraged, and promised a battle to keep the canvases from being carted off to the Museo de Arte Moderno in Madrid – plans are underway to exhibit over a hundred of the paintings in an as yet undecided location in Catalunya.

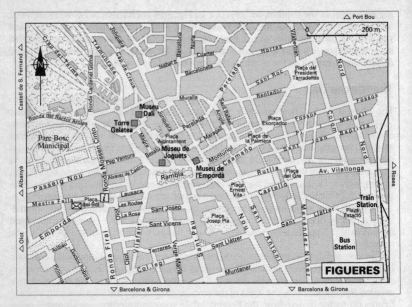

FIGUERES

▽ Barcelona & Girona   ▽ Barcelona & Girona

Around the rest of town

After the museum, the main sight in town is the huge seventeenth-century **Castell de Sant Fernand**, 1km northwest of the centre – follow Pujada del Castell from just beyond the Dalí museum. This was the last bastion of the Republicans in the Civil War, when the town became their capital after the fall of Barcelona. Earlier in the war, it had been used as a barracks for newly arrived members of the International Brigades before they moved on to Barcelona and the front: the sculptor Jason Gurney, in his *Crusade in Spain*, recorded how he slept in the dungeons but was still excited enough to describe it as the "most beautiful barracks in Spain . . .the building, and its setting in the Pyrenean foothills . . .exquisite". The castle is still in use by the military, but the five-kilometre circuit around the outside of the star-shaped walls makes a good walk.

Back in the centre pavement cafés line the Rambla, and you can browse around the art galleries and gift shops in the streets and squares surrounding the church of Sant Pere. There are two more museums, too. The **Museu de l'Empordà** at Rambla 1 (Tues–Sat 11.30am–1.30pm & 4.30–8pm, Sun 11am–2pm; free) has some local Roman finds and work by local artists, and the **Museu de Joguets** (Mon–Sat 10am–12.30pm & 4–7.30pm, Sun 11am–1.30pm & 5–7.30pm; closed Tues from Sept–June and all Feb; 400ptas, children 250ptas), further up the Rambla on the same side, is a toy museum with over 3000 exhibits from all over Catalunya. The statue at the bottom of the Rambla is a monument to Narcis Monturiol, a local who distinguished himself by inventing the submarine.

Practicalities

Arriving at the **train station**, you reach the centre of town by simply following the "Museu Dalí" signs. The **bus station** is just a couple of minutes' walk up on the left, at the top of Plaça Estació above the train station. There's a small **tourist information** booth just outside the bus station (June–Sept Mon–Sat 9.30am–1pm & 4.15pm–7pm), and a full-blown **Turismo** at the other end of town, on Plaça del Sol, in front of the Post Office building (June–Sept Mon–Sat 9am–9pm; Oct–May Mon–Fri 9am–7pm, Sat 9am–2pm; ☎972/503155). Both dish out a town map, handy hotel lists, and timetables for all onward transport.

Accommodation

The best place to start looking for budget **accommodation** is at the *Pensión Bartis*, c/ Méndez Nuñez 2 (☎972/501473; ①), fairly close to bus and train stations, which has perfectly reasonable, and absolutely the cheapest, rooms. Otherwise, you could try the streets at the top right-hand corner of the Rambla: there are two places on c/Pep Ventura, including the friendly *Venta del Toro* (☎972/510510; ②). Further down around the Dalí museum, several bars offer *habitaciones* – *Bar Ringo*, c/de la Muralla 4 (②) is a real spit-and-sawdust place; further along at no.12 *Bar Brindis* (☎972/500004; ②) is slightly more expensive but more welcoming. More regular *hostales* are difficult to recommend since many lie on the main roads out of town, but some fairly central ones include *Isabel II*, c/Isabel II 16 (☎972/504735; ③); *Fenix*, Via Emporitana 3 (☎972/503185; ②); and *España*, c/Jonquera 26 (☎972/500869; ④), this last with good discounts out of the summer season.

There's a good **youth hostel, the** *Tramuntana* (☎972/501213; closed Sept; ①), at c/Anicet Pages 2, off Plaça del Sol at the top of town, while the local **campsite**, *Pous* (☎972/500014), is on the road to La Jonquera – sadly, it's rather dirty and overpriced. Don't, whatever you do, opt to sleep in the municipal park instead: it's a dangerous place to be at night.

Eating and drinking

A gaggle of tourist **restaurants** is crowded into the narrow streets around the Dalí museum, particularly along c/Jonquera. Here you'll be able to find a decent *menú del día*, while the cafés on the Rambla are good for snacks and sandwiches. For a food treat, head for the *Hotel Duran*, at c/Lausaca 5, at the top of the Rambla, where they serve generous regional dishes with a modern touch; it's expensive but has an excellent reputation. Eating aside, Figueres is generally fairly comatose **at night**: on weekend evenings there are traffic jams on the road to Roses as everyone heads out there instead to let their hair down.

North of Figueres: the Albères mountains

The region north of Figueres, which encompasses the **Albères mountains**, is virtually unknown to foreigners; a slow-moving mix of semi-ruined villages hidden among resin-scented hills, dotted with occasional vineyards, olive groves and shady cork plantations. During World War II the area was so deserted that there were no *Guardia Civil* stationed in the area, which made the eastern Albères a favoured escape route from France. These days, local bus services from Figueres can take you to a few of the more accessible villages, though as departures are only once or twice a day you may have to stay overnight.

The Maçanet region

One of the best routes is to **SANT LLORENÇ DE LA MUGA**, 15km northwest of Figueres, near the shore of a reservoir that looks huge on the map but turns out to be less impressive in the flesh. Across the other side of the reservoir, **MAÇANET DE CABRENYS** (linked to Sant Llorenç by a long hiking trail) looks down on wetlands that are a haven for herons. There are two or three *hostales* here, including the *Cal Ratero* – also known as *Hostal Oliveros* – c/de les Dòmines 6 (☎972/544068; ③), just off the main square. The village is also linked directly with Figueres by bus – the service passing through **DARNIUS**, where there's another (more expensive) place to stay, the *Darnius*, c/Maçanet 17 (☎972/535117; ④–⑤). Maçanet is much the livelier of the two places.

The Espolla region

Northeast of Figueres, a daily bus heads for **ESPOLLA**, which boasts at least ten prehistoric sites in the immediate area. Easiest to find is the **Dolmen de la Cabana Arqueta**, dating from around 2500 BC; from Espolla take the **SANT CLIMENT** road, and at the rising bend 1km beyond the village turn down the farm track to the right – the dolmen is ten minutes' walk on. The most important, however, is the **Dolmen del Barranc**, the only carved tomb yet found in the area; it lies 3km from the village off the track leading north to the Col de Banyuls.

Espolla itself is an authentic Alt Empordà village, its shuttered houses crammed into a labyrinth of streets that buzz each year with the flurry of the grape harvest. The only accommodation here is the friendly, family-run *La Manela*, at Plaça del Carmé 7 (☎972/563065; ②), which also cooks good, inexpensive meals if you need them. There's also the more upmarket *Can Calau* **restaurant** on the edge of the village.

The Golfo de Roses

The **Golfo de Roses** stretches between L'Escala and Roses, a wide bay backed for the most part by flat, rural land, well-watered by the Muga and Fluvia rivers. Left to its own, quiet devices for centuries, it's quite distinct from the otherwise rocky and touristy Costa Brava, and has really only suffered the attention of the developers in towns at either end of the bay, most notably in the few kilometres between the marina-cum-resort of Ampuriabrava and Roses. Probably the most you'll do is cross the attractive farmlands on your way to or from Figueres, but there are a couple of specific targets if you want to avoid the beach for a while, as well as the excellent beach itself at the resort of Roses.

Parc Natural dels Aiguamolls de l'Empordà

Halfway around the bay is one of Spain's newest and most accessible nature reserves, the **PARC NATURAL DELS AIGUAMOLLS DE L'EMPORDÀ**. Made up of two blocks of land, one on either side of Ampuriabrava, it encompasses what's left of the Empordà marshland, which once covered the entire plain of the Golfo de Roses, but has gradually disappeared over the centuries as a result of agricultural developments and cattle-raising. Relying heavily on the botany students of Barcelona University and volunteers, the park looks a little raw in places, but attracts a wonderful selection of birds to both its coastal terrain and the paddy fields typical of the area. There are several easy paths around lagoons and marshes, and hides have been created along the way: morning and early evening are the best times for bird-watching in the marshes and you'll see the largest number of species during the migration periods (March–May and August–October).

Entrance to the park is free, and routes to follow around it are all marked on a brochure that you can pick up at the **information centre** at El Cortalet (June–Sept daily 9.30am–2pm & 4.30–7.30pm; Oct–May daily 9.30am–2pm & 3.30–6pm; ☎972/ 454222), on the road between Castelló d'Empúries and Sant Pere Pescador (see below). To get the most out of the park, take a pair of binoculars – and in summer and autumn you'll need mosquito repellent. The only **camping** allowed within the park is at the massive "first-class" *Nautic Almata* (☎972/454477; May–Sept).

Sant Pere Pescador and Torroella de Fluvià

The nearest village to the park is **SANT PERE PESCADOR**, 3km south of the information centre. The village is easily reached by *SARFA* bus from Figueres and there are also services from Palafrugell, L'Escala and (once-daily) Girona. Despite being a drab place in the middle of nowhere, the village is relatively developed, and this does at least mean that there's plenty of choice if you need to spend the night here: there are half a dozen *hostales* and hotels (most open only from June–Sept), and several bars and restaurants. There's also a bike rental shop.

The Figueres–Palafrugell bus also makes a stop in the little village of **TORROELLA DE FLUVIÀ**, 4km southwest of Sant Pere, where there's a lovely country house, *El Sugué*, at c/de Sant Pere Pescador 1 (☎972/550067; ③), which takes guests. You can cook for yourself here if you wish, though the owners will provide good Catalan and vegetarian meals for anyone who wants them.

Castelló d'Empúries

The delightful small town of **CASTELLÓ D'EMPÚRIES**, halfway between Roses and Figueres and connected to both by very frequent buses, makes a much more attractive base for the park – and indeed is worth a stop in passing anyway. Five minutes' walk off the main road, where the bus drops you, transports you into a little medieval conglomeration, astride the Riu Muga, that's lost little of its genteel charm despite being so close to the beach-bound hordes. Formerly the capital of the Counts of Empúries, the town's narrow alleys and streets conceal some fine preserved buildings, a medieval bridge, and a thirteenth-century battlemented church, **Santa María**, whose ornate doorway alone is reward enough for the trip.

The nature reserve lies around 5km south, reached on the minor road to Sant Pere Pescador, and the beach at Roses is also close by – only fifteen minutes away by bus. There are several **places to stay** and while prices are a little higher here than usual, it's a price worth paying for the peace and quiet when the day-trippers have all gone home. On the way into the village, *Fonda Cal Avi*, c/Muralla 23 (☎972/250507; ②), is the least expensive option, while *Hostal Canet* (☎972/250340; ④) enjoys a fine position on Plaça Joc de la Pilota. Both these places serve food – a meal on the terrace of the *Canet* is particularly good value. There are also two places next to each other on the main road, near where the bus stops, which are much nicer than their position suggests. The *Hostal Ca L'Anton* (☎972/250509; ③) has rooms with and without bath available, and an attached restaurant with a fine *menú del día* and plenty of locally inspired dishes. The slightly pricier, very smart, *Fonda Serratosa* (☎972/250508; ④) also has a dining room.

Roses

ROSES itself enjoys a brilliant situation, beneath ruined medieval fortress walls at the head of the grand sweeping bay. It's a site that's been inhabited for over three thousand years – the Greeks called the place *Rhoda*, when they set up a trading colony around the excellent natural harbour in the ninth century BC – but apart from the castle, the extensive ruined citadel (daily 9am–8pm, closes at 5pm in winter) and the surviving sections of the city wall, there's little in present-day Roses to hint at its long history. Instead, the town trades exclusively on its four kilometres of sandy beach, which have fostered a large and popular water-sports industry. Roses is a full-blown resort, with the usual supermarkets, discos and English breakfasts: if you're staying, apart from the beach action one of the better entertainments is to take the bus ride to more attractive Cadaqués, which runs across the plain and up over the bare hills giving superb views back over the resort and bay. Another option is a **boat trip**: there are regular excursions to Cadaqués or the Illes Medes throughout the summer.

Buses stop outside the post office, with the town centre and restaurants to the left, hotel blocks to the right. There's a **Turismo** on the seafront promenade, and any number of **hotels** and *hostales* in the town; all are marked on the map given away by the Turismo, but as ever, many are likely to be booked solid throughout the summer. Out of town, there are several enormous **campsites** on the road between Roses and Figueres.

Cadaqués

CADAQUÉS is a far more pleasant place to stay, accessible only by the steep winding road over the hills behind and consequently still retaining an air of isolation. With box-like, whitewashed houses lining the narrow, hilly streets, a tree-lined promenade and craggy bays on either side of a harbour that is still a working fishing port, it's genuinely picturesque. Sitting on the seafront, you can watch the fishermen take their live catches straight to the restaurant kitchens. In the 1960s Salvador Dalí built a house on the outskirts of the town (at Port Lligat) and for some years Cadaqués became a distinctly hip place to be, hosting an interesting floating community. Over the last few years though, it has been "discovered" and is now too trendy for its own good. Nonetheless, Cadaqués remains accessible. There are beautiful people around and more than a few Mercedes, but it all falls far short of, say, a South-of-France snobbery. Out of season Cadaqués could be great and even in midsummer – if you can bear the company and the high prices – you'll probably have fun.

The **beaches** are all tiny and pebbly, but there are some fine local walks around the harbour and nearby coves, while the town itself makes for an interesting tour, clambering around the streets below the church. The number of private art galleries here has mushroomed since the monied set began stopping by, and a couple of good museums soak up browsers, too: the **Museu Perrot-Moore**, in the middle of town at c/Vigilant 1 (daily 10.30am–1.30pm & 4.30–8.30pm; 400ptas, students 250ptas) has paintings, drawings and graphics by Dalí and Picasso; while the **Museu Municipal d'Art** on c/ Monturiol (daily 10.30am–1pm & 5–9pm; 100ptas) features work by local artists whose efforts are mostly inspired by the spectacular local coastline.

Practicalities

Buses stop at the little *SARFA* bus office on c/Sant Vicens, on the edge of town. It's less than ten minutes from here, following c/Unió and c/Vigilant, to the central beach and square. Just off the square, the **Turismo** is at c/des Cotxe 2 (Mon–Sat 10am– 1.30pm & 4–9pm, winter 5–7pm, Sun 10am–noon; ☎972/258315).

Accommodation

Finding **rooms** is likely to be a big problem unless you're here outside peak season: a town plan posted at the bus stop marks all the possibilities. The cheapest rooms are at one of three *fondas* scattered about the town: *Fonda Velí*, c/de l'Esglesia 6 (☎972/ 256470; ③), has the best position, just below the church; it's only open in summer. Just back from the main square, very close to the seafront, the *Hostal Marina* (☎972/ 258199; ③) and *Hostal Cristina* (☎972/258138; ③) are the next step up – similarly priced, with more expensive rooms with bath, too, and discounts out of season. The *Cristina* won't accept reservations, either, so there's usually a good chance of a room in high season if you arrive early enough. *Hostal Ubaldo* on the way into town from the bus stop at c/Unió 13 (☎972/258125; ④) has recently refurbished its rooms; they're an even better bargain outside high season. There's a noisy **campsite** (☎972/258126; mid-April to Sept) on the road to Port Lligat, a steep 1km out of town; it also rents out cabins for around 3500ptas double, with shower.

Eating

The harbourside promenade is lined with pizzerias and **restaurants** all offering the same kind of deals. If you're not sick of it yet, then Cadaqués is a nice place to sit outside and dive into a paella, which most places offer as part of a *menú del día*. One very attractive possibility is *El Pescador* on c/Nemesi Llorens, which is around the harbourside, to the right as you face the water. There's an elegant two-floored dining room, or seats outside, an authentic Catalan paella (with seafood, sauasage and spare ribs) and an 1100ptas *menú del día*. On Avda. Caritat Serinyana, which is the main road running away from the water, the *Don Quijote* (no. 6), has pleasant courtyard seating and a *menú del día* for 1200ptas.

El Port de la Selva and Sant Pere de Rodes

Inexplicably, there is no bus service north of Cadaqués and you are forced to backtrack to Figueres for onward transport. Alternatively, you can venture to make the relatively easy 13-kilometre walk/hitch across the cape, **Cap de Creus**, from Cadaqués to **EL PORT DE LA SELVA**, at which point you're back on a bus route. An intensive fishing port set on the eastern side of a large bay, El Port de la Selva isn't terribly enticing, its beaches and campsites mainly used by families who retire early for the night. The town does, however, allow access to Sant Pere de Rodes (see below), the most important monastery in the region. From Selva de la Mar, 2km above the port, a good dirt road takes you right there (a further 4km), or you can approach from Vilajüiga on the Figueres–Port Bou rail line, an eight-kilometre walk from the monastery.

If you need to **stay** there are a few choices: the *Fonda Sol y Sombra*, c/Nou 8 (☎972/ 387060; ③), requires you to take half-board, while the more expensive *Hotel Porto Cristo*, at c/Major 59 (☎972/387062; ⑤), is about twice the price, though good value out of season. Perhaps the most attractive place is the *Hostal L'Arola* (☎972/387005; ④), right on the beach opposite the turning to Selva de la Mar. The views from the *hostal* are unbeatable, and it's not too expensive for a room without a bath; there's also a **campsite** here, on the beach.

Sant Pere de Rodes

The Benedictine monastery of **Sant Pere de Rodes** (July & Aug Tues–Sun 10am–7pm; Sept–June Tues–Sun 9am–1.30pm & 3–6pm; 150ptas; free on Tues) was one of the many religious institutions founded in this area after the departure of the Moors. Legend has it that, with Rome threatened by barbarians, Pope Boniface IV ordered the Church's most powerful relics – including the head of St Peter – to be hidden. They were brought to this remote cape for safe-keeping and hidden in a cave, though when the danger had passed the relics couldn't be found. A monastery was duly built on the site and dedicated to Saint Peter. More certainly, the first written record of the monastery dates back to 879, and in 934 it became independent, answerable only to Rome: in these early years, and thanks especially to the Roman connection, the monks became tremendously rich and powerful, administrating huge territories. At the same time they aroused local jealousy, so that from the beginning there were disputes between the monastery and the feudal lords of the surrounding country. As the monastery was enlarged it was also fortified against attack, starting a period of splendour that lasted four hundred years before decadence set in. Many fine treasures were looted when it was finally abandoned in 1789, and it was also pillaged by the French during the Peninsular War; some of the rescued silver can be seen in Girona's Museu d'Art.

The monastery may originally have been built over a pagan temple dedicated to the Pyrenean Venus, *Afrodita Pyrene* – a theory based on a second- or first-century BC Egyptian map, written narratives of the third and fourth centuries AD, and the discovery of fragments of pagan sculptures and Corinthian capitals in the area. Whatever its origins, the daunting ruins are a splendid sight, with the monastery-church universally recognized to be the precursor of the Catalan Romanesque style. The eleventh-century columns in the barrel-vaulted nave are decorated with wolves' and dogs' heads, and there's an irregular cloister adjacent to the church.

Nearby is the pre-Romanesque church of **Santa Elena**, all that stands of the small rural community which grew up around the monastery. Above the monastery (and contemporary with it) stands the very ruined **Castell de Sant Salvador**, of which only the walls remain. This provided the perfect lookout site for the frequent invasions (French or Moorish), which normally came from the sea. In the event of attack, fires were lighted on the hill to warn the whole surrounding area.

Llançà

The train line from Barcelona finally joins the coast at **LLANÇÀ**, 8km north of El Port de la Selva (regular daily buses link the two) and a handier base for touring. Once a small fishing town, Llançà has been opened up to the passing tourist trade by the road and rail route to France – and is shameless in its attempts to cash in. Unlike many such towns, however, it does have compensatory attractions. The beach is a good 2km from the train station (the buses stop outside), but the **old town** is much closer, just off to the right – set back so far from the water to escape the attentions of pirates. A tiny Plaça Major houses an outsize medieval church (currently under restoration) and the renovated remains of a later defensive tower, which houses an exhibition (Sat & Sun 4–6pm) of photograps of bygone Llança.

On the road down to the **port**, where there's a market each Wednesday, are lined dozens of restaurants, souvenir shops and miniature golf courses. At the end, though, you'll still find a proper working port and a coarse sandy beach, all reassuringly undeveloped and concrete-free.

Practicalities

There are five buses a day to Llançà from El Port de la Selva; the **Turismo** (June–Sept daily 9.30am–9pm; open sporadically in winter; ☎972/380855) is on the road into town. For **accommodation**, there are some cheap *habitaciones* and *hostales* in the old town, or you can stay down at the harbour. Try the pleasant *Habitaciones Can Pau*, c/Afora 22 (☎972/380271; ②), as an example of the former; or the harbourside *Hostal Miramar*, Passeig Maritim 7 (☎972/380132; ③). There are two **campsites** signposted on the way in from the train station: *L'Ombra* (☎972/380335; open all year) and the smaller *Camping Llança* (☎972/380485; mid-June–Aug).

A couple of recommended **restaurants** are *La Brasa*, Plaça de Catalunya 6 (closed Dec–Feb), which specializes – as its name sugggests – in grilled meat and fish, and a seafood restaurant, *Can Manel*, Plaça del Port 5 (closed Thurs in winter).

Colera

At Llançà you can pick up trains heading for Port Bou. At several, usually inconvenient, times throughout the day these will also stop at **COLERA**, only a few kilometres to the north. One of the smallest villages left on this coast, it seems little frequented by passing drivers – partly, one suspects, because it's easy to miss; you need to turn off at the sign to Sant Miquel, Colera's official name. There's only fitful development here, and it's mostly locals using the very pebbly beaches. The water is clean and clear (despite the town's name), and quite safe for children to splash about in. For all these reasons it makes a pleasant stop, at least for lunch: there are a couple of pricey **restaurants** overlooking the beach and harbour, or some more reasonable, equally congenial, alternatives in the village square, Plaça Pi i Margall.

Just off the square, *Hostal Bon Repos*, at c/Francesc Ribera 12 (☎972/389012; ③), is an adequate place to sleep and eat, while you've also the choice of a couple of more upmarket *hostales* down by the two small beaches. The well-kept *Hostal Gambina* (☎972/389014; ③) is right on the seafront, and discounts its rooms out of season. There's also a good **campsite** (*Sant Miquel*; ☎972/389018; April–Sept), set well back from the beach, just off the main road.

Port Bou

PORT BOU, 7km further north, and only 3km from the French border, is a fine place to approach by road, over the hill and around the bay. It's even worth walking from Colera (it takes around two-and-a-half hours) and suffering the initial steep climb to enjoy the view down over the green hills, deep blue water and small, pebbled beach. Close up, it's still a very pretty place, with a natural harbour and stone beach used by the local fishermen to mend their nets. There are some excellent outdoor **restaurants**, both in the back streets of the old town and lining the quay, none of them outrageously expensive; you can get an excellent meal here for around 1200ptas. And you can spend the rest of your day pottering around the little coves nearby, all reached on footpaths scratched out of the rocks, all clean and relatively uncrowded.

If you arrive on the **train** the massive station with its souvenir stalls creates entirely the wrong impression, although it is true that the railway has transformed the place. Before the Barcelona–Cerbère line came into operation, Port Bou was a small fishing village; now it's a stop on the dash in and out of Spain, getting much of its trade from French tourists who come to stock up on booze and souvenirs before crossing straight back into France. Other visitors include those killing the afternoon hours before the night train from Cerbère to Paris, certainly a better way to pass the time than sitting in the Cerbère station bar.

Practicalities

There's a **Turismo** (June to mid-Sept daily 9am–8pm; ☎972/390284) right at the harbour, which has a map and list of **hotels** to give away; staff here are friendly and more than willing to help with recommendations. The rock-bottom choice in town is the *Hostal Comercio*, Rambla de Catalunya 16 (☎972/390001; ②), on the pleasant rambla close to the beach – friendly, welcoming and utterly run-down, with no hot water. Around the harbour, and just back from the sea, *Hostal Juventus*, Avda. Barcelona 3 (☎972/390241; ②), has small, basic quarters, or there are much better rooms with bath at the pleasant *Hostal Plaza*, c/Mercat 15 (☎972/390024; ②), on the street leading down from the station. If you want to overlook the sea, you're going to have to pay a little more: try the attractive *Hotel Bahia*, c/de Cervera 1 (☎972/390196; ③), which also has rooms with bath available that are in the next price category.

There's a similarly wide choice when it comes to **eating**. Of the restaurants along the seafront promenade, Passeig de la Sardana, *L'Ancora* serves a fabulous seafood paella; it also serves beer in virtual buckets if you're set for an afternoon's chat with the barman. Other great seafood establishments are at the *Hostal de Francia*, c/del Mar 1, and the *Tauro*, on Avda. de Barcelona (the Figueres road). A particularly attractive setting for a meal is in the garden-courtyard of the *Hotel Comodoro*, one block from the beach at c/Méndez Nuñez 1 – good local food in relaxed surroundings. For sandwiches, or just a drink, *Casa David* in the main Plaça del Mercat has popular outdoor seating, and over the road is the little **market** hall itself, open in the mornings for picnic fixings.

The road **border crossing** into France is open 24 hours from mid-June to September, but closes from midnight until 7am for the rest of the year.

GIRONA AND AROUND

Just an hour inland from the coast, the city of **Girona** with its medieval core provides a startling and likeable contrast to the wilder excesses of the Costa Brava. It's easy to make the day trip here from the coast, or from Barcelona (to which it's connected by regular trains and buses), but it really warrants more time than that – two or three nights in Girona would show you the best of the city and let you enjoy some of the striking surrounding countryside. The quickest trip is to the lakeside town of **Banyoles**, only half an hour from Girona, and it's not much further on to beautiful **Besalú**, one of the oldest and most attractive of Catalan towns.

To see more of the province of which Girona is capital you have to head for **Olot**, an hour and a half west of the city, at the heart of the **Garrotxa** region. Much of this is an ancient volcanic area, now established as the **Parc Natural de la Zona Volcanica**, whose rolling, fertile countryside is pitted with spent craters. Some of these are within the town boundaries of Olot itself, but the best of the scenery is around the village of **Santa Pau**, just to the east. North of here, and also close to Olot, **Castellfollit de la Roca** is the starting point for several good treks which take you into the foothills of the nearby Pyrenees.

In the other direction, south towards Barcelona, those with a little more time can veer off into the mountainous **Serra del Montseny**, whose spa towns and precipitous roads are a restful diversion – though one you'll find easiest to see if you have your own transport, since buses are infrequent.

Girona

The ancient, walled city of **GIRONA** stands on a fortress-like hill, high above the Riu Onyar. It's been fought over in almost every century since it was the Roman fortress of *Gerunda* on the Via Augusta, and perhaps more than any other place in Catalunya, it retains the distinct flavour of its erstwhile inhabitants. Following the Moorish conquest of Spain, Girona was an Arab town for over two hundred years, a fact apparent in the maze of narrow streets in the centre, and there was also a continuous Jewish presence here for six hundred years. The intricate former Jewish quarter of houses, shops and community buildings is now visible again after centuries of neglect. By the eighteenth century, Girona had been besieged on twenty-one occasions, and in the nineteenth it earned itself the nickname "Immortal" by surviving five attacks, of which the longest was a seven-month assualt by the French in 1809. Not surprisingly, all this attention has bequeathed the city a hotch-potch of architectural styles, from Roman classicism to *modernisme*, yet the overall impression for the visitor is of an overwhelmingly beautiful medieval city, whose attraction is heightened by its river setting.

Considering Girona's airport serves most of the Costa Brava's resorts, the city can seem oddly devoid of tourists, which makes browsing around the streets and cool churches doubly enticing. It's a fine place, full of historical and cultural interest, and one where you can easily end up spending longer than you'd planned. There are two or three excellent museums and a cathedral that's the equal of anything in the region. Even if these leave you unmoved it's hard to resist the lure of simply wandering the superbly preserved medieval streets, fetching up now and again at the river, above which high blocks of pastel-coloured houses lean precipitously on the banks.

Arriving, information and getting around

Girona's **airport**, 13km south of the city centre, is used mainly for Costa Brava charter flights; there's no bus into town, so you'll have little choice but to take a taxi. Most arriving passengers are bussed direct to their resorts, an hour away to the east.

The **train station** is at Plaça d'Espanya, across the river in the new part of the city – from here, it's a twenty-minute walk into the old centre, where you're most likely to want to stay. The **bus station** is around the back of the train station, with frequent services to the Costa Brava and inland to towns in Girona province and beyond. This is also where international buses from London and other parts of western Europe stop. For route information, phone the numbers given in "Listings", p.604.

Information

There's a **Turismo** inside the train station (Mon–Sat 9am–2pm; ☎972/216296), while the main office is at Rambla de la Llibertat 1 (Mon–Fri 8am–8pm, Sat 8am–2pm & 4–8pm; also July & Aug Sun 9am–2pm; ☎972/419419), right on the river at the eastern end of the old town. Both offices have useful maps and up-to-date accommodation lists, English-speaking staff, and bus and train timetables for all onward services. If you need city information outside these hours, give the **city information service** a try – ring ☎972/419010 and expect to have to communicate in Spanish.

Getting around

As for **getting around the city**, you'll probably do it exclusively on foot, since the old town area where you'll want to spend most time is compact and ideal for strolling. There is a bus service whose six routes cover the greater city; you're more likely to use a **taxi** for short hops – there are ranks at the train station, Plaça Catalunya and Plaça Independencia.

Accommodation

There are plenty of **places to stay** in Girona, including one or two *hostales* near the train station, though if you arrive at any reasonable time during the day it's much better to look for a place in or near the old town, which is also where you'll find the youth hostel. The nearest **campsite** is at Fornells de la Selva, 8km south of town and open all year (☎972/476117), though you might prefer to stay at livelier Banyoles, half an hour by bus to the west (see p.605).

Albergue Juvenil, c/dels Ciutadans 9, off Plaça del Vi (☎972/218003 or ☎972/201554). Girona's youth hostel has a good old town location and smart new facilities, including laundry, TV and video; reception open 8–11am and 6–10pm, breakfast included in the price, dinner available. But note that it's hardly any better value than the very cheapest of the *hostales*, and if you're over 25 it's actually more expensive. ①–②.

Fonda Barnet, c/Santa Clara 16 (☎972/200033). In a shambolic old block facing the river from the south side, near the Pont de Pedra. Basic, workaday rooms above the *comedor*, separate showers. ②.

Hostal Bellmirall, c/Bellmirall 3 (☎972/204009). An attractive old town choice, close to the cathedral and very pleasantly turned out, with stone walls and awash with artefacts and paintings. There are only seven rooms (with and without bath), so book ahead. The price includes breakfast. ④.

Hostal Brindis, Avda. Ramón Folch 13 (☎972/203039). Near the post office in the modern part of town, this two-star *hostal* keeps its prices fairly low, and has rooms with and without bath. ②–③.

Pensión Gerunda, c/de Barcelona 34 (☎972/202285). Just to the right of the train station, on the main road, this reasonably priced standby is handy for late arrivals. ③.

Hotel Peninsular, c/Nou 3 (☎972/203800). A large hotel on a busy shopping street. What it lacks in charm it makes up for in location, just a stride away from the bridge and river. Less expensive rooms also available without bath. ④.

Habitaciones Perez, Plaça Bell-lloc 4 (☎972/224008). The most basic rooms (mainly singles) in Girona, in a very gloomy building in an even gloomier part of town. It's off c/Nou del Teatre, just over Pont de Pedra. ②.

Hostal Reyma, Pujada Rei Martí 15 (☎972/200228). The best choice at the budget end of the scale. Surprizingly good value, nice rooms (some with balcony) with and without shower, and an excellent location very near the archaeological museum. ③.

Pension Viladomat, c/Ciutadans 5 (☎972/203176). Popular place whose airy rooms (with bath) fill quickly in July and August due to its very central location. At the bottom end of its price category; breakfast available for 350ptas. ③.

Around the city

Although the bulk of modern Girona lies on the south side of the Riu Onyar, bordered to the west by the large riverside Parc de la Devesa, most visitors spend nearly all their time in the **old city**, over the river. This thin wedge of land, tucked under the hillside, contains all the sights and monuments, and as it takes only half an hour or so to walk from end to end it's easy to explore thoroughly. A zone of high walls, stepped streets, closed gates and hidden courtyards, the old city has been zealously preserved. Recent restorations mean that many of the oldest buildings and arcades now house trendy galleries, exclusive shops, restaurants and bars. But here and there – around a corner or up a side alley – real life goes on much as it's always done, in local bars and shops.

The Catedral

The centrepiece of the old city is Girona's **Catedral** (daily 10am–6pm), a mighty Gothic structure built onto the hillside and approached by a magnificent flight of seventeenth-century Baroque steps. This area has been a place of worship since Roman times, and a Moorish mosque stood on the site before the foundation of the cathedral in 1038. Much of the present building dates from the fourteenth and fifteenth centuries, but a few earlier parts can still be seen – including the eleventh-century north tower, the *Torre de Carlomagno*, and the Romanesque cloisters with their exquisite sculpted capitals.

The main facade, remodelled in the eighteenth century, bursts with exuberant decoration: faces, bodies, coats-of-arms, and with Saints Peter and Paul flanking the door. Inside, the cathedral is awesome – there are no aisles, just one tremendous single-naved Gothic vault with a span of 22m, the largest in the world. This emphasis on width and height is a feature of Catalan Gothic with its "hall churches", of which, unsurprizingly, Girona's is the ultimate example. Contemporary sceptics declared the vault to be unsafe, and building only went ahead after an appeal by its designer, Guillermo Bofill, to a panel of architects. The huge sweep of stone rises to bright stained glass, the only thing obstructing the grand sense of space being the enormous organ, placed there a century ago.

You can visit the cloisters by buying a ticket to the **Museu Capitular** (Tues–Sat 10am–2pm & 4–7pm, Sun 10am–2pm; 300ptas), inside the cathedral, which in this case is certainly a good idea. The museum is rich in religious art, including a perfect *Beatus* illuminated by Mozarabic miniaturists in 975, and the famous eleventh- to twelfth-century *Creation Tapestry* in the end room – the best piece of Romanesque textile in existence, depicting in strong colours the months and seasons, and elements of the earth. The irregularly shaped **cloisters** themselves (1180–1210) boast minutely carved figures and scenes on double columns, while steps lead up to a chamber above full of ecclesiastical garb and adornments.

The Museu d'Art

If you find the collection in the cathedral's museum remotely interesting, the large **Museu d'Art** (Tues–Sat 10am–7pm, winter closes at 6pm, Sun 10am–2pm; 100ptas)

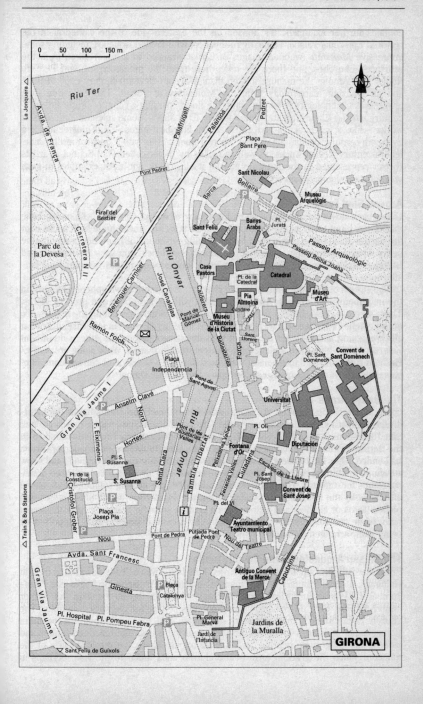

GIRONA

contains further examples; it's housed on the eastern side of the cathedral in the restored Episcopal Palace. The early rooms deal with Romanesque art, including some impressive *Majestats* (wooden images of Christ wrapped in a tunic) taken from the province's churches, and there are relics here from the monastery of Sant Pere de Rodes, too. Among the manuscripts on display are an eleventh-century copy of Bede and an amazing martyrology from the Monastery of Poblet. The collection then progresses chronologically as you climb the floors, passing a room of bright fifteenth-century *retables* (their intricate scenes almost 3D in effect), some splendid *Renaixement* works – like a lovely set of sixteenth-century liturgical items – and nineteenth- and twentieth-century Catalan art on the top two floors. Here you'll find some fine nineteenth-century Realist works, as well as pieces by the so-called Olot School of artists (better represented in the museum at Olot itself; p.611), and even examples of local *modernista* and *noucentista* art.

Around Sant Feliu

Climb back down the cathedral steps for a view of one of Girona's best-known landmarks, the blunt tower of the large church of **Sant Feliu**, whose huge bulk backs onto the narrow main street. Shortened by a lightning strike in 1581 and never rebuilt, the belfry tops a hemmed-in church that happily combines Romanesque, Gothic and Baroque styles; you can usually get in for a look around in the morning and late-afternoon.

The streets behind the church, by the river, are a bit more down-at-heel than most in the neighbourhood; **c/de la Barça** is typical, with its bare bars and grocery stores. There's even a red-light area of sorts, though that's rather overstating the importance of the couple of hidden stairways and the odd loitering person. In any case, it's not at all threatening and provides a contrast with the streets just on the other side of Sant Feliu church, which have undergone a genteel transformation. Walk along arcaded **c/Ballesteries** and you'll immediately see the difference – the ancient houses along here have been converted into swish gallery space and antique shops.

The Banys Arabs

Close to Sant Feliu, through the twin-towered Portal de Sobreportas below the cathedral, are Girona's so-called **Banys Arabs** (Tues–Sat 10am–7pm, winter closes at 6pm, Sun 10am–2pm; 100ptas), a civil building probably designed by Moorish craftsmen in the thirteenth century, a couple of hundred years after the Moors' occupation of Girona had ended. They are the best preserved baths in Spain after those at Granada and show a curious mixture of Arab and Romanesque styles. The layout, a series of three principal rooms for different temperatures, with an under-floor heating system, is influenced ultimately by the Romans. The cooling room (the *frigidarium*) is the most interesting; niches (for your clothes) and a stone bench provide seats for relaxation after the steam bath, while the room is lit, most unusually, by a central skylight-vault supported by octagonally arranged columns.

The Museu Arqueològic and the city walls

From the cathedral square, the main street, Pujada Rei Marti, leads downhill to the Riu Galligans, a small tributary of the Onyar. The **Museu Arqueològic** (Tues–Sat 10am–1pm & 4.30–7pm, Sun 10am–1pm; 100ptas) stands on the far bank in the former church of Sant Pere de Galligans, a harmonious setting for the varied exhibits. The church itself holds Roman statuary, sarcophagi and mosaics, while the beautiful Romanesque cloisters contain the heavier medieval relics, like inscribed tablets and stones, including some bearing Jewish inscriptions. These are the best parts of the museum, since the graceful form of the church adds much to the visit; perhaps in recognition of this, there's a full-size copy of the church's ornate twelfth-century rose window planted amidst the Roman finds. The extensive rooms above the cloisters go on to outline rather methodically the region's history from Paleolithic times to the Romanization of the area: unless you read Spanish or Catalan you'll get little out of the lines of exhibit-filled cases and explanatory maps.

From the museum you can gain access to the **Passeig Arqueològic**, where steps and landscaped grounds lead up to the walls of the old city. There are fine views out over the rooftops and the cathedral, and endless little diversions into old watchtowers, down blind dead-ends and around crumpled sections of masonry. The walls and the little paths lead right around the perimeter of the city, with several other points of access or egress along the way: by the Banys Arabs, behind the Sant Domènec convent, and down by Plaça Catalunya at the eastern end of the old city.

Carrer de la Força and the Call

Quite apart from its Roman remains and Arab influences, Girona also contains the best preserved **Jewish quarter** in western Europe. There is evidence that Jews settled in Girona before the Moorish invasion, although the first mention of a real settlement – based in the streets around the cathedral – dates from the end of the ninth century. Gradually, the settlement spread, having as its main street the **c/de la Força**, which in turn followed the course of the old Roman road, Via Augusta. The area was known as the **Call** and at its height was home to around three hundred people who formed a sort of independent town within Girona, protected by the king in return for payment. From the eleventh century onwards, however, the Jewish community suffered systematic and escalating persecution, with attacks on them and their homes by local people: in 1391 a mob killed forty of the Call's residents, while the rest were locked up in a Roman fortress until the fury had subsided. For the next hundred years, until the expulsion of the Jews from Spain in 1492, the Call was effectively a ghetto, its residents restricted to its limits, forced to wear distinguishing clothing if they did leave, and prevented from having doors or windows opening onto c/de la Força.

For an idea of the layout of this sector of tall, narrow houses and maze-like interconnecting passages, visit the **Centre Bonastruc Ça Porta**, formerly the *Centre Isaac el Cec* (June–Oct Mon–Sat 10am–6pm, Sun 10am–2pm; Nov–May Tues–Sun 10am–2pm; free), which is signposted (to *Call Jeue*) up the skinniest of stepped streets off c/de la Força. Opened to the public in 1975, the complex of rooms, staircases, a courtyard and adjoining buildings off c/de Sant Llorenç is an attempt to give an impression of the cultural and social life of Girona's medieval Jewish community – this was the site of the synagogue (though the exact spot hasn't yet been identified), the butcher's shop and the community baths. Work is still going on here, with other nearby alleys currently sealed off but awaiting reopening, and there's an information office on the site, a café and a quiet place just to sit and contemplate the difficulties of a life confined to these dark nooks and crannies.

The Museu d'Historia de la Ciutat

A little way back up c/de la Força, at no. 27, the **Museu d'Historia de la Ciutat** (Tues–Sat 10am–2pm & 5–7pm, Sun 10am–2pm; free) completes Girona's set of museums. For casual, non-specialist browsing it's the most rewarding of the lot, housed in an eighteenth-century convent. Remains of the convent's cemetery are visible as you enter, with niches reserved for the preserved bodies of the inhabitants. The rest of the collection is fascinating, less for the insights into how Girona developed as a city – though this is explained efficiently through text, exhibits and photos – than for the strange, miscellaneous bits and pieces displayed. A circuit of the rooms shows you old radios from the 1930s, a 1925 Olivetti typewriter, a printing press, cameras, machine tools, engines and a dozen other mechanical and electrical delights.

Eating and drinking

Girona's chic **bars** and **restaurants** are grouped on c/de la Força, on and around the riverside Rambla Llibertat and on the parallel Plaça del Vi – the last two places being where you'll also find the best daytime cafés with outdoor seating. Another little enclave of restaurants with good *menús del día* is over the river in Plaça de la Independencia. For something less touristy – and much less expensive – explore the streets near Sant Feliu church, where there's a run of old-men's bars and some inexpensive *comedors*. Carrer Ballesteries, nearby, is more upmarket: there's a trendy un-named bar at no. 23, with window seats looking out over the river, typical of the places Girona's youth frequent.

Restaurants

Fonda Barnet, c/Santa Clara 16. The *comedor* of this *fonda* is the best value in Girona, and the food is much better than the fairly basic surroundings suggest (though it's not going to win any prizes).

Boira, Plaça de la Independencia 17. The best food on the square and very popular with locals and visitors alike – 1100ptas or so buys a very Catalan *menú*.

Can Lluis, c/dels Alemanys 3. Pizzas and salads, just around the corner from the *Hostal Bellmirall*. It's a good choice for vegetarians. Closed Mon.

Bar-Restaurant Los Jara, c/de la Força 4. The best value on this central street, with a big budget *menú del día* served in the stone-walled *comedor* behind the bar. The waiter rattles off plenty of choices to hungry local workers from 1–4pm and also in the evening.

La Penyora, c/Nou del Teatre 3. Staunchly Catalan restaurant hidden away and worth seeking out. There's a 1500ptas *menú del día* and a reasonable if limited à la carte choice. Closed Tues.

El Pou del Call, c/de la Força 14. Good local food and wine right in the Jewish quarter in a very pleasant and friendly restaurant. Around 2000ptas a head. Closed Sun night.

Bars and cafés

Antiga, Plaça del Vi 8. Marble-tabled *xocolateria*, with a good line in cakes, *orxata* and other delights.

L'Arcada, Rambla Llibertat 38. Bar-restaurant situated underneath the arcade with a pleasant old-time interior, and serving good breakfast pastries in the morning. Outdoor tables are a good place to relax in summer.

Café Bistrot, Pujada de Sant Domènec. Snacks, crèpes and drinks either outside on the steps below the church, or inside in cool, jazzy surroundings.

Cafeteria Sol, Plaça del Vi. Stylish hang-out for *tapas* and snacks, with seats inside or in the arcade.

Listings

Airport Call ☎972/202350 for flight information.

Banks and exchange There's an exchange office at the train station, and you'll find banks along the Rambla Llibertat.

Buses From the bus station (☎972/212319), there are *Rafael Mas* services (☎972/213227) to Lloret de Mar; *SARFA* (☎972/201796) to Tossa, Palafrugell and Sant Feliu; *Teisa* (☎972/200275) to Olot; and express services to Barcelona and Figueres.

Car rental Most agencies are close to the train station on c/Barcelona: *Avis* (☎972/206933) and *Hertz* (☎972/210108).

Car trouble Contact *Reial Automobil Club de Catalunya*, c/de Barcelona 30 (☎972/200868).

Emergencies Dial ☎092 or contact the *Cruz Roja* (☎972/222222).

Hospital *Hospital de Girona*, Avda. França 60 (☎972/202700).

Newspapers British and American newspapers available at the train station and at shops along Rambla Llibertat.

Police *Policia Municpal* at c/Bacià 4 (☎972/204526); *Guardia Civil* (☎972/201100).

Post office At Avda. Ramón Folch 2; Mon–Sat 8am–9pm.

Telephone office At Gran Via de Jaume I 58; Mon–Sat 9am–9pm.

Trains *RENFE* information on ☎972/207093.

Banyoles

For an escape into the countryside around Girona, take a bus to **BANYOLES**, half an hour (17km) north of the city. Here, the Pyrenees are on the horizon and the town basks around its greatest attraction – the lake, famed for its enormous carp. The lake has been under state protection since 1951, something that kept Banyoles little developed until it was announced that the 1992 Olympic rowing events would be held here. Most of the lakeside closest to town was consequently redeveloped, with tourist boats, new hotels and fancy restaurants much in evidence. Even so, it remains an attractive place to visit, with an old town which has escaped much of the recent building and plenty of opportunities for walking around the lake on shaded footpaths, beyond the new development.

The town and lake

Banyoles grew up around a monastery originally founded by Benedictines in 812. This, the **Monestir de Sant Esteve** at the eastern end of town, is still easily the biggest structure in old Banyoles, and though it's usually locked, you might try asking around for the key holder who lives nearby. If you do get in, don't miss the magnificent fifteenth-century retablo by Joan Antigo. The medieval streets which lead back into town from here are full of other ancient buildings, including an almshouse and a dye market. In the end, all streets lead to the central **Plaça Major**, a lovely tree-lined, arcaded space with several café-bars and a Wednesday market that has been held here since the eleventh century.

From the square, signs point the way to the **Museu Arqueològic Comarcal** (July & Aug daily 10.30am–1pm & 4.30–8pm; Sept–June Tues–Sun 10.30am–1.30pm & 4–6.30pm; 250ptas), installed in a fourteenth-century poorhouse in Plaça de la Font. The museum used to contain the famous jawbone of a pre-Neanderthal man found in the nearby Serinya caves, but nowadays you have to make do with a replica: authentic specimens include Palaeolithic tools, and bison, elephant and lion bones, all found locally. The **Museu Municipal Darder d'Historia Natural** (same hours and combined ticket with the Museu Arqueològic), in nearby Plaça dels Estudis, has a useful display of local flora and fauna.

The Estany de Banyoles

The lake itself – the **Estany de Banyoles** – is a fifteen-minute walk from Plaça Major. It's long been used for water sports, so the Olympic choice wasn't surprizing, and although there's little distinctive or attractive about the area nearest the centre, a thirty-minute walk through the woods around the southern edge takes you to the tiny hamlet of **PORQUERES**, where the water is at its deepest (63m). Here the elegant Romanesque church of **Santa Maria** was consecrated in 1182 and has a barrel-vaulted interior, and unusual capitals with plant and animal designs. The lake itself boasts a whole series of **boating** options – cruises, rowing boats and pedaloes – all of which run to a few hundred pesetas for an hour's fooling about on the water.

Practicalities

Buses all stop on Passeig de la Industria, with the bus office (where you buy onward tickets) nearby at the corner of the main road, c/Alvarez de Castro. Cross this road and signs point you down to Plaça Major, two minutes' away. The **Turismo** is in the other direction, along Passeig de la Industria at no. 25 (Mon–Fri 10am–3pm & 5–7pm, Sat 10am–1pm; June–Aug also open Sat afternoon & Sun; ☎972/575573) – and the lake ten minutes' further away. For local **trekking information**, the *Centre Excursionista de*

Banyoles, c/del Puig 6, near Sant Esteve, seems to be open most evenings and has a wide range of maps available and tips on local routes.

With Girona so close, there is no advantage in staying in Banyoles, whose **hotels** are expensive anyway. If you do want to stay – and the prospect of a lakeside hotel in summer might persuade you – the **Turismo** can give you an accommodation list. The most pleasant old town hotel is *Fonda Comas*, c/del Canal 19 (☎972/570127; ③), off Plaça dels Estudis, near the Darder museum: this immaculate building, with stone staircases and its own courtyard and restaurant, has nice rooms with and without bath (closed Sat in winter).

Camping is perhaps a more attractive proposition here than in most places. There's a large site, *El Llac* (☎972/570305), which you'll pass on the walk to Porqueres, just before the church, and another three in the vicinity. All of them are included on the tourist office's accommodation list.

There are plenty of places to **eat and drink** in the old town. The *menú del día* at the *Fonda Comas* is 1400ptas, and usually very good, while cheaper meals are served at *Les Olles*, Plaça dels Estudis 6 – whose main attraction is an English-language menu offering such rare treats as "Coptel Toad Fish" and "Pork Cheeks". Eating in the hotel-restaurants overlooking the lake is more expensive, though the *Mirallac*, Passeig Darder 50, won't break the bank as long as you eat meat rather than fish. Best place for an evening **drink** or just a sandwich is Plaça Major, whose café-bars spill under the medieval arcades.

Besalú

From the road, the imposing eleventh-century bridge by the confluence of the Fluvià and Capellada rivers is the only sign that there is anything remarkable about BESALÚ, 14km north of Banyoles (and connected by regular daily buses). But walk a couple of minutes into the town and you enter a medieval settlement virtually untainted by tourism – probably the most attractive and interesting small town in Catalunya, perfect for a half-day's outing.

Although the restorers' cement is barely dry in places, the steep narrow streets, dusty squares and dark archways exude a sense of history. Besalú was an important town from early times, and when the Moors were expelled from this corner of Spain, it was one of several independent kingdoms that arose to fill the vacuum. Despite a total population of just eight hundred it prospered, as it had done in a small way since Roman times, and remained a place of importance well into the fourteenth century. In appearance the town is almost completely medieval, boasting some striking monuments quite out of proportion to its current humble status. Unfortunately, most of the churches and sights in Besalú are firmly locked – not a great disappointment in a place where strolling around is a real pleasure. However, if you ask at the Turismo, they'll either arrange a guided tour for you or have them unlocked so that you can visit them properly.

Around town

The most striking reminder of Besalú's grandeur is the splendid eleventh-century **Pont Fortificat** – fortified bridge – over the river Fluvià. In the middle stands a fortified gatehouse complete with portcullis. Down to the left beyond the bridge the **Miqwé**, or Jewish bath-house, was originally attached to a synagogue positioned in the old Jewish quarter in the heart of the lower town, along the riverbank.

Plaça Llibertat, in the centre of Besalú, is entirely enclosed by medieval buildings, including the elegant thirteenth-century Casa de la Vila, which now houses the *Ajuntament*. There's a weekly market in the square each Tuesday. The majestically porticoed c/Tallaferro leads up from here to the ruined shell of **Santa María** (you can't get inside), which for just two years (1018–20) was designated Cathedral of the Bishopric of Besalú; union with Barcelona meant the end of its short-lived episcopal independence.

In the other direction, the twelfth-century monastery church of **Sant Pere** is the sole remnant of the town's Benedictine community, which was founded in 977. It stands in its own square, El Prat de Sant Pere, from where the most eye-catching feature is the window in the otherwise severe main facade, flanked by a pair of grotesque stone lions. Across the square – almost all of which has been heavily restored over the last few years – is the **Casa Cornellà**, a rare example of Romanesque domestic building which houses a museum of assorted antique domestic and agricultural implements. Elsewhere in the web of cobbled streets radiating from Plaça Llibertat, you'll come across other attractive buildings – many sporting stone flourishes, ornate windows and columns. Finally, you can work your way around to the delightful little church of **Sant Vicenç**, close to the main Olot–Banyoles road in a plant-decked square with a café-restaurant and outdoor seating. The church (its entrance arches decorated with mythical monsters) is a lovely example of Catalan Romanesque.

Practicalities

The **bus** stop is on the main Olot–Banyoles road, from where the quickest way into the centre is to walk down the main road towards the *Fonda Siqués* (see below) and then turn right down the little street that leads past the back of Sant Vicenç straight into Plaça Llibertat. The **Turismo** is on c/Major (June–Sept Mon–Sat 9.30am–2pm & 3.30–7pm, Sun 10am–2pm & 4–7pm; ☎972/591240), where you can pick up a map and fix up your tour.

The town has three very comfortable and quite reasonable **places to stay** and making use of one of them is a very attractive proposition as in the daytime Besalú is prey to whirlwind coach parties, while by early evening it has settled down to its own infinitely preferable pace of life. The *Fonda Siqués* (☎972/590110; ④) is at Avda. Lluis Companys 6, on the main road just down from the bus stop; the *Residencia Maria* (☎972/590106; ③) is better positioned, right on Plaça Llibertat; while the best budget choice is perhaps the *Fonda Venencia*, opposite the Turismo at c/Major 8 (☎972/591257; ③), which is very spick and span and at the lower end of the price scale.

The first two of these places serve **food**: the *Fonda Siqués* has a *menú del día* for around 1000ptas (Nov–Easter, closed Mon), while the *Curia Reial* (closed Tues and Jan) can seat you on the outdoor terrace next to the square, and has a beautiful patio at the rear overlooking the bridge. Eating at both places can lead to rather large bills if you don't have the *menú del día*. Cheaper meals can be found at the *Can Quei*, Plaça Sant Vicenç 4, outside the church of the same name, where there's an 900ptas *menú del día*, as well as sandwiches and *platos combinados*. *Pont Vell*, c/Pont Vell 28, is much more expensive (around 3000ptas a head), but beautifully situated, with outdoor tables more or less under the bridge.

The Garrotxa region

Besalú is on the eastern edge of the lush and beautiful **Garrotxa region**, bisected by the Fluvià river and the main C150 road. The northern part – the **Alta Garrotxa** – is an area of deserted farms set amid low mountains, bursting with attractive trekking possibilities. The bus runs through Alta Garrotxa on its way from Besalú to Olot, and in parts the route is spectacular – as at **Castellfollit de la Roca**, where the houses peer over a sheer basalt cliff. South of the Fluvià lies volcanic **Baixa Garrotxa**, where over ten thousand years of erosion have moulded the dormant cones into rounded and fertile hills. The tiny C524, from Banyoles to Olot via **Santa Pau** (an infrequent bus route), takes in the terrific walking in the **Parc Natural de la Zona Volcanica** and the remnants of the great beech wood known as **La Fageda d'en Jorda**.

Alta Garrotxa: around Castellfollit de la Roca

Fourteen kilometres west of Besalú, along the C150, **CASTELLFOLLIT DE LA ROCA** presents its best aspect as you climb up the main road to the village. It's built on the edge of a precipice that falls sixty metres sheer to the Fluvià river, with the church crowded by houses onto the very rim of the cliff. It's an impressive sight from a distance (even more so at night, when spotlights play on the natural basalt columns), but as you pass through the village itself on the busy main road you could be forgiven for wondering what happened to it: it's a dirty, dangerous bottleneck, with tightly packed rows of grubby brown buildings which give no hint of anything out of the ordinary.

If you're in no hurry to reach Olot, however, you can get off the bus to take in the view from the top of the village over the edge of the cliff. Walk down past the clock tower, by the *fonda* on the main road, and you'll come out by the church at the head of the cliff, which juts out above the valley for a kilometre or more. Having gasped at the drop, and poked around the huddled houses, you can simply hang around for the next bus to Olot, or you could walk on to nearby Sant Joan les Fonts. Thrill-seekers will also want to stay long enough to view Castellfollit's unlikely **Museum of Sausages** (Mon–Sat 9.30am–1.30pm & 4–8pm, Sun 9.30am–2pm & 4.30–8pm), which celebrates the local Sala family's 150 years in the skin-stuffing business. The family is almost certainly right in claiming the museum as unique.

Castellfollit is the starting point for some of the region's best **treks** (see below), heading north and northeast through the Alta Garrotxa. You could easily enough stay in Olot, but if you want an early start then the *Fonda Ca La Paula*, Plaça de Sant Roc 3 (☎972/294015; ③), on the main road through Castellfollit, is very reasonable and has a restaurant and a decent bar attached.

Alta Garrotxa treks

The **Alta Garrotxa** stretches north from the main C150 road as far as the peaks along the French border. For speleologists, the region is amost inexhaustible, with more than a hundred catalogued caves, and for walkers it's a fabulous area as well. Whichever of the three routes given below you follow (all begin just outside Castellfollit), the *Editorial Alpina* "Garrotxa" map is an invaluable aid.

It's around 7km from Castellfollit up the **Llierca valley** past **MONTAGUT DE FLUVIÀ** and another 6km on to **SADERNES** (minor road all the way), from where you can continue on the trail to the *Refugi de Santa Aniol*, right on the northern edge of the Garrotxa. From here, the Col de Massanes (1126m) border-crossing can be reached by continuing north on the footpath from the refuge, spending the next night at Coustouges or Saint-Laurent-de-Cerdans, both French villages in the Tech Valley.

Staying in Spain, two more routes head northeast into the **Ripoll region**. If you take the paved road to **OIX** (9km), you've a choice of tracks towards Camprodon, either passing just north of the summits of El Tallo (1288m) and Puig Ou (1306m), or going on through the hamlet of Beget. The route continues through Rocabruna to Camprodon (see p.619), a day's hike all told. Alternatively, there's the shorter **Carreras valley** track to **SANT PAU DE SEGURIES** via the Col de Collcarrera; the only facility en route is the *Can Planes* (☎972/294478; ④ b&b, ⑤ half-board), well before the pass, where you might be able to get a snack at short notice. At Sant Pau, you're on the Ripoll–Camprodon bus route.

Sant Joan les Fonts

For less energetic souls, **SANT JOAN LES FONTS** is no more than a three-kilometre walk from Castellfollit, along the less direct road to Olot. You'll soon see its enormous monastery-church in the distance, high above the river, and although on a main road, the walk is scenic and enjoyable. Once in the village follow the signs to the *Columnes Basaltiques* – basalt cliffs – and you'll cross the restored medieval bridge, which stands beneath the massive twelfth-century walls of the Romanesque Sant Esteve (usually locked). From the bridge, a path leads up along the right-hand side of the church and then snakes down to the impressive basalt cliffs, part of the *fonts*, or waterfalls, which give the village its name. It all makes for a very pleasant diversion, splashing around the rocks and river, having a drink in one of the small village bars – and afterwards you can either walk or hitch the 4km on to Olot, or wait for the bus, which passes through Sant Joan on its way from Besalú.

Baixa Garrotxa: along the C524

Most of the **Baixa Garrotxa** region – accessible on the minor C254 which runs between Banyoles and Olot – is volcanic in origin, and has been within the **Parc Natural de la Zona Volcanica de la Garrotxa**, which covers almost 12,000 hectares, since 1985. It's one of the most interesting such areas in Europe, the road passing through a beautiful wooded landscape, climbing and dipping around the craters, offering some lovely valley views. It's not, however, a zone of belching steam and boiling mud. It's been 11,500 years since the last eruption, during which time the ash and lava have weathered into a fertile soil whose luxuriant vegetation masks the contours of the dormant volcanoes. There are thirty cones in all in the area, the largest of them some 160m high and 1500m across the base.

If you don't have your own transport, you'll find **access** a little problematic, since the only **bus** is the twice-weekly Olot–Mieres–Banyoles service (currently Wed & Sat at 12.45pm from Banyoles, 7.15am from Olot) to Santa Pau, the central village of the volcanic zone. As it's certainly worth making the effort to see the region, you might consider instead **staying in Olot** (see below) and walking to Santa Pau from there – it's three hours by track and trail, with the added bonus of passing through the beautiful Fageda d'en Jorda beech forest.

Santa Pau

Medieval **SANTA PAU** presents to the outside world a defensive perimeter of continuous and almost windowless house walls. Inside the village, balconies drip with flowers, steps and walls are tufted with grass and huge potted plants line the pavement arcades – it's a village positively reeking with atmosphere, that would make a smashing base for some gentle local walking. Santa Pau is usually quiet, busy only on Sunday with trippers, who crowd into the local restaurants. The rest of the time you're likely to be on your own as you negotiate the cobbled alleys, which converge on the thirteenth-century, arcaded Plaça Major, with its dark Romanesque church of Santa María and an **information centre** that's only open sporadically, but which is good for trekking information and for a free map of the volcanic zone.

In the square adjacent to Plaça Major, Plaçeta dels Balls, you'll find the *Cal Sastre* (☎972/680421; ④, ⑤ half-board), which has seven **rooms** available in the summer, a decent restaurant, and tables outside in the medieval arcade which are just right for a beer. There are a couple of other places to eat in the village, but nowhere so nice to stay. If the *Cal Sastre* is full, you'll have to fall back on the less desirable alternative out of the village on the main road, or **camp**: *Lava* (☎972/680358; open all year) is 3km up the road towards Olot, a large, well-positioned site in the shadow of two volcanic cones.

THE GARROTXA REGION'S FLORA AND FAUNA

The lower slopes of the Garrotxa region's distinctive hills are clothed with evergreen oak **forests**, grading into deciduous oak and beech woods, with sub-alpine meadows and pastures at higher altitudes. More than 1500 species of vascular plant have been recorded within the park, ranging from typical **forest herbs** like snowdrops, yellow wood anemones and rue-leaved isopyrum to high-altitude specialities like ramonda and Pyrenean saxifrage. In addition, the Garrotxa contains a number of Iberian rarities, several of which are found nowhere else in the world: the white-flowered *Allium pyrenaicum*, typical of rocky limestone cliffs, Pyrenean milkwort (*Polygala vayredae*), a woody species with large pinkish-purple flowers, and shrubby gromwell (*Lithodora oleifolia*), a scrambling plant with pale pink flowers that turn blue with age.

A phenomenal 143 species of **bird** have been observed in the region. Since three-quarters of the park is covered with forest, goshawks, tawny owls, short-toed treecreepers, great spotted woodpeckers and nuthatches are common. Flocks of bramblings and hawfinches take refuge in the beech woods during winter, while the more barren volcanic summits support alpine choughs and alpine accentors. Summer visitors include short-toed eagles, hobbies, wrynecks, red-backed shrikes and Bonelli's warblers, along with Mediterranean species such as sub-alpine warblers, golden orioles and bee-eaters.

Forest-dwelling **mammals** include beech martens, wildcats, genets, badgers and wild boar, as well as a number of small insectivores – common, pygmy and Etruscan shrews – and the noctural oak dormouse, characterized by its "Lone Ranger" mask and long, black-tufted tail. Otters are also sighted along the rivers from time to time.

A loop walk

An excellent way to get acquainted with the Baixa Garrotxa is to take a **loop walk** out of Olot which almost totally avoids paved roads and can easily be completed by any reasonably fit person in a single day. If you're not up for the full distance, you could arrange to be fetched at Santa Pau, roughly half way.

Begin in Olot by following the multiple signposts directing you across the Riu Fluvià, from where it's an hour south along surfaced country lanes, equally suited to horse-riding or mountain-biking (as is most of this circuit), to the **Fageda d'en Jordà**. Although much reduced, this beech forest is still a treat in the autumn when the leaves are turning; it takes about half an hour more to emerge on the far side of the spooky, maze-like groves, deserted except for the tourist *carruatges* (horsecarts) visiting from Santa Pau.

Turn left when you meet the helpfully marked **GR2** long-distance trail, then right twice in succession when you encounter the track to Sa Cot. Follow the signposts to stay on the GR2, soon becoming a proper path as it heads east for thirty minutes to the medieval chapel of **Sant Miquel de Sa Cot**, a popular weekend picnic spot.

The **Volcà Santa Margarida** is visible just behind and within forty minutes more, you should be up on its rim and then down into its grassy caldera, where another tiny chapel sits at the bottom. From the turn-off to the cone – just 15 minutes from Sant Miquel – you descend to the **Font de Can Roure**, source of the only water en route, before skirting Roca Negra with its disused quarry, then entering Santa Pau 45 minutes from the shoulder of Santa Margarida, and some three hours from Olot (not counting the detour to the caldera).

From Santa Pau the GR2 continues north towards the scenic **Serra de Sant Julià del Mont**, just east of which are two places to stay: *Can Jou* (☎908/137096; ③ B&B, ④ half-board), over two hours from Santa Pau, and *Rectoria la Miana* (☎972/223959; ③ B&B, ④ half-board), further east and housed in a twelfth-century monastery.

However for day-trekkers this would inconveniently lengthen the circuit, so you're best advised to bear west at **Can Mascou** and approach **Volcà Croscat** via the *Lava* campsite (see "Santa Pau" above). You skirt the northeast flank of Croscat, badly scarred by quarrying, and from the campsite it's another hour, along a progressively narrowing track unsigned except for 'BATET' painted on hunting-zone signs, to the high (720m) plateau of **Batet de la Serra**, scattered with handsome farms.

Here you meet a marked path-and-track coming west from the Serra de Sant Julià, turning west yourself to follow the road briefly before adopting the well-marked *camí* – beautiful and partly cobbled in basalt – which passes the hamlet of Santa Maria de Batet on its way down to Olot. It takes just under another hour of downhill progress, or a total of something less than seven hours in total, to emerge at the top of c/Sant Cristòfor, which runs right down to the main boulevard through Olot.

Olot

OLOT, the main town of the Garrotxa region, is a far nicer place than first impressions suggest. As you penetrate towards the centre, the industrial outskirts and snarling through roads give way to a series of narrow, old town streets and a pleasant rambla where the inhabitants go about their prosperous business. The centre is largely made up of attractive eighteenth- and nineteenth-century buildings, evidence of the destructive geological forces that surround the town: successive fifteenth-century earthquakes levelled the medieval town, and – thankfully dormant but easily accessible – three small volcanoes can be seen just to the north, reminders of the volcanic zone beyond.

Olot makes a good base for the Garrotxa: Santa Pau, Sant Joan les Fonts and Castellfollit are all easily reached, and there's a good choice of food and accommodation. It's a position not lost upon the local authorities who have done their best to counter Olot's previously rather dour tourist image – *Olot és natural* proclaim the noticeboards and, off the main roads, so it is.

The town

If you arrived by bus on the busy main through road, the older streets nearby, between Plaça Major and Sant Esteve church, are a revelation. Filled with fashionable shops, art galleries and smart patisseries, they tell of a continuing wealth, historically based on textiles and the production of religious statuary. **Sant Esteve** lies right at the heart of town, built high above the streets on a platform, its tower a useful landmark. Beyond the church, the central **rambla**, Passeig d'en Blay, is lined with pavement cafés and benches, and adorned by the delightful nineteenth-century Teatre Principal. Between 6pm and 8pm, this whole area teems with life as the well-dressed *passeig* swings into action.

Museu Comarcal de la Garrotxa

The substantial cotton industry that flourished here in the eighteenth century led indirectly to the emergence of Olot as an artistic centre: the finished cotton fabrics were printed with coloured drawings, a process that provided the impetus for the foundation of a Public School of Drawing in 1783. Joaquim Vayreda i Vila (1843–94), one of the founders of the so-called **Olot School** of painters, was a pupil of the school, but it was his trip to Paris in 1871 that was the true formative experience. There he came under the spell of Millet's paintings of rural life and scenery, and must have been aware of the work of the Impressionists. From these twin influences, and the strange Garrotxa scenery, evolved the distinctive and eclectic style of the Olot artists.

Some of the best pieces produced by the Olot School can be seen in the town's excellent museum, the **Museu Comarcal de la Garrotxa** (daily except Tues 11am–2pm & 4–7pm, also closed Sun afternoon; 200ptas), which occupies the third floor of a converted eighteenth-century hospital at c/Hospici 8, a side street off c/Mulleras. The first part of the museum traces the development of Olot through photos and models of its industries. The bulk of the collection, though, is work by local artists and sculptors, and it's an interesting and diverse set of paintings and figures. There's characteristic work by Ramon Amadeu, whose sculpted rural figures are particularly touching; Miquel Blay's work is more monumental, powerfully influenced by Rodin; while Joaquim Vayreda's *Les Falgueres* is typical of the paintings in its recreation of the Garrotxa light. By way of contrast – and indicative of a continuing artistic tradition in the town – there's also a room of modern ironwork sculpture and a few striking post-war paintings.

Jardí Botànic and the Casal dels Volcans

A twenty-minute walk from the centre are the town's landscaped botanical gardens, the **Jardí Botànic** (winter daily 10am–2pm & 4–6pm; summer 10am–2pm & 5–7pm; free); follow the signs for *Casal dels Volcans*. They're worth walking out to, not least because they contain the fascinating **Casal dels Volcans** itself (Mon–Fri 10am–2pm & 4–6pm, Sat 10am–2pm & 5–7pm, Sun 10am–2pm; free with Museu Comarcal ticket), a small museum devoted to the local volcanic region and housed in a Palladian building. Even if you don't speak Catalan or Castilian, you'll get a pretty good idea of the displays: there are photos and maps of the local craters, rock chunks and a seismograph, and even a "what to do in an earthquake" series of explanatory drawings (the answer appears to be to run like hell). The building also houses an information centre on activities in the Garrotxa volcanic zone.

Practicalities

The **bus station** is on the main road through town and there's a **Turismo** right opposite on c/Bispe Lorenzana (Mon–Fri 9am–2pm & 3–7pm, Sat 10am–2pm; ☎972/260141), and another, privately funded, one further down at at c/Mulleras 33 (Mon–Fri 9am–1pm & 4–7pm; ☎972/270242) – take your pick. Both have English-speaking staff, contain a good stock of local brochures, maps and timetables, and hand out accommodation lists and information on the volcanic zone. More local **trekking information** can be had from the *Centro Excursionista de Olot*, irregularly open, next to the theatre on the Passeig d'en Blay; maps and guides are sold at the *DRAC* bookshop, at the bottom of the *passeig*.

Accommodation

There are several reasonable *hostales* in the centre of town. Least expensive is the *Hostal Stop*, c/Sant Pere Màrtir 29 (☎972/261048; ②), which looks a bit decrepit but is fine – large rooms with separate shower. *La Garrotxa*, Plaça Móra 3 (☎972/261612; ②), is just a little pricier but better placed, just past the museum entrance above a tiny square. More expensive all round, though very pleasant and in a better position yet, just off Plaça Major, the *Pension Narmar*, c/Sant Roc 1 (☎972/269807; ③), has clean modern rooms with sinks, and its own restaurant-patisserie on the ground floor.

Hostal Sant Bernat, Ctra. de les Feixes 31 (☎972/261919; ②) is a bit out-of-the-way towards the northeast end of the town, but is quiet and friendly, with some rooms with bath. It's a good alternative to the *Narmar*, and with its locking garage the best choice if you've a car or bike. The **youth hostel**, *Alberg Torre Malagrida* (☎972/264200; closed Sept and Sun–Mon in winter; ①) is southwest of the centre on Passeig de Barcelona, overlooking the river, about halfway to the Casal dels Volcans; it's open 8–10am and 1pm–midnight. Closest **campsites** are *Les Tries* (☎972/262405), 2km east of town on the way to Girona, or *La Fageda* (☎972/271239), 4km out on the minor road to Santa Pau.

Eating, drinking and nightlife

For **Catalan food**, look no further than *Can Guix*, c/Mulleras 3 (closed Sun), a cheery bar-restaurant where lines form for the large servings. It's all well-cooked, and you can eat mightily for just over 1000ptas – the local wine is served in a *porrón*, but you get a glass to decant it into if you chicken out. Middling- to high-priced Catalan dishes are served at *Ramon*, Plaça Clara 10, and even if you don't eat here, the bar under the arches is a good vantage point for a drink. Don't forget the restaurant at the *Narmar* (see above), while *Font de l'Angel* on Plaça Móra is a snack-bar/café with garden seating and inexpensive *menús*; it closes on Sunday after characteristically lively Saturday nights. If you're in need of a change of diet, Olot has a health-food store and **vegetarian restaurant**, *La Vegetal*, at c/dels Sastres 43 (open noon–7pm, closed Tues and Sun) – tasty if slightly on the expensive side. Finally, at Passeig d'en Blay 49, the *Set al Gust* **pizzeria** is smart and trendy, though it includes things you hoped you'd never see on a pizza (like *bacalau*...); pizza and local wine runs to around 1500ptas a head.

More than a dozen **bars and cafés** are scattered between the bullring and Plaça Carme at the eastern end of the Barri Antic. Aside from some obvious ones on the Passeig d'en Blay (itself the best place for an outdoor drink), choose among genteel artiness (*Cocodrilo*, on c/Sant Roc), grunge (a raucous bar in an apparently abandoned store on Plaça Móra), post-modernism (the *crêperie* on Plaça del Mig) or just plain passé (*Disco Up*, just off Passeig d'en Blay). There are even two **cinemas**, *Colom* on the *passeig* being classier than *Nuria* near Plaça Carmé. Most events of the **summer festival** take place in the Plaça del Mig, behind the museum.

The Montseny region

South of Girona, the train line and main road to Barcelona both give a wide berth to the province's other great natural attraction, the **Serra del Montseny**, a chain of mountains that rises in parts to 1700m. It's a well-forested region, and from it comes the bulk of Catalunya's mineral water, which is bottled in small spa villages. You can approach either from Girona or Barcelona, though if you're using public transport you'll have to be prepared to stay the night in whichever village you aim for, since the infrequent services rarely allow for day trips. The company which operates most of the routes below is *La Hispano Hilariense*, whose buses leave from the bus station in Girona or from the *Bar La Bolsa*, c/Consolat 45, in Barcelona's Plaça de Palau.

Breda and Riells

The bus route from Girona into the region passes through **HOSTALRIC**, an old walled village in the heart of a cork-oak growing district, but **BREDA**, about 6km further on, is a better place to call a halt – known for its ceramic shops, and adorned by a Gothic church with an eleventh-century tower.

There's a fork at Breda, with a minor road (and occasional local bus) running the 7km up to **RIELLS**, which provides your first real glimpse of the hills. There's not much to Riells, and not much to do except stroll around the pretty surroundings, but there is a good place to stay just before the village: *Hostal Marlet* (☎972/870943; ③), with a garden and restaurant. It's open July and August and weekends throughout the year, and you have to take full board.

Sant Hilari Sacalm

The main bus route continues up the other road, past Arbúcies, with the views getting ever more impressive as you approach **SANT HILARI SACALM** (1hr 20min from Girona, 2hr from Barcelona). Perched at around 800m above sea level, Sant Hilari is a pleasant spa town that could make an enjoyable base for a couple of days. It's big enough to support a whole range of hotels and *hostales* – many catering for people taking the curative local waters, and consequently open only during the summer (July–Sept). The central *Hostal Torras*, Plaça Gravalosa 13 (☎972/868096; ③–④), seems to stay open most of the year, and serves good food, as does the excellent *Hostal Brugués*, c/Valls 4 (☎972/868018; ③), which conjures up delicious Catalan cooking. A **Turismo** (July–Sept Mon–Sat 10am–2pm & 4–6pm, Sun 10am–2pm; ☎972/868826), at the junction of the main roads through town, has details of all bus connections in the area.

Viladrau

If you're driving, it's a splendid, winding twelve-kilometre ride southwest to **VILADRAU**, another spa town set slightly higher in the mountains though not as large as Sant Hilari. By public transport, you have to approach from the other side of the range, by taking the train from Barcelona to Balenyá (on the line to Vic) and connecting with the local bus from there for the twenty-kilometre ride to Viladrau. Even this is not easy, as there are currently only two services a week from Balenyá; check first in Barcelona.

Being more difficult to reach, Viladrau manages to preserve a very tranquil feel within its old streets and attractive surrounding countryside. There are plenty of local wooded walks, and half a dozen places to stay should the area appeal to you. *Fonda La Moderna*, c/Pare Claret 1 (☎93/8849061; ③) is about the least expensive.

THE CATALAN PYRENEES

Away from the coast and city you don't have to travel very far before you reach the foothills of the **Catalan Pyrenees**, the easternmost stretch of the mountain chain that divides Spain and France. From Barcelona, you can reach **Ripoll** by train in just a couple of hours. The area north of here has been extensively developed as a skiing centre: out of season (in summer) it's much quieter, which is all to the good if you just want some gentle rambling in and around places like **Camprodon**. A longer trip can take in the private train line up to **Núria** (itself a major ski centre), one of the most stunning rides in Catalunya. Further north, by the French border, **Puigcerdà** boasts the only surviving train link with France over the Pyrenees; while wholly enclosed within France lies the odd Spanish enclave of **Llívia**.

For serious Pyrenean walking – and a wider range of scenery, flora and fauna – you need to head further west, beyond **La Seu d'Urgell** and the adjacent duty-free principality of **Andorra**, which mark roughly the middle of the Catalan Pyrenees. Although more developed (with hydroelectric projects in particular) than, say, the Aragonese stretch to the west, the trekking is some of the best in the whole Pyrenees. The **Noguera Pallaresa** valley, the **Vall d'Aran** and the superbly scenic **Parc Nacional d'Aigües Tortes** are all reasonably accessible, containing routes and treks that novices will be able to follow as well as more specialist terrain. A further lure is the **Boí** valley, on the western edge of the national park, which has a magnificent concentration of **Romanesque churches**.

One complication that faces anyone intent upon seeing more than a small part of the Catalan Pyrenees in one go is the geographical layout of the region. The central Aran valley (Vall d'Aran), in the northwestern corner of Catalunya, lies east–west in orientation, but most of the others run north–south, which means that connecting between them is not always easy. Determined hikers and climbers can follow various passes between the valleys, but most visitors will have to content themselves with **approaching** from the towns and villages to the south of the range, and heading out of the mountains each time before they venture up a new valley.

SKIING IN THE PYRENEES

If you want to go **skiing** in the Catalan Pyrenees – still relatively undeveloped compared to the French side – it will almost certainly prove cheaper to buy an inclusive package from a travel agency than turn up at the resort and do it yourself. The main destination on offer is Andorra (p.632), though some agents do offer Spain, too; you'll get most choice if you go through a travel agency in Barcelona.

The best resorts are those around the La Molina-Super Molina complex (p.626), including Masella, which have a more extensive terrain and more challenging pistes than most. And even in summer, it's possible to see how good Núria (p.622) is for skiing, with a whole range of graded terrain. For **cross-country skiing**, the whole of the Cerdanya (p.629) and much of the Cadí (p.624) are covered with trails, which are drenched with sunshine in spring.

The system for **grading pistes** used in local ski literature is based on a colour code: green for beginner, blue for easy, red for intermediate and black for difficult. It's not a completely dependable system – black in one resort might be red in another – but it does give a fair idea of what to expect.

This section is arranged accordingly, starting in the east, closest to Barcelona, and moving west; it details the easiest approaches and emphasizes the routes that can be followed by **public transport**. Obviously if you have your own transport you've more freedom, and you're helped in your travels by an increasing number of road tunnels, which are being built to connect the valleys.

Vic

The quickest approach to the mountains from Barcelona is to take the train north to Ripoll. About an hour out of the city, the route passes through **VIC**, a handsomely sited small town with a long history, whose few well-preserved relics are worth stopping to see. Capital of an ancient Iberian tribe, Vic was later a Roman settlement (part of a second-century temple survives in town) and then a wealthy medieval market centre. The **market** continues to thrive here, taking place twice weekly (Tuesday and Saturday) in the enormous arcaded main square. Vic is also renowned for its excellent sausages, especially those known as *fuet* and *butifarra*, which you'll see on sale in the market and throughout the town.

Beyond and to the right of the square lies the old quarter of town, dominated by a reworked late-eighteenth-century **Catedral**. A rather dull, Neoclassical edifice, this doesn't make much of a claim on your attention, though it does retain its original Romanesque bell-tower and, inside, impressive wall paintings by Josep María Sert. Sert completed two original sets, both of which were lost during the Civil War when the church was burned down, and these date from his third attempt, just before he died in 1945.

Perhaps most interesting in Vic, though, is the **Museu Episcopal** (Tues–Sat 10am–1pm & 4–7pm, Sun 10am–1.30pm), next door in Plaça del Bisbe Oliba. As well as the usual local archaeological finds, and some early Catalan paintings, this museum houses the second most important collection of Romanesque art outside Barcelona's Museu d'Art de Catalunya, featuring a wealth of eleventh- and twelfth-century frescoes and wooden sculptures rescued from local Pyrenean churches. As with the Barcelona collection, you don't need to be a specialist to appreciate the craft that went into these objects, and the work here is likely to set you off on the trail of other similar pieces scattered throughout the region.

Practicalities

From the **train station**, walk straight up the road opposite to reach the main market square. This is where the **Turismo** is (at Plaça Major 1) if you need to pick up a map. There's a handful of small **hotels** should you want to stay – though you're close enough to either Barcelona or Ripoll to make it unnecessary. A good place for **lunch** or dinner is the renowned *La Taula*, Plaça Miquel Clariana 4 (☎93/886 32 29; closed Sun night, Mon, and Feb), a restaurant in an old mansion, with fine local food at around 3000ptas a head, and exceedingly slow service.

If you have transport (and plenty of cash), you might be tempted to drive the 14km north to the Embalse de Sau reservoir, overlooking which is the grand **Parador Nacional de Vic** (☎93/888 72 11; ⑥). The converted country house has all the upmarket facilities you'd expect, including a good Catalan restaurant.

Ripoll

At **RIPOLL**, an hour or so up the train line, you're between the foothills and the peaks, perfectly poised for walking in the surrounding green countryside. Most of the town itself, at the confluence of the Ter and Freser rivers, is modern and industrial, but at its heart it boasts an old quarter containing one of the most famous and beautiful monuments of Romanesque art, the monastery of Santa Maria. Ripoll is refreshingly free of other tourists, save for the odd coachload that descends upon the monastery and then departs, and it's also small enough to get to intimate grips with quickly; all of which makes it an attractive base.

Around the town

An obvious landmark in the centre of town, the Benedictine **Monestir de Santa Maria** was founded in 888 by Guifré el Pilós (Wilfred the Hairy), Count of Barcelona, as a means of resettling the surrounding valleys after the expulsion of the Moors. Guided by one Olivia, a cousin of the Counts of Besalú, the monastery rose to prominence as a centre of learning in the eleventh and twelfth centuries. Under Olivia and succeeding abbots it was completely rebuilt, using some of the finest craftsmen of the age.

Sadly, much was destroyed by a fire in 1835, though some of the original work can still be seen intact in the **west portal** (presently the main entrance to the church), which is protected from the elements by a sort of glass-fronted conservatory. The delicate columns and arches of the portal contain ornamental designs, zodiac signs and an agricultural-year calendar. These are enclosed by a tremendous sculpted facade of biblical scenes, historical and allegorical tales, and symbols of the Evangelists. The portal and the lower gallery of the adjacent two-storey **cloister** (June–Aug daily 9am–1pm & 3–7pm; Sept–May Tues–Sun 9am–1pm & 3–7pm; 50ptas), with its rhythmic arches and marvellous capitals, both date from the twelfth century, probably the greatest period of Spanish Romanesque. With their monks and nuns, beasts mundane and mythical, plus secular figures of the time, the capitals completely overshadow the works on display in the cloisters' own museum, the **Museu Lapidari**, which displays assorted stonework, masonry, sarcophagi and funerary art laid out along the walls. The monastery **church** itself (open all day for prayer) is less compelling, heavily restored over the years though still with an impressive barrel-vaulted nave.

Sant Pere

Adjacent to the monastery in Plaça Abat Oliba is the rather severe facade of the fourteenth-century church of **Sant Pere**. Inside, on the top floor, is the rambling and eclectic **Museu dels Pirineos** (Tues–Sun 9.30am–1.30pm & 3.30–7pm; 200ptas), detailing – among other things – Ripoll's history as an important seventeenth-century arms-producing and metal-working centre. There's a whole room of pistols and rifles, along with exhibits ranging from old coins through to ancient clothing, church art, archaeology and folkloric items. Incidentally, the church is also the venue for Ripoll's music festival, staged on scattered weekends during July and August – providing the only opportunity to see the interior of the church itself.

The rest of town

Once you've seen the monastery and church you've exhausted the real sights of Ripoll, though it's worth taking the time to climb up around the back of Sant Pere church to the **terrace** from where you can overlook the monastery. There's a bar here, too, which is much the nicest place in town to sit.

Beyond these few old town streets there's little temptation to wander; the river, certainly, is resolutely dirty. A **street market** on Saturday mornings fills up the town centre, while the only other gleam of interest is to track down the several *modernista* buildings found in Ripoll, perhaps the last place you'd expect to come across them. The most notable is the tiny church of **Sant Miquel de la Roqueta**, built in 1912 by Gaudí's contemporary, Joan Rubió – it looks like a pixie's house with a witch's hat on top. You'll pass this on the way to or from the train station, as you will the more easily found **Can Bonada**, c/del Progrés 14, with its sprouting stone flourishes and battlements.

Practicalities

The **train station** and **bus station** are close together, from where it's a ten-minute walk into town, over the Pont d'Olot and up to Plaça Ajuntament; the adjacent Plaça Abat Oliba is where you'll find the monastery as well as the **Turismo** (Mon–Fri 10am–1pm & 5–7pm, Sat 10am–1pm; ☎972/702351), just to the left of the Museu dels Pirineos, underneath the sundial. No English is spoken here, but the office has maps, lots of pamphlets and local transport timetables posted on the wall.

Leaving Ripoll, **trains** continue to Puigcerdà and the French border, which is also the way you have to go if you're heading for Andorra. Transport elsewhere is by **bus**: either with *Autos Güell Camprodon*, heading northeast to Sant Joan (7 daily) and Camprodon (5 daily); or east to Olot (4–5 daily) with *Teisa*, or west to Guardiola (Mon–Fri 1 daily); all departures from the bus station.

Accommodation

The handiest **places to stay** are in the old streets close to Santa María, but none are particularly inspiring. Least expensive is the *Fonda Cala Paula*, Plaça de l'Abat Arnulf 6 (☎972/700011; ②), which, if you face the Turismo, is above a bar-restaurant just thirty seconds' walk beyond, to the left. Some of the rooms are fairly small and windowless, however, so be sure to ask to see yours first. You could also try the *Hotel Payet*, Plaça Nova 2 (☎972/700250; ③), 300m south of the Turismo (with your back to it), off Plaça Sant Eudald, halfway down c/Sant Pere: this is a rambling old place with some dreadful singles, largish double rooms with and without bath, and an all-pervading mustiness, not least between the ears of the proprietress. There's a better alternative further down on the arcaded Plaça Gran, where the more upmarket *Hotel Monasterio* (☎972/700150; ④) has comfortable rooms with bath. *La Trobada*, Passeig Honorat Vilamanya 4 (☎972/714353; ③), across the Pont d'Olot, is perhaps the best of all: quiet rooms with bath, with a view of town over the river and a bar-restaurant on the ground floor.

The local **campsite**, *Solana del Ter* (☎972/701062; closed Nov), is 2km south of town on the Contrada Barcelona.

Eating and drinking

The **restaurant** attached to the *Fonda Cala Paula* is pretty popular, serving Catalan dishes with wonderful *canelones* and trout the specialities. Note that it's never open before 9pm. The *Restaurant Perla*, Plaça Gran 4, has a filling, if limited, 1000ptas *menú del día* (wine extra) and the other Catalan dishes are more adventurous than usual. The adjacent *Hotel Monastir* has an altogether more expensive menu, but also sports an affordable snack bar.

Two other places to try are the *Restaurant El Passeig*, Passeig Ragull 10, open for lunch only except at weekends, and the *Cafetería*, c/Berenguer el Vell, opposite the monastery, a bright, modern bar with outdoor seating, sandwiches and the best array of **tapas** in town. There's more of the same (and traffic-free outdoor tables) at the *Bar Stop*, on Plaça Tomàs Raguer, just to the south.

Northeast: the Romanesque Trail

From Ripoll an important **Romanesque Trail** of beautiful churches and monasteries leads northeast into the mountains. To follow the whole route by public transport you'll have to be prepared to wait (sometimes overnight) for buses, which get more scarce the further north you go. The first two towns, Sant Joan de les Abadesses and Camprodon, are easy to reach on day trips from Ripoll or from Olot (see p.611). The other, more distant villages take more time and effort but are correspondingly less developed; **trekking** between them is a real pleasure.

Sant Joan de les Abadesses

SANT JOAN DE LES ABADESSES lies just 11km from Ripoll and is connected to it by a regular twenty-minute bus ride. The small town owes its existence to the foundation of another convent by Count Guifré el Pilós, whose daughter became the first abbess here. Later, the convent was turned into a canonical monastery, and the surviving building is still the main reason to make a stop in town; even today the austerity of its single-nave twelfth-century church makes a powerful impression.

This **Monestir** (mid-June–mid-Sept daily 10am–2pm & 4–7pm; rest of the year daily 11am–2pm & 4–6pm, except Nov–mid-March Mon–Fri 11am–2.30pm, Sat & Sun 11am–2pm & 4–6pm; 200ptas), which replaced the original ninth-century foundation, was built in a Latin cross shape and has five apses, seen to their best effect from outside. Inside, the central apse houses a famous wooden sculpture group, the *Santíssim Misteri* of 1251, depicting Christ's deposition from the Cross. It's a fine work of simple proportions and, if the literature you're given on the way in is to be believed, "On Christ's forehead a piece of Holy Bread has been preserved untouched for 700 years."

Your admission ticket also covers entry to the fifteenth-century Gothic cloisters and the **Museu del Monestir**, whose oldest item is a page from an eleventh-century sacramental book. If that doesn't sound like much, you'll probably be more impressed by the other well-presented exhibits, which include a fine series of Renaissance and Baroque altar pieces, plenty of medieval statuary, ornate chalices, and curiosities such as a crucifix in rock crystal.

The monastery apart, there's not much to Sant Joan, but it's quiet and relaxing – a more attractive (and only slightly less convenient) base than Ripoll for touring the area. The slender twelfth-century **bridge** sets the tone, with the wide valley below terraced and farmed as far as the eye can see. The bridge was destroyed in fierce fighting in February 1939 during the final Republican retreat in the Civil War, and was only fully restored in 1976. Set back from the river there's a fair-sized cluster of ancient houses, where the street names are longer than the streets themselves, centred on a lovely, arcaded **Plaça Major**, west of the rambla. Having strolled around and scared the pigeons out of the abandoned shell of the Sant Pol church in the centre, you've pretty much exhausted the excitements in town.

Practicalities

The **bus terminal** (a grand name for a couple of bus shelters in a car park) is opposite the monastery and just around the corner from the town's main rambla, Passeig Comte Guifré, with the **Turismo** at no. 5 (Mon–Sat 11am–1pm & 5–7pm, Sun 11am–1pm; ☎972/720092).

Accommodation is easy to find, not least because it's all signposted throughout town. *Hostal Ter*, overlooking both the new and old town bridges from c/Vista Alegra 2 (☎972/720005; ③), is a good first choice, genuinely family-run and with decent meals. Otherwise, *Hostal Casa Nati*, on the road leading down from the bus terminal (c/Pere Rovira 3; ☎972/720114; ②), has large, bright rooms (separate showers): ask in the bar on the ground floor. Nearby, one block below the bus terminal, the *Hostal Janpere*, c/del Mestre Josep Andreu 3 (☎972/720077; ③), has rooms at slightly higher prices, though some come with shower or bath, too. *Habitacions Mateu* is almost next door on the corner, at c/Mossen Masdeu 10 (☎972/720186; ②), but it's fairly unprepossessing.

Possibilities for **eating and drinking** are a little limited, though there are a couple of pleasant cafés along the rambla where you can sit outside – at the *Cafeteria La Rambla* you can enjoy the 1000ptas *menú del día* or a *plato combinado* at a pavement table. The restaurant at the back of the *Hostal Casa Nati* is the most economical choice, with a full 800ptas *menú del día* on offer at lunch and dinner; you can also pick a dish from the pictures on the wall. The food isn't spectacular by any means, but it's a friendly enough place. *Hostal Janpere*'s attached diner promises better gastronomic treats, with a *menú del día* at around 1000ptas.

Camprodon

It's another twenty minutes by bus from Sant Joan to **CAMPRODON**, 14km further to the northeast, and the drive is promising – a gradual climb into the low hills alongside the lively Ter river. Coming this way, Camprodon – at 950m – is the first place with the character of a real mountain town, something that was exploited in the nineteenth century by the Catalan gentry who arrived by the (now defunct) railway to relax in the hills. The town still retains the prosperous air of those times, with ornate villas set amongst rows of towering trees, and high town houses embellished now and again with striking *modernista* flourishes.

Like Ripoll, Camprodon is at the confluence of two rivers, this time the Ter and the Ritort, and is knit together by little bridges. The principal one, the sixteenth-century **Pont Nou**, still has a defensive tower. From here you can follow the narrow main street, c/València, to the restored Romanesque monastic church of **Sant Pere** (first consecrated in 904), at the top of town, and complete your sightseeing. There *is* a small castle above the confluence of the two rivers, but no apparent way up.

More important is Camprodon's character as a mountain town: the shops are full of leather goods, ski gear, and mounds of local sausage and cheese. In winter it's packed with skiers, and in summer the countryside is ideal for walking (see below); in autumn, when the woods are ablaze with the different hues of turning trees, it is more scenic still.

Practicalities

Buses stop some way south of the centre at the *Teisa* terminal: there are two to three daily services to Olot, one daily (not Sun) to and from Molló, and two daily to and from Setcases. Walk up to the central Plaça d'Espanya, where the *Ajuntament* building houses the **Turismo** (Tues–Sat 11am–1.30pm & 5–7.30pm, Sun 11am–2pm;

☎972/740010). You can pick up a map here, though you'll hardly need it, and some information about the surrounding area (in English if you're lucky).

Accommodation in Camprodon is pricier than back down the valley, and you should consider booking in advance if you want to stay. The town is often as busy in summer as in the winter ski season. Best budget option is *Can Ganansi* at c/Josep Morera 9 (☎972/740134; ②), a street that leads off Plaça d'Espanya, though rooms here are much in demand – and those with bath are twice the price of those without. *Hostal Sayola*, on the same street at no. 4 (☎972/740142; ③), also has some cheaper rooms without bath. A couple of other choices can be found in Plaça del Carme, the first square as you come into town, which lies east of c/Josep Morera: *Hostal Sant Roc* (☎972/740119; ②) and *Habitacions La Placeta* (☎972/701520; ④). Or simply head for the best-placed of the town's hotels, the *Hotel Güell* (☎972/740011; ④), right on Plaça d'Espanya, where the well-appointed rooms justify the expense. There's also a local **campsite**, *Els Solans* (☎972/740012), on the Molló road.

There are several places in and around Plaça d'Espanya where you'll get good **food**, including the excellent *Bar-Restaurant Núria* at no. 11, which has a dining room that backs onto the river and a hearty 900ptas *menú del día*, though at night you have to choose from the more expensive *à la carte* menu. *Habitacions La Placeta* has a good attached restaurant (dinner only), or alternatively, try the restaurant at the *Can Ganansi*, which features lots of differently priced *menús del día* and local dishes. The latter include *pinyes*, extremely rich and dense pine-nut balls, which you can find on sale at bakeries throughout town.

Trekking and skiing: the Ter and Ritort valleys

Beyond Camprodon you have to rely more and more on your own transport and, ultimately, on your own legs. It's not all hard-core trekking by any means, though, and there are a couple of nearby targets which you could reach quite easily in a day trip from Camprodon – or even from Sant Joan or Ripoll if you timed the transport right. The basic choice is between heading northwest up the **Ter Valley**, which is the route most skiers follow since it ends at the resort of Vallter 2000, or northeast up the **Ritort Valley**, better if you just want some medium-grade hiking.

Llanars, Vilallonga and Tregurà

A couple of kilometres northwest of Camprodon, the first potential stop on the Ter Valley route is **LLANARS**, where there's a fine twelfth-century church. From here it's only three or four kilometres more to **VILALLONGA DE TER**, set in lovely green surroundings and with a couple of mid-range *hostales* and a year-round campsite to tempt you to stay. Two or three times a day a bus from Camprodon passes through both places on its way to Setcases.

A couple of kilometres past Vilallonga, there's a turn-off for **TREGURÀ DE DALT**, standing on a sunny shelf at 1400m. The upper part of the village has a church dating from about 980 and there are a few small hotels here, too. From Tregurà, serious hikers have the option of making the all-day **walk to Queralbs**, across to the west on the Núria rack-railway line. From the village, a path climbs to Puig Castell (2125m) and then through the Col dels Tres Pics (2hr) to the *Refugi Coma de Vaca* (4hr) at the top of the Gorges del Freser. From just before the *refugi*, on the south side of the Freser river, a path drops westwards through a stunning gorge to Queralbs (7hr), from where you can pick up the train down to Ribes de Freser or up to Núria.

Setcases

Back in the Ter Valley, beautifully sited **SETCASES**, 11km from Camprodon, is a strange mixture of the moderately chic and the decrepit. It was once an important agricultural village but was almost totally abandoned in the years before the ski station brought in a new wave of hoteliers and second-home owners. The bus from Camprodon takes just thirty minutes to get here, so it's one of the few mountain villages that sees much casual trade. If you want to **stay** there's plenty of choice, though again it makes sense to book ahead. Try the *Can Japet* (☎972/740612; ②), *Ter* (☎972/74 05 94; ④) or *Nova Tiranda* (☎972/740574; ③), all right in the centre.

Vallter 2000

Situated at the head of the Ter Valley right on the French border, **VALLTER 2000** (no public transport) is the most easterly ski resort in the Pyrenees. Despite the altitude its snow record isn't particularly reliable, but if the snow is good it's worthwhile for the range of pistes laid out in its glacial bowl – three green runs, three blue, five red and four black. There are also plenty of options for ski mountaineers, with possible routes west to Núria or east via the 2507-metre-high Roc Colom to the French *Refuge de Mariailles* (1718m). Less ambitious off-piste skiers can traverse from Vallter's top lift to the **Portella de Mantet** (2415m), dropping down to the French village of Mantet: it takes about three hours to get there and twice that to return the next day.

The Ritort Valley

Heading northeast from Camprodon, one daily bus (not Sun) makes the short ride up the Ritort Valley to **MOLLÓ**, 8km away, whose slight attraction is the Romanesque church of Santa Cecilia with its skinny four-storey bell-tower. If you're heading for France by road, over the Col d'Ares, Molló has virtually the only food or accommodation en route to the pass in its two hotel-restaurants, the *Calitxó* (☎972/740386; ③) and the *Francois* (☎972/740388; ④); rooms in both are discounted outside July and August.

Rocabruna and Beget

There's more attraction, for hikers at least, in turning off the road about halfway to Molló and following the minor road to **ROCABRUNA**. Here you'll find another small twelfth-century church, plus a couple of good restaurants with simple Catalan food.

From Rocabruna, a tortuous road winds down and down again through terraced slopes to the tiny rustic village of **BEGET**, 12km from Camprodon. Like so many villages in this area it has suffered crippling depopulation, coming to life only in summer when it's a popular Spanish holiday destination. There are two impressive medieval bridges, but the jewels are the late-twelfth-century church of **Sant Cristofor** (two distinct construction periods can be distinguished in the bell-tower) and the *Majestat* it houses. Many of the best of these Romanesque wooden images, portraying Christ fully clothed, were produced in this region, though most were destroyed in 1936. This is a particularly solemn and serene example, dating from the late twelfth or early thirteenth century, and is one of the very few that can still be admired in its original setting. If the church is locked, ask in the souvenir shop opposite.

Beyond Beget, it's possible to continue walking on tracks which lead southeast to Oix, from where a road runs the 9km down to Castellfollit de la Roca – a trek that takes a whole day and puts you within striking distance of Olot and the Garrotxa region.

The Upper Freser Valley and Núria

From Ripoll, the striking **Freser Valley** rises to the town of Ribes de Freser and then climbs steeply to Queralbs, where it swings eastwards through a gorge of awesome beauty. Just above Queralbs, to the north, the Riu Núria has scoured out a second gorge, beyond which lies the sanctuary and ski station of Núria.

THE *FERROCARRIL CREMALLERA*

Services on the train line to Núria, the *Ferrocarril Cremallera*, depart Ribes-Enllaç every day in summer (July–mid-Sept), hourly on the quarter-hour from 9.15am through to 5.15pm (*not* at 2.15pm; 23min past the hour at Ribes-Vila); there's a final summer departure at 9.30pm; in winter the weekday outbound service ends at 11.15am but the last return is at 6pm, and extra trains run at weekends and on holidays all year round. Return **tickets** to Núria cost around 1800ptas (one-ways available) and rail passes are *not* valid.

You can take the **train** all the way from Barcelona on this route, one of Catalunya's most extraordinary rides. The first stretch is by *RENFE* train to Ribes de Freser, about a two-and-a-half-hour ride (or just 20min from Ripoll). From there, the *Cremallera* (Zipper) rack-railway takes over: the small trains of this private line, built in 1931, take another 45 minutes to reach Núria.

Ribes de Freser

The simple riverside town of **RIBES DE FRESER** is invariably bypassed in the rush to Núria, no great shame since it has little to offer beyond a few uninspiring hotels and a quiet country town atmosphere. Its shops sell sacks of grain, seeds, oils and other agricultural and domestic paraphernalia, and there's an important weekly market, too (on Saturday).

You probably won't see any of this: the train from Barcelona/Ripoll stops at the station of Ribes de Freser-Renfe, ten minutes' walk from the centre, and if you're heading for Núria you simply cross the platform to Ribes-Enllaç, where you catch the *Cremallera*, which makes a stop in the middle of town (Ribes-Vila) before heading up into the mountains.

Taking the *Cremallera*: Queralbs

The *Cremallera* is a fabulous introduction to the mountains. After a leisurely start through the lower valley, the tiny train lurches up into the Pyrenees, following the river between great crags before starting to climb high above both river and fir forests. Occasionally it stops, the track only inches from a drop of hundreds of metres into the valley, a sheer rock face soaring way above you.

One such halt about twenty-five minutes into the journey, is at **QUERALBS**, an attractive stone-built village, sympathetically renovated and suffering from the attentions of too many tourists only in peak season. Reasonable **accommodation** and **eating** here is provided by the recommended *Fonda Can Constans*, 200 metres above the village on the Fontalba road (☎972/727370; ②); the village's other place to stay, the *Hotel Rialp*, on Contrada de Núria, is currently closed.

Núria

Beyond Queralbs, the train hauls itself up the precipitous valley to **NÚRIA**, twenty minutes further on. The views are dramatic and the drop sometimes terrifying, the impact being enhanced by a sequence of tunnels. Through a final tunnel the train emerges into a south-facing bowl containing a small lake and, at the far end, the one giant building that constitutes Núria, the **Santuario de Nuestra Senyora de Núria**. This "Sanctuary of Our Lady of Núria" was originally founded in the eleventh century on the spot where an image of the Virgin was said to have been found. Believed to bestow fertility, the Virgin of Núria is the patroness of shepherds of the Pyrenees, and local baby girls are often named after her. The main **religious celebrations** in Núria are on 8 September every year.

A severe stone structure, the sanctuary combines church, Turismo, café, hotel and ski centre all in one. The **hotel**, the *Hotel Vall de Núria* (☎972/730326; ⑤), is expensive (though at the bottom of its price category, and discounted in winter) but the sanctuary maintains a few simple former cells as a kind of budget hostel. In addition, there's an official **youth hostel** at the top of the cable car above Núria: the *Alberg Pic de l'Aliga* (☎972/730048; ①–②) – make reservations in advance to stay here. There are also several bunk-bedded refuges around, though these are often full of Spanish school groups, or you might want to **camp**; a site has been prepared behind the sanctuary complex.

A shop in the hotel sells **food**; fresh bread arrives by train every day. You can also buy hot snacks or breakfast at the *Bar Finestrelles* and there's a self-service place for midday or evening meals. The hotel dining room provides a not-too-expensive set meal.

Trekking and skiing

Despite the day-trippers and hordes of kids, solitude is easily found amid the bleak, treeless scenery. Serious **walkers** and **climbers** can move on from Núria to the summit of **Puigmal** (2909m), a four-to-five-hour hike: the 1:25,000 "Puigmal-Núria" *Editorial Alpina* contoured map/guide is recommended. The **skiing** here is usually more reliable than at Vallter 2000, but the lift system is very limited (passes cost around 1200ptas) and the top station is at only 2262m, so it's best for beginners and intermediates. There are two green runs, two blue, four red and one black. Off-piste, the summits of Pic de Finistrelles (2829m) and Puigmal are both fairly easy, each ascent taking three to five hours depending on conditions.

Most people, in fact, aren't this committed, but a good **trekking** option if you're reasonably energetic is to look around for a while and then walk back down, at least as far as Queralbs. This is the best part of the route and more than half the total distance: you trek along a beautiful, mostly marked four-hour mountain path down in the river valley below the train line.

Berguedà

An alternative approach to this eastern section of the Catalan Pyrenees is to aim initially for the *comarca* (district) of **Berguedà**, west of Ripoll. It's easiest with your own transport: from Barcelona, the road (the C1411) runs through Manresa and then heads due north to Puigcerdà, via the **Tunel del Cadí**, Spain's longest tunnel. You can come this way by bus, too – heading first for **Berga**, the region's main town, from Barcelona – though this approach is much slower than the train journey to Puigcerdà, via Ripoll.

In this region there's nothing as immediately spectacular as the Núria train journey, though northeast of Berga there's plenty of straightforward trekking at hand, in and around villages like La Pobla de Lillet and Castellar de N'Hug. To the west, the vast **Serra del Cadí** contains more serious walks, including treks around (and a possible ascent of) the twin peaks of that most recognisable of Catalan mountains, **Pedraforca**.

Berga

The centre of the *comarca* is **BERGA**, where the Pyrenees seem to arrive with an amazing abruptness. You can get here by bus from Barcelona, a two-hour ride, and though it's a fairly dull place it does have a ruined castle, a well-preserved medieval centre and – more importantly – connections on to more interesting villages.

There's one other reason to come to Berga, and that's at Corpus Christi when the town hosts the **Festa de la Patum**, one of the most famous and grandest of Catalunya's festivals. For three days, it features huge figures of giants and dwarves processing to hornpipe music along streets packed with red-hatted locals. A dragon attacks onlookers in the course of a symbolic battle between good and evil, firecrackers blazing from its mouth, while the climax comes on the Saturday night, when a dance is performed by masked men covered in grass.

Not surprisingly, **accommodation** is impossible during the festival unless you've booked weeks in advance. At other times you should have few problems. There are at least eight places to stay, all reasonably priced: try *Fonda Catalunya*, c/Ciutat 35 (☎93/821 00 77; ②); *Residencia Paseo*, Passeig de la Pau 12 (☎93/812 04 15; ③), which has some less expensive rooms without bath, too; and *Hostal del Guiu*, c/Queralt (☎93/821 03 15; ③). The local **campsite** (☎93/821 12 50; open all year) is out on the C1411. If you need help, try the **Turismo** at Plaça de Sant Pere 1 (Mon–Sat 9am–3pm; ☎93/821 03 04).

Northwest of Berga: the Serra del Cadí

If you're a fully equipped and experienced trekker, the **Serra del Cadí** range to the northwest of Berga potentially offers three or four days' trekking through lonely areas not served by public transport. There are a number of paths and tracks crossing the range, though the favourite excursion remains the ascent of Pedraforca. As with other limestone massifs, finding fresh water is a problem, and that – combined with intense summer heat at the relatively low altitude – means the peak visitors' season is during May–June and September. In recognition of its unique landscape, the Cadí was declared a national reserve some years ago, and it maintains two fairly well-placed refuges, accessible from a number of foothill villages – themselves served poorly, or not at all, by bus, so you'll have to walk or hitch to them from the larger towns down-valley. Extended explorations of this region imply possession of the *Editorial Alpina* 1:25,000 "Serra del Cadí/Pedraforca" and "Moixeró" maps and guide.

Guardiola de Berguedà, Bagà, Saldes and Gòsol

The best approaches to the Cadí are from **GUARDIOLA DE BERGUEDÀ**, 21km north of Berga (1 daily bus in summer) or the equally small town of Bagá (see below), another 5km further north. If you get stuck in Guardiola – likely if you've just arrived on the afternoon bus from Ripoll – places to stay include the *Fonda La Llobregat* (☎93/824 01 56; ②), within sight of the bus terminal, or *Fonda Guardiola* (☎93/824 00 01; ②), on the way south out of town. There are no proper buses from here west towards the mountains, though the mailman stops at the *Bar L'Avellaner* at 11am on weekdays; if you don't have too much equipment you can hitch a ride with him as far as Gòsol (see below). Otherwise, you'll have to hitch from the crossroads 1500 metres south of town, along the secondary paved road up the Saldes river valley.

The first significant habitation along this, after 18km, is the small village of **SALDES**, set dramatically at the foot of Pedraforca. Here, you'll find two stores with staple provisions suitable for trekking, and two *fondas* at which rooms must be reserved in advance: the *Carinyena* near the church (☎93/824 00 08; ①), and the pricier *Cal Manuel* (☎93/822 73 41; ②), serving meals.

GÒSOL, 10km further, is an ancient stone village whose peaceful surroundings attracted Picasso back from Paris in 1906: he stayed for several weeks, in fairly primitive conditions, inspired to paint by the glorious local countryside. There are a handful of *hostales* here – more expensive than in Saldes – the bars on the square serve food, and you'll have passed a couple of campsites along the way from Saldes.

From **BAGÀ** (*hostal* and campsite – the *Bastareny*, ☎93/824 44 20, open all year), you have a slightly shorter but steeper tramp or hitch 12km west to **GISCLARENY**, not really a village, but rather a pair of campsites and a primitive refuge amidst scattered farms. From here it ultimately takes longer to get to grips with the mountains, which require a further five-hour contour walk to the base of Pedraforca, or a sharp drop into the Gresolet valley followed by an equally hard climb up to Saldes, all of this on jeep tracks.

Up Pedraforca – and beyond

Most people tackle **Pedraforca** (the "stone pitchfork") from Saldes: a good ninety-minute path shortcuts the road up, which passes fifteen minutes below the **Refugi Lluís Estasen** (staffed most of the year; ☎93/822 00 79; advance booking recommended). From here the ascent of the 2491-metre peak is a popular outing, steep but not technically demanding if you approach clockwise via the scree-clogged couloir heading up the "fork"; at the divide between the two summits you'll meet a proper path coming up from Gòsol. The anti-clockwise climb from the refuge via the Canal de Verdet is harder; descent that way is almost impossible, and however you do it count on a round trip of five to six hours.

From the *Estasen* refuge, a day's walk separates you from the Segre valley to the north. The easiest traverse route, on a mixture of jeep tracks and paths, goes through the Pas dels Gosolans, a notch in the imposing, steeply dropping north face of the Cadí watershed. An hour below, the *Refugí Prat d'Aguiló* (primitive facilities, always open) is well placed near one of the few springs in these mountains; from here it's best to hitch a ride along the 18km of dirt track down to Martinet on the main valley road linking La Seu d'Urgell with Puigcerdà.

Around La Pobla de Lillet

From Berga a daily bus heads northeast to **LA POBLA DE LILLET**, an hour away, picturesquely situated with two ancient bridges arching a shallow river and the snowy peaks of the Pyrenees framing the whole. You can also get here by afternoon bus from Ripoll, 28km to the east.

The village is handily placed for some gentle local trekking; otherwise, apart from taking a turn around a couple of minor Romanesque churches – ruined, monastic Santa María and circular Sant Miquel, both 1500m east of town – you're really only here to find overnight **accommodation**. Neither of the two *hostales* – Pericas, c/Furrioles Altes 3 (☎93/823 61 62; ③) and *Cerdanya*, c/Pontarró 3 (☎93/823 61 07; ③) – is particularly good value, but **camping** nearby presents no problems.

The route to Castellar de N'Hug

From La Pobla it's a steady twelve-kilometre ascent to Castellar de N'Hug, and since you can't really leave the road, except for short sections at the beginning and at the end, you miss little by hitching if you get the chance. A little way out of La Pobla de Lillet, on the left, is a disused **cement factory**, a flamboyant *modernista* building designed by Rafael Guastavino in 1901; it looks like a stack of cave dwellings, now eerily empty.

Approaching Castellar, you'll come to the **Fonts del Llobregat**, source of the river which divides Catalunya in two, entering the sea at Barcelona. The *fonts* receive many Catalan visitors, who come here almost as a pilgrimage. Summer droughts frequently beset Catalunya, temporarily drying up many of the rivers, so there's great pride in any durable source of water, even if it's only a trickle by outsiders' standards.

To reach the village from here you can stay with the road or take a steep climb up the back way. **CASTELLAR DE N'HUG** is magnificently situated, an old place heaped up the sides of a hill at the base of the Pyrenees. It makes a good base for some splendid local treks, while a farm beyond the village, on the path going into the mountains, has a couple of horses which are available for treks. There's good local **accommodation** too. First choices are *Fonda Fanxicó* (☎93/823 60 15; ③) and *Fonda Armengou* (☎93/823 60 94; ③), both in Plaça Major. Or there's the slightly more expensive *Hostal Alt Llobregat* in c/Portell (☎93/823 61 64; ③).

Sant Jaume de Frontanyà

The beautiful eleventh-century church at **SANT JAUME DE FRONTANYÀ** is a ten-kilometre trek southeast from La Pobla. Again, it's wonderfully sited at the foot of a naturally terraced cliff, and is the finest Romanesque church in the region, built in the shape of a Latin cross, with three apses.

Around it are just a few scattered stone houses, a couple of restaurants and a *hostal*, and a road that leads 10km south to **BORREDÀ**, where it joins the main road (C149) back to Berga, 21km away. There's no public transport on any part of this route.

To the French border: the Cerdanya

The train from Barcelona, via Ripoll and Ribes de Freser, ends its run on the Spanish side of the border at Puigcerdà, having cut through the historical region of the **Cerdanya**. A wide agricultural plain, ringed by mountains to the north and south, the region shares a past and a culture with French Cerdagne over the border. The division of the area followed the 1659 Treaty of the Pyrenees, which also gave France control of neighbouring Rousillon, but left Llívia as a Spanish enclave just inside France. Today, the **train** continues over the border into France (the only surviving trans-Pyrenean rail route), providing a good alternative method of leaving or entering Spain. Note that if you're heading to France by train, via Puigcerdà, it's wise to reserve a seat in advance in Barcelona.

From Ripoll to Puigcerdà by train

The railway (and road) **from Ripoll** follows the Freser river north to Ribes de Freser (p.622), and cuts west, climbing gradually up the Rigart river valley. **PLANOLES**, 7km from Ribes de Freser in the valley bottom, has a **youth hostel** (☎972/736177; closed Sept–Oct; ①). Road and rail then enter Cerdanya at the **Collada de Toses** (1800m) – the railway by tunnel – and the views to the west begin a breathtaking sequence, over bare rolling mountains and swathes of deep green forest.

Beyond, the broad meadows of Tossa d'Alp form the pistes of **LA MOLINA/SUPER MOLINA** and **MASELLA**, adjacent ski resorts strung out along the north-facing slopes. By Spanish Pyrenean standards, the skiing here is impressive, both resorts having lifts almost to the top of the 2537-metre-high peak, while in summer all the resorts become upmarket holiday camps for organized activities like riding, archery and trail-biking. There are lots of **places to stay**, both in La Molina and nearby **ALP**, but prices are high. If all you want to do is come out to La Molina for a walk among the trees and hills, you're better off staying in Puigcerdà and making a day trip of it.

Puigcerdà

Although it was founded as long ago as 1177 as a new capital for the Cerdanya, **PUIGCERDÀ** (pronounced "Poo-eeg-chair-dah") retains no very compelling attractions, partly due to the heavy bombing it suffered in the Civil War. One of the few things in the centre that survived the bombs was the forty-metre-high **bell-tower** in

Plaça de Santa Maria. The other end of town, down the pleasant, tree-lined Passeig de 10 Abril, escaped more lightly. Here, the church of **Sant Domenèc**, the largest in the Cerdanya, is enveloped in an interior gloom that has helped preserve what little is left of some medieval murals. The only other interesting building, the thirteenth-century convent next door, has been recently renovated and is now used as a local cultural and youth centre. Work is still going on to restore what's left of the medieval cloisters to the rear.

The best thing about Puigcerdà, though, is the atmosphere of the place itself. Certainly if you've just arrived from France, or are just leaving, the attractive streets and squares with their pavement cafés and well-to-do shops are worth allowing at least enough time for lunch, if not an overnight stop. Lots of French trippers think the same, so in summer there's a decidedly lively ambience in the bars and restaurants. The most enjoyable of the outdoor **cafés** are in the Plaça de Santa María and adjacent Plaça dels Herois – both fine places to rest up over a beer. Between drinks, you can stroll the narrow old town streets between Plaça Ajuntament and Passeig de 10 Abril, or amble up to the small recreational **lake**, five minutes from the centre.

Arriving and accommodation

From the **train station** (buses stop outside), it's a seriously steep climb up to the centre: take the steps in front of you, go right at the top and up more steps, and then left and up even more steps, to arrive at Plaça Ajuntament, which has superb views over the hills to revive you. The **Turismo** is on the right, behind the *Casa de la Vila* at c/Querol 1 (June–Aug daily 10am–8pm; Sept–May Tues–Sat 10am–1pm & 4–7pm, Sun 10am–2pm; ☎972/880542), and has plenty of printed information to give away.

There's lots of **accommodation**, including two hotels right outside the station, but unless you're at death's door and can't face the climb into town there's absolutely no advantage in staying down here. Instead, try one of a dozen *hostales* and *pensiones* in town. *Hostal La Muntanya*, c/Coronel Morera 1, at Plaça Barcelona (☎972/880202; ③), is one of the best value, comfortable enough and close to all the bars. *Fonda Lorens*, c/Alfons I 1 (☎972/880486; ③), next to the *Madrigal* bar, is slightly more expensive but also friendly and clean, as is the very central *Hotel Alfonso*, c/Espanya 5 (☎972/880246; ③–④). *Pension Núria*, Plaça Cabrinetty 18 (☎972/881756; ③–④), is in one of the town's nicest squares, down from the Turismo, but costs more than its hand-written *habitaciones* sign suggests. Or splash out on the *Hostal del Lago*, Avda. Dr Puiguillém (☎972/881000; ④), off Plaça Barcelona, just a short walk from the lake – this is the most pleasant large hotel in Puigcerdà and superbly appointed.

The **campsite**, *Stel* (☎972/882361; open all year), is 1km out of Puigcerdà on the road to Llívia, just before you cross into France; and there's another, *Pirineus*, 3km out of town in the opposite direction, beyond the *RENFE* station.

Eating and drinking

Passing French tourists are responsible for the bilingual menus and relatively high prices in Puigcerdà, but there are still plenty of reasonable places to eat. At the budget end, *Sant Remo* at c/Ramon Cosp 9 is a straightforward bar that serves large, freshly cooked meals for 900ptas and 1300ptas. *La Cantonada*, c/Major 48, beyond the belltower, has more attractive surroundings and a 900ptas *menú*, while at *Cris Bar*, Passeig de 10 Abril, the *tapas* are typically Catalan – wash them down with home-made red wine that packs a serious punch.

A little more expensive (though by no means as grand as it sounds), the *Montserrat* restaurant at the back of the *Hotel Alfonso*, c/Espanya 5, is a good find, despite the fading decor. It has fish and shellfish on the menu, including fine local trout. Further up the same street, the *Bar-Restaurant Kennedy*, c/Espanya 33, serves *tapas* at the bar and meals from 1000ptas at the tables – all cooked in view at the rear kitchen.

The three **bars** with outdoor seats in Plaça de Santa María and Plaça dels Herois – the *Miami, Kennedy* and *Sol i Sombra* – are usually busy; the *Sol i Sombra* does a fine side-line in cured meat and serves up that most degenerate of Catalan breakfasts, *pa amb tomàquet* with slices of meat, washed down with local wine. The *Cervesseria* on Plaça Cabrinetty fancies itself as a beer specialist, and if that's your scene you can sit outside, drinking your way around the world.

Moving on: west to Andorra and north to France

If you're heading **west towards Andorra**, you may have to spend the night in Puigcerdà as there are only three buses a day to La Seu d'Urgell, via Bellver de Cerdanya (see below): currently at 7.30am, 2.30pm and 5.30pm. Heading into **France**, three trains daily cross the border to **LA TOUR DE CAROL**, five minutes away, where you change for Toulouse (4hr) and Paris (12hr). If you're **driving**, you enter France at the adjacent town of **BOURG-MADAME**; the **border** is open 24 hours, all year round, and formal checks here are almost non-existent – the French don't bother much and the Spanish just want see that you have a valid passport. It's also a simple matter to walk across to Bourg-Madame, 2km maximum from the centre of Puigcerdà.

Llívia

The Spanish enclave of **LLÍVIA**, 6km from Puigcerdà but completely surrounded by French territory, is a curious place indeed. There are only a couple of buses a day (from in front of the train station), but the walk isn't too strenuous: bear left at the junction 1km outside Puigcerdà and keep to the main road.

French **history** books claim that Llívia's anomalous position is the result of an oversight. According to the traditional version of events, in the exchanges that followed the Treaty of the Pyrenees the French delegates insisted on possession of the thirty-three Cerdanya villages between the Ariège and newly acquired Rousillon. The Spanish agreed, and then pointed out that Llívia was officially a town rather than a village and was thus excluded from the terms of the handover. Llívia had, in fact, been the capital of the Cerdanya until the foundation of Puigcerdà, and Spain had every intention of retaining it at the negotiations, which were held in Llívia itself.

The town

Once in Llívia, and off the built-up main road, things become positively medieval. Although there's lots of new building throughout the nucleus of the town itself, it's mostly sympathetic, done in local stone and wood. The narrow streets wind up to a solid fifteenth-century fortified **church** (daily 10am–1pm & 3–7pm; winter closed Mon), with an older defensive tower. On the hill behind are the remains of an even earlier castle, destroyed on the orders of Louis XI in 1479.

It's claimed that the **Museu Municipal** (Tues–Sun 10am–1pm & 3–7pm; 100ptas), opposite the church, occupies the site of the oldest pharmacy in Europe. The display features pots, powders and jars of herbs, plus a reconstruction of the dispensary, while the rest of the museum is given over to various local finds – Bronze Age relics, maps, and even the eighteenth-century bell mechanism from the church. The ticket also includes entry to the fifteenth-century tower adjoining the church, the *Tour Bernat*. The Turismo is sited in the tower as well: if it's not open (quite probable), the museum may have a little pamphlet about the town to give you.

Practicalities

Most people just stay long enough for **lunch**, not a bad idea. In the main square, Plaça Major, there's the upscale *Can Ventura* restaurant (the building dating from 1791), as well as an excellent *xarcuteria* if you're making your own picnic. The *Fonda-Restaurant Can Marcel.li*, visible just up the street, has a pleasant dining room above the bar with a 1300ptas *menú del día*. In the *Bar Esportiv*, below the church, the most athletic item in evidence is a rickety pool table, though the one-armed bandit may help generate a bit of excitement. Just behind here, *Can Francesc* at c/Forns 7 has probably the least expensive food in town – not bad for all that – with courtyard dining during the summer.

There are a few **places to stay** if you're so minded. The *Can Marcel.li* (☎972/896394; ③) has reasonable rooms; ask at the bar. Or there's the similarly priced *Fonda Merce*, c/d'Estavar 31 (☎972/896040; ③), down c/Raval from the main square and on the left at the end. A couple of much more expensive hotels are on the main road below town, but there's little attraction in staying down here.

Bellver de Cerdanya

Three daily buses run between Puigcerdà and La Seu d'Urgell, and although there's no real reason to get off in this part of the Cerdanya, you might be sufficiently taken by the sight of **BELLVER DE CERDANYA**, 18km west of Puigcerdà, to do so. A trout-fishing centre, standing on a low hill on the left bank of the Segre river, Bellver is a fine example of a mountain village, with a ruined castle and a sprinkling of old, balconied houses. The Romanesque church of **Santa María de Talló** is a short stroll south of the town. Known locally as the "Cathedral of the Cerdanya", this is a rather plain building, but has a few nice decorative touches in the nave and apse, and contains a wooden statue of the Virgin that's as old as the building itself.

The **Turismo** at Plaça Sant Roc 9 (July–Sept Mon–Fri 10am–1pm & 4–7pm, Sat & Sun 10am–1pm) can fill you in on **accommodation** details, but if it's closed, the *Vianya*, c/Sant Roc 11 (☎973/510044; ②), and the *Hostal Pendis*, Avda. Cerdanya 36 (☎973/510479; ③), are the budget choices; *Casa Martí*, c/Martí de Bares (☎973/510022; ④), and *Mesón Matía*, Contrada Puigcerdà (☎973/510039; ④), have slightly more expensive rooms, available with and without bath.

Towards Andorra and the west

The semi-autonomous principality of Andorra (p.632) is not much of an end in itself, and you'll get immeasurably better trekking (if that's what you're after) in the Pyrenees to either side. However, if you're curious – or travelling back through France – the route there is a reasonably interesting one, covered regularly by buses **from Barcelona**. These end their run in La Seu d'Urgell, the last Spanish town before Andorra. You can also approach Andorra **from Puigcerdà**, by taking the bus west along the C1313 to La Seu d'Urgell; see p.631 for details.

Ponts, Cardona and Solsona

The bus service from Barcelona to La Seu d'Urgell is run by the *Alsina Graells* company (Ronda Universitat 4), and takes three-and-a-half to four hours. There are two different routes: travelling either via **PONTS**, an undistinguished, fly-blown town where there's a drinks stop and a chance to stretch your legs, or the more interesting journey via Cardona and Solsona on the C1410 (see below). The two eventually converge when the buses join the C1313 for the final run up the Segre valley to La Seu. These same routes are the quickest if you're driving towards Andorra or the western Pyrenees, though less attractive than the roads further east.

Cardona

CARDONA lies about halfway between Barcelona and Andorra, and is dominated by a medieval hillside castle, whose eleventh-century chapel contains the tombs of the Dukes of Cardona. The castle has been converted into a *parador* (☎93/869 12 75; ⑥), which as a luxurious overnight stop would be hard to beat, particularly since it also contains an excellent Catalan restaurant, where dinner runs to around 3500ptas a head. Perhaps the most remarkable thing about Cardona, however, is its salt "mountain", the *Salina*, close to the river – a massive saline deposit which has been in existence since ancient times.

Solsona

Twenty kilometres further on, **SOLSONA** is a smallish, ramshackle town of considerable charm, with medieval walls and gates, and a ruined castle. The **Catedral** here is gloomy and mysterious, in the best traditions of Catalan Gothic, and has fine stained glass and a diminuitive twelfth-century Virgin, reminiscent of the Montserrat icon. Inside the adjacent seventeenth-century Bishop's Palace is the **Museu Diocesano** (Tues–Sun 10am–1pm & 4–8pm), a collection of Romanesque frescoes, altar panels and sculpture taken from local churches.

If you want to **break the journey** to Andorra without splashing out for the *parador*, Solsona is probably the best place. There's a good *fonda* (the *Vilanova*; ②) just off the cathedral square, and the even more reasonable *Pensio Pilar* nearby (①), with a *comedor* attached. Or try the *Sant Roc*, Plaça de Sant Roc 2 (☎973/480827; ③), just off the road to La Seu opposite the *Bar San Fermin* (where most of the buses stop).

The Segre valley: Organyà

Once you've left Solsona, and the bus has edged its way onto the main highway from Lleida (the C1313), the drama begins. Amid tremendous mountain vistas the road plunges through a great gorge, lined with terraces of rock jutting to over 600m above. This journey through the **Segre valley** alone makes the trip worthwhile, and Andorra starts to seem an exciting prospect by the time you reach La Seu d'Urgell.

There's only one reason to stop on the way, and that's at **ORGANYÀ** – some 20km short of La Seu – for the small, round building on the main road which contains what is possibly the oldest document in the Catalan language. Written in the twelfth century, the *Homilies d'Organyà* are annotations to some Latin sermons, discovered in a local presbytery at the beginning of this century. Opening times for the *Homilies* and the adjacent **Turismo** are the same (Mon–Sat 11am–2pm & 5–7pm, Sun 11am–2pm). There's a reasonable **hostal** on the bend of the road almost opposite, or if you want something smarter go to *La Cabana*, Avda. de Montaña 2 (☎973/383000; ②), which also has more expensive rooms with bath available.

La Seu d'Urgell

The historic town of **LA SEU D'URGELL,** capital of the Alt Urgell region, provides the best base for the area if you don't want to stay in Andorra itself. For years a run-down sort of place, with a neglected medieval quarter, La Seu has undergone a mild transformation since the 1992 Olympic canoeing competitions were held nearby. There are two or three new hotels, as well as the purpose-built canoeing facilities by the River Segre, but as the greater part of the new development is outside the old centre, you should still be able to enjoy a fairly relaxed stay before heading off for the wild excesses of Andorra.

Around the town

Named after the imposing twelfth-century cathedral at the end of c/Major, La Seu has always had a dual function – as an episcopal seat and commercial centre. A bishopric was etablished here as early as 820, and it was squabbling between the Bishops of La Seu d'Urgell and the Counts of Foix over local land rights that led directly to the independence of Andorra in the thirteenth century. Although consecrated at the time of the foundation of the episcopal see, the **Catedral** (Mon–Sat 9.30am–1pm & 4–6pm, Sun 9.30am–1pm) itself was completely rebuilt in 1175, and has been restored several times since. Nevertheless, it retains some graceful interior decoration and fine cloisters with droll capitals, which you can see by buying an inclusive ticket around the back of the church – 250ptas gets you into the cloisters, the adjacent eleventh-century church of Sant Miquel and the **Museu Diocesano** (Mon–Sat 10am–1pm & 4–7pm, Sun 10am–1pm), containing a brightly coloured tenth-century Mozarabic manuscript with miniatures, the *Beatus*. To see only the cloister and church costs 125ptas.

Other than these few sights, time is most agreeably spent strolling the dark, cobbled and arcaded **old town streets** below the cathedral, which is where you'll find many of the town's best bars and restaurants. There's a strong medieval feel here, accentuated by the fine buildings lining c/dels Canonges (parallel to c/Major), and it seems appropriate that the town's fourteenth-century stone corn measures should still stand under the arcade on c/Major.

Castellciutat

Fine views of the whole valley can be enjoyed from the village of **CASTELLCIUTAT**, just 1km out of town, and its nearby ruined castle. Follow c/Sant Ermengol, cross the river and climb up to the village, which glories in the views that La Seu never gets. There's still some farming going on here, on the slopes below the tiny stone church, and a *hostal* in the square (see "Accommodation" below) which makes a nice retreat from La Seu. To continue your walk from Castellciutat, follow the path around the base of the castle and cross the main road for the nearby **Torre Solsona**. A sign here says "danger" and the scanty remains of the old fortifications are indeed crumbling away, assisted by the quarry below – take care at the edges. You can vary your route there or back by following the walkways through the post-Olympic Valira riverside park: from La Seu, head west from Avda. de Pau Claris (north of c/Sant Ot) to intercept it.

Practicalities

The **bus station** is on c/Joan Garriga Masso, just north of the old town: *Alsina Graells* buses connect La Seu with Puigcerdà (at 9.30am, 12.30pm & 7pm), Lleida and Barcelona; more frequent *La Hispano-Andorrana* services run to Andorra. The **Turismo** (Mon–Sat 10am–2pm & 5–8pm; ☎973/351511) is on the main road coming into town, Avda. del Valira, not far from the campsite, but if all you want is a brochure and map try the *Ajuntament* behind the cathedral first.

Accommodation

There's not much decent budget **accommodation** available in La Seu, the standard set by the *Habitaciones Palomares*, c/dels Canonges 38–40 (③), in the old town, a warren of chipboard, windowless closets rented out as rooms, tolerable only if you can obtain one of the multi-bedded front rooms with balcony. At least in the *Fonda Urgell*, c/Capdevila 30 (☎973/351078; ②), close to the bus terminal, all the rooms have windows. If you're counting every *peseta*, you're probably best off in the *La Valira* **youth hostel** (☎973/353897; closed Sept; ①), at the western end of c/Joaquim Fuerza, by the Valira riverside park.

There are a few more expensive hotels on the main road through town, best placed is the one-star *Hotel Andría*, Passeig Joan Brudieu 24 (☎973/350300; ④), full of faded elegance, which means things don't always run as smoothly as they should. Top-of-the-range places include the modern *Parador* (☎973/352000; ⑤), very near the cathedral at c/Sant Domènec 6, and the better-sited *El Castell* (☎973/350704; ⑥), which is on the main Lleida road and incorporated within the Castell de Castellciutat. Or you might consider staying in the village of **Castellciutat** itself, though without your own transport there's no alternative but to walk there with your luggage or take a taxi: the *Pensió Fransol* in the main Plaça de l'Arbre (☎973/350219; ③) is nicely positioned.

The nearest **campsite** is *En Valira* (☎973/351035; open all year), just out of town on the Lleida road at Avda. del Valira 10.

Eating and drinking

Lively **tapas bars** are plentiful in La Seu's old town: try *Bar Lalin*, c/Major 24, one of the best, or *Bodega Fabrega*, c/Major 81. For **restaurant meals**, and excellent value, *Restaurant Cal Pacho*, c/la Font 11 (at the southern end of c/Major, to the east), has a very Catalan menu, worth trying for lunch or dinner.

Out of the old town there are plenty of choices too. *Palace*, out by the bus station, at the corner of c/Joan Garriga Masso and the highway, has an all-you-can-eat buffet for 1200ptas. More centrally, *Bambola Pizzeria-Creperia*, c/Andreu Capella 4 (east of the main Passeig) serves – no surprizes here – tasty and reasonable pizzas and crepes. The *Nazario*, next door, is a good *orxateria/gelateria* with outdoor seating, though it's rather dear. For budget Catalan food, the bustling *Restaurant Canigó*, c/Sant Ot 3 (at the north end of the Passeig), has a 900ptas *menú del día* and a fistful of *platos combinados*. Much more expensive is the restaurant of the *Hotel Andría*, on the Passeig: the food is no great bargain but it's an attractive venue for a drink, with a terrace-garden.

Andorra

After 700 years of feudalism, the twentieth century has finally forced itself upon the **PRINCIPALITY OF ANDORRA**, 450 square kilometres of mountainous land between France and Spain. A referendum held in March 1993 produced an overwhelming vote to accept a democratic constitution, replacing the semi-autonomous system in place since 1278, when the Spanish Bishops of La Seu d'Urgell and the French Counts of Foix settled a long-standing quarrel by granting Andorra independence under joint sovereignty. Despite a certain devolution of powers – the Counts' sovereignty passed successively to the French king and then the French President – the principality largely managed to maintain its independence over the centuries. The bishops and counts, and later the French king and President, appointed regents who took little interest in the nitty gritty of day-to-day life in the principality. The country was run instead by the *Consell General de les Vals* (General Council of the Valleys), made up of appointed representatives from Andorra's seven valley communes, who ensured that the principality remained well out of the European mainstream – it even managed to maintain its neutrality during the Spanish Civil War and World War II.

It was during these conflicts that Andorra began its meteoric economic rise, as locals first smuggled in goods from France during the civil war and, later, goods from Spain during the occupation of France. After the war, this trade was largely replaced by the legitimate duty-free business in alcohol, tobacco and electronics, and by the money generated by the huge demand for winter skiing. Much of the principality became little more than a drive-in supermarket, with the main road through the country and into France clogged with French and Spanish visitors after cut-price hi-fi and electrical gear, mountain bikes, ski equipment, car parts and a tankful of discount petrol. Seasoned Spain-watcher John Hooper has called Andorra "a kind of cross between Shangri-La and Heathrow Duty Free". Ironically, though, this tax-free status held the seeds of Andorra's belated conversion to democracy. Although the inhabitants enjoyed one of Europe's highest standards of living, the twelve million visitors a year began to cause serious logistical problems: the country's infrastructure was sorely stretched, the valleys increasingly laid open to speculative blight, while the budget deficit grew alarmingly. Spanish entry into the EC in 1986 only exacerbated the situation, affecting the difference in price of imported goods in Spain and Andorra.

The 1993 referendum was an attempt to come to terms with the economic realities of twentieth-century Europe. Or rather, some of the economic realities, since none of the parties involved in the negotiations and arguments seriously suggested that the solution would be to introduce direct taxation: there is still no income tax in Andorra, and barely any indirect taxes either. Instead, the idea is to transform Andorra into a kind of "offshore" banking centre, to rival the likes of Gibraltar, Lichtenstein and Luxembourg.

Following the referendum, the state's first **constitutional election** was held in December 1993. Only the 10,000 native Andorrans were entitled to vote (out of a total population of 60,000) and an 80 percent turn-out gave the outgoing head of the *Consell General*, Oscar Ribas Reig the biggest share of the vote. His *Agrupament Nacional Democratic* took eight seats in the new 28-seat parliament and formed a coalition with other right-wing parties to usher in the new democratic era. For the first time, Andorrans (ie, those born there, or who have lived there for over 20 years) can vote freely, and join trades unions and political parties, while their government now has the

ANDORRA PRACTICALITIES

Getting there

From Spain, there are two daily direct buses from Barcelona (4hr 30min), and regular buses from La Seu d'Urgell, at 8am, 9.30am, 12.15pm, 2pm, 3.20pm, 6pm and 7.15pm (Sun at 8am, 9.30am, 12.15pm, 2pm, 4.15pm and 7.15pm), which take 40 minutes to reach the capital, Andorra la Vella.

From France, the bus leaves L'Hospitalet at 7.50am and 1pm (12.30pm from Ax-les-Thermes), arriving at Pas de la Casa thirty minutes later; summer service from La Tour de Carol at 10.35am and 5.45pm, taking 1hr 10min to Pas de la Casa.

If you're **driving** you might as well leave the car behind and take the bus – in high season (summer or winter) the traffic is so bad that the bus isn't much slower, and parking in Andorra la Vella is an ordeal.

Currency and Post

Andorra has no money of its own, so both pesetas and French francs are accepted; prices in shops and restaurants are quoted in both currencies. There's also a dual-operation postal system, with both a French and Spanish post office in Andorra la Vella.

Language

Catalan is the official language, but Spanish and, to a slightly lesser extent, French are widely understood.

Leaving Andorra

Buses back to La Seu d'Urgell leave from Plaça Guillemó in Andorra la Vella, parallel to the main road. Departures are Monday–Saturday 8am, 9am, 11.30am, 1.30pm, 4pm, 6pm and 8pm (Sunday 9am, 11.30am, 1.30pm, 4pm and 6pm).

right to run its own foreign policy and establish its own judicial system: the principality has already been accepted as a full member of the United Nations.

For many visitors, though, the attractive quaintness stops at the border. As little as thirty years ago Andorra was virtually cut off from the rest of the world – an archaic region which, romantically, happened also to be a separate country. There are still no planes and no trains, but the rest of the development has been all-encompassing: it can take an hour in packed traffic to drive the few kilometres from La Seu d'Urgell to Andorra la Vella, the main town; while the large-scale ski resorts have already taken up much of the most attractive corners of the state – another is currently planned in the beautiful Prat-Primer upland. If you're curious, it can be worth a day or so for the cheap shopping and eating, and it's worth getting at least a little way out of the capital to see some of the scenery that brought the early visitors here. Don't expect to find an unspoiled spot anywhere, though, unless you're prepared to strike off up the mountains on foot – and if you are, there are much more rewarding places on either side of Andorra where you could spend time.

Andorra la Vella

At just over 1000m, **ANDORRA LA VELLA**, with its stone church, river and enclosing hills, must once have been an attractive little town. Now it's ghastly; a seething mass of electrical hardware stores, tourist restaurants (six-language menus a speciality), tacky discos and parked cars. It's consumerism gone mad, which is a shame in light of the spectacular setting, with crags and green *sierra* to either side. There's a partial respite in the old quarter, the **Barri Antic**, which lies on the heights above the river, to the south of the main through road, Avda. Princep Benlloch. But even here, the sole monument is the sixteenth-century stone **Casa de la Vall** in c/de la Vall (free guided tours Mon–Fri 10am–1pm & 3.30–6.30pm, Sat 10am–1pm), once a family house, but now housing the *Sala de Sessions* of Andorra's parliament and a small museum on the top floor.

The **Turismo** is east of the Barri Antic, closer to the river, on c/Dr. Vilanova (Mon–Sat 9am–1pm & 3–7pm) and has complete lists of local accommodation, restaurants, bus timetables and sells a good topographical map of the principality.

Accommodation and eating

Most of the two dozen or so modest **hotels** here are reasonably priced, but there's absolutely no reason to stay. If you're at all taken with the old quarter, the only place within it is *Racó d'en Joan*, c/de la Vall 20 (☎9738/20811; ③), which is quiet enough.

A better plan is to stick around just long enough for something to eat, since there's no shortage of **restaurants** and competition fosters low prices, and then head out into the more attractive rural surroundings. *Pizzeria Primavera*, c/Dr. Nequi 4, near the Barri Antic, and *Restaurant Macary*, c/Mossen Tremosa 6, are both fine. For filling combo specials, *Les Arcades*, Plaça Guillemó 5, is the place – it's a hotel, too (☎9738/21355; ③). South of the centre, on the far side of the river, *Pizzeria Taverneta*, in an alley off Avda. Tarragona, is good but has shoved up its prices a lot recently; *El Viet Nam* in the same block provides the only Asian food for miles around.

Up the Valira d'Ordino

It's hard to convince yourself that not all of Andorra is like this (sadly, much of it is) but with a bit of effort you can effect a partial escape into the magnificent mountain scenery by heading up the **Valira d'Ordino**. At **LA MASSANA**, 7km out of Andorra la Vella, the road splits, the left-hand fork climbing the 4km up to the ski resorts of **ARINSAL** and **PAL**. The former is the most developed (with a bus from Andorra la Vella in season), while the latter is a pretty stone-built village with limited skiing.

The right fork at La Massana is for **ORDINO** itself (regular buses from Andorra la Vella; catch them from where the La Seu bus sets you down, near the church), an intriguing and steep eight-kilometre climb from Andorra la Vella. Construction work is rapidly making its small-village existence a thing of the past, but Ordino still retains a handful of old stone buildings and some infinitely quieter surroundings.

El Serrat and Ordino-Arcalis

From Ordino it's an easy eight-kilometre (two-hour) walk up the gently undulating valley towards El Serrat; there are also three buses daily from Andorra la Vella. The views get better and better as you go and there are several tiny hamlets on the way, mere clusters of houses built over the river. Given its proximity to the main road it's all remarkably pleasant, but even here the excursion trade is beginning to make itself felt: a suspiciously good restaurant here, a tourist bar there, and everywhere the foundations and works that tell of another nascent hotel or apartment block.

At **EL SERRAT** there are some tumbling waterfalls and a couple of hotels offering tea and views from their restaurant terraces. If you wanted to **stay** (and these parts are certainly attractive enough), then there's the odd *hostal* on the Ordino–El Serrat road, as well as hotels in both Ordino (*Montana*, c/Coll d'Ordino, ☎9738/35056; ③) and El Serrat (*Hotel Tristaina*, ☎9738/35081; ③), and two **campsites**; the first and nicest 2km beyond Ordino, the second just before El Serrat.

From El Serrat, the road climbs steeply to the new ski resort of **ORDINO-ARCALIS**, probably the best place to ski in Andorra, set in remote high-mountain scenery, above the Tristaina lakes. In season, three ski buses a day run there from Sant Julia through Andorra la Vella.

The road to France: the Valira del Orient

It's around 35km from Andorra la Vella to the French border at Pas de la Casa, a route you can follow by bus, in which case you're unlikely to be tempted to get off anywhere en route. If you're driving, it's easier to stop off at the couple of places of minor interest.

Just a few kilometres northeast of Andorra la Vella, **ESCALDES** is little more than a continuation of the capital – all cars, coaches, hotels and restaurants. On a shelf of land just to the north is **Sant Miquel d'Engolasters**, one of Andorra's most attractive Romanesque churches. Its frescoes, like those of many Andorran churches, have been taken to the Museu d'Art de Catalunya in Barcelona, but this eleventh-century chapel is still an evocative sight. To get there, take the road that climbs to the dammed lake of Engolasters, passing the church after 4km.

Beyond Encamp, **CANILLO** is one of the best compromise bases in Andorra – fairly close to the shops of Andorra la Vella, but far enough away to retain some dignity and character. On the eastern fringe of town, the bell-tower of the Romanesque church of **Sant Joan de Caselles** is original, but the porch is a fifteenth-century addition. Just short of Canillo, a small road climbs to **Notre-Dame-de-Meritxell**, the ugly new sanctuary designed by architect Ricardo Bofill to replace a Romanesque building that burned down in 1972. Five kilometres on, **RANSOL** is set just above the main road, at the start of the Ransol valley – one of the few pleasant villages left in Andorra, with apartments available for rent if you fancied overnighting here.

SOLDEU, three kilometres further on, is one of Andorra's biggest ski resorts and has plenty of hotel accommodation, but here you're fast entering the built-up area close to the French border. You can escape the development by heading off up the lovely **Vall d'Incles**, at the head of which is a campsite (about an hour's walk from the·main road). Once over the **Port d'Envalira**, the road tumbles down to the border town of **PAS DE LA CASA**, a combination of duty-free bazaar and ski-station and, again, of no more than passing interest.

The Noguera Pallaresa Valley

The **Noguera Pallaresa**, the most powerful river in the Pyrenees, was once used to float logs down from the mountains to the sawmills at La Pobla de Segur, a job now done by truck. These days, the river is known for its river-rafting opportunities, while for those with less specialized enthusiasms its primary interest is as a way of getting into the high Pyrenees, particularly to the celebrated Vall d'Aran.

Getting there: Artesa de Segre and Tremp

Access to the valley is easiest through La Pobla de Segur (see below), which can be reached direct from Barcelona or Lleida. Approaching from the east, there's a road from La Seu d'Urgell to Sort, at the northern end of the valley (see below), through 53km of gorgeous scenery; no buses run this way, though, and hitching can be very slow – you do so from the turn-off at Adrall, 7km southwest of La Seu.

One **bus** a day (run by *Alsina Graells*) leaves Barcelona (from Plaça de la Universitat) for La Pobla de Segur, a three-and-a-half-hour ride. It passes through **ARTESA DE SEGRE** (on the C1313), a town which also lies on the bus route between La Seu d'Urgell and Lleida, and therefore can provide a roundabout connection if you're coming from La Seu or Andorra. Unless you have to change here, don't even think of stopping in dismal Artesa de Segre – you can hear jaws drop at the very thought as you make your way to the front of the bus.

After Artesa, the first major halt in the Noguera Pallaresa valley itself is at **TREMP**, which can also be reached on a spectacular **train** ride direct from Lleida. Tremp is at the centre of the huge hydroelectric project that supplies much of Catalunya's power, and although it's a distinct improvement on Artesa de Segre – people here walk around with their mouths closed – there's still no real reason to delay, since the best of the scenery is yet to come. If you do get stuck, there are a few places to stay, a pleasant central square, and even a tourist office. With your own transport, though, and a big **meal** in mind, you can do immeasurably better by heading north a few kilometres to the small town of **TALARN**, where the *Casa Lola* (c/Soldevilla 2; ☎973/650814) is widely recognized as providing abundant portions of superb local food – from around 3000ptas a head.

La Pobla de Segur

Thirteen kilometres further north, **LA POBLA DE SEGUR** sits on the Noguera Pallaresa river, at the head of the Embalse de Talarn. You only come to La Pobla really because all the region's transport connects here, but it's lively enough if you want to break your journey. **Trains** from Lleida terminate here, while **buses** run from La Pobla to El Pont de Suert, Boí and Capdella for the western side of Aigües Tortes (see p.642), and direct to Viella via the Túnel de Viella for the Vall d'Aran (p.639). Most excitingly, though, the bus from Barcelona continues from La Pobla **up the Noguera Pallaresa valley**, travelling through Sort and Llavorsí (see below) and passing within 7km of Espot, the major entry point to the Aigües Tortes national park – from June to October, the bus continues to Viella in the Vall d'Aran, during the winter it stops short of the pass at Esterri d'Aneu. Arriving from Lleida, morning train and bus services should connect with the onward bus up the Noguera Pallaresa (it leaves at around 11.40am; there's another at 6.30pm).

Trains arrive in the new town, from where you must walk up the road, cross the bridge and head along the main street to the *Alsina Graells* **bus terminal**, at c/Sant Miquel de Puy 3, next to the *Hostal La Montaña*. Should you miss your connection, there are a few reasonably cheap **places to stay**; try the *Torrentet*, Plaça Pedrera 5 (☎973/680352; ②), or *Roy*, Avda. de la Font (☎973/680031; ③).

Gerri de la Sal and around

From La Pobla de Segur, the road threads through the spectacular **Desfiladero de Collegats**, a mighty gorge forged by the Noguera Pallaresa through 300-metre-high cliffs. Stalactites hang heavy here in huge caves gouged out of the rock. Unfortunately, since a new tunnel has been blasted through part of the defile, drivers see little of the spectacular valley, though the abandoned old road is still a marvellous route for walkers.

As the defile widens you come suddenly upon the rickety village and enchanting twelfth-century Benedictine monastery of **GERRI DE LA SAL** – "de la Sal" because of the local salt-making industry. You'll see the surviving salt pans at the side of the river as you pass by. Village and monastery are linked by an ancient stone bridge, and though the monastery, Santa María, is normally closed, it's worth a look even from outside, where an arched hay-loft runs the entire length of the building. If you have your own car this is a fine place for a short break, but it's inconvenient without transport: there are only a handful of bars, and the nearest accommodation is 4km north, at the tiny village of **BARO**, where there are two or three places to stay strung along the main road, a riverside campsite (the *Pallars Sobirà*, ☎973/662030; open all year) and a supermarket.

West to Pobleta de Bellveí

The minor road from Gerri to **POBLETA DE BELLVEÍ**, 17km west, is a pristine and tranquil run, passing the idyllic little Estany de Montcortès, and providing wonderful views of the Collegats gorge from the village of **BRETUI** (10km). The chances of a lift are remote, but at Pobleta de Bellveí you can pick up the Capdella bus (see p.646).

Sort, Rialp and Llavorsí

SORT, 30km from La Pobla de Segur, has an attractive old centre of tall, narrow houses, now hemmed in by modern apartment blocks. The main reason for this rapid development is that Sort and its neighbouring villages have suddenly found themselves among the premier **river-running** spots in Europe. After spring snowmelt the area swarms with canoeists and rafters, mostly foreign and encumbered with hi-tech gear. And every year in late June/early July, the communities in the valley stage their own festival of the *Raiers* (Rafters), re-enacting the exploits of the old-time timber pilots who still put the slick new daredevils to shame.

Because of the upmarket sports types it attracts, Sort has priced itself out of any casual trade, and in any case it's not a place to linger unless you're here for the action (which can be exhilarating; see feature above): its main street is almost exclusively devoted to rafting/adventure shops and information centres, and there's nowhere cheap to stay or eat, unless you get a sandwich in one of the bars. The bus stops outside the *Bar Cayote* on the main road.

RIALP, 3km north, is a similarly uninviting mix of new buildings and boutiques; the bus stop/office is next to the *Hotel Victor*. **LLAVORSÍ**, 10km further, would be the most attractive place to stay on this stretch if you were determined to do so. Despite extensive renovation, and a scattering of new bar-restaurants and rafting paraphernalia, this tight huddle of stone-built houses at the meeting of the Noguera Pallaresa and Cardós rivers still retains much of its character. There's a riverside **campsite** 1km out of town, and any number of **hostales** catering for the new trade. In rafting season (April to end–August), reserve in advance: try the *Hostal Lamoga*, Avda. Pallaresa 1 (☎973/630006; May–Sept only; ③), or the *Hostal Del Rey*, right on the riverfront at c/Santa Ana 7 (☎973/630011; ③).

The Vall d'Àneu

From Llavorsí the bus from Barcelona/La Pobla de Segur continues along the Noguera Pallaresa, past the turning for Espot and the artificially placid lake of Panta de la Torrassa, to **LA GUINGUETA D'ÀNEU**. This is the first of three villages that incorporate the name of the local valley, the **Vall d'Àneu**, and it has a small cluster of roadside **accommodation** (a couple of *fondas* and one hotel) and a decent **campsite** across from the lake.

Esterri d'Àneu

ESTERRI D'ÀNEU, 4km on at the head of the lake, has changed so quickly that the former farming community doesn't know what's hit it. Taken in isolation, the few huddled houses between the road and the river, the arched bridge and slender-towered Sant Vicenç church are as graceful an ensemble as you'll see, but the new apartment blocks on the north side of the village, the sports shops, fancy hotels and "pub", have altered its once somnolent character irretrievably. Which is not to deny that it's a pleasant place to fetch up in the evening if you're looking for an overnight stop. There are several **places to stay**, the pick of which (and easily the best value) is the delightful *Fonda Agustí* (☎973/626034; ③) in Plaça de l'Església, just behind the church. This serves meals, too, and has an inexpensive bar. You can also get a drink and a good *bocadillo* at *Els Cremalls*, on the main street. The **campsite**, *La Presalla* (☎973/626031; open April–Sept), is 1km south of the village.

Esterri has a couple of banks, three or four supermarkets for provisions, and a building at the end of the village that houses a post office, *Ajuntament* and **Turismo** (Mon–Sat 9.30am–2pm & 4.30–8pm, Sun 10am–2pm). From November to May, the village is also the end of the line for the bus from Barcelona: the pass itself is closed throughout the winter.

València d'Àneu and the Port de la Bonaigua

A few minutes further up the hill, **VALÈNCIA D'ÀNEU** is a village of traditional stone and rendered houses that has been far less disrupted by development. There are two places to stay here, *La Morera* (☎973/626124; ③) and the more reasonable *Cortina*

(☎973/626107; ②). If you're staying in Esterri, it's a pleasant three-kilometre walk: there's a restaurant, a bar for drinks and the small Romanesque church of Sant Andreu to explore.

Soon after València, the road starts to climb away from the river and the quilt of green and brown fields that mark the valley. The views get ever more impressive as it heads above the treeline, passing an isolated *bar-restaurant* and *refugi* before reaching the bleak pass of **Port de la Bonaigua** (road closed in winter). Near the top (2072m) snow patches persist year-round, and you get a brief glimpse of half-wild horses grazing and simultaneous panoramas of the valley you've just left and the Vall d'Aran to come.

The Vall d'Aran

The **Vall d'Aran**, with its majestic alpine feel, is completely encircled by the Pyrenean mountains. Although it has belonged to Spain since 1192, the valley, with the Garonne river cleaving down the middle, opens to the north, and is actually much more accessible from France. Like Andorra, it was virtually independent for much of its history, and for centuries it was sealed off from the rest of Spain by snow for eight months of the year. But in 1948 the Viella tunnel was cut to provide a year-round link with the provincial capital of Lleida along the N230 highway.

In recent years, life in the valley has changed beyond recognition. The old scythe-wielding hay-reapers of summer have been replaced by Massey Ferguson balers, overlooked by holiday chalets for city folk, which have sprouted at the edge of each and every village. Although the development is undeniably sympathetic – the new Aranese-style stone buildings fit closely with the originals – the increasing number of restaurants and sports shops sit uneasily with the dark little villages they surround. By getting off the main road through the valley and trekking it's still possible to get some idea of the region as it was fifty years ago, but on the whole the Vall d'Aran has lost its claim to be one of the most remote, unspoiled valleys in the Pyrenees. If all you're doing is making the bus ride to Viella you shouldn't expect great undiscovered rural expanses – generally speaking, someone's been there first and has built an apartment.

The valley's legendary greenness derives from the streams that drain into it, mostly from lakes on the south side, and this means that hikers have a better than even chance of enjoying the region's **wildlife** at first hand. When the weather is wet, black and yellow fire salamanders move with unconcerned slowness on the damp footpaths; before and after the rain, there are the equally brilliant butterflies, for which the Vall d'Aran and Aigües Tortes are both famous; and on the heights you should see izards (chamois).

Among themselves the inhabitants speak Aranés, a **language** (not a dialect, as a glance at the bizarre road signs will tell you) apparently consisting of elements of Catalan and Gascon with a generous sprinkling of Basque. *Aran*, in this language, means "valley"; *Nautaran*, "High Valley", is the most scenic eastern portion. The Aranese spelling of local place names is given in parentheses below.

Baqueira-Beret

The ride down from Port de la Bonaigua is adventurous, to say the least – and often plain scary as you contemplate the choice between the terrifying drop on one side and the sheer rock wall on the other. The first place you encounter coming down from the pass is **BAQUEIRA-BERET**, a mammoth skiing development, much frequented by the French. This is the biggest engine of change in the region, and the surrounding land is virtually all divided into lots waiting to be sold off. No doubt in winter the skiing fraternity have a ball (the resort is a favourite of the Spanish royal family), but in summer – as W.C Fields said of Philadelphia – Baqueira-Beret is closed. Stay on the bus.

Salardú

SALARDÚ, a few kilometres further west, is the biggest of the villages of the *Nautaran* and the obvious base for visiting the others, being large enough to offer a reasonable choice of accommodation and food, but small enough to feel pleasantly isolated (except in August or in peak ski season). With its steeply pitched roofs clustered around the church, it still retains some of its traditional feel, though the main attraction in staying is to explore the surrounding villages, all – like Salardú – centred on beautiful Romanesque churches. Salardú's is the roomy, thirteenth-century church of **Sant Andreu**, at the top of the village. The doors here are usually open, and you'll be able to see the *Sant Crist de Salardú*, a detailed wooden crucifix contemporary with the church. The church grounds are a pleasant place for a picnic.

Even at the height of the summer you should be able to find a bed (if not a room) easily enough in Salardú. If you need any help, there's a wooden **Turismo** hut (Mon–Fri 9.30am–1.30pm & 4.30–7.30pm, Sat 10am–1pm & 4–7pm, Sun 10am–1pm) just off the main road at the turning for Bagergue. The one **bank** in the village has normal opening hours throughout the year, plus 4.30–7.45pm in the ski season.

Accommodation

The cheapest **place to stay** is the *Era Garona* **youth hostel** (☎973/645271; ①), where you'll need a *IYHF* card and a reservation; it's above the village on the main road to Baqueira. The hostel serves evening meals (bed and breakfast only in September), and also rents out mountain bikes to all-comers (under 2000ptas a day). This is followed by the very central *Fonda Barbara*, c/Major 15 (☎973/645083; ②), and the lovely little wood-furnished rooms above the *Bar Muntanya*, at c/Major 4 (☎973/645008; ②) – both fill quickly in summer. The other central budget choice is one of the rooms above the *Supermercado Solei* (②) – ask in the bar, marked *Bar Comidas*.

Accommodation aimed at **trekkers** includes the *Refugi Rosti*, Plaça Major 4 (☎973/64 53 08; July to mid-Sept; rooms ③, dorms ①), in a 300-year-old building on the main square, and *Refugi Juli Soler Santaló* (☎973/645016; ①) in c/del Port, close to the youth hostel on the main Baqueira road. In addition to these, five more expensive **hostales** and **hotels** advertise themselves around the village. In any of these you can expect to pay at least 5000ptas for a double.

Eating and drinking

Most of the places to stay in the village serve good-value **meals**: non-guests can eat at the rated *Fonda Barbara*, provided they book in advance; while meals at the *Refugi Juli Soler Santaló* receive good reports, too. Alternatives are scarce, especially as the couple of village restaurants are overpriced for what you get: the *Bar Montaña* does a basic eggs-and-bacon meal or sandwiches (and has a pool table); there's a smart pizzeria on the main road; and the *Granja Era Lera*, on c/Major, is a fine *creperie* and sweet shop. While the restaurant at the *Refugi Rosti* is decent enough, too, its main draw is the nicest **bar** in town: *Delicatesen*.

Villages around Salardú

The Barcelona bus gets into Salardú at around 2pm, leaving plenty of time to find accommodation and then strike off into the surrounding villages. Houses here are traditionally built sturdily of stone, with slate roofs, and there's surprizingly little to distinguish a 400-year-old home from a four-year-old one. Fortunately, many display dates on the lintels – not of the same vintage as the churches but respectable enough, with some going back as far as the sixteenth century.

UNYA (UNHA), 700m up the hill, boasts a shrine of the same age as the church in Salardú, as does **BAGERGUE**, 2km higher up the road. Bagergue is the most countrified of the *Nautaran* settlements, sheltered from the view of Baqueira by the rounded contours of Roc de Macia. In the other direction, the church at **GESSA** (1km downhill, towards Arties) has a square, keep-like belfry. A signposted two-kilometre walk from Salardú runs along a delightful country lane into the heart of **TREDÒS**, a small village overlooked by a neglected church impressive mostly for its massive bulk and separate bell tower. A river runs through the middle of the old village, and once you've fooled around in this, and stopped for a drink in the village bar-restaurant, there's nothing to stop you from walking back to Salardú.

In terms of **trekking**, there are no really hard-core walks in the valley except for the eight-hour (round-trip) excursion up to the Liat lakes (2130m) by the French border, starting from Bagergue. This doesn't have many fans – the way up is along a steep, rutted track through shadeless, bleak scenery, more suited for jeeps or mountain bikes than walkers. The local paths joining Unya with Gessa, and Salardú with Tredòs, are only short, but everywhere – even from the asphalt road up to Bagergue – the scenery and views are spectacular. On a clear day, **Aneto**, highest peak in the Pyrenees at 3404m, looms snowcapped to the west.

Arties

ARTIES, the next valley community of any size, features the usual complement of new holiday homes. Nevertheless, if you're driving and can afford the time, it has some attraction, particularly in its Romanesque church which has fine furnishings, including a delightful painted screen. The village is otherwise known for its hot springs, but these are currently shut down. However, the *camí* leading past them cuts out 3km of the busy main highway, rejoining it at the river bridge below Garòs, a boon if you're cycling.

There's **accommodation** in Arties, too, which takes up the overflow from Salardú. Besides the very comfortable *Parador Don Gaspar de Portolà* (☎973/640801; ⑤), there are two or three hotels and a few places with rooms, like the *Bar Consul* (☎973/640803; ②) on the main road; *Portolà*, Plaça Ortau 4, in the village (☎973/640828; ②); or *María Jesús* (☎973/641472; ③). The *Montarto*, also on the main road (☎973/641602; ③), has a decent bar-restauarant, and there's a **campsite** (*Era Yerla d'Arties*: ☎973/641602; closed mid-Sept–Nov) just below the village on the main road to Viella.

Viella

From *Nautaran*, the highest of the three divisions of the Vall d'Aran, you move into *Mijaran* (Mid-Aran), whose major town is **VIELLA** (VIELHA), the end of the line for the bus from Barcelona/La Pobla de Segur in summer. This arrives at 2.30pm, with the daily service in the opposite direction leaving at about 11.30am. You may also arrive in Viella on the more direct run from Lleida, via El Pont de Suert, a spectacular route in its final stages that culminates in the awesome **Túnel de Viella**, nearly 6km long. This brings you right out at the southwest corner of the valley, the road swirling down to the town below.

In truth, the ride to Viella from either direction is more attractive than the town itself, and there's no great reason to stay, particularly if you can make a bus connection onwards. Viella has become intensely developed and smartened up of late, a trend aggravated by French day-trippers who patronize the numerous supermarkets, gift shops and restaurants. Yet some old smallholdings still lurk by the side of the Garona river as it runs through town, and the parish **church** in the central square is as decrepit as ever. There's a pleasant little café with outdoor seats just outside the church, and if you've got more time to kill, the **Museu Etnológico** (Mon–Sat 10am–1pm & 5–8pm, Sun 10am–1pm), on c/Major, west of the river, is worth a look for its coverage of Aranese history and folklore.

Practicalities

Buses stop next to the *Teléfonos* office, on the roundabout at the west end of town; information and tickets from inside the booth. The **Turismo** (Mon–Sat 9am–1pm & 4–8pm, Sun 10am–1pm & 5–7.30pm) is near the post office at c/Sarriulera 6, just off the church square; it has maps and accommodation lists.

As you might expect there's no shortage of **accommodation** in Viella, though little of it is particularly good value. Starting at the church, you'll find the best of the budget places by turning left along the main street and then right down the lane just across the bridge. Just off to the left, at c/Cardenal Cassanyas 6, is the *Hostal El Ciervo II* (☎973/640165; ③); *Pensío Puig*, c/Camí Reiau 6 (☎973/640031; ②), has rock-bottom prices and consequently is often full; or there's also the tiny *Pension Casa Vicenta* at c/Camí Reiau 7 (☎973/640819; ③). You'll find other inexpensive *habitaciones* at c/Major 5 and c/Major 9, across from the museum. Otherwise, the *Verneda* **campsite** (☎973/641024; March–Oct) is 5km away on the road towards France.

Meals aren't particularly memorable in Viella either. About the best you can do without excessive spending is to eat at the *Et Curné* bar on Passeig dera Llibertat which serves menus from 1000ptas to 2100ptas. Or you can get an authentic snack in the *Era Puma* on the main Avda. Pas d'Orro, or a good sandwich at the nearby *Frankfurt Aran*.

Les Bordes, Arròs and Bossost

You can continue from Viella by bus, through **LES BORDES** (6km) and **ARRÒS** (9km), two places that play a key role in Aranese domestic architecture. Les Bordes supplies the granite for the walls and Arròs the slates for the slightly concave roofs that the planners generally demand in *Nautaran* and *Mijaran*. Arròs itself, though, is almost in the lower *Baixaran* region, and the balconied houses here, around the octagonal bell-tower, have rendered white walls and red-tiled roofs. There are two **campsites** at Arròs – the *Artigane* (☎973/640189; June–Sept) and the *Verneda* (see Viella, above) – and another just past Les Bordes.

The focus of *Baixaran* is the large village of **BOSSOST**, 18km from Viella, where the houses are strung out along the main road and on both sides of the curving river. This being the direct road between France and the Viella tunnel, accommodation is highly priced, but there's no real reason to stop: it's only around 10km to the **French border**, and 20km to the first significant French town, Saint-Béat.

Parc Nacional d'Aigües Tortes i Sant Maurici

The most popular target for trekkers in the Catalan Pyrenees is the **Parc Nacional d'Aigües Tortes i Sant Maurici**, a vast and beautiful mountainous area constituting Catalunya's only national park. Established in 1955, and covering some 130 square kilometres, it is a rock- and forest-strewn landscape of harsh beauty, including spectacular snow-spotted peaks of up to 3000m, cirques and dramatic V-shaped valleys. For the less adventurous, there are any number of mid-altitude rambles to be made through some lovely scenery. The Sant Nicolau valley (in the west) has many glacially-formed lakes and cirques, as well as the Aigües Tortes (Twisted Waters) themselves; in the east, the Escrita valley, slightly craggier, contains the Sant Maurici lake.

The most common **trees** are fir and Scotch pine, along with silver birch and beech, especially on north-facing slopes. There's also an abundance of flowers in spring and early summer (don't forget that when spring is in the air lower down, winter still has a grip on the higher slopes). As for the **fauna**, wild boar apparently roam here and at the very least you should see izards (chamois); **birds** you might spot include the golden eagle, ptarmigan and black woodpecker.

Which **approach** to the park you use rather depends upon which zone you intend to explore, and how strenuous you want your walking to be. Access to the Sant Maurici zone is via the village of **Espot**, just beyond the eastern fringes of the park and within 7km of the La Pobla de Segur–Viella bus route. Quickest access to the high and remote peaks is via **Capdella**, south of the park at the head of the Flamicell river – this is the next valley west from Noguera Pallaresa, served by bus from La Pobla de Segur. Finally, for the western Aigües Tortes zone, the entrance is from **Boí**, approached via **El Pont de Suert** which has a bus service from La Pobla de Segur and Viella.

If you can only afford a day or two, then Boí is probably the best place for which to aim. It's easy to reach, and though the village itself is some 7km from the park entrance, there's enough mountain grandeur in the immediate surroundings to compensate if you're not going all the way into the park. All the approaches – and details of how to move on into the park – are dealt with fully below, while for **practical details** about the park itself check the boxed feature below.

AIGÜES TORTES: PRACTICALITIES

• **Entry** to the park is free, but private cars are prohibited between 10am and 6pm, and only 175 vehicles are allowed in before 10am. A total access ban for vehicles except for the jeep-taxis into the park from Espot and Boí is under consideration. You can get **information** at one of the summer park information offices in Espot or Boí (see text for details); or contact the park's administration office at c/Camp de Mart 35, 25004 Lleida (☎973/246650).

• **Accommodation in the park** is limited to four mountain refuges (with a warden during the summer – you'll need sleeping bags at all of them), but there are several more in nearly as impressive alpine areas just outside the park boundaries. Each refuge has a kitchen, emergency transmitter and bunk beds. **Camping** in the park (and in a peripheral "zone of influence") is officially forbidden, but there are campsites close to Caldes de Boí and at Taüll in the west, and at Espot in the east. All the approach villages have *hostales* and hotels.

• The region is covered by three *Editorial Alpina* **map/booklets**: the two you'll need for walking any of the routes described below are "Sant Maurici" for the east, and "Montardo" for the west, both 1:25,000 and available in Boí, Espot and good bookshops throughout the Pyrenees and in Barcelona. An English-language leaflet/map about the park is also available from park information offices. Beware some of the "paths" marked on maps: even where a *bona fide* trail exists, you may eventually find yourself at the base of steep, snowed-in passes which require special equipment to negotiate – check routes with information offices and refuge wardens.

• Be aware of **weather conditions**. In winter the park is covered in snow. In mid-summer many rivers are passable which are otherwise not so, but temperature contrasts between day and night are still very marked and you should always be prepared for foul weather higher up. Local summer patterns in recent years have alternated between daily rain showers throughout July and August, or prolonged drought – the general trend is towards drier summers. The best time to see the wonderful colour contrasts here are in autumn or early summer.

• In winter, the park is excellent for cross-country and high-mountain **skiing**, though there are no marked trails. There are two ski resorts on the fringes of the park: Boí-Taüll in the west and Super Espot in the east.

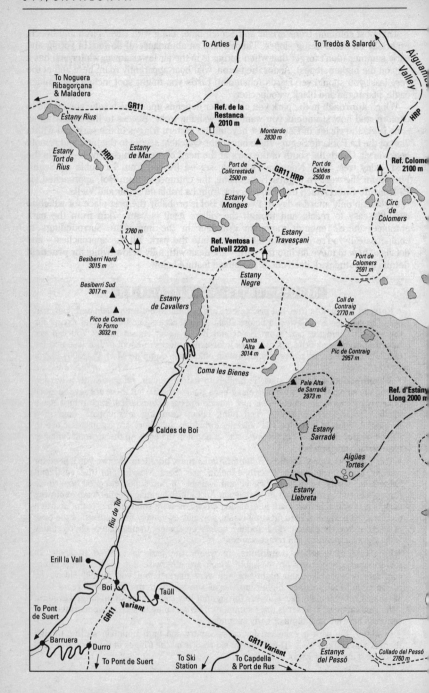

To Arties

To Tredòs & Salardú

Aiguamòg Valley

HRP

To Noguera
Ribagorçana
& Maladera

GR11

Estany Rius

Ref. de la
Restanca
2010 m

Montardo
2830 m

Ref. Colome
2100 m

HRP

Estany
Tort de
Rius

Estany
de Mar

Port de
Collcrestada
2500 m

GR11 HRP

Port de
Caldes
2500 m

Circ
de
Colomers

Estany
Monges

2760 m

Ref. Ventosa i
Calvell 2220 m

Estany
Travesçani

Besiberri Nord
3015 m

Port de
Colomers
2591 m

Besiberri Sud
3017 m

Estany
Negre

Coll de
Contraig
2770 m

Pico de Coma
lo Forno
3032 m

Estany
de Cavallers

Punta
Alta
3014 m

Pic de Contraig
2957 m

Ref. d'Estàny
Llong 2000 m

Coma les Bienes

Pala Alta
de Sarradé
2973 m

Estany
Sarradé

Caldes de Boí

Aigües
Tortes

Riu de Tor

Estany
Llebreta

Erill la Vall

Boí

Taüll

To Pont
de Suert

GR11

Variant

Barruera

Durro

To Ski
Station

To Capdella
& Port de Rus

GR11 Variant

Estanys
del Pessó

Collado del Pessó
2760 m

To Pont de Suert

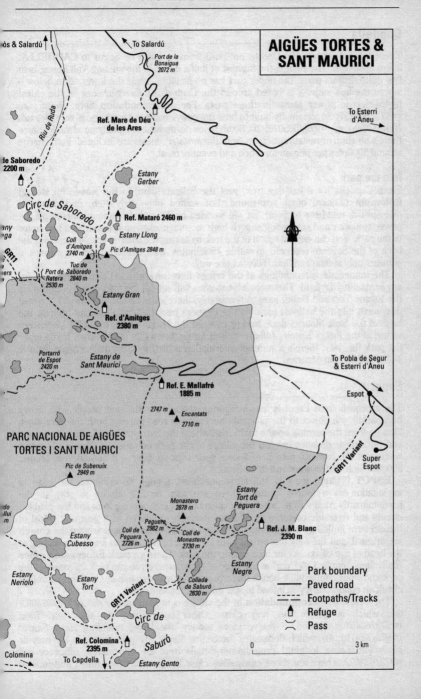

AIGÜES TORTES & SANT MAURICI

To Salardú

Port de la Bonaigua 2072 m

ò & Salardú

To Esterri d'Aneu

Riu de Ruda

Ref. Mare de Déu de les Ares

de Saboredo 2200 m

Estany Gerber

Circ de Saboredo

Ref. Mataró 2460 m

any ga

Estany Llong

GR11 ers

Coll d'Amitges 2740 m

Pic d'Amitges 2848 m

Tuc de Saboredo 2840 m

Port de Ratera 2530 m

Estany Gran

Ref. d'Amitges 2380 m

Portarró de Espot 2420 m

Estany de Sant Maurici

Ref. E. Mallafré 1885 m

To Pobla de Segur & Esterri d'Aneu

Espot

2747 m

Encantats 2710 m

PARC NACIONAL DE AIGÜES TORTES I SANT MAURICI

GR11 Variant

Super Espot

Pic de Subenuix 2949 m

Monastero 2878 m

Estany Tort de Peguera

Peguera 2982 m

Coll de Peguera 2726 m

Coll de Monastero 2730 m

Ref. J. M. Blanc 2390 m

do lui m

Estany Cubesso

Estany Tort

Estany Neriolo

Estany Negre

Collada de Saburó 2630 m

GR11 Variant

Circ de

Saburó

Ref. Colomina 2395 m

Colomina

To Capdella

Estany Gento

	Park boundary
	Paved road
	Footpaths/Tracks
	Refuge
	Pass

0   3 km

Capdella

There's one daily bus (*La Ocense*; not Sun) from La Pobla de Segur to **CAPDELLA**, 30km upstream. The village, the highest of half a dozen in the unsung Vall Fosca, is in two quite distinct parts: the upper part has no facilities, while the lower, 2km below – where the bus stops – is based around the *Central (de Energia)*, one of the oldest hydro-electric power plants in these parts. For **accommodation** here, *Hostal Leo* (☎973/663157; ③), originally built to host the power company workers, is very elegant; *Hostal Monseny* (☎973/663079; ③), 800m below, is newer but equally good value. Since there's no shop or restaurant (apart from the *hostales*), meals are included: both charge around 3000ptas per person for a bed and evening meal.

Into the park

From Capdella it's a half-day trek, past the Sallente dam, to the wonderful **Refugi Colomina** (2395m; open year-round, but staffed only early Feb, mid-March to mid-April & mid-June to Sept), an old wooden chalet ceded to mountaineers by the power company and set among superb high mountain lakes on the southern perimeter of the park. You can cut out much of the trek by taking the *teléferic* (cable car) from the back of the Sallente reservoir to within 45 minutes' walk of the refuge: departures in summer only at 9am and 3pm, 500ptas one-way.

The immediate surroundings of the refuge have several short outings suitable for any remaining daylight. The more adventurous will set out the following day to Boí via the Estany Tort and Dellui pass. Alternatively, there's the classic (if difficult) traverse due north into the national park via the Peguera pass (2726m). You end up near the base of the Sant Maurici dam, having covered the length of the beautiful Monastero valley, at the *Refugi Ernest Mallafré*, poised for further walks (see below). If you enter the park this way, there's a summer information post (July–Sept daily 9.30am–2pm & 4–6.30pm) at Sant Maurici.

Espot

The approach from Espot is less strenuous, though purists (and people with heavy backpacks) will object to the probable necessity of road-walking both the very steep 7km up from the turning on the main road where the Barcelona–Viella bus drops you, and the similar distance beyond the village to the park entrance. If there's a jeep-taxi waiting at the turn-off, take it and save your legs for later – it should cost around 300ptas each for the short run up to Espot.

ESPOT (1430m) itself is still fairly unspoiled, though hovering on the edge of exploitation as a tourist centre. There are four or five places to stay in the predominantly rural village, where hay spills out of neighbouring lofts and the cobbled streets and riverside pastures are still reassuringly splattered with goat shit. Most of the old farm buildings downstream from the La Capella bridge and around the church are original, and the only discordant note is struck by the rank of jeep-taxis waiting at the head of the village, all for hire on into the park. There's a **park information office** (daily 9am–1pm & 3.30–7pm) at the edge of Espot, where you can pick up **maps** of the park and wonderful wildlife books (unfortunately only in Spanish or Catalan), as well as check on conditions if you intend to stay and trek for some time.

The best-value **accommodation** in the village is at *Residencia Felip* (☎973/624093; ③), which is simple but very clean. Other possibilities are the *Hotel Roya* (☎973/624040; ③) and, if you've more money, the large, rambling *Hotel Saurat* (☎973/624162; ④), which dominates the centre. Espot also participates in the *casa de pagès* (old house lodging) programme; details from the information office or call ☎973/624072. There are three **campsites** close by: the *Sol i Neu* (open mid-June to mid-Sept; ☎973/624001) is excellent and just a few hundred metres from the village; *La Mola* (July–Sept; ☎973/624024), 2km further down the hill, has a swimming pool. At the far (upstream) edge of Espot, beyond the old bridge, the *Solau* (☎973/624068), in the *bairro* of that name, isn't a brilliant campsite, but it also rents out rooms (②), a good fallback if the village itself is full.

As for **eating**, you pay for the fact that you're in a tourist mill, miles from anywhere; there are no *menús del día* for less than 1000ptas. Most of the bars serve sandwiches and *platos combinados*, though the surly *Cabana d'Espot* is worth avoiding. In contrast, the adjacent *L'Isard* is welcoming and as fair value as you'll find in the village. There are also two well-stocked **supermarkets** and another shop selling maps, camping gas cartridges, and the like.

Walks from Espot

Coming from Espot, you see clearly how development is starting to encroach on the park. Two kilometres above the village, **SUPER ESPOT** is already established as a substantial ski-resort, and a recent road also leads to the park boundary (3km) and from there to the end of the tarmac at the **Estany de Sant Maurici** (a further 4km). The jeep-taxis from Espot run this far: they carry eight people and cost around 5000ptas, so if you can share a full one it's not a terribly expensive way to cut out the initial, fairly dull, road-walking.

One of the classic walks – demanding but realistic for anyone in reasonable shape – is right across the park from east to west, starting at Espot, or further in at the Sant Maurici lake: Espot to Boí is about 30km, or around twelve hours' walking. The Sant Maurici lake itself, beneath the twin peaks of Els Encantats (2749m), is one of the most beautiful spots in the Catalan Pyrenees and the **Refugi Ernest Mallafré** (open early June–mid-Oct) offers the chance to stay here. There's another refuge, **Refugi d'Estany Llong** (mid-June–mid-Oct; ☎973/696284 for reservations) at **Estany Llong**, three or four hours along the wide track, with Caldes de Boí then within easy reach.

Heading north from Sant Maurici, you can reach a couple the **Refugi-Xalet Amitges** (mid-June–Sept; ☎93/318 15 05 for reservations) with a couple of hours' walking up the Ratera valley. The fourth of the park's refuges, **Refugi Josep Mariá Blanc** (mid-June–Sept), in the Peguera valley, is reached by a direct trail from Espot in around three-and-a-half hours. You can continue to the Colomina refuge in another three-and-a-half to four hours from here: this is a well-travelled route, marked as a variant of the GR11 trail. Unless you're very committed to trekking, and proficient and well-equipped, the east–west traverse described above is the best option. Really serious walkers regard it as altogether too easy, but if you spread it over two or three days there are some excellent day-treks to be enjoyed from the refuges at which you'll stay.

El Pont de Suert: the route to Boí

The route into the western area of Aigües Tortes begins at **EL PONT DE SUERT**, a small town 41km northwest of La Pobla de Segur: currently, there's a *La Ocense* bus at 2pm from La Pobla, as well as services from Viella (2 daily) and from Lleida. The buses all stop close to the church on the main road through town, with timetables posted in the window of the adjacent *Las Cumbres* bar-restaurant.

El Pont de Suert is pleasant enough if you have to spend the night before catching the bus north to Boí the next day (which operates June–Sept only). There are several **cafés** with outdoor tables, and places doing sandwiches and *platos combinados*, while you can stock up in the supermarkets and bakeries for the days ahead. **Rooms** are available at *Habitaciones Gállego* (☎973/690242; ②), which is opposite where the bus stops. There are also a few places in the next price category, including the *Can Mestre* at Plaça Major 8 (☎973/690306; ③), which has a good dining room.

Coll, Barruera, Durro and Erill la Vall

From El Pont de Suert, a bus (June–mid-Sept once daily, currently at 11.15am) runs north up the Noguera de Tort valley towards Caldes de Boí, passing Boí on the way. It's an area crammed with **Romanesque churches** and is far from an impossible route to walk or hitch: Boí is 21km away, and there's some local traffic to the villages on the way.

After about 8km the twelfth-century church of Santa María appears on the hillside to the left at **COLL** (the village is 2km off the main road); the ironwork on the door is particularly fine, but you're in for a long walk afterwards if you get off the bus to see it. **BARRUERA**, 4km further on and much larger, has several places to stay, the least expensive being the *Noray* (☎973/694021; June–Sept only; ③), right on the main road. For a bit more of an outlay, the *Farre d'Avall* (☎973/694029; ③–④), in the village centre, is much more pleasant and quiet. Barruera also boasts the main **Turismo** for the entire valley (Mon–Fri 10am–2pm & 4–7pm, Sat 10am–1pm & 4–6pm; ☎973/694000), right opposite the not-so-nice *Camping Boneta* (☎973/696086; April–Sept). And there's also a **riding stable** – the *Hípica Casa Coll* (☎973/694072) – if you fancy saddling up.

There are two Romanesque churches hereabouts: the eleventh-century Sant Feliu, down by the river and campsite, and La Nativitat de la Mare de Déu at the small village of **DURRO**, 3km away by road, on the hillside to the east, with a massive bell-tower. Here, you can stay and eat at *Casa Ioquim* (☎973/696059; ③). Finally, just before the turn-off for Boí, you pass **ERILL LA VALL**, whose twelfth-century church of Santa Eulalia has an attractive arcaded porch and a six-storey tower.

Boí

BOÍ lies 1km off the main road, which continues up to Caldes de Boí (see below): if you're dropped at the turn-off instead of being taken into the centre, it's a twenty-minute walk. With a few stone houses clinging to steep mud-spattered alleys, the core of Boí remains attractive despite the inevitable surrounding development. This amounts to extensive parking facilities, several new (overpriced) hotels and a choice of restaurants, though if you've just walked across the park and want to rest up for a couple of days this kind of development is most welcome. If you're on your way in, there's plenty of chance to get used to the stunning scenery first with some lovely local walks, on relatively gentle, green slopes beneath the peaks.

Prime **accommodation** is at the splendid *Hostal Pascual* (☎973/696014; ③), at the turn-off from the main road, 1km below the village by the bridge. This has cheaper rooms without bath, is open out of season, and has helpful owners and a decent menu in its dining room. In the village, more expensive and similarly endowed choices include the *Pensió Pey* (☎973/696036; ④), in the square; *Hostal Beneria* (☎973/696030; ④), just off the square; and *Hostal Fondevila* (☎973/696011; ④), 200m down towards the main road. There are also some clean, modern rooms (②) just through the stone archway from the village square – look for the *habitacions* sign.

For **eating**, you'll not do better than the *Casa Higinio*, 200m up the road to Taüll, above the village. Its wood-fired range produces excellent grilled meat dishes, or try the fine local trout – a big meal accompanied by the local *vi negre* comes to around 1500ptas, but there's no *carta* advising you of this, so don't order separate items unecessarily. Other restaurants in the village also have ranges; and the *Hostal Pascual* serves hearty *menús del día*.

The **park information office** is in Boí's square (daily 9am–1pm & 3.30–7pm), and you can buy an *Editorial Alpina* map in the **supermarket** (open Sun morning too) behind the *Hostal Beneria*. The **bank**, around the back of the supermarket, is open in the summer, on Monday, Wednesday and Thursday only, from 5–7pm.

Into the park

It's 6km from Boí to the **park entrance**, and another 4km to the scenic springs of **Aigües Tortes**, where there's yet another park information office (July–Sept daily 9.30am–2pm & 4–6.30pm). Jeep-taxis from Boí's village square run as far as this, past the artificial Llebreta reservoir, and, as at Espot, this will cost around 5000ptas per vehicle. You can either wander around for an hour or so, or forfeit your return ticket and walk back down later (no great hardship). If you walk on further into the park, it's relatively level as far as **Estany Llong**, but beyond that point the ascent to the pass overlooking Sant Maurici begins.

Around Boí: Taüll and Caldes de Boí

The added advantage of approaching (or leaving) the park via Boí is that you get the chance to visit the area's numerous **Romanesque churches**. Only one original apse and the bell-tower remain of the renovated twelfth-century church of Sant Joan in Boí village, but within reasonable walking distance are the churches at Erill la Vall, Barruera and Durro (see above). The path to Erill la Vall from Boí, across the valley, takes half an hour; the best route to Durro is the well-signposted path which you can pick up behind Boí village – it starts just over the little bridge at the back of the village and takes around an hour to follow.

Taüll

The most popular local excursion, however, is the walk to **TAÜLL**, three or four kilometres by road above Boí (or there's a steep forty-minute path from the village that cuts across the road). Either way, you arrive at the six-storeyed tower of Romanesque **Sant Climent** (10.30am–2pm & 4–8pm; 50ptas), whose interior is like a dusty junk shop. The ticket lets you climb the rickety wooden steps to the top of the bell-tower for scintillating village and valley views. There's an appealing bar with a garden, the *Mallador*, just outside the church, run by nice folks with a good taste in music; it's the only place in the village that serves any sort of to-order breakfast (pricey, like their lunches and dinners). Up in the village, the church of **Santa María** was consecrated, like Sant Climent, in 1123, though its belfry only has four storeys. After a millennium of subsidence, there's not a right angle remaining in the building. Admission is by the same ticket as for Sant Climent, and it's nominally open the same hours, but as it's also the parish church it may in fact be open longer.

Accommodation options, mostly under the *casa de pagès* scheme, include *La Coma* (☎973/696025; ③), at the village entrance, with *Sant Climent* (③) and *Casa Barò* (③) across the way. Budget rooms are either at *Casa Llovet*, Plaça Franc 5 (☎973/696032; ②), or *Casa Chep* (☎973/696054; ②), just below Plaça Santa María – information from the adjacent supermarket. A **campsite** (☎973/696082) perches on the hill below Sant Climent. *La Coma*'s **restaurant** is very good, if a bit on the expensive side; *El Caliu*, at the top of Taüll in a new apartment block, is also fine, though tending towards *cuisine minceur* in its portions.

Boí-Taüll and Caldes de Boí

The character of both Taüll and Boí has been changed by the ski resort – known as **BOÍ-TAÜLL** – established on the mountains above them. Even in summer, Taüll is prey to tour coaches and drivers seeking out panoramic picnic spots, and there's a new and enormous holiday complex 1500m beyond the village, en route to the ski station. Even before the ski resort was built, one other local place that had already seen radical transformation is the spa resort of **CALDES DE BOÍ**, 5km above the park entrance, built below the highest peaks in the immediate area and within sight of one of the highest dams, at the southern end of Estany de Cavallers. This is where the bus that passes Boí ends its run, but there's no budget accommodation here.

THE SOUTH

The great triangle of land **south** of Barcelona is not the first place you think of going when you visit Catalunya. It's made up of the province of Tarragona and part of the province of Lleida (the rest of which takes in the western Pyrenees) and, with the exception of the obvious attractions of the coast and one medieval monastery, almost all the interest lies in the provincial capitals themselves.

The main target is the **Costa Daurada** – the coastline that stretches from Barcelona to Tarragona and beyond – which is far less exploited than the Costa Brava. Although this might be reason in itself to visit, it is easy enough to see why it has been so neglected. All too often the shoreline is drab, with beaches that are narrow and characterless, backed by sparse villages overwhelmed by pockets of villas. There are exceptions, though, notably vibrant **Sitges**, which is just forty minutes from Barcelona. This is one of the great Spanish resorts, bolstered by its reputation as a major gay summer destination. If all you want to do is relax by a beach for a while, there are several other less trendy and perfectly functional possibilities, ranging from tiny **Cunit** to the region's biggest holiday resorts at **Salou** and **Cambrils**.

The Costa Daurada really begins to pay dividends, however, if you can forget about the beaches temporarily and plan to spend a couple of days in **Tarragona**, the provincial capital. It's a city with a solid Roman past – reflected in an array of impressive ruins and monuments – and it makes a handy springboard for trips inland into Lleida province. South of Tarragona, Catalunya peters out in the lagoons and marshes of the **Delta de l'Ebre**, a riverine wetland that's rich in bird life: perfect for slow boat trips, fishing and sampling the local seafood.

Inland attractions are fewer, and many travelling this way are inclined to head on out of Catalunya altogether, not stopping until they reach Zaragoza. It's true that much of the region is flat, rural and dull, but nonetheless it would be a mistake to miss the outstanding monastery at **Poblet**, only an hour or so inland from Tarragona. A couple of other nearby towns and monasteries – notably medieval **Montblanc** and **Santa Creus** – add a bit more interest to the region, while by the time you've rattled across the huge plain that encircles the provincial capital of **Lleida** you've earned a night's rest. Pretty much off the tourist trail, Lleida makes a very pleasant overnight stop: from here, it's only two and a half hours to Zaragoza, or you're at the start of dramatic road and train routes into the western foothills of the Catalan Pyrenees.

Sitges

SITGES, 40km from Barcelona, is definitely the highlight of the Costa Daurada. Established in the 1960s as a holiday town whose loose attitudes openly challenged the rigidity of Franco's Spain, it has now become the great weekend escape for young Barcelonans, who have created a resort very much in their own image. It's also a noted **gay** holiday destination, with a nightlife to match: indeed, if you don't like vigorous action of all kinds, you'd be wise to avoid Sitges in the summer: staid it isn't. As well as a certain style, the Barcelona trippers have brought with them the high prices from the Catalan capital – the bars, particularly, can empty the deepest wallets – while finding anywhere to stay (at any price) can be a problem unless you arrive early in the day or book well in advance. None of this deters the varied and generally well-heeled visitors, however, and nor should it, since Sitges as a sort of Barcelona-on-Sea is definitely worth experiencing for at least one night.

The town itself is reasonably attractive – a former fishing village whose pleasing houses and narrow streets have attracted artists and opted-out intellectuals for a century or so. The beaches, though crowded, are far from oppressive, and Sitges even

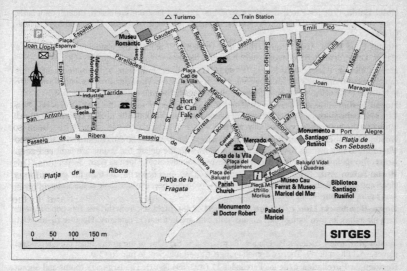

has a smattering of cultural interest – though no one is seriously suggesting you come here just for that.

Arrival, information and accommodation

Trains to Sitges leave Barcelona-Sants every 30 minutes throughout the day; the station is about ten minutes' walk from the town centre and seafront. **Buses** stop in front of the train station. If you're driving, it's probably best to pay for a **car park** rather than leave your vehicle on the street: there are car parks at Plaça Espanya (open air), c/Sant Francesc (covered) and at the *Mercat Nou*, c/Artur Carbonell (covered).

On arrival you may as well drop in at the **Turismo** (July–mid-Sept daily 9am–9pm; mid-Sept–June Mon–Fri 9.30am–2pm & 4–6.30pm, Sat 10am–1pm; ☎93/894 12 30), at the *Oasis* shopping mall, which is a right turn out of the train station and then right again up Passeig Vilafranca. It has a useful free map with local listings on the back, and all sorts of English-language information about the town. From July to September, there's also tourist information available from a building on Plaça Ajuntament (Tues–Sun 10am–1pm & 5–9pm) and from an office inside a double-decker bus parked on Passeig Maritim (Tues–Sun 6–9pm).

Accommodation

If you're offered a **room** by someone as you get off the train, take it: if it's sub-standard, you can always look for a better one later. Otherwise, try one of the places listed below, though note that in July and August they are all liable to be full; it's always best to book ahead. If you arrive without a reservation, a short walk through the central streets and along the front (particularly Passeig de la Ribera) reveals most of the possibilities – places near the station are not exactly glamorous, but are more likely to have space. Come **out of season** (after October and before May) and the high prices tend to soften a little, though in mid-winter you may have real difficulty finding anywhere that's open, especially at the budget end of the scale.

The nearest local **campsite** is *El Roca* (☎93/894 00 43), well signposted north of the Turismo under the railway bridge.

Hotel Bahia, c/de les Parellades 27 (☎93/894 00 12). Not far from the beach, though on a fairly noisy street, this comfortable hotel-restaurant drops its prices out of season. Open mid-April to mid-Oct. ④.

Hostal Casa Bella, Avda. Artur Carbonell 12 (☎93/894 27 53). On the main road down from the station. Large, spartan rooms: some have balconies but these are noisy. Open May–Oct. ③.

Hotel Celimar, Passeig de la Ribera 18 (☎93/811 01 70). Seafront hotel at the bottom end of this range, worth trying early on for a balconied room with a view. These, and rooms with shower, are in the next price category up, though you may get a small discount outside high season. ④.

Hostal Ferbor, Passatge Termes (☎93/894 23 43). Hidden up one of the back streets off Plaça Espanya, and consequently a fair chance of a room, with or without bath. In high season, prices can lurch into the next category. Open all year. ③.

Hostal-Residencia Internacional, c/Sant Francesc 52 (☎93/894 26 90). Clean and simple place where the family owners have made a bit of effort with the decor; the rooms are light and crisp. Nearer the station than the beach, but not massively inconvenient. Open all year. ③–④.

Hostal Julian, Avda. Artur Carbonell 2 (☎93/894 03 06). Just down the hill from the station, this is clean and more likely than most to have room – probably because one look at the wallpaper puts many off. Open June–Sept. ③.

Hostal-Residencia Lido, c/Bonaire 26 (☎93/894 48 48). Just back from the sea, this popular, well-kept place has its own lounge-bar. Rooms with bath are in the next category. Open April–mid-Oct. ③.

Hostal Mariangel, c/de les Parellades 78 (☎93/894 13 57). One of the town's most popular budget places, so it fills quickly. There's a small lounge. Closed mid-Sept to mid-Nov. ③.

Residencia Parellades, c/de les Parellades 11 (☎93/894 08 01). The large airy rooms and decent location make this a good first choice. Open April–Sept. ③.

Hotel Romantic, c/Sant Isidre 33 (☎93/894 83 75). Attractive, old converted nineteenth-century villa in the quiet streets away from the front, not far from the train station. It's a favourite with gay visitors. Many rooms have a terrace overlooking the gardens; those with showers are in the next category. Open April–mid-Oct. The similar *La Renaixença* is owned by the same management (same telephone number and prices), but is open all year. ④.

Hotel Terramar, Passeig Maritim 30 (☎93/894 00 50). Superb position at the end of the long promenade, and splendid views from its large balconied rooms, but a bit dated in style and decor. Open April–Dec. ⑥.

Hotel El Xalet, c/Illa de Cuba 35 (☎93/811 00 70). Charming, discreet hotel in a beautiful *modernista* house near the train station. There are only 10 rooms – booking ahead is a necessity in summer. It's at the bottom end of this price category. ⑤.

Around the town

It's the **beach** that brings most people to Sitges, and it's not hard to find, with two strands right in town, to the west of the church. From here, a succession of beaches of varying quality and crowdedness stretches west as far as the *Hotel Terramar*, a couple of kilometres down the coast. A long seafront promenade, the **Passeig Maritim**, runs all the way there, and all along there are beach bars, restaurants, showers and water sports facilities. Beyond the hotel, following the train line, you eventually reach the more notorious nudist beaches, a couple of which are exclusively gay. It's worth noting that as the town's popularity has increased, petty crime seems to have been exported from Barcelona to Sitges. Watch your possessions on the beaches and exercise care at night.

Back in town, make the effort at some stage to climb up the knoll overlooking the beaches, topped by the Baroque parish church – known as *La Punta* – and a street of old whitewashed mansions. One contains the **Museu Cau Ferrat** (Tues–Sat 9.30am–2pm & 4–6pm, Sun 9.30am–2pm; 200ptas, free on Sun), an art gallery for want of a better description. Home and workshop to the artist and writer Santiago Rusiñol (1861–1931), its two floors contain a massive jumble of his own paintings, as well as sculpture, painted tiles, drawings and various collected odds and ends – like the decorative ironwork Rusiñol brought back in bulk from the Pyrenees. Two of his better buys were the minor El Grecos at the top of the stairs on either side of a crucifix. The museum also contains works by the artist's friends (including Picasso) who used to meet in the *Els Quatre Gats* bar in Barcelona.

Two other museums are worth giving a whirl on a rainy day. The **Museu Maricel de Mar** (Tues–Sat 9.30am–2pm & 4–6pm, Sun 9.30am–2pm; 200ptas, free on Sun), next door to the Museu Cau Ferrat, has more minor artworks, medieval to modern, and maintains an impressive collection of Catalan ceramics and sculpture. More entertaining is the **Museu Romantic** (Tues–Sat 9.30am–2pm & 4–6pm, Sun 9.30am–2pm; 200ptas, free on Sun), which aims to show the lifestyle of a rich Sitges family in the eighteenth and nineteenth centuries by displaying some of their furniture and possessions. It's full of nineteenth-century knick-knacks, including a set of working music boxes and a collection of antique dolls. The museum is right in the centre of town, at c/Sant Gaudenci 1, off c/Bonaire.

Eating

International tourism has left its mark on Sitges: multilingual menus and "English breakfasts" are everywhere. Fortunately there are reasonable **restaurants** among them, and though you're unlikely to be sampling Catalan cuisine at its finest you'll find plenty of good *menús del día* on offer. Some suggestions appear below, but good general areas to explore are the side streets around the church, or the beachfront for more expensive seafood restaurants. For picnic supplies, the town's **market** – the *Mercat Nou* – is very close to the train station, on Avda. Artur Carbonell. **Ice cream** fiends should check out the stuff at *Ribera*, Passeig de la Ribera 5, *Italiana*, c/Jesús, or *Heladeria* and *Il Gelatieri*, both on c/Parellades.

Calitja, c/Marquès de Montroig 3. Catalan place open in the evenings that's well thought of and reasonably priced by Sitges standards. There's not a wide choice of dishes, though.

Chez Nous, Passeig Vilafranca 2. Moderately priced Swiss-French food in a restaurant popular with Sitges' gay crowd.

El Cisne, c/Sant Pere 4 (junction with c/de les Parellades). Nothing adventurous here, but you'll get well-cooked food in a dining room at the back of the bar – around 1100ptas for a four-course *menú del día*.

Dubliner, c/Illa de Cuba 9. It's bold and it's tacky, but this pub-restaurant knows its clientele – it offers two aspirins with its full English breakfast.

Flamboyant. c/Pau Barrabeig, off c/Carreta. Rather expensive, but with a beautiful garden setting. There's a 1550ptas *menú del día*.

Mare Nostrum, Passeig de Ribeira 60. Long-established fish restaurant situated on the seafront, with a menu that changes according to the catch and season. Around 3000ptas a head, though you may find a *menú del día* for half that.

Nieuw Amsterdam, c/de les Parellades 70. The "English Chef" can recommend what he likes, but the only real reason to come is for the medium-priced Indonesian and Indian specialities – not spectacular, but then you're not in Indonesia.

Olivers, c/Illa de Cuba 39. A mid-priced Spanish, rather than Catalan, restaurant, but the menu has some interesting flourishes that make a meal memorable. Meals from around 2000ptas a head.

El Superpollo, c/Sant Josep 8 (opposite Museu Romantic). Functional, stainless steel diner that's super value: terrific roast chicken and a glass of *cava* for just over 300ptas, or around 450ptas with french fries. Open daily until midnight.

El Trull, c/Mossèn Felix Clara 3, off c/Major. Fairly pricey French-style restaurant in the old town, though with a 1200ptas *menú del día* of mainly Spanish food (drinks excluded).

Los Vikingos, c/Marquès de Montroig 7–9. Good cheap restaurant right on the main tourist drag serving anything and everything (including fresh fish) accompanied by loud music.

Bars and nightlife

The main part of the action in Sitges is concentrated in a block of streets just back from the sea in the centre of town. Late-opening bars started to spring up here in the late-1950s: today, **c/1er (Primer) de Maig** (marked as c/Dos de Mayo on some old maps) and its continuation, **c/Marquès de Montroig**, are fully pedestrianized, while c/de les Parellades and c/Bonaire complete the block – not somewhere to come if you're looking for a quiet drink. This is basically one long run of disco bars, pumping music out into the late evening, interspersed with the odd restaurant or fancier cocktail bar, all with outdoor tables vying for your custom. The bars are all loud and their clientele predominantly young, and you can choose from just about any style you care to imagine: pool hall chic, colonial cane, Costa Brava excess or sleek dance-party. The best policy is to browse and sluice your way around until you find a favourite, though a few are picked out below. More **genteel bars** are not so easy to come by, though the places right on the seafront are generally quieter.

Afrika, c/1er de Maig. One of the best of the music bars.

Atlántida, Sector Terramar, 3km out of town. The town's favourite club, the clifftop *Atlántida* can be reached on regular buses which run there and back all night from the bottom of c/1er de Maig.

Bar Bodega Talino, c/de les Parellades 72. That rare thing in Sitges – a real *tapas* bar.

Café-Bar Roy, c/de les Parellades 9. An old-fashioned café with dressed-up waiters and marble tables. It's good for breakfast, or for a glass of *cava* and a fancy snack.

Parrots Pub, Plaça de la Industria. Stylish bar at the top of c/1er de Maig that's a required stop at some point of the day; it's just one place you can pick up the free gay map of Sitges (see below).

The gay scene and Carnaval

The **gay scene** in Sitges is frenetic and ever-changing, but chronicled on a gay map of town available from *Parrots Pub*, in Plaça de la Industria, as well as from several other bars and clubs.

During the day, current favourite hang-outs include the *Picnic Bar* on Passeig de la Ribera (opposite *Les Anfores* restaurant in the *Calipolis* hotel), popular for its sandwiches, and the terrace of the *Hotel Bertran*, at c/Marquès de Montroig 11–13. By early **evening**, everyone's moved on to *Parrots Pub* for cocktails. The best concentration of bars and discos is in c/Bonaire and c/Sant Buenaventura: at *Bourbons*, c/Sant Buenaventura 9, gay women are especially welcome, as they are in the *Bar Azul* (at no. 10), where happy hour is from 9–10.30pm. The best gay disco is at *Trailer* at c/Angel Vidal 14, in the old town. *Bar el 7*, at c/Nou 7, is a bar serving late breakfasts before an afternoon on the beach.

Carnaval

Carnaval in Sitges (February/March) is outrageous, thanks largely to the gay populace. The official programme of parades and masked balls is complemented by an unwritten but widely recognized schedule of events. The climax is Tuesday's late-night parade (not in the official programme), in which exquisitely dressed drag queens swan about the streets in high heels, twirling lacy parasols and coyly fanning themselves. Bar doors stand wide open, bands play, and processions and celebrations go on until four in the morning; *Bar el 7* has photos of parades from days gone by if you miss the action.

Listings

Banks *Banco Central*, c/de les Parellades 42; *Banco Español de Credito*, Plaça Cap de Vila 9; *Banco de Sabadell*, Plaça Cap de Vila 7; *La Caixa*, c/de les Parellades 16.

Cinema Movies are shown at *Casino Prado*, c/Francesc Gumà 6, and *El Retiro*, c/Angel Vidal 13.

Hospital *Hospital Sant Joan Baptista*, c/Hospital (☎93/894 00 03); in emergencies, call *Ambulatorio*, Plaça del Hospital (☎93/894 31 49).

Pharmacist Two central *farmacias* are *Ferret de Querol*, c/de les Parellades 1, and *Planas*, c/Artur Carbonell 30.

Police Plaça Ajuntament (☎93/811 76 25).

Post office Plaça Espanya, open Mon–Fri 9am–2pm.

Sports Other than in the sea, there's swimming in the *Piscina Municipal*, on Passeig Marítim; there's a windsurf school at Platja Riera Xica, a beach about 500m west of the church; and ten-pin bowling at the *Oasis* commercial centre.

Taxis There's a rank outside the train station (☎93/894 13 29), and you should find someone prepared to take you to/from Barcelona airport, which is 30km away.

Telephone office At c/Jesus 10, open daily 10am–10pm; c/Sant Pau, daily 11am–3pm & 5–11pm.

Train information Call ☎ 93/894 98 89.

Travel agencies *Viajes Sitges*, c/Marquès de Montroig 21 and Plaça Cap de Vila 19; *Viajes Playa de Oro*, c/de les Parellades 22. For train tickets and local tours.

Vilanova i la Geltrú

Eight kilometres south down the coast is the large fishing port of **VILANOVA I LA GELTRÚ**. Sitges gets most of its fish from here, but Vilanova borrows little in return – this is a real working port, whose quayside is lined with great refrigerated trucks waiting to load the catches from the hundreds of boats moored alongside. Although the town itself is nothing special, it's fascinating to wander along the docks through the scattered fishing nets, and when you tire of this there's a tourist side to Vilanova which is a pleasant contrast to the excesses of Sitges. There are two **beaches**: one beyond the port, the second – better – at the end of the seafront promenade. This road changes its name: near the port it's Passeig Marítim, while beyond, up by the Turismo, it becomes the Passeig de Ribes Roges, a palm-lined stretch with some nice café-bars open to the pavement.

You might be tempted by Vilanova's fair smattering of **museums**, two of which are found straight out of the train station door: one of Spain's few railway museums to the right (June–Aug Tues–Fri 10am–2pm & 5–7pm, Sat & Sun 10am–2pm; Sept–May Tues–Fri 10am–5pm, Sat & Sun 10am–2pm; 200ptas), probably best left to the specialists, and the **Biblioteca Museu Balaguer** (Tues–Sat 10am–2pm & 4–7pm, Sun 10am–2pm; free) to the left, founded by a local nineteenth-century politician. This is actually a quite rewarding stop, featuring pieces loaned from the Prado alongside a hoard of Catalan nineteenth- and twentieth-century paintings. Best of all, though, is the town's **Museu Romantic Casa Papiol**, behind the church at the very top of the Rambla Principal (Tues–Sat 10am–2pm & 4–6pm, Sun 10am–2pm; 200ptas). It's the sister museum to the one in Sitges, and the entrance fee includes a guided tour around the lavishly furnished eighteenth-century town house in which the collection is housed.

Practicalities

Trains and **buses** run about every twenty to thirty minutes from Sitges, and there are daily bus connections between Vilanova and Vilafranca del Penedés if you want to take an inland loop back to Barcelona. The bus might drop you off on the seafront, otherwise the main stops are in front of the train station – from here, cross the tracks by turning left out of the station, left again and heading under the tunnel. The port is on the left, while to the right is the Passeig Marítim. Further up, in the tower on Passeig Ribes Roges, is the **Turismo** (Mon–Sat 9.30am–1.30pm & 4.30–8.30pm, Sun 9.30am–1.30pm; ☎93/815 45 17).

There are a few **hotels** opposite the tourist office – and the town's best beach just beyond – though a less expensive *hostal*, the *Costa d'Or*, is at Passeig Maritím 49 (☎93/815 55 42; ③). If you want to pitch a tent, Vilanova might be a better bet than Sitges as it has three **campsites**, including the beach-based *Platja Vilanova* (☎93/895 07 67; April–Sept). There are a dozen or so **restaurants** along the seafront *passeig*, which on the whole are better value than the equivalents in Sitges. All have outdoor seating and while the views may not be quite so special as further up the coast, the atmosphere is a lot more down to earth. A good choice is the *Casa del Mar*, at no. 63, which has an excellent four-course *menú del día*; the restaurant doubles as the local fishermen's social club.

Cunit, Puerta Romana and Torredembarra

If the Costa Daurada beaches so far seem too crowded and frenetic – a distinct possibility in high season – there are a couple of other possible stops before Tarragona. Travelling by train, make sure you catch a local and not an express which will run straight through.

Cunit
CUNIT, about 15km south of Sitges, is the first stop inside Tarragona province. Rather soulless – more a collection of villas than a village – nonetheless it has a good, long beach. There's a **campsite**, *Mar de Cunit* (☎977/674058; June–Sept), behind the beach and a few good places **to stay**: *Los Almendros* (☎977/675437; ③), at the top of the village, but cut off from it by the highway, or the more pricey *Hostal La Diligencia* at Plaça Major 4 (☎977/674081; ④; Easter–Oct only), opposite the church in the centre. The former has an outdoor grill and a decent menu, while *La Diligencia* has a particularly good restaurant, with a 1300ptas *menú del día*.

Puerta Romana and Torredembarra
Again little more than a few streets of villas, the hamlet of **PUERTA ROMANA**, 15km before Tarragona, has perhaps the best swimming and sunbathing on this stretch of coast, with clean sand and clear water. It's not on the map or signposted from the main road, and the nearest train station is at the small resort of **TORREDEMBARRA** (a few hotels here), from where you could walk the 4km north. Ask to be put down at *Camping Sirena Dorada* (☎977/801103 or 801303), by the main road; this is open all year, changes money and has huts to rent. From there walk straight towards the sea, across the railway line, and you'll reach Puerta Romana, where there's another campsite – *Gavina* (☎977/801503; April–Sept) – slap bang on the beach. The nearest village is **CREIXELL**, a small place on a hill among olive groves, but the closest place to eat is at the *Puerta Romana*, a bar serving basic meals, on the street just back from the beach.

Tarragona

Majestically sited on a rocky hill, sheer above the sea, **TARRAGONA** is an ancient place. Settled originally by Iberians and then Carthaginians, it was later used as the base for the Roman conquest of the peninsula, which began in 218 BC with Scipio's march south against Hannibal. The fortified city became an Imperial resort and, under Augustus, *Tarraco* became capital of Rome's eastern Iberian province – the most elegant and cultured city of Roman Spain, boasting at its peak a quarter of a million inhabitants. Temples and monuments were built in and around the city and, despite a history of seemingly constant sacking and looting since Roman times, it's this distinguished past which still asserts itself throughout modern Tarragona.

Time spent in the handsome upper town quickly shows what attracted the emperors to the city: strategically – and beautifully – placed, it's a fine setting for some splendid Roman remains and a few excellent museums. There's an attractive medieval part, too, while the rocky coastline below conceals a couple of reasonable beaches. If there's a downside, it's that Tarragona is today the second largest port in Catalunya, so the views aren't always unencumbered – though the fish in the Serrallo fishing quarter is always good and fresh. Also, the city's ugly outskirts to the south have been steadily degraded by new industries which do little for Tarragona's character as a resort: chemical and oil refineries, and a nuclear power station.

Arrival and information

The city divides clearly into two parts, on two levels: a predominantly medieval, walled upper town (where you'll spend most time), and a prosperous modern extension below. Heart of the upper town is the sweeping **Rambla Nova**, a sturdy provincial rival to Barcelona's, lined with fashionable cafés and restaurants. Parallel, and to the east, lies the **Rambla Vella**, marking – as its name suggests – the start of the old town. To either side of the *ramblas* are scattered a profusion of relics from Tarragona's Roman past, including various temples, and parts of the forum, theatre and amphitheatre.

The **train station** is in the lower town: when you arrive, turn right and climb the steps ahead of you and you'll emerge at the top of the Rambla Nova, from where everything is a short walk away. The **bus terminal** is at the other end of the Rambla Nova, at Plaça Imperial Tarraco. Tarragona is well-provided with **tourist information** outlets, with main offices at Rambla Nova 46 (Mon–Sat 9.30am–8.30pm) and c/Major 39 (July–Sept Mon–Sat 10am–2pm & 4–8pm, Sun 10am–2pm; Oct–June Mon–Fri 9am–2pm & 4–7pm, Sat 10am–2pm, Sun 11am–2pm); and there are also seasonal information booths (July–Sept) at Plaça Imperial Tarraco and at the beginning of Via Augusta. The telephone number for tourist information is ☎977/232143.

You're unlikely to use the city's **local bus** network, other than for trips out to the campsite or to the aqueduct (the relevant details are given below), but the Turismos can give you a map showing the routes if you're interested.

Accommodation

Tarragona makes a great stopover, and is certainly less exhausting than Sitges. The nicest **rooms** in town, or at least the ones in the best location, are in the Plaça de la Font, just in the old town off Rambla Vella. If these are full, there are a couple of less desirable places near the train station. The pick of the city's pensions and hotels is reviewed below. Cheapest lodgings are at the *Sant Jordi* youth hostel (see list below for details), while down towards the beach, Platja Rabassada, a few kilometres out of town, are **campsites** and some more small hotels. *Camping Tarraco* here (☎977/239989) is open all year; office 9am–1pm & 4–7pm; 450ptas per person plus 450ptas per tent. Take bus #1, #3 or #9 (every 20min; 75ptas) from Plaça de Corsini, near the market and local forum.

Hotel España, Rambla Nova 49 (☎977/232712). Affordable mid-range hotel on the *rambla*, with bath in every room. ④.

Imperial Tarraco Hotel, Passeig de Palmeres (☎977/233040). The city's best and most expensive hotel, modern but beautifully positioned, sitting on top of the cliff and facing out to sea. ⑥.

Hotel Lauria, Rambla Nova 20 (☎977/236712). Posh three-star hotel on the main *rambla*. Outside July and August, room prices here become eminently reasonable. ⑤.

Pensión Mar i Flor, c/General Contreras 29 (☎977/238231). Only two blocks from the train station, and much less shifty than its location suggests. Housed in a modern apartment block, this has fairly large rooms and is clean and friendly; hot showers cost extra. ②.

Pensión Marsal, Plaça de la Font 26 (☎977/224069). Above the *Bar/Restaurante Turia*, this is the square's best-value choice, with modern, well-kept rooms at the bottom of this price range. Bathrooms are separate and spotless. Ask for one with a view of the square. ③.

Hostal Noria, Plaça de la Font 53 (☎977/238717). Smarter and more upmarket than most around the plaça, but good value out of season. Ask inside the bar/cafeteria. ③.

Pensión Sant Jordi, Plaça de la Font 37 (☎977/238358). Long-standing favourite that recently moved from its previous berth across the square into these more roomy premises. Well run and friendly; all rooms have bath. ③.

Sant Jordi youth hostel, Avda. President Companys 5 (☎977/240195 or 210195). An *IYHF* hostel with four- or six-bedded rooms (over 26s pay 50 percent more) and sports facilities; breakfast included in the price. Reception open 7–10am & 2–8pm; reservations advised in July and August, closed Sept. ①–②.

The city

Much of the attraction of Tarragona lies in the **Roman remains** dotted around the city. Some of the most impressive monuments are a fair way out (see "Out of the centre" below), but there's enough within walking distance to occupy a good day's sightseeing and to provide a vivid impression of life in Tarragona in Imperial Roman times. It's worth noting in advance, though, that almost all Tarragona's sights and museums are **closed on Mondays**; while the admission price to the Passeig Arqueologic buys a **combined ticket** which also allows entry to the Circ Roma, the Amfiteatre, the Casa Museu de Castellarnau and Museu d'Historia, all of which are covered below.

Passeig Arqueologic

For an overview of the city and its history, start at the **Passeig Arqueologic** (July–Sept Tues–Sat 10am–midnight; Oct–March Tues–Sat 10am–5.30pm; April–June Tues–Sat 10am–8pm; Sun all year 10am–3pm; 400ptas combined ticket), a promenade which encircles the northernmost half of the old town. From the entrance at the Portal del Roser, a path runs between **Roman walls** of the third century BC and the sloping, **outer fortifications** erected by the British in 1707 to secure the city during the War of the Spanish Succession. Megalithic walls built by the Iberians are excellently preserved in places, too, particularly two awesome gateways; the huge blocks used in their construction are quite distinct from the more refined Roman additions. Vantage points (and occasional telescopes) give views across the plain behind the city and around to the sea, while various objects are displayed within the Passeig – several Roman columns, a fine bronze statue of Augustus, and eighteenth-century cannons still defending the city's heights.

Roman Tarragona: the Necropolis, Forum and Amphitheatre

The most interesting remains in town are those of the ancient Necropolis, a twenty-minute walk out of the centre down Avda. Ramon i Cajal, which runs west off Rambla Nova. Here, both pagan and Christian tombs have been uncovered, spanning a period from the third to the sixth century AD. They're now contained within the fascinating **Museu i Necropolis Paleocristians** (mid-June to mid-Sept Tues–Sat 10am–1pm & 4.30–8pm, Sun 10am–2pm; rest of the year Tues–Sat 10am–1.30pm & 4–7pm, Sun 10am–2pm; 100ptas), whose entrance is on Passeig de la Independencia. The museum is lined with sarcophagi and displays a few fragmented mosaics and photographs of the site, but it's outside in the covered trenches and stone foundations that you get most sense of Tarragona's erstwhile importance. Scattered about are amphorae, inscribed tablets and plinths, rare examples of later Visigothic sculpture, and even the sketchy remains of a mausoleum. Most of the relics attest to Tarragona's enthusiastically

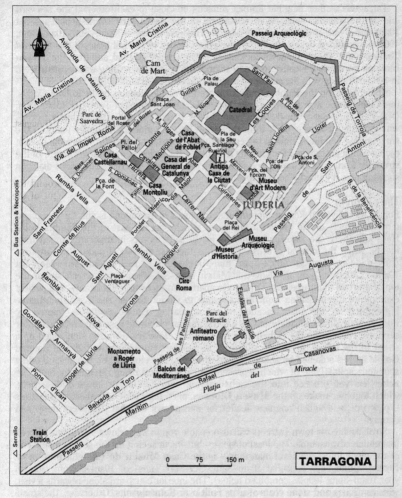

Christian status: Saint Paul preached here, and the city became an important Visigothic bishopric after the break-up of Roman power. Back in the centre, the Roman forum has survived too. Or rather forums, since – as provincial capital – Tarragona sustained both a ceremonial **provincial forum** (the scant remnants of which are close to the cathedral) and a **local forum**, whose more substantial remains are on the western side of Rambla Nova, near the market hall and square. Located on the flat land near the port, this was the commercial centre of Imperial *Tarraco* and the main meeting place for locals for three centuries. The site (April–Sept Tues–Sat 10am–8pm, Sun 10am–3pm; Oct–March Tues–Sat 10am–5.30pm, Sun 10am–3pm; free), which contained temples and small shops ranged around a porticoed square, has been split by a main road: a footbridge now connects the two halves where you can see a water cistern, house foundations, fragments of stone inscriptions and four elegant columns.

Tarragona's other tangible Roman remains lie close to each other at the seaward end of the Rambla Vella. Most rewarding is the **Amfiteatre** (April–Sept Tues–Sat 10am–8pm, Sun 10am–3pm; Oct–March Tues–Sat 10am–5.30pm, Sun 10am–3pm; 400ptas combined ticket), built into the green slopes of the hill beneath the *Imperial Tarraco* hotel. The tiered seats backing on to the sea are original, and from the top you can look north, up the coast, to the headland; the rest of the seating was reconstructed in 1969–70, along with the surviving tunnels and structural buildings.

Above here, on the Rambla Vella itself are the visible remains of the Roman Circus, the **Circ Roma**, also known as *Las Voltas del Circ* (June–Sept Tues–Sat 10am–8pm; Oct–May Tues–Sat 10am–5.30pm; Sun all year 10am–3pm; 400ptas combined ticket), whose vaults disappear back from the street into the gloom and under many of the surrounding buildings. Built at the end of the first century AD, this is where the chariot racing which entertained the citizens took place. If it's closed, you can get a view of the structure from outside the Museu d'Historia (see below), where there's also a diagram showing how it looked when complete.

The old town

For all its individual Roman monuments, the heart of Tarragona is still the steep and intricate streets of the medieval **old town** which spreads east of the Rambla Vella. Here and there the towering mansions in the side streets incorporate Roman fragments, while the central c/Major climbs to the quarter's focal point, the **Catedral** (July–mid-Oct Mon–Sat 10am–7pm; mid-March–June & mid-Oct–mid-Nov Mon–Sat 10am–12.30pm 4–7pm; mid-Nov–mid-March Mon–Sat 10am–2pm), which sits at the top of a broad flight of steps. This, quite apart from its own grand beauty, is a perfect example of the transition from Romanesque to Gothic forms. You'll see the change highlighted in the main facade, where a soaring Gothic portal is framed by Romanesque doors, surmounted by a cross and an elaborate rose window. Except for services, entrance to the cathedral is through the **cloisters** (*claustre*; signposted up a street to the left of the facade; 300ptas), themselves superbly executed with pointed Gothic arches softened by smaller round divisions. The cloister also has several oddly sculpted capitals, one of which represents a cat's funeral being directed by rats. The ticket lets you proceed into the cathedral, and into its chapter house and sacristy, which together make up the **Museu Diocesa**, piled high with ecclesiastical treasures – pick up the English-language leaflet for a rundown of what's in every nook and cranny.

Strolling the old town's streets will also enable you to track down Tarragona's excellent clutch of museums. The least obvious – but worth seeing for the setting inside one of the city's finest medieval mansions – is the **Casa Museu de Castellarnau** on c/ Ferrers (June–Sept Tues–Sat 10am–8pm; Oct–May Tues–Sat 10am–5.30pm; Sun all year 10am–3pm; 400ptas combined ticket). The interior courtyard alone rewards a visit, with its arches and stone coats-of-arms built over Roman vaults. Otherwise, the small-scale collections are largely archaeological and historical (coins and jars), rescued from banality by some rich eighteenth-century Catalan furniture and furnishings.

Museums of archaeology and history

The most stimulating exhibitions in town are in adjacent buildings off Plaça del Rei at the edge of the old town. The splendid **Museu Nacional Arqueologic** (mid-June to mid-Sept Tues–Sat 10am–1pm & 4.30–8pm; rest of the year Tues–Sat 10am–1.30pm & 4–7pm, Sun all year 10am–2pm; 100ptas, free on Tues) has a mutual admission ticket with the Necropolis and shouldn't be missed. The huge collection is a marvellous reflection of the richness of Imperial *Tarraco*, and admirably laid-out, starting in the basement with a section of the old Roman wall preserved *in situ*. On other floors are thematic displays on the various remains and buildings around the city, accompanied by pictures, text and relics, as well as whole rooms devoted to inscriptions, sculpture, ceramics, jewellery – even a series of anchors retrieved from the sea. More importantly, there's an unusually complete collection of mosaics, exemplifying the stages of development from the plain black-and-white patterns of the first century AD to the elaborate polychrome pictures of the second and third centuries.

Just around the corner, in the former residence of the Aragonese kings in Tarragona, is the **Museu d'Historia** (June–Sept Tues–Sat 10am–8pm; Oct–May Tues–Sat 10am–5.30pm; Sun all year 10am–3pm; 400ptas combined ticket), built over Roman vaults. The content here is less compelling, especially since you need to read Spanish or Catalan to make much of its storyboard approach to the city's history. Where it scores highly, though, is with the building itself – a tower whose enormous vaults, part of the Circ Roma, are spooky and silent, followed by a staircase that cuts right up through the building and on to the roof for the best views in Tarragona.

Out of the centre: ruins, seafood and beaches

Tarragona is compact enough not only to be able to walk everywhere in the city, but to reach most of the outlying districts on foot, too. It's less than half an hour to either the port area of **Serrallo** or, across town, to the best local beach at **Rabassada**. The Roman **Aqueduct**, 4km inland, is best reached by bus, but for most of the other Roman remains dotted around the surrounding countryside you'll need transport of your own.

Other Roman remains

Perhaps the most remarkable (and least visited) of Tarragona's monuments stands outside the original city walls. This is the **Roman Aqueduct**, which brought water from the Riu Gayo, some 32km distant. The most impressive extant section, nearly 220 metres long and 26 metres high, lies in an overgrown valley, off the main road in the middle of nowhere: take bus #5, marked *Sant Salvador* (every 20min from the stop outside Avda. Prat de la Riba 11, off Avda. Ramon i Cajal) – a ten-minute ride. The trip is undoubtedly worthwhile; the utilitarian beauty of the aqueduct is surpassed only by those at Segovia and the Pont du Gard, in the south of France. Popularly, it is known as *El Pont del Diable* (Devil's Bridge) due, remarked Richard Ford, to the Spanish habit of "giving all praise to 'the Devil', as Pontifex Maximus".

Other local Roman monuments of similar grandeur are more difficult to reach: in fact, without your own transport, almost impossible. If you're determined, keep a wary eye out for directional signs, and expect to have to ask directions locally from time to time. The square, three-storeyed **Torre dels Escipions**, a funerary monument built in the second century AD and nearly ten metres high, stands just off the main Barcelona road, the N340, 6km northeast up the coast. A couple of kilometres further north, the **Pedrera del Medol** is the excavated quarry that provided much of the stone used in Tarragona's constructions, while 20km from the city, after the turn-off for Altafulla, is the triumphal **Arc de Bera**, built over the great Via Maxima in the second century AD.

Serrallo

A fifteen-minute walk west along the industrial harbourfront from the train station (or the same distance south from the Necropolis) takes you right into the working port of **SERRALLO**, Tarragona's so-called "fisherman's quarter". Built a century ago, the harbour here is authentic enough – fishing smacks tied up, nets laid out on the ground for mending – but the real interest for visitors is the line of **fish and seafood restaurants** which fronts the main Muelle Pescadores. You'll get something to eat, somewhere, on most days, though the weekend is when the locals descend and then you'll need to arrive early to grab a table. None of the restaurants are designed for budget eaters, but there are a couple of more basic joints hidden in the parallel back street, and it's also worth checking the *menús del día*. Where these are available you should be able to eat for around 1500ptas a head; otherwise, commit yourself to the higher *à la carte* prices in the knowledge that the fish is as fresh as can be. *La Puda* (no. 25), at the far end, has tables overlooking the harbour inside and out, a short selection of seafood *tapas*, and a main menu that's overpriced but very good – the full three-course seafood works for two, plus wine, will cost around 8000ptas.

After your meal, you can walk back to Tarragona through the tangle of boats and nets, following the rail lines – or wait on the main road for one of the city buses (#1) back up to the old town.

Tarragona's beaches

The closest beach to town is the long **Platja del Miracle**, over the rail lines below the amphitheatre. The nicest, though, is a couple of kilometres further up the coast, reached by taking Via Augusta (off the end of Rambla Vella) and turning right at the *Hotel Astari*. Don't despair upon the way: the main road and railway bridge eventually give way to a road which winds around the headland and down to **Platja Rabassada**, an ultimately pleasant walk with gradually unfolding views of the beach. There are regular buses in summer (#1, #3, or #9) from various points throughout town.

Rabassada isn't anything very special, though it's roomy enough and has a few other diversions that make it worthwhile. Top of the list is the *Brasilmos* beach **bar-restaurant**, at the far end by the headland, which features seafood *tapas*, Latin American sounds, a pool table and occasional live music on summer evenings. There are a couple of other beach bars, too, and under the railway line, by *Brasilmos*, tiny **RABASSADA** village itself, which boasts two or three restaurants, a couple of hotels and *hostales*, a supermarket and two **campsites**, including *Camping Tarraco* (see "Accommodation", above).

Eating and drinking

There are plenty of good **restaurants** in the centre of Tarragona, as well as the fish and seafood places down in Serrallo. Many – particularly in and around Plaça de la Font – have outdoor seating in the summer. *Pescado Romesco* (fish with *romesco* sauce) is the regional **speciality** and you'll find it on several *menús del día* around town: *Romesco* sauce has a base of dry pepper, almonds and/or hazelnuts, olive oil, garlic and a glass of Priorato wine. Beyond this, there are many variations, as cooks tend to add their own secret ingredients. Good **bars** are less in evidence in Tarragona, though there are a few recommended ones listed below. Instead, you can join the locals in their nocturnal search for **cakes and ice-cream**: Rambla Nova particularly is groaning with pavement cafés, all doing a roaring trade. For the location of Tarragona's **markets**, see "Listings", below.

Bars and cafés

Café L'Antiquari, c/Santa Anna 3. Laid-back café-bar with funk and rock sounds and a liberal use of borrowed religious artefacts and statues, including a confessional box converted into a telephone cabin. A noticeboard at the entrance has details of events around town.

Café Cantonada, c/Fortuny 23. Civilized café-bar whose roomy interior and pool table encourage extended visits. Breakfast served from 8.30am to midday; closed Mon.

Frankfurt, c/Canyelles (off Rambla Nova, on the left before the fountain). A bar with good hot and cold sandwiches prepared in front of you – a wide selection for 200–350ptas a go.

Bar Frankfurt el Balcon, Rambla Nova 1. Outdoor tables in the best spot on the rambla, on the balcony of land next to the statue of Roger de Lluria. Sandwiches and *tapas*.

La Geladeria, Plaça del Rei 6. Popular ice-cream parlour outside the archaeological museum.

Patisseria Granta, c/Major 32. Cakes and pastries in a swish, modern *patisseria*. Counter or table service; popular on Sundays.

Moto Club Tarragona, Rambla Nova 53. Busy *rambla* bar with televised soccer if it's on. Open daily from 7am to midnight for drinks and snacks.

Bar Neftys, Plaça de la Font 9. Excellent *tapas*, freshly cooked, at a long steel bar on the town's prettiest square.

Restaurants

Can Llesques, c/Natzaret 6, on Plaça del Rei. Cramped, atmospheric restaurant with low stone arches serving endless variations of *Pa amb tomaquet*, accompanied by drinks dished up in ceramic pitchers. It's amazingly popular; go early or prepare to hang around for a table. Sitting outside attracts a 10 percent surcharge.

El Caseron, c/de Cos del Bou 9. Small restaurant just off Plaça de la Font, with a decent menu of staples – rabbit, paella, grills and fries – and a very good value *menú del día*. Closed Sun in winter.

Les Coques, c/de les Coques. Fine dining in an upmarket Catalan restaurant, just off Plaça de la Seu. Around 3000ptas a head. Closed Sun.

Mistral, Plaça de la Font 17. Pizzas around the 500ptas mark, plus the usual (Spanish) menu, including pricey *Pescado Romesco*. Tables on the square in summer are its main attraction, though. Closed Sun.

La Pizzeria, c/Cos del Bou 6. Averagely priced pizza and pasta. Closed Sun and Mon lunch.

El Plata, c/August 20. Summer outdoor dining in the pedestrian zone between the two *ramblas*. A decent *menú del día* at 1000ptas and a wide *tapas* selection.

Bar-Restaurant Turia, Plaça de la Font 26. Basic *comedor* with home-cooked food. No great choice, just the daily 700ptas *menú del día*, but as cheap as it comes, and not at all bad.

Listings

Airlines *Iberia*, Rambla Nova 116 (☎977/230512 or 212710).

Banks and exchange Many banks have offices along Rambla Nova. Outside banking hours you can exchange money and travellers' cheques at *Viajes Eurojet*, Rambla Nova 30; Mon–Fri 9am–1.30pm & 4.30–8.30pm, Sat 9am–1pm. This agency also handles *American Express* matters, and will exchange cheques and hold mail.

Buses Local bus information is available from the tourist offices or the cabin on c/Cristòfor Colom (☎977/549480). Bus station information on ☎977/229126.

Car rental *Atesa*, at *Viatgens Marsans*, c/Lleida 11 (☎977/219867); *Auto Sport* in the *Imperial Tarraco* hotel (☎977/211894); *Avis*, at *Viatges Vibus*, Rambla Nova 125 (☎977/219156); *Hertz*, Via Augusta 91 (☎977/238003).

Car trouble Contact *Reial Automòbil Club de Catalunya*, Rambla Nova 114 (☎977/245876).

Cinemas Movies are shown at *Oscars*, c/Ramon i Cajal 15, and *Catalunya*, Rambla Vella 9. Listings from the tourist offices or in the local newspaper.

Consulates *Denmark*, c/Apodaca 32 (☎977/234111); *France*, c/Armanyà 2 (☎977/237950); *Germany*, Avda. President Companys 14 (☎977/230398); *Italy*, c/Portalet 4 (☎977/234318); *Netherlands*, c/Reial 38 (☎977/240720); *Norway*, c/Apocada 32 (☎977/234111); *UK*, c/Reial 33 (☎977/220812). The nearest consulates for citizens of other countries are all in Barcelona; see p.568.

Emergencies Call ☎092 or ☎977/222222 for an ambulance.

Hospitals *Hospital de Sant Pau i Santa Tecla*, Rambla Vella 14 (☎977/235012); *Creu Roja Espanyola*, Avda. M. Cristina 17 (☎977/236505).

Markets Daily food market (not Sun) on and around c/Merceria, near the provincial forum; indoor food market at Plaça de Corsini (Mon–Thurs 7am–1pm, Fri & Sat 7am–1pm & 7–9pm). On Sundays, there's an antiques market at the top of the cathedral steps, with jewellery, bric-a-brac, ornaments and antiques spilling over into the arcades along c/Merceria.

Newspapers Foreign newspapers are on sale at the kiosks on Rambla Nova.

Post office At Plaça de Corsini (Mon–Fri 8am–9pm, Sat 9am–2pm).

Taxis There are ranks on Rambla Nova (at the *Moto Club*), in Plaça del Font, and at the bus and train stations. Or call ☎977/221414; 236064 or 215656.

Telephone office At Rambla Nova 74 (junction with c/Fortuny); Mon–Sat 9am–10pm, Sun 11am–2pm & 5–9pm.

Trains Information on ☎977/240202. *RENFE* has an office at Rambla Nova 40 for tickets and enquiries (Mon–Fri 9am–1pm & 4–7pm; ☎977/232534).

Travel Agencies For local tours, train and bus information, and tickets, contact *Viajes Eurojet*, Rambla Nova 30; *Viatgens Marsans*, c/Lleida 11; *Vibus*, Rambla Nova 125; or *Wagon Lits*, c/Cristòfor Colom 8.

Salou-Cambrils

The coast south of Tarragona is an uninspiring prospect. The occasional beaches are not easily reached by public transport, and few of them have anything to encourage a stop: long thin strips of sand, they are almost universally backed by gargantuan caravan-camping grounds, packed full and miles from anywhere. This part of the Costa Daurada also boasts one of Catalunya's biggest tourist developments, the extended coastal stretch that is the resort of **Salou-Cambrils**. It's actually two separate towns, but the few kilometres between them have long been filled and stacked with holiday apartments, bars and restaurants. You may wish to give them a miss altogether – understandable in high summer when every inch is block-booked and smothered in sunscreen – though Cambrils does have its good points, especially out of season.

Salou

The ten-minute train ride from Tarragona to **SALOU** makes an unpromising start, passing through a mesh of petro-chemical pipes and tanks before rounding on the resort itself – an almost entirely unrelieved gash of apartment blocks and hotels spilling down towards the sea. There are three or four separate beaches here, ringed around a sweeping bay and backed by a promenade studded with palms. From the seafront it's quite an attractive prospect, but the town is resolutely downmarket and stuffed to the gills in summer, the streets back from the sea teeming with "English pubs" and poor restaurants serving overpriced food and beer.

If you're thinking about staying in the area – it's certainly lively enough in the summer – you're much better off at Cambrils, 7km south. Buses regularly ply the coastal road between the two, or it's one more stop on the train.

Cambrils

Smaller **CAMBRILS** is nicer in every way, the town set back from a large harbour which still has working boats and fishing nets interspersed among the restaurants and hotels. In summer it's as full as anywhere along the Catalan coast, and Cambrils is probably better seen as a day trip from Tarragona, only fifteen minutes to the north. Out of season, though, it's more relaxed and while inexpensive accommodation isn't easy to come by it might be worth persevering for a night to eat in the good fish restaurants and amble around the harbour and nearby beaches. There's a **market** in town every Wednesday (the one in Salou is on Monday).

Arriving by bus from Tarragona, you'll pass through Salou and can ask to be dropped in Cambrils on the harbour front. By **train**, you're faced with a fifteen-minute walk from the inland part of town down to Cambrils-Port and the harbour: from the station, turn right and then right again at the main road, heading for the sea. Across the bridge on your left is the main **Turismo** (Mon–Fri 9am–2pm & 4–7pm; ☎977/361159), which has free maps, local bus and train timetables posted on the door, and may be able to help find a room. From here, Cambrils-Port is straight ahead, down any of the roads in front of you; at the seafront, there's another Turismo (daily 10am–2pm & 5–8pm).

Accommodation

Finding **rooms** can be a problem, since accommodation in town is mainly in apartments. The hotels that exist are pricey, and not inclined to reduce their rates out of season. On the square outside the train station, and on the way to the harbour, a few places advertize *habitaciones*: you'd probably do best to take whatever's going in summer, even though here you're fifteen minutes or so from all the action.

Down at the harbour, hotels mingle with places just offering rooms. Try the *Restaurant Platja*, c/Roger de Lauria 16 (☎977/360029; marked *CH*; ②–③), whose clean, bright rooms (without bath) are about the best value in town. The *Hotel-Restaurant Miramar*, Passeig Miramar 30 (☎977/360063; ④), is a deal more expensive, but nicely positioned overlooking the sea; the price here includes breakfast.

There are no less than eight **campsites** in and around Cambrils, and the Turismo has a free map showing where they all are. Closest to the centre is *Camping Horta* (☎977/361243; April–Oct), north of the harbour at the top of Rambla Regueral; the others are spread up and down the coast in both directions.

Eating

Food prices in Cambrils are on the steep side, but there's plenty of choice and some splendid fish **restaurants** along the harbour if you're prepared to dust off your wallet. The *Restaurant Platja* (see above) makes a good start, with three variously priced *menús del día*, the most expensive of which – at around 1500ptas a head – guarantees you a fine feast. Elsewhere, you're looking at a *menú del día* for around 1200ptas in most of the restaurants, though *à la carte* seafood at one of the harbour front restaurants comes in at considerably more than that.

Less expensive meals are found at one of several pizzerias, or go for the modestly priced *platos combinados* at *Cafeteria La Sirena*, c/Sant Pere 2 (entrance also on c/ Roger de Lauria; closed Thurs). The bar opposite the train station has seafood *tapas* and the usual *comedor* standbys.

South of Cambrils

Beyond Cambrils the train shoots past a scrappy coastline that resolutely fails to impress. The sporadic concrete development is punctuated by campsites and beaches that might tempt drivers but shouldn't persuade you off the infrequent trains. If disaster strikes, or the fancy takes, the only place even to consider delaying your progress is at **L'AMETLLA DE MAR**, a tourist town of rooms and restaurants but of no other intrinsic interest. Once you're past here, the landscape of the Delta de l'Ebre (see below) soon begins to make itself felt, before the train suddenly cuts inland to Tortosa, framed by the mountains behind.

Tortosa

The only town of any size in Catalunya's deep south is **TORTOSA**, slightly inland astride the Riu Ebre. In the Civil War the front was outside Tortosa for several months until the Nationalists eventually took the town in April 1938. The battle cost 35,000 lives – a traumatic event that is commemorated by a gaunt metal monument standing on a huge stone plinth in the middle of the river in town. The fighting took its toll in other ways, too: there's little left of the medieval quarter in the few old streets around the **cathedral**, though the building itself is worth a look. Founded originally in the twelfth century on the site of an earlier mosque, it was rebuilt in the fourteenth century, and its Gothic interior and quiet cloister – although much worn – are very fine. Several *modernista* houses around town (marked on the Turismo map) also add a bit of interest.

Tortosa's brightest point is also its highest. **La Suda**, the old castle, sits perched above the cathedral, glowering from behind its battlements at the Ebre valley below and the mountains beyond. Like so many in Spain, the castle has been converted into a luxury *parador*, but there's nothing to stop you climbing up for a magnificent view from the walls, or even from marching into the plush bar and having a drink. From the cathedral, c/de la Suda takes you straight there.

On the other side of La Suda, a garden beneath the castle houses a collection of **sculptures** (April–Sept Tues–Sat 10am–1pm & 4.30–7.30pm; Oct–March Tues–Sat 10am–1pm & 3.30–5.30pm, Sun all year 10am–2pm; 300ptas) by Santiago de Santiago. Human figures based loosely on themes such as "Ambition" and "Love", the central feature here is a ten-metre-high tower of seething bodies apparently depicting the struggle of humanity.

Practicalities

Tortosa is the main transport terminus for the region: in particular, regular buses run from here out to the principal towns and villages of the Delta de l'Ebre (see below). This, really, is the main reason to come, since the town is otherwise hardly an inspirational stopover, unless you stay at the *parador*. Moving on **out of Catalunya**, regular **buses** run from Tortosa to Vinaròs (in Castellón province to the south), from where you can reach the wonderful inland mountain town of Morella; and less regularly west to Alcañiz (in Aragón). **Trains** head south, passing through Vinaròs, on their way to Valencia.

The main **Turismo** (Mon–Sat 10am–1pm & 4–7pm, Sun 10am–1pm; closed Sat afternoon in winter; ☎977/442567) is on the main road into town, Avda. de la Generalitat, in the park on the left-hand side. To get there from the bus or train stations, follow the train tracks towards the river and turn left – away from the centre – under the bridge. Further out of town along here is the *Pensión Virginia*, at no. 133 (☎977/444186; ②), a good place to stay if your budget doesn't run to the **Parador** (☎977/444450; ⑥) at La Suda. If you do stay at the *parador* you should eat there as well, since it has the best **restaurant** in town, open to non-guests. The *Virginia* also has a decent restaurant, but other good places to eat are thin on the ground in Tortosa.

The Delta de l'Ebre

In the bottom corner of Catalunya is the **Delta de l'Ebre** (Ebro Delta), 320 square kilometres of sandy delta constituting the biggest wetland in Catalunya and one of the most important aquatic habitats in the western Mediterranean. Designated a natural park, its brackish lagoons, marshes, dunes and reedbeds are home to thousands of wintering birds and provide excellent fishing; around fifteen percent of the total Catalan catch comes from this area. The delta has been inhabited since the time of the Moorish conquest – some of the local names are Arab-influenced – but endemic malaria and heavy flooding kept the population in check for centuries, and only comparatively recently has there been any stability in the various settlements within the delta.

Much of the area of the **Parc Natural de Delta de l'Ebre** is a protected zone and hence access is limited. It's also difficult to visit without your own transport, though the effort of doing so is rewarded by tranquillity and space. If you're relying on buses, aim for one of the three main towns – Amposta, Sant Carles de la Ràpita or Deltebre – where you'll find accommodation and boat services on into the delta. Outside the towns, camping is allowed in certain areas.

Amposta

AMPOSTA, at the far western edge of the delta, is the largest and least attractive of the towns in the region, and not really somewhere you need to stay long. There are a couple of places to stay on the edge of town and a **Turismo** at Plaça Espanya 1, which can advise you about the possibility of renting a boat to take you down to the river mouth: with costs shared between a group of people, this is not too expensive.

Sant Carles de la Ràpita

SANT CARLES DE LA RÀPITA, to the south, is a more inviting place, with regular daily buses from Tortosa and another **Turismo** (Mon–Fri 9am–2pm & 4–9pm, Sat & Sun 10am–1pm & 5–8pm; winter morning only; ☎977/740100). It's quite a busy town in summer, drawing families to the several campsites stretching away down the coast – prepare to fend off swarms of mosquitoes if you stay at them – and to the dozens of restaurants which are said to serve the best prawns in the Med. Unless you've access to a car, though, you'll only be able to explore the immediate surroundings.

For **rooms** in town, try the large *Pensión Roca Mar*, Avda. Constitucío 8 (☎977/740458; ③), whose rooms without bath are fine, or *Pensión Agusti*, c/Pilar 2 (☎977/740427; ③), whose rooms with bath are only a shade dearer. The latter also has some rooms with air-conditioning, a rare treat in these parts. The *Agusti*'s excellent **restaurant** is much frequented by locals, as is the *Can Victor*, signposted from all over town, whose position right beneath the market guarantees the freshest of produce. Throughout July, local restaurants take turns to lay on special promotional menus, at the end of which you'll either have turned into a prawn or be off seafood for life.

Deltebre, Sant Jaume d'Enveja and around

From Amposta, road and river run to **DELTEBRE** (buses from Tortosa), at the centre of the delta. The **park information office** here, on the edge of town at c/Ulldecona 22 and well-signposted (Mon–Fri 10am–2pm & 3–6pm, Sat 10am–1pm & 3.30–6pm, Sun 10am–1pm; ☎977/489679), can provide you with a map of the delta, and has information about tours and local walks. At the same place there's an interesting **Ecomuseum** (100ptas), which has an aquarium displaying (non-edible) species from the delta, and also maintains hides for birdwatchers which overlook a pond. There are three or four places to stay in Deltebre, all reasonably priced, as well as a **youth hostel** (☎977/480136; ①) at Avda. de les Goles del Ebre, and a ferry across to **SANT JAUME D'ENVEJA** on the opposite shore. The local restaurants serve wonderful fish dishes, the speciality being *arròs a banda*, similar to *paella* except that the rice is brought before the seafood itself.

Three islands lie between Amposta and the open sea, the biggest being the **Illa de Buda** just by the river mouth. It's covered with rice fields (the main local crop) and you can reach it on excursion boats from Deltebre or by scheduled ferry from Sant Jaume. The road which runs along the south bank of the river leads to the so-called *Eucaliptus* **beach**, where there's a campsite, *Mediterrani Blau* (☎977/468212). Sunbathers should be careful not to burn in these flat, windy zones.

Inland: the route to Lleida

The train line from Barcelona forks at Tarragona, and the choice is either south towards Tortosa or **inland** for the fairly monotonous three-hour ride northwest across the flat lands to Lleida. The Tarragona–Lleida bus is a slightly more attractive proposition than the train, if only because it climbs the odd bluff and ridge on the way for good views over the plain. The bus also takes you directly to the region's only major attraction, the monastery of Poblet, which you could see in half a day and then move on to Lleida. Access to the monastery by train is possible, but means walking some of the way – not an unpleasant task by any means if the weather's fine since the surroundings are lovely.

Montblanc

The walled medieval town of **MONTBLANC**, 8km before the turning to the monastery at Poblet, is also on the train line to Lleida, so it's easy enough to see both on the same trip. It's a surprizingly beautiful place to discover in the middle of nowhere, and astonishingly lively during the evening *passeig* around the picturesque Plaça Major. There are many fine little Romanesque and Gothic monuments contained within a tight circle of old streets; all are marked on a map attached to the town's medieval gateway, the **Portal de Boue**, which is just a hundred metres or so up from the train station.

The grand Gothic parish church of **Santa Maria**, just above the central square, is perhaps the first thing to look out for: its elaborate facade has lions' faces on either side of the main doorway and cherubs swarming up the pillars. There's a fine view from the once-fortified mound that rises behind the church – over the rooftops, defensive towers and walls, and away across the plain. A couple of other churches to track down are Romanesque Sant Miquel (usually locked) and Sant Marcel, on the other side of the mound, which contains the **Museu Marès** (June–Sept Tues–Sat 10am–2pm & 4–8pm, Sun 10am–2pm; Oct–May Sat & Sun only). Like the one in Barcelona (p.531), it's an eclectic collection of sculpture and art. Montblanc also has a fine local history museum, the **Museu Comarcal de la Conca de Barberà** (June–Sept Tues–Sat 10am–2pm & 5–8pm; Oct–May Tues–Sat 10am–1pm & 4–7pm, Sun all year 10am–2pm; 200ptas), just off Plaça Major below the church, which is bright and informative, although all annotated in Catalan.

Practicalities

There's a very friendly and helpful **Turismo** inside the *Casa de la Vila* building in the arcaded Plaça Major. When it's closed, the policeman on the door should hand over a map if he's asked nicely. If you're driving, Montblanc would make a fine base for visiting Poblet – even on foot, it's only 8km to the monastery. The friendliest place to stay is the *Fonda dels Àngels*, Plaça Àngels 1 (☎977/860173; ③), in the first square you reach after passing through the town gate; it also serves meals.

The Monestir de Poblet

There are few ruins more stirring than the **MONESTIR DE POBLET**. It lies in glorious open country, vast and sprawling within massive battlemented walls and towered gateways. Once *the* great monastery of Catalunya, it was in effect a complete manorial village and enjoyed scarcely credible rights, powers and wealth. Founded in 1151 by Ramón Berenguer IV, who united the kingdoms of Catalunya and Aragón, it was planned from the beginning on an immensely grand scale. The kings of Aragón Catalunya chose to be buried in its chapel and for three centuries diverted huge sums for its endowment, a munificence that was inevitably corrupting. By the late Middle Ages Poblet had become a byword for decadence – there are lewder stories about this than any other Cistercian monastery – and so it continued, hated by the local peasantry, until the Carlist revolution of 1835. Then, in a passionate frenzy of destruction, a mob burned and tore it apart, so remorselessly that Augustus Hare, an English traveller who visited it 36 years later, recorded that "violence and vengeance are written on every stone".

The monastery was repopulated by Italian Cistercians in 1940 and over the past decades a superb job of restoration has been undertaken. Much remains delightfully ruined but, inside the main gates, you are now proudly escorted around the principal complex of buildings. As so often, the **cloisters**, focus of monastic life, are the most evocative and beautiful part. Late Romanesque, and sporting a pavilion and fountain, they open on to a series of rooms: a splendid Gothic **chapter house** (with the former abbots' tombs set in the floor), wine cellars, a parlour, a **kitchen** equipped with ranges and copper pots, and a sombre wood-panelled **refectory**.

Beyond, you enter the **chapel** in which the twelfth- and thirteenth-century tombs of the Kings of Aragón have been meticulously restored by Frederico Marès, the manic collector of Barcelona. They lie in marble sarcophagi on either side of the nave, focusing attention on the central sixteenth-century altarpiece. You'll also be shown the vast old **dormitory**, to which there's direct access from the chapel choir, a poignant reminder of Cistercian discipline. From the dormitory (half of which is sealed off since it's still in use), a door leads out on to the cloister roof for views down into the cloister itself and up the chapel towers.

Entry to the monastery costs 300ptas, and it's **open** daily from 10am–12.30pm and 3–6pm (closing 30min earlier in the winter). Officially, it can only be toured as a member of a **guided group**. The tours take an hour and depart roughly every half-hour (every 15min Sun and holidays). However, the porter may let you in to walk around alone if there aren't enough people within a reasonable period of time.

Getting there by bus

Three **buses** a day run to Poblet from Tarragona or Lleida, passing right by the monastery. It's an easy day trip from either city, or can be seen on the way between the two – the gap between buses is roughly three hours, which is enough time to get around the complex. You could also **stay overnight** at Poblet, an even more attractive proposition if you have your own transport, since there are several pleasant excursion targets in the surrounding countryside (see below). The solitary *Hostal Fonoll* outside the main gate of the monastery (☎977/870333; ②; March–Oct only) has a decent restaurant and bar, functional standard rooms and more expensive rooms with bath; while 1km up the road, around the walls, the hamlet of **LES MASIES** has a couple more hotels and restaurants.

By train: L'Espluga de Francolí

The approach by **train** is much more atmospheric. You get off at the ruinous station of **L'ESPLUGA DE FRANCOLÍ**, from where it's a beautiful three-kilometre walk to the monastery. Unfortunately there's no baggage *consigna* at the station, and L'Espluga itself is such a one-horse town that there's not much to do when it's not your turn with the horse. However, there are a couple of places to stay, including the *Hostal Senglar* (☎977/870121; ④), a very comfortable set-up with a decent restaurant on the main road through town that leads to Poblet.

You can of course vary your approach to the monastery, taking the bus one way and choosing to walk to or from L'Espluga (3km), Montblanc (8km) or even Vimbodí (5km), at all of which the Tarragona–Lleida train stops.

Around Poblet: excursions

If you have time and transport, a couple of excursions into the countryside surrounding Poblet are well worth making. The red-stone walled village of **PRADES**, in the Serra de Prades, 20km from the monastery, is a beautifully sited and tranquil place that needs no other excuse for a visit. The *Pensión Espasa*, c/Sant Roc 1 (☎977/868023; ③), offers simple accommodation if you decide you like it enough to stay on.

The other option is to take in two more twelfth-century Cistercian monasteries. **Santes Creus** (summer daily 10am–1.30pm & 3–7pm; winter Tues–Sun 10am–1.30pm & 3–6pm; 300ptas) is the easier to reach, northeast of **VALLS** on the other side of the Tarragona–Lleida highway. It's built in Transitional style, with a grand Gothic cloister and some Romanesque traces, and you can explore the dormitory, chapter house and royal palace. There's a once-daily bus from Tarragona to Valls, which connects with a local service to Santa Creus, but check on return times because you don't want to get stranded in these parts. Trickier to find, though worth the drive, is the monastery of **Vallbona de les Monges** (Mon–Sat 10am–1.30pm & 4.30–6.45pm, Sun noon–1.30pm & 4.30–6.45pm), north of Poblet, reached up the C240 from Montblanc. This has been occupied continuously for 800 years, and the church is particularly fine.

Lleida

LLEIDA (Lérida in Castilian Spanish), at the heart of a fertile plain near the Aragonese border, has a rich history. First a *municipium* under the Roman Empire and later the centre of a small Arab kingdom, it was reconquered by the Catalans and became the seat of a bishopric in 1149. Little of those periods survives in today's pleasant city but there is one building of outstanding interest, the old cathedral, which is sufficient justification in itself to find the time for a visit. If you have to spend the night in Lleida – and you will if you're heading north to the Pyrenees by train or bus – there are a couple of museums and a steep set of old town streets to occupy any remaining time. Little known it may be, but Lleida certainly isn't dull, and the lack of visitors makes an overnight stop doubly attractive: rooms are easy to come by, and the students at the local university fill the streets and bars on weekend evenings in good-natured throngs.

Around the city

The **Seu Vella** (Tues–Sat 9.30am–1.30pm & 3–6.30pm, 5.30pm in winter, Sun 9.30am–1.30pm; 150ptas), or old cathedral, is entirely enclosed within the walls of the ruined castle (*La Suda*), high above the Riu Segre, a twenty-minute climb from the centre of town. It's a peculiar fortified building, which in 1707 was deconsecrated and taken over by the military. It remained in military hands until 1940 since, wrote Richard Ford, "in the piping times of peace the steep walk proved too much for the pursy canons, who, abandoning their lofty church, built a new cathedral below in the convenient and Corinthian style!" Enormous damage was inflicted over the years (documented by photos in a side chapel) but the church remains a notable example of the Transitional style, similar in many respects to the cathedral of Tarragona. Once again the Gothic cloisters are masterful, each walk comprising arches different in size and shape but sharing delicate stone tracery. They served the military as a canteen and kitchen. Outside, the views from the walls, away over the plain, are stupendous.

You can climb back down towards the river by way of the aforementioned new cathedral, the **Seu Nova**, a grimy eighteenth-century building only enlivened inside by a series of minuscule, high stained glass windows. Nearby, halfway up the steep c/ Cavallers at no. 15, is the **Museu Morera** (on the second floor; Mon–Sat 11am–2pm & 6.30–9pm; free), a permanent display of contemporary art by local artists, housed in an old monastery building. On the other side of the cathedral, on Avda. de Blondel, the **Museu Arqueologic** (Tues–Sat noon–2pm & 6–9pm; free) is a fairly negligible collection, but again is housed in an interesting building, this time the fifteenth-century Santa Maria hospital.

Once you've seen the cathedral and museums, you've just about seen the lot that Lleida has to offer, though its central pedestrianized shopping streets are good for a browse, and you can wind up in the **Plaça de Sant Joan** for a drink in one of the outdoor cafés. This square has been in the throes of regeneration for years, the last addition being a lift from the plaça to the Seu Vella. Much of the new stone and concrete infrastructure is already in place, and according to your point of view it's either making bold use of new materials to link the lower town with *La Suda*, or making a pig's ear of the square and its surroundings – so far the town seems unable to decide whether to love it or hate it.

Practicalities

Plaça de Sant Joan is a fifteen- to twenty-minute walk from the **train station**, with the **bus station** a few minutes' beyond the square, down Avda. de Blondel. The **Turismo** (June–Sept Mon–Sat 9am–8pm, Sun 9am–2pm; Oct–May Mon–Fri 9am–7pm, Sat 9am–2pm; ☎973/870333) is in the Edificio Pallas, on Plaça de la Paeria, the small square next to Plaça Sant Joan. Pick up a map and a brochure, but don't expect too much English to be spoken.

Accommodation

There are a couple of **places to stay** right outside the train station, and more along the road straight ahead – Rambla Ferrán – which leads into the centre. Or press on to the central Plaça Sant Joan, around which there are several possibilities.

Along Rambla Ferrán, *Habitaciones Ana* (no. 26, 4th floor; ②), *Habitaciones Gilabert* (no. 24; ☎973/249802; ①) and *Hostal España* (no. 20; ☎973/240200; ②) are virtually next door to each other, but choose rooms carefully as this is a very busy main road; the *España* is the most upmarket and some of its rooms come with a shower.

The best central choice is *Residencia Mundial*, Plaça de Sant Joan 4 (☎973/242700; ②–③), which is friendly and not as posh as it looks from outside – it has a breakfast-bar and some of its rooms (with and without bath) overlook the square. There are a couple more places in and just off the square, including the more luxurious *Hotel Principal* (☎973/230800; ④), otherwise you could try *Habitaciones Brianso*, c/de Pi i Maragall 22 (☎973/236339; ①), in a modern apartment block along the continuation of c/Magdalena.

Lleida has a **youth hostel,** the *Sant Anastasi* – open July and August only – at Rambla d'Aragón 11 (☎973/266099; ①) and a **campsite** (*Les Basses*, ☎973/235954; mid-May to Sept), a couple of kilometres out of town on the Huesca road. Take the bus labelled *BS* or *Les Basses* (every 45min from Rambla Ferrán).

Eating and drinking

Finding anything to **eat** or **drink** can be surprisingly difficult in the evening in Lleida, particularly on Sunday when many places are closed (including most of those detailed below). For **breakfast** and *platos combinados*, *Café Triunfo* on the edge of Plaça de Sant Joan is good – step inside anyway for a look at the photographs of old Lleida. The very cheapest meals are at *Casa José*, c/Botera 17 (off c/Magdalena), basic to the point of being positively grim. Nearby *Casa Marti*, c/Magdalena 37, is much more pleasant: the restaurant above the bar serves fine, locally inspired food at very reasonable prices – 1200ptas or less for a full meal. The other place for budget dining is along c/de Cavallers, on the way up to the Seu Vella, where a string of rickety bars serve *tapas* (including snails, the local speciality) and meals. The **market** is just at the top of this street (Mon–Sat 9am–2pm), in Plaça dels Gramàtics.

If you're looking for more variety and better **restaurants**, head for the block of streets north of the church of Sant Marti. The university is close by, and this is where the students come to eat and hang out, in the restaurants and loud **music-bars** along the block formed by c/Sant Marti, c/Camp de Marti, c/Balmes and Avda. Prat de la Riba. As well as a couple of budget Catalan places, there are several pricier pizzerias here, including the popular *Restaurant-Pizzeria Travestere*, c/Camp de Marti 27. The *Marisquería Bar Lugano*, close by at Plaça Ricard Viñes 10, has a strong seafood *tapas* menu. Finally, one place that is definitely **open on Sunday** is *Snoopy*, Avda. de Blondel 9, on the main road close to the bus station. Ignore the naff name and the pink-bowed interior: inside, there are good *platos combinados*, reasonable pizzas and a friendly English-speaking proprietor.

LLEIDA

0   400 m

travel details

For services from Barcelona to destinations in Catalunya, see p.570.

Trains

Blanes to Figueres (2 daily; 1hr 30min); Girona (4 daily; 45min).

Figueres to Barcelona (19 daily; 1hr 30min–2hr); Colera (5 daily; 25min); Girona (20 daily; 45min); Llançà (10 daily; 15min); Port Bou (10 daily; 20min).

Girona to Barcelona (hourly; 1hr 20min); Blanes (5 daily; 40min); Figueres (hourly; 35min); Port Bou (hourly; 1hr 10min).

Lleida to Barcelona via Valls or Reus/Tarragona (10 daily; 2–3hr); Barcelona via Manresa (6 daily; 3hr); La Pobla de Segur (4 daily; 2hr); Tarragona (3 daily; 2hr); Zaragoza (11 daily; 1hr 40min).

Puigcerdà to La Tour de Carol (4 daily; 5min).

Ribes de Freser to Núria (9–10 daily; 45min); Queralbs (9–10 daily; 25min).

Ripoll to Barcelona (6 daily; 2hr); Puigcerdà (7 daily; 1hr 45min).

Sitges to Barcelona (every 10–15min; 25–40min); Cunit (12 daily; 20min); Tarragona (12 daily; 1hr); Vilanova (12 daily; 10min).

Tarragona to Barcelona (every 30min; 1hr 30min); Cambrils (14 daily; 20min); Cunit (10 daily; 40min); Lleida (5 daily; 2hr); Salou (14 daily; 10min); Sitges (direct every 30min; 1hr); Tortosa (hourly; 45min); Valencia (15 daily; 4hr); Vilanova i la Geltrú (10 daily; 50min); Zaragoza (5 daily; 3hr 30min).

Buses

Banyoles to Besalú (Mon–Sat 8 daily, Sun 3; 15min); Olot (Mon–Sat 8 daily, Sun 3; 45min); Santa Pau/Olot (2 weekly; 45min/1hr).

Cadaqués to Barcelona (2–4 daily; 2hr 20min); Castelló d'Empúries (5 daily; 1hr); Figueres (5 daily; 1hr 15min); Roses (5 daily; 35min).

Camprodon to Molló (Mon–Sat 1 daily; 15min); Olot (1–2 daily; 1hr); Setcases (1–2 daily; 30min).

L'Escala to Barcelona (July–Sept 1–2 daily; 2hr 40min); Figueres (5 daily; 45min); Girona (2 daily; 1hr); Palafrugell (3 daily; 45min); Pals (3 daily; 35min); Sant Pere Pescador (5 daily; 20min); Torroella de Montgrí (3 daily; 20min).

Figueres to Barcelona (3–8 daily; 1hr 30min); Cadaqués (4 daily; 1hr 15min); Castelló d'Empúries (every 30min; 15min); El Port de la Selva (Mon–Fri 1 daily; 40min); L'Escala (5 daily; 45min); Espolla (1 daily; 35min); Girona (3–8 daily; 1hr); Llançà (Mon–Fri 1 daily; 20min); Olot (2–3 daily; 1hr 30min; Palafrugell (3 daily; 1hr 30min); Pals (3 daily; 1hr 20min); Roses (every 30min; 40min); Sant Pere Pescador (5 daily; 25min); Torroella de Montgrí (3 daily; 1hr).

Girona to Banyoles (Mon–Sat 13 daily, Sun 4; 30min); Barcelona (Mon–Sat 6–9 daily, Sun 3; 1hr 30min); Besalú (Mon–Sat 7 daily, Sun 3; 45min); Figueres (Mon–Sat 6–10 daily, Sun 4; 50min); Olot (Mon–Sat 7 daily, Sun 3; 1hr 15min); Palafrugell (hourly; 1hr 15min); Palamós (4 daily; 1hr); Platja d'Oro (4 daily; 45min); Sant Feliu (hourly; 1hr 45min); Sant Hilari Sacalm (Mon–Sat 1 daily; 1hr 20min); Tossa de Mar (July–Sept 3 daily; 1hr).

Lleida to Artesa de Segre (2 daily; 1hr); Barcelona (Mon–Sat 12 daily, Sun 2; 2hr 15min); Huesca (2 daily; 2hr 30min); La Seu d'Urgell (2 daily; 3hr 30min); Montblanc (1 daily; 1hr 30min); Pobla de Segur (2 daily; 2hr); Poblet (3 daily; 1hr 15min); Tarragona (3 daily; 2hr); Viella, via Túnel de Viella (Mon–Sat 2 daily; 3hr); Zaragoza (Mon–Sat 4 daily, Sun 1; 2hr 30min).

Lloret de Mar to Barcelona (July to mid-Sept 10 daily; 1hr 15min); Blanes (every 15min; 15min); Girona (5 daily; 1hr 20min); Palafrugell (2 daily; 1hr 30min); Palamós (2–4 daily; 1hr); Platja d'Oro (2–4 daily; 50min); Sant Feliu (2–4 daily; 40min); Tossa de Mar (every 30min; 15min).

Olot to Banyoles (Mon–Sat 8 daily, Sun 3; 50min); Barcelona (2–3 daily; 2hr 10min); Besalú (Mon–Sat 8 daily, Sun 3; 30min); Camprodon (1 daily; 1hr); Figueres (2–3 daily; 1hr); Girona (Mon–Sat 8 daily, Sun 3; 1hr 20min); Ripoll (3–4 daily; 1hr 10min); Sant Joan les Abadesses (1 daily; 50min); Santa Pau/Banyoles (1–2 weekly; 15min/1hr).

Palafrugell to Barcelona (8 daily; 2hr); L'Escala (3 daily; 45min); Figueres (3 daily; 1hr 30min); Girona (13 daily; 1hr); Lloret de Mar (2 daily; 1hr 30min); Pals (3 daily; 10min); Sant Feliu (hourly; 45min); Sant Pere Pescador (3 daily; 1hr); Torroella de Montgrí (3 daily; 25min).

La Pobla de Segur to Caldes de Boí (July to mid-Sept 1 daily; 2hr); Capdella (Mon–Sat 1 daily;

1hr); El Pont de Suert (Mon–Sat 1 daily; 1hr); Viella (Mon–Sat 1 daily; 2hr).

El Port de la Selva to Figueres (Mon–Fri 1 daily; 40min); Llança (July–mid-Sept 7 daily, rest of the year 2–4 daily; 25min).

Ripoll to Camprodon (3–5 daily; 40min); Olot (3–4 daily; 1hr 10min); Sant Joan de les Abadesses (7–9 daily; 20min).

Sant Feliu to Barcelona (8 daily; 1hr 30min); Girona (July–Sept 10 daily; 2hr); Lloret de Mar (July & Aug 4 daily; 40min); Palafrugell (hourly; 45min); Palamós (hourly; 30min); Platja d'Oro (hourly; 15min).

La Seu d'Urgell to Andorra la Vella (6–7 daily; 1hr); Artesa de Segre (2 daily; 2hr); Lleida (2 daily; 3hr); Puigcerdà (3 daily; 1hr).

Tarragona to Andorra (1–2 daily; 4hr 30min); Barcelona (18 daily; 1hr 30min); Berga (July & Aug 1 daily, rest of the year Sat & Sun only; 3hr 10min); L'Espluga (3 daily; 1hr); La Pobla de Lillet (July & Aug 1 daily, rest of the year Sat & Sun only; 4hr 15min); La Seu d'Urgell (daily at 8am; 3hr 45min); Lleida (3 daily; 2hr); Montblanc (3 daily; 50min); Poblet (3 daily; 1hr 5min); Salou-Cambrils (every 30min; 20min); Valencia (7 daily; 3hr 30min); Zaragoza (4 daily; 4hr).

Tortosa to Deltebre (Mon–Fri 5 daily, Sat 2; 1hr); Sant Carles de la Ràpita (Mon–Sat 5 daily, Sun 1; 40min); Tarragona (Mon–Fri 1 daily; 1hr 30min).

Tossa de Mar to Barcelona (July–Sept 10 daily; 1hr 35min); Girona (July–Sept 3 daily; 1hr); Lloret de Mar (every 30min; 15min).

Viella to Lleida (Mon–Sat 2 daily; 3hr); Salardú (Mon–Sat 1 daily; 30min).

Cruceros boats

Calella to Palamós and vice versa, stopping at all intermediate ports (June–Sept 1 daily; 4hr).

Blanes to Lloret de Mar/Tossa de Mar (June–Sept 9 daily; 20min/45min).

Tossa de Mar to Sant Feliu/Platja d'Oro/Sant Antoni de Calonge/Palamós (June–Sept 4 daily; 45min/1hr 15min/1hr 25min/1hr 45min).

CHAPTER TWELVE

VALENCIA AND MURCIA

The area known as the **Levante** (the East), combining the provinces of Valencia and Murcia is a bizarre mixture of ancient and modern, of beauty and beastliness.

The rich *huerta* of **Valencia** is said to be the most fertile slab of land in Europe, crowded with orange, lemon and peach groves, and with rice fields still irrigated by systems devised by the Moors. Unsurprisingly, a farmhouse is the most characteristic building of the Valencian *huerta:* called a *barraca*, its most striking feature is its steeply pitched thatched roof. *Valenciano*, a dialect of Catalan, is spoken in some parts of the region and, as it's been recently revived in schools, it now receives a higher profile in the capital. There's even an extreme nationalist group who deny the dialect's Catalan origins, but they haven't managed to convince anyone else. Evidence of the lengthy Moorish occupation can be seen throughout the province, in the castles, irrigation systems, crops and place names; Benidorm, Alicante, Alcoy, all come from Arabic.

Murcia is quite distinct, a *comunidad autónoma* in its own right, and there could hardly be a more severe contrast with the richness of the Valencian *huerta*. This southeastern corner of Spain is virtually a desert and is some of the driest territory in Europe. Fought over for centuries by Phoenicians, Greeks, Carthaginians and Romans, there survives almost no physical evidence of their presence – or of 500 years of Moorish rule, beyond an Arabic feel to some of the small towns and the odd date palm here and there. As if the sterility of the land weren't enough, the unfortunate Murcians rank lowest in the popularity stakes in Spain, according to a survey taken in the 1970s of where people would prefer their son- or daughter-in-law to come from. The prejudice probably originated in the 1920s, when Murcians flooded into Catalunya in search of work and later spread to the entire country.

Much of the region's **coast**, despite some fine beaches, is marred by the highway to the south, the industrial development which has sprouted all around it (with consequent pollution), and of course the heavy overdevelopment of villas and vacation homes. The coves around **Denia** and **Jávea** in Valencia are the prettiest beach areas, but access and accommodation are difficult. The resorts of the **Mar Menor** in Murcia are similarly attractive, but again don't even think of turning up in season if you don't have a reservation. For the "wild" beaches of **southern Murcia**, transport is the major hurdle, but crowds won't be a problem. **Valencia** and **Alicante** are the major urban centres, and there are several historic small towns and villages a short way inland, such as **Játiva**, **Orihuela** and **Lorca**. Throughout the region, trains are usually less expensive and faster than buses on shorter journeys.

There's no shortage of **culinary pleasures** in the region. Gourmets tend to agree that the best *paellas* are to be found around (but not *in*) Valencia, the city where the dish originated. It should be prepared fresh, and cooked over wood (*leña*), not scooped from some vast, sticky vat; most places will make it for a minimum of two people, with advance notice. Of the region's other rice-based dishes, the most famous is *arròs a banda*, which is served in two stages: first the rice, then the fish. Another speciality is eels served with piquant *all i pebre* (garlic and pepper) sauce. The sweet-toothed should try *turrón;* made of nuts and honey, it traditionally comes in a soft, flaky variety or very hard like a nougat (the *turrón* from Jijona is the finest). You could follow it with an *horchata*, a milky drink made from tiger nuts (*chufas*) or almonds (*almendras*).

February

2–5 Moors and Christians battle for the castle in Bocariente, with wild firework displays at night.

Carnaval (40 days before Easter Week) in Águilas is one of the wildest in the country after Tenerife and Cádiz. Good carnival celebrations also in Cabezo de Torres.

March

12–19 *The Fallas de San José* in Valencia is by far the biggest of the bonfire festivals, and indeed one of the most important fiestas in all Spain. The whole thing costs as much as 200 million ptas, most of which goes up in smoke (literally) on the final *Nit de Foc* when the grotesque cardboard and wooden caricatures are burned. These *fallas* may be politicians, film stars or professional athletes, and anyone else who may be a popular target for satirical treatment. Throughout, there are bullfights, music and stupendous fireworks.

The middle of the month, especially around the **19th** (*San José*) also sees smaller *fallas* festivals in Játiva, Benidorm and Denia.

Third Sun of Lent *Fiesta de la Magdalena* in Castellón de la Plana is marked by major processions and pilgrimages.

April

Holy Week is celebrated everywhere. In Elche there are, naturally, big Palm Sunday celebrations making use of the local palms, while throughout the week there are also religious processions in Cartagena, Lorca, Orihuela, Moncada and Valencia. The **Easter processions** in Murcia are particularly famous and they continue into the following week with, on the Tuesday, the *Bando de la Huerta*, a huge parade of floats celebrating local agriculture and, on the Sat evening, the riotous "Burial of the Sardine" which marks the end of these spring festivals.

23 Famous *Moros y Cristianos* in Alcoy.

25 Morella holds the traditional fiesta of *Las Primes*.

May

1–5 *Fiestas de los Mayos* in Alhama de Murcia, and *Moros y Cristianos* in Caravaca de la Cruz.

The Valencia area has a powerful tradition of **fiestas** and there are a couple of elements unique to this part of the country. Above all, throughout the year and more or less wherever you go, there are mock battles between Moors and Christians (*Moros y Cristianos*). Recalling the Christian Reconquest of the country – whether through symbolic processions or recreations of specific battles – they're some of the most elaborate and colourful festivities to be seen anywhere. The other recurring feature is the *fallas* (bonfires) in which giant carnival floats and figures are paraded through the streets before being ceremoniously burned.

Valencia

Valencia, the third largest city in Spain, may not approach the cosmopolitan vitality of Barcelona or the cultural variety of Madrid, but boasts some of the best nightlife of mainland Spain. *Vivir Sin Dormir* (live without sleep) is the name of one of its bars, and could be taken as the Valencian motto. The city is alive with noise and colour throughout the year, with unexpected explosions of gunpowder, fireworks and festivities. Although in summer the air becomes heavy with pollution, the clear Levante light, special to the area, flatters the city. The traffic is certainly the least attractive aspect of the city, but new metro lines are being built in an effort to reduce the congestion in the city centre.

Third Sun Moors and Christians battle in Altea.

June

24 *Día de San Juan* Magnificent *fallas* festival around this date on the beaches of San Juan de Alicante. Similar to the March *fallas* of Valencia, with processions and fireworks, and celebrated on a smaller scale on the beaches of Valencia (Malvarossa), with bonfire-jumping.

July

Early July *Fiestas de la Santísima Sangre* in Denia with dancing in the steets, music and more mock battles.

12–20 *Moros y Cristianos* in Orihuela.

16 In San Pedro del Pinatar a maritime *Romería* in which an image of the Virgin is carried in procession around the Mar Menor.

Second week *Feria* in Valencia with much music and above all fireworks, ending with the Battle of the Flowers in the Alameda. Festival of music in Valencia throughout the month, featuring open-air concerts in Viveros park.

25–31 *Moros y Cristianos* battle in Villajoyosa by both land and sea.

August

1–15 Local *Fiesta* in Sagunto and at the same time the great Moors and Christians and a mystery play in Elche. *La Tomatina* in Buñol, a tomato-throwing fiesta.

15 Local festivities in Denia, Jumilla,and Requena.

September

4–9 *Moros y Cristianos* in Villena.

7–17 *Feria* in Albacete.

8 *Mare de Deu de la Salut* – colourful folkloric processions in Algemesi.

10–13 International Mediterranean Folk Festival in Murcia.

11 Rice festival in Sueca includes a national *paella* contest.

22 Fiesta of *Santo Tomás* in Benicasim with bands and a "blazing bull".

October

Second Sunday Benidorm celebrates its patron saint's day.

December

6–8 *La Fiesta de la Virgen* in Yecla when the effigy of Mary is carried down from the sanctuary on top of the hill amid much partying.

It has always been an important city, fought over for the agricultural wealth of its surrounding *huerta*. After Romans and Visigoths, it was occupied by the Moors for over four centuries with only a brief interruption (1094-1101) when El Cid recaptured it. He died here in 1099 but his body, propped on a horse and led out through the gates, was still enough to cause the Moorish armies – previously encouraged by news of death – to flee in terror. It wasn't until 1238 that Jaime I of Aragón permanently wrested Valencia back. It has remained one of Spain's largest, richest and most stylish cities ever since. Despite its size, however, Valencia retains a strong feeling of *pueblo*. You won't hear much English spoken here and there are as yet few tourists outside *Fallas* time.

Valencia's **fiestas** are some of the most riotous in Spain. The best is *Las Fallas*, March 12–19 (see box), which culminates in a massive bonfire when all the processional floats are burned. In July the city celebrates the *Feria de Julio* with bullfights, concerts, the "battle of the flowers" and fireworks. In September, there's a spectacular fireworks competition held in the river-park.

Arrival, information and accommodation

Arriving by train at Valencia's beautifully tiled **Estación del Nord**, you're very close to the town centre; walk down Avda. Marqués de Sotelo to the Plaza del Ayuntamiento, the central square. The **bus station** is some way out, take local bus #28, or allow 15 minutes if you decide to walk. The **Balearic ferry terminal** connects with the central plaza via bus #4 and with the train station via the #19 bus.

VALENCIA

LAS FALLAS

From 12–19 March, around the saint's day of San José, Valencia erupts in a blaze of colour and noise for the **Fiesta de Las Fallas**. During the year, each *barrio* or neighbourhood builds a satirical caricature or **falla**. These begin to appear in the plazas of each *barrio* at the beginning of March and are judged and awarded prizes before being set alight at midnight on March 19 the *Nit de Foc*. The festival takes its name from the Valencian word for torch. Traditionally, carpenters celebrated the day of San José and the beginning of spring with a ritual burning of spare wood. They would decorate the torches used over the winter and add them to the bonfire. This simple rite of spring has become an international tourist attraction, and it's an extraordinary sight to watch these painstakingly constructed models, some as tall as buildings, some big enough to walk inside, be strung with firecrackers and literally go up in smoke. The *fallas* are ignited in succession; the last to go up are the prize winners. Each *falla* has a small model or **ninot** beside it, usually created by the children of the *barrio*. The *ninots* are exhibited in La Lonja before the fiesta begins, and the best is added to the Museu Faller; the rest are burnt with the *fallas*. Finally, around one o'clock, the *falla* of the Plaza Ayuntamiento goes up in flames, set off by a string of firecrackers, followed by the last thunderous firework display of the fiesta.

During the fiesta, processions of *falleros*, dressed in traditional costume and accompanied by bands, carry flowers to the Plaza de la Virgen, where the flowers are massed to create the skirt of a huge statue of La Virgen. The daily **Las Mascaletas** firecracker display takes place at 2pm in the Plaza Ayuntamiento – for a reputedly unpunctual race, the Valencians observe the timing of this celebration religiously. Traffic comes to a standstill, streets are blocked and the whole city races to the central square for a ten-minute series of body-shuddering explosions. There are nightly fireworks, bullfights, *paella* contests in the streets and *chocolate y buñuelos* stalls selling fresh doughnuts. On March 20th, Valencia returns to normality - the streets are cleaned overnight, and the planning begins for the next year's Fallas.

On the **Plaza del Ayuntamiento**, you'll find the **correos** crowned with trumpeting angels, and the **Turismo** (Mon–Fri 9am–1.30pm & 4.30–7pm, Sat 9.30am–1.30pm), which gives out an excellent map. There's another Turismo in c/de la Paz (Mon–Fri 9am–2pm & 5–7pm, Sat 9am–1pm) and an information point with a hotel reservation service at the **train station**.

Accommodation

Valencia's budget accommodation is centred around the train station, in c/Bailén and c/Pelayo, parallel to the tracks off c/Játiva. C/Pelayo is the quieter of the two streets, but the area is not the most salubrious and there are plenty of good places nearer the centre of town, around the market and out near the beach. There are **campsites** all along the coast, but none less than 10km from the city.

Albergue Juvenil Colegio Mayor "La Paz", Avda. del Puerto 69 (☎96/361 74 59). Valencia's youth hostel is out of town halfway to the port. Inexpensive but not too attractive, with a midnight curfew. Open July–Sept only. Bus #19 from Plaza Ayuntamiento. ①.

Hotel Alcázar, c/Mosén Femades 11 (☎96/352 95 75). Dependable and well cared for town centre hotel, near the post office. All rooms with shower. ④.

Hostal Aparicio, Torno del Hospital 3, west of the *Ayuntamiento* (☎96/331 52 80). Bottom of the range, but convenient. ②.

Habitaciones Australia, c/Conde Montornes 16. A useful fall-back if the *Gran Glorieta* is full. Rock-bottom prices. ①.

Hotel Bristol, c/Abadía San Martin 3 (☎96/352 11 76). Central and very comfortable. ④.

Hostal Residencial Don Pelayo, c/Pelayo 7 (☎96/352 11 35). A basic *hostal* with shared bathrooms. ②.

Hostal España, Embajador Vich 5 (☎96/352 93 42). A small selection of rooms from the bare bathless minimum to reasonable standards of comfort. ②.

Hostal Gran Glorieta, c/Conde Montornes 22, just off Plaza Tetuán, up c/de Colón (☎96/352 78 85). Friendly, popular place away from the noise of the station. Often full, so arrive early. ①–②.

Hotel La Marcelina, Paseo de Neptuno 72, near the sea (☎96/371 31 51). Pleasant, comfortable rooms with bath. ④.

Hotel La Pepica, Avda. Neptuno 2, near the beach (☎96/371 41 11). More upmarket place offering good value rooms with bath. ③.

Hospedería del Pilar, Plaza Mercado 19 (☎96/331 66 00). Crumbling, safe and central. ②.

Hostal del Rincón, c/Carda (which leads into c/Murillo) 11, near Plaza Mercado (☎96/331 60 83). Popular place with clean, spacious rooms and excellent location by the market. ②.

Hostal Residencial San Vicente, c/San Vicente 57 (☎96/352 70 61). Clean, reasonable rooms, no private bathrooms. ②.

CAMPING

El Salér, Mata del Fang (☎96/367 04 11). On a good beach, 10km south of Valencia. Bus from the Puerta del Mar at the end of Glorieta Park, leaving from just next to the newspaper kiosk (in summer on the hour and half-hour, out of season on the hour). Open all year.

El Palmar, Carretera Valencia–Cullera (☎96/161 08 53). 16km out, by La Albufera; same bus as for *El Salér*. Open July–August.

The city

The most interesting area for wandering around is undoubtedly the mazelike **Barrio del Carmen** (the oldest part of town), roughly between c/de Caballeros and the Río Turia around the Torres de Serranos. In c/de Caballeros, look for the old door knockers placed high up for the convenience of the horse-borne gentlemen residents (hence the name of the street). The **city walls**, which judging from the two surviving gates must have been magnificent, were pulled down in 1871 to make way for a roundabout; and the church of **Santo Domingo**, said to be the city's most beautiful, has been converted into a barracks – the very barracks from which General Milans del Bosch ordered his tanks onto the streets during the abortive coup of 1981. This fact, however, isn't representative of the city's political inclination, which has always been to the left – Valencia was the seat of the Republican government during the Civil War after it fled Madrid, and the last city to fall to Franco.

The oldest part of the city is almost entirely encircled by the **Río Turia**, which is now a **river-bed park**. The river was diverted in 1956 after serious flooding which damaged much of the old town. The ancient stone bridges remain, and the riverbed houses cycle and footpaths, football pitches, a stadium, a giant Gulliver for children to climb on and also the **Palau de la Musica**, a striking greenhouse style glass concert hall, which offers daily classical and jazz concerts.

Around the Plaza del Ayuntamiento

Within the **Plaza del Ayuntamiento** is a central square lined with flower stalls, and an impressive floodlit fountain. The *Ayuntamiento* houses the **Museo Historico**

Municipal (Mon–Fri 9–2pm; free) whose library has an impressive eighteenth-century map of Valencia showing the city walls intact.

The distinctive feature of Valencian architecture is its wealth of elaborate Baroque facades – you'll see them on almost every old building in town, but none so extraordinary or rich as the **Palacio del Marqués de Dos Aguas**. Hipólito Rovira, who designed its amazing alabaster doorway, died insane in 1740, which should come as no surprise to anyone who's seen it. Inside is the **Museo Nacional de Cerámica** (closed for restoration until 1996, but there are temporary exhibitions on the ground floor) with a vast collection of ceramics from all over Spain. Valencia itself was a major ceramics centre, largely owing to the size of its *morisco* population. Apart from an impressive display of *azulejos*, the collection contains some stunning plates with gold and copper varnishes (*reflejos*), a trio of evocatively ornate eighteenth-century carriages and, on the top floor, some fine fifteenth-century furniture. In the same decorative vein as the *palacio* is the church of **San Juan de la Cruz** (or San Andrés) next door.

Nearby, in the Plaza Patriarca, is the neoclassical former university with lovely cloisters where free classical concerts are held throughout July, and the beautiful Renaissance **Colegio del Patriarca**, whose small **art museum** (daily 11am–1pm) includes excellent works by El Greco, Morales and Ribalta. Another Ribalta, *The Last Supper*, hangs above the altar in the college's chapel; in the middle of the Miserere service at 10am on Friday mornings it's whisked aside to reveal a series of curtains. The last of these, drawn at the climactic moment, conceals a giant illuminated crucifix. The whole performance is amazingly dramatic, and typical of the aura of miracle and mystery which the Spanish church still cultivates. The University library contains the first book printed in Spain, *Les Trobes*, 1474.

The Cathedral

North from the University, along c/de la Paz, is the **Plaza Zaragoza** (sometimes still known as Plaza de la Reina) and Valencia's **Catedral**. The plaza is dominated by two octagonal towers, the florid spire of the church of **Santa Catalina** and the **Miguelete** (fourteenth–fifteenth century), the unfinished tower of the cathedral itself. You can make the long climb up to the roof for a fantastic view over the city with its many blue-domed churches. Entrance to the tower from inside the cathedral costs 100ptas; hours are not fixed but it's usually open in the morning until about 1pm and again from about 5 to 8pm. The church's most attractive and unusual feature is the lantern above the crossing, its windows glazed with sheets of alabaster, a popular material in the region as it lets in the Valencian light. The process of removing the later Baroque additions from the original Gothic structure of the main body of the building has been halted by lack of funds.

In the **Museu de la Seu**, the cathedral museum (Mon–Sat 1–2pm & 4–6pm) is a gold and agate cup (the *Santo Cáliz*) said to be the one used by Christ at the Last Supper – the Holy Grail itself. It's certainly old and, hidden away throughout the Dark Ages in a monastery in northern Aragón, it really did inspire many of the legends associated with the Grail. Other treasures include two Goyas, one of which depicts an exorcism (the corpse was originally naked, but after Goya's death a sheet was painted over it), a 2,300 kilo tabernacle made from gold, silver and jewels donated by the Valencian people. Made in 1939, it is paraded through the streets at Corpus Christi. The bells actually ring, and the silver figures of saints have removeable clothes.

Leaving the cathedral through the **Puerta de los Apóstoles**, you enter the **Plaza de la Virgen**. Here the *Tribunal de las Aguas*, the black-clad regulatory body of Valencia's water users, meets at noon every Thursday to judge grievances about the water irrigation system of the *huertas*. Blasco Ibáñez (1867–1928) describes their workings in detail in his novel *La Barraca*, which is about peasant life in the Valencian *huerta* and remains the best guide to the life of that region.

Two footbridges allow the clergy (only) to go straight from the cathedral into the Archbishop's Palace and the tiny chapel of **Nuestra Señora de los Desamparados**, also on the Plaza de la Virgen, where thousands of candles constantly burn in front of the image of the Virgin, patron of Valencia.

From the plaza, c/Caballeros leads to the **Palau de la Generalitat**, built in 1510. The courtyard can be visited Monday to Friday, 9am-8pm, but to see inside you need to make an appointment (Mon-Fri 9-2pm; ☎96/386 34 61; English-speaking guide available). It's worth the phone call to see the beautifully painted ceilings and frescoes depicting a meeting of the assembly (1592) in the Salón Dorado and Salón de Cortes.

Silk exchange and markets

If you tire of Baroque excesses, visit the beautifully elegant Gothic **Lonja de la Seda** (the Silk Exchange; Tues–Sat 10am–1.30pm & 5–9pm, Sun & holidays 10am–2pm) in the Plaza del Mercat. On weekdays it still operates as a commercial exchange. Opposite is the enormous **Mercado Central**, a modernist iron, girder and glass structure built at the beginning of the century and crowned with swordfish and parrot weathervanes. It's one of the biggest markets in Europe, fitting for *huerta* country, with amazing local fruit and vegetables, as well as hard-to-find herbs, health foods and dried goods. It closes around 2pm every day. Valencia's other spectacular market is the Mercado Colon on c/Cirilo Amoros.

Valencia's museums and the Jardines del Turia

The **Museo de Bellas Artes** (Tues–Sat 10am–2pm & 4–6pm, Sun 10am–2pm) on the far side of the river has one of the best general collections in Spain with works by Bosch, El Greco, Goya, Velázquez, Ribera and Ribalta as well as quantities of modern Valencian art. Outside is the largest of Valencia's parks – the **Jardines del Turia** (also called the Viveros Gardens) – in the centre of which is a small zoo. The gardens are the site of various events during the summer: a book fair in May and a music fair in July with open-air concerts.

As you head back into town don't miss the fourteenth-century **Torres Serranas**, an impressive gateway defending the entrance to the town across the Río Turia. The other remaining gateway is the **Torres de Quart**, a simpler structure but equally awesome in scale. Along with the **Museos de Etnología y Prehistoria**, c/Corona 36, another minor museum that calls for a visit is the **Museo Paleontológico** in c/Arzobispo Mayoral 3. It's in a building called the *Almudí*, a former grain storehouse built in the thirteenth century and rebuilt in the sixteenth century, now housing an awesome collection of bones and a magnificent collection of shells. Check opening times with the Turismo as both have been closed for restoration. If you're interested in bullfighting, the **Museo Taurino** is behind the bull ring on Pasaje Doctor Serra (Mon–Fri 10.30am–1.30pm).

Eating, drinking and nightlife

Home of **paella**, the city of Valencia doesn't offer the best opportunities to sample it. The best places are out of town in Perellonet or El Palmar (see p.690), or along the city beach, *Playa Levante;* Paseo Neptuno is lined with small hotels all with their own *paella* and *marisco* restaurants.The Barrio del Carmen is the best area for *tapas* and inexpensive meals.

Valencia has two weekly **listings guides**, *Qué y Dónde*, and the slightly less comprehensive, *Cartelera Turia*. If you don't know where to go, the city can seem dead at night as the action is widely dispersed, with many locations across the Turia. To get there, or go from one zone to another as the Spanish do, you'll either have to do a lot of walking or take taxis. The area immediately around the cathedral, where you might expect some action, is dead after dark.

VALENCIAN CUISINE

Gastronomy is of great cultural importance to the Valencians. Rice is the dominant ingredient in dishes of the region, grown locally in paddy fields still irrigated by the Arabic canal system (*acequias*). The genuine **Paella Valenciana** doesn't mix fish and meat. It typically contains chicken, rabbit, green beans, *garrofón* (large butter beans), snails, artichokes and saffron. Shellfish are eaten as a starter.

Rice dishes vary around the region: *arroz negro* is riced cooked with squid complete with ink which gives the dish its colour, and served with *all i oli*, a powerful garlic mayonnaise. *Arroz al horno* is drier, baked with chickpeas. *Fideuá* is seafood and noodles cooked *paella*-style.You'll find *arroz a banda* further south on the coast around Denia – it's rice cooked with seafood, served as two separate dishes, soup then rice. Around Alicante you can try *arroz con costra*, which is a meat-based *paella* topped with a baked egg crust. Apart from rice, vegetables (best *a la plancha*, brushed with olive oil and garlic) are always fresh and plentiful.

Restaurants and tapas bars

Bar Almudín, c/Almudín. Situated just behind the cathedral and renowned for its good seafood *raciones*.

Bar Ancoa, Plaza San Lorenzo at c/Novellos. A mid-range place on the pedestrianized streets between the *Ayuntamiento* and the Turia. Also serves inexpensive *platos*.

Barbacoa, Plaza del Carmen 6 (☎96/392 24 48). Serves a wonderful *menú del día* including barbecued meat for 1500ptas. Be prepared to wait as it's small and very popular.

Bar Cánovas, Plaza Cánovas Castillo. One of the city's best *tapas* bars.

Civera, C/Visitación (☎96/347 59 17). The best seafood restaurant in Valencia, situated across the river from the Torres de Serranos.

Comidas Eliseo, c/Conde Montornes. Basic and very inexpensive meals on one of Valencia's main budget accommodation streets.

Gargantua, c/Navarro Reverter 9. A good Valencian restaurant serving regional specialties. Closed Sunday evening and all day Monday.

Bar Glorieta, Plaza Alfonso Magnánimo. A large old bar serving *tapas* and excellent coffee (closes about 9pm).

La Hacienda, c/Navarro Reverter 12 (☎96/3731859). The best and most expensive restaurant in town where the speciality is bull's tail Cordoban-style. Closed Saturday lunchtime, all day Sunday and Easter.

La Lluna, c/San Ramón. A good vegetarian restaurant right in the heart of the Barrio del Carmen.

El Mesón, corner of Plaza del Carmen and c/Roteros. Once a famous political bar, now an upmarket restaurant.

Mey Mey, c/Historiador Diago (☎96/384 07 47). A popular Chinese restaurant where you'll need to book at weekends.

Restaurante Patos, Plaza San Vicente Ferrer. Handy if you're staying in c/Conde Montornes, this small, quiet restaurant has reasonably priced, interesting dishes.

Bar Pilar, on the corner of c/Moro Zeit, just off Plaza del Esparto. A traditional place for *mejillones* (mussels), where they serve them in a piquant sauce and you throw the shells into buckets under the bar.

Rotunda, Plaza Redonda. Moderately priced restaurant, superbly situated on Valencia's distinctive round plaza.

Bars

Valencia takes its nightlife very seriously and has one of the liveliest bar scenes in mainland Spain. Make sure you try an authentic Valencian cocktail while you're here.

BARRIO DEL CARMEN

In town, the youngest crowd and loudest music are to be found on c/Bailén and c/ Pelayo. The **Barrio del Carmen** has dozens of small café-bars and is one of the liveliest areas at night, especially around Plaza San Jaume. The popular *La Marxa* is worth searching out, located in an imaginatively decorated town house, with a small, sweaty dance floor and varied music. You'll find plenty of other good options along c/ Serranos, c/de Quart (running into c/de Caballeros), c/Alta and c/Baja, c/ Beneficiencia, and the four parallel streets of Na Jordana, San Ramón, de Ripalda and Dr. Chiarri. Good *salsa* bars include *Rincón Latino*, c/Gobernador Viejo 10 and the nearby *Azucar Mareno*.

ACROSS THE RÍO TURIA

You'll also find plenty of bars on the **other side of the river** beyond the Barrio (around c/Ruaya, c/Visitación and c/Orihuela), and behind the Gran Vía de Fernando el Católico (along c/Juan Llorens and c/Calixto). In the latter area, the *Café Carioca* and *Café La Habana*, at c/Juan Llorens 52 and 41 are currently in favour, as are *La Torna* at c/Carmen 12 and *Bésame Mucho* in Ciudad Jardín at c/Explorador Andrés 6, which has live music.

Most of the "in" places are across the Turia in the new **university** region. The trendiest bars are on Avda. Blasco Ibáñez – the *Público* at no. 111, the *Metro* at no. 97, *Hipódromo* and *El Asesino*. The bars of Plaza Xuquer, just off the Blasco Ibáñez, are popular meeting places – *Cuba Litro*, in the corner, serves litre plastic cups of *combinados* (see box), while the *Pan de Azúcar* serves snack food until late. Wherever you look around here there's a bar worth calling in at – they're particularly thick on the ground in c/Artes Gráficas, c/Rodrigo Poros, c/Alfonso de Córdoba (the town side of Blasco Ibáñez, towards the Jardín del Real) and c/Menéndez Pelayo (on the opposite side).

MALVARROSA BEACH

In summer, the bars lining the **Malvarrosa beach** are the place to be, in particular the *Genaro* and *Tropical*, large bar-discos on c/Eugenio Vines (the beach road). To get there, take bus #1 or #2 from the bus station, or #19 from Plaza del Ayuntamiento. All three buses go along the Avda. del Puerto and turn into c/Dr. Lluch; get off about halfway along and go down to the beach along c/Virgen del Sufragio – *Genaro* is on your right, *Tropical* is along on the left. The stop for the return bus is one road back from where you got off. You'll probably need a taxi late at night. There are also several bars between Paseo Neptuno and the new Paseo Maritimo next to the port which are less rowdy. The best is *Vivir sin Dormir*, where you can play pool or sit at candlelit tables.

HORCHATA

Valencia is also known for its **horchata** – a drink made from *chufas* (tiger nuts) served either liquid or *granizada* (slightly frozen). It is accompanied by *fartóns* (long thin cakes). Legend has it that the name "horchata" was coined by Jaume I, shortly after he conquered Valencia. He was admiring the *huerta* one hot afternoon, and an Arab girl offered him a drink so refreshing that he exclaimed, "Aixó es or, xata" (this is gold, girl).

You can get *horchata* all over the city but the best traditionally comes from Alboraya, formerly a village in the Valencian suburbs, now absorbed into the city. The oldest *horchatería* in town is the *Santa Catalina* on the bottom corner of Plaza Zaragoza. The various *horchaterías* and *heladerías* on Plaza San Lorenzo, just in from the Torres de Serranos, are excellent and very good value. To get to **Alboraya**, take the #70 bus, or metro line 3 from Estación Puente de Madera (across the river from Torres de Serranos). The most renowned *horchatería* is *Daniel*, where you can sit on the terrace and escape from the summer heat of the city.

COMBINADOS VALENCIANOS

The *Valencianos* seem to really like *combinados*, or **cocktails**, which don't necessarily have the upmarket connotation they have elsewhere. The *Rincón Latino*, c/Gobernador Viejo 10, off c/Conde Montornes, near Plaza San Vicente Ferrer, is a smoky cellar where the speciality is inexpensive Nicaraguan drinks – order a rum and pineapple cocktail and you'll get a tiny glass of each, the idea being to toss back all the rum in one go, quickly followed by the juice. A classic cocktail goes under the name of *Agua de Valencia* and is served by the jug in a series of old bars. The *Cervecería de Madrid*, c/de la Abadía de San Martín, just below Plaza Zaragoza, is a popular old-fashioned bar with walls crammed full of paintings, where they serve the orthodox *Agua de Valencia* made with orange juice, champagne and vodka. The *Café Malvarrosa*, c/Ruíz de Lihoro, off c/de la Paz, has its own *Agua de Malvarrosa*, made with lemon instead of orange. The nearby cafés *Paris* and *Madrid* also have their own versions of the same.

PLAZA CÁNOVAS CASTILLO

Another fashionable area is the **Plaza Cánovas Castillo** and the side streets off it, full of *pubs* (music bars) where people go to see and be seen. The bars along c/Serrano Morales and c/Grabador Esteve are yuppie haunts (the cars outside are a good indicator), but those off the opposite side, down c/Salamanca, c/Conde de Altea and c/Burriana are more mixed. In both cases, each bar has its own particular age group and style – there's something for everyone from *salsa* to *flamenco* to *bacalao*. In many of the bars around Plaza Cánovas you can ask the waiters for discount/free entrance cards for discos, but these will only be available early in the evening. One of the more unusual places in this area is *Johan Sebastian Bach* in c/del Mar (1500ptas entry charge). They used to keep a lion in a cage in the bar, but even without the lion, it's impressive.

Discos

Most discos play exclusively rave techno music. Known as **bacalao** or *makina* (machine) music, this scene has ruled in Valencia since the late 1980s. One of the best *bacalao* spots is *Calcatta*, in a converted old house in c/Reloj Viejo off c/Caballeros. There's plenty of alternative music around, however; try *La Marxa* off c/Caballeros, *Un Sur* in c/Maestro Gozalbo, *Época* in c/Cuba, *Raza* in c/Pedro III El Grande (often with live music) and *Jerusalem*, c/Jerusalem off Pl. de España, all in or near the city centre.

There are also lots of good venues in the university area: *Distrito 10*, c/Gen. Elio, just over the Puente del Real, the slick *Jardines del Real* (in the same block), *Acción* in Blasco Ibañez, the teenage *Woody*, c/Menéndez Pelayo and *Arena*, c/Emilio Baró, which as well as a disco is a venue for visiting bands.

Valencia has a thriving **gay culture**, and there are scores of bars and discos, varying from "mixed" to a heavier, gay male only scene. Most of the gay bars/discos are found around Central Market and c/Quart. *Venial*, c/Quart, is young and trendy, and you only pay to get in at weekends. Or try the very popular *Dakota*, c/San Martir, near Plaza de la Reina; a bar with a wild west theme. A couple of other discos worth trying are *Balkiss* at c/Dr. Monserrat 23, near the Torres de Quart and *Ales*, behind the old bar *Barrachina* in Plaza del Ayuntamiento.

The rest of the discos are out of town on the main road heading south along the coast. *Spook Factory* on Carretera El Salér and *Dreams* are near each other, on the Playa de Pinedo, Camino Montañares. Further down, on the Playa Recati (El Perellonet, below the Albufera), are *Saliter* and *Pomelo* – the former funky, the latter new wave. In Las Palmeras, *La Barraca* is a pop disco and *Chocolate* is pop-rock. For **jazz**, the favourite is the *Perdido Club Jazz* at c/Sueca 17.

Listings

Airlines *Iberia* and *Aviaco*, c/de la Paz 14 (☎96/352 05 00); *British Airways*, Plaza Rodrigo Botet 6 (☎96/351 22 84).

Airport Manises, 15km away; ☎96/370 95 00; bus #15 from bus station (hourly).

Balearic ferries Leave daily for Mallorca (9hr) and twice weekly for Ibiza (7 hr); information and tickets from *Transmediterránea*, Avda. Manuel Soto 19, but it's a long trip out and you may as well buy tickets from any of the half-dozen travel agents on the *Ayuntamiento* plaza.

Banks Main branches of most banks are around the Plaza del Ayuntamiento or along c/Játiva. There's a *Barclays* at c/Correos 10, and a *Londres y América Sur* at Plaza Rodrigo Botet 6. Outside banking hours, two branches of the *Caja de Ahorros* are open Mon–Sat 9am–8pm: one at c/Játiva 14, to the left as you come out of the train station, and the other in the *Nuevo Centro*, near the bus station. As savings banks, they can only do certain transactions. *Banco de Valencia*, Division Internacional, c/Colon 20, charges one of the lowest commission rates for changing money.

Beaches The city beach, Malvarrosa, is polluted, but is being cleaned up and does have an elegant promendade. It's best go to El Salér, a long, wide stretch with pine trees and a campsite behind it. A bus goes from the Puerta del Mar at the end of Glorieta Park, leaving from just next to the newspaper kiosk (in summer on the hour and half-hour, out of season on the hour). The ride takes 20min and it stops in the village before heading down to the beach and then turning back.

Bookstores English books are available from the *International Bookshop* on c/Ruzafa, the *English Book Centre* on c/Pascual y Genis and *Crisol*, Antic Regne de Valencia.

Buses Main station is at Avda. Menéndez Pidal 13, across the Turia (☎96/349 72 22). Regular services to northern Europe and to London leave from here – offices in the station.

Car rental Best value is probably *Cuñat Car Hire*, c/Burriana 51 (☎96/374 85 61). Otherwise, there's *Avis* at the airport and at c/Isabel la Católica 17 (☎96/351 07 34), *Hertz* at the airport and c/Segorbe 7 (☎96/341 50 36), *Atesa* at the airport and Avda. del Cid 64 (☎96/379 91 08) and many more.

Cinema Original-language films are shown regularly at the subsidized municipal *Filmoteca*, Plaza del Ayuntamiento, and are sometimes also shown at *Albatros Mini-Cines*, Plaza Fray Luis Colomer, and *Xerea*, c/En Blanch 6.

Consulates *Holland*, *Belgium* and *Luxembourg*, c/G.V. Germanias 18 (☎96/341 46 33); *Sweden*, c/Pintor Sorolla 4 (☎96/352 41 54); *USA*, c/Ribera 3 (☎96/351 69 73). No British consulate, but there is a British Institute at c/Gen. Sanmartín 7 (☎96/351 88 18).

Cyclists There are various cycle paths (marked in green) running through the city; watch out for straying pedestrians. For info on the excursions and longer routes organized by the *Consellería de Cultura, Educación y Ciencia de la Generalitat de Valencia*, ask at *ITVA* (*Institut Turistic Valencia*) Avda. Aragón 30 (☎96/398 60 00).

Hospital Avda. Cid, at the Tres Cruces junction (☎96/379 16 00). First-aid station at Plaza América 6 (☎96/352 67 50).

Left Luggage Self-store lockers at *RENFE*; 24-hr access, 150ptas a day.

Markets Check out the crowded **flea market** around the Plaza Redonda (off Plaza Zaragoza) and also Plaza San Esteban behind the cathedral. There are also a few stalls alongside the cathedral – best for crunchy sugar cane. Every day except Sun and Tues there are stalls selling jewellery, clothes and knick-knacks off c/de la Paz in Plaza Alfonso Magnánimo. On Sundays it's held in Plaza de la Virgen, and on Tuesdays in Plaza España.

Police Headquarters are on Gran Vía Ramón y Cajal 40 (☎96/351 08 62).

Post Office Main *Correos* is at Plaza del Ayuntamiento 1 (Mon–Sat 9am–9pm & Sun am.)

Telephones Plaza del Ayuntamiento 27 (Mon–Sat 9am–1pm & 5–9pm).

Trains *RENFE* is on c/Játiva (☎96/351 36 12). Several each day to Barcelona, Madrid and Málaga. For destinations around Valencia, there's the *FGV* (metro) from Plaza España (lines 1 & 2) and Puente de Madera (line 3).

Trekking Treks through various mountain areas in the region are organized year-round. You can either join a guided group or, if you want to go it alone, they'll provide route maps and info. Details from *Per les Nostres Muntanyes* at c/Caballeros 21 near the Plaza del Virgen (Mon–Fri 6–10pm), or *ITVA* (see "Cyclists").

Outside the city

There are a number of good **day trips** to be made from the city including visits to the region's very best *paella* restaurants at El Palmar, El Perello and Perellonet. Valencia can get extremely hot in the summer and the cool mountains of the Alto Turia are an enticing option.

La Albufera and the paella villages

La Albufera is a vast lagoon separated from the sea by a sandbank and surrounded by rice fields. Being one of the largest bodies of freshwater in Spain it constitutes an important wetland, and attracts tens of thousands of migratory birds – a throng composed of 250 species, of which 90 breed here regularly. In the Middle Ages it was ten times its present size but the surrounding paddies have gradually reduced it. Experts, having detected growing contamination by industrial waste, domestic sewage and insecticide pollution, have recently made it a natural park.

Whether you're into birdwatching or not, it's a relaxing change from the city and you can eat *paella* in the nearby villages of El Palmar and El Perelló. **EL PALMAR** was formerly a settlement of fishing huts, now packed with **restaurants** as struggling fishing families turn to the catering business. One of the better restaurants is *Mateu* (☎96/161 09 72). El Palmar celebrates its **fiesta** on 4 August. The image of Christ on the cross is taken out onto the lake in a procession of boats to the *Illuent*, or centre, of the lake, where hymns are sung.

Further along the road to El Perelló is the small village of **PERELLONET**, where you can eat some of the best *paella* around. Try *Vert i Blau* for *patatas Amparín* – a potato *tapa* with a kick – and *Blayet* or *Gaviotas* (☎96/177 75 75), where you need to book, for *paella*, *mariscos* and *all i pebre* (piquant eels). Regular buses run from the city via El Salér and on to the lagoon, El Palmar and El Perelló.

Manises

Fifteen kilometres south west of the city at **MANISES**, where Valencia's airport is located, is the centre of the region's ceramics business. Look out for the internationally renowned Lladró figures. The *Museo de Cerámica*, c/Sagrario 22 (Mon-Sat 10-1pm, 4-7pm, Sun 11-2pm) has displays of ceramics from medieval blue and metallic varnishes to award-winning modern examples, and a demonstration of the traditional process of ceramic-making.

The Alto Turia

The mountains and vineyards of the **Alto Turia** can be reached by direct bus from Valencia. There are several reservoirs in this region, and areas set aside for Sunday paella-makers. At the reservoir *Domeño* you'll find a ghost town, the remains of a village that was flooded to create the reservoir. It's said that on windy nights, you can hear the church bells ringing. Further along this road is **CHELVA**. Turn right in the village for the *Peña Cortada* where, at the end of a very rough track, there is a Roman aqueduct which is tunnelled into the mountain – an ambitious plan the Romans thought up to carry water across the mountains to the arid central plains, but they didn't stay in Spain long enough to complete it.

On from Chelva on the same road you reach **TUÉJAR** and the **Mancomunidad del Alto Turia**, where the Río Turia begins. Walks in this area are signposted – follow the red and white stripes (another part of the *Gran Recorrido*). There's a decent hotel in Tuéjar, and a *posada* in Chelva (☎96/210 01 04; ③) if you want to spend more time in the area.

North of Valencia – the Costa del Alzahar

The best **beaches** along the Costa del Alzahar are around **Benicasim**, north of the rather grim provincial capital, **Castellón de la Plana**. Further north, **Peñíscola**, a historic town with good beaches and seafood restaurants, is worth a visit, and **Benicarló** is pleasant too. Perhaps the best place to stop en route to Catalunya or Morella is **Vinaroz** at the mouth of the tiny Río Servol – a real town, not developed exclusively for tourists.

Sagunto

Twenty kilometres north of Valencia are the fine Roman remains of **SAGUNTO**. This town passed into Spanish legend when, in 219 BC, it was attacked by Hannibal in one of the first acts of the war waged by Carthage on the Roman Empire. Its citizens withstood a nine-month siege before burning the city and themselves rather than surrendering. When belated help from Rome arrived, the city was recaptured and rebuilding eventually got under way. Chief among the ruins is the second-century **Roman amphitheatre**, the basic shape of which survives intact. Debate continues about its restoration: it's now functional and covered in marble, but for many people, has lost its authenticity. Plays are performed here during the summer. The wonderful views from its seats take in a vast span of history – Roman stones all around, a ramshackle Moorish castle on the hill behind, medieval churches in the town below, and, across the plain towards the sea, the black smoke of modern industry. Further Roman remains are being excavated within the walls of the huge **acropolis-castle**, and numerous smaller finds are on show in the small museum (summer Mon–Sat 10–8pm, Sun 10–2pm; winter Mon–Sat 10–2pm & 4–6pm, Sun 10–2pm) almost next to the theatre on the road up to the site.

The main road, with frequent buses from Valencia, passes below, as do the main Valencia–Barcelona and Valencia–Zaragoza rail lines, with fifteen trains per day. If you want to **stay near Sagunto**, try the inexpensive *La Pinada* (☎96/246 04 50; ②) which has a pool. It's 3km out of town on the CN234, the road to Teruel.

Segorbe and Montanejos

About 30km inland from Sagunto is **SEGORBE**, the Roman Segóbriga, which is worth a visit more for its tranquillity than its sights. It lies in the valley of the Río Palancia, among medlar and lemon orchards. Segorbe's cathedral was begun in the thirteenth-century, but suffered in the neoclassic reforms and only the cloister is original. The museum (daily 11am–1pm) contains a few pieces of Gothic Valencian art, with a *retablo* by Vicente Maçip. Only part of the old city wall remains, but the views are more rewarding. One kilometre outside Segorbe on the road to Jérica, you'll find the "fountain of the provinces" which has 50 spouts, one for each province of Spain, each labelled with the coat of arms. If you want **to stay**, the only option is the *Fonda Aparicio* (②) next to the bus stop. Segorbe lies on the main **train** line from Valencia to Teruel and Zaragoza and there are seven trains a day. Segorbe has its **fiestas** at the beginning of September, when *La Entrada* takes place and bulls are run through the town by horses.

From Segorbe, its an easy trip to **MONTANEJOS**. Turn off at Jérica for the road to Montanejos, or catch the bus in Segorbe. This tiny village has three hotels and rents out apartments, as it's popular with visitors to the hot springs, **Fuente de Baños**; the water emerges at 25°C and has medicinal properties. Walks around the village join up with the *Gran Recorrido*, the walkers' route that crosses the whole peninsula. If you want to stay here, there's *Rosaleda del Mijares*, Carretera de Tales (☎964/131079; ③), or *Hostal Gil Navarro*, Avda Fuente de Baños (☎964/131063; ②).

Castellón de la Plana

Continuing north along the coast, **CASTELLÓN DE LA PLANA** is in itself singularly
unattractive, but there are a couple of good reasons for stopping here. It's one of the
least expensive places to stay along this stretch of coast and there are some
surprisingly good beaches within easy reach. In the town there's really only one thing
worth seeing, the **Museo de Bellas Artes** on c/Caballeros, between Plaza Mayor and
Plaza Aulas (10am–2pm & 4–6pm, Sat 10am–12.30pm; free). It displays ceramics and
work by local artists. For budget **rooms** make straight for *Bagán*, c/Pérez Galdós 13
(☎964/213905; ①); for something a little less basic check out the beachfront *Martí*,
c/Herrero 19 (☎964/224566; ② or ③ with bath); or look on c/Trinidad and c/Navarra
near the Puerta Sol. You'll find the **youth hostel** at c/Orfebrer Santalínea 2
(☎964/202300). For the best *arroz negro*, try the *Tasca del Puerto*, Avda. del Puerto 13
(☎964/236018).

The **beaches** are at Grao de Castellón (*grao* simply means port) and all along the
coast to Benicasim. Buses for both leave regularly from the Plaza Hernán Cortés, heading down to the port and then turning north.

Villafames

VILLAFAMES, 24km inland from Castellón, is an attractive hill town which successfully mixes the medieval, renaissance and modern. In the highest part of the town
there's an ancient ruined castle, conquered by Jaime I in 1233. The fifteenth-century
Palacio del Batle houses the **Museo Popular del Arte Contemporáneo** (daily 11am–
1pm & 5–7pm), a collection of over 500 sculptures and paintings including works by
Miró, Lozano and Mompó. There are good **rooms** at *El Rullo*, c/de la Fuente (③),
which also has a restaurant.

Benicasim

BENICASIM, a few kilometres north of Castellón, is heavily developed and budget
accommodation is scarce – the **Turismo** (9am–2pm & 4–6pm) at Plaza María
Agustina 5 has a list of *hostales*. Several of the better-value *fondas* are in the old village
near the train station; try *Fonda Garamar*, c/Queipodellano (☎964/300011; ②) or
Fonda Chiva, c/Santo Tomás (☎964/300905). The *Buenavista*, c/San Antonio 13
(☎964/300905; ②, closed winter) is large and inexpensive for rooms with bath. More
expensive is the *Hostal Montreal-76*, in the town at c/Barracas 5 (☎964/300681; ③)
which has lots of facilities and even a swimming pool. There's also a year-round **youth
hostel** on Avda. de Ferrandiz Salvador (☎964/300949) and at least seven **campsites** in
the area.

Six kilometres inland from Benicasim is the **Desierto de las Palmas**, a Carmelite
monastery in an idyllic setting which dates from 1694. The Carmelites run meditation
courses here and there is also a museum of religious history (daily 10am–1pm & 4–
7pm). Climb the nearby Monte Bartolo for a great view across the plains. Parts of the
mountain were unfortunately stripped of trees by a forest fire in 1992 – a serious problem throughout the whole of Valencia and often caused by arsonists.

Peñíscola

There's not much else along this stretch until you reach Peñíscola, although the resort
of **OROPESA** just beyond Benicasim does have reasonable beaches, good campsites
and a lively atmosphere in the summer.

PEÑÍSCOLA occupies a heavily fortified promontory jutting out into the
Mediterranean. There was a Phoenician settlement here, and later it saw Greek,
Carthaginian, Roman and Moorish rulers, but the present castle was built by the
Knights Templar with alterations by Pedro de la Luna. Pope Benedict XIII, Pedro

(*Papa Luna*) lived here for six years after he had been deposed from the papacy during the fifteenth-century church schisms. The castle today (where part of *El Cid* was filmed) is heavily restored and largely a museum to *Papa Luna*, but it's impressive from a distance and the old town that clusters around its base is extremely picturesque, if heavily commercialized. There are small **beaches** on either side of the castle but the best one is on the town side, even though it's accordingly more crowded. Peñíscola is best visited off-season to avoid the crowds and to make sure of finding **accommodation** in the old town. For sea views, try *Chiqui Bar*, c/Mayor 3 (☎964/480284; ②), run by a friendly couple. The magnificent *Hostería del Mar*, Avda. Papa Luna 18 (☎964/480600; ⑤) offers more luxury and also specializes in medieval banquets with music and dancing. There are several reasonably priced **hostales** near the base of the castle and along the beach road, and it's here that you'll find the town's many restaurants, although the atmosphere is rather staid in the evenings. Buses run down the coast from Vinaros and Benicarló hourly from 8am to 9pm.

Benicarló

BENICARLÓ, seven kilometres further along the coast, boasts a church with a fine octagonal tower and blue-tiled dome and a small but tranquil beach. There are several inexpensive places to **stay** right in the centre – the *Monte Casino*, c/Doctor Ferrer 2 (☎964/471010; ②) should be first on the list for budget rooms with bath – plus there's a **youth hostel** at Avda. de Yecla 4 (☎964/470500) and, **campsites** on the coast nearby. The docks are important for shipbuilding and worth a look.

Vinaroz

The **beaches** of VINAROZ, next along the coast, are small but rarely packed and in town there's an elaborate Baroque church, with an excellent local produce market nearby. The **Turismo** (9am–1pm & 6–8pm), close to the church, can help you to find accommodation. Perhaps the best place to try is the *Fonda Centro* – from the Turismo, bear right over the roundabout and it's in the first street on the left. You can eat well there for very little, too. Otherwise, the *Salom*, Plaza de San Antonio 13 (☎964/455849; ②) is good value if you're not looking for private facilities; the small *El Pino*, c/San Pascual 47 (☎964/450553; ③) is the least expensive *hostal* with bathrooms.

Anywhere in town the **fish** is locally caught and excellent; go down to the dockside market in the early evenings to watch the day's catch being auctioned and packed off to restaurants all over the region. *Bar Neus* (which makes excellent iced coffee), opposite the bus terminal, is the main source of information for all timetables or routes from the town; the bus to Morella currently leaves at 4pm. The town's **train station** is a good 2km from the centre.

Morella

MORELLA, 60km inland on the road from the coast to Zaragoza, is the most attractive town in the province of Castellón and one of the most remarkable in the entire area. A medieval fortress town, it rises from the plain around a small hill crowned by a tall, rocky spur and a virtually impregnable **castle** which dominates the countryside for miles around. A perfectly preserved ring of ancient walls defends its lower reaches. The city was recovered from the Moors in the thirteenth century by the steward of Jaime I. He was reluctant to hand it over to the crown, and it is said that the king came to blows with him over the possession of the city.

Chief among the monuments, apart from the castle, is the church of **Santa María la Mayor** (*Iglesia Arciprestal*, 11am–2pm & 3.30–6pm), a fourteenth-century Gothic construction with beautifully carved doorways (*dels Apòstols*) and an unusual raised *coro* reached by a marble spiral stairway. A few minutes' walk to the left, at the foot of the castle, is the ruined **Monasterio de San Francisco** (10am–2pm & 3–8pm), currently being rebuilt. Its elegant cloister houses a museum of sorts – a strange collection of curios from the area – and you pass through to approach the **fortress**, itself in ruins but still impressive. It's a tiring climb but there are tremendous views in every direction from the crumbling courtyard at the top – down over the monastery, bullring and town walls to the plains. In the distance are the remains of the weird Gothic **aqueduct** which once supplied the town's water.

Not far from the monastery is a curious private **museum**, nearly all of whose exhibits (painted tiles, fragments of jewellery, broken clocks, fossils and aged ploughs) are for sale. In the c/de la Virgen de Villavana is a house where San Vicente Ferrer performed the prodigious miracle of resurrecting a child who had been chopped up and stewed by its mother – she could find nothing else fit for a saint to eat. There's an annual **festival of classical music** in Morella in the last week of August.

Practicalities

The **Turismo** is a five-minute walk from the bus station, inside the Torres de San Miguel, the main double gate-tower into town; little useful information is on offer, but it does have a small and interesting exhibition of muskets, bullets and pictures from the Carlist Wars.

The best of Morella's budget **accommodation** is the excellent and welcoming *Elías*, c/Colomer 7 (☎964/160092; ②). *Hostal El Cid*, Puerta San Mateo 2 (☎964/160125; ②) is right by the bus stop and town gate and has views of the plain and the distant hills from its balconied rooms, but its traffic hub location tends to make it noisy – not really worth the small saving. There's also a basic *fonda,* the *Moreno* (☎964/160105; ①) at c/San Nicolás 12. During fiestas and national holidays, you should book accommodation in advance, as Morella is very popular with Spanish holidaymakers. If you are stuck without accommodation, there's a good *hostal, Guadalupe* (☎964/856005; ②) in **MONROYO**, a neighbouring village. Be prepared for lower temperatures in Morello than elsewhere in the province, and for snow in winter.

The main porticoed street, **Els Porxos**, bisected by steep steps leading down to the lower walls, is the place to focus on for food, a good source of **bars, bakeries and cafés**. *Vinatea* and *Rovera* are both excellent bars for *tapas.* Below the monastery are a couple of small plazas where you can sit at outdoor cafés – especially pleasant in the evening.

Morella is one possible approach to the Maestrazgo region of southern Aragón. Daily **buses** leave for Alcañiz, (at 10am) and Cantavieja/Villafranca del Cid (6.30pm), as well as to Vinaroz (4pm) and Castellón (7.30am).

The Costa Blanca

South of Valencia stretches a long strip of country with some of the **best beaches** on this coast, especially betwen Gandía and Benidorm. Much of it, though, suffers from the worst excesses of **package tourism** and in the summer it's hard to get a room anywhere – in August it's virtually impossible. Campers have it somewhat easier – there are hundreds of campsites – but driving can be a nightmare unless you stick to the dull highway.

Leaving Valencia, both road and rail pass the vast **Ford factory**, one of the Spanish government's earliest successes in persuading multinational companies to invest in the country's cheap labour and favourable tax measures. If you're taking the inland route as far as Gandía, you'll get the opportunity to see the historic town of **Játiva**.

Játiva

The ancient town of **JÁTIVA** (Xátiva), 50km south of Valencia was probably founded by the Phoenicians and certainly inhabited by the Romans. Today it's a scenic, tranquil place to kill a few hours in the relative coolness of the hills, and makes a good day out from the capital. Medieval Xátiva was the birthplace of Alfonso de Borja, who became Pope Calixtus III, and his nephew Rodrigo, father of the infamous Lucrezia and Caesar Borgia. When Rodrigo became Pope Alexander VI, the family moved to Italy. **Fiestas** are held during Holy Week and in the second half of August when the *Feria de Agosto* is celebrated with bullfights and livestock fairs, but beware, it can get unbearably hot at this time of year.

Játiva has a fine collection of mansions scattered around town, but most are private and cannot be entered. Many of the churches are in a state of disrepair and are closed, but the **old town** is a pleasant place to wander. If you arrive by train, follow c/Baixada Estació up towards the central tree-lined Alameda, and then keep heading up towards the castle. Just off the Alameda, you'll find the post office, *Ayuntamiento* (or *Casa de la Ciutat*) and the **Turismo**, on c/Noguera, in a beautifully restored *botica* (apothecary). They have a leaflet showing a suggested walk (corresponding numbers are marked on street signs themselves) but it's not necessary to follow it slavishly since the place is tiny and you're better off discovering things for yourself.

It's a fairly long walk up the hill to the **castle** (Tues–Sun 10.30am–2pm & 4.30–8pm in summer) – follow signposts from the Plaza del Españoleto. On the way, you'll pass the thirteenth-century **Ermita de San Feliu** (Mon–Sat 10am–1pm & 3–6pm), a hermitage built in transitional Romanesque-Gothic style; ancient pillars, fine capitals and a magnificent Gothic *retablo* are the chief attractions of the interior.

The **Museo Municipal** (Tues–Fri 11am–2pm & 4–8pm; Sat & Sun 11am–2pm) consists of two separate sections, one an archaeological collection, the other an art museum. The latter includes several pictures by José Ribera (who was born here in 1591) and engravings by Goya – *Caprichos* and *Los Proverbios*. A portrait of Felipe V is hung upside down in retribution for his having set fire to the city in the War of Succession and his having changed its name.

It doesn't take long to see Játiva, but if you're enjoying the peace and quiet and want to **stay**, the best place is the *Hostal Margallonero*, Plaza Mercat 42 (☎96/227 66 77; ②) – they also serve food. Also worth trying is the *Casa Isabel* (☎96/227 67 77; ②) next to the Turismo. Keep an eye open for *arnadí* in the bakeries – it's a local speciality of Moorish origin, a rich (and expensive) sweet made with pumpkin, cinnamon, almonds, eggs, sugar and pine nuts.

Játiva is served by buses and trains from Valencia; the train (1hr) is half the price of the bus and leaves every half-hour. There are also connection to Gandía by bus and to Alicante by train.

Gandía

There's not much along the coast until you get to **GANDÍA**, the first of the big resorts. A few kilometres inland from the modern seafront development, the old town is quiet and provincial, with one sight that's well worth seeing, and some good inexpensive accommodation.

The town of Gandía was once important enough to have its own university but the only real testimony to its heyday is the **Palacio Ducal de los Borja**, built in the fourteenth century but with Renaissance and Baroque additions and modifications. There are regular guided tours (daily 11am–noon & 6–7pm) throughout the year. Tours are in Spanish, but photocopied translations are available at the reception and it is essential

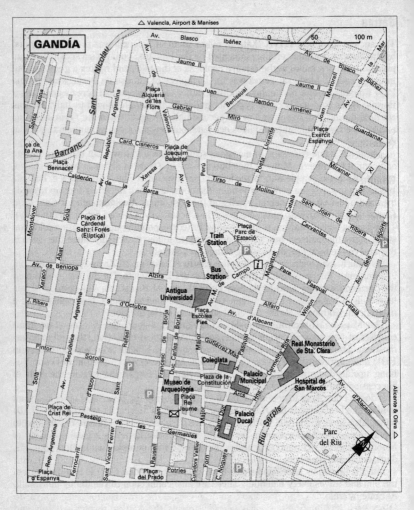

to book (☎96/287 12 04). The lifetime of duke Francisco de Borja coincided with the golden age of the town (late fifteenth to early sixteenth century) in terms of urban and cultural development, a process in which he played an important part; learned and pious, the Duke opened colleges all over Spain and Europe, and was eventually canonized. The palace contains his paintings, tapestries and books, but parts of the building itself are of equal interest, such as the *artesonado* ceilings and the pine window shutters, so perfectly preserved by prolonged burial in soil and manure that resin still oozes from them when the hot sun beats down. There are also several beautiful sets of *azulejos*, but these are outshone by the fourteenth-century Arab wall tiles, whose brilliant lustre is now unattainable, derived from pigments of plants that became extinct soon after the Moors left.

Practicalities

Both **buses** and **trains** arrive on Marqués de Campo. The **Turismo** (Mon–Fri 10am–2pm & 4–8pm, Sat & Sun 10am–2pm) occupies a brown hut, cleverly camouflaged behind some trees opposite the train station. There are a handful of **pensiones** in town; try the clean and spacious *Requena* at c/Tirso de Molino 28 (☎96/286 58 63; ②), close to the train station, or the nearby *Pepita*, c/Cardenal Cisneros 10 (☎96/287 34 88; ②). For a bit more luxury, there's *Clibomar* (☎96/284 32 37; ③) in c/Alcoy by the Playa de Gandía or the *Duque Carlos* in c/Duque Carlos de Borja 34 (☎96/287 28 44; ③). The exceptionally nice **youth hostel** is on the beachfront at **Playa de Piles**, 5km down the coast (☎96/289 34 25; ①) and there are buses every hour from outside the train station (8am–8pm). Gandía's best **restaurants** and **bars** are ten minutes from town at the beach. *Flash* and *Fakata* discos are also out of town on the Carretera de Valencia.

Gandía beach

Buses run regularly from the Turismo down to the enormous **beach**, *Gandía Playa*. The beach is packed in summer (especially with Spanish families) and lined with high-rise apartments which out of season can be remarkably good value. The beach zone is a good place for **seafood** and *paellas*. Try *fideua*, a local speciality with a strong seafood flavour, cooked with vermicelli instead of rice. *La Gamba* (☎96/284 13 10), Carretera Nazaret-Oliva, a few blocks back from the beach is one of the best places to eat here.

Gandía to Altea – around the cape

A string of lovely little towns and beaches stretches from Gandía to Altea before you reach the developments of Benidorm and Alicante, but your own transport is essential to enjoy the best of them and accommodation can be pricey. The most inexpensive option along this coast is to camp. There are scores of decent campsites and a useful booklet listing them is available from local Turismos. Try *La Merced* in Calpe, Carretera La Cometa (96/583 00 97) and *El Naranjal* in Jávea, Carretera Cabo de la Nao, 96/579 29 89).

Oliva

OLIVA, 8km south beyond Gandía, is a much lower-key development. Again the village is set back from the coast and although the main road charges through its centre, it's relatively unspoiled and there's a number of **hostales and fondas**. *La Tropical* is a rather upmarket *hostal* on Avda. del Mar 9 (☎96/285 00 20; ③) with seasonal reductions and a variety of rooms. The beach, served by frequent buses, stretches a long way to the south, almost as far as Denia, so if you're prepared to walk, or better still if you've got transport, you can escape the crowds altogether. **Playa de Oliva** itself has hundreds of villas and apartments (booked up throughout July and Aug) but is refreshingly free of concrete and tackiness.

Denia

DENIA is a far bigger place, a sizable town even without its summer visitors, and operates a daily **boat to Palma**, Mallorca. A rattling narrow-gauge railway (*FEVE*) runs down the coast from Denia to Alicante, with an hourly service throughout the day. Beneath the wooded capes beyond, bypassed by the main road, stretch probably the most beautiful beaches on this coastline – but you'll need a car to get to most of them, and there's little inexpensive accommodation. If you want to stay, try the *Hostal Residencial Llacer*, Barrio de la Xara (☎96/578 51 04; ③), first – this is about the lowest price you'll find.

Jávea

At the heart of this area, very near the easternmost Cabo de la Nau, is **JÁVEA**, an attractive village surrounded by hillside villas, and with two smallish beaches hemmed in by hotels. In summer both Denia and Jávea are lively in the evenings, especially at weekends, as they're popular with young people from Valencia. One of Jávea's best-value *hostals* is the *Hostal Residencial La Favorita*, c/Magallanes 4 (☎96/579 04 77; ③). There is also a *parador*, the modern *Parador de Jávea* (☎96/579 02 00; ⑤) at Playa del Arenal 2, which has good low season rates at around 12,000ptas for two nights' half board. **Nightlife** is centred around the beach; good bars include *Mongo di Bongo* and *Terra*. Later in the evening, the crowds move to *La Hacienda* on the Jávea–Denia road, *Trance* on the road to Calpe and *Moli Blanc* in Jávea itself.

Calpe

If you have a car, you could make a detour to the quiet family resort of **CALPE** and the dramatic rocky outcrop known as the **Peñón de Ifach**. The *Peñón* has been declared a national park to prevent encroaching tourist development. The harbour at its foot is used by a small fleet of fishing vessels. *Hostal Peñón de Ifach* (☎96/583 03 00; ③) offers low-priced rooms, but it's only open in the summer.

Altea

Back on the main road again is **ALTEA**, set on a small hill overlooking this whole stretch of coastline. Restrained tourist development is centred on the seafront, and being so close to Benidorm it does receive some overspill. In character, however, it's a world apart. The old village up the hill is picturesquely attractive with its white houses, blue-domed church and profuse blossoms. You can eat and drink well here: the main square has a host of bars; pizzerias are lined up along the front, and at the *L'Obrador*, c/Concepción 8, they serve some of the best pasta in the whole area. There are two or three budget **hostales** at the back of the main square, or try *Hostal Paco* on c/Fermín Sanz Orrio 7-A (☎96/584 05 41; ③). A sandy **beach** has recently been artificially created right in front of the town; more spacious is the stony and windy natural beach to the south – it's a twenty-minute walk, or you can take a bus.

Benidorm

Beyond Altea there's nothing between you and the packed beaches of **BENIDORM**. Only thirty years ago Rose Macaulay could describe Benidorm as a small village "crowded very beautifully round its domed and tiled church on a rocky peninsula". The old part's still there, but so overshadowed by the miles of towering concrete that you'd be hard-pressed to find it. If you want hordes of British and Scandinavian sunseekers, scores of "English" pubs, at least seventy discos, and bacon and eggs for breakfast, this is the place to come. The beach – nearly 6km of it, regularly topped up with imported Moroccan sand – is undeniably impressive, when you can see it through the roasting flesh.

Surprisingly, except in August, you can usually find a **room** in Benidorm, but it takes a lot of walking. The budget places are all near the centre and away from the sea, but out of season many of the giant hotels and apartment blocks slash their prices drastically. Some of the least expensive places are *Primo*, c/Antonio Ramos Carratala 1 (☎96/585 06 26; ②); *Sanpol*, c/Santa Faz 44 (☎96/586 12 02; ③); *Stop*, Plaza de la Cruz 5 (☎96/585 26 00; ②); *El Trovador*, c/Maren de Comillas 23 (☎96/586 07 24; ②); and *Tabarca*, c/Ruzafa 9 (☎96/585 70 80; ②). The **Turismo** (☎96/585 32 24), at the bottom of c/Martínez Alejos, near the old village is also helpful in finding accommodation.

Going on to Alicante, you can get either a bus or train – both leave hourly; the bus is slightly more expensive.

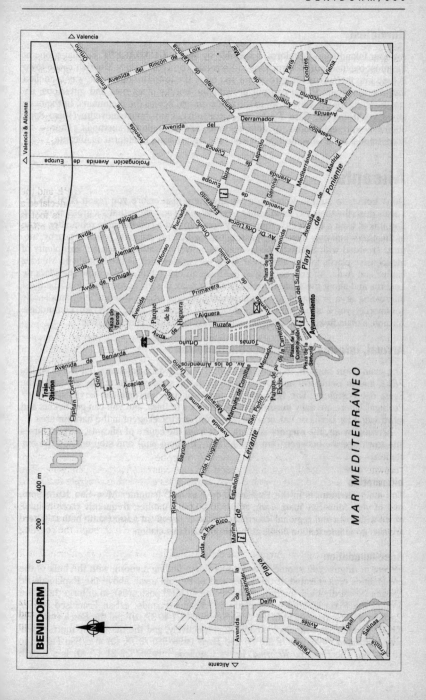

BENIDORM

Guadalest

An hour inland from Benidorm, accessible by bus, is **GUADALEST**, justifiably one of the most popular tourist attractions in Valencia. The 16th-century Moorish castle town is built into the surrounding rock and you enter the town through a gateway tunnelled into the mountain. If you can put up with the hordes of tourists and gift-shops, it's worth visting for the view down to the reservoir and across the mountains. In the main street you'll find the *Casa Típica*, an eighteenth-century house-museum (10am–8pm; 300ptas) with exhibitions of antique tools and agricultural methods. There's no accommodation in Guadalest, but it's an easy daytrip from Benidorm or Alicante.

Alicante

Don't bother to stop in Villajoyosa, or anywhere else before you reach **ALICANTE**. Locals describe their city as *la millor terra del mond* and while that's a gross exaggeration it is at least a living city, thoroughly Spanish, and a considerable relief after some of the places you may have been passing through. There are good beaches nearby, too, most crowded with Spanish holiday-makers, a lively nightlife in season, and plenty of inexpensive places to stay and to eat. Wide esplanades such as the Rambla de Méndez Núñez and Avda. Alfonso Sabio give the town an elegant air, and around the Plaza de Luceros and along the seafront *paseo*, you can relax in style at terrace cafés. The most interesting area is around the *Ayuntamiento*, where, among the bustle of small-scale commerce, you'll see plenty of evidence of Alicante's large Algerian community. Alicante's main **fiesta**, the *fallas*, second only to Valencia's, is held in June.

Arrival, information and accommodation

The main **train station**, Estación de Madrid is on Avda. Salamanca, but trains on the *FEVE* line to Benidorm and Denia leave from the small station at the far end of the Playa del Postiguet. The **bus station** for local and international services is in c/ Portugal. There are daily **summer boat services** to Ibiza, and you can get tickets and information for Denia or Valencia services from any travel agent in the harbour area.

Arriving by air, the **airport** is 12km west from the centre of Alicante. Airport buses into town operate between 7am and 9.20pm (10.30pm Sun) and stop outside the bus station.

Information

The main **Turismo** is in the Explanada de España 2 (summer Mon–Sun 10am–9pm; rest of year Mon–Sat 10am–7pm; ☎96/520 00 00). Another, frequently more helpful, office with town and regional information is on the seafront *paseo* (same hours). There are also good information desks at the airport and bus station.

Accommodation

Except in August you should have little problem finding a **room**, with the bulk of the possibilities concentrated at the lower end of the old town, above the Explanada de España (a weirdly tiled seafront walk seen on all local postcards), in c/Jorge Juan and around the Plaza Gabriel – especially on c/San Fernando, c/San Francisco and c/ Castaño. Places to try include the *Olimpia* (☎96/521 40 37; ②) and the *Bosch* (☎96/520 63 00; ②) at c/San Francisco 60 and 12 respectively, and the marginally more expensive *Larensana* (☎96/520 78 20; ②) and *París* (☎96/520 73 78; ②) at c/San Fernando 10 and 56. The *Hotel La Reforma*, Reyes Católicos 7 (☎96/522 21 47; ④) is a superb mid-range place close to the town centre and bus station and within a few minutes's walk of the beach. There's a **youth hostel** on Avda. Orihuela 59 (☎96/528 12 11) and several **campsites**; two in the Albufereta to the north, one open all year, the other summer only; and one at La Marina, south of town in woods on a good beach.

The town and its beaches

The rambling **Castillo de Santa Bárbara**, an imposing fortress on the bare rock behind the town beach, is Alicante's only real "sight" – with a tremendous view from the top. It's best approached from the seaward side where a shaft has been cut straight up through the hill to get you to the top. The lift (Mon–Fri 9am–8.30pm, 7.30 in winter, Sat 9am–1.30pm) is directly opposite Meeting Point 5 on the other side of the road from Playa Postiguet. Drivers can reach the castle from the other side. Iberian and Roman remains have been found on the site, but most of the present layout dates from the sixteenth century. The **Museo de las Hogueras** (museum of fiesta floats) at the top is a highly odd collection, but well worth a look.

The other main attraction is a remarkably good **Museo de Arte Siglo 20** (May–Sept Tues–Sat 10.30am–1.30pm & 6–9pm, Sun 10.30am–1.30pm; Oct–Apr Tues–Sat 10am–1pm & 5–8pm, Sun 10am–1pm; free), behind the *Ayuntamiento* and opposite the church of Santa María, with works by Picasso, Tapies, Miró and Dalí.

The town also has a small **Museo Arqueológico** in the *Palacio de la Diputación* on Avda. de la Estacíon which is well laid out, though you have to be a real buff to enjoy it (Mon–Fri 9am–1.30pm, bring your passport, sign the book and get security clearance!).

Beaches

For the best local beaches head for **San Juan de Alicante**, about 6km out, reached either by bus from the Plaza del Mar (half-hourly) or on the *FEVE* Alicante-Denia railway. The town beach – **Playa del Postiguet** – is crowded and none too clean. Between Playa Agua Amarga and Playa del Saladar/Urbanova, there's a *playa libre* (nudist beach), take the Line A bus for El Palmeral or the airport bus. You can also take a day trip to the **island of Cantera (Tabarca)** to the south – boats leave from the Explanada de España daily in summer, Sunday and Thursday in winter, weather permitting – but a good deal of rubbish has been dumped on the beaches here in recent years and the current is extremely strong for swimming.

Eating, drinking and nightlife

Inexpensive **restaurants** are clustered around the *Ayuntamiento*, including a couple of places on c/Miquel Saler where you can eat couscous, and a couple of excellent *churrerías*; try *La Madrileña* in c/San José. Over on the other side of town c/San Francisco, leading off a square near the bottom end of the Rambla, has a group of restaurant/*tabernas* with seats outside. For *tapas* try the *Taberna Castellana* on c/Loaces, on the other side of Avda. Dr. Gadea – sample their *montaditos* (tiny bread rolls), *croquetas* and *patatas bravas* (spicy potatoes). Further along the road at no. 15 is the smarter *Museo del Jamón* – the restaurant is expensive but they also serve *tapas*. On the waterside *paseo*, near the Turismo, the *Boutique de Jamón* also specializes in *jamón serrano*. On c/S. Fernando the *Venta del Lobos* does very low-priced *carnes a la brasa* (barbecued meats), and in Plaza Santa María, opposite the gothic portico of the church, you'll find a good vegetarian restaurant, *Mixto Vegetariano*.

If you want to buy your own food, visit the enormous **Mercado Central**, housed in a wonderful old Art Deco-meets-Modernism building, recently renovated, on Avda.

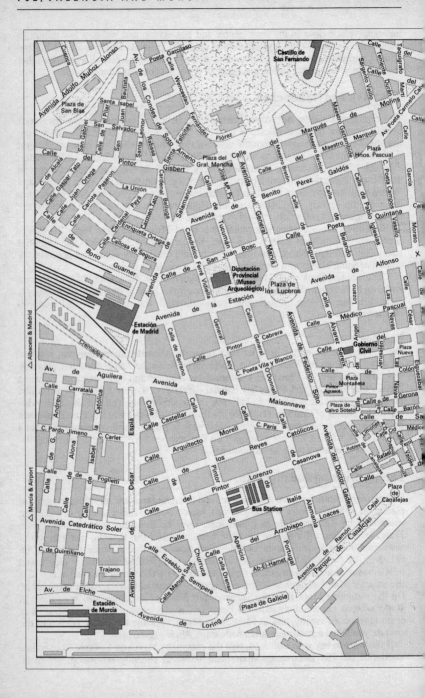

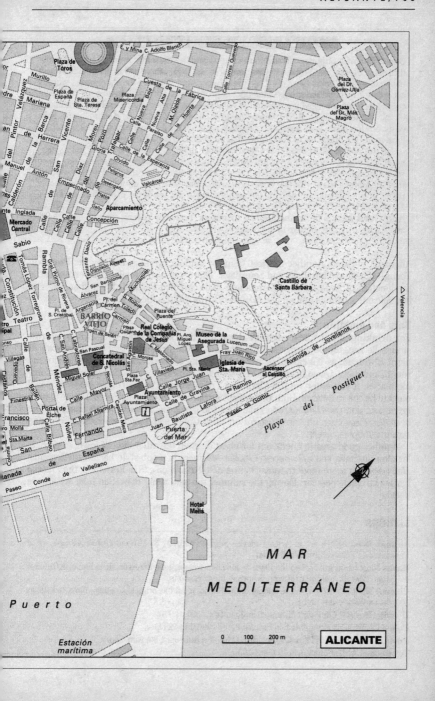

ALICANTE

FIESTA DE MOROS Y CRISTIANOS

One of the most important fiestas in the region and the most important of its kind is the three-day **Fiesta de Moros y Cristianos** in **ALCOY**, about 60km from Alicante. It happens around Saint George's Day (*San Jorge*, April 23), but the date varies slightly according to when Easter falls. Magnificent processions and mock battles for the castle culminate in the decisive intervention of Saint George himself — a legend that originated in the Battle of Alcoy (1276) when the town was attacked by a Muslim army. New costumes are made each year and prizes are awarded for the best which then go into the local museum, *Museu de la Festa Casal de San Jordi* in c/San Miguel 60.

On day one the Christians make their entrance in the morning, the Moors in the afternoon; day two is dedicated to Saint George, with several religious processions; day three sees a gunpowder battle, leading to the saint's appearance on the battlements. Access from Alicante is easy, with five buses a day. You may have to commute since reasonably priced accommodation in Alcoy is not plentiful; try *Hotel San Jorge*, c/San Juan de Ribera 11 (☎96/554 32 77; ④) and *Hostal Savoy*, c/Casablanca 5 (☎96/554 21 02; ③ without bath). After Alcoy's fiesta, the *Moros y Cristianos* fiestas in **Villena** (beginning of Sept) and **Elche** (August) are two of the best.

Alfonso X el Sabio. Another **market** (a major outdoor event) is held by the **Plaza de Toros**, 9am–2pm Thursdays and Saturdays. There's also an excellent **supermarket** at the junction of Avda. Alverez Serena and Avda. Médico Pasqual. It's a good place to buy Alicante's famous nougat-like *turrón* – *Turrón 1880* is the best.

Bars and nightlife

For **drinking** and the best **nightlife**, head into the Barrio Santa Cruz, whose narrow streets lie roughly between the cathedral, Plaza Carmen and Plaza San Cristóbal. At night *El Barrio*, as it's called, is avoided by many of the locals, but it's really not too rough, and there are so many bars here that you can easily steer clear of the questionable places. If you enter via the Plaza San Cristóbal or c/Santo Tomás below it, you'll quickly hit the main area. Both the *Armstrong* bar and *Desafinado*, Santo Tomas 6, have great jazz, and the *Doñana*, on c/San Fernando, is a *sevillanos* bar with dancing. The best *discotecas* currently are *Histeria* on c/de Colón and *Bugati* on c/San Fernando (around 700ptas cover).

Another good area to check out for nightlife is on the other side of town, in particular along c/Italia and c/Lohaces. *El Lobo Marinero* is a pub-style bar on c/Alemania; *Hollywood* is a more modern music bar on c/Italia; and on c/San Fernando, the *Plátano* bar is extremely popular. During the summer the bars along Playa San Juan are always packed.

Listings

Airlines *Iberia* offices are at Avda. Federico Soto 9 (☎96/521 85 10) and *British Airways* are at Explanada de España 3 (☎96/520 05 94).

Banks Most banks are around the Plaza de los Luceros and along the Avda. de la Estación/Alfonso del Sabio. *Caja Alicante* on c/Mayor, is open in the afternoons.

Cinema The *Cine Astoria*, in the middle of the Barrio, often has original-language films (all shows 100ptas on Wednesday nights).

Hospital Hospital Clinico, c/Alicante Sant Joan (☎96/590 83 00).

Police Commisaría is at c/Médico Pascual Pérez (☎96/514 22 22).

Post Office *Correo* is in Plaza Gabriel Miró (Mon–Fri 8am–9pm, Sat 9am–2pm).

Telephones Avda. Constitució 10 (9am–10pm).

Inland – Elche and Orihuela

ELCHE, 20km inland and south from Alicante, is famed throughout Spain for its exotic **palm forest** and for the ancient stone bust known as *La Dama de Elche* discovered here in 1897 (and now in the *Museo Archeológico*, Madrid). The palm trees, originally planted by the Moors, are still the town's chief industry – not only do they attract tourists, but the female trees produce dates, and the fronds from the males are in demand all over the country for use in Palm Sunday processions and as charms against lightning. You can see the forest, unique in Europe, almost anywhere around the outskirts of the city; the finest trees are those in the specially cultivated **Huerto del Cura** on c/ Federico García Sánchez.

Elche is also the home of a remarkable **fiesta** in the first two weeks of August which culminates in a centuries-old mystery play – the celebrations include one of the best examples of the mock battles between Christians and Moors. Over several days the elaborately costumed warriors fight it out before the Moors are eventually driven from the city and the Christian king enters in triumph.

There are buses more or less hourly from Alicante to Elche. Outside fiesta time you should have no problem finding somewhere to stay. The *Bar Águila* on c/Dr Coro 31 is highly recommended for convivial drinking and good *tapas*. The restaurant in the park, *Parque Municipal*, serves *arroz con costra*, the delicious local rice dish.

Elche is also regularly connected with **SANTA POLA** on the coast – previously a village but now quite developed, with good rooms to let, clean beaches, and ferries to **Tabarca** on the Islote de la Cantera, a strange little islet offshore. Inland, the road continues to Orihuela.

Orihuela

You wouldn't guess it from the shabby overhanging houses, but **ORIHUELA** had a very aristocratic past – in 1488 *Los Reyes Católicos* held court here. Today many buildings are half-demolished or half-built, with palm trees stranded in the middle of them, and yet at the same time the place has a provincial bustle to it. Though it doesn't take long to see Orihuela's monuments, it's worth spending a whole day (and maybe even a night) to enjoy its pace – you're unlikely to run into other tourists here. Orihuela also has a natural attraction in **El Palmeral**, the second largest palm forest in Spain – walk out beyond Colegio de Santo Domingo or take the Alicante bus (from the centre) and ask to be dropped off. Many of the town's seventeenth- and eighteenth-century mansions are closed to the public, however, you can roam around the one occupied by the **Turismo** (Mon–Fri 8am–3pm & 4–7pm, Sat am only).

Opposite the Turismo is one of the town's three medieval churches, all of which are Catalan Gothic (subsequently altered), a style you won't find any further south. The oldest part of the **Iglesia de Santiago** (10am–1pm & 5–7pm) is the front portal, the *Puerta de Santiago*, a spectacular example of the late fifteenth-century Isabelline style. Inside, the furniture is baroque but the whole is gloomily sombre. Heading back down towards the town centre, just past the *Ayuntamiento* (a former palace) you'll see the **Iglesia de Santas Justa y Rufina** – its tower is the oldest construction in the parish and has excellent gargoyle sculptures.

Right in the centre of the old town is the **Catedral** (daily 10.30am–1.30pm & 4–6pm), no bigger than the average parish church, built with spiralling, twisted pillars and vaulting. A painting by Velázquez, *The Temptation of St Thomas,* hangs in a small museum in the nave of the cathedral – and don't overlook the Mudéjar-influenced, four-teenth-century *Puerta de las Cadenas*. The **Museo Diocesano de Arte Sacro**, above the cloister, contains an unexpectedly rich collection of art and religious treasures (including a painting by Ribera), many of which are brought out during *Semana Santa*, the town's most important fiesta. There's also a **Museo Semana Santa** (daily 10am–1pm & 5–7pm) not far from the cathedral.

The other main sight in Oriheula is the Baroque **Colegio de Santo Domingo** (10am–1pm & 6–8pm), out towards the palm forest. It's now in a pretty bad state but has two interior patios and some fine eighteenth-century Valencian tiles in the refectory. For a view of the town and surrounding plains, walk up to the seminary on top of the hill. From Plaza Caturla in the centre of town, take the road leading up on the right; not far from the top, there are a couple of steeper short cuts to the right.

Practicalities

The best **hostal** in town, *Rey Teodomiro* (☎96/530 03 48; ③) is at the top of the long avenue from the train station – it's clean, showers are free, and there are plenty of rooms. Alternatively, there are some good budget places a bit further into town: try the friendly *Pensión Versalles*, c/San Cristobal (☎96/530 29 61; ①); *Pensión Ros*, c/Luis de Rojas 52 (①); or *Pensión Joaquina*, c/del Río 23 (①). There are a few more out by the Palmeral, *Casa Corro* (☎96/530 29 63; ②) and *El Palmeral* (☎96/530 25 00; ②), but neither is very convenient.

Cross over the road from the *Rey Teodomiro* and take the first right, and you'll come to the best **place to eat** – *Mesón Don Pepe* at c/Valencia 3. It has great *tapas* and a good lunch menu during the week – try the *consomé al Jerez* (soup with sherry) or the region's speciality, *arroz y costra* (literally "rice and crust", made with rice, eggs, *embutidos*, chicken and rabbit). **Nightlife** is surprisingly good in Oriheula. In the early evening head for the bars along c/Duque de Tamanes, and later on try the c/Castellon, c/Valencia area. There are also a lot of big *bakalao* discos just outside the town, but you'll need a car to get to them. These include *Thamesis* (one of the biggest discos in Europe) in Redovan, *The End* in Bigastro and *Blue Sky* in Benijofar.

Frequent trains and buses go on to Murcia. **Buses** for Torrevieja on the coast are run by *Costa Azul* – they leave four times a day from outside *Confitería Bécquer* on c/Duque de Tamames, which runs along the bottom of Glorieta Park.

Murcia

MURCIA, according to the nineteenth-century writer Augustus Hare, would "from the stagnation of its long existence, be the only place Adam would recognize if he returned to Earth". Things have changed slightly – there is industrial development on the outskirts and a gathering movement to spruce up the centre – but it remains basically a slow-moving city. Founded in the ninth century on the banks of the Río Segura (no more than a trickle now), by the Moors, Murcia soon became an important trading centre and, four centuries later, the regional capital. It was extensively rebuilt in the eighteenth century, and the buildings in the old quarter are still mostly of this era.

Today it's the commercial centre of the region and most of the industry is connected with the surrounding agriculture. There are very few tourists and a refreshing lack of tawdry souvenir and postcards stands. Surrounded by mountains, Murcia has a tranquility and unspoilt air impossible to find in most modern cities.

Arrival and accommodation

Both bus and train stations are on the edge of town. If you're arriving by **bus**, either walk down to the Plano de San Francisco, then follow the river until you see the cathedral or take bus #3 to the town centre. The **train station** is across the river at the

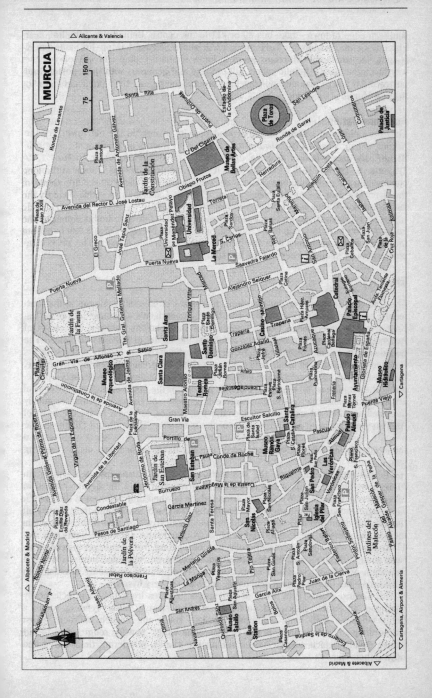

MURCIA

southern edge of town – take bus #9 or #11 to the centre. Behind the cathedral, near Plaza de Cetina, is Murcia's **Turismo** at c/Alejandro Seiquer 4 (Mon–Fri 9am–2pm & 5–8pm, Sat 9am–1pm). Murcians seem to know it's hard to find and will tell you the way; it's an unusually helpful office, full of ideas and generous with their posters and postcards. If you're planning on travelling around the region, their publication *A Day Around Murcia* is excellent.

Accommodation

There are plenty of *hostales* dotted around the city, mainly in the old town. Try the *Aitana*, c/San Nicolás (②); *Alejandro VI*, c/Literato Andrés de Claramonte 6 (☎968/231087; ②); *Desvio-Rincón de Paco*, c/Cortés 27 (☎968/218436; ②) or *Hispano 1*, c/Trapería 8 (☎968/216152; ②–④) which has bathless budget rooms or more comfortable self-contained ones. There are a couple more choices on the other side of the river, just over the *puente viejo: Segura*, Plaza de Camachos 19 (☎968/211281; ②) and *Avenida*, c/Canalejas 10 (☎968/215294; ③).

For Murcia's **youth hostel** – a beautiful one located in fine surroundings in a *parque natural* – you have to go up to La Alberca, 5km outside Murcia. Catch a #29 bus from the Jardín de Floridablanca over the bridge on the south side of town. The YH is signposted about a kilometre beyond the last stop.

The city

The **Catedral** towers over the mansions and plazas of the centre. Begun in the fourteenth century and finally completed in the eighteenth, it's a strange mix of styles. Known as "Mediterranean Gothic" because of the relations between the crown of Aragón and the Kingdom of Murcia, it follows the model of Valencia cathedral. The outside is more interesting architecturally, particularly the south side, with its Romanesque facade and tower which you can climb for great views of the city. Inside, the most remarkable aspect is the florid Plateresque decoration of the chapels – particularly the *Capilla de los Vélez* (1491–1505). It's one of the finest examples of Medieval art in Murcia and one of the most interesting pieces of Hispanic Gothic, originally designed as a funeral area but never completed. It does, however, house the heart of Alfonso the Wise in an urn in the niche of the main altar. The museum (10am–1pm & 5–7pm) has some fine primitive sculptures and above all, a giant processional monstrance – 600 kilos of gold and silver twirling like a musical box on its revolving stand.

The **Museo Salzillo**, near the bus station (Tues–Sat 10am–1pm & 4–7pm, Sun 11am–1pm; closed August), has an extraordinary collection of the figures carried in Murcia's renowned Holy Week procession (which is when they are seen at their best). They were carved in the eighteenth century by Francisco Salzillo and they display all the cloying sentimentality and delight in the "rustic" of that age. Other museums include the **Museo de Bellas Artes** on c/Obispo Frutos (Mon–Fri 9am–2pm, Sat 11am–2pm), with a representative collection of local art from medieval to contemporary, some of it good; and the **Museo Arqueológico** on Avda. de Jaime 1 (Mon–Fri 9am–2pm & 5–8pm, Sat 11am–2pm), for which you should be keenly interested in potsherds – but there's a great deal to see and staff are very friendly.

The **Casino** (9am–11pm; free) at c/Trapería 22 dates from 1847, and eclectically combines an Arabic patio and vestibule, an English-style library-reading room, a Pompeian patio with Ionic columns, a billiard room and French ballroom. Most extraordinary of all perhaps, is the Neo-Baroque ladies' powder room (open to all) whose ceiling depicts angelic ladies among the clouds, powdering their noses and tidying their hair.

Eating, drinking and nightlife

Murcia is known as *La Huerta de Europa* (the Orchard of Europe), and although this might be a slight exaggeration, you'll find local produce in all the city's restaurants. Murcia is an important rice-growing region, and the local variety, *Calasparra*, is renowned in Spain. It's the vegetables though, that the area is really known for, and you'll find that vegetable soups, grills and *paellas* are a speciality.

Restaurants and tapas bars

At **lunchtime**, the whole of the Gran Vía Alfonso X is packed with people drinking apéritifs in outdoor cafés. The *Bar de las Tapas*, Plaza de las Flores, down towards the river end of Gran Vía Salzillo, is also very popular for midday *tapas* and a drink – there are several similar bars in the same streeet. Although rather grim from the outside, *Casa Nicholas*, c/Raimundo de los Reyes, serves excellent, inexpensive meals and home-made puddings. A few doors down, *Mesón Sevillano*, has reputedly the best *patatas bravas* in town. There are plenty of reasonably priced Spanish restaurants for a good **evening meal**. Try *Pacos*, Alfaro 7, just behind the theatre or *Mesón del Corral de José Luis*, Plaza Santa Domingo 23. If you want to splurge, a nationally renowned and traditional restaurant is the four-forks-grade *Rincón de Pepe*, c/Apostoles 34 (☎968/212239; closed all Sun from June–Aug and Sun night from Oct–May), between the cathedral and the *Palacio Episcopal*. *La Barra del Rincón* opposite has a superb 1000ptas *menú* and shares the same chef as the *Rincón de Pepe*. There's also a café and restaurant in the *Casino*, c/Trapería where you can get an 800ptas *menú*.

Bars and nightlife

Being a university town, Murcia has a pretty good **nightlife** during semesters. The liveliest area is around the university, near the Museo de Bellas Artes, in particular the c/de Saavedra Fajardo and the side streets off it. There is also a big gay scene in Murcia, unusual for a provincial Spanish town.

Good **bars** for an evening drink include *Tropico*, c/Vara de Rey 2 which serves the local equivalent of *Agua de Valencia*, made with limes rather than oranges; *Gad*, c/Azarde which has good music and bizarre decor; and the mixed/gay bar *Mare Mia*, Plaza de la Universidad. Amongst the **disco-bars**, the best are *Ocio*, c/Victorio 20 with inexpensive drinks and indie music; *Piscis*, Plaza Santa Domingo, predominantly gay, and *Telegrama* on c/Trinidad. If you're looking for late-night venues and dancing, head for the streets off Gran Vía Alfonso X, below Plaza Circular near the *Museo Archeológico*. Here you'll find the salsa clubs, *Salsa*, *Cha Cha Cha* and *Codigo*. *Pacha*, Plaza Santa Gertundis (12–6am; free) has the usual mix of chart sound and *bakalao*, while the almost exclusively gay, *Metropol*, c/San Andres, near the bus station, plays excellent music until around 8am.

Listings

Airlines *Iberia*, Avda. Alfonso X, Edif. Velázquez (☎968/240050). Most of the others are represented by travel agencies. The airport is at San Javier on the Mar Menor. There are limited internal flights to Almería, Barcelona and Madrid.

Banks All the big ones, with foreign exchange desks, are on the Gran Vías.

Bus station c/Sierra Nevada (☎968/264366).

Car rental *Hertz* is next to the train station on Plaza de la Industria (☎968/268938), *Eurocar*, c/Primo de Rivera 10 (☎968/249215), *Ital*, c/Doctor Fleming 10 , and *Avis*, Florida Blanca 26 (☎968/264366).

Hospitals The General Hospital is near the river on Avda. del Intendente Jorge Palacios (☎968/256900). Red Cross (☎968/222222).

Market Mercado Municipal, c/Verónicas has stacks of wonderful local produce including kiwi fruits, dates, bananas and, of course, citrus fruit.

Police, Avda. San Juan de la Cruz (☎968/266600).

Post Office *Correos* is at Plaza de Ceballos (Mon–Fri 9am–2pm & 5–8pm, Sat 9am–2pm.

Shopping *El Corte Inglés* is on Gran Vía Salzillo. The main shopping area is around the Gran Vías.

Trains *RENFE*, Plaza de la Industria (☎968/252154).

Telephones *Telefónica* is on c/Jeronimo de Roda, off Gran Vía Salzillo.

The coast south of Torrevieja

The stretch of coast around and south of **Torrevieja** is just beginning to be exploited – over the last ten years it has developed at an alarming rate and Torrevieja itself has become a real blot on the landscape. Just to the south is a series of pleasant, small beaches called **Las Playas de Orihuela** (as they come within Orihuela's provincial boundary) which is being developed as villa/apartment territory. Four soulless *urbanizaciones* spread from Punta Prima to Campo Amor, the latter seeming the most established and least unattractive.

The Murcian *Costa Cálida* starts at the **Mar Menor** (Lesser Sea), a broad lagoon whose shallow waters (ideal for kids) warm up early in the year, making it a good out-of-season destination. With its high-rise hotels, the "sleeve" (*la manga*) looks like a diminutive Miami Beach; the upmarket resorts on the land side of the lagoon are more appealing, and they do have a few *hostales*. The main problem is getting a room in season – the area is immensely popular with Spaniards and by April all the cheaper places could be booked up for the summer.

San Pedro del Pinatar

SAN PEDRO DEL PINATAR, the first resort, is probably your best bet in season as it's not as polished-looking as the others, and is actually more pleasant as a result. The **bus station** is up in the old town, but it's not worth spending much time here. Head down Avda. de Generalissimo or take a bus straight to the seafront. On Monday there's a big market (on the inland side of the main road) with food, clothes and a stand where you can swap, buy or sell English paperbacks.

Much of the town **beach** area, called *Lo Pagán*, was reconstructed after terrible floods in 1986. Year after year people return to *La Puntica* beach to coat themselves in its **therapeutic mud**, a product of the salt pools behind, which reputedly relieves rheumatism and is good for the skin. The best beach near here is *Playa de las Llanas*, the other side of the salt pool area; it's a long way to walk though – from town, go down Emilio Castelar and turn off into Avda. Salinera Española (*puerto* direction).

Practicalities

If you do get stuck in the old town and need a bed for the night, try *Hostal Mariana*, Avda. Dr Arturo Guirao (☎968/181013; ④). There are plenty of **hostales** down at the resort including: *Pensión Katherine*, c/Emilio Castelar (☎968/180276; ④); *Pensión Alas Playa* (☎968/181017; ③), very good value and virtually on the beach but only open April–October; *Casa Lucrecia*, c/Caserío de los Sáez (☎968/181928; ③ with bath); *Hostal Mariana*, on the main Avda. Dr Arturo Guirao (☎968/181013; ④ with bath); and *Hotel Arce*, C/Tervel (☎968/182247; ④), just off the road to *Lo Pagán*.

Places to **eat** are in good supply – the *Hogar del Pescador* is an inexpensive seafood restaurant at c/Lorenzo Morales 2, near the main square; *Restaurante La Pradera*, c/Emilio Castelar is ranch-style, good for barbecues; *Mesón La Panocha*, c/Muñoz Delgado, near the seafront, has excellent *tapas;* and *El Venezuela* is a high-quality if rather expensive seafood place virtually on the beach. Most of San Pedro's bars and discos are along Avda. de Generalissimo.

Santiago de la Ribera

The next town on the Mar Menor, and within walking distance, is **SANTIAGO DE LA RIBERA**, a fancy resort that's popular with *Madrileños*. There's an important sailing club here, as the calm sea is perfect for novices.

One of the best budget **hostales** is *Hostal Manida*, near the sea at c/Muñoz 11 (☎968/570011; ②), with a range of rooms and good full-board deals. Alternatively, *Hostal K Hito*, c/Maestre 9 (☎968/570002; ② without bath, closed in winter) and *Hostal Trabuco*, Avda. Mar Menor 1 (☎968/570051; ③) are close together at the back of the town. More expensive is *Hostal Don Juan*, Avda. Nuestra Señora de Loreto 2 (☎968/571043; ④). Also worth trying on c/Zarandona are *La Obrera Fonda*, at no. 7 (☎968/570042; ③ with bath) and *Hotel Madrid* at no. 18. (☎968/570504; ③). If you're looking for seafood, you'll get the best in town at *Mesón El Pescador* on Explanada Barnuevo. There are three **campsites** in the area: *Alcázares* (Málaga–Valencia road) with pool, *San Javier* (Balsicas road), and *Mar Menor* (Alicante–Cartagena road).

From the military airport at San Javier you can get **flights** to Madrid and Barcelona (and in summer there are some *Iberia* flights to London, but no cheap charters). The nearest **train station** for this area is Balsicas (connected with San Pedro and Santiago by bus). A train called the *Costa Cálida* runs direct to here from Barcelona and Madrid in summer. There are daily buses from San Pedro to Cartagena and Murcia.

Cartagena

Whether you're approaching **CARTAGENA** from one of the numerous resorts along Mar Menor, inland from Murcia, or from Almería to the south, it's not a pretty sight. Scrub and semi-desert give way to a ring of hills littered with disused factories and mines, eventually merging into the newer suburbs. It's only when you reach the old part of town down by the port, with its narrow medieval streets, packed with bars and restaurants, that the city's real character emerges.

Hannibal's capital city on the Iberian peninsula, named after his Carthage in North Africa, and a strategic port and administrative centre for the Romans, Cartagena is still overrun with sailors. International Nautical Week is celebrated here in June, and in November, the city hosts an International Festival of Nautical Cinema. The **fiestas** of *Semana Santa* are some of the most elaborate in Spain with processions leaving from the church of Santa María de Gracia in the early hours of Good Friday morning.

The city

Cartagena does not have an excess of sights and much of what it does have is in ruins or not open to the public. The vast military **Arsenal** that dominates the old part of the town dates from the mid eighteenth century and, like the Captaincy General building, is still in use, heavily guarded and not open to the public. However, you can visit the **Naval Museum** (Tues–Sat 10am–1pm & 4–6pm, Sat 10am–1pm), c/Menéndez Pelayo 6, set in the walls of the Arsenal, and the **National Museum for Underwater Archeology** (Tues–Sat 10am–3pm) which is a long walk round the outer walls of the Arsenal on the way to the lighthouse, and has a reconstructed Roman galley and a lot of interesting exhibits salvaged from shipwrecks. The **Museo Arqueológico**, c/Ramon y Cajal 45 (Tues–Fri 10am–1pm & 4–6pm, Sat & Sun 10am–1pm) in the new part of town is built on a Roman burial ground and has an excellent collection of Roman artefacts and a good introduction to the ancient history of the city.

The best of Cartagena's churches is **Santa María de Gracia** on c/San Miguel which contains various works by Salzillo, including the figures on the high altar. There are more works by Salzillo and a fine art collection in *La Caridad* on c/la Caridad. You'll see a large number of Art Nouveau buildings around the city. Most of these are the work of former Cartagenian and disciple of Gaudí, Victor Beltri (1865–1935). In particular, have a look at *Casa Maestre* in Plaza San Francisco, *Casa Cervantes*, c/ Mayor 15 and the *Hotel Zapata*, Plaza de España.

To get a feel of the city's distinguished past, wander along the sea wall towards the old military hospital. It's a huge, empty, but evocative building, now falling into disrepair and no-one will mind you looking around. From the lighthouse there are great views of the harbour and city, but perhaps the best **city views** are from Torres Park, reached along c/Gisbert. Past the ruins of the old cathedral, the road winds down back into Plaza del Ayuntamiento.

There are numerous castles in the hills around the city. The easiest to get to on foot is the **Castillo de los Moros**, built on the site of a former mosque, though it's still a half day's trek to the east of the city. The castle has been the scene of various uprisings from Roman times and today is not the safest part of town, so don't go there alone or at night.

Practicalities

Cartagena has two **bus** stops: buses from Alicante, Barcelona and Valencia will set you down just behind the Captaincy General Residence opposite the big orange walled Arsenal, in c/Real. Murcia and Almeria buses arrive at c/Angel Bruna in the new part of town. The **train** stations, both *RENFE* and *FEVE*, are in Plaza Mexico. The **Turismo** is at the corner of the *Ayuntamiento* and produces the curiously over-enthusiatic publication, *Cartagena – An Artistic Guide*.

Rooms are not plentiful or particularly low in price. Try *Pensión Pabelita* (③), Plaza María José Artes adjacent to Plaza del Ayuntamiento (ask in *El Puerto* restaurant); *Pensión Rosa*, Plaza San Agustin 6 (☎968/520028; ③), or, the best value and most central, *Hostal Peninsular*, c/Cuatro Santos 3 (☎968/500033; ③), just off c/Mayor. There are also two places on c/Jara; *Pensión Garrido* at no. 27 (☎968/503736; ③), a homely place but noisy, and as a last resort, *Hotel Cartagenero* (☎968/502500; ④), almost opposite.

There are plenty of unexploited **bars** and **restaurants** in the old town with Spanish-only menus and uninflated prices. The best places to look for food are Plaza del Ayuntamiento and Plaza María José Artes – best value is *Casa Pedrero* on the corner of Plaza María José Artes with very low-priced *platos combinados* and a 700ptas *menú del día*. *Mesón Artes*, opposite, has a vast range of *tapas*, and the popular *El Mejilloneria*, c/ Mayor 4, just off Plaza del Ayuntamiento, is definitely worth trying to squeeze your way into. The side streets around the squares also contain plenty of good places: on c/ Escorial, *El Bahia* is a tiny seafood restaurant with meals cooked straight from its tanks of live fish, and the more expensive *Mare Nostrum*, down by the port, also offers excellent seafood dishes as well as *tapas*.

In the evening, try *El Macho*, corner of c/Aire and c/del Cañon which specializes in *pulpo* and *patatas bravas*; *Mi Bodega* has excellent *tortilla;* and *La Uva Jumillana* on c/ Jara, serves extremely strong wines from the barrel. You'll find Cartagena's **discos** and late-night bars on c/del Cañon and the streets of Plaza de San Agustín.

The Golfo de Mazarrón

South of Cartagena, on the coast of the **Golfo de Mazarrón**, only Mazarrón and Águila are easily accessible. Very little building has been allowed around the beaches between these two towns, because the area is a breeding ground for **tortoises** and a species of **eagle** – for the last decade there have been plans to make it a nature reserve. The few roads that lead down to the better beaches usually end up as tracks.

Mazarrón and around

The inland village of **MAZARRÓN** is small and peaceful with an attractive plaza, and a few places to stay; both *Calventus II*, Avda. de la Constitución 60 (☎968/590054; ③), and *Guillermo II*, c/Carmen 3 (☎968/590436; ③), are worth trying. The resort, Puerto de Mazarrón is 6km away, served by three daily buses from Cartagena.

Despite a fair amount of development, **PUERTO DE MAZARRÓN** is pretty quiet even in season, but most of the **accommodation** is in expensive resort hotels. If you're looking for something a little less expensive, *Hostal Delfín*, c/Mayor (☎968/594639; ③) and *La Línea*, c/San Isidro (③) are both clean and reasonable, or try the smarter *Hostal Duran*, Playa de la Isla (☎968/594050; ④). The massive **campsite**, *Playa de Mazarrón*, on Carretera Puerto de Mazarrón Bolnuevo, is open year round. The better **beaches**, *Cabo Tiñoso* to the north and *Punta Calnegre* to the south, are not served by public transport, but the best one, *Bol Nuevo*, is just about walkable from Puerto de Mazarrón. Nearby is the "Enchanted City of Bol Nuevo", a small area of weird-eroded rocks. If you get tired of sunbathing, the nature reserve at **La Albufera de las Morenas**, has a lagoon which attracts a variety of migratory birds.

Totana and Aledo

Inland from Mazarrón is the town of **TOTANA**, at the foot of the Sierra Espuña, home to wild boars and royal eagles. The strange stone domes dotted around in the mountains are "snow wells", used to store snow before the thaw. The sanctuary *La Santa*, 7km outside the town has a beautifully carved wooden ceiling, and houses a collection of sixteenth- and seventeenth-century paintings. Totana is served by buses and trains from Murcia, and buses continue on to **ALEDO**, another ancient mountain town with Arabic walls and a tower. Medieval traditions are still strong here and on January 6 it hosts the **Auto Sacramental** (mystery play). Just outside the town is the *Hotel El Pinito de Oro* (☎968/421036; ③–④) with magnificent views.

Águilas

ÁGUILAS lies at the southern end of the Golfo de Mazarrón, bordered inland by fields of tomatoes, one of the few things that can grow in this hot, arid region. Fishing, along with the cultivation of tomatoes, is the mainstay of the economy here, and a fish auction is held at around 5pm every day in the port's large warehouse. **Carnival** is especially wild in Águilas, and for three days and nights the entire population lets its hair down with processions, floats and general fancy-dress mayhem.

Águilas is a popular spot as the beaches are plentiful, reasonably served by public transport and the area has a superb year-round climate. **Hostales** tend to be full from mid-July to mid-August. *Hostal Cruz del Sur* is the best of the budget places, with its seafront position on Levante beach, c/Constitución 38 (☎968/410171; ③, with or without bath). In the centre of town, *Hostal La Aguileña* at c/Isabel la Católica 8 (☎968/410303; ③ without bath) is also very good, as is *Hostal Mar y Sol* near the station at c/Aire 107 (☎968/410000; ③). The **youth hostel** is 4km out of town at Calarreona along the Carretera Almería, and there is no bus out this way. You'll find the **Turismo** (8.30am–2pm & 6–9pm in summer; 9.30am–1.30pm & 5–7pm rest of year) on Plaza de Antonio Cortijos, near the port. **Buses** stop at the *Bar Peña Aguileña*, with services to Almería, Cartagena, Murcia and Lorca. There are **trains** to Murcia and Lorca.

The Águilas beaches

The town itself has two fine **beaches**, but there are about twenty small beaches in the vicinity. In general, those to the north are rockier and more often backed by low cliffs; to the south they are grittier and more open. The attraction, however, is the lack of development around them – some are totally wild, others have a smattering of villas, others have only a bar. Beaches are cleaned daily from May onwards as a lot of seaweed is washed up. Car rental is available in Águilas from *Seat*, c/Barcelona 4 (☎968/410750) for those who want to explore all the options fully.

Heading north from Águilas, *Playa Hornillo* (on the summer-only Calabardina bus route) is a nice beach with a couple of bars nearby. From here, it's possible to walk round to *Playa Amarillo*, probably the most secluded and beautiful of the beaches. A string of beaches are served by the Calabardina bus; *Playa Arroz*, *La Cola* and *Calabardina* itself (7km from town). If you feel energetic you could walk across Cabo Cope to yet another chain of beaches beginning at Ruinas Torre Cope, but there's really no need to go so far.

South of Águilas, the *Las Lomas* bus serves the rocky *Playa Las Lomas* from where you can walk to *Playa Matalentisco* with shallow stretches, ideal for kids. The Almería bus will drop you off anywhere you ask further along the coast and you can flag it down on the way back anywhere on the main road – it currently leaves Águilas at 10am, returning at 3pm. The *Las Palomas* beach (known locally as *La Cabaña*) has the added attraction of a restaurant; beside it is *Calarreona* beach, then comes *La Higuérica*, 5km from town. Further south, *Playa Cuatro Calas* has a drinks stall, but no other unnatural presence, and by the time you get to *La Carolina*, on the border of Andalucía, the shore is completely wild.

Inland to Lorca

Many of the historic villages of inland Murcia are accessible only with your own transport, but one place you can reach easily is **Lorca**, a beautiful former frontier town. The villages around all have their share of Renaissance and Baroque architecture and are surrounded by stunning countryside.

Lorca

Despite being slowly shaken to pieces by the traffic that hammers straight through its centre, **LORCA** still has a distinct aura of the past. For a time it was part of the caliphate, but it was retaken by the Christians in 1243, after which Muslim raids were a feature of life until the fall of Granada, the last Muslim stronghold. Most of the town's notable buildings – churches and ancestral homes – date from the sixteenth century onwards. Many are, unfortunately, closed for restoration and some are permanently shut.

Arriving by **train**, get off at *Lorca Sutullera*; buses will also drop you at the station, but the bus stop before is closer to town. The **Turismo** is on c/López Gisbert (☎968/466157; summer 9am–2pm & 5.30–7pm; winter 10am–2pm & 5.30–7pm). They provide a good map and an excellent guided architectural walk of about an hour around the town. Next door to the Turismo, is the **Centro de Artesanía**, displaying and selling work combining traditional crafts with avant-garde design (Tues–Sat 11am–2pm & 5–8pm, Mon 5–8pm, Sun 11am–2pm).

The old part of town lies up the hill from c/López Gisbert. The **Casa de los Guevara**, above the Turismo is an excellent example of civic Baroque architecture from the end of the seventeenth century and the best mansion in town. On the corner of Plaza San Vicente and c/Corredera, the main shopping artery, is the **Columna Milenaria**, a Roman column dating from around 10 BC: it marked the distance between Lorca and Cartagena on the *Vía Heraclea*, the Roman road from the Pyrenees to Cádiz. The Gothic **Porche de San Antonio**, the only gate remaining from the old city walls, lies at the far end of the Corredera. On Plaza de España, the focal point of the town, and seemingly out of proportion with the rest, you'll find the imposing

Colegio de San Patricio (10am–1pm & 6–8pm), with its enormous proto-Baroque facade, built between the sixteenth and eighteenth centuries – there's a marked contrast between the outside and the sober, refined interior, which is largely Renaissance. Nearby is the *Casa Consistorial*, now the **Ayuntamiento**, with its seventeenth- to eighteenth-century facade. An equally impressive front is presented by the sixteenth-century **Posito**, down a nearby side street – originally an old grain storehouse, it's now the municipal archive.

The thirteenth- to fourteenth-century **Castillo** overlooking the town seems an obvious destination but it's a very hot walk and not really worth it, as the two towers of interest are open only on November 23, the day the fortress was recovered from the Moors. The impoverished *barrio antiguo*, huddled below the castle, can be a little dangerous at night, but it's worth wandering around it in daylight.

Lorca is famed for its **Semana Santa** celebrations which out-do those of Murcia and Cartagena, the next best in the region. There's a distinctly operatic splendour about the dramatization of the triumph of Christianity, with characters such as Cleopatra, Julius Caesar and the royalty of Persia and Babylon attired in embroidered costumes of velvet and silk. The high point is the afternoon and evening of Good Friday.

Practicalities

Even though it really only takes an hour or two to look around Lorca, it's still a good place to stop overnight, with inexpensive **rooms** all along the highway. Try *Hostal del Carmen*, c/Rincón de los Valientes 3 (✆968/466459; ③), *Casa Juan*, c/Guerra 10 (✆968/468006; ③), *Ciudad del Sol*, c/Galicia 9 (✆968/467872; ② with bath) or *Hotel Felix*, Avda. Fuerzas Armadas 146 (✆968/467650; ③), an old-fashioned place and very good value. If you have trouble finding a room, the enormous *La Alberca*, Plaza Juan Moreno 1, is clean and friendly and is likely to have space. If you're coming for Holy Week you'll have to book at least a month in advance, or stay in Murcia or Águilas.

A good place to **eat** is the *Restaurante El Teatro*, Plaza Colón 12 (closed Sun & Aug) – the square is on the same road as the Turismo. Also try the *Restaurante Barcas Casa Cándido*, c/Santo Domingo 13 for their very good 800ptas *menús*. Up the road from here in c/Tintes, on the corner of Est. Cava is a great, seedy **bodega**, where they serve powerful shots of port-like *vino tinto* for next to nothing.

Both trains and buses connect Lorca with Murcia; the train is cheaper and quicker. Heading south to Granada there are two buses daily, at 10.40am and 4pm.

Caravaca de la Cruz and Moratalla

CARAVACA DE LA CRUZ, an important border town, can be reached from Lorca by daily bus, although there are more direct buses from Murcia. The town is dominated by the castillo which contains a beautiful marble and sandstone church, **El Santuario de Vera Cruz**. The church houses the cross used in the Easter celebrations, and on May 3, the cross is "bathed" in the temple at the bottom of town to commemorate the apparition of a cross to the Moorish king, Ceyt Abuceit, in 1231. Just outside the church, cloisters lead to the museum (Tues–Sat 10am–1pm & 4–8pm, Sun 11am–2pm, closed Wed; 250ptas) which concentrates on religious art and history. The churches that tower over the rest of the town, **La Iglesia del Salvador** and **La Iglesia de la Concepción** are also worth a visit. The latter contains some excellent examples of carved Mudéjar wood.

Moratalla

Fourteen kilometres on is **MORATALLA**, a pretty village spread around the foot of a fortress. The steep, winding streets of the old town lead up to the castle from where there are stunning views of the surrounding countryside and its vast forests.

It's a lovely place to stay if you want to relax: *Pensión Alhameda*, Carretera de Caravaca (☎968/730057; ③) on your left as you come into town has lots of rooms and a good restaurant below; and *Pensión Levante* (☎968/730454; ③), Carretera del Canal 21, although slightly out of town has comfortable rooms and modern bathrooms. There is a **campsite** 8km out of town in La Puerta (☎968/730008; open all year). Moratalla is full of little **bars**; the *Alhameda* is one of the best for food.

travel details

Trains

Alicante to: Madrid (4 daily; 6–10hr); Murcia (10 daily; 6–10hr).

Murcia to: Águilas (3 daily, 1 on Sunday; 2hr); Barcelona (2 daily; 7hr); Cartagena (6 daily; 1hr); Granada (2 daily; 8hr); Lorca (14 daily; 1hr); Madrid (3 daily; 6–8hr).

Valencia to: Alicante (5 daily; 2–3hr); Barcelona (8 daily; 5hr); Castellón (11 daily; 1hr 30min); Gandía (12 daily; 1hr); Játiva (16 daily; 1hr); Madrid (3 daily via Cuenca; 6–7hr, 5 daily via Albacete; 7hr); Zaragoza (3 daily; 6hr).

Buses

Alicante to: Albacete (2 daily; 2hr 30min); Almería (2 daily; 7hr); Barcelona (5 daily; 10hr); Cartagena (8 daily; 2hr); Granada (4 daily; 12hr); Madrid (3 daily; 6hr); Málaga (4 daily; 9hr); Murcia (7 daily; 2hr); San Pedro del Pinatar (8 daily; 1hr 15min); Torrevieja (8 daily; 1hr).

Murcia to: Águilas (daily Mon–Fri, 2 daily Sat & Sun; 2hr); Albacete (2 daily; 2hr 30min); Alicante (8 daily; 2hr); Almería (4 daily; 4hr); Barcelona (5 daily; 8 hr); Cartagena (14 daily; 1hr); Granada (5 daily; 6hr); Lorca (11 daily; 1hr 15min); Madrid (6

daily; 8 hours); Málaga (4 daily; 8hr); Mazárron (8 daily; 1hr 30min); Valencia (6 daily; 4hr 30min).

Valencia to: Alicante (6 daily, 10 in summer; 4hr); Barcelona (7 daily; 6hr); Benidorm (6 daily, 10 in summer; 3hr 15min); Castellón (9 daily; 1hr 30min); Cuenca (3 daily; 4hr); Gandía (6 daily, 10 in summer; 1hr), Madrid (6 daily; 6hr); Murcia (3 daily; 4hr 30min); Oliva (6 daily, 10 in summer; 1hr 30min); Sevilla (1 daily; 12hr).

Balearic Connections

From Valencia *Transmediterránea* **sailings** to: Palma, Mallorca (9hr) daily except Sun at 11.30pm; Sun service in summer; Ibiza (7hr) Tues & Thurs at 11.45pm, Sat & Sun too in summer. At least 4 **flights** daily to Palma (40min), at least 2 daily to Ibiza (30min).

From Denia *Flebasa/Isnasa* **ferries** to Ibiza Wed & Thurs at 8am, other days (except Tues) at 4pm (3hr). *Ubesa* runs connecting buses to/from Valencia and Alicante.

From Alicante Summer only daily boat service to Ibiza. Year-round, at least 2 **flights** daily to Palma (40min) and (summer only) 3 per week to Ibiza (30min).

CHAPTER THIRTEEN

THE BALEARIC ISLANDS

T he four chief **Balearic islands** – Ibiza, Formentera, Mallorca and Menorca – maintain a character distinct from the mainland and from each other. **Ibiza**, firmly established among Europe's trendiest resorts, is wholly unique with an intense, outrageous street life and a floating summer population that seems to include every club-going Spaniard from Sevilla to Barcelona. It can be fun, if this sounds your idea of island activity, and above all if you're gay – Ibiza is a very tolerant place. **Formentera**, small and a little desolate, is something of a beach-annexe to Ibiza, though it struggles to present its own alternative image of reclusive artists and "in the know" tourists. **Mallorca**, the largest and best-known Balearic, also battles with its image, popularly reckoned as little more than sun, booze and high-rise hotels. In reality you'll find all the clichés, most of them crammed into the mega-resorts of the Bay of Palma, but there's certainly much else besides: mountains, lively fishing ports, some beautiful coves and the Balearics' one real city, **Palma**. Mallorca is in fact the one island in the group you might come to other than for beaches and nightlife, with scope to explore, walk and travel about. And last, to the east, there's **Menorca** – more subdued in its clientele, and here at least, the grim modern resorts are kept at a safe distance from the two main towns, the capital **Maó**, and **Ciutadella**. Few people have ever heard of them, but there are actually eleven other islets in the group – all uninhabited rocks which can be visited, if at all, only as a day trip from one of the main islands.

Access to the islands is easy from Britain or northern Europe, with charter **flights** and complete package deals dropping to absurd prices out of season or with last-minute bookings. From mainland Spain, too, there are charters, though believe it or not these can often cost as much or even more. **Ferries** – from Barcelona, Valencia, Denia (and Marseilles) – are less expensive but still severely overpriced for the distances involved: Denia–Ibiza for example, will set you back some 5200ptas. Likewise, rates for **inter-island** ferries are also high, and for journeys like Ibiza–Mallorca or even Mallorca–Menorca it can actually be better value to fly. The catch here is that in midseason seats are often unavailable: the solution is to get up before dawn, head for the airport and get yourself on a waiting list for the first flight of the day – someone always oversleeps. For fuller details on **routes** see "Travel details" at the end of this chapter.

Expense and **overdemand** can be crippling in other areas, too. As "holiday islands", each with a buoyant international tourist trade, the Balearics charge considerably above mainland prices for **rooms** – which from mid-June to mid-September are in very short supply. If you go at these times, and you're not into camping, it's sensible to try to fix up some kind of reservation in advance or at least get a bag of small change and phone round before tramping the streets (though some places accept only agency bookings). If you plan to rent a **car**, these are also in short supply in season. **Mopeds** are a good option on the islands but be sure to check your insurance policy: it should definitely include theft (*seguro de robo*) as well as accident. To avoid the latter, store most of your baggage somewhere before setting out – riding with a pack is both exhausting and dangerous. Without your own transport, there are reasonable bus services, and these are detailed in the text for the specific islands.

As elsewhere, the Balearics have revived their own **dialects** over the last few years. Throughout the islands a dialect of Catalan is spoken, a result of the conquest by the Catalan-Aragonese confederation in the thirteenth century. Each of the three main islands has a different subdialect, and many inhabitants object to their language being called Catalan at all. For the visitor, confusion arises from the difference between the islands' road signs and street names – which are almost exclusively in Catalan – and most of the maps on sale, which are in Castilian. In particular, note that Menorca now calls its capital *Maó* rather than Mahón, while both the island and town of Ibiza are usually referred to as *Eivissa*. In speech, though, Castilian Spanish is dominant, and for once in Spain you'll find no shortage of people with perfect English or French. In this chapter we give the Catalan name for towns, beaches and streets with the Castilian name in brackets where helpful, except for Ibiza and Ibiza Town which are not widely known by their Catalan names outside Spain.

FIESTAS

January

17 *Día de Sant Antoni de Portmany* is marked by fiestas in several Mallorcan villages, and in Palma itself with bonfires (*foguerones*) in the streets and the blessing of animals. Also celebrated of course, in Sant Antoni de Portmany (Ibiza) and in Ciutadella (Menorca) where the Reconquest is commemorated.

19 Palma (Mallorca) has more bonfires, singing and dancing for *San Sebastián*.

March/April

Holy Week *Semana Santa* is as widely observed as everywhere. Maó (Menorca) sees a big celebration on **Good Friday**, but the larger ceremonies are all on Mallorca, especially at Palma and Pollença on Good Friday and the *Romerías* from Sa Pobla, Llubi and Montuiri the **following Tuesday**.

May

Second Sunday *Fiesta de Nuestra Señora de la Vitoria* in Sóller (Mallorca) spreads into the next week's *Fiestas de Mayo*, with battles between Moors and Christians.

30 *Fiesta de San Fernando* celebrated in Sant Ferran (Formentera).

June

23–26 In Ciutadella (Menorca), the major midsummer festival of *San Juan*, with jousting tournaments. Also wildly celebrated in Ibiza.

July

9 *Fiesta Patriótica* in Ciutadella (Menorca) celebrates the resistance to the Turks.

Second Sunday The Reconquest of Menorca is celebrated in a fiesta in Mercadal.

28 The monastery at Valldemossa (Mallorca.), where Chopin stayed, celebrates *Santa Catalina's* day appropriately enough with a piano concert.

August

2 Moors and Christians battle, Pollença (Mallorca).

5 *Día de la Virgen de las Nieves* in Ibiza; festivities spill over into the next few days.

Second week *Fiesta de San Lorenzo* in Alaior (Menorca), high jinks on horseback through the streets of the town.

23–25 San Luis (Menorca) has a similar equine *jaleo* for the festival of *Sant Genis*.

28 Felanitx (Mallorca) starts the *Cavallets*, a major week-long festival.

International Festival at Pollença: art and sculpture exhibitions, chamber music, etc.

September

7–8 *Fiestas de Gracia* in Maó (Menorca).

Second week *La Diada de Lluc*, traditional and religious festivities in Escorca (Menorca.).

December

3 *Día de San Francisco* celebrated in Sant Francesc Xavier (Formentera).

Christmas is especially picturesque in Palma (Mallorca) where there are Nativity plays in the days leading up to the 25th.

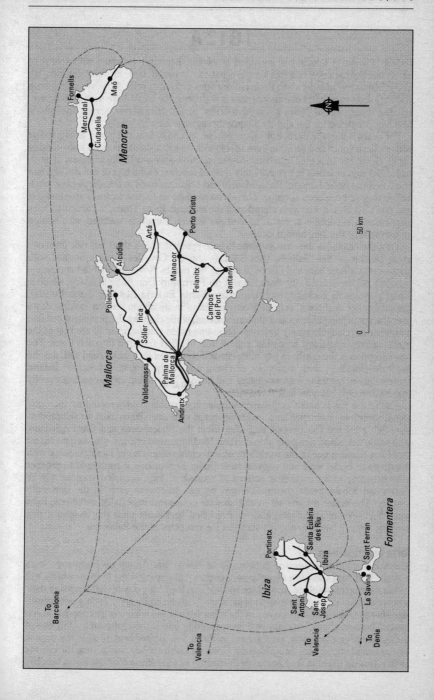

IBIZA

IBIZA (Eivissa in Catalan) is an island of excess. Beautiful, indented with scores of barely accessible cove beaches that are not too crowded even in high summer, it's nevertheless the islanders and their visitors who make it special. However outrageous you may want to be (and outrageousness is the norm) the locals have seen it all before. By day thousands of Nivea-smeared tourists spread themselves across the nudist beaches, preparing for the nightly flounce through the bars and clubs.

For years it was *the* European hippie escape, but nowadays the island is as popular with modern youth and sociable gays as it is with its 1960s denizens (who keep coming back). Germans, squeezed into their *lederhosen*, rub bottoms with the trimmest of international designer labels in a remarkably relaxed meeting of the hippie and the hip, and you'll find the latest London, Paris, Madrid and Milan fashions in the shops here, often before they've been seen at home. There's no need for an excuse to dress up – in fact if you don't it'll be *you* who gets stared at in the evening. **Ibiza Town**, in particular, lives glamorously, especially at night; an endless fashion parade is watched with benign amusement by the long-inured locals.

This, the capital, is the obvious place to base yourself: only a short bus ride from two great beaches – **Ses Salines** (Las Salinas) and **Es Cavellet** – and crammed with shops, restaurants, bars and discos to occupy the nights. Nowhere else can compare – certainly not the second city, **Sant Antoni de Portmany** (San Antonio Abad), which is a highly avoidable package resort nightmare. **Santa Eulària des Riu** (Santa Eulalia), the only other real town, retains a certain charm in its hilltop church looking down over the sprawling old town and modern seafront, while close by the persistent can find a number of relatively empty beaches. The same holds true for most of the rest of the coast – plenty of golden sands but a good deal of effort required to reach them. The one exception is the northern bay of **Portinatx**, connected by a major road and, despite hotel development, with a number of clean, not overly populated beaches. **Inland** there's little of anything – a few villages and holiday homes that are exceedingly pretty to drive through but offer little if you stop.

The island has a harsh landscape of tinder-dry scrubland interrupted by the occasional stretch of productive land, and is peppered with small lakes used for salt production. Salt attracted the Greeks, and after them the Phoenicians and **Carthaginians**, who made the island a regular stop on their Mediterranean cruises – to such an extent that Ibiza remains one of the world's most important reliquaries of Punic remains, with hundreds of burial sites still unexcavated. Under Roman rule it continued to prosper until dropping into the familiar pattern of Spanish history, occupied successively by Goths and Moors before being liberated by the Aragonese early in the thirteenth century. Thereafter decline set in and, despite occasional imperialist ambitions, Ibiza was effectively an abandoned and impoverished backwater until the middle of this century, when it began to acquire status as the most chic of the Balearics.

Ibiza practicalities

There is a good **bus service** between Ibiza Town, Sant Antoni de Portmany, Santa Eulària, Portinatx and a few of the larger beaches, but renting some form of **vehicle** will widen your options no end (though be warned that the traffic cops delight in using their wheel clamps). Your own transport is particularly useful on Ibiza for finding **accommodation** – as difficult here as on any of the other islands and even more expensive. If you haven't booked ahead, you may well be reduced to one of the **campsites**. Only one of these, *Camping d'en Bossa*, on the road to Platja d'en Bossa, is at all near the capital; others include three near Santa Eulària: *Payes*, on Portinatx bay, and among the crowds at *San Antonio* (right in Sant Antoni de Portmany) or *Cala Bassa* (on Cala Bassa beach).

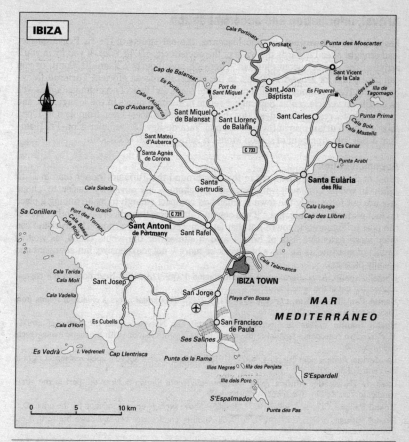

IBIZA

Cala Portinatx
Portinatx
Punta des Moscarter
Cap de Balansat
Es Portixol
Sant Vicent
de la Cala
Port de
Sant Miquel
Sant Joan
Baptista
Es Figueral
Illa de
Tagomago
Pou des Lleó
Cap d'Aubarca
Sant Miquel
de Balansat
Sant Llorenç
de Balàfia
Sant Carles
Punta Prima
Cala Boix
Cala Mastella
Sant Mateu
d'Aubarca
C 733
Es Canar
Santa Agnès
de Corona
Punta Arabí
Cala Salada
Santa
Gertrudis
Santa Eulària
des Riu
Sa Conillera
Cala Gració
Port des Torrent
Cala Bassa
Cala Roja
C 731
Sant Antoni
de Portmany
Sant Rafel
Cala Llonga
Cap des Llibrel
Cala Talamanca
Cala Tarida
Cala Molí
Sant Josep
IBIZA TOWN
MAR
MEDITERRÁNEO
Cala Vadella
San Jorge
Playa d'en Bossa
Cala d'Hort
Es Cubells
San Francisco
de Paula
Es Vedrà
I. Vedrenell
Cap Llentrisca
Ses Salines
Punta de la Rama
Illes Negres
Illa des Penjats
S'Espardell
Illa dels Porc
S'Espalmador
Punta des Pas

0   5   10 km

Ibiza Town

In physical terms as well as in its atmosphere and adventure, **IBIZA TOWN** (Eivissa Town) is the most attractive place on the island. Most people stay in rented apartments or small *pensiones* which means fewer hotels to ruin the skyline and no package incursions. Approach by sea and you'll get the full frontal effect of the old town's walls rising like a natural extension of the rocky cliffs which protect the port. Within the walls, the ancient quarter is topped by a sturdy cathedral, whose illuminated clock shines out across the harbour throughout the night.

Daylight hours are usually spent on the **beaches** at Ses Salines and Es Cavellet or the nearer (but not so nice) Figueretes. At night, before the discos open their doors, the shops stay open until 11pm – on c/D'Enmig you'll find stalls six nights a week selling everything from earrings and accessories through naive paintings and tawdry souvenirs. Afterwards the groove goes on till dawn and beyond, the last port of call being *Amnesia*, which keeps going till 6am. As a break from the stress of sunbathing and the simple pleasures of wandering the streets, there are two good archeological museums and a fancy modern art gallery with prices that will amaze you even if the displays don't.

Arrival, information and accommodation

From the **ferry terminal**, Estació Marítima, the old streets of the Sa Penya quarter lead straight ahead towards the walls of the ancient city (*D'Alt Vila*). If you fly in you'll arrive at the **airport** about 6km out. There's a bus (hourly 7.30am–10.30pm), or you can take a taxi for around 1800ptas. In the airport there's an efficient **Turismo** (May–Sept daily 10am–midnight) which can provide maps and lists of accommodation as well as details on vehicle rental. Several car rental firms have desks in the lounge, too, and there's a hotel reservations desk (for more expensive places) open from 8am to 10pm. Ibiza's main **Turismo** is in the new town at Vara de Rey 13 (summer Mon–Fri 10am–7pm & Sat 9am–1pm; out of season Mon–Fri 9am–1pm; ☎971/301900).

Accommodation

Most of the **budget places** are in the area around the Turismo (rather than in *D'Alt Vila*). If you're confident with Spanish telephones, it's obviously easier to phone around, but fortunately the town is small and compact enough to make finding a place on foot perfectly feasible. Even if you stay in Talamanca, though, or on the other side of the port in Figueretes, you're not that far removed from the action. The Turismo can offer more extensive lists of **hotels and hostales** for the whole island, as well as details of apartments for stays of a week or more – not inexpensive, but abundant and usually pleasant.

Hostal España, Avda. Bartolomeu Vicente Ramón 1 (☎971/311317). Next door to the popular Muñoz, but not in the same league. ③.

Hostal Estrella del Mar, c/Felipe II (☎971/312212). This *hostal* offers a choice of rooms from basic to relative luxury. ②/③.

Hostal Juanito, c/Joan de Austria 17 and **Hostal Las Nieves**, c/Joan de Austria 18 (☎971/315822). Two reasonable *hostales* in the street below Vicente Ramón, with the same management and prices. ②.

La Marina, Andenes del Puerto 4 (☎971/310172). Rooms to rent above a good restaurant right in the centre of the action. ③.

Casa de Huéspedes Muñoz, Avda. Bartolomeu Vicente Ramón 3. Near the port in the street parallel to Vara de Rey. Worn but comfortable. ③.

Hostal Parque, Cayetano Soller (☎971/301358). Above average accommodation for the price. ③.

Hostal Pitiusa, c/Galicia 29 (☎971/301905). Another comfortable two-star place but further out from the centre. ④.

Hostal El Puerto, c/Carles III 22 (☎971/313827). Good two-star *hostal* with pool and bar. Less expensive off-season. ④.

Hostal Sol y Brisa, Avda. Bartolomeu Vicente Ramón 15 (☎971/310818). In the centre of the budget accommodation close to the port; excellent value. ②.

The town

The capital is a simple enough place to find your way around. An excellent waterside walk leads from the **D'Alt Vila** (old town) past bars and restaurants to the harbour wall from where the entire bay can be surveyed. Continue past the port and you'll be in the **new town**, below the old to the west.

D'Alt Vila

Traffic enters the walled citadel through the **Portal de Ses Taules** and leaves by the **Portal Nou**. The main gate – Taules – leads into the great space of the **Plaça Desamparados** which is packed with restaurants and bars, as is the path towards the top of the town and the Plaça de Vila. The **Museu d'Art Contemporani** (summer

△ Santa Eulària d'es Riú & Portinatx

MAR MEDITERRÁNEO

Port de Eivissa

IBIZA TOWN

Mon–Fri 10am–1.30pm & 6–8pm, Sat 10am–1.30pm; winter Mon–Fri 10am–1pm, Sat 10am–1.30pm; 200ptas) is here as well, above the arch of the Portal de Ses Taules. Inside are held bimonthly exhibitions of contemporary artists from around the world: most of the art is for sale, though not at prices you're likely to want to pay.

Heading uphill along the main street, **Sa Carrossa**, you'll find some of the better restaurants, easy access to the top of the walls (*murallas*) and some great views down over the town. In the **Plaça de Espanya**, the sixteenth-century church of San Domingo – with added Baroque facade – stands next to its former monastery, converted in 1838 into the **Ayuntamiento**. Across the road a long, dark tunnel leads through the walls to a severe cliff walk that eventually takes you to a beachfront bar in the *Molinos* area, re-entering the walls at the Baluard de Santa Tecla cathedral square.

The **Catedral** (daily except Sat 10am–2pm), dedicated to Santa María la Mayor, is hardly more interesting than any of the other island churches. Its whitewashed interior is picked out in burnt-red vertical stripes and there are a few small murals on the walls of the single nave. A plaque commemorates the massacre of churchmen, soldiers and ordinary *ibizeños* at the hands of "Marxists" during the Civil War. The **museum**, however, is considerably better value than most, especially in its display of luxuriant bishops' regalia: mitres, sandals, gloves, cloaks and some nifty red-and-white velvet slippers which were obviously of great comfort to ecclesiastical feet on the stone floors. Pictures of past incumbents line the walls, along with a depiction of the Christian Reconquest of the island.

Across the square is the **Museu D'Alt Vila** (summer 10am–2pm & 6–8pm; winter 10am–1pm & 4–7pm), currently closed for refurbishment, with a collection of local archeological finds. The majority of the objects on display are from Phoenician and Carthaginian (Punic) sites, but there are also some bones from Formentera that date back to 1600 BC, and various Arab and Roman curiosities. Just outside the walls, along Via Romana, the **Puig des Molins Museu** (summer daily 10am–2pm & 6–8pm; out of season daily 10am–1pm & 4–7pm) contains many finds from a huge Punic **necropolis** that was excavated here. Among the objects discovered in graves are some splendidly decorated terracotta pieces, clay figurines, amphoras and amulets depicting Egyptian gods. There are tours of the necropolis itself at fifteen minutes past the hour. So many funerary sites have been found on Ibiza that it was long assumed to be some kind of burial island, and although this theory is no longer accepted the finds are still impressive.

One step further up the hill are the ruins of the thirteenth-century **castle**, but little remains to be seen apart from the view.

Outside the walls

Not quite as grand, nor as ancient as the *D'Alt Vila*, the **Sa Penya** quarter snuggles between the harbour and the ramparts, a maze of raked passages and narrow streets of balconied, whitewashed houses constructed virtually on top of one another. Here, especially along the waterside promenade and c/D'Enmig, the evening *paseo* reaches its peak and everyone – local and visitor alike – gravitates towards the bars and restaurants. Ibizan characters dress up to roam the streets or decorate the clubs and are generally appreciative of enthusiastic support, while c/D'Enmig, above all, is lively until well after midnight. This is where many of the shops are too, occupying almost every doorway that isn't a bar.

For a stroll after supper, head along the waterfront to observe the antics outside the *Zoo* bar. The *Bar Mariano*, on the corner of c/D'Enmig, may not look like much, but its sidewalk seating offers front-row viewing of the parade.

The **new town** is generally of less interest, but there's activity here too, centred on the Passeig de Vara de Rey. At dusk the air is filled with birds swooping in and out of the trees that line the pedestrian square, and the *Café-Hotel Montesol* becomes a popular meeting place. The *Café Mar y Sol* on the opposite corner, towards the waterfront, is another ideal vantage point from which to enjoy the nightly show, though it isn't terribly friendly. Worth seeing, too, if only as a curiosity, is the church of **El Salvador** in Plaça Canalejas: its modern interior boasts a huge pine Christ, looking like Roger Moore in discreet sauna wrap and 1965-vintage haircut.

Eating, drinking and nightlife

Despite catering for the mass holiday crowd, Ibiza does have some good traditional restaurants particularly in *D'Alt Vila*. But it's the bars and clubs that the town is known for – you come to Ibiza to party.

Restaurants and markets

The **Sa Penya** quarter is the place to head for for reasonably priced **restaurants** and **bars**. One of the best bets for simple dishes of good, fresh food is smoky *C'an Costa* at c/Cruz 19; along the road on the corner, *La Victoria*, c/Riambau 1, is another popular and long-established eatery. *Los Pasajeros* is perhaps the trendiest place to dine, with a limited menu and more people-watching than eating going on. It's on the first floor in c/Vicent Soler, an unmarked street connecting c/D'Enmig with the waterfront – ask for the restaurant by name.

Down by the waterside, or up in the walled town, you'll be paying a lot more. There are several extremely classy restaurants in **D'Alt Vila**: *El Portalón* and *D'Alt Vila* both have four-fork ratings with menus and prices to match. Nearby *El Mesón* also serves very good food but at much lower prices. *Mr Hotdog*, by the **port**, is popular among the less adventurous (and passing US Marines), while *San Juan*, off La Marina at c/Montgri 8, is inexpensive and worth seeking out. Other good places include *La Marina*, Andenes del Puerto 4 (☎971/310172), where the seafood is excellent; *El Proverone Trattoria*, c/ Mar de Deu, an economical Italian restaurant without a pizza in sight; and the *Café Vara Rey* opposite the Turismo which serves tasty *tapas*. A more expensive option is the Basque cuisine of *S'Oficina*, Avinguda d'Espanya 6 (☎971/300016)

You'll find all sorts of other possibilities, and in particular loads of **pizzerias**; unfortunately almost all of these seem to rely heavily on microwave ovens with erratic timer controls, although *Pizzeria Pinocchio*, c/D'Enmig 18, has the added compensation of being a good place to watch the world go by. You can get **early breakfast** in Passeig de Vara de Rey, next to *Montesol*, or at the new Estació Marítima, on the west side of the harbour.

If you plan to do it yourself, or want to gather ingredients for a picnic, the covered **market** at the bottom of the ramp into the Portal de Ses Taules is not bad, if not quite a match for the main market in the new town between Avingudas Espanya and Isidor Macabich. Be warned, though, that prices are double what they would be in a mainland market and that the selection is not all that great.

Bars and clubs

Ibiza's bars and clubs keep the place alive twenty-four hours a day – with money and mobility the night is yours, and there's a lot of it. The best places to begin your night out are around the port and along c/D'Enmig. There are a few **gay bars** here including *Bobby's*, *Teatro* and *JJ's*, but the most crowded ones are found up by the city walls – *Incognito's* and *Angelo's* are neighbours nestling by the Portal de Ses Taules. This is a good area to hang out in any case, with loads of basic stand-up drinking places. Just inside the D'Alt Vila you can watch in rather more style from the patio of *La Muralla*, with tables looking out over the walls.

As for **clubs**, even if you haven't heard of *Amnesia* or *Pacha*, you'll certainly be made aware of them during your wanderings round the port in the evening. Each – and many of their younger rivals – employs teams of PR artistes who descend on the town in a whirl of enthusiasm to drum up business for their respective establishments. Competition is fierce and you emerge from their assault like a piece of well-spattered flypaper, covered in sticky badges promoting the discos. None of them really gets going much before midnight, and the dancing goes on until dawn. You should also check out *Ku* (May–Sept), 6km out on the road to San Antonio; this is one of *the* places to be, and the sole reason why some people come to Ibiza.

Amnesia, also on the San Antonio road, charges around 3000ptas entry, stays open till 6am, and not surprisingly can get pretty wild. **Pacha** is around the bay near the casino, and is perhaps slightly tamer: certainly it's glossier and even more expensive (an outrageous 4000ptas; closes around 4am). Younger rivals which can't quite match the kudos of these two, though they might turn out to be more fun, include *Space*

BUSES AND BOATS FROM IBIZA TOWN

The main **bus routes**, departing from Avda. Isidor Macabich, are:

Sant Antoni de Portmany, every half-hour.

Ses Salines, every hour.

Santa Eulària des Riu, every half-hour.

Sant Joan, Cala Sant Vicent, Platja d'en Bossa, Figueretes and Sant Miquel, several daily departures each.

Portinatx, 2–6 services daily.

Boats run from the Estacio Marítima to:

Santa Eulària des Riu, 7 daily.

Cala Llonga, 7 daily.

Es Canar, 7 daily.

Platja d'en Bossa, 6 daily.

(2500ptas; till around 3.30am) and *Kiss*, with a considerably younger crowd (about 2000ptas, often free for women; till 2am), both at Platja d'en Bossa. There's just one exclusivcly **gay disco** in town – *Anfora* in the upper part of the D'Alt Vila, a walk away from the popular *Crisco* leather bar. For **jazz**, try *Excis* (*God's Love Bar*) on c/Mar de Deu which is painted with a 15ft-high mural of a nun.

Listings

Airport information (☎971/302200). The *Iberia* office is at Vara de Rey 15 (☎971/301368).

Ferry offices These are located near the Estació Marítima (☎971/304096 for information). *Transmediterránea* is at Avda. Bartolomeu Vicente Ramón 2 (☎971/314173), *Transmapi* (☎971/310711; for Formentera) and local services along the coast actually at the port.

Hospital Hospital Can Mises, Avda Espanya 49 (☎971/397000).

Laundry *Masterclean*, close to *Hostal El Puerto* on c/Felip II.

Moped rental *Ribas*, c/Vicent Cuervo 3 (☎971/301811) situated behind the main Turismo; *Motos Valentin*, Avda. Vicent Ramos 19 (☎971/310822); and *Motosud*, Avda. d'Espanya (☎971/302442), which is a 1-km walk west of the centre.

Post office The main *Correos* (Mon–Fri 8.30am–2pm; ☎971/311380) is at c/Madrid 23.

Telephones Telefónica is at Avda. de Santa Eulària (April–Oct 10am–2pm & 4–10pm).

Around Ibiza Town: the beaches

The closest sea and sand to Ibiza Town are at **Figueretes**, a built-up continuation of the capital concentrated round a small and rather overexploited bay, and at the neighbouring **Platja d'en Bossa**, but it's worth going a little further afield to escape the high-rise hotels.

Ses Salines and Es Cavallet

To the **south of Ibiza Town**, stretching from the airport to the sea, are thousands of acres of **salt flats**. Ibiza's history, and its powerful presence on ancient trade routes, was based on these salt fields (*salinas*), a trade vital, above all, to the ancient Carthaginians. Salt remained an important economic resource until comparatively recently; the island's only rail line ran from the middle of the marshes to **La Canal**, a dock where an enormous container ship would arrive weekly to be loaded with the bright white sea salt. Even now, though tourism brings in far more money and the rail line has been torn up, salt production continues.

There are two beaches here, **SES SALINES** and, on the other side of the dunes, **ES CAVALLET**. Although Platja d'Es Cavallet is the official nudist beach, full-frontal tanning seems just as common at Ses Salines (in high season at least). Both beaches have a couple of *chiringuitos* (beach bars). Near the entrance to the beach road, at the start of Es Cavallet you can also have a shiatsu massage. *Hostal Mar y Sol* (②) offers basic rooms above a bar behind Ses Salines beach.

Northeast to Santa Eulària

Heading **northeast from Ibiza Town**, the road to Portinatx and the coastal route to Santa Eulària diverge at the small crossroads of **JESÚS**. There are a couple of excellent bars here: the *Bar Casablanca* which serves a cheap *menú del día*, and the *Bar Bon Lloch* with a marvellous array of *tapas*. Follow the coast road towards Santa Eulària and you'll pass an uninspired development area at **CALA LLONGA**. A small sandy beach saddled with package hotels, it's to be avoided unless you're looking for a **campsite**; the one here is at least in pleasant surroundings, with a pool, about 500m from the sea. For a swim en route, the **Platja Sol Den Serra**, a one-bar cove just before you reach Cala Llonga, is far more attractive.

Santa Eulària des Riu

The town of **SANTA EULÀRIA DES RIU** has at least a modicum of interest – it's situated on the only river in the Balearics and has, nearby, the dwarfed remains of the island's only **Roman aqueduct** (a tiny wall which takes some finding, by the *Hotel S'Argamassa*). There's a family atmosphere here, though still with a scattering of fashion victims and ageing hippies, and it's close enough to Ibiza Town to be visited for the day or the evening. The hilltop church, approached up a slope lined with the Stations of the Cross, is whitewashed and bare except for a garish, glass-encased Christ – typical, in other words. The Museu Barcau by the church seems permanently closed.

Down by the sea you'll find a short, modern, tree-lined seafront promenade with a seasonal **Turismo** (☎971/330728), *Telefónica*, a clutch of pavement cafés and craft stalls, and **restaurants** which are renowned on the island. *El Naranjo*, c/Sant Josep 31, has a lovely patio full of orange trees; for livelier action you could try the *Harlequin* or *Mozart* bars, or *Estudio 64* disco.

If you want to **stay** there are any number of possibilities: try *Hostal Central* (☎971/330043; ③) or *Sa Rota* (☎971/☎330022; ③) on c/Sant Vicent; *Hostal Rey* (☎971/330210; ③) on c/Sant Josep; or *Cala Boix* (②) on c/Sant Carles. There's a daily **boat** from here to Formentera, and also regular services to the beaches nearby, which are better than Santa Eulària's own.

The northern beaches

Just north of Santa Eulària, the beach at **S'ARGAMASSA** is notorious for its yahoo package tourists, who spend their sober hours waterskiing around the bay or windsurfing – sports which can easily be arranged here. There's a very pleasant **campsite**, *Florida* (☎971/331154) at **PUNTA ARABI**, at the end of the bay, which also rents chalets – they're good value if you can fill all six beds. **ES CANAR**, beyond the point, has a sailing club and boats back to Santa Eulària or across to Formentera. There's a long-established "hippie market" here, too.

Continuing to the north, you'll find another **campsite**, *Es Canar* (☎971/332117) at **PLATJA CALA NOVA**. It wins no prizes for beauty, but the amenities are good and it's close to a fine sandy beach. **CALA LENA**, another 2km along the coast, offers a pretty, small sandy beach with a bar and only private apartments nearby. **CALA MASTELLA**, the next bay, is still more secluded and still harder to get to, but it does offer a bar with food cooked over a wood fire, a tiny beach in the rocky cove, and a restaurant on the approach road.

Inland, a road heads from Santa Eulària to Es Figueral via **SANT CARLES**, a one-horse town where Es Canar hippies congregate to socialize. **FIGUERAL** itself consists almost entirely of a holiday complex known as *Club Figueral*, with a supermarket, disco and phone box. Its beach – just a short walk from this development and the holiday villas – is always busy, with a windsurfing school that runs well-supervized classes. If you want to **stay**, there are a couple of reasonably priced choices: *Es Alocs* (☎971/330179; ③) right on the beach or the *Fonda Figueral*. Out in the bay, seen from the road at the top of the cliffs, is the uninhabited island of **Tagomago**.

Finally in this direction, and around the edge of the same large bay, lies **CALA SANT VICENT**, which would be exceptionally pretty were it not for gross overcrowding from five large hotels serving the British package tour market and an ugly hillside *urbanización*. As things stand it's best avoided – the bars and restaurants, despite their quantity, are expensive.

The north coast

Cutting straight across the island towards the north coast, the road branches about 6km out of Ibiza Town, with the right fork heading for **Portinatx**, the left to **Sant Miquel**. Taking either route, you'll pass through some of the island's finest countryside, burnt-red fields of olive, almond and carob trees, and occasionally a plantation of melons or vines. On the way to Sant Miquel there's another fork at **Santa Gertrudis**; bearing left will take you to Sant Mateu and eventually around to Sant Antoni de Portmany.

Sant Miquel

At **SANT MIQUEL**, on top of a low hill, there are two artist's studios (worth at least a quick visit) in the square beside the church. There's folk dancing here, too, every Thursday evening at 6pm (a bus leaves Ibiza Town to see this at 5pm, returning at 7.30pm). The old **port** is 4km beyond – once an attractive small bay, now rather spoilt by the scourges of development. The deluxe *Hotel Hacienda* (☎971/333031; ⑨) is perched spectacularly above here, up a private road to the west; it's a favourite of holidaying sheiks and honeymooning couples, and has one of the island's best restaurants to boot. There's waterskiing and motorboat hire around the bay, and you can visit the recently opened **caves** with some spectacular lighting effects and an artifical waterfall cascading over fossil-rich rocks.

More adventurous souls might attempt to follow the rough path over the hills to **CALA BENIRRÀS**, which saves a tedious journey along the signposted tarmac road to this magnificent and, as yet, unspoiled cove. At present, there are just two bars and a beach where you can hire pedal-boats and other small craft. Catch it while you can.

Portinatx

Portinatx is approached, in a final twisting stretch of road, through a beautiful, fertile valley lined with olive-terraced hills and orderly groves of almond and pine. After rain, in particular, there's a distinctive brightness to the air here and a delightful burgundy glow to the soil. At **CALA XARRACA** you emerge above the sea with a path leading down to a tiny sandy beach, sparklingly clear water, rocks to dive off and a lone bar. **CALA XULA**, next along, is in much the same mould, reached by an even steeper track. The **campsite**, *Camping Payés*, is further along, on the left-hand side of the Portinatx road; you can rent tents, it's friendly and open all year.

PORTINATX is nowadays purely a vacation resort. Once you've walked the length of its three beaches, tried the harbour sports and purchased your quota from the souvenir shops, there's little left to do. The beaches – **Big Beach**, **Little Beach** and **Es Port Beach** – have to serve several medium-sized hotels and there's barely room to squeeze a towel in between the sunbeds, all rotated hourly to follow the path of the sun. In the port area you'll usually find a couple of elegant yachts anchored offshore, and climbing up beyond the *Holiday Club* chalets to the old watchtower (one of very few which survive intact and accessible), there's a great view down across the town and its bay and back into the hills. A constant symphony of cicadas buzzes its appreciation of the panorama.

If you're looking for a **room**, and the hotels are all agency-booked to capacity (as they probably will be), try the *Hostal Portinatx* (☎971/333043; ②), the *Se Vinye* (same management and phone; ③) or the *Hostal La Cigüeña* (☎971/333044; ③). **Bike rental** is available from *Betacar Edifico Banksa* (☎971/333069) next to the *Hotel Portisol* apartments.

The west coast: Sant Antoni de Portmany

SANT ANTONI DE PORTMANY is seriously out of place on Ibiza. Its total lack of charm, allure or style would make it more at home among the worst excesses of Mallorca. This is where you'll find the *Club 18–30* patrons practising their projectile vomiting from fifth-floor balconies and letting it all hang out at beach party orgies. Restaurants along the quay dish up sausage, chips and beans.

The **Turismo** (☎971/343363) is in the park at the beginning of the waterfront Passeig de Ses Fonts; they can provide information on **places to stay**. Probably the best place to look is around c/Soledad and c/Prim, but watch out for tour-company stickers which mean crowds and inflated prices. Reasonable options include *Hostal Tumas* (c/Soletat 49; ☎971/342826; ③), *Hostal Cisne* (Vara de Rey 13; ☎971/340093; ②), *Flores* (c/Rossell 26; ☎971/341129; ③), *Roig* (c/Progres 44; ☎971/340483; ②) and *Horizonte* (c/Progres 62; ☎971/340333; ③). There are also a couple of **campsites** nearby, *San Antonio* (☎340536), a couple of kilometres out on the Ibiza road, and *Cala Bassa*, round the coast at Cala Bassa (see below).

Eating is no problem, but on the whole food here is either dull or expensive: try *Rías Baixas* in c/Ignasi Riquer or *Grill San Antonio* in c/Bisbe Torres both of which are better than average. **Nightlife** consists of a string of discos with such thrillingly original names as *Playboy, Manhattan, San Francisco* or the *Starclub*, and music to match: one of the best is a new one, *Es Paradis Terrénal*, with action till 3 or 4am. **Bike rental** outlets include *Autos Reco*, c/Ramon y Cajal (☎971/340388) and on Avda. Dr Fleming, *Moto Rent* (☎971/340981) and *Autos Portmany* (☎971/340673).

There are several daily **boat journeys** across the bay to the beaches of **CALA BASSA** and its high-rise hotels; glass-bottomed boat tours of the harbour; and, twice weekly, a complete circuit of the island by boat, calling in at the "hippie market" (now a historical curiosity) at Es Canar. You can also sail round to Portinatx, or across to Formentera or the mainland (6 sailings weekly with *Flebasa*; ☎971/342871) at Denia and Gandia. **Buses** leave for Ibiza Town every half-hour, four times daily to Santa Eulària and frequently along local routes to Cala Conta (a pretty beach, also accessible by boat) and Port d'es Tourrent.

Around Sant Antoni

Heading away from Sant Antoni, you'll find more promising **beaches**, and fewer people, in just about any direction. Some 4km to the north lies the small beach of **CALA SALADA**, easily accessible if you've got a vehicle, with fewer crowds, a small friendly restaurant and pedalos to rent. Nearby **CALA GALERA** looks promising, but the *urbanización* here is determined to maintain its privacy, and the small beach really doesn't merit the effort of getting past the barricaded gate.

Further north, and inland, the **Chapel of Santa Inés** (in the village of the same name although the Catalan signposts curiously mark it as Santa Agnés) is the last point of any interest, with a subterranean gallery in which local Christians worshipped secretly during the Moorish occupation. Lately this has been closed, however, so check with the Turismo before making a special trip.

Sant Antoni to Ibiza Town

Beyond the boat trip destinations to the south of Sant Antoni, there are several more excellent beaches. **CALA BASSA** is packed, but it does have a well-equipped **campsite**. More promising still is **CALA D'HORT** in the southwest corner of the island, approached either along the twisting minor road from Sant Josep (San José) or via the new coastal road. Both routes end at a lovely quiet beach with two excellent seafood **restaurants**, *Es Boldado* and *Can Jaime*, as well as a good-value café-restaurant, the *Cala Hort*. Alll three have views over **Es Vedra**, a canine tooth of rock stabbing through the bay just offshore. Ibiza's highest peak, it starred in the film of *South Pacific* as the mysterious island of Bali Hai. The sea looks dirty, but it's natural muck and perfectly safe and pleasant to swim in.

Heading back towards Ibiza Town by the southern route, it's possible to cut down from Sant Josep to the coast at **ES CUBELLS**. The road that links the two is an engineering marvel sliced out of the cliff edge, but it's not enough to make the journey worthwhile – there are no beaches to speak of and a couple of remarkably unattractive developments, with further building clearly planned.

Head on towards the capital, and you'll pass the **Covas Santas** (Holy Caves), with some impressive drippy stalactites 17m underground, just off the main road. Unfortunately there are no set opening hours – you just have to turn up and hope you're lucky. Follow the track south of the caves and you'll get to **CALA JONDAL**. Fields of tempting melons and grapes greet your arrival and you can get delicious seafood at the bar, but the beach itself, despite its popularity with the islanders and lizards, is pebbly and uncomfortable. The trip is worth doing once, maybe, but you're unlikely to want to return to disturb the peace.

FORMENTERA

Just three nautical miles south of Ibiza, **FORMENTERA** (population 4000) is the smallest of the inhabited Balearics. It's actually two small islets joined together by a narrow sandy isthmus and is just 14km long from east to west. The crossing from Ibiza is short, but strong currents ensure that it's slow – over an hour – and rough: keep the seasickness pills handy. Fares are about 2000ptas (3000 on the hydrofoil, which is quicker but less enjoyable) and there are usually rival sailings to choose from: check the return times before deciding. Sailing from Ibiza Town there's a stupendous view of the citadel astride its cliff and you'll also pass the **Illa Ahorcados** – "Hanged Men's Island", once the last stop for Ibiza's criminals – and the sand-fringed **Illa Espalmador**.

Formentera's history more or less parallels that of Ibiza, though for nearly 300 years – from the early fifteenth century to the end of the seventeenth – it was left uninhabited for lack of water and fear of Turkish pirate raids. Under the Romans it had been a major agricultural centre (its name derives from *frumentaria*, "granary") and when repopulated in 1697 the island was again divided up for cultivation. It never regained its original level of productivity, however, and nowadays is largely barren, the few crops having to be protected, as on Menorca, against the lashing of winter winds. Most of the island is now covered in rosemary, growing wild everywhere, and crawling with thousands of brilliant green lizards.

Modern income is derived from tourism (especially German and British), taking advantage of some of Spain's longest, whitest and least-crowded beaches. The shortage of fresh water continues to keep away the crowds – there's nowhere for them to stay – and for the most part visitors are seeking escape with little in the way of sophistication. It is however, becoming increasingly popular, and is certainly not the "paradise" it once was. Nude sunbathing is tolerated – indeed the norm – just about everywhere.

Formentera practicalities

Most people treat Formentera as a day trip from Ibiza, and if you want to be one of the few who **stay** you may have difficulty finding anywhere not given over to agency reservations. If you're stuck, it's also worth asking in bars, many of which have attached rooms at government-controlled prices. Each town also has at least one letting agency dealing with apartments and villas, often not badly priced. There's a **laundry** in La Savina, on the right as you head out towards Sant Francesc.

Although Formentera has no official **campsite**, finding a secluded spot should not prove too difficult. Many people camp in the pine woods behind Platja de Mitjorn, though the police do occasionally swoop down to clear them off. There is a basic bus service from La Savina but journeys rarely keep to timetables, and they connect only the towns, leaving you long, hot walks to the beaches. **Taxis** are cheap, though, with ranks at La Savina, Sant Francesc and Es Pujols; it's best to book one the day before you need it. If you're staying on the island, buy the 1:25,000 map which shows the dirt tracks as well as the tarmac roads.

There aren't many inexpensive places to eat on the island. All the *hostales* serve **food**, or you can get your own supplies from the market and supermarket in Sant Francesc. Generally speaking, **beach bars** serve better food than the resorts. There are two **discos** in Es Pujols, the *Tipic* and the *Magoo*, the latter the best and staying open until 5am. Both are fairly expensive. The *Disco Vedra* at the large *Club Hotel de la*

Mola complex at Platja de Mitjorn is also open to non-residents. Resident hippies of Es Pujols set up stalls and sell jewellery each evening.

La Savina and Sant Francesc Xavier

Boats from the various Ibiza ports head for the tiny but functional harbour of **LA SAVINA**, where the two waterside streets are lined with places offering cars, mopeds or bicycles for rent, interspersed with the odd bar and café. This is the place to get yourself mobile, but if possible phone ahead, certainly if you want a car (try *MotoRent*, ☎971/322255, or *Autos Formentera*, ☎971/322156); mopeds and bicycles are much less expensive and easier to come by and there are lots of outlets to choose from. Check with the **Turismo** (☎971/322057) by the harbour if you need help with this, or with island accommodation, maps and walking or cycling routes. The best place to stay is *Hostal La Savina* (☎971/322279; ③), 1km outside La Savina. Hemming the town in are two lagoons: the **Estany d'es Peix**, once used for fish farming but now devoted to watersports, and the aptly named **Estany Pudent** (Stinking Pond). Neither offers much incentive to hang around.

The capital, **SANT FRANCESC XAVIER**, is just a couple of kilometres away, easily reached on foot or by local bus or taxi if you're not planning to rent a vehicle. From here, the island's roads and tracks fan out. As well as the whitewashed fortified church – now stripped of its defensive cannon – this metropolis has several restaurants and cafés, at least three banks, four bars, a hotel, supermarkets, a pharmacist, a doctor, a *Telefónica* for international calls and its own open-air market. If you want to **stay**, try the *Casa Rafal*, near the church (☎971/322205; ③).

Around the island

Formentera's main road continues from Sant Francesc to the island's easternmost point at La Mola. Along it, or just off it, are concentrated almost all of the island's habitation and most of the beaches. The next largest town, **SANT FERRAN** – with a bar, a church and the *Hostal Pepe* (☎971/322031; ②) – serves the beach of **ES PUJOLS** where Formentera's package tour industry, such as it is, is concentrated (the town itself totally lacks character). Despite relative crowding, this is a beautiful coast with clear water and pure white sand dunes backed by low pines. Windsurfing is taught here in German and Spanish, and there are two *hostales* worth trying: *Hostal Bar Los Rosales* (☎971/328123; ③) and *Tahiti* (☎971/328122; ③). Es Pujols has the most **restaurants** on the island, including one Chinese, *Capri* (☎971/328352), which specializes in fish. The *Café de la Ópera* is also very popular. For something less expensive, *Pizza Pazza* does the best pizzas and *Bar Escobar* is good for other food.

Northwest, on the **Es Trucadors** peninsula, are the **Platja de Ses Illetes** (on the west) and the nudist **Platja de Llevant** (on the east), lovely beaches with soft white sand, backed by stunted pine trees and supplied with a number of bars. They're an easy bike ride from La Savina.

Heading east, the caves at **D'EN XERONI** are less than a kilometre outside Sant Ferran; wait in the bar by the entrance and there'll be a guided tour as soon as a few people have turned up. The caves were discovered quite by accident in 1975. **PLATJA DE MITJORN**, on the south side of this narrow stretch of the island, is an enormous stretch of sand broken only by the occasional bar or hotel. If you're looking for accommodation, try *Hostal Sol y Mar* (☎971/328180; ③). At the western end of Mitjorn is the *Lagartija*, an excellent open-air **restaurant** run by Belgians serving French cuisine. There is often a singer and the atmosphere is very relaxed. Further east is the cheerful

Sol y Luna which offers good Spanish food at terrific prices. Formentera's strict regulations on new building means that this area will remain relatively undeveloped: rather soulless, but definitely the place to head for total isolation, and the main area for nude sunbathing. East and west of the Platja de Mitjorn, beaches stretch out along the island's south coast almost without interruption, shadowed by the main road.

On the north coast, near the east end of the isthmus, **ES CALÓ** has several *hostales* including *Hostal Pascual* (☎971/328309; ③), somewhat incongruously located around a tiny harbour that seems more adapted to its fishing activities. Beyond, the island cantilevers up in a great wedge of rock. At this eastern extremity, the island's highest point, stands the lighthouse of **La Mola** (which features in Jules Verne's *Hector Servadac, or The Career of a Comet*) – with views right across to Mallorca – and in the cool mountain pines there's a long-established, and now thoroughly assimilated, settlement of hippies.

South to Cap de Berberia

To the south of the capital a second track, in bad condition, leads towards the lighthouse on **Cap de Berberia**. It's an arduous trek and barely merits the effort, but **CALA SAONA**, a short way down and then off to the right, certainly does. A beautiful cove, among the best on the island, this is a popular place for passing pleasure crafts to drop anchor for a while; unfortunately an enormous, ugly hotel rather spoils it. There are also a couple of bars, a small restaurant among the sand dunes, and an intriguingly well-guarded private villa not far from the beach. One of the best places to **stay** here is the pleasant *Hostal Cala Saona* (☎971/322030; ⑤) with its own pool.

MALLORCA

MALLORCA, perhaps more than anywhere in Spain, has a split identity. So much so, in fact, that there's a long-standing joke here about a fifth Balearic island, *Majorca*, a popular sort of place that pulls in an estimated three million tourists a year. There are sections of coast where high-rise hotels and shopping centres are continuous, wedged beside and upon one another and broken only by a dual carriageway down to more of the same. But the spread of development, even after 25 years, is surprisingly limited; occupying only the Bay of Palma, a forty-kilometre strip flanking the island capital. Beyond, to the north and east, things are very different. Not only are there good cove beaches (spared the interminable rows of plastic sunbathing trays), but there's a startling variety and physical beauty to the land itself. It's this which drew the original Mallorcan tourists – the nineteenth-century Habsburg archdukes, and later George Sand and Chopin – and it's this which makes the island many people's favourite in the group.

Less known to most people is the **archeological interest**. Dating from around 5000 BC, the rock shelter of **Son Matge**, near Valldemossa, is the oldest discovered site of human occupation in the Balearics, whilst the people of the Beaker culture (dating from about 2500–1400 BC) studded the islands with crude stone remains – most notably the *talayots*, cones built to cover funeral chambers, and *taulas*, upright altar stones similar to the ones at the prehistoric villages of Ses Paisses near Artá and Capicorp Vell, 12km south of Llucmajor on the road to Cala Pi. These sites are only of passing interest, and devotees of prehistoric remains usually stick to the more substantial sites on Menorca (see p.752).

Mallorca practicalities

It's possible you'll **arrive** by boat from Menorca at **Port d'Alcúdia** in the north of the island, but you're most likely to find yourself in **Palma de Mallorca**, the capital and

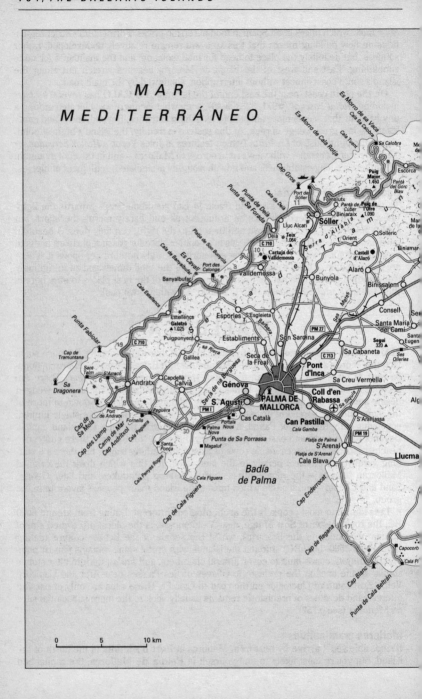

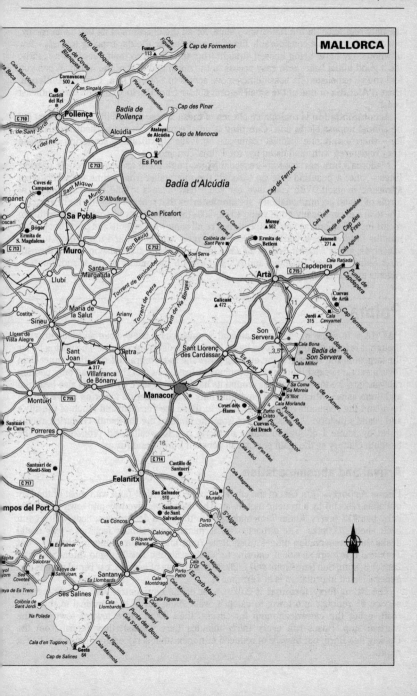

the only real "city" in the Balearics. Palma, for all the disasters of its bay, is an earthy, bustling place with a considerable life of its own despite the day-tripping tourists – few of whom stay here, being bussed straight from the airport to their out-of-town resorts. It's a good initial base, with easy access to the north and east of the island. When you feel you've exhausted its possibilities move across to **Sóller/Deià**, **Port de Pollença**, **Port d'Alcúdia** or one of the small resorts not far from **Porto Cristo** on the southeast coast.

Accommodation is reasonable at each of these towns, though in July or August it'll be almost impossible to find. **Camping** is an alternative but not particularly provided for – there's only one "official" campsite (at Platja Brava) and a scattering of private ones registered with (and listed by) the Palma Turismo.

Mallorca's **bus services** are reasonably good and there are even a couple of **train lines** – one, a beautiful ride up through the mountains from Palma to Sóller, is an attraction in itself. With your own car you'll have access to one of the more offbeat forms of island accommodation – six **monasteries** that rent cells for the night or week. These are exceptionally good value (from 500–1500ptas for two people, often with two meals included) but, as you'd expect, they're all somewhat remote and often booked up months in advance. If you're interested, the most accessible, and most likely to have vacancies, are at *Nuestra Señora del Puig* (near Pollença), *Lluc* (also in the northwest), *Sant Salvador* (near Felantix) and *NS de Cura* (in the middle of the island, between Algaida and Llucmajor).

Palma

PALMA is in some ways like a mainland Spanish city – lively, solid and industrious – though it is immediately set apart by its insular, Mediterranean aura. The port is by far the largest in the Balearics, the evening *paseo* the most ingrained (if rather tamer than Ibiza's exotic events), and, in the evenings at least, you feel the city has only passing relevance to the tourist enclaves around its bay. Arriving here by sea, it is also beautiful and impressive, with the grand limestone bulk of the cathedral towering above the old town and the remnants of medieval walls. In these are encapsulated much of the city's and island's history: Moorish control from the ninth to the thirteenth centuries, reconquest by Jaime I of Aragón and a meteoric rise to wealth and prominence in the fifteenth century as the main port of call between Europe and Africa.

Arrival and accommodation

Palma airport is 7km east of the city and connected with it (and with most of the Bay of Palma resorts) by a frenetic motorway. The least expensive way into town from here is by bus #17 (every 30min 7am–midnight) to the Plaça de Espanya; taxis will set you back about 2000ptas. The airport's two terminals have similar facilities – car rental desks, hotel reservation offices (daily 9am–7pm) and 24-hour money exchange – but Terminal B is more seasonal, catering for charter flights. The Turismo (Mon–Sat 9am–2pm & 3–8pm; Sun 9am–2pm; ☎971/260803) with lists of *hostales*, car rental outlets and general island information is in Terminal A.

The Palma **ferry terminal** is 3.5km west of the city centre, with connecting bus service #1 running into town; to catch it, walk 200m out of the terminal to the main road, using the cloverleaf ramp for access, then 200m more toward town for the marked stop. Buses run every thirty minutes (fare 75ptas); they return from the Passeig des Born, but beware of reduced or nonexistent services on Sunday and late at night.

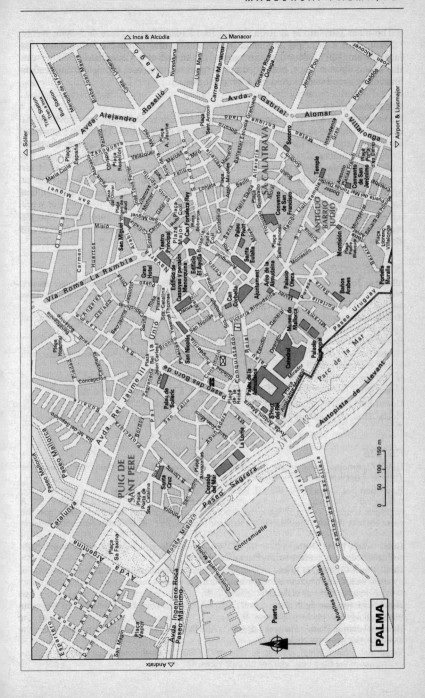

The main **Turismo** is at Avda. Jaume III 10 (daily 9am–2.30pm & 3–8pm; ☎971/712216), with a principal sub-office beneath c/Victoria (Mon–Fri 9am–8.30pm; Sat 9am–1.30pm; ☎971/724090) in the subway at the end of c/Conquistador. Either can also supply various maps, bus schedules, ferry timetables, boat trip details and leaflets (including a good one on trekking around the island).

Accommodation

There are hundreds of *pensiones* and hotels in Palma, and your first move in the summer should be to pick up the official lists from the Turismo. They won't however, book accommodation for you, leaving that to the city's many travel agents; *Ultramar Express* has offices all over the city including one just a few doors down from the Turismo on Avda. Jaume III.

Best initial areas to look for yourself are along the Passeig Mallorca, on c/Apuntadors or c/Sant Feliu running west from Passeig des Born (budget places), and on c/Sant Jaume at the top of the Passeig des Born (mid-range). Fancier places are largely to the west in the hotel area, especially along Avda. Joan Miró. Specific recommendations are probably futile in summer, but out of season the following are likely to have vacancies:

BUDGET OPTIONS

Albergue Juvenil, c/Costa Brava 13 in El Arenal (☎971/260892). A clean youth hostel situated very near the beach, but well out of town and invariably booked en masse by school groups. Take bus #15 from Plaça de Espanya and get off at the *Aptos Royal Plaza* hotel block.

Hostal Apuntadors, c/Apuntadors 8 (☎971/215910). One more star than the popular *Ritzi*, but lower prices and quality. ③.

Hostal Bahía de Palma, c/Bosc 14 (☎971/237480). Standard, central *hostal*. ③.

Hostal Borne, c/Sant Jaume 3 (☎971/712942). Comfortable mid-price choice, very popular, with its own courtyard café. ③.

Hostal Goya, c/Estanc 7 (☎971/726986). Very basic, but just off Passeig Des Born. ①.

Hostal Pons (☎971/722658), c/VI (General Barceló) 8. A basic *hostal*, but clean and friendly. ①.

Hostal Ritzi, c/Apuntadors 6 (☎971/714610). Friendly and comfortable. ③.

Hostal Tirol, c/Apuntadors 19 (☎971/211808). Large, so likely to have space, but check the room. ②.

HOTELS

Hotel Almudaina, Avda. Jaume III 9 (☎971/727340). Located right in the centre opposite the Turismo with every modern convenience and comfort. ⑤.

Hotel Bon Sol, Illetes (☎971/402111). Situated in Illetes, a 20-min bus ride west of the city centre, this curious hotel, with its own tiny artificial beach, tumbles down a steep seashore cliff. A family-run concern, it's got all the conveniences you could want and the better rooms have fine views out over the bay. The clientele are staid and steady rather like the antique-crammed interior. ⑥.

Hotel Drach, Font i Monteros 23 (☎971/723146). Centrally located, old-fashioned hotel with high-ceilinged bedrooms, not far from the Placa d'Espanya. ④.

Hotel Royal Cristina, El Arenal (☎971/492550). Luxury apartments and hotel rooms a couple of minutes' walk from the crowded sandy beach that fronts El Arenal, a predicatable tourist resort about 20-min bus ride east of the centre. Bus #15. ⑥.

Hotel Saratoga, Passeig Mallorca 6 (☎971/727240). Above average new hotel with roof top swimming pool. Most rooms have balconies. ⑤.

Hotel Sol Jaime, Passeig Mallorca 14B (☎971/725943). Straightforward, modern 3-star hotel overlooking a wide and busy boulevard. ⑤.

Valparaiso Palace Hotel, c/Francesc Vidal (☎971/400411). Plush hotel, located 1km west of the centre; one of the city's best, with fine harbour views. ⑥.

The city

Finding your way around Palma is fairly straightforward once you're in the centre. Around the **cathedral** – *La Seu* – is the **Portela quarter**, "Old" Palma, a cluster of alleyways and lanes that becomes more spacious and ordered as you move towards the zigzag of avenues built beside or in place of the city walls. Cutting up from the sea, beside the cathedral, is Avda. D'Antoni Maura, a garden promenade as well as boulevard, and way up the hill to the northeast lies the **Plaça Mayor**, mecca for most of the day-tripping tourists.

The Cathedral

Palma's **Catedral** (Mon–Fri 10am–6.30pm, Sat 10am–2.30pm; 300ptas; also open for services), five hundred years in the making, dominates the old city from a hill above the seafront. It's a magnificent building – the equal of almost any on the mainland – and a surprising one, too, with *modernista* interior features designed by Antoni Gaudí. Its original foundation came with the Christian Reconquest of the city, and the site taken, in fulfilment of a vow by Jaime I, was that of the Moorish Great Mosque. Essentially Gothic, with massive exterior buttresses to take the weight off the pillars within, the church derives its effect through its sheer height, impressive from any angle but startling when glimpsed from the waterside esplanade. The *reconquista*-era builders had a point to make, and they didn't hold back.

Inside the nave, you are immersed in a dappled kaleidoscope of light, for once untrapped by the central *coro* (choir) that normally blocks the centre of Spanish cathedrals. This innovation, and the fantastic forms of the lighting system above the altar, were Gaudí's work, completed in 1904 under the patronage of an inspired local bishop. At the time, these measures were deeply controversial; no *coro* had ever before been removed in Spain. The artistic success of the project, though, was undeniable, and it was immediately popular. Compared to Gaudí's designs in Barcelona, everything here is simple and restrained but there are touches of his characteristic fantasy. The wrought-iron contraption above the altar resembles a giant tiara and, elsewhere, there are railings twisted into forms inspired by Mallorcan window-grilles. For those who want to take photos inside, only the altar is properly illuminated, and the lights are switched on automatically for three minutes every few minutes, so have your camera ready.

If you can coincide with it, the *Missa solemne* at 10.30am on Sunday is magnificent. Chanting is in Latin, the choir is small but competent, and the curé seems rather enlightened judging by his homily. Also of possible interest are the *Missa cantada* (Sat 9am) and the *mallorquin* mass (Sun 1pm).

Before you enter the nave, you pass through three rooms of assorted ecclesiastical bric-a-brac, amongst which you'll find a couple of paintings by the fourteenth-century Majorcan Primitives. Leaving the cathedral, it's a short signposted walk round to the **Museo Diocesano** (200ptas), where there are more religious artefacts, but, with the exception of the Moorish tiles, it's not very exciting.

Palau de L'Almudain and La Llotja

Opposite the cathedral entrance is the imposing **Palau de L'Almudain** (June–Sept Mon–Fri 10am–7pm; Oct–May Mon–Fri 10.30am–2pm & 4–6pm; 500ptas), originally the residence of the Moorish *walis* and later of the Mallorcan kings. Visits here are guided, with energetic commentaries repeated in three languages, and it's well worth a look. Most of what you see – and there are considerable parts cordoned off as the island's official State Apartments – dates from a thirteenth- to fifteenth-century reconstruction under Christian rule. The Council Room, which is normally on view, is pressed into service once a year when King Juan Carlos convenes the Mallorcan assemblies; the small chapel across the court is used by the army's officers for their Masses and weddings. The ordinary soldiers, rigged out in toy-town costume to stand guard, are ferociously camera-shy.

If none of this sounds too inspiring, there are some pleasant gardens attached to the palace and you can stroll down through these to the grand fifteenth-century **Llotja**, the city's former stock or commodities exchange. This is now home to frequent and occasionally excellent temporary exhibitions (Tues–Sat 11am–2pm & 4–8pm).

The rest of the city

More traditionally rewarding is the *medina*-like maze of streets at the back of the cathedral, and here, at Can Serra 7, you'll come upon the **Banys Àrabs** (daily 10am–1.30pm & 4–6pm; 100ptas). One of the few genuine reminders of the Moorish presence, this *hamam* is an elegant, horseshoe-arched and domed chamber. But if you've been to the ones in Girona or Granada, these are anticlimactic; the garden outside, with tables where you can picnic, is perhaps nicer. Nearby, in c/Portella, the **Museu de Mallorca** (Mon–Sat 10am–2pm & 4–7pm, Sun 10am–2pm; 200ptas), occupying one of the many fifteenth- and sixteenth-century patrician mansions that fill out this part of town, has extensive local archeology exhibits and some exceptionally fine medieval religious paintings.

A five-minute walk away along Pont i Vich and Pare Nadal, and occupying, oddly enough, the site of the old Moorish soap factory, the **Basilica de Sant Francesc** (Mon–Sat 9.30am–1pm & 3.30–6.45pm) is the finest among a host of worthy medieval churches. A vast building founded towards the end of the thirteenth century, it boasts a cavernous interior dominated by the gilt mass of its gaudy altar, and a fine Gothic cloister. The strange-looking statue outside the church – of a Franciscan monk and a native American Indian – celebrates the misssionary work of Junipero Serra, a Mallorcan priest who took charge of the Californian missions in 1768, subsequently founding San Diego and Monterey. Nearby **Santa Eulària**, the first church to be built after Jaime's arrival, is in a similar vein, airy and high-roofed, and haunted by a history of mass executions of the island's Jews. Just to its west, the **Ajuntament** is an elegant example of pure Renaissance style with a grand and self-assured foyer.

Eating, drinking and nightlife

Eating in Palma is less expensive – or can be – than anywhere else in the Balearics. Some of the lowest-priced places are the cramped cafés and *cantinas* crowded on or near c/Apuntadors at the lower end of Passeig des Born, whilst, rather surprisingly, the restaurants aimed at tourists nearby along Avda. D'Antoni Maura are reasonably priced too. But Palma's tourist-oriented cafés and restaurants are only part of the picture and, dotted across the city centre, are several excellent establishments where you can enjoy the very best of Spanish cuisine. If you're looking for breakfast, scores of downtown cafés, particularly at the top of Passeig des Born, serve up a mean *café con leche*.

Restaurants and tapas bars

L'Angel Blau, c/Del Capiscolat. Chic bar-restaurant with classical music and smooth-tasting *tapas*. You'll walk past the place en route from the cathedral to the Museo Diocesano. Moderately expensive.

Asador Tierra Aranda, Concepció 4, off Avda. Jaume III (☎971/714256). High-class restaurant housed within an old mansion. Specializes in roasted suckling lamb from Aranda. Expensive.

Bon Lloc, c/Sant Feliu 7 (☎971/718617). One of the few vegetarian restaurants on the island, centrally situated off the Passieg des Born. Informal atmosphere and good food at low prices.

Mesón Carlos I, c/Apuntadors 15. Traditional Spanish food in timber-vaulted old house – steaks are good here. Moderately expensive.

Cellar Sa Premsa, Bisbe Berengues de Palou 8 (☎971/723529). Immensely, and justifiably so, popular restaurant with delicious seafood situated 5min walk west of the Plaça d'Espanya. There are old bull fighting photos and posters on the walls, and you'll probably share a table with other diners. Surprisingly low prices.

Chez Sophie, c/Apuntadors. Stick to the crepes, of which there are a wide range from 400ptas.

Orient Express, Llotja De Mar, behind La Lotja. Idiosyncratic café-restaurant with an interior built like the inside of a railway carriage. Its slightly overpriced salads are its speciality, and you'll have to wait for a seat at lunchtime.

El Parlament, Conquistador 11 (☎971/726026). All gilt-wood mirrors and chandeliers, this old and polished restaurant specializes in *paella*. Expensive.

Raixa, Can Sayella 8 (☎971/711711). Wholesome, good-value vegetarian food, near Sant Eulària.

El Rey, Avda. Jaume III, opposite the Turismo. The best take-away pizza slices in town. Inexpensive.

La Bodega de Santurce, Concepió 34 (☎971/710801). Serves Basque dishes, but open lunch time only.

La Zamorama, c/Apuntadors 14. Inexpensive *tapas* in stucco cellar with hocks of meat hanging from the ceiling. One of several bars on this stretch of c/Apuntadors.

Bars and clubs

Just off c/Apuntadors is one of the world's most unusual **bars**. Called the *Abaco*, this offers an experience beyond mere drinking, with an interior like a Busby Berkeley musical: fruits cascading down its stairway, caged birds hidden amid patio foliage, elegant music and a daily flower bill you could live on for a month. Drinks, as you might imagine, are extremely expensive but you're never hurried into buying one. The entrance, easy to miss, is at c/Sant Joan 1.

Conventional **nightlife** takes place along the hotel mile of Avda. Joan Miró. This is not very promising, and can be ludicrously expensive (beware of eating *tapas* in the Plaça Gomila bars), but there's a fair selection of **discos** – both straight and gay – amid the souvenir shops and *hamburguesa* bars. Many of these are free to get in, though they make up for it behind the bar. US Navy personnel provide a rather bizarre leavening to Palman nightlife and two of their favourite haunts (one below the *Hostal Ritzi*, and *Texas Jack's* on Sant Feliu) are best avoided.

Listings

Banks are plentiful on and around the Passeig des Born and Avda. Jaume III. *American Express* is at *Viajes Iberia* at Passeig des Born 14.

Car rental Most car-rental companies have information desks at the airport and many have their main offices on Paseo Maritimo, out towards the port. These include *Betacar* (☎971/455111) at no. 20; *Avis* (☎971/730720) at no. 19 and *Iber-Auto* (☎971/285448) at no. 13. More central is *Rossello Moll*, c/Apuntadors 6; ☎971/721231).

Consulates The British Consulate is at Plaça Major 3 (☎971/712445); USA at Avda Jaume III 26 (☎971/722660); Irish at c/Sant Miquel 68A, 8° (☎971/719244); German at Passeig des Born 15, 6° (☎971/722371).

Laundry The most convenient self-service laundry is *Self-Press* at c/Anníbal 14, off Paseo Sagrera.

Post office The central *Correos* is at c/de la Constitució 6.

Telephones *Telefónica* is at c/de la Constitució 2.

Around Palma

For a **day out** from Palma, anywhere in the west or centre of the island is accessible, but if you're just after a quick **swim** you'll probably want to stick to the city's suburbs and its bay. From the Plaça d'Espanya and Avda. D'Antoni Maura there are almost continuous buses shuttling down to the big resorts. Locals tend to go east on the #15 bus to the individual *balneario* sections of **ARENAL**, where there's an enormously long if crowded sandy beach. Alternatively, you might conceivably be tempted by the Terreno suburb, 4km west of the centre, for its attractively ruined circular **Castell de Bellver**, set in a large park high above the sea and containing an archeological museum (Mon–Sat 8am–6pm).

Andratx, San Telm and Port d'Andratx

Inland from Palma bay, you could certainly find worse ways to spend an afternoon than hopping on a bus to **ANDRATX**, a small, unaffected town huddled among the hills to the west. From here one of the Turismo's easiest and most enjoyable **treks** will take you on through the village of S'Arraco to the ruinous castle of Sant Telm, and eventually into the tiny port of **SANT TELM**. From the pretty little harbour, boat trips shuttle up and down the coast and across to the rocky, off-shore islet of *Illa Dragonara*. Boats from Sóller dock here too, so the island can get pretty crowded, especially its finest fish restaurants, the *Garangol*, *Panoramic* and the *Vistamar*, which features a particularly good *menú del día*. There are just two *hostales*, the *Aquamarin* (☎971/671075; ④), a package tour destination, and the *Dragonera* (☎971/671886; ③), close to the sandy beach.

Also from Andratx, buses make the five-kilometre trip west to **PORT D'ANDRATX**, a working port with a good selection of expensive seafood restaurants spread out along the gritty waterfront. There are less expensive places round the main square too – try *La Café* or the *tapas* at the bar *Garcia*. If you want to stay, try *Hostal Bellavista* (☎971/671625; ③), *Catalina Vera* (☎971/671918; ③) or *Los Palmeras* (☎971/672078; ③).

Banyalbufar

Eighteen kilometres northwest from Palma, **BANYALBUFAR** is a small village clinging to the cliffs over the sea (you need your own vehicle to get there). The small beach is framed by tidy terraces that have existed since Moorish times and there are a couple of family-run hotels, *Baronia* (☎971/610121; ③) and *Sa Coma* (☎971/618034; ④), whose restaurants also serve tasty seafood. From the village, it's a strenuous trek north along the coast to **Port d'es Canonge**, a miniscule harbour where local fishermen unload their daily catches.

Algaida and the monastery of Nostra Senyora de Cura

Heading east of Palma, out towards Manacor, **ALGAIDA** also offers an attractive day trek. Taking the 4km-long minor road leading southeast from the town, you reach the village of **RANDA** at the start of a winding track up the **Puig Randa**, the highest mountain in this part of the island. Near the top, a fifteen-minute drive or two-hour trek, is the **monastery of Nostra Senyora de Cura** (Nuestra Señora de Cura), an active Franciscan monastery which lets out basic cells with amazing views (☎971/660994).

Western Mallorca

The 36-kilometre journey from **Palma to Sóller** is enjoyable in itself, especially if you do it on the train (*Autocares Llompart* also provides an indirect, slightly less scenic bus service 5 times daily). The rail line, constructed on the profits of the nineteenth-century orange and lemon trade, is a delight, dipping and cutting through the mountains and fertile valleys of the **Sierra de Tramuntana**. In January and February, the first half-hour is spent passing through vast almond groves in full bloom. The rolling stock, too, is tremendous: narrow carriages which in the first-class sections seem straight out of Agatha Christie novels. There are five departures daily (six from Sóller), the whole ride taking just under an hour and a half.

Sóller

At **SÓLLER** the tracks end, and a tram – another open, wooden thing which looks like
a refuge from a theme park (in fact it's ex-San Francisco rolling stock from the
Thirties) – takes over for a rumbling, five-kilometre journey down to the **port** (24 daily
each way from 6am–9pm, roughly every 30min). Sóller town is a pretty place of eighteenth-century town houses, very much in keeping with its transport, with a small,
newly restored **Museu Municipal** and a few small **hotels**. *El Guía*, c/Castañer 3, a
beautiful one-star hotel, just west of the station; (☎971/630227; ③), *Hostal Nadal*, c/
Romaguera 27; (☎971/631180; ②) and *Casa de Huéspedes Margarita Trías Vives*, c/
Real 3, near *El Guía* (②) are all worth trying, and all are more likely to have room than
anywhere down at the port. If you're desperate, the local *Associao Sóllerica* (Social
Club) also lets out hostel-type beds. Lowest priced **meals** are served at the *Bar Oasis*,
below the Plaça Constitucio by the tram tracks, though the best **eating** for miles
around is again at *El Guía*, even if the conversation (when in English) at adjoining
tables tends to outdo Noel Coward. There are also several good cafés and bars
surrounding the main square: in particular – *Es Firo* and *Café Paris*. If you're staying
here for a few days, you can sign up (two days in advance) for a guided walk; these
leave from the *Ajuntament* on the Plaça Constitucio and are graded from "easy" (8km)
to "tiresome and difficult" (18km).

Port de Sóller

PORT DE SÓLLER, however, is where most people head for, and its curling picture-
postcard bay must be about the most photographed spot on the island after the package hangouts of Magalluf. *Club 18–30* antics are about the last thing imaginable down
here, though; the place is almost stiflingly staid. There's no point in staying just for the
swimming either, since although the water is warm and calm, it's surprisingly murky
(courtesy of the yachts at anchor), and the beach is overlooked on all sides – by the
road, hotels and restaurants. If you can, it's better to base yourself in Deiá or Sóller
proper and bus it to better beaches.

Outside of peak season there's a chance of a reasonably priced **room** at the *Hotel
Miramar*, c/Marina 12 (☎971/631350; ③) opposite the tram stop, and at the *Generoso*,
c/Marina 12 (☎971/631450; ②). One of the best places, with a laid-back atmosphere
and enormous help-yourself breakfasts, is the *Primavera*, c/Puerto (☎971/630184; ③),
about 3km out of town towards Sóller town. In July or August you've little hope. As far
as **food and fun** go, Port de Sóller has lots of fine seafood restaurants overlooking the
bay; try the *Es Raco*. *Bar Piata* offers its own herbal liqueur as well as a range of
Mallorcan dishes, whilst the young (at heart) congregate at the noisy *Bar El Bianco*
before pressing on to even livelier bars such as *Patio*, *St Germain* and *Altamar*.

There are regular **boat trips** along the coast - south to Sant Telm and Illa Dragonera
(1 daily) and north to Sa Calobra (3 daily) – as well as frequent glass-bottom boat
cruises and excursions to Deià.

Biniaraix and Fornalutx

The most obvious excursions from Sóller are to two villages to the east. **BINIARAIX**,
just 2km away, is tiny – virtually a hamlet – but self-contained and large enough to have
a small central square, off which is a *mallorquín* rarity: a *taberna*. Here the proprietor
squeezes fresh orange juice and sells (factory) ice cream. You can sit at wooden tables
watching the sun stream in the windows; no video games, no TV, no hulking *señoritos*
smoking at the bar – altogether a nice change.

FORNALUTX, reached from Biniaraix via a narrow backroad, is touted as the most attractive village on the island, and unfortunately is beginning to realize it. You'll find an expensive restaurant or two, numerous bars, and as many postcards for sale as in Sóller, plus *Hostal Fornalux*, c/de L'Arba (⑤), a relaxing and comfortable place to stay. Almost a quarter of the village's three hundred houses are foreign-owned, but it's still worth coming this far just to wander the streets between the honey-coloured stone houses, and to watch the fish swimming in the orange-grove irrigation tanks on the way up. The stream beds run, as do most of the watercourses in the Sóller valley, until midsummer.

Deià and around

Southwest of Sóller, **Route 710** rambles through orchards of fruit, almond, olive and carob trees, occasionally plummeting down to the sea. You briefly skim the coast at Lluc-Alcari and then climb up to the village of **DEIÀ**, high in the hills and tucked at the base of formidable cliffs. Famed in every guidebook as the former home of Robert Graves (his grave, marked simply *"Robert Graves: Poeta"*, is in the churchyard at the top of the hill). Much later, Deià was also a focus for British hippie rock bands in the 1960s. The village itself is very much the haunt of long-term expatriates, mostly ex-flower children and artistes living on ample trust funds, judging from the sorts of monthly rents charged.

Of the two places catering to overnighters, *Fonda Villa Verde* (☎971/639037; ② including breakfast) has beautiful premises on the edge of the church-hill cluster; *Pensión Miramar* is situated up the hill on the far side of the road (☎971/639084; ②) with huge suppers included.

Deià has a beach of sorts, the **Cala de Deià**, some 200m of pebbles with two good café-bars. It's beautiful for a swim, the water clean, deep and cool, but it often gets crowded, and you may have to sit on the boathouse ramps to either side of the cove. The fastest way to get there from Deià proper is to take the stepped street down from the wash trough on the main road to the archeological museum, then follow the road beside the stream bed until this ends at a private gate. The well-marked onward path begins just to the right; it's less than half an hour's walk down to the water, as opposed to over an hour on the ugly new road. There's also a boat from Sóller.

You may have better luck with rooms and swimming at **LLUC-ALCARI**, which is in any case the best local beach for Deià. The hotel here, *La Costa d'Or* (☎639025; ③), is reasonably priced by island standards, especially considering it has a pool, and the beach is reached through a gate marked "No Entry" at the bottom of its garden. A bizarre but very wonderful feature of the Lluc-Alcari beach is its natural mud bath, formed by a pure mountain stream trickling through the rich red earth. You can coat yourself in this and later wash the sun-dried mud pack off in the sea.

ROBERT GRAVES IN DEIA

Robert Graves lived in Deià from the end of World War II until his death in 1985. This was his second stay, the first – in the 1930s – was when he shared his house at the edge of the village with Laura Riding, co-author of *A Survey of Modernist Poetry*. American-born, Riding came to England in 1926 and, after she become Graves's secretary and collaborator, the two of them had an affair. The tumultuous course of their relationship created sufficient furore for them to decide to leave England and they supposedly chose Mallorca on the advice of Gertrude Stein. Graves and Riding were forced to leave Mallorca in 1936, and their relationship ended in 1939.

Walking in the Tramuntana

These few coves apart, Mallorca's northwest coast, from Banyalbufar to Cala Sant Vicenç, is mostly sheer, with the gnarled ridge of the **Sierra de Tramuntana** dropping straight to the sea. The ridge provides the best walking on Mallorca, with Sóller (or alternatively Deià) ideally positioned as overnight bases about midway along. It's a trekker's paradise as long as you don't venture out in midsummer, when water is scarce.

If you're interested, there's a plethora of **information for walkers** available in various languages and paths are well marked (though apt to be thornbush-clogged). Useful books available locally include *Twelve Classic Hikes on Mallorca* (sold in the Sóller bookshop) and *Guía de Sóller* from the Turismo.

Short walks from Sóller

The **Cornadors circuit**, starting from Sóller, is an easy introduction, climbing up via the S'Arrom farm to the Cornadors *mirador* and from there down to the L'Ofre plateau, followed by a descent along wonderful old steps through the Es Barranc canyon. You finish in Biniaraix in just under five hours, with an option to continue to Fornalutx on the signposted *Cami d'es Marroig*.

Leaving Sóller in almost the opposite direction, you can follow the **Camino Viejo to Cala Tuent**. The first leg involves climbing up to C'an Costure, and from there past the Mirador de Ses Barcs (also on Route 710 heading northeast) to the enchanted Balitx valley. After dropping down to the lowest of three farms there, you toil briefly up to the Coll de Biniamar, where you can detour to Sa Costera villa on a cliff, for spring water and views over the most spectacular portion of the northwest coast.

The main route continues parallel to the shore until **Cala Tuent**, one of the sandiest and quietest of the northern beaches, though also rather dirty. There's a single bar-restaurant, and it's possible to continue another hour to Sa Calobra (see p.746). It will take four hours to reach Cala Tuent, unless you cheat and take a bus to Mirador de Ses Barcs.

You can also take a scenic route **from Sóller to Deià** in just under three hours by following the rather complicated but accurate instructions in the *Guía de Sóller*. The trail, a real beauty with stunning views over the ocean and intervening farms, winds along a few hundred metres inland from the coast road. The path finally intersects the highway between Lluc-Alcari and Deià, giving you a choice of swimming spots and easy access to buses back to Sóller.

The Camino del Archiduque and more ambitious treks

By using the morning bus south to Valldemossa, the famous **Camino del Archiduque** is easily accessible. After an initial ascent to the Mirador de Ses Puntes, you turn right and take the ridge above Deià to follow the stone-laid *camino*, a gem of romantic nineteenth-century engineering commissioned by an eccentric Austrian aristocrat whose villa at Son Marroig below is now on the bus tour circuit. His private promenade ends after traversing the rather bleak "roof of the island" on the edge of 400m drops, at the start of the detour east to **Teix peak**. The main route dips down into the Cairats valley, past a hut and the only water since the start, to finish in Valldemossa (5–6hr, including detour up Teix) in time for the afternoon bus back to Sóller.

The descent of the **Torrent de Pareis** is perhaps the most popular "stunt" on Mallorca. From the restaurant at **Escorca**, where the bus drops you, you traverse an awesome limestone gorge, emerging at the seaward end on the touristified beach of Sa Calobra. This outing is not practicable in winter or spring, when the river can be waist-high; otherwise high-school groups do it regularly, and its difficulty has been somewhat exaggerated in most of the existing literature. Some Class 3 scrambling and a head for boulder hopping is required, as there are half a dozen places where ten-foot drops require nerve and suppleness, but it's not too much of a problem as long as the rocks are dry. **Sa Calobra**, where you arrive after four or more hours, is a bit of a letdown (busloads of tourists) but at least you can have a swim while awaiting the boat back to Sóller.

Now that Puig Major has a radar station on top and is off-limits, **Puig de Massanella** (1349m) is the highest peak that can be climbed on Mallorca. On the Pollença-bound bus from Sóller ask to be set down as close as possible to the service station before Lluc, from where it's a four-and-a-half-hour round trip, with no complications and a permanent spring near the summit. Northern Mallorca is prone to mists, which may spoil the view, but they usually lift at some point in the day. Catch the same bus on its way back to Sóller.

Transport to trailheads

Two **buses**, run by different companies, ply Route 710. They are invaluable to trekkers, though some of their daily frequencies leave a bit to be desired. *Autocares Llompart* serves the line Sóller–Deyá–Valldemossa five times a day in each direction year-round; in Sóller town the terminal is on the round Plaça América, 600m down the Gran Vía from the post office. Another line leaves here daily at 9am (except Sunday) going via the Port to the Mirador de Ses Barcs, Escorca, the foot of Puig Massanella and Lluc monastery before finishing at Pollensa. The same vehicle turns round at 4pm in Port de Pollença to retrace its route, arriving in Sóller just after 6pm.

The Cartuja de Valldemossa

The **Cartuja de Valldemossa** (Mon–Sat 9.30am–1pm & 3–6.30pm) – the island's most famous building after Palma Cathedral – owes its notoriety almost entirely to the novelist George Sand who, with her companion Frédéric Chopin, made her home here for four months from 1838 to 1839. Their stay in the monastery is commemorated in Sand's *Winter in Majorca*, a book that tends to be a little overplayed here, being available in just about every European language. The couple were hardly appreciative of their Spanish neighbours. In the book, Sand explains that their nickname for Mallorca, "Monkey Island", was coined for its "crafty, thieving and yet innocent" inhabitants. By the time the pair arrived, the *Cartuja* had been abandoned by its monks, and the cells in which they stayed can hardly have been spartan, judging by present standards. Bright, sizeable rooms, they all look out onto a private garden and magnificent views, a fact that's been rather cleverly exploited, along with the romantic connotations, in selling various nearby holiday villas. The grounds of the *Cartuja* are peaceful and there's an obvious curiosity in looking round Sand and Chopin's quarters, with their miscellaneous collections of manuscripts and, of course, Chopin's piano. After three months of unbelievable complications, the piano arrived, less than three weeks before they both left for Paris. Also on display is the old **monastic pharmacy**, decked out in slightly bogus fashion, and a small **municipal museum** with displays on Mallorcan social history.

The *Hostal C'Am Mario* is the only affordable place to stay in Valldemossa (☎971/ 612122; ④), and even this charges pretty steeply – though the price does include breakfast. There are regular buses (*Autocares Llompart*) up from Palma, and you can take these onward – or hitch, or walk – to Deià (10km), Lluc-Alcari and Sóller; one bus a day also comes from Peguera. The closest spot for a swim is **Port de Valldemossa**, but it's a rocky shore and no public transport covers the 5km down to the water. Near Valldemossa is the site of **Son Matge**, a rock shelter used by Stone Age people around 8500 years ago. Initially home to a succession of prehistoric families, it later became a cemetery.

Northern Mallorca

Beyond a doubt the most interesting approach to the northern tip of the island – to Pollença, Lluc and Alcúdia – is the continuation of **Route 710 beyond Sóller**, skirting the edge of the Sierra de Tramuntana. If you've rented a vehicle, or if you're taking this in two stages, you'll be able to stop along the way at the **Monastery of Lluc** (see p.748).

The more direct **central route**, which the rail line follows as far as Inca and Sa Pobla, is rather less memorable. **Inca** itself is heavily promoted for its distilleries, leather factories and Thursday market – all called to your attention on a series of billboards along the way, but it's an ugly town that's best avoided unless you're a devotee of leather goods. Beyond, around **Sa Pobla**, there's a more attractive look to the landscape – arable land liberally scattered with windmills – and at **Muro** is one of Mallorca's more interesting crafts museums, complete with an original Moorish patio and water wheel, and comprehensive exhibits from forge and field.

Badia de Pollença

Development in this northern corner of Mallorca has focused on the beach of **Cala De Sant Vicenç**, once among the best on the island. **Pollença bay**, across the peninsula (and the last reach of the Tramuntana), is surprisingly unspoiled. Much of its coast is inaccessible – like so much of the north – but by no means all of it. At both **PORT DE POLLENÇA** and **CAP DE FORMENTOR** there are excellent sandy coves.

As a base for these beaches, you've a choice between the quiet inland town of **POLLENÇA** and its port, 7km distant. The town is dominated by a striking **shrine of Calvary**. It's reached by 365 steps which the faithful and penitent climb on their knees past the various stations of the Cross, though the unrepentant can now drive up in a couple of minutes. The only other attraction is a small museum dedicated to local artist **Miguel Costa Lloberra**, in the street of the same name, but to visit you have to have had the foresight to write in advance. From the 250-metre-high summit there's a tremendous view over the coast, all the way up to both northern capes. Perhaps better than the view is the **monastery** attached to the shrine, constructed in 1348 and alternately abandoned and restored by both monks and nuns of various orders. Unfortunately the rooms here no longer seem to be rented out – but it's worth enquiring, as this used to be one of the most attractive places to stay on the island (albeit a little spartan).

As such, there's little to halt your onward or upward progress, though Pollença is a pleasant enough place to stop off and **eat**. The restaurant by the Torrente San Jordi, still crossed by a Roman bridge, is good and economical; much more expensive, but with well-prepared food and a spectacular herbal liqueur is the *Daus* on the steps to the Calvary. Nearby, *Bar Elgallitos* has live jazz every Tuesday night. There are no hotels in Pollença, until the *Hostal Juma* (☎971/530007; ③) reopens for business after its refurbishment.

Three kilometres to the south is the superb *Sanctuario Puig de María* (☎971/530235; ①), where the original monks' cells have been renovated to provide simple accommodation. Founded in 1348, the monastery has ben alternately abandoned and restored by both monks and nuns of various orders. Today's premises include a small basilica, refectory and the cells, all perched on top of a hill with great views out along the coast, and the food is great too. To get there, cut off the main Pollença–Palma road south of town and head up the steep two-kilometre track which leads to the cobbled path winding up to the monastery entrance. The proposed funicular will soon open up this quiet spot.

Port de Pollença

Over at **PORT DE POLLENÇA** things are a little more lively, though still pleasantly low-key. The port has something of a split personality: the bad points are the *Pollença Park Hotel* complex (airport lounge-style), the considerable development going on at the edge of town, and the noisy Alcúdia road which runs along the seaside area. Overall, however, the place is very appealing, especially the pedestrianized Avda. Anglada Camarasa, along the waterside. Once again there's a minor art museum, devoted this time to the Chagallish daubings of the Catalan **Anglada Camarasa** (d. 1959); it's at Passeig D'Anglada Camarasa 87, open afternoons except Wednesday and Sunday. But the sea and the **coves** are the main attraction, reached either by road or by one of the regular boat-taxis that ply their way down to Cap de Formentor and one of the island's best beaches at **Platja de Formentor**. On the Formentor road you'll soon come to the *Hotel Formentor*, with a good sandy beach but crowds of Pollença-based tourists. Back in town, the beaches are narrow but not too crowded except near *Pollença Park*.

Places to stay here are slightly expensive but there are several reasonable options: the *Hostal Coro* (☎971/865005; ②) and the *Hostal Banza* (☎971/865474; ②) are in the town centre, and, a few minutes' walk along the Alcúdia road is *Hostal Galeon* (☎971/865703; ③), which has sea views. The **Turismo** (☎971/207470) in Plaça Miguel Capllond, has local information and accommodation lists. You can rent **mopeds** and **motorcycles** from *March* on c/Juan XXIII (☎971/864784) and **mountain bikes** from *María's*, Roger de Flor, off c/Juan XXIII.

There are plenty of **restaurants**: the best and most expensive is the *Becfi* on Avda. Anglada Camarasa, apparently visited by both Pete Townshend and King Juan Carlos. The *Pizzeria Llenaire* on the Alcúdia road serves good, inexpensive pizzas and is better than the *Cafetería Mestral* on the front. *Bar-Restaurante Mibar*, on the way to Formentor, has a reasonably priced *menú*. The night scene is gentle – there's a poor **disco** at the *Pollença Park Hotel* and another, the *Chivas*, on Metge Llopis off the main square, which is free (expensive drinks). The best place to hang out, though, is the *Bar Pascalinos* on Avda. Anglada Camarasa: beachfront location, reasonable prices and a young clientele (many Palmese spend the summer in Port de Pollença). The place swings until around 3am.

The Boquer Valley

The road on to the cape is spectacular, passing through a totally uninhabited area with beautiful views. After a kilometre or two, keep an eye out for a farm perched above on the left, with a track up to it starting opposite Avda. Bocharis. An obvious path, beginning from a nearby iron gate, leads through the **Boquer Valley**, a favourite of ornithologists and a possible place to camp if Port de Pollença is full. After about 45 minutes you reach a small, shingly **beach** offering good swimming in clean water (though the shore may be rubbish-strewn). For triathlon trainees, there's a **grotto**, on the right as you face the sea but not visible from the shore, which takes almost half an hour to reach – with flippers. Look for a black discolouration on the cliffs; close up, the entrance is a mere 4m wide with perhaps a foot of clearance above sea level. Once inside, and accustomed to the unearthly light, you find yourself in a cavern some 7m by 15m, with the ceiling 10m high. This can be a risky adventure though, and you shouldn't attempt it unless you know what you're doing.

Monastery of Lluc

From Pollença, its port or from Sóller, the **MONASTERY OF LLUC** is an easy excursion. The largest monastic complex on the island, its thirteenth-century statue of the Virgin, *La Moreneta*, also makes it Mallorca's principal place of pilgrimage. The big attraction for the less devout is the site – a spectacular outreach of the Tramuntana – and the individualist contributions of **Antoni Gaudí**. Gaudí was responsible for the monuments marking the stations of the Cross on the route to the shrine, and also for some imaginative adaptations to the Baroque interior of the main church. This is open daily from around 10am to 7pm, along with a splendidly eclectic **museum**, mixing displays of Bronze Age pots and artefacts with an episcopal fashion show to rival Fellini's *Roma*.

Accommodation at the monastery is highly organized, featuring self-contained **apartment cells** with the use of a kitchen and dining room; in summer they're becoming popular so phone ahead if you want to be sure of space (☎971/517025; ②), or settle for the monastic **campsite**. Stay here between mid-September and early June and you'll also catch a **boy's choir** performance, as remorselessly touted as Sand and Chopin are at Valldemossa, and constantly piped in to greet new arrivals in the car and coach park. In addition to the daily bus from Sóller (leaving 9am, returning from Port de Pollença at 4pm), there's a further April–October bus service from Port de Pollença. This leaves at 10am, returning from Sóller at 4.30pm, allowing you ample time at the monastery and its surroundings.

Badia d'Alcúdia

The beaches around the **Badia de Alcúdia** are longer and more numerous than Pollença's, and shoreline developments reflect this – not to any disastrous extent, however. Again, both town and port make good bases and are regularly served by buses from Palma.

PORT D'ALCÚDIA is inevitably where the action is – a growing resort whose clutch of discos and bars attracts crowds from the high-rise hotels and *urbanizaciones* off to the south. Should you want to stay at the port, there's a vague chance of a bed in three reasonably priced **hostales**: *Calma* (☎971/545343; ③), *Puerto* (☎971/545447; ②) and *Vista Alegre* (☎971/547347; ②). If these are full you could try 1km east at Aucanada – *Hostal Aucanada*, c/S'Illot (☎971/545402; ③), or at Alcúdia town (see below), or you could **camp** – the island's one official ground is only 8km down the coast at **Platja Brava**, on the road, and bus route, to Ca'n Picafort (☎537863), and is well equipped, with a pool, though more expensive than most. The local **Turismo**, Avda. Pere Mas Reus (Mon–Sat 8.30am–1.30pm & 4–7pm, summer only) is a mine of information on just about all possible activities – moped and car rental, windsurfing and waterskiing sessions – all of which vary from one season to the next. The Alcúdia **beach** is pretty good, or for a little variety walk round the bay to Aucanada with its offshore island and abandoned lighthouse, swimmable from the shore. Don't forget, too, that Port d'Alcúdia has **ferries** to Ciutadella on Menorca (four daily); tickets are best booked in advance from *Flebasa* down at the harbour (☎971/546454, 546655).

Alcúdia town and around

Remains of Spain's smallest **Roman theatre** can be visited if you turn sharply to the left just before arriving at **ALCÚDIA** town, twenty minutes' walk from the port. This apart, you're most likely to come here in a quest for **accommodation**. The best budget option is the *Fonda Llabres* (☎545000; ②), above a pastry shop in the main plaza. An alternative is to make for the **Santuario La Vittoria**, an hour or so's walk towards Cab d'es Pinar, with a sporadically operating café-restaurant. The Santuario – or *Ermida* as it's known in *mallorquín* – is in any case an enjoyable walk. So are the marshes of **S'Albufera** immediately south of Alcúdia, seasonal home to over 200 different species of migratory birds. You need a permit to visit; further information from one of the Turismos in Palma.

Heading southeast from Alcúdia town and port, it's about 12km round the Badia d'Alcúdia to **Son Real**, an Iron Age cemetery dating from 600 BC; dozens of tombs cling to the seashore where part of the site has been swamped by the rising Mediterranean. If you have transport, **COLÒNIA DE SANT PERE** at the far end of the bay is a fishing village situated beneath the Artá mountain range; an hour's walk from here is the hillside hermitage of **Betlem**, but there's no accommodation, just picnic tables.

Eastern Mallorca

With more easily accessible beaches and an efficient public transport network from Palma, Mallorca's **east coast** is predictably developed. If you're after more than a metre of sand – or a bed for the night – stay away from mid-June until mid-September. On the other hand, if you're lucky enough to be here in spring or late autumn there are a handful of tempting propositions: **Canyamel** in the north, **Porto Cristo** and **Porto Petro** in the south. Inland, too, there are attractions in the hill town of **Artá**, the region around **Felanitx** and the packaged but impressive caves of **Drach**.

Manacor, Artá and the upper coast

MANACOR declares its business long before you arrive – vast roadside hoardings promote its furniture and artificial pearl factories. On the strength of these, the city has risen to become the second urban centre of Mallorca, a far smaller place than Palma but sprawling into suburbs on all sides. It's not exactly compelling, but this "life after tourism" does give Manacor an industrial independence distinctly lacking elsewhere. If you want to **stay** and commute to the sea (to Cala Millor, for example) there are a couple of reasonably priced possibilities: *Hostal Jacinto*, across from the cathedral (☎971/550124; ①) and *Can Guixa*, c/Alfareros 15 (②). Be warned, though, that others have the same idea.

Following the train line or main highway north brings you to a pair of hill towns: Artá and Capdepera. **ARTÁ**, where dilapidated streets of grandee mansions slope up towards the old fortress-hermitage of San Salvador, is worth a few minutes, and there are a couple of grisly **bars** here to delay your progress to the coast (buses leave from outside the *Bar Ca'n Balague*). After Artá, the main road cuts through the village of **CAPDEPERA** – a dusty, elongated village, crouched below a fine crenellated castle en route to the **Cap de Capdepera** and the massive and massively ugly resort of **CALA RATJADA**, whose excellent beach is a favourite haunt of German package tourists. What you won't find is a room. Almost every bed is agency-booked from Munich or Bonn, and though the Turismo is happy to give out lists of *hostales*, even they admit that these are useless in midsummer.

Beaches and caves south of Ratjada

The succession of **coves south** of Ratjada, notching the coast for 25km to **Porto Cristo**, are all touristified to some degree, usually for the worse. Finding a room in season is a problem almost anywhere and, to complicate matters further, the main road runs for the most part some way inland and even with transport, it's a time-consuming business getting from one cove to the next; if you're hitching or relying on buses you'll do best to pick one spot and stick with it.

Playa de Canyamel

PLAYA DE CANYAMEL, some 11km from Ratjada and 10km east of Artá, is the prettiest of these cove resorts, its neat modern villas draped around a pine-backed sandy beach. There's no high-rise here and the resort is of manageable proportions. Canyamel's principal **hostal** is the *Laguna* (☎971/563400; ④) stuck right against the beach. For **food**, try the *Isabel* restuarant. There's also a local sight, the **Cuevas de**

Artá (guided tours daily 9.30am–7pm, winter 10am–5pm; 600ptas), one of the best of numerous eastern Mallorcan caves, high up in the cliffs above the bay and with a majestic Gothic-horror stairway.

Porto Cristo

Moving further down the coast, past vineyards and groves of almonds, various roads converge on **PORTO CRISTO**, once an attractive fishing harbour but now a busy and cramped resort near the region's two big excursions. These, announced by multicoloured, multilingual billboards, are the **Cuevas del Hams** (summer only 10.30am–1.20pm & 2.45–4.30pm) and **Cuevas del Drach** (regular guided tours summer daily 10am–5pm; winter 10.30am–4pm; 700ptas), each of which includes underground concerts (more Chopin) in the price and endurance of a visit. You'd hardly want to see them both; opt for the *Drach* (Dragon) caverns. The lighting here is really very impressive, focused as it is on what the leaflet asserts is "Europe's largest underwater lake", and musicians drift about in boats playing harmoniums (performances at 10am, 11am, noon, 2pm, 3pm, 4pm & 5pm). If you have kids to entertain, Porto Cristo offers one further attraction, a well-stocked **aquarium** (daily 9am–7pm) where the glass tanks magnify such exotic horrors as electric eels, piranhas and stinging fish. If you want to **stay** in Porto Cristo, there are several hotels and *hostales* – try the *Estrella*, Currican 16 (☎971/820833; ④) or the *Felip*, Burdils 61 (☎971/820750; ④).

Felanitx and around Cap de Ses Salines

FELANITX, "capital" of the southeastern corner of the island, is an industrious town. It bottles wine, produces ceramics and manufactures pearls. If you stop – and you may need to change buses here if coming from Palma – sample the local *Ilet*, a wonderful pick-me-up made from milk, sugar and cinnamon, and served in most of the bars. If you're into walking, take the road out towards Porto Colom and turn off along the mountain road to the **Ermita de Sant Salvador** – another of the Palma Turismo's *Twenty Hiking Excursions*. You can rent **rooms** at the thirteenth-century monastery (☎971/827282) – which is recognizable from miles around by its massive *Creu* (Cross) *de Picot* and equally vast monument of Christ – and with a car this could make an interesting base for a few days. In any case, it's a magnificent location. You can usually get a meal at the hostelry and the monks will point you toward the path to the **Castillo de Santueri**, another good walk. From there you can loop back towards Felanitx or down towards the flower-dense village of **Cas Concos**.

Porto Colom to Cala Figuera

Down on the coast, northeast of Cap de Ses Salines, there's a string of resort-villages extending from Porto Colom in the north to Cala Figuera in the south. The largest is **PORTO COLOM**, a desultory fishing port looped around a deep bay, but this unenticing sprawl is only partly redeemed by its proximity to a couple of good **beaches**.There are a couple of non-agency-booked **hostales** here: *Porto Colom* (☎971/825323; ②) and *Bahía Azul* (☎971/575180; ③), with an excellent, not too pricey restaurant.

Heading south, past highly exploited **Cala Ferrera** and **Cala d'or**, **PORTO PETRO** is much smaller and far more attractive, its rocky harbour framed by hills and plush villas. **Rooms** here, though, are sparse; the only real possibility is the two-star *Hostal Nereida* (☎971/657223; ③/④), a comfortable place with pool, though you might also try the simpler *Hostal Roca Blanca* (☎971/657521; ③).

At **CALA FIGUERA** development is considerably more advanced, but the adjoining coves of **Llombards** and **Santanyi** give reasonable escape from the crowds and good access to camping spots. Official **accommodation** is harder to come by and slightly more expensive, though *Hostal Oliver* (☎971/645127; ③) does have some non-agency rooms. Inland lie the main vineyards of Felanitx's wine industry, with high stone walls enclosing narrow straight roads, vines and almond trees. The mustard-yellow stone quarried round here was used for several Palmese buildings, including the cathedral.

The southern shore

Past **Cap de Ses Salines** there's less of promise. The entire southeastern tip of the island is owned by the Spanish banking magnate Joan March, who preserves much of it as a private nature reserve. At **COLÓNIA DE SANT JORDI**, reached from the inland village of Ses Salines (which is itself owned by March), there's a new and growing *urbanización* – not much fun. **SA RAPITA**, with the best beach on this stretch, **Es Trenc** reached by road from Campos, is mainly holiday villas. So too is **CALA PÍ**, whose chalets are clustered above hard to reach coves. From here, a rough minor road leads the 4km northwest to the prehistoric remains of **Capicorp Vell** before joining the main coastal route at Capicorp itself. Beyond lies the dreary 24-km trip along the empty southeast shore of the Badia de Palma – meeting the teeming hotel strip at **S'Arenal**.

MENORCA

Second largest of the Balearics, **MENORCA** has the greatest number of reminders of its prehistoric past (see introduction to "Mallorca"): crude stone remains that litter much of the landscape. The island also has its share of modern crudity in its tourist villages and resorts that lie dotted along the coast. Fortunately, there's still the occasional undeveloped cove or beach and, more distinctive still, are the two main towns, **Maó** in the east and **Ciutadella** in the west, which have preserved much of their seventeenth- and eighteenth-century appearance.

Little is known of the island's prehistory, despite the omnipresent physical evidence; the monuments are thought to be linked to those of Sardinia and representative of the second-millennium BC Talayot culture. **Talayots** are the rock mounds found all over the island – popular belief has it that they functioned as watchtowers, but it's a theory few experts accept. They have no interior stairway, and only a few are found on the coast. Even so, no one has come up with a much more convincing explanation. The megalithic **taulas** – huge stones topped with another to form a T, around 4m high and unique to Menorca – are even more puzzling. They have no obvious function, and they are almost always found alongside a *talayot*. The best preserved *talayot* and *taula* remains are on the edge of Maó at the **Trepuco** site. Then there are **navetas** (dating from 1400 to 800 BC), stone-slab constructions shaped like an inverted loaf tin. Many have false ceilings, and although you can stand up inside they were clearly not living spaces – communal pantries, perhaps, or more probably tombs.

In more recent history, the deep-water channel of the port of Maó promoted Menorca to an important position in European affairs. The **British** saw its potential as a **naval base** during the War of the Spanish Succession and achieved their aim in having the island handed over to British rule under the Treaty of Utrecht (1713). Spain regained possession in 1783, but with the threat of Napoleon in the Mediterranean, a new British base was temporarily established under admirals Nelson and Collingwood. The British influence is still considerable, especially in architecture: the sash windows so popular in Georgian design are still sometimes referred to as *winderes*, locals often part with a fond *bye-bye*, and there's a substantial expatriate community (with several English-language magazines). The British also moved the capital from Ciutadella to Maó and constructed the main island road. More importantly they introduced the art of distilling juniper berries: Menorcan **gin** (*Xoriguer, Beltran* or *Nelson*) is renowned.

Before much of it was killed off by tourism, Menorcan **agriculture** had become highly advanced. Every field was protected by a dry stone wall to prevent the

tramóntana (the vicious north wind) from tearing away the topsoil; even olive trees have their roots individually protected in a little stone well. Nowadays, apart from a few acres of rape and corn, many of the fields are barren, but the walls survive. Any vegetation that dares to emerge above their safety is instantly swept away by the gusts.

Menorca practicalities

Menorca is boomerang shaped, stretching from the enormous natural harbour of Maó in the east to the smaller port of Ciutadella in the west. **Bus routes** are distinctly limited, adhering mostly to the main central road between these two, occasionally branching off to the larger coastal resorts. You'll need your own vehicle to get to any of the more attractive beaches. There are one or two points to remember, though. To reach any of the emptier sands you'll probably have to drive down a track fit only for four-wheel drive – and the wind, which can be very helpful when it's blowing behind you, is distinctly uncomfortable if you're trying to ride into it on a moped. Bear in mind too that petrol stations are strategically placed (ie few and far between) across the island. After 10pm and on Sundays and fiestas, you'll be lucky to find anywhere open so plan ahead: it's no fun to be stuck in Mercadal if you're staying in Maó and the only *gasolinera* open is in Ciutadella.

Accommodation is at an exploited premium, with little of anything outside the bigger coastal resorts and towns. Once you find something reasonable, stay there. Advance booking is essential in August.

Maó

MAÓ (MAHÓN), the island capital, is likely to be your first port of call. It's a respectable, almost dull little town, the people restrained and polite. So is the architecture: an unusual hybrid of classical Georgian sash-windowed town houses and tall, gloomy Spanish apartment blocks shading the narrow streets. Port it may be, but there's no seamy side to Maó – and the harbour is home to a string of restaurants and cafés that attract tourists in their droves.

Arrival, information and accommodation

The **airport** (short on amenities and served only by taxi, 800ptas) is just 5km out. If you arrive by **ferry** from Barcelona or Palma you'll sail straight into Maó's vast natural harbour here. The **ferry** offices are down at the port (*Transmediterránea* ☎971/362950) and the **airlines** are basesd at the airport (☎971/360150). **Turismo** (Mon–Fri 9am–2pm & 5–7pm, Sat 9.30am–1pm) in the Plaça Esplanada can provide maps of Maó, Ciutadella and the island, and should also have leaflets giving details of accommodation, car rental, banks, beaches and so on.

Maó is linked by **bus** to Ciutadella via Alaior and Ferreríes (6 daily); to Es Mitjorn and Sant Tomás (1 a day); to Es Castell (every 30min, 7.20am–8.45pm); to Sant Climent and Cala En Porter (10 daily); to Punta Prima via Sant Luis (9 a day); to Son Bou via Alaior (5); to Fornells (3); and to Arenal d'en Castell (3). This sounds like plenty, but to get to the really good beaches you still need your own transport; there are abundant **car rental** places around the centre, but even so it's very hard to get anything in August. It may prove marginally easier to find a **Vespa** or **Mobylette** – try *Gelabert*, Avda. J A Clavé 12 (☎971/360614)). For car rental, try *Autos Confort*, Avda. J A Clavé 56 (☎971/369470), *Autos Pons*, Avda. J A Clavé 157 (☎971/366879); or *Ibercars*, Vasallo 44 (☎971/364208).

Accommodation

If possible you should fix up **a room** in advance – certainly in August – and be prepared to pay over the odds as island prices, thanks to excessive demand, tend to be inflated. On the other hand Maó, along with Cuitadella, is your best bet for bargain accommodation, and those possibilities that exist are all fairly central. The best place to start looking is around Plaça Reial: try c/Infanta with *Hostal Orsi* at no. 19 (☎971/364751; ③) or c/Comerç just off here where you'll find *Hostal Reynes* at no. 26 (☎971/364059; ②). Calle del Carme is another good bet, off Plaça Princep; *Hostal Roca* is at no. 37 (☎971/350839; ②) and *Sa Roqueta* at no. 122 (☎971/364335; ②), or there's *Sheila*, at c/Santa Cecilia 41, just off Carme (☎971/64855; ③). There's not a lot to choose between these *hostales*, and they do tend to be rather basic, but Maó also has pricier alternatives, including the *Noa*, Cos de Gracia 157 (☎971/361200; ④), though this is further from the centre, and the unimaginatively modern *Capri* (☎971/361400; ⑤), a three-star hotel at Sant Estebe 8.

The town

While you'll need transport to get around the island, Maó itself is best seen on foot. Its compact centre, with its deep streets rising high above the water's edge, is no more than ten minutes' walk from top to bottom. Maó's fine setting and its crowded old mansions are its charm – rather than any specific sight – and you can explore the place thoroughly in a day. From near the ferry terminal, set beneath the cliff that supports the remains of the city wall, a generous stone stairway leads up to four small squares that are practically adjacent to each other. The first, the **Plaça d'Espanya**, offers views right across the port and bay. Immediately to the left is the **Plaça del Carme**, with a simple Carmelite church whose cloisters have been adapted to house the town's fresh fish, fruit and vegetable **market**, where you can also sample local cheeses including *queso de Mahón* .They're made from cow's milk, with a touch of ewe's milk to add extra flavour, and sold at various stages of maturity: young (*tierno*); mature (*curado*); and very mature (*anejo*). The museum at the back of the cloister is hopeless. In the other direction from Plaça d'Espanya lie the Plaça de la Conquesta and the Plaça de la Constitució.

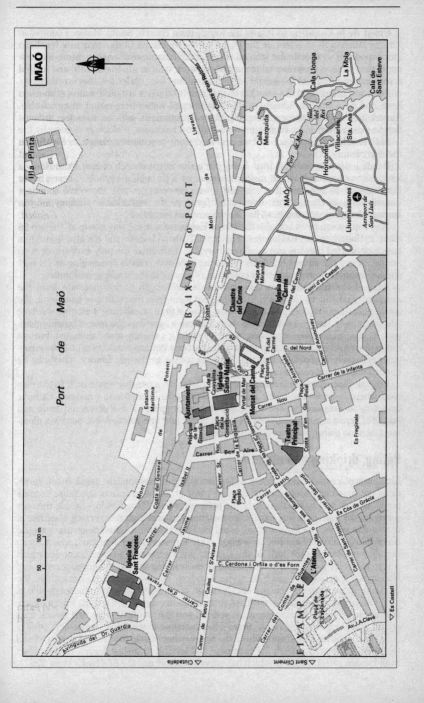

Plaça de la Constitució boasts the town's main church, **Santa María**. Founded in 1287 by Alfonso III to celebrate the island's Reconquest, its Gothic structure has been much modified – in particular with an unremarkable Baroque altarpiece. More interesting is the organ, a monumental piece of woodwork built in Austria in 1810 and lugged across half of Europe at the height of the Napoleonic wars under the concerned charge of Admiral Collingwood. Its four keyboards and 3000 pipes are quite out of proportion here, and it's a pity the Admiral couldn't have found somewhere rather more suitable. Almost next door is the seventeenth-century **Ajuntament**, with an attractive arcaded facade dating from 1788, handsome wrought-iron balconies, a clock presented by the island's first British governor and an inscribed stone proclaiming Roman occupation in the first century AD.

Heading down c/Isabel II from here, you arrive at the church of **San Francesc** – a long, narrow approach which makes it appear as if through a keyhole. There's a fine Romanesque facade, but the confined space prevents its full appreciation. Inside (usually Sun 8–11am, other days after 6pm) is the remarkable **Chapel of the Immaculate Conception** in all its *Churrigueresque* splendour.

Maó's main square is actually the **Plaça Esplanada**, some way above all the streets along c/Hannover and c/Moreres. The main Turismo is here and it's also home to a bunch of overfed pigeons and a military barracks. Otherwise the only excitement is on Sunday, when the square becomes the social hub, with crowds converging on its bars and ice cream parlours, and street entertainers playing to the strolling multitudes.

Back at the **harbour**, you can walk the entire length of the quayside from the *Xoriguer* gin distillery (Mon–Fri 8am–7pm, Sat 9am–1pm; free with free samples in the shop) near the ferry dock to the southeast edge of town, a half-hour walk that will take you past a long string of restaurants, bars and cafés as well as the town's bulging marinas. By day, this makes a relaxing stroll; at night it's slightly more animated, but not much. Alternatively, a **boat trip** around the harbour (for around 800ptas) can be enjoyable, especially if you take one that includes a visit to the gin factory. They can be booked at most travel agents.

Leaving Plaça Esplanada along Avda. J A Clavé, it's a twenty-minute walk to the ring road where – across the traffic island – a twisting lane leads past a massive Catholic cemetery to **Trepuco**, a prehistoric site that incorporates a well-preserved *taula* and *talayot*. There's a certain excitement if this is the first one you've seen, but it's a pleasure that soon palls if you repeat the exercise.

Eating, drinking and nightlife

Maó has a place in culinary history as the birthplace of **mayonnaise** (*mahonesa*), something not much in evidence these days, as most of the **restaurants** specialize in traditional Spanish and Italian dishes. In the town centre, on Plaça Bastió – beside the only surviving city gate, Sant Roc – there are two friendly bar-restaurants serving basic fare at reasonable prices; the *Pigalle* at no. 4 and *Sa Placeta* at no. 14. Just below the gate, *La Dolce Vita* pizzeria at Sant Roc 25 is good value and serves excellent food, whilst, down the alley on the opposite side of the square, there's the *Mos i Glop*, Alaior 10, which serves mediocre food, but its outdoor tables overlooking the paved shopping area of c/Nou make it a pleasant place to nurse a coffee. The *Nou Bar* and, beneath it, the *S'Oficina*, close by, on the corner of c/Nou and c/Hannover, are lively and enjoyable as well. Other than these, the majority of restaurants are down by the port, where expensive French cuisine, local *tapas*, good seafood and the standard steak and french fries are all available. Amongst many, there's the excellent *Roma*, Moll Llevant 295 (☎971/353777), a popular tourist spot where the Spanish and Italian food is well prepared and the menu reasonably priced; the expensive and lavishly furnished *Jagaro*, further down Moll Llevant (☎971/362390), which has superb seafood: and the *El Alsador* at no. 225.

Nightlife

Other forms of **nightlife** are fairly limited. The liveliest **bars** in town are down by the harbour, staying open till 3am at weekends. **Discos** worth checking out are *Spiral*, *Andy's* and *Coco's* all by the ferry dock. There's also *Sí* (open till the early hours) on c/ Santiago Ramón y Cajal.

Around Maó

It's an easy trip across to Ciutadella (45min by bus), where ferries leave for Alcudia, on Mallorca, and it's also comparatively simple to reach the larger resorts. Emptier **beaches**, however, will be beyond your reach without your own transport. Given the difficulites with accommodation, destinations on the eastern half of the island are best treated as **day trips** from the capital.

Southeast: Es Castell and Cala En Porter

ES CASTELL (Villa Carlos) barely counts as being outside Maó, since it overlooks the capital's main road, a virtual continuation of the city. Nevertheless its appearance is very different, and it's far quieter. Originally called Georgetown, Es Castell was built by the British in the 1770s, in a militaristic and very English style: sash windows, doors with glass fanlights, and wrought-iron work adorn many of its older houses, while the huge parade ground/plaza is lined with what remains of the old barracks buildings. Worth a brief wander, the town's at its prettiest around the **harbour**, Cales Fonts cove, and here you'll find a string of **restaurants** – try *La Caprichosa*, at no. 44, where a decent pizza will set you back around 600ptas. If you decide to **stay**, the basic *Hostal Toni* at c/Castillo 3 (☎971/365999; ②) is close to the main square right by where the bus stops, or you could try the staid-looking, agency-booked hotel, the *Hamilton*, looking out across the channel at Passeig de Santa Agueda 6 (☎971/362050; ④–⑤).

Es Castell faces the **Isla Del Rey** with a hospital built during the British occupation. Nowadays this is a resort for Spanish health workers. **Llatzaret**, the rocky islet further along, was cut off from the mainland in 1900 by a canal in order to establish an isolated leper colony. On the headland behind is the fortress of **La Mola**, still in use and inaccessible, opposite the site of **Fort San Felipe**, now nothing but ruins with rumours of secret tunnels.

Heading southwest from Es Castell, a narrow country lane snakes its way to **SANT LUIS**, a trim and proper-looking village – a one-square, one-church town with blank windowless houses and a huge sports centre. Beyond, arcing round the coast, are hundreds of holiday villas, disfiguring the landscape from **Punta Prima** west to the uglist place of all, **CALA EN PORTER**. This shabby *urbanizacióne* does, however, have one notable attraction, the **Covas d'en Xoroi**, stuck high above the bay, their natural beauty exploited by a local businessman who has installed a bar and disco. The latter opens nightly at 10pm (around 1000ptas for the disco, where the action doesn't really start till midnight, continuing to dawn) but loud music thunders out, and you can visit, all day: 200ptas entrance includes a drink under the dripping ceilings.

North to Fornells

North of Maó, the road to Fornells runs through some of Menorca's finest scenery – the fields are cultivated and protected by great stands of trees, and the land rises as it approaches Monte Toro and skirts around it to the north. There's very little along the way, but at regular intervals you can turn off towards a series of beachside communities.

CALA MESQUIDA is the first of these, a tatty little place reached by turning right at the end of Maó harbour, a 5-km trip. The village tumbles over a series of rough and rocky hills that rise above the ocean, and there's a ruined fortress here too. Further along the main road, the next fork takes you to **ES GRAU** past the salt marshes of **S'Albufera** (rich in migrant bird life). Es Grau is short on beauty, and the beach is hardly memorable but you can reach the quiet **Illa d'en Colom** by boat: the island's just offshore. Further north, the next turning leads to **Cap de Favàritx**, whose lighthouse shines out over an extraordinary, almost lunar landscape: slate rocks surround a series of jagged inlets, like layers of *millefeuille* stubbled with red and green shrubs. Back on the main road, there are turnings to several tourist settlements, the largest of which is **ARENAL D'EN CASTELL**, a monstrosity sandwiched between the coast and the barren, windswept hills behind.

Better than any of these options is to continue all the way to **FORNELLS**, a low-rise, classically pretty harbour town edging a broad bay. Though it's been popular with tourists for years, above all for its **seafood restaurants** (*caldareta*, the speciality, is a fabulously expensive lobster stew), there's been little development. Two ruined fortresses protect the harbour, and the sweeping inlet provides ideal conditions for **windsurfers**; accordingly there's a residential windsurfing school offering one- or two-week courses. It's pretty good for simple beach-lovers too, and you can easily escape the crowds by walking along the rocky shoreline behind the town. Such is the renown of local restaurants that King Juan Carlos regularly calls in here on his yacht, and many people phone up days in advance with their orders – prices, though, are regal to match; along the seafront, you could try the *Sibaris*, S'Algaret 1 or *El Pescador* next door, whilst the *Es Port*, nearby at Rosario 17 (☎971/376644), is excellent too. There's only one central *hostal*, the two-star *S'Algaret* (☎971/376674; ④), a neat little place on the main square at Placa S'Algaret 7.

For less popular **beaches**, you can continue round to the north. At **CALA TIRANT** there's a good value semi-official **campsite** with a bar and cold showers, more windsurfing, and pedal-boats for rent. Beyond the next cape is the **Platja de Binimel'la** – an unofficial nudist beach with dark red sand. There are no trees or shade, and the tortuous track down is appalling, but the surrounding cliffs make for good walks, and a stream running across the beach provides mud which you can plaster all over when you feel the need for protection against the sun.

Across the island

The road from Maó to Ciutadella forms the backbone of Menorca, and what little industry the island enjoys – a few shoe factories and producers of the island's famous cheeses – is concentrated along it.

Alaior

Cheese is the main reason for stopping at **ALAIOR**, a market town some 12km out of Maó. En route you pass two *taulas* and a *talayot* at **Talati de Dalt**, and a couple of *navetas* at **Rafal Rubi**. The centre of Alaior is a tangle of narrow streets and bright white houses tumbling down the hillside beneath the imposing church of Santa Eulària which is on a rise behind the main square. There's also a cheese factory in town (*Quesos Coinga*) producing the open-textured white cheese which is sold throughout Spain. On the coast, 9km to the south, is the long, sandy beach of **Son Bou**, one of the island's best, though the scrubland behind accommodates a massive, and massively ugly, tourist development. Next to the beach are the ruins of a paleo-Christian basilica.

In the second weekend of August, Alaior lets loose for the **Fiesta de San Lorenzo** – a drunken display of horsemanship and general celebration. As its highlight, with the tiny town square packed, a procession of horses tears through the crowd, bucking and rearing, with their riders clinging on for dear life. Although no one seems to get hurt, you'd probably be best to join the privileged townspeople and witness the spectacle from the safety of an overlooking balcony.

Mercadal

Nine kilometres further along you arrive at **MERCADAL**, at the very centre of the island. Another old market town, it's cramped and rather dreary, but it's the point from which you can set off on the ascent of **Monte Toro**, the island's highest point. This is a steep four-kilometre climb (by road) but there are wonderful vistas from the top: on a good day you can see the entire coastline, on a bad one at least to Fornells in the north. Also at the summit is an old **convent** – now used as a short-stay Catholic retreat – its roof-line bristling with the aerials and radar dishes of *Radio Menorca*. The well in its patio provides wonderfully cool, fresh water, and there are picnic tables and a **café**. The church contains the remains of an earlier structure, and outside the whole place is dominated by a huge statue of Christ built to commemorate Civil War dead.

Ferreríes and Cala Santa Galdana

FERRERÍES is the next town along the route, though there's little to detain you here unless you're interested in the guided tour of the *Rubrica* shoe factory. It's a strange place, little more than a village really, which seems even more insignificant because it's hidden at the bottom of a dip in the road – no sooner do you leave than it has disappeared. One definite plus is the *Vimpi* bar on the plaza at the entrance to town, which serves some of the tastiest *tapas* on the island.

South from here, an excellent road will get you the 7km down to **CALA SANTA GALDANA**, once an island beauty spot. The road is new, and along with it has come development; arriving, the first thing you see is a twelve-storey hotel, *Hotel Sol*, built high above the beach. But although it's become a busy resort, the development is of manageable proportions, and the place preserves a semblance of its original charm, its curving sandy beach framed by a rocky promontory; there's a restaurant built into this and if you climb up behind you can still enjoy the sensation of being alone. In season, small boats ply regularly to other local beaches.

Getting back, you've no choice but to head through Ferreríes again – a picturesque drive through undulating, wooded scenery. The road to **Es Mitjorn** and **Sant Tomás** is equally pretty, but there's little reason to take it. Despite a reputation for folk dancing you won't find much in Es Mitjorn, while Sant Tomás, with a sandy beach and good windsurfing, is spoiled by an uninspiring mass of apartments and hotels. Heading west from Ferreríes, you'll find one of the best examples of a *nayeta* – the **Nayeta des Tudous** – beside the main road as you near Ciutadella: just watch for the sign.

Ciutadella and around

Like Maó, **CIUTADELLA** (Ciudadela) sits high above its harbour. Here, though, navigation is far more difficult, up a narrow channel which ends in the silted-up estuary of a dried-up river. If you're driving in, it also suffers from a horribly complex, one-way traffic flow, the legacy of a particularly crazed traffic engineer.

Until 1722 and the British intervention, this was the capital of the island, and its history is considerably richer than Maó's. Under Muslim rule it was known as *Medina Minurka*, and there are still a few Moorish traces, including parts of the old mosque, now converted to Christian use. In 1558 the city was invaded by the Turks with considerable destruction, especially of old records and documents, and decline was completed by the transferral of the capital to the more strategic setting of Maó.

Nevertheless it remains the seat of Menorca's bishopric, and a thoroughly attractive city. There's far less British influence here; instead, the narrow, cobbled streets lined with vaulted arches have a very Moorish/Andalucian feel to them.

The town

Ciutadella's compact centre crowds around the fortified cliff face shadowing the south side of the harbour. The main plazas and points of interest are within a few strides of each other, on and around the Plaça d'es Born, which overlooks the port from the south. This is the **main square**, packed with fluttering pigeons and built around an obelisk commemorating the futile defence against the Turks. Flanking the western side is the **Ajuntament**, whose nineteenth-century arches and crenallations hide a Gothic reception hall with wrought-iron lamps and a heavy, panelled ceiling reflecting the self-confident prosperity that was a key product of the British occupation. Opposite, across the square, the **Palacio de Torre-Saura**, also built in the nineteenth century but looking far older, is the grandest of several aristocratic mansions edging the plaza, its frontage, proclaiming the family coat of arms, is pierced by a giant wooden door through to the patio. Like most of its neighbours, this is still owner-occupied, so the impressively luxurious interior is off-bounds, one exception being the residence of the **Salort** family (daily 10am–2pm; 250ptas), round the corner on Major del Born. The entry fee is steep, but the house is worth a look for its high-ceilinged rooms redolent of nineteenth-century bourgeois life.

Many of Ciutadella's churches suffered heavy damage in the Civil War and have never been restored; **Sant Francesc**, in the southwest corner of the Plaça d'es Born, is an exception. A clean-lined, airy, fourteenth-century Gothic building, it contains some superb, carved wood altars and a lovely little domed manger scene as well as the more usual polychromatic saints. There's also an ancient **opera house** in the square – now reduced to showing reruns of old movies, and from here you can walk round to the steep steps leading down to the harbour, where the waterside restaurants, pleasure boats and remains of the old city walls present one of Menorca's most attractive scenes.

Past the Palau Salort , is the **Catedral**, built by Alfonso III on the site of the chief mosque. So soon after the Reconquest, its construction is fortress-like and Gothic, its windows set high and impregnably above the ground. Inside, this gives a beautiful lighting effect, with rays filtering down from the narrow recesses. There's also a wonderfully kitschy, pointed altar arch and a wealth of ornately decorated chapels. Nearby, along c/Roser, the church of **Nuestra Señora del Rosario** (in which British troops were briefly, and unpopularly, quartered) has a heavy golden facade.

Beyond the cathedral, heading east, c/Quadrado boasts a block of *voltes* or whitewashed arches, distinctly Moorish in inspiration, and a suitable setting for several attractive period shops and cafés. Nearby, one little street, a narrow, balconied cul-de-sac, is known simply and understandably as *Que no Pasa* (The One that Doesn't Go Through). Carrer Quadrado leads into the Plaça Nova and, continuing east along c/Carme, you leave the narrow alleys of the old town at Plaça Alfons III.

In the other direction from the Plaça d'es Born, rounding the northern edge of the Plaça Dels Pins (L'Esplanada), Cami Sant Nicolau runs straight out to the **Castell Sant Nicolau**, a pint-sized octagonal fortress standing on unwelcoming rocks looking out towards Mallorca.

Practicalities

Most mornings, during the season, a **Turismo** bus is parked outside the *Ajuntament*, and can supply helpful lists of **hostales** and **casas de huéspedes** – though be warned that the realistic choices are extremely limited. Among the more reasonably priced and

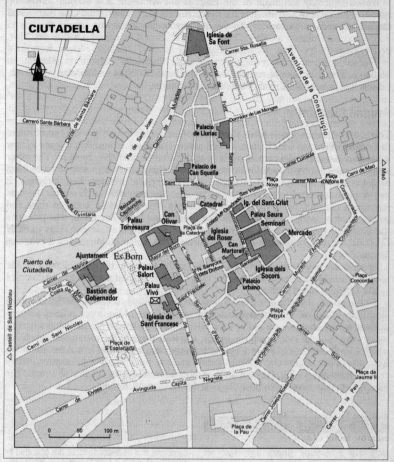

comfortable options, there's a cluster in the vicinity of Plaça Alfons III, at the end of the main road from Maó. These include: *Oasis*, c/Sant Isidre 33 (☎971/382197; ③); *Ciutadella*, Sant Eloy 10 (☎971/383462; ④); and *Alfonso III*, Cami de Maó 53 (☎971/380150; ④); or there's the basic *París*, c/Santandria s/n (☎971/381622; ②), not far from where most buses stop; and, on the same street, the two-star hotel *Ses Voltes* (☎971/380400; ④). Out towards the Castell Sant Nicolau, you could also try the *Patricia*, Cami Sant Nicolau 90 (☎971/385511; ⑥) or best of all, the *Esmeralda* (☎971/380250; ⑤), where most of the bedrooms have balconies looking out to sea.

There are several inexpensive **café-restaurants** dotted around the city centre – try along c/Quadrado, where you'll find the *Tascasa Barreta*, or on Plaça Alfons III, home to the *C'as Quintu* seafood restaurant. But most of Ciutadella's better places are down by the harbour, including the *Casa del Mar* and the *Café Balear*, great for a drink or a coffee. Here too, the *Es Moll* serves fine seafood, as does the *Casa Manolo*, at Marina 117, off the Plaça dels Pins.

Buses generally terminate in the Plaça dels Pins; there is a service across the island, of course, but also south to the beach resorts of Santandria and Cala Blanca and the *urbanización* at Tamarinda. To the north, you can take a bus around the bay to Forcat and Els Dolfins via Cala En Blanes and Cala Brut. **Car rental** is widely available, or for **mopeds** try *Motos Genestar*, Barcelona 24 (☎971/82282). *Flebasa* **ferrylines** (☎971/480012) run a twice-daily service from Ciutadella harbour to Alcudia on Mallorca. The trip takes about four hours and costs 3000ptas or 6950ptas with a car. Connecting buses take arrivals from Alcudia to Palma.

Around Ciutadella

There are two roads **south from Ciutadella**. One, which follows the west coast round to **TAMARINDA** via Cala Blanca, is well paved – an obvious sign that it leads to new *urbanizaciónes* and hotel complexes (and in this case to little else; avoid it). The other sets off cross-country toward the south coast, branching after about 4km into two 7-km long tracks which both lead through leafy countryside to **unspoiled beaches**. If you've hired a moped then be prepared for a bumpy ride and watch out for the dust and muck churned up by passing cars. There's little to choose between their end points – lovely sandy coves at **Platja Son Saura** and **Cala Turqueta**, where there's the tiniest of villages. Beside the road to Son Saura, are the *talayotic* ruins of **SON CATLAR** village, including 800m of defensive walls, some buildings and a religious sanctuary.

Around the bay to the **west of Ciutadella**, the terse coastline is followed by the road, but this is villa country that ends up at the whitewashed modern tourist complex of **Els Dolfins** – don't bother.

To the **north**, if you can find and follow the limited signs to **CALA MORELL**, some 7km from town, you'll be rewarded by the sight of one of the more refined *urbanizaciónes*, whose streets – named in Latin after the constellations – lead round a narrow rocky bay. You can swim from the beach, and visit some of the man-made **caves**, for which Cala Morell is well known. Dating from the late Bronze and Iron Ages, the caves form one of the largest necropolises known and are surprisingly sophisticated, with a central pillar supporting the roof and, on occasions, windows cut into the rock. The most spectacular caves even have classical designs carved in relief.

travel details

Note that inter-island **flights** can work out cheaper than **ferries**; so too, at times, can some charters between the Spanish mainland and Balearics. Check in an hour early or risk losing your seat. All schedules below are for **summer service** – slightly reduced out of season.

Mainland ferry connections
Barcelona to: Ibiza (6 weekly; 9–10hr); Mahón (6 weekly; 9hr); Palma (1 daily; 8hr).
Denia to: Ibiza (1 daily; 4hr).
Valencia to: Ibiza (2 weekly; 7hr); Mahón (1 weekly, via Palma); Palma (6 weekly; 8–9hr).

Barcelona and Valencia services are operated by *Transmediterránea*, which has offices in Barcelona at Estación del Mar 1, Muelle Barcelona (☎93/412 25 24) and VALENCIA at Estació Maritima (☎96/367 65 12) and agents in all the island capitals. The Denia service is run by *Flebasa* (Denia office: ☎96/578 40 11).

Mainland flights
There are flights to the Balearics on **Iberia** and on the Spanish charter airline, **Aviaco**. For details of tickets and special deals stop in at any Spanish travel agent – in summer well in advance.

Charters and reduced Iberia flights are most regularly operated between **Barcelona**, **Valencia** or **Madrid**, and **Palma** or **Ibiza**.

Inter-island ferries and flights

Alcúdia to: to Ciutadella (2 daily ferries; 4hr).

Ibiza to: Formentera (9 daily hydrofoils and ferries; 30min –1hr); Mahón (1 flight daily); Palma (2 ferries a week; 4hr 30min; 5 flights daily).

Palma to: Mahón (1 ferry weekly; 6hr 30min; several daily flights).

PART THREE

THE

CONTEXTS

THE HISTORICAL FRAMEWORK

EARLY CIVILIZATIONS

The first Spanish peoples arrived on the Iberian peninsula from southern France towards the close of the Palaeolithic age. They were cave dwellers and hunter-gatherers and seem to have been heavily concentrated in the north of the country, around the modern province of Santander. Here survive the most remarkable traces of their culture (which peaked around 15,000 BC), the deftly stylized cave murals of the animals that they hunted. The finest examples are at Altamira – now closed for general visits, though you can see similar paintings at Puente Viesgo, also near Santander.

Subsequent prehistory is more complex and confused. There does not appear to have been any great development in the cave cultures of the north. Instead the focus shifts south to Almería, which was settled around 5000–4000 BC by the "Iberians", **Neolithic** colonists from North Africa. They had already assimilated into their culture many of the changes that had developed in Egypt and the Near East. Settling in villages, they introduced pastoral and agricultural ways of life and exploited the plentiful supply of copper. Around 1500 BC, with the onset of the **Bronze Age**, they began to spread outwards into fortified villages on the central meseta, the high plateau of modern Castile. At the turn of the millennium they were joined by numerous waves of **Celtic** and **Germanic** peoples. Here, Spain's divisive physical make-up – with its network of mountain ranges – determined its social nature. The incoming tribes formed distinct and isolated groups, conquering and sometimes absorbing each other but only on a very limited and local scale. Hence the Celtic "urnfield people" established themselves in Catalunya, the **Vascones** in the Basque Country, and near them along the Atlantic coast the **Astures**. Pockets of earlier cultures survived, too, particularly in Galicia with its "*citanias*" of beehive huts.

THE FIRST COLONISTS

The Spanish coast meanwhile attracted colonists from different regions of the Mediterranean. The **Phoenicians** founded the port of Gadir (Cádiz) in 1100 BC and traded intensively in the metals of the Guadalquivir valley. Their wealth and success gave rise to a Spanish "Atlantis" myth, based around Huelva. Market rivalry also brought the **Greeks**, who established their trading colonies along the eastern coast – the modern Costa Brava. There's a fine surviving site at Empúries, near Barcelona.

More significant, however, was the arrival of the **Carthaginians** in the third century BC. Expelled from Sicily by the Romans, they saw in Spain a new base for their empire, from which to regain strength and strike back at their rivals. Although making little impact inland, they occupied most of Andalucía and expanded along the Mediterranean seaboard to establish a new capital at Cartagena. Under Hannibal they prepared to invade Italy and in 214 BC attacked Saguntum, a strategic outpost of the Roman Empire. It was a disastrous move, precipitating the **Second Punic War**; by 210 BC only Cádiz remained in their control and they were forced to accept terms. A new and very different age had begun.

ROMANS AND VISIGOTHS

The **Roman colonization** of the peninsula was far more intense than anything previously experienced and met with great resistance from the Celtiberian tribes of the north and centre. It was almost two centuries before the conquest was complete and indeed the Basques, although defeated, were never fully Romanized.

Nonetheless, Spain became the most important centre of the Roman Empire after Italy itself, producing no less than four emperors, along with the writers Seneca and Lucan. Again, geography dictated an uneven spread of influence, at its strongest in Andalucía, southern Portugal and on the Catalan coast around Tarragona. In the first two centuries AD the Spanish mines and the granaries of Andalucía brought unprecedented wealth and Roman Spain enjoyed a brief "**Golden Age**". The finest monuments were built in the great provincial capitals – Córdoba, Mérida (which boasts the finest remains) and Tarragona – but all across the country more practical structures were undertaken: roads, bridges and aqueducts. Many were still used well into recent centuries – perhaps the most remarkable being the aqueducts of Segovia and Tarragona – and a few bridges remain in use even today.

Towards the third century, however, the Roman political framework began to show signs of decadence and corruption. Although the actual structure didn't totally collapse until the Muslim invasions of the early eighth century, it became increasingly vulnerable to **barbarian invasions** from northern Europe. The Franks and the Suevi (Swabians) swept across the Pyrenees between 264 and 276, leaving much devastation in their wake. They were followed two centuries later by further waves of Suevi, Alans and Vandals. Internal strife was heightened by the arrival of the **Visigoths** from Gaul, allies of Rome and already Romanized to a large degree. The triumph of Visigothic strength in the fifth century resulted in a period of spurious unity, based upon an exclusive military rule from their capital at Toledo, but their numbers were never great and their order was often fragmentary and nominal, with the bulk of the subject people kept in a state of disconsolate servility and held ransom for their services in time of war. Above them in the ranks of the military elite there were constant plots and factions – exacerbated by the Visigothic system of elected monarchy and by their adherence to the heretical Arian philosophy. In 589 **King Recared** converted to Catholicism but religious strife was only multiplied: forced conversions, especially within the Jewish enclaves, maintained a constant simmering of discontent.

MOORISH SPAIN

In contrast to the long-drawn-out Roman campaigns, **Moorish conquest** of the peninsula was effected with extraordinary speed. This was a characteristic phenomenon of the spread of Islam – Muhammad left Mecca in 622 and by 705 his followers had established control over all of North Africa. Spain, with its political instability, its wealth and its fertile climate, was an inevitable extension of their aims. In 711 Tariq, governor of Tangier, led a force of 7000 Berbers across the straits and routed the Visigoth army of King Roderic: two years later the Visigoths made a last desperate stand at Mérida and within a decade the Moors had conquered all but the wild mountains of Asturias. The land under their authority was dubbed "**al-Andalus**", a fluid term which expanded and shrunk with the intermittent gains and losses of the Reconquest. According to region, the Moors were to remain in control for the next three to eight centuries.

It was not simply a military conquest. The Moors (a collective term for the numerous waves of Arab and Berber settlers from North Africa) were often content to grant a limited autonomy in exchange for payment of tribute; their administrative system was tolerant and easily absorbed both Jews and Christians, those who retained their religion being known as "Mozarabs". And al-Andalus was a distinctly Spanish state of Islam. Though at first politically subject to the Eastern Caliphate (or empire) of Baghdad, it was soon virtually independent. In the tenth century, at the peak of its power and expansion, Abd ar-Rahman III asserted total independence, proclaiming himself Caliph of a new **Western Islamic Empire**. Its capital was Córdoba – the largest, most prosperous and most civilized city in Europe. This was the great age of Muslim Spain: its scholarship, philosophy, architecture and craftsmanship were without rival and there was an unparalleled growth in urban life, in trade, and in agriculture aided by magnificent irrigation projects. These and other engineering feats were not, on the whole, instigated by the Moors who instead took basic Roman models and adapted them to a new level of sophistication. In **architecture** and the **decorative arts**, however, their contribution was original and unique – as may be seen in the incredible monuments of Sevilla, Córdoba and Granada.

The Córdoban Caliphate for a while created a remarkable degree of unity. But its rulers were to become decadent and out of touch, prompting the brilliant but dictatorial **al-Mansur** to usurp control. Under this extraordinary ruler Moorish power actually reached new heights, pushing the Christian kingdom of Asturias-León back into the Cantabrian mountains and sacking its most holy shrine, Santiago de Compostela. However, after his death the Caliphate quickly lost its authority and in 1031 disintegrated into a series of small independent kingdoms or "*taifas*", the strongest of which was Sevilla.

Internal divisions amongst the *taifas* offered less resistance to the Christian kingdoms which were rallying in the north, and twice North Africa had to be turned to for reinforcement. This resulted in two distinct new waves of Moorish invasion – first by the fanatically Islamic **Almoravids** (1086) and later by the **Almohads** (1147), who restored effective Muslim authority until their defeat at the battle of Las Navas de Tolosa in 1212.

THE CHRISTIAN RECONQUEST

The **reconquest** of land and influence from the Moors was a slow and intermittent process. It began with a symbolic victory by a small force of Christians at Covadonga in the Asturias (727) and was not completed until 1492 with the conquest of Granada by Fernando and Isabella.

Covadonga resulted in the formation of the tiny Christian **Kingdom of the Asturias**. Initially just 65 by 50km in area, it had by 914 reclaimed León and most of Galicia and northern Portugal. At this point, progress was temporarily halted by the devastating campaigns of al-Mansur. However, with the fall of the Córdoban Caliphate and the divine aid of Spain's Moor-slaying patron, Saint James the Apostle (see "Santiago de Compostela"), the Reconquest moved into a new and powerful phase.

The frontier castles built against Arab attack gave name to **Castile**, founded in the tenth century as a county of León-Asturias. Under Fernando I (1037–65) it achieved the status of a kingdom and became the main thrust and focus of the Reconquest. Other kingdoms were being defined in the north at the same time: the Basques founded Navarra (Navarre), while dynastic marriage merged Catalunya with Aragón. In 1085 this period of confident Christian expansion reached its zenith with the capture of the great Moorish city of Toledo. The following year, however, the Almoravids arrived on invitation from Sevilla, and military activity was efféctively frozen – except, that is, for the exploits of the legendary **El Cid**, a Castilian nobleman who won considerable lands around Valencia in 1095.

The next concerted phase of the Reconquest really began as a response to the threat imposed by the Almohads. The Kings of León, Castile, Aragón and Navarra united in a general crusade which resulted in the great victory at **Las Navas de Tolosa** (1212). Thereafter Muslim power was effectively paralyzed and the Christian armies moved on to take most of al-Andalus. Fernando III ("El Santo", the saint) led Castilian soldiers into Córdoba in 1236 and twelve years later into Sevilla. Meanwhile, the Kingdom of Portugal had expanded to more or less its present size, while Jaime I of Aragón was to conquer Valencia, Alicante, Murcia and the Balearic Islands. By the end of the thirteenth century only the Kingdom of Granada remained under Muslim authority and for much of the following two centuries it was forced to pay tribute to the monarchs of Castile.

Two factors should be stressed regarding the Reconquest. First, its unifying religious nature – the **spirit of crusade**, intensified by the religious zeal of the Almoravids and Almohads, and by the wider European climate (which in 1085 gave rise to the First Crusade). This powerful religious motivation is well illustrated by the subsequent canonization of Fernando III, and found solid expression in the part played by the military orders of Christian knights, the most important of which were the **Knights Templar** and the Order of Santiago. At the same time the Reconquest was a movement of **recolonization**. The fact that the country had been in arms for so long meant that the nobility had a major and clearly visible social role, a trend perpetuated by the redistribution of captured land in huge packages, or "*latifundia*". Heirs to this tradition still remain as landlords of the great estates, most conspicuously in Andalucía. Men from the ranks were also awarded land, forming a lower, larger stratum of nobility, the *hidalgos*. It was their particular social code that provided the material for Cervantes in *Don Quixote*.

Any spirit of mutual cooperation that had temporarily united the Christian kingdoms disintegrated during the fourteenth century, and independent lines of development were once again pursued. Attempts to merge **Portugal** with Castile foundered at the battle of Aljubarrota (1385), and Portuguese attention turned away from Spain towards the Atlantic. Aragón experienced a similar pull towards the markets of the Mediterranean, although pre-eminence in this area was soon passed to the Genoese. It was **Castile** that emerged as the strongest over this period: self-sufficiency in agriculture and a flourishing wool trade with the Netherlands enabled the state to build upon the prominent military role played under Fernando III. Politically, Castilian history was a tale of dynastic conflict until the accession of the Catholic monarchs.

LOS REYES CATÓLICOS

Los Reyes Católicos – the **Catholic Monarchs** – was the joint title given to **Fernando V of Aragón and Isabella I of Castile**, whose marriage in 1479 united the two largest king-doms in Spain. Unity was in practice more symbolic than real: Castile had underlined its rights in the marriage vows and Aragón retained its old administrative structure. So, in the beginning at least, the growth of any national unity or Spanish – as opposed to local – sentiment was very much dependent on the head of state. Nevertheless, from this time on it begins to be realistic to consider Spain as a single political entity.

At the heart of Fernando and Isabella's popular appeal lay a **religious bigotry** that they shared with most of their Christian subjects. The **Inquisition** was instituted in Castile in 1480 and in Aragón seven years later. Aiming to establish the purity of the Catholic faith by rooting out heresy, it was directed mainly at Jews – resented for their enterprise in commerce and influence in high places, as well as for their faith. Expression had already been given to these feelings in a pogrom in 1391; it was reinforced by an edict issued in 1492 which forced up to 400,000 Jews to flee the country. A similar spirit was embodied in the reconquest of the **Kingdom of Granada**, also in 1492. As the last stronghold of Muslim authority, the religious rights of its citizens were guaranteed under the treaty of surrender. Within a decade, though, those Muslims under Christian rule had been given the choice between conversion or expulsion.

The year 1492 was symbolic of a fresh start in another way: it was in this year that Columbus discovered America, and the Papal Bull that followed, entrusting Spain with the conversion of the American Indians, further entrenched Spain's sense of a mission to bring the world to the "True Faith". The next ten years saw the systematic conquest, coloniza-tion and exploitation of the **New World** as it was discovered, with new territory stretching from Labrador to Brazil, and new-found wealth pouring into the royal coffers. Important as this was for Fernando and Isabella, and especially for their prestige, priorities remained in Europe and strategic marriage alliances were made with Portugal, England and the Holy Roman Empire. It was not until the accession of the Habsburg dynasty that Spain could look to the activities of Cortés, Magellan and Pizarro and claim to be the world's leading power.

HABSBURG SPAIN

Carlos I, a Habsburg, came to the throne in 1516 as a beneficiary of the marriage alliances of the Catholic monarchs. Five years later, he was elected Emperor of the Holy Roman Empire as Carlos V (**Charles V**), inheriting not only Castile and Aragón, but Flanders, the Netherlands, Artois, the Franche-Comté and all the American colonies to boot. With such responsibilities it was inevitable that attention would be diverted from Spain, whose chief function became to sustain the Holy Roman Empire with gold and silver from the Americas. It was only with the accession of **Felipe II** in 1556 that Spanish politics became more centralized. The notion of an absentee king was reversed. Felipe lived in the centre of Castile near Madrid, creating a monument to the values of medieval Spain in his palace, El Escorial.

Two main themes run through his reign: the preservation of his own inheritance, and the revival of the crusade in the name of the Catholic Church. In pursuit of the former, Felipe successfully claimed the Portuguese throne (through the marriage of his mother), gaining access to the additional wealth of its empire. Plots were also woven in support of Mary Queen of Scots's claim to the throne of

England, and to that end the ill-fated Armada sailed in 1588, its sinking a triumph for English naval strength and for Protestantism.

This was a period of unusual religious intensity: the **Inquisition** was enforced with renewed vigour, and a rising of Moriscos (subject Moors) in the Alpujarras was fiercely suppressed. Felipe III later ordered the expulsion of half the total number of Moriscos in Spain – allowing only two families to remain in each village in order to maintain irrigation techniques. The **exodus** of both Muslim and Jew created a large gulf in the labour force and in the higher echelons of commercial life – and in trying to uphold the Catholic cause, an enormous strain was put upon resources without any clearcut victory.

By the middle of the seventeenth century, Spain was losing international credibility. Domestically, the disparity between the wealth surrounding Crown and Court and the poverty and suffering of the mass of the population was a source of perpetual tension. Discontent fuelled regional revolts in Catalunya and Portugal in 1640, and the latter had finally to be acknowledged as an independent state in 1668.

BOURBONS AND THE PENINSULAR WAR

The **Bourbon dynasty** succeeded to the Spanish throne in the person of Felipe V (1700); with him began the War of Spanish Succession against the rival claim of Archduke Charles of Austria, assisted by British forces. As a result of the Treaty of Utrecht which ended the war (1713), Spain was stripped of all territory in Belgium, Luxembourg, Italy and Sardinia, but Felipe V was recognized as king. Gibraltar was seized by the British in the course of the war. For the rest of the century Spain fell very much under the French sphere of influence, an influence that was given political definition by an alliance with the French Bourbons in 1762.

Contact with France made involvement in the **Napoleonic Wars** inevitable and led eventually to the defeat of the Spanish fleet at Trafalgar in 1805. Popular outrage was such that the powerful prime minister, Godoy, was overthrown and King Carlos IV forced to abdicate (1808). Napoleon seized the opportunity to install his brother, Joseph, on the throne.

Fierce local resistance was eventually backed by the muscle of a British army, first under Sir John Moore, later under the Duke of Wellington, and the French were at last driven out in the course of the Peninsular War. Meanwhile, however, the **American colonies** had been successfully asserting their independence from a preoccupied centre and with them went Spain's last claim of significance on the world stage. The entire nineteenth century was dominated by the struggle between an often reactionary monarchy and the aspirations of liberal constitutional reformers.

SEEDS OF CIVIL WAR

Between 1810 and 1813 an ad hoc Cortes (parliament) had set up a **liberal constitution** with ministers responsible to a democratically elected chamber. The first act of Fernando VII on being returned to the throne was to abolish this, and until his death in 1833 he continued to stamp out the least hint of liberalism. On his death, the right of succession was contested between his brother, Don Carlos, backed by the Church, conservatives and Basques, and his infant daughter, Isabel, who looked to the Liberals and the army for support. So began the **First Carlist War**, a civil war that divided Spanish emotions for six years. Isabel II was eventually declared of age in 1843, her reign a long record of scandal, political crisis and constitutional compromise. Liberal army generals under the leadership of General Prim effected a coup in 1868 and the queen was forced to abdicate, but attempts to maintain a Republican government foundered. The Cortes was again dissolved and the throne returned to Isabel's son, Alfonso XII. A new constitution was declared in 1876, limiting the power of the Crown through the institution of bicameral government, but again the progress was halted by the lack of any tradition on which to base the constitutional theory.

The years preceding World War I merely heightened the discontent, which found expression in the growing **political movements** of the working class. The Socialist Workers' Party was founded in Madrid after the restoration of Alfonso XII, and spawned its own trade union, the UGT (1888), successful predominantly in areas of high industrial concentration such as the Basque region and Asturias. Its anarchist counterpart, the CNT, was founded in 1911, gaining substantial support among the peasantry of Andalucía.

The loss of **Cuba** in 1898 emphasized the growing isolation of Spain in international affairs and added to economic problems with the return of soldiers seeking employment where there was none. A call-up for army reserves to fight in **Morocco** in 1909 provoked a general strike and the "Tragic Week" of rioting in Barcelona. Between 1914 and 1918, Spain was outwardly neutral but inwardly turbulent; inflated prices made the postwar recession harder to bear.

The general disillusionment with parliamentary government, together with the fears of employers and businessmen for their own security, gave **General Primo de Rivera** sufficient support for a military coup in 1923. Dictatorship did result in an increase in material prosperity, but the death of the dictator in 1930 revealed the apparent stability as a facade. New political factions were taking shape: the Liberal Republican Right was founded by Alcalá Zamora, while the Socialist Party was given definition under the leadership of Largo Caballero. The victory of anti-monarchist parties in the 1931 municipal elections forced the abdication of the king and the **Second Republic** was declared.

THE SECOND REPUBLIC

Catalunya declared itself a republic independent of the central government and was conceded control of internal affairs by a statute of 1932. **Separatist movements** were powerful too in the Basque provinces and Galicia, each with their own demands for autonomy. Meanwhile, the government, set up on a tidal wave of hope, was failing to satisfy even the least of the expectations which it had raised. Hopelessly divided internally and too scared of right-wing reaction to carry out the massive tax and agrarian reforms that the left demanded and that might have provided the resources for thoroughgoing regeneration of the economy, it had neither the will nor the money to provide what it had promised.

The result was the increasing polarization of Spanish politics. **Anarchism**, in particular, was gaining strength among the frustrated middle classes as well as among workers and peasantry. The **Communist Party** and left-wing **Socialists**, driven into alliance by their mutual distrust of the "moderate" socialists in government, were also forming a growing bloc. There was little real unity of purpose on either left or right, but their fear of each other and their own exaggerated boasts made each seem an imminent threat. On the right the **Falangists**, basically a youth party founded in 1923 by **José Antonio Primo de Rivera** (son of the dictator), made uneasy bedfellows with conservative traditionalists and dissident elements in the army upset by modernizing reforms.

In an atmosphere of growing confusion, the left-wing Popular Front alliance won the general election of **February 1936** by a narrow margin. Normal life, though, became increasingly impossible: the economy was crippled by strikes, peasants took agrarian reform into their own hands and the government failed to exert its authority over anyone. Finally, on July 17, 1936, the military garrison in Morocco rebelled under **General Franco**'s leadership, to be followed by risings at military garrisons throughout the country. It was the culmination of years of scheming in the army, but in the event far from the overnight success its leaders almost certainly expected. The south and west quickly fell into Nationalist hands, but Madrid and the industrialized north and east remained loyal to the Republican government.

CIVIL WAR

The ensuing **Civil War** was undoubtedly one of the most bitter and bloody the world has seen. Violent reprisals were taken on their enemies by both sides – the Republicans shooting priests and local landowners wholesale, the Nationalists carrying out mass slaughter on the population of almost every town they took. Contradictions were legion in the way the Spanish populations found themselves divided from each other. Perhaps the greatest irony was that Franco's troops, on their "holy" mission to ensure a Catholic Spain, comprised a core of Moroccan troops from Spain's North African colony.

It was, too, the first modern war – Franco's German allies demonstrated their ability to wipe out entire civilian populations with their bombing raids on Gernika and Durango, and radio proved an important weapon, as Nationalist propagandists offered the starving Republicans "the white bread of Franco".

Despite sporadic help from Russia and thousands of volunteers in the International Brigades, the Republic could never compete with the professional armies and the massive assistance from Fascist Italy and Nazi Germany enjoyed by the Nationalists. In addition, the left was torn by internal divisions which at times led almost to civil war within its own ranks. Nevertheless, the Republicans held out in slowly dwindling territories for nearly three years, with **Catalunya** falling in January 1939 and armed resistance in **Madrid** – which never formally surrendered – petering out over the next few months. As hundreds of thousands of refugees flooded into France, General Francisco Franco, who had long before proclaimed himself Head of State, took up the reins of power.

FRANCO'S SPAIN

The early reprisals taken by the victors were on a massive and terrifying scale. Executions were commonplace in town and village and upwards of two million people were put in concentration camps until "order" had been established by authoritarian means. Only one party was permitted and censorship was rigidly enforced. By the end of World War II, during which Spain was too weak to be anything but neutral, **Franco** was the only fascist head of state left in Europe, one responsible for sanctioning more deaths than any other in Spanish history. Spain was economically and politically isolated and, bereft of markets, suffered – almost half the population were still tilling the soil for little or no return. When General Eisenhower visited Madrid in 1953 with the offer of huge loans, it came as water to the desert, and the price, the establishment of American nuclear bases, was one Franco was more than willing to pay. However belated, economic development was incredibly rapid, with Spain enjoying a growth rate second only to that of Japan for much of the 1960s, a boom fuelled by the tourist industry and the remittances of Spanish workers abroad.

Increased **prosperity**, however, only underlined the bankruptcy of Franco's regime and its inability to cope with popular demands. Higher incomes, the need for better education and a creeping invasion of western culture made the anachronism of Franco ever clearer. His only reaction was to attempt to withdraw what few

signs of increased liberalism had crept through, and his last years mirrored the repression of the postwar period. Basque Nationalists, whose assassination of Admiral Carrero Blanco had effectively destroyed Franco's last hope of a like-minded successor, were singled out for particularly harsh treatment. Hundreds of so-called terrorists were tortured, and the Burgos trials of 1970, together with the executions of August 1975, provoked worldwide protest. Franco finally died in November 1975, nominating **King Juan Carlos** as his successor.

SPAIN IN THE 80s

On October 28, 1982, Felipe González's Socialist Workers' Party – the PSOE – was elected with massive support to rule a country that had been firmly in the hands of the right for forty-three years. The Socialists captured the imagination and the votes of nearly ten million Spaniards with the simplest of appeals: "for change". It was a telling comment on just how far Spain had moved since Franco's death, for in the intervening years change seemed the one factor that could still threaten the new-found democracy.

Certainly, in the Spain of 1976 the thought of a freely elected left-wing government would have been incredible. **King Juan Carlos** was the hand-picked successor of Franco, groomed for the job and very much in with the army – of which he remains official Commander in Chief. His initial moves were cautious in the extreme, appointing a government dominated by loyal Francoists who had little sympathy for the growing opposition demands for "democracy without adjectives". In the summer of 1976 demonstrations in Madrid ended in violence, with the police upholding the old authoritarian ways.

To his credit, however, Juan Carlos recognized that some real break with the past was now urgent and inevitable, and, accepting the resignation of his prime minister, set in motion the process of **democratization**. His newly appointed prime minister, Adolfo Suárez, steered through a Law of Political Reform, allowing for a two-chamber **Cortes** (parliament). He also legitimized the Socialist Party and, controversially, the Communists. When elections were held in June 1977, Suárez's own centre-right UCD party was rewarded with a 34 percent share of the vote, the Socialists coming in second with 28 percent, and the Communists and Francoist **Alianza Popular** both marginalised at 9 percent and 8 percent. It was almost certainly a vote for democratic stability rather than for ideology and this was reflected in the course of the parliament, with Suárez governing through "consensus politics", negotiating settlements on all important issues with the major parties. The king, perhaps recognizing that his own future depended on the maintenance of the new democracy, lent it his support – most notably in February 1981 when Civil Guard Colonel Tejero stormed the Cortes and, with other officers loyal to Franco's memory, attempted to institute an army **coup**. The crisis, for a while, was real. Tanks were brought out onto the streets of Valencia, and only three of the army's ten regional commanders remained unreservedly loyal to the government. But as it became clear that the king would not support the plotters, most of the rest affirmed their support.

Tejero's continued role as a figurehead for the extreme right is evidenced by the graffiti proclaiming his name everywhere. But for most Spaniards his attempted coup is now an irrelevant and increasingly distant concern. Spanish democracy – even in army circles – has become institutionalized. And in **Felipe González** (known always as "Felipe") and the PSOE it has found, at least until the last couple of years and the ongoing economic crisis, a party of enduring stability, and to the left of exasperating moderation.

CONTEMPORARY POLITICS

Significant "change", even well into González's third term (he was convincingly re-elected in 1986, but lost an overall majority in the Congress of Deputies in 1989, and stayed in by the skin of this teeth in 1993), has yet to be seen. Indeed in most political spheres – and above all in their economic policy – the PSOE are hardly distinguishable from the previous UCD administration, or even from the present conservative governments of Britain or Germany. Control of inflation has been a more urgent target than employment, for all the manifesto promises. Loss-making heavy industries – steel and shipbuilding especially – have been ruthlessly overhauled, and industries held or taken over by the state have been speedily reprivatized. **European Community** membership, which became a reality in 1986, has in the government's eyes increased the need to put industrial and economic efficiency above social policies: at the same time the pride which most Spanish people felt at this tangible proof of their acceptance by the rest of Europe bought the Socialists more valuable time.

On the issue of **NATO** (or *OTAN* as Spaniards know it), perhaps more than any other, Felipe's personal pragmatism was apparent. During the 1982 election campaign the largest rally he attended was against NATO, and he made the closing speech. When the promised referendum was finally held four years later – and to the surprise of almost everyone turned out marginally in favour of staying in – his was one of the main voices in favour of continued membership. Nonetheless, the American presence is being cut (albeit largely for world strategic reasons rather than as a result of Spanish pressure), most obviously with the closure of the huge Torrejon air base near Madrid. These days army **conscription** is becoming a bigger issue than NATO membership – certainly among the young.

Autonomy has remained a major stumbling block. The system of granting varying degrees of self-rule to the regions has had no consistency and little effect on the separatist movements. In Catalunya and the Basque country elections have consistently been won by nationalist parties (Catalan Nationalists form the equal third-largest group in the national Congress of Deputies), and in the latter sporadic terrorism continues – despite an amnesty, talks with ETA and an increased military presence.

But for all this, Felipe has remained the most popular figure on the political scene, partly because he has had no real competitors for the job from within the ranks of his own party and partly due to the fact that the **opposition** has been hopelessly divided. In the last few years, however, things have been changing considerably, with re-alignments on right and left. Former prime minister Adolfo Suárez's Christian Democrats merged with the Alianza Popular to form the new right-wing **Partido Popular**, which came a respectable second in the 1989 elections; a new far-left coalition, Izquierda Unida (United Left), came third, albeit with only eighteen seats in the Congress of Deputies (the same number as the Catalan Nationalists), barely a tenth of the PSOE's representation.

The increasing rise to prominence since then of **José María Aznar** as leader of the Partido Popular (PP) and his relentless criticism of government incompetence in dealing with the growing economic crisis debilitated the PSOE's position still further in the build-up to the 1993 elections. With opinion polls showing both parties standing neck and neck, it looked like the favourable coverage Aznar and the PP were getting in Spain's predominantly right-wing press and on TV might well swing the balance in favour of the opposition, especially since the government appeared to offer no concrete approach in dealing with official unemployment figures of 24 percent and was becoming increasingly discredited due to a series of financial scandals. As it turned out, there was a last minute swing back towards the socialists, due in part, to the the fact that the shadow of far-right politics in Spain was perhaps still too recent in many voters' minds and despite a concerted attempt by Aznar to claim (not totally convincingly) that his party had evolved into a fully centrist one.

Nonetheless, a **hung Parliament** ensued, with the PSOE having to rely on the support of the Catalan Nationalists in order to gain the necessary majority. Whether they will survive next time around remains to be seen – the election result certainly gave Felipe a severe jolt and at times during the campaign he appeared very drawn. A second general strike in January 1994 in response to recent further cuts in unemployment benefits, a wage freeze for civil servants and a new law enabling employers to contract under-25s on ridiculously low wages just six months after elections provides strong evidence of the flagging support and **discontent** generally felt in Spain over domestic policies (especially among Felipe's own supporters, who see him abandoning his principles – the strike was backed by the PSOE's own trade union, the powerful UGT). Internationally, his record has remained a good one, and on balance it is undeniable that the **Spanish economy** has grown rapidly under his leadership, consistently among the fastest growing in western Europe, and top of the list for much of the Eighties. At a local level there has been a flourishing of **cultural activity** of every kind, much of it sponsored by enlightened and revitalized local councils – especially in Madrid and Barcelona. On an international level, the British have agreed to discuss the sovereignty of **Gibraltar** and the border has been reopened. Most significantly for Spaniards, perhaps, the Spanish government's voice is now one which is taken seriously at an international level, acknowledged as having a role in the Latin American peace process, and in the councils of Europe.

In **1992** the **Olympics** were held in Barcelona, **Madrid** was European City of Culture, **Sevilla** hosted EXPO'92, and the 500th anniversary of Columbus's discovery of the Americas was celebrated. The Spanish have undeniably been making their mark in a big way, and within the country this has been viewed as a return to the big league. Sceptics would also add, however, that the Spanish love of grandiose celebrations as experienced on such a massive scale in the space of a mere twelve-month period certainly stretched things a bit, at a time when there is such an urgent need for investment in all sectors. While the traditional powerhouse of Catalunya may be better equipped than most areas to face up to the current crisis and build on the impetus created in the wake of the Olympics, the abandoned EXPO pavilions in Sevilla, a place with chronic unemployment and huge disparities of wealth, provide evidence of the need to concentrate on the more mundane day-to-day issues – how the country deals with the post-1992 blues brought on by present economic conditions will determine whether it remains counted among the leading European nations.

CHRONOLOGY OF MONUMENTS

25,000 BC	Prehistoric settlements, mainly around Santander.	Cave paintings at Altamira and Puente Viesgo; also Las Piletas (near Ronda).
1100 BC	**Phoenicians** found Cádiz.	
C9th–4th BC	**Celts** settle in the north.	Celtic dolmens and "*citania*": both can be seen at La Guardia (Galicia).
	Greeks establish trading posts along east coast.	Empuries, near Barcelona (Greek site).
C3rd BC	**Carthaginians** occupy Andalucian and Mediterranean coast.	**Celto-Iberian** culture develops, with Greek influence: busts of "La Dama de Elche", etc in Museo Nacional Arqueológico, Madrid.
214 BC	Second Punic War with Rome.	
210 BC	**Roman colonization** begins.	Important **Roman sites** at Mérida, Tarragona, Itálica, Carmona, Sagunto, Segovia, etc.
414 AD	**Visigoths** arrive.	Sculpture and jewellery (in museums at Madrid and Toledo); also isolated churches.
711	**Moors** from North Africa invade, and conquer peninsula within seven years.	
718	Battle of Covadonga: Christian victory leads to formation of **Asturian kingdom**.	Asturian **pre-Romanesque** churches in and around Oviedo and the Picos de Europa.
756	Abd ar-Rahman I proclaims **Emirate of Córdoba**.	Great Mosque (Mezquita) begun at Córdoba, climax of **early Moorish architecture**.
812	Christians discover body of Santiago (St James) at Compostela.	**Mozarabic** churches built by Arabized Christians in Andalucía – and in the north a century later.
C9th	Kingdoms of **Catalunya** and **Navarra** founded.	
939	Abd ar-Rahman III adopts title "Caliph".	Medina Azahara palace and extensions to Mezquita at Córdoba in the **Caliphal style**.
967	**Al-Mansur** usurps Caliphal powers, and forces Christians back into the Asturias.	
1013	Caliphate disintegrates into *taifas*, petty kingdoms.	Alcazabas built at Málaga, Granada, Almería, Sevilla, Carmona, Ronda, etc.
1037	Fernando I unites kingdoms of Castile and León-Asturias. Ramón Berenguer I extends and strengthens Catalan kingdom.	**Romanesque architecture** enters Spain along the pilgrim route to Compostela. Superb examples throughout Castile and the north – especially at Salamanca, Segovia, Burgos, Ávila and Santillana.
1085	Christians capture Toledo.	
1086	**Almoravids** invade Spain.	
1147	**Almohads** restore Muslim authority in Andalucía.	Sevilla becomes new Moorish capital in Spain: **Almohad minarets** include Giralda and Torre del Oro.
1162	Alfonso II unites kingdoms of Aragón and Catalunya.	**Cluniac monasteries** built along pilgrim route to Santiago; **Cistercian abbeys** at Poblet and elsewhere.
1212	Almohad advance halted at Las Navas de Tolosa.	**Mudéjar** style emerges through Moorish craftsmen working on Christian buildings: good examples in Aragón at Teruel and Tarazona.

1213	Jaime I "El Conquistador" becomes king of Aragón. **Christian Reconquest** of Balearics (1229), Valencia (1238), Alicante (1266).	First **Gothic cathedrals** built at Burgos (1221), Toledo (1227) and León (1258). Catalan Gothic also develops in 1220s, best seen in Barcelona's Barri Gòtic and Girona.
1217	Fernando III "El Santo," king of Castile and retakes Córdoba (1236), Murcia (1241) and Sevilla (1248).	Granada's **Alhambra** palace constructed under Ibn Ahmar (1238–75) and his successors. Craftsmen from Granada also construct Sevilla Alcázar for Pedro the Cruel (1350–69).
1479	Castile and Aragón united under **Isabella and Fernando**.	Sevilla Cathedral (1402–1506). **Isabelline** style of late Gothic age of castle building: Coca and Segovia are outstanding.
1492	**Fall of Granada**, the last Moorish kingdom. **Discovery of America** by Columbus.	Last Gothic cathedrals built at Salamanca (1512) and Segovia (1522).
1516	**Carlos V** succeeds to throne and (1520) becomes the Holy Roman Emperor. "**Golden Age**.'	**Renaissance** reaches Spain. Elaborate early style is known as Plateresque (best represented at Salamanca). Later, key figures include Diego de Siloé (1495–1563; Burgos, Granada, etc) and Andrés de Valdelvira (d. 1565; Jaén, Úbeda and Baeza).
1519	Cortés lands in Mexico.	
1532	Pizarro "discovers" Peru.	
1556	**Felipe II** (d. 1598).	Juan de Herrera (1530–97) introduces new austerity in the Escorial.
1588	Sinking of the Armada.	**Painters** include: El Greco (1540–1614; Toledo), Ribalta (1551–1628), Ribera (1591–1652), Zurbarán (1598–1664), Alonso Cano (1601–67) and Velázquez (1599–1660). Best collections of all at Madrid's Prado.
1609	Expulsion of Moriscos, last remaining Spanish Muslims.	
1700	War of Spanish Succession brings Felipe V (1713–46), a Bourbon, to the throne. British seize Gibraltar.	**Baroque** develops in reaction to the severity of High Renaissance and reaches a flamboyant peak in the Churrigueresque style of the C18th. (Salamanca's Plaza Mayor, and altarpieces throughout Spain, and above all the Obradoiro facade at Santiago.) Last great cathedrals built at Valencia, Murcia and Cádiz.
1808	**French occupy Spain**.	Francisco de Goya (1746–1828). Royal Palaces of Madrid and Aranjuez.
1811	Venezuela declares independence: others follow.	
1835	**First Carlist War**.	**Dissolution of monasteries**.
1874	**Second Carlist War**.	
1898	Loss of Cuba, Spain's last American colony.	Antoni Gaudí (1852–1926) and **Modernisme**, or *Modernista* (Art Nouveau) movement in Barcelona.
1923	Primo de Rivera dictatorship.	Pablo **Picasso** (1883–1973; museum in Barcelona, *Guernica* in Madrid); Joan **Miró** (1893–1982; museum in Barcelona); Salvador **Dalí** (1904–89; museum at Figueres).
1931	Second Republic.	
1936–9	**Spanish Civil War**.	
1939	**Franco dictatorship** begins.	
1953	US makes economic deal with Franco in return for military bases.	
1975	Death of Franco; **restoration of democracy**.	Antonio Saura and **abstract artists** (Museum of Abstract Art, Cuenca).
1982	Election of socialist government under Prime Minister Felipe González.	
1992		Much new building in Barcelona for the Olympics and in Sevilla for Expo '92.

ARCHITECTURE

Spain's architectural legacy is a highly distinctive one, made up of a mixture of styles quite unlike anything else in Europe. The country was usually slow to pick up on the main currents of European architecture, and when a new style was adopted it was often in an extreme or stylized form. There are French, Dutch, German and Italian currents, but all were synthesized into something uniquely Spanish. Centuries of Moorish occupation have left an indelible mark, too, manifested both in the handful of wonderful buildings which represent the highpoint of Moorish civilization in Anda-lucía, and in a powerful influence on Christian and secular architecture, including the layout of entire towns.

There has been less of the wanton destruction of old buildings in Spain than in most other countries, and in general the architecture here is astonishingly well preserved. There's perhaps less purity of form than elsewhere in Europe – additions over the years have left many buildings with a medley of different styles – but no other country can boast quite as many old churches, castles and unspoiled towns and villages.

At the risk of making generalizations, it's possible to identify a number of **trends** in the buildings of Spain. As a rule, there is an emphasis on the longitudinal, and on solidity of construction. A heavy use of surface ornament is often popular, with elaborate doorways and rich decoration. Because of the warm climate there is an interest in outdoor living and a need for cool and open space, which accounts for the prevalence of patios in civic buildings and cloisters in religious edifices, including those which were not monastic. There is also a tendency to break up long vistas by various means, creating a variety of compartments within a large space.

THE ROMAN PERIOD

Although fragments of earlier civilizations do exist, Spain's architectural history (in terms of surviving buildings) begins in the **Roman** period, from which there remain a number of remarkable structures. These have no particular Spanish flavour, nor were they to prove as influential on subsequent developments as in some other countries, but nonetheless the aqueduct at **Segovia**, the bridge at **Alcántara** (the highest in the Roman world), and the theatre and associated remains at **Mérida** belong among the first rank of Roman survivals anywhere. There's another fine group in and around **Tarragona**, with walls, a necropolis, an arena, a forum and a praetorium in the city itself, and more notably an aqueduct, the Centcelles Mausoleum, the Arco de Bar and the Torre de Scipio all within a radius of a few kilometres.

Other Roman monuments worthy of special note include the walls of Lugo, the amphitheatre and castle at Sagunto, and the three-span triumphal arch at Medinaceli. Excavations of complete towns can be seen at Empuries, Itálica, Numancia and Bilbilis.

THE VISIGOTHIC AND ASTURIAN PERIODS

The **Visigothic** period, which succeeded the Roman, bequeathed a small number of buildings of uncertain date. Visigothic buildings have simple exteriors, and were the first in Spain to adopt the horseshoe arch (later to be altered and used widely by the Moors). They also developed elements from Roman buildings, the most refined example of which is at **Quintanilla de las Viñas** in Old Castile, a church whose exterior is enlivened by delicately carved stone friezes set in bands; inside there's a triumphal arch over the apse, carved with the earliest surviving representation of

Christ in Spain. Other remnants of the era survive at the modern industrial town of **Tarrasa** in Catalunya, formerly Egara, in the shape of three churches, one of which – the Baptistery of San Miguel – dates from the fifth or sixth century; the other two have apses that are probably of ninth-century construction. Other Visigothic buildings include part of the crypt of Palencia Cathedral, and the nearby basilica of San Juan at Baños de Cerrato, documented as seventh century.

Hard on the heels of the Visigothic epoch was the **Asturian** period, named after the small kingdom on the northern coast, which developed its own style during the ninth century. This retained Visigothic elements alongside technical developments that anticipated the general European trends still to come. A little group of buildings centred around **Oviedo** – the Cámara Santa, the church of Santulano in the city itself, San Miguel de Lillo and Santa María de Naranco on the slopes of Monte Naranco nearby – are, unusually in Spanish history, clearly superior to and more highly developed than any contemporaneous work in Europe. The last represents the pinnacle of the style, a perfectly proportioned little building with barrel vaulting and arches supported on pilasters, as well as delicate decoration using Roman and Byzantine elements. The isolated surrounding countryside holds a few similar buildings from the succeeding century, but the Asturian style was soon to be swallowed up by the new Romanesque movement which swept across the north of Spain from France and Italy.

THE MOORISH PERIOD

By this time most of Spain was under Muslim domination. It remained so, at least in part, until the final defeat of the Moors in 1492. During this period Moorish architecture did not develop in the way we understand the word, and it is best to consider the different epochs of building separately.

The first real style was the **Caliphate**, centred around Córdoba, whose great surviving monument – the **Mezquita** – was built and added to over a period from the eighth to the tenth centuries. The Caliphate style demonstrates most of the vocabulary used by Moorish builders over the years – horseshoe, cusped and multifoil arches, the contrasting use of courses of stone and brick, the use of interlacing as a particular feature of design, doors surmounted by blind arcades, stucco work, and the ornamental use of calligraphy along with geometric and plant motifs. Various technical innovations, too, were introduced in the construction of the Mezquita, from the original solution of two-tiered arches to give greater height to the ribbed dome vaults in front of the *mihrab* (prayer-niche).

Another example of the Caliphate style, the (now ruined) palace-city of **Medina Azahara**, just outside Córdoba, was no less splendid than the Mezquita. Many of its buildings were produced according to the descriptions of Solomon's temple. In **Toledo**, El Cristo de la Luz is a small-scale Caliphate mosque, and the old Bisagra Gate was part of the fortifications of that time. As the Reconquest progressed, other fortifications went up. Gormaz was begun in around 965. Only part of the original Moorish building has survived, including two gateways. Calatayud, in the north, holds more fortifications of the period, probably of an even earlier date.

With the fall of the Caliphate at the end of the eleventh century, Moorish Spain was divided into independent kingdoms or *taifas*, giving rise to the *alcazabas* or castles at Granada, Málaga, Guadix, Almería, Tarifa and Carmona. The Aljafería palace in Zaragoza also dates from this period, much altered over the years but preserving its mosque and a tower. The strongest *taifa* was at Sevilla, where later the **Almohad** dynasty created an art of refined brickwork and left behind the Patio de Yeso in the Alcázar, the Torre del Oro, which originally formed part of the city's fortifications, and the Giralda – former minaret of the mosque and arguably the finest tower ever built in the Arab world.

The apotheosis of pure Muslim art came, however, with the **Nasrid** dynasty in Granada, the last city to fall to the Christians. The gorgeously opulent palace of the **Alhambra** went up between the thirteenth and fifteenth centuries. Built on a hill against the romantic backdrop of the Sierra Nevada, this structure provided the necessary partner in the union between art and nature sought by the Moorish architects, especially in the lush gardens of the more modest Generalife section. As for the palace itself, the buildings are structurally very poor, with no exterior features of note; yet the interior, around the two great courtyards, is one of the most intoxicating creations in the world, the culminating ideal of Moorish civilization, built when it was already in irreversible decline.

MOZARABIC AND MUDÉJAR

The Moorish occupation had an indelible influence on the architecture of Spain, and led directly to two hybrid architectural styles unique to the country – **Mozarabic** and Mudéjar. The former was the style of Christians subjugated by the Moors who retained their old religion but built in the Arabic style. Their churches are mostly in isolated situations – San Miguel de Escalada east of León, Santa María de Lebena near the Picos de Europa and San Baudelio near Berlanga de Duero in Soria Province are the finest examples.

Mudéjar is far more common, the style of the Arabs who stayed on after their homelands had been conquered, or who had migrated to the Christian kingdoms. Often they proved to be both the most skilful builders and the cheapest workforce, and they left their mark on almost all of the country over a period of several centuries. They continued to build predominantly in brick, mainly working on the construction of parish churches, resulting in an odd – though unmistakably Moorish – Christian-Islamic hybrid that some claim is barely a distinct architectural style at all. There are details of Mudéjar buildings under the relevant European headings, below, although a number deserve inclusion here as being more firmly within the Arab tradition. Among these are the palaces of Tordesillas and the Alcázar in Sevilla; various secular buildings in Toledo; the Chapel of the Assumption of Santiago at Las Huelgas; and the synagogues of Toledo and Córdoba.

THE ROMANESQUE

Back in the mainstream of European architecture, the **Romanesque** style in Spain is most associated with the churches, bridges and hospices built along the **pilgrim road** to Santiago de Compostela. None of the hospices has survived, but the Puente la Reina in Navarra is the most famous of a number of Romanesque-era bridges. The churches come in various shapes and forms, but all include beautiful sculpture. The Cathedral of Jaca, the monasteries of Santa Cruz de la Seros, San Juan de la Peña and Leyre, and the churches of Santa María la Real at Sanguesa, San Miguel at Estella, San Martín at Fromista and San Isidoro at León are the most notable examples, but the climax, of the style as of the pilgrimage, came with the great **Cathedral of Santiago** itself. This is now almost entirely encased by Baroque additions, but preserves the original shape of the interior. Begun around 1070, it was built to allow as much space as possible for the pilgrims to circulate – hence the large triforium gallery, and the ambulatory with radiating chapels. Santiago's cathedral also served as a model for many contemporary derivations, particularly the nearby cathedrals of Lugo, Orense and Tuy.

Elsewhere, the influence of the great Burgundian abbey of Cluny, which so influenced the development of the pilgrimage, can be seen most clearly at **San Vicente** in Ávila. Another building closely related to the pilgrimage churches is the monastery of **Santo Domingo de Silos**, where the architecture and superb bas-reliefs of the cloisters, the only surviving part of the original building, are clearly derived from French models. There's an additional ingredient, too: most of the capitals here show an unmistakable Moorish influence – a very early example of the mix of East and West to be found in Spain.

Other Romanesque buildings tend towards regional variants. In **Catalunya**, whose architectural history so often diverges from that of the rest of Spain, the influence was more from Lombardy than France, with tall, square bell towers, prominent apses, blind arcading and little sculptural detail – although this last was later to become important, for example in the cloisters of the Cathedral and San Pedro in Girona.

Belfries were a dominant feature in **Segovia**, where the main innovation was the construction of covered arcades in the manner of cloisters built against the sides of this building, making the parish churches of this city amongst the most distinctive in Spain. **Soria's** churches, particularly San Domingo, recall those of Poitiers, although the fantastic cloister of San Juan de Duero defies classification in its combination of the round-headed Romanesque, early pointed Gothic, and Moorish horseshoe and intersecting arches in one extraordinarily capricious composition. **Zamora** was unusual in having a Byzantine influence; also its portals tended to lack tympana, but had richly carved archivolts. Finally, there are a number of churches in a crossover *Mudéjar*/Romanesque style in such places as Toledo, Sahagún, Cúellar and Arévalo.

Military architecture of this period is dominated by the complete walls of Ávila, the best preserved in Europe, and by the castle at Loarre, the most spectacular of the early Christian castles built to defend the conquered lands. Survivors of civil buildings are few and far between, but there are precious examples in the form of the palaces of Estella and Huesca.

THE TRANSITIONAL STYLE

With the advent of the Cistercian reforms, the **Transitional** style was introduced to Spain in the middle of the twelfth century, first in a series of monasteries – La Oliva, Veruela, Poblet, Santes Creus, Las Huelgas and Santa María la Huerta – that are notable for massiveness of construction combined with the introduction of such Gothic characteristics as the pointed arch and the ribbed vault.

In some ways, **La Oliva** can claim to be the first Gothic building in Spain, although in both its solidity and ground plan it is still Romanesque in spirit. The severe, unadorned style of the Cistercians was to have a great impact at a time when the rest of Europe was moving towards an appreciation of the structural advantages of Gothic, not quickly realized in Spain. The late twelfth and early thirteenth century saw the construction of a number of cathedrals in the Transitional style – Siguenza, Ávila, Santo Domingo de la Calzada, Tarragona and Lleida – all of which had fortress-like features and were indeed at times used for defensive purposes. Similar is the Collegiate church at Tudela, although the sculpture here, in direct contravention of Cistercian rules, is among the richest in Spain.

A few buildings of the same period show clear **Byzantine** influence – the Old Cathedral of Salamanca, Zamora Cathedral and the Colegiata at Toro – each with a distinctive central dome, although their design otherwise shows normal Transitional elements. Closely related are the Cathedral of Ciudad Rodrigo and the often octagonally shaped buildings

associated with the Knights Templar: La Vera Cruz in Segovia, and two mysterious buildings on the pilgrim route whose exact nature is uncertain – Eunate and Torres de Río.

THE GOTHIC STYLE

Examples of the early **Gothic** style in Spain are rare, and those that there are seem to derive from French and English sources. The refectory of Santa María la Huerta is as pure and elegant as the best in France; Cuenca Cathedral, begun about 1200, seems to derive from a Norman or English model. Later, buildings began to develop a more specifically Spanish style, eschewing any notions of purity of form.

Three great cathedrals commenced in the 1220s best exemplify the increasingly Spanish features of the churches of the time. Of these, the overall plans and building of **Burgos** and **Toledo** are obviously indebted to French models, but they are far from the grace and lightness of the great French Gothic cathedrals. The windows are much smaller – partly, perhaps, to cut down on excessive sunlight, partly to preserve a greater sense of mystery than their French equivalents did. Both were also given the rich interior decoration that soon became the norm for Spanish cathedrals, most characteristic of which was the *coro*, an elaborate set of choir stalls often enclosed by a *trascoro* or retrochoir, situated in the nave – a feature that looks odd to those used to the chancel-based choirs of northern Europe. The reasons for this are unclear, but it seems it was associated with the predominance of the choir services of the clergy, which meant that the construction of the *coro* made the best use of the space; it may also have been felt that the chancel should be reserved solely for the Holy Sacrament, and not downgraded for any other purpose.

Equally typical are the giant *retablos*, the most important of which are situated over the high altar, again masking the architecture. Generally these were carved and multicoloured, and contained a series of scenes from the life of Christ and of the Virgin, perhaps along with statues of saints. Basically their function was similar to that of stained-glass windows in the cathedrals of France, providing pictorial representation of the Bible to an illiterate population. Smaller *retablos*, either painted or carved, were placed over smaller altars. In addition, tombs of monarchs, aristocratic families, bishops and saints were often placed in specially built chapels, and sometimes enclosed by iron gates or grilles (*rejas*) which were often of a highly elaborate workmanship and would enclose the entrances to the *coro* and the chancel too. The overall effect of all this decoration can appear oversumptuous to the modern eye, but it gives a better impression of a medieval cathedral than anything that can be found in Northern Europe, where reformation, revolution, war and restoration have combined to leave buildings that are architecturally far purer but spiritually far less authentic.

The third great cathedral of the 1200s, **León**, was the only one to adopt the normal French system of triple portal, prominent flying buttresses and large windows filled with brilliantly coloured stained glass. Even here, however, there were Spanish touches, such as the cloister and its dependencies, and the later construction of a *coro*.

All the other cathedrals followed the model of Burgos and Toledo. **El Burgo de Osma** is in a way a miniature version of them, although it's purer Gothic in form. **Palencia**, built in the fourteenth and fifteenth centuries, is unusual in that most of its decoration is roughly contemporary with the architecture, with very few later additions. At **Pamplona** and **Huesca**, the architects built in the knowledge that there would be a *coro* in the nave – though ironically these were removed relatively recently by restorers. Pamplona's cloister, the earliest part of the building, is perhaps the most beautiful Gothic cloister in Spain. It has several fine doorways and a chapel with an exquisite star vault, a feature that was to be Spain's main contribution to the vocabulary of Gothic architecture, as characteristic as fan vaulting in England, although far more common – and with an obvious debt to Moorish models. There are other, equally grand examples of the national Gothic style: **Murcia** and **Oviedo** are two, **Sevilla** a more spectacular one, its vast size determined by the ground plan of the mosque that preceded it.

REGIONAL STYLES

Regional forms of Gothic are found in Catalunya and Aragón. In **Catalunya**, churches were built with huge arcades, omitting the triforium and including only a small clerestory. Long spans were also common; aisles, if there were any, were very nearly the same height as the nave; buttresses were internalized by the construction of tall, straight-walled chapels built between them, lending a rather sober appearance to the outside. Barcelona's **Cathedral of Santa María del Mar** is a good example of all these features, as is **Palma Cathedral**, although the most spectacular of the Catalan cathedrals is **Girona** – so daring structurally as to be admired more for its engineering than its aesthetic appeal.

In **Aragón** there was strong Mudéjar influence, which extended even to the cathedrals of **Zaragoza**, **Tarazona** and **Teruel**. The towers of these cities, and of **Calatayud**, tend to be either square in shape and decorated with ceramic tiles that glisten in the sun, or else octagonal and of brick only. Both show a virtuoso skill in decoration with what appear to be very basic and unpromising materials. Each of the cathedrals has a central cupola, while Tarazona has an amazing cloister filled with Mudéjar ornament. There's another unusual cloister far away in Guadalupe, while more orthodox Mudéjar Gothic churches are all over, though there's a fine concentration in **Toledo**.

MILITARY ARCHITECTURE

Turning to **military architecture**, a number of fortified towns from the Gothic period still survive. Toledo has several gateways and two bridges of the era, and there are fine examples of walls at Albarracín, Daroca, Morella, Berlanga de Duero, Madrigal de las Altes Torres and Montblanch. Spain's castles of this period are without parallel in Europe. However, those that had a genuine function in the Reconquest are as a rule in the poorest condition, while those that look most impressive today often had little if any defensive purpose. It should be remembered that there is no Spanish equivalent at any time to the English or French country house. Where great houses were built by the nobility in Spain, they often resembled castles, even if they were never used for military purposes.

Perhaps the finest fourteenth-century castle is that of **Bellver** near Palma, a circular structure built as a summer residence by the kings of Mallorca. The great fifteenth-century castle at **Olite** is a palace in the pastiche form on a grand scale. For all the monumentality of its towers, many are wholly ornamental and would have been quite useless in time of war. Unfortunately, what you see today gives little hint of the richness of the former interior decoration.

Along the banks of the Duero are castles which were genuinely in action at the time of the Reconquest. **Gormaz** is particularly interesting, showing how an originally Moorish building was adapted by the Christians after its capture. **Peñafiel's** fifteenth-century castle is actually the successor to the one that was built as protection against the Moors; apart from its own severe beauty, it clearly shows the importance of a strong strategic location. The many brick castles in the **area of Segovia and Valladolid** should be thought of more as expressions of the wealth and power of the nobility than as genuine military constructions of the time. These often incorporated Mudéjar features, and their construction was often in reality rather delicate: **Coca** is the best example of this.

CIVIL BUILDINGS AND LATE GOTHIC

The legacy of **Gothic civil architecture** is also impressive. Large numbers of towns preserve their medieval character in layout and design, even if many of the houses are not, strictly speaking, original. Important town mansions survive all over the country, often characterized by the carving of a coat of arms on the facade. **Cáceres**, in Extremadura, is probably the richest place for seigneurial houses, although most of the other towns in this province are also notable for vernacular architecture of this, and later dates. Elsewhere, the shipyards of **Barcelona** constitute a unique survival from the Gothic period, as do parts of the Barri Gotic, which contains a number of original municipal buildings. Barcelona also has the earliest *lonja*, or exchange – later and more exotic examples of which can be found in Valencia, Palma and Zaragoza.

Spanish **late Gothic** architecture is particularly spectacular, the increasing ornamentation partly the result of the mid-fifteenth-century influx of artists from Germany and the Netherlands to Spain. **Burgos** and **Toledo** were the centre of the developing style. Juan de Colonia built the superb openwork spires of Burgos Cathedral, modelled on those of his native Cologne – which themselves, ironically,

existed only on paper until the nineteenth century. His son, Simon, was responsible for other work on the same building, particularly the Capilla del Condestable at the east end, and worked with his father on the Cartuja de Miraflores. At the same time, Anequin de Egas from Brussels began a series of additions to Toledo Cathedral.

A little later the focus shifted to **Valladolid** and became increasingly florid – the **Isabelline** style – reaching its most extreme in the facades of San Pablo and the Colegio San Gregorio. It's not known who was responsible for these, or for the equally ornate facade of Santa María in Aranda de Duero, though a variety of people have been suggested, not least Juan Guas, who is known to have built San Juan de los Reyes in Toledo, the gallery of the castle at **Manzanares el Real** and perhaps the Palacio del Infantado in **Guadalajara**. The Isabelline style, at its best, combined the Moorish penchant for hanging decoration with standard European motifs, and has been seen by some commentators as the one chance Spain had to create its own special, unified architectural style. However, Isabelline had a very short life. The queen after whom it was named became more enchanted by the Italians before long, and encouraged the adoption of the Renaissance in Spain.

There was also a counter-movement towards a purer Gothic form. The New Cathedral of **Salamanca** and the Cathedral of **Segovia** were both begun in the sixteenth century in what was then a wholly archaic language by Juan Gil de Ontañón, and continued by his son Rodrigo. Juan de Álava also built a number of monuments in this style – San Esteban in Salamanca, part of the cathedral at Plasencia, and the cloisters at Santiago. **Segovia Cathedral**, too – unusually for Spain – displays a remarkable unity of form, using the traditional Gothic elements rejected by earlier builders.

THE RENAISSANCE

Oddly enough, the **Renaissance** was introduced to Spain with the **Collegio Santa Cruz** in Valladolid, just a few hundred metres from the simultaneous construction of two Isabelline facades. The architect, Lorenzo Vázquez, for all his historical importance, remains a rather shadowy figure. (Later, he was to build an

Italian Renaissance palace at La Calahorra in Andalucía.) Enrique de Egas, who built the hospitals at Toledo (Santa Cruz), Granada and Santiago, and who also worked in a late Gothic style, as witnessed by his Capilla Real in Granada and his design for the adjoining cathedral, is much better documented.

Much early Spanish Renaissance architecture is termed **Plateresque**, from the profusion of carving which allegedly resembled the work of silversmiths. The term is now applied rather loosely, but it is most associated with **Salamanca**, which is built of an extremely delicate rose-coloured sandstone. The supreme masterpiece of the style is the facade of the **University** here, where instead of the wild and irregular carvings of Valladolid, a generation before, all is order and symmetry while equally ornate. The motifs used in Plateresque carving are wholly Italianate – figures in medallions, *putti*, candelabra, grotesques, garlands of flowers and fruit, scrollwork and coats of arms. No convincing attribution has been made for the university facade, but one Plateresque architect whose work can be traced is **Alonso de Covarrubias**. He built the Capilla de los Reyes Nuevos in Toledo Cathedral, part of the Alcázar and probably the Hospital de Tavera in the same city, and worked on Sigüenza Cathedral, particularly the amazing sacristy. The facade of the University of Alcalá de Henares is a more severe Plateresque masterpiece by Rodrigo Gil de Ontañón; other important works are San Marcos in León by Juan de Badajoz, and the Hospital del Rey near Burgos.

The **High Renaissance**, by contrast, centred around **Andalucía**, the part of the country that was most lacking in Christian architecture following its liberation from the Muslim powers. The real masterpiece of the style is the **Palace of Carlos V** in Granada – incongruously located in the Alhambra, but a superbly pure piece of architecture. It is rare in being based on a round courtyard, and is the only surviving building by Pedro Machuca. As for churches, the leading architect of the Andalucian Renaissance in this field was Diego de Siloé, who began his career as a sculptor in Burgos under his father, Gil, and built the marvellous Plateresque *Escalera Dorada* in the cathedral there. Following study in Italy, he worked as an architect, devising an ingenious east end for the cathedral at Granada, and

designing Guadix Cathedral and El Savador at Úbeda. The last-named was actually built by his pupil, Andrés de Vandelvira, whose own main work is the monumental Cathedral of Jaén. All these buildings show a strongly classical influence.

The severest, purest and greatest Spanish Renaissance architect was **Juan de Herrera**, who succeeded Juan Bautista de Toledo as architect of **El Escorial**, to which he devoted much of his working life. To many, this vast building is excessively sober, particularly in a country where ornamentation has so often reigned supreme. However, it does have a unique grandeur, and illustrates the Spanish penchant for taking any style to its extremes. Herrera's other main building is the **Cathedral of Valladolid**, though sadly only half of this was ever built, and some of that well after Herrera. In this truncated form it can appear rather cold and sombre, although the model for the complete building shows what a well-proportioned, harmonious and majestic edifice it might have become.

THE BAROQUE

For a time, Herrera's style was to spawn a number of imitations, and early **Baroque** architecture was remarkably restrained – Madrid's early seventeenth-century **Plaza Mayor** by Juan Gomez de Mora being a case in point. In the east, Neapolitan influence was paramount, and led to the building of a large number of dignified churches.

Before long, however, this early phase gave way to an exuberant, playful and confident style that is perhaps Spain's most singular contribution to European architecture, the **Churrigueresque** – taken from the name of the family of architects, the Churrigueras, with whom the style was most associated. Ironically, their own work in architecture was far less ornate than that of many of their successors, although they also designed *retablos*, which are as embellished as anything that followed, so large as to seem almost pieces of architecture in themselves. These were typically of carved wood, painted and gilded, with twisted columns populated by saints in visionary or ecstatic mood and swirling processions of angels. *Retablos* of this type were soon to be found in churches all over Spain. Often the work of far cruder imitators, they raised the ire of visiting Protestant travellers, who used the term "Churrigueresque" to signify all that was basest in art. It's still a pejorative term, although the Churrigueras did actually create a number of masterpieces.

José, the eldest brother, created a complete planned town in **Nuevo Baztán**, not far from Madrid. Alberto, the youngest and most talented, laid out the **Plaza Mayor** in Salamanca in collaboration with Andrés García de Quiñones – a superb and harmonious piece of town planning, integrated wonderfully with the town's older buildings, and with the plain sides enlivened by carvings deriving from Plateresque work, and the rhythmic facade of the *Ayuntamiento* providing a central focus on the north side.

The Churrigeras' contemporaries were more profusely ornate, often imitating the form of the *retablos* in their portals, perhaps the finest example of which is the **Hospicio San Fernando** in Madrid by Pedro de Ribera. Another new architectural feature was the *transparente*, in which a lavish altarpiece is lit from above by a window cut in the vault, giving a highly theatrical effect. The most famous example is that in **Toledo Cathedral** by Narciso Tomé, a brilliant piece of illusionism when the sun shines through, though in an utterly incongruous setting.

The Baroque style was also, of course, used when making additions to existing buildings, something you see all over Spain. Sometimes the merging of Baroque and medieval was triumphantly successful, as in the mid-eighteenth-century Obradoiro facade of **Santiago Cathedral** by Fernando Casas y Novoa, the climax of about a century's work, encasing the old Romanesque building in a lively Baroque exterior. While the loss of the Romanesque exterior is regrettable, particularly as some of the Baroque building is mediocre, the facade ranks as one of the most joyous creations in all architecture, and the ultimate triumph of Spanish Baroque. Other notably successful Baroque additions are the towers of the cathedrals of El Burgo de Osma, Santo Domingo de la Calzada and Murcia, which all harmonize surprisingly well with the existing structures, and give them a dimension they previously lacked. Many other additions, however, were far less fortunate: much of the time Baroque builders paid insufficient atten-

tion to the scale, style and materials of the existing work, and even when each is a competent piece of work in its own right, old and new scream at each other in horror.

Because of the trend towards enlivening old buildings, only one complete Baroque cathedral was built in Spain, at **Cádiz**. Nor are there many notable Baroque monasteries, although a number of charterhouses (*cartujas*) were built, not least at **Granada**, which became more and more extreme as construction progressed, culminating in the outrageous *sagrario* (sacristy) by Francesco Hurtado Izquiero. However, Spanish Baroque never found favour at court, where Italian and French models were preferred, and architects and decorators were imported from these countries, producing the Bourbon palaces of Aranjuez, La Granja de San Ildefonso and Madrid, which stand apart from Spanish buildings of the period. Filippo Juvara, the famous architect of Turin, was summoned to Spain in the penultimate year of his life to design the garden front of La Granja and the overall plan for Madrid, although both were executed by his pupil, Giovanni Battista Sachetti.

NEOCLASSICISM

In time, the court taste changed to **Neoclassical**, enforced by the mid-century establishment of academies, and the presiding architectural style became heavy and monumental in scale. The dominant figure was **Ventura Rodríguez**, a technically competent architect who built a lavish Augustinian church in **Valladolid** and completed **Basílica del Pilar** in Zaragoza – a colossal building with elements drawn from a variety of styles that is more notable for its grandiose outline than for any other feature. But Rodríguez's talents were not put to their best use: his facade for **Pamplona Cathedral** would look fine on a bank but is wholly incongruous for a church, and a serious distraction in what is otherwise a fine building; and his plain, rather nondescript church at **Santo Domingo de Silos** is a similarly poor partner for the great cloister there. Another leading Neoclassical architect was **Juan de Villaneuva**, who built the **Prado** (actually as a natural history museum) and the two **Casitas** at El Escorial.

Spain's subsequent provincial history is mirrored in the paucity of buildings of much consequence. The slow process of industrial and social change meant that there were few of the self-confident expressions of prosperity found all over northern Europe. There were a host of imitative styles, but it is really only on the small scale that they give much pleasure. **Neo-Gothic**, also, was nowhere near as vital or as prevalent as elsewhere: the cathedrals built in this style, at **San Sebastián** and **Vitoria**, are not especially notable, and the most satisfying work was probably the completion of **Barcelona Cathedral**, which was actually accomplished according to a fifteenth-century plan.

MODERNISME

Barcelona provides the one bright spot in Spain's otherwise gloomy architectural history of the past two centuries, showing once again how distinctive Catalunya's heritage is. The last quarter of the nineteenth century was a turbulent time there – a fact mirrored in the **Modernisme** (or *Modernista*) movement in architecture, which created a remarkable number of challenging, art nouveau-type buildings until well into the present century.

The dominant genius was **Antoni Gaudí**, one of the most distinctive voices of the age – indeed, of any age. He was interested not merely in architecture but also in sculpture and interior design, including lighting. His main architectural influences were Moorish and Gothic, which he considered the greatest European style. From the former he took towers, trompe l'oeil effects, repeated elements, ceramics, cornices, dragons and the use of water, all employed, like his Gothic influences, in a free and fantastic way. He was also influenced by the natural world: trees, rocks, embankments, animals, birds, eroded and organic forms. He combined all these elements in an amazing – and distinctive – architectural vocabulary. Some of his projects were almost impossibly ambitious. He worked for over forty years on the **Sagrada Familia**, yet only built a small portion. The **Parc Güell** was another vast project for a complete garden city, a commercial failure that has become a successful public park. Still, many less grandiose plans in a variety of forms were completed in Barcelona, and his work can also be seen in Astorga, León and Comillas.

Gaudí stands out among his **contemporaries**, but there are a number of other architects of the time worthy of note, such as Lluis Domanech y Montaner, who was responsible for the sumptuous Palau de la Musica in Barcelona and who, with Juan Martorell, built at Comillas. These other architects, though, came nowhere near to developing the personal style of Gaudí and were far less utopian in their thinking.

MODERN

Beyond the Modernisme movement, much of Spain's **modern architecture** is best passed over. The buildings for the abortive "Fair of the Americas" in Sevilla in 1929 do have a certain period charm, but there's not much that's good about the bloated public buildings that went up in Madrid before and after the Civil War. The last thirty years have seen the wholesale destruction of large sections of the coast, particularly the south and east, as Spain led the way in speculative building projects, wiping out old communities in order to develop the country's tourist facilities; in addition, many of the larger cities have been spoiled by ugly and unchecked modern sprawl – Valladolid and Zaragoza are particularly good examples of irretrievably damaged cities.

The most prestigious (if politically obnoxious) building project of recent years was Franco's **Valley of the Fallen** outside Madrid, which commemorates the dead of the Civil War, and also houses the Generalíssimo's own tomb. It's a typical example of the sort of building favoured by dictators – classical in inspiration, overbearing in style.

More exciting is the project to complete Gaudí's **Sagrada Familia**, which is likely to take a century or more. It remains to be seen whether the finishing process will take the form of pastiche of the master or modern innovation. Regrettably, the continuing construction of **Madrid Cathedral** is another opportunity missed. The Neo-Romanesque crypt built at the end of the last century has been succeeded by a dull medley of Neo-Gothic and Neoclassical, unlikely to produce anything very challenging.

Only in Catalunya was modern architecture kept alive at all, through the work of local architects such as Oriol Bohigas, Ricardo Bofill and Federico Correa. Here too, the first signs of a new style have emerged, in a series of massive projects undertaken for the 1992 Olympics. A similar process took place in Sevilla in preparation for the World Fair.

Away from the big cities, and to Spain's further credit, most of the smaller towns have been untouched by modern building programmes, and remain delightfully unspoiled. There has grown up, since the return to democracy, a genuine concern about the country's heritage, which was pretty much taken for granted in the past, and a good deal of restoration work is now underway. Spain's great monuments remain, but there are still equally potent joys to be found in the country's townscapes, whether they be simple agricultural villages, complete small towns such as Santillana del Mar and Covarrubias, or formerly important cities such as Toledo, Segovia, Salamanca and Santiago.

Gordon McLachlan

SPANISH PAINTING

From the Middle Ages to the present day, the history of Spanish painting is a chequered one, more a series of high spots – El Greco, Velázquez, Goya, Picasso – than a continuous process of development. Influence from abroad has often been a factor, with somewhat mixed results. Yet at its best Spanish painting can stand comparison with that of any other country, not least in its intensity: the great masterpieces of Spain have a power that has seldom been equalled elsewhere.

BEGINNINGS

Early examples of this strength of expression can be found in the **illuminated manuscripts** and **mural paintings** of the eleventh and twelfth centuries. Dominant among the manuscripts are the many versions of Beatus's *Commentaries on the Apocalypse*, the original text of which, written by an eighth-century Spanish monk, inspired a whole series of versions illuminating the text with brilliantly coloured miniatures. These books have found their way into libraries all over the world, but many still remain in Spain, with those in Girona and El Burgo de Osma particularly worthy of note.

The great decorative plans of village churches are also characteristic of the period, especially in Catalunya, though for the most part these are no longer in situ; many were

saved earlier this century, just in time to prevent them from deteriorating irrevocably, and have been removed to museums, of which Barcelona's have by far the finest collection. The most imposing example of this style is by the so-called **Master of Tahull**, whose decoration of the apse of the church of San Clemente combines a Byzantine hierarchical composition with the vibrant colours and strong outlines of the manuscript illuminators. His overall rawness and monumentality seem strangely anticipatory of much of the best modern art.

Amazingly, two other highly talented painters also worked in the village of Tahull in the 1120s: art historians have christened them the **Master of Maderuelo** and the **Master of the Last Judgement**. Another notable artist of the period is the **Master of Pedret**, who incorporated scenes of everyday and natural life into his paintings.

Catalan studios also produced painted wooden altar frontals, often based on a central figure of a saint, surrounded by scenes from his life. In time, this grew in scale into the large *retablo* over the high altar – a key feature of Spanish churches for centuries. The most remarkable frescoes outside Catalunya are those of the Panteón de los Reyes in San Isidoro in León. These date from the second half of the twelfth century, and show a softer, more courtly style, perhaps influenced by French models.

THE CATALAN SCHOOL

In the Gothic period, Catalunya's predominance continued, rivalled only by Valencia. The leader of the school was **Ferrer Bassa** (c.1285–1348), court painter to Pedro IV of Aragón and a manuscript illuminator. Unfortunately, his only certain surviving work comes from late in his long career – a series of murals in the Convent of Pedralbes in Barcelona. These are charming, notable for their colouring and descriptive qualities, along with a sense of movement and skilled draughtsmanship, and are clearly influenced by the paintings of the Sienese school, though they're freer and less refined. Bassa may also have been influenced by the rounder qualities of Giotto and the Florentine school – Italian currents that are also found in the work of the artist's followers, along with various French trends.

The most notable names of this school were **Jaume Serra** (d. 1395), his brother, **Pere Serra** (d. 1408), **Ramón Destorrents** (1346–91), **Luis Borrassa** (d. 1424) and **Ramón de Mur** (d. 1435). **Bernat Martorell** (d. 1452) is perhaps the most appealing of the group, a notable draughtsman who worked very carefully and deliberately, striving to give character to faces in his paintings. **Luis Daimau** (d. 1460) came strongly under the influence of contemporary Flemish painting, in particular that of Jan van Eyck, and no other foreign currents are discernible in his work. **Jaume Huguet** (c.1414–92) blended this new realism to the traditional forms of the Catalan school, and can thus be seen as a representative of the International Gothic style of painting.

THE VALENCIAN SCHOOL

The Valencian school tended towards a more purely Italian influence, although one of its main painters, **Andrés Marzal de Sax** (d. 1410), may have been German. Other notable names are **Pedro Nicolau** (d. 1410), **Jaime Baco** ("Jacomart") (d. 1461), **Juan Rexach** (1431–92) and **Rodrigo de Osona** (d. 1510), the last of whom was influenced by the Renaissance. The greatest of all the Spanish Primitives, however, was **Bartolomé Bermejo** (d. 1495/8), originally from Córdoba, who worked in both Valencia and Barcelona. He seems to have had a fairly long career but only a few works, of a consistently high quality, survive. His earlier paintings, of which the Prado's *Santo Domingo de Silos* is a good example, are sumptuous; the later works, particularly the *Pietà* in Barcelona Cathedral, are altogether more complex, with a haunting sense of mystery and a Flemish and French influence that marks the introduction of oil painting to Spain.

THE CASTILIAN SCHOOL

In Castile, artists of foreign origin predominated – **Deillo Delli** ("Nicolas Florentino") (d. 1470) in Salamanca, **Nicolás Frances** (1425–68) in León, **Jorge Inglés** (dates unknown) in Valladololid, and **Juan de Flandes** (d. 1514) in Salamanca and Valencia. The last became court painter to Isabella la Católica and introduced a Renaissance sense of space along with the beautiful modelling

and colouring typical of the Flemish school. There was a rustic local school active in Ávila, however, and towards the end of the century native artists came increasingly to the fore. Particularly notable is **Fernando Gallego** (c.1440–1507), who worked in Zamora and Extremadura. Superficially, his paintings seem strongly reminiscent of Flemish types, but his exaggerated sense of drama – manifested in distorted expressions, strange postures and movements frozen in mid-course – is far removed from these models. Nonetheless, the garments are correctly drawn, and landscape is often a feature of the backgrounds.

Pedro Berruguete (c.1450–1504) was originally trained in the Flemish style, but spent an extended period in Italy at the court of Urbino, where he remained until 1482. His productions from this period are so close to those of the Fleming Justus van Gent that art historians have frequently been unable to distinguish between them. On his return to Spain, Berruguete worked in a hybrid style: although his drawing was precise and he introduced chiaroscuro to Spanish art, he persisted in using the traditional gold backgrounds – an anachronistic mixture that is surprisingly satisfying. Berruguete was never a slavish imitator of Italian models, like too many of his successors, and his most impressive works are those with crowd scenes, where the differentiation of types and attitudes is remarkable. **Alonso Berruguete** (1486–1561), his son, also went to Italy, and his paintings are heavily Mannerist in style, with strong drawing and harsh colours. His work as a sculptor is more significant: uneven in quality but sometimes truly inspired, with many powerful and intensely personal images. Certainly, he was the most distinctive and arguably the greatest native Spanish artist of the Renaissance.

THE LATE RENAISSANCE

Too often the quality of Italian art was diluted in Spain: neither nudes nor mythological subjects – both of crucial importance in Italy – had any attraction here, and there is hardly an example of either. Instead, there was a sweetening and sentimentalization of religious models. In Valencia, **Fernando Yáñez** (d. 1531) and his collaborator **Fernando de los Llanos** (dates unknown) adopted this facet of the art of Leonardo da Vinci, while **Juan Vicente Masip** (c.1475–1550) and his son of the same name, usually referred to as **Juan de Juanes** (1523–79), drew more from Raphael, becoming ever more saccharine as time went on.

Sevilla also had a school of painters, beginning with **Alejo Fernandez** (d. 1543), but although less slavishly imitative of Italian models than the Valencian, it also failed to produce an artist of the very first rank. The Extremaduran **Luis Morales** (c. 1509–86) is more notable: he was revered by the common people, who referred to him as "El Divino", but he never found favour with authority, and much of his work is still in village churches. He is at his best with such small-scale subjects as *Madonna and Child*, which he repeated many times with slight variations. Strongly Mannerist in outlook, his drawing is rather stiff and his colours often cold, but he has a genuine religious feeling.

Ironically enough, it took a foreigner, Domenico Theotocopoulos (1540–1614), universally known as **El Greco**, to forge a truly great and quintessentially Spanish art in the late Renaissance period. He arrived in Toledo in 1575, having come from his native Crete via Italy. Presumably he hoped to find favour at court, particularly in the decoration of El Escorial, but was soon disappointed, and spent the rest of his life painting portraits of the nobility, along with a host of religious works for the many churches and monasteries of Spain's ecclesiastical capital. Having shown himself adept at both the Byzantine and Venetian styles of painting, he drew from both to create a highly idiosyncratic art that was ideally suited to the mood of Spain at the time. Distinguished features of his style include elongated faces and bodies, together with a sense of spiritual ecstasy that gives a strong feeling of the union of the terrestrial and the celestial. El Greco's gift for portraiture, too, is shown not only in his paintings of real-life sitters, but also in those of historical subjects, most notably in the several series of Apostles he was required to produce. His greatest work, *The Burial of the Count of Orgaz*, in Santo Tomás in Toledo, displays all the facets of his genius in a single canvas. Later, El Greco's style became increasingly abstract, with a freeing of his brushwork that anticipates many subsequent developments in the history of art. Sadly, although he maintained a flourishing studio which produced many replicas, none of El Greco's followers picked up much on his master's style. Most talented was **Luis Tristán** (1586–1624), whose own output was very uneven.

At court, a school of portraiture was founded by a Dutchman, **Antonio Moro** (1517–76), who emphasized the dignity of his sitters in their facial expressions and by giving prominence to clothes and jewellery – a style that was followed by two native artists, **Alonso Sanchez Coello** (1531–88) and **Juan Pantoja de la Cruz** (1553–1608). At El Escorial, minor Italian Mannerists were imported in preference to native artists. An exception was the deaf-mute **Juan Navarret** (1526–79).

In Valencia, **Francisco Ribalta** (1565–1628) began working in a similar Mannerist style, but soon came under the influence of Caravaggio and introduced naturalism and the sharp contrasts of light associated with "tenebrism" into Spain. He was followed by a yet more significant painter, **Jusepe (Jose) de Ribera** (1591–1652). Ribera spent nearly all his career in Naples under the protection of the Spanish viceroys, who sent many of his works back to his native land. He had two distinctive periods: early on in his career he used heavy chiaroscuro and small, thick brushstrokes; later he brightened his palette considerably. Above all he was interested in the dignity of human beings, and whether he painted ancient philosophers in contemplation, saints in solace, or martyrs resigned to their fate, his art is a concentrated one, with the spotlight very much on the main subject. His subjects at times can appear gruesome, but they are very much of their period in that respect, and the treatment is never mere sensationalism. For a long time out of critical favour, Ribera now appears as one of the most accomplished artists of European Baroque.

THE SEVENTEENTH CENTURY

In the early seventeenth century, Sevilla and Madrid replaced Valencia and Toledo as the main artistic centres of Spain. **Francisco Pacheco** (1564–1654) was the father figure of the Sevillan school, although nowadays his work as a theorist is more significant than his paintings. He adopted a naturalistic approach as a reaction against Mannerism, and was followed in this by **Francisco Herrera** (c.1590–1656) and his son of the same name (1622–85), who painted in an increasingly bombastic and theatrical manner.

Towering high above these, Pacheco's son-in-law, **Diego Velázquez** (1599–1660), is probably the artist the Spanish people take most pride in. Velázquez was a stunning technician. His genre scenes of Sevillan life, painted while he was still in his teens, have a naturalistic quality that is almost photographic. In contrast to many of his fellow countrymen, Velázquez was a slow and meticulous worker: he probably painted less than 200 works in his entire career, some 120 of which survive, almost half of them in the Prado.

In 1623 Velázquez went to Madrid to work for the court, a position he retained for the rest of his life. As well as the many royal portraits, he portrayed the jesters and dwarfs of the palace, giving them a Spanish sense of dignity. In *The Surrender of Breda* he revolutionized history painting, ridding it of supernatural overtones. His greatest masterpieces, *Las Hilanderas* and *Las Meninas*, date from near the end of his life, and are remarkable for the way they immortalize fleeting moments, as well as for their absolute technical mastery, particularly of aerial perspective.

Juan Bautista del Marzo (c.1615–67), son-in-law and assistant to Velázquez, was so adept at imitating his style that it is often difficult to determine which works are the originals and which are copies. His independent work, however, is altogether of inferior quality. **Juan Carreno de Miranda** (1614–85) also followed Velázquez's portrait style very closely, and was very active as a painter of religious subjects, a field largely abandoned by Velázquez in his maturity.

In Sevilla, the greatest painter was **Francisco de Zurbarán** (1598–1664), who is best known as an illustrator of monastic life of the times. He painted mainly for the more austere orders, such as Carthusians and Hieronymites, and many of his portraits of saints are modelled on real-life monks, some of them single figures of an almost sculptural quality. Zurbarán's palette was a bright one, his lighting effects are subtle rather than dramatic, and he ranks as one of the supreme masters of still lifes, which have a frequent presence in his larger paintings as well as in a few independent compositions. A complete example of one of his decorative schemes is still extant at Guadalupe, but sadly his later work sometimes shows a fall-off in quality: to pay off his debts he was forced to produce a large number of works for export to religious foundations in Latin America.

Zurbarán also sentimentalized his style in order to meet the competition of his highly successful younger contemporary, **Bartolomé Esteban Murillo** (1618–82), who spent his entire career in Sevilla. Murillo's light, airy style was in perfect accord with the mood of the Counter-Reformation, and he was to have an important impact on Catholic imagery. His versions of subjects such as the Immaculate Conception, Madonna and Child, and the Good Shepherd, became the norm in terms of the portrayal of traditional dogma. His genre scenes of street urchins and portraits in the manner of van Dyck made him popular in northern Europe too, and for a long time he was considered one of the greatest artists of all time. His reputation slumped considerably in the nineteenth century, and it is only in the last few years that critical opinion has turned again in his favour. Certainly his subject matter can seem cloying to modern tastes, but Murillo nearly always painted beautifully, and he was a marvellous storyteller. His later works were particularly successful, employing the *vaporoso* technique of delicate brushwork and diffuse forms, and there's no doubt that he was a substantial influence on much subsequent eighteenth- and nineteenth-century painting in Spain, France and England.

In complete contrast to Murillo, **Juan Valdés Leal** (1622–90) preferred the violent and macabre side of the Baroque. His work was very uneven in quality; the paintings in the Hospital de la Caridad in Sevilla are the most celebrated. **Alonso Cano** (1601–67) was the leading painter of Granada and also active as an architect and sculptor. He led a rather dissolute life, and changed his working style abruptly several times. Perhaps the most successful of his paintings are the mature, pale-coloured religious works, which reveal debts to van Dyck and Velázquez.

A large number of artists can be grouped together under the **Madrid school**. One of the earliest was the Florentine-born **Vicente Carducho** (1576–1638), who painted large-scale works in sombre colours for the

Carthusians and other orders. **Fra Juan Rizi** (1600–81) illustrated contemporary monastic life in a different and less mystical way than Zurbarán. His brother, **Francisco Rizi** (1614–85), favoured full-blown canvases of Baroque pomp. **Fra Juan Bautista Maino** (1578–1649) was more influenced by the classical aspects of seventeenth-century art; he painted some notable religious and historical canvases with strong colouring, but with little interest in lighting effects. **Juan de Arellano** (1614–76) and **Bartolomé Pérez** (1634–93) worked mainly with landscape and historical religious works, while **José Antolínez** (1635–75) was particularly renowned for his versions of the Immaculate Conception. **Mateo Cerezo** (1626–66) painted fluid religious canvases under the influence of the works by Titian and van Dyck in the royal collections. The last major figure was probably also the most accomplished: **Claudio Coello** (1642–93), who was a master of the large-scale decorative style, using techniques of spatial illusion and very complicated arrangements of figures. His work at El Escorial shows his style at its best.

THE EIGHTEENTH AND NINETEENTH CENTURIES

The late seventeenth century and the first half of the eighteenth century was a very thin time in the history of Spanish painting: even the French and Italian artists imported by the Bourbon court were seldom of great merit. One native artist worthy of mention, however, is **Luis Meléndez** (1716–80), a master of still-life subjects. **Anton Raphael Mengs** (1728–79) came to Spain from Bohemia in 1761 as court painter, and in this capacity was a virtual dictator of style for a while, spearheading the adoption of an academic, Neoclassical tone, particularly in portraiture. His assistant, **Francisco Bayeu** (1734–95), was a prolific fresco painter for both royal and religious patrons, and was also in charge of the cartoons for the Royal Tapestry Factory. His brother, **Ramón Bayeu** (1746–93), worked on similar projects but was far less accomplished.

It was the Bayeus' brother-in-law, however, **Francisco Goya** (1746–1828), who was the overwhelmingly dominant personality of the period. Goya's output was prolific and his range of subject matter and style so immense that it is hard to believe one man was responsible for so much. Interestingly, he was no prodigy. In his twenties he became a highly competent painter of religious murals, his work at Zaragoza and Aula Dei already surpassing that of his contemporaries. After moving to Madrid, he worked for many years on tapestry cartoons (preparatory drawings), which in their graceful handling and skilful grouping made the most of their rather frivolous subject matter and gave Goya an entry into court circles, after which he became a fashionable portrait painter. It was in this role that his originality began to show through: his portraits eschew any attempt at flattery, and it's clear that he was less than impressed by his sitters. A serious illness in the early 1790s left him deaf and led to a more bitter and sarcastic art; his increasingly fantastic style may have emerged from his developing interest in witchcraft, which resulted in many paintings and two series of etchings: *Los Caprichos* and, later, *Los Disparates.* The marvellous frescoes in San Antonio de la Florida in Madrid are the exception here, among his most beautiful creations ever and containing a remarkable representation of the various social types of the day. But the Peninsular War further darkened Goya's mood, as shown by *May 2nd* and especially *May 3rd,* and by the engravings *The Disasters of War.* The last paintings are probably his most remarkable, especially those of bullfights, in which he showed an extraordinary visual perception, the exactness of which was proved only with the development of the slow-motion camera. Finally, there were the despairing "black paintings" made on the walls of his own house, the Quinta del Sordo, now detached and hung in the Prado.

Of Goya's contemporaries, the most interesting are **Luis Paret y Alcázar** (1746–99), who painted Rococo scenes under French and Italian influence, and **Vicente López** (1772–1850), an academic portrait painter in the manner of Mengs whose severe portrait of Goya hangs in the Prado. The nearest artist to Goya in style was **Eugenio Lucas** (1824–70), who followed his interest in bullfighting and Inquisition scenes, but did little of stylistic advance. Indeed, most of the nineteenth century was extremely barren in Spanish art history, a period of imitation, largely of French models, at least twenty years late. The most gifted painter was perhaps

Mariano Fortuny (1838–74), who specialized in small, very highly finished canvases, often of exotic subjects. Other artists worthy of mention are **Dario de Regoyos y Valdés** (1857–1913), the nearest thing to an Impressionist working in Spain at the time; **Joaquín Sorolla** (1863–1923), who was noted for his beach scenes; and **Ignacio Zuloaga** (1870–1945), who painted portraits against landscape backgrounds.

THE TWENTIETH CENTURY

As with architecture, it was Catalunya that took the lead in painting towards the end of the nineteenth century. **Isidoro Nonell** (1873–1911) was best known as a naturalistic painter of the poor. In contrast, **Jose María Sert** (1874–1945) was at his best in large-scale mural decorations, particularly in the powerful sepia and grey frescoes he produced for Vic Cathedral, replacements for two earlier sets.

Although born in Málaga, **Pablo Picasso** (1881–1973), the overwhelmingly dominant figure in twentieth-century art, spent many of his formative years in Barcelona, achieving great technical facility at a very early age, and creating many accomplished works in a representational style before the age of twenty. In 1900 he first visited Paris, where the influence of Toulouse-Lautrec made itself felt in the "blue period" of 1901–4, during which he depicted many of society's victims in Paris and Barcelona, following the lead of Nonell. The "rose period" of 1904–6 was perhaps Picasso's most "Spanish" phase (although by now he was living in Paris). Actors, clowns and models featured among his subjects, and his interest turned to the work of El Greco and ancient Iberian sculpture. The following "Negro period" of 1907–9 marked the break with traditional forms, as manifested in the key work, *Les Demoiselles d'Avignon*. After this Picasso returned to representational painting only for a short time in the 1920s, and from 1910 onward developed Cubism in association with Frenchman Georges Braque.

The movement's first phase, analytical Cubism, was largely concerned with form, with being able to depict objects as if seen from different angles at the same time. This was followed by synthetic Cubism, which showed a revival of interest in colour and handling. For a time in the 1920s and 1930s, Picasso combined Cubism with Surrealism, inventing a new anatomy for the human form, and eventually becoming noted as a painter of protest, most markedly in *Guernica*, a cry of despair about the Civil War in his native land (which he had by then left for good). Until his death, Picasso worked in a variety of styles, active in sculpture and ceramics as well. He was prolific to an almost unimaginable degree – in 1969 alone he produced almost as many canvases as Velázquez did in his lifetime, among the most notable of which were variations on well-known paintings such as *Las Meninas*.

One of the most faithful Cubists was **Juan Gris** (1887–1927), who favoured stronger colours and softer forms than others in the group. In **Surrealism**, two Catalans were among the leading figures: **Joan Miró** (1893–1983) and **Salvador Dalí** (1904–1989). Miró created the most poetic and whimsical works of the movement, showing a childlike delight in colours and shapes, and developing a highly personal language that was freer in form and more highly decorative than that of the other Surrealists. One of his favourite techniques during the Thirties was to spill paint on the canvas and move his brush around in it. He was also active in a variety of artistic media besides paint and canvas: collage, murals, book illustrations, sculpture and ceramics. Aside from an early period as a Futurist and Cubist, Dalí was more concerned with creating his own vision of a dream world. He was particularly interested in infantile obsessions and in paranoia, and his works often showed wholly unrelated objects grouped together, the distortion of solid forms, and unrealistic perspectives. He also worked on book illustrations, some of them his own texts, and on films. In later years he looked for other stimuli and painted a number of religious subjects. Few other artists in history have shown such talent for self-publicity. There are few artists, either, who have been so easily forged: in his later years Dalí reputedly made millions by signing thousands of blank pieces of paper.

Artists of the same generation include **Óscar Domínguez** (1906–57), who used both the Cubist and Surrealist idioms, at times combining the two in a wholly individualistic way. Another isolated figure of note was **José Gutiérrez Solana** (1885–1945), whose impoverished background led him to seek out his subjects amongst the low-life of Madrid he knew so well, adopting a realist approach with strong use of colour.

THE PRESENT DAY

Among the most important living Spanish artists are the members of the "abstract generation", who run a museum at Cuenca devoted solely to their works. By far the most individual figure of the group is **Antonio Saura** (b. 1930), whose violently expressive canvases, the earlier of which are painted in black and white only, are overtly political in tone, showing Man oppressed but unbowed. He uses religious themes in a deliberately humanist or even blasphemous way in his triptychs of crowd scenes, and transformation of the Crucifixion into a parable of secular oppression. The Catalan **Antoni Tàpies** (b. 1923) is an abstractionist in the tradition of the *Dada* movement; he began

by making collages out of newspaper, cardboard, silver wrapping, string and wire. For a period he turned to graffiti-type work with deformed letters, before returning to experiments with unusual materials, particularly oil paint mixed with crushed marble.

For those who despair of the theoretical and iconoclastic side of the modern movement, **Antonio López García** (b. 1936) comes as a refreshing change. Whilst obviously using modern idioms, he is a representational painter of landscapes, cityscapes, still lifes and nudes of an immediately appealing effect which clearly have their roots firmly in artistic tradition. **Eduardo Arroyo** (b. 1937) is a follower of the Pop Art movement, with its emphasis on large-scale depictions of familiar everyday faces and objects.

Gordon McLachlan

WILDLIFE

Despite its reputation as the land of the package holiday, you can't beat Spain for sheer diversity of landscape and wildlife. When the Pyrenees were squeezed from the earth's crust they created an almost impenetrable barrier stretching from the Bay of Biscay to the Mediterranean Sea. Those animals and plants already present in Spain were cut off from the rest of Europe, and have been evolving independently ever since. In the same way, the breach of the land bridge at what are now the Straits of Gibraltar, and the subsequent reflooding of the Mediterranean basin, stranded typical African species on the peninsula. The outcome was an assortment of wildlife originating from two continents, resulting in modern-day Iberia's unique flora and fauna.

Spain is the second most **mountainous** country in Europe after Switzerland. The central plateau – the *Meseta* – averages 600–700m in elevation, slopes gently westwards and is surrounded and traversed by imposing *sierras* and *cordilleras*. To the north, the plateau is divided from the coast by the extensive ranges of the Cordillera Cantábrica, and in the south the towering Sierra Nevada and several lesser ranges such as the Serranía de Ronda run along the Mediterranean shores (where these southern sierras continue across the Mediterranean basin, the unsubmerged peaks are today known as the Balearic Islands). The Pyrenean chain marks the border with France,

and even along Spain's eastern shores the narrow coastal plain soon rises into the foothills of the Sierras of Montseny, Espuña and los Filabres, among others. The ancient sierras de Guadarrama and Gredos cross the Meseta just north of Madrid, and the Sierra Morena and the Montes de Toledo rise out of the dusty southern plains. So it is not surprising to find that both flora and fauna of Spain possess a distinctly alpine element, with many species adapted to high levels of ultraviolet light and prolonged winter snow-cover.

The centre of Spain lies many kilometres from the coast, and thus the **climate** is almost continental in character. The summers are scorching, the winters bitter, and what rain there is falls only in spring and autumn. Moving eastwards, the Mediterranean Sea has a moderating effect on this weather pattern, favouring the coastal lands with mild winters and summers which become progressively hotter as you move south towards Africa. What most people tend to forget, however, is that the northern and western parts of the country are endowed with a climate that, if anything, is even worse than that of Britain! Depressions coming in from the Atlantic Ocean are responsible for almost continual cloud cover, high rainfall and persistent mists along the appropriately named Costa Verde; when the sun does show its face the high humidity can make life very uncomfortable.

These climatic variations have produced a corresponding diversity in Spanish wildlife. The wet, humid **north** is populated by species common throughout Atlantic Europe, especially Ireland, whilst the **southern** foothills of the Sierra Nevada, situated only a stone's throw from Africa, have an almost subtropical vegetation. The continental weather pattern of much of the **interior** has given rise to a community of drought-resistant shrubs, together with annual herbs which flower and set seed in the brief spring and autumn rains, or more long-lived plants which possess underground bulbs or tubers to withstand the prolonged summer drought and winter cold.

LANDSCAPE

The Iberian peninsula was once heavily forested, although it is estimated that today only about ten percent of the original **woodland** remains, mostly in the north. Much of the

Meseta was covered with evergreen oaks and associated shrubs such as laurustinus and strawberry tree, but the clearance of land for arable and pastoral purposes has taken its toll, as have the ravages of war. Today tracts of Mediterranean woodland persist only in the sierras and some parts of Extremadura. When it was realized that much of the plateau was unsuitable for permanent agricultural use, the land was abandoned, and is now covered with low-growing, aromatic scrub vegetation, known as *matorral* (maquis). The southeastern corner of the Meseta is the only part of Spain which probably never supported woodland; here the arid steppe **grasslands** – *calvero* – remain basically untouched by man. In northern Spain, where vast areas are still forested, the typical tree species are more familiar: oak, beech, ash and lime on the lower slopes, grading into pine and fir at higher levels.

Much of the *Meseta* is flat, arid and predominantly brown. Indeed, in Almería, Europe's only true **desert** is to be found, such is the lack of rainfall. But the presence of subterranean water supplies gives rise to occasional **oases**: flashes of green and blue, teeming with wildlife. The numerous tree-lined **watercourses** of the peninsula also attract birds and animals from the surrounding dusty plains. The great Ebro and Duero rivers of the north, and the Tajo and Guadiana in the south have been dammed at intervals, creating **reservoirs** which attract wildfowl in winter.

The Spanish **coastline** has a little of everything: dune systems, shingle banks, rocky cliffs, salt marshes and sweeping sandy beaches. In Galicia, submerged river valleys, or *rías*, are reminiscent of the Norwegian fjords, and the offshore islands are home to noisy seabird colonies; the north Atlantic coast is characterized by limestone promontories and tiny, sandy coves; the Mediterranean coast, despite its reputation for wall-to-wall hotels and beach towels, still boasts many undeveloped lagoons and marshes, and west of Gibraltar lies perhaps the greatest of all coastal marshlands: the Coto Doñana.

The Spanish **landscape** has changed little since the early disappearance of the forests. While the rest of Europe strives for agricultural supremacy, in Spain the land is still **farmed** by traditional methods. The olive groves of the south, the extensive livestock-rearing lands of the north and even the cereal-growing and wine-producing regions of the plains are still havens for the indigenous wildlife of the country. It is only since Spain joined the European Community that artificial pesticides and fertilizers and huge machines have made much impact. Even so, Spain is still essentially a wild country compared to much of Europe. Apart from a few industrial areas around Madrid and in the northeast, the landscape reflects the absence of modern technology, and the low population density means that few demands are made of the wilderness areas that remain.

FLOWERS

With such a broad range of habitats, Spain's **flora** is nothing less than superb. Excluding the Canary Islands, about 8000 species occur on Spanish soil, approximately ten percent of which are endemic: that is, they are found nowhere else in the world. Due to the plethora of high **mountains**, an alpine flora persists in Spain well beyond its normal north European distribution, and because of the relative geographical isolation of the mountain ranges, plants have evolved which are specific to each (there are about 180 plants which occur only in the Pyrenees, and over forty species endemic to the Sierra Nevada).

The **buttercup** family makes a good example. In the Pyrenees, endemic species include the pheasant's-eye *Adonis pyrenaica* and the meadow-rue *Thalictrum macrocarpum*; the Sierra Nevada has *Delphinium nevadense* and the monkshood *Aconitum nevadense*, and of the columbines *Aquilegia nevadensis* occurs here alone. *A. discolor* is endemic to the Picos de Europa, *A. cazorlensis* is found only in the Sierra de Cazorla and *A. pyrenaica* is unique to the Pyrenees. Other handsome montane members of this family include alpine pasque flowers, hepatica, hellebores, clematis and a host of more obvious buttercups.

The dry Mediterranean grasslands of Spain are excellent hunting grounds for **orchids**. In spring, in the meadows of the Cordillera Cantábrica, early purple, elder-flowered, woodcock, pink butterfly, green-winged, lizard and tongue orchids are ten a penny, and a little searching will turn up sombre bee, sawfly and Provence orchids. Further into the Mediterranean zone, exotic species to look for include Bertoloni's bee, bumblebee and mirror orchids. Lax-flowered orchids are common on the Costa Brava and high limestone areas will reveal black vanilla orchids, frog orchids and summer lady's tresses a bit later in the year.

The Mediterranean **maquis** is a delight to the eye and nose in early summer, as the cistus bushes and heaths come into flower, with wild rosemary, thyme, clary and French lavender adding to the profusion of colour. The *dehesa* grasslands of southwest Spain are carpeted with the flowers of *Dipcadi serotinum* (resembling brown bluebells), pink gladioli and twenty or so different trefoils in May. In the shade of the ancient evergreen oaks grow birthworts, with their pitcher-shaped flowers, bladder senna and a species of lupin known locally as "devil's chickpea".

Even a trip across the **northern Meseta**, although apparently through endless cereal fields, is by no means a dull experience: arable weeds such as cornflowers, poppies, corncockle, chicory and shrubby pimpernel are sometimes more abundant than the crops themselves. Where the coastal **sand dunes** have escaped the ravages of the tourist industry you can find sea daffodils, sea holly, sea bindweed, sea squill and the large violet flowers of *Romulea clusiana*.

MAMMALS

Spain's mammalian fauna has changed little since the Middle Ages: only the beaver has been lost since that time. Unfortunately, that doesn't mean that the remaining creatures are easy to see. Although still quite common in the mountains of the north and west, **wolves** keep out of man's way as much as possible (they're sporadically protected in Spain, but are widely regarded as a threat to livestock; the shepherds complain that wolves seem to know when a man is carrying a rifle and react accordingly). Neither are you likely to come across any of the few remaining brown **bears**. In fact, of Spain's enormous wealth of mammals, only a few species are active during the day and present in sufficient numbers for regular sightings to be made.

In the **northern mountains** – the Pyrenees and the Cordillera Cantábrica – you should get at least a glimpse of chamois, roe and red deer, and possibly wild boar, which can be seen at dusk during the winter when they conduct nightly raids on village potato patches.

Wildcats sometimes cross the road in front of you, and red squirrels are quite common, especially in the pine forests. Ibex, with robust scimitar-shaped horns, are common in the Sierras de Cazorla and Gredos, and marmots can occasionally be seen in the Pyrenees.

The typical mammals of **southern Spain** are seldom seen, but include the pardel lynx (a paler animal than the north European one), the Egyptian mongoose, the Mediterranean, or blind mole, and fallow deer in the umbrella pine woods of the Coto Doñana. No less than 27 species of **bat** occupy caves and woodlands throughout Spain, including four types of horseshoe bat. Over a score of **whale** and **dolphin** species frequent Spanish waters and the Mediterranean shores are still home to some of the last remaining Mediterranean **monk seals**.

BIRDS

If you care to spend your vacation with binoculars trained on the sky, trees or marshes, then Spain is one of the best venues in Europe for **birdwatching**. Most people head for the Coto Doñana National Park if it's birds they're after, but other parts of the country are just as rewarding, even if the list of sightings isn't quite so long at the end of the day.

If you have the patience to search out and identify **birds of prey**, Spain is an ideal destination, especially in **summer**, as about 25 species breed here. Some, such as red kites, goshawks, Bonelli's and golden eagles, griffon vultures, peregrine falcons and marsh harriers can be seen at all times of year in almost any part of the country. Others are confined to certain parts of the peninsula, where climate, landscape and vegetation combine to provide the right environment in which to raise their young. You will only see the rare black-shouldered kite, for example, in the southwest, or the majestic lammergeier in the high Pyrenees (and sometimes in the peaks behind the eastern coast), while black vultures (about 240 pairs) and the rare Spanish race of the imperial eagle are restricted to the southern half of the country.

Some of these raptors visit Spain only in the **winter**; these are best seen in late autumn or early spring on migration, and include the kestrel-like red-footed falcon and magnificent spotted eagle. By contrast, when these birds

ENVIRONMENT AND CONSERVATION

Protecting the environment of a country which encourages well over forty million tourists to leave their footprints in the sand each year could easily be perceived as a lost cause. But since most of these visitors flock to, and stay on, a comparatively narrow coastal strip, the damage is contained.

The environmental impact of "**costa**" tourism, with its pressures on water supply, sewage disposal and landscape, is a specialist subject in its own right, and one in which the battles are by no means over. According to the Barcelona-based environment group *DEPANA*, there is cause for worry over the second boom in coastal tourism as foreigners start to buy holiday homes. Meanwhile in inland, rural areas encroachment is fostered by domestic second-home buyers.

Concerned people in Spain have a common complaint: while there may be lip service paid to environmental matters, actually goading bureaucracy into action is a different matter. The only language understood by all sides is an economic one, the good news being that the value of the environment to tourism is becoming increasingly evident and important in bargaining terms.

Protection, then, is the name of a game increasingly played in the political arena, in which environmental benefit becomes almost incidental. Spain is still one of the wilder places of Europe, and wilderness can be found surprisingly close to some of the major urban and touristic centres. There are about a dozen *Parques Nacionales* (national parks) with a total protected area of more than 17,000 square kilometres, or 3.4 per cent of Spain's total land area. This, of course, is chicken feed compared to the level of ecological threat, but protection of the environment isn't yet on the worry list of the average Spaniard, and doesn't attract priority spending.

The stirrings of a movement towards environmental education can be seen in the creation of regionally nominated and managed *Parques Naturales*. So far the majority of these are in Catalunya, Galicia and Andalucía, but they now exist in every part of the country, and natural parks, with their fairly comprehen-

sive protection, already cover an area some three times larger than national parks.

Even Spain's highest profile national park, though, the **Coto Doñana**, was recently in the headlines for an ecological disaster in which 30,000 birds including coots, spoonbills, pintails and mallards died as a result of a combination of drought and the toxic cocktail of seven pesticides used illegally in adjacent areas. The **Parque Nacional de Aigües Tortes**, too, has lost international recognition as a national park because of continuing hydro-electric exploitation of its lakes.

WETLANDS

In 1980 Spain had 10,852 square kilometres of wetlands, six times more than France. It has not been so ready as some other nations to condemn wetland out of hand and rush to get it drained. Spain was an early signatory of the Ramsar Convention, an international agreement (the only one of its kind) to protect wetland. Three Spanish sites of international importance had been nominated by 1985. None of this, however, has prevented the steady decline of wetland areas, either by pollution or indirect draining.

The **Coto Doñana**, perhaps the most important wetland, is facing chronic drought and is suffering both from chemical run-off pollution (which caused the disaster mentioned above) and from detrimental agricultural practices. Just across the Río Guadalquivir from the Doñana, the last remaining unprotected wetland of the region has been drained and converted into farms.

The **Tablas de Daimiel** in La Mancha, too, are well known in conservationist circles for their deteriorated condition. Once recognized as being one of Europe's most important wetlands, and designated *Reserva Nacional* in 1966, then *Parque Nacional* in 1973, the area has nonetheless suffered terribly. Most blame is put on local viniculture upstream, with its irrigation and resultant heavy demand on artesian water. The Río Guadiana dried up in 1982 and the nearby Cigüela is heavily polluted. In the summer months particularly, the region can hardly support wildlife at all and certainly no longer attracts the once fabulous amounts of waterfowl which earned it worldwide fame.

There is some comfort in knowing that the plight of the Tablas has been officially recognized, with the launch of a project aimed at restoring former water levels. Naturalists are certain that if the water returns so will the birds and ditto the visitors. **La Albufera de Valencia** was once one of the largest bodies of fresh water in Spain, but it too is shrinking rapidly and is now ten times smaller than it was in the Middle Ages. On a more positive note, the most accessible wetland of the lot, **Aiguamolls de L'Emporda**, just behind the tourist beaches of the Costa Brava, has very recently been established as a *Parque Natural*.

HUNTING

The greatest confrontation over environmental issues in Spain involves hunting and farming groups. Many middle-aged and older men in Spain believe a shotgun is an accessory that they shouldn't be seen without in the countryside, and feel personally threatened at the news of the establishment or expansion of protected areas. One of the most emotive subjects is the protection of **wolves**. In areas where they have been protected, in the north especially, numbers have grown rapidly. Over recent years, outraged farmers have taken to increasingly militant demonstrations in an attempt to "protect" their land.

The figures speak for themselves. Although national parks protect more than 1200 square kilometres, **hunting reserves** (*reservas nacionales de caza*) cover a vastly greater area – almost four million acres to date. Largest is Saja in Cantabria, which is larger than all the mainland national parks put together. And although more species than ever before are protected and now forbidden to the hunter (ibex, bears, capercaillie and most of the major birds of prey, for instance) there is no shortage of demand for other hunting trophies such as wild boar, deer and chamois. Supermarkets stock all hunting gear, including shotgun cartridges, and walkers have to take care not to look shootable on weekends in season, when the hills are alive with the sound of double barrels.

As long ago as 1970 there were well over a million hunting licences issued annually, and exceeding quotas or **poaching** is considered virtually normal procedure, especially in areas where shooting and trapping provide an extra source of income for the poor. **Waterfowl** is a popular target, with huge numbers being killed each year.

The shooting and netting of **common birds** is also a major problem, as it is in much of southern Europe and North Africa. The annual slaughter of migrating birds in the Pyrenees, for a start, contributes substantially to the overall global figure of 900 million bird deaths each year. Latest European estimates for Spain are that about 30 million birds, often accused of being agricultural pests, are caught each year.

ACID RAIN

Spain was among the first countries to sign and ratify the UN's Convention on Long Range Transboundary Pollution, which came into effect in 1983, claiming that: "Spain recognises the need to take the prevention of air pollution into account in overall energy policies". However, as the time for accession to the European Community in 1986 drew near, the tone changed. There were strong political hints at this stage that the adoption of environmental policies was going to prove "difficult and costly". Spain's rapid growth as an industrial nation is a further blow to the environment.

In 1983, 235 square kilometres acres of Spanish forests were showing signs of damage from acid rain. But most of this is homeproduced: as far as Europe is concerned, Spain is one of the six countries receiving the least acid rain (18 percent of its total) from foreign sources. On the other hand Spain's domestic sulphur pollution accounts for 63 percent of its total. The country is the sixth largest source of sulphur in western Europe. Worst affected by acid deposition are parts of the north coast downwind from major industrial centres such as **Bilbao** and **Avilés**, and around the power stations of **Serchs** (Barcelona), **Andorra** and **El Serrallo** (Castellon). It is believed that industry in Avilés alone has been generating 24,000 metric tons of SO annually. A technical commission established to study pollution in the forests of **El Maestrazgo** and **El Port de Tortosa-Beseit**, which spread over three provinces, blamed emissions from Andorran industry for the damage, which seems, on the face of it, like an attempt to whitewash Spain's own problem.

Paul Jenner and Christine Smith

are leaving for their African and Asian nesting sites, others, like Montagu's harriers, short-toed and booted eagles, Eleonora's falcons and Egyptian vultures are coming the other way, having spent the winter in warmer climes, but returning to breed in Spanish territory.

There is no less variety in other types of birds; woodpeckers, for example, are most abundant in the extensive forests of the **northern mountain ranges.** White-backed woodpeckers are confined to the Pyrenees, other such rarities as black and middle-spotted woodpeckers may also be seen in the Cordillera Cantábrica, and the well-camouflaged wryneck breeds in the north and winters in the south of the country. Other typical breeding birds of these northern mountains are the turkey-like capercaillie, tree pipits, wood warblers, pied flycatchers, ring ouzels, alpine accentors, citril and snow finches, ptarmigan in the Pyrenees, and that most sought-after of all montane birds: the wallcreeper.

In the open **grasslands** and cereal fields of the Meseta, larks are particularly common. Look out for the Calandra lark, easily identified by the trailing white edge to the wing, although loads of patience and good binoculars are needed to distinguish between short-toed, lesser short-toed, crested and Thekla larks. Other small brown birds of the plains are rock sparrows and corn buntings, but more rewarding, and a lot easier to identify, are great and little bustards – majestic at any time of year, but especially the males when they fan out their plumage during the springtime courtship display. Look out also for the exotically patterned pin-tailed sandgrouse, the only European member of a family of **desert-dwelling birds**, as well as stone curlews and red-necked nightjars, the latter seen (and heard) mainly at dusk.

If you come across an ancient olive grove, or an area of southern Spain where the evergreen oak **forests** are still standing, then stop! A colourful assemblage of birds is typical of such oases of natural vegetation: hoopoes, azure-winged magpies, golden orioles, great grey and woodchat shrikes, bee-eaters, rollers, greater-spotted cuckoos, redstarts and black-eared wheatears. On a sunny summer's day, these birds are active and easy to spot.

Natural inland bodies of **water** often have wide marshy borders owing to the fluctuating water level. In these rushy margins look out for water rail and purple gallinule, as well as the diminutive Baillon's crake, and scrutinize reed-beds carefully for signs of penduline and bearded tits. The airspace above the water is usually occupied by hundreds of swifts and swallows; you should be able to pick out alpine, pallid and white-rumped swifts and red-rumped swallows if you are in the southern half of the country, as well as collared pratincoles. These lakes are also frequented by wintering waterfowl (although Spain has no breeding swans or geese), European cranes and sometimes by migrating flamingos.

The **coastal wetlands** are certainly a must for any serious birdwatcher, with common summer occupants including black-winged stilts, avocets and most members of the heron family: cattle and little egrets, purple, squacco and night herons, bitterns and little bitterns. On the Mediterranean coast, especially in low-growing scrub, keep an eye out for a small quail-like bird called the Andalucian hemipode: strangely enough it is closely related to the graceful crane. Wintering waders are not outstandingly distinctive, though wherever you go, even on the Atlantic coast, spoonbills are frequently encountered. Grey phalaropes visit the northwest corner, as do whimbrel, godwits, skuas and ruff, taking a break from their northern breeding grounds.

The **Balearic Islands** can provide you with a few more exotic cliff-nesting species, such as Cory's shearwater and storm petrels; and the Islas Cíes, off the Galician coast, provide breeding grounds for shags, the rare Iberian race of guillemot and the southernmost colony of lesser black-backed gulls in the world.

Hundreds more birds could be listed: with a good field guide you should find many of them for yourself.

REPTILES AND AMPHIBIANS

As with other types of wildlife, Spain is especially rich in amphibians and reptiles, with about sixty species in total. Some of the easiest to see are **fire salamanders**, which occur throughout Spain, albeit with colouration varying from yellow stripes on a black background to vice versa, depending on the exact locality. The best time to see them is in cool, misty weather in the mountains, or immediately after rain.

Three other species of **salamander** live in Spain. The golden-striped salamander (a slender, rather nondescript beast, despite its name) is endemic to northwest Iberia; the large sharp-ribbed salamander is found only in the south-west of the peninsula; and the Pyrenean brook salamander is confined to the Pyrenees.

Closely related to the salamanders are the **newts**, of which there are only four species in Spain. If you take a trip into the high mountain pastures of the Cordillera Cantábrica, where water is present in small, peaty ponds all year round, you should see the blackish alpine newt; marbled newts can be seen round the edges of many of Spain's inland lakes, and reservoirs. Midwife **toads** strike up their chorus at dusk, and can often be heard well away from water, sometimes causing confusion with the call of the Scops owl. If you search through tall water-side vegetation you may be rewarded by the sight of a tiny, lurid-green tree-frog: striped in the north and west, but stripeless along the Mediterranean coast.

Two species of **tortoise** occur in Spain; spur-thighed tortoises can still be found along the southern coast and on the Balearic Islands, which are also the only Spanish locality for Hermann's tortoise. European pond terrapins and stripe-necked terrapins are more widely distributed, but only in freshwater habitats.

Perhaps the most exotic reptilian species to occur in Spain is the **chameleon**, although again this swivel-eyed creature is confined to the extreme southern shores. **Lizards** are numerous, with the most handsome species being the ocellated or eyed lizard – green with blue spots along the flank. Some species are very restricted in their range, such as Ibiza, Italian and Lilford's wall lizards, which live only in the Balearic Islands.

Similarly, **snakes** are common, although few are venomous, and in any case it's some-times quite difficult to spot them before they spot you and take evasive action themselves. Asps and western whip snakes occur in the Pyrenees, but you are only likely to see horse-shoe whip snakes and false smooth snakes in the extreme south.

INSECTS

Almost 100,000 insects have been named and described in Europe and an untold number await discovery. In Spain, with areas where no one knows for sure how many bears there are, insects have barely begun to be explored.

From early spring to late autumn, as long as the sun is shining, you will see **butterflies**: there are few European species which do not occur in Spain, but by contrast there are many Spanish butterflies which are not found north of the Pyrenees. These seem to be named mostly after obscure entomologists: Lorquin's blue, Carswell's little blue, Forster's furry blue, Oberthur's anomalous blue, Lefèbvre's ringlet, Zapater's ringlet, Chapman's ringlet, Zeller's skipper, and many others. You need to be an expert to identify most of these, but the more exciting butterflies are in any case better known ones: the Camberwell beauty, almost black and bordered with gold and blue; swal-lowtails, yellow and black or striped like zebras, depending on the species, but always with the distinctive "tails"; the lovely two-tailed pasha, which is often seen feeding on the ripe fruit of the strawberry tree; and the apollo (papery white wings with distinctive red and black eyespots), of which there are almost as many varieties as there are mountains in Spain. Other favourites include the small, be-jewelled blues, coppers, fritillaries and hair-streaks that inhabit the hay meadows.

Aside from the butterflies, keep an eye open for the largest **moth** in Europe, the giant peacock, which flies by night but is often attracted to outside lights, or the rare, green-tinted Spanish moon moth, a close relative of tropical silk moths. During the day, take a closer look at that hovering bumble bee, as it may be a hummingbird hawkmoth, or a broad-bordered bee-hawk, flying clumsily from flower to flower. Oleander and elephant hawkmoths (resplendent in their pink and green livery) are often seen around flowering honeysuckle bushes at dusk. Many moths have bizarre cater-pillars, for example the lobster moth, which feeds on beech, or the pussmoth, found on willows and poplars, although the adults may be quite nondescript in appearance.

Grasslands and arid scrub areas are usually good hunting grounds for **grasshoppers and crickets**, which you can locate by following their calls. Mole crickets and field crickets live in burrows they have excavated themselves, but look to the trees for the adult great green bush cricket, about 7–8cm long. French laven-der bushes in the maquis are a favourite haunt of the green mantis *Empusa pennata*, identified by a large crest on the back of the head (the nymphs are brown, with a distinctive curled-up abdomen). **Stick insects** are harder to spot, as they tend to sit parallel with the stems of grasses, where they are well camouflaged.

Members of the *Arachnidae* (**spiders**) to be found include two species of **scorpion** in the dry lands of southern Spain. Look out also for long-legged *Gyas*, the largest harvest-spider in Europe, which can be about 10cm in diameter, although the body is little larger than a pea. Spanish **centipedes** can grow to quite a size too: *Scutigera coleoptata*, for example, often live indoors – they have fifteen pairs of incredibly long, striped legs, which create a wonderful rippling effect when they move across walls.

WHERE AND
WHEN TO GO

Virtually anywhere in Spain, outside the cities and most popular tourist resorts, rewards scrutiny in terms of wildlife. Perhaps the best thing about this country is that so much wilderness remains to be discovered on your own, without guidebooks to tell you where to go.

The main drawback, however, is getting anywhere on public transport, which often doesn't stop between departure point and destination. There is rarely any problem getting off a bus when you feel the urge, but you may have problems stopping the next one, which in any case may not arrive until the following day.

The following suggestions, then, are largely limited to those which are easily accessible by public transport. Inevitably this means that other people will be there, too: you'll have to head off into the hills on foot in order to experience the best of Spanish wildlife.

Southern Spain is a good choice for any **time of year**, since even in the depths of winter the climate is mild and many plants will be in full bloom. If you decide on the **northern mountain ranges**, spring and early summer are best. The weather can be temperamental, but for the combination of snowy peaks and flower-filled meadows, it's worth taking the risk. The **interior** of Spain is freezing in winter and almost too hot to bear in midsummer, so

spring or autumn – to coincide with the occasional rains and the flowering of the maquis and steppe grasslands – are best. Again, if your real interest is the **coastal bird life** of Spain, visit in spring or autumn, not only to catch the phenomenal migrations of birds between Africa and northern Europe, but also because accommodation in the resorts can be incredibly low-priced outside the tourist season.

THE PYRENEES

The Moors called these mountains *El Hadjiz* – the barricade – which is effectively what they are, isolating Spain from the rest of Europe. The Spanish flanks of the Pyrenees are somewhat hotter and drier than their northern counterparts, but the high passes are nevertheless snowbound for several months in the winter.

If you avoid the ski resorts there are still many unspoiled valleys to explore, with their colourful alpine meadows studded with Pyrenean hyacinths and horned pansy, and some of the highest forests in Europe, extending up to 2500m in places. The **Vall d'Aran**, close to Pico de Aneto (the highest point of the chain, at 3408m), is a botanical paradise at any time of year. Go in spring and you will find alpine pasque flowers, trumpet gentians and sheets of daffodils, among them pale Lent lilies and pheasant's-eye narcissi. A little later in the year sees the flowering of Turks'-cap lilies, dusky cranesbill and Pyrenean fritillaries, sheltering among the low-growing shrubs on the hillsides; while in autumn, following the annual hay-making, the denuded meadows shimmer with a pink-purple haze of merendera and autumn crocuses.

Farther west, the **Parque Nacional de Ordesa y Monte Perdido** in the Aragonese Pyrenees shelters valleys clothed in primeval pine, fir and beech forests which are home to pine martens, wildcats, genets, red squirrels, polecats and wild boar among the 32 mammal species that live within the Park boundaries. Dominating the forests are sheer cliffs with spectacular waterfalls and towering rock formations, the haunt of the sprightly chamois which thrive here in profusion. Although these antelope-like creatures are easily spotted, you will need to have your sights set firmly on the heavens to see the most renowned occupant of Ordesa: the lammergeier. A vulture of splendid proportions, it is now almost completely confined to the Pyrenees and a few eastern ranges in Spain. Its Spanish name – *quebranta-huesos*, or "bone-breaker" – refers to its habit of dropping animal bones from great heights to smash on the rocks below, exposing the tender marrow.

The second national park in the Spanish Pyrenees is that of **Aigües Tortes**, centred on the glacial hanging valleys and impressive cirques of northern Catalunya. The extensive coniferous forests of Scots pine and common silver fir are populated by capercaillie and black woodpeckers. Just above the timberline, early purple orchids and alpine and southern gentians flourish in the superb alpine meadows, and the rocky screes conceal pale, delicate edelweiss and yellow mountain saxifrage. The fast-flowing mountain rivers are home to otters; and the tiny secretive Pyrenean desman, Pyrenean brook salamanders and alpine newts live in the clear waters of the glacial lake of San Mauricio. In the airspace above the peaks look out for honey buzzards and golden eagles soaring on the thermals, and if you scrutinize the cliff faces you might be rewarded with the sight of a wallcreeper.

CORDILLERA CANTABRICA

This mountain chain runs more or less parallel to the north coast from the Portuguese border eastwards into the Basque country. It has long formed a barrier between the northern coast and the rest of Spain since there are few crossing points, of which a good proportion are impassable during the winter. The vegetation is clearly affected by the rain-laden clouds which constantly sweep in from the Atlantic, as can be seen by the extensive oak and beech forests that shroud the slopes. Extensive beef and dairy farming is the traditional way of life, and the majority of the flower-filled meadows have never been subjected to artificial fertilizers and pesticides. One of the most fascinating aspects is the abundance of meadow flowers now rarely found in northern Europe: lizard orchids, heath lobelia, greater yellow rattle, moon carrot, Cambridge milk-parsley, galingal and summer lady's-tresses – a delicate, white-flowered orchid.

The high point of the Cordillera Cantábrica is the small limestone mountain range of the **Picos de Europa**, visible from miles offshore in the Bay of Biscay. Over sixty species of mammal have been recorded here, ranging from such typical wilderness creatures as brown bears and wolves to snow voles, tiny denizens of the high peaks. Red squirrels, roe deer and chamois are easy to see, but many of the mammals which haunt these mountains, such as genets, beech martens and wildcats, are secretive nocturnal beasts.

One of the most outstanding landscape features of the Picos de Europa is the **Cares gorge**, where the river bed lies almost 2000m below the peaks on either side. The sheltered depths of the gorge are home to a number of shrubs more typical of Mediterranean Spain – figs, strawberry trees, wild jasmine and barberry – and the sheer rock-faces are home to the exotic wallcreeper, a small ash-grey bird with splashes of crimson under the wings, the sight of which is highly coveted by bird-watchers.

The **Covadonga National Park** covers much of the western massif of the Picos de Europa, its focal point being the glacial lakes of Enol and Ercina. In spring the verdant pastures which surround the lakes are studded with pale yellow hoop-petticoat daffodils and tiny dog's-tooth violets, but a visit later in the year will be amply rewarded by the discovery of hundreds of purple spikes of monkshood and the steel-blue flowers of Pyrenean eryngo. A few hours scrambling across the limestone crags away from the lake should be sufficient for excellent views of griffon and Egyptian vultures, or you don't even have to leave the small café in the car park to see alpine choughs scavenging among the litter-bins.

For those who prefer a more gentle scenery, **Galicia**, with its green rolling hills and constant mists, is hard to beat. Few people live in the countryside, which as a consequence is teeming with wildlife. The oak and beech woods of Ancares provide shelter for deer and wild boar; although the chamois were hunted to extinction for food during the Civil War. The meadows benefit from the frequent rains and you can find all manner of wet-loving plants, such as large-flowered butterwort, bog pimpernel, globe flowers, marsh helleborines, whorled caraway and early marsh orchids.

THE INTERIOR

If you believed everything you read you'd be tempted to regard inland Spain as a flat, barren plain covered with mile after mile of bleached cornfields. But the wildlife is there – if you know where to look.

A good place to start is the **central sierras**. Just to the north of Madrid, almost bisecting the vast plain of the Meseta, run several contiguous mountain ranges which are well worth a visit. They may not have the rugged grandeur of the Pyrenees but there is plenty of wildlife to be found on the rocky, scrub-covered slopes. Venture into the extensive pine forests of the **Sierra de Guadarrama** to see Spanish bluebells and an unmistakable toadflax, *Linaria triornithophora*, which has large snapdragon-like flowers each with a long tail, sometimes pink, sometimes white. Birds of prey are abundant, and not too difficult to tell apart; both red and black kites can be seen, easily distinguished from other raptors by their distinctly forked tails (the red kite has clear white patches under its wings). Booted eagles are identified by the black trailing edge to their wings, and the Spanish short-toed eagle, here known as *aguila culebrera*, the "snake eagle", is almost pure white below, with a broad, dark head.

Farther west the granite bulk of the **Sierra de Gredos** boasts some of the highest peaks in Spain after the Sierra Nevada and the Pyrenees. Scots and maritime pines occur in the higher levels, sweet chestnut and Pyrenean and cork oaks on the southern slopes. The springtime flora is superb, including lily-of-the-valley, conspicuous St Bernard's and martagon lilies, and several species of brightly coloured peonies. On some of the drier slopes, where the trees have been cleared, the aromatic gum cistus forms a dense layer up to 2m high. There is no need to fight your way through their sticky branches to discover the delights of the flora here: even the edges of the shepherds' tracks are ablaze with asphodels, French lavender, a strange-looking plant called the tassel hyacinth and the closely related grape hyacinth. But best of all in the Gredos are the ibex, very common in the pine zones between the cirques of Laguna Grande and Cinco Lagunas. Look out also for Egyptian and

griffon vultures, red and black kites and Bonelli's eagles overhead, crossbills and firecrests in the coniferous forests, and rock buntings, identified by their striped heads, almost everywhere.

Moving away from the mountains there are still sights to be seen in the plains. *Dehesa* parkland is the best habitat, especially for birds: **Monfragüe Natural Park**, in Extremadura, contains some excellent areas of *dehesa*. Golden orioles, woodchat and great grey shrikes, hoopoes and bee-eaters are impossible to miss, and you might even see a roller. In winter about 7000 common cranes descend on the Monfragüe grasslands, and the flooded river valleys which are an integral part of this park are good viewing points for red-rumped swallows and collared pratincoles in summer.

Monfragüe is perhaps best known for its breeding population of the endangered Spanish **imperial eagle**, easily identified by the distinct white shoulder markings. The central reserve where this raptor nests is open only to permit holders, but you may see them soaring over the *dehesa*. The same can be said for the rare black vulture: a huge bird which is impossible to miss. Monfragüe has the largest known breeding colony (about sixty pairs). Most people head for the huge rock outcrop known as Peñafalcón, where black storks, now extremely rare as a breeding bird in Spain, can be seen perched up on the cliff face, and the sky is constantly filled with griffon vultures coming and going. And look out for a smallish, light-coloured hovering bird – it might be a rare black-shouldered kite, which you certainly won't see elsewhere in Europe.

Heading in the other direction, towards Zaragoza in the northeastern corner of the plains, you might consider visiting the **Laguna de Gallocanta**. This is Spain's largest natural inland lake, and has a lot to recommend it. Look out for birds more typical of the arid plains – pin-tailed sandgrouse and stone curlews – as well as those usually associated with fresh water. Gallocanta is a national stronghold for red-crested pochard.

MEDITERRANEAN COAST

Spain's Mediterranean coast conjures up visions of sandy beaches packed with oiled bodies and a concrete wall of hotels stretching from the French border to Gibraltar. Even in the heart of the Costa Brava, though, there's rich wildlife to be found. The **Parc Natural dels Aiguamolls de L'Empordá** in Catalunya is a salt marsh and wetland reserve sandwiched between the A7 motorway and the hotel developments in the Gulf of Roses. It is the nearest thing in Spain to a British nature reserve, with signposted nature trails, a well-equipped information centre and several bird hides. This rather detracts from the wilderness aspect of the site, but it is nevertheless a good place to watch out for the 300 species of birds that have been observed here. Apart from the more typical water birds look out for little bittern, black-winged stilt, bearded tit and purple heron, all of which breed here. Spring is perhaps the best time, when flamingos, glossy ibis and spoonbills drop in on migration.

If you can't stand the mosquitos from the marshes, try the drier, Mediterranean scrub areas nearby, which are ideal for spotting red-footed falcons on migration, breeding lesser grey shrikes (the only Spanish locality), stone curlews, great spotted cuckoos and moustached and Marmora's warblers in summer. And of course, marsh and Montagu's harriers are always present.

Other promising wildlife locations include the fan-like **Delta de L'Ebre** (Ebro Delta), with up to 100,000 wintering birds and a large colony of purple herons. Again isolated from the mainland by the A7 motorway, the lagoons and reed-beds here attract squacco and night herons, avocets and red-crested pochard, with isolated islands providing nesting areas for the rare Audouin's and slender-billed gulls. Look out, too, for lesser short-toed larks, and a multitude of terns, including gull-billed, whiskered, roseate and Sandwich.

Further south again lies a smaller coastal wetland known as the **Albufera de Valencia**. It is so close to the city of Valencia that to learn it supports a breeding colony of the rare ferruginous duck is quite a surprise. Other water birds to look out for are red-crested pochard and, during the winter, the extremely rare crested coot, as well as cattle and little egrets, breeding night, purple and squacco herons, little bitterns, black-necked grebes and bearded and penduline tits.

SOUTHERN SPANISH SIERRAS

Stretching for miles behind the coastal metropolises of the Costa del Sol, these lofty mountains are a complete contrast with the sun-and-sea image of southern Spain. Perhaps the best-known is the **Sierra Nevada** at the eastern end of the range, which peaks at Mulhacén (3482m), the highest mountain in mainland Spain. Snow persists for much of the year at the highest levels, but the south-facing foothills are only about 150km from Africa. Environmental conditions thus range from alpine to almost tropical. Not surprisingly there is an incredible range of plant and animal life. If you are equipped to visit the high mountains when the snow is starting to melt you should see such attractive endemic plants as glacier eryngo, looking not unlike its Pyrenean counterpart, and Nevada daffodils, saxifrages and crocuses. Later on in the year there is still plenty to see, including the strange, spiny mountain tragacanth, wild tulips, peonies, pinks, alpine gentians, the Nevada monkshood and columbine, and the white-flowered rockrose *Helianthemeum apenniunum*.

Owing to the extreme altitude of the Sierra Nevada, birds more commonly found further north – crossbills, alpine accentors and choughs – have a final European outpost here. You should also see many of the smaller birds which favour dry, rocky hillsides. Perhaps the most distinguished of these is the black wheatear, the males identified by their funereal plumage and white rump. Farther north, in the limestone **Sierras de Cazorla y Segura**, raptor-watching will be amply rewarded. Cazorla is the only Spanish locality outside the Pyrenees where lammergeiers regularly breed, and the smaller Egyptian vultures are common here. Small numbers of golden and Bonelli's eagles nest in the peaks and goshawks frequent the extensive forests (black, maritime and Aleppo pines at high levels and holly, holm and Lusitanian oaks, with narrow-leaved ash and strawberry trees, on the lower slopes).

These mountain ranges, birthplace of the great Río Guadalquivir, are rather unusual in Spain in that they run approximately north–south rather than east–west. They also have a flora of some 1300 unique species including such handsome rock-dwelling plants as the crimson-flowered Cazorla violet (*Viola cazorlensis*), the columbine *Aquilegia cazorlensis*, a relict carnivorous butterwort (*Pinguicula vallisneriifolia*) and several endemic narcissi.

To the west lie some extraordinary Jurassic limestone ranges, eroded over centuries into formations known collectively as *torcales*. One of the more famous of these is at **Grazalema**, renowned for its Spanish fir forest. This tree (*Abies pinsapo*) is now restricted to just a handful of localities in southern Spain, including the **Serranía de Ronda**, and a specialized flora has evolved to cope with the dense shade that the trees cast. You should be able to find the colourful peonies *Paeonia coriacea* and *P. broteri*, as well as paper-white daffodils and the winter-flowering *Iris planifolia*, with a large, solitary flower on a ridiculously short stem. A whole range of typical Mediterranean shrub species grow here, including laurustinus, grey-leaved and poplar-leaved cistus, Spanish barberry, Etruscan honeysuckle, the nettle tree (*Celtis australis*) and *Acer granatense*, a maple species confined to the mountains of southern Spain. Also in these woods the eagle owl breeds: the largest in Europe, it even preys on roe deer and capercaillie.

As a break from the mountains you might consider a visit to **Fuente de Piedra**, the largest inland lagoon in Andalucía (about 15 square kilometres). Partly because the water is never more than 1.5m deep (the level being further reduced by intense evaporation in summer) and also due to the lack of pollution, large numbers of flamingos construct their conical mud nests here every year. Fuente de Piedra is thus one of only two regular breeding places for greater flamingos in Europe, and has recently been declared a *Reserva Integral*, the most strictly protected type of nature reserve in Spain. Altogether about 120 species of bird, 18 mammals and 21 reptiles and amphibians have been recorded here.

SOUTHERN ATLANTIC COAST

The more or less tideless Mediterranean ends at Gibraltar, so the coast stretching westwards up to the Portuguese border is washed by the Atlantic Ocean. Here, the low-lying basin formed by the Río Guadalquivir contains one of Europe's finest wetlands: the **Coto Doñana**, Spain's most famous national park.

Perhaps the most renowned spectacles are the breeding colonies of spoonbills and herons in the cork oaks which border the marshes, but equally impressive are the huge flocks of **waterfowl** which descend on the lagoons during the winter. As for breeding ducks, Doñana is the European stronghold for the marbled teal, a smallish, mottled-brown dabbling duck which rarely breeds in Europe outside Spain. Ruddy shelduck – large, goose-like birds, generally confined to the eastern Mediterranean – are also present throughout the year, but breeding has not yet been proved. White-headed ducks definitely nest and rear their young here, although the more renowned nursery for this is at the Lagunas de Córdoba in central Andalucía. One of Europe's rarest birds is the crested coot, distinguished from the common coot only at close range by two small red knobs on its forehead, or in flight by the absence of a white wing-bar. It breeds in Morocco, migrating northwards into southern Spain for the winter; Doñana is the only Spanish locality where this species is resident all year round, although again no one is quite sure whether it breeds here or not.

Water birds aside, keep an eye out for large flocks of pin-tailed sandgrouse, which perform prodigious aerobatics in perfect time, rather like a shoal of fish; and, at ground level, cattle egrets in the grasslands, usually in the company of some of the renowned black bulls of the region. Cattle egrets are most easily distinguished from other egrets by their pinkish legs (black or yellow in all other species). A smaller bird to watch out for is the Spanish sparrow, which commonly makes its home in the nether regions of the large, untidy nests of the white stork. Doñana also boasts an impressive roll call of birds of prey, including imperial eagle and black vulture.

Some large **mammals** are relatively easy to see in Doñana: red and fallow deer and wild boar display an inordinate lack of fear when approached by people, despite the fact that this area was a Royal Hunting Reserve until quite recently. The same, unfortunately, cannot be said for Doñana's pardel lynxes, of which there are some 25 pairs, estimated to represent about half the total Spanish population. Egyptian mongooses also frequent the dry, scrubby areas, and genets are occasionally seen by day in the more remote, forested parts of the national park. If you can drag your eyes from the veritable feast of bird life you might spot a curious creature known as Bedriaga's skink. Endemic to Iberia, this small lizard has only rudimentary legs; you are most likely to see it burrowing rapidly into the sand in an effort to escape detection.

The nearby **Marismas de Odiel**, which lie within the boundaries of the city of Huelva a little to the west, are also very worthwhile. Apart from the flamingos, which are increasingly preferring these saline coastal marshes as breeding grounds to the nearby Doñana, you will also be rewarded by the sight of large numbers of spoonbills, purple herons and other typical southern Spanish waterbirds.

THE BALEARIC ISLANDS

Despite the sun-seeker image of the Balearic Islands, there are many remote spots which have escaped the ravages of the tourist industry. Even on the big ones you can escape easily enough, and in total there are fifteen islands (most uninhabited).

One of the wilder regions is the **Sierra de Tramuntana** which runs along the northern coast of Mallorca, dropping abruptly into the sea for much of its length. It is a good place to see the diminutive Eleonora's falcon and enormous black vulture. Around your feet you can feast your eyes on an array of exotic plants such as *Cyclamen balearicum*, an autumn-flowering crocus (*Crocus cambessedesii*), *Helleborus lividus* (a rare member of the buttercup family), the pink-flowered *Senecio rodriguezii*, and many other endemic species of peony, birthwort and hare's ear. Even in January many plants are in flower, but the best time of year to see the blossoming of the islands is from March to May.

Away from the mountains, other wildlife refuges are the low-lying coastal marshes which have to date defied the hotel trade. On Mallorca that of **S'Albufera** is a birdwatcher's paradise. The maze of tamarisk-lined creeks and lagoons is the summer haunt of water rail, spotted crake and little egrets, and a little careful scrutiny may reveal more secretive denizens: Savi's, Cetti's, Sardinian, moustached, fan-tailed and great reed warblers. Also easy to get to are the saltpans known as **C'an Pastilla**, close to the airport at Palma, where whiskered and white-winged black terns, as well as Mediterranean and Audouins's gulls (this latter bird is the rarest breeding gull in Europe), are frequently seen.

The Balearics are also ideal places for watching the endemic races of lizards; they are usually quite undeterred by your presence, and make excellent subjects for portrait photography! If you are keen on marine life, don't forget your flippers and snorkel, as the underwater scenario is superb.

Teresa Farino

MUSIC

Music in Spain is going through some good times, and has been since the return to democracy. In the past decade home-grown talent has flourished as never before in most fields, from traditional regional music, through new jazz and salsa-influenced flamenco, to experimental rock.

The main problem facing musicians – as everywhere – is a record industry dominated by multinational companies. Reaching a wide audience or getting decent record distribution is virtually impossible for anyone out of the mainstream. The media seems interested only in pop. Artists in other areas, whether folk, jazz, *flamenco* or traditional, have difficulty getting their records reviewed in the press let alone played on radio or TV.

Nevertheless, at a local and live level almost every type of music can be heard, the performers sustained by enthusiastic groups of aficionados. Only in one area has Spanish music noticeably declined of late – the songs of political protest which were so successful in the early 1970s have now all but disappeared.

FLAMENCO

Flamenco is undoubtedly the most important musical-cultural phenomenon in Spain, and the most defined in the sense that a racial aspect (gypsy/non-gypsy) plays an important role. Although it's linked fundamentally to Andalucía, the *flamenco* map also covers parts of Madrid, Extremadura and the Levante. Where *flamenco* came from and how it began is a source of considerable controversy around

Sevilla and Cádiz, its centre of gravity. But its "laws" were established in the nineteenth century. There is a classical repertoire of more than sixty *flamenco* songs and dances – some solos, some group numbers, some with instrumental accompaniment, others a cappella. The prevailing sentiment, with few exceptions, is one of suffering and pain.

At present there are some good singers and fantastic guitarists around, and although the record industry doesn't take much notice of them, there are albums on the market by both old masters and contemporary artists. The former can be heard on many *flamenco* anthologies, as well as on their own records. Of the latter, the following **guitarists** are worth special mention: Paco de Lucía, Manolo Sanlúcar, the Habichuelas, Tomatito, Paco Cepero, Gerardo Núñez, Enrique de Melchor, Vicente Amigo and Rafael Riqueni. Among **singers**, the most important (and most popular) figure in recent years was **Camerón de la Isla**, who died in 1992: he had raised *cante jondo*, the virtuoso "deep song" to a new art, accompanied by Paco de Lucía and, latterly, Tomatito. Other singers to look out for too include Enrique Morente, El Cabrero, Juan Peña El Lebrijano, the Sorderas, Fosforito, José Menese, Carmen Linares and Fernanda and Bernarda de Utrera. Don't forget the **dancers**, either – who are an important part of *flamenco* culture. The two top figures of the moment are Antonio Gades and Cristina Hoyos, co-stars of Carlos Saura's films, *Blood Wedding* and *Amor Brujo*, but there are dozens more superb dancers emerging from the Madrid *flamenco* school.

The best known of all contemporary *flamenco* musicians is **Paco de Lucía**, who, from the late 1970s, introduced jazz rhythms and instruments to create an entirely new *flamenco* sound, to the outrage of purists. Other artists experimented, too, through the 1980s. **Lolé y Manuel** updated the *flamenco* sound with original songs and huge success; Jorge Pardo followed Paco's jazz direction; Salvador Tavora and Mario Maya staged *flamenco*-based spectacles; and Enrique Morente and Juan Peña El Lebrijano both worked with **Andalucian orchestras** from Morocco, revealing a perhaps unsurprising stylistic unity.

There was crossover with rock and blues, too, through bands like **Ketama** and **Pata**

Negra, forerunners of what has become known, in the 1990s, as **nuevo flamenco**, associated particularly with the label Nuevos Medios and a club, Revolver, in Madrid. Bands and singers to look out for include *La Barbería del Sur* (who add a dash of salsa), Aurora (who prefers rumba), Wili Gimenez and Raimundo Amador. *Radio Tarifa* are an exciting new trio from Andalucía, mixing Arabic and pop sounds onto a *flamenco* base.

FOLK

Folk music as it might be understood in the rest of Europe or in North America never had much of a chance to develop in Spain. In the 1970s, when Francoism's end began to look conceivable, political songs were all-important. They didn't leave much room for a movement of folk music to take shape, and only a few groups survive from that era: *Oskorri*, *Al Tall* and *Nuevo Mester*.

What folk music there is is at its most developed in the northwest of the peninsula, from Galicia to Euskadi. The *Festival del Mundo Celta* at Ortigueira played a leading role in the early 1980s, bringing together musicians from Wales, Ireland, Scotland and Brittany with those from Galicia and Asturias. It was followed by other **festivals** in Galicia (Vigo, Moañas, Lugo) and in Asturias (Oviedo), though none of these have yet established themselves as regular events. Two folk festivals which have the Mediterranean as a reference point, and in which the countries bordering it participate, are the *Trobada de Música del Mediterráneo* in Valencia and the *Cançons de la Mediterranía* in Palma, Mallorca.

Perhaps the most accessible Spanish folk music is from **Galicia**, where groups include *Milladoiro*, well known in Celtic circles throughout Europe. Others worth a hearing include *Na Lua* (who combine saxophone with bagpipe); *Doa*, *Citania*, *Trisquell*, *Fía Na Roca* and *Xorima* (all traditional and acoustic); *Palla Mallada* (hyper-traditional); and *Alecrín*, *Brath* and *Matto Congrio* (electric folk).

The Celtic movement in **Asturias** centres around two festivals in Oviedo (*Oviedo Folk* and *Noche Celta*). Most Asturian groups are fairly traditional, especially *Ubiña* (who have great excellent bagpipe-players) and *Lliberdón*; Llan de Cubel is a little more adventurous. Look out, too, for the excellent harpists Herminia Álvarez

and Fernando Largo. In **Cantabria**, *Cambrizal* and *Luétiga* are names to watch out for.

In terms of local support, **Euskadi** heads the league, with the benefit of Basque-language radio stations, and it shows. Oskorri, an excellent electro-acoustic group, has been mentioned above. Also impressive are *Ganbara* and *Azala*; the singer-songwriter Benito Lertxundi, whose energies generally go into traditional Basque music but who has also recently branched off into a Celtic sound; and the fantastic *trikitixa* (accordeon) player, Kepa Jukera.

Catalunya generally lags behind where folk is concerned. The only reliable names are *La Murga* and the young and promising Tradivarius. Vaguely related, though not strictly folk, are a series of orchestras who play traditional **dance music**: some closer to salsa like the *Orquesta Platería* and the *Salseta del Poble Sec*, others more traditional like *Tercet Treset* and the *Orquesta Galana*.

In the **Balearics**, despite geographical isolation, several groups have formed: *Musica Nostra*, *Sis Som*, *Calitja* and *Aliorna*, who are traditional, and *Coanegra* and *Siurell Electric*, more progressive. *Calabruix*, is an electro-acoustic duo.

From **Valencia**, *Al Tall* are an interesting band whose last project was a joint effort with *Muluk El Hwa*, a group from Marrakesh; *Alimara* are involved with both music and traditional dance; *Salpicao* experiment with flamenco-based fusions; and *La Vella Banda* are an innovative horn band.

Aragón, after years in the wilderness, is beginning to see a bit of a folk revival under the auspices of groups like *Hato de Foces*, *Cornamusa* and the *Orquestina del Fabriol*. The scene in **Castile** has for many years been dominated by the activity of Joaquín Díaz, a phenomenally hard-working and prolific artist, and by *Nuevo Mester de Juglaría*. Manuel Luna and *La Musgaña* are also worth listening out for, as is the singer María Salgado, and the Segovian group, *Rebolada*, who include eight *dulzainas* in their line-up.

In **Andalucía** there are just two folk groups of much interest: the highly traditional *Almadraba* from Tarifa, and the more revivalist *Lombarda* from Granada. Folk festivals are held in Tarifa and in the **Alpujarras**; the latter, catering for this region's particular musical

SELECT DISCOGRAPHY

All the recommendations below are CDs, which in Spain, as elsewhere, have virtually taken over from records.

CLASSIC FLAMENCO

Magna Antología del Cante Flamenco (Hispavox; 10 volumes).

Noches Gitanas (EPM; 4CDs).

Sevillanas: the soundtrack of Carlos Saura's film (Polydor).

Agustín Carbonell Bola *Carmen* (Messidor).

Camarón de la Isla *Una leyends flamenca, Vivire* and *Autorretrato* (Philips).

Carmen Linares *La luna en el río* (Auvidis).

Duquende (Nuevos Medios).

El Indio Gitano *Nací gitano por la gracia de Dios* (Nuevos Medios).

Enrique de Melchor *Cuchichi* (Fonodisc).

Paco de Lucía *Siroco* (Philips).

Paco de Lucía y Paco Peña *Paco Doble* (Philips).

José Menese *El viente solano* (Nuevos Medios).

Moraíto *Morao y oro* (Auvidis).

Enrique Morente *Negra, si tú supieras* (Nuevos Medios).

Ramón el Portugués *Gitanos de la Plaza* (Nuevos Medios).

Tomatito *Barrio Negro* (Nuevos Medios).

NUEVO FLAMENCO

Los Jóvenes Flamencos Vol I & II (Nuevos Medios).

Amalgama y Karnataka College of Percussion (Nuba).

La Barbería del Sue (Nuevos Medios).

Chano Dominguez *Chano* (Nuba).

Ray Heredia *Quien no corre, vuela* (Nuevos Medios).

Jazzpaña (Nuevos Medios).

Ketama *Canciones hondas* (Nuevos Medios) and *Ketama* (Hannibal).

Lole . . . y Manuel (Gong Fonomusic).

Paco de Lucía Sextet *Solo Quiero Caminar* and *Live in America* (Philips), *Live . . . . One Summer Night* (Phonogram).

Juan Peña Lebrijano y Orquestra Andalusi de Tanger *Encuentros* (Ariola/Globestyle).

Pata Negra *Blues de la Frontera* (Nuevos Medios/Hannibal).

Radio Tarifa *Rumba argelina* (Música Sin Fin).

Songhai: Ketama/Toumani Diabate/Danny Thompson (Nuevos Medios/Hannibal).

ROCK

Arrajatabla *Sevilla blues* (Fonomusic).

Celtas Cortos *Tranquilo majete* (Dro).

Ciudad Jardin *Ojos mas que ojos* (Hispavox).

Corcobado *Tormenta de tormento* (Triquinoise).

Fangoria *Una ola cualquiera en Vulcano* (Gasa).

Héroes del Silencio *El espíritu del vino* (Hispavox).

---

tradition of *trovos* – dirge-like songs, with guitar accompaniment.

Sephardic (medieval Iberian Jewish) music can be included here as a cross between folk and traditional styles. Two female singers – Rosa Zaragoza and Aurora Moreno – are the most interesting in this field; Moreno is also involved in Mozarabic *jarchas* (Arabic verse set to music). Two other "medieval" groups are *Els Trobadors* and *Cálamus*.

ROCK

Even when it comes to **rock and pop** music, it is hard to talk of Spain as a single entity. In the 1970s Madrid was dominated by heavy rock,

with a series of groups whose fans lived in the working-class districts of the capital and in the dormitory towns of the outskirts. Meanwhile, in Barcelona, the scene was split between musicians who were producing a very cool jazz-rock and those into a warmer Catalan salsa, or Barcelona's own gypsy music – **Catalan rumba** – popularized by Peret, a Barcelona musician with a liking for Elvis Presley. On the fringes were the singer-songwriters and the Latin American groups who, despite Franco, managed to tour Spain.

At the end of the 1970s, the **punk** reaction began to take hold among teenagers just as it did in Britain and the US. Some of the older

Illegales *Regreso al sexo químicamente puro* (Hispavox).

Luz *A contraluz* (Hispavox).

Negu Gorriak *Borreroak baditu milaka aurpegi* (Esan Ozanki).

Presuntos Implicados *Alma de blues* (WEA).

Radio Futura *Tierra para bailar* (Ariola).

Los Rebeldes *La rosa y la cruz* (Epic).

Os Resentidos *Están aqui* (Gasa).

Miguel Ríos *Así que pasen 30 años* (Polydor).

Los Rodriguez *Sin documentos* (Gasa).

Rosario *De Ley* (Epic).

Los Secretos *Cambio de planes* (Dro).

Seguridad Social *Furia Latina* (Gasa).

Tam Tam Go! *Vida y color* (Hispavox).

Manolo Tena *Sangre Española* (Epic).

El Ultimo de la Fila *Astronomía razonable* (EMI).

Antonio Vega *El sitio de mi recreo* (Polygram).

Kiko Veneno *La Pequeña Salvaje* (Nuevos Medios) and *Échate un cantecito* (BMG).

FOLK

Charo Centenera *No soy la Piquer* (RNE).

Llan de Cubel *L'otru llaou de la mar* (Fono Astur).

Fía na Roca (Arpafolk).

Kepa Junkera *Trikitixa zoom* (Nuba).

Benito Lertxundi *Hyunkidura kuttunak* (Elkar).

La Musgaña *El Diablo Cojuelo* (Sonifolk).

Manuel Luna *Como hablan las sabinas* (RNE).

Mestisay *El cantar viene de lejos* (Manzana).

Milladoiro *Galicia no temp* (Discmedi).

Aurora Moreno *Aynadamar* (Saga).

Oskorri *Badok hamahiru* (Elkar).

Maria Salgado *Mirándote* (Ediciones Cúbicas).

Salpicão (RNE).

Al Tall y Muluk el Hwa *Xarq al-Andalus* (RNE).

Els Trobadors *Et ades sera l'Alba* (Lyricon).

SINGER-SONGWRITERS

Rafael Alberti y Paco Ibañez *A galopar* (PDI).

Luis Eduardo Aute y Silvio Rodriguez *Mano a mano* (Ariola).

Ana Belen *Veneno para el corazón* (Ariola).

María del Mar Bonet *Gavines y Dragons* (Ariola).

Carlos Cano *Quedate con la Copla* (CBS).

Vainica Doble *1970* (RNE).

Pablo Guerrero *Todo la vida es ahora* (Polygram).

Imanol *Alfonsina, viaje de mar y luna* (Ediciones Cúbicas).

Lluis Llach *Astres* (CBS).

Ruper Ordorika *Ez da posible* (Gasa).

Albert Pla *No solo de rumba vive el hombre* (Ariola).

Marina Rossell *Marina* (PDI).

Joan Manuel Serrat *Utopia* (Ariola).

REGIONAL TRADITIONS

Magna Antología del Folklore Musical de España (Hispavox; 17 LPs).

rockers, like Ramoncín, attempted to take punk on board, but punk broke up the old order and set the scene for the future, with an explosion of myriad groups. These days, in every Spanish city there are dozens of them, all making demotapes and looking for a break. Straightforward pop is the main area of activity, but there have been various phases in which punks, *tecnos*, *garajistas*, *siniestros*, Romantics and rockabillies and others have succeeded and overlapped one another. All the following bands are reasonably established, have cut records and are currently active. The list also includes the odd older rocker who still manages to play the part with dignity!

Madrid has the most active scene, with bands covering a wide range of styles and stances. Since the punk days, a key figure on the scene has been **Alaska** – a club owner and one-time muse of modernity – whose records are a little forgettable, but who is always brilliant live. Then there is **Mecano**, a girl singer and two male musicians, who have become the most successful Spanish pop group ever, popular in Latin America, France and Italy, as well as Spain. Other established bands include the country-influenced *Los Secretos*; the futuristic *Aviador Dro*; Miguel Ríos and Ramoncín, both of whom stick to classic rock; and the heavy metal groups, *Rosendo*, *Obús* and *Barón Rojo*.

A slightly younger generation includes *Gabinete Caligari* (macho Hispano-pop), *Los Coyotes* (Latin rockabilly) and *La Frontera* (cowboy), while the big new stars are Luz – a kind of Spanish Nina Hagen – and **Rosario**, an interesting and original singer from a *flamenco* family (she is the daughter of Rosa Flores). *Radio Futura* , who split up recently, were one of the best bands of the 80s.

In **Barcelona** three different groups stand out: the most interesting band, by some way, is **El Ultimo de la Fila**, a duo with good lyrics and a sophisticated Mediterranean sound, who have recently recorded at Peter Gabriel's studio. Equally enjoyable are *Los Rebeldes*, former rockabilly heroes, now seeking new directions.

The **Basque Country** scene is divided into two. Radical rock is represented by *Negu Gorriak*, *Potato*, *Hertzainak* and *La Polla Records*, who use hot rhythms, reggae, ska, etc, as a base for their political message. On a more straightforward rock level, the best bands are *21 Japonesas* and *La Dama se Esconde*.

From **Galicia** (especially Vigo) has emerged a surprising number and diversity of bands. *Siniestro Total* and *Os Resentidos* are the best from the 1980s, with Os Diplomaticos an interesting new arrival. **Asturias** can offer just one reasonably well-known group, *Los Ilegales*, powerful rockers with a strong live set. **Aragón** has **Heroes del Silencio**, who are one of the major chart rock groups in the 1990s.

From **Andalucía** there's the Malagueño combo *Danza Invisible*, and a Sevillan mafia made up of *Martirio* (who combine pop and traditional songs), *Pata Negra* (see also "Flamenco"), *Arrajatabla* and **Kiko Veneno**. Veneno started out working in *flamenco* and wrote Camarón de la Isla's best-known and most hummable song, "Volando Voy". His own sporadic albums are clever, literate and utterly Spanish rock songs – highly recommended.

SINGER-SONGWRITERS

There's a long history of **singer-songwriters** in Spain, but few have managed to adapt themselves to the times. In **Catalunya**, where the *Nova Cançó* (New Song) until recently had a wide base of appeal, many singers have simply dropped out of sight. Among those still going strong are Joan Manuel Serrat, one of the big record sellers in Spain, who sings both in Catalan and Castilian; Marina Rossell, searching for "a Mediterranean music without frontiers"; the lyrical Lluis Llach; and Albert Pla, who now sings rather paranoid songs in Castilian. The biggest name of all is **María del Mar Bonet**, a Catalan singer from the **Balearics**, who also dabbles in folk and jazz.

Euskadi has a similar situation to Catalunya. Mikel Laboa is an old name going strong but not producing anything new, while younger artists like Txomin Artola and his former companion Amaia Zubiría have yet to establish themselves. Other names include Imanol (sophisticated), and Ruper Ordorika (rocky). In **Galicia**, Emilio Cao switches back and forth between traditional folk and more modern singer-songwriting.

Madrid is again the centre of the scene, even if few of the performers are native. Names you're likely to see include Luis Eduardo Aute, who has a huge following; Joaquín Sabina, an Andaluz who plays a catchy simple rock with lyrics younger musicians can identify with; the Asturian Víctor Manuel; Javier Batanero (of *Academica Palanca*); and Javier Bergia, the best and most original of the latest generation.

Andalucía has two further excellent singer-songwriters, the popular Carlos Cano, who has revived the traditional Andalucian *copla*, and Javier Ruibal.

JAZZ

Jazz in Spain always had loyal fans tucked away in small clubs, but since the end of the 1970s it has really taken off. There are many festivals and a good number of established groups. Bop and hard bop predominate, but there are also many experiments with fusion and traditional jazz.

Three great musicians exemplify the best in current Spanish jazz: the Catalan pianist **Tete Montoliu** and the Madrid saxophonists **Pedro Iturralde** and **Jorge Pardo**. All three head their own groups and Jorge is also working on *flamenco* projects with Paco de Lucía. Other combos that stand out are the Madrid-based *Canal Street Band* and *Clamores Band*, both trad; the ultramodern *O C Q*; Vlady Bas's group; and the groups led by Tomás San Miguel, José Antonio Galicia and Gerardo Núñez; all of them in Madrid.

The country's biggest **jazz festival** is held at San Sebastián in July. Vitoria celebrates one in the same month, and there are two in Madrid: one in May (*Fiestas de San Isidro*), the other in November. November is jazz month in Spain, when there's also a festival in Barcelona and many smaller events which take the opportunity of featuring some of the artists who are playing in the two major cities. Other worthwhile events are the *Festival de Jazz* in the streets of Murcia and the *Muestra de Jazz* for young exponents, organized by the *Instituto de la Juventud* in Ibiza.

Manuel Domínguez

CINEMA

The vast majority of Spanish films remain unseen in the rest of Europe. In recent years the films of **Pedro Almodóvar** have become part of the staple diet of repetory cinemas, while before Almodóvar Spanish films would periodically appear on the film festival circuit and, on occasions, be taken up by the odd art-house cinema. One director in particular, **Carlos Saura**, achieved international prestige even while working under the restrictions of the Franco regime; from an earlier generation, another Spanish film-maker, **Luis Buñuel**, has been generally accepted as one of the major figures in the history of cinema. Saura was, however, something of an exception, Almodóvar is hardly typical, and Buñuel made almost all his films in either France or Mexico.

Beyond Almodóvar, Saura and Buñuel exists a large body of Spanish films including "boulevard comedies" aimed at a purely domestic audience and low-budget horror films. Cinema has not always found it easy to take root in Spain: the country's rural basis, the devastation of the Civil War, and the restrictions of the Franco regime all meant that film-makers had to struggle to get films made in Spain, and then struggle again to get them released. Yet a Spanish film industry and film culture has developed, and in recent years Spain has provided some of the most exciting examples of European cinema.

THE EARLY DECADES

The history of Spanish film goes back to the last century, and in **Segundo de Chomón**,

Spain even produced one of the pioneers of early cinema, a man whose use of trick photography rivalled that of the French director, Georges Mélière.

Overall, however, Spanish cinema developed slowly. Spain entered the twentieth century lacking the technology, the capital and the audience that produced a thriving film industry in neighbouring France. "In my own village of Calanda," wrote Luis Buñuel in his autobiography, "...the Middle Ages lasted until World War I." Like Buñuel, Segundo de Chomón spent much of his career abroad; he ended up producing special-effects for other directors In Italy and France. By the 1920s, a Spanish film industry had been established, but its modest scale and pretensions are the reason that one film of 1925 was promoted with the catchy slogan – "It's so good that it doesn't seem Spanish".

Without a strong production base, cinema in Spain was particularly susceptible to the rapidly developing economic power of **America**. In the early 1930s "Spanish" films were being produced, but often in Paris or Hollywood rather than Madrid, as the major American film companies dealt with the coming of sound (and the threat that an indigenous Spanish film industry might have provided) by producing Spanish-language versions of their English-speaking product. The importance of this short-lived phenomenon rests not so much in the films that were made – though it has been claimed that in instances such as the Spanish-language version of *Dracula* (1931) the copy was somewhat better than the original – but in the fact that it deprived Spain of a number of film-makers.

However, in 1934, a major production and distribution company, **CIFAS**, was founded in Madrid. With a degree of support from the Republican government, and with the native product proving more popular than subtitled American movies (though dubbing was gradually adopted as a standard practice), the Spanish film industry began to appear relatively healthy. Luis Buñuel returned to Spain from France – where, with fellow Spaniard Salvador Dalí, he had directed a couple of surrealist classics, *Un Chien Andalou* (1928) and *L'Age d'Or* (1930) – to make *Land Without Bread* (1932). This film, an unremitting documentary about rural poverty, was promptly banned, but Buñuel stayed on, dubbing films for *Warner Brothers*, and working as executive producer (and reputedly occasional director) on four more mainstream projects.

The **Civil War** and the eventual Nationalist victory drove Buñuel into exile. It also ended the brief flowering of popular Spanish cinema that had been exhibited in films such as *Paloma Fair* (1935) and *Clara the Brunette* (1936), the latter featuring the first "star" of Spanish cinema, Imperio Argentina.

During the conflict, the Communists and the anarcho-syndicalists used film as one of the weapons of war, producing numerous shorts extolling their cause, while there were also appeals for international support for the Republican cause in films such as Joris Ivens' *The Spanish Earth* (1937). In 1937, the **Supreme Board of Film Censorship** was established by the Nationalist government, and inaugurated four decades in which censorship was the strongest force in Spanish cinema.

THE FRANCO YEARS

Under Franco, both scripts and completed films had to be submitted for approval. Taboo subjects ranged from sex to the Civil War; no actual **code of censorship** was laid down until 1963, but this only gave greater freedom to the censors. Film-makers had no power of redress, and also needed to placate the Catholic Church – in 1950 the Church established the **National Board of Classification of Spectacles** which made its own "recommendations". Foreign films that were not banned could be made more acceptable through the dubbing process; as late as the 1970s a voice-over was added to Sam Peckinpah's *The Getaway*, assuring the audience that the criminals in the film were later captured and brought to justice.

Some directly **propagandist** films were produced by the new regime, for instance *The Madrid Front* (1939) and *Race* (1941), the latter an adaptation of Franco's own novel. More generally, the 1940s brought a series of films glorifying the Spanish past and presenting **idealized images** of the state, the Church and the family.

Efforts were made to support an indigenous Spanish film industry. In 1947 a **film school** was established in Madrid, and in 1952 state subsidy regulations were changed to allow for the awarding of fifty percent of the estimated cost of films of "national interest". In practice, however, the interpretation of 'national interest' tended to mean a bias against nonconformity.

It was against this background that a group of **left-wing film-makers** met in 1955, declaring contemporary Spanish cinema to be "1. Politically futile. 2. Socially false. 3. Intellectually worthless. 4. Aesthetically valueless. 5. Industrially paralytic." Inspired by the example of Italian neo-realism such film-makers were, in fact, beginning to present a less idealized picture of Spanish society. Films such as Luis Berlanga's *Welcome Mr Marshall* (1953), a satire about the effect of America's Marshall Plan on a Spanish village, and Antonio Bardem's *Main Street* (1956) suggested that there was at least some room for alternative voices in the Spanish film industry.

The restrictions continued (in 1956 Bardem was briefly imprisoned for his political views) but the Spanish government did institute a more **flexible policy**, if largely to attract international support and investment. While American film companies were being persuaded to use relatively inexpensive **Spanish locations** for the filming of "epics" such as *Alexander the Great* (1955), the prestige offered by the international film festival circuit meant that even films offering a critical view of Spanish institutions could be used as a means of "selling" Spain abroad.

The **contradictions** inherent in this policy were shown up most blatantly when **Buñuel** was invited back to Spain to make a film for the production company *UNINCI*, which had been formed by a group of film-makers including Bardem, Berlanga and Carlos Saura. *Viridiana* (1961) revealed that the director of *L'Age d'Or* could be as uncompromising and irreverent as ever.

Astonishingly, *Viridiana* was initially passed by the censor, despite scenes such as one that looked uncannily like a debauched parody of Leonardo's *The Last Supper*. The film was only banned after it had been attacked in the Vatican newspaper. The result was that Bunuel resumed his career in Mexico and France, and the promise and short life of *UNINCI* was brought to a close.

Buñuel returned to Spain to make *Tristana* in 1970 and *That Obscure Object of Desire* in 1977, though both were French-Spanish co-productions rather than exclusively Spanish films. *Viridiana* was not shown in Spain until 1977. In the meantime what Spain got was the so-called **New Spanish Cinema**, a government-sponsored film movement based on broadly realist principles.

In this slightly liberalized but still restictive atmosphere some directors managed to develop the problem of getting round the censor into something of a fine art. **Carlos Saura**, in particular, who had quickly left behind the naturalism of his earliest films, used the power of **suggestion**, **allegory** and **symbol** to attack Francoist pretensions in films such as *The Hunt* (1965) and *The Garden of Delights* (1970). Working in association with the actress Geraldine Chaplin and the producer El Ras Querjeta he also used his developing international prestige to retain a remarkable degree of control over his own films.

Other directors lacked Saura's prestige, though the loose movement known as the **Barcelona School** attempted to challenge the dominance of Madrid and the lack of adventurousness in New Spanish Cinema. Meanwhile, another side of Spanish cinema was revealed in the developing market for **low-budget horror** films, capitalizing on the fact that violence was less censored than sex.

If in the 1960s a Spanish new wave had essentially failed to develop, the **1970s** proved a **more exciting period**, both politically and culturally. In the last years of the Franco regime, Saura continued to maintain his independence, exploring the scars of the Civil War in *Cousin Angelica* (1973) and the consequences of repression in *Raise Ravens* (1975). The aftermath of the Civil War also provided the theme of Victor Erice's debut feature, *The Spirit of the Beehive* (1973), a lyrical film set in a bleak Castilian village and featuring, like *Raise Ravens*, the young **Ana Torrént**.

A more violent picture of rural Spain was presented in Ricardo Franco's *Pascale Duarte* (1975) and also in José Luis Borau's *Poachers* (1975). In its story of **disintegrating authority** the latter film, released shortly before Franco's death, seemed almost to anticipate the demise of the dictatorship.

POST FRANCO

Franco's death was followed by the lifting of censorship in 1977, but initially also by the **withdrawal of government subsidies**, while the same law that removed censorship also removed the restrictions on foreign blockbusters. The problems of the Spanish film industry were by no means over, they had simply become those of **economics** rather than those of direct political control.

"It really takes a miracle to make a film in Spain," Pedro Almodóvar has stated. "It's a miracle that Spanish cinema exists at all." Such miracles have, however, occured, and they were helped by the enactment of the so-called **Miró Law** – named after the then director general of cinema – which reintroduced generous government subsidies. Support from regional authorities, and the move away from Franco's exclusive emphasis on Spain's Castilian heritage, have also assisted the development of a more decentralized Spanish film industry. Films using the Catalan language, for example, became possible for the first time, following the establishment in 1975 of the **Institute of Catalan Film**, while the Basque government has also financed feature films such as the recent *Vacas* (1992), a story of a feud between two family clans set against the Basque mountains.

For directors who had mastered the art of indirect statement the post-Franco era necessitated a **change of direction**. For **Carlos Saura** such a change bore fruit in the form of *Blood Wedding* (1981), a filmed record of a company rehearsing a ballet version of Frederico Garcia Lorca's play, and *Carmen* (1983), in which a similar treatment was given to Prosper Mérimée's novel. If Saura's subsequent films have largely failed to gather similar audiences or praise, he did achieve a popular and critical success with *Ay, Carmela* (1990), a return to the Civil War, this time as a subject of both comedy and tragedy.

Since *The Spirit of the Beehive* **Victor Erice** has directed just two films: *The South* (1983) and *The Quince Tree Sun* (1991). *The South* is, like his first film, a poetic and unsentimental exploration of a father-daughter relationship under the shadow of the Civil War, while *The Quince Tree Sun* is a "film diary" recording the meticulous preparations made by the Spanish artist Antonio López as he waits to capture the exact light needed for his painting - a very slow but potentially rewarding study of an artist at work.

A more overtly **political subject matter** provided the basis of a number of Spanish films during the changes that took place in the late 1970s. *Black Brood* (1977), directed by Manuel Gutiérrez Aragón, dealt with right-wing terrorists, *The Truth About the Salvatore Affair* (1978), directed by Antonio Drove, returned to history (Barcelona in the years between 1917 and 1923) to examine the economic roots of political change, while veteran of the left Juan Bardem contributed to the debate with the political thriller *Seven Days in May* (1978).

A **new generation** of film-makers and performers have risen to prominence in the post-Franco era. Almost all Spanish directors have been men, but one woman, Pilar Miró, has been both director general of cinema and in charge of the state-run national television network. She has also made her own films, courting controversy with *The Engagement Party* (1976) and *The Cuena Crime* (1980) (both of which were initially banned despite the more liberal atmosphere of the time), and examining the experience of a woman working in a male-dominated industry in *Gary Cooper, Who Art in Heaven* (1980).

Vicente Aranda began directing in 1964. He went on to make a series of stylish horror films, thrillers and the odd political satire, and also, in 1976, to introduce **Victoria Abril** to cinema audiences. Abril later appeared in the film with which Aranda achieved his international breakthrough, *The Lovers* (1991), a highly charged story of fatal attraction in 1950s Madrid. But by that time she had gone on to achieve fame within and beyond the borders of Spain, through her appearances in Almodóvar's *Tie Me Up, Tie Me Down* (1990) and *High Heels* (1991).

Pedro Almodóvar has himself become the most famous, if also at times the most notorious, of contemporary Spanish film-makers. He began making Super-8 movies in 1974, switch-

ing to 35mm. In the middle of making the cheap and cheerfully transgressive *Pepi, Luci and Bom* in 1980. He achieved instant cult status in Spain with *Labyrinth of Passion* (1982) and an international reputation with the more sophisticated comic style of *Women on the Edge of a Nervous Breakdown* (1988). His prodigous output in the 1980s also included *What Have I Done To Deserve This?* (1984), a black comedy about drugs, prostitution and the forging of Hitler's diaries, *Matador* (1986), a very dark thriller linking sexual excitement with the violence of the bullfight, and *The Law of Desire* (1987), a story involving a gay film director with a transsexual brother/sister and a further variation on the theme of sex and death. Most of these films were further enlivened by the presence of Carmen Maura.

Almodóvar's cinema seems to be a world away from the censorship of the Franco regime, and also a world away from earlier Spanish films characterized by a careful evasion of censorship or the investigation of Spain's rural past. "I never speak of Franco; I hardly acknowledge his existence", he has stated. "I start after Franco."

The influence of the past continues to be felt in contemporary Spanish cinema, and, in marked contrast to Almodóvar, directors such as **Pedro Olea** have continued to concentrate on a cinema of literary adaptation and careful period reconstruction: Olea's *The Fencing Master* (1993), for example, returned to nineteenth-century Madrid to produce a more restrained variation on the recurring theme of fatal passion. Other important contemporary Spanish film directors include Mario Camus, Jaime Chávarria, José Juan Bigas Luna, Fernando Trueba and Imanol Uribe.

1994 has begun as a promising year for Spanish cinema on the international circuit with **Fernando Trueba**'s *Belle Epoque*, a film about the difficulty of choosing and the limits of happiness, winning an **Oscar** for best foreign film.

Guy Barefoot

BOOKS

Listings below represent a highly selective reading list on Spain and matters Spanish, especially in the sections on history. Most titles are in print, although we've included a few older classics, many of them easy enough to find in second-hand bookshops and libraries. For all books in print, publishing details are in the form (UK publisher/US publisher), where both exist; if books are published in one country only, this follows the publisher's name (eg Serpent's Tail, UK). University Press has been abbreviated as UP.

IMPRESSIONS, TRAVEL AND GENERAL ACCOUNTS

THE BEST INTRODUCTIONS

Ian Gibson *Fire in the Blood: the New Spain* (Faber/BBC, UK). Gibson is a Madrid-based writer, resident since 1978, and a Spanish national since 1984. He is a passionate enthusiast and critic of Spain and the Spanish, both of which he gets across brilliantly in this 1993 book – the accompaniment to a gripping TV series – in all their mass of contradictions, attitudes, obsessions, quirks and everything else. Hugely recommended, but did receive flack from outraged Spanish reviewers.

John Hooper *Spaniards: A Portrait of the New Spain* (Penguin, UK/US). Excellent, insightful portrait of post-Franco Spain and the new generation by *The Guardian*'s correspondent there for the last decade; written in 1986 and updated in 1993. Along with Ian Gibson's book (above), this is the best possible introduction to contemporary Spain.

RECENT TRAVELS

David Gilmour *Cities of Spain* (Pimlico/Ivan R Dee). A modern cultural portrait of Spain, but very much in the old tradition; it is a little fogeyish at times but excellent, nonetheless, in its evocation of history, especially on the Moorish cities of Andalucía.

Adam Hopkins *Spanish Journeys: A Portrait of Spain* (Penguin, UK). Published in 1993, this is an enjoyable and highly stimulating exploration of Spanish history and culture, weaving its (considerable) scholarship in an accessible and unforced travelogue form, and full of illuminating anecdotes.

Robert Hughes *Barcelona* (Harvill/Vintage). This is the best of the 1992 books on the Olympic city: a text that, in the author's stated ambition, "explains the zeitgeist of the place and the connective tissue between the cultural icons".

Michael Jacobs *Between Hopes and Memories: A Spanish Journey* (Picador, UK). The thorough and entertaining account of a journey through Spain in 1992 with lively digressions on food, art, literature and the characters met along the way.

Paul Richardson *Not Part of the Package* (Macmillan, UK). Published in 1993, this is the best account yet of tourism in Spain – in this case a year's hedonism on Ibiza, which emerges in all its disco-dazzled lights.

Ted Walker *In Spain* (out of print). The poet Ted Walker has lived and travelled in Spain on and off since the 1950s. This is a lyrical and perceptive account of the country and people, structured around his various sorties.

James Woodall *In Search of the Firedance: Spain through Flamenco* (Sinclair Stevenson, UK). This is a terrific history and exploration of *flamenco*, and as the subtitle suggests it is never satisfied with "just the music" in getting to the heart of the culture.

EARLIER TWENTIETH-CENTURY WRITERS

Gerald Brenan *South From Granada* (Penguin/CUP). An enduring classic. Brenan lived in a small village in the Alpujarras in the 1920s, and records this and the visits of his Bloomsbury contemporaries Virginia Woolf, Lytton Strachey and Bertrand Russell.

Camilo José Cela *Journey to the Alcarria* (Penguin/Wisconsin UP). A Nobel Prize winner for literature, Cela explored a hidden corner of New Castile in 1946 – a study of a rural world that no longer exists.

Nina Epton *Grapes and Granite* (out of print). This is one of the few English books on Galicia – full of folklore and rural life in the 1960s – and well worth hunting down in libraries or second-hand bookshops.

Laurie Lee *As I Walked Out One Midsummer Morning, A Rose For Winter* (Penguin, UK), *A Moment of War* (Penguin/New Press). *One Midsummer Morning* is the irresistibly romantic account of Lee's walk through Spain – from Vigo to Málaga – and his gradual awareness of the forces moving the country towards Civil War. As an autobiographical novel, of living rough and busking his way from the Cotswolds with a violin, it's a delight; as a piece of social observation, painfully sharp. In *A Rose For Winter* he describes his return, twenty years later, to Andalucía, while in *A Moment of War* he looks back again to describe a winter fighting with the International Brigade in the Civil War – by turns moving, comic and tragic.

Rose Macaulay *Fabled Shore* (out of print). The Spanish coast as it was in 1949 (read it and weep), travelled and described from Catalunya to the Portuguese Algarve.

James A. Michener *Iberia* (Corgi/Crest). A bestselling, idiosyncratic and encyclopedic compendium of interviews and impressions of Spain on the brink – in 1968 – looking forward to the post-Franco years. Fascinating, still.

Jan Morris *Spain* (Penguin/Prentice-Hall). Morris wrote this in six months in 1960, on her (or, at the time, his) first visit to the country. It is an impressionistic account – good in its sweeping control of place and history, though prone to see everything as symbolic. The updated edition is plain bizarre in its ideas on Franco and dictatorship – a condition for which Morris seems to believe Spaniards were naturally inclined.

George Orwell *Homage to Catalonia* (Penguin/Harvest Books). Stirring account of Orwell's participation in the early exhilaration of revolution in Barcelona, and his growing disillusionment with the factional fighting among the Republican forces during the ensuing Civil War.

OLDER CLASSICS

George Borrow *The Bible in Spain* and *The Zincali* (both out of print). On first publication in 1842, Borrow subtitled *The Bible in Spain* "Journeys, Adventures and Imprisonments of an English-man"; it is one of the most famous books on Spain – slow in places but with some very amusing stories. *Zincali* is an account of the Spanish gypsies, whom Borrow got to know pretty well.

Richard Ford *A Handbook for Travellers in Spain and Readers at Home* (Centaur Press/ Gordon Press); *Gatherings from Spain* (out of print). The *Handbook* must be the best guide ever written to any country and stayed in print as a *Murray's Handbook* (one of the earliest series of guides) well into this century. Massively opinionated, it is an extremely witty book in its British, nineteenth-century manner, incredibly knowledgeable, and worth flicking through for the proverbs alone. Copies of *Murray's* may be available in second-hand bookshops – the earlier the edition the purer the Ford. The *Gatherings* is a rather timid abridgement of the general pieces.

Washington Irving *Tales of the Alhambra* (originally published 1832; abridged editions are on sale in Granada). Half of Irving's book consists of oriental stories, set in the Alhambra; the rest of accounts of his own residence there and the local characters of his time. A perfect read in situ.

George Sand *A Winter in Majorca* (Academy Press, US). Sand and Chopin spent their winter at the monastery of Valldemossa. They weren't entirely appreciated by the locals, in which lies much of the book's appeal. Local editions, including a translation by late Mallorcan resident Robert Graves, are on sale around the island.

ANTHOLOGIES

Jimmy Burns (ed) *Spain: A Literary Companion* (John Murray, UK). A good anthology, including nuggets of most authors recommended here, amid a whole host of others.

David Mitchell *Travellers in Spain: An Illustrated Anthology* (Cassell, UK). A well-told story of how four centuries of travellers – and most often travel-writers – saw Spain. It's intersting to see Ford, Brenan, Laurie Lee and the rest set in context.

HISTORY

EARLY, MEDIEVAL AND BEYOND

Manuel Fernández Álvarez *Charles V* (out of print); **Peter Pierson** *Philip II of Spain* (Thames & Hudson, UK). Good studies in an illustrated biography series.

James M. Anderson *Spain: 1001 Archaelogical Sites* (Hale/Calgary UP). A good guide and gazeteer to 95 percent of Spain's archeological sites with detailed illustrations of how to get there.

John A. Crow *Spain: The Root and the Flower* (California UP, US/UK). Cultural/social history from Roman Spain to the present.

J.H. Elliott *Imperial Spain 1469–1716* (Penguin, US/UK). The best introduction to "the Golden Age" – academically respected and a gripping tale. The new *The Hispanic World*, edited by Professor Elliott, is a weighty (and expensive) history of Spain with particular reference to Spanish influence in the Americas.

Richard Fletcher *The Quest for El Cid* (OUP, UK) and *Moorish Spain* (Weidenfeld & Nicolson/California UP). Two of the best studies of their kind – fascinating and highly readable narratives. The latter has a suitably iconoclastic conclusion to the history of Moorish Spain.

L.P. Harvey *Islamic Spain 1250–1500* (Chicago UP, US/UK). Comprehensive account of its period – both the Islamic kingdoms and the Muslims living beyond their protection.

David Howarth *The Voyage of the Armada* (Penguin, US). An account from the Spanish perspective of the personalities, from king to sailors, involved in the Armada.

S.J. Keay *Roman Spain* (British Musuem Publications/California UP). Relatively new and definitive survey of a neglected subject, well illustrated and highly readable.

Elie Kedourie *Spain and the Jews: The Sephardi Experience, 1492 and After* (Thames & Hudson, UK/US). A collection of essays on the three million Spanish Jews of the Middle Ages and their expulsion by the Catholic kings.

THE 20TH CENTURY AND THE CIVIL WAR

Gerald Brenan *The Spanish Labyrinth* (CUP, US/UK). First published in 1943, Brenan's account of the background to the Civil War is tinged by personal experience, yet still an impressively rounded account.

Raymond Carr *Modern Spain 1875–1980* (OUP, US/UK) and *The Spanish Tragedy: the Civil War in Perspective* (Weidenfeld, UK). Two of the best books available on modern Spanish history – concise and well-told narratives.

Ronald Fraser *Blood of Spain* (Pantheon, US). Subtitled "The Experience of Civil War, 1936–39", this is an equally impressive piece of research, constructed entirely of oral accounts. *In Hiding*, by the same author, is a fascinating individual account of a Republican mayor hidden by his family for thirty years until the Civil War amnesty of 1969.

Ian Gibson *Federico García Lorca* (Faber & Faber/Pantheon), *The Assassination of Federico García Lorca* (Penguin, UK) and *Lorca's Granada* (Faber & Faber, US/UK). The biography is a compelling book and *The Assassination* a brilliant reconstruction of the events at the end of his life, with an examination of fascist corruption and of the shaping influences on Lorca, twentieth-century Spain and the Civil War. *Granada* contains Lorca's fascinating tours around the town.

Robert Low *La Pasionaria* (Hutchinson, UK). Dolores Ibarurri – La Pasionaria – coined the battle cry "*¡No Pasaran!*" during the siege of Madrid and was a crucial figure in the leadership of the Spanish Communist Party during the Civil War and in subsequent exile. This is a skilful tale of her sad and extraordinary life.

Paul Preston *Franco* (Harper Collins, UK). A penetrating – and monumental – biography of Franco and his regime, which provides as clear a picture as any yet published of how he won the Civil War, how he survived in power so long, and what, twenty years on from his death, was his significance.

Hugh Thomas *The Spanish Civil War* (Penguin/Touchstone). This exhaustive study is regarded (both in Spain and abroad) as the definitive history of the Civil War.

ART AND ARCHITECTURE

Marianne Barrucand and Achim Bednoz *Moorish Architecture* (Taschen, Cologne). A beautifully illustrated guide to the major Moorish monuments.

Titus Burckhardt *Moorish Culture in Spain* (out of print). An outstanding book which opens up ways of looking at Spain's Islamic monuments, explaining their patterns and significance and the social environment in which, and for which, they were produced.

Jerrilyn D. Dodds *Al-Andalus* (Abrams, UK/US). An in-depth study of the arts and monuments of Moorish Andalucía, put together as a catalogue for a major exhibition at the Alhambra.

Godfrey Goodwin *Islamic Spain* (Chronicle Books, US). Architectural guide with descriptions of virtually every significant Islamic building in Spain, and a fair amount of background.

Meyer Schapiro *Romanesque Art* (Thames & Hudson/Braziller). An excellent, illustrated survey of Romanesque art and architecture – and its Visigothic and Mozarabic precursors.

Sacheverell Sitwell *Spanish Baroque* (Ayer, US). Published in 1931, this is interesting mainly for the absence of anything better on the subject.

Anatzu Zabalbeascoa *The New Spanish Architecture* (Rizzoli, UK/US). A superb, highly illustrated study of the new Spanish architecture of the 1980s and 1990s in Barcelona, Madrid, Sevilla and elsewhere.

Numerous **individual studies** of Picasso, Miró, Dalí and Gaudí as well as the classic Spanish painters are, of course, also available.

FICTION AND POETRY

SPANISH CLASSICS

Pedro de Alarcón *The Three-Cornered Hat and Other Stories* (out of print). Ironic nineteenth-century tales of the previous century's corruption, bureaucracy and absolutism.

Leopoldo Alas *La Regenta* (Penguin, US/UK). A more involved nineteenth-century novel with sweeping vision of the disintegrating social fabric of the period.

Ramón Pérez de Ayala *Belarmino and Apolonio* (Quartet/California UP) and *Honeymoon, Bittermoon* (Quartet/California UP). A pair of tragi-comic Picaresque novels written around the turn of the century.

Miguel de Cervantes *Don Quixote* (Penguin/Signet) and *Exemplary Stories* (Penguin, UK). *Quixote* is of course the classic of Spanish literature and still an excellent read. If you want to try Cervantes in a more modest dose, the *Stories* are a good place to start.

Benito Pérez Galdós *Torquemada* (Columbia, US) and *Misericordia* (Dedalus, UK). Galdós wrote, in the last decades of the nineteenth century and the first of this, of life in Madrid, combining comic scenes and social realism; he is often characterized as a "Spanish Balzac". *Torquemada* is an epic tale of a Madrid moneylender, as vicious as his famous namesake. *Misericordia* is the tale of a good woman trying to stop her family falling into destitution.

Saint Teresa of Ávila Saint Teresa's autobiography is said to be the most widely read Spanish classic after *Don Quixote*. Takes some wading through, but fascinating in parts. Various translations, but easiest to find is *The Life of Saint Teresa of Ávila by Herself*.

MODERN FICTION

Felipe Alfau *Locos: A Comedy of Gestures* (Penguin/Vintage), *Chromos* (Viking/Vintage). Though Alfau emigrated to New York and wrote in English (in the 1930s and 1940s), his recently republished novels are very Spanish; also well ahead of their time in terms of style, so perhaps not the easiest of reads.

Bernardo Atxaga *Obabakoak* (Vintage/Pantheon). This challenging novel by a Basque writer won major prizes on its Spanish publication. It is a sequence of tales of life in a Basque village and the narrator's search to give them meaning.

Arturo Barea *The Forging of a Rebel* (out of print). Superb autobiographical trilogy, taking in the Spanish war in Morocco in the 1920s, and Barea's own part in the Civil War. The books are published under the individual titles *The Forge*, *The Track* and *The Clash*.

Michel del Castillo *The Disinherited* (Serpent's Tail/Consort). Gripping tale of Madrid during the Civil War, written in 1959.

Víctor Català (Caterina Albert i Paradís) *Solitude* (Readers International, UK/US). This tragic tale of a woman's life and sexual passions in a Catalan mountain village is regarded as the most important pre-Civil War Catalan novel.

Juan Luis Cebrián *Red Doll* (Grove-Atlantic, US). Easy-to-read thriller set in post-Franco years, involving Basque terrorists, the KGB, right-wing backlash and, of course, romance.

Camilo José Cela *The Family of Pascual Duarte* (Little, Brown, US/UK). Cela should be the grand old man of Spanish fiction – a Nobel prizewinner and integral to the revival of Spanish literature after the Civil War – though his reputation in Spain is compromised by his involvement with Franco's government. *Pascual Duarte*, his first and best-known novel, portrays a family in the aftermath of the war.

Juan Goytisolo *Marks of Identity* (Serpent's Tail/Consort), *Count Julian* (Serpent's Tail, UK/US), *Juan the Landless* (Serpent's Tail, UK/US), *Landscapes after the Battle* (Serpent's Tail/Seaver Books). Born in Barcelona in 1931, Goytisolo became a bitter enemy of the Franco regime, and has spent most of his life in self-exile, in Paris and in Morocco. He is perhaps the most important modern Spanish novelist, confronting, above all ·in his great trilogy (comprising the first three titles listed above), the whole ambivalent idea of Spain and Spanishness. His writing is difficult, modernist prose, full of interior monologue and wrestling with the conventions of language. Goytisolo has also written an autobiography, *Forbidden Territory* (Serpent's Tail, UK).

Ana María Matute *School of the Sun* (Quartet/Columbia UP). The loss of childhood innnocence on a Balearic island, where old enmities are redefined during the Civil War.

Manuel Vazquez Montalban *Murder in the Central Committee, Southern Seas, An Olympic Death* and *The Angst Ridden Executive* (all Serpent's Tail, UK). Montalban is one of Spain's most influential writers, through his weekly political column in *El Pais* newspaper. A long-time member of the Communist Party, he lives in Barcelona, like his great creation, the gourmand private detective Pepe Carvalho, who stars in all of his wry and racy crime thrillers. The one to begin with – indeed, a bit of a classic – is *Murder in the Central Committee*, where the lights go down on a session of the Committee and the General Secretary of the party is found murdered. Read on . . .

Julián Ríos *Larva* (Quartet/Dalkey Archive). Subtitled "Midsummer Night's Babel", *Larva* is a large, complex, postmodern novel by a leading Spanish literary figure, originally published to huge acclaim in Spain.

Mercé Roderada *The Time of the Doves* (*La Plaza del Diamante)* (out of print). A working-class woman in the Barcelona suburb of Gracia struggles to survive amid the pressures and poverty of the post-Civil War years. The book is lucid and lyrical – as was the film of the novel – and much acclaimed when it emerged in the 1970s.

Javier Tomo *The Coded Letter and Dear Monster* (Carcanet, UK). A pair of Kafkaesque tales from one of Spain's leading post-Franco era novelists.

Maruja Torres *Desperately Seeking Julio* (4th Estate, UK). The Julio is of course Iglesias (the original Spanish title – "*It's Him!*" – had no need for names) in this enjoyable romp of a novel. Torres is quite a name in Spain, writing for gossip magazines, as well as a regular opinion column in *El Pais*. Her last novel, as yet untranslated, featured the replica of Columbus's boat sinking at the Sevilla Expo – an event that promptly came about.

Llorenç Villalonga *The Doll's Room* (out of print). Nobility in decline in nineteenth-century Mallorca lyrically depicted by a Mallorcan/Catalan writer.

If you can read **Spanish**, the following modern novelists are also of interest: **Luis Martín Santos** (*Tiempo de Silencio*); **Alfonso Grosso** (*Con Flores a María*); **Mariano Antolín** (*Wham!, Hombre Araña!* – the Spanish William Burroughs); **Montserrat Roig** (best of contemporary feminist writers); **Rafael Sánchez Ferlosio** (*El Jarama, Alfanhui*); **Pío Baroja** (*El Arbol de la Ciencia*); and **Miguel Delibes** (*El Camino*, or any others).

PLAYS AND POETRY

Pedro Calderón de la Barca *Life is a Dream and other Spanish Classics* (Nick Hern Books/Players Press), *The Mayor of Zalamea* (Absolute Press/Dramatic Publications). Some of the best works of the great dramatist of Spain's "Golden Age".

Federico García Lorca *Five Plays: Comedies and Tragicomedies* (Penguin/New Directions). The great pre-Civil War playwright and poet. Arturo Barea's *Lorca: the Poet and His People* is also of interest.

Lope de Vega. The nation's first important playwright wrote literally hundreds of plays, the best of which remain standards of classic Spanish theatre.

J.M. Cohen (ed.) *The Penguin Book of Spanish Verse* (Penguin, UK/US). Spanish, British and American poets, including many combatants, record or recall their Civil War experiences.

SPAIN IN FOREIGN FICTION

Harry Chapman *Spanish Drums* (Mainstream, UK). An engaging thriller, telling of an Englishwoman outsider's entry into the life of a family in Teruel – and her discovery of all the terrible baggage of its Civil War past.

Douglas Day *Journey of the Wolf* (Penguin, UK). Outstanding first novel by an American writer, given the seal of approval by Graham Greene ("gripping and poignant"). The subject is a Civil War fighter, "El Lobo", who returns to his village in the Alpujarras as a fugitive, forty years on.

Graham Greene *Monsignor Quixote* (Penguin/ Pocket Books). The journey of a small-town priest around modern Spain; Greene at his comic best.

Ernest Hemingway *Fiesta/The Sun Also Rises* (Cape/ Scribner) and *For Whom the Bell Tolls* (Cape/Scribner). Hemingway remains a big part of the American myth of Spain – *Fiesta* contains some lyrically beautiful writing while the latter is a good deal more laboured. He also published an enthusiastic and not very good account of bullfighting, *Death in the Afternoon*.

Arthur Koestler *Dialogue with Death* (out of print). Koestler was reporting the Civil War in 1937 when he was captured and imprisoned by Franco's troops – this is essentially his prison diary.

Norman Lewis *Voices of the Old Sea* (Penguin, US/UK) and *The Day of the Fox* (Robinson Publishing, UK). Lewis lived in Catalunya from 1948 to 1952, just as tourism was arriving. These two books are each ingenious blends of novel and social record, charting the breakdown of the old ways in the face of the "new revolution".

Amin Malouf *Leo the African* (Quarter, UK). A wonderful historical novel, recreating the life of Leo Africanus, the fifteenth-century Moorish geographer, in the last years of the kingdom of Granada, and on his subsequent exile in Morocco and world travels.

SPECIALIST GUIDEBOOKS

TREKKING AND CYCLING

Robin Collomb *Picos de Europa, Sierra de Gredos* and *Sierra Nevada*, plus others (West Col, UK). Detailed guides aimed primarily at serious trekkers and climbers.

Valerie Crespi-Green *Landscapes of Mallorca* (Sunflower Books, UK). One of a reliable and well-put together series, aimed at fairly casual walkers and picnickers.

Marc S. Dubin *Trekking in Spain* (Lonely Planet, UK/US). A detailed and practical trekking guide by a *Rough Guide* author moonlighting for the opposition. It covers the most interesting mainland *sierras*, plus Mallorca.

Kev Reynolds *Walks and Climbs in the Pyrenees* (Cicerone Press, UK). User-friendly guide for trekkers and walkers, though half devoted to the French side of the frontier.

In Spanish, look out for the excellent series of guides published by **Sua Edizioak** of Bilbao. These include *Topoguias* and *Rutas y Paseos* covering most of the individual **Spanish sierras and mountain regions**, and a superb range of **regional guides for cyclists**, *En Bici*, functionally ring-bound, with detailed maps and route contours. **Penthalol** guides available from major bookshops in Spain detail walks in various regions throughout the country.

THE PILGRIM ROUTE TO SANTIAGO

Abbé G. Bernes, Georges Veron and L. Laborde Balen *The Pilgrim Route to Compostela* (Robertson-McCarta, UK). This is the most practical of the many guides to the route – thorough on the paths, clear on maps and with basic details of accommodation. It is translated from the French, however, and is not that inspiring a read.

Michael Jacobs *The Road to Santiago de Compostela* (Penguin, UK). An architectural guide, excellent on the buildings but with no practicalities.

Edwin Mullins *The Pilgrimage to Santiago* (out of print). This is a travelogue rather than a guide, but is by far the best book on the Santiago legend and its fascinating medieval pilgrimage industry. Mullins follows the route, points out churches along the way, and gives incisive accounts of their social and architectural history.

Pilgrim Guide to Spain (Confraternity of Saint James, UK). A pamphlet, revised annually, with information on the routes and places to stay and eat. The confraternity can also supply many other relevant publications, as well as pilgrim accreditation. Their address is: c/o Marion Marples, 45 Dolben St, London SE1 0UQ, UK.

WILDLIFE

Frederic Grunfeld and Teresa Farino *Wild Spain* (Sheldrake Press/Sierra). A knowledgable and practical guide to Spain's national parks, ecology and wildlife. Highly recommended.

Heinzel, Fitter and Parslow *Collins Guide to the Birds of Britain and Europe* (Collins, UK). Alternative to the other Collins guide below. Also includes North Africa and the Middle East.

John Measures *The Wildlife Travelling Companion* (Crowood Press, UK). Clearly laid-out field guide to specific wildlife areas complete with an illustrated index of the most common flora and fauna.

Peterson, Mountfort and Hollom *Collins Field Guide to the Birds of Britain and Europe* (Collins Reference/Houghton Mifflin). Standard reference book – covers most birds in Spain though you may find yourself confused by the bird-song descriptions.

Oleg Polunin and Anthony Huxley *Flowers of the Mediterranean* (Chatto, UK). Useful if by no means exhaustive field guide.

FOOD AND WINE

Coleman Andrews *Catalan Cuisine* (Headline, UK). Best available English-language book dealing with Spain's most adventurous regional cuisine.

Nicholas Butcher *The Spanish Kitchen* (Macmillan, UK). *A* practical, unstuffy guide to creating Spanish food when you get back. Informative detail on olive oil, *jamón serrano* and herbs.

Penelope Casas *The Foods and Wines of Spain* (Penguin/Knopf). Superb Spanish cookbook, covering classic and regional dishes with equal, authoritative aplomb. Easy to use; highly recommended.

Mark and Kim Millon *Wine Roads of Spain* (HarperCollins, UK/US). Everything you ever wanted to know about Spanish wine and sherry: when it's made, how it's made and where to find it, with a good array of useful maps.

PHOTOGRAPHY

Cristina García Rodero *Festivals and Rituals of Spain* (Abrams, US), *España Oculta* (Little, Brown, US). *Festival and Rituals* is a mesmerizing photographic record of the exuberance and colour of Spain's many fiestas; *Oculta* is an atmospheric black and white collection of pictures celebrating the country's religion and mysticism.

LANGUAGE

Once you get into it, Spanish is the easiest language there is – and you'll be helped everywhere by people who are eager to try and understand even the most faltering attempt. English is spoken, but only in the main tourist areas to any extent, and wherever you are you'll get a far better reception if you at least try communicating with Spaniards in their own tongue. Being understood, of course, is only half the problem – and getting the gist of the reply, often rattled out at a furious pace, may prove far more difficult. Nevertheless, you'll be getting there.

The rules of **pronunciation** are pretty straightforward and, once you get to know them, strictly observed. Unless there's an accent, words ending in d, l, r, and z are **stressed** on the last syllable, all others on the second last. All **vowels** are pure and short; combinations have predictable results.

A somewhere between the "A" sound of back and that of father.
E as in get.
I as in police.
O as in hot.
U as in rule.
C is lisped before E and I, hard otherwise: *cerca* is pronounced "thairka".
G works the same way, a guttural "H" sound (like the *ch* in loch) before E or I, a hard G elsewhere – *gigante* becomes "higante".
H is always silent.
J the same sound as a guttural G: *jamón* is pronounced "hamon".
LL sounds like an English Y or LY: *tortilla* is pronounced "torteeya/torteelya".
N is as in English unless it has a tilde (accent) over it, when it becomes NY: *mañana* sounds like "manyana".
QU is pronounced like an English K.
R is rolled, RR doubly so.
V sounds more like B, *vino* becoming "beano".
X has an S sound before consonants, normal X before vowels. More common in Basque, Gallego or Catalan words where it's *sh* or *zh*.
Z is the same as a soft C, so *cerveza* becomes "thairvaitha".

A list of a few essential words and phrases follows which should be enough to get you started, though if you're travelling for any length of time a dictionary or phrasebook obviously a worthwhile investment. If you're using a **dictionary**, bear in mind that in Spanish CH, LL, and Ñ count as separate letters and are listed after the Cs, Ls and Ns respectively.

SPANISH WORDS AND PHRASES

BASICS

Yes, No, OK	*Sí, No, Vale*	With, Without	*Con, Sin*
Please, Thank you	*Por favor, Gracias*	Good, Bad	*Buen(o)/a, Mal(o)/a*
Where, When	*Dónde, Cuando*	Big, Small	*Gran(de), Pequeño/a*
What, How much	*Qué, Cuánto*	Cheap, Expensive	*Barato, Caro*
Here, There	*Aquí, Allí*	Hot, Cold	*Caliente, Frío*
This, That	*Esto, Eso*	More, Less	*Más, Menos*
Now, Later	*Ahora, Más tarde*	Today, Tomorrow	*Hoy, Mañana*
Open, Closed	*Abierto/a, Cerrado/a*	Yesterday	*Ayer*

Continues overleaf

GREETINGS AND RESPONSES

Hello, Goodbye	Hola, Adiós
Good morning	Buenos días
Good afternoon/night	Buenas tardes/noches
See you later	Hasta luego
Sorry	Lo siento/disculpéme
Excusé me	Con permiso/perdón
How are you?	¿Como está (usted)?
I (don't) understand	(No) Entiendo
Not at all/You're welcome	De nada

Do you speak English?	¿Habla (usted) inglés?
I don't speak Spanish	(No) Hablo español
My name is . . .	Me llamo . . .
What's your name?	¿Como se llama usted?
I am English/	Soy inglés(a)/
Australian/	australiano(a)/
Canadian/	canadiense(a)/
American/	americano(a)
Irish/	irlandes(a)

NEEDS – HOTELS AND TRANSPORT

I want	Quiero
I'd like	Quisiera
Do you know . . . ?	¿Sabe . . . ?
I don't know	No sé
There is (is there)?	(¿)Hay(?)
Give me . . .	Deme . . .
(one like that)	(uno así)
Do you have . . . ?	¿Tiene . . . ?
. . . the time	. . . la hora
. . . a room	. . . una habitación
. . . with two beds/ double bed	. . . con dos camas/ cama matrimonial
. . . with shower/bath	. . . con ducha/baño
It's for one person (two people)	Es para una persona (dos personas)
. . . for one night (one week)	. . . para una noche (una semana)
It's fine, how much is it?	¿Está bien, cuánto es?
It's too expensive	Es demasiado caro
Don't you have anything cheaper?	¿No tiene algo más barato?
Can one . . . ?	¿Se puede . . . ?
. . . camp (near) here?	¿ . . . acampar aqui (cerca)?
Is there a hostel nearby?	¿Hay un hostal aquí cerca?

How do I get to . . . ?	¿Por donde se va a . . . ?
Left, right, straight on	Izquierda, derecha, todo recto
Where is . . . ?	¿Dónde está . . . ?
. . . the bus station	. . . la estación de autobuses
. . . the railway station	. . . la estación de ferrocarril
. . . the nearest bank	. . . el banco mas cercano
. . . the post office	. . . el correos/la oficina de correos
. . . the toilet	. . . el baño/aseo/ servicio
Where does the bus to . . . leave from?	¿De dónde sale el autobús para . . . ?
Is this the train for Mérida?	¿Es este el tren para Mérida?
I'd like a (return) ticket to . . .	Quisiera un billete (de ida y vuelta) para . . .
What time does it leave (arrive in . . .)?	¿A qué hora sale (llega a . . .)?
What is there to eat?	¿Qué hay para comer?
What's that?	¿Qué es eso?
What's this called in Spanish?	¿Como se llama este en español?

NUMBERS AND DAYS

1	un/uno/una	13	trece	90	noventa	third	tercero/a
2	dos	14	catorce	100	cien(to)	fifth	quinto/a
3	tres	15	quince	101	ciento uno	tenth	décimo/a
4	cuatro	16	diez y seis	200	doscientos		
5	cinco	20	veinte	201	doscientos uno	Monday	lunes
6	seis	21	veintiuno	500	quinientos	Tuesday	martes
7	siete	30	treinta	1000	mil	Wednesday	miércoles
8	ocho	40	cuarenta	2000	dos mil	Thursday	jueves
9	nueve	50	cincuenta	1992	mil novecientos	Friday	viernes
10	diez	60	sesenta		noventa y dos	Saturday	sábado
11	once	70	setenta	first	primero/a	Sunday	domingo
12	doce	80	ochenta	second	segundo/a		

SPANISH TERMS: A GLOSSARY

ALAMEDA park or grassy promenade.

ALCAZABA Moorish castle.

ALCÁZAR Moorish fortified palace.

ARTESONADO inlaid wooden ceiling of Moorish origin or inspiration.

AYUNTAMIENTO town hall (also CASA CONSISTORIAL).

AZULEJO glazed ceramic tilework.

BARRIO suburb or quarter.

BODEGA cellar, wine bar or warehouse.

CALLE street.

CAPILLA MAYOR chapel containing the high altar.

CAPILLA REAL Royal Chapel.

CARTUJA Carthusian monastery.

CASTILLO castle.

CHURRIGUERESQUE extreme form of Baroque art named after José Churriguera (1650–1723) and his extended family, its main exponents.

COLEGIATA collegiate (large parish) church.

CONVENTO monastery or convent.

CORO central part of church built for the choir.

CORO ALTO raised choir, often above west door of a church.

CORREOS post office.

CORRIDA DE TOROS bullfight.

CUSTODIA large receptacle for Eucharist wafers.

IGLESIA church.

ISABELLINE ornamental form of late Gothic developed during the reign of Isabella and Fernando.

LONJA stock exchange building.

MERCADO market.

MIHRAB prayer niche of Moorish mosque.

MIRADOR viewing point (literally balcony).

MODERNISME (MODERNISTA) Catalan/Spanish form of Art Nouveau, whose most famous exponent was Antoni Gaudí.

MONASTERIO monastery or convent.

MORISCO Muslim Spaniard subject to medieval Christian rule – and nominally baptized.

MOZARABE Christian subject to medieval Moorish rule; normally allowed freedom of worship, they built churches in an Arabinfluenced manner (MOZARABIC).

MUDÉJAR Muslim Spaniard subject to medieval Christian rule, but retaining Islamic worship; most commonly a term applied to architecture which includes buildings built by Moorish craftsmen for the Christian rulers and later designs influenced by the Moors. The 1890s to 1930s saw a Mudéjar revival, blended with Art Nouveau and Art Deco forms.

PALACIO aristocratic mansion.

PARADOR luxury hotel, often converted from minor monument.

PASEO promenade; also the evening stroll thereon.

PATIO inner courtyard.

PLATERESQUE elaborately decorative Renaissance style, the sixteenth-century successor of Isabelline forms. Named for its resemblance to silversmiths' work (*platería*).

PLAZA square.

PLAZA DE TOROS bullring.

POSADA old name for an inn.

PUERTA gateway, also mountain pass.

PUERTO port.

REJA iron screen or grille, often fronting a window.

RETABLO altarpiece.

RÍA river estuary in Galicia.

RÍO river.

ROMERÍA religious procession to a rural shrine.

SACRISTÍA, SAGRARIO sacristy or sanctuary of church.

SEO, SEU, LA SE ancient/regional names for cathedrals.

SIERRA mountain range.

SILLERÍA choir stall.

SOLAR aristocratic town mansion.

TAIFA small Moorish kingdom, many of which emerged after the disintegration of the Córdoba caliphate.

TELEFÓNICA the phone company; also used for its offices in any town.

TURISMO tourist office.

POLITICAL PARTIES AND ACRONYMS

CNT anarchist trade union.

CONVERGENCIA I UNIO conservative party in power in Catalunya.

ETA Basque terrorist organization. Its political wing is *Herri Batasuna*.

FALANGE Franco's old fascist party; now officially defunct.

FUERZA NUEVA descendants of the above, also on the way out.

IU *Izquierda Unida*, broad-left alliance of communists and others.

MC *Movimiento Comunista* (Communist Movement), small radical offshoot of the PCE.

MOC *Movimiento de Objeción de Conciencia*, peace group, concerned with NATO and conscription.

OTAN NATO.

PCE *Partido Comunista de España* (Spanish Communist Party).

PNV Basque Nationalist Party – in control of the right-wing autonomous government.

PP *Partido Popular*, the new right-wing alliance formed by Alianza Popular and the Christian Democrats.

PSOE *Partido Socialista Obrero Español*, the Spanish Socialist Workers' Party – currently in power under Prime Minister Felipe González.

UGT *Unión General de Trabajadores*, the Spanish TUC.

DIRECT ORDERS IN THE UK

Title	ISBN	Price
Amsterdam	1858280869	£7.99
Australia	1858280354	£12.99
Barcelona & Catalunya	1858280486	£7.99
Berlin	1858280338	£8.99
Brazil	0747101272	£7.95
Brittany & Normandy	1858280192	£7.99
Bulgaria	1858280478	£8.99
California	1858280907	£9.99
Canada	185828001X	£10.99
Corsica	1858280893	£8.99
Crete	1858280494	£6.99
Cyprus	185828032X	£8.99
Czech & Slovak Republics	185828029X	£8.99
Egypt	1858280753	£10.99
England	1858280788	£9.99
Europe	185828077X	£14.99
Florida	1858280109	£8.99
France	1858280508	£9.99
Germany	1858280257	£11.99
Greece	1858280206	£9.99
Guatemala & Belize	1858280451	£9.99
Holland, Belgium & Luxembourg	1858280877	£9.99
Hong Kong & Macau	1858280664	£8.99
Hungary	1858280214	£7.99
Ireland	1858280958	£9.99
Italy	1858280311	£12.99
Kenya	1858280435	£9.99
Mediterranean Wildlife	0747100993	£7.95
Morocco	1858280400	£9.99
Nepal	185828046X	£8.99
New York	1858280583	£8.99
Nothing Ventured	0747102082	£7.99
Paris	1858280389	£7.99
Peru	0747102546	£7.95
Poland	1858280346	£9.99
Portugal	1858280842	£9.99
Prague	185828015X	£7.99
Provence & the Côte d'Azur	1858280230	£8.99
Pyrenees	1858280524	£7.99
St Petersburg	1858280303	£8.99
San Francisco	1858280826	£8.99
Scandinavia	1858280397	£10.99
Scotland	1858280834	£8.99
Sicily	1858280370	£8.99
Spain	1858280818	£9.99
Thailand	1858280168	£8.99
Tunisia	1858280656	£8.99
Turkey	1858280885	£9.99
Tuscany & Umbria	1858280915	£8.99
USA	185828080X	£12.99
Venice	1858280362	£8.99
West Africa	1858280141	£12.99
Women Travel	1858280710	£7.99
Zimbabwe & Botswana	1858280419	£10.99

Rough Guides are available from all good bookstores, but can be obtained directly in the UK* from Penguin by contacting:

Penguin Direct, Penguin Books Ltd, Bath Road, Harmondsworth, West Drayton, Middlesex UB7 0DA; or telephone our credit line on 081-899 4036 (9am–5pm) and ask for Penguin Direct. Visa, Access and Amex accepted. Delivery will normally be within 14 working days. Penguin Direct ordering facilities are only available in the UK.

The availability and published prices quoted are correct at the time of going to press but are subject to alteration without prior notice.

* For USA and international orders, see separate price list

DIRECT ORDERS IN THE USA

Title	ISBN	Price			
able to Travel	1858281105	$19.95	Italy	1858280311	$17.95
Amsterdam	1858280869	$13.95	Kenya	1858280435	$15.95
Australia	1858280354	$18.95	Mediterranean Wildlife	1858280699	$15.95
Berlin	1858280338	$13.99	Morocco	1858280400	$16.95
Brittany & Normandy	1858280192	$14.95	Nepal	185828046X	$13.95
Bulgaria	1858280478	$14.99	New York	1858280583	$13.95
California	1858280907	$14.95	Paris	1858280389	$13.95
Canada	185828001X	$14.95	Poland	1858280346	$16.95
Corsica	1858280893	$14.95	Portugal	1858280842	$15.95
Crete	1858280494	$14.95	Prague	185828015X	$14.95
Cyprus	185828032X	$13.99	Provence & the	1858280230	$14.95
Czech & Slovak	185828029X	$14.95	Côte d'Azur		
Republics			St Petersburg	1858280303	$14.95
Egypt	1858280753	$17.95	San Francisco	1858280826	$13.95
England	1858280788	$16.95	Scandinavia	1858280397	$16.99
Europe	185828077X	$18.95	Scotland	1858280834	$14.95
Florida	1858280109	$14.95	Sicily	1858280370	$14.99
France	1858280508	$16.95	Spain	1858280818	$16.95
Germany	1858280257	$17.95	Thailand	1858280168	$15.95
Greece	1858280206	$16.95	Tunisia	1858280656	$15.95
Guatemala & Belize	1858280451	$14.95	Turkey	1858280885	$16.95
Holland, Belgium	1858280877	$15.95	Tuscany & Umbria	1858280915	$15.95
& Luxembourg			USA	185828080X	$18.95
Hong Kong & Macau	1858280664	$13.95	Venice	1858280362	$13.99
Hungary	1858280214	$13.95	Women Travel	1858280710	$12.95
Ireland	1858280958	$16.95	Zimbabwe & Botswana	1858280419	$16.95

Rough Guides are available from all good bookstores, but can be obtained directly in the USA and Worldwide (except the UK*) from Penguin:

Charge your order by Master Card or Visa (US$15.00 minimum order): call 1-800-255-6476; or send orders, with complete name, address and zip code, and list price, plus $2.00 shipping and handling per order to:
Consumer Sales, Penguin USA, PO Box 999 – Dept #17109, Bergenfield, NJ 07621.
No COD. Prepay foreign orders by international money order, a cheque drawn on a US bank, or US currency. No postage stamps are accepted. All orders are subject to stock availability at the time they are processed. Refunds will be made for books not available at that time. Please allow a minimum of four weeks for delivery.

* The availability and published prices quoted are correct at the time of going to press but are subject to alteration without prior notice. Titles currently not available outside the UK will be available by January 1995. Call to check.

For UK orders, see separate price list